NEUROPSYCHOLOGICAL AND COGNITIVE PROCESSES IN READING

PERSPECTIVES IN
NEUROLINGUISTICS, NEUROPSYCHOLOGY, AND
PSYCHOLINGUISTICS: A Series of Monographs and Treatises

Harry A. Whitaker, Series Editor
DEPARTMENT OF PSYCHOLOGY
THE UNIVERSITY OF ROCHESTER
ROCHESTER, NEW YORK

HAIGANOOSH WHITAKER and HARRY A. WHITAKER (Eds.).
Studies in Neurolinguistics, Volumes 1, 2, 3, and 4

NORMAN J. LASS (Ed.). Contemporary Issues in Experimental Phonetics

JASON W. BROWN. Mind, Brain, and Consciousness: The Neuropsychology of Cognition

SIDNEY J. SEGALOWITZ and FREDERIC A. GRUBER (Eds.). Language Development and Neurological Theory

SUSAN CURTISS. Genie: A Psycholinguistic Study of a Modern-Day "Wild Child"

JOHN MACNAMARA (Ed.). Language Learning and Thought

I. M. SCHLESINGER and LILA NAMIR (Eds.). Sign Language of the Deaf: Psychological, Linguistic, and Sociological Perspectives

WILLIAM C. RITCHIE (Ed.). Second Language Acquisition Research: Issues and Implications

PATRICIA SIPLE (Ed.). Understanding Language through Sign Language Research

MARTIN L. ALBERT and LORAINE K. OBLER. The Bilingual Brain: Neuropsychological and Neurolinguistic Aspects of Bilingualism

TALMY GIVÓN. On Understanding Grammar

CHARLES J. FILLMORE, DANIEL KEMPLER, and WILLIAM S-Y. WANG (Eds.).
Individual Differences in Language Ability and Language Behavior

JEANNINE HERRON (Ed.). Neuropsychology of Left-Handedness

FRANÇOIS BOLLER and MAUREEN DENNIS (Eds.). Auditory Comprehension: Clinical and Experimental Studies with the Token Test

R. W. RIEBER (Ed.). Language Development and Aphasia in Children: New Essays and a Translation of "Kindersprache und Aphasie" by Emil Fröschels

GRACE H. YENI-KOMSHIAN, JAMES F. KAVANAGH, and CHARLES A. FERGUSON (Eds.). Child Phonology, Volume 1: Production and Volume 2: Perception

FRANCIS J. PIROZZOLO and MERLIN C. WITTROCK (Eds.). Neuropsychological and Cognitive Processes in Reading

In preparation

JASON W. BROWN (Ed.). Jargonaphasia

NEUROPSYCHOLOGICAL AND COGNITIVE PROCESSES IN READING

EDITED BY

Francis J. Pirozzolo

GRECC/Neurology Service
Minneapolis Veterans Administration Medical Center
Minneapolis, Minnesota

Merlin C. Wittrock

Graduate School of Education
University of California, Los Angeles
Los Angeles, California

 1981

ACADEMIC PRESS
A Subsidiary of Harcourt Brace Jovanovich, Publishers
New York   London   Toronto   Sydney   San Francisco

ACADEMIC PRESS, INC.
111 Fifth Avenue, New York, New York 10003

United Kingdom Edition published by
ACADEMIC PRESS, INC. (LONDON) LTD.
24/28 Oval Road, London NW1 7DX

Library of Congress Cataloging in Publication Data
Main entry under title:

Neuropsychological and cognitive processes in
    reading.

    (Perspectives in neurolinguistics, neuropsychology,
and psycholinguistics: A series of monographs and treatises)
    Includes bibliographies and index.
    1. Reading, Psychology of. I. Pirozzolo, Francis J.
II. Wittrock, Merlin C. [DNLM: 1. Cognition. 2. Models,
Psychological. 3. Reading. 4. Dyslexia--Psychology.
5. Dyslexia--Physiopathology. 6. Neurophysiology.
WM 475 N494]
BF456.R2N43   153.6   80-29246
ISBN 0-12-557360-X

CONTENTS

I

MODELS OF READING AND READING DISABILITIES

1

2

ALEXIA AND THE NEUROANATOMICAL
BASIS OF READING

D. Frank Benson

DYSLEXIA SYNDROMES IN CHILDREN:
TOWARD THE DEVELOPMENT OF
SYNDROME–SPECIFIC TREATMENT PROGRAMS

Steven Mattis

5

LEARNING DISABILITY SUBTYPES: A REVIEW

Paul Satz and Robin Morris

II

PERCEPTUAL AND IMAGINAL PROCESSES
IN READING COMPREHENSION

6

EYE MOVEMENTS AND THE PERCEPTUAL SPAN
IN READING

Keith Rayner

7

PERCEPTUAL PROCESSES IN READING:
AN ANALYSIS–BY–SYNTHESIS MODEL

Lyn R. Haber and Ralph Norman Haber

III

VISUAL AND LINGUISTIC PROCESSES
OF READING

8

ON FUNCTIONS OF PICTURES IN PROSE

Joel R. Levin

12

RECOVERY FROM ALEXIA: FACTORS INFLUENCING
RESTORATION OF FUNCTION AFTER
FOCAL CEREBRAL DAMAGE

Francis J. Pirozzolo and Kathryn Lawson-Kerr

LIST OF CONTRIBUTORS

Numbers in parentheses indicate the pages on which the authors' contributions begin.

D. Frank Benson (69), Department of Neurology, University of California, Los Angeles, Los Angeles, California 90024

Rita Sloan Berndt (297), Department of Psychology, The Johns Hopkins University, Baltimore, Maryland 21218

Robert C. Calfee (3), School of Education, Stanford University, Stanford, California 94305

Alfonso Caramazza (297), Department of Psychology, The Johns Hopkins University, Baltimore, Maryland 21218

Peter Eisenberg (31), Department of Educational Psychology, School of Education, University of Minnesota, Minneapolis, Minnesota 55455

Jack M. Fletcher (261), Neuropsychology Research, Texas Research Institute of Mental Sciences, Texas Medical Center, Houston, Texas 77030

Lyn R. Haber (167), Department of Psychology, University of Illinois—Chicago Circle, Chicago, Illinois 60680

Ralph Norman Haber (167), Department of Psychology, University of Illinois—Chicago Circle, Chicago, Illinois 60680

John Hart (297)*, Department of Psychology, The Johns Hopkins University, Baltimore, Maryland 21218

Kathryn Lawson-Kerr (319), GRECC/Neurology Service, Minneapolis Veterans Administration Medical Center, Minneapolis, Minnesota 55417

Joel R. Levin (203), School of Education, University of Wisconsin—Madison, Madison, Wisconsin 53706

*Present address: School of Medicine, University of Maryland, Baltimore, Maryland 21201

Steven Mattis (93), Department of Neurology, Montefiore Hospital and Medical Center, Bronx, New York 10467

Robin Morris (109), Department of Clinical Psychology, University of Florida, Gainesville, Florida 32610

Francis J. Pirozzolo (319), GRECC/Neurology Service, Minneapolis Veterans Administration Medical Center, Minneapolis, Minnesota 55417

Keith Rayner (145), Department of Psychology, University of Massachusetts, Amherst, Massachusetts 01003

S. Jay Samuels (31), Department of Educational Psychology, School of Education, University of Minnesota, Minneapolis, Minneapolis, Minnesota 55455

Paul Satz (109), Department of Psychology, University of Victoria, Victoria, British Columbia V8W 2Y2

Janet E. Spector (3), School of Education, Stanford University, Stanford, California 94305

Merlin C. Wittrock (229), Graduate School of Education, University of California, Los Angeles, Los Angeles, California 90024

PREFACE

Reading and reading disabilities are areas of vital interest in cognitive psychology and neuropsychology. Since about 1955, the widespread public interest in the socially significant problems relating to learning to read has been matched by sustained research on the processes of reading and by continued attempts to understand and to model them. This recent congruity of interests in reading is reminiscent of a similar interest that existed late in the nineteenth century. From about 1890 to 1910, experimental psychologists frequently studied the cognitive and neural processes of reading, examining perception, inner speech, the nature of meaning, serial processing, parallel processing, imagery, and verbal processes as they relate to reading. For example, in his laboratories at Leipzig, James M. Cattell studied individual differences in reaction time and in the recognition of letters and words.

Shortly after the turn of the century, the flurry of research on the cognitive and neural processes of reading subsided. For the next 50 years, research in reading eschewed mentalistic processes and focused on observable behavior and methods of learning to read. With the recent resurgence of interest in cognition and in neuropsychology, research on the cognitive and neural processes of reading increased markedly. Once again, reading comprehension, information processing, attention, and the neural substrates of reading disabilities were mentioned frequently in journal articles about the processes of reading, and with them emerged new areas of interest in reading research, including neurolinguistics. These old and new topics comprise the subject matter of this book.

The present volume is designed to bring together the most recent findings regarding the roles of brain mechanisms in reading and reading disturbances from the areas of neuropsychology and cognitive psychology. The volume's treatments of the literature in the areas of perception and cognition will use theoretical models of the reading process to give the reader an understanding of the various psychological processes involved in the act of skilled reading.

Chapters in this volume are written to convey, in an organized way, the significant findings and models emerging from the recent research on the neural and cognitive processes of reading. The volume is organized to bring together many of the recent and complementary findings and models developed from the two different levels of studying reading; neuropsychology and cognitive psychology. We intended to show that these findings and models, although they developed from two different and productive lines and levels of research, often complement each other and provide a useful understanding of the function of processes of reading and their neural substrates.

Robert C. Calfee and Janet E. Spector, in Chapter 1, introduce a model of the fundamental processes of reading. They begin the chapter by presenting a psychological theory that leads to concrete and testable predictions about the basic processes of reading. Their theory builds on two concepts: (a) that the fundamental processes of reading are few in number; and (b) that they are separable from one another. The chapter results in a useful and testable information-processing model of reading that consists of three separable, fundamental processes: decoding, word meaning, and sentence comprehension. Each process is defined by its unique factors and appropriate measures for testing the model.

S. Jay Samuels and Peter Eisenberg, Chapter 2, specify some of the external and internal factors involved in reading. They begin the chapter with a discussion of the external factors of reading: the physical characteristics of the text and the environment, the readability of the text, the content area of the text, and the goals imposed on the reader by other people. The authors then discuss the internal factors of reading: the reader's propositional and procedural knowledge base, the reader's energy and attention, visual memory, phonological memory, episodic memory, and feedback mechanisms from semantic memory to visual and phonological memories. The chapter culminates in a discussion of the comprehension process, which combines the factors of the authors' model of reading and leads to implications about the teaching of reading.

Chapter 3 presents a model of disorders of reading comprehension (the alexias) by D. Frank Benson. His discussion of the three major forms of alexia is preceded by a historical introduction to the problem of reading disorders caused by brain damage and by a review of the neuroanatomy of reading disturbances. Benson discusses the pathophysiology of posterior alexia, a disconnection of the left hemisphere's language mechanisms from visual information coming from the left and right visual cortex. Central alexia is a disturbance caused by lesions directly involving the language cortex. Anterior alexia, which is the most poorly understood reading disorder, often occurs in patients with Broca's aphasia. The causal mechanism is unclear, although evidence suggests that these patients may be agrammatic readers or that they suffer from a gaze paresis.

Steven Mattis, Chapter 4, describes a study he and his colleagues carried out comparing the neuropsychological test performance of brain-damaged and non-brain-damaged dyslexic children. An important conclusion of that study was that there were no significant differences in the patterns of impairment between the two groups. In addition, the authors showed that 90% of their clinical population of dyslexic children could be easily classified into one of the three dyslexia subgroups. The three syndromes of dyslexia to be identified were: language disorder dyslexia, articulatory–graphomotor dyscoordination dyslexia, and visual–perceptual disorder dyslexia. Mattis concludes that these syndromes can be reliably detected, and that assessment techniques and selection criteria exist for differentiating these reading disturbances. Finally, he presents a syndrome-specific treatment program based on clinical findings in each of the dyslexia groups.

In Chapter 5, Paul Satz and Robin Morris present another view of the problem of subtypes of learning disability. As in the previous chapter, they argue that reading disability is not a single, homogenous diagnostic entity and that, contrary to the suggestion of early investigators in the field, it is probably not caused by a single defect. They also argue that the failure to agree on an operational definition of learning disabilities has resulted in, among other things, a variability in the prevalence estimates of learning and reading disabilities. Satz and Morris present an alternative to the clinical inferential approach to the subtyping of learning disabled children in their application of multivariate analysis.

Next, Keith Rayner (Chapter 6) reviews the basic facts about eye movements and perceptual spans in reading. He discusses the various techniques that have been employed to study the information that is available to the reader from outside the fovea. He shows that different types of information (e.g., featural, semantic, etc.) are obtained from different regions of the perceptual span. In addition, Rayner presents evidence that the perceptual spans are asymmetric around the fovea.

The span from which useful information can be apprehended is biased to the right for English readers and biased to the left for Hebrew readers, suggesting that an underlying attentional mechanism accounts for this perceptual asymmetry.

Lyn R. Haber and Ralph Norman Haber, in Chapter 7, present an analysis-by-synthesis model of the reading process. This model is based on the notion that fluent reading requires an interaction between the visual features of words and the expectancies that readers have about the text. It emphasizes the role of redundancies, visual–featural, grammatical, and semantic. The good reader relies on the context to extract meaning from words. Only when the readers' hypotheses or expectancies about the syntax and semantics have not been met did they deploy their attention to identification of the smaller units of text (i.e., letter identification).

In Chapter 8, Joel R. Levin studies pictures and imagery in children's learning from prose. In this chapter he presents a model of the functions of pictures in prose learning that provides a new interpretation of the research literature on pictures and imagery in prose learning.

With very few exceptions notwithstanding, pictures positively, potently, and pervasively influence children's learning from prose. Relevant illustrations facilitate learning of the content of a story, usually by 40% or more. Visual imagery, or more precisely, instructions to learners to construct visual images, show lesser positive effects on learning. Children under 8 years of age show no positive effect on learning from these instructions.

Merlin C. Wittrock, Chapter 9, presents a model of reading comprehension. Comprehension is the process of generating meaning for text from one's experience and knowledge. The generation of meaning involves the processes of *attention, encoding,* and *memory*. According to the generative model, the most useful procedures for enhancing comprehension depend on the learner's abilities to attend and to generate representations or elaborations. With those learners who cannot generate relations between text and knowledge, the model predicts that pictures, verbal descriptions, statements of the rules, examples, inferences, analogies and metaphors, and goals and objectives given to the learner facilitate comprehension. For those learners who can, but do not, spontaneously construct mental representations, the model predicts that instructions to construct inferences, analogies, metaphors, meanings, images, to draw pictures, to relate text to kowledge, and to construct higher order concepts facilitate reading comprehension.

For those learners who can and do generate mental representations for the text, the model predicts that subtle instructions to direct attention, questions, discussions, and related procedures to induce verbal and imagined elaborations enhance reading comprehension.

In Chapter 10, Jack M. Fletcher argues that developmental changes in linguistic function play an important role in reading acquisition. The strategies that younger readers employ to extract meaning from text are, in large part, different from those employed by older, more fluent readers. Developmental changes in the ability to make use of visual–featural, syntactic, and semantic redundancies also undoubtedly affect a readers' strategy in processing text. Finally, Fletcher reviews studies of reading disability, concluding that a single-deficit causal model is incompatible with the evidence showing that developmental changes in language functioning interact with the cognitive strategies that children use to learn to read.

In Chapter 11, Alfonso Caramazza, Rita Sloan Berndt, and John Hart analyze the problem of agrammatism and how it affects oral language and reading comprehension in Broca's aphasia. Broca's aphasics produce speech that is faulty by virtue of its articulatory struggle, dysprosody, the predominant use of uninflected substantives, and the omission of grammatical morphemes. Not only do Broca's aphasics not use function words in their expressive speech, but recent evidence suggests that they have difficulty understanding these grammatical words. Although Broca's aphasics do show asyntactic comprehension of written material, their reading impairment is not specific to grammatical words, but also to abstract nouns and nonwords, suggesting a failure in the grapheme-to-phoneme translation process as well.

In the final chapter, Francis J. Pirozzolo and Kathryn Lawson-Kerr analyze the factors that influence recovery from alexia. They discuss the general principles that govern the brain's reaction to injury, including the appearance of edema, changes in the flow of blood and cerebrospinal fluid in the brain, and diaschisis. The authors analyze factors that reputedly underlie restoration of function, such as age of the patient, type of language disturbance, and treatment effects. Although there is relatively little data available on the recovery of reading ability, the authors review the existing literature beginning with the observations of Schmidt in 1673, Charcot in 1877, and Franz in 1918, all of who made early contributions to the recovery literature. The authors suggest that an information-processing approach, or an analysis of the component processes in reading, may more clearly elucidate the stages in recovery of reading ability.

NEUROPSYCHOLOGICAL AND COGNITIVE PROCESSES IN READING

I

MODELS OF READING AND READING DISABILITIES

1

Robert C. Calfee
Janet E. Spector

SEPARABLE PROCESSES IN READING[1]

What happens in the mind of the student during a careful reading of a prose passage? In our opinion, the answer to this question necessarily takes the form of a psychological theory—a theory that guides the investigator through an examination and an analysis of observable performance to gain insight into unobservable thought processes. This position is by no means novel; others have argued for the importance of theory in reading research (e.g., Gibson &˙Levin, 1975). Such pronouncements, however, have been primarily exhortative and have not necessarily resulted in the desired action. Our objective in this chapter is to exemplify, rather than to exhort. We will describe a theoretical approach that has advantages both in research and in practice. The models we present are not only heuristic; they are formal and testable. Although our approach is not intended to supplant all other theoretical efforts, we think that it yields a general, but powerful technique for building and testing comprehensive models of "natural reading."

In the first section of the chapter, we present the theoretical position on which we base our models of reading. The concept of process independence is described in the context of Sternberg's (1969) additive-factor method for testing process independence in performance of cognitive tasks. Then we present the multifactor–multimeasure method (Calfee, 1976), which is an extension of independent-process

[1] This research is supported by grants from the U.S. Office of Education (Bureau of the Educationally Handicapped) and the National Institute of Education.

NEUROPSYCHOLOGICAL AND COGNITIVE
PROCESSES IN READING

theory more suited to measurement of performance on educational tasks. In the second section, the development and evaluation of independent-process models are illustrated for two reading tasks: sentence reading and passage comprehension. Finally, we summarize our discussion of independent-process models of reading, stressing the implications for practice and research.

Independent-Process Theory

The theoretical approach described here builds upon the concept of *process independence*. This idea, originally proposed by Sternberg (1963), begins with the assumption that the mental activities that underlie performance on a task comprise a relatively small set of independent and separable cognitive processes. Then it is assumed that, for each process, the theorist can identify a set of *factors* that uniquely influence the process, and a set of *measures* that are unique indicators of the process (Calfee & Drum, 1978; Calfee, Spector, & Piontkowski, 1979). This second proposition operationalizes the concept of process independence.

The Additive-Factor Method

Sternberg (1969) proposed the *additive-factor method* for testing the concept of process independence.

> The basic idea is that a stage is one of a series of successive processes that operates on an input to produce an output, and contributes an additive component to the RT [reaction time]. The concept of "additivity" here entails a property of independence for mean stage-durations: the mean duration of a stage depends only on its input and the levels of factors that influence it, and not directly on the mean durations of other stages [pp. 282–283].
>
> Suppose that stages a, b, and c [shown in Figure 1.1, this volume] are among a series of stages between stimulus and response. Suppose further that there are three experimental factors, F, G, and H, such that factor F influences only the duration of stage a, factor G influences only the duration of stage b, and factor H influences stages b and c, but not a. By a "factor" here is meant an experimentally manipulated variable, or a set of two or more related treatments called "levels"; the "effect" of a factor is the change in the response measure induced by a change in the level of that factor. What are the most likely relations among the effects of the three factors on mean RT? These relations are shown above the broken line. The general idea is that when factors influence no stages in common, their effects on mean RT will be independent and additive because stage durations are additive. That is, the effect of

one factor will not depend on the levels of the others. Thus, factors F and G should have additive effects on mean RT. On the other hand, when two factors, G and H, influence at least one stage in common (stage b) there is no reason to expect their effects on RT to add; the most likely relation to some sort of interaction [pp. 281–282].

The first step in the additive-factor method is to specify the underlying cognitive operations required to perform a task and to order the tasks serially, thereby developing a rudimentary information-processing model.

The second step in this method is to specify one or more factors that can be uniquely linked to each cognitive operation. These factors are combined into a factorial design.

The subject then performs the task under each of the factorial variations, and RT (or some other additive index of performance) is measured. If the model is a reasonable account of the thought processes, and if the factors are properly chosen, the total time to perform the task under each factorial combination will be the sum of the times taken by each stage. In other words, factors associated with different processes will not interact with one another.

The additive-factor method has seen extensive application in laboratory research in experimental psychology, where precise control over factorial variations and careful measurement of RTs are possible. The procedure is less readily applicable to complex tasks in real-world settings, where measures other than RT are more appropriate, and where the assumption of serial processing may be challenged.

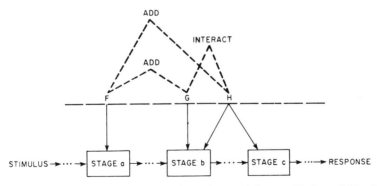

FIGURE 1.1. *Arrangement of stages* (a, b, *and* c) *and factors* (F, G, *and* H) *allows testing of stage independence. Horizontal arrows represent inputs and outputs of stages; time proceeds from left to right. Arrows indicate the stages assumed to be influenced by specific factors.* (After Sternberg, 1969.)

The Multifactor–Multimeasure Method

Calfee (1976) proposed an extension of independent-process theory more suited to measurement of performance on educational tasks. This generalization is shown in Figure 1.2. Processes A, B, and C are cognitive operations assumed to underlie the performance of some task. To establish the independence of these processes, the theorist links a *factor set* and a *measure set* to each process. A factor set consists of one or more independent variables, each of which is presumed to influence the corresponding process and that process only. A measure set consists of one or more dependent variables, each of which reflects the operation of the corresponding process and that process only.

In spelling out these specifications, we touch on the essence of the independent-process approach: For a process model to serve a useful purpose, theoretically or practically, we should be able to specify the input–output features of each process. We should be able to state what variables affect each process, and how the operation of each process can be measured most directly. By contrast, if every factor interacts with every other factor, if we have no clear-cut way of measuring the underlying processes, or if every measure correlates with every other measure, it is questionable whether we gain much understanding no matter how elaborate our flow charts may be.

The evaluation of a model such as the one depicted in Figure 1.2 requires a *multifactor experiment* with *multivariate measures;* each subject must be assessed under combinations of factors from each factor set, and a variety of measures must be taken under each combination.

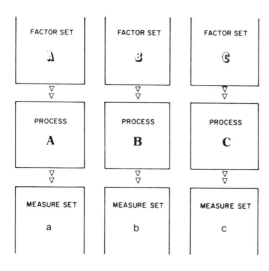

FIGURE 1.2. A generalization of the independent-process model. Associated with each component process is a set of factors and a set of measures each assumed to be uniquely linked to the process. (After Calfee, 1976.)

The multifactor–multimeasure method resembles the additive-factor technique in its strong reliance on a carefully planned factorial design for observing each subject's performance under different testing conditions. Unlike a strictly empirical investigation, however, the variables are not arbitrary; each factor must be justified on the basis of a clear and well defined link to one of the underlying processes.

The distinctive feature of the multifactor–multimeasure technique is the requirement of a unique measure set for each process. The additive-factor technique relies on the decomposition of a single index (e.g., RT) into derived parameters, each assumed to be linked to a given process. In the multifactor–multimeasure approach, the researcher selects one or more direct measures appropriate to each of the processes.

The analysis of the data from a multifactor–multimeasure design is fairly straightforward. The analysis of variance for each measure determines which factors affect that measure. If students are thinking as predicted by independent-process theory, the analysis of variance should confirm the linkages predicted by the model, and *only* those linkages. The analysis of variance on measure A, which is assumed to be linked to process A, should reveal significant effects of variables in factor set A, but no effects of the variables from any other factor set.

Independent-Process Models of Reading

Models generated by the independent-process approach are task specific and normative. That is, the creation of each model begins with a description of the kind of reading task that the student is to undertake and a specification of the boundary conditions within which the model is to be applicable. The model is best understood as a description of how an *ideal* reader thinks under the specified conditions. We think that it is quite conceivable that different groups of people may be taught to read in substantially different ways, and hence that more than one model may be called for. We think, however, that the number of distinctive models is likely to be small, two or three models are apt to account for how most people read in a given context.

In this section, we apply the independent-process approach to two reading situations. The first is one in which the student is asked to read aloud and to try to understand a relatively simple sentence. In the second case, the student attempts to comprehend a narrative passage. For each situation, we describe the development of an independent-process model for an effective reader performing in a context that stresses careful, accurate reading, and we demonstrate a plan for testing the model.

An Independent-Process Study of Sentence Reading

Juel (1977) investigated the applications of the independent-process approach to a sentence reading task. The plan of the study is shown in Figure 1.3. Three processes were included in the model: *decoding, word meaning,* and *sentence comprehension.* Simply put, Juel's analysis was that the reader had to (*a*) translate the printed letter symbols into a spoken word equivalent; (*b*) find a definition for each word in semantic memory; and then (*c*) apply knowledge of grammar and word associations to make sense of the sentence.

It is not assumed that these processes operate in a straight-line fashion. For instance, suppose the student cannot understand the sentence, even though he has decoded each word, found a plausible meaning, and analyzed the syntax. He may go back and search for another definition for a word. Such interplay among processes does not in itself counter the predictions of the independent-process model. Moreover, it should be obvious that a breakdown in any one of the processes may jeopardize the flow of information to other processes. If a word cannot be decoded, then the lexical process has nothing to work on; a mistranslation may cause the lexical process to come up with an uninterpretable meaning. Such interplay is expected, and does not violate any assumptions of the model.

The factors chosen for each process in Juel's design are shown in Figure 1.3. Each factor was selected on the basis of previous research results, for its direct relevance to the corresponding process, and for its strength of effect. Figure 1.3 also shows the measures chosen for each process. Once again, these were chosen for their direct relevance to the process, and for their uniqueness; each measure and the overall context of measurement were arranged to represent the corresponding process, and to be minimally influenced by any other processes. Sentence reading time is an exception; this index is closer to the additive-factor paradigm, and will be discussed later in the section.

Juel was especially interested in comparing the reading performance of different groups of students—she wanted evidence about patterns of reading skill and reading style. Accordingly, she arranged for a careful selection of students in the study. Students were sampled from two grade levels (second and fifth), both sexes (boys and girls), and two reading ability levels (relatively good readers and relatively poor readers).

It will help to understand the task if we describe the experience of a typical student during the experiment. The basic task was to read and understand 32 sentences. The student was taken through six steps during the testing of each sentence.

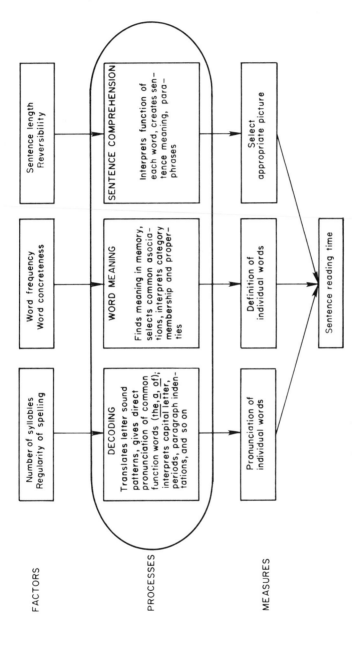

FIGURE 1.3. Application of independent-process approach to a sentence reading task. (From Juel, 1977.)

Step 1.	**Pronounce** all the words in the sentence.
Step 2.	**Define** all nouns and verbs in the sentence.
Step 3.	Training on any words missed in Steps 1 and 2.
Step 4.	Retest on any words missed in Steps 1 and 2.
Step 5.	Read each test sentence aloud.
Step 6.	Show **understanding** of sentence by pointing to test picture that best illustrates meaning.

Each step was planned to measure a unique process, and to ensure that the measures for one process would not be affected by the operation of the other processes. A few test sentences will illustrate the variations in the design used to test the model:

The *bus* hits the *car*.
   (One syllable, regular spelling, high frequency, concrete target words; reversible, short sentence)
The fat *bear* bites the *wolf* on the back.
   (One syllable, irregular spelling, high frequency, concrete target words; reversible, long sentence)
The small *group* makes a *choice* about the food.
   (One syllable, irregular spelling, high frequency, abstract target words; nonreversible, long sentence)
The *owl* sees the *field*.
   (one syllable, irregular spelling, high frequency, concrete target words; nonreversible, short sentence)
The happy *pair* see the *prey* on the hill.
   (One syllable, irregular spelling, high frequency, abstract target words; reversible, long sentence)
The *tiger* sees the *rabbit*.
   (Two syllables, regular spelling, high frequency, concrete target words; reversible, short sentence)

The target words, which are italicized, change according to the Decoding and Word Meaning factors in the design. These same words are then incorporated into the test sentences, which vary according to the Sentence Comprehension factors.

The design of the experiment was somewhat complicated, and each student was tested quite intensively. If reading is a combination of several processes, it should not be surprising that a complex design is needed to untangle this system. Fortunately, the theoretical model provided guidance in handling the data structure. To analyze the results, the researcher determined the effect of each factor for each measure. The model predicted which factors would affect each measure, so the researcher was not simply looking for "needles in haystacks."

The plan of the analysis is shown in Figure 1.4. The boxes in heavy frames show where we should "see some action" according to the predictions of the independent-process model. The comments in each box summarize the actual results of the statistical analysis used to test the findings.

A quick glance at Figure 1.4 suggests some general conclusions:

1. Decoding and Word Meaning factors have the strongest effects.
2. The relation between factors and measures follow the theoretical predictions, by and large.

FACTOR SETS

	DECODING	WORD MEANING	COMPREHENSION
PRONUNCIATION	a. Decodability and Syllables and the interaction of the two factors affect Pronunciation ($p < .001$) b. The effects of Decodability ($p < .001$) and Syllables ($p < .001$) depend on Reading Ability	a. Concreteness and Frequency and the interaction of the two affect Pronunciation ($p < .001$) b. Concreteness and Frequency interact with Reading Ability c. Frequency affects the influence of both Decodability and Syllables on Pronunciation	
WORD MEANING	a. Decodability and Syllables both affect Word Definition performance ($p < .001$)	a. Frequency and Concreteness both affect Word Definition performance ($p < .001$)	
COMPREHENSION			a. Reversibility affected Sentence Understanding ($p < .001$)

(MEASURE SETS)

FIGURE 1.4. *Overall plan of analysis and major results.*

3. There is some "cross talk" between the Decoding and Word
   Meaning processes

Figure 1.4 shows the statistically significant effects. To gain a
better understanding, we must examine the descriptive statistics. Let us
look first at the results for the Decoding process in the upper left
segment of Figure 1.5. The Decodability and Syllable factors both affect
the Pronunciation Measure, and strongly so. Regularly spelled one-
syllable words are mispronounced about one in six times, whereas
two-syllable words are missed almost half the time. Irregularly spelled
words, whether of one or two syllables, are mispronounced more than
two-thirds of the time. These data reveal effects on the Decoding process that are both statistically and practically important influences on
the rate of pronunciation errors.

Also shown in the panel is the standard deviation of the residual
scores for each factor, which is an index of the variability among
individual students in their response to the factor. Two-thirds of the
students will generally fall within one standard deviation on either
side of an average. For instance, easy words are missed about 30% of
the time, hard words are missed about 70% of the time, so the average
impact of the Decodability factor is 40% difference. The standard deviation (SD) for this factor is about 13%. Two-thirds of the students
will fall within 1 SD of the average difference of 40%. Thus, at the
lower bound, a typical student should mispronounce hard to decode
words about 27% more often than easy to decode words (average
difference minus standard deviation equals 40 − 13 = 27), and, at the
upper bound, a typical student should mispronounce hard words about
53% more often than easy words (average difference plus standard
deviation equals 40 + 13 = 53).

The next two panels along the diagonal contain additional factor
effects that are predicted by the model. Word Frequency and Concreteness both affect Word Definition skill. Sentence Reversibility and
Length have only negligible effects on Sentence Understanding. Students apparently read the sentences carefully with virtually complete
understanding.

Now let us examine the off-diagonal graphs, where the independent-process model predicts no effects. One set of findings stands in
noticeable contradiction to the model—Word Meaning factors affect
Pronunciation (top row, middle column). The effects are fairly large,
although somewhat smaller than the predicted effects of the Decoding
factors on Pronunciation. Word Familiarity also interacts with Decodability and Syllables. Rare words are more likely to be mispronounced,

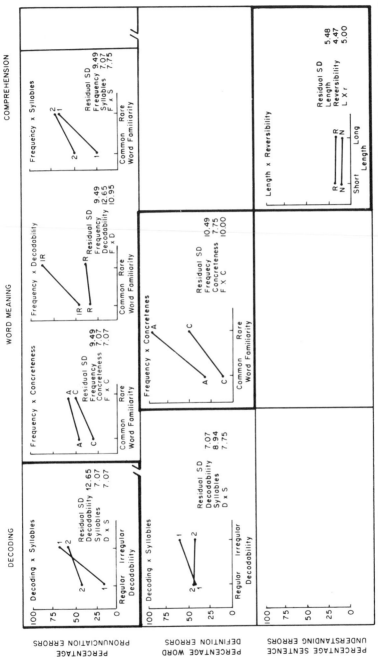

FIGURE 1.5. Results of Juel (1977) study, arranged according to multifactor–multimeasure plan. Residual standard deviation is shown for each source.

13

unless they have simple spelling patterns—the model predicts that Pronunciation should not be influenced, either directly or indirectly, by Word Frequency.

Looking over the results as a whole, the greatest departures from the predictions of the independent-process model are the strong effects of Familiarity and Concreteness on the Pronunciation measure. One might simply reject the model, but Juel considered instead the possibility that the model was appropriate for some students but not for others.

The critical data for testing this hypothesis were to be found in the relation between Reading Ability, the Familiarity and Concreteness factors, and the Pronunciation measure. Figure 1.6 shows the details of this relationship, where the findings are given separately for good and for poor readers.

The data in the panels on the main diagonal indicate that both good and poor readers are affected by the factors where the model predicts such effects. However, the unpredicted effects of Familiarity and Concreteness on Pronunciation occur mainly among the poor readers. Unfamiliar but regularly spelled words such as *sod*, *rig*, and *mole* are correctly pronounced by good readers. But poor readers have as much trouble with these words as they have with less regularly spelled words such as *squid*, *fiend*, and *grouch*. Good readers' Pronunciation is only slightly influenced by Familiarity. A plausible interpretation of this result is that when poor readers encounter difficulty in decoding words they rely on guesses based on inadequate spelling cues (word length, the initial letter). If a word is a familiar one, the guess may be correct. Unfortunately, it is harder to make good guesses when the word is rare and unfamiliar.

Putting these findings together, what can we say about the separability of processes in the sentence reading task? The more able readers appear to think in the manner described by the model. One can imagine conditions in which these students might adopt other reading strategies, but when careful and precise reading is stressed, these students perform the task as if by a set of independent, separable processes. These processes are those that appear as distinctive elements in many reading curricula. The less able readers, however, perform in a much more holistic fashion, especially in the decoding task. It is as if their translation of print to spoken language is complexly and ineffectively interwoven with other processes. One suspects that instruction for these students might also have been rather complicated. If students are encouraged to try phonics or to guess from context or to ask another student when they encounter words they cannot pronounce, the

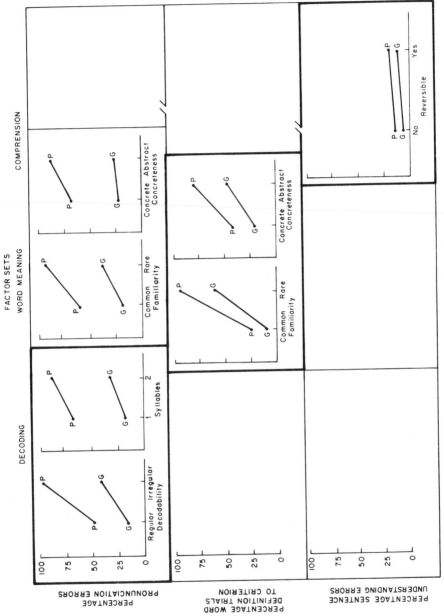

FIGURE 1.6. Results of Juel (1977) study for good (G) and poor (P) readers.

15

teacher may leave them thoroughly confused about effective word attack and word meaning strategies.

Juel's study also provides an opportunity to apply the additive technique for evaluation of the independent-process model. Each student was asked to read each sentence well enough to understand it, and the tester measured the time required to read the sentence. The prediction of the additive-factor model is that factors associated with different processes should not interact with one another.

Figure 1.7 shows that the findings for Sentence Reading Time support this prediction. All six factors have substantial inpact on Reading Time. These results are along the main diagonal. The off-diagonal panels display interactions contrary to those predicted by the model—for instance, Decodability with Familiarity, or Syllables with Sentence Length. These panels are all empty—none of these effects were large enough to warrant attention.

INDEPENDENT PROCESSES IN PROSE COMPREHENSION

In the preceding section, we focused on prerequisite skills in reading—word attack, word meaning, and sentence-level grammar. In this section, we address the application of the independent-process approach to the understanding of larger chunks of written material—paragraphs and stories. The emphasis is on the experimental design and instrumentation of studies for evaluating an independent-process model of comprehension. The purpose is not to present data for or against the model; our intent is to illustrate an approach to developing and evaluating such a model.

A Brief Review of Comprehension Research

A substantial amount of research on comprehension has been conducted during the past decade under the information-processing banner (e.g., Anderson, Spiro, & Montague, 1977; Just & Carpenter, 1977; Lindsay & Norman, 1972; Norman & Rumelhart, 1975). This approach attempts to describe the activities (processes) that mediate the exchange of information between a person and a message, often by analogy to the operations of digital computers.

Much of the research has been conducted with college-level materials, tasks, and subjects—the findings apply with safety to the skilled adult reader working under laboratory conditions. In the typical prose recall study, students are asked to read a passage, and some time later are tested for recall. They may be asked simply to recount the passage, or a more elaborate probing procedure may be used.

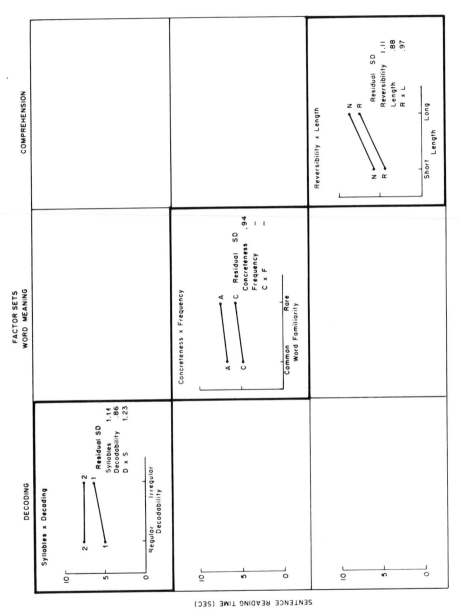

FIGURE 1.7. Additive factor analysis of Sentence Reading Time. (From Juel, 1977 study.)

The research suggests a number of general conclusions. We learn that competent readers recall mainly the substance of a passage—the textual base (Kintsch, 1976a), or the hierarchical structure (Meyer, 1975, 1977). Omissions and distortions increase with passage length (Cofer, 1941; Gomulicki, 1956) and with the amount of time between the original reading and the test (Kintsch, 1976b, 1977; Perfetti & Goldman, 1974; Sachs, 1967). At longer time intervals, the gist of the text is more likely to be recalled than the details (Kintsch & van Dijk, 1978).

A fuller understanding of specific characteristics of passage recall has been made possible by developments in case and text grammars. The analysis of semantics and syntax is conjoined in these grammars. "The case notions comprise a set of universal presumably innate concepts which identify certain types of judgments human beings are capable of making about such matters as who did it, whom it happened to, and what got changed [Fillmore, 1968, p. 24]." Case grammars specify relations that may exist among sentence constituents (Anderson, 1971; Fillmore, 1968, 1970). Text grammars treat paragraphs as concatenations of sentences (Grimes, 1975; Petöfi & Rieser, 1973; van Dijk, 1977). They serve to categorize relations that may exist among sentences in a passage.

To deal with the understanding of higher level organization of prose, psychologists have called upon a broader theory of comprehension based on the notion of frames (Minsky, 1975), scripts (Schank & Abelson, 1977), macrostructure (Bower, 1976; Kintsch, 1977; Kintsch & van Dijk, 1978), and schemata (Anderson, 1977; Rumelhart & Ortony, 1977). A prose type that has received considerable attention from researchers in this area is the *story*. The story, or narrative form, is one of the most commonly occurring frameworks for communication appearing in conversation, in television, and in fiction.

It is believed that through repetition of similar sequences of experiences, events, or actions, the individual abstracts a framework or "stereotype" of how stories are organized (Thorndyke, 1977). This framework comprises a set of related categories or slots to be filled by specific objects or events in a particular story. Researchers have proposed various grammars to represent the story. The details vary, but the grammatical structure of the prototypic story generally includes an introductory *setting*, one or more *episodes*, and a *resolution*. Each episode is further divided into a *beginning*, in which a problem is posed, a *reaction* by the character to the problem, an *attempt* to deal with the situation, and an *outcome* of the attempt.

Research on story grammar shows that passages that conform to the prototypic story grammar are easier to recall than passages that are incomplete or jumbled (Glenn, 1978; Mandler, 1978; Stein & Nezworski, 1978; Thorndyke, 1977). Furthermore, readers appear to construct an interpretation of a story to fit culturally determined notions of what is most sensible in a particular situation. When a story departs from cultural expectations, distortions are likely to occur (Bartlett, 1932; Kintsch & Greene, 1978; Mandler & Johnson, 1977). We also know that, although children recall fewer propositions from a story than do adults, the recall of story elements resembles the pattern of adult recall. Children's recall, however, is more adversely affected when a story deviates from the standard grammar (Stein & Glenn, 1978).

A Model of Text Comprehension

It is most usual to view comprehension as a complex tangle of interrelated operations. LaBerge and Samuels (1974) suggest that "the complexity of the comprehension operation appears to be as enormous as that of thinking in general [p. 320]." This definition strikes us as unworkable, and we agree instead with Kintsch and van Dijk (1978):

> As long as one accepts this viewpoint, it would be foolish to offer a model of comprehension processes. If it were not possible to separate aspects of the total comprehension processes for study, our enterprise would be futile. We believe, however, that the comprehension process can be decomposed into components, some of which may be manageable at present, while others can be put aside until later [p. 364].

In our opinion, the existing research provides the basis for describing comprehension as a small set of separable processes. We think that, with suitable design and analysis, it is possible to identify a set of comprehension processes that operate in a functionally autonomous fashion. In this section, we describe the application of the independent-process approach for evaluating a simple model of reading comprehension.

Figure 1.8 displays a model of the independent processes in text comprehension, with subsidiary processes discussed in the preceding section (i.e., decoding, word knowledge, sentence grammar). In essence, we are proposing that text comprehension entails two independent processes—microanalysis and macroanalysis. Microanalysis handles detail, and macroanalysis operates on structures at the discourse level (Kintsch & van Dijk, 1978, have made a similar proposal about the information processing of text). The decomposition of such a "complex" system as comprehension into only two processes may

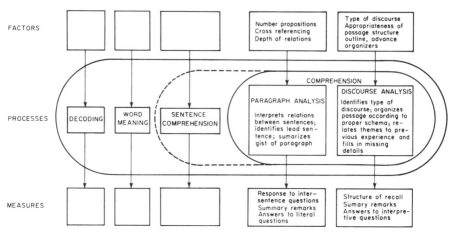

FIGURE 1.8. *Independent processes in text comprehension.*

seem a gross oversimplification. However, we think that the hypothesis is consistent with available findings (cf. Kintsch & van Dijk, 1978), is robustly testable, and has significant implications for both theory and practice. We acknowledge that other comprehension processes besides the two being proposed may come into play (e.g., inferential processes), and we are certain that these two can be decomposed further. Nonetheless, postulating the independence of the macro- and microanalysis processes is a strong hypothesis in its own right. Simple models like the one shown in Figure 1.8 provide the necessary empirical and theoretical foundation upon which more complex models can be built.

Let us describe briefly what we envisage as the operation of the two text comprehension processes as a basis for selecting factors and measures. Macroanalysis is the process for detecting the thematic structure of a text, for organizing the details of the text according to this structure, for linking previous experiences to the theme, and for guiding the reproduction of the text during recall. This process leads the student to identify a text as a narrative, rather than as an expository passage, and thus to use knowledge of story grammar to organize information from the text in memory.

Microanalysis is the process for untangling and reweaving the web of details within the primary structural elements of a text. In a passage of any complexity, the syntactic and semantic relations within each element comprise a complex network. Sorting out the threads is the task of the microanalysis process, which works primarily at the sentence and paragraph level. The operations may be idiosyncratic to the paragraph, guided by the local associative and referential cues. For instance, within a sentence, the student must figure out who or what performed the action, what the action was, when and how it took place, and so on. Answers to these questions require implicit knowledge of a case grammar. Between sentences within the paragraph, it is important for the student to be able to identify the referents of pronouns and definite articles (who is "he," which boat was "the boat," and so on); to focus on the topic sentence to make sense of the paragraph; and to search out the multitude of cues that allow the student to link the sentences into a meaningful whole. These tasks require implicit knowledge of something like a text grammar.

The concept of a two-stage analysis finds support in several places in the literature. As noted earlier, it parallels quite closely the recent analysis of Kintsch and van Dijk (1978), who also point to factors likely to influence each of these processes, and to their potential independence (cf. p. 392). Kintsch and van Dijk restrict themselves to narrative prose, where they can call upon the relatively extensive research on story grammars to identify macrostructural factors. Their discussion of microanalysis research, especially studies of the effects of variation in propositional factors, is quite detailed and comprehensive. We mentioned some of the findings from story grammar research earlier. Relatively little research is to be found on other types of discourse structures. To be sure, the texts on rhetoric discuss various types of prose models (Levin, 1978), and psychologists have investigated the comprehension of certain kinds of descriptive–topical passages (Frase, 1969; 1973; Friedman & Greitzer, 1972).

The taxonomy of structural models for prose remains largely undeveloped. Recently, one of our colleagues, Robert Curley, suggested that the author's treatment of a topic may be a key to the underlying discourse structure—the topic may be treated as an *event*, an *object*, or an *idea*. Events require sequential, historical accounts. Narratives are specific instances of this treatment. Objects require attributive accounts. The examples here include most of what we think of as "descriptive" writing. Ideas are forms of argument, logical or analogical. Expositions that aim to persuade are part of this genre, along with other forms of abstract essays. This taxonomy is sketchy, but it seems to us to be a useful guide in otherwise uncharted territory. It may be possible to identify optimal structures for each of these treatments, and to generate appropriate grammars to handle them.

Evaluation of the Two-Stage Comprehension Model

A serious evaluation of the two-stage model of text comprehension requires that the student read a series of passages, each incorporating variations in factors associated in turn with the macro- and microanalysis stages. After reading each passage, the student is tested by a multi-stage procedure that allows separable measurement of each process.

Arranging the multifactorial variations for each process is relatively straightforward. Kintsch and van Dijk (1978; also cf. Kintsch, Kozminsky, Streby, McKoon, & Keenan, 1975) have proposed some factors that appear to be quite robust. Most of the factors on their list apply to the microanalysis process. Among the relevant factors are propositional density, propositional complexity, number of unique propositional arguments, and clarity of anaphoric reference. We think that a macrostructural variation of especial significance might build upon the differences between event, object, and idea treatments of the same topic. Within a particular treatment (e.g., narrative–event structure), three factors that we would expect to influence the macroanalysis process include the completeness of the discourse grammar, the typicality of familiarity of the grammar, and the appropriateness of relational markers between elements of the grammar (e.g., temporal links for event structures, spatial markers for object structures, and logical connectives for idea structures).

In any event, it seems to us relatively simple to specify factorial variations that correspond to macro- and microanalysis of prose. A more difficult task is to measure the processes in a separable fashion. One possibility is to use a free recall task, such as the one that we have used to assess comprehension as part of an individually administered reading test (Calfee & Calfee, 1979).

Figure 1.9 shows a passage used to test story comprehension at an early level of skill, about halfway through first grade. Shown beside the story is a structural analysis of the passage. The analysis has two parts that correspond to the macro- and microlevels of the story. The headings in the center column are the elements of the narrative grammar. To the right is the breakdown into a propositional analysis.

This simple story consists of a single episode, along with the setting and resolution. The propositional analysis, which shows the syntactic–semantic relations within each element represents the microstructure for that element. From the listing, one gains an idea of the number of propositions, the complexity or embedding of propositions, and the amount of cross-referencing from one element to another.

The student reads the story (or listens to the story if his decoding skills are poor) and is then asked to recall the story. The analysis of the recall protocol is arranged in two levels. First, a sequence number is recorded by each story element according to the order in which the element is first mentioned. For instance, suppose the student says, "Tom wanted to play ball with Bob, but Bob wanted to ride his bike."

Story analysis		Text	Propositional analysis	
Setting	1	The sun is out.	Sun is out	X
Initiating event		Tom wants to play ball.	Tom wants play	X
			play ball	X
		He asks Bob to play with him.	Tom asks X₁	—
			X₁ = Bob play	X
			play with Tom	
Development	2	Bob is on his bike.	Bob is on bike	—
		He will not play ball now.	Bob will not play	X
			play ball	X
			play now	—
Reaction	3	Tom is sad.	Tom is sad	X
Attempt		He asks Bob, "Can we take a ride and then play ball?"	Tom asks X₂	—
			asks Bob	X
			X₂ = X₃ then X₄	—
			X₃ = take a ride	X
			X₄ = play ball	—
Outcome		"Yes," says Bob. "It is fun to ride and play."	Bob says X₅	—
			X₅ = X₆, X₇, and X₈	—
			X₆ = Yes	—
			X₇ = ride	—
			X₈ = play	—
Resolution	4	So Tom goes home to get his bike.	Tom goes	X
			goes home	X
			goes to get bike	X
			bike is his	X

Episode

FIGURE 1.9. Macro- and microstructural analysis of simple one-episode story.

23

This protocol approximates the narrative sequence, with a few elements deleted. The numbers on the solid lines in the center column of Figure 1.9 show how the student's recall is recorded with reference to the macrostructure. At this level of analysis, the amount of detail in the mention of an element is disregarded. The main criterion is the degree to which the student recapitulates the thematic elements of the story and the ordering of that recapitulation as temporal organization is basic to the narrative form.

The *microstructural analysis* is then recorded by checking off those propositions in each element that were actually mentioned by the student. In Figure 1.9 we have shown how we would record the propositions in the preceding example. This example should be taken with a grain of salt; we have not attempted a formal analysis here. However, whenever recall is abbreviated or paraphrasic, we suspect that some degree of subjective judgment is entailed. Several systems have been developed for handling propositional analysis of prose, and for the scoring of protocols (e.g., Grimes, 1975; Kintsch & Vipond, 1977), and these references may be consulted for technical details.

Figure 1.10 presents an example of an object treatment. The passage follows a model typically found in the social studies and in science. A general characteristic is postulated, substantiated by a series of specific attributes. We do not have much systematic data on the comprehension and recall of such passages, but a number of informal observations reveals what appears to be a common pattern of results. We find that students often cannot reproduce the basic structure of passages like the one appearing in Figure 1.10. The statement of the

---

The cat has greater endurance than other animals of similar size. Although its bones are light and small, the cat is tough and solidly put together. It has about 230 bones and more than 500 voluntary muscles. Its spine is flexible, with 48 vertebrae, including its tail, which has between 18 and 21 vertebrae. It can leap several times its body length—up and forward at the same time.

A cat salesman would be sure to point out the equipment included in the model: retractable claws, about 30 whiskers that help the animal sense its surroundings in the dark, 30 teeth, eyes with protective membranes and vertical pupils that increase in size for better vision in near darkness, and a raspy tongue for self-grooming.

A cat can quickly get itself out of trouble. Sometimes it has to use psychological warfare: hissing, snarling, arching its back, and raising its hair until it looks twice its size. A cat's ability to emerge a winner accounts for its legendary nine lives.

FIGURE 1.10. *Example of object treatment in prose passage consisting of general characteristic and substantiating attributes.*

general characteristic is frequently left out. Recall tends to focus on the first and last attributes mentioned in the passage, on the concrete elements, and on exceptional details. If there is a structure to the recall, it is often best described as an attempt to fit the information into a narrative format.

The similarity between recall protocols from expository passages like the one shown in Figure 1.10 and those obtained from paradigmatic studies of short-term verbal memory is striking. The amount of information recalled is relatively small and is forgotten within a relatively short time. Primary and recency effects are apparent, as is remembrance of striking and unusual detail. When there is no guiding structure the student must rely on the limited capacity "tape recorder" memory.

Such a pattern of findings might well be expected. Few reading programs train the student to identify and make use of prose models. The emphasis in many curricula is on literal comprehension—the memorization and recollection of detailed facts and simple relations. Students, when asked direct questions of this sort, are provided the cues needed to give a reasonable answer. One can respond to literal questions without necessarily having a well-organized store of knowledge. The free recall task, which teachers are not trained to use, gives a more sensitive portrayal of the student level of comprehension. Under this condition, the student who lacks a structural framework to guide systematic retrieval of information can produce only the "first things that come to mind."

The separability of the two processes we have proposed as fundamental to text comprehension remains to be established—we know of no published research that bears directly on the model. The work of Kintsch & van Dijk (1978) is supportive, but it does not provide a clear test of the independence of the two processes. We have proposed factors that are good candidates for separable effects. The separability of outcomes is more problematic, although we think that the analysis of recall protocols along the lines we have suggested is quite workable. We expect the conditions of presentation (listening, oral reading, silent reading) and of testing (free production, probe recall, recognition) to have separable effects on the two processes. We are currently undertaking studies that will provide some evidence about the applicability of the model. We suspect that it will undergo considerable revision over time. The important point, however, is not whether it is right or wrong; the value of the model is its role in simplifying what is an otherwise overwhelming task—the design, analysis, and interpretation of research on reading comprehension.

Conclusions

We have explored two applications of independent-process analysis. Juel's (1977) study suggests that, under certain conditions, more able readers perform as though their minds operate in the clockwork fashion represented by the model. In a sense, this finding should come as no surprise—several reading curricula are designed to produce just this result. Under conditions stressing careful reading and comprehension, the capable student should behave as he has been taught. When the conditions stress speed over accuracy, skimming over studying, then a different model may be called for. An appropriate "high speed" model may also be quite systematic, or it may describe a jumble of thought—it depends on how the student has learned to think under these circumstances.

Independent-process models are inherently simple, much too simple to comprise completely adequate descriptions of any behavior. However, psychology is beset with complicated models. We think that the concept of separable processes provides the basis for constructing normative models that are testable, and that provide the foundation upon which more complex ideas may be built. We find the Juel study encouraging in that it demonstrates that one can establish conditions under which the individual student performs a nontrivial task, and the results can be described by a parsimonious model.

The key to the independent-process approach is design. Having specified the processes underlying performance on a task, the researcher must then plan how to vary factors associated with each process in a well-controlled fashion. The notion of achieving experimental control in real-world settings may seem to be "pie in the sky," but engineers, agricultural researchers, and medical scientists have succeeded in accomplishing this job in the past few decades. Educational tests, on-the-job training, opinion surveys, and simulation tasks all represent situations in which human performance can be measured under controlled variations to gain insight into the nature of underlying cognitive processes. Snow (1974), among others, has called for research with greater ecological validity. We agree with this call, and believe that the designs generated by independent-process theory represent a response to the challenge.

On the practical side, teachers and other practitioners are overrun with extensive lists of reading objectives. These lists tend to be relatively disorganized and undisciplined. What shall be the names for the various "strands"? How does one decide which strand is the proper assignment for an objective, or whether to divide it and put the pieces into two strands, or perhaps to combine it with another objective? What is a reasonable level of detail for stating an objective? Despite various "how to" books on the writing of objectives, it is clear that we lack guidance in specifying objectives for reading instruction.

We think that the concept of independent processes in reading, and research based on this concept, are likely to provide guidance in organizing reading instruction. Separate strands make sense only if we can identify the nature of the cognitive processes that are engaged by those strands, if we can influence by instruction and context the operation of those processes, if we can state a set of appropriate measures of the outcomes of the instruction, and if we can demonstrate the separability of the strand from other strands. If this application of the independent-process concept proves workable, we will have indeed realized Gibson and Levin's (1975) adage that "nothing is so practical as a good theory."

References

Anderson, J. M. The grammar of case: Towards a localistic theory. London and New York: Cambridge Univ. Press, 1971.

Anderson, R. C. The notion of schemata and the educational enterprise. In R. C. Anderson, R. J. Spiro, & W. E. Montague (Eds.), Schooling and the acquisition of knowledge. Hillsdale, New Jersey: Erlbaum, 1977.

Anderson, R. C., Spiro, R. J., & Montague, W. E. (Eds.). Schooling and the acquisition of knowledge. Hillsdale, New Jersey: Erlbaum, 1977.

Bartlett, F. C. Remembering: A study in experimental and social psychology. Cambridge, Eng.: The University Press, 1932.

Bower, G. H. Experiments on story understanding and recall. Quarterly Journal of Experimental Psychology, 1976, 28, 511–534.

Calfee, R. C. Sources of dependency in cognitive processes. In D. Klahr (Ed.), Cognition and instruction. Hillsdale, New Jersey: Erlbaum, 1976.

Calfee, R. C., & Calfee, K. H. Interactive reading assessment system (IRAS) (rev.). Unpublished manuscript. Stanford, California, 1979.

Calfee, R. C., & Drum, P. A. Learning to read: Theory, research, and practice. Curriculum Inquiry, 1978, 8(3), 183–249.

Calfee, R., Spector, J., Piontkowski, D. An interactive system for assessing reading and language skills. Bulletin of the Orton Society, 1979.

Cofer, C. N. A comparison of logical and verbatim learning of prose passages of different lengths. American Journal of Psychology, 1941, 54, 1–20.

Fillmore, C. J. The case for case. In E. Back & R. T. Harms (Eds.), Universals in linguistic theory. New York: Holt, 1968.

Fillmore, C. J. Subjects, speakers, and roles. Working Papers in Linguistics. (Tech. Rep. 70–20). Ohio: Ohio State University, Computer and Information Science Research Center, 1970.

Frase, L. T. Paragraph organization of written materials. *Journal of Educational Psychology*, 1969, *60*, 394–401.

Frase, L. T. Integration of written text. *Journal of Educational Psychology*, 1973, 65(2), 252–261.

Friedman, M. P., & Greitzer, F. L. Organization and study time in learning from reading. *Journal of Educational Psychology*, 1972, *63*, 609–616.

Gibson, E. J., & Levin, H. *The psychology of reading*. Cambridge, Massachusetts: The MIT Press, 1975.

Glenn, C. G. The role of episodic structure and of story length in children's recall of simple stories. *Journal of Verbal Learning and Verbal Behavior*, 1978, *17*, 229–247.

Gomulicki, B. R. Recall as an abstractive process. *Acta Psychologica*, 1956, *12*, 77–94.

Grimes, J. E. *The thread of discourse*. The Hague: Mouton, 1975.

Juel, C. L. *An independent-process model of reading for beginning readers*. Unpublished doctoral dissertation, Stanford University, 1977.

Just, M., & Carpenter, P. (Eds.). *Cognitive processes in comprehension*. Hillsdale, New Jersey: Erlbaum, 1977.

Kintsch, W. Reading comprehension as a function of text structure. In A. S. Reber & D. Scarborough (Eds.), *Proceedings of the Symposium on Reading*, Brooklyn College, March 1974. Hillsdale, New Jersey: Erlbaum, 1976. (a)

Kintsch, W. Memory for prose. In C. N. Cofer (Ed.), *The structure of human memory*. San Francisco: Freeman, 1976. (b)

Kintsch, W. On comprehending stories. In M. A. Just & P. Carpenter (Eds.), *Cognitive processes in comprehension*. Hillsdale, New Jersey: Erlbaum, 1977.

Kintsch, W., & Greene, E. The role of culture-specific schemata in the comprehension and recall of stories. *Discourse Processes*, 1978, *1*, 1–13.

Kintsch, W., Kozminsky, E., Streby, W. J., McKoon, G., & Keenan, J. M. Comprehension and recall of text as a function of content variables. *Journal of Verbal Learning and Verbal Behavior*, 1975, *14*, 196–214.

Kintsch, W., & van Dijk, T. A. Toward a model of text comprehension and production. *Psychological Review*, 1978, 85(5), 363–394.

Kintsch, W., & Vipond, B. *Reading comprehension and readability in educational practice and psychological theory*. Paper presented at Conference on Memory, University of Upsala, 1977.

LaBerge, D., & Samuels, S. J. Toward a theory of automatic information processing in reading. *Cognitive Psychology*, 1974, *6*, 293–323.

Levin, G. *Prose models* (4th ed.). New York: Harcourt Brace Jovanovich, 1978.

Lindsay, P. H., & Norman, D. A. *Human information processing: An introduction to psychology*. New York: Academic Press, 1972.

Mandler, J. M. A code in the node: The use of a story schema in retrieval. *Discourse Processes*, 1978, *1*, 14–35.

Mandler, J. M., & Johnson, N. S. Remembrance of things parsed: Story structure and recall. *Cognitive Psychology*, 1977, 9(1), 111–151.

Meyer, B. J. F. Identification of the structure of prose and its implications for the study of reading and memory. *Journal of Reading Behavior*, 1975, 7(1), 7–47.

Meyer, B. J. F. The structure of prose: Effects on learning and memory and implications for educational practice. In R. C. Anderson, R. J. Spiro, & W. E. Montague (Eds.), *Schooling and the acquisition of knowledge*. Hillsdale, New Jersey: Erlbaum, 1977.

Minsky, M. A. A Framework for representing knowledge. In P. Winston (Ed.), *The psychology of computer vision*. New York: McGraw-Hill, 1975.

Norman, D. A., & Rumelhart, D. E. *Explorations in cognition*. San Francisco: Freeman, 1975.

Perfetti, C. A., & Goldman, S. R. Thematization in sentence retrieval. *Journal of Verbal Learning and Verbal Behavior*, 1974, *13*, 70–79.

Petöfi, J. S., & Rieser, H. *Studies in text grammar*. Dordrest, Holland: D. Reidel, 1973.

Rumelhart, D., & Ortony, A. The representation of knowledge in memory. In R. C. Anderson, R. J. Spiro, & W. E. Montague (Eds.), *Schooling and the acquisition of knowledge*. Hillsdale, New Jersey: Erlbaum, 1977.

Sachs, J. S. Recognition nemory for syntactic and semantic aspects of connected discourse. *Perception and Psychophysics*, 1967, *2*, 437–442.

Schank, R., & Abelson, R. P. *Scripts, plans, goals, and understanding: An inquiry into human knowledge structures*. Hillsdale, New Jersey: Erlbaum, 1977.

Snow, R. E. Representative and quasi-representative designs for research on teaching. *Review of Educational Research*, 1974, *44*, 265–292.

Stein, N. L., & Glenn, C. G. An analysis of story comprehension in elementary school children. In R. Freedle (Ed.), *Multidisciplinary perspectives in discourse comprehension*. Norwood, New Jersey: Ablex, 1978.

Stein, N., & Nezworski, T. The effects of organization and instructional set on story memory. *Discourse Processes*, 1978, *7*, 177–193.

Sternberg, S. Retrieval from recent memory: Some reaction-time experiments and a search theory. Psychonomic Society, Niagra Falls, August 1963.

Sternberg, S. The discovery of processing stages: Extensions of Donders' method. In W. G. Koster (Ed.), *Attention and performance II*. Amsterdam: North-Holland, 1969.

Thorndyke, P. W. Memory for narrative discourse. *Cognitive Psychology*, 1977, *9*(1), 77–110.

van Dijk, T. A. Macro-structures, knowledge frames, and discourse comprehension. In M. A. Just & P. Carpenter (Eds.), *Cognitive processes in comprehension*. Hillsdale, New Jersey: Erlbaum, 1977.

2

S. Jay Samuels
Peter Eisenberg

A FRAMEWORK FOR UNDERSTANDING THE READING PROCESS

Comprehension is a process that requires the translation of written language into a form that is usable by the reader's cognitive system. It requires the integration of that information into the network of existing knowledge stored in the reader's long-term memory system. At the risk of oversimplification, one can say that the ease and extent of comprehension is related to the degree to which there is a match between the incoming information from the text and the knowledge and information stored in the reader's mind.

Any model that can describe the comprehension process fully would have to take into account a great number of the cognitive faculties available to the human mind. It would also have to deal with the many different types of information that may be available and useful to the cognitive system during reading. Perhaps even more important is that the model would have to be able to describe the complex interactions that occur between these faculties and sources of information. It is these interactions that enable the reader to perform the large amount of cognitive information processing that must occur in a normal reading situation.

The purpose of this chapter is to give the reader a perspective on how one might first approach the problem of modeling the reading process; and, second, how one can apply aspects of such a model to the teaching and development of reading skills. What follows is by no means a model of the reading process, per se, but is more a framework that specifies what some of the factors involved in the process of

NEUROPSYCHOLOGICAL AND COGNITIVE
PROCESSES IN READING

comprehending text are; it describes some of the relations between these factors, and gives an overview of how parts of the cognitive system involved in reading might be modeled. To set up this framework, we will use some of the theoretical notions of other researchers along with some of our own ideas about how to put the parts of the process together.

Although it is impossible to give a truly comprehensive account of the reading process, it is useful to attempt to bring together some ideas about the parts of the process that have been modeled in near isolation from the other components. For example, a word recognition model may be described without describing how the decoded words are comprehended in semantic memory, or a text comprehension model might be given that does not deal with the difficulties of decoding visual information into some usable form. Each of the models of the component processes of reading as well as models of word recognition and models of comprehension are important and give us a great deal of information. Our attempt here will be to see how this information can fit into a framework for modeling the reading process as a whole.

There is a danger, however, in trying to describe the reading process as a whole. In the past, comprehensive descriptions of the reading process have attempted to explain so much that they suffered from the serious flaw of being untestable. The partial models, on the other hand, sacrificed comprehensiveness, but they were testable. Thus, the partial models were altered as new information became available so that the models more accurately reflected nature. Like the inventor who may put together a series of components to form a new system, we will be putting together several partial models that we hope will help us to gain a better understanding of the reading process as a whole.

In putting together these different notions, we will try to relate the component parts to two main ideas that are possible to overlook when dealing with an isolated part of the system. One is stressing the interactive nature of the components and the sources of information upon which they operate. In fluent reading, no part of the process works completely independently of the others. Information does not flow through the system in a simple serial fashion. The other idea is that of relating the component parts of the process to the primary goal of reading, which is comprehension. Comprehension of text is implied in any fluent reading situation. All of the parts of the process are ultimately working toward this goal. The interaction of components and their relationships to comprehension are essential elements in any description of the reading process.

This framework of the reading process will begin with a listing and brief description of some of the factors that are involved in fluent reading. Included in the list are factors that are external to the reader, such as the physical characteristics and subject matter of the text, and factors that are internal to the reader, such as the depth and breadth of the reader's stored information. It will be shown how these factors can relate to comprehension and how the factors that are internal and external to the reader interact.

Following this description of factors influencing comprehension, we will present a modified version of the LaBerge–Samuels (1974) model of reading. Like all models of the reading process, this model has its weaknesses. A weakness of the LaBerge–Samuels model is its lack of description of the comprehension process. Gough's (1972) reading model also suffers in this way. Although there is a detailed explanation of how the visual stimuli from print are transformed, there comes a point in the processing where the transformation has to be understood, and it is at this point that Gough resorts to magic, calling upon *Merlin* and *tpwsgwtau* (the place where sentences go when they are understood). In the not too distant past when these models were devised, our knowledge of comprehension was too meagre to venture a guess as to the nature of that process, but during these last few years, enough progress has been made regarding the nature of text processing that we can be brave enough to venture what one might call a first approximation. Thus, we are able to utilize the earlier models and add to them what we have learned about comprehension to describe the nature of the reading process in a more comprehensive manner.

This description of the reading process must be able to take the information that has been translated from its written form and must be able to integrate some part of it into a network of already stored information. This system must provide for those higher level comprehension processes like syntactic analysis and inferring. Some recent notions of how these processes might operate will be described and fit into the framework.

The last section of the chapter will give a brief account of how we might use such a framework in applying our knowledge of the reading process to education. At some point in the development of reading skills, the emphasis on single isolated components will reach a point of diminishing returns. At this point, it is necessary to know how these parts of the process interact in building up fluent reading skills.

Factors Influencing Comprehension

Fluent reading is an extremely complex process. Much of this complexity is due to the large number of factors that feed into and affect the process. These factors that influence the process range from the ambient illumination of the reading environment to the abstract reasoning ability of the reader. We will give a brief description of the more important factors involved in fluent reading. We can classify these factors into two broad categories: those that are external to the reader, such as the amount of illumination, and those that are internal to the reader, such as the kinds of information the reader processes. As will be seen, these internal and external factors are not independent of each other. To specify the real effect of any one of these factors in a normal reading situation, it would be necessary to know how it interacts with all of the other factors involved. At this time, it is nearly an impossible task to describe all of these interactions, although such a description will eventually be needed for any complete model of the reading process. We will describe here how these factors might show themselves in a simple situation, and also give examples of how interactions between these factors can more fully describe the reading process.

External Factors

PHYSICAL CHARACTERISTICS OF THE TEXT AND ENVIRONMENT

There are a number of physical characteristics of text materials and the reading environment that can affect the reading process. These include illumination of the text, orthography, size of the print, and format of the text.

Obviously, we need a certain amount of light to read. In reading isolated characters or words, an optimum level of stimulus light intensity can be determined using recognition latency tasks. This optimum level is not as meaningful when dealing with a normal reading situation or even when dealing with single word recognition when the words are presented with some amount of contextual information (Becker & Killion, 1977). In normal reading situations, the intensity will have small or no effects on recognition time or reading when it is within a fairly broad, moderate range of values. This will hold true for other types of physical degradation of stimuli, such as placing words in a field of random lines or dots (e.g., Meyer, Schvaneveldt, & Ruddy, 1975). The negative effect of degrading stimuli seems to be reduced when contextual information is given with the stimuli to be read. Thus, the fact that text has been degraded will not matter much to a fluent reader in a fairly normal, moderately illuminated reading situation. It may, though, have an effect on the inexperienced reader who cannot yet use contextual information as readily as can the good reader.

The size, style, and legibility of print can have an effect on reading speed. There are optimum type sizes that may vary with the experience of the reader. A relationship probably exists between the optimum size of type for an individual reader and the amount of information that can be dealt with during a single eye fixation. Coordinating size, spacing, and stroke width enhances legibility of print, but, within moderate ranges, will not affect fluent readers much, although it can influence a beginning reader (Tinker, 1966). In general, nearly all common typefaces are equally legible to the experienced reader (Tinker, 1966).

Other physical characteristics contribute to a factor we refer to as text format. This would include things like column width, page size, and margin size. A novel and a newspaper look very different and can produce differences in the way each is read. For instance, the narrow column width of a newspaper will cause the reader to make fewer fixations per line of print but will require more line shifts than the same amount of material covered in the usual format of a novel.

Information given from the gross physical character of the text can be used in determining how the material is going to be read. If people use different types of strategies for reading different types of text material, then any information that can be ascertained about the text may be useful in deciding on and implementing a particular strategy. For example, one's strategy for reading a newspaper may be to skim very quickly over most of the material until something of interest is found. The features of the text format can tell readers whether or not they are going to be reading a newspaper. This information can then feed into any kind of strategy decision-making process the reader may go through. In many cases, this particular type of information can be evaluated before the actual reading of the text begins.

In general, physical characteristics of a text can affect the speed of reading, the nature of eye movements, and the overall reading strategy implemented. For fluent readers with normal text materials, interference caused by changes in physical variables will not occur over a fairly wide range of values. These variable changes will have a greater effect on less experienced readers or in situations where nonnormal reading materials are provided (such as for contextually unrelated strings of words). Any facilitation that can be derived from the gross physical characteristics of a text should be seen more with experienced readers who have learned how to use this information to their advantage.

READABILITY—STYLE

A second group of external factors are those that influence the readability of text materials. *Readability* will be defined here as the linguistic ease with which a text can be comprehended. Many readability formulas have been derived during the past 50 years, but they are nearly all based on correlational data, giving us little information as to what really makes a text difficult or easy to understand (Kintsch & Vipond, 1978; Smith & Dechant, 1961). These formulas use measures such as word length, word frequency, sentence length, and number of syllables per word. These factors can be measured simply and objectively and are fairly highly correlated with reading speed and scores on comprehension tests. However, the factors used in the readability formulas cannot tell us why texts having the same readability levels may vary widely in the degree to which they can be comprehended. We must look at the text characteristics from a more theoretical standpoint and search for those factors that have a real effect on the cognitive processes involved in reading a text. We must also take the individual reader into consideration, bringing in influences from factors that will be discussed more in the section on internal factors.

The following are brief descriptions of some of the more important external factors that theoretically will affect the readability or comprehensibility of text materials.

Word Frequency. One should be wary of treating word frequency purely as an external factor. For any individual, it is not just how many times the word has been seen, but the circumstances of seeing it, and how that word has been represented in memory, that will determine any kind of frequency effect. Over a population, one might generalize and say that the more frequently a word is in print the greater the chance that it has been read and encoded by an individual. Taking this reasoning another step, it might be postulated that the more times a word has been read, the greater the chance that it has been processed in a way that will facilitate subsequent recognition of the word. If word frequency is going to be used as a measure, it should be remembered that this last step may not follow for individual words or for individual readers. The generalization made will only be usable over a population of words presented to a population of readers. Given that all other factors are equal, including individual reader and word characteristics, a statement might be made that a text with a higher average word frequency count will be easier to read than one with a lower average.

Sentence Construction. Very similar or identical ideas can be presented in syntactically different ways. Sentences or groups of sentences can vary in construction and length and convey the same meaning. Sentence length has been used in a number of readability formulas as a measure of the difficulty of sentence construction. Again, this is just a correlational measure. For modeling purposes, one needs to determine why it is easier to convert some surface forms into a representation of their meaning than it is others. Any description of this process will have to account for the effects of two important internal factors, that of the knowledge base of the reader related to the content of the material and the linguistic competence of the reader.

In a normal reading situation, the conversion from surface to deep representation does not take place in isolation. The nature and amount of contextual information present can make the task more or less difficult. Changing the form of a sentence can make its meaning less ambiguous and comprehension easier even though the new form might intuitively be judged as syntactically more difficult when presented in isolation. Sometimes a longer and syntactically complex sentence can express the same meaning as two shorter, simpler sentences, but be able to do it in a more efficient, easier to understand manner (Pearson & Johnson, 1978). It is possible that people set up strategies to handle different syntactic styles. If this is the case, any abrupt change in style, even if it is to an intuitively easier form, might be disruptive to the reader and make comprehension more difficult.

There are limits to the complexity of syntactic structure that can be used before comprehension processes break down. We are limited by the immediate processing resources of the cognitive system and also by lack of experience in dealing with such structures. For example, in the following sentence, we can only keep track of the embedding up to a point, beyond which the sentence can turn into what seems like a string of unrelated words: *The red ball the little girl the boy kissed liked was stolen.* In summary, there is no easy way to describe the effects of sentence construction on comprehension. We must know many other things about the text material and the reader to give a causal description of its effects on overall readability.

Another factor that will influence ease of comprehension is the use of referring terms or, as they are also called, *deixis*. The four types of deitic terms are sources of confusion, especially to the beginning reader.

1. *Person deixis* may create problems in understanding when passages contain first- and second person pronoun substitutions of the *I, you, my,* and *your* type. For example, "Bill said to John, 'Come over to my house tomorrow.'"
2. *Time deixis* may create problems when the passage contains temporal references such as *the next day* or *before he entered the castle.*

3. *Place deixis* may create problems when locational references such as *under, behind,* or *inside* are made.
4. *Discourse deixis* may create problems when third person pronouns stand for things in a passage such as "Give *this* to *them.*" Unless children are given explicit instruction on how to interpret these deitic types, these referring expressions may continue to create confusion for many readers.

Density of Propositions. An important variable in comprehension is the number of ideas presented in a given length of text. Kintsch (1974; Turner & Greene, 1979) analyzes text material by breaking it down into idea units, or propositions. A proposition contains a relation with one or more arguments, where an argument is a concept represented by a word or group of words, and a relation gives predicate information (how the argument is being used or acted on). An example from Kintsch (1974) would be in representing the sentence *George hit John* as the proposition (*hit, George, John*), where *hit* is the relation and *George* and *John* are agent and object arguments respectively. This is a simple case where there is only a single proposition in the sentence. The sentence *George apologized for hitting John* contains two propositions, with one embedded in the other, and would be represented as (*apologize, George,* (*hit, George, John*)) where the proposition representing *George hit John* serves as one of the arguments for the proposition with *apologize* as the relation and *George* as an agent argument. By breaking down text in this manner, it is possible to get a measure of the number of ideas that a reader will encounter in the text. Kintsch and Keenan (1973) have shown that people have a harder time understanding text that has a large number of propositions for a given length of text. The reason is that there is a greater amount of relevant or important information entering the cognitive system in a densely packed text than in a loosely packed one. The resources of the system will be taxed to a greater degree by this density factor, making comprehension more difficult.

Overall Text Construction. This factor deals with how the text, as a whole, is organized. This includes the coherence of text from word to word or proposition to proposition up to a text's conformity with common text grammars. Coherence of the elements of a text is one of the most important aspects of readability. One proposition should lead into or be related to the next. One sentence should lead into the next one. Consecutive paragraphs should have some common thread between them. Kintsch, Kozminsky, Streby, McKoon, and Keenan (1975) have studied coherence at the propositional level and, as might be expected, have found that texts containing consecutive propositions with shared arguments are easier to read than are those containing unconnected propositions. The redundancy of words and ideas provides for continuity between consecutive pieces of text. This finding should easily extend to larger elements of text such as paragraphs or even chapters of a book.

Another way to provide organization to a text is by the use of titles, chapter headings, section headings, and other advance organizers, such as outlining a section of text in an introduction. These organizers provide useful contextual information to the reader. This information can be used to prime or prepare a part of the reader's knowledge base that can facilitate the integration and understanding of the text to follow. This, of course, assumes the existence of some stored representation of the information in the reader's mind. The extent of the reader's knowledge base is an internal factor that interacts with this notion of advance organizers. It will be discussed in a later section.

One other general text factor is that of the conformity of the text to common text grammars. A text grammar represents a common syntax used for writing a particular type of text. Examples are the story grammars that have been the object of some recent research (Mandler & Johnson, 1977; Stein & Glenn, 1978). For different types of stories, different rules are followed or certain elements are used to describe the flow of action in the story. For instance, in some types of fairy tales there will be a heroic knight who will save a beautiful princess and they will live happily ever after. Some version of these elements will be found in an example of that class of story. The action will follow one or another path from a set of common paths. The fact that a story follows a common route cannot by itself have an effect on comprehension. Once again, it depends upon what the reader knows. With some experience, a reader will have some representation of such a grammar stored in one's knowledge base. When reading such a story, one will come to expect to see the elements and action organized according to the rules of the story grammar. The further the story deviates from the rules, the less predictable it will be, and the less contact it will have with the part of the knowledge base currently being used to interpret the story.

Text grammars can be constructed for nearly any type of text material and can be at any level of detail. By constructed, we mean constructed in the mind of the reader. We can derive the nature of these grammars in a number of ways including the analysis of recall data, as was done in much of the story grammar research, and perhaps also from introspective accounts. For instance, Figure 2.1 shows a text

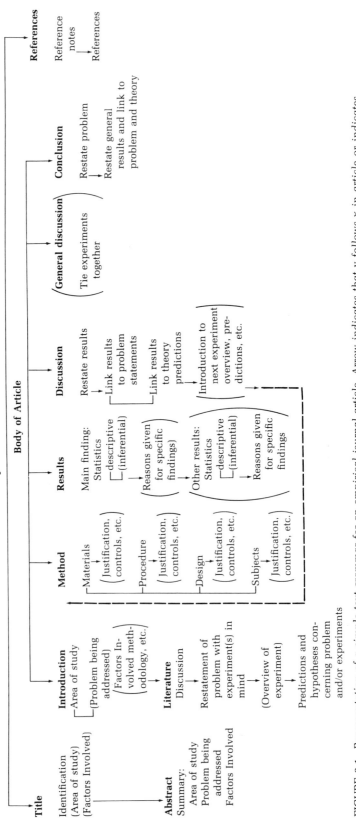

FIGURE 2.1. Representation of a simple text grammar for an empirical journal article. Arrow indicates that y follows x in article or indicates iteration in multiple experiment articles; brackets indicate that order of x and y may vary between articles; parentheses indicate optional section or variable between articles.

grammar of a typical article published in an experimentally oriented psychology journal. This example shows the reader's expectations of specific elements and their order. If these elements are not found, or are found in unexpected places, there will be some interference with comprehension. This explanation brings us into consideration of the reader's knowledge base, an internal factor that plays an important role in comprehension of psychological journal articles.

There are other factors that can influence the readability of a text. A list of 16 factors compiled by Smith and Dechant (1961, p. 251) follows:

1. Word length and frequency
2. Percentage of different words
3. Sentence length
4. Personal references
5. Number of syllables
6. Number of pronouns
7. Number of affixes
8. Number of prepositional phrases
9. Number of difficult words according to word lists
10. The use of simple or complex sentences
11. Density and unusualness of the facts
12. Number of pictorial illustrations
13. Interest and purpose
14. Concept load—abstractness of words
15. Organization of the material and format
16. Interrelationship of the ideas

Most of the factors discussed are included here with correlational factors commonly used in readability formulas. We would like to stress again that these factors cannot be examined in isolation. They all interact with each other and with other external and internal factors in influencing the reading process. The only factors that are really useful in modeling this process are those that can be used to explain the workings of the system rather than those that can only be correlated to any of various reading measures.

CONTENT AREA OF THE TEXT

Whereas the factors described under the heading *Readability* affect the linguistic difficulty of a text, other factors influence the content difficulty. The subject matter or content of a text is of critical importance in the comprehension of it. At least three factors determine content difficulty. The first is the specific subject area itself. This cannot really be considered an external factor because its effect is almost entirely dependent upon the reader's knowledge base. The more a person knows about a particular subject, the easier it will be for him to assimilate new information about it from reading. As with text grammars, the reader has stored representations, or schemata, of some organized knowledge about the particular content area. The closer the text material fits in with what one knows, the easier it will be to understand.

A second external factor is that of the generality of the material. The same subject matter can be presented in a broad general manner by specifying the most important aspects of the area or by giving summary information about an area. This is in contrast to a very detailed, specific account of the material. For example, an introductory college text on perception might describe the events of neural transmission of information in a very general way, giving the reader a good enough idea of how it occurs. It is only detailed enough to give readers the information they need to understand how sensory signals can travel through the body. On the other hand, a text on physiology, written for the same type of reader, will give a very detailed, step-by-step account of the process. The inherent difficulty of comprehending either text may be the same, but the level of specificity used to describe the subject matter is very different. Chances are that the physiology text will be more difficult, but the cause of this difficulty is more likely to be the result of the density of propositions of this specific text compared to the more general one.

A third content factor is that of the abstractness of the material. In most cases, a more concrete presentation of a subject area will be easier to understand than an abstract one. Reasons for this may be that representations of concrete concepts are easier to grasp and to use, and that fewer inferences and other cognitive strategies need to be implemented to integrate the more concrete information. This will not always hold, though. Something written at a very concrete level can lose readability and coherence, especially to a fluent reader familiar with the content area. Also, some things require explanations given in abstract terms or can best be described abstractly or metaphorically. At this point, we cannot specify a measure of abstractness or an optimal level of abstraction to use. Once again, any measure would have to take into account other factors such as the specific content area, the reader's knowledge base, and also the abstract reasoning ability of the reader.

THE EXTERNAL GOAL SET

The last external factor is that of the goal set imposed on the reader from an outside source. For example, instructing a person to read for detail, as opposed to reading for an overview, produces large differences in rate of reading. Other examples of an external goal set occur in school or work settings where the reader is instructed to read something because he will be tested on it or because he will have to give a report on it. Obviously an external goal is not a necessary input to the reading process. If an external goal set is imposed, its effect will be a function of how it is interpreted when the reader forms an internal goal set.

Internal Factors

THE KNOWLEDGE BASE

Internal factors are those that can be accounted for by the content and activity in the reader's mind. The contents of the reader's mind, or the knowledge base of the reader, interacts with nearly all of the external factors described earlier. It is the storehouse of information needed to interpret what is read and contains the means for performing these interpretations. In other words, the knowledge base of the reader includes both the *propositional knowledge* and the *procedural knowledge* needed to manipulate the propositional knowledge stored in the reader's memory.

Propositional Knowledge. Propositional knowledge is knowledge of the things in our world and in our minds. These things range from very simple physical features of objects in the world to very abstract concepts that may only exist in an individual's mind. In reading, the type of information needed runs the gamut from simple perceptually based representations to high-level cognitive schema information. At the lower end are representations of simple features that would be needed to construct letters. These primitive representations are probably not normally used by experienced readers. There is much evidence to suggest that experienced readers have stored perceptually based representations of whole letters. Instead of having to construct letters from features while they read, they only have to access this whole letter information, cutting down on the processing resources required for the task.

The recognition system of experienced readers appears to go beyond the efficiency of processing just letters with perceptually based representations. There is strong evidence that familiar groups of letters, whole words, and perhaps even short common phrases may be represented in a similar manner. Beyond this point, we probably do not have perceptually based representations of linguistic information. There are two factors that contribute to making this assumption. One is that we can only form perceptual representations of those things that we see frequently appearing as a whole unit. Although we may see the individual words in a longer phrase many times, the number of times that we see the whole phrase is low. The second reason is that we can only have a perceptually based representation of information that can enter the system, clearly resolved, in a single fixation. Anything that needs more than one fixation to be seen must be perceptually coded in parts, instead of as a whole unit.

Of course, we cannot go very far in comprehension with just perceptually based representations of letters and words. We need some form of semantic information linked to these representations. This may be in the form of specific meanings, associations to other stored representations of words or concepts, or associations to representations of episodic or schematic information.

By a concept, we mean a collection of semantic information that may represent the meaning of a word or a number of different words. A single word may be connected to a number of different concepts, one of which will be used depending upon the context. To be able to select which concept to use we need some way to represent the current context in which the word is being interpreted. This type of information can be represented in schemata, which we define as organized groups of concepts. Schemata represent things that we have experienced within the world. "They exist for generalized concepts underlying objects, situations, events, sequences of events, actions, and sequences of actions [Rumelhart & Ortony, 1977, p. 101]." The word generalized is important. That is, schemata do not represent single instances of information (actions, events, etc.), but contain information that is common to or generalized from experience with that information.

One example of a schema can be taken from Schank's (1975) work. He refers to schemata as scripts. He represents scripts of everyday situations on a computer so that they can be used by cognitive processing simulation programs. One of these scripts is the restaurant script frequently cited in psychology literature. Schank specifies the characters that might be included in a restaurant script: the customer, waitress, chef, and cashier. We know that restaurants provide hungry people with food and provide wages for people that work there. We know what sequence of events to expect when going to a restaurant. Upon entering a restaurant, one finds a table and sits down. Then, a menu is obtained. We look at the menu and decide what to order. We convey the order to the waitress; the waitress conveys the order to the chef; the chef prepares the food; the waitress obtains the food, serves it, and ultimately we eat. Furthermore, a sequence for leaving includes: asking for a check, leaving a tip, going to the cashier, paying the bill, and departing from the restaurant.

This schema is an action-oriented one. It is one that serves computer programs quite well. More descriptive information can also be included, so that restaurants are identified as places with tables and chairs or where waiters wear uniforms. Schemata can exist at all levels of complexity or completeness. After going to an amusement park once or twice, you may have some ideas of what to expect the next time, but your expectations could not be as complete and detailed as those of the person who goes to one every week. The experienced person may not use all that information, but it is there and available if it is needed. In this case, the too-detailed schema may not be as much fun if surprise is an important element in going to amusement parks! In most situations, however, the more information we have, the better we can cope.

An important characteristic of schemata is that more than one can be invoked concurrently (Rumelhart & Ortony, 1977). Any one schema will most likely not have all of the information in it that might be useful to any particular situation. If schemata did contain all possible useful information, they would have to be much too large, or contain too many concepts for a person to handle with a resource-limited processing system. A more efficient way to organize the information would be to store only that information that is peculiar to a particular situation in a schema and to allow for other schemata containing information that might be usable in a number of different situations to be used concurrently. For example, the restaurant schema described earlier would not have information that might be useful if you ordered fried chicken. From your experience in eating fried chicken, you have a separate schema built up around this activity. The information contained in it might include things about how messy chicken can be and ways of eating it politely. Another example is that your restaurant schema contains the information that you have to pay for your meal, but does not tell you anything about using a check to do this. In such a situation it would be useful to use the information stored in a separate check-writing schema.

Because schemata are generalized knowledge and because they can be embedded within one another, we must specify that they can accept variable information in parts of their organization. The types of variables that may be required can range from needing a single word to complete the organization to needing another fairly extensive schema to fill a space in the original schema. In our restaurant schema, there is the information that we must pay for the meal, but there might be a variable slot that would represent a method of payment. A number of separate schemata may fit into this slot, including payment by cash, credit card, washing dishes, or, by check.

Schemata are idiosyncratic. For any particular situation, people will have schemata that are based on their own experiences. One person's experiences will be different from another's in both variability and extent, which will affect both what goes into the organization and ease of access to the schema. For example, the more a person performs an activity, the more specific will be the details stored in the schema, and the easier it will be to gain access to the schema from memory. A person with a lot of experience in an activity in which many things may vary would be more likely to build up a very flexible schema. This schema would lack specific details and would contain a number of variable slots.

Another factor in building up an individual's schema involves the rest of the knowledge base. A schema is not constructed in isolation of what else is known by the person. There is no reason to represent a lot of knowledge in a particular schema if that knowledge is stored elsewhere in a manner that can be used concurrently with that schema. For example, if a person is able to both drive a car and ride a bicycle, there is much overlapping information for each activity that needs only to be stored in a schema (e.g., a schema for dealing with stop signs) that can be used for either situation. For the bicycle rider who does not drive a car, this same information may be included in a bicycle riding schema. If the bicycle rider learns to drive a car, this information may then become more general to both situations rather than be stored again within a car driving schema. This is a rather obvious type of example. It is likely that any type of knowledge we already have can affect the building and restructuring of schemata. Even for the most common situations, there should be at least subtle differences in the ways that individuals organize the information contained in their own schemata.

Schemata have two very important roles in fluent reading. The first is to provide some organization to the information that will be used in understanding the text. This organization can provide structure for a detailed set of factual information or can provide as general an organization as that from a stored representation of a text grammar. To read as fast as we do, it is necessary to have this organization in some previously stored and easy to retrieve form. Otherwise the reader would have to structure all this information as an on-line operation, a process that can be painfully slow and can use up a great deal of available cognitive resources. In reading, we want to expend this energy on placing new text information into the networks of our previously stored schemata.

The second important role of schemata is that of providing information not given by a text. This type of information is assumed by the writer to exist in some form in the reader's mind. This means that we must make inferences when we read—we must make use of information that is not given, and we must get this information from memory. For instance, if we are given the information that a person went to a restaurant, paid the bill, and left, we will infer that a number of other things took place in this episode. We will infer that this person ordered food, had it served, and ate the food. This information has come from memory and would have to have been stored in some organized fashion along with the given information in order for the inferences to have been made. This organization is in the form of a restaurant schema.

Procedural Knowledge. If all of the information we had available were in the form of propositional knowledge, and if we only had a simple recognition mechanism that could inform the system when a match between text and the knowledge base occurs, we would not be able to get very far in actually understanding that text. Even if this matching of information could go a step further by activating information highly associated with what was recognized, we would still be at a loss to comprehend the text. To be able to analyze and integrate text, or any other form of language, we need a way to go beyond these simple forms of activating the various parts of our stored knowledge base.

The means for going beyond this simple form of activation is contained in parts of the knowledge base that we will refer to as procedural knowledge. Procedural knowledge is used to gain access to information not given directly from the text. This is essential at all levels of processing information. The printed representation of an unfamiliar word does not give explicit instructions as to how it should be decoded. Nor does an allegorical story give a detailed account of its symbolism. In both cases, we must go beyond the text information, and we need a way to select which indirect information should be retrieved.

At lower levels of processing, we need some method for consolidating individual elements into higher order units. For example, one can construct a word from a series of recognized letters or letter clusters. This type of decoding process is essential, especially in dealing with unfamiliar or uncommon words. This is the normal case with beginning readers. For these readers, the accessibility and use of the procedural information needed for blending individual letters into words may be a conscious experience that requires a considerable amount of attention. For the fluent reader, the activation of the same type of decoding procedures will be automatic. Although the actual decoding of the unfamiliar word may require some attention, the activation of the decoding procedure may not require any attention.

One form of higher level procedural knowledge includes the tools for parsing the results of the lower-level recognition and decoding processes. The sentences formed by the decoding words cannot be matched directly to some already stored propositional information. The inefficiency of storing whole sentences as propositional knowledge is obvious (except perhaps for special purposes such as memorizing the lines of a play). A bigger problem is caused by the fact that nearly anything we read or hear will be novel to us. It would be impossible to have any kind of stored, complete representation for this incoming information. We have to be able to parse the incoming text. The rules and heuristics needed to perform this analysis are stored as procedural knowledge. We can think of this knowledge as being in the form of programs that are activated as needed for particular situations. These programs set up syntactic frameworks to accommodate upcoming text information, and then verify that this information fits into the set-up structure. Reconstructing the framework and verification occurs constantly as new text is read.

When we perform this parsing process, we are going beyond the information given directly by the text. Although recognition of a word might activate associated information that might convey some semantic information or might label the word as a particular part of speech, this is not enough to comprehend strings of words held together by syntactic relationships. Procedural knowledge that represents syntactic processes contains the means of relating the elements of a group of words in a way that it becomes useful to the system in its ultimate goal of comprehending the text.

Syntactically parsed representations of text serve the system only if some meaning can be derived from the combination of words just analyzed. Again, the recognition of words may activate associated information representing a meaning of the word or even other words and meanings that are associated with it, but this is not necessarily enough to make the text understandable. We need a form of procedural information that can take these meanings and associations and relate the information to other currently activated information or to other stored information that must now be activated. In short, we must go beyond the semantic information given directly by the text. We must have a form of procedural knowledge that can make inferences or indirect activation of stored knowledge. Again, this type of information will be activated as a function of the current input and state of the system. We can extend this type of knowledge to include any representation of the processes we use for problem solving, abstract reasoning, and other high-level cognitive tasks. The basis of these processes are procedures that can assess the current context or state of the system, and be able to activate other, possibly distantly related, parts of the knowledge base that would be relevant to the current situation.

The distinction we have made between propositional and procedural knowledge is mainly descriptive. These types of knowledge are probably not completely separable. Concepts, plans of action, words, and other entities can all be represented in some form in our minds. These representations are, for the most part, the result of experience. We can activate and make use of these representations as a result of the current incoming information and current state of the system.

COGNITIVE RESOURCES

A second internal factor is that of the cognitive processing resources available to the reader. In simple terms, this would be the amount of cognitive energy or attention available within a unit of time. In terms of the previously discussed descriptions, it could be the extent of the knowledge base (propositional and procedural parts) that can be kept in an active, usable state over a unit of time. Another term that may be used for this is attentional capacity.

What we consider to be cognitive energy is a more basic thing. It is, in part, an innate aspect of the system, but it can also be changed to some extent by both long-term and immediate environmental factors. Examples of these might be illness or just simply fatigue. It seems obvious that we cannot think as well late at night when we are physically and mentally exhausted as we can during a "good" hour of the day. There is some evidence that processing resources do not even increase much after the first few years of life. This means that the apparent changes seen with development are those caused by an increase in the extent and efficiency of the organization of the stored information available to the system.

The LaBerge–Samuels Reading Model

We have described a number of factors that are important to consider if one is to model the reading process. The descriptions of the various factors give an indication of how each factor will interact with any number of other factors. What is missing is an overall organizational framework with which we can give a more coherent, procedural account of how these factors fit into the reading process.

There are a number of benefits in trying to account for these factors in a single model, or at least a framework for modeling the process. Some of the complexity of dealing with a large number of different components and factors can be eliminated by placing them in a single organization. This simplification will help in understanding the process as an entity. We should be able to make well-formed predictions because we have a better overall understanding of how the system might be organized. If the model is to be truly useful, we should be able to test these predictions. We can then evaluate aspects of the model and either keep using it in its present form, modify it, or throw it out in favor of a different one. Any model that is adopted should have some practical implications. It would be useless if we could not apply what we have learned from the modeling process to some real-world setting. This is especially true in dealing with a task as prevalent and important for everyday living as reading is.

Our intention in this chapter is to present a framework for modeling the reading process rather than to give a single specific model. Successful presentation of a complete specific model is a formidable task, beyond the scope of the present paper. It is hoped that this framework will show an organizational theme and give an idea of the direction we are going in constructing more specific models of the process.

To present this framework, a short description will be given of an earlier model postulated to explain some aspects of the reading process. From there, we will show some of the shortcomings of this model in line with accounting for the factors just described. Then we will give examples of how we can pick up where this model leaves off to give a broader based account of reading. This is where the idea of a framework is important. The extentions described are, at this point, not as detailed and specific as a true model should be, but only give a good idea of the type of approach we think it will be necessary to take to achieve the ultimate goal of adequately modeling the whole process. The last section of the chapter will go a step further than this by describing potential practical implications of such an approach.

The LaBerge–Samuels (1974) model of automatic information processing in reading is shown in modified form in Figure 2.2. As seen in this figure, there are five main components labeled VM, PM, SM, EM,

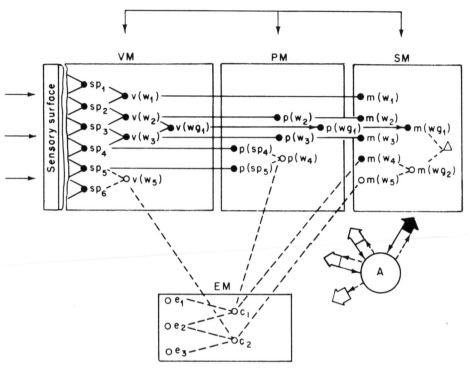

FIGURE 2.2. *The Laberge–Samuels model of automatic information processing in reading, showing feedback loops.*

and A. These symbols stand for *visual memory, phonological memory, semantic memory, episodic memory,* and *attention,* respectively.

Attention

Because attention lies at the heart of the model, this component will be described first. The model assumes that attention is required to derive meaning, and that the amount of attention that any individual possesses for processing text is limited. This does not mean that the amount of attention one has is limited to some finite amount and once it is used up it is gone forever, but rather, for any given interval of time, there seems to be a limit to the amount of attention we have available. In other words, attention is a renewable resource but at any given moment there is a limit to how much attention is available for text processing.

As there is a limit to the amount of attention available over any unit of time for comprehending text, attention, like any other scarce resource, must be allocated with care. How attention is allocated during reading is important if we are to understand this necessary aspect of the reading process.

To understand how attention is used in reading we must consider two tasks we perform when we read. These two component tasks are decoding and comprehension. By *decoding* we mean visually analyzing the printed word either with or without articulatory, phonological, or semantic representation of the word. By *comprehension* we mean deriving meaning from the material we have decoded.

Both decoding and comprehension require attention. How much attention is required depends upon a number of factors. For example, the amount of attention required for decoding depends on the skill of the reader as well as the reader's familiarity with the words in the text. The amount of attention required for comprehension depends upon factors such as the number of propositions or ideas contained in a sentence as well as the degree to which the ideas presented by a writer are matched by the knowledge contained in the reader's head. Thus, we see that both decoding and comprehension require attention and the amount of attention required varies with the reader's decoding skill, familiarity with the words in the text, as well as the topic and density of idea units found in the text.

For the beginning reader, decoding the text is a difficult task. Consequently, the combined demands of decoding and comprehension may exceed the limited attention capacity of the student. When the combined demands from these two essential tasks exceed the student's attentional capacity, the tasks cannot be performed simultaneously. To overcome this apparent impass, the beginning reader uses a simple strategy, namely that of attention switching. First, attention is used for decoding. After decoding is done, attention is switched to the comprehension task. This alternative switching of attention from decoding to comprehension is similar to the strategy used by beginning students of a foreign language who first go through a novel written in the foreign language translating all the difficult words and then rereading the text in order to understand it. In beginning reading, the switching of attention allows the student to comprehend but it comes at a cost. Attention switching is time consuming, puts a heavy demand on short-term memory, and tends to interfere with recall.

With practice, there is a transition from the attention switching characteristic of the beginning stage to the skilled stage where attention switching is not required. The skilled stage occurs when the decoding task can be performed with little or almost no attention. When almost no attention is required, we can think of the student as being automatic at the decoding aspect of reading. The skilled reader who is automatic at decoding can do two things simultaneously—decode and comprehend—whereas the beginning reader who is nonautomatic, can do only one thing at a time, either decode or comprehend. The reason the skilled reader can do two things at the same time is that the decoding task requires so little attention that nearly all of the available attention can be allocated to the task of comprehension. Consequently, attention switching is not necessary in fluent reading.

It would be wrong to think, once the skilled reading stage was reached, that all decoding would be automatic. There are several special circumstances that require additional amounts of attention. For example, when words are encountered that are rare or unfamiliar, or when words are printed in an unfamiliar orthography, additional amounts of attention are required for decoding.

Having explained the differences between how attention is allocated by beginning and by skilled readers, one additional point needs to be made, which is that attention can be allocated in a variety of ways. If, for example, a skilled reader is proofreading a manuscript, then attention may be directed on spelling patterns while ignoring meaning. If one is looking at a handwritten manuscript to see if it is legible, attention may be directed at the distinctive features of each letter. If one is reading a text for a fast general overview, attention would be directed at meaning, while spelling errors would probably go unnoticed. Depending upon the skill of the reader and the kind of task undertaken, attention can be directed at distinctive features embodied within letters, at each letter as a unit, at the spelling patterns within words, or at the entire word itself. This freedom to allocate attention to visual units that vary in size from individual letters to the whole word or to put a major portion of attention on meaning rather than on decoding suggests that, for the skilled reader at least, there is no fixed pathway that must be followed to process a text.

Visual Memory

As seen in Figure 2.3, it is at the visual memory component that the visual stimuli from the printed page are processed. Exactly what size unit is selected for processing, whether it is a distinctive feature, letter, spelling pattern, or word, depends upon several factors such as the reader's skill, orthographic features such as familiarity, and purpose for reading.

As Figure 2.3 shows, stimuli from the sensory surface of the eye can be represented at any one of several levels. Thus, stimuli from letters could be analyzed into distinctive features, represented by f_3 through f_8. For example, letters b, d, p, and q could be analyzed into verticals, circles, and a relational dimension such as up–down and left–right. Letter b would be represented as a vertical element with a circle on the lower right, whereas letter d would be represented as a vertical with a circle on the lower left. It is highly probable that noting the distinctive features of letters is an early stage in letter recognition.

With practice, the distinctive features would be unitized into a letter code, represented by ℓ in Figure 2.3. Thus, the student who is able to recognize letters with speed and accuracy sees the letter as a single unit and not as a set of distinctive features. In fact, as skilled readers, it is hard to imagine any letter of the alphabet in separate components because, with practice, the separate components are unitized or welded together. Of course, for purposes of analysis, we can separate the components, but that is not how we tend to see them.

Again, with sufficient practice and exposure to certain recurrent letter combinations, we begin to see them as spelling patterns. These spelling patterns are represented as sp in Figure 2.3. The recurrent patterns of letters would not be processed by experienced readers as separate letters but as a single visual unit. For example, recurrent

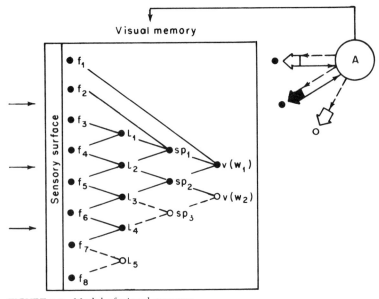

FIGURE 2.3. *Model of visual memory.*

spelling patterns such as *sch* as in *school, gh* as in *ghost, anti* as in *antiestablishment,* or the *ed* or *ing* in *jumped* and *jumping* would be processed as a single visual unit.

At still a higher level of organization, as seen in Figure 2.3, spelling patterns are combined so that the word itself is processed as a single visual unit. This is represented by $v(w)$ in the model of visual memory.

Before leaving the model of visual memory, several additional points should be made. Thus far, we have shown how visual stimuli from printed words can be processed at the distinctive feature, letter, spelling pattern, and word level. There are still two other routes to the word. As indicated by f_1, features such as word length, word contour, and the internal visual patterns (of one letter seen next to another one) may be used in word recognition. In words such as

fat and friend   pay and penny

we see how word length and contour may possibly serve as cues for recognition. As f_2 indicates, these may be a combination of letter cues as well as word length and contour cues that are used in word recognition as in

f⊏⊐ or p⊏⊐⟍.

These cues would be most useful when there is some context available as in

Because of overeating he became f⊏⊐
or
He was broke and down to his last p⊏⊐⟍.

Before leaving the visual memory component, for purposes of clarification, one important point should be made. This point relates to what some have wrongly interpreted in the LaBerge–Samuels model as an obligatory bottom–up hierarchy that one goes through from distinctive features, to letters, to spelling patterns, and finally to the identification of the word. These visual units that increase in size should not be thought of as representing an obligatory sequence. Because attention can be allocated in a variety of ways according to particular task demands such as fast reading for meaning as opposed to proofreading for spelling errors, skilled readers can process words using visual units that vary in size. Research on the size of the visual unit used in word recognition indicates that fluent readers use the entire word when it is a common word in regular orthography but when the word is in mirror image, they use letter-by-letter decoding strategies (Terry, Samuels, & LaBerge, 1976). In another study, using second-, fourth-, and sixth-grade subjects as well as college students, we found a developmental trend in the size of the visual unit used for word recognition (Samuels, LaBerge, & Bremer, 1978). The younger students were using component letter-by-letter strategies and, with increasing skill, the size of the unit increased so that by grade six the unit of recognition was the word. Another study demonstrated that when subjects had to process mirror image text, the size of the visual processing unit increased rather quickly within one testing session for words shown over and over, but there was no increase in the size of the unit for words presented only once (Samuels, Miller, & Eisenberg, 1979). In summary, then, the size unit one uses depends upon one's reading skill, the kinds of tasks being performed, and familiarity.

Phonological Memory

As seen in Figure 2.2 all the other components in the system feed information into phonological memory. It is assumed that phonological memory contains units that are related to acoustic and articulatory inputs. Although the presence of acoustic codes in a phonological system seems logical, one wonders why there would be articulatory codes. The reason is that in recent years evidence has been gathered to the effect that certain kinds of articulatory—motor responses made in programming a speech sound may also be involved in the perception of that sound.

The organization of codes in phonological memory is somewhat similar to the organization of codes in visual memory. The units in visual memory increase in size from the distinctive features to the word level. Similarly, the size of the units represented in phonological memory increases in size. The units in phonological memory include distinctive features, phonemes, syllables, and morphemes.

Phonological memory serves an important function in any system that attempts to explain how meaning is derived while reading. Its importance is underscored when one considers that phonological memory provides a mediating link between visual and semantic memory. In other words, whatever size unit is selected from visual memory for processing, it must be recoded and a counterpart found in phonological memory. For instance, the units in visual memory may be letters, spelling patterns, or words, and these would be recoded in phonological memory into letter sounds, syllables, or morphemes. Once the visual unit is recoded into a phonological unit, the phonological information is passed on to semantic memory where it is processed into meaning. Despite claims that skilled readers may be able to go directly from input to meaning without the need for a phonological recoding stage, there seems to be common agreement that beginning readers as well as skilled readers who are reading difficult text engage in phonological recoding.

Episodic Memory

Episodic memory is involved in the recall of specific events related to people, objects, location, and time. Information in episodic memory might well be organized around *wh* words such as *wh*en (time), *wh*ere (location), *wh*o (people), and *wh*at (objects). When we attempt to answer questions such as "Who was my first grade reading teacher?" or "What reading series did I use in first grade?" we are using episodic memory. There are special conditions under which episodic memory can be used in the reading process, as, for example, when a student uses a mnemonic such as the long word is *hippopotamus* or the word with the tail on the end is *monkey*. Obviously, this type of recognition strategy and the use of episodic memory, in general, is not a major factor in fluent reading.

Semantic Memory

Semantic memory is involved in the recall of general knowledge such as how to program computers, drive cars, or act in restaurants, regardless of whether they are fast food or high cuisine establishments. In a reading situation, semantic memory is used when we apply our knowledge of letter–sound correspondences and sound blending to decode unusual words or when we process text for meaning.

It is in semantic memory that our general information about the world is stored. At the risk of oversimplification, the comprehension process seems to work in the following manner. To make sense of what we are experiencing—or reading—we attempt to match the incoming information from outside the head with the knowledge stored in memory that is inside the head. To the extent that there is a good match between the two sources of information, we are able to comprehend and make sense of the world.

Feedback Loop

The model of information processing shown in Figure 2.2 has an important modification when compared with the LaBerge–Samuels (1974) model. The earlier model did not have a feedback loop from semantic to visual and phonological memory, whereas the present model does contain this change. This modification allows information contained in semantic memory to influence the manner in which information is processed in the earlier stages. For example, if the reader knows that the text topic is about precious jewels, and the reader has already read *Father cut the green*————, decoding the next word in the sentence may be simplified. Information provided by semantic memory would suggest that the next word is probably *emerald*. Thus, if there is a match between the first few letters of the word in print and the predicted word, instead of having to visually analyze the entire word, the reader would identify the word based on a partial perception. In this manner, the feedback loop allows information from a processing stage that occurs later in the system to influence the processing of information that occurs earlier in the system.

Semantic Memory Network

Since the LaBerge–Samuels (1974) model of reading was developed, we have increased our understanding of how knowledge is represented in memory and how we use this knowledge to make sense of our experiences.

Our knowledge base is stored in a memory network. This network contains representations of any kind of information, from low-level visual representations of letters to high-level procedural information of the kind used in abstract reasoning or problem solving. We will not specify any single mode of representing this information, because several of the notions postulated recently could fit into our network with some modifications.

It seems obvious that there is a great deal of complexity in the way that we store and remember the things we know about, and consequently, any representational scheme used for modeling this will be a simplification. Examples that can be given of such a representation will only cover a minuscule portion of the knowledge base and even this small domain cannot be accurately portrayed for any individual. For our purposes we will just use a simple idea of a network composed of nodes and links. The nodes of the network represent pieces or chunks of information. A node can be thought of as representing a concept. These nodes are linked to a large number of other nodes. For example, the concept "dog" includes the information: animal, warm blooded, feeds its young with milk, walks on four legs, barks, has fur, and Collies and German Shepards are examples. Embedded within the concept are still other concepts such as "leg," "mouth," and "eyes." Thus, a simple concept contains a network of other kinds of information that help to define the concept.

Because concepts are not necessarily single bits of information, they must represent a consolidation of information. One can think of this consolidation as being a group of nodes being bound so closely together that the group can be considered as being nearly the same thing as a single node. This consolidation would be brought about by a learning process, with the easiest example due to repetition of dealing with the element nodes concurrently. An instance of this type of learning is the case where the beginning reader sees the three letters *c, a,* and *t* a number of times until he gradually can process them all together as *cat*. In this case, nodes representing the letters have become tied closely enough together to form a single representation of the whole word. Similarly, the information contained in a schema might be represented as a fairly tightly bound network of concepts. Schemata may be thought of as the concepts underlying objects, actions, and sequences of actions. The essential characteristics of schemata are that they have: (a) variables or slots that have to be filled, much like filling in the defining characteristics of the concept "dog"; (b) schemata can be embedded one within the other as, for example, the concept "arm" includes other concepts such as "hand" and "finger"; and (c) schemata are abstract and generic rather than specific (Rumelhart & Ortony, 1977). Schemata representations also include procedural and relational information. For instance, in the restaurant schema, we might have concepts for *waiter* and *food*. We would also need an intervening node or concept that represents *serves* and perhaps also a node containing directional information making it clear that the *waiter*, not the *food*, *serves*.

A problem with any open-ended node and link network model is that it is too powerful to be properly tested. It would be a simple matter to explain anything we wanted to within such a system but it would be difficult to prove or disprove our hypothesis.

The Comprehension Process

Having described one notion of how knowledge is represented in semantic memory, it is important to describe the process one goes through in comprehending written discourse. As mentioned previously, we experience the "click" of comprehension when there is a match between textual information coming from outside the head and concepts stored inside the head. If this is true, it is likely that our ability to understand the ideas in a text, as well as our attitudes about this information is limited and colored, to a large degree, by the concepts already stored in memory. Thus, contrary to conventional wisdom, which states that comprehension is the process of getting meaning from a page, it is viewed here as an interactive process of bringing meaning to a text as well as getting meaning from the text. It is this process of bringing meaning to a text that accounts for the fact that the same text can be interpreted so differently by so many people.

Because comprehension entails a link-up between incoming information and knowledge stored in memory, one might inquire about the mechanism that guides this process. What we are trying to explain is the process that allows us to search through our memory network of concepts and schemata for the appropriate knowledge that will account for and make comprehensible the information coming in from the outside. To a considerable extent, it is the context and the environment surrounding the object, text, or event we are trying to understand that guides us in the search for concepts that will give meaning to our experience. For example, a textbook provides a variety of cues that facilitate this search through memory for appropriate concepts. On a desk is a book with the title *Educational Psychology*. Inside the cover is a "Table of Contents" listing topics including "Basic Processes in Infancy," "Curiosity and Exploratory Behavior," "Transfer," "Memory," and "Forgetting." Each of the chapters contains side headings in bold type indicating the major topics to be covered in that subsection, and many of the paragraphs in the book contain topic sentences that signal what kind of information will be presented.

Each of the contextual cues found in a textbook, ranging from titles to side headings, guide the reader in the selection of concepts that can be used to interpret what is being read. To illustrate this process with a simple case, the ambiguous sentence *The shooting of the hunters was terrible* becomes clear as soon as we add contextual cues such as *marksmanship* or *murder*. Still another example is the ambiguous sentence: *Reading teachers are novel lovers*. The critical word here is *novel* and the meaning is changed depending on whether we add a cue indicating that it is used as an adjective or as a noun. These examples illustrate that decontextualized sentences often appear to be ambiguous, and it is the addition of contextual cues that allows us to remove the uncertainty and interpret the sentence in a particular way. Similarly, it is through the addition of contextual cues found in a textbook that we are aided in the activation of those concepts and schemata that facilitate text comprehension.

Inference as a Basis for Comprehension

The difference between literal and inferential comprehension is that, with the former type, all the information requested is contained in the text, whereas, in the latter type, the information requested goes beyond the information contained in the text. For example, when given a sentence such as *John kicked Mary*, one can ask "Who kicked Mary" or "Why did John kick Mary?" The answer to the first question involves literal comprehension, whereas the answer to the second question involves inferential comprehension.

In this section, we would like to make two points: The first is that teachers are in error when they think that they can get an adequate measure of a student's comprehension when only literal questions are asked, and the second point is that even literal comprehension requires some degree of inference to understand the text.

Let us begin with the first point, which states that literal comprehension questions are not an adequate test of comprehension. Assume that a text states that *X pligumed Y for Z.* We can ask questions such as "What did X pligume?" (The answer is Y.) or "For whom was Y pligumed?" (The answer is Z.) or "When did this action take place?" (The answer is in the past.) All of these literal comprehension questions can be answered without a shred of real understanding of what is involved.

It is not until we ask some inferential questions that we realize that no real understanding of the nonsense sentence occurred. For example, when we ask questions such as "Where did the action probably take place?" or "What tools or utensils were used?" or "How did Y feel?" we discover that it is virtually impossible to answer these inferential questions with any degree of certainty about the truth value. Thus, the ability to answer literal questions does not necessarily mean that the student understood the text and that the ability to answer inferential questions may indicate if, indeed, there was any real comprehension.

The nonsense sentence *X pligumed Y for Z* can be changed to a meaningful sentence of the same syntactic form by stating that *Mother cooked breakfast for Bill.* Now we can ask inferential questions such as:

Question	Answer
Where was breakfast cooked?	Probably in the kitchen, but it could have been at a campfire if they were on a camping trip.
What utensils were used?	Probably a stove, pots, and pans.
How did Bill feel?	He was probably hungry and after eating he was not hungry.

It is the ability to make reasonable inferences that go beyond the actual information contained in the sentence that indicates that the student comprehended the text.

Our second point is that even the simplest type of literal comprehension requires that we engage in inferencing. The reason for this is that there is an unwritten contract between a writer and a reader—or, for that matter, between a speaker and a listener. This contract specifies that, as writers, we should provide no more information than the reader needs to make sense of what we are expressing. Thus, the writer must assess the potential audience and provide no more information than what is needed. To violate this contract leads to some problems. If we provide too much detail, the reader may become bored, the text seems redundant, and the author appears to be condescending. However, if we provide less detail than the reader needs, the text appears to be incomprehensible. Thus, the writer provides only as much detail as the reader needs and the writer relies on the stored knowledge of the reader to fill in the gaps left vacant in the text.

Let us look at two examples of inferring that we must engage in to fill in information gaps in the text. Although the sentence, *The hiker's carelessly dropped cigarette led to one of the worst fires in the state's history* is easily understood, it requires considerable inference to understand it. This inference is made possible by the rich network of associations that we have about key words such as *hiker* and *cigarettes*. For example, to comprehend this sentence, we have to make two assumptions, first, that the hiker was probably in a wooded area, and that we are describing a forest fire, and second, that the cigarette was lit. Both of these assumptions enable us to make sense of the sentence although neither fact was expressly stated.

The second example of how inferring is required in literal comprehension may be illustrated with a sentence such as *Mr. Smith drank a quart of vodka in less than an hour.* Although the sentence does not specifically state how this was done, we can make some highly probable guesses. Mr. Smith is a human being. Consequently, he probably used his arm, hands, and fingers to grasp a bottle, or the contents of the bottle, to bring the liquid to his mouth to ingest it. We also know the probable condition of Mr. Smith after drinking the vodka. Again, we must use our knowledge of what kind of liquid vodka is, as well as our knowledge of the physical capacity of human beings to ingest alcoholic beverages, to judge the probable condition of Mr. Smith. If we apply this knowledge, we assume that Mr. Smith is currently in poor health, and may well be at death's door.

Solving Practical Problems

Theoretical models of reading can serve a variety of useful functions such as providing a rationale for diagnosing reading problems, devising methods of instruction, and testing. This section will indicate some specific ways in which the ideas presented earlier can be used.

Automaticity theory may be used to diagnose certain kinds of common reading problems. For example, some teachers have observed that students may be able to recognize words accurately but may not be able to comprehend with ease. Teachers call this problem "barking at print." Automaticity theory would suggest that one possible reason for the student's problem is that the decoding is requiring too much attention and that the act of decoding is interfering with comprehension.

Another common problem one can observe occurs when skilled readers, often college students, claim that, even though they read the text with care, they cannot remember what was read. Because the students are skilled readers, the actual decoding of the words on the page can take place without much attention. Thus attention is free to be directed elsewhere. Instead of focusing attention on deriving meaning from the text and understanding and recalling the author's viewpoints, the students' attention wanders elsewhere, to matters entirely unrelated to the text. Thus the students decode the text but are thinking about that Saturday night date or misunderstandings with roommates.

These problems require quite different remedies. For students whose attention is on decoding rather than on comprehension, one solution is to give them a text that is easier to read. Another solution is to suggest that they read the text several times until the meaning becomes clear. This practice is often followed in beginning stages of reading. The first time or two, students read the text, emphasizing decoding. Once they are able to decode the words, the students switch their attention to meaning. A third solution is for the teacher to realize that more than accuracy is needed for students to become skilled readers. One must go beyond accuracy to automaticity. In human activities that require high levels of proficiency and skill, a considerable amount of time must be spent in practicing the skills leading to mastery. Only by spending a great deal of time in actual reading will the student develop beyond the level of mere accuracy. This practice may be directed toward important subskills in reading, but it must also include time spent on reading easy and interesting meaningful material. At one time, teachers felt guilty about having students spend time on a task at which the students had exhibited some minimal level of proficiency. What the teachers were afraid of was being accused of giving the students "busy work" assignments. Teachers should realize that to go beyond accuracy to automaticity in reading requires practice. So what may appear to be "busy work" to some is actually "automaticity training" to others. Time spent in reading simple meaningful material, however, is a good way to give the student the practice necessary for building the necessary skills for automatic decoding.

For students who are skilled readers but have poor recall, it is often helpful to explain that the poor recall is due, not to a memory deficit, but to lack of attention directed toward processing the text. Although the mere understanding of the nature of the problem is often helpful to the student, additional aid is frequently needed. To help students focus attention on text meaning, they should be taught how to engage in self-testing. Asking "What ideas were expressed on this page?" at the end of each page helps students in the areas of comprehension and recall.

The next suggestion grows directly out of automaticity theory. An interesting question is what can be learned about how to teach reading from areas of human performance requiring extraordinarily high levels of proficiency (e.g., music and sports). Both of these areas have similarities in training methods that differ from those generally used in reading. For example, let us compare the teaching of reading and music.

In music, the teacher may assign one or two pieces of music and tell the beginning student to practice these pieces for a week. The student's goal is to play the pieces accurately and fluently. Thus the student practices the same pieces over and over, trying to reduce errors and to blend the notes into a smooth rendition. A somewhat different situation exists in beginning reading. Although the goals in both music and reading are accuracy and fluency, the beginning reader is seldom encouraged to read and reread a passage until these goals are achieved. Instead, teachers tend to move many students too rapidly through the pages in the reading text before any degree of mastery has been reached.

For several years, we have been using a technique that we call "the method of repeated readings" with enough improvement in students' comprehension and reading speed to justify suggesting it here. It is not a total method, but is used in conjunction with whatever the ongoing reading method happens to be. Of course, many teachers will probably want to alter this method of repeated readings somewhat to fit particular classroom needs.

1. Have the student select a short reading selection that is neither so hard that the student cannot read any of the words nor so easy that the student can read it with high accuracy and speed.

The selection can be as short as 50 words or as long as 500 words, depending on the skill of the reader.

2. In addition to the reading selection, you will need a chart for recording word recognition errors and speed, as well as a stopwatch.

3. The student reads the selection aloud to a helper—a teacher, teacher aide, parent, or student tutor. The helper counts the number of errors and records the time in seconds. These data on errors and speed are put on the chart of each testing.

4. The student sits down again and rereads the selection until called to read again by the helper. It may be necessary to write the words the student cannot read on a sheet of paper and have the student study these words in addition to rereading the selection.

5. The testing–rereading cycle is repeated until the student can read the selection with some degree of fluency. It is *not* important to eliminate all word recognition errors, but it is important to have the student read the selection with fluency. When this goal is reached, a new selection is chosen and the process is repeated. The charts provide feedback to the student to indicate the rate of progress.

A useful modification of this technique is to have the helper dictate the story onto a tape recorder. While listening to the story on the tape recorder, the student is silently reading along. Then, as soon as possible, the student practices rereading the story silently without the tape recorder. Thus there is a progression from reading with auditory support to reading without support. The practice is continued until the student can orally read the selection with fluency.

The last two suggestions are about comprehension. The first has to do with diagnosing if a student has a comprehension problem, a decoding problem, or both. A simply way to make this diagnosis is to have two passages available that are written at what is called a "recreational" level available on a topic with which the student has some familiarity. One of the passages will be used to measure reading comprehension. Obviously, the degree of difficulty of the questions used to measure comprehension should be the same for the listening and the reading conditions and the student should be told beforehand that immediately following reading and listening a test will be administered. For the reading condition, the reading should be oral and the student should not be permitted to preview the material. The rationale for this is that oral reading with no chance to preview the material forces the student to decode and comprehend simultaneously. If the

decoding uses up too much attention, there will not be enough attention left over to comprehend. If the listening comprehension score is
satisfactory but the reading comprehension score is not, the student has
a decoding problem. If, however, listening comprehension is unsatis-
factory and the reading comprehension score is even lower, the student
has both a comprehension and a decoding problem.

The final suggestion has to do with testing for comprehension. As
suggested earlier, if the instructor asks only literal comprehension
questions, it is not clear to what extent the student understood the
material. It is primarily through the ability to answer both literal and
inferential questions that we may conclude that the student did, indeed, have more than a superficial understanding of the material.

References

Becker, C. A., & Killion, T. H. Interaction of visual and cognitive effects in word
recognition. *Journal of Experimental Psychology: Human Learning and Memory*,
1977, 3(3), 389–401.

Gough, P. B. One second of reading. In J. F. Kavanagh & I. G. Mattingly, (Eds.), *Language
by ear and by eye*. Cambridge, Massachusetts: The MIT Press, 1972.

Kintsch, W. *The representation of meaning in memory*. Hillsdale, New Jersey: Erlbaum,
1974.

Kintsch, W., & Keenan, J. M. Reading rate as a function of the number of propositions in
the base structure of sentences. *Cognitive Psychology*, 1973, 5, 257–274.

Kintsch, W., Kozminsky, E., Streby, W. J., McKoon, G., & Keenan, J. M. Comprehension
and recall of text as a function of content variables. *Journal of Verbal Learning and
Verbal Behavior*, 1975, 14, 196–214.

Kintsch, W., & Vipond, D. Reading comprehension and readability in educational practice and psychological theory. In L. G. Nilsson (Ed.), *Memory, processes, and problems*. Hillsdale, New Jersey: Erlbaum, 1978.

LaBerge, D., & Samuels, S. J. Toward a theory of automatic information processing in
reading. *Cognitive Psychology*, 1974, 6, 293–323.

Mandler, J. M., & Johnson, N. S. Remembrance of things parsed: Story structure and
recall. *Cognitive Psychology*, 1974, 9, 111–151.

Meyer, D. E., Schvaneveldt, R. W., & Ruddy, M. G. Loci of contextual effects of visual
word recognition. In P. Rabbitt & S. Dornic (Eds.), *Attention and performance V*.
New York: Academic Press, 1975.

Pearson, P. D., & Johnson, D. D. *Teaching reading comprehension*, New York: Holt, 1978.

Rumelhart, D. E., & Ortony, A. The representation of knowledge in memory. In R. C.
Anderson, R. J. Spiro, & W. E. Montague (Eds.), *Schooling and the acquisition of
knowledge*. Hillsdale, New Jersey: Erlbaum, 1977.

Samuels, S. J., LaBerge, D., & Bremer, C. Units of word recognition: Evidence for developmental change. *The Journal of Verbal Learning and Verbal Behavior*, 1978, 17,
715–720.

Samuels, S. J., Miller, N., & Eisenberg, P. Practice effects on the unit of word recognition.
The Journal of Educational Psychology, 1979, 4, 514–520.

Schank, R. C. The structure of episodes in memory. In D. G. Bobrow & A. Collins (Eds.), *Representation and understanding*. New York: Academic Press, 1975.

Smith, H. P., & Dechant, E. V. *Psychology in teaching reading*. Englewood Cliffs, New Jersey: Prentice-Hall, 1961.

Stein, N. L., & Glenn, C. G. An analysis of story comprehension in elementary school children. In R. Freedle (Ed.), *Multidisciplinary approaches to discourse comprehension*. Hillsdale, New Jersey: Erlbaum, 1978.

Terry, P., Samuels, S. J., & LaBerge, D. The effects of letter degradation and letter spacing on word recognition. *The Journal of Verbal Learning and Verbal Behavior*, 1976, *15*, 577–585.

Tinker, M. A. Annotated bibliography: Legibility of print. *Reading Research Quarterly, 1*, 1966.

Turner, A., & Greene, E. The construction of a propositional text base. *JSAS Catalog of Selected Documents in Psychology*, 1979.

3

D. Frank Benson

ALEXIA AND THE
NEUROANATOMICAL BASIS
OF READING

As literacy has become widespread in the twentieth century, disorders of written language have become increasingly disabling. As a consequence, disorders of reading have come under increasing clinical, educational, and psychological scrutiny. Among the many avenues of investigation, one approach, the study of acquired loss of written language comprehension (alexia) will be the focus of the present chapter. Clinically separable syndromes of alexia will be outlined, correlated with their consistent anatomical features, and, based on these data, a neuroanatomical structure for some of the functions underlying reading will be proposed.

Definitions

As a term to denote acquired reading impairment (inability to comprehend written or printed language material), *alexia* is of comparatively recent origin. Older terms such as *word blindness*, while still in use, are being replaced. One artificial differentiation in terminology is becoming widely used but is still not universally recognized. The term *dyslexia* has often been used to denote an incomplete impairment of reading ability. In the past decade, however, many investigators have used the term only in reference to an innate inability to learn to comprehend written or printed language. Strictly speaking, the use of *dyslexia* to indicate a partial loss of reading ability is correct philology.

NEUROPSYCHOLOGICAL AND COGNITIVE
PROCESSES IN READING

Operationally, however, the second use makes considerable sense. The child innately unable to learn to read presents a very different problem, anatomically, physiologically, psychologically, and behaviorally, when compared to the individual who has been able to read but has lost the ability through brain damage. For this chapter, the two conditions will be distinguished; *alexia* will refer to all acquired reading impairments, and *dyslexia* will be reserved for the innate, inborn inability to learn to read. *Alexia* will have no quantitative connotation; it will represent all degrees of acquired reading loss.

One crucial point deserves emphasis. *Alexia* refers to an impairment of the *comprehension* of written material, not to an inability to read aloud. In most instances, disturbance of the ability to comprehend written material is accompanied by a similar problem in reading aloud but important exceptions exist. The term *alexia* should be used only for acquired deficiencies in the comprehension of written material.

Several other terms deserve mention. For instance, *literal alexia* (letter blindness) refers to an inability to read individual letters, whereas *verbal alexia* (word blindness) indicates an inability to read words. *Agraphia*, a disability in production of written or printed language, is analogous to disturbances in the production of spoken language. Variations of agraphia have been recognized but remain poorly understood (Hecaen & Albert, 1978; Leichsner, 1957; Luria, 1966; Nielsen, 1936), and the differences will not be reviewed in this presentation. *Agraphia* will be used to denote all disturbances of written production. This is misleading, but descriptions and separation of the varieties of agraphia are beyond the scope of this chapter.

Other terms will appear in this presentation, usually specific to the problems under discussion. Inasmuch as possible, definitions will be offered in the context in which the term is used.

Historical Background

Although recognized for centuries, alexia has become a major medical and social problem only as literacy has become widespread. Reviews of early medical writings (Benson & Geschwind, 1969; Benton, 1964) reveal that a variety of reading disturbances have been noted through the centuries. With the blossoming of interest in aphasia following the demonstration of a neuroanatomical correlation with language disturbance by Broca (1861), additional cases of alexia were reported sporadically until the early 1890s. At that time, Dejerine presented two well-documented cases with detailed clinical evaluation, definitive postmortem findings, and good theoretical discussions of the reading disturbances. Dejerine's first report (1891) described an individual who became aphasic, alexic, and agraphic following a cerebral vascular accident. Over a period of several years, the aphasia cleared almost entirely but the patient remained incapable of comprehending or producing written language. At postmortem, a large, dominant hemisphere, parietal (angular gyrus) infarct was present. The second report, published the following year, featured an individual who suddenly lost the ability to comprehend written material but could still write. There were no associated language findings and the only major neurologic disturbance was a right homonymous hemianopia. The patient was not aphasic and produced written language without difficulty. Postmortem examination revealed occlusion of the left posterior cerebral artery causing infarction in the left medial occipital region, destroying the pathways carrying stimuli to the left visual cortex, plus destruction of the splenium of the corpus callosum. Dejerine conjectured that the individual discussed in the second report could receive visual stimuli (written language) in the right visual cortex but this information could not be transferred to the dominant left hemisphere for language interpretation. Dejerine conjectured that, in the first case, in contrast, the infarction destroyed an area necessary for both interpretation and production of written language and had, in effect, produced an acquired illiteracy.

Dejerine's carefully described cases and lucid explanations were readily accepted and, within a decade, numerous cases substantiating his findings had been reported. Dejerine's theoretical explanations were republished and supported by many eminent clinicians of the day (Bastian, 1898; Hinshelwood, 1900; Wylie, 1894).

The clinically distinct and anatomically separate types of alexia were widely recognized and accepted at the turn of the century, but this differentiation was nearly lost in the twentieth century. A unitary or holistic approach to language and language disturbances had been proposed by Jackson (1932), championed by Marie (1906), and promoted by numerous investigators (Bay, 1964; Head, 1926; Lashley, 1929; Pick, 1913, 1931; Schuell, Jenkins, & Jimenez-Palson, 1964; Wepman, 1951). As the holistic approach was advanced, reading disturbance came to be regarded as a focal side effect of an overall language defect. Separation of varieties of reading disturbances became unnecessary.

Dejerine's dichotomy of alexia was rediscovered, refurbished, and promoted in the early 1960s, largely through the efforts of Norman Geschwind (1962, 1965), who used alexia without agraphia to illustrate his disconnection theory of higher cortical function. Geschwind's efforts renewed interest in alexia, particularly as a model for the study of abnormal reading.

Whereas the two classic varieties of alexia are again generally accepted, it is obvious that many individuals who lose reading ability have neither of these disturbances. It has long been recognized that alexia could occur with anterior (frontal) aphasia (Benson & Geschwind, 1969; Freud, 1891; Lichtheim, 1885; Nielsen, 1938). In these cases, there is no pathology in the areas outlined by Dejerine and yet the patients suffer a significant impairment of reading. A study by Benson (1977) correlated alexia with Broca's aphasia, a disturbance associated with frontal language area pathology, and suggested that a separate and distinct reading problem was present. Alexia appears to be better understood if three different clinical entities are recognized.

The ultimate correlation of the clinical and anatomical basis of alexia has yet to be presented. Additional observations and appropriately directed investigations will be necessary to clarify and enhance the present clinical knowledge. Nonetheless, sufficient information is available to allow some anatomical–psychological speculations. These will be presented following a description of the three alexias.

The Three Alexias

There is little agreement on the terminology designating these entities. Table 3.1 illustrates the diversity of terminology that has been used in the past to differentiate variations in reading disturbance. Terms have been based on anatomical (occipital, parietal–temporal, frontal), functional (receptive, associative, syntactic), operational (literal alexia, total alexia, verbal alexia) and other features. Some of the terms imply underlying causes for the reading problems that are not fully supported; others suggest clinical differentiations that are incomplete. To date, no single classification or set of terms has proved to be acceptable. For this chapter, a simple, comparatively nonspecific classification will be used. This terminology should not be considered preferable, however, nor is it even the terminology favored by the author. It will suffice, however, for presentation of clinical, anatomical, and functional views of the brain's involvement in the act of reading.

Central Alexia

The term *central alexia* has been selected to designate a clinical disturbance often called alexia *with* agraphia (a term that fails to differentiate two clearly different types of alexia) but also known as parietal–temporal alexia, associative alexia, and aphasic alexia (see Table 3.1). Central alexia occurs frequently and presents striking clinical features but, not frequently, there are so many neighborhood clinical findings contaminating the picture that the diagnosis is obscured.

The major features of central alexia are, of course, impairment of reading and writing (alexia and agraphia). The impairment is often total but may occur in degrees of completeness. The ability to comprehend both letters and words is impaired and, as a rule, there is an equal difficulty in the comprehension of numbers and musical notations. Both the ability to read aloud and the ability to comprehend written language are disturbed. Prompting is of little help. Thus, tracing the letters with the finger, using embossed letters or spelling the word aloud fail to aid the patient.

The writing disturbance in central alexia is usually severe, almost always as severe as the reading disturbance. The patient may produce real letters or even combinations of letters in a caricature of real words, but many of the letter combinations are meaningless. The ability to copy written and printed words is far better. Copying is performed, however, in a slavish manner, similar to copying a language that is not understood. Transposition of cursive (script) writing to printed form and vice versa is a failure. The patient with central alexia can be considered illiterate, an acquired illiteracy.

Noteworthy neurologic and neurobehavioral abnormalities are often present in individuals with central alexia. Right hemiparesis may be present in early stages but is usually transient so that most patients with central alexia have little or no paralysis. Right-sided sensory loss is more frequent, often remains as a permanent problem and, in some instances, appears to be a major factor in the agraphia (Albert, Yamadori, Gardner, & Howes, 1973). A right-sided visual field defect may be

TABLE 3.1
Terminology of the Three Alexias

Posterior Alexia	Central alexia	Anterior Alexia
Occipital alexia	Parietal–temporal alexia	Frontal alexia
Alexia without agraphia	Alexia with agraphia	
Sensory alexia	Associative alexia	Motor alexia
Agnosic alexia	Aphasic alexia	
Optic alexia	Cortical alexia	
Word blindness	Letter and word blindness	Letter blindness
Verbal alexia	Total alexia	Literal alexia
Syntactic alexia	Semantic alexia	

present but is not a constant feature. A variety of aphasic findings may be present; these may include an empty paraphasic verbal output, defective comprehension of spoken language, an inability to repeat, or a serious word finding problem. In rare instances, however, aphasia may be absent. The Gerstmann syndrome (finger agnosia, right–left disorientation, acalculia, and agraphia) and constructional disturbance are seen frequently with central alexia. Similarly, a significant disturbance of intellectual capability is often present. None of these findings are consistently present, however, and none are necessary to make a diagnosis of central alexia.

The course in central alexia varies, dependent on the underlying etiology and size of the lesion. A rapid recovery of some or all reading skills is not uncommon. More often, a slow, partial recovery permits limited comprehension of written material. Not infrequently, however, the acquired illiteracy remains unaltered from the day it begins. The degree of recovery may be influenced by the premorbid literacy level and, to a somewhat lesser degree, by the importance of reading in the life style of the patient. Many patients have never been regular readers and are unconcerned by their acquired illiteracy. Unfortunately, many individuals for whom reading was an important activity remain permanently impaired.

Central alexia may result from a number of different disease processes. The most common, at least in current civilian practice, is cerebral vascular disease, most often occlusion of the angular branch of the middle cerebral artery. Not infrequently, central alexia is caused by arterial-venous malformation or an infiltrating brain tumor of the glioma series. Trauma, particularly gunshot wound, abscess, and metastatic tumor are all recognized as causes of central alexia, although less frequent ones.

Anatomical localization of central alexia has been accomplished by a variety of techniques. The original case reports featured autopsy demonstration. In more recent years, the pathology has been localized by surgical exploration, EEG, skull x-ray, radioisotope brain scans, and, most recently, computerized tomogram (CAT scan). All methods of localization have consistently demonstrated that the pathology involves the dominant parietal lobe. Dejerine's original case had focal pathology in this area and innumerable reports of well-studied cases of central alexia subsequently reported have had pathology involving the dominant parietal area (Benson & Geschwind, 1969; DeMassary, 1932; Leichsner, 1957; Starr, 1889). Thus, strong clinical evidence demonstrates that central alexia, an acquired illiteracy, indicates pathology involving the dominant parietal region and, by implication, that this area (the dominant angular gyrus) plays a crucial role in the interpretation of written language symbols.

Posterior Alexia

The syndrome most often called alexia *without* agraphia but also called occipital alexia, agnosic alexia, posterior alexia, and other terms is clinically spectacular and anatomically specific, but not common. The major feature is a serious disability in comprehending written material contrasted with an apparently uncanny preservation of writing ability. The patient with posterior alexia actually finds himself unable to read a letter or paragraph that he has just written. Most patients with posterior alexia can read a few letters of the alphabet and also recognize a few letter combinations such as their own names, the names of their cities and states, U.S.A., Men (or Ladies) and other frequently used language symbols but cannot understand most words. With improvement, a number of individual letters can be recognized and read aloud. This process is performed slowly and uncertainly but, if the word is short and the letters read accurately, the word spelled aloud can be interpreted. Retention of the ability to recognize words spelled aloud can be demonstrated easily. Patients with posterior alexia perform this task at a near normal level in sharp contrast to their failure or long latency in grasping the same word when written (verbal alexia, an inability to read words). This capability also contrasts strongly with the total failure of patients with central alexia to decipher orally spelled words. Just as the patient with posterior alexia recognizes words spelled aloud, words spelled letter by letter in the palm, or with embossed anagram blocks, and, in fact, written material presented in any manner except visually can be comprehended. The process of pronouncing individual letters aloud and then comprehending the word thus spelled is inefficient and open to error, particularly on longer words dependent on specific suffixes for exact meaning. Thus *national* may be read as *nation, refrigeration* as *refrigerator*, and so on. With continued improvement, the recognition of individual letters becomes more rapid and secure and can be performed silently. A gestalt interpretation of many common words (*and, if, it,* etc.) is developed, and reading ability improves in speed and accuracy, but remains slower and more difficult than before onset of the alexia.

The neurologic and behavioral complications of posterior alexia are fairly consistent. These patients usually write without difficulty, even full-length personal letters, or long, complicated, and accurate descriptive paragraphs. It has been noted, however, that with time the writing deteriorates. The handwriting slants and becomes messy and inaccurate over the years (Adler, 1950), presumably because of the long absence of visual monitoring of their own written output. Patients with posterior alexia have greater difficulty copying written material than writing to dictation or on command, the opposite of central alexia, where copying is the only successful writing task. Similarly, patients with posterior alexia spell aloud with ease, unlike patients with central alexia.

Most individuals with posterior alexia have a right homonymous hemianopia, although some cases of posterior alexia without hemianopia have been recorded (Ajax, 1967; Goldstein, Joynt, & Goldblatt, 1971; Greenblatt, 1973). There is no aphasia, although one language oriented finding, a color naming problem, is common. The difficulty with color naming is a two-way defect, failure both to name colors when presented and to point to colors when the name is given. The problem is not related to color perception; the patient can easily match similarly colored items. The difficulty with color names is not aphasic either. If asked to tell the color of an object (fire engine, banana, etc.), the patient gives a correct verbal response. Only tasks requiring association between visual and verbal modalities are failed; this has been defined by Teuber (1968), accurately, as a "percept stripped of its meaning," and fits his definition of an agnosia. The disturbance of color naming in patients with posterior alexia is a true *color agnosia*. Not all patients with posterior alexia have color agnosia, however. In one large series of posterior alexia cases (Gloning, Gloning, & Hoff, 1968), color naming disturbance was present in about 70% of the cases, and individual case reports of posterior alexia without color naming disturbance are not uncommon (Ajax, 1964; Stackowiack & Poeck, 1976).

Other neighborhood findings occur with less consistency. Individuals with posterior alexia may have a mild degree of anomia, less pronounced than the color naming disturbance but occasionally appreciable. Some have difficulty with number reading, others have a true acalculia. Muscial notation reading is lost by some, not by others. The limited extent of musical literacy has frustrated investigation of whether musical notation and language reading losses run parallel.

Far more significant is the fact that patients with posterior alexia show few basic neurologic disturbances except for the right visual field loss. Most have no paralysis, major sensory deficit, or aphasia. The loss of reading ability is all the more striking when contrasted to the otherwise intact behavior functions and makes this a readily recognized syndrome.

The course of posterior alexia is variable, but a slow, persistent improvement is usual. Improved reading ability follows increased skill in recognizing individual letters. Improvement is often sufficient to permit functional reading although reading is never as facile or as pleasurable as before.

Many localizing techniques have successfully demonstrated the site of pathology in posterior alexia. Starting with Dejerine's anatomical demonstration, a number of autopsy cases have been recorded. Laboratory techniques now localize the pathology in many living patients. These include the EEG, the radioisotope brain scan, and the CAT scan. Even cerebral angiography, a technique with limited usefulness for localizing most language disturbances, may demonstrate occlusion of the dominant posterior cerebral artery in cases of posterior alexia.

General agreement exists as to the site of pathology in posterior alexia. The anatomical defect described by Dejerine has been demonstrated in almost every case recorded. Most frequently the defect follows cerebral vascular accident (occlusion of the left posterior cerebral artery) but it has been described with tumors and arterio-venous (AV) malformation. Cerebral destruction usually involves the posterior medial cerebral cortex, usually the white matter of the fusiform and the lingual gyri of the dominant occipital lobe. In addition to the dominant occipital lobe pathology, most carefully studied cases show involvement of the splenium (posterior aspect) of the corpus callosum. Posterior alexia without splenial pathology can· occur if the pathological process involves the white matter deep in the left parietal–occipital junction area destroying fibers traversing the splenium (Ajax, 1964). Destruction of the left hemisphere visual sensory pathways and connections from the right hemisphere visual area can be surmised if posterior alexia is present (Benson & Geschwind, 1969).

Subangular Alexia

A separate entity, closely related but slightly different from the two types of alexia just mentioned, has been described by Greenblatt (1976), who suggested the term *subangular alexia*. His patient had alexia but neither agraphia nor hemianopsia. Similar cases were quoted from the literature, and Greenblatt suggested that the common denominator was pathological involvement of white matter deep in the dominant parietal cortex undercutting the angular gyrus. He further suggested that this subangular lesion disconnected the intact dominant hemisphere angular gyrus from equally intact cortical visual areas bilaterally. In a later publication, Greenblatt (1977) presented additional cases that showed a mixture of the clinical findings of posterior and central alexia.

He contended that much of the variability in alexia symptomatology reflects pathology located between the classic localizations of posterior and central alexia. Subangular alexia, then, does not refer to a separate variety of alexia but, rather, represents symptomatology part way between the two classic syndromes.

Anterior Alexia

A third variety of alexia has only recently been established (Benson, 1977) but this disturbance has a long and controversial history. For almost a century, investigators have noted that many patients with Broca's aphasia lose the ability to read. A frontal reading disturbance was not readily explained by the anatomical theories emanating from Dejerine's two cases, and it was generally suspected that in these cases the frontal lobe pathology producing Broca's aphasia extended posteriorly to involve the dominant parietal lobe and cause a central alexia, an explanation that has not been entirely acceptable. Alexia is frequently present in individuals whose pathology is located exclusively in the dominant frontal lobe (Nielsen, 1938). Of 61 cases of Broca's aphasia studied at the Boston Veterans Administration Medical Center, 51 showed a significant degree of reading impairment (Benson, 1977). Most had few findings suggesting posterior extension of pathology and, in many, the localizing information pointed exclusively to frontal destruction. A third (anterior) locus for alexia deserves recognition.

The clinical features of frontal alexia are sufficiently distinctive to allow differentiation from the two classic varieties. Most patients with frontal alexia do comprehend some written material, usually nouns, action verbs, or significant modifiers, the substantive words of a sentence, but they may fail to maintain this information in correct sequence (Albert, 1972). More important, they fail to understand the syntactic, grammatically significant relational words of a sentence. Many patients with frontal alexia can decipher a newspaper headline but cannot comprehend the article itself. Asked to read aloud, they only produce isolated words, almost exclusively substantives. If a word can be read aloud it will be understood (the opposite is not necessarily true). If the meaning of a sentence or a phrase is conveyed by one or even two substantive words, the patient may accurately interpret the entire production. If, however, relational words such as adjectives, prepositional phrases, possessives, and so forth, are important for the meaning of the sentence, misinterpretation or complete failure to comprehend is likely. Thus, although comprehending some written words, patients with anterior alexia insist that they cannot read and consistently avoid reading. In sharp contrast to posterior alexia, individuals with anterior alexia read words but fail to read (name) the individual letters of the word. They can be said to show a severe literal alexia and a lesser degree of verbal alexia (Benson, Brown, & Tomlinson, 1971). These patients recognize very few words spelled aloud and can spell few words; production in these spheres is far below that of posterior alexia and resembles that of central alexia (acquired illiteracy).

A severe writing disturbance is almost constant in frontal alexia. Often the writing must be performed by the left hand because of right hemiplegia. The graphic problems are greater than can be explained only by forced use of the nondominant hand, however. The written output is crude, poorly formed, often contains faulty spelling, including omission of letters, and is agrammatic (absence of most nonsubstantive words). Although patients with frontal alexia can copy written language, they have greater difficulty in this task than patients with either central or posterior alexia. Attempts to copy printed or cursive script also demonstrate badly formed production and a tendency to omit letters.

The associated findings in frontal alexia are distinct and help confirm the diagnosis. First, a nonfluent aphasia, most often Broca's aphasia, is present. The verbal output of patients with anterior alexia is notably limited, although comprehension of spoken language remains comparatively well preserved, appearing better than the ability to comprehend written language. As already noted, a right hemiplegia is usually present; some patients show sensory loss, and a few have a visual field defect (Benson, 1977).

The course of anterior alexia is variable. Many show no distinct improvement in reading whatsoever. Others, however, improve over time, mirroring the improvement in spoken language. The pathology is variable. Although many reported cases have been based on trauma, far more are caused by cerebral vascular accident; tumor, abscess, and gunshot wounds are less common causes of anterior alexia.

The neuroanatomic location of pathology in anterior alexia has been demonstrated by post mortem examination, EEG, radioisotope brain scan and CAT scan and is fairly consistent. Almost invariably, the posterior inferior portion of the dominant (left) frontal gyrus is involved. In addition, extension deep into the subcortical tissues, particularly in the anterior insula, is common. To date, study of the pathoanatony of anterior alexia is not sufficiently exact to tell whether involvement of other portions of the frontal language area (anterior or superior to Broca's area) will also produce alexia. Some suggest that patients with transcortical motor aphasia do not have a significant alexia (Hecaen & Albert, 1978) but this observation demands additional support.

Anterior alexia differs from the two classic alexias. The patient with this problem can read and extract meaning from some words, but, nonetheless, has a very real problem in reading. There is a definite impairment of the ability to comprehend written or printed language, and the disturbance deserves to be called alexia. These patients do not have the illiteracy of central alexia and many clinical features separate this problem from posterior alexia. A table of clinical features differentiating the three major varieties of alexia (Table 3.2) highlights the distinction between the three types of alexias.

A final note should be made emphasizing that anterior alexia causes greatest disturbance in the ability to utilize relational (syntactic) language structures and to maintain sequences. In this light, anterior alexia mirrors the language problems of anterior aphasia. Not only are anterior aphasics agrammatic in verbal output (Goodglass & Berko, 1960), but they have distinct problems in the comprehension of syntactical structures (Samuels & Benson, 1979; Zurif, Caramazza, & Myerson,

TABLE 3.2
Clinical Features of the Three Alexias

	Anterior	Central	Posterior
Written language			
1. Reading	Primarily literal alexia	Total alexia	Primarily verbal alexia
2. Writing to dictation	Severe agraphia	Severe agraphia	No agraphia
3. Copying	Poor	Slavish	Slavish (poorer than writing to dictation)
4. Letter naming	Severe anomia	Severe anomia	Relatively intact
5. Comprehension of spelled words	Partial success	Failed	Good
6. Spelling aloud	Poor	Failed	Good
Associated findings			
1. Language	Nonfluent aphasia	Fluent aphasia	Non aphasic
2. Motor	Hemiplegia	Mild paresis	No paresis
3. Sensation	Mild sensory loss	Hemisensory loss	No sensory loss
4. Visual fields	Usually normal	Hemianopia may or may not be present	Right hemianopia
5. Gerstmann syndrome	Absent	Frequently present	Absent

1972), and they often fail to maintain language information in correct sequence (Albert, 1972). The disability in the handling of relational, syntactic, and sequential language appears to be the major feature of anterior alexia. Combinations of anterior and central alexia almost undoubtedly exist just as the work of Greenblatt demonstrates that combinations of posterior and central alexia can occur. The three major types of alexia presented here appear distinct, however, and most variations in clinical features probably represent partial combinations of the three major varieties.

Other Varieties of Reading Disturbance

Hemialexia

A few cases have been reported where the splenium of the corpus callosum was surgically severed and consequent reading problems studied, but rather divergent results have been recorded. Akelitis (1943) studied a group of such cases and reported no difficulty with reading. From this observation, he suggested that both hemispheres could comprehend written material. Others however, have reported abnormal comprehension of written material in similar circumstances. In particular, Trescher and Ford (1937), Maspes (1948), and Gazzaniga and Sperry (1967) all demonstrated alexia in the left visual field (right hemisphere) with preservation of reading in the right visual field, a condition called *hemialexia* (Benson & Geschwind, 1969). The disturbance is rare and appears functionally related to posterior alexia. Hemialexia has only been reported following neurosurgical severence of the splenium of the corpus callosum; theoretically, however, the disturbance could occur with pathology that destroys the splenium alone.

Aphasic Alexia

Impairment of reading ability (alexia) is a feature of many aphasic syndromes, and many observers suggest that the alexia merely reflects the disturbance of language comprehension and does not warrant distinction. Thus, anterior alexia is not accepted as a distinct type of alexia by many contemporary investigators. Similarly the alexia consistently present in two posterior aphasic syndromes, Wernicke's aphasia and transcortical sensory aphasia is often considered only a side effect of the basic language disturbance. In transcortical sensory aphasia, the clinical features of the reading disturbance are identical or very similar to central alexia, and the pathology almost invariably involves the dominant parietal lobe. The alexia of transcortical sensory aphasia appears identical to central alexia. However, Wernicke's aphasia follows destruction of the posterior superior temporal lobe, an area immediately adjacent to, but separate from, the angular gyrus. Many cases of Wernicke's aphasia with severe alexia have had no pathological encroachment on parietal tissue (Nielsen, 1939). It has been suggested that auditory language is thoroughly mastered before learning a visual language; visual language is then learned through association with the already overlearned auditory language. Pathology disturbing auditory comprehension could therefore interfere with the associations established for the interpretation of written language. Although this explanation is not universally accepted, it is recognized that pathology limited to the dominant temporal lobe can produce an alexia that is either identical to or very similar to central alexia. In fact, the two alexias cannot be separated by clinical features and central alexia is often called parietal–temporal alexia (Benson & Geschwind, 1969).

Alexia in Oriental Languages

Until recently, almost all reported studies of alexia have concerned Indo-European languages. There has been good reason to believe that acquired disturbances of written languages may be quite different in the Oriental languages where ideographic characters are utilized rather than phonetic letters. Although reports of alexia in Oriental languages are relatively rare, the few reports, particularly those emanating from Japan, have been of considerable interest. The Japanese learn two forms of written language, *Kana*, a phonetic (syllabic) form of writing and *Kanji* which utilizes nonphonetic (logographic or ideographic) characters. That reading may be lost in one while maintained in the other has been reported (Sasanumo & Fujimura, 1971; Yamadori, 1975) and the reports of alexia primarily involving either *Kana* or *Kanji* suggest specific neuroanatomical correlations. Although the number of cases studied to date remains limited, those patients with the most posterior dominant hemisphere lesions (parietal–occipital) appear to have greater disturbance in comprehending *Kanji*, whereas patients with more anterior (temporal–parietal) pathology have greater problems understanding *Kana*. In addition, several reports suggest that *Kanji* is more disturbed by right hemisphere damage, *Kana* by left hemisphere destruction (Halta, 1977; Sasanumo, Itoh, Mori, & Kabayaski, 1977). Both of these findings correlate with the stronger visual aspects of the *Kanji* and the stronger auditory aspects of the *Kana* characters. The separable disturbances of reading reported in the Oriental languages appear to have a neuroanatomical basis.

Reading with the Right Hemisphere

Some of the preceding discussion, particularly the discussion of hemialexia, implies that most individuals read with the left hemisphere only. Following corpus callosum sectioning (hemialexia), patients apparently could not read with their right hemisphere. Similarly, almost all cases of alexia reported to date have had left hemisphere pathology and show little evidence of transfer of reading ability to the right hemisphere. The few cases of alexia following right hemisphere pathology have been in strongly left-handed individuals (Gloning, Gloning, Seitelberger, & Tschabitscher, 1955) implying that reversed language dominance was present. Clinical observation, therefore, indicates that comprehension of written language demands an intact language-dominant hemisphere and, conversely, the presence of alexia indicates dominant (almost always left) hemisphere pathology.

In recent years, however, accumulated evidence suggests that the right hemisphere may comprehend some written language. Most evidence comes from patients whose corpus callosum was sectioned for control of epilepsy (Bogen & Vogel, 1962). A limited ability of the isolated right hemisphere to read (interpret written material) has been demonstrated by tachistoscopic presentation of written words to the left visual field in some of these patients (Bogen, 1969; Gazzaniga, 1970; Gazzaniga & Sperry, 1967). The patient may state that no word has been seen (the left hemisphere gives the oral response and it has not seen any word), but the left hand often reaches out and picks up the object named in the written presentation. This experiment clearly demonstrates that the right hemisphere of these patients has the ability to comprehend written material designating concrete, picturable objects. Some clinical features of these cases, however, deserve attention. In particular, each patient demonstrating comprehension of written language with the right hemisphere had a serious seizure problem dating from early childhood. Whether or nor they had ever achieved a full lateralization of language function can be questioned. In the face of the strong clinical evidence that alexia improves far less than aphasia, it must be assumed that the right hemisphere's ability to read is limited.

One piece of clinical information, however, suggests that the right hemisphere may eventually assume some reading capability. Following destruction of the dominant parietal–temporal region producing central alexia, some patients may, after a number of years, comprehend some written language. Their "reading" is limited to picturable words, most often high frequency words. Thus, a housewife, alexic for many years, reported that she could recognize words such as *milk* and *bread* because she had seen the printed word so often in the context of the actual object. A large number of individual words may be identified by such patients but characteristic errors occur frequently. Thus, the printed word *infant* may be read as *baby*, *restaurant* as *cafe*, *automobile* as *car*, and so on. One such patient identified the printed word *living room* as *the place that my husband and I go after dinner to drink our coffee and talk*. This condition has been called *paralaxia* and it can be suggested that the right hemisphere visualizes the written material, associates the written symbols with a visual image (note that all of the words are picturable) and then names or describes the visual image. The name may be the same as the written name and can be interpreted as reading; the name produced may be a synonym, however, giving the appearance of misreading. The phenomenon of paralexia demonstrates that the right hemisphere can develop (or always maintains) some ability to interpret (picture) written material; the clinical observation that full comprehension of written material demands dominant hemisphere function is also supported.

Pseudoalexia

Some disturbances of reading may resemble alexia but, with careful testing, do not fulfill the criteria presented in the definition of alexia. These disorders have been called *pseudoalexia* (Benson & Geschwind, 1969). They can mislead the evaluation or distort the picture of alexia and, as such, deserve careful attention.

READING ALOUD

Without much question, the most common source of apparent, but not real, alexia stems from failure to test reading beyond the ability to read aloud. A fairly sizable number of aphasic patients, particularly those with Broca's or conduction aphasia, will fail to read aloud but comprehend silently read material. Only if such patients fail to comprehend can the term *alexia* be considered.

UNILATERAL PARALEXIA

Unilateral paralexia is easily mistaken for alexia. Following an acute homonymous visual field loss, the patient may fail to read (neglect) one side of a word or sentence. Thus, a patient with right visual field defect may read the word *basketball* as *basket*, whereas a patient with acute left visual field loss may read the same word as *ball*. The patient may substitute (confabulate) the portion of the word that falls in the neglected visual field (e.g., *baseball* for *basketball*). Unilateral paralaxia can cause considerable difficulty in comprehending written material, particularly sentence length written material, and is easily mistaken for alexia. That this is not a true alexia can be demonstrated rather easily. If the misread word or sentence is presented in a vertical rather than the traditional horizontal fashion, the patient comprehends with ease (Kinsbourne & Warrington, 1962). Similarly, Rubens and Butler (1974) were able to correct the unilateral paralexia seen in a series of patients with acute conjugate deviation of gaze by appropriate cold water caloric injections. Unilateral paralexia is a disturbance of conjugate visual gaze, not an inability to comprehend written material.

MENTAL RETARDATION AND DEVELOPMENTAL DYSLEXIA

A great number of mentally retarded individuals never learn to read, and if such an individual suffers an acute cerebral lesion in adult life, examination will demonstrate the inability to comprehend written material. This is easily misinterpreted as alexia unless a carefully taken history reveals that the patient's reading capabilities were always negligible.

Similarly, some individuals have never learned to read (dyslexia) despite otherwise normal mental capabilities. Many dyslexics are sensitive about their defect and will not admit that they cannot read. If such an individual suffers an acute cerebral disturbance, the behavioral examination will demonstrate inability to comprehend written material. Again, unless a specific history is obtained from the patient or the family, this is easily misdiagnosed as alexia.

PSYCHOGENIC PSEUDOALEXIA

Loss of the ability to comprehend written material is rarely presented as a psychogenic symptom. Acutely anxious, seriously depressed, or deteriorated schizophrenic patients may refuse to read and can be mistaken for alexics. Almost never does the alexia in these conditions stand out in comparison to other behavioral symptomatology, however; alexia is usually part of a far more extensive pseudodementia picture. If the clinician is aware of the language characteristics and common associated findings of the varieties of alexia there should be little difficulty in recognizing psychogenic pseudoalexia.

Theoretical Considerations

In recent presentations, the neuroanatomical sites underlying a number of different disturbances of language have been outlined (Benson, 1977; Benson, 1979a), and the neuroanatomical correlations of varieties of anomia were used as a foundation to postulate the portions of the brain necessary for the act of finding a specific word (Benson, 1979b). A similar postulation of the activities performed by various portions of the brain in the comprehension of written language will be presented here.

The three varieties of alexia have clinical distinctions that are obvious and significant (Table 3.2). Posterior alexia can be considered a primary disturbance of either the reception or the transmission of the visual language signals (or both). In fact, posterior alexia is not a true loss of reading ability but, rather, an impairment of the ability to utilize visually presented language stimuli. Written material presented through any modality other than vision is successfully comprehended. Anterior alexia, in contrast, features a significant disturbance of the ability to comprehend specific language structures. Thus, syntactically and relationally important words such as prepositions, possessives, modifiers, verb tenses, and plurals are poorly recognized (and often ignored) by the anterior alexic, whereas semantically meaningful substantive words are understood. Finally, central alexia appears to be a true loss of reading ability, an acquired illiteracy that involves all language functions. Central alexia features serious disturbance of semantic activities (the lexicon) and has been called semantic alexia, but the term is misleading as it emphasizes only one portion of the total disturbance of reading ability present in central alexia. The difference between anterior and central alexia was graphically demonstrated in an investigation by Samuels and Benson (1979). Three groups of patients, Broca's aphasia, Wernicke's aphasia and matched controls were given sentences for comprehension in both auditory and written form. Half of the sentences were answered with true–false responses; the other half by selecting, from a list of words, the word omitted from the sentence. The key word was semantic in half of the sentences, relational in the other half. The normal control group performed perfectly, making no errors on any sentence. The anterior aphasics scored as well as the normal controls on the sentences dependent upon semantic information but were only 50% accurate (barely above chance) on the sentences with key relational words. The posterior aphasic group (central alexia) performed as poorly as the anterior aphasics with syntactic material and performed just as poorly with the semantic material. The results were similar for both written and oral presentations. A functional difference between the two types of comprehension disability, and thus between the two types of alexia, was clearly demonstrated.

In league with these operational differences in reading impairment is the difference in the anatomical locus of pathology. The neuroanatomical localizations are schematically illustrated in Figure 3.1. Posterior alexia almost invariably indicates pathology involving the dominant hemisphere medial occipital and splenial region; central alexia indicates involvement of the parietal and/or temporal regions; anterior alexia indicates pathology of the dominant hemisphere posterior–inferior frontal lobe, primarily Broca's area, and subcortical tissues deep in this region. On the basis of the clinical and anatomical differentiations, the neuroanatomical basis of reading can be hypothesized.

The cornerstone of the proposed theory of reading rests on the human brain's ability to transfer material from one sensory modality into another, a process called cross-modal or intermodal association. Recent investigations (Butters & Brody, 1969; Ettlinger, 1960, 1967; Geschwind, 1964, 1965) have demonstrated the importance of intermodal synthesis for human language function and a number of investigators have demonstrated that the major cross-modal link takes place in the parietal lobe (Butters & Brody, 1968; Hecaen, Penfield, & Malmo, 1956). The portion of the parietal lobe known as the angular gyrus is a phylogenetically recent acquisition and appears unique in that it lies between, and has direct connections with, the association cortex of each of the major sensory modalities (visual, somesthetic, and audi-

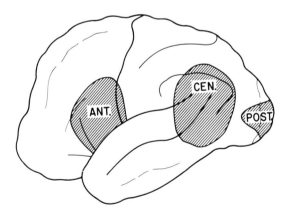

FIGURE 3.1. *Lateral view of left hemisphere indicating the anatomic sites of pathology underlying the three alexias. Ant. = anterior alexia, Cen. = central alexia, Post. = posterior alexia.*

tory). Much clinical evidence suggests that the dominant hemisphere angular gyrus is essential for language; a similar case can be made for the importance of the nondominant parietal lobe in complex visual–spatial associations (Butters, Barton, & Brody, 1970). The ability of the human brain to associate a stimulus received by one sensory modality (for instance a visual stimulation like a written word) with material learned through another sensory medium (for instance, the verbalization of the word) is almost uniquely human and is crucial for language. The angular gyrus appears essential for the association of the written language symbol with a meaningful auditory language entity and thus appears essential for the act of comprehending written language; not all reading disturbances point to angular gyrus pathology, however. In particular, the clinical evidence cited earlier demonstrates that reading disturbance can follow disruption of the transmission of the written symbols to the angular gyrus (posterior alexia) or inability to utilize syntactic language structures as seen in anterior alexia.

Based on these observations, a hypothesis of the neuroanatomical structures active in written language comprehension becomes rather obvious. When a written word is visualized, the primary visual cortex and the visual association areas (Brodmann's areas 17, 18, and 19) receive the stimulation. Visual sensory stimuli, following appropriate analysis and alteration, are transmitted to the angular gyri for association with other modalities. Cross-modal association in the angular gyri allows linkage between the visualized written symbol and multiple sensory associations previously associated with the written symbol. It would appear, however, that cross-modal association is not sufficient by itself to allow comprehension of the written material (data is too scanty to allow more than speculation on this point); other steps appear to be necessary. Transfer of stimuli from the angular gyrus to the adjacent temporal language area (Wernicke's area) is probably necessary to allow correlation of the printed language symbol to the highly overlearned auditory language symbols. Even this step does not appear sufficient for full language comprehension. Association between the parietal–temporal language areas and the frontal language area appears essential for understanding of the grammatic structures (relationships) of a sentence. Thus, although individual, semantically distinct words may be understood by an individual with anterior language area pathology, comprehension of sentence length material is often failed.

Clinical observations suggest that both the right and left angular gyri carry out cross-modal associations of the visualized written word. Most of the speculations in the previous paragraph concerned the activities of the dominant (left) angular gyrus in reading conprehen-

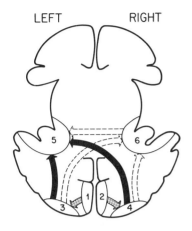

FIGURE 3.2. *Highly schematized horizontal view of brain suggesting visual sensory and associative connections for the process of reading. (1) and (2) indicate the left and right primary visual cortices, (3) and (4) indicate the visual association cortices, and (5) and (6) indicate the areas of cross-model association. The heavy line indicates the pathway for verbal–visual associations, the stippled line indicates the pathway for nonverbal–visual associations.*

sion. The nondominant (usually right) angular gyrus appears to be just as active in this process but its efforts are masked unless there is destruction of the dominant angular gyrus or the corpus callosum is severed (Benson & Geschwind, 1969; Gazzaniga & Sperry, 1967; Landis, Regard, & Serrat, 1979). In these situations, comprehension of selected written words can be demonstrated. It can be suggested that the right hemisphere makes an association between the visualized written word and an image (or an object or action) and the image is then identified (named or described). This same process probably occurs during normal reading also. As the reader translates written language into the auditory form, a simultaneous translation into visual imagery is probably occurring. Introspection suggests that this is true. Descriptive narrative (unlike abstract or philosophical material) does not appear to be comprehended solely as combinations of auditory linguistic symbols; most readers experience simultaneous visual imagery. Figure 3.2 presents a highly diagrammatic scheme of the bi-parietal activity thought to be occurring with reading. It can be suggested that both parietal lobes carry out cross-modal associations of visually presented language symbols, although with different end points. This hypothesis appears consistent with the clinical syndromes, with clinical observations, and with experimental data.

Summary

Three clinically distinct varieties of alexia (impaired ability to comprehend written or printed language) are associated with pathology involving distinctly different anatomical regions. One variation of alexia that follows dominant hemisphere occipital plus posterior callosal pathology produces a receptive disturbance and has been termed *posterior alexia*. A second, involving the parietal–temporal junction area, damages the brain's ability to interpret written or printed symbols. Called *central alexia*, this type appears to disturb essential associative activities. The third variety features specific problems with syntactical, relational, and sequential language structures, follows dominant frontal pathology, and can be called *anterior alexia*. Study of a number of other reading disturbances such as pseudoalexia, alexia in Oriental languages, and the reading ability (or disability) of the nondominant hemisphere support the anatomical correlations suggested by the major alexia syndromes. From this information, an anatomical–functional correlation of the process of reading can be proposed and supported.

References

Adler, A. Course and outcome of visual agnosia. *Journal of Nervous and Mental Disorders*, 1950, *3*, 41–51.

Ajax, E. T. Acquired dyslexia. *Archives of Neurology*, 1964, *11*, 66–72.

Ajax, E. T. Dyslexia without agraphia. *Archives of Neurology*, 1967, *17*, 645–652.

Akelaitis, A. J. Studies on the corpus callosum, VII—Study of language functions (tactile and visual lexia and graphia) unilaterally following section of the corpus callosum. *Journal of Neuropathology and Experimental Neurology*, 1943, *2*, 226–262.

Albert, M. L. Auditory sequencing and left cerebral dominance for language. *Neuropsychologia*, 1972, *10*, 245–248.

Albert, M. L., Yamadori, A., Gardner, H., & Howes, D. Comprehension in alexia. *Brain*, 1973, *96*, 317–328.

Bastian, H. C. *Aphasia and other speech defects*. London: H. K. Lewis, 1898.

Bay, E. Principles of classification and their influence on our concepts of aphasia. In A. V. S. De Reuk & M. O'Connor (Eds.), *Disorders of language*. Boston: Little Brown, 1964.

Benson, D. F. Neurologic correlates of aphasia and apraxia. In W. B. Matthews & G. Glaser (Eds.), *Recent advances in neurology*. London: Churchill, 1977.

Benson, D. F. *Aphasia, alexia and agraphia*. London: Churchill, 1979. (a)

Benson, D. F. Neurologic correlates of anomia. In H. Whitaker & H. Whitaker (Eds.), *Studies of neurolinguistics* (Vol. 4). New York: Academic Press, 1979. (b)

Benson, D. F., Brown, J., & Tomlinson, E. B. Varieties of alexia. *Neurology*, 1971, *21*, 951–957.

Benson, D. F., & Geschwind, N. The alexias. In P. J. Vinken & G. W. Bruyn (Eds.), *Handbook of clinical neurology* (Vol. 4). Amsterdam: North-Holland, 1969.

Benson, D. F., & Geschwind, N. Aphasia and related cortical disturbances. In A. B. Baker & L. H. Baker (Eds.), *Clinical neurology*. New York: Harper, 1971.

Benton, A. L. Contributions to aphasia before Broca. *Cortex*, 1964, *1*, 314–327.

Bogen, J. E. The other side of the brain I: Dysgraphia and dyscopia following cerebral commissurotomy. *Bulletins of the Los Angeles Neurological Society*, 1969, *34*, 73–105.

Bogen, J. E., & Vogel, P. J. Cerebral commissurotomy: A case report. *Bulletin of the Los Angeles Neurological Society*, 1962, *27*, 169.

Broca, P. Remarques sur le siege de la faculte du langage articule, suives d'une observation d'aphemie. *Bulletin of the Society Anatomie*, 1861, *2*, 330–357 (Paris).

Butters, N., Barton, M., & Brody, B. A. Role of the right parietal lobe in the mediation of cross-modal associations and reversible operations in space. *Cortex*. 1970, *6*, 174–190.

Butters, N., & Brody, B. The role of the left parietal lobe in the mediation of intra- and cross-modal associations. *Cortex*, 1968, *4*, 328–343.

Butters, N., & Brody, B. Familiarity as a factor in the cross-modal associations of brain-damaged patients. *Perceptual and Motor Skills*, 1969, *28*, 68.

Dejerine, J. Sur un cas de cecite verbale avec agraphie, suivi d'autopsie. *Memoires de la Society Biologie*, 1891, *3*, 197–201.

Dejerine, J. Contribution a l'etude anatomo-pathologique et clinique des differentes varietes de cecite verbale. *Memoires de la Societie Biologie*, 1892, *4*, 61–90.

DeMassary, J. L'alexie. *Encephale*, 1932, *27*, 134–164.

Ettlinger, G. Cross-modal transfer of training in monkeys. *Behavior*, 1960, *16*, 56–65.

Ettlinger, G. Analysis of cross-modal effects and their relationship to language. In C. Millikau & F. Darley (Eds.), *Brain mechanisms underlying speech and language*. New York: Grune & Stratton, 1967.

Freud, S. *[On aphasia.]* (E. Steng, trans.) New York: International University Press, 1953. (Originally published, 1891.)

Gazzaniga, M. S. *The bisected brain*. New York: Appleton, 1970.

Gazzaniga, M. S., & Sperry, R. W. Language after section of the cerebral commissures. *Brain*, 1967, *90*, 131–148.

Geschwind, N. The anatomy of acquired disorders of reading. In J. Money (Ed.), *Reading disability*. Baltimore: Johns Hopkins Press, 1962.

Geschwind, N. The development of the brain and the evolution of language. *Monograph series on languages and linguistics, No. 17*. Report of the 15th Annual R.T.M. on Linguistic and Language Studies. (C. I. J. M. Stuart, ed.) April, 1964.

Geschwind, N. Disconnexion syndromes in animals and man. *Brain*, 1965, *88*, 237–294.

Gloning, I., Gloning, K., & Hoff, H. *Neuropsychological symptoms and syndromes in lesions of the occipital lobe and the adjacent areas*. Paris: Gonthier Villar, 1968.

Gloning, I., Gloning, K., Seitelberger, F., & Tschabitscher, H. Ein fall von reiner Wortblindheit mit obduktionsbefund. *Wiener Zeitschrift fur Nervenheilkunde un der Grenzgebiek*, 1955, *12*, 194–215.

Goldstein, J., Joynt, R., & Goldblatt, D. Word blindness. *Neurology*, 1971, *21*, 873–876.

Goodglass, H., & Berko, J. Agrammatism and inflectional morphology in English. *Journal of Speech and Hearing Research*, 1960, *3*, 257–267.

Greenblatt, S. H. Alexia without graphia or hemianopia. *Brain*, 1973, *96*, 307–316.

Greenblatt, S. H. Subangular alexia without agraphia or hemianopia. *Brain and Language*, 1976, *3*, 229–245.

Greenblatt, S. H. Neurosurgery and the anatomy of reading: A practical review. *Neurosurgery*, 1977, *1*, 6–15.

Halta, T. Recognition of Japanese Kanji in the right and left visual fields. *Neuropsychologia*, 1977, *15*, 685–688.

Head, H. *Aphasia and kindred disorders* (2 vols.). London and New York: Cambridge Univ. Press, 1926.

Hecaen, H., & Albert, M. L. *Human neuropsychology*. New York: Wiley, 1978.

Hecaen, H., Penfield, W., Bertrand, C., & Malmo, R. The syndrome of apractagnosia due to lesions of the minor cerebral hemisphere. *Archives of Neurology and Psychiatry*. 1956, *75*, 400–434.

Hinshelwood, J. *Letter-word and mind-blindness.* London: H. K. Lewis, 1900.

Jackson, J. H. *Selected writings* (J. Taylor, Ed.). London: Hodder & Stoughton, 1932.

Kinsbourne, M., & Warrington, E. K. A variety of reading disability associated with right hemisphere lesions. *Journal of Neurological Neurosurgery Psychiatry,* 1962, *25,* 339–344.

Landis, T., Regard, M., & Serrat, A. Iconic reading in a case of alexia without agraphia caused by a brain tumor. *Brain and Language,* 1980, *11,* 45–53.

Lashley, K. S. *Brain mechanisms and language.* Chicago: Univ. of Chicago Press, 1929.

Leischner, A. *Die storungen der schriftsprache (agraphie and alexie)* Stuttgart: Georg Thieme Verlag, 1957.

Lichtheim, L. On aphasia. *Brain,* 1885, *8,* 434–484.

Luria, A. R. *Higher cortical functions in man.* New York: Basic Books, 1966.

Marie, P. Revision de la question de l'aphasie. *Semaine Medicine,* 1906, *26,* 241–247; *26,* 493–500; *26,* 565–571.

Maspes, P. E. Le syndrome experimental chez l'homme de la section du splenium du corps calleux alexie visuelle pure hemianopsique. *Revue Neurologique,* 1948, *2,* 101–113.

Nielsen, J. M. *Agnosia, apraxia and aphasia: Their value in cerebral localization.* New York: Hafner, 1936.

Neilsen, J. M. The unsolved problems in aphasia: Alexia in motor aphasia. *Bulletin of the Los Angeles Neurological Society* 1938, *4,* 114–122.

Neilsen, J. M. The unsolved problems in aphasia: Alexia resulting from a temporal lesion. *Bulletin of the Los Angeles Neurological Society* 1939, *4,* 168–183.

Pick, A. *Die agrammatischen sprachstorungen.* Berlin: Springer, 1913.

Pick, A. *Aphasia.* Springfield, Illinois: Thomas, 1973. (Originally published, 1931.)

Rubens, A. B., & Butler, R. B. Correction of conjugate gaze defect with cold water calorics. Personal communication, 1974.

Samuels, J., & Benson, D. F. Some aspects of language comprehension in anterior aphasia. *Brain and Language,* 1979, *8,* 275–286.

Sasanuma, S., & Fijimura, O. Kanji versus Kana processing in alexia with transient agraphia: A case report. *Cortex,* 1971, *7,* 1–18.

Sasanuma, S., Itoh, M., Mori, K., & Kabayaski, Y. Tachistoscopic recognition of Kana and Kanji words. *Neuropsychologia,* 1977, *15,* 547–553.

Schuell, H., Jenkins, J. J., & Jimenez-Pabon, E. *Aphasia in adults–diagnosis, prognosis and treatment.* New York: Harper, 1964.

Stackowiak, F. J., & Poeck, K. Functional disconnection in pure alexia and color naming deficit demonstrated by deblocking methods. *Brain and Language,* 1976, *3,* 135–143.

Starr, A. The pathology of sensory aphasia, with an analysis of fifty cases in which Broca's centre was not diseased. *Brain,* 1889, *12,* 82–99.

Teuber, H. L. Alterations of perception and memory in man. In L. Weiskrantz (Ed.), *Analysis of behavioral change,* New York: Harper, 1968.

Trescher, J. H., & Ford, F. R. Colloid cyst of the third ventricle. *Archives of Neurology and Psychology,* 1937, *37,* 959–973.

Wepman, J. M. *Recovery from aphasia.* New York: Ronald, 1951.

Wylie, J. *The disorders of speech.* Edinburgh: Oliver and Boyd, 1894.

Yamadori, A. Ideographic reading in alexia. *Brain,* 1975, *98,* 231–238.

Zurif, E. B., Caramazza, A., & Myerson, R. Grammatical judgments of agrammetic aphasics. *Neuropsychologia,* 1972, *10,* 405–417.

4

Steven Mattis

DYSLEXIA SYNDROMES IN CHILDREN:
Toward the Development of Syndrome-Specific Treatment Programs

In a study that compared the results of the neuropsychological evaluation of brain-damaged and developmentally dyslexic children to that of brain-damaged children who read adequately, Mattis, French, and Rapin (1975) reported isolating three independent dyslexia syndromes. From 252 children referred by pediatric neurologists to the Neuropsychology Division of the Montefiore Hospital and Medical Center and the Albert Einstein College of Medicine, 113 children with a chief complaint of learning disability were selected and studied between 1969 and 1971. All those selected were between the ages of 8 and 18, had a Verbal or Performance IQ greater than 80, normal visual and auditory acuity, adequate academic exposure, and showed no evidence of psychosis or thought disorder. Eighty-four of the children were diagnosed as brain-damaged by the referring pediatric neurologists on the following findings: (a) a history of an encephalopathic event and subsequent abnormal development; (b) abnormal findings on clinical neurological examination; (c) significant abnormalities on electroencephalogram or skull X-rays; and, in some cases, (d) abnormality on special neuroradiographic study (pneumoencephalogram or arteriogram). Eighty-two children were classified as dyslexic as defined by a score on the Wide Range Achievement Test (Jastak, Bijou, & Jastak, 1965) two or more grades below the level appropriate for their ages. The children were therefore classified as belonging to one of three groups: (a) brain-damaged dyslexic children (N = 29); (b) non-brain-

NEUROPSYCHOLOGICAL AND COGNITIVE
PROCESSES IN READING

damaged dyslexic children ($N = 53$); and (c) brain-damaged children who read adequately ($N = 31$). Of the 29 non-brain-damaged dyslexic children, 27 had a clear genetic history of learning disabilities (there were several siblings in this group) suggesting that this group was composed primarily of developmental or primary dyslexic children (Critchley, 1964). There was not a sufficient number of non-brain-damaged readers (i.e., "normal children" older than 8 years) to be included for study. No differences existed between groups in mean age (11–12) and full scale IQ (98–99). More importantly, no significant differences were found between the brain-damaged and non-brain-damaged dyslexic children on an extensive battery of neuropsychological tests. Both dyslexic groups presented with patterns of deficits in higher cortical and motor functions consonant with focal neocortical damage in adults and associated with multifocal damage in children. Both dyslexic groups presented findings indicative of cerebral dysfunction that lead to a conclusion similar to Knights' (1973), that the patterns of resulting cognitive defects rather than the etiology of such deficits are the more significant factors in learning disabilities. It appeared, clinically, that the dyslexic children, regardless of etiology, presented with several differing patterns of cognitive strengths and deficiencies (i.e., syndromes). However, many dyslexics presented findings also observed in our brain-damaged reader group. It appeared that the dyslexic children presented with some deficits that, although associated with brain damage, were not necessarily directly related to reading disabilities. To isolate those critical factors, the authors excluded as causes of dyslexia those deficiencies observed in the brain-damaged reader group. Three separate clusters of deficits were operationally defined. Each cluster, independent of the etiology of the deficits, appeared to limit the development of a different subprocess critical to the acquisition of reading skill. The criteria for each syndrome are presented in Table 4.1.

Of the dyslexic children, 90% presented with one of the dyslexia syndromes. None presented with more than one syndrome. It should be noted that many disorders frequently observed in large populations of "poor readers" were not included as syndrome criteria because of their frequent occurrence in our brain-damaged reader group. Among the more significant findings in our brain-damaged readers were hyperkinesis, poor gross and fine motor dyscoordination, mixed dominance (hand, eye, and foot in all combinations), sinistrality without a family history of sinistrality, ambidexterity, poor lateral awareness for per-

TABLE 4.1
Quantitative Criteria for Each Dyslexia Syndrome[a]

I. Language disorder
  A. Anomia—20 % or greater proportion of errors on the Naming Test and one of the following:
  B. Disorder of comprehension:
     performance on Token Test at least 1 *SD* below the mean; or
  C. Disorder of imitative speech: performance greater than 1 *SD* below the mean on the Sentence Repetition Test; or
  D. Disorder of speech sound discrimination:
     10% or greater proportion of errors on discrimination of 'e' rhyming letters.
II. Articulatory and graphomotor dyscoordination
  A. Performance on ITPA Sound Blending subtest greater than one standard deviation below the mean; and
  B. Performance on graphomotor test greater than 1 *SD* below the mean; and
  C. Acousto–sensory and receptive language processes within normal limits.
III. Visual–spatial perceptual disorder
  A. Verbal IQ more than 10 points above Performance IQ; and
  B. Raven's Coloured Progressive Matrices percentile less than equivalent Performance IQ; and
  C. Benton Test of Visual Retention (10-sec exposure immediate reproduction) score at or below the borderline level.

[a] From Mattis *et al.*, 1975.

sonal and extrapersonal space, poor intersensory transfer of information, defective construction of puzzles and dyscalculia.

The Mattis *et al.* (1975) study clearly supported the view that dyslexia can result from a defect in any one of several independent processes. The *several independent causal defects* model of dyslexia had been suggested by Applebee (1971) as one of several logical alternatives to the *single causal defect* model proposed by many investigators until the early 1960s. This alternative view of dyslexia implies: (*a*) that the acquisition of reading skill requires the integration of specific, albeit moderately complex, input, output, and mediating processes; and (*b*) that a deficit in any one of these critical processes results in distorted or atypical reading development. The results of our first study indicated that adequate development of language skills, motor–speech fluency, and visual–spatial perception are each critical to the acquisition of reading skill. A child presenting a deficit in any one of these processes will by dyslexic despite the relative intactness, or even superior development, of all other cognitive skills.

These three syndromes do not exhaust the list of possible critical defects. Indeed Martha Denckla (1977a,b) has provided convincing evidence for an additional critical defect she terms a "phonemic sequencing" disorder. A recent study of 168 dyslexic children out of 263 school-aged children referred to a multidisciplinary diagnostic center in a disadvantaged area of the South Bronx found 10% of the children presented findings consonant with the phonemic sequencing disorder, 60% presented the language disorder syndrome, 10% the articulatory–graphomotor dyscoordination syndrome, and 5% the visual–perceptual disorder syndrome (Mattis, Erenberg, & French, 1978). In addition, 10% were found to have two syndromes, a phenomena not observed in the earlier study but reported by Denckla (1977a). The cluster of deficits critical to the phonemic sequencing disorder has not as yet been isolated: A matched contrast group of brain-damaged readers has not been studied to exclude associated but dyslexic-irrelevant deficiencies. All the school-aged children seen at the South Bronx clinic were referred because their academic achievement was glaringly discrepant from their peers. Thus, a sizable population of brain-damaged readers matched for age, socioeconomic status, and ethnic background has not as yet accrued.

The existence of dyslexic types had been previously suggested by others (e.g., Bateman, 1968; Boder, 1973; Ingram, Mason. & Blackburn, 1970; Kinsbourne & Warrington, 1966; Myklebust & Johnson, 1962), the typology derived from patterns of disorders in higher cortical function, developmental and medical history, and/or patterns of reading and spelling errors observed in populations of dyslexic children. However, in these earlier reports, the failure to introduce a contrast group of neurologically impaired children who could read severely limited the specificity with which the investigators could delineate the critical factors.

More recent studies by Rourke (1978a,b) included a contrast group of children with specific dyscalculia but with intact reading. Factor analysis of the result of a comprehensive neuropsychological test battery demonstrated three dyslexia types similar to those we reported. Satz (see Chapter 5), who did not include a brain-damaged reader group but utilized cluster analysis techniques, generated four cluster types clearly supporting the model of several independent causal defects and specific clusters of deficits consonant with our findings.

At this time, it seems evident that (a) the three syndromes reported can be reliably detected; (b) assessment techniques and criteria exist for homogeneously grouping dyslexic children as a function of their pattern of critical deficiencies; and (c) the prevalence of these three syndromes are of sufficient magnitude to warrant the development of syndrome-specific treatment programs.

Syndrome-Specific Treatment Programs

In proceeding from the clinical diagnostic findings to the logical development of several syllabi for remediation, it was necessary to survey existing programs. It was found that there are many schools of thought about remedial procedures for dyslexia, each school assuming that a different single causal defect is responsible for reading disabilities. Thus, each generated one program purporting to be "the" treatment program for dyslexia. From our findings as to the differing clusters of deficits underlying dyslexia, it appeared that a portion of some given programs seemed appropriate for a specific syndrome. Other programs, which one might characterize as "ortho–neuro–perceptual–optico–motor–dominance" programs, appeared to focus undue attention on processes not found to be directly related to reading disability. No one program in its entirety appeared satisfactory as a "package" to be used for a given syndrome. What I wish to present, therefore, is a clinical description of the children who present with each syndrome, observations as to the relationship between their cognitive deficits and their inability to acquire reading skill, and proposed treatment procedures for each dyslexia syndrome.

Implicit in the suggested treatment procedures are several guidelines that should be made explicit. Of the various treatment strategies possible it was decided that the proposed programs should capitalize on the child's assets avoiding direct involvement of deficient processes. This does not imply that a direct attempt to enhance a specific cognitive deficit would not be a valuable complement to any reading program. Capitalizing on the child's strength, in my experience, has the highest probability of initial success. This initial success is of inestimable importance to the dyslexic child in enhancing his self-esteem and willingness to pursue a learning experience for which he subjectively holds a high expectancy of humiliating failure. A second consideration derives from the observation that published basal readers and manuals contain a wealth of material and procedures. It was therefore decided that, whenever possible, suggested procedures and materials should be gleaned from the armamentarium already at the disposal of the learning disability and reading specialist. Two minor considerations were that undue attention should not be given to the associated deficiencies often found in dyslexic children that are not directly relevant to their reading disability, and, whenever possible, a suggested procedure should have potential for adaption for small groups.

Language Disorder Syndrome

The children with this syndrome present with intact visual and constructional skills, and adequate graphomotor coordination. Blending of speech sounds per se is generally intact. Often when there is speech-sound discrimination difficulty, the misperceived phonemes are adequately blended in their correct sequence and without intrusion and omissions. Performance IQ is within normal limits. In most, although not in all children, the Verbal IQ is statistically significantly poorer than Performance IQ. This Verbal–Performance IQ discrepancy is not in itself of clinical significance: We have observed many disadvantaged and disturbed children who present with sizable Verbal–Performance differences but with no anomia and with intact reading skills. This dyslexic child presents, in brief, a specific language disorder in which the anomia is viewed as the major critical factor.

The instability of verbal learning and verbal retrieval directly impedes the acquisition of a "look–say" vocabulary. The children respond to sight words in a manner similar to their misnaming of objects, colors, and body parts. Those who are more severely impaired have not as yet learned the names of the letters. In most basal reader series, the sound referent for each letter is anchored in the name of the letter or a word that begins with this letter. In practice the child is required to know the name of the letter and to use this knowledge as the major clue to its sound. The language disordered child, unable to retrieve the cue words reliably, arrives at faulty letter–sound associations. There are some children who, by prior training or by idiosyncratic strategies, have managed to learn several grapheme–phoneme associations. They are often hampered in elaborating this approach because of a relative inability to judge when they have blended a real word. Although most beginning readers will utter neologisms while using their new phonic skills, they will self-correct especially when challenged. During out diagnostic evaluation, the aphasic dyslexic children produce neologisms as a final judgment more frequently than normal or other dyslexics and more often report being satisfield that their utterance is a real word when they are challenged.

The anomia had a secondary effect on the development of a phonic attack. In many basal readers series, children are not introduced to phonics until a modest recognition vocabulary has been established. A "look–say" vocabulary is quite difficult for these children to acquire, and thus most of the children in this group are delayed before starting a good phonic program.

SUGGESTED TREATMENT PROGRAM

The overall treatment strategy is to capitalize on the child's sound-blending skills and ability to make letter–sound associations while minimizing the need for verbal labeling of letters and whole words and paying scant attention to the meaning of a blended word. The initial goal for this group is to aid the child in breaking the word code. The first step, therefore, is to teach the sounds to be associated with letters and letter groups without teaching letter names and without imbedding the sound referent in a word cue. In a small pilot study with four dyslexic children with moderate to severe language impairments, this initial stage was accomplished with simple drill obeying the laws of contiguity. The grapheme was drawn by the therapist while uttering its speech sound, elongating the liquid sounds, long vowels, and so on, and repetitively clipping hard consonants and short vowels. The children in a similar fashion drew the letter or observed the letter while uttering the appropriate speech sound. For the therapist, there are two difficult aspects in this stage of training. First, one must withhold giving the child a word cue. Second, one must avoid giving a nominative connotation to the sound reference. That is, the type of instructions one should avoid are "O.K., now let's draw an 'mm-mm-mm-mm'," and "What is the sound of this letter?"

Once a modest core of sound referents has been learned, the letters can be presented in sequence as consonant–vowel–consonant series or words to be blended. At this point, one might employ material derived from phonic programs relying heavily on compelling visual stimuli (e.g., Gettagno, 1964) to further differentiate grapheme–phoneme associations. However, once several sound referents have been mastered, the basal readers of any rigorously synthetic program (e.g., Rasmussan & Goldberg, 1966) would be appropriate.

Once the initial hurdle of learning the sounds and blending them is over, the language disordered dyslexic would make rapid gains in decoding skill in the first year with spelling errors being phonetically precise. A small proportion of language disordered dyslexic children, those with severe language comprehension deficits but adequate decoding skill, will appear to be hyperlexic. This may not become very apparent until third- and fourth-grade material is introduced. When the goal is to use reading as a tool to gain further information rather than merely to break the letter code, these children's poor paragraph comprehension markedly impedes further achievement. At about this same level of achievement, once the full flush of the child's victory over the letter code has receded, a second problem arises, one that is common to all dyslexic children. That is, the content of the basal readers that accompany most phonic programs, although appropriate for the child's level of reading competence, is inappropriate for his or her age and interest.

To augment the reading texts and attack the problem of stabilizing word and sentence meaning, a second procedure might be introduced concurrent with third- or fourth-grade material. This technique is called the Language Experience Method (Chall, 1967, p. 40). This is the general term for methods that use the child's own words and stories as the material to be written and read. This approach is difficult to present systematically because it does not follow a set lesson plan. A given treatment session depends very much on what the child brings to the session and the teacher's creative abilities in using the material. The procedure can be as straightforward as asking the child to relate an experience in one or two sentences or to describe a picture he has drawn. This is written down by the therapist along with other reported experiences. A reading text is soon developed whose content is of intrinsic interest to the child—always a good pedagogical gambit. More importantly, however, the text that evolves will contain a large sample of words that are reliably retrieved and have stable meaning. The therapist will thus have accrued a sufficient number of words with high reliability of recall to provide material for new blends and eventually a small recognition vocabulary. It is common at some point in the Language Experience approach for the child to write his own text, with the editorial comments of the therapist serving as the lesson for that session. It is at this point that syntax and finer semantic distinctions can be broached.

In summary, the proposed treatment program for the language disorder syndrome begins with the development of letter–sound associations without regard to letter naming and proceeds to a highly synthetic phonic program without undue attention to word meaning. The purposeful development of a recognition vocabulary is avoided. Once this word attack skill has been partially mastered, phonic readers are used concurrently with ongoing phonic training. In an effort to stabilize word meaning, present more age-appropriate content, and augment comprehension, a Language Experience program is introduced once the child has achieved third- to fourth-grade material.

Articulation and Graphomotor
Dyscoordination Syndrome

These children present with intact visual–spatial perception, language, and constructional skills. Verbal IQ approximates Performance IQ. There may be an assortment of gross or fine motor coordination findings, however, the critical deficiencies are a buccal–lingual dyspraxia with resultant poor speech, and graphomotor dyscoordination. Even the poorest readers in this group, in our studies, were aware that letter sequences stood for words and had a modest recognition vocabulary. No child in this group had a phonic attack skill. Reading and spelling was dysphonetic as described by Boder (1973) with consonant and syllable omissions, and perseveration or confusion of articulemes like *t, l, n,* and *d*. Handwriting, of course, was poor, but more important than the sloppiness of the final product, a child in this group did not appear to draw a given letter the same way two times in succession. It is felt that the children presenting with this syndrome are initially handicapped by their inability both to utter reliably or to blend phonemes and reliably reproduce the appropriate graphemes. The smooth motor coordination of speech musculature necessary to effectively sequence individual phonemes is not yet available to these children. Among those with severe difficulty, it is impossible to produce a stop consonant without uttering an associated vowel. Thus a word like *cat* might be part of a given child's spontaneous vocabulary and he can repeat the word on request. However, when aurally presented with *c-a-t* as on the Illinois Test of Psycholinguistic Abilities (ITPA) sound blending task (Kirk, McCarthy, & Kirk, 1968) he would respond *cuh-a-tuh* and attempt to blend to a polysyllabic word. Frequent repetition of the three sounds in an attempt to blend them often results in perseveration of a given phoneme, substitution of irrelevant phonemes, and omission or transposition of vowels and consonants.

PROPOSED TREATMENT

The treatment program capitalizes on the child's intact visual–spatial perception and language skills and minimizes the necessity for a phonic approach. The initial phase begins with two separate procedures, a two-prong attack on both handwriting and reading. We have found that these children respond well to penmanship drill. Attention is paid not necessarily to the neatness of the final product but rather to the consistency with which a given letter is drawn. Indeed, many of the older children who have been taught script in their normal class settings show dramatic differences between the legibility of their script as contrasted with the unevenness in spacing and size of their block letters. Reading is approached initially through the development of a sizable recognition vocabulary. This is done for two reasons. First, this method results in immediate gains bolstering self-confidence. Second, a look–say approach can be exceedingly useful in and of itself. Almost all clinicians working with dyslexic children have encountered several late adolescents or adults presenting with this syndrome who have amassed a huge sight vocabulary. They generally do not read for pleasure but can with tremendous effort plow through the necessary texts, reports, and articles to achieve a fair degree of academic success. Reading is tedious because it requires frequent guessing and successive approximations of unfamiliar words primarily based on contextual cues. Spelling and handwriting is abysmal but by dictating reports to be typed by others, course work and business can be completed. Initially any "whole word" program can be used if the basal reader series is designed with an initial emphasis on meaning and appreciation of story line (e.g., The Bank Street Readers, 1965). These series introduce phonics and word analysis skill later but generally through analysis of known words. It seems necessary in the initial phase to divorce writing exercises from the process of acquiring new words until graphic production is stable.

Although reliance on a look–say approach is appropriate for the initial phase, amassing a useful recognition vocabulary past fourth-grade requires an unusually high level of sustained motivation. It is, therefore, necessary to teach the child word attack skills that will enable him or her to comprehend unfamiliar words without undue reliance on blending ability. A linguistic approach (Chall, 1967, p. 24) might therefore be introduced once a modest lexicon of sight words has been accrued. The linguistic method is viewed as a word analysis process in contrast to the phonics approach that teaches word synthesis. When encountering a new word, the phonic reader might proceed from left to right blending sounds until he has synthesized the word. The linguistic reader might instead scan the word to detect recognizable chunks representing a prefix, suffix, and root. Initially in the linguistic method, for example, one does not teach an s sound in initial, final, and medial position, but as a letter that might signify plurality or possession (e.g., Hall, 1964). Letters and letter series such as ed for the past tense and ing can be taught as a chunk similar to a whole word.

In summary, the children presenting with the articulation and graphomotor dyscoordination syndrome manifest a buccal–lingual dyspraxia that is the major limiting factor in developing a phonic attack. The suggested treatment program initially embarks upon a two-prong attack emphasizing the development of a look–say vocabulary in conjunction with basal reader material, and penmanship drill with attention to consistency of letter production rather than neatness of the final product. At a later phase, word analysis skills using methodology and material from a linguistic approach might be introduced.

Visual–Perceptual Disorders

The children presenting with this syndrome demonstrate intact language, graphomotor coordination, and speech-blending skill. Although constructional ability is poor, visual–spatial perception is decidedly poorer when measured by tests requiring visual discrimination without complex motor manipulation of stimuli. Perception, storage, and/or retrieval of visual stimuli are so poorly processed that letters and letter sequences cannot be efficiently associated with their sound or linguistic referents. Those who are most severely affected cannot discriminate letters, although many can recite the alphabet, isolate a sound in initial and final placement in an orally presented word, and blend sounds adequately.

SUGGESTED TREATMENT

Most of the children referred to the Neuropsychology Division have already experienced programs designed to train perception via an approach of seeing, naming, feeling, and drawing the letter (VAKT) or programs emphasizing tracing letters and then fading the visual cues. A few have been engaged in direct perceptual training exercises utilizing tachistoscopic presentation of stimuli and various reward schedules for correct discrimination. It is possible that we see a biased sample of such patients, that is, those who are referred because they have been unresponsive to such treatment. In any event, the suggested treatment strategy capitalizes on the child's intact linguistic abilities to aid in stabilizing the identification of letters.

The initial procedure is to present a letter, usually one in the child's first name, and ask the child to describe it. This verbal description is then used as the clue for graphic reproduction. For example, the letter T might be presented and described as a *line going up and down and a line going across*. The letter is then removed, and the child is asked to draw what he has just said. The therapist at this stage might amend a verbal description if it is inaccurate or if it is not specific enough. For example, the description of the capital letter A as *two lines going up and down and one going across* is also appropriate for the letter *H*. The therapist might direct the child's attention to the fact that the two lines join at the top. With oblique lines and curves, *body English* is often an integral part of the description.

In the first phase, the lessons consist of drills emphasizing memorization of the description and reliance on the description for reproduction. As the child demonstrates reliability in *drawing* a letter, its name and sound referent is introduced. Eventually, the description is faded rather concretely by having the child gradually decrease the amplitude of his vocalization when drawing. Toward the conclusion of this procedure, a casual observer would judge that the children are writing letters to dictation although there appears to be an inordinate frequency of body tics that eventually abate. Letters that are reliably drawn to dictation are reliably discriminated by these children. At this point, a phonics program is embarked upon. However, the children are still rather easily perceptually flooded and material that minimizes the visual impact of the letters is more appropriate than those contained in color phonics programs. There is minor dispute within the education literature as to the role of pictures in early basal readers. One camp feels that they are distractions diluting concentration from the task of learning the code, and the other feels that the pictures enhance word meaning, and therefore facilitate learning. In some series, the pictures are delightful and attractive but would be decidedly disruptive. Others using pastels and grays are more subdued. If one wishes to be most cautious, the Carden series (1966), which can be used in conjunction with a phonics program, is recommended because it excludes pictures.

In summary, the children in this group present with inefficient processing of visual–spatial arrays: Letters and letter sequences cannot be associated with their sound and linguistic referents. Stable letter identification is developed with a procedure that requires the child to describe a letter and then reproduce it using these verbal and kinesthetic cues. When discrimination is reliable, a phonics program is introduced.

It would seem reasonable to assume that an effective treatment program for a dyslexic child should reflect (*a*) an understanding of the child's cognitive strength and weaknesses; (*b*) the causal relationship between the profile of neuropsychological functioning, the processes disrupting the acquisition of reading skill, and the pattern of reading and spelling errors manifested; and (*c*) experience with pedagogical methods and materials appropriate to the child's given deficits and abilities. Unfortunately, the clinical skills required for each determination reside within the purview of several separate disciplines whose members rarely share the same training, theoretical framework, or vocabulary, and who rarely converse directly.

Quite often the elegant comprehensive multidisciplinary differential diagnostic evaluation of cognitive processes conducted in hospital based facilities results in recommendations that are naive as to their practicability or so obfuscated in technical jargon as to be of limited value to the school based reading specialist responsible for the treatment. Frequently, logical gaps exist between the detection of cognitive defects and the inferences made as to their effect on reading. A crevass of ignorance must be traversed as the hospital based clinician leaps from the familiarity of clinical findings and inferences to their implications for programmatic treatment by the school. Similarly, heroic inferential leaps are made without trepidation by school based personnel in inferring patterns of cognitive deficits from observed patterns of reading and spelling errors. For example, it is not at all clear that a child's difficulty in look–say vocabulary is referrable to a disorder of visual processing nor is a difficulty in phonic attack reflective of a disorder in auditory processing. Distortions in the development of both a phonic attack and a whole word approach are each referrable to several etiological factors. That is, the development of phonic skills may be independently impaired by receptive difficulties in speech-sound discrimination and sequencing or expressive difficulties in motor–speech coordination. Similarly, recognition vocabulary can be impaired by visual- perceptual disorders or deficient verbal labeling of whole words.

The dyslexia programs outlined are derived from our understanding of the clusters of deficits critical to normal acquisition of reading skill and our observations of the relationship between these deficits and patterns of reading and spelling errors. Although the suggested sequence of procedures and rationale may be novel, the specific material and methods are within the armamentarium of most reading specialists. It should be noted that the efficacy of these programs has not been tested and that it is expected that, with experience, materials and procedures other than those suggested will be substituted as more optimally effective in reaching the goal of a given sequence in treatment.

Most of the suggested procedures are easier to outline than they are to implement, and treatment specialists among the readers of this chapter may find that the recommendations for treatment still sound somewhat naive. However, it was not the purpose of this chapter to present the treatment programs for dyslexia. Rather, it was hoped that delineating some of the logical processes by which specific treatment programs (to be implemented within the school) may be developed from clinical diagnostic findings would underscore the necessity for the active participation of both hospital-based and school-based specialists in planning dyslexia treatment and serve as a focus for renewed discourse between diagnostic and treatment clinicians.

References

Applebee, A. N. Research in reading retardation: Two critical problems. *Journal of Child Psychological Psychiatry* 1971, *12*, 91–113.

Bank Street College of Education. *The Bank Street readers*. New York: Macmillan, 1965.

Bateman, B. D. *Interpretation of the 1961 Illinois Test of Psycholinguistic Abilities*. Seattle: Special Child Publication, 1968.

Boder, E. Developmental dyslexia: Prevailing diagnostic concepts and a new diagnostic approach. *Bulletin of the Orton Society*, 1973, *23*, 106–118.

Carden, M. *The Carden method*. Glenrock, N.J.: Mae Carden, 1966.

Chall, J. S. *Learning to read: The great debate*. New York: McGraw-Hill, 1967.

Critchley, M. *Developmental dyslexia*. London: Heinemann, 1964.

Denckla, M. B. Minimal brain dysfunction and dyslexia: Beyond diagnosis by exclusion. In M. E. Blaw, I. Rapin, & M. Kinsbourne (Eds.), *Topics in child neurology*. New York: Spectrum, 1977. (a)

Denckla, M. B. The neurological basis of reading disability. In F. G. Roswell & G. Natcher (Eds.), *Reading disability: A human approach to learning*. New York: Basic Books, 1977. (b)

Gattegno, C. *Words in color*. Chicago: Encyclopedia Brittanica, 1964.

Hall, F. A. *Sounds and letters*. Ithaca, New York: Linguistica, 1964.

Ingram, T. T. S., Mason, A. W., & Blackburn, I. A retrospective study of 82 children with reading disability. *Developmental Medium and Child Neurology*, 1970, *12*, 271–281.

Jastak, J., Bijou, S. W., & Jastak, S. R. *Wide Range Achievement Test*. Wilmington, Delaware: Guidance Associates, 1965.

Kinsbourne, M., & Warrington, E. K. Developmental factors in reading and writing backwardness. In J. Money (Ed.), *The disabled reader: Education of the dyslexic child*. Baltimore: Johns Hopkins Press, 1966.

Kirk, S. A., McCarthy, J. J., & Kirk, W. D. *Illinois Test of Psycholinguistic Abilities*. Urbana: Univ. of Illinois Press, 1968.

Knights, R. M. Problems of criteria in diagnosis: A profile similarities approach. *Annals of the New York Academy of Sciences*, 1973, *205*, 124–131.

Mattis, S., Erenberg, G., & French, J. H. *Dyslexia syndromes: A cross validation study*. Paper presented at Sixth Annual Meeting, International Neuropsychological Society, Minneapolis, Minnesota, 1978.

Mattis, S., French, J. H., & Rapin, I. Dyslexia in children and young adults: Three independent neuropsychological syndromes. *Developmental Medicine and Child Neurology*, 1975, *17*, 150–163.

Myklebust, H. R., & Johnson, D. J. Dyslexia in children. *Exceptional Children*, 1962, *29*, 14–25.

Rasmussen, D., & Goldberg, L. *SRA basic reading series*. Chicago: Science Research Associates, 1966.

Rourke, B. P., & Finlayson, M. A. J. Neuropsychological significance of variations in patterns of academic performance: Verbal and visual–spatial abilities. *Journal of Abnormal Child Psychology,* 1978, 121–133.

Rourke, B. P., & Strong, J. D. Neuropsychological significance of variations in patterns of academic performance: Motor, psychomotor and tactual–perceptual abilities. *Journal of Pediatric Psychology,* 1978, 3(2), 62–66.

Paul Satz
Robin Morris

LEARNING DISABILITY SUBTYPES:
A Review

In recent years, considerable efforts have been made to identify more specific subtypes of learning disabled children who share common attributes that distinguish them from other subtypes. These attributes have been based on etiological inferences (e.g., neurological or genetic), performance on psychometric measures of ability (e.g., language, memory, perception), and/or direct measures of achievement (i.e., word recognition, comprehension, spelling, arithmetic). The search for homogeneous subtypes has been fostered largely by an increasing awareness of the heterogeneity of the term *learning disabilities* and the failure to define operationally what is meant by the term (Applebee, 1971; Benton, 1978; Gaddes, 1976; Rourke, 1978; Rutter, 1978; Spreen, 1976). This latter failure may well explain the persistent variability in prevalence estimates of learning disabilities in this country and abroad (Applebee, 1971; Gaddes, 1976).

At the present time, there is increasing recognition that "reading or learning disability" is not a homogeneous diagnostic entity (Benton, 1978; Rutter, 1978). In fact, such disabilities may take several forms in terms of achievement patterns and/or associated cognitive information-processing abilities that may additionally vary as a function of etiology or age. This position bears some resemblance to Applebee's Model 2 (1971), one of several statistical models proposed as logical alternatives to the theory of a single causal defect. Proponents of the single defect model, in contrast, would tend to subsume learning disabled children within a unitary framework that disregards heterogeneity at the level of

NEUROPSYCHOLOGICAL AND COGNITIVE
PROCESSES IN READING

classification, type of information-processing ability and/or cause. Such examples include the synaptic transmission theory of Smith and Carrigan (1959), Delacato's (1959) central neurological organization theory, Bender's (1958) maturational lag hypothesis, Cruickshank's (1977) perceptual deficit hypothesis, and Vellutino's (1978) verbal mediation hypothesis; according to Applebee (1971), research in reading retardation was, for too long, focused on these simplistic models. His recommendations are prophetic:

> Research has been successful only in showing that these simplest models do not fit the problem with which we are dealing: and that if we hope in the future to add anything of significance to our understanding of the problem, we must concentrate on new models which correspond more closely to the heterogeneity of the disorder. Such a shift will require more sophisticated methods of analysis than have been employed in the past, and will probably bring with them a whole new set of problems of interpretation and design. Nevertheless, to continue any longer with models which have outlived their usefulness seems as foolish as to abandon any attempts at resolution of the problem whatsoever [p. 112].

The identification of subtypes has traditionally been based on clinical–inferential approaches that group learning disabled children according to various a priori considerations, theoretical or otherwise. As stated earlier, these groupings have been based on one of three attributes: (a) etiology (often inferred); (b) performance on psychological cognitive measures; and/or (c) direct measures of reading and learning (achievement variables). Regardless of the attribute type, these approaches, as will be seen, have attempted to reduce complex data sets of subjects into presumably homogeneous classes based largely upon a priori considerations and visual inspection techniques. Despite inherent flaws in this type of clinical–inferential approach, the results have provided heuristic insights on different subtypes of learning disabled children.

More recently, attempts have been made to apply descriptive multivariate statistics in the search for meaningful learning disability subtypes. These statistical approaches, in contrast to clinical–inferential ones, create classifications through the search for the hidden structure of complex multidimensional data sets. The data sets have generally comprised measures of cognitive linguistic skills or direct measures of achievement. The following section will briefly review and critically evaluate the strengths and weaknesses of both approaches. Within each approach, representative studies will be cited for each method of classification.

Clinical–Inferential Classification Approaches

Classification by Etiology

One of the classic subtype approaches involves the postulate that, although there are many causes of reading disability, there is one specific syndrome (i.e., developmental dyslexia) in which the reading difficulties are due to an intrinsic constitutional deficit. The term is defined as "A disorder manifested by difficulty in learning to read despite conventional instruction, adequate intelligence, and socio-cultural opportunity. It is dependent upon fundamental cognitive disabilities which are frequently of constitutional origin [Critchley, 1970, p. 11]."

Special interest in dyslexia as opposed to other forms of reading disability seems to have come about for several reasons. The primary basis for its long history of investigation, however, is the promise it holds as a distinct subtype of reading disability. Because undifferentiated groups of disabled readers exhibit deficits along multiple dimensions (Bell & Aftamas, 1972; Belmont & Birch, 1966; Rourke, 1975), they likely represent conglomerates of various types of reading disorders. Accordingly, studies of such undifferentiated groups can contribute little to the identification of crucial antecedents responsible for an individual child's problem or to judgments regarding course, outcome, or preferred treatment. The major impetus for studying dyslexia thus stems from an implicit need to form more homogeneous subgroups of disabled readers, comprising more meaningful diagnostic entities.

Despite the appeal of this approach, the term *dyslexia* is essentially a diagnosis by exclusion and the presumption of a neurological or constitutional basis is just that—namely, a presumption (Benton, 1975). According to Rutter (1978), this definition, as a piece of logic, is a nonstarter and replete with vague and circular reasoning. Unfortunately, definitions of this type have long plagued research in the area of learning disabilities. As Ross (1976) has aptly stated

Stripped of those clauses which specified what a learning disability is not, this definition is circular, for it states, in absence, that a learning disability is an inability to learn. It is a reflection of the rudimentary state of knowledge in this field that every definition in current use has it focus on what the condition is not, leaving what it is unspecified and thus ambiguous. Furthermore, when defined in this manner, 'learning disability' is a heterogeneous category: progress in this field demands further refinement of the definition and an identification of subcategories [p. 11].

Rutter (1978) has also argued convincingly against exclusionary definitions such as dyslexia:

A negative definition of this kind not only fails to aid conceptual clarity but also it implies that dyslexia cannot be diagnosed in a child from a poor or unconventional background. In short it suggests that if all the known causes of reading disability can be ruled out, the unknown (in the form of dyslexia) should be invoked. A counsel of despair indeed [p. 12].

It seems ironic that a term that was used to identify subgroups of the general population of disabled readers should still include such an indeterminate and heterogeneous subset of children. Equally perplexing is the acceptance that this term has enjoyed in medical, psychological, and educational settings. The presumption of a constitutional basis associated with "fundamental cognitive disabilities" has generally been accepted despite the exclusionary and circular nature of the definition. Even more striking is the presumption that children diagnosed as dyslexic are distinguishable from other failing readers along several academic, neurological, familial, and psychological dimensions. The point is this: If a term is used to define a subset of the population of disabled readers, this subset should differ from the remaining subset on at least some of the dimensions subsumed under the term. This statement speaks to the issues of utility and validity that must be addressed in any approach involving subtypes, whether derived from clinical or statistical methods. In other words, one must determine whether a subtype is meaningful and distinguishable from other subtypes in the population.

The concept of developmental dyslexia was recently subjected to such a test by Taylor, Satz, and Friel (1979). Using the World Federation definition of specific developmental dyslexia (Waites, 1968), this study had two major aims: (a) to identify the number of failing readers who met the criteria for this diagnosis selected from a total school population of white boys (N = 570); and (b) to compare this subgroup with the remaining subset of failing readers on a number of academic, neuropsychological, medical, psychological, and prognostic dimensions. The first objective was designed to obtain prevalence estimates of the disorder, whereas the second was addressed to the utility or meaningfulness of the concept. This study represented the first attempt to address either objective. The subjects were derived from a population of white males who were followed from the beginning of Grade K (1970) to the end of Grade 5 (1977). The disabled readers represented a unique and unselected sample not biased by referral status. They were in Grades 2–5 at the time of the various assessment probes.

Objective 1: The results revealed that 14% of the population ($N = 80$) were reading approximately two grades or more below expectation at the end of Grade 2 (ages 7–8). Of these children, 50% ($N = 40$) met the criteria for specific developmental dyslexia. This represents an incidence of 7% (40/570), which, when corrected for a combined sex sample favoring males (4:1), would yield an estimate of 4.4% in the general school population (Taylor et al., 1979). This estimate closely approximates earlier clinical estimates (Benton, 1975; Critchley, 1970).

Objective 2: The results showed that the dyslexic subgroup could not be distinguished from the nondyslexic poor readers along any of several dimensions, including the initial severity and progression of the reading disturbance, frequency of reversal errors, familial reading and spelling competencies, math skills, neurobehavioral performance, or personality functioning. As these represent most of the dimensions along which dyslexics have been traditionally viewed as "distinctive," the present results raise serious doubts as to the clinical or research value of this diagnosis, at least as applied to the general population of white male school children. One might therefore conclude, according to Taylor et al. (1979), that reading failure associated with low intelligence, sociocultural inopportunity, emotional disturbance, or physical handicap may be no different from reading failure in the absence of these factors, and that the study of reading disabilities in the general population may not be facilitated by focusing on children whose reading problems are "unexpected."

The formation of subgroups based on exclusionary and etiological criteria is not idiosyncratic to the concept of specific developmental dyslexia. Early examples can also be seen in attempts to differentiate children with primary and secondary reading retardation (Rabinovitch, 1968; Rabinovitch, Drew, DeJong, Ingram, & Withey, 1954). Conceptually, the primary reading retardation group fits the criteria for the definition of specific developmental dyslexia. Secondary reading retardation implies that the disorder is the result of other factors—encephalopathy, emotional disturbance, deficient language experience, or educational–motivational deprivation. This latter group of children was shown to have a better prognosis than the primary reading retardation group who were hypothesized to suffer from an underlying neurological–genetic disturbance. Unfortunately, this method of classification is also weakened by the presumption of an underlying cause

that is couched in vague and circular language. Furthermore, by exclusion, it assumes that each of the groups share common attributes that
distinguish them on the basis of etiology, cognitive abilities, and/or
patterns of academic performance. This assumption, although seldom
tested, can also be criticized for definitional ambiguity and logical
inconsistency (Rutter, 1978). Similar criticisms could also be advanced
at the classification system of Bannatyne (1971) based on presumed
causal events.

Classification on Performance Variables (Nonreading)

Numerous attempts have been made to classify learning disabled
children on the basis of various neuropsychological–psychometric performance patterns. The rationale for this approach is that reading is a
highly complex activity that utilizes a great number of cognitive and
linguistic skills known to be altered not only in reading disabled
children, but in children with central nervous system injuries
(Maliphant, Supramaniam, & Saraga, 1974; Rourke, 1975; Rutter, 1978;
Satz & Van Nostrand, 1973). In fact, Mattis, French, and Rapin (1975)
have stated that "almost every disorder of higher cortical functioning
recognized in children has been found with greater frequency in dyslexic children than in normal controls [p. 150]." These authors further
suggest "that the processes critical to reading are adequate development of language, motor–speech blending fluency and visuospatial
perception, and that disruption in any one of these skills will result in
atypical reading [p. 158]."

Mattis et al. (1975) and Mattis (1978) have advanced the most
formal theory in the search for homogeneous subtypes of learning
disabled children. However, because of this theory and the method of
classification employed (visual inspection techniques), this work is
subsumed under clinical–inferential approaches. Their position (1975)
is that

> The underlying assumption is that if the development of fluency in reading re-
> quires the complex integration of several input, output and mediating processes,
> then a deficit in any given critical process would impair the learning of this
> complex skill. There should therefore exist separate subgroups of dyslexic children
> who manifest differing clusters of deficiencies, each of which limits the develop-
> ment of a specific, subprocess necessary for the acquisition of reading skill [p. 151].

Based on this rationale, Mattis et al. (1975) proceeded to search for
distinct and homogeneous subtypes in a sample of 82 dyslexic children
(developmental dyslexic = 29; brain-damaged dyslexic = 53) who

were selected from a much larger group of clinic-referred children (N = 252). This reduced subset of children (mean age = 11.5) was selected on the basis of exclusionary criteria to conform generally to the concept of developmental dyslexia. However, the selection process was strengthened by the inclusion of a comparison group of brain-damaged normal readers (N = 31). This comparison group was then used to isolate syndromes within the two dyslexic groups whose deficiencies were unrelated to brain complications in normal readers. The classification process was based on the children's performance on a wide variety of language, speech, motor, and perceptual tasks. The method of classification involved a set of a priori rules designed to identify three distinct and nonoverlapping syndromes: (a) a language disorder subtype; (b) an articulatory and graphomotor dyscoordination subtype; and (c) a visual–spatial perceptual disorder subtype. It is unclear as to whether the rules were derived after visual inspection of the data sets or before, in accordance with their theoretical expectations. If the former, the results are subject to many of the flaws inherent in attempts to reduce multidimensional data sets based on visual inspection techniques. If the latter, the results could be criticized for attempts to fit complex data sets into predetermined theoretical classes (Cormack, 1971).

Nevertheless, on the basis of these decision rules, Mattis et al. (1975) identified three syndrome types that varied in frequency: (a) a language disorder subtype (39%); (b) an articulatory and graphomotor dyscoordination subtype (37%); and (c) a visual–perceptual disorder subtype (16%). This grouping method classified 90% of the subjects, none of whom "demonstrated findings consonant with more than one syndrome [1975, p. 155]." The authors concluded that these subtypes had both etiological and educational implications.

Further support for these subtypes was recently reported by Mattis (1978) on a cross-validation sample of younger black and hispanic school children (mean age = 9). This study was strengthened by the use of a larger sample (N = 400) that was unbiased by clinic referral. Results again revealed the presence of these subtypes in 78% of the subjects; however, the frequencies within each subtype varied from the original study: (a) language disorder subtype (63%); (b) articulatory graphomotor dyscoordination subtype (10%); and (c) visual–perceptual disorder subtype (5%). These differences in the percentage of subjects classified within types may be due to sample differences or limitations of the classification method.

Despite the appeal that these subtypes hold for clinical and educational practice, they should be viewed with caution on the basis of the preceding criticisms. One should also note that a set of subtype patterns that conform to a set of a priori decision rules need not reflect the true hidden structure of the data, especially complex data sets. Determination of the latter problem may be accomplished through the use of computers employing multivariate statistical techniques to describe data in multidimensional hyperspaces. This approach will be discussed in the subsequent section.

Another issue regarding the Mattis et al. (1975) approach is the statement that homogeneous and nonoverlapping subtypes emerged on the basis of their analysis. With respect to the principles of taxonomic classification (Bailey, 1973; Sneath & Sokal, 1973), this may mean that monothetic groups were formed. Such groups in biology are formed by rigid and successive logical divisions so that the possession of a unique set of features is both necessary and sufficient for membership in the group thus defined. According to Sneath and Sokal (1973),

> they are called monothetic because the defining set of features is unique. That is, all the members of any group possess all of the features that are used to define the group. Such groupings will always carry the risk of serious misclassification if we wish to make natural phenetic groups. By contrast, in a polythetic group organisms are placed together that have the greatest number of shared character states and no state is either essential to group membership or is sufficient to make an organism a member of the group [pp. 20–21].

Polythetic groups have greater application in the behavioral sciences because class membership is defined in terms of highly common or shared attributes (i.e., members of a group possess most, but not necessarily all attributes in common). This taxonomic concept conforms more readily to psychological phenomena in which classifications are based more on achievement or ability distributions that contain typical variances. Polythetic classification allows for the inclusion of more subjects (coverage) in a classification schema.

One should note that in the Mattis et al. (1975) studies, subjects were classified into three distinct homogeneous subtypes in which all members of each group possessed the same exact features, none of which was shared by the other groups. Puzzling is the fact that no subjects had features common to more than one subtype that would have possibly generated at least one additional subtype (e.g., a language and perceptual disorder subtype). This latter subtype would certainly conform to clinical and empirical reports of learning disabled children who show a mixed pattern of performance or achievement deficits (Boder, 1973; Denckla, 1972; Ingram, Mann, & Blackburn, 1970; Keeney & Keeney, 1968; Owen, 1978; Petrauskas & Rourke, 1979; Rourke &

Finlayson, 1978; Smith, 1970). Mattis (1978) does state that, in the "cross-validation study, 9% (of the children) presented with two syndromes (although none presented with all three [p. 50]." Mattis goes on to report that he is "reluctant to affirm" a new deficit cluster. It seems reasonable to suggest that these children with "two syndromes" could represent another subtype(s) (mixed?) that is obscured due to the classification criteria used (monothetic).

With respect to performance patterns, Smith (1970) identified, by visual inspection, three subtypes of retarded readers on the basis of WISC profiles; these types were not observed in a comparison group of good readers. Pattern I was characterized by deficient symbol manipulation and auditory sequencing in the presence of intact spatial ability. Pattern II was deficient in spatial–perceptual ability with intact symbol manipulation and auditory sequencing. Pattern III, in particular, was composed of subjects who showed deficiencies common to Patterns I and II (i.e., a mixed category).[1]

Using identical measures, Kinsbourne and Warrington (1966) attempted to divide their children on the basis of extreme discrepancy scale scores on the Wechsler Intelligence Scale for Children (WISC) (> 20 IQ points). This a priori method produced two small subtypes: (a) a disabled group (N = 6) with depressed verbal IQs and delayed speech and comprehensional vocabulary; and (b) a disabled group (N = 7) with depressed performance IQs and poor arithmetical and constructional ability. Unfortunately, children were excluded who showed a mixed pattern of impaired verbal and spatial performance. Also, no comparison group of good readers was employed to ensure that these performance patterns were idiosyncratic to the failing readers.

Using neuropsychological data, Denckla (1972) identified three clinical syndromes in a clinic sample of learning disabled children: (a) a specific language disturbance subtype; (b) a specific visuo–spatial disability subtype; and (c) a dyscontrol subtype. Although these syndromes resemble those reported by Mattis et al. (1975) and Mattis (1978), it should be noted that Denckla found that approximately 70%

---

[1] It is interesting to note that the proportion of Pattern I individuals (verbal defect) increased as the age of the children increased. In contrast, the proportion of Pattern II individuals (spatial defect) decreased significantly as the age of the children increased. This finding is compatible with the theory advanced by Satz and Sparrow (1970) that predicts two subtype patterns in reading disabled children: a predominantly visual–perceptual pattern at younger ages and a predominantly language disorder pattern at older ages. Unfortunately, this formulation can also be criticized for its reliance on rather simplistic a priori notions of dyslexia subtypes and its failure to withstand more recent follow-up tests (Fennell & Satz, 1979; Satz & Morris, this chapter).

of the disabled learners either produced mixed deficits or did not fit into any of the three categories.

The preceding studies, in summary, highlight many of the problems inherent in the clinical–inferential method of subtype classification. Although much of this research has contributed to our knowledge of potential subtype divisions within the concept of learning disabilities, the validity, reliability, and utility of these subtypes have seldom been tested. More seriously, the methods used to derive these subtypes have relied solely on visual inspection of complex, multidimensional data sets often based on predetermined a priori divisions that usually result in rigid monothetic groups. In addition, comparison groups of good readers, both normals and brain damaged, have seldom been employed in the search for distinctive subtypes of learning disabled children.[2] It will be shown that many of these same problems exist in those clinical–inferential approaches that employ more direct measures of reading and achievement skill in the subdivision process. Some of these studies will be reviewed next.

Classification on Achievement Variables

One of the landmark studies in this area is the paper by Elena Boder (1973). This study is distinguished by its perceptive analysis of quantitative and qualitative achievement patterns in a preselected group of children who met the World Federation definition of specific developmental dyslexia. This group of children (92 boys and 15 girls) was selected from a larger group of 300 children who also met the World Federation definition. The 107 children ranged in age from 8 to 16, were currently enrolled in school, and were 2 or more years behind in reading and spelling.

Within this preselected group of children, Boder proceeded to search for distinctive patterns of reading and spelling that might further subdivide her sample into distinctive subtypes. Particular emphasis was given to a qualitative analysis of how the child reads and spells rather than the grade level obtained. This clinical approach was felt to offer additional guidelines for remedial teaching. Based on this approach, she identified three subtypes in 100 of the 107 children. *Subtype 1* was defined as a dysphonetic group who had selective impairments in analyzing the phonetic properties of words and syllables. These children lacked word analysis skills and were unable to

---

[2] An exception is the study by Mattis *et al.* (1975), which employed a brain-injured sample of normal readers as the comparison group.

sound out and blend component letters and syllables. Because of this deficiency, they approached written material in a global fashion, relying on sight alone. They were also unable to analyze the auditory gestalt of a spoken word into its component sounds and syllables. The dysphonetic group comprised the largest number of children (67%). Subtype 2 was defined as a dyseidetic group who had selective impairments in remembering and discriminating visual gestalts. These children tended to read laboriously as if seeing each word for the first time. Because of this deficiency (i.e., "letter blind"), they tended to adopt an analytic strategy of phonetic analysis rather than whole word visual gestalts. Only 10% of the children were classified within this subtype. Subtype 3 was defined as a mixed dysphonetic–dyseidetic group who had deficiencies in both phonetic analysis and discrimination of visual gestalts. Educationally, they were also more severely handicapped. Because of these multiple handicaps (visual and auditory), their word attack skills were fragmented, unpredictable, and often bizarre. Children in this subtype also showed more striking signs of emotional frustration and defeat. Of all the children, 23% were classified in this mixed subtype group.

The strength of this study inheres largely in the detailed clinical analyses of each child's approach to written material. It is difficult to fault the rich clinical impressions that can be derived from this type of approach or from that employed by Mattis et al. (1975). Yet one must still address the questions or validity, reliability, and utility of the subtypes derived from these clinical impressions. Lacking replication, statistical derivation, or verification, these subtypes perforce represent abstractions based on the clinician's visual inspection of complex data sets and patterns. As such, the terms used to denote the subtypes may contain much surplus meaning (McCorquodale & Meehl, 1948).

Boder (1973) attempted to address these questions indirectly by asking whether the subtype divisions were compatible with other studies. She reported that her subtypes were consistent with other reports using either achievement or cognitive measures. Her dysphonetic subtype, in particular, was felt to be consistent with a growing number of observations on the importance of audiophonic deficits as a basic underlying "cause" of developmental dyslexia (Bateman, 1968; Ingram et al., 1970). This subtype also bears some resemblance to the language disorder subtype identified by Mattis et al. (1975). In both studies, this subtype comprised the largest number of children. Similar subtypes have also been reported by Myklebust (1968) with reference to his concept of audiophonic dyslexia and by Quiros (1964) with reference to his concept of a central auditory processing defect. This subtype has also been observed in retarded readers on the basis of WISC profile scores. Kinsbourne and Warrington (1966) identified a language retardation subtype and Smith (1970) identified a subtype that was selectively impaired in symbol manipulation and sequencing ability.

Boder (1973) also found indirect support for her dyseidetic subtype from other reports in the literature. Myklebust (1968) referred to the concept of a visual dyslexia subtype and Quiros (1964) referred to a subgroup of dyslexic readers who were impaired in visual–perceptive processes. Similar subtypes have also been reported on the basis of WISC subtype profiles. Kinsbourne and Warrington (1966) identified a subtype that had selective impairments in nonverbal performance skills and Smith (1970) identified a subtype that had selective impairments in visuospatial ability. One should note that Mattis et al. (1975) also identified a subtype referred to as visuospatial–perceptual disorder. This subtype comprised the smallest number of children in both the Mattis et al. (1975) and Boder (1973) studies.

Boder (1973) also claimed that her mixed dysphonetic–dyseidetic subtype was similar to other reports in the literature (Bateman, 1968; Denckla, 1972; Ingram et al., 1970; Smith, 1970). A tally of this literature generally reveals a subgroup that is distinguished by a mixed pattern of verbal and perceptual deficits. Unfortunately, the proportion of children classified within these subtypes vary markedly between studies. In some studies, the majority of dyslexic children produce either mixed deficits or do not fit neatly into any of the clinical categories (Denckla, 1972). This variability can spring from several sources, including differences in subject selection criteria, sample size, the type and number of tests employed as well as the method of classification used, especially if monothetic groups are formed. When visual inspection techniques are employed, these problems are likely to lower the reliability and validity of the subtypes. The attempt to validate subtypes by reference to other studies, although commendable as a beginning step, is nevertheless subject to errors of interpretation and logic.

What Boder (1973) refers to as a dysphonetic subtype may be quite different from what Mattis et al. (1975) refer to as a language disorder subtype, Myklebust (1968) as auditory dyslexia, or Smith (1970) as a symbol manipulation–sequencing pattern on the WISC. The methods used in each of these studies, including subject selection, sample size, tests, and observer rules are quite different. Also, the terms used to describe the subtypes represent abstractions that may be derived from observer bias and need not conform to the true hidden structure of the data. Furthermore, these abstractions may contain surplus meaning that may mask more refined categories within the subtype. This is especially likely to be the case for global terms such as *language disorder*. Of course, the creation of a hierarchical classification schema could include increasingly refined categories of subtypes.

Whereas Boder's (1973) subtypes have an intuitive appeal and "resemblance" to reports in the clinical literature, they must be viewed with caution until the rules for subtype classification are more clearly operationalized and validated against external criteria. For example, are there differences or similarities in the phonetic analysis skills of dysphonetic (Group 1) and mixed dysphonetic and dyseidetic dyslexics (Group III)? If differences, are they in terms of levels or patterns? Are the differences scalar? Similar questions might also be asked with respect to the visual gestalt deficits between the dyseidetic (Group II) and mixed dysphonetic–dyseidetic (Group III) subtypes. Although Boder recognizes some of these problems, the basis for classification remains obscure. One might also ask whether the subtypes vary by age, IQ, sex, neurological status, or performance on nonreading measures of ability.

Another point to consider in any subtype study, regardless of the classification method, is whether a comparison group of good readers was also employed. If not, one cannot be sure that the subtypes are idiosyncratic to the target group (i.e., failing readers). This point becomes even more poignant when the target group is already preselected on the basis of various exclusionary criteria (e.g., developmental dyslexia). In this case, the investigator would be wise to employ two independent comparison groups, normal readers and nondyslexic retarded readers—particularly if the derived subtypes are extrapolated to these populations. Other comparison group alternatives could employ normal or retarded readers who were brain-damaged (Mattis *et al.*, 1975). In the Boder (1973) study, such extrapolations were made without the utilization of these control groups. For example, she stated: "A child with nonspecific reading disorder reads poorly but has normal reading potential, the reading and spelling performance of such a child is quantitatively, but not qualitatively, different from that of a normal reader, whereas a dyslexic child, as has been noted, reads differently, both quantitatively and qualitatively [p. 700]."

This interpretation, although probably based on sound clinical impression, must nevertheless be viewed with caution until comparison profiles are presented for normal and nonspecific reading disorder groups. One might recall the study by Taylor, Satz, & Friel (1979), which failed to identify distinctive performance patterns of "dyslexic" children when a comparison group of nonspecific reading retarded children was employed. Also, a study addressed to different patterns of spelling errors in a reading retarded and normal control group failed to substantiate the existence of subtypes as hypothesized by Boder (1973). The groups differed only in terms of the total number of errors (Holmes & Peper, 1973). These findings only serve to reinforce the cautions advanced by Meehl (1954) in his classic book on clinical versus statistical prediction. All too often instances of presumed clinical "truth" pale in the light of statistical fact.

The preceding section provided a brief, though critical, review of some of the representative subtype studies that employed clinical rather than statistical methods of classification. An attempt was made to address both the strengths and weaknesses of each study within the identified categories (etiology, ability patterns, and achievement skill). Despite the clinical and heuristic value of many of these studies, weaknesses in experimental design and data reduction were shown to limit some of the conclusions that might be derived from these subtype patterns. One might argue, however, that even with adequate designs, the search for subtypes based on visual inspection of complex data sets is limited and may not generate optimal and valid subgroups. What is additionally needed is the application of more powerful statistical methods that may allow one to validate these clinical models, or isolate new models that correspond more closely to the heterogeneity of learning disabled children.

The following section provides a brief review of some representative studies that have employed multivariate statistical techniques in the search for learning disability subtypes.

Statistical Classification Approaches

The application of statistical techniques in the search for homogeneous subtypes of learning disabled children is of recent origin. This may be due to the fact that only recently have major strides been made in high-speed computer technology and multivariate statistical techniques. However, note should be given to two earlier studies that employed cluster analytic techniques for classifying subtypes of reading disabled children (Naidoo, 1972; Smith & Carrigan, 1959). These studies, although subject to criticisms of small sample size (Smith & Carrigan, 1959), lack of normal comparison groups, and unsophisticated use of cluster analysis, represent timely and innovative forerunners of the studies that will now be discussed.

Classification on Achievement Variables

The study by Doehring and Hoshko (1977) represents one of the first major attempts to apply statistical techniques in the search for homogeneous subtypes of learning disabled children. The uniqueness of this study is its attempt to derive homogeneous subtypes, based on statistical techniques without recourse to a priori decision rules regarding subtype divisions. Two separate groups of children were selected from somewhat different populations. Group R (reading problems, N = 34) included children 8 years and older who were seen in a summer program. There were 31 boys and 3 girls ranging in age from 8.8 to 17.4 years, and in IQ from 71 to 125. Group M (mixed problems, N = 31) included children 8 years and older who were seen in a summer program. This group included children with learning disorders, language disorders, and mental retardation. There were 10 girls and 21 boys with ages ranging from 8.2 to 12.5 and IQ from 79 to 105.

A total of 31 tests of reading-related skills was administered to each child. Following this, the results were subjected to a Q-technique factor analysis (Nunnally, 1967) for each group separately. The Q-technique is a "transposed" or "inverted" method that groups children together (not test variables as in factor analysis) who show similar patterns of performance. Three subtypes emerged for each group.

Group R. The profile for Subtype 1 revealed good performance on all the visual matching tests and on three of the auditory–visual matching tests, and poor performance on the oral reading tests (words and syllables). The authors felt that these children (N = 12) had more of a linguistic defect. The profile for Subtype 2 revealed good performance on visual scanning tests (letters and numbers), poor performance on auditory–visual letter matching, and poor performance on two other auditory–visual tests and on four oral reading tests (words). Doehring and Hoshko (1977) felt that these children (N = 11) had more of a phonological defect marked by difficulty in associating printed and spoken letters. The profile for Subtype 3 revealed good visual and auditory–visual matching of single letters but poor visual and auditory–visual matching (words and syllables). The authors referred to these children (N = 8) as deficient in intersensory integration. The Q-technique managed to classify 31 of the 34 children.

An interesting and important feature of this study was the attempt to use external criteria for validating the three subtype patterns. Teacher recommendations were used for this comparison and provided preliminary support for these subtypes. In addition, most of the children in Subtype 1 were labeled as distractable and all but one were in regular classes; most of the children in Subtype 2 were in regular classes, whereas most of the children in Subtype 3 were in special classes, had repeated a grade and had some kind of family reading problem.

Group M. Three independent subtypes emerged in this analysis, two of which (1 and 2) were also observed in the primary reading group (Group R). Subtype 3, however, bore no resemblance to the other subtype patterns in Group R. This subtype (N = 7) was largely characterized by deficient performance on most of the visual–perceptual tests. When the Q-technique was applied to combined Groups R and M, only Subtype 1 of Group R retained its separate identity and Subtype 3 of Group M disappeared.

With respect to further validation of the subtypes, Doehring and Hoshko (1977) made comparative reference to other subtype studies. They felt that Subtype 1 of Group R was most similar to the language disorder subtype of Kinsbourne and Warrington (1966) and Mattis et al. (1975). This subtype had a trend toward higher performance IQs along with naming and language comprehension problems. They also felt that Subtype 3 of Group R, which included selective difficulties in auditory–visual word matching and letter–sound blending, was compatible with the auditory dyslexia subtype of Myklebust (1968) and the dysphonetic subtype of Boder (1973). The profile of Subtype 2 of Group R proved more difficult to interpret. They suggested, with caution, that "the accompanying oral expression difficulty in the Group R children could be indicative of a language disorder involving naming [p. 290]."

The preceding statements again highlight some of the problems of subtype validation based on comparison with other studies. Such comparisons are subject to errors of interpretation and logic. This point was made earlier with respect to the Boder (1973) paper. For example, what Boder (1973) refers to as a dysphonetic subtype may be quite different from what Mattis et al. (1975) refer to as a language disorder subtype or what Myklebust (1968) refers to as auditory dyslexia. These terms represent abstractions and as such are imbued with surplus meaning. Note that Doehring and Hoshko (1977) fall prey to this definitial ambiguity. For example, they liken their Subtype 1 to Mattis et al.'s (1975) language disorder subtype and their Subtype 2 to Boder's (1973) dysphonetic and Myklebust's (1968) auditory dyslexia subtype. However, Boder (1973) likens her dysphonetic group to Mattis et al.'s (1975) language disorder subtype. In fact, all three of Doehring and Hoshko's

(1977) subtypes refer to some type of loosely formulated "language" disorder that may in part be due to the nature of the tests employed.

The preceding criticisms address only the use of comparative studies in subtype validation. They do not question the intrinsic validity of the subtypes that Doehring and Hoshko (1977) attempted to validate by comparison with independent teacher recommendations. However, this phase of the study would have been strengthened by the use of more objective statistics (e.g., ANOVA, MANOVA, etc.) to test for subtype differences on external criteria not used in the classification process.

Additional concerns may also be raised with respect to the selection procedures and statistical analysis employed. No comparison group of normal readers was used to determine whether the subtypes were idiosyncratic to the failing readers–learners. One could argue that a comparison group of normal readers is less mandatory when achievement rather than ability tests are employed. However, without such a group, one could not be sure that scalar or configural patterns in the normal readers would not alter the subtype derivations. This problem was corrected in a recent replication study by the authors (Doehring, Hoshko, & Bryans, 1979). Using the same sample of 31 reading disabled children (Group R) plus 31 normal readers matched on both age and sex, they reported that the original three subtypes remained stable and distinct from the normal readers who were evenly distributed among the high positive and high negative loadings. Unfortunately, this latter reference to normal readers remains unclear.

A more serious concern could be raised with respect to the statistical technique used. The Q-technique is controversial. This technique produces product–moment correlations between subjects, and a matrix of these coefficients is then factored and sometimes rotated. If each subject has a high factor loading on only one factor, subjects with similar high loadings on the same factor can be classified in the same group. However, if a subject has significant loadings on more than one factor, problems of classification occur. There are no objective rules for how such multiple loadings should be dealt with.

Other problems with this technique have been noted by Fleiss and Zubin (1969) and by Fleiss, Lawlor, Platman, and Fieve (1971). They object to the use of the correlation technique as a measure of similarity between subjects. The correlation coefficient provides no measure of elevation that could obscure potential subtypes in dimensional data. In addition the technique is invalid for data in which the assumption of linearity is questioned. One must consider the meaning of linear composites of children. It has also been pointed out that the number of subtypes, given a set of variables, can never be more than one less the number of variables ($p - 1$). Thus, the data description is restricted by the method's limitations. One might also question the use of Q-technique on such a small sample ($N = 31$) involving multiple variables ($N = 18$). The subject–variable relationship's effect on Q-technique's results is also a matter of controversy. The small sample size also prevents a subdivision of the subjects into randomized groups to check reliability of the subtypes. Finally, the use of this statistical technique lacks the advantages inherent in other techniques (e.g., cluster analysis), that can utilize distance functions and were created for the purpose of classification.

Some of these concerns are not intended to question the validity of subtypes derived from the Doehring et al. studies. Inspection of their data reveals that only a few of the subjects had loadings on more than one factor (subtype). Also, the subtypes remained relatively stable when recomputed on combined retarded and normal readers. However, inattention to these problems could flaw subsequent applications of the method.

The Doehring et al. studies (1977, 1979) are unique in showing the potential application of statistical methods in the search for homogeneous subtypes of learning disabled children. Criticisms can still be leveled at some of the sampling methods employed, the statistical methods used, and, more importantly, the external validation criteria employed. Nevertheless, the study represents a novel departure from earlier approaches that could be used as a model for future studies. The following section provides an example of an application using neuropsychological data as the basis for classification.

Classification on Neuropsychological Variables

One of the major extensions of the Q-technique was conducted by Byron Rourke and colleagues at the University of Windsor (Petrauskas & Rourke, 1979). Forty-four neuropsychological tests assessing a wide variety of cognitive, motor, and tactile skills were administered to 160 children between the ages of 7 and 9. The sample was preselected on the basis of Wide Range Achievement Test (WRAT) scores that yielded two groups, retarded readers ($N = 133$) and normal readers ($N = 27$). The retarded readers were further selected to exclude children with low IQs (< 80), cultural deprivation, and visual or hearing problems. These selection criteria were apparently imposed to obtain cases of specific reading retardation. The 44 tests were then grouped into various skill areas based on a grouping procedure advocated by Reitan

(1974). From these, 20 tests were selected on the basis of low intertest correlations, skill area, and test interpretability. A unique feature of this study is that it divided the 160 subjects randomly into two subsamples of 80 subjects each to determine the reliability of the factor subtypes.

The results of the Q-technique factor analysis revealed five subtypes, only three of which were replicable across samples. Only 50% of the subjects were classified into the three subtypes. Subtype 1, which contained the largest number of subjects (N = 40), encompassed those having mild impairments in concept formation, word blending, immediate memory for digits, and moderate to severe impairments in verbal fluency and sentence memory. These subjects (3:1, males:females) also showed the largest verbal–performance IQ discrepancies on the WISC (lower VIQ) and lower WRAT scores in reading and spelling than in arithmetic. The authors considered subjects in this subtype as having a language disorder commonly "observed in adults with actively debilitating lesions of the left temporal lobe [p. 31]." They also felt that this subtype was similar to the language disorder subtype described by Mattis et al. (1979).

Subtype 2, which contained 26 subjects (12:1, males:females), showed mild impairment in verbal fluency and concept formation, moderate impairment in sentence memory, and moderate to severe impairment in finger recognition and immediate visual–spatial memory. Children in this subtype revealed no WISC verbal or performance scale discrepancies, but they exhibited uniformly poor performance on the WRAT reading, spelling, and arithmetic subtests. The authors hypothesized "that the combination of linguistic, sequencing, and finger localization deficiencies evident in type 2 are reflective of compromised functional integrity of the posterior regions of the left cerebral hemisphere [p. 32]." Petrauskas and Rourke (1979) were unable to compare this subtype with other reports in the literature.

Subtype 3, which contained 13 subjects (2:1, males:females), showed mild impairment in finger recognition (right hand), mild to moderate impairment in verbal fluency, sentence memory, and immediate visual–spatial memory, and moderate to severe impairment in concept formation (verbal coding). This subtype also had lower verbal than performance IQ scores on the WISC. No information, however, was presented on the WRAT scores. It should be noted that two subjects from the normal reading group loaded highly on this factor. With respect to interpretation of this subtype, the authors felt that the presence of intact visual–spatial abilities and verbal comprehension with impaired verbal coding made this subtype similar to the articulation and graphomotor dyscoordination group of Mattis et al. (1975, 1978). They also hypothesized a similarity between this subtype and adults who have sustained injury to the left parietal region of the brain.

The final two subtypes were found to be unreliable and therefore will not be discussed. However, it should be pointed out that only eight children fell within Subtype 4, seven of whom were normal readers. No mention is given as to the number of normal readers in Subtype 5.

The strengths of this study include the large number of carefully selected retarded readers, the broad range of neuropsychological functions assessed, the derivation of subtypes based on combined reading groups, the use of a split-sample reliability method for measuring subtype stability and the attempt to validate the subtypes on external criteria.

The weaknesses of this study also deserve mention. First, a larger number of normal readers should probably have been employed. It is unclear from the results whether a clearly definable normal subtype(s) emerged. In fact, Subtype 4, which contained mostly normal readers, accounted for only 26% of the normal readers (7/27). Second, the presence of some normal readers in Subtype 3 raises a question of whether the reading groups (good and poor) should be preselected prior to the subtype analysis. This issue has not been addressed up to this point. However, it may be a crucial issue. One could argue that the method also be used to define reading groups (prior to the subtype analyses) rather than relying on arbitrary and/or exclusionary criteria in the preselection of these groups. If the rationale behind these methods is to identify the hidden structure of the complex data sets, then logic would dictate that the techniques be applied initially to a representative sample of children across various achievement distributions. This approach would therefore provide a more objective criteria for identifying subgroups within the achievement distribution. If, on this basis, a subgroup(s) of retarded readers emerged, this subgroup(s) could be further analyzed, using neuropsychological data, to search for meaningful or homogeneous subtypes. This criticism is directed to the subtype literature in general, which has consistently disregarded the issue. At least Petrauskas and Rourke (1979) attempted to pool their good and poor readers prior to the subdivision analyses.

A third weakness in the Petrauskas and Rourke (1979) study was the failure to apply a factor analysis on their initial test battery ($N = 44$). Such an analysis could have validated their test groupings, possibly reduced their error and redundancy variance, and allowed them to find possible factor differences between subsamples. This procedure, in turn, could have greatly simplified interpretability of their subtypes.

Due to the problem of subject–variable ratio necessary in Q-technique, such a process may not have been practical or useful in this particular study.

A fourth weakness concerns the use of Q-technique method and has already been discussed in the previous section. One should note that the technique managed to classify only half of the subjects into replicable subtypes. This means that coverage was limited and a major part of the data set was lost.

A fifth weakness concerns the method employed for testing the validity of the subtypes. Apparently IQ and WRAT data were not tested across subtypes, a technique which would have provided a more significant test of group differences. The reader is merely told that various corresponding WISC or WRAT patterns were observed. Even with such an analysis, the use of external criterion variables is required. Variables used in the classification process should not be confounded with the validation criteria.

A final concern relates to the interpretations made on each of the subtypes. These concerns were discussed in some detail in the preceding section and will not be repeated. However, one should be wary of inferences alluding to brain abnormalities based on these preliminary, unvalidated behavioral subtypes.

*Classification on Achievement and
Neuropsychological Variables*

One of the recent applications of this approach was conducted by the present authors using data from the Florida Longitudinal Project. This study followed some of the earlier work by Darby (1978). A unique feature of this study was the use of cluster analysis to initially identify the learning disabled group. This was accomplished by first analyzing the WRAT achievement scores on a large and generally unselected sample (N = 236) of white boys who remained in Alachua County at the end of Grade 5 (6 years later).[3] The sample (mean age = 11) included children at all levels of achievement. This approach represents the first attempt to use cluster analysis to define the target subgroup and comparison subgroups prior to the search for subtypes. The advantages of this approach are as follows: (a) it avoids the use of

---

[3] The sample comprised all learning disabled boys from the original standardization population (6 years earlier) who continued to reside in Alachua County, plus their respective matched controls (primary and often secondary). In this respect, only the learning disabled children were really unselected although they had been earlier defined on an a priori basis.

exclusionary criteria in the selection of learning disabled subjects; and (b) it provides a more objective and statistical classification of probands. Cluster analysis is a procedure designed to facilitate the creation of classification schemes. It has been defined as procedure that groups individuals into homogeneous clusters based on each subject's performance on the clustering variables.

CLASSIFICATION ON ACHIEVEMENT VARIABLES

The WRAT reading, spelling, and arithmetic subtests were first converted into discrepancy scores by comparing a child's grade level with the grade-equivalent score obtained on each subtest. These scores were then subjected to cluster analysis to group individuals most similar to each other on these discrepancy scores.

The WRAT data were subjected to a hierarchical agglomerative analysis utilizing an average linkage method and squared Euclidian distance similarity measure. The average linkage method combined with the Euclidean distance measure was used because of the high correlation among the WRAT subtests (Jastak & Jastak, 1976), and its sensitivity to elevation in a data set. This method was likely to permit clusters that are different on their levels of achievement to emerge.

Nine clusters (subgroups) emerged, which were then subjected to a K-means iterative partitioning clustering method. This additional method was used because of the fact that an individual, once placed in a given cluster by a hierarchical agglomerative method, is not able to be reassigned to a later forming cluster, even if its similarity to the latter cluster is greater.[4] This method attempts to reduce within-cluster variance (increase homogeneity) while increasing between-cluster variance (decrease overlap), thus attempting to clarify the cluster solution. The clusters (achievement subgroups) were then subjected to a multivariate analysis of variance (MANOVA) using the WRAT subtests as the dependent variable. Robust differences among cluster groups emerged from this analysis, further confirming the solution of the cluster analysis. It should be noted, though, that the use of the actual clustering variables in testing cluster solutions by various statistical means (ANOVA, MANOVA, discriminate analysis) is not a validation process. One expects these significant differences from a majority of the clustering algorithms in use and nonsignificance is an important sign that something is wrong with one's computer program.

The nine subgroups, which included 230 of the 236 subjects,

---

[4] During each iterative partioning phase, each individual is statistically removed from its parent cluster and its similarity to all other clusters is computed. If its similarity to another cluster is greater than its similarity to the parent cluster, the individual is placed in that cluster and the centroids (cluster centers) are immediately recomputed.

revealed a number of interesting patterns of reading, spelling, and arithmetic skill.[5] Subgroups 1 and 2 both obtained superior scores in reading, but Subgroup 2 exhibited only average performance in arithmetic. Subgroup 3 achieved high reading, spelling, and arithmetic scores. Subgroup 4 emerged as a group with adequate reading and spelling scores, but standard performance in arithmetic. Subgroup 5 constituted a unique group by virtue of its average reading, slightly below average spelling, and severely depressed arithmetic scores. Subgroup 6 showed average reading and spelling, but was superior in arithmetic. Subgroup 7's performance in all areas was the most nearly average of all the subgroups.

At the lower end of the achievement spectrum, Subgroups 8 and 9 each contained a large number of children. Reading and spelling scores for these three subgroups could be arranged according to decreasing levels of performance. Arithmetic scores were below average for both subgroups. The overall achievement of Subgroups 8 and 9 were sufficiently depressed (2-year deficit) to suggest that these children could be labeled as learning disabled. There were 89 boys in these two subgroups.

The validity of the cluster subgroups was examined by asking whether any group differences existed in terms of IQ (PPVT), neuropsychological performance, neurological status and socioeconomic level (SES). Robust differences (MANOVA) were shown for each of these analyses. For example, the PPVT IQ scores ranged from 90 (Subgroup 9) to 116 (Subgroup 1) with an overall sample mean of 103, which closely approximates the standardization mean for this test. Similar subgroup differences were also found for the language and cognitive–perceptual tests of the neuropsychological battery; again, Subgroups 8 and 9 showed lower performances on each of these tests. Chi-square tests of independence were also significant between subgroups in terms of neurological and socioeconomic status. Subgroups 8 and 9 contained a much larger proportion of children with "soft" neurological signs and lower SES.

CLASSIFICATION ON NEUROPSYCHOLOGICAL VARIABLES

In view of the preceding differences between subgroups on a wide range of external criteria, it was decided to further subdivide Sub-

---

[5] Three small clusters, consisting of only six subjects, showed extremely high and deviant reading scores and resisted incorporation into the larger clusters until a four-cluster solution. Following the recommendation of Everitt (1974), they were considered "outliers" and were dropped from further analysis. Outliers can be viewed as resulting from measurement errors, or unique individuals for which there are few, if any, similar individuals with which to cluster in a given sample.

groups 8 and 9 in the search for possible subtypes of learning disabled children. These two subgroups, it will be remembered, were severely impaired on all of the WRAT subtests.

The children in these two subgroups (N = 89) were then subjected to cluster analytic techniques based on their performance on four neuropsychological tests administered at the end of Grade 5. These tests (clustering variables) were selected from a larger group of measures based on high factor loadings on a language factor (WISC similarities, verbal fluency) and a perceptual factor (Berry test of visual–motor integration, recognition–discrimination). A discussion of the tests and factor analyses can be found in Fletcher and Satz (1979). The rationale for this procedure was to restrict the number of tests to a few highly independent factors that would reduce test redundancy, random error variance, and increase subtype interpretability. Reliable variables were therefore expected to yield a more reliable classification. These variables also provided the opportunity to employ a number of clustering techniques to ensure that the subtypes were replicable across different clustering methods. Replication at this level was felt to be mandatory in view of the controversy surrounding the potential uses and misuses of cluster analysis (Everitt, 1977).

Four hierarchical agglomerative techniques were employed, including complete linkage, average linkage, centroid, and Ward's methods. With each of these methods, squared Euclidian distance and error sum of squares similarity coefficients were used, yielding eight different methods. Following each cluster analysis, the individual solutions were subjected to a K-means iterative partitioning method.

Five distinct clusters (subtypes) emerged from each of the cluster analytic techniques. In fact, the subtypes were virtually identical (only 5–9 subjects changed clusters) in terms of profile elevation, pattern, and sample sizes. Subtype 1 was severely impaired on both of the language measures (similarity and verbal fluency) and in terms of PPVT IQ (used as a marker variable). The latter test purports to measure comprehensional vocabulary. In contrast, performance on the nonlanguage perceptual tests was within normal limits for this subtype (normal defined in terms of the scaled mean for the total sample, N = 236). Twenty-seven children were classified within this subtype, which was defined as a global language impairment type. Subtype 2 was selectively impaired on only the verbal fluency test. Performance on the remaining neuropsychological tests, including the PPVT, was within normal limits. Fourteen children were classified within this subtype, which was defined as a specific language (naming) type. Subtype 3 was severely impaired on all of the neuropsychological tests (language and perceptual), including PPVT IQ. Ten children were classified in this subtype, which was defined as a global language and perceptual impaired type (mixed). Subtype 4 was selectively impaired on only the nonlanguage perceptual tests. In contrast, their performance on the language tests, including PPVT IQ, were within the normal range. Twenty-three children were classified within this subtype, which was defined as a visual–perceptual–motor impaired type. Subtype 5, in contrast to the preceding four subtypes, showed no impairment on any of the neuropsychological tests; in fact, their subtype profile was characterized by average to superior performance on each of the cognitive tests, including PPVT IQ. As such they were defined as an unexpected learning disabled subtype. Twelve children were classified in this group.

VALIDATION OF SUBTYPES

Separate analyses were then conducted on each of the subtypes against various external criteria including WRAT scores, SES level, neurological status, and parental reading levels. A multivariate analysis of variance (MANOVA) was first run on the WRAT scores to see whether the subtypes varied by achievement level. This analysis was prompted in part by the high neuropsychological performance of children in Subtype 5 (unexpected). No significant main effect was found, which again supports the clustering solution for Subgroups 8 and 9, which identified the learning disabled probands. Significant differences between subtypes were observed, however, in terms of neurological status and parental reading levels.

In terms of neurological status (including birth histories), children in Subtypes 1 (global language), 3 (global language and perceptual) and 4 (visual–perceptual–motor) had a significantly higher proportion of positive findings (soft neurological signs). There was also a trend (nonsignificant) favoring a higher proportion of low SES children in two of these subtypes (1, 3). In contrast, Subtypes 2 (specific language-naming) and 5 (unexpected) had a lower proportion of children with positive neurological findings and a trend toward higher SES levels. When parental reading levels were examined across subtypes, it was found that the blood parents of the two latter subtypes (2 and 5) achieved higher scores than those of the other subtypes (1, 3, 4): In fact, their WRAT scores, when adjusted for education and SES level, were shown to be higher than the total sample mean (Subgroups 1–9). This latter finding further underscores the need for subdividing learning disabled children into more homogeneous subtypes in the search for familial–genetic determinants (Owen, 1978; Taylor et al., 1979). Sampling variations in the composition of heterogeneous groups could obscure or spuriously inflate the relationship between learning disabilities and parental reading levels.

On the basis of the preceding analyses, one might conclude that the subtypes represent distinctive clusters of children who share a number of unique and common attributes; furthermore, that these subtypes remain relatively distinct when compared with various external criteria. However, the interpretation one assigns to these subtypes is another matter. At this level, caution should be exercised. Intuitively, the subtypes, at least Types 1–4, are compatible with other reports in this review that typically refer to a language, perceptual, or mixed subgroup of learning disabled children. Within these reports, the language disordered subtype has more frequently been observed (Boder, 1973; Doehring & Hoshko, 1977; Mattis, 1978; Mattis et al., 1975; Petrauskas & Rourke, 1979). In the present study, at least 60% (51/86) of the children evidenced some type of language difficulty on the neuropsychological tests (Subtypes 1–3). However, the clustering method classified these children into different types of language disordered groups, some with more global difficulties (Subtype 1), some with more selective difficulties (Subtype 2) and some with both global language and perceptual handicaps (Subtype 3). Such profile differences are not uncommon to clinicians working with learning disabled children. Moreover, the production difficulties in Subtype 2 and the global language difficulties in Subtype 1 have features in common with adult aphasia models. However, reference to these adult models should be treated as speculation and not as fact. Lacking additional clinical or neuroradiographic information on these various language disordered subtypes both cautions and restricts premature inferences concerning etiology. However, any advances in the etiology or causes of learning disabilities must first rest on a firm basis of classification and definition. The present results provide some beginning steps in this direction.

The derivation of Subtype 4 (visual–perceptual–motor) and especially Subtype 5 (unexpected) should caution those advocates who postulate a unitary language deficit model for learning disabled children (Vellutino, 1978). At least 40% of the children in this relatively unselected school sample of disabled readers showed no impairment in language skills—at least as assessed by the present measures. Rather, one of the subtypes (4) showed a selective impairment in nonlanguage cognitive skills (visual perception), and the other subtype (5) showed average average–superior performance on all of the neuropsychological measures. The former subtype (4) also conflicts with the early formulation of Satz and Sparrow (1970), who postulated two general subtypes, a predominantly language disorder type seen at older ages (11–12) and a predominantly spatial–perceptual disorder type seen at younger ages (5–7). The presence of Subtype 4, which was derived on children at the end of Grade 5 (age = 11), lends little support for this hypothesis. In fact, this subtype, in contrast to previous studies (Boder, 1973; Mattis et al., 1975), contained the second largest number of children (N = 23). Despite these differences, most subtype studies have identified a subgroup of learning disabled children who continue to show selective cognitive differences in processing visual information—even at older ages (11–12 years). To ignore this subgroup of learning disabled children could retard progress in the search for differential causes as well as to subject these children to inappropriate methods of remediation.

The identification of Subgroup 5 was totally unexpected—hence its name. The potential significance of this subtype, however, should not be dismissed. Virtually no attention has been given in the subtype literature to those learning disabled children who are seemingly free of neuropsychological deficits. In fact, they would be completely missed by methods (clinical or statistical) that excluded direct measures of achievement to subdivide the children.

One could argue, of course, that this subtype was an artifact of the clustering method employed or of the variables used for clustering. This explanation, however, is unlikely, in view of the stability of this subtype across each of the different clustering methods used. A more reasonable explanation is that this group of children had motivational and/or emotional problems. For this reason, a separate analysis (MANOVA) was conducted across subtypes on the children's personality questionnaire (CPQ) (Porter & Cattell, 1972), which was administered to the total sample at the end of Grade 5. The CPQ assesses 14 independent factors or traits presumed to underlie the normal personality. Results, however, failed to differentiate subtypes on this measure.[6] Nor did this subtype reveal a familial association with reading failure; in fact, the blood parents of these children and those of Subtype 2 (specific language-naming) revealed a higher level of WRAT reading and spelling scores than did the children in the remaining subtypes or subgroups (1–9).

The failure to explain the nature of this unexpected subtype should not be viewed as a limitation. The purpose of the study was addressed primarily to the search for stable and homogeneous subtypes

---

[6] These negative results, however, could be due to limitations in the sensitivity of the CPQ to emotional difficulties.

in a relatively unselected school sample of children. In this respect, the objectives were more descriptive than explanatory. However, lack of an objective and valid classification of these subtypes could retard future progress in the search for explanatory causes of these disabilities.

Despite the promise that this study holds, particularly for establishing an approach for subtype classification, the results should be viewed as preliminary. None of the studies reviewed in this chapter were free from criticism. The present study is no exception. One should note the following concerns.

First, one must continue to question the use of achievement measures that sample such a restricted range of reading skills. The WRAT is notoriously limited in this respect. In fact, it provides no measure of reading comprehension that would have improved the search for subgroups and subtypes in this study. Also, the subtests are highly intercorrelated.

Second, one could fault the use of such a small number of neuropsychological tests as clustering variables in the search for subtypes. Despite the logic argued in defense of this approach, one must still ask whether the same subtype clusters would have emerged with a larger number of neuropsychological variables. One might predict a similar subtype division if similar factor-loaded tests were clustered. However, this prediction remains to be confirmed empirically. More difficult to predict is the cluster typing that would emerge with other factor tests. The study also would have been strengthened by the use of more formal psycholinguistic measures that came into use after the Florida Longitudinal Project was launched (1970).

Third, one should note that the subtype analyses were conducted on only Subgroups 8 and 9, both of whom showed marked and uniform impairment on each of the WRAT subtests. However, Subgroup 5 showed a severe although selective impairment in arithmetic, which would have justified their inclusion in the learning disability subgroups. Such analyses are now underway.

Fourth, each of the subtypes was derived on a highly homogeneous group of children with respect to age (11 years), sex (male) and race (white). This factor significantly restricts any extrapolation to disabled learners in the population. The age restriction, while reducing heterogeneity in the data during the initial analyses, should be expanded in future analyses. This is particularly crucial if developmental factors are hypothesized to underlie different stages in the reading process (Fletcher & Satz, 1980; Rourke, 1981; Satz & Fletcher, 1980). Such subtype analyses are now being explored on data from the Florida Longitudinal Project (Satz & Morris, in preparation; Schauer, 1979).

Also, Fisk and Rourke (1979) have recently addressed this using the Q-technique of factor analysis.

Fifth, the validity of the subtypes would have been strengthened by the use of additional criterion measures. For example, the relationship between subtypes and teacher observations, remedial programs, and developmental histories may have provided additional insights concerning the nature of the five subtypes; also, more sensitive measures of personality functioning than the CPQ would have proved helpful in understanding Subtype 5.

Sixth, the use of the PPVT as a measure of intellectual level could be criticized on the basis of its restricted assessment of intellectual abilities. Also, its measure of comprehensional vocabulary would warrant its insertion as a clustering variable in the subtype analysis.

Finally, the use of cluster analysis as a multivariate classification method has its own inherent limitations. Its limitations are somewhat different from those of Q-technique factor analysis but are no less important to examine. Cluster analysis includes numerous methods, many of which have never been critically examined nor clearly defined. These problems have only served to increase confusion and communication in the area. Different classification problems require different methods, which can create problems not always apparent. There are also many different algorithms and computer software packages that may yield different results from the same procedures. In general, clustering methods are not built upon a firm statistical foundation and are basically only heuristic. In addition, only limited attempts have been made to validate cluster results. Thus, validation of cluster solutions is especially critical because most methods will "find" solutions in random data. A more critical review of these issues specific to this research is under preparation (Morris, Blashfield, & Satz, 1980).[7]

The preceding comments, in summary, complete this review of the subtype literature. To date, this literature has not been subjected to any comprehensive or critical evaluation. An attempt has been made to examine the strengths and weaknesses of some of the representative studies and approaches in this area in hopes that future studies will avoid some of the pitfalls mentioned in this review. The future will certainly see an increasing recognition of the subtype problem and a rejection of old models that no longer serve any usefulness (Applebee,

[7] Investigators planning to conduct future research on subtype classification, using multivariate statistical methods, are advised to explore the theoretical foundations underlying the various methods (cluster analysis or Q-technique) as well as their potential uses and misuses. Caution is urged in this endeavor and the results should be viewed with skepticism until issues of reliability and validity are established.

1971). It is only hoped that such studies reflect an awareness of the complexity of the problems being addressed and do not represent premature exercises using techniques that obscure rather than elucidate one's understanding of these children.

References

Applebee, A. N. Research in reading retardation: Two critical problems. *Journal of Child Psychology and Psychiatry and Allied Disciplines*, 1971, *12*, 91–113.

Bailey, K. D. Monothetic and polythetic typologies and their relation to conceptualization, measurement, and scaling. *American Sociological Review*, 1973, *38*, 18–33.

Bannatyne, A. *Language, reading and learning disabilities*. Springfield, Illinois: Thomas, 1971.

Bateman, B. C. *Interpretation of the 1961 Illinois Test of Psycholinguistic Abilities*. Seattle: Special Child Publications, 1968.

Bell, A E., & Aftamas, M. S. Some correlates of reading retardation. *Perceptual and Motor Skills*, 1972, *35*, 659.

Belmont, L., & Birch, H. G. The intellectual profile of retarded readers. *Perceptual and Motor Skills*, 1966, *22*, 787–816.

Bender, L. Problems in conceptualization and communication in children with developmental alexia. In P. H. Hock & J. Zubin (Eds.), *Psychopathology of communication*. New York: Grune & Stratton, 1958.

Benton, A. L. Developmental dyslexia: Neurological aspects. *Advances in Neurology*, 1975, *7*, 1–41.

Benton, A. L. Some conclusions about dyslexia. In A. L. Benton & D. Pearl (Eds.), *Dyslexia: An appraisal of current knowledge*. New York and London: Oxford Univ. Press, 1978.

Boder, E. Developmental dyslexia: A diagnostic approach based on three atypical reading–spelling patterns. *Developmental Medicine and Child Neurology*, 1973, *15*, 663–687.

Cormack, R. M. A review of classification. *Journal of the Royal Statistical Society (Series A)*, 1971, *134*, 321–367.

Critchley, M. *The dyslexic child*. Springfield, Illinois: Thomas, 1970.

Cruickshank, W. M. Some issues facing the field of learning disabilities. *Journal of Learning Disabilities*, 1977, *10*, 57–64.

Darby, R. O. *Learning disabilities: A multivariate search for subtypes*. Unpublished doctoral dissertation, University of Florida, 1978.

Delacato, C. H. *The treatment and prevention of reading problems*. Springfield, Illinois: Thomas, 1959.

Denckla, M. B. Clinical syndromes in learning disabilities: The case for "splitting" vs. "lumping". *Journal of Learning Disabilities*, 1972, *5*, 401–406.

Doehring, D. G., & Hoshko, I. M. Classification of reading problems by the Q-technique of factor analysis. *Cortex*, 1977, *13*, 281–294.

Doehring, D. G., Hoshko, I. M., & Bryans. Statistical classification of children with reading problems. *Journal of Clinical Neuropsychology*, 1979, *1*, 5–16.

Everitt, E. *Cluster analysis*. London: Heineman, 1974.

Fennell, E., & Satz, P. *A multivariate test of the maturational lag hypothesis*. Paper presented at the International Neuropsychological Society, New York, 1979.

Fisk, I. L., & Rourke, B. P. Identification of subtypes of learning-disabled children at three age levels: A neuropsychological, multivariate approach, 1979, in press.

Fleiss, J. L., Lawlor, W., Platman, S. R., & Fieve, R. R. On the use of inverted factor analysis for generating typologies. *Journal of Abnormal Psychology*, 1971, *77*, 127–132.

Fleiss, J. L., & Zubin, J. On the methods and theory of clustering. *Multivariate Behavior Research*, 1969, *4*, 235–250.

Fletcher, J. M., & Satz, P. Developmental changes in the neuropsychological correlates of reading achievement: A six-year longitudinal followup. *Journal of Clinical Neuropsychology*, 1980, *2*, 23–37.

Gaddes, W. Learning disabilities: Prevalence estimates and the need for definition. In R. Knights & D. J. Bakker (Eds.), *The neuropsychology of learning disorders: Theoretical approaches.* Proceedings of NATO conference. Baltimore, Maryland: University Park Press, 1976.

Holmes, C. L., & Peper, R. J. An evaluation of the use of spelling error analysis in the diagnosis of reading disabilities. *Child Development*, 1977, *48*, 1708–1711.

Ingram, T. T. S., Mann, A. W., & Blackburn, I. A retrospective study of 82 children with reading disability. *Developmental Medicine and Child Neurology*, 1970, *12*, 271–

Jastak, J. F., & Jastak, S. R. *The Wide Range Achievement Test manual of instruction* (rev.). Wilmington: Guidance Associates of Delaware, 1976.

Keeney, A. H., & Keeney, V. T. *Dyslexia: Diagnosis and treatment of reading disorders.* St. Louis: Masky, 1968.

Kinsbourne, M., & Warrington, E. K. Developmental factors in reading and writing backwardness. In J. Money (Ed.), *The disabled reader: Education of the dyslexic child.* Baltimore: John Hopkins Press, 1966.

Maliphant, R., Supramaniam, S., & Saraga, E. Acquiring skill in reading: A review of experimental research. *Journal of Child Psychology and Psychiatry and Allied Disciplines*, 1974, *15*, 175–185.

Mattis, S. Dyslexia syndromes: A working hypothesis that works. In A. L. Benton & D. Pearl (Eds.), *Dyslexia: An appraisal of current knowledge.* New York and London: Oxford Univ. Press, 1978.

Mattis, S., French, J. H., & Rapin, I. Dyslexia in children and adults: Three independent neuropsychological syndromes. *Developmental Medicine and Child Neurology*, 1975, *17*, 150–163.

McCorquodole, K., & Meehl, P. E. On a distinction between hypothetical constructs and intervening variables. *Psychological Review*, 1948, *55*, 95–107.

Meehl, P. E. *Clinical versus statistical prediction: A theoretical analysis and a review of the evidence.* Minneapolis: Univ. of Minnesota Press, 1954.

Morris, R., Blashfield, R., & Satz, P. Neuropsychology and cluster potentials and problems, 1980, in preparation.

Myklebust, H. R. (Ed.). *Progress in learning disabilities* (Vol. 1). New York: Grune & Stratton, 1968.

Naidoo, S. *Specific dyslexia.* New York: Pitman, 1972.

Nunnally, J. C. *Psychometric theory.* New York: McGraw-Hill, 1967.

Owen, F. W. Dyslexia—genetic aspects. In A. L. Benton & D. Pearl (Eds.), *Dyslexia: An appraisal of current knowledge.* New York and London: Oxford Univ. Press, 1978.

Petrauskas, R., & Rourke, B. Identification of subgroups of retarded readers; a neuropsychological multivariate approach. *Journal of Clinical Neuropsychology*, 1979, *1*, 17–37.

Porter, R. D., & Cattell, R. B. *Handbook for the Children's Personality Questionnaire (the CPQ).* Champaign, Illinois: Institute for Personality and Ability Testing, 1972.

Quiros, J. B. Dysphasia and dyslexia in school children. *Folia Phoniatrica*, 1964, *16*, 201.

Rabinovitch, R. D. Reading problems in children: Definitions and classifications. In A. H. Keeny & J. C. Keeny (Eds.), *Dyslexia: Diagnosis and treatment of reading disorders.* St. Louis: Mosby, 1968.

Rabinovitch, R. D., Drew, A. L., Dejong, R., Ingram, W., & Withey, L. A. A research approach to reading retardation. *Association for Research in Nervous and Mental Disease*, 1954, *34*, 363–396.

Reitan, R. M. Psychological effects of cerebral lesions in children of early school age. In R. M. Reitan & L. A. Davison (Eds.), *Clinical neuropsychology: Current status and applications.* Washington, D.C.: Winston, 1974. (New York: Wiley.)

Ross, A. O. *Psychological aspects of learning disabilities and reading disorders.* New York: McGraw-Hill, 1976.

Rourke, B. P. Brain–behavior relationships in children with learning disabilities: A research program. *American Psychologist*, 1975, *30*, 911–920.

Rourke, B. P. Reading, spelling, arithmetic disabilities: A neuropsychological perspective. In H. R. Myklebust (Ed.), *Progress in learning disabilities* (Vol. 4). New York: Grune & Stratton, 1978.

Rourke, B. P., & Finlayson, M. A. J. Neuropsychological significance of variations in patterns of academic performances, verbal and visual–spatial abilities. *Journal of Abnormal Child Psychology*, 1978, *6*, 121–133.

Rourke, B. P. Reading and spelling disabilities: A developmental neuropsychological perspective. In H. Kirk (Ed.), *Neuropsychology of language, reading, and spelling.* New York: Academic Press (in press), 1981.

Rutter, M. Prevalence and types of dyslexia. In A. L. Benton & D. Pearl (Eds.), *Dyslexia: An appraisal of current knowledge.* New York and London: Oxford Univ. Press, 1978.

Satz, P., & Fletcher, J. M. Early screening tests: SCME uses and abuses. *Journal of Learning Disabilities*, 1979, *12*, 43–50.

Satz, P., & Sparrow, S. Specific developmental dyslexia: A theoretical formulation. In D. J. Bakker & P. Satz (Eds.), *Specific reading disability.* Rotterdam: Rotterdam Univ. Press, 1970, 41–60.

Satz, P., & Van Nostrand, G. Developmental dyslexia: An evaluation of a theory. In P. Satz & J. Ross (Eds.), *The disabled learner; early detection and intervention.* Rotterdam: Rotterdam Univ. Press, 1973.

Satz, P., Morris, R., & Darby, R. O. Subtypes of learning disabilities: A multivariate search. Paper presented to the IYC symposium, Vancouver, B.C., Canada, March, 1979.

Schauer, C. A. *The developmental relationship between neuropsychological and achievement variables: A cluster analytic study.* Unpublished doctoral dissertation, University of Florida, 1979.

Smith, M. M. *Patterns of intellectual abilities in educationally handicapped children.* Unpublished doctoral dissertation, Claremont College, California, 1970.

Smith, D. E. P., & Carrigan, P. M. *The nature of reading disability.* New York: Harcourt Brace World, 1959.

Sneath, P. H. A., & Sokal, R. R. *Numerical taxonomy: The principles and practice of numerical classification.* San Francisco: Freeman, 1973.

Spreen, O. Neuropsychology of learning disorders: Post conference review. In R. Knights & D. J. Bakker (Eds.), *The neuropsychology of learning disorders: Theoretical approaches.* Proceedings of NATO Conference, Baltimore, Maryland: University Park Press, 1976.

Taylor, H. G., Satz, P., & Friel, J. Developmental dyslexia in relation to other childhood reading disorders; significance and utility. *Reading Research Quarterly*, 1979, *15*, 84–101.

Vellutino, F. R. Toward an understanding of dyslexia: Psychological factors in specific reading disability. In A. L. Benton & D. Pearl (Eds.), *Dyslexia: An appraisal of current knowledge*. New York and London: Oxford Univ. Press, 1978.

Waites, L. *World Federation of neurology: Research group on developmental dyslexia and world illiteracy*. Report of proceedings, 1968, p. 22.

Wishart, D. *Clustan user manual* (3rd ed.). London: Computer Centre, Univ. of London, 1975.

PERCEPTUAL AND IMAGINAL PROCESSES IN READING COMPREHENSION

6

Keith Rayner

EYE MOVEMENTS AND THE PERCEPTUAL SPAN IN READING[1]

How much information can a reader obtain during an eye fixation in reading? This question has intrigued psychologists for many years because the answer would provide a fundamental fact about the reading process that is essential in the construction of a model of reading. Huey (1908) and Woodworth (1938) both devoted a considerable amount of attention to this question in their classic reviews of the early research on reading, and recent work on reading has also included a fair amount of research on the topic. In this chapter, I will (a) briefly review some basic facts about eye movements in reading; (b) discuss various techniques that have been utilized to investigate the perceptual span and also discuss the results obtained with each; and (c) make some summary statements about the perceptual span in reading based on the available data.

Eye Movements in Reading

One of the most well-established facts about reading is that we abstract information from the text during the fixational pauses of the eye. Each fixation is separated by saccades that serve the function of bringing a new region of text into foveal vision for detailed analysis.

[1]Preparation of this chapter was supported by Grant HD12727 from the National Institute of Child Health and Human Development to Keith Rayner.

NEUROPSYCHOLOGICAL AND COGNITIVE
PROCESSES IN READING

Saccades take up about 10% of the total reading time and are regarded as ballistic movements whose trajectories cannot be influenced once the movement has begun. On the average, each saccade covers about 7 or 8 character positions. Fixational pauses average approximately 200–250 msec. The third major component of eye movements during reading is the regression, which occurs about 15–20% of the time. An important point that should not be overlooked is that all of these values represent averages and there is a considerable amount of variability in each of these measures (Rayner, 1978; Rayner & McConkie, 1976). Thus, for normal reading rates of 200–500 words per minute (wpm), the range of saccade lengths within and between subjects is from 1 to over 20 characters and the range of fixation durations is from 100 to over 500 msec. The frequency of regressions between readers ranges from 0 to 40%. Generally speaking, for each of these measures, there will be a somewhat normal shaped distribution around the mean values described here. However, the variability both within and between readers is very evident; the most striking characteristic of the eye movement records is not the regularity of the pattern for good readers, but the variability.

It is beyond the scope of the present chapter to discuss in detail how the eye movements are guided and what determines how long the eye will remain fixated. However, it appears (Rayner, 1978; Rayner & Inhoff, 1981) that eye movements are made on a nonrandom basis in that certain patterns emerge from the data. For example, the length of the word to the right of the word currently fixated influences the length of the following saccade (O'Regan, 1975; Rayner, 1979) and the frequency of fixation on letters within words of different lengths is rather systematic (Rayner, 1979). Spacing between words also affects saccade length (McConkie & Rayner, 1975), and if extra spaces are added between words, the eye tends to jump over those blank areas (Abrams & Zuber, 1972). In addition, certain short function words in text are fixated less frequently than one would predict (O'Regan, 1979), and areas marking the end of one sentence and the beginning of the next are likewise skipped quite frequently (Rayner, 1975a). These data all suggest that the location of the eye fixation is determined by visual characteristics of the text or the cognitive processing state of the reader (Rayner, 1979).

Just as it appears that eye movements are made on a nonrandom basis, it also appears that the length of time the eye remains fixated is determined in a nonrandom manner (Rayner, 1977, 1978). For example, fixation durations are longer on certain grammatical elements than on other elements within a passage, and infrequent words receive longer fixations than frequent words (Rayner, 1977). In addition, fixation durations differ on lexically ambiguous words according to the meaning demanded by the context of the passage (McConkie, Hogaboam, Wolverton, Zola, & Lucas, 1979). Again, these data indicate that the length of time the eye will remain in any location is related to the cognitive processing state of the reader and the difficulty of the material being fixated. Researchers interested in eye movements in reading will, however, have to specify more completely how eye location and fixation duration are related to textual characteristics and/or the processing state of the reader. For a more comprehensive review of eye guidance and determinants of fixation duration, the interested reader is invited to consult the reviews by Rayner (1978) and Rayner and Inhoff (1981).

Techniques to Study the Perceptual Span

A number of techniques have been used to investigate the perceptual span in reading. The complexity of the techniques varies considerably as do the results obtained using the different methods. In this section, each of the techniques will be described as well as the characteristics of the results obtained using each method. First, however, it is important to make a distinction between (a) information *seen* during a single eye fixation; and (b) information *used* during a single eye fixation. During an eye fixation, the reader has information about the location of the text in the visual field and other gross information from the surrounding scene. However, the specific information necessary for reading has to be confined to a general region around the center of vision called the foveal region. The foveal region extends 2 degrees (six to eight characters) around the center of fixation. Beyond the fovea, acuity decreases rather dramatically as a word is presented further from fixation. In the parafoveal region (extending 10 degrees around fixation), acuity is better than in the peripheral region, but vision is markedly poorer than in the foveal region. On the line being looked at, it may well be that different types of information can be obtained from different regions; although clear detail of letters is available only near the fovea, other more gross types of information may be obtained from the parafoveal and peripheral regions. For example, word length, word shape, information about where sentences begin and end, and so on, may be obtained from nonfoveal vision. Thus, in one sense, it may be more appropriate to talk about the perceptual spans in that different types of information may be obtained from different parts of the visual field. However, the crucial distinction is between information seen during an eye fixation and information actually used during a single eye fixation. Many of the types of gross information just described may well be seen during an eye fixation, but the important information is that which the reader actually uses to facilitate reading.

Tachistoscopic Presentations of Words and Letters

Perhaps the oldest technique used to investigate the perceptual span is to simply present letters or words at different distances from the fixation point and ask the subject to name the word or to make a lexical decision. The stimuli are presented for rather brief durations (200 msec or less) so that subjects cannot make eye movements. Figure 6.1 shows typical data obtained when subjects are asked to make lexical decisions on five-letter words. In the experiment, vowels in the words were replaced by visually similar consonants to form the nonword stimuli. Figure 6.1 clearly shows that, as the stimuli are presented further from fixation, the probability of correct identification decreases. In fact, subjects perform at no better than chance performance when the stimuli are presented 5 degrees from fixation. If we extrapolate to the reading situation, these data would imply that readers are not able to obtain the type of information necessary for word identification for words beginning 15–20 or more character positions to the right of the fixation point. Unfortunately, it is not all that simple. Although such experiments

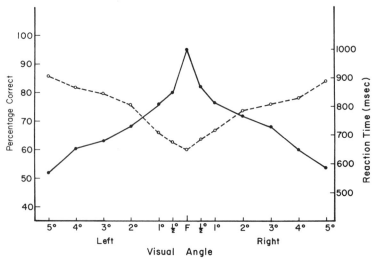

FIGURE 6.1. *Percentage correct and average reaction times (RTs) for correct decisions in a lexical decision task as a function of eccentricity of stimulus.*

provide information about visual acuity and may effectively place an upper bound on the area from which a reader can get information to identify words, the generalizability to reading is questionable at best. How, for example, are we to evaluate performance in such a task for stimuli presented 2 degrees from fixation with respect to reading? Subjects were accurate in making lexical decisions approximately 70% of the time. Although such performance is better than chance, it is not overly impressive. Do these results necessarily mean that a reader gets little information necessary for word identification from words beginning only 2 degrees away from the current fixation? Taylor (1965) concluded, on the basis of similar extrapolations, that the answer to the question just posed must be yes; he argued that readers cannot identify words beginning 2 degrees from fixation. However, as I have pointed out elsewhere (Rayner, 1975b), there are definite problems associated with this technique that makes the generalizability to reading very questionable. One limitation of the method is that subjects are able to see much more than they can retain and later report (Sperling, 1960). Thus, what subjects report from a brief presentation cannot be taken as a complete specification of what they actually see. Furthermore, and more central to the topic of the present chapter, Geyer (1970) has pointed out that even if the verbal report coincided with what the subject actually saw, there is no particular reason to believe that the perceptual span obtained in a tachistoscopic study actually coincides with that of a fixation in reading. It is likely that normal reading and tachistoscopic report vary enough to induce different strategies in different subjects. The tachistoscopic studies generally involve the isolated presentation of stimuli, whereas reading involves fixations at the rate of four or five per second, with a very complex stimulus pattern having a great deal of redundancy. Because of these differences, the perceptual span in reading could be either larger or smaller than that found with tachistoscopic presentations. It could be larger because the contextual constraint allows a reader to identify words with less visual information, or it could be smaller because of the rapid sequence of fixations and the complexity of the surrounding stimulus pattern that may lead to tunnel vision (Mackworth, 1965).

Tachistoscopic Presentations of Sentences

A technique very similar to that just described involves the presentation of stimuli tachistoscopically to simulate the time period of an average fixation in reading, but to present sentences rather than isolated letters or words. The classic studies of Cattell (described by

Woodworth and by Huey), were essentially experiments of this type. As is well known, Cattell found that, with a single, brief tachistoscopic exposure, subjects could report three to four unrelated letters, one to two unrelated words, or three to four short related words that went together as a phrase. The major problem with Cattell's experiments and others like it is that, as Henderson (1977) and others have pointed out, there is no correction for guessing and subjects will be able to remember words that go together better than words that do not. Likewise, memory for unrelated letters should be considerably poorer than memory for letters making up words because there is no easy way to chunk the unrelated letters in memory. Experiments dealing with subjects' performance in identifying unrelated letters in comparison to letters in words have used a more sophisticated procedure in which subjects are required to make forced choices of what they saw (Reicher, 1969; Wheeler, 1970).

Other experiments utilizing tachistoscopic exposures of sentences are subject to the same type of criticism concerning guessing. For example, Marcel (1974) had subjects read aloud passages of text in one field of a tachistoscope. When the subjects read the last word aloud, they were to fixate on a dot, and 100 msec later a continuation of the sequence appeared for 200 msec. In reality, the continuation was an approximation to English (ranging from first- to sixth-order approximation) and subjects were to verbally report as much of what they had seen as they could in words and letters. Then they were asked to write down as much as they could remember. Marcel tested average readers (reading speed of 305 wpm) and fast readers who had just completed a speed reading course (879 wpm). As would be expected, subjects were able to report more words and letters correctly as the approximation to English increased. With sixth-order approximations to English, the normal readers were able to report 3.2 words on average correctly and the fast readers were able to report 4.1 words correctly. In addition to the fact that there was no control over guessing in the experiment, it is also true that there was no actual control over where subjects fixated. In a very interesting experiment dealing with determinants of reading speed, Jackson and McClelland (1975) presented 5-word sentences for a 200 msec exposure. They also tested normal readers (260 wpm) and fast readers (586 wpm) and reported that the normal readers reported on average 16% of the words from the sentence, whereas the fast readers reported 39%. In a forced choice task, in which subjects were shown 5-word sentences for 200 msec and then chose between two different word alternatives that could have occurred in the same word position, normal readers were correct 71% of the time, and the fast readers were correct 76% of the time. In another task relevant to this discussion, the two groups of subjects were shown individual letters at different eccentricities from fixation. There were no differences in accuracy between the two groups at any of the eccentricities tested (range, 2.3 degrees–5.9 degrees). In summary, both the Marcel (1974) and the Jackson and McClelland (1975) experiments imply that redundancy influences what can be reported from a brief array. The general implication from the research is that readers (particularly fast readers) are able to identify 2 or 3 words to the right of the currently fixated word. However, as indicated, Marcel did not control for guessing strategies, and neither study actually controlled for fixation location so that the results have to be considered marginal for understanding the nature of the perceptual span in reading. The studies are important, however, in that they indicate some potential characteristics of individual differences in reading skill, an area of research that has been largely overlooked.

Eye Movement Determinants of the Perceptual Span

Another technique that has been used to determine the perceptual span in reading is to have subjects read passages of text and divide the number of letters per line by the number of fixations per line (Taylor, 1965). This is clearly one of the simplest techniques that has been used to investigate the perceptual span. Using this technique, Taylor (1965) found that the average span of perception was one and one-tenth words for skilled adult readers. Spragins, Lefton, and Fisher (1976) reported similar results in that they found the mean number of character spaces per fixation to be approximately five and two-thirds for adult readers. However, Taylor's assumption that the perceptual span corresponds to just over one word per fixation cannot be taken at face value. That is, this method of estimating the perceptual span is based on the assumption that, on successive fixations, the perceptual spans do not overlap from fixation to fixation or that they overlap the same amount. This assumption is false, as we shall see, as there is overlap of information from fixation to fixation.

At this point, it is probably worthwhile to return to a point made earlier. As I indicated previously, in some sense, it is probably more accurate to talk about the perceptual *spans* rather than a single span. That is, the perceptual span can be thought of as composed of different subspans with different types of information obtained from different regions. If information acquired from parafoveal vision were limited to gross characteristics such that the type of information necessary for word identification was not available, this gross information obtained from parafoveal vision could be stored and would be useful to the reader on the following fixation. But, it would still be necessary to bring the word into foveal vision for identification. In this manner, there would be overlap of information, but it would be necessary for the reader to fixate the partially processed word. On some level, Taylor's notion that the perceptual span is limited to just over one word makes sense. That is, if readers can identify two or three words to the right of the word currently fixated, why would they bother to fixate those words after they have already identified them? Thus, the perceptual span area containing information necessary for word identification (termed the semantic span by Rayner & Inhoff, 1981) may well be rather small, whereas the perceptual span containing more gross types of information about parafoveal words might be considerably larger. In effect, that is precisely what I shall argue later in this chapter.

Varying the Amount of Text Visible to the Reader

The fourth technique used to identify the perceptual span is to manipulate the amount of text that is visible to a subject at a given moment. Poulton (1962) had subjects read aloud from text over which a mask containing a window was passed. The speed and size of the window varied systematically on different trials, and subjects' eye movements were recorded. In Poulton's study, the text was immobile, and the window passed over it allowing only a certain amount to be seen at once. Newman (1966) kept the window stable and passed the text beneath it. He presented text on a screen, with the letters moving from right to left, and varied the number of letters on the screen at any moment, the number of new letters that were added at once, and the rate at which they were added. In a similar type of study, Bouma and deVoogd (1974) required subjects to hold fixation and text was moved from right to left across the visual field in jumps simulating the distance of normal eye saccades in reading. Bouma and deVoogd varied the duration that a given region was in foveal vision and also the number of letters that were included in a shift. Bouma and deVoogd referred to their method as *linestep reading* and found that the limits of shift extent in the task were one and a half to two times the average values of saccade extents in normal reading. They suggested that this value (about 14–18 characters to the right of fixation) represents a conservative estimate of the horizontal span of vision during normal reading. Although these studies are interesting attempts to deal with the nature of the perceptual span, they can be criticized because a reader's normal eye movements are disrupted; the reader must either move the eyes so as to keep up with the moving window or else hold fixation.

Another attempt to determine the perceptual span that involved varying the amount of text that could be clearly seen during a fixation has been reported by Patberg and Yonas (1978). Readers of varying skill were asked to read normal passages of text or passages with 13 letter spaces between the last letter of each word and the first letter of the subsequent word. For skilled readers, it was found that the added spacing significantly decreased reading speed. However, if one assumes that the perceptual span for word identification is approximately one and one-third words per fixation (or about the size Taylor argued for), their data can be accounted for as the mean reading time was 69 sec for normal reading and 90 sec for spaced text. This study also represents an interesting attempt to investigate the perceptual span, but it is somewhat artificial in that we seldom read text in which words are widely spaced.

Summary of Research on the Perceptual Span

Prior to considering the most recent technique used to study the perceptual span, it is probably instructive to pause for a moment and consider the results of studies dealing with the perceptual span in reading that have been discussed up to this point. It should be obvious from the preceding review that it is difficult to get a clear-cut picture of the size of the perceptual span. Depending upon the method used, one can obtain estimates that the span is as small as a single word or as large as three or four words. As I have indicated, there are problems associated with each of the techniques that makes it difficult to interpret the results. Furthermore, it is not at all clear whether various techniques are yielding information about what information a reader actually uses during an eye fixation. In addition, some of the approaches suffer, because it appears likely that subjects are able to guess on the basis of rather incomplete information. In the next section, a newer, more sophisticated, and accurate technique for studying the perceptual span in reading will be described.

Controlling the Amount of Text Visible to the Reader via Eye Movements

A number of recent experiments have utilized a technique that involved controlling the characteristics of the reading display by the reader's eye movements with display changes in the text made contingent upon eye position. These studies have provided data on the perceptual span in reading in a more ecologically valid situation than the earlier studies were able to do because the subject controlled when, where, and how long to look at different parts of the text. The technique involves monitoring readers' eye movements as they read text displayed on a computer controlled cathode-ray tube (CRT). The signal from the eye movement sensors is then fed into the computer so that moment-to-moment information about the location of the gaze can be obtained.

McConkie and Rayner (1975) asked subjects to read text as their eye movements were monitored. Initially, a passage of mutilated text was presented on the CRT. In one condition in the experiment, for example, every letter from the original text was replaced by an x. However, when the reader fixated on the first line of text, the display changed so that within a certain area (eight character spaces to the left and right of the fixation point, for example) the xs were replaced by corresponding letters from the original text. This area within which normal text appeared was called the *window*. When the reader made an eye movement, those letters became xs once again, and the xs within the window area around the new fixation point were replaced by the corresponding letters from the original text. Thus, wherever the reader fixated, there was readable text, while the mutilated text appeared outside of the window area. The experimenters varied the size of the window area and the characteristics of the mutilated text. That is, the experimenters were able to specify what aspects of the original text were present in the parafovea and periphery by preparing mutilations of the original text in specific ways. Some of the mutilations preserved both word length and word shape information, and other mutilations altered one or both of these aspects of the original text. Thus, although the area within the window always contained normal text, the area beyond the window did or did not contain certain aspects of the original. A major assumption in the study was that if the information that was removed was information the reader used, the result should be some sort of change in reading behavior such as shorter saccades, longer fixations, and/or more regressions. The study indicated that readers do not obtain useful information more than 12–15 characters to the right of the fixation point. Word length information affects reading further into parafoveal vision than does word shape or specific letter information and appears to be used in determining where to look next. It appeared that letter and word shape information is obtained from a rather limited area during a fixation, only 8 or 9 character spaces to the right of the fixation point at most. However, it is clear from the experiment that useful information is obtained further to the right of fixation than would be represented by the average saccade length. That is, the average saccade length was 8 characters, but useful information was obtained from an area extending at least 12–15 characters away from fixation. Thus, there must be some overlap of information from fixation to fixation. A study by Ikeda and Saida (1978), in which the area of clear vision was restricted, also yielded the conclusion that there is overlap from fixation to fixation. It is difficult to compare directly the results of this study with the McConkie and Rayner (1975) study because Ikeda and Saida used Japanese subjects and prose; Japanese text is composed of both ideographic and alphabetic characters making the comparison difficult. The average length of saccade for Japanese readers is somewhat shorter than it is for English readers, but the results appear somewhat comparable in indicating that there is overlap of information from fixation to fixation.

McConkie and Rayner (1976) also varied certain characteristics of the window area so that it was either symmetrical (20 characters left and right of fixation) around the fixation point or asymmetrical around fixation. In the asymmetric conditions, the window contained 20 characters to the right of fixation and only 4 characters to the left of fixation or it contained 4 characters to the right of fixation and 20 characters to the left. They found that readers acquire more information to the right of the fixation point than from the left. In fact, there was no difference between the symmetric condition and the asymmetric condition in which the window extended further to the right than to the left; the left-shifted asymmetric condition resulted in considerable difficulty in reading for all of the subjects.

Rayner (1975b) also used the technique of making display changes in the text contingent on the location of the subject's eye. In this experiment, however, rather than each saccade resulting in a display change, only a single display change occurred at predetermined locations in the passage. Thus, if the display changes that occurred each time the eye moved in the window study somehow reduced the span of effective vision, the technique used in the study reported by Rayner (1975b) should make it apparent that the technique used in the window studies artificially created a type of tunnel vision. The results of the study were quite consistent with the results of the window study and indicated that subjects identify the semantic content of words falling on the fovea and just to the right of it. Beyond that area, however, readers were able to obtain information about the terminal letters of words and the overall word shape. However, the size of the area from which they were able to obtain this information was rather small; the subjects were able to obtain the type of information studied from words beginning less than 12 character spaces from fixation.

These experiments (see McConkie, 1976; Rayner & McConkie, 1977 for a general discussion of the series of experiments) suggest that readers obtain different types of information from different regions within the perceptual span during a fixation in reading. Rayner and McConkie (1977) concluded that information falling on the fovea and just to the right of it is processed for its semantic content and information from parafoveal vision is limited to rather gross featural information such as word shape and word length. Interestingly, they also reported that there was no evidence that word shape information was obtained further from fixation than was specific letter information (beginning and ending letters of words), and there was no evidence that information beyond the parafoveal region was useful to a reader during a particular fixation. Generally, they found that changes in word shape affected fixation durations, and changes in word length affected saccade length.

McConkie and Zola (1979) and Rayner, McConkie, and Zola (1980) have reported that the type of information from parafoveal vision that is combined across eye movements during reading is information about the beginning letters of words. McConkie and Zola (1979) had subjects read text presented in alternating case. However, on each fixation, a display change occurred so that if the word appeared as cHeSt prior to the saccade, after the saccade it appeared as ChEsT. Thus, the shape of every letter on the line of text changed during the saccade. McConkie and Zola found that these display changes were not disruptive to reading and that there were no differences in eye movement data between the condition in which there was a display change and a condition in which no display change occurred. Rayner, McConkie and Zola (1980) have also found that case changes during an eye movement were not disruptive to word identification and further reported that information about the beginning letters of parafoveal words is obtained and stored in an abstract form independent of its visual representation and is useful in identifying words. Thus, these experiments imply that it is specific letter information that is being acquired from words in parafoveal vision during reading.

In summary, these experiments imply that information necessary for semantic identification of words is obtained from a rather restricted range around foveal vision and the near parafovea. Information about beginning letters of words and word length information is acquired from parafoveal vision. The information about word length seems to be useful in guiding eye movements to the next location (Rayner & Inhoff, 1981).

Recent Experiments on the Perceptual Span

In our laboratory, we have recently conducted a number of experiments dealing with the perceptual span using techniques very similar to that used by McConkie and Rayner (1975). In the first of these studies (Rayner & Bertera, 1979), a window moved across a sentence and subjects were asked to read the sentence and push a button when they had completed reading. Then they reported the sentence to the experimenter. Figure 6.2 shows the results of the study. As can be seen, the window varied in size from 1 to 29 characters. A window of 21 characters meant that the character in the center of vision and 10 characters left and right of fixation were visible. Reading performance improved with increasing window size, and there was no difference between the condition in which the window was 29 characters and the condition in which a sentence was displayed without a window. Hence, the results of the study are consistent with McConkie and Rayner's (1975) finding that information that is useful to a reader during a fixation is confined to an area extending about 15 characters to the right of the fixation.

In another study, we (Rayner & Bertera, 1979) asked subjects to read sentences, and a visual mask moved in synchrony with the eye across the text. The size of the mask was varied so that, in some cases, it was as small as 1 character (the character the fixation point fell on) and in other cases it was as large as 17 characters (the character in the center of vision and 8 characters to the left and right of the centrally fixated character). When the mask covered the 7 characters in the center of vision, foveal vision was completely masked. Figure 6.3 shows the results of the experiment. As mask size was increased, reading became increasingly difficult. When foveal vision was masked, subjects were able to report about 75% of the words from the sentences, but it required a great deal of effort for them to do so as can be ascertained from an examination of the data shown in Figure 6.3. As the masks became rather large (over 13 characters), reading performance was dramatically affected so that subjects could report only about 20% of the words. Most of the words that could be reported accurately were short words, particularly when they began and ended the sentence (and were not subject to lateral masking to such great extents as were words in the middle of the line). Most of the errors that the subjects made in reporting words from the sentence were highly consistent with the

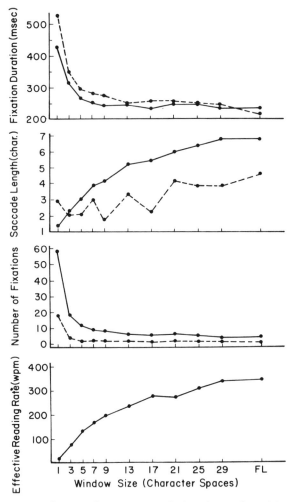

FIGURE 6.2. *Average fixation duration, saccade length, number of fixations, and effective reading rate as a function of the size of the window of readable text. (Reproduced from Rayner & Bertera, 1979, by permission of the American Association for the Advancement of Science.)*

visual information that was available from the sentence. Subjects seemed to be acquiring information about the beginning (and ending) letters of words and trying to construct coherent sentences out of the information available. The errors made tended also to be very consistent with the word shape and word length of the words that were in the sentences. Thus, for example, the sentence *The pretty bracelet attracted much attention* was read as *The priest brought much*

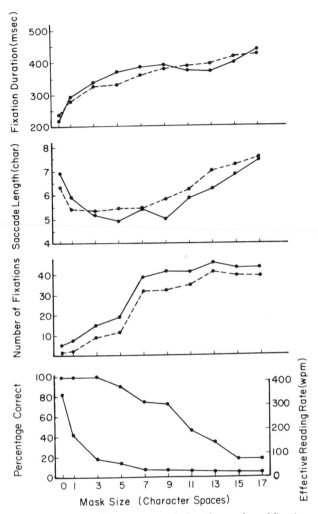

FIGURE 6.3. *Average fixation duration, saccade length, number of fixations, percentage correct, and effective reading rate as a function of mask size. In the bottom panel, the upper curve represents percentage correct and the lower curve represents effective reading rate. (Reproduced from Rayner & Bertera, 1979, by permission of the American Association for the Advancement of Science.)*

ammunition. The following types of errors were very consistent in the data: *rusted* was read as *raised*, *frosty* as *family*, *recruits* as *relatives*, *fuzzy* as *funny*, *satisfaction* as *accommodation*, and *sanctioned* as *sentenced*. With the large masks, on 20% of the trials, subjects could report nothing from the display even though they were able to make up to 100 eye movements on the sentence. In these cases, they were well aware that there were words in parafoveal and peripheral vision, but were unable to report them.

The results of these two experiments are very consistent with results we have reported previously (McConkie & Rayner, 1975; Rayner, 1975b) and indicate that the information necessary for semantic identification is obtained from a small area around foveal vision and that other types of information useful in reading are obtained from the parafovea.

In the final experiments to be described here, we asked subjects to read sentences with asymmetric windows and have replicated the findings of McConkie and Rayner (1976) that the most useful information is obtained from the right of the fixation. In fact, we (Rayner, Well, & Pollatsek, 1980) have found that the region of useful vision extends from the beginning of the currently fixated word (but no further than 4 characters to the left of fixation) to about 14–16 characters to the right of fixation. We (Pollatsek, Bolozky, Well, & Rayner, 1981) have also asked native Israeli subjects to read Hebrew and English with symmetric and asymmetric windows. Because Hebrew is read from right to left, an interesting question concerns whether or not Israeli readers' perceptual span is symmetric or asymmetric to the left. That is, for readers of English, the useful information is to the right of fixation and information to the right of fixation gets to the left hemisphere of the brain more rapidly than information to the left of fixation. In Hebrew text, the useful information is to the left of fixation for Israeli readers and information left of fixation would get most rapidly to the nonlanguage (right) hemisphere of the brain. Figure 6.4 shows the results of some pilot experiments we have carried out. The absolute wpm value for the Hebrew text should be interpreted cautiously, as it is based on the number of words per sentence prior to translation to Hebrew, and, in Hebrew, there are differences in structure (many vowels are deleted and some function words become prefixes and suffixes) that resulted in the sentences being shorter (in terms of the number of characters per sentence). However, the general trend is that it takes Israeli readers longer to read Hebrew when the window is shifted to the right than when it is symmetrical or shifted to the left. However, when the Israeli subjects read English, their perceptual span was asymmetric to the right. The fact that they were so much slower reading English stems from the fact that English is not their native language. These findings are consistent with an interesting case history reported by Dessoff (1957) of a patient with a paracentral homonymous hemianopic scotoma such that vision to the right of fixation in both eyes was affected, but not to the left. The patient was Jewish, and although he could not

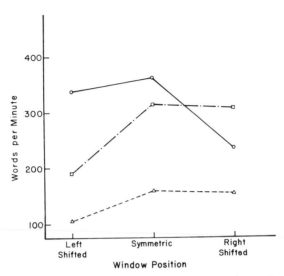

FIGURE 6.4. *Reading rate for native Israeli readers when reading Hebrew and English with symmetric and asymmetric windows. The symmetric window extended 14 characters to the left and to the right of fixation. The asymmetric window was 4 characters left and 14 characters right of fixation (right-shifted) or 14 characters left and 4 characters right of fixation (left-shifted). Reading rates of American subjects reading English are also shown.*

read English after the onset of the scotoma, he could read Hebrew. In summary, our studies indicate that the asymmetry of the perceptual span seems to be determined by attentional factors related to where the most useful information can be obtained as we read and not by structural factors associated with bilateral functions of the brain.

Summary

In the present chapter, I have attempted to review the techniques that have been used to identify the size of the perceptual span and the characteristics of the data obtained using each technique. As indicated previously, the estimate of the size of the perceptual span depends very much on the technique used and the values range from three or four words down to a single word. However, the crucial issue, as I have pointed out a number of times, is not what information a reader sees in a single fixation, but what information is used for reading purposes in a single fixation. Another very important issue is that different types of information are obtained from different regions within a fixation. Thus, the perceptual span for information necessary for semantic identification (referred to as the semantic span by Rayner & Inhoff, 1981) appears to be rather small, limited to a word or two around fixation. In fact, the data seem to suggest that the word currently fixated and perhaps the next word can be identified if they are both short words or if one of the words is five to eight letters and the other word is very short (three letters or less). If the word being fixated is rather long (over nine letters), there is a very high probability that the next word will be fixated. In particular, the experiments that have utilized rapid on-line computer display changes in text (Rayner, 1975b; Rayner & Bertera, 1979) seem to make the conclusion inescapable that the area from which information necessary for semantic identification can be obtained is limited to a region close to foveal vision.

However, these same types of experiments (Ikeda & Saida, 1978; McConkie & Rayner, 1975; Rayner, 1975b; Rayner & Bertera, 1979; Rayner, Inhoff, Morrison, Slowiaczek, & Bertera, 1981) also indicate that other types of information useful during a fixation can be obtained from words further into parafoveal vision. Some of this information can be used for identifying words more rapidly following the eye movement bringing the word into foveal vision (Rayner, 1975b; Rayner, McConkie, & Ehrlich, 1978; Rayner, McConkie, & Zola, 1980) and other information can be used in guiding the eye movement to a new location (McConkie & Rayner, 1975; Rayner & Bertera, 1979; Rayner & McConkie, 1976). The area from which these types of information useful in reading (although not directly used for semantic identification) can be obtained, however, seems to be limited to a region extending about 14–18 characters to the right of the fixation (Bouma & deVoogd, 1974; McConkie & Rayner, 1975; Rayner & Bertera, 1979).

The notion that different types of information are obtained from different regions of the perceptual span when combined with the fact that some experiments have not controlled for guessing strategies accounts for all of the discrepancies concerning the size of the perceptual span. Because the area for obtaining semantic information is small, the average saccade length would correspond to this area yielding an estimate of the span of about one and one-tenth words (Taylor, 1965). However, as partial information can be obtained further into the parafovea, the combination of the partial information with guessing strategies would lead to larger estimates.

Finally, there is evidence indicating that information that is useful in reading English is obtained to the right of the fixation and that information useful for reading Hebrew is obtained to the left of fixation. Thus, the perceptual span is asymmetric and biased in the direction from which the useful information can be obtained. When reading English, it may well be that attention is directed to the left of the fixation following return sweeps of the eye from the end of one line to the beginning of the next and also following certain types of regressive eye movements (Rayner, 1979). In conclusion, the area of effective vision during an eye fixation appears to extend from the beginning of the currently fixated word (but no further than 4 characters to the left of fixation) to about 14–16 characters to the right of fixation. These findings have important implications for a theory of reading and must be accounted for by models attempting to explain the reading process.

Acknowledgments

I would like to thank Albrecht Werner Inhoff and Robert Morrison for their valuable comments on an earlier draft of the chapter.

References

Abrams, S. G., & Zuber, B. L. Some temporal characteristics of information processing during reading. *Reading Research Quarterly*, 1972, *12*, 41–51.

Bouma, H., & deVoogd, A. H. On the control of eye saccades in reading. *Vision Research*, 1974, *14*, 273–284.

Dessoff, J. Paracentral homonymous hemianopic scotoma. *Archives of Ophthalmology*, 1957, *58*, 452–454.

Geyer, J. J. Models of perceptual processes in reading. In H. Singer & R. B. Ruddell (Eds.), *Theoretical models and processes of reading*. Newark, Delaware: International Reading Association, 1979.

Henderson, L. Word recognition. In N. S. Sutherland (Ed.), *Tutorial essays in experimental psychology*. Hillsdale, New Jersey: Erlbaum, 1977.

Huey, E. B. *The psychology and pedagogy of reading*. New York: Macmillan, 1908.

Ikeda, M., & Saida, S. Span of recognition in reading. *Vision Research*, 1978, *18*, 83–88.

Jackson, M. D., & McClelland, J. L. Sensory and cognitive determinants of reading speed. *Journal of Verbal Learning and Verbal Behavior*, 1975, *14*, 565–574.

McConkie, G. W. The use of eye-movement data in determining the perceptual span in reading. In R. A. Monty & J. W. Senders (Eds.), *Eye movements and psychological processes*. Hillsdale, New Jersey: Erlbaum, 1976.

McConkie, G. W., Hogaboam, T. W., Wolverton, G. S., Zola, D., & Lucas, P. A. Toward the use of eye movements in the study of language processing. *Discourse Processes*, 1979, *2*, 157–177.

McConkie, G. W., & Rayner, K. The span of the effective stimulus during a fixation in reading. *Perception and Psychophysics*, 1975, *17*, 578–586.

McConkie, G. W., & Rayner, K. Asymmetry of the perceptual span in reading. *Bulletin of the Psychonomic Society*, 1976, *8*, 365–368.

McConkie, G. W., & Zola, D. Is visual information integrated across successive fixations in reading? *Perception and Psychophysics*, 1979, *25*, 221–224.

Mackworth, N. H. Visual noise causes tunnel vision. *Psychonomic Science*, 1965, *3*, 67–68.

Marcel, T. The effective visual field and the use of context in fast and slow readers of two ages. *British Journal of Psychology*, 1974, *65*, 479–492.

Newman, E. B. Speed of reading when the span of letters is restricted. *American Journal of Psychology*, 1966, *79*, 272–273.

O'Regan, J. K. Structural and contextual constraints on eye movements in reading. Unpublished doctoral dissertation, University of Cambridge, England, 1975.

O'Regan, J. K. Saccade size control in reading: Evidence for the linguistic control hypothesis. *Perception and Psychophysics*, 1979, *25*, 501–509.

Patberg, J. P., & Yonas, A. The effects of the reader's skill and the difficulty of the text on the perceptual span in reading. *Journal of Experimental Psychology: Human Perception and Performance*, 1978, *4*, 545–552.

Pollatsek, A., Bolozky, S., Well, A. D., & Rayner, K. Asymmetries in the perceptual span for Israeli readers. *Brain and Language*, 1981, in press.

Poulton, E. C. Periperhal vision, refractoriness and eye movements in fast oral reading. *British Journal of Psychology*, 1962, *53*, 409–419.

Rayner, K. Parafoveal identification during a fixation in reading. *Acta Psychologica*, 1975, *39*, 271–282. (a)

Rayner, K. The perceptual span and peripheral cues in reading. *Cognitive Psychology*, 1975, *7*, 65–81. (b)

Rayner, K. Visual attention in reading: Eye movements reflect cognitive processes. *Memory and Cognition*, 1977, *5*, 443–448.

Rayner, K. Eye movements in reading and information processing. *Psychological Bulletin*, 1978, *85*, 618–660.

Rayner, K. Eye guidance in reading: Fixation locations within words. *Perception*, 1979, *8*, 21–30.

Rayner, K., & Bertera, J. H. Reading without a fovea. *Science*, 1979, *206*, 468–469.

Rayner, K., & Inhoff, A. W. Control of eye movements during reading. In B. L. Zuber (Ed.), *Models of oculomotor behavior and control*. West Palm Beach, Florida: CRC Press, 1981.

Rayner, K., Inhoff, A. W., Morrison, R., Slowiaczek, M. L., & Bertera, J. H. Masking of foveal and parafoveal vision during eye fixations in reading. *Journal of Experimental Psychology: Human Perception and Performance*, 1981, in press.

Rayner, K., & McConkie, G. W. What guides a reader's eye movements? *Vision Research*, 1976, *16*, 829–837.

Rayner, K., & McConkie, G. W. Perceptual processes in reading: The perceptual spans. In A. Reber & D. Scarborough (Eds.), *Toward a psychology of reading*. Hillsdale, New Jersey: Erlbaum, 1977.

Rayner, K., McConkie, G. W., & Ehrlich, S. Eye movements and integrating information across fixations. *Journal of Experimental Psychology: Human Perception and Performance*, 1979, *4*, 529–544.

Rayner, K., McConkie, G. W., & Zola, D. Integrating information across eye movements. *Cognitive Psychology*, 1980, *12*, 206–226.

Rayner, K., Well, A. D., & Pollatsek, A. Asymmetry of the effective visual field in reading. *Perception and Psychophysics*, 1980, *27*, 537–544.

Reicher, G. Perceptual recognition as a function of meaningfulness of stimulus material. *Journal of Experimental Psychology*, 1969, *81*, 274–280.

Sperling, G. The information available in brief visual presentations. *Psychological Monographs*, 1960, *74*(1, Whole No. 11).

Spragins, A. B., Lefton, L. A., & Fisher, D. F. Eye movements while reading spatially transformed text: A developmental study. *Memory and Cognition*, 1976, 4, 36–42.

Taylor, S. E. Eye movements while reading: Facts and fallacies. *American Educational Research Journal*, 1965, 2, 187–202.

Wheeler, D. D. Processes in word recognition. *Cognitive Psychology*, 1970, 1, 59–85.

Woodworth, R. S. *Experimental psychology*. New York: Holt, 1938.

7

Lyn R. Haber
Ralph Norman Haber

PERCEPTUAL PROCESSES
IN READING:
An Analysis-by-Synthesis Model

We define reading as the process of extracting information from printed text. Although all models that describe the reading process recognize that information can be extracted from the visual features of the printed page, there is considerable disagreement regarding the role played by information already available to the reader before his eyes fall on the text. Wildman and Kling (1978) have recently reviewed models of reading in light of the degree to which they depend on the reader's expectancies. At one extreme, best exemplified by Gough (1972), visual features are the foundation on which the entire structure is built. Just as the roof cannot be put on before the walls are made, neither can a word be processed until all the letters have been identified, nor a sentence, until the words are examined and named. For a model such as this, expectancies play no role at all. At the other extreme (Smith, 1971, probably comes closest) the reader might be compared to a writer: He begins with a complete anticipatory idea of what the text must be, and then tests his expectancies, starting with the most general, as he goes along. For reading models somewhere between these extremes (such as those of Gibson & Levin, 1975; or of Rumelhart, 1977), the reading process requires a continuous interaction between the visual features on the page (or on the retina), and the expectancies or hypotheses in the reader's head. For models such as these, the building analogy is meaningless: The ceiling and floor may be constructed simultaneously and be mutually determined. The critical element in this processing combination of sensory information with

NEUROPSYCHOLOGICAL AND COGNITIVE
PROCESSES IN READING

expectancies (see Lindsay & Norman, 1977, for the clearest discussion of the principles of analysis-by-synthesis) is that it leads to a set of clear, testable predictions that may be formulated as a general hypothesis: When expectancies are strong, less visual information should be needed to arrive at the resultant understanding of the text; whereas when the reader has fewer expectancies about what might be in the text, he has to be more dependent on the visual features on the page. We will attempt to show how existing research literature, conflicting as it is, supports this general notion of reading as analysis by synthesis.

If the amount of expectancy and reliance on visual features interact, models of reading should not only include an interaction of expectancies and visual feature testing, but also provide a way for that interaction to be highly flexible and changing. Failure to recognize this flexibility has led some theorists to reject the role of expectancies because they found no evidence of their presence. Thus, under some circumstances of text and task (especially those often found in highly constrained and controlled laboratory studies), no evidence for expectancies should be found at all.

Those models that do emphasize expectancies face a different and more serious problem: imprecision. Such models have been vague about what these expectancies are, how they are generated, and particularly as to the mechanism by which having an expectancy facilitates the extraction of information from text. Wildman and Kling (1978) recognize this problem, and are frequently critical of the research on this account. The major purpose of this chapter is to clarify both the bases upon which readers form expectancies, and the mechanisms by which such expectancies can aid information extraction.

For the reader to have an expectancy, there has to be some redundancy available. Shannon (1948) began the task of describing the redundancies in language in mathematical terms, and his procedures have been used in a number of early experiments on language processing (for example, Miller, Heise, & Lichten, 1951). Since that time, a number of kinds of redundancies beyond those described by Shannon have been identified (see Massaro, 1975, for some of these; Haber, 1978; and Haber & Hershenson (1980) for a more complete description). Shannon's notion, as applied to language processing of any kind, is that there are rules that restrict the alternative forms or sequences that are permissible in a language signal. If the listener–reader knows any of these rules, he has fewer alternatives to process. There is overwhelming evidence (see Miller, 1956, for an early review) that information processing of any kind is more accurate and faster when possible alternatives about the content to be processed are restricted. The types of rules we will define and examine all enable the reader to predict upcoming text, permitting him or her to generate information about material ahead of where he is looking at any one instant.

We discuss in the first section of this chapter three types of rules: (a) those that pertain to the features of the printed page; (b) syntactic rules of language structure; and (c) the reader's knowledge of the world. These independent knowledges share a characteristic: Once any knowledge is present, it reduces subsequent alternatives. In the second section, we examine the evidence that readers know these redundancies and that they actually use these rules during the process of reading normal text.

The demonstration that readers know and use rules that create redundancies to generate hypotheses about upcoming text represents an explication of an analysis-by-synthesis model of reading. However, the explication cannot be sufficient unless a description of the mechanism is provided. How does knowledge of rules help with information extraction? In the last section, we suggest how knowledge of rules that produce redundancies can directly enhance the reading process.

What Readers Might Know: Types of Knowledge Available for the Generation of Expectancies

We will first consider three overlapping kinds of knowledge that, in the abstract, readers could use to generate predictions about text as yet unseen. The first pertains to purely visual input, ranging from information available from printing conventions to word shape. The second concerns syntactic knowledge, or the rules by which language is organized; and the third is world knowledge, or experience. Although we discuss these three kinds of knowledge separately, they are interdependent.

Knowledge Available from Visual Input

Independent of his or her knowledge of language, the world, or the general content of the text to be read (story, news report, cake recipe), the reader has available for processing a considerable amount of knowledge from visual features alone. *Visual features* refer not only to distinctive features of single letters, but also to word shape and to printing conventions, all of which can provide substantial information about content further ahead.

REDUNDANCY AMONG LETTER FEATURES

Regardless of typeface, once readers know the names of the letters of the alphabet, they know, in effect, the general rules for how the letters are shaped. This means that, given partial visual features, they can predict the rest of the features and be able to recognize the letter. There are several different ways of describing this type of redundancy. Figure 7.1 shows one example, in which a brief paragraph is printed with either all the tops of the letters removed or all the bottoms. It is clearly easier to read the passage when the bottoms of letters are missing than when the tops are, which suggests that more information (that is, less redundancy) is contained in the tops. (These passages, of course, are in context, so other redundancies are present besides the visual features. The top and bottom differences occur even when the letters are presented out of context.)

Most attempts to describe the visual features that compose letters have looked at different kinds of line elements in terms of their length, orientation, degree of closure or circularity, their general size, their position in relation to the line or to the center of the letter (see Gibson & Levin, 1975, for a review). Figure 7.2 illustrates a visual feature list for upper-case letters in English. A slightly different featural set is necessary for lower-case letters. The 26 letters, each of which can appear in upper and lower case, plus 10 numbers, as well as the standard punctuation marks, make about 75 characters. If a feature set is created that uniquely distinguishes these 75 characters with a minimum number of binary features (that is, features that are either present or absent in

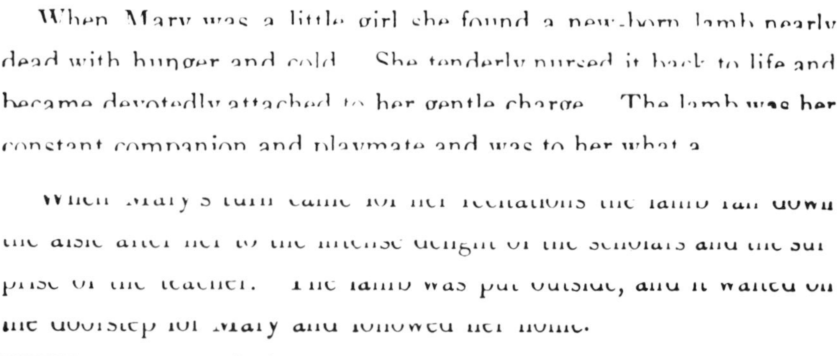

When Mary was a little girl she found a new-born lamb nearly dead with hunger and cold. She tenderly nursed it back to life and became devotedly attached to her gentle charge. The lamb was her constant companion and playmate and was to her what a

When Mary's turn came for her recitations the lamb ran down the aisle after her to the intense delight of the scholars and the surprise of the teacher. The lamb was put outside, and it waited on the doorstep for Mary and followed her home.

FIGURE 7.1. An example, from Huey (1908) in which either the tops or the bottoms of each letter are omitted in printing a paragraph. It is much easier to read the version with the bottoms missing, suggesting that more information (less redundancy) is contained in the upper parts of the visual feature, at least for English print of this type face.

Features	A	E	F	H	I	L	T	K	M	N	V	W	X	Y	Z	B	C	D	G	J	O	P	R	Q	S	U
Straight																										
horizontal	+	+	+	+		+	+								+				+							
vertical		+	+	+	+	+	+	+	+	+				+		+		+				+	+			
diagonal /	+							+	+	+	+	+	+	+	+											
diagonal \	+							+	+	+	+	+	+	+	+								+	+		
Curve																										
closed																+		+			+	+	+	+		
open V												+														+
open H																	+		+							+
Intersection	+	+	+	+		+	+				+					+						+	+	+		
Redundancy																										
cyclic change		+							+		+					+									+	
symmetry	+	+		+	+	+	+	+	+	+	+	+	+	+		+	+	+			+					+
Discontinuity																										
vertical	+		+	+	+		+	+	+	+				+								+	+			
horizontal		+	+			+	+								+											

FIGURE 7.2. A visual feature list from Gibson (1969), in which each capital letter is described by the presence or absence of a set of 12 visual features.

each character), 7 features would be needed. The estimate from current research (Gibson & Levin, 1975) is that about 20 features are used to differentiate among the 75 characters, or nearly three times the minimum number. The independent combination of 20 different features specifies slightly over 1 million letters if there is no redundancy. Thus, it is clear that the features that distinguish among English letters are highly redundant.

Figure 7.3 provides examples of a number of typefaces of English. Although superficially different from each other, the features that comprise each of the typefaces are virtually identical. There are several letters, such as a lower-case *a* or lower-case *g*, each of which can be printed quite differently, but other than those, one set of visual features accounts for almost all the common typefaces in English. A few typefaces are very difficult to read (see the last two lines of Figure 7.3); these use quite a different set of visual features.

The implication of the very high redundancy among the visual features of alphabetic characters is that relatively little visual information is necessary from a letter to determine its identity. Picking up only one or two features is usually all that is needed. For example, if all that has been detected of a capital letter is a diagonal, from that one feature the reader can eliminate more than half of the 26 possible alternatives: Only the 11 capital letters *A, K, M, N, Q, R, V, W, X, Y,* and *Z* contain this feature. If all that he or she picks up is a horizontal line at the bottom of the letter, then all alternatives except *E, L,* and *Z* can be eliminated. If both a diagonal and a lower horizontal line are seen, the letter must be *Z*. Although each letter may be made up of 5 or 6 features

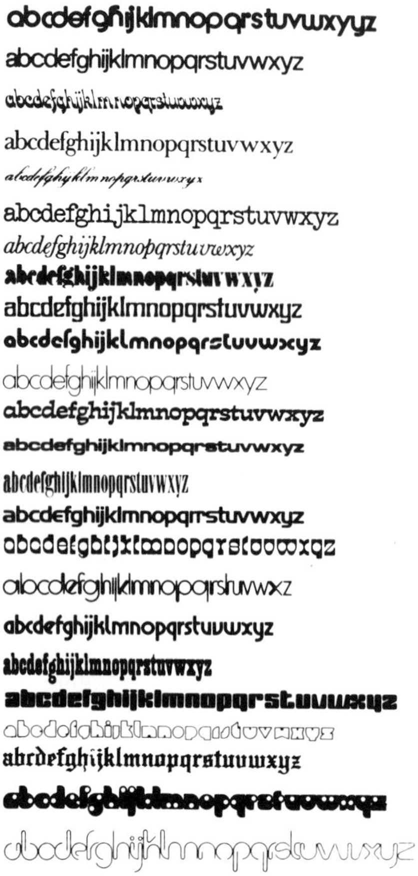

FIGURE 7.3. Examples of a number of different English typefaces for lower case print. Whereas most of these appear to be different, careful comparison across all of them for each letter reveals great similarity of features (check Figure 7.2).

drawn from a set of as many as 20, it is usually necessary to detect only 2, or, at most, 3 of those features in any single letter to determine its identity. As we will show in what follows, in combination with knowledge of spelling rules, only 1 feature of a letter is sufficient to specify the letter.

REDUNDANCY IN THE SHAPES OF WORDS

If an envelope is drawn around the outline of a lower-case word, different words have characteristic shapes and lengths. This profile is independent of the particular letters and, as such, provides visual information as to what the word is without the identification or processing of the individual letters. Figure 7.4 illustrates a passage in which every instance of the 100 most common words in English has been

FIGURE 7.4. *A passage in which each instance of each of the 100 most frequent words found in English print (Carroll, Davies, & Richman, 1971) is replaced by its outline shape. With only a little practice, it is easy to read passages printed in this form, suggesting that at least for these very high frequency words, we are able to read them by their outline shapes alone, without access to any specific letters.*

replaced simply by its outline shape. This passage is relatively easy to read and, with a little practice at this task, most readers can proceed almost at a normal rate of reading.

Figure 7.5 provides the profiles for these 100 most frequently used words. These words account for almost 50% of all the words that appear in normal print (*American Heritage Word Book*, Carroll, Davies, & Richman, 1971): They account for half the words in this chapter. These 100 words contain virtually no nouns nor verbs, but consist mainly of functors. Because these words appear so frequently in print, it seems quite likely that readers learn their shapes rather early in their reading experience, and are frequently able to recognize them by their shape alone. However, the redundancy of shape is by no means perfect. As can be seen from Figure 7.5, there are 40 different shapes represented by these 100 most frequent words, and for nearly all these shapes, there is more than 1 word that possesses that shape. Thus, whereas knowing the shape greatly reduces the number of alternatives, thereby increasing the redundancy, it does not eliminate all alternatives. Hence, for many words this source of redundancy cannot predict exactly which word it is without other information from the context (that is, information about language structure, specific information

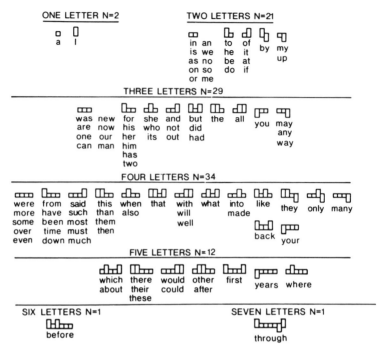

FIGURE 7.5. *The outline shape profiles for the 100 most frequent words in English. These 100 words are less than .1% of all the different words in English, but account for slightly over 50% of all the occurrences of words in print.*

about the preceding content of the passage, and more general world knowledge). The reason it is possible to read the passage in Figure 7.4 so easily is that, in addition to word shape, the full context is available.

REDUNDANCY FROM PRINTING CONVENTIONS

Figure 7.6 lists some examples of various kinds of printing conventions used for English prose. Even if all the individual letters were replaced by a common symbol (such as Xs in Figure 7.13), punctuation alone enables the reader to extract a great deal of information about the locations of words, sentences, paragraphs, and even structure of sentences. General spacing and arrangement of text on the page can provide additional information.

Redundancy for Language Rules

The types of redundancies described so far have been derived solely from visual information. However, readers normally have other

End-of-line conventions:	Right and left justified Hyphen indicates word division
Paragraph conventions:	Indentation Skip a line Bold face, initial character enlarged, etc.
Sentence boundary conventions:	Initial capitalization Final punctuation marks Extra space
Phrase boundary conventions:	Punctuation Extra space
Transformation conventions:	Question has question mark at end (some languages at beginning) Imperatives and exclamations have exclamation mark Statements have periods Emphatics have italics or boldface
Direct speech conventions:	Quotation marks Paragraphing for change of speaker
Word conventions:	Space before and after Initial capitalization for proper nouns

FIGURE 7.6. *Several examples of printing conventions used for English prose.*

sources of redundancies available to draw upon. One of these is knowledge of the linguistic and semantic structure of the text. Thus, there are restrictions among letter co-occurrences, so that letters do not freely combine. Further, there are syntactic limitations, such that given a preceding string of words, the part of speech possibilities for the next word are few or even limited to only one; and there are ongoing semantic restrictions, so that only certain kinds of words can occur later in a sentence.

SPELLING RULES

Spelling rules restrict the sequences among letters. A fluent speaker of the language who does not know how to read knows nothing about spelling rules (although several theories about reading have linked the rules underlying letter restrictions to phoneme restrictions that exist for speech [see Gibson & Levin, 1975]). As an alphabetic language, English has a very small number of separate letters that can be combined in a relatively large number of ways to make up an enormously large set of words. However, if it were permissible to combine the 27 characters (including the space character) randomly (that is, if any character could follow or precede any other character including itself), there would be no redundancy within an English letter sequence. Given any one of the 27 characters of English, there would be 27 possibilities for the next letter. To decode a sequence would then require specific identification of each and every character in the sequence.

English, however, has very specific rules that restrict the combinations of letters. When these rules are known, the identification of one or several letters of a word means that the letters that can follow are not all the possible letters of the language, but only a very small subset of them. For example, consider the spelling rules for monosyllables. Starting from the vowel, the maximum number of consonants that can precede it is only three. If there are three consonants, the first must be an S or a T. Figure 7.7 lists all the consonant combinations that can precede the nuclear vowel in an English syllable. There are no instances in which four consonants can precede the nuclear vowel and there are only 9 instances of combinations in which three consonants can precede it. As there are over 9000 possible ways to combine the 21 consonants in all possible combinations of three and yet only 1% of

FOUR INITIAL CONSONANTS- NONE ALLOWED-0 OUT OF 193,481 ALTERNATIVES
THREE INITIAL CONSONANTS-9 COMBINATIONS ALLOWED OUT OF 9261 ALTERNATIVES

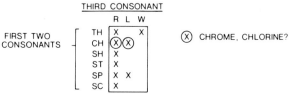

TWO INITIAL CONSONANTS-28 COMBINATIONS ALLOWED OUT OF 441 ALTERNATIVES

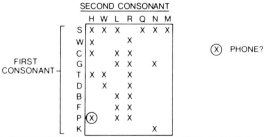

ONE INITIAL CONSONANT-ALL 21 COMBINATIONS ALLOWED OUT OF 21 ALTERNATIVES

FIGURE 7.7. *Initial consonant letter combinations that are found preceding the nuclear vowel in English words (Haber & Haber, 1980). No English words are spelled with four initial consonants. Less than 10 different spellings occur with three initial consonants (out of nearly 10,000 different ways three consonants could be combined if all combinations were used). Less than 30 different spellings with two initial consonants occur, out of 441 possible combinations. The difference between the few combinations found, as compared to the large number theoretically possible suggests the great restrictions (redundancy) among letter combinations found in English.*

those are permissible, the redundancy is impressively large. There are 441 possible combinations of two consonants, and yet only 30 of those are found in English words. All 21 consonants can appear singly.

Because English is an Indo-European language, polysyllabic words are typically composed of monosyllabic content words, to which affixes are added. Affixes conform to the same spelling co-occurrence restrictions as monosyllables, but are subject to a critical further limitation: placement within the word. Thus prefixes such as *pre-* and *un-* begin words; suffixes such as *-ing* or *-ion* end words—a further source of redundancy that identifies parts of speech as well.

A few letter combinations found in an English dictionary are absent from Figure 7.7. For example, the initial *cz* as in *czar*, *ps* as in *psychology*, or *ph* as in *phone*, do not appear. It is not clear what to do with such combinations psychologically. The letter combinations themselves have come into English from other languages, and, in some cases, represent non-English spellings and non-English pronunciations. In a few cases, the words appear very frequently, such as the initial *ps* combination in the chapters in this book. Psychologically, however, such spelling combinations are not considered productive, in that, if a person were asked to spell the initial consonant in the pronounced word *sigh*, it would be a rare English speller who would use an initial *ps*. On these grounds, such spelling combinations are not included in Figure 7.7. Even if they were, they might add only another dozen or so entries to Figure 7.7. The same impressive limitations are found for final consonant clusters.

Figure 7.8 shows all the spelling combinations of vowels found in English monosyllables. The five vowels (plus *y* when it follows a consonant) can all occur by themselves. Many of them appear in two-letter combinations. If the six vowels, taken one or two at a time, could be randomly combined, there would be 42 different nuclear vowel spellings; most of these can be found in English spellings. This may be one reason these vowel spellings are so hard to learn. (*Ieu* and *eau* are the only three-letter vowel combinations found in English. Both are imported from the French, and are not used productively.) (Final *-e*, as in *breathe*, is not discussed here because it does not affect co-occurrence restrictions.)

It is clear, then, that familiarity with the spelling rules for the letter combinations in the language provides a tremendous amount of redundancy, enabling prediction of letter sequences. Thus, if a reader sees that the initial letter of a word is a *t*, he or she can tell by reference to Figure 7.7 (or the equivalent knowledge that adult readers carry around in their heads) that all six vowels can follow or the consonants *h*, *r*, or

	A	E	I	O	U
A			AI		AU
E	EA	EE	EI	EO	EU
I	IA	IE		IO	
O	OA	OE	OI	OO	OU
U	UA	UE	UI		

FIGURE 7.8. *Spelling combinations of the nuclear vowel found in English words (Haber & Haber, 1980). All the vowels can appear singly, and of the 25 combinations of two spelled vowels, 18 occur. Thus, there is much less restriction of alternatives with spelled vowels, which may be one reason for the greater difficulty children have in learning the spelling of vowel sounds (Haber & Haber, 1979). There are no English words with three spelled vowels (with a few exceptions such as eau in beau which is not an English word).*

w. If Figure 7.7 also included the frequencies with which each of these combinations occur, it would be obvious that the most likely alternative is *h*: Of all nine combinations of initial *t* followed by any other letter, *th* accounts for 65% of the words in English (Haber & Haber, 1980).

RULES OF SYNTAX

Syntactic rules are descriptions of the structural regularities among the words of the language. In most circumstances, syntactic rules are identical for print and for speech. Figure 7.9 provides one example of syntactic redundancy given simply by the identification of word class for functors (pronoun, preposition, etc.). Whenever a reader encounters one of these functors in a sentence, he can also predict the class of word (and often the class of the entire clause) that follows it. Figure 7.10 provides a different example, based upon more general syntactic rules. If the reader has identified the syntactic form of the words up to each point in a sentence, there are great restrictions on the syntactic class of the words to come.

Determiners (*a, an, the*) and quantifiers (*some, all, many, two, six,* etc.) begin a new Noun Phrase.

Definite Pronouns (*I, you, he, she, it,* etc.) begin a new Noun Phrase.

Prepositions (*to, at, in*) begin a new Prepositional Phrase.

Verb Auxiliaries with Tense (*is, are, was, have, can,* etc.) begin a new Verb Phrase.

Relative Pronouns (*that, which, who, when*) begin a new Clause.

Complements (*for–to, that,* etc.) begin a new Clause.

Subordinating Conjunctions (*because, when, since, if,* etc.) begin a new Clause.

Coordinating Conjunctions (*and, or, but nor*) begin a new Constituent similar to preceding one.

FIGURE 7.9. *Syntactic restriction on clauses following different classes of functors (From Clark & Clark, 1977).*

Syntactic rules interact with other types of redundancies. For instance, a syntactic rule governing WH questions is marked both syntactically and visually by beginning with a WH word (*what, why,* etc.), again, visually, by ending with a question mark, and, syntactically, by fronting the tense carrier portion of the auxiliary verb before the subject noun phrase. These multiple markings, of course, further increase the redundancy, thereby restricting the information in the text.

This short sentence demonstrates syntactic redundancy

1. If restrictions are only from the left side:

    _____ can be anything.

    This _____ can be adjective, noun, or quantifier (adverb).

    This short _____ can be noun or adjective.

    This short sentence _____ can be verb, time adverb, or new clause.

    This short sentence demonstrates _____ can be noun phrase, adverb, or new clause.

    This short sentence demonstrates syntactic _____ must be noun or adjectival phrase.

2. If restrictions are in both directions:

    _____ short sentence demonstrates syntactic redundancy. Must be article.

    This _____ sentence demonstrates syntactic redundancy. Must be adjective.

    This short _____ demonstrates syntactic redundancy. Must be noun.

    This short sentence demonstrates _____ redundancy. Must be article or adjective.

    This short sentence demonstrates syntactic _____ . Must be noun.

FIGURE 7.10. *Two examples of syntactic word choice restrictions. The first is based upon specification of the parts of the sentence preceding the word but without any restriction based on words to the right of the word to be specified. As can be seen, there is a substantial amount of restriction of syntactic class. However, when all the words except one is specified, that one word is nearly always restricted to a single syntactic class.*

SEMANTIC FEATURES OF WORDS

Closely tied to the syntactic properties displayed in Figures 7.9 and 7.10 are the restrictions created by semantic features. Consider the word *visit*. Normal use of this word (that is, nonmetaphorical) requires an animate, mobile subject—trees, while animate, cannot move of their own volition, so the phrase, *the tree visited* . . . does not occur in nonmetaphoric parlance. *Visit* also requires an object whose referent is either a person or a place: we visit *someone*, or *somewhere*. Among these possibilities, word shape information would quickly identify the presence or absence of a pronoun or a locative adverb such as *there*. In the same way, the subject of a sentence, be it *rock* or *Harry*, limits the kinds of activities available to the following verb: Whereas Harry is likely to go visiting, the rock is not.

Limitations of possibilities, or redundancies, based on language structure are like spelling rules in that they represent a kind of knowledge the reader presumably carries around in his head independent of any specific text. Once the reader has a particular text in hand, such knowledge interacts with information extracted from the visual features of the text. For example, visual information about word shape may define a functor; syntactic information may dictate a preposition rather than an article of the same shape: Thus, *He was sitting **on** a barstool*, not *He was sitting **an** a barstool*.

Figure 7.11 provides examples of several categories of restrictions, in which syntactic and semantic features of words combine to delimit the way the rest of the sentence can be constructed.

Linguists have thus far been unsuccessful in mapping the rules underlying semantic organization, yet semantic knowledge is undoubtedly a major source of redundancy for the fluent reader. Psychologists have focused mostly on vocabulary—a more limited view of semantics—and have successfully demonstrated through studies of associations that, where associations are strong, pick-up is facilitated. Thus, *He opened the door* is easier than *He opened the dance*, in that *door*, as the expected word in this context, apparently requires less processing. Extreme cases of semantic predictability are provided by "mother's-milk" quotations and fixed phrases. Thus, a reader will be at .9 in predicting the text following the sequences *four score and* . . . , or *dead as* . . . or *he stuck out like*. . . .

Redundancies Based on World Knowledge

The third broad category of knowledge available to readers stems from their own experiences. This includes general knowledge of world

Grammatical

Plural: The cat climbing my leg has <u>twenty</u> sharp claw <u> s </u>.
Past: <u>Yesterday</u> he verb <u> ed </u> something unprintable.

Functional

Verbs requiring two following noun phrases
  Put, shove (object noun + location): Put <u>the cat down</u>.
                                          *Put the cat.

Verbs requiring one following noun phrase
  Require (object noun): 'Require' <u>requires</u> an <u>object noun</u>.
  Fix (object noun): He <u>fixes</u> <u>broken machines</u> permanently.
                   *It requires.

Verbs obligatorily without following noun phrase
  Die: He died.
       *He died the parking attendant.

Categorical

Animate verb requires animate subject: The man walked
                                      *The table walked
Adjective of measure requires a measurable noun: Tall building
                                      *Tall democracy
                                      Green wall
                                    *Green ghost

Semantic
  Noun: <u>son of</u> requires a noun phrase with a person old enough
  Adverb: <u>quickly</u> requires a verb of movement
  Verb: <u>waltz</u> requires a subject noun phrase with legs

FIGURE 7.11. *Some examples of syntactic and semantic restriction that limit construction of sentences.*

events: that water makes things wet, it can freeze and make things cold; that it is hot near the Equator; and that stars are far away. World knowledge also includes the readers' general perceptions of the text in hand; their suppositions about type of text, author's style, and topic.

FAMILIARITY OF TOPIC

It is clearly easier to read text on a topic with which one is familiar. It seems reasonable that, when a reader knows something about the topic, the choice of vocabulary items is more predictable; the purpose that the writer has in communicating is more predictable; and the kind of new information is more predictable. The title or headline will often indicate what the text contains: the topic, the probable noun in the first sentential noun phrase. Often, the semantic field of the modifiers may be predicated as well: A text about pirates probably includes robbery, ships, and treasure; a weather report in Rochester,

New York probably refers to precipitation. Such knowledge interacts with semantic associations and syntactic rules. As a complex instance, consider the reader's knowledge, often held prior to reading the text at hand, of the many terms that may name one referent. For example, *the professors in the Psychology Department, the faculty, the staff, the tenured members,* and *we* may all refer to the identical collection of bodies. Readers usually maintain and predict the proper referent (Haber, Haber, & Furlin, 1981) despite the many forms in which it is realized. Pronoun substitution is the most common (and least understood) instance of this type.

REDUNDANCIES GIVEN BY THE TYPE OF TEXT

Once writers commit themselves to particular forms, the structure of that form greatly limits alternatives at all levels of text. For example, one can describe a murder in the form of a detective story, or in the form of a newspaper article. One can describe a loan as a legal document or as an IOU. One can tell an improbable happening as a fairy story, or as a story in a first-grade reading book. One can write a sonnet or a nursery rhyme, and so forth. In each case, the form chosen places restrictions on the structure of the text. For example, Figure 7.12 shows the kinds of restrictions that are placed on a fairytale in terms of the structure of the story, the choice of words, grammar, the format, its length, the way it is printed, the types of characters, and so forth. If the reader is familiar with the genre, and therefore with these restrictions, the redundancies that the restrictions create substantially reduce alternatives at all levels of language processing.

1. Opens: "Once upon a time . . .
        "Long, long ago there lived . . .
   Closes: "And they lived happily ever after."
2. Characters: Stereotyped as particular extremes: good/wicked, kings/paupers, beautiful/ugly.
3. Normal rules of reality are suspended. There are impossible beings (dragons and witches), impossible places (ice palaces and gingerbread cottages), impossible objects (magic swords), and impossible events (people turn into toads).
4. Time: Remote
5. Place: Remote or unreal (Never-Never Land, deep forest)
6. Language: Coordinate. This and this, then this happened. Events unfold but do not cause each other, so because (subordination) is rare. Little conversation. Often meter is poetic as in nursery rhymes: "And over the bridge and up the hill and under the deep green wood . . . we wove."

FIGURE 7.12. *Restrictions of various kinds on the content of a fairy story based upon the genre for fairy stories.*

FAMILIARITY WITH THE AUTHOR'S STYLE

A related source of redundancy is knowledge of the author's style. A short story by Hemingway shares few characteristics with a short story by Mark Twain. This is true even if the contents of the stories are similar. Obviously, this type of redundancy is of no use if one is not familiar with the different stylistic qualities of authors. But if these are known to the reader, there are severe restrictions on the alternatives that could occur.

The Interaction of Redundancies

We have sorted redundancies into categories of: (a) those available from the visual input; (b) those based on the reader's language system, independent of the text; and (c) those pertaining to experience, or to world knowledge. These redundancies, of course, interact. The reader not only sees the text, but uses his linguistic and experiential knowledge at each instant in processing. Visual features and these other knowledges combine to limit the possible alternatives, thus increasing predictability down the line.

In this discussion, we have distinguished three sources of redundancy: those that pertain to regularities in the visual input; those that stem from the language system being used; and those that result from the reader's experience. These redundancies are relevant to reading, however, only if they are known and used by the reader. Thus, implicit in this description is the assumption that one of the things acquired with the skill of reading is the knowledge of these redundancies. We turn now to the kinds of evidence that show that readers, in fact, know and use these regularities.

Evidence of Knowledge and Use of Redundancies by Readers

The foregoing is a theoretical armchair description of redundancy based upon an examination of the co-occurrence restrictions among the elements of printed language.

It is logically possible (if intuitively and linguistically nonsensical) that all these lovely redundancies exist in language and in print, but readers are ignorant of them. Fortunately, there is a growing body of evidence that, whereas readers may not be able to verbalize the regularities we have described, they do exhibit knowledge of them. However, the demonstration of such redundancies or even the demonstration that readers know of them, does not in itself show that readers use any of them in the reading process.

For some of the redundancies, a large, although highly varied, literature already exists. Others have never been studied. In little of this research is the nature of the redundancies carefully defined, and seldom is a single source of redundancy isolated. Even more rarely is the distinction between knowledge and actual use explored. Even so, substantial hints already exist of the importance of the use of redundancies in reading.

Knowledge versus Use of Redundancies

It is impossible to separate studies that merely provide evidence of knowledge of redundancy rules from evidence that a reader actually uses such rules in normal reading. Even the criteria specifying evidence of use have not been carefully spelled out before. Merely showing that reading performance improves when some redundancy is added is not sufficient. This is no more than saying that easy text is easier to read.

The most powerful evidence for the use of redundancy in reading would be to show that the productive errors made by the reader in misreading the visual features are exactly predictable by the redundancies present. As one example, failure to detect misprints in the visual features, but reading the words as they are expected to be, shows that the reader is, at that point, using his expectations about spelling configuration and word sequences rather than attending entirely to the visual features themselves. Such evidence further requires error analyses that relate the specific pattern of errors made to the specific redundancies present. Unfortunately, not very many studies have reported appropriate error analyses, nor could they do so unless they also precisely spelled out the particular redundancies being manipulated.

A second kind of evidence for the use of redundancies would be based upon an analysis of individual differences in reading performance. If error analyses are made, those readers who know a particular redundancy should be those most prone to make productive errors that can be predicted by the nature of the redundancy rather than by the visual features. Individual differences are useful even in the absence of an error analysis. Readers who know a particular redundancy should be those most debilitated if that redundancy is altered or removed. Thus, filling in the spaces between words should affect all readers, but it should hurt the better readers most, as they are the ones using word length redundancies (Hochberg, 1970). Such evidence is particularly powerful because of the counterintuitive findings that better readers are hurt more than are poorer readers by a manipulation.

The more typical evidence offered in support of the use of redundancies in normal reading is to show that reading performance changes when the presence of a redundancy is altered. We consider this to be weak evidence at best, because no converging operation is offered that it was the manipulated redundancy that accounted for the change, and not some other correlated variable. Even so, most of the evidence is of this form, and we shall include some of it with the less frequent but more powerful examples. This review is by no means complete. In fact, allowing the weaker criterion to be used, the list of relevant studies would be enormous. Examples of all three criteria (failures to detect misprints, analyses of individual differences, and correlations between reading performance and amount of redundancy) can be found in the Wildman and Kling (1978) review of evidence of anticipatory processes in reading.

Visual Feature Redundancies. Examples of evidence of the use of visual redundancies include Hochberg's finding (see 1970 for a description) that skilled readers are affected more than poor readers when spaces between words are filled; evidence that it takes about 10% longer to read all upper-case print, which removes word shape information (see Fisher, 1975); McConkie and Rayner's (1976) finding that word length information is used by readers up to 12 spaces beyond fixation position, and word shape and individual letter shape up to 9 spaces beyond fixation; and Haber, Haber, and Furlin's (1981) evidence that readers can use word shape information in predicting upcoming material.

In that study, college students were asked to read passages displayed on a cathode-ray tube (CRT). A few lines would appear ending in the middle of a sentence. The subject had to read the text and to guess the next word. After the subject's guess, another line or two of the passage appeared ending in the middle of a sentence and the next word had to be guessed. This procedure continued to the end of the passage. In the blank condition, no information about each of the words to be guessed was provided, except, of course, all of the previous context. In the length condition, the number of letters in each word to be guessed was specified by xs. In the shape condition, the envelope shape of the word was drawn. We found that accuracy of guesses increased substantially from the blank to the length condition, and again from the length to the shape conditions respectively. Furthermore, even when wrong, the errors were more likely to match the correct word in length or shape when that information was supplied. We concluded that subjects were able to use the length and shape information in this task to generate expectancies about what was coming in the text. Detailed analyses of parts of speech and the nature of the errors supported this conclusion, and   the separation of semantic and syntactic accuracy also supported this conclusion.

Language Redundancies. Evidence for the use of language redundancies is more varied. In a misprint detection task, Haber and Schindler (1981) found detection less likely in misprinted functors as compared to misprinted high-frequency content words, and R. N. Haber (1980) found misprint detection to be much faster in sentences with high as compared to low semantic redundancy. Klein and Klein (1973) printed text with equal spaces between letters and words and asked readers to mark out the word boundaries, and found they are faster as the semantic redundancy of the sentences increases. Kolers (1970) showed that nearly all substitution errors made in reading geometrically transformed text are semantically appropriate; Haber, Haber, and Furlin (1981) found the same result in their Cloze test (see L. R. Haber, 1980). Kolers (1970) found that when bilinguals read texts that alternate in language, they often translate the ends of phrases to match the language of the beginning, even when this unwitting translation requires violation of the physical ordering of the words. Isakson and Miller (1976) created semantic and syntactic violations in sentences and found these produce disruption in reading, with better readers suffering more than poor readers. A number of studies (see Wildman & Kling, 1978, for a review) have shown that the presence of semantically ambiguous words in a sentence affects, among other dependent measures, decision time in a phoneme monitoring test, paraphrase accuracy in a dichotic listening test, and decision time in a word–nonword classification test. These results all indicate that readers are sensitive to the alternative meanings that affect the subsequent processing of the text.

Several studies using eye–voice span have shown that grammatical redundancies affect the size of the span (Levin & Kaplan, 1970, 1971; Wanat, 1976). Oral reading errors are shown to reflect syntactic constraints (Isakson & Miller, 1976; Kolers, 1970; Weber, 1970), and Stevens and Rummelhart (1975) showed, via a quantitative description of grammaticality, that they could accurately predict readers' Cloze-type responses as a function of grammatical constraints.

Finally, there is an enormous literature on spelling and related orthographic constraints. Haber and Haber (1979) used a Cloze-type spelling task in which children had to insert an acceptable letter in a blank space of a six-letter word, and showed a steady increase in acceptable responses from ages 5 to 12. They also showed that different spelling rules are acquired at different times and by readers of different skills. Acceptability was determined according to a complete spelling canon of English (Haber & Haber, 1980) in which all spelling clusters in the 80,000 different words found in the 5-million-word corpus of the *American Heritage Word Book* (Carroll *et al.*, 1971) were tabulated by position, co-occurrence restriction around the nuclear vowel, and frequency of occurrence. Without this analysis, most of the literature studying spelling rules has used other, less accurate indices of orthographic constraints (see Haber & Haber, 1975). Whereas most studies do show a positive effect of constraint on whatever dependent measure is used, many make erroneous claims about the units involved in processing these constraints.

World Knowledge Redundancies. Although common sense argues that relevant background knowledge would make a text easier to read, or more redundant, the relation between prior knowledge and the reading process has received little attention. Although it was done for a different purpose, Kolers (1975) studied the savings in speed and errors when various forms of the same passage are read a second time. Gibson and Levin (1975) neither discuss the topic nor mention a single study that manipulated any of the world knowledge variables. However, they do include a tangential literature review on the effects of posing questions to the reader to facilitate retention. In some studies, these questions may have sensitized the reader to prior knowledge about the topic, style, or author (see Gibson & Levin, 1975, pp. 392–437). Anderson, Reynolds, Schallert, and Goetz (1977) found that subjects' background knowledge, as well as the testing conditions, are highly related to their comprehension and recall of passages containing two interpretations; Bransford and McCarnell (1974) also used ambiguous passages, attaching one or another title, and found that subjects remembered propositions consistent with whichever theme they had been given.

A direct and recent study of the effect of prior knowledge on reading has been made by Pearson, Hansen, and Gordon (1979). Second graders of average intelligence, reading at grade level or just above, were tested for their knowledge of spiders. The 10 most knowledgeable, and 10 least so, read a text about spiders and then answered six explicit and six implicit questions (categories defined in Pearson & Johnson, 1978). The implicit questions are intended to require reference to prior knowledge for the generation of an answer. The two groups were found to differ significantly in their performance on implicit questions, but not on explicit questions. Both groups did better on explicit than on implicit questions. These results suggest that background knowledge enables the reader to draw wider inferences from a passage: to general-ize, and to test broader expectancies.

To summarize, a growing body of experimental literature demon-strates that readers know and use a number of the redundancies we have described, ranging from redundancies based on visual features on the printed page to those based on knowledge—both linguistic and ex-periential—in the reader's head independent of the text at hand.

The Information Processing of Feature Extraction and Hypothesis Testing

If we stopped here in the chapter, we would have made a case for the plausibility of an analysis-by-synthesis approach to reading, with-out offering any ideas on how it works. To say that readers use redun-dancies does not specify how that use supplants visual feature process-ing. This last section provides some suggestions.

Briefly, our argument is that, for an expectancy model to function, there has to be evidence that the visual system has access to more visual information than the features that cover the center of the fovea during each fixation. If the only features that can be picked up are the few letters in clearest central vision, it would be difficult to imagine how expectancies could be generated or tested about the text being read. Thus, we need evidence to show that featural, spelling, and syntactic information, especially, are available beyond the center of each fixation area. If this is the case, it is possible to explain how expectancies that encompass more of the text than a few letters at a time can be generated and tested.

Therefore, in this last section, we shall first review evidence to show that information about the text can be picked up in peripheral vision—that is, beyond the center of each fixation. Then we will show, with such evidence in hand, that it explains how we can have percep-tual access to large segments of each line of text at each moment, and, most important, how the size of that segment varies with redundancy. With higher redundancy, greater amounts of text are perceptually ac-cessible for processing. It is this relationship of redundancy to the size of the field of view that provides the mechanism by which expectancies operate in and facilitate the fluent reading process.

*Information Available from outside the Central
Area of Vision*

The kinds of information that reasonably could be picked up in peripheral vision are the positions of words (given by detecting the spaces between words), length of words, ends of sentences or clauses (given by detecting punctuation and extra spaces following punctuation), beginnings of sentences (given by detecting capitalization), end of line (given by white margin around the printed area of the text), shapes of the words (given by the pattern of ascending or descending letters in the word), and, of course, the actual letters in the words (given by their distinctive visual features). It is likely that the distance into the peripheral visual field at which each of these sources of information can be picked up depends on the size of the visual feature conveying the information. Hence, resolving individual letters may be difficult in the far periphery, whereas word shape and word length would be easier, and end of line easiest.

Rayner (1978), in his review of eye movements in reading, describes several kinds of evidence to show that the reader is sensitive to information in the text to the right of the current fixation, that is, information that has not yet been fixated.

One experimental procedure has manipulated the amount of text the reader can see. If a reader normally picks up no information from peripheral vision, and can see only the word over the fovea (plus all those previously fixated) when extracting meaning from text, then reading performance would not be impaired if the reader was never able to see any of the words to the right of fixation until he actually moved his eyes over them. However, if he did normally pick up information from the next few words to the right of fixation, denying the reader access to them would slow down or otherwise impair performance. Several experiments have examined these possibilities (Newman, 1966; Poulton, 1962). In general, the reader is presented with text generated by a camera with a restricted angle of view, which moves over the line of print just as the eye would do. The number of character spaces visible at any time to the camera is restricted, so that only part of a line can be seen at any one instant. Using reading performance with no restricted line length as a baseline, all these studies have shown disruption of performance as soon as the visible area of text is restricted to below 25–50 character spaces. Thus, they provide one kind of evidence that readers use text well beyond the center of fixation.

These studies, although persuasive, have been criticized because the disruption could be due to the unusualness of the task. The saccades normally made by a reader are simulated by the camera. Hence, it is not a natural way to read.

McConkie and Rayner (1975) repeated the experiment using a somewhat more natural procedure. The text to be read was displayed on a television screen controlled by a digital computer. The reader's eye movements were simultaneously recorded and measured by the same computer, which was programmed to make the appearance of the text contingent upon the position of the eyes while reading. Figure 7.13 illustrates the nature of the task. Part (a) is a sample of the text to be read. The computer displays the text on the television screen so that each letter and space has been replaced by a capital X. When the reader begins, and the computer determines that his eye is fixated near the beginning of the first line, all of the Xs around the center of fixation are replaced with the actual letters, so that the reader can process them. When he moves his eyes to the next fixation position, the earlier part of the text reverts to Xs and the letters around the new fixation are "uncovered." Part (b) of Figure 7.13 illustrates how the text would look for a window 17 character spaces wide. The window size—the number of letters uncovered in each glance—is determined by computer control. McConkie and Rayner used window sizes from 1 to 21 letters. In addition, they had the window either centered on the center of fixation, to the right of fixation, or to the left of fixation.

Figure 7.14 shows the results of several experimental conditions. In general, restricting viewing to less than three or four words disrupted performance, in that the distance the eyes moved decreased.

By far the single most abundant substance in the biosphere is the familiar but unusual inorganic compound called water. In nearly all its physical properties water is either unique or at the extreme end of the range of property. It's extraordinary

(a)

XXXXXXXXXXXXXXXXXXXXXXXXXXXXXXXXXXXXXXXXXXXXXXXXXXXXXXXXXX
XXXXXXXXXXXXXXXXXXXXXsual inorganic coXXXXXXXXXXXXXXXXXXXXXXXX
XXXXXXXXXXXXXXXXXXXXXXXXXXXXXXXXXXXXXXXXXXXXXXXXXXXXXXXXXX
XXXXXXXXXXXXXXXXXXXXXXXXXXXXXXXXXXXXXXXXXXXXXXXXXXXXXXXXXX

(b)

Xx xxx xxx xxxxxx xxxx xxxxxxxx xxxxxxxxx xx xxx xxxxxxxxx
xx xxx xxxxxxxx xxx xxxsual inorganic coxxxxxxx xxxxxx xxxxx. Xx
xxxxxx xxx xxx xxxxxxxx xxxxxxxxxx xxxxx xx xxxxxx xxxxx xx xx
xxx xxxxxxx xxx xx xxx xxxxx xx x xxxxxxxx. Xx'x xxxxxxxxxxxxx

(c)

FIGURE 7.13. *Different examples of the computer generated display used by McConkie and Rayner (1975). The top is the normal text. In the middle, all of the text including spaces is replaced with capital Xs, except for a "window" of 17 character spaces, centered on a fixation in its middle, through which the normal text is visible. In the bottom example, the same window is illuminated, but in the rest of the text, the space character is not replaced by an X.*

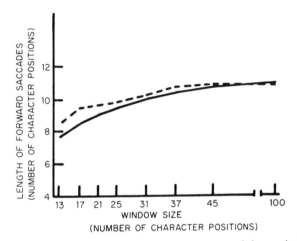

FIGURE 7.14. *Changes in average distance the eyes moved for each fixation as a function of window size (data from McConkie & Rayner, 1975). The solid line corresponds to text like that in the middle example of Figure 7.13; the dashed line corresponds to text with the space character preserved (bottom example of Figure 7.13). For windows less than about 25 character spaces—about 4–5 words—the larger distance moved in the space condition suggests that the spaces between words is being used from peripheral vision to provide added information about the text being read.*

McConkie and Rayner (1975) also manipulated the information outside the window. In general, the greater the amount of information contained outside the window area, the less important was the size of the window. For example, Figure 7.14 contains the results from the displays shown in Conditions B and C in Figure 7.13. Saccade distance is greater when word length information is preserved outside of the window as compared to when the spaces are filled in so that the position of the words cannot be seen in peripheral vision. Word length specification seems to be effective only for windows of 25 spaces or less—about 12 spaces from the center of fixation, or two to three words, as shown by the difference between the two curves in Figure 7.14. The same effect occurs when word shape information is preserved outside of the window. Specifically, outside of the window, when ascenders are replaced with ascenders, descenders with descenders, and so forth, saccade distance is greater, showing that readers are sensitive to shape information beyond the word in the center of fixation. Word shape information is only effective for about one to two words beyond the center.

These studies provide strong evidence that the reader does attend to information well to the right of the center of the current fixation and that the distance over which information is obtained can be as large as several words.

Rayner (1974) reported a different type of experiment that also used a gaze-contingent display system. Several lines of text appeared on a screen, under computer control. The computer also monitored eye movements and was programmed to change one word in the text when the reader's eyes were fixated at some point on the text that preceded that word. The change occurred during the saccade that carried the eye over the trigger position, so that the reader could not notice the actual change in the display as it occurred. An example of one of the passages follows.

> A. *The robbers guarded the pcluce with their guns.*
> B. *The robbers guarded the palace with their guns.*

Rayner's argument was that if the reader has not picked up any information about the word to be changed prior to the change, then after it was changed, it would take no longer to read that part of the text than if the word were left unaltered. If, on the contrary, the reader had picked up some information in peripheral vision, then, when he encountered the new word it should slow him down, require extra fixations, or in some other way disrupt the normal reading process. To test this, Rayner made several types of changes, including ones that preserved word shape and length (such as changing *police* to *palace*), length but not shape (*palace* to *hostel*), and neither length nor shape (*palace* to *home*). He also varied the semantic meaning of the sentence. For each variation, he manipulated the distance at which the change was made.

Rayner found that when word shape and length are preserved, reading is affected only if the change is made within about five spaces, or one word away, and only when the change is from nonsense to sense. If the original word is a real word, no affect on reading is detected. However, if the change alters word length or shape, the distance over which the effect occurred was larger. For example, if the change altered shape, then it was noticed up to about two words away, and changing length was noticed up to three words away. These affects obtained for both nonsense to sense and real word changes. Again, these results show that readers do pick up information beyond the center of the current fixation. If the change preserves shape and length, then the change can be determined only by noticing the changes in the individual letters, and this can only be done one word away. Letter information is picked up from the next word beyond the fixation, but not farther. Shape information is perceived about two words away.

Word length is picked up as far as three words away. Rayner did not test for punctuation changes, sentence boundaries, or length of lines, but presumably these could be noticed even farther than letter shape and length information.

One last study also bears on this question. Haber, Haber, and Furlin (1981), in their study described earlier, found that supplying either word length alone or word length and shape improved readers' accuracy in guessing the next word in a text. Regardless of the difficulty of the text, letting the reader know the correct number of letters improved his guessing accuracy by about 10%, and if he also knew the shape of the word, accuracy increased another 10%. These results indicate that readers usually and typically are able to make use of word length and word shape information in extracting the meaning of the text.

All of this evidence suggests that the eye picks up information beyond the center of the current fixation. Therefore, while processing during a given fixation, the reader has available not only all the material he has read up to that point and that currently is before his fovea, but at least information about word shape, word length, and printing format further down the line.

The Effect of Redundancy on the Size of the Visual Field

The size of the visual field at any one instant is specified by the area over which useful visual information can be extracted (Mackworth, 1976). One assessment procedure is to measure visual acuity for targets as a function of target distance from the fovea. Figure 7.15 from Alpern (1962) is a typical result, showing very high acuity for targets presented within the foveal region, but rapidly falling recognition accuracy as the target is presented farther and farther into the periphery. For normal sized alphabetic characters (about 15 min of visual angle), recognition acuity drops sufficiently that a single letter presented in isolation would not be recognizable even 2 degrees from the center of the fovea (less than eight character spaces, or slightly more than the length of one word in typical text).

However, there is now substantial evidence that acuity goes up (as measured by increased recognition accuracy) when the redundancy of the target increases. Thus, at any retinal location, accuracy is higher if the number of alternatives from which the target letter is to be selected is restricted, or if the target letter is part of a familiar letter sequence or a word (e.g., Reicher, 1969). What this implies is that Alpern's acuity

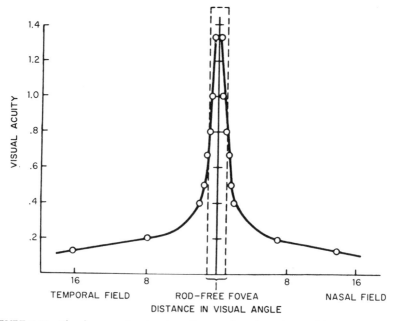

FIGURE 7.15. *The decrease in visual acuity as a function of retinal location (Alpern, 1962). Acuity is maximal in the center of the fovea and falls off rapidly for targets presented to the side of straight ahead. Since a six- to seven-letter word covers the entire fovea at normal reading distance with normal print, acuity for letters of adjacent words is less than one-fourth that for a centrally fixated word, and for a letter farther from the center of fixation, acuity is less by at least a factor of 10.*

curve is really only one curve among many, each of which differs as a function of the predictability or redundancy of the target.

This relation is sketched in Figure 7.16 as a family of curves. They can be read in two ways. First, at any particular retinal location, recognition accuracy varies directly as a function of redundancy. Second, these curves also suggest that, as redundancy increases, the same level of acuity can be found farther from the fovea. In other words, the size of the effective field of view changes with the redundancy of the targets being recognized. It is not a fixed value, determined only by the receptor mosaic, or the neural coding network of the retina, but also by the amount of prior information the perceiver has about what the target might be.

This variability in the effective field of view as a function of redundancy is the basis of the mechanism by which redundancy can effect reading. When redundancy is low, the effective field of view is narrow, and the reader has access only to those visual features near the

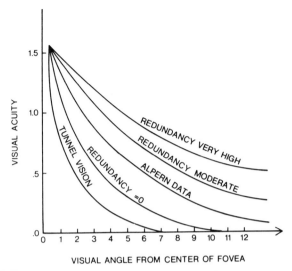

VISUAL ANGLE FROM CENTER OF FOVEA

FIGURE 7.16. *A schematic representation of a family of acuity curves across retinal position. Each curve results from a different amount of redundancy in the target display, such that as redundancy increases, the functional amount of acuity, for any retinal position also increases.*

center of fixation. However, when redundancy is high, the reader has access to the same fineness of visual features but much farther from fixation—that is, more of the line of print is perceptually available.

This variability also permits the size of the visual field to change from moment to moment in reading, rather than being fixed by characteristics of retinal sensitivity or neural coding. In general, the amount of redundancy is lower at the beginning of a paragraph than in the middle, and this implies that the size of the effective field of view is smaller. There already is evidence (Buswell, 1937) that fixations are closer together at the beginning of a paragraph than they are in the middle. A reasonable corollary to this is that if the size of the effective field of view is large, so are the saccade distances. Thus, with larger effective fields of view, reading speeds can be higher. In his work on eye–voice span, Geyer (1968) showed that the eye–voice span was larger for easy as compared to difficult text. Although difficulty of text is a crude way of expressing redundancy, Geyer does have some evidence that the size of the effective field of view covaries with redundancy.

Overlap of Successive Effective Fields of View. In the evidence just reviewed, we showed that the effective field of view extends well beyond the few letters covering the fovea, and that this area varies with the amount of redundancy available to the reader. The analysis that follows provides one additional insight about the reading process, one that also implicates the role of redundancy. Because the distance moved by the eyes between each fixation is relatively small in relation to the size of the effective field of view, each portion of the text being read is available several times for processing, not just once as is traditionally assumed.

For example, average college student readers move their eyes about seven character spaces between each fixation when reading typed material (Rayner, 1978)—about one word. But the peripheral vision and the acuity–redundancy relationships just reviewed suggest that the effective field of view at any one moment is much larger, at least for the recognition of some visual features. The overlap that results is illustrated in Figure 7.17. The implication of overlap is that each area of the text is looked at several times, initially by the peripheral retina, then by the parafoveal retina, then by the fovea itself, and then by the parafoveal retina on the other side.

Recognizing this multiplicity of views helps to understand three critically important theoretical problems underlying the reading process. First, overlapping fields of view promote a perceptual integration of the whole line of print in the same way that integrating all of the views of a picture can lead to a constructed picture. Most readers report introspectively that they "see" a whole line even though their acuity would never permit that kind of clarity.

Second, successive overlap provides the basis for peripheral vision to work. Parts of the sentence first come into view peripherally, then become available more centrally. This permits a time sharing of different levels of processing from different parts of the phrase or to different depths. When a part of the text first comes into view in the periphery, only the most general and higher-level redundancies can be used. The reader certainly cannot see letter features of even whole letters at those distances. But he can be testing out semantic and syntactic hypotheses. What kind of a phrase is he in? Where are the punctuation marks located? How long is the phrase? Where are the sentence boundaries? With the next fixation, this same area of text can

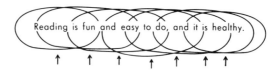

FIGURE 7.17. *A schematic representation of the overlap of the effective fields of view from successive fixations along a line of print.*

now be seen with greater clarity and the reader can pick up word length and word shape, so that he gets some general idea of the nature of the words. Syntax is very powerful in isolating the functors from the content words. With these high-frequency words, particularly the functors, shape and length are probably sufficient to provide exact identification. If the functors are identified, then the syntactic information that follows from them provides the reader with further information about what is coming in the text. The next fixation will bring that portion of the text directly over the fovea and now letter features themselves can be processed if needed, but in many cases there is already sufficient information (see Figure 7.10, Example (2) for an example of how extensively alternatives are restricted when information about larger chunks of text is available). Some of Rayner's data have already shown this process.

A third benefit of successive overlap is particularly important for English. English is notoriously difficult to process word by word, for nearly every word in English has multiple meanings and some have several pronunciations. Consequently, when the reader encounters a word, it is not always possible to determine which meaning is the appropriate one unless he has the context, including some of the text to the right of the word. Some of the ambiguity disappears from text seen prior to the word to be identified, but it is a rare English sentence in which any ambiguity is left once the reader has the full syntax of the phrase.

To delay the final assignment of meaning until the entire phrase is available, the reader needs a way to pick up information from the right side of the phrase without losing what has been seen on the left side. One way of doing this is to take in all the words in a phrase and hold them in some unprocessed buffer storage until the entire phrase has been looked at. Then the phrase can be examined as a whole and meanings assigned to each of the words. But if the words in the phrase are stored in unprocessed form, unrelated to each other, as soon as a phrase exceeds several words, the short-term memory is overloaded and some of the content is forgotten. Successive overlap, however, means that the reader does not need to depend on an uncoded memory; rather the successive overlap allows him to see the whole phrase. This notion is consistent with the large eye–voice spans that occur with high redundancy. It is a technique for getting lots of text to look at before final processing and pronunciation of it are completed.

Just as the presence of redundancy can alter the effective field of view, it can increase the amount of effectively available processing "space." Miller (1956) showed that roughly seven isolated elements can be maintained in short-term memory. Greater reader expectations mean that more text material can be chunked and briefly stored for processing.

This general discussion of redundancy has attempted to show how knowledge of the structure of the language, of the spelling conventions, of the individual letter features, and of the topic being read all have direct perceptual implications for the reading process. Redundancies improve effective acuity; they enlarge the effective field of view; they create successive overlap: all of which are direct aids in extracting meaning from text.

The Importance of Context

Because the reading process is so complex, the majority of researchers have attempted to tease apart its component parts. Thus letter features have largely been studied within the context of single letters; word recognition has been tested using isolated words or single sentences. Subjects can and do read in such impoverished conditions; but, we suggest, the normal reader resorts to letter identification only when more general hypotheses about syntax or semantics have failed him. These general hypotheses or expectancies require context for their generation. Specifically, the mechanism of overlap of fixations virtually disappears as the reader is forced to entertain and test ever narrower hypotheses.

Our discussion has focused on the fluent reader. Do beginning readers depend on context? Should they? Although we expect individual differences in reading performance to be highly related to use of redundancies, this does not imply a necessary causal relation between them. It is a question for careful research.

Finally, the demonstration that readers use redundancies to generate expectancies does not in itself provide a complete model of the reading process. Although Gough's bottoms-up approach becomes untenable, the degree to which expectancies govern eye movements, how they affect which aspects of the input are tested, or whether they are subjugated to or elevated above visual input actually tested, all remain to be explored. However, our description of the relation between amount of redundancy and size of field of view has provided a piece of the processing mechanism used in reading.

References

Alpern, M. Movements of the eyes. In H. Davson (Ed.), *The eye (Vol. 3): Muscular mechanism.* New York: Academic Press, 1962.

Anderson, R. C., Reynolds, R. E., Schallert, D. L., & Goetz, E. T. Frameworks for comprehending discourse. *American Educational Research Journal*, 1977, 4, 367–381.

Bouma, H., & Legein, C. P. Foveal and parafoveal recognition of letters and words by dyslexics and by average readers. *Neuropsychologia*, 1977, *15*, 69–79.

Bransford, J. D., & McCarrell, N. S. A sketch of a cognitive approach to comprehension. In W. Weimer & D. Palermo (Eds.), *Cognition and the symbolic processes*. Hillsdale, New Jersey: Erlbaum, 1974.

Buswell, G. T. How adults read. *Supplementary Educational Monographs*, No. 45, Chicago: Univ. of Chicago Press, 1937.

Carroll, J. B., Davies, P., & Richman, B. *The American Heritage word frequency book.* Boston: Houghton, 1971.

Clark, H., & Clark, E. *Psychology and language.* New York: Harcourt, 1977.

Fisher, D. F. Reading and visual search. *Memory and Cognition*, 1975, *3*, 188–196.

Geyer, J. J. Perceptual system in reading: The prediction of a temporal eye–voice span. In H. K. Smith (Ed.), *Perception and Reading*. Newark, Delaware: International Reading Association, 1968.

Gibson, E. J. *Principles of perceptual learning and development.* New York: Appleton, 1969.

Gibson, J., & Levin, H. *The psychology of reading.* Cambridge, Massachusetts: MIT Press, 1975.

Gough, B. One second of reading. In J. F. Kavanagh & I. G. Mattingly (Eds.), *Language by ear and by eye*. Cambridge, Massachusetts: MIT Press, 1972.

Haber, L. R. *A syntactic and semantic scoring manual for Cloze data*. Manuscript in preparation, 1980.

Haber, L. R., & Haber R. N. *Acquisition of spelling rules by children.* (Presented at the Psychonomic Society Annual Convention, Phoenix, Arizona, November 1979.) Manuscript in preparation.

Haber, L. R., & Haber, R. N. *Restrictions on letter co-occurrences: The spelling rules of English*. Manuscript in preparation, 1980.

Haber, L. R., Haber, R. N., & Furlin, K. R. *Word length and word shape as sources of information in reading.* Manuscript in preparation, 1981.

Haber, R. N. Visual perception. In M. R. Rosensweig (Ed.), *Annual Review of Psychology*, 1978, *29*, 25–59.

Haber, R. N. *Detection of misprint errors: Evidence of semantic control over reading.* Manuscript in preparation, 1980.

Haber, R. N., & Haber, L. R. What language do approximations to English approximate? (Presented at Psychonomic Society Annual Convention, Denver, November, 1975.) Manuscript in preparation.

Haber, R. N., & Hershenson, M. *The psychology of visual perception* (2nd ed.). New York: Holt, 1980.

Haber, R. N., & Schindler, R. Errors in proofreading: Evidence of syntactic control of letter processing? *Journal of Experimental Psychology: Human Perception and Performance*, 1981, *7*, in press.

Hochberg, J. Components of literacy: Speculations and exploratory research. In H. Levin & J. P. Williams (Eds.), *Basic studies on reading*. New York: Basic Books, 1970.

Isakon, R. L., & Miller, J. W. Sensitivity to syntactic and semantic cues in good and poor comprehenders. *Journal of Educational Psychology*, 1976, *68*, 787–792.

Klein, G. A., & Klein, H. A. Word identification as a function of contextual information. *American Journal of Psychology*, 1973, *86*, 399–406.

Kolers, P. A. Three stages of reading. In H. Levin & J. P. Williams (Eds.), *Basic studies on reading*. New York: Basic Books, 1970.

Kolers, P. A. Specificity of operations in sentence recognition. *Cognitive Psychology*, 1975, *7*, 289–306.

Levin, H., & Kaplan, E. Grammatical structure and reading. In H. Levin & J. P. Williams (Eds.), *Basic studies on reading*. New York: Basic Books, 1970.

Levin, H., & Kaplan, E. Listening, reading, and grammatical structure. In D. L. Horton & J. J., Jenkins (Eds.), *Perception of language*. Columbia, Ohio: Merrill, 1971.

Lindsay, P., & Norman, D. *Human information processing* (2nd ed.). New York: Academic Press, 1977.

McConkie, G. W., & Rayner, K. The span of the effective stimulus during fixations in reading. *Perception and Psychophysics*, 1975, *17*, 578–586.

McConkie, G. W., & Rayner, K. Identifying the span of the effective stimulus in reading: literature review and theories of reading. In H. Singer & R. B. Ruddell (Eds.), *Theoretical models and processes of reading*. Newark, Delaware: International Reading Association, 1976.

Mackworth, N. H. Stimulus density limits the useful field of view. In R. A. Monty & J. W. Senders (Eds.), *Eye movements and psychological processes*. Hillsdale, New Jersey: Erlbaum, 1976.

Massaro, D. Primary and secondary recognition in reading. In D. Massaro (Ed.), *Understanding language: An information processing analysis of speech, reading, and psycholinguistics*. New York: Academic Press, 1975.

Miller, G A. The magical number seven, plus or minus two. *Psychological Review*, 1956, *63*, 81–97.

Miller, G. A., Heise, G. A., & Lichten, W. The intelligibility of speech as a function of the context of the text materials. *Journal of Experimental Psychology*, 1951, *41*, 329–335.

Newman, E. B. Speed of reading when the span of letters is restricted. *American Journal of Psychology*, 1966, *79*, 272–278.

Pearson, P. D., Hansen, J., & Gordon, C. *The effect of background knowledge on young children's comprehension of explicit and implicit information*. (Center for The Study of Reading. Tech. Rep. No. 116). Cambridge, Massachusetts: Bolt, Beranek, and Newman, 1979.

Pearson, P. D., & Johnson, D. D. *Teaching reading comprehension*. New York: Holt, 1978.

Poulton, E. C. Peripheral vision, refractoriness and eye movements in fast oral reading. *British Journal of Psychology*, 1962, *53*, 409–419.

Rayner, K. The perceptual span and peripheral cues in reading. *Reading and learning series research report*. Ithaca, New York: Department of Education, Cornell University, 1974.

Rayner, K. Eye movements in reading. *Psychological Bulletin*, 1978, *85*, 1–50.

Reicher, G. Perceptual recognition as a function of meaningfulness of stimulus materials. *Journal of Experimental Psychology*, 1969, *81*, 274–280.

Rummelhart, D. E. Toward an interactive model of reading. In S. Dornic (Ed.), *Attention and performance VI*. Hillsdale, New Jersey: Erlbaum, 1977.

Shannon, C. E. A mathematical theory of communication. *Bell Telephone Technical Journal*, 1948, *27*, 379–423.

Smith, F. *Understanding reading*. New York: Holt, 1971.

Stevens, A., & Rummelhart, D. E. Errors in reading: An analysis using an augmented transition network model of grammar. In D. A. Norman & D. E. Rummelhart (Eds.), *Explorations in cognition*. San Francisco: Freeman, 1975.

Wanat, S. F. Relations between language and visual processing. In H. Singer & R. B. Ruddell (Eds.), *Theoretical models and processes of reading*. Newark, Delaware: International Reading Association, 1976.

Weber, R. First-graders' use of grammatical context in reading. In H. Levin & J. P. Williams (Eds.), *Basic studies on reading*. New York: Basic Books, 1970.

Wildman, D., & Kling, M. Semantic, syntactic and spatial anticipation in reading. *Reading Research Quarterly*, 1978–1979, *14*, 128–164.

VISUAL AND LINGUISTIC PROCESSES OF READING

8

Joel R. Levin

ON FUNCTIONS OF PICTURES
IN PROSE[1]

In this chapter, I will provide evidence that pictures can facilitate children's prose learning. Included in my purview of "pictures" are both visual illustrations that physically accompany a prose passage and analogous visual images that take shape only inside a learner's head. The evidence will be presented in the context of a conceptual framework that, at this writing, seems to account well for the various findings in the relevant prose-learning literature. As will be seen, this framework assumes that pictures in prose can serve multiple functions, two of which will receive special attention here. A consideration of these functions, with selected text and learner characteristics, makes it possible to specify the conditions under which picture effects would be expected to be nonexistent or minimal, on the one hand, and maximal, on the other. Findings thought to provide critical support for the framework's assertions are then indicated.

The first part of the chapter includes a summary of what has recently been concluded about picture effects in children's prose learning. The second part of the chapter presents the conceptual framework and its components, with the available empirical evidence reevaluated in light of these components.

[1]This research was funded by the Wisconsin Research and Development Center for Individualized Schooling, supported in part as a research and development center by funds from the National Institute of Education (Center Grant No. OB–NIE–G–78–0217). The opinions herein do not necessarily reflect the position or policy of the National Institute of Education and no official endorsement by the National Institute of Education should be inferred.

NEUROPSYCHOLOGICAL AND COGNITIVE
PROCESSES IN READING

Pictures and Children's Prose Learning

Are Visual Illustrations Helpful?

Levin and Lesgold (1978) have examined children's prose-learning studies in which experimenter-provided pictures accompany a text. Their conclusions will provide us with a convenient point of departure.

One of the most salient discoveries in the Levin and Lesgold review is surely the inadequacy of researchers' operationalizations of the question, Do pictures facilitate children's prose learning? In some studies, comprehension has been confounded with word recognition. In other studies, the pictures used seem to bear little or no relationship to the story content. In still others, the specific prose passages presented—and the associated comprehension assessment devices—appear less than optimal for answering basic questions about picture facilitation. For these reasons, Levin and Lesgold had to delineate a number of side conditions, or "ground rules," associated with the conclusions they reached. The ground rules functionally eliminated from consideration any study suffering from one or more inadequate operationalizations of the kind just described.

Levin and Lesgold (1978) were able to identify nearly 20 experiments that incorporated their methodological ground rules. Several recent ones can now be added to that list. The results of these experiments clearly permit the conclusion that picture effects in children's prose learning are positive, potent, and pervasive. In particular, visual illustrations constructed to be relevant to (indeed, overlapping with) a story's content have been found invariably to facilitate children's learning of that content. Although the magnitude of facilitation varies across experiments, a figure of 40% represents an apparent lower limit. That is, children exposed to story-relevant pictures may be expected to recall at least 40% more of that information in comparison to no-picture controls.[2]

---

[2]Of course, in specifying such a figure, one must assume that the results are based on passages for which there is plenty of "room" for pictures to show their worth. That is, with extremely simple or memorable passages that produce near ceiling-level performance in a control condition, obviously pictures cannot produce 40% improvement. Picture–control differences could alternatively be expressed in within-group standard deviation units (e.g., Levin, 1975)—which would help alleviate this problem somewhat— but percentage facilitation is reported here because most readers probably are more used to thinking in those terms.

EXTENSIONS TO OTHER PROSE TYPES

Levin and Lesgold's (1978) conclusions were derived almost exclusively from studies in which children were presented fictional narrative passages to learn. Such passages are the kind that would likely appear in children's story books. However, the picture facilitation effects discussed so far would take on added significance if they extended to other classes of prose material. The results of a number of studies suggest that they might. For example, visual illustrations have been found to facilitate elementary school children's learning of historical and scientific content (DeRose, 1976; Schallert, 1980). And, in a series of experiments recently completed in our laboratory (Levin, 1980, to be detailed later), we found that a special kind of picture dramatically improved junior high school students' learning about the accomplishments of famous people. Finally, a generalization of the visual illustration findings to an important "everyday" class of prose materials was accomplished in a study by Jill Berry and myself.

In that study (Levin & Berry, 1980), fourth-grade students were read a series of passages. The passages consisted of human interest and novelty stories that had been gleaned from local newspapers. Consider, for example, the following passage:

> The honey bee, Wisconsin's official insect, is dying. It is dying from a poisonous spray that farmers use to destroy bugs on their crops. The farmers don't mean to kill the bees, but some spray they use gets carried through the air to the hives of neighboring beekeepers. These beekeepers want the farmers to stop spraying their crops so the bees won't die. If the farmers won't stop spraying, the beekeepers want the farmers to tell them when and where they will be spraying so the beekeepers can move their bees away from sprayed crops.

As each passage was read, half of the children were shown a colored line drawing that captured the main idea of the passage. For the present example, the picture in Figure 8.1 was displayed. The other half of the children simply listened to the passages without pictures. In one experiment, the children's recall of passage content was tested immediately; in a second experiment, it was tested after a 3-day delay. In both experiments, children who were shown the pictures remembered more of that information in comparison to children who were not shown the pictures. Thus, it appears that the consistently positive effects of pictures on children's recall of fictional narratives do indeed generalize to their recall of illustrable real-life incidents.

In summary, to answer the question posed at the beginning of this

FIGURE 8.1. *Example of a picture used to improve children's recall of newspaper content. (From Levin & Berry, 1980.)*

section—Are visual illustrations helpful?—one can respond with confidence, Yes, very!

Are Visual Imagery Instructions Helpful?

ILLUSTRATIONS VERSUS IMAGES

A review of the imagery and learning literature reveals that many researchers do not attend much to the distinction between externally presented illustrations, on the one hand, and internally generated images, on the other. Indeed, the two picture types are often referred to interchangeably. Why, then, should we bother to make the distinction here? There are two related reasons, one basically empirical and the other theoretical.

The empirical reason for distinguishing between illustrations on the page and images in the head is a simple one. The findings associated with the two types of manipulation are often not identical. In particular, if one operationalizes the imagery generation process in terms of explicit instructions to learners to generate mental pictures, with accompanying practice at doing so or training in the process, then—as will soon become apparent in this section—the consistently positive effects obtained with illustrations are not nearly so consistently positive with imagery. This discrepancy, in fact, substantially shaped the conceptual framework to be developed later.

The theoretical reason behind the distinction relates to speculations about what goes on inside a learner's head when looking at an illustration, as opposed to when creating an original image. Although it might be argued that, once an illustration has been internalized, it resembles a visual image, the two types of pictures are most certainly associated with different companion cognitive processes and abilities. Visual perception and interpretation skills are required in internalizing an illustration, whereas cognitive constructions and elaborations are required in creating imaginal representations of verbal messages. Assuming that the illustrations provided are well drawn, easily interpreted, and appropriate to the verbal message, it might be expected that, at least in certain populations, picture effects would be more uniformly positive when they are associated with ready-made illustrations than when they are associated with self-generated visual imagery. This is because, with good illustrations, individual differences in the requisite perception and interpretation skills should play less of a role than would individual differences in the cognitive skills underlying visual imagery creation.[3]

I will now attempt to summarize the evidence pertaining to visual imagery effects in children's prose learning. Wittrock's chapter in this volume (Chapter 9), as well as Pressley's (1977) review article, should be consulted for additional information on the topic. Three main points, bolstered by relevant references, will be made here: (a) positive effects associated with visual imagery manipulations often do not materialize; when positive effects do occur, they are typically (b) small in magnitude; and/or (c) limited in generality. These points are offered in striking contrast to the previously discussed illustration effects, which have been found to be both ubiquitous and of impressive magnitude. This is not to suggest, however, that visual imagery must always retain a second-class citizen status as far as children's prose learning is concerned. Rather, as detailed in our framework to be presented later, a certain kind of learner-generated visual imagery may not have to take a back seat to anything.

---

[3]Competing explanations of such a finding are possible, one of which will be highlighted later in this chapter.

REVIEW OF THE EVIDENCE

All the studies reviewed here involve at least two basic conditions. In one condition (control), students simply listen to or read a prose passage. In the other condition (imagery), students are given explicit instructions (with varying degrees of practice or training) to create internal visual representations of the passage's content while processing it. The evidence to be summarized will be framed in terms of the three points mentioned earlier.

No Positive Effects of Visual Imagery. A number of prose-learning studies conducted with elementary school children have found no statistical difference between imagery and control groups (e.g., DeRose, 1976; Heckler, 1975; Johnson, 1975; Kulhavy & Swenson, 1975; Lesgold, McCormick, & Golinkoff, 1975; Levin & Divine-Hawkins, 1974, Experiment 2; Pierce, 1980; Steuck, 1979; Triplett, 1980). The Kulhavy and Swenson (1975) study is noteworthy because no imagery effect was detected on an immediate test, even though a slight effect appeared on a test administered a week later. Steuck (1979) could not replicate this delayed finding, however. The Triplett (1980) study is noteworthy because students (fourth graders) who received considerable practice at generating images to prose passages produced no hint of facilitated performance.

At this point, it should be mentioned that the children in the previously mentioned studies were all at least 9 years of age (i.e., at least third graders). Why is this consideration an important one? It is important because some have speculated that the ability to profit from visual imagery instructions is developmentally sensitive (Lesgold, Levin, Shimron, & Guttmann, 1975; Levin, 1976; Pressley, 1977). That is, a child's age—chronological, mental, or both—appears to be an important determinant of whether or not *any* benefits from visual imagery instructions will occur. Supporting data related to a chronological age interpretation may be found in the studies of Dunham and Levin (1979), Guttmann, Levin, and Pressley (1977), Ruch and Levin (1979), and Shimron (1974), where children less than 9 years of age experienced no facilitation whatsoever from prose-learning imagery instructions. Supporting data related to a mental age interpretation may be found in the studies of Bender and Levin (1978) and Wasserman (1979), where educable mentally retarded (EMR) children did not benefit from visual imagery instructions. Moreover, within an EMR student population that varied considerably in chronological age, Wasserman found that mental age was moderately related to students' prose recall in the imagery condition ($r = .53$), but not in the control condition ($r = .16$).

Small Positive Effects of Visual Imagery. There is no getting around the conclusion that the positive effects of visual imagery reported to date have generally been small in magnitude. The tiny effect of imagery on Kulhavy and Swenson's (1975) delayed test, mentioned earlier, is one example. Similarly unimpressive imagery effects were found in the very carefully controlled study by Pressley (1976). Even with conditions designed to be extremely hospitable to imagery generation, children (second graders) in the imagery condition statistically outperformed controls by only a small amount (62% versus 53% correct, on the average). Bender (1977) also reported a small positive effect of visual imagery in his sample of normal (i.e., non-EMR) third-grade children (averages of 73% and 63% correct for imagery and control subjects, respectively). These latter figures are almost identical to those of Guttmann et al.'s (1977, Experiment 1) third graders (74% and 62%).

Limited Positive Effects of Visual Imagery. The previously cited Lesgold, McCormick, and Golinkoff (1975) study will be used to illustrate a situational limitation associated with visual imagery instructions. In that study, third and fourth graders were given extensive training in cartooning and imagery generation. Following the training, however, modest prose recall gains were found only when the children read "homemade" stories similar in form to those given during training *and* were reminded to use an imagery strategy while reading them. Without the imagery reminder and/or for passages taken from a standardized reading test, no positive effect of imagery training was observed. Moreover, students who were given just imagery instructions (i.e., without the special training) showed no improvement, even on the homemade passages.

The variables of chronological and mental age discussed earlier certainly restrict one's ability to generalize about visual imagery effects across subject populations. As has already been shown, with younger or cognitively less advanced subjects, positive effects of visual imagery instructions have not emerged in the prose-learning literature. This is in sharp contrast to the positive effects of visual illustrations, which emerge with regularity even in such populations (Bender & Levin, 1978; Dunham & Levin, 1979; Guttmann et al., 1977; Lesgold, Levin, Shimron, & Guttmann, 1975; Shimron, 1974).

Apart from age and intellectual development indicators, interactions of selected individual differences and the ability to profit from visual imagery instructions are suggested in the literature. For example, in an experiment with fourth graders, Levin (1973) found that imagery instructions improved the reading comprehension of below-average readers with adequate vocabulary–decoding skills. In contrast, imagery instructions were not helpful to below-average readers with inadequate vocabulary–decoding skills. In another study, Levin, Divine-Hawkins, Kerst, and Guttmann (1974) found that fourth-grade students who were relatively adept at pictorial paired-associate learning benefited from prose-learning imagery instructions. Students whose pictorial paired-associate learning performance was relatively low did not benefit from prose-learning imagery instructions. Finally, Pierce (1980) recently attempted to relate imagery strategy effectiveness to the cognitive style variable of field independence, but with only marginal success.

Thus, based on the evidence reported in the literature, as well as that related at conventions or via personal communications of (typically nonsignificant) results, I am reluctantly forced to respond to the initiating question of this section—Are visual images helpful?—with, Slightly, perhaps! Because of this, some of my initial enthusiasm directed toward visual imagery as an effective—and teachable—prose-learning strategy (e.g., Levin, 1972) must surely be dampened. However, there is no justification for across-the-board pessimism. Some types of students seem to profit substantially from visual imagery instructions: for example, those with adequate word recognition skills who, nonetheless, exhibit comprehension failure (Levin, 1973). For such students, generating images of the passage content may be just the organizational strategy they need to foster comprehension. Thus, the potential of visual imagery to assist poor comprehenders should not be minimized. At the same time, and as has been alluded to already, the deployment of a different kind of visual imagery strategy may be required to produce more globally positive effects.

A Conceptual Framework for Prose-Learning Pictures

Can we account for the fact that, in the prose-learning studies considered so far, text-relevant provided illustrations invariably facilitate children's recall of passage content to a nontrivial degree, whereas instructions to generate visual imagery are not nearly so consistent in producing positive effects? Or, better yet, can we begin to specify the prose-learning conditions under which illustrations and images would be expected to yield the greatest returns? By the phrase "prose-learning conditions," I am referring to learner and text characteristics, both of which are likely to interact with picture manipulations. I think we can respond affirmatively to each of these questions. To do so, however, requires that we give consideration to a variety of functions that pictures might be presumed to serve.

Two prefatory comments need to be made with respect to the conceptual framework proposed here. First, some of the functions listed will apply more (or even exclusively) to pictures as visual illustrations, and others to pictures as visual imagery. Which is for which should be clear by context, however, and no special problems seem to have been created by incorporating the two types of pictures into a single table. Second, even though the functions are discussed separately, it is not reasonable to regard them as mutually exclusive competitors (i.e., one function is "right" and the others are "wrong"). In all probability, multiple aspects of pictures contribute to improved prose learning. These effects could be additive or interactive depending on the prose-learning conditions alluded to earlier. For purposes of the present discussion, however, the several picture functions will be treated as separate components, each contributing to prose-learning facilitation. The necessary component-isolating research has not yet been conducted to allow for definitive statements concerning additive and interactive effects.

Hypothesized Functions of Prose Pictures

As has already been claimed, a variety of functions can be served by prose pictures. Table 8.1 summarizes eight that come to mind, arranged in their likely increasing order of prose-learning benefits. By "benefits," I consider here only improved recall of explicitly stated text information. Other benefits such as improved recall of implied text information (i.e., inferences derived from text information, or inferences about the text's theme) and improved student affective characteristics (i.e., attitudes toward the specific text or toward prose in general) are beyond the scope of the present chapter. We now examine the eight proposed functions of Table 8.1, some in more detail than others.

Decoration Function. This function is listed strictly as a courtesy to those who believe that visual illustrations should be included in text simply because they enhance a book's attractiveness. Because this aesthetic motive has no obvious bearing on the present criterion of enhanced prose recall, however, the function will not be considered further.

TABLE 8.1
Proposed Functions of Prose Pictures

Function	General operating principle	Anticipated contribution to improved prose learning
1. Decoration	Pictures increase a text's attractiveness	Not applicable
2. Remuneration	Pictures increase publishers' sales	Not applicable
3. Motivation	Pictures increase children's interest in the text	Little or none
4. Reiteration	Pictures provide additional exposures of the text	Little
5. Representation	Pictures make the text information more concrete	Moderate
6. Organization	Pictures make the text information more integrated	Moderate to substantial
7. Interpretation	Pictures make the text information more comprehensible	Moderate to substantial
8. Transformation	Pictures make the text information more memorable	Substantial

Remuneration Function. This is the commercial by-product of the decoration function. That is, as many book purchasers share the decoration function view, if book publishers include visual illustrations in their books, sales will increase. In this sense, then, increased decoration leads to increased remuneration. But just as the former is irrelevant to increased recall of text information, so is the latter. Let us, therefore, resolve to dismiss this pecuniary function forthwith.

Motivation Function. Some people believe that prose illustrations serve to increase children's interest in the text. The empirical data related to this belief are, however, far from conclusive (e.g., Samuels, 1970). Moreover, even if children's interest, motivation, and the like are positively affected by illustrations, there exist no convincing data to relate increased motivation per se to increased prose recall. In a study by Heckler (1975), for example, increased motivation defined in terms of monetary incentives for learning did not improve children's prose recall. Moreover, if illustrations are purely motivators, then their specific relationship to the information presented in the text should make little difference as far as text recall is concerned. Some unpublished data by Michael Pressley, D. J. Hope, and myself show that this is simply not the case.

When 4-year-old children were explicitly instructed to remember information presented in a text, providing illustrations per se was not sufficient to improve text recall. When the illustrations conveyed the same information as the text, recall was indeed enhanced, but when the illustrated information contradicted that in the text, recall suffered. Children continued to recall the illustrated content rather than the text they were told to remember. A strict (content-free) motivation function of illustrations would be hard pressed to account for these findings (see also Peeck, 1974).

My best guess about the role of illustrations as motivators in children's prose-learning situations is that, in general, they have little effect. As long as the passages presented are sufficiently interesting, there is no reason to believe that illustrations increase children's interest in the text. Even if they do, how much does this increased interest (however slight) contribute to improved prose recall? Perhaps with extremely dull passages, illustrations serve to keep the learner awake, thereby improving recall. But such an antisoporific explanation is merely a sophomoric explanation until the relevant data have been collected.

Reiteration Function. A fourth proposed function of prose pictures is that they simply repeat the information presented in the text. This would be especially true of illustrations that are substantially redundant with the text content (Levin & Lesgold, 1978). According to this explanation, illustrations provide additional exposures of the text (especially in comparison to single auditory receptions). Because learning theorists subscribing to such notions as *repetition, exercise,* and *frequency* would advocate that more is better, the contribution of illustrations to improved prose recall can be accounted for in purely quantitative terms: Providing illustrations guarantees a second exposure of the prose content, and two exposures are better than one.

There may well be some truth to this picture function. For example, Levin, Bender, and Lesgold (1976) found that children who were presented each sentence of a prose passage twice in succession recalled more passage content in comparison to children who were presented each sentence only once. That is, repetition per se did elevate recall. But illustrations have been found to afford something more than a simple repetition of the prose content. In the first place, children in the Levin et al. (1976) study who viewed story-relevant illustrations recalled more prose content in comparison to children in the just-described repetition condition. Second, Ruch and Levin (1977) found pictures and repetition to produce qualitatively different recall patterns: Pictures facilitated recall of prose content cued by both verbatim and paraphrased questions, whereas repetition only facilitated recall of prose content cued by verbatim questions. Moreover, a repetition procedure is sometimes not facilitative at all, even though providing illustrations produces striking gains (Bender & Levin, 1978).

Thus, although something akin to a repetition component may underlie the positive prose-learning effects that are attributable to illustrations, such a component can account for neither the magnitude nor the generality of illustration effects. In short, to view a text-relevant illustration is to do more than simply "play it again, Sam."

The final four proposed functions of prose pictures constitute a more serious attempt to understand exactly what effect pictures have on the learner. This is not to say that the third and fourth proposed functions ought to be readily dismissed; rather, they are comparatively less interesting according to the cognitive–psychological perspective adopted by the present author. In particular, the final four functions focus on the *concreteness, relatedness, meaningfulness,* and *memorableness* of pictures. Moreover, as will become apparent, none of these specific functions is necessarily unique to pictures. Rather, each may be thought of as a general strategy for improving children's prose learning (Levin & Pressley, in press), which in turn subsumes such alternative techniques as question answering, paraphrasing, classifying, note taking, and verbal analogues to the pictorial strategies discussed here.

Representation Function. This function and the next assume that prose content presented in a format or mode that is different from that of the original will aid learning. Tabular, graphic, or taxonomic representations of a text, and underlining, segmenting, or summarizing important text sections constitute commonly applied format changes that characterize the present intent. In terms of the representation function as applied to pictures, text relevant illustrations and images take information that was represented in one mode (verbal) and represent it in another (pictorial). Enhanced recall of such pictorially represented information would be anticipated from a number of theoretical perspectives (cf. Ghatala, Levin, & Wilder, 1973; Nelson, Reed, & McEvoy, 1977, Paivio, 1971), which will not be detailed here. Suffice it to say that pictures make the to-be-learned information more *specific*. They also provide a *second modality* through which the text information can be directly represented in the brain (i.e., visually in the right hemisphere in addition to verbally in the left). For present purposes, however, we will regard the representation function of pictures as one of simply rendering the prose content more *concrete*.

According to the representation function, pictures lay down a "memory trace" that—for any or all of the theoretical reasons just alluded to—is stronger than that associated with a strict verbal representation of the text. This greater trace strength is assumed to pay off both during initial storage of the passage content and during subsequent retrieval of that content. More about these notions will be presented in the next section.

Organization Function. The assumption underlying this function is that well-organized text information will be better recalled than loosely organized or fragmented text information. In most of the children's pictures-in-prose studies reviewed by Levin and Lesgold (1978), concrete narrative passages were used. Such passages are typically straightforward and well structured. For less than optimally structured passages, however, pictures may help to organize the content. This is essentially the rationale adopted by Steingart and Glock (1979). In their study, it was expected that a visual imagery strategy would serve an important organization function for passage content that was potentially classifiable but that was not presented according to its optimal structure. Unfortunately, a number of methodological difficulties compromise interpretation of the results, but application of pictures to the kind of texts used by Steingart and Glock illustrates the present organization function.

The organization function was also assumed to be operative in the previously mentioned Levin (1973) study. In that study, well structured narrative passages were used. However, some of the children were poor comprehenders, for whom it could be reasoned that effective encoding of passage content did not occur during the normal reading process. When these students were instructed to apply a visual imagery strategy, their prose recall increased dramatically. A plausible interpretation of this finding is that the imagery strategy forced integration of information that otherwise would have been encoded only in fragments. Thus, one of the few impressive demonstrations of imagery strategy effects in the children's prose-learning literature is believed to have capitalized primarily on the organization function of pictures. The results of a recent study by Dillingofski (1980) are similarly consistent with an organization function account.

The amount of facilitation anticipated from this function is likely to be intimately connected to specific text and learner characteristics of the kind discussed here. The corresponding entry in Table 8.1 reflects the variable benefits assumed to be associated with the organization function.

Interpretation Function. Arguments similar to those just presented also characterize the interpretation function. That is, in comparison to the representation function (where easy to follow text is represented literally), a greater amount of facilitation would be expected when relatively abstract or difficult to comprehend information is made more understandable. In general, such an interpretation function would reflect content clarifications that are directed toward enhancing the student's understanding of that content. In some cases, the clarifications may be substantial, as when the provision of an advance organizer or analogy permits apparently incomprehensible prose (or poetry!) to be understood, or when these same devices contribute to one's processing of text from a totally new, extraliteral, perspective. One of the basic premises associated with the interpretation function is that to understand new information, one must relate it to existing knowledge. Given this description, the reader should have little difficulty incorporating contemporary *schema theory* notions (cf. Anderson, Spiro, & Montague, 1977) into what is intended by the interpretation function.

A case for pictures in this regard can be found in Levin and Pressley's (in press) discussion of *stage-setting* and other content-clarifying strategies used to enhance children's prose learning. The reader is referred to the Levin and Pressley chapter for illustrations of the kinds of strategies that have proven successful. The dependence of each of these strategies upon the student's prior knowledge is obvious. What needs to be reiterated here, however, is that the amount of success to be expected from any of these strategies probably depends upon the familiarity and/or complexity of the material being learned. With easy to understand materials, pictures would not serve an interpretation function; whatever benefits are observed would have to be associated with one or more of the other Table 8.1 functions. In contrast, when content-clarifying pictures accompany difficult to understand prose passages, the role played by the interpretation function of pictures becomes preeminent, with correspondingly substantial recall gains anticipated as a result. The position in Table 8.1 occupied by this function is based on the assumption that the type of text being studied merits the use of content-clarifying pictures.

Transformation Function. If the interpretation function is associated with prose materials that are difficult to comprehend, the transformation function is reserved for prose passages whose constituents may not be that difficult to comprehend, but that contain information that is difficult to remember. Examples of such texts include historical passages where names, events, sequences, and dates are important to remember; and medical and other scientific texts, where easily identified concepts, principles, and functions have to be associated with unfamiliar technical terminology. According to the transformation function, the existing content must be changed into a form that promotes better long-term memory for that content. Such changes also include the creation of new (extratextual) information to aid in storage and retrieval of the passage content. Although appropriate verbal transformations of the passage can certainly be prescribed, pictorial transformations are viewed here as being especially helpful. As will be argued shortly, illustrations' representation and transformation functions can be effectively combined to produce a powerful effect on students' prose recall.

As will also be seen, maximum prose-learning facilitation is believed to occur when the transformation function, rather than just the representation function, is operative. That is, pictures serving as mnemonic devices are hypothesized to yield the very greatest prose-learning benefits. Until only recently, however, little if any attention has been paid to pictures serving in this capacity. Indeed, the hypothesized transformation function holds the key to understanding why the prose-learning imagery effects reported to date have been singularly unimpressive. This key will now be used to unlock the illustration versus imagery dilemma that has surfaced repeatedly throughout the chapter.

"Functional" Analysis of Illustrations versus Imagery

The general analysis to be presented here can perhaps best be captured by the graph that is Figure 8.2.[4] The basic message conveyed by that figure is twofold: First, the major impact of pictures on prose-learning facilitation is derived from their transformation function rather than from their representation function. Second, much larger facilitation differences between visual illustrations and visual imagery are associated with the representation function than with the transformation function. The figure as drawn applies not only to the children's prose-learning literature of present concern, but to more fundamental studies of associative learning as well. Let us briefly consider the figure in that latter context first.

---

[4]Note that only two of the eight functions of Table 8.1 are included in this analysis. This is reflected in the author's bias that the two included are most directly related to the issue at hand. The organization and interpretation functions, although omitted here, obviously play an important role with certain classes of prose material and for certain kinds of students (see our previous discussion and Levin & Pressley, in press.)

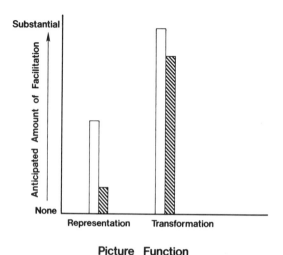

Picture Function

FIGURE 8.2. *Anticipated learning benefits associated with illustrations and imagery. Blank columns represent illustrations; shaded columns represent imagery.*

ASSOCIATIVE-LEARNING FINDINGS

The basic findings in this literature, following over 10 years of experimental investigation (see Bower, 1972; Levin, 1976; Paivio, 1971; and Pressley, 1977) are accurately reflected by Figure 8.2. In particular, consider the task of associating arbitrarily paired concrete nouns. It is well established that if the experimenter provides pictorial representations of those nouns (i.e., two pictures side by side), associative recall is moderately increased (relative to associating just the verbal labels). In contrast, instructing subjects to generate side-by-side imaginal representations has little or no effect on performance. Such a finding can be explained in terms of our previously discussed memory trace notions. First, it was argued in an earlier section that the process of perceiving illustrations results in a more reliable encoding of that information, in comparison to the process of generating images. Second, illustrations are more concrete than visual images in the Paivio (1971) sense. As a result, in comparison to visual imagery, the trace laid down by pictures is a stronger and more reliable one. According to present terminology, the representation function is more effectively realized by illustrations than it is by imagery. Corroborative data in support of these assumptions are provided by Ghatala et al. (1973), and will not be reviewed here.

Equally well established in the basic associative-learning literature is the finding that facilitation produced by providing illustrations per se is not nearly as great as that produced by creating a meaningful associative link between the paired items. Such linkings invariably involve *elaborations* (Rohwer, 1973) or—adopting the present terminology—*transformations* of the nominal stimuli to render them more memorable. An illustration or image in which the two items are interacting in a meaningful way has been found to constitute a highly effective mnemonic strategy. When purposeful mnemonic activity is involved, the difference between illustration and imagery efficacy diminishes, especially when cognitively advanced (older and intellectually more capable) students represent the target population. A small difference between illustration and imagery variations has been retained in Figure 8.2 to remind us of the potentially weaker and more variable trace associated with the latter. Note, however, the much greater amount of facilitation expected from the two strategies capitalizing on the transformation function (likely representation plus transformation) than from the two strategies capitalizing simply on the representation function. Now, with the associative-learning findings in mind, let us consider the extant prose-learning findings from a similar perspective.

PROSE-LEARNING FINDINGS

An important distinction between basic associative learning and prose learning needs to be made at the outset. Whereas the former is inherently arbitrary and rote in nature, the latter is usually thematic and meaningful. Certainly the distinction appears to be a valid one when distinguishing between the task of recalling noun pairs and that of recalling narrative prose. With few exceptions, it can be stated that most of the pictures-in-prose literature is derived from what will be described here loosely as fairly straightforward, concrete narrative passages. That is, the passages are comprehensible, they describe concrete (visualizable) incidents, and they follow a logical sequence with a prevailing theme, to name a few salient characteristics.

Pictures as Literal Representations. Consider the role played by visual imagery instructions in the vast majority of children's prose-learning studies. With the concrete narrative passages employed, it is probable that a great many effective comprehension activities are being carried out spontaneously by those who are asked to process the story content. Exactly what kind of strategies are employed by normal prose comprehenders is not relevant to the present discussion. Quite possibly, however, visual imagery is involved to some extent. The point here is that explicit visual imagery instructions are not likely to promote much effective information processing beyond that which students normally do. As we have already argued that the representation function associated with visual imagery instructions is not a potent one, certainly one cannot expect much help in that regard. In contrast, the more potent representation function of illustrations might be expected to give prose recall somewhat of a boost. This is the usual empirical result, as has been discussed throughout the chapter.

Additional data support the notion of representation strength differences between illustrations and imagery in prose-learning contexts. Guttmann et al. (1977) devised a special kind of pictorial aid to increase the potency of visual instructions. These "partial pictures" were illustrations that contained some, but not all, of the story's content. What was not depicted, however, was hinted at by being just outside the picture frame or obscured by an object in the illustration. Consider, for example, the partial picture of Figure 8.3, where children heard the accompanying sentence, *One evening Sue's family sat down to eat a big turkey for dinner*. It is important to note that in each partial picture, the information that was later asked for (e.g., *What did Sue's family eat for dinner one evening?*) was not visible. Students who viewed such pictures were instructed to create images of the missing content. Guttmann et al. found that partial pictures produced an intermediate level of performance in second-grade children, falling somewhere between complete imagery instructions, on the one hand, and complete illustrations, on the other. In a follow-up study, Ruch and Levin (1979) found

FIGURE 8.3. *Example of a partial picture. (From Guttmann et al., 1977.)*

that still younger children (first graders) could benefit from partial pictures only as long as they were reinstated during testing.

Although not previously discussed in exactly these terms, it could be argued that partial pictures serve as aids in strengthening an imagery representation. For some children, the increased concreteness afforded by partial pictures may succeed where straight imagery instructions would fail. And for still other (younger) children, the provision of partial pictures as concrete imagery-retrieval cues may serve to reevoke an otherwise forgotten representation. Ruch and Levin (1977, 1979) have documented that retrieval pictures per se (i.e., without prior study pictures) or verbal retrieval cues do not produce comparable recall benefits. This suggests that a concrete representation must first be established before it can be reevoked by a similarly concrete retrieval cue.

Pictures as Mnemonic Transformations. With prose that does not leap out in easy to process narrative fashion, the strain on one's comprehension and memory facilities can be considerably increased. Processing difficult to comprehend information falls under the aegis of the interpretation function that is not considered further here. But what about easily comprehended information that is difficult to code for future retrieval? As mentioned previously, such content is perhaps best represented by science and social studies passages, where much new information (names, dates, events, terminology) is presented. Such information is likely to require more than a passive, effortless encoding. Enter the transformation function. Here, the idea is to construct pictures that transform information that is only weakly connected into more memorable representations. In the associative-learning literature, arbitrarily paired objects were placed in a meaningful relational context. With factual prose passages, analogous importations may well be required. Let us consider an effort by Linda Shriberg, Christine McCormick, Michael Pressley, and myself to get at some of these notions (summarized by Levin, 1980).

Shriberg, Levin, and McCormick (1980) constructed passages that told about "famous" people and their accomplishments. The people's names were actually randomly drawn from the phone book and paired with fictitious accomplishments. Twelve name–accomplishment pairs were generated in this fashion, with each person's accomplishment described in a three-sentence passage. In addition to the critical name–accomplishment information, each accomplishment was further detailed by two pieces of incidental information in each passage. Consider, for example, the following passage: *Animal lovers all over the world are impressed that Charlene McKune has taught her pet cat how to count. The cat can count to 20 without making any mistakes. Moreover, the remarkable cat can do some simple addition.* The critical name–accomplishment information is that Charlene McKune's claim to fame is her counting cat. All students (eighth graders) were told explicitly to learn that information. The passage also states that the cat can both count to 20 and do some simple addition. These are the two incidental details that students were not told explicitly to learn.

Control students simply listened to the passages. Picture students were shown illustrations in which each person's name was mnemonically linked to his or her accomplishment. The illustrations conformed to the requisites of the transformation function, as described in this chapter. That is, they took the initial information and transformed it into something more memorable. For the present example, *McKune*, which is not picturable, sounds something like *raccoon*, which is. The resulting illustration capitalized on the picturable name derivative, linking it to the picturable accomplishment—see Figure 8.4. Finally, it should be mentioned that, although students in the picture condition had previously learned name derivatives (e.g., *McKune = raccoon*) for all 12 people, they were shown actual illustrations for only the first six passages. For the second six, they were told to use the same method to make up their own internal pictures (visual images).

Consistent with the present conceptualization summarized in Figure 8.2, both illustrations and visual imagery instructions substantially facilitated students' name–accomplishment recall (e.g., *What*

FIGURE 8.4. *Example of a transformational picture used to improve name–accomplishment recall. (From Shriberg et al., 1980.)*

was Charlene McKune famous for?). On the first six passages, students shown illustrations recalled about three times as much of that information in comparison to controls; on the last six passages, imagery instructions produced about a 2 to 1 advantage. Of course, picture type (illustrations versus imagery) and order (first six passages versus last six) are confounded in this study, so no direct comparison of illustrations and imagery could be made. Such was not the case in a second study, however, where subjects were given either illustrations, imagery instructions, or printed texts for all 12 passages. Despite this change in procedure, illustrations and imagery again produced about 3 to 1 and 2 to 1 advantages, respectively, relative to the no-picture control group. Thus, in both studies, very impressive gains in name–accomplishment recall were effected by mnemonic imagery instructions, as well as by actual mnemonic illustrations (just as in the associative-learning literature). This is in striking contrast to previous prose-learning studies, based on simple narrative passages, where imagery instructions do little in the way of enhancing recall. Of course, the transformation versus representation function distinction presumably is involved, which was the focus of a third study.

In that study, children were again told that they would be learning the accomplishments of "famous" people. Half the students were given the famous person's name, and half were given that person's occupation, to be linked to the appropriate accomplishment. Thus, for example, students heard that either *Larry Taylor* (name passages) or *a tailor* (occupation passages) had invented a house on a turntable. All surnames selected could be alternatively interpreted as occupations when processed auditorially (e.g., *Plummer, Shepard, Gardner*). For each type of passage, half the students were given imagery instructions and half were not. Imagery students given name passages were told to create transformational pictures of the kind generated in the previous two experiments. An example for the Larry Taylor passage is shown in Figure 8.5. In contrast, imagery students given occupation passages were told simply to visualize the contents of the passage as presented (i.e., a representational picture without accompanying transformation). Thus, for the tailor passage, they were told to visualize a tailor associated with a house on a turntable, also as in Figure 8.5. The critical outcome needed to support the transformation–representation distinction was obtained: The imagery-control difference was far greater for the name passages than it was for the occupation passages. In particular, for the name passages (where transformational imagery was applied), the imagery advantage was better than 2 to 1 and statistically significant, whereas for the occupation passages (where only represen-

and minimal or even nonexistent for visual imagery. This latter set of findings very accurately captures the differing representation strengths assumed to be served by illustrations and imagery when applied to literally encoded (rather than transformed) text.

Summary

I conclude this chapter by reiterating and expanding upon the pictures in prose observations of Levin and Lesgold (1978). Visual illustrations definitely *do* help children recall prose information. Just how much depends, of course, upon the kind of illustrations provided, as well as upon a number of other previously stated ground rules. Included in these rules is the type of prose passage presented. A very large number of studies support the conclusion that, with simple narrative prose, illustration effects are moderate, amounting to at least 40% facilitation. The Levin and Berry (1980) study mentioned here suggests that illustrations, used in conjunction with simple newspaper articles, also produce moderate recall benefits. In contrast, with passages containing difficult to remember information, the advantages associated with mnemonic illustrations can be even greater. In the "famous people" studies reviewed here, illustrations improved eighth graders' recall of important information by about 200%.

With pictures defined as visual imagery, however, about the safest conclusion is that prose facilitation is only a "sometime thing." With simple narrative passages, instructions to generate corresponding visual images often do not improve recall, and, when they do, the amount of facilitation produced is small. Moreover, the prose-learning conditions under which visual imagery would even be expected to facilitate recall have not been carefully delineated. For example, researchers have barely scratched the surface in capitalizing on the integrative character of imagery or on its potential, through concrete analogy, to serve as a useful interpretive vehicle. Optimism stems, however, from the "famous people" studies in which students applying a mnemonic imagery strategy were able to increase their recall of prose information by 100% or more. It is clear that a good deal of careful thinking needs to be done about what visual imagery can and cannot be expected to accomplish in various prose-learning situations.

As an initial attack on that problem, a conceptual framework was presented to permit a formal distinction among the several functions that prose-learning pictures probably serve. Two of these functions (the representation function and the transformation function) proved useful in differentiating among the magnitude and consistency of picture effects that can be anticipated from one prose-learning study to the next. The functional analysis also proved helpful in identifying both the kinds of variables that need to be controlled when looking for pictures in prose effects, as well as the kind of research that still needs to be conducted to isolate the contributions of specific picture components.

Acknowledgments

The chapter benefited greatly from my continuing collaboration and discussion with Michael Pressley of the University of Western Ontario. I am also grateful to Jean Padrutt for her helpful editorial suggestions and to Lynn Sowle for typing the manuscript.

References

Anderson, R. C., Spiro, R. J., & Montague, W. E. (Eds.). *Schooling and the acquisition of knowledge.* Hillsdale, New Jersey: Erlbaum, 1977.

Bender, B. G. *The effects of imposed and induced visual elaboration on EMR children's learning from oral prose.* Unpublished doctoral dissertation, University of Wisconsin, Madison, 1977.

Bender, B. G., & Levin, J. R. Pictures, imagery, and retarded children's prose learning. *Journal of Educational Psychology,* 1978, *70,* 583–588.

Bower, G. H. Mental imagery and associative learning. In L. Gregg (Ed.), *Cognition in learning and memory.* New York: Wiley, 1972.

DeRose, T. M. *The effects of verbally and pictorially induced and imposed strategies on children's reading comprehension.* Unpublished doctoral dissertation, University of Wisconsin, Madison, 1976.

Dillingofski, M. S. *The effects of imposed and induced visual imagery strategies on ninth-grade difference-poor readers' literal comprehension of concrete and abstract prose.* Unpublished doctoral dissertation, University of Wisconsin, Madison, 1980.

Dunham, T. C., & Levin, J. R. Imagery instructions and young children's prose learning: No evidence of "support". *Contemporary Educational Psychology,* 1979, *4,* 107–113.

Ghatala, E. S., Levin, J. R., & Wilder, L. Apparent frequency of words and pictures as a function of pronunciation and imagery. *Journal of Verbal Learning and Verbal Behavior,* 1973, *12,* 85–90.

Guttmann, J., Levin, J. R., & Pressley, M. Pictures, partial pictures, and young children's oral prose learning. *Journal of Educational Psychology,* 1977, *69,* 473–480.

Heckler, J. H. *Some factors involved in the comprehension of prose materials.* Unpublished doctoral dissertation, University of Wisconsin, Madison, 1975.

Johnson, H E. *A developmental study of imagery and oral prose comprehension.* Unpublished honors thesis, Department of Psychology, University of Minnesota, 1975.

Krebs, E. W., Snowman, J., & Smith, S. H. Teaching new dogs old tricks: Facilitating prose learning through mnemonic training. *Journal of Instructional Psychology,* 1978, *5,* 33–39.

Kulhavy, R. W., & Swenson, I. Imagery instructions and the comprehension of text. *British Journal of Educational Psychology*, 1975, *45*, 47–51.

Lesgold, A. M., Levin, J. R., Shimron, J., & Guttmann, J. Pictures and young children's learning from oral prose. *Journal of Educational Psychology*, 1975, *67*, 636–642.

Lesgold, A M., McCormick, C., & Golinkoff, R. M. Imagery training and children's prose learning. *Journal of Educational Psychology*, 1975, *67*, 663–667.

Levin, J. R. Comprehending what we read: An outsider looks in. *Journal of Reading Behavior*, 1972, *4*, 18–28.

Levin, J. R. Inducing comprehension in poor readers: A test of a recent model. *Journal of Educational Psychology*, 1973, *65*, 19–24.

Levin, J. R. Determining sample size for planned and post hoc analysis of variance comparisons. *Journal of Educational Measurement*, 1975, *12*, 99–108.

Levin, J R. What have we learned about maximizing what children learn? In J. R. Levin & V. L. Allen (Eds.), *Cognitive learning in children: Theories and strategies*. New York: Academic Press, 1976.

Levin, J. R. *Pictures and children's prose learning: State of the "art."* Paper presented at the annual meeting of the American Educational Research Association, Boston, April, 1980.

Levin, J. R., Bender, B. G., & Lesgold, A. M. Pictures, repetition, and young children's oral prose learning. *AV Communication Review*, 1976, *24*, 367–380.

Levin, J. R., & Berry, J. K. Children's learning of all the news that's fit to picture. *Educational Communication and Technology*, 1980, *28*, 177–185.

Levin, J. R., & Divine-Hawkins, P. Visual imagery as a prose-learning process. *Journal of Reading Behavior*, 1974, *6*, 23–30.

Levin, J. R., Divine-Hawkins, P., Kerst, S., & Guttmann, J. Individual differences in learning from pictures and words: The development and application of an instrument. *Journal of Educational Psychology*, 1974, *66*, 296–303.

Levin, J. R., & Lesgold, A. M. On pictures in prose. *Educational Communication and Technology*, 1978, *26*, 233–243.

Levin, J. R., & Pressley, M. Improving children's prose comprehension: Selected strategies that seem to succeed. In C. Santa & B. Hayes (Eds.), *Children's prose comprehension: Research and practice*. Newark, Delaware: International Reading Association, in press.

Nelson, D. L., Reed, V. S., & McEvoy, C. L. Learning to order pictures and words: A model of sensory and semantic encoding. *Journal of Experimental Psychology: Human Learning and Memory*, 1977, *3*, 485–497.

Paivio, A. *Imagery and verbal processes*. New York: Holt, 1971.

Peeck, J. Retention of pictorial and verbal content of a text with illustrations. *Journal of Educational Psychology*, 1974, *66*, 880–888.

Pierce, J. W. Field independence and imagery-assisted prose recall of children. *Journal of Educational Psychology*, 1980, *72*, 200–203.

Pressley, G. M. Mental imagery helps eight-year-olds remember what they read. *Journal of Educational Psychology*, 1976, *68*, 355–359.

Pressley, M. Imagery and children's learning: Putting the picture in developmental perspective. *Review of Educational Research*, 1977, *47*, 585–622.

Rohwer, W. D., Jr. Elaboration and learning in childhood and adolescence. In H. W. Reese (Ed.), *Advances in child development and behavior* (Vol. 8). New York: Academic Press, 1973.

Ruch, M. D., & Levin, J. R. Pictorial organization versus verbal repetition of children's prose: Evidence for processing differences. *AV Communication Review*, 1977, *25*, 269–280.

Ruch, M. D., & Levin, J. R. Partial pictures as imagery-retrieval cues in young children's prose recall. *Journal of Experimental Child Psychology*, 1979, *28*, 268–279.

Samuels, S. J. Effects of pictures on learning to read, comprehension and attitudes. *Review of Educational Research*, 1970, *40*, 397–407.

Schallert, D. L. The role of illustrations in reading comprehension. In R. J. Spiro, B. C. Bruce, & W. F. Brewer (Eds.), *Theoretical issues in reading comprehension: Perspectives from cognitive psychology, linguistics, artificial intelligence, and education*. Hillsdale, New Jersey: Erlbaum, 1980.

Shimron, J. Imagery and the comprehension of prose by elementary school children. (Doctoral dissertation, University of Pittsburgh, 1974). *Dissertation Abstracts International*, 1975, *36*, 735A. (University Microfilms No. 75–18, 254).

Shriberg, L. K., Levin, J. R., & McCormick, C. B. *Learning about famous people via the keyword method*. Paper presented at the annual meeting of the American Educational Research Association, Boston, April 1980.

Steingart, S. K., & Glock, M. D. Imagery and the recall of connected discourse. *Reading Research Quarterly*, 1979, *15*, 66–83.

Steuck, K. W. *The effects of pictures, imagery, and a change of context on young children's oral prose learning* (Working Paper No. 264). Madison: Wisconsin Research and Development Center for Individualized Schooling, 1979.

Triplett, D. G. *A test of two prose-learning strategies: Imagery and paraphrase*. Unpublished doctoral dissertation, University of Wisconsin, Madison, 1980.

Wasserman, B. L. *Incomplete pictures and retarded children's oral prose learning* (Working Paper No. 268). Madison: Wisconsin Research and Development Center for Individualized Schooling, 1979.

9

Merlin C. Wittrock

READING COMPREHENSION

When people read with comprehension they generate meaning for written language. To construct meaning for written or printed words and sentences, readers employ complex psychological processes.

Readers attend to the text. They create images and verbal transformations to represent its meaning. Most impressively, they generate meaning as they read by constructing relations between their knowledge, their memories of experiences, and the written sentences, paragraphs, and passages.

In this chapter, we will discuss these complex processes of reading comprehension. I will begin the discussion with an introduction to a model of reading comprehension as a generative process. After the introduction of the model, we will discuss several of the fundamental processes of reading comprehension, attention, encoding, and memory. Last of all, throughout the chapter, we will elaborate relations between the model, the research on these processes, and the facilitation of reading comprehension.

Reading Comprehension as a Generative Process

In our recent research studies, we find that children and adults read with comprehension when they generate meanings for written language by relating it to their knowledge and memories of experience.

NEUROPSYCHOLOGICAL AND COGNITIVE
PROCESSES IN READING

By this constructive process, they make sense of prose and connected discourse. I find that comprehension involves more than reading an author's syntactically correct, semantically plausible sentence or passage. The generation of literal or inferential meanings for written language involves the reader's organized knowledge and memories of experience. Apparently the reader's active construction of verbal, imaginal, and related representations for the text, using knowledge, experience, and context, produces or enhances the understandings that comprise reading comprehension. In brief, to comprehend a text, we not only read it, in the nominal sense of the word, we construct a meaning for it.

To comprehend written language we must do more than read it, and more than construct a meaning for it. We must derive the constructed or reconstructed meaning or meanings from the syntactic and semantic characteristics of the written language that we read. These meanings include the author's intended messages, their extensions, inferences, and embellishments. These generated meanings, which can be constructions at different levels of abstraction, also include alternative, unintended, text-derived interpretations and understandings, even when they contradict the writers' intentions. For example, modern-day meanings children construct as they read fairy tales, such as the Cinderella story, might differ substantially either from the meanings children constructed for this story many years ago, or from the author's intended meaning. If the unintended literal or inferential constructed meanings are derived from the text, they too evidence reading with comprehension. We might say, then, that reading with comprehension is the disciplined generation of meaning for written language.

We do not know if reading comprehension consists of a distinctive set of psychological processes, or if it consists of a great variety of psychological processes. In one study, Kintsch and Kozminsky (1977) found that reading comprehension shared a common core of psychological processes with listening comprehension. However, LaBerge and Samuels (1974) believe that the process of reading comprehension may be as complicated as thinking itself.

In the generative model, we incorporate the previously introduced common core of psychological processes of reading comprehension, and we expect to find a variety of currently unknown processes used differently by different people, depending upon the context, the readers' intentions, plans, expectations, purposes, knowledge, and experience. The reading of a poem, a narrative, a description, a word problem, a cookbook, a repair manual, a lesson in a reader, or of individual sentences involves more than an essential core of grammatical, syntactic, and semantic processes of comprehension. They involve different contexts, vocabulary, background knowledge, rules, and distinctive, relevant experiences in unknown ways in the transformation of written linguistic symbols into meaningful mental representations.

The reading of a single word, as different from a sentence, a paragraph, or a passage, also involves the generative process of comprehension discussed here. We usually think of reading comprehension occurring with sentences and larger units of written language. However, the generative model implies that learners construct word meanings as well, again using context and other cues in the process.

In brief, then, reading comprehension involves, differently for different people and contexts, the psychological processes involved in generating meaning by relating the parts of the text to one another and to stored information such as rules, schemata, and memories of events. The model was introduced earlier (Wittrock, 1974) and supported in several studies of reading comprehension (Doctorow, Wittrock, & Marks, 1978; Wittrock, Marks, & Doctorow, 1975), which will be discussed in this chapter.

The model implies some changes in the teaching of reading comprehension to children and young people. The teaching of reading comprehension in elementary schools usually entails teaching the central idea of each paragraph of a text and the construction of literal meanings for the texts, often without the active development of cognitive interactions between the text and the learner's experience, schemata, events, and rules. Reading in secondary schools also often involves the isolation of ideas in the text from the learners' experience and knowledge, in an effort to obtain accurate recall and understanding. As a result, students learn to reproduce information for the examination, but not to relate experience to it, or to reorganize it into more coherent or more useful schemata. The active generation of meaning by relating the text to memories and schemata, that is, the generative model, leads to different ways for teachers to facilitate comprehension.

Early Research on Reading Comprehension

We will now selectively examine the research literature in cognition and neuropsychology that involves reading comprehension. We will begin with a brief look at the history of the scientific study of reading comprehension. It will be followed by a discussion of recent research on the processes of reading comprehension and its measurement.

Gesture language and picture language date to the antiquity of civilizations. Babylonian writing had passed beyond pictographs 6000 years ago, as had Egyptian writing (Huey, p. 187, reprinted in 1968). Reading as thought-getting is also centuries old. Mathews (1966, p. 193) quotes a third- or fourth-century Latin source in which Cato tells his son to read with understanding, "for to read and not understand is not to read at all."

In Europe in the sixteenth and seventeenth centuries it became imperative for people to learn to read. The Protestant reformation emphasized the importance of each person learning to read the Bible. The common methods used to teach beginning reading were similar to those used by the Greeks and the Romans. Drill on the names of the letters followed by the sounding of combinations of consonants, vowels, and syllables often comprised initial reading instruction. Comprehension apparently was not stressed.

In the late nineteenth century in Europe and America, scientists who studied reading and experimental psychologists often shared some interests, at least in the area of reaction time studies. At Wundt's experimental psychology laboratory in Leipzig, James M. Cattell studied individual differences in the recognition of letters, words, and print. In one experiment, he found that people read the letters in words twice as fast as they read comparable groups of letters not connected into words. Subjects also read words grouped into sentences twice as fast as they read comparable words not grouped into sentences. Although comprehension was not the focus of early research in experimental psychology, Cattell pioneered the study of reading. He showed some of the effects upon reading produced by the meaningful grouping of letters and words. E. L. Thorndike and A. I. Gates, both prominent figures in reading research, studied with James Cattell.

From about 1890 to about 1910, research in reading was a central theme in psychological laboratories. Some of the then-current topics resemble contemporary subjects once again under study in the laboratory. Perception, inner speech, and the nature of meaning in reading were all frequently studied. In his book on reading, Huey (1908) wrote a chapter on each of these subjects, along with chapters on the pedagogy of reading. Huey discussed serial processing, parallel processing, imagery, verbal processes, and meaning, as an active process reflecting the readers' knowledge and cognition, all topics that have present day counterparts. In his discussions of these topics, he believed that people, especially adults, use auditory images or word sounds more than visual images to represent word meanings. With a model of word meaning reminiscent of James' theory of emotion, Huey concludes that meanings in reading were mostly feelings, motor responses, and movements associated with the sentences. However, he tempered his associationistic analysis of word meaning by noting that the speaking of a sentence "comes at some distance behind the eye [p. 167]." That is, the lag in time between the looking at the words and the speaking of them implied that people constructed their meaning by cognitively processing the visual stimuli and the feelings associated with them.

In contrast to these early interests in cognitive and neuropsychological processes, from about 1910 until about 1955, many experimental psychologists became interested in behaviorism. As a result, they largely abandoned studies of the cognitive processes of reading. Unfortunately, only a few examples of important studies of the processes of reading exist in the literature for that period.

However, during that same interval of time, the centuries-old debate about the teaching of initial reading continued unabated among educators. Should children first learn to comprehend words and sentences, or should they first learn to pronounce letters, and to speak words and sentences? With the decline of interest in the study of the psychological processes of reading comprehension, that question remained unanswered.

When the study of cognitive psychology returned to prominence, about 1955, reading comprehension again became an acceptable topic to research and to theorize about. Imagery and verbal processes, eye movements, attention, and perception, to name a few, once again became important topics that interested educators and psychologists alike. Some new and important findings about the psychological processes of reading comprehension have come from these recent studies and from attempts to theorize about reading with comprehension. We will now discuss some of these studies with the intent of building an understanding of some of the cognitive processes involved in reading comprehension. Although the processes of reading comprehension involve vocabulary, syntax, grammar, and decoding, we will concentrate on the research that deals directly with the semantic processes in the construction of meaning. Most of these studies deal with written language, but some of them deal with spoken language because it shares with reading some of the processes of comprehension.

The Measurement of Reading Comprehension

Before we begin to examine the recent research, we will discuss the measurement of reading comprehension. I will indicate a new and unusual measure appropriate for measuring comprehension as a generative process. Researchers, commercial test makers, and teachers usually measure reading comprehension without regard to any single conceptualization or theory of reading. In one commonly used method of measuring reading comprehension, after reading the text, the student answers multiple choice questions about the facts and the concepts in the sentences and paragraphs of the passage just read. The researchers who designed and conducted the recent international study of reading comprehension in 15 countries (Thorndike, 1973) used this technique, as did the makers of the commercially published tests used in this massive study.

Another commonly used method of measuring reading comprehension involves the Cloze test, in which the student encounters reproduced segments of the original text modified by the deletion of every fifth or tenth or so word. The student attempts to insert in the blanks, which occur where words have been deleted, the words originally used in the text. The number of words correctly inserted in the blanks measures comprehension.

Neither of these useful techniques necessarily measures reading as a generative process, which involves the cognitive interactions between the readers' knowledge and experience, the context, and the text itself. To measure these processes, we need tests that delve beyond the surface structure of a passage into its meaning. The measurement of comprehension involves transfer of learning (Wittrock, 1968), rather than the measurement of behavior specific to the surface structure of the message.

To measure the generative processes of reading comprehension, a test must go beyond the verbatim recall of information. Tests that involve the construction or identification of paraphrases, inferences, summaries, examples, applications, analogies, and metaphors change the surface structure while holding constant the meaning of the written language. These tests can measure the generative processes of reading comprehension.

The differences between tests that measure the generative processes of reading and more conventional tests of reading comprehension deserve further comment. Correct answers on tests of verbatim memory such as *Did this sentence appear in the text?* do not necessarily indicate comprehension. However, discounting the effects of guessing, some incorrect answers on the same type of test do indicate comprehension; for example, an affirmative answer to the previous question when the surface structure of the test sentence has been changed although the meaning of the test sentence remains the same as the meaning of its counterpart in the text.

Correct answers to questions about the similarity in surface structure of text sentences and test sentences do not measure generative processes in comprehension. Instead, recognition of similarity or identicality of sentence meaning across changes in surface structure does indicate comprehension. Text-derived meanings that incorporate the learners' knowledge and experience index generative processes in comprehension. Inferences, elaborations, and applications often involve and measure these generative processes.

From this analysis, I infer that teachers of reading sometimes measure reading comprehension in ways that discourage students from relating their experience and knowledge to the text. Teachers often ask the student to report the main idea of a paragraph or a story, which is an acceptable measure of reading comprehension. However, that technique may sometimes discourage relating the paragraph to knowledge or to experience, evaluating it, applying it, and elaborating it. These generative processes might reduce performance on tests that emphasize literal summaries not confounded with relations between the learners' everyday activities and beliefs and the information in the book. The teaching technique encourages abstract learning that may not function or transfer outside the classroom. The learning may not become associated with the learners' activities and experience.

Now that we have introduced measures of reading comprehension, we will discuss the recent research on the psychological processes of reading comprehension. We begin with attention, then turn to encoding and memory. As mentioned previously, these are not the only psychological processes involved in reading comprehension, but they comprise a common core of important generative processes. In each of the following sections, the active role of the individual in the construction and the reconstruction of meaning provides the theme that organizes the research and emphasizes its meaning for understanding reading comprehension.

Attention

Selective attention, and methods of influencing it, interests many cognitive psychologists and neuropsychologists who study reading, including reading comprehension. In a study of selective attention in good and poor sixth grade male readers, Willows (1974) inserted an irrelevant text into a written passage. He found the poor readers were distracted by the surface structure, the appearance, of the inserted irrelevant text. The good readers were distracted by the meaning of the inserted irrelevant text. The good readers automatically decoded the text and attended to its meaning, while the poor readers attended to the visual qualities of the stimulus and decoded them. The study implies that, to comprehend a text, one must attend to its meaning. Different meanings can be constructed from the text by directing the learners to different information in it, and by giving the learners different goals for reading the text, such as to learn its meaning or to remember the facts in it.

Adjunct Questions

Pre- and post adjunct questions, which are questions inserted into a text either before or after the paragraphs relevant to answering the respective questions, influence reading comprehension. Questions about the meaning of the material tend to facilitate a broad, conceptually oriented learning. Prequestions tend to direct attention to the specific information, fact, or idea relevant to the answer to the question. As well as stimulating a broad learning of relevant, previously read information, postquestions direct attention in subsequent paragraphs to the broad type of information relevant to answering previous postquestions.

With college undergraduates, Sagaria and Di Vesta (1978) found that prequestions led to a narrowly focused, sometimes verbatim, processing, while postquestions led to a broader, sometimes more meaningful processing that resulted in the learning of a variety of information. Boyd (1973) also reported that prequestions enhanced selective attention. Boker (1974) found that prequestions facilitated learning of the specific answers to the questions, whereas postquestions facilitated nonverbatim learning as well as verbatim learning.

Prequestions inserted in the text enhance learning or comprehension of the questioned material, but often reduce learning of other material. Because they appear in the text after the relevant paragraph, postquestions cannot narrow attention to a specific answer in a previously read paragraph, at least not as it is initially read. Postquestions can direct attention in subsequent paragraphs to the types or the classes of material probably useful for answering later postquestions. Consequently, postquestions enhance comprehension and broaden learning.

When we interpret the effects of pre- and postquestions, we should remember that the distinction between them is somewhat artificial. Each of them occurs between paragraphs. Postquestions can work forward, influencing the processing of following paragraphs. Prequestions can also work backward, influencing rehearsal of previous paragraphs. The distinction between pre- and postquestions holds only with regard to a given paragraph, not to a given passage. The major finding is that they influence retention.

Questions constructed by children also influence retention. Ross and Killey (1977) studied the effects on retention produced when fourth-graders asked and received answers to their own questions about pictures they saw. Compared with questions asked by other children, asking their own questions facilitated memory.

Inserted questions can also enhance comprehension as well as retention. Andre and Womack (1978) found that, compared with verbatim questions, paraphrased adjunct questions facilitated comprehension among college students. The comprehension tests consisted of paraphrased questions not seen earlier in the study. Mayer (1975, 1978) found that meaningful learning increased with the insertion in the text of adjunct questions or testlike events that directed the readers toward understanding information or to applying principles, rather than to rote learning.

There are developmental differences in the ability to control attention and to construct meanings for sentences. Brown and Smiley (1978) found that young children often do not know the important units of information in a text. Those children who spontaneously attended to the important units in the text, who underlined and took notes, improved their comprehension. Another study (Myers & Paris, 1978) showed that young children often do not know the semantic structures of paragraphs, the strategies for comprehending meaning, or the objectives for reading a text. Young children have not yet learned to control their attention, to set goals for reading, and to view reading as the construction of meaning instead of the verbatim recall of written material. Perhaps some young children can profit from instruction in the constructive processes of reading and in the control of attention. The development of strategies for reading texts might well begin with teaching children to generate their own questions that will help them to attend selectively to the meaning of the prose.

Goals and Objectives

Another way to influence attention when reading is to give the learner objectives to be attained. Duell (1974) found that behaviorally defined objectives directed the readers' attention to material that is often ignored. Kaplan and Simmons (1974) found that information not specific to a given objective was best learned when the objective appeared after the text was read. Information specific to the objective was learned well either when the objective came before or after the text was read. Royer (1977) gave college students a passage on the development of computers to read. Either specific or general objectives were given either before or after the students read the passage. Compared with objectives given after the passage was read, objectives given before the passage was read enhanced the learning of information directly relevant to the objectives. The objectives given after the passage was read enhanced the learning of information not directly relevant to the objectives, compared with the learning of information directly relevant to the objectives.

Duchastel (1979) found that objectives given to Swiss college students reading passages on energy facilitated their memory of the passage. He reports that "This finding lends further support to the view that objectives influence learning through a process of selective attention [p. 106]." The objectives increased free recall primarily when they called attention to paragraphs low in structural importance to the text. Either high structural salience in the organization of the text or a high salience stimulated by objectives and goals enhances selective attention to the meaning of the passage.

These results parallel the findings reported for inserted questions. Goals and objectives given to learners before they read a text focus attention, and thereby enhance comprehension and memory of information relevant to the goal. Goals and objectives given to learners after, compared with before, they read a text focus attention less narrowly, and consequently enhance comprehension or memory more broadly.

The Mechanisms of Attention

We are beginning to get data that describe some of the mechanisms involved in goal-mediated learning. Rothkopf and Billington (1979) studied inspection times and eye movements of high school students given specific goals before reading a passage about oceanographic data. The goal-relevant sentences of the text doubled eye fixations and increased their length by 15 msec, yet total time to read the passage was not increased. Apparently, less time was devoted to the reading of the remaining sentences.

The study cannot show conclusively that the increased number and length of eye movements caused increased comprehension and retention. Selective attention implies more than looking at a target, and more than additional eye fixations. Although time and frequency of looking at the surface features of the text may correlate with attention, it is attention to the meaning of the text that is crucial.

Neuropsychologists also study the mechanisms of selective attention, albeit at a different level. Teyler, Megela, and Hesse (1977) measured brain wave responses evoked by visually different stimuli with identical meanings, or by visually similar stimuli with different meanings. The meaning of the stimuli, not their appearance, determined the responses. In another study, the contexts of ambiguous words determined their meaning and also evoked different forms of brain waves (Brown, Marsh, & Smith, 1973).

Components of brain wave responses index different types of attention. A brain wave component at 100 msec after a stimulus is presented indexes attention to external stimuli. Later components (200–300 msec latency) index internal events, such as expectations, short-term memory, and response sets. Expectancy also produces a change in wave forms, called the contingent negative variation (CNV), that occurs after a warning stimulus but *before* a stimulus that elicits a response.

Conners (1970) found a correlation of $-.6$ between a left parietal lobe brain wave component at 200 msec latency and reading achievement among third and fourth graders. With 9-year-old poor readers, compared with good readers of comparable age, Preston, Guthrie, and Childs (1974) found a brain wave component of reduced amplitude at 180-msec latency only in response to light flashes, not in response to words. The implication is that the good and poor readers in their study differed in ability to attend, but not in ability to read words.

Some of the most dramatic findings regarding attention and reading comprehension involve research with hyperkinetic children, who sometimes improve in ability to learn when given the proper dosage of a stimulant drug, such as Ritalin. The paradoxical effect of a stimulant drug reducing hyperactivity sometimes results from the medicine's influence upon arousal and attention. Hyperkinetic children sometimes are less aroused than normal children. More importantly, hyperkinetic children sometimes have a relatively flat gradient of attention across distracting, task-relevant, contextual stimuli. The stimulant drugs increase arousal somewhat. More significantly, in one study, the drugs increased the voluntary control of attention, which enabled children to inhibit their responses to distracting contextual stimuli (Conners, 1976). The drugs produce attentional effects among hyperkinetic children similar to the attentional effects produced among many children by instructions, objectives, and inserted questions.

The deficit of attention shown by hyperactive children occurs primarily in voluntary rather than in involuntary sustained attention (Krupski, 1980). With measures of skin conductance, hyperactive children showed deficits of attention only with active tasks, not with passive tasks. Again, voluntary attention seems to be implicated in some problems of learning, such as reading with comprehension.

Within the framework of attention described in this section, a group of psychologists developed an intervention program to improve reading comprehension among hyperactive children. Douglas, Parry, Martin, and Garson (1976) used cognitive training techniques developed by Donald Meichenbaum to teach 18 hyperactive children in 3 months to control their impulses and to regulate their problem-solving strategies. Even though the cognitive training program was not aimed directly at reading, the intervention did increase scores on some reading achievement tests, on tests of organization and planning, and on the Matching Familiar Figures Test, which measures analytic ability. Malamuth (1977) also used self-management, cognitive training techniques with poor readers. The training increased ability to sustain attention and also improved reading performance among these children, who were not hyperactive.

Before we discuss encoding, let us summarize the research on attention as a process involved in reading comprehension. In this section on attention we found evidence to indicate that selectively attending to the meaning of a text, rather than to its surface structure, enhances comprehension. Reading with goals or specific objectives in mind directs attention and facilitates comprehension of relevant information. Inserted questions also direct attention and, consequently, often enhance the comprehension of meanings relevant to the answers to questions.

Good and poor readers sometimes differ in brain waves that index attention. Further, stimulant drugs that enhance attention sometimes facilitate learning among children. At a cognitive level and again at a neural level, the data indicate that attention is one of the important psychological processes involved in different types of comprehension of different types of reading materials, and different comprehension strategies.

Encoding and Memory

In this section on encoding and memory, we will examine other fundamental psychological processes involved in reading comprehension. To comprehend written information, a reader does more than attend to it. In 1974, I reported that people often understand or comprehend information by relating it to their knowledge and experience.

From these cognitive interactions between incoming information, knowledge, and memories of experience, they generate meanings and encode them into memory.

To facilitate comprehension, the model implies that we should stimulate the active generation of relations between knowledge, experience, and written stimuli. We can enhance the construction of these interactions in numerous ways, such as by stimulating (a) the strategies or processes learners use to comprehend text; (b) the knowledge base or experience of the learner; and (c) the characteristics and organization of the text. These three types of components involved in reading comprehension have been frequently studied. A discussion of results obtained in some of these recently conducted studies in each of these three categories follows.

Generative Processes

Wittrock and Carter (1975) asked college students to read hierarchically arranged words either by generatively processing them, that is, by constructing relations involving them, or by reproductively processing them, that is, by copying them. Whether the words were properly or randomly arranged in the hierarchy, even when the words were not conceptually related to one another, generative processing of them resulted in substantial increases in memory.

Doctorow, Wittrock, and Marks (1978) asked 400 sixth-graders of three different reading ability levels to read a story, taken from a commercially published reader, and to write, in their own words, a sentence about each paragraph immediately after reading it. In addition, some groups of students were given paragraph headings, either to be incorporated into their sentences or omitted from them. The generation of their own sentences was hypothesized to facilitate the construction of relations between experience, knowledge, and the story. The paragraph headings were intended to serve as cues for the relevant schema, that is, for relevant, organized knowledge stored in memory. The data closely supported the predictions. As predicted, in each of the two experiments, in ascending order, the insertion of headings, the student generation of sentences for paragraphs, and the combination of headings and generated sentences enhanced retention and comprehension. The abstract paragraph headings were relatively more effective with the better readers, while the generated sentences were relatively better with the poor readers, although each condition facilitated comprehension with each group. The combination of the generation of sentences and the insertion of paragraph headings doubled comprehension for each group of learners at each level of reading ability. The effect was replicated across three different stories and three different tests.

Kathryn Au (1977) reported the results of a cognitive training program used to teach reading comprehension to native Hawaiian children in the first, second, and third grades. In the program, the teacher actively involves the children in the verbalization of their experience and knowledge as they read each story. The teacher's frequent questions emphasize that, in their own words, the children express ideas about the reading material, recall events that relate to the story, and make inferences from the ideas in the text. Instead of grapheme–phoneme correspondences, the program emphasizes the construction of meaning for the text by elaborating upon it. Compared with comparable classes not given the year-long cognitive training program, as measured by the Gates-MacGinite Reading Test, reading achievement substantially improved as a result of the instruction. In the first grade, the average percentile rank for the cognitive training class was 69, and, for the three control classes, the averages were 8, 21, and 27. In the second grade, the percentile ranks were 42 for the experimental group and 8 and 10 for the control groups. In the third grade, the average percentile ranks were 27 for the experimental group and 7 for the control group. In all grades, the experimental program had existed for only 1 year.

From those data, it seems that children do not always understand that reading involves bringing knowledge and experience to bear on the text. More encouraging, it also seems that young children performing at very low percentile rankings in reading can learn to construct relations between the text and their own experience and knowledge.

With college students, Kane and Anderson (1978) found that students who completed the missing last word of the sentences they read increased their learning and, to a lesser extent, their retention as compared with students who only read the sentences. The effects held whether the written words were correct or incorrect, although the incorrect words apparently reduced retention somewhat.

Rickards and August (1975) studied college students reading sentences in which some words were either underlined for them or were to be underlined by them. The highest average learning occurred when the readers underlined any words they wished, and the second highest average learning occurred when the learners underlined words of structural importance. The underlining of words of high or low structural importance by the experimenter did not influence learning. When the readers underlined words of low structural importance, learning decreased.

Note-taking is another way of inducing learners to generate elaborations and inferences. Peper and Mayer (1978) compared the generative functions of note-taking, in the sense that it increased the construction of relations between new information and experience, with the less integrative activity of remembering information by keeping it separate from experience. Note-taking facilitated assimilative encoding and supported a generative model of comprehension.

Another way to facilitate a cognitive interaction between knowledge and text is to ask learners to take a point of view or perspective as they read a story; for example, to take the point of view of a burglar or a home buyer as they read a story about a house (Pichert & Anderson, 1977). The significance of the information for the perspective adopted by the learners influenced their learning and their recall of it 1 week later.

In a later study, using essentially the same materials, Anderson, Pichert, and Shirey (1979) found that among undergraduates, the home buyer and the burglar perspectives, when given before reading, selectively enhance encoding. When given after reading, they selectively enhance retrieval.

Paris, Lindauer, and Cox (1977) taught young children to construct paragraphs about sentences they read. The children's goal was to construct a story. The generation of stories facilitated comprehension and memory of the sentences by allowing the child to construct inferences about them. Apparently young children, ages 7 and 8 years, can compose effective inferences about sentences, but they rarely spontaneously construct inferences to achieve goals, such as the remembering of information.

Kail, Chi, Ingram, and Danner (1977) also studied children's construction of inferences in reading comprehension. Second graders and sixth graders both learned to build inferences from sentences, but the older children were no more accurate than the younger children. Di Vesta, Hayward, and Orlando (1979) investigated generative processes in reading comprehension among good and poor readers in the sixth, seventh, and eighth grades. Poor readers tended to use a strategy called "running text," that is, to read the sentences strictly in the order in which they were written. The good readers tended to use a different strategy called "searching subsequent text." The good readers showed substantial control over their processing of text, knowledge about comprehension as the goal of reading, and a realization that the text, and the order in which its ideas are presented, is not the only source of information available to them for comprehending its meaning.

In sum, a wide variety of data indicate that reading comprehension is a generative process. Good readers often engage in the constructive processing of text. A number of techniques, including simple directions, increase generative processing and consequently reading comprehension.

The studies of generative processes reviewed in this section have emphasized verbal elaborations. We will now discuss imagery as a cognitive strategy in reading comprehension. Especially important for the purposes of this chapter are procedures, such as instructions, that lead to self-generated images as they relate to reading comprehension. The effects of pictures given to the learners will be discussed in a later section. Because Levin discusses imagery at length in Chapter 8 of this volume, we will mention only several studies here to depict some of the nonverbal generative processes of reading comprehension.

Self-generated images facilitate reading and reading comprehension somewhat, although young children, less than 8 years old, frequently do not spontaneously generate effective images. One way to stimulate the generation of images for words or texts is to ask children to draw simple pictures of them as they read. Bull and Wittrock (1973) found that the meanings of words were better learned and remembered when fifth graders drew pictures of the definitions of terms rather than when they rehearsed or copied the words.

Levin (1973) gave fourth graders who were poor readers an imagery organizational strategy before they read a story. Only the poor readers who had good vocabulary increased their comprehension of the story with the imagery strategy. Pressley (1976) taught 8-year-old children to construct mental images of the sentences and the paragraphs of the stories they read. Compared with a control group that only read the story, the imagery group comprehended or remembered better the events of the story. With learners younger than 8 years, induced imagery usually fails to facilitate comprehension or retention.

Wolff and Levin (1972) studied the development of the ability to generate images with paired associate tasks. They found that kindergartners could not, but third graders (i.e., 8-year-olds) could construct images to help them remember associations among words. Although that study does not deal directly with reading comprehension, it does help to establish the time when imagery ability is rapidly increasing in children.

Several studies have attempted to stimulate the generation of images by giving children within the age range of 5–8 years partial pictures while they listen to or read a story. Guttman, Levin, and Pressley (1977) found that the partial pictures or imagery instruction facilitated reading comprehension for the third graders but not for the kindergartners (see their Experiment 2). Dynamic partial pictures, that is, pictures illustrating motion, increased the learning of propositions. In another study (Ruch & Levin, 1977), partial pictures presented with the passage but not presented with the text again facilitated comprehension among third graders listening to a story. In another study, 10–16-year-old mentally retarded children did not increase their recall of story information when given instructions to generate images as they listened to the passage as it was read to them (Bender & Levin, 1978). Ability to construct images as a way to read with comprehension develops at about 8 years of age. Prior to that age, asking children to construct their own images often does not enhance reading comprehension or memory.

Most recently, newly defined types of processes of reading comprehension differentiate readers from one another. We will mention one of these processes. Individuals differ substantially in their styles of comprehension. Spiro (1979) reports that some individuals rely heavily on a "top-down" process of comprehension, in which they use their knowledge base to infer meaning for text. Other individuals use a "bottom-up" process, in which they emphasize the text and its meaning with little reliance upon their schemata or knowledge base. These "top-down" and "bottom-up" processes may actually be different emphases within the process of generating relations between knowledge, experience, and the text. In either case, relations between internal processes and the text influence comprehension, whether one starts to build associations from the inside–out or from the outside–in.

From these studies of verbal processes and imagery in encoding, it is clear that comprehension and retention often increase when readers generate cognitive representations for the information they read. We also learned several points about the delicate relations between the learners' individual differences, in age and ability, and the effectiveness of different procedures for stimulating generative processing of written or spoken language.

Effective techniques for stimulating constructive elaborations by learners sometimes interact with the learners' cognitive abilities (Delaney, 1978) and depend upon the developmental level or the age of the learner (Tirre, Manelis, & Leicht, 1978). With college undergraduates learning foreign language vocabulary words, Delaney found that verbal elaborations would be better than visual elaborations for learners with high verbal fluency, while visual elaborations would be better than verbal elaborations for learners with low verbal fluency.

Tirre *et al.* (1978) asked adults reading abstract and concrete passages from textbooks of mammalogy and archaeology to construct conceptual relationships among words in text using either a verbal strategy or an imagery strategy. The verbal strategy produced greater comprehension than did the imagery strategy for both concrete and abstract words.

We are also beginning to see the development of cognitive training programs for the teaching of reading comprehension. Meichenbaum and Asarnow (1978) report that Bommarito and Meichenbaum taught seventh- and eighth graders with comprehension levels 1 or more years below their grade level to organize their reading habits and, as they read a story, to ask themselves questions about its main idea, its important details, its sequence of events, and its characters' feelings. Compared with a control group who did not get the self-instructional training, but who did receive the training sessions and reading materials, the experimental group averaged greater mean change scores: 11.5 months gain on the Nelson Reading Test and 13.5 months gain on a Cloze Exercise Test. These results indicate that at least some poor readers read passively without actively searching for the meaning or the meanings of the text. Their results imply that the skills of active reading can be taught to some readers at least, and that reading comprehension can improve as a result of a cognitive training program.

Knowledge Base of the Learner

In the previous section we discussed cognitive processes learners use to comprehend information as they read. We emphasized studies designed to stimulate people to use effective comprehension strategies, which often involve the construction of relations between knowledge, experience, and the reading material.

In this section on the knowledge base of the learner, we will examine studies that show a different approach to stimulating the generation of relations between text and knowledge and experience. The difference in approach emphasizes the knowledge and the information, rather than the comprehension strategy, that the learner brings to the task of making sense of the written language. One obvious way to try to enhance the relation between text and knowledge is to provide the learner with relevant background information, advance organizers, and useful schemata. Another way cues the readers to remember previously learned information relevant to comprehending the text.

Dooling and Christiaansen (1977) varied the influence of the reader's knowledge upon the comprehension of a story read by college undergraduates by telling one group of them, and not telling another group, that the story was about a famous person, for example, Helen Keller. Information about the theme of the story led to thematic errors later. The errors evidenced the use of their knowledge about the famous person to construct or to reconstruct information not contained in the passages they read.

Royer, Perkins, and Konold (1978) told groups of undergraduates that a biographical passage was about either a famous person known to them, for example, Winston Churchill, or a fictitious person unknown to them. The groups given the name of the famous person made many false positive errors on sentences thematically related to the famous person.

Brown, Smiley, Day, Townsend, Michael, and Lawton (1977) gave second grade through seventh grade children appropriate frameworks for comprehending ambiguous passages read to them. The framework enhanced recognition and comprehension and produced intrusion errors consistent with the orientation provided by experimenter-given schemata. There were very few developmental trends in these effects of frameworks upon comprehension. As did the adults, the children had difficulty distinguishing between the information in the text and their own elaborations upon it, although the older children made substantial use of their background information in the recall of text. They also made many thematically relevant intrusion errors. Again, it is clear that meaning is not specified wholly by the written language. The learner's background knowledge, and the ways it relates to the text, contribute to the construction of meaning by the learner.

Pearson (1979) studied reading comprehension among second graders given a passage to read about spiders. The readers with greater prior knowledge about spiders performed better than readers with less knowledge about spiders on items involving inferential comprehension. No difference between the groups occurred on items testing the specific information stated in the written passage. The data imply that background knowledge is especially important in going beyond the literal comprehension of the text. Recall of information stated in the text can be achieved, apparently, in a more rote, less integrative fashion than can inferential comprehension.

It is appropriate to conclude this section with several references to David Ausubel's extensive work on advance organizers. Nearly two decades ago he showed (Ausubel & Fitzgerald, 1962) that background knowledge enhances learning of new material, and that advance organizers provide subsuming concepts that facilitate learning and retention of conceptual material (Ausubel, 1960).

More recently, advance organizers again enhanced comprehension of written materials. Mayer (1978) gave undergraduates a text on computer programming that was either scrambled or logically ordered. An advance organizer facilitated learning of the scrambled text, but not of the logically organized text. Advance organizers can compensate for poorly organized text. They seem to increase the utility of relevant background knowledge.

Text and Its Context

In addition to the readers' strategies of comprehension and background knowledge, the characteristics of the text itself can be used to enhance the relations between knowledge and experience and written language. In a study of Wittrock's model of generative learning, Wittrock, Marks, and Doctorow (1975) showed that 10–12-year-old children sizably enhanced their comprehension and retention of unfamiliar and undefined words when these words were embedded in familiar stories. These results held for children of low, middle, and high reading ability, whether they read the stories or listened to them being read aloud. The familiar story provided the context used to generate meaning for the unfamiliar words.

The generative model of learning also predicts that substituting one higher frequency word for one lower frequency word in each sentence enhances the comprehension of sentences difficult to understand. In three experiments with sixth-grade children, the substitution of a familiar word for an unfamiliar word in each sentence of a text taken from a commercially published reader substantially increased comprehension, frequently by 50%, for readers of high, middle, and low ability levels reading materials at and above their reading level. The effect occurred across three different levels of reading ability, six different stories, and six different tests of comprehension.

In a previously mentioned study (Doctorow et al., 1978), paragraph headings inserted into the text facilitated reading comprehension among junior high school students, apparently by stimulating use of relevant knowledge to construct interpretations of the meanings of the paragraphs. These results occurred across different levels of reading ability, different stories, and different types of comprehension.

Tenenbaum (1977) studied the effects of text organization upon reading comprehension among high school seniors. A hierarchical organization of the passage enhanced learning of the main idea and of facts.

Glynn and Di Vesta (1977) gave undergraduates a structural outline of the passage they were to read about minerals and varied the logical sequencing of the text. Compared with a scrambled order of the paragraphs of the text, a logical order enhanced comprehension, but not recall of unique or isolated facts. The structural outline given during retrieval enhanced elaborations and inferences upon the text.

McClure and Mason (1979) gave third-, sixth-, and ninth graders six-sentence-long scrambled stories to reorder in their correct sequences. The results indicate that the surface features of the story are far less important than the deep structure of the story for the comprehension of its meaning and for the reordering of its parts into a proper sequence. In an extensive study, Marshall and Glock (1978) examined the effects of four text characteristics, such as where the main idea was placed in a paragraph, upon the reading comprehension of undergraduate learners from an Ivy League university and a community college. The surface text characteristics influenced the learning of the community college students but not the Ivy League students, who attended to the intended meaning of the text. The authors infer that highly able readers attend primarily to the meaning of the text, not to its surface characteristics.

Pictures and high imagery words facilitate paired-associate learning and memory among children and adults. Standing, Conezio, and Haber (1970) found that people recognized 90% of the 2500 pictures they saw 3 days earlier. In paired-associate learning, pictures and high imagery stimulus terms often facilitate performance (Paivio, 1971). With children and adults, Wittrock and Goldberg (1975) found that high imagery words facilitated free recall of words.

Pictures and words of high imagery value enhance memory. But what are the effects of pictures upon reading comprehension? Some authors (Willows, 1978) maintain that pictures distract readers' attention from the meaning of the text. However, his pictures, for example, of a cat presented alongside the word *dog*, provided an inappropriate context for facilitating comprehension. His results indicate that pictures can affect comprehension as well as memory.

In studies where pictures are used to represent the objects and events presented in the text, the data often indicate a facilitative effect on listening comprehension or reading comprehension. Bransford and Johnson (1972) studied comprehension among high school students given ambiguous passages to decipher. When appropriate pictures or verbal headings were given to the learners before they heard the stories, their comprehension of them sizably improved. Much lower comprehension was obtained when the pictures or the story headings were given to the students after they had heard the passages. Arnold and Brooks (1976) gave pictures or verbal organizers to elementary school children before they read paragraphs to them. The organizers that presented the relationships among the ideas in the text enhanced comprehension. The pictures were more effective than the verbal organizers with the fifth graders.

Rohwer and Matz (1975) read stories to middle-class white and lower class black fourth graders, who simultaneously viewed either printed or pictorial versions of the texts. Although the results are open to alternative interpretations, it seems that both groups of fourth graders comprehended more information in the pictorial version than in the printed version. Guttman et al. (1977) found that pictures, when compared with partial pictures, instructions to construct images, and a control condition, produced the greatest listening comprehension among kindergartners and second graders. Bender and Levin (1978) found that the listening comprehension of mentally retarded children rose from 40 to 60% when pictures were provided to them as they heard stories read aloud.

From these data, pictures appropriate for the text enhance comprehension among adults and among children of different ages, abilities, and socioeconomic levels. Pictures seem to work well with young children as early as kindergarten age at least, which is younger than the ages, about 7–8 years, when children can construct images to enhance comprehension.

Words of high frequency value or of high imagery value also facilitate reading comprehension. Marks, Doctorow, and Wittrock (1974) facilitated reading comprehension among sixth graders, often by 25%, by substituting in each sentence of the text one high frequency synonym for a word of lower frequency. Jorm (1977) found that good and poor readers, 8–11 years old, could read high frequency words better than low frequency words. Only the poor readers read the high imagery words better than they read the low imagery words.

The meaningfulness of words, the imagery of the words, and the use of appropriate pictures each influences reading comprehension. Each type of stimulus seems to facilitate the construction of representations for the ideas and the information contained in the written passages.

Discussion

To construct meaning for a text involves a set of complex psychological processes. Readers attend to the text. They perceive its written symbols as characters in a language. They decode or transform these linguistic representations into semantic units that can have meaning for them—morphemes, words, sentences, paragraphs, and passages. At each of these levels, the readers can encode the language by relating it to their knowledge and to their memories of experience. From the construction of these relationships comes reading comprehension. It is the process of going from the surface structure of a text to its meaning or meanings.

Each level or unit of language introduces new variables into the construction of meaning for a text, when compared with the units that comprise it. For example, compared with words, sentences introduce syntax and parts of speech. As a result, readers can acquire meanings about events, states of being, principles, and abstractions.

In every case, the meaning of the language representation is not printed on the pages of the text. Reading comprehension occurs only when the readers use their psychological processes—perception, attention, encoding, and memory—to transform the printed symbols into meanings reflective of their knowledge and experience. These psychological processes, along with linguistic, neurological, and situational or contextual variables influence the meanings people construct as they read.

Reading comprehension consists of more than a reconstruction of the authors' intended meaning. Within the constraints of the vocabulary and syntax of the sentences of a passage, a reader can legitimately construct meanings at multiple levels of abstraction, or with reference to multiple issues of interest to the reader. The context and the reader's background of information and mental set contribute significantly to reading comprehension. If these multiple constructed meanings derive from the text, or are permissible transformations or inferences from it, then they evidence comprehension. Reading comprehension is not an idiosyncratic, anarchic phenomenon. But neither is it a monolithic, unitary process where only one meaning is correct. Instead, it is a generative process that reflects the reader's disciplined attempts to construct one or more meanings within the rules of language.

In this chapter, we began with a brief discussion of my model of reading comprehension as a generative process. We focused upon a minimal set of these processes, attention, encoding, and memory, that define the model more precisely. At length we discussed recent research on ways to facilitate reading comprehension by influencing these psychological processes.

In the study of attention and its facilitation, we found that good readers attend primarily to the meaning of the text, while poor readers attend more to its surface characteristics. The meaning of irrelevant sentences inserted into a text distracted good readers, while the surface structure of these same sentences distracted poor readers. Differences in ability to decode text does not adequately explain these results. The readers differed in attention and in their goals for reading. The so-called good readers concentrated on the construction of meaning.

We also discussed ways to facilitate attention to the construction of meaning. Adjunct questions, often studied during the last 15 years, direct attention. Questions about the underlying principles, models, and concepts facilitate broad, conceptual learning. Questions about facts facilitate memory of specific information.

Objectives given to learners also direct attention. Especially when the structurally important information in the text is not made salient by its organization, objectives enhance selective attention to its meaning. Either well-chosen conceptually oriented objectives or careful organization of the structurally important information enhances attention to the meaning of the text and facilitates reading comprehension and retention.

From neurological research, we have important information about the mechanisms of attention. Brain wave components differentiate between attention to environmental stimuli and to internal events, such as expectations, response sets, and short-term memory. Some learning disabilities, such as hyperactivity, seem to be, at least in part, a deficit in attention, an inability to ignore contextual, task-relevant, but distracting stimuli. When stimulant drugs are given in correct dosage to hyperactive children, they sometimes steepen the gradient of attention to the learning task. As a result, learning improves.

Most impressively, cognitive training programs designed to increase and to sustain attention enhanced reading comprehension in two studies, with hyperactive children in one study and with normal children in the other study. The cognitive training programs taught the children to control their impulses, to manage their activities, and to rehearse self-instructions that directed their energies to effective comprehension strategies and away from distractions.

In the research on encoding and memory, we found that reading comprehension consists of more than attention to the meaning of the text. The active generation of relations between the learner's knowledge and experience and the text comprises an important part of reading comprehension. Several researchers, including my students and myself, report ways to facilitate these active constructions of relations between text and learner. One approach emphasizes learner-generated verbal elaboration. In several studies, reading comprehension sizably increased, 50–100%, when learners constructed sentences about each paragraph of a text immediately after they read it. Inserted paragraph headings facilitated reading comprehension, especially when the learners incorporated these headings into their constructed sentences.

Reading comprehension increased markedly when primary school children expressed in their own words, and related to their experience, the meaning of familiar folk stories read to them by their teachers. When children make inferences from stories and recall incidents in their lives that relate to the text, their comprehension of the text sometimes improves, as well as their ability to read with comprehension.

When the learner has appropriate experience and adequate ability, completing missing last words in sentences, underlining words in sentences, taking a given perspective while reading a story, constructing inferences, and even taking notes facilitate reading comprehension. In each case, the facilitation seems to involve active learner generation of relations between the text and the reader's knowledge and memories of experience.

Developmental differences in ability to construct verbal elaborations also exist. Prior to about 5 or 6 years, many children can profit from verbal elaborations given to them by another person. But they cannot often construct verbal elaborations to facilitate reading or listening comprehension. Beginning at about 5 or 6 years of age, with careful guidance, many children can construct verbal elaborations that facilitate comprehension of text and stories. After this age children can, but usually do not, spontaneously construct the verbal elaborations and inferences that facilitate comprehension. In this situation, directions to construct elaborations and inferences often produce marked improvements in reading comprehension. We do not know when, if ever, the ability to produce verbal elaborations becomes automatic. Even college undergraduates often profit from instructions to comprehend text by constructing verbal elaborations and inferences about its meaning.

With imagery, the effects upon reading comprehension are also significant, although the developmental progression in ability to construct images differs from its counterpart with verbal stimuli. Although a few authors agree that pictures distract readers from the meaning of the text, the overwhelming results of relevant empirical studies indicate that pictures often facilitate reading comprehension, even among children 3–4 years of age. Directions to construct pictures or images also facilitate reading comprehension and retention. However, the facilitative effect of these learner-generated elaborations does not occur until about 8 years with most children, which is about 2–3 years later than the effect with directions to construct verbal elaborations.

Individual differences in ability to generate verbal elaborations or imagery influence the process of constructing meaning for text. The research on this issue shows promising results, but it is only beginning to appear in the literature. In the next few years we expect to see research on cognitive styles, information-processing strategies, and individual differences in generative processes relate more closely to research in reading comprehension.

The knowledge base of the learner, as it differs from cognitive style or ability to construct verbal or imaginal representations, affects reading comprehension. A well-organized and relevant background of knowledge facilitates reading comprehension and recall. Advanced organizers can enhance comprehension of text, especially when it is poorly organized. The organizers emphasize relations between the text and the reader's abstract relevant knowledge.

The characteristics of the text and its context also influence reading comprehension. Children comprehend unfamiliar words when they are embedded in a meaningful context. As we mentioned earlier, appropriate pictures clearly facilitate reading comprehension and retention, as do high imagery words under some conditions. High frequency words enhance comprehension among good readers and poor ones. From the generative model of reading comprehension, the facilitative effects of these characteristics of text and its context occur spontaneously because of the same processes, such as attention and encoding, that are stimulated externally by instructions to relate print to knowledge or experience.

In summary, reading comprehension is the generation of meaning for written language. At least several psychological processes contribute to the construction of meaning. In this chapter, we discussed several of these processes—attention, encoding, and memory—and research about them. We found that reading comprehension can be facilitated by several different procedures that emphasize attention to the text and to the construction of verbal or imaginal elaborations.

The generative model of reading comprehension, as supported by the research data reviewed here, implies the following conditions for facilitating reading comprehension. When the readers cannot adequately attend to the text, cognitive training in attention, rehearsal strategies, and self-management techniques seems appropriate. When the readers attend to the text but cannot generate elaborations for it, then elaborations, such as verbal statements and pictures to represent its meaning or possible meanings, are appropriate for facilitating comprehension.

When readers attend to the text and can, but do not, spontaneously generate a meaning for it, instructions to elaborate it verbally, to create images, to draw pictures, to construct inferences, applications, and analogies, or to assimilate it with higher order concepts seems appropriate. The objective is to induce the readers to construct these relations between the text and their knowledge and experience. The specific type of direction best for the reader depends upon many variables, including the nature of the text, the objectives for the reading, and the individual differences among the readers.

When the readers attend to the text and construct meaning for it, reading comprehension can be influenced subtly by directions, questions, discussions, and the like chosen to induce and enhance meanings or inferences that might otherwise be ignored.

As research on reading comprehension proceeds, we should learn more about these processes and about additional but as yet not understood neural and psychological processes people use to generate understanding from words on pages.

References

Anderson, R. C., Pichert, J. W., & Shirey, L. L. Effects of the reader's schema at different points in time (Technical Report No. 119). University of Illinois, Urbana, Center for the Study of Reading, April 1979.

Andre, T., & Womack, S. Verbatim and paraphrased adjunct questions and learning from prose. Journal of Educational Psychology, 1978, 70, 796–802.

Arnold, D. J., & Brooks, P. H. Influence of contextual organizing material on children's listening comprehension. Journal of Educational Psychology, 1976, 68, 711–716.

Au, K. Cognitive training and reading achievement. Paper presented at the meeting of the Association for the Advancement of Behavior Therapy, Atlanta, Georgia, December 1977.

Ausubel, D. P. The use of advance organizers in the learning and retention of meaningful verbal material. Journal of Educational Psychology, 1960, 51, 267–272.

Ausubel, D. P., & Fitzgerald, D. Organizer, general background, and antecedent learning variables in sequential verbal learning. Journal of Educational Psychology, 1962, 53, 243–249.

Bender, B. G., & Levin, L. R. Pictures, imagery, and retarded children's prose learning. Journal of Educational Psychology, 1978, 70, 583–588.

Boker, J. R. Immediate and delayed retention effects of interspersing questions in written instructional passages. Journal of Educational Psychology, 1974, 66, 96–98.

Boyd, W., McK. Repeating questions in prose learning. *Journal of Educational Psychology*, 1973, *64*, 31–38.

Bransford, J. D., & Johnson, M. K. Contextual prerequisites for understanding: Some investigations of comprehension and recall. *Journal of Verbal Learning and Verbal Behavior*, 1972, *11*, 717–726.

Brown, A. L., & Smiley, S. S. The development of strategies for studying texts. *Child Development*, 1978, *49*, 1076–1088.

Brown, A. L., Smiley, S. S., Day, J. D., Townsend, M. A. R., & Lawton, S. C. Intrusion of a thematic idea in children's comprehension and retention of stories. *Child Development*, 1977, *48*, 1454–1466.

Brown, W. S., Marsh, J. T., & Smith, J. C. Contextual meaning effects on speech-evoked potentials. *Behavioral Biology*, 1973, *9*, 755–761.

Bull, B. L., & Wittrock, M. C. Imagery in the learning of verbal definitions. *British Journal of Educational Psychology*, 1973, *43*, 289–293.

Conners, C. K. Cortical visual evoked response in children with learning disorders. *Psychophysiology*, 1970, *7*, 418–428.

Conners, C. K. Learning disabilities and stimulant drugs in children: Theoretical implications. In R. M. Knights & D. J. Bakker (Eds.), *The neuropsychology of learning disorders*. Baltimore, Maryland: University Park Press, 1976.

Delaney, H. D. Interaction of individual differences with visual and verbal elaboration instructions. *Journal of Educational Psychology*, 1978, *70*, 306–318.

Di Vesta, F. S., Hayward, K. G., & Orlando, V. P. Developmental trends in monitoring text for comprehension. *Child Development*, 1979, *50*, 97–105.

Doctorow, M. J., Wittrock, M. C., & Marks, C. B. Generative processes in reading comprehension. *Journal of Educational Psychology*, 1978, *70*, 109–118.

Dooling, D. J., & Christiaansen, R. E. Episodic and semantic aspects of memory for prose. *Journal of Experimental Psychology: Human Learning and Memory*, 1977, *3*, 428–436.

Douglas, V. I., Parry, P., Martin, P., & Garson, C. Assessment of a cognitive training program for hyperactive children. *Journal of Abnormal Child Psychology*, 1976, *4*, 389–410.

Duchastel, P. Learning objectives and the organization of prose. *Journal of Educational Psychology*, 1979, *71*, 100–106.

Duell, O. K. Effect of type of objective, level of test questions, and the judged importance of tested materials upon posttest performance. *Journal of Educational Psychology*, 1974, *66*, 225–232.

Glynn, S. M., & Di Vesta, F. J. Outline and hierarchial organization as aids for study and retrieval. *Journal of Educational Psychology*, 1977, *69*, 89–95.

Guttman, J., Levin, J. R., & Pressley, M. Pictures, partial pictures, and young children's oral prose learning. *Journal of Educational Psychology*, 1977, *69*, 473–480.

Huey, E. B. *The psychology and pedagogy of reading*. Cambridge, Massachusetts: The MIT Press, 1968 (reprinted).

Jorm, A. F. Effect of word imagery on reading performance as a function of reader ability. *Journal of Educational Psychology*, 1977, *69*, 46–54.

Kail, R. V., Jr., & Marshall, V. Reading skill and memory scanning. *Journal of Educational Psychology*, 1978, *70*, 808–814.

Kail, R. V., Jr., Chi, M. T. H., Ingram, A. C., & Danner, F. W. Constructive aspects of children's reading comprehension. *Child Development*, 1977, *48*, 684–688.

Kane, J. H., & Anderson, R. C. Depth of processing and interference effects in the learning and remembering of sentences. *Journal of Educational Psychology*, 1978, *70*, 626–635.

Kaplan, R., & Simmons, F. G. Effects of instructional objectives used as orienting stimuli or as summary/review upon prose learning. *Journal of Educational Psychology*, 1974, *66*, 614–622.

Kintsch, W., & Kozminsky, E. Summarizing stories after reading and listening. *Journal of Educational Psychology*, 1977, *69*, 491–499.

Krupski, A. Sustained attention: Research, theory and implications for special education. In B. K. Keogh (Ed.), *Advances in special education* (vol. 1). Greenwich, Connecticut: JAI Press, 1980.

LaBerge, D., & Samuels, S. J. Toward a theory of automatic information processing in reading. *Cognitive Psychology*, 1974, *6*, 293–323.

Levin, J. R. Inducing comprehension in poor readers: A test of a recent model. *Journal of Educational Psychology*, 1973, *65*, 19–24.

McClure, E., Mason, J., & Barnity, J. *Story structure and age effects on children's ability to sequence stories* (Technical Report No. 122). University of Illinois, Urbana, Center for the Study of Reading, May 1979.

Malamuth, S. *Self-management training for children with reading problems: Effects on reading performance and sustained attention*. Unpublished doctoral dissertation, University of California, Los Angeles, 1977.

Marks, C. B., Doctorow, M. J., & Wittrock, M. C. Word frequency and reading comprehension. *Journal of Educational Psychology*, 1974, *67*, 259–262.

Marshall, N., & Glock, M. V. Comprehension of connected discourse: A study into the relationships between the structure of text and information recalled. *Reading Research Quarterly*, 1978, *14*, 10–56.

Mathews, M. M. *Teaching to read*. Chicago: Univ. of Chicago Press, 1966.

Mayer, R. E. Different problem-solving competencies established in learning computer programming with and without meaningful models. *Journal of Educational Psychology*, 1975, *67*, 165–169.

Mayer, R. E. Effects of prior test-like events and meaningfulness of information on numeric and comparative reasoning. *Journal of Educational Psychology*, 1978, *70*, 29–38.

Mayer, R. E. Advance organizers that compensate for the organization of text. *Journal of Educational Psychology*, 1978, *70*, 880–886.

Meichenbaum, D., & Asarnow, J. Cognitive–behavior modification and metacognitive development: Implications for the classroom. In P. Kendall & S. Hollen (Eds.), *Cognitive–behavioral interventions: Theory, research, and procedures*. New York: Academic Press, 1978.

Miller, R. B., Perry, F. L., & Cunningham, D. J. Differential forgetting of superordinate and subordinate information acquired from prose material. *Journal of Educational Psychology*, 1977, *69*, 730–735.

Myers, M. II, & Paris, S. G. Children's metacognitive knowledge about reading. *Journal of Educational Psychology*, 1978, *70*, 680–690.

Paivio, A. *Imagery and verbal processes*. New York: Holt, Rinehart & Winston, 1971.

Paris, S. G., Lindauer, B. K., & Cox, G. L. The development of inferential comprehension. *Child Development*, 1977, *48*, 1728–1733.

Pearson, P. D., Hansen, J., & Gordon, C. *The effect of background knowledge on young children's comprehension of explicit and implicit information* (Technical Report No. 116). University of Illinois, Urbana Center for the Study of Reading, March 1979.

Peper, R. J., & Mayer, R. E. Note taking as a generative activity. *Journal of Educational Psychology*, 1978, *70*, 514–522.

Pichert, J. W., & Anderson, R. C. Taking different perspectives on a story. *Journal of Educational Psychology*, 1977, *69*, 309–315.

Pressley, G. M. Mental imagery helps eight-year-olds remember what they read. *Journal of Educational Psychology*, 1976, *68*, 355–359.

Preston, M. S., Guthrie, J. T., & Childs, B. Visual evoked responses in normal and disabled readers. *Psychophysiology*, 1974, *11*, 452–457.

Rickards, J. P., & August, G. J. Generative underlining strategies in prose recall. *Journal of Educational Psychology*, 1975, *67*, 860–865.

Ross, H. S., & Killey, J. C. The effects of questioning on retention. *Child Development*, 1977, *48*, 312–314.

Rothkopf, E. Z., & Billington, M. J. Goal-guided learning from text: Inferring a descriptive processing model from inspection times and eye movements. *Journal of Educational Psychology*, 1979, *71*, 310–327.

Rohwer, W. D., Jr., & Matz, R. Improving aural comprehension in white and black children: Pictures versus print. *Journal of Experimental Child Psychology*, 1975, *19*, 23–36.

Royer, P. N. Effects of specificity and position of written instructional objectives on learning from lecture. *Journal of Educational Psychology*, 1977, *69*, 40–45.

Royer, J. M., Perkins, M. R., & Konold, C. E. Evidence for a selective storage mechanism in prose learning. *Journal of Educational Psychology*, 1978, *70*, 457–462.

Ruch, M. D., & Levin, J. R. Pictorial organization versus verbal repetition of children's prose: Evidence for processing differences. *AV Communication Review*, 1977, *25*, 269–280.

Sagaria, S. D., & Di Vesta, F. J. Learner expectations induced by adjunct questions and the retrieval of intentional and incidental information. *Journal of Educational Psychology*, 1978, *70*, 280–288.

Spiro, R. J. *Etiology of reading comprehension style* (Technical Report No. 124). University of Illinois, Urbana, Center for the Study of Reading, May 1979.

Standing, L., Conezio, J., & Haber, R. N. Perception and memory for pictures: Single-trial learning of 2500 visual stimuli. *Psychonomic Science*, 1970, *19*, 73–74.

Tenenbaum, A. B. Task-dependent effects of organization and context upon comprehension of prose. *Journal of Educational Psychology*, 1977, *69*, 528–536.

Teyler, T. J., Megela, A., & Hesse, G. Habituation and generalization of the ERP to linguistic and non-linguistic stimuli. In D. Otto (Ed.), *Perspectives in event-related brain potential research*. Washington, D.C.: Government Printing Office, 1977.

Thorndike, R. L. *Reading comprehension education in fifteen countries*. New York: Halsted, 1973.

Tirre, W. C., Manelis, L., & Leicht, K. L. *The effects of imaginal and verbal strategies on prose comprehension in adults*. (Technical Report No. 110). University of Illinois, Urbana, Center for the Study of Reading, December 1978.

Willows, D. M. A picture is not always worth a thousand words: Pictures as distractors in reading. *Journal of Educational Psychology*, 1978, *70*, 255–262.

Willows, D. M. Reading between the lines: Selective attention in good and poor readers. *Child Development*, 1974, *45*, 408–415.

Wittrock, M. C. Learning as a generative process. *Educational Psychologist*, 1974, *11*, 87–95.

Wittrock, M. C. Three conceptual approaches to research on transfer of training. In R. Gagne (Ed.), *Learning research and school subjects*. Itasca, Illinois: Peacock Press, 1968.

Wittrock, M. C., & Carter, J. Generative processing of hierarchically organized words. *American Journal of Psychology*, 1975, *88*, 489–501.

Wittrock, M. C., & Goldberg, S. Imagery and meaningfulness in free recall: Word attributes and instructional sets. *Journal of General Psychology*. 1975, *92*, 137–151.

Wittrock, M. C., & Lutz, K. Reading comprehension and the generation of verbal analogies and summaries, in preparation.

Wittrock, M. C., Marks, C. B., & Doctorow, M. J. Reading as a generative process. *Journal of Educational Psychology*, 1975, *67*, 484–489.

Wolff, P., & Levin, J. R. The role of overt activity in children's imagery production. *Child Development*, 1972, *43*, 537–547.

10

Jack M. Fletcher

LINGUISTIC FACTORS IN READING ACQUISITION: Evidence for Developmental Changes

Wohlwill (1973) described the study of behavioral change as the primary task of developmental psychology. For cognitive development, part of this task includes the scientific analysis of the characteristics of the developing behavior, such as the nature of cognitive structures at different developmental periods. More important, however, is the scientific analysis of behavioral change as an entity in itself. This analysis would include the study of characteristics such as the rate, degree, and sequence of development for various cognitive structures. In this respect, the study of cognitive development would emphasize age-dependent relationships, with chronological age as the primary unit of analysis for developmental changes. From Wohlwill's (1973) point of view, chronological age would represent a dependent variable marking developmental changes in the organization of cognitive skills.

Recent theory and research on the acquisition of reading skills constitutes one area that has begun to emphasize developmental changes. For example, Gibson and Levin (1975) provided a general theory of reading acquisition that emphasized developmental changes in the nature of the fundamental attributes processed by the developing reader. As the reader develops, increased skill is represented by the capacity to process larger and more complex sources of written information. Analysis of the relationship between those attributes processed and reading proficiency requires direct reference to chronological age so that developmental changes can be specified.

The analysis of developmental change is also important for the

NEUROPSYCHOLOGICAL AND COGNITIVE
PROCESSES IN READING

study of children who fail to acquire proficiency in some aspect of cognitive development. Recent reviews on mental retardation (Weitz & Zigler, 1979) and learning disabilities (Satz & Fletcher, 1980) have emphasized the heuristic value of studying developmental changes for understanding the cognitive nature of these disabilities. These reviews suggest that the exploration of age-dependent relationships between disabled and nondisabled children is one way of generating and testing hypotheses about these disabilities. Inherent within this approach is the assumption that basic developmental models can be fruitfully applied and evaluated with disabled populations such as the mentally retarded and the learning disabled.

This commentary on the importance of developmental change is prefatory to the purposes of this chapter. Whereas the material reviewed will concern the relationship of language and reading, the major purpose is to illustrate the importance of developmental change for understanding reading acquisition and reading failure. One of the problems with much of the research on reading acquisition and reading failure is that a developmental model (e.g., Wohlwill, 1973) is seldom employed, particularly in the reading disability literature. There is a dearth of cross-sectional and longitudinal research, with many studies actually using groups composed of heterogeneously aged children (Satz & Fletcher, 1980). Consequently, the present chapter will attempt to organize research on linguistic factors in reading acquisition in an attempt to provide evidence for developmental changes. These changes can be predicted according to the size and type of linguistic attribute characterizing the reading process at different ages. Age-dependent relationships are particularly evident when disabled and nondisabled readers are compared. Differences in linguistic processing characterize disabled and nondisabled readers at various chronological ages. The nature of these differences are consistent with developmental studies of nondisabled readers, which show that disabled populations can be used to test basic developmental theories. Such an approach is heuristic for the study of both normal and disabled children.

Three areas of research provide information on the relationship of language and reading acquisition. The first area concerns the nature of the reading process. This area is primarily concerned with how the fluent reader processes the attributes of written language. The second area of research concerns the acquisition of reading skills in normal children. The major research emphasis in this area concerns the nature of the attributes that the learning reader processes at different periods during the acquisition process. The third area of research focuses on children who experience difficulty learning to read. Although this area is difficult to characterize, it will be suggested that its concerns have been similar to developmental studies of reading acquisition in normal children, namely the nature of the attributes that the reader can or cannot process.

Organizing research in these three areas from the perspective of developmental change suggests a general model of the developing reader. This model, based on Zigler's (1969) *similar sequence theory* of differences in cognitive performance between familially retarded and nonretarded children, helps explain performance differences between at least some disabled and nondisabled readers. The model is also useful for understanding the relationship of the three areas of research to the reading process, normal reading acquisition, and reading disabilities. Summarily, although the material for this chapter will be linguistic, attempts will be made to describe a more general model of the developing reader from three sources of research.

Developmental Changes in Reading Acquisition

Developmental changes can be approached from a perceptual model similar to *attribute dominance* theories of memory (Hagen, Jongeward, & Kail, 1975; Underwood, 1969). In these theories, memory stores are assumed to be formed of distinctive elements (attributes) that discriminate different memories and serve as cues for retrieval and storage. Children at different ages may form memories based on different attributes. For younger children, acoustic and spatial attributes may be more dominant than higher order linguistic attributes. Older children form memories based on higher order linguistic attributes that help to organize information in larger units for more efficient storage. Consequently, at different ages, children's memories are composed of those stimulus attributes that are more dominant. Developmental changes are most apparent in the nature of memory strategies used by children at different ages (Hagen *et al.*, 1975).

Words can also be considered to be collections of attributes. Gibson and Levin (1975) argued that the fundamental unit of visual information in reading is the word. Individual words are composed of different types of distinctive features (attributes): graphic features, orthographic regularities in letter combinations, phonological correlates of letter combinations, and syntactic and semantic characteristics of words and groups of words. These constraints form patterns of invariance to which the reader must selectively attend to obtain meaning from print. Learning to read involves developing strategies for processing increasingly larger units of information. However, developmental changes in the *type* and *size* of the attribute processed may be observed. Beginning readers attend primarily to graphological and phonological attributes of words. More experienced readers attend to syntactic and semantic regularities within connected text. In part, these changes reflect the child's developing capacity for abstracting meaning from text. For example, once strategies for decoding single words are mastered, the need for selective attention to single word attributes is reduced. These processes may become automatized (LaBerge & Samuels, 1974) such that attention can be distributed to higher-order linguistic redundancies in text. When a child is able to process these larger units of information, comprehension is no longer a word-for-word process. More efficient use of short-term memory is made, such that reading becomes faster and comprehension continues to improve (Smith, 1971). These changes parallel the increased use of higher-order linguistic skills for organizing information in memory as children develop (Hagen *et al.*, 1975).

Doehring (1976) evaluated developmental change hypotheses in a study of the rapid visual processing of different types and sizes of information in children from kindergarten to Grade 11. Speed of response to written letters, syllables, words, and word sequences were measured for visual matching, visual–auditory matching, oral reading, and visual scanning tasks. Response speed improved systematically as age increased in the children. In the early grades, rapid processing was observed for smaller units of information. Phonological attributes were the most important determinant of speed. Several years were required before units of a size characteristic of skilled readers were processed rapidly. Although children as early as the first grade attempted to use syntactic and semantic attributes to group words, rapid processing of these units was apparent only in relatively older children. In a subsequent study of sentence comprehension, Doehring and Hoshko (1977) employed a Cloze procedure requiring children from Grades 1–11 to identify a word missing from a sentence as rapidly as possible. Older children identified the word much more rapidly than younger children. Doehring and Hoshko hypothesized that, whereas sentence comprehension involves several operations, one important factor involved "processing of the logical–semantic–grammatical relationships among words [p. 313]." Processing of these relationships was more characteristic of older children.

This research shows that developmental changes occur in the acquisition of reading-related skills. These changes are most apparent in the reader's ability to process increasingly larger units of information. In terms of language, it is clear that there are multiple linguistic (and nonlinguistic) attributes embedded in written language. Linguistic attributes vary from small phonetic segments to larger grammatical phrases. At different phases of the reading acquisition process, the child selectively processes different linguistic attributes to obtain meaning from written language. Changes can be observed in the size and type of linguistic attributes processed at these different phases, representing developmental shifts in reading acquisition (Gibson & Levin, 1975). These shifts suggest different characterizations of children as readers depending on their proficiency. For example, younger children may be characterized as decoders, employing strategies designed for single word recognition. Older, more fluent readers may be characterized as comprehenders, employing strategies designed to access meaning directly from units of information larger than a single word. The next two sections will consider research on linguistic attributes involved in decoding and comprehension. By focusing on the age of the children included in different studies, evidence for developmental changes in the attributes characterizing decoding and comprehension will be provided.

Linguistic Attributes and Decoding Processes

Pronouncing and recognizing single words involves the joint operation of a number of cognitive skills for identifying single word constraints. These constraints comprise graphological, phonetic, and orthographic sources of redundancy in print. Two issues will be considered in relating language development to single word recognition. The first is the extent to which the phonological correlates of words are necessary for decoding. Basic research on the reading process is unclear regarding the relative contribution of graphological and phonological units for word recognition (Bradshaw, 1975). Whereas some research seems to show that the visual information of a word must be translated to a speech code (Meyer, Schvaneveldt, & Ruddy, 1974; Rubenstein, Lewis, & Rubenstein, 1971), other research suggests that word recognition can occur directly on the basis of the visual information alone (Baron, 1973). Furthermore, cases of acquired aphasia with alexia (phonemic alexia) can be described in which word recognition proceeds despite disruption of the phonological system (Saffran & Marin, 1977). In children, strategies based on the phonological correlates of words facilitate word recognition (Doehring, 1976). Whereas processing of these phonological correlates may be *sufficient* for word recognition, it is not clear that they are *necessary* for decoding. This issue is particularly critical for studies of reading failure, where some children may master word recognition skills but fail to acquire comprehension skills (Smith, 1971).

A second issue pertains to the child's increasing capacity for processing intraword redundancies through visual and orthographic regularities and through letter-cluster–sound correspondences. Developmental shifts in the size and type of the stimulus attributes processed during single word recognition can be demonstrated. Furthermore, children less proficient in reading process smaller attributes less efficiently. Research pertaining to both these issues will be reviewed.

Phonology and Decoding

In the early stages of reading acquisition, children employ different types of linguistic skills and strategies. In establishing the link between oral and written language for early decoding, the child may apply his understanding of the acoustic structure of speech to the phonological correlates of letters and words. This is a new task for the child, requiring him to apply what he has learned through an auditory modality to visual information. Although the basic framework has been acquired, the capacity to process the phonological correlates of letters and words requires new learning that generally persists until age 8 (Gibson & Levin, 1975).

Linguistic skills that the child has already acquired may transfer more directly to the reading process. Both Weber (1970) and Biemuller (1971) compared the oral reading errors of first grade children. Weber found that these errors generally conformed to syntactic and semantic constraints provided by prior grammatical context. Thus, beginning readers applied their knowledge of language to the new problem of word identification. In addition, Weber (1970) and Biemuller (1971) found no differences between good and poor readers in the number or type of these contextual errors. In terms of correcting these errors, however, good readers were distinctly superior (Weber, 1970). Biemuller (1971) described three stages in the initial process of learning to read. The first phase was characterized by an emphasis on use of *contextual* information. In the second phase, an increase in the number of *graphically* constrained errors was observed, and the third phase was marked by a co-occurrence of contextual and graphically constrained errors. Most important, however, was Biemuller's finding that the early reader's ability to use *graphic* information for word identification differentiated good and poor achievers.

Difficulties in processing the visual features of letters and words could reflect problems with graphological and/or phonological correlates of visual information. In particular, insufficient development of the child's knowledge of the acoustic structure of speech could hamper the early reader's ability to deal with the graphic features processed during decoding. Two classes of studies regarding the child's capacity for using his knowledge of the acoustic structure of speech for decoding will be reviewed, pertaining to phonetic segmentation and intraword redundancies.

Phonemic Segmentation

Most of the research on phonemic segmentation stems from work by Liberman and Shankweiler (cf. Liberman, Shankweiler, Liberman, Fowler, & Fischer, 1977). This work is based on the "assumption that reading is somehow parasitic on speech. . . . In order to learn to read, the child must map the written word to the spoken word . . . in order to do this, he must have some recognition of the phonetic structure of his spoken language [Liberman & Shankweiler, 1976, p. 2]." In this quotation, the importance of mastering the phonological correlates of words is clearly recognized. Liberman, Shankweiler, and associates have investigated three aspects of this relationship as it pertains to reading acquisition: (a) awareness of phonetic segments; (b) phonetic representations in short-term memory; and (c) oral reading errors.

Awareness of Phonetic Segmentation

The syllable, not the phoneme, is the minimal unit of articulation. Consequently, learning to read by sounding letters one by one is impossible. Reading analytically implies the discovery of how letter segments (sounds) can be simultaneously blended to arrive at the correct phonetic representation of each syllable. Therefore, knowing how many phonemic segments form a unit of articulation is vital to relating speech and written language (Liberman et al., 1977).

Liberman, Shankweiler, Fischer, and Carter (1974) explored the ability of 4-, 5-, and 6-year-olds (prekindergarten to Grade 1) to identify the number of phonemic and syllabic segments in spoken utterances. The task required the child to tap a wooden mallet for each of the segments in a list of test utterances. At age 4, no children could identify phonemic segments, although half could identify syllabic segments. At age 6, however, 70% could identify phonemic segments and 90% could identify syllabic segments.

Using their first grade sample, Liberman et al. (1977) also contrasted good and poor readers on their segmentation skills about 4 months after initial testing (beginning of Grade 2). Half of the children in the lowest third of the reading achievement distribution had failed the phonemic segmentation task, but all of the top third of the distribution had passed the task.

More rigorous investigations have strengthened the relationship of phonemic segmentation and early reading achievement. Helfgott (1976) measured segmentation and blending skills in kindergarten children in an attempt to predict first grade reading achievement. Segmentation of spoken consonant–vowel–consonant (CVC) words in kindergarten correlated at .75 with the first grade word recognition score from the Wide Range Achievement Test. Zifcak (1976) found a significant correlational relationship between phonemic segmentation on the dowel tapping task (described earlier) and reading achievement in first grade children. Treiman (1976), in a study of first and second grade inner city children (largely blacks), also found a high correlational relationship between phonemic segmentation (measured by a variation of the tapping task) and reading ability. These results, on diverse samples with different criterion reading measures, suggest that the child's ability to decompose linguistic units into phonemic segments has a high relationship with early reading achievement.

Phonemic Recoding

A second set of studies concerns phonemic recoding in short-term memory. These studies are predicated on the assumption that, before longer segments of speech, oral and written language can be processed, a temporary acoustic store must be established. This acoustic store takes the form of a phonemic representation. Therefore, if poor readers have trouble forming phonemic representations of language, as indicated by the segmentation studies, differences between good and poor readers should be observed in the amount of coding used for short-term memory tasks (Liberman & Shankweiler, 1976).

Experiments pertaining to this hypothesis were summarized by Liberman and Shankweiler (1976). Two experiments (Liberman et al., 1977; Shankweiler & Liberman, 1976) compared recall of phonetically confusable (rhyming) and nonconfusable (nonrhyming) strings of letters in second grade reading groups. Results from both studies indicated that, regardless of presentation modality, the interference effect of confusable stimuli was more apparent for good readers than for poor readers. No disruptive effects were observed on nonconfusable stimuli for either reading group. Thus, tasks requiring a phonemic strategy had a greater disruptive effect on recall in good readers than in poor readers, indicating more consistent application of phonemic recoding strategies in the good reader group.

A more rigorous experiment (Mark, 1977) gave beginning readers (age unspecified) a list of 28 words to be read aloud, followed by a recognition list containing the original words and 28 new distractor words. Half the distractors were phonetically confusable but visually dissimilar from an original test word. The other 14 words were not confusable (i.e., did not rhyme). Again, the interference effect of confusability on recall was more pronounced in good than in poor readers.

Oral Reading Errors

The third approach to early phonemic encoding is based on research addressing phonemic analysis of reading errors made by second grade (and older) disabled and nondisabled readers. Shankweiler and Liberman (1972) found a distinct pattern of oral reading errors showing that errors on the final consonant of a CVC syllable were twice those on the initial consonant, whereas medial vowel errors exceeded both possible consonant errors. In other words, more errors were observed on medial vowel and final position consonants. These results were interpreted as revealing incomplete understanding of the phonological segments of language in these children. When scanning from left to right, a child with incomplete phonological awareness will search for any lexical word beginning with the initial sound. As such, errors later in the word would be more frequent because the child failed to process the remainder of the word. These interpretations were buttressed by recent phonemic analyses of the oral reading errors of second, third, and fourth grade readers (Fowler, Liberman, & Shankweiler, 1977). Although the number of errors decreased with increased age, the error pattern remained the same.

These latter studies have led Liberman and Shankweiler (1976) to argue against the importance of direct visual encoding of graphological information because the difference in vowel and consonant errors is difficult to explain in terms of distinctive features (e.g., physical shape) of letters. The absence of errors (e.g., reversals) presumably reflecting perceptual anomalies is also cited as substantiating this argument (Fischer, Liberman, & Shankweiler, 1978). Liberman and Shankweiler (1976) concluded that the problems of beginning and disabled readers reflect phonemic segmentation difficulties as opposed to visual–perceptual difficulties. It should be noted, however, that both the oral reading error and the phonemic recoding studies that support this hypothesis are based on null (not negative) data obtained from relatively older (second grade and above) readers, an age where visual–perceptual problems are expected to be less prominent (Benton, 1962; Fletcher & Satz, 1979a,b). Therefore, whereas the present series of studies provides strong support for the role of phonological factors in early reading, generalizations regarding other types of skills are inappropriate because of the restricted age range. The next set of studies will illustrate clearly that some beginning readers employ strategies that are not necessarily phonologically mediated.

Intraword Redundancies

Decoding for older readers is characterized by the use of higher order intraword relationships. In this respect, factors such as pronounceability, orthographic structure (e.g., spelling patterns), letter correspondences, and visuospatial sources of redundancies are important for decoding strategies. For earlier phases of reading, lower level analyses (e.g., sequential letter recognition and spelling–sound correspondences) may characterize decoding strategies. With age and experience, higher levels of analysis, including the use of orthographic structures for identifying clusters of letters, become more characteristic (Doehring, 1976).

An earlier developing source of intraword redundancy is letter–sound correspondence. Calfee, Venezky, and Chapman (1969) explored the relationship of the child's knowledge of letter–sound correspondences with reading achievement. Synthetic words incorporating regular and irregular letter–sound patterns were presented for pronunciation to good and poor readers in third grade, fifth grade, high school, and college. Correlations between pronunciation and reading achievement were highest in third graders, decreasing substantially after that age as intelligence test scores accounted for more of the variability in reading achievement. Differences between good and poor readers were larger at the third grade level, decreasing with age except on more complex patterns. A subsequent study (Venezky & Johnson, 1973) gave similar synthetic words to first, second, and third grade reading groups. Correlations with word recognition scores were at .77 for the first grade readers, dropping to .63 for third grade readers.

In these studies, the use of letter–sound correspondences for pronouncing pseudowords is correlated with reading achievement in Grades 1–3, diminishing after this age. Whether this relationship reflects phonological or orthographic sources of redundancy is unclear. Tasks that do not require pronunciation show that the use of spelling patterns for word identification emerges after Grade 2 (Gibson & Levin, 1975). Rosinski and Wheeler (1972) showed that third and fifth graders could use spelling patterns to discriminate the closeness of nonsense words to real words. First grader performance was at the chance level. A reaction time study (Santa, 1976–1977) compared first, second, and fifth grade children and adults in the rapid visual recognition of different reading units: single letters, initial and final letter clusters, and whole words. Fifth graders and adults were faster processors for all these units. First graders processed single letters most rapidly, whereas second graders processed initial letter clusters as rapidly as single letters.

Developmental changes in the use of intraword structures can also be described for groups differing in reading ability. Calfee et al. (1969) and Venezky and Johnson (1973) found larger correlations with word recognition in younger reading groups (Grades 1 and 3) than in older reading groups (Grade 6) on the ability to use letter–sound correspondences for word recognition. Santa (1976–1977) showed that poor second grade readers were attempting to process smaller units of information based on sequential letter analysis, whereas achieving second graders were using strategies based on higher order units of information.

Katz and Wicklund (1972) found no differences in search time for single letters embedded in random letter strings between good and poor readers in Grades 2 and 6. However, good and poor first grade readers may differ on the use of strategies based on letter and word shapes for word identification. Rayner and Hagelberg (1975) compared strategies based on letter shapes and whole word shapes in kindergarten and good and poor first grade readers. Results indicated that poor first grade readers employed strategies based on initial letter shape less consistently than their same-aged counterparts, though both reading groups preferred letter shape (and not word shape) as a word recognition cue. Expanding this study to the sixth grade, Rayner (1976) revealed that the first-letter strategy was important until Grade 4, at which time whole word shape became the more important cue. Although good and poor readers were not employed in this study, Rayner and Kaiser (1975) compared sixth grade reading groups on reading text mutilated by altering first and last target letters. Good readers were better at identifying the mutilated word irrespective of the location of the mutilation.

Some studies have explored the use of more complex sources of intraword redundancy. In a variant of the Katz and Wicklund (1972) study, Mason (1975) found differences between good and poor sixth grade readers in single letter search time when the letters were embedded in highly redundant strings. Mason, Katz, and Wicklund (1975) showed that this improvement also reflected differences between reader groups for remembering spatial order. Katz and Wicklund (1971) found no differences in the ability of fifth grade reading groups to identify target words embedded within grammatical and nongrammatical sentences, with grammaticity facilitating identification for both groups. In contrast, Samuels, Begy, and Chen (1975–1976), comparing fourth grade reading groups, showed that good readers identified words faster when the target words were embedded within contextual (and orthographic) sources of redundancy. This finding was apparent when the groups were equated on visual word recognition ability.

Developmental Change: Preliminary Conclusions

These studies show that processing of the phonological correlates of letters and words facilitates word recognition. Furthermore, poor readers are less proficient in learning to process these correlates. However, word recognition can also proceed according to the graphological correlates of letters and words. These correlates can be primarily visuospatial (e.g., letter shape versus whole word shape), implying that phonological processing is not always necessary for word recognition. Attempts to characterize younger disabled readers as primarily language disabled on the basis of null results is not consistent with this research on reading acquisition in mostly normal children. In addition, this research also shows that some poor readers experience difficulties with the graphological correlates of words (Mason, 1975; Rayner & Hagelberg, 1975). This finding is consistent with neuropsychological research that shows a strong relationship between measures of visuospatial processing and reading achievement primarily in younger children (Fletcher & Satz, 1980; Rourke, 1978).

The second point concerns the evidence for developmental changes. Reading strategies based on higher order intraword units characterize older children. Younger children use smaller phonological and graphological units for word recognition. Consequently, the size and type of linguistic units processed changes as the child learns to read. Furthermore, reading group differences may be age-dependent. For example, while Katz and Wicklund (1972) found no differences in the ability of second and sixth grade reading groups to recognize single letters, Rayner and Hagelberg (1975) found differences in first grade reading groups' use of initial letter shape as a word recognition cue.

It should be noted that problems with decoding seem to persist in disabled readers throughout development. For example, Calfee, Linda-mood, and Lindamood (1973) measured performance of kindergarten through twelfth grade children on three subtests of the Lindamood Auditory Conceptualization Test, a variation on phonetic segmentation, as a function of reader ability. On the easier task, the largest differences emerged between kindergarten achievement groups, with differences persisting until Grade 4. The two more difficult tasks may have been too difficult for children prior to Grade 2, at which point large differences between achievement groups up to Grade 10 were obtained. However, it should be noted that even good readers did not fully master these tasks at the high school level.

Studies examining general decoding skills in relatively older poor readers also found deficits. Perfetti and Hogaboam (1975) measured oral response latencies to tachistoscopically presented pseudoword stimuli. Reaction time differences were observed between both third and fifth grade reading groups. Similar results were reported by Vellutino, Smith, Steger, and Kaman (1975) for second and sixth grade reader groups for the simple pronunciation of visually presented words. More specific studies of decoding ability and access of single word meanings show that relatively older reading groups defined on the basis of comprehension scores still differ on decoding skills. Golinkoff and Rosinski (1976) found that both third and fifth grade poor readers had longer latencies than their respective controls for identifying visually presented trigrams. Pace and Golinkoff (1976) extended this finding to more difficult real words. Interestingly, in this latter study, the difference was larger between third grade than fifth grade reading groups.

One common aspect of all the studies cited as evidence for the later decoding problems concerns task requirements for pronunciation of visually presented stimuli. This may reflect a confounding because the pronunciation requirement corresponds with criteria (word recognition scores) used to define disabled readers. A variety of factors underlie reading disabilities, so that conclusions are confounded by these task requirements. Age-dependent relationships between reading groups on the use of intraword structure are more apparent when a pronunciation response is not required (Rosinski & Wheeler, 1972; Santa, 1976–1977). Moreover, deficits in the use of later developing higher order intraword sources of redundancy can be described, which could also explain the persistence of these deficits.

Linguistic Attributes and Comprehension

Acquisition of comprehension strategies characteristic of fluent reading requires the capacity to extract written information in units larger than the single word (Gibson & Levin, 1975; Smith, 1971). For example, syntactic rules can be viewed as a system of constraints that increases the redundancy in a string of words. By developing strategies for processing these redundant units, fluent readers can handle larger units of information. This processing reduces the load on short-term memory and enables more efficient extraction of information from text (Gibson & Levin, 1975; Smith, 1971).

The influence of grammatical constraints on the extraction of information can be demonstrated in a variety of contexts. The large number of studies on eye–voice span (summarized by Gibson & Levin, 1975) show that older readers are progressively more sensitive to syntactically constrained units of text. Moreover, older good readers have larger eye–voice spans than younger and/or poor readers. Rode (1974–1975) explored the relationship of syntactic structure and the eye–voice spans of third, fourth, and fifth grade readers. Although younger readers had shorter eye–voice spans, they also attempted to use syntactic constraints for reading. Older readers, however, tended to use the clause as the basic unit of processing, while younger readers used a smaller unit, the phrase.

Previously cited studies by Weber (1970) and Biemuller (1970–1971) revealed that first grade beginning readers were sensitive to grammatical context. Sawyer (1976) evaluated the ability of adults to recognize target phrases in tachistoscopically produced sentences differing in the amount of grammatical redundancy. Recognition was facilitated when the grammatical structure of the sentence was highly constrained. Wisher (1976) examined the role of syntactic expectations during adult reading. He showed that more rehearsal for recalling a string of numbers occurred while reading a sentence if the reader knew the syntactic structure prior to reading the sentence. Summarizing this interesting area, Gibson & Levin (1975) concluded that by the fourth grade, children regularly use grammatical constraints for reading comprehension.

Grammatical Processing in Good and Poor Readers

In the preceding section on decoding, it was shown that reading group differences tend to emerge as a function of the size and type of the linguistic unit processed. This section will review research on the processing of grammatical constraints by good and poor readers to see what relationships emerge. Several different types of studies have been attempted, based on (a) oral reading errors; (b) oral language performance; (c) syntactic comprehension; and (d) semantic organizational constraints.

Oral Reading Errors

Two oral reading studies that failed to find differences in the linguistic error patterns of good and poor first grade readers were described earlier (Biemuller, 1970–1971; Weber, 1970). In both studies, 90% of the oral reading errors "made sense" given preceding grammatical context. Somewhat different results were reported by Little (1975), who analyzed oral reading errors of third grade average and disabled readers. These errors were also compared with performance on the Developmental Sentence Scoring Test (Lee & Canter, 1971). Although no relationship between oral reading errors and syntactic development was evident, the errors of average readers conformed more to grammatical constraints within stimulus sentences than they did for poor readers. Isakson and Miller (1976) defined groups of fourth grade children equivalent on word recognition skills but differing in comprehension ability. Results, based on oral reading errors at the verb position, revealed that poor comprehenders were less disturbed by syntactic (and semantic) violations of sentence structure than were good comprehenders, in whom error rates increased. This study replicated similar findings by Clay and Imlach (1971) and Weinstein and Rabinovitch (1971) showing that (relatively older) poor readers seemed insensitive to grammatical constraints, processing words one at a time. Less use was made of syntactic (and semantic) context cues necessary for processing groups of words. Oakan, Weiner, and Cromer (1971) and Steiner, Weiner, and Cromer (1971) provided different types of comprehension training for good and poor fifth grade comprehenders. Again, oral reading errors indicated that performance was disrupted only in good comprehenders.

Oral Language

Several studies have examined the relationship of syntactic characteristics of oral language and reading achievement. From a correlational paradigm, Bougere (1969–1970), Ribovitch (1975), and Mahaffey (1975) all correlated different measures of oral syntax (sentence length, number of kernal phrases, transformational complexity, etc.) with reading achievement in first grade samples. Only Ribovitch (1975) obtained even a moderate correlation with reading achievement, which was lower than the correlation with intelligence and other linguistic and nonlinguistic measures. Mahaffey (1975) found letter naming skills to be more predictive, and Bougere (1969–1970) found Metropolitan Readiness Test subtests to be more highly correlated with reading achievement. Bougere (1969–1970) concluded that, although different measures of oral syntax were not correlated with Grade 1 reading achievement, they may be more important in later grades. Hensley (1974) provided similar results by finding no oral syntax differences between poor, average, and superior first grade readers.

Correlational studies of older readers provide different results. Second grade (Harris, 1975) and seventh grade (Kuntz, 1975) correlations of reading achievement and oral syntax (using Falk Sentence Construction Test) were quite high (.68 – .70). Experimental studies of oral syntax between relatively older reading groups provide similar results. Fry, Johnson, and Muehl (1970) found differences on a variety of oral language measures between second grade good and poor readers. Similar findings were reported by Dumas (1976) with third grade reading groups. Calvert (1973) found that the oral language of good fifth and sixth grade readers was syntactically more complex and mature than in comparably aged poor readers. Summarily, these oral language studies show that oral syntax is less related to the discrimination of first grade reading ability, and more related to the discrimination of reading ability in second grade and older children.

Syntactic Comprehension

The age effects described for oral reading and oral syntax were largely based on measures of language production. The present section will examine studies based on the comprehension of sentences to see if a similar generalization is possible.

For younger reading groups, two studies are quite pertinent. Falk (1977) compared the ability of good and poor first and second grade readers to answer questions about 23 spoken sentences varying in syntactic complexity. A significant age effect was observed, but reading group differences were apparent only for second grade (not first grade) readers. Taylor (1977) dichotomized first and second grade readers on the basis of Metropolitan Achievement Test scores. He then asked these children to judge the grammatical acceptability of disrupted sentences. Correct judgments increased with age, with semantic disruptions more easily identified and correlated with achievement at both grade levels. Syntactic disruptions, however, were correlated with reading achievement only at the second grade level (not the first grade).

With older reading groups, Vogel (1975) failed to find differences in second grade readers on the Northwestern Syntax Screening Test (Lee, 1971), a task requiring picture selection on the basis of different sentence types. In contrast, Semel and Wiig (1975) found differences on this measure between reading groups sampled across a broader age range (7–11.5 years) and therefore slightly older (about 1 year).

Berger (1978) and Wiig and Semel (1976) examined comprehension of different sentence types in good and poor readers about 11 years old using sentence repetition tasks. Differences in sentence comprehension were found in both studies. Finally, Guthrie (1973) examined the relationship between sentence comprehension and the use of syntactic cues during silent reading. Disabled readers, about 10 years old, were selected across a broad age range, with younger (7.5 years) and older (10 years) control groups employed. The task required children to read silently and select different words from contrasting syntactic classes that would make the sentence passages acceptable. Results indicated that, although comprehension was much lower in disabled readers, the pattern of errors was quite similar. These results are similar to those obtained by Oaken et al. (1971) and Steiner et al. (1971) for older readers. Rabinovitch and Strassberg (1968) also showed that syntactic cues did not facilitate comprehension in fourth grade poor readers using sentence repetition and sentence learning tasks.

A variety of methodological problems are apparent in the syntactic comprehension studies. First, few studies have examined syntactic aspects of language in preschool children (age 5) prior to the measurable onset of reading disabilities (age 7). This earlier time period is when many of these linguistic skills undergo primary development (Bloom, 1975). Second, like much of the research on reading disabilities, the age variable has been poorly controlled (Satz & Fletcher, 1980; Torgesen, 1975). Children of varying ages are often placed together in reading groups (e.g., Semel & Wiig, 1975). Third, the measures used to assess syntactic comprehension are often confounded with several linguistic skills that may develop at different rates. For example, the Northwestern Syntax Screening Test used in several studies (Semel & Wiig, 1975; Vogel, 1975) requires comprehension of sentences differing not only syntactically, but also lexically. Comprehension problems could reflect difficulty processing either the syntactic structure or the major lexical items of the sentence. Finally, many of these studies (e.g., Guthrie, 1973) have assessed language performance with a test requiring reading. Although these studies are important, a variety of linguistic and nonlinguistic problems may be involved in reading disabilities. Conclusions regarding language skills and their role in reading failure may be confounded by these procedures.

These problems, apparent for much of the research reviewed in this chapter, were addressed in a study by Fletcher, Satz, and Scholes (in press). A measure of syntactic comprehension was administered to good and poor readers at 5.5-, 8.5-, and 11-year mean age levels. The 5.5-year-old groups were composed of children ($N = 40$) who received the syntactic measure in kindergarten, with groups formed 3 years later at the end of Grade 2. The 8.5- and 11-year-old children (disabled and nondisabled readers), were selected according to similar criteria.

The syntactic comprehension measure, presented in Table 10.1, comprised a set of sentences assessing the child's ability to understand the relationship of direct and indirect objects. The child heard the sentence and was asked to select a picture depicting the correct relationship of direct and indirect object. Several different grammatical forms of each base sentence (Reading I and Reading II) were used. Several studies with normal children revealed that the capacity of the child to comprehend these forms varies with age (Scholes, 1978). For example, children attain proficiency on Reading II sentences much earlier than on Reading I sentences. Because Reading I and II sentences can be represented by pictures that do not differ in the major lexical items, incorrect picture selection implies inaccurate processing of the sentence structure. The results of this study revealed an age × group interaction showing group differences between disabled and nondisabled readers only at age 11. There was no evidence for ceiling or floor effects. Furthermore, the degree to which the different linguistic forms contributed to this interaction corresponded almost exactly with the developmental sequence of acquisition defined by the studies on normal children. In this respect, no differences were apparent on linguistic forms that developed earlier. Rather, group differences were apparent only on linguistic forms with a later development. This finding is consistent with research suggesting that the use of higher order linguis-

TABLE 10.1
Examples of Stimulus Sentences for Double-Object Comprehension Test (DOCT)

Reading	Clue	Sentence
I	B	*He showed pictures to the girls' baby.*
I	A	*He showed the girl's baby the pictures.*
I	D	*He showed the girl's baby / pictures.*
I	AT	*It's the girl's baby the pictures were shown to.*
I	DT	*It's the girl's baby / pictures were shown to.*
II	B	*He showed baby pictures to the girls.*
II	A	*He showed the girls the baby pictures.*
II	D	*He showed the girls / baby pictures.*
II	AT	*It's the girls the baby pictures were shown to.*
II	DT	*It's the girls / baby pictures were shown to.*
Ambiguous		*He showed the girls baby pictures.*

tic attributes for reading is more characteristic of older children (Doehring, 1976; Gibson & Levin, 1975).

Semantic Organizational Constraints

Several studies have investigated the role of conceptual–semantic organization in facilitating short-term retention of disabled and nondisabled readers. These studies are reminiscent of Clay and Imlach (1973), who manipulated variables more syntactic in nature. Freston and Drew (1974) provided a group of disabled readers (mean age about 11 years) with free recall lists of paradigmatic associations. These lists were either unorganized or organized via retrieval cues (conceptual categories) embedded within the list. Material organization had no effect on recall. Parker, Freston, and Drew (1975) expanded this experiment by including a control group. Free recall lists were again provided to reading groups (mean age about 10 years) and two variables were manipulated: material organization and difficulty level. Although difficulty level influenced performance for both groups, material organization facilitated recall only for the control group.

A study by Waller (1976) employed a semantic integration task (Paris & Carter, 1973) to explore differences in sentence recognition memory between fifth grade reading groups. Each subject read a series of "acquisition" sentences. After an interference task, a recognition test composing either original sentences or different transformations of the acquisition sentences was presented. The child was required to respond yes or no if he recognized the sentence as being identical to the original acquisition sentence. No group differences were observed if the new sentence was a true or false premise, or a false inference. If the sentence was a true inference, that is, derived directly from the acquisition list, or if it changed number or tense, poor readers performed more poorly.

Three studies (Golinkoff & Rosinski, 1976; Pace & Golinkoff, 1976; Rosinski, Golinkoff, & Kukish, 1975) summarized in Golinkoff (1975–1976), are quite pertinent here. These studies employed good and poor comprehenders in Grades 3 and 5. Single word access was measured with a series of picture–word interference tasks and timed sets of decoding tests. Interference tasks required children to label common pictures as rapidly as possible while ignoring printed words and trigrams superimposed on the pictures. Group differences were obtained on the decoding tasks, but the effects of semantic interference were equal for the two groups. Rosinski et al. (1975) interpreted these results as indicating that decoding and semantic access skills are independent, with minimal decoding skills required for accessing single word meanings. Golinkoff (1975–1976) summarized these findings by noting that "poor comprehenders may readily obtain the meaning of common printed words [p. 639]." However, Perfetti (1977) found fifth grade poor readers to be deficient on other types of semantic skills (e.g., semantic categorization). This suggests that, along with deficiencies in semantic knowledge, poor comprehenders are less proficient in the use of semantic cues than are good comprehenders.

Conclusions: Age-Dependent Relationships

Some evidence is apparent for age-dependent relationships in the development of the child's capacity for processing the linguistic attributes of oral and written language. In terms of the size of the unit, children clearly learn to process larger units of information over time. In this way, reading strategies change from those necessary for decoding single words to strategies necessary for comprehending meaning from groups of words. Different linguistic attributes, however, are involved in decoding and comprehension. The proficient decoder utilizes information contained in the graphological, phonological, and orthographic correlates of letters and words. The proficient comprehender, however, minimizes these sources of information, relying instead on high-order sources of linguistic redundancy embedded in print. This evidence is derived from studies of both oral and written language attribute processing.

Age-dependent relationships emerge most clearly when performance is compared between good and poor readers. In younger reading groups, the oral and written language patterns of disabled readers reflect the use of smaller units that are characteristic of beginning reading. Differences in the use of higher order units of information are less apparent. For older readers, the oral and written language patterns of disabled readers reflect difficulties with the use of higher-order sources of invariance (syntactic and semantic units) and with more complex intraword redundancies.

It should be noted that few of the studies interpreted as showing developmental changes were designed to test this hypothesis. In addition, major methodological differences were apparent among these studies, including the criteria for forming reading groups, age of the groups, and type of task employed. Nonetheless, the few cross-sectional and longitudinal studies included in this review did reveal evidence for developmental changes in the linguistic performance correlates of reading achievement. There are additional cross-sectional studies of the relationship of other cognitive skills with reading achievement that also provide evidence for developmental changes (Satz & Fletcher, 1980).

The importance of the developmental change issue has to do with the clear illustration that good and poor readers change with age. Consequently, those studies that form single groups combining children across several ages may have inherent flaws because of the failure to adequately control for age differences. Furthermore, the age variable should be manipulated so that the process of change can be studied. The value of the manipulation is that factors related to change (i.e., rate, sequence, and degree of development) can be studied, shedding light on the acquisitional process. This type of research emphasis could lead to a model of the developing reader with clear implications for understanding reading failure. The next section presents a simplistic and heuristic model that incorporates the developmental change data reviewed in this chapter into a more general characterization of the developing reader.

Similar Sequence Model of the Developing Reader

Zigler (1969) presented a model of cognitive development addressing performance differences between familially retarded and nonretarded children. This model, based on the "similar sequence hypothesis" (Weitz & Zigler, 1979) suggests that these children differ primarily in terms of their *rate* and absolute *level* of cognitive development. The sequence of acquisition is predicted to be invariant between groups, such that retarded and nonretarded children at the same stage of cognitive development should not differ in performance on other measures of cognitive development. Consequently, familially based retardation represents a normal variation in cognitive development. Theories positing that cognitive organization was fundamentally *different* in these children were contrasted with this *developmental* model, which does not view cognitive performance differences as *deficits* implying defective cognitive organization in these children.

Zigler (1969) described his model as follows:

> Employing a stage or levels approach to cognitive development, the normal variation viewpoint generated in my thinking the rather parsimonious view that the cognitive development of the familially retarded is characterized by a slower

progression through the same sequence of cognitive stages (a rate phenomenon) and a more limited upper stage of cognition (a levels phenomenon) than is characteristic of the individual of average intellect [p. 537].

Figure 10.1 provides a representation of the similar sequence model. Three intellectual outcomes are presented, each representing a different rate of cognitive development. Whereas the overall *level* of development is different for each outcome, the *sequence* of development is the same, regardless of outcome. Consequently, *same aged* comparisons of retarded and nonretarded individuals will inevitably produce cognitive performance differences because the groups are at different stages of development. Matching different aged retarded and nonretarded children at the same developmental stage should reduce cognitive performance differences. Weitz and Zigler (1979) reviewed 3 longitudinal and 28 cross-sectional studies of Piagetan developmental phenomena in retarded and nonretarded children. They concluded that "while more information is needed, . . . it seems clear from our review that evidence from the 31 studies currently available offers consistent support for the similar sequence hypothesis [p. 848]."

Attempts to characterize the disabled reader have invariably involved variations of developmental versus deficit theories that underlie Zigler's (1969) model. For example, Cromer (1970) described four models of the disabled reader: defect, deficit, disruption, and difference. Cromer noted that most reading disability research employs a *deficit* model that explains poor reading as "the absence of an ability which must be added before adequate reading can occur [p. 471]." In contrast, the *difference* model explains poor reading in terms of "a mismatch

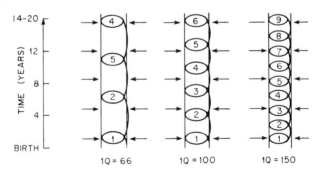

FIGURE 10.1 *Developmental model of cognitive growth. The single vertical arrow represents the passage of time. The horizontal arrows represent environmental events impinging on the individual who is represented as a pair of vertical lines. The individual's cognitive development appears as an internal ascending spiral, in which the numbered loops represent sucessive stages of cognitive growth (Zigler, 1969).*

between the individual's typical mode of responding and the pattern of responding assumed necessary for adequate reading to occur [p. 471]." One interpretation of a difference model is that a poor reader may not possess the cognitive skills necessary to master age-appropriate levels of instructional curriculum. More recently, Rourke (1976) evaluated evidence for developmental lag theories of reading disabilities. Rourke concluded that, although some evidence supported the developmental lag theory, especially for earlier developing skills, the preponderance of evidence supported a deficit model in which "catching up" was not apparent.

Rourke (1976) emphasized the question of whether disabled readers eventually attained age-appropriate levels of performance in reading and reading-related skills. While this is one component of a developmental model, the implications of Zigler (1969) suggest that other factors must be considered when making chronological age comparisons of good and poor readers. Three sets of component hypotheses can be evaluated for developmental versus deficit characterizations of the developing reader pertaining to (a) chronological age comparisons; (b) degree of development; and (c) reading level comparisons.

The chronological age component predicts that cognitive performance differences will emerge on any comparison of same-aged disabled and nondisabled children. However, a similar sequence model predicts that the magnitude of these differences will vary with chronological age according to the developmental rate of the attribute processed. Figure 10.1 shows that any comparison of same-age disabled and nondisabled readers will produce differences because the two groups develop at different rates. However, older children will be at different developmental stages, such that comparisons between older and younger reading groups will yield differences varying in magnitude.

The degree of development component addresses catching-up phenomena emphasized by Rourke (1976). A similar sequence model predicts that in the absence of a limited upper level of development, disabled readers will ultimately attain age-appropriate achievement levels. Figure 10.1 shows how the degree of development component could explain why some poor readers do not catch up. The rate of development is hypothesized to diminish over time, with stability appearing in adolescence. Consequently, disabled readers would not be expected to acquire age-appropriate achievement levels because sufficient development would not occur prior to the onset of stability.

The reading level component compares older disabled and younger normal readers. A similar sequence model predicts no differences in cognitive performance when older disabled and younger normal children are matched for reading level. This hypothesis is similar to Zigler's (1969) contention that familial retarded and nonretarded children matched on mental age will have corresponding levels of cognitive development, hence reducing performance differences on cognitive tasks.

Research on reading disabled children can be employed to test each of these component hypotheses. This research helps evaluate the utility of a similar sequence model of the developing reader, with direct application to reading failure.

Chronological Age Component

Much of the literature reviewed in this chapter provided evidence for age-dependent relationships predicted by this component. However, few of these studies employed cross-sectional and longitudinal designs necessary for an adequate test of this component. One exception comes from the Florida Longitudinal Project (Satz, Taylor, Friel, & Fletcher, 1978). The Florida Longitudinal Project was a 7-year longitudinal study of reading achievement that followed large samples of white males entering kindergarten in 1970 and 1971 until Grade 5 (1976 and 1977). Neuropsychological and cognitive measures were obtained at the beginning of kindergarten and at the end of Grades 2 and 5. Achievement criteria were also selected concurrently at the end of Grades 2 and 5. Fletcher and Satz (1980) employed data from the Florida Longitudinal Project to test two developmental change hypotheses. Hypothesis 1 predicted that measures of earlier developing skills important for beginning reading (sensorimotor–perceptual) contribute more to variation of reading achievement at younger ages (5–7) than at older ages (10–12). Hypothesis 2 predicted that measures of later developing skills important for more advanced phases of reading acquisition (verbal–conceptual) contribute more to variation of reading achievement at older ages (10–12) than at younger ages (5–7). Results based on repeat assessments of the same children over time were in substantial agreement with these hypotheses. Factorial measures of sensorimotor–perceptual skills accounted for more of the predictive variation of reading achievement at younger ages (e.g., kindergarten to Grade 5). In contrast, factorial measures of verbal–conceptual skills accounted for more of the concurrent variation of reading achievement at older ages (e.g., Grade 5 performance–Grade 5 criteria). These results emerged despite clear univariate differences between groups at each age assessed, providing strong support for developmental change and the first component of the model.

Degree of Development

This component predicts that disabled readers eventually attain age-appropriate achievement levels. Follow-up studies clearly show that few children with reading problems earlier in life attain age appropriate achievement levels later in school (Rourke, 1976; Satz et al., 1978). It might be speculated that continued poor achievement reflects the secondary effects of academic failure such as poor self-esteem, reduced motivation, and alienation. Consequently, catching up may occur only on reading-related skills that do not directly measure reading. Fennell and Satz (1979) tested this hypothesis with data from the Florida Longitudinal Project. Results revealed no evidence for catching up except on measures with ceiling effects. Interestingly, the results of the Fletcher and Satz (1980) study also held for this analysis. Consequently, although disabled readers clearly acquired cognitive skills more slowly than normal readers, the nature and extent of performance differences could be predicted according to their sequence of acquisition.

Reading Level Component

More direct evaluation of the similar sequence model requires confirmation of the reading level component. If disabled readers differ in rate but not in sequence of acquisition, older disabled children should display cognitive performance patterns similar to those characteristic of younger normal children. Consequently, older disabled and younger normal children matched on reading level should display similar patterns on other reading-related skills.

Research by Guthrie (1973); Guthrie and Tyler (1975); Guthrie and Seifert (1977); and Steinhauser and Guthrie (1977) addresses this possibility. In each study, matching older disabled and younger normal children diminished group differences on nonreading tasks. For example, Guthrie (1973) showed that reading disabled children differed from both reading level matched younger controls and age matched controls in oral reading comprehension. However, differences were not apparent between younger controls and disabled readers on the use of syntactic and semantic cues during silent reading and in the pattern of reading errors. Guthrie and Tyler (1975) compared groups composed of younger normal and older disabled readers matched on reading comprehension scores. The tasks measured comprehension of syntactic and semantic clues in oral and written sentences. Whereas results revealed comprehension differences in written language, there were no oral language differences.

Both of these studies show that group differences between younger normal and older disabled readers are apparent in written language but not in oral language. A third study (Guthrie & Seifert, 1977) further clarified this relationship with a longitudinal study of the acquisition of letter–sound correspondence rules in good and poor readers in the first, second, and third grades. Children were matched only on reading level, so that the disabled reader group (age = 9.35 years) was substantially older than the control group (age = 6.3 years). During the course of the year, children were evaluated three times with different word identification tasks. Results revealed a definite sequence in the acquisition of letter–sound correspondence rules based on the complexity of the rules. For our purposes, the important finding was that "Good and poor readers manifested similar developmental phases [p. 695]." In other words, the developmental sequence governing the acquisition of these rules was similar. Both groups acquired simpler rules before they learned more complex rules, although disabled readers acquired the rules more slowly.

Neuropsychological Implications of the Model: Integrating Research Areas

The neuropsychologist may experience some difficulty with this model of the developing reader. This difficulty may stem from two factors. The first is the assumption that performance differences between disabled and nondisabled readers represent normal variations of the acquisition process. The second is the emphasis on cognitive development as opposed to an emphasis on the nature of disordered brain functioning characterizing disabled readers. These two areas of difficulty are related because the assumption of normal variation implies that the organization of the central nervous system of disabled readers is less mature than that of normal readers at a given age, but not fundamentally different. Reading disability research in general employs a deficit model (Doehring, 1978; Satz & Fletcher, 1980), with neuropsychologists typically inferring disordered brain functioning in terms of a deficit model (e.g., Denckla, 1979).

The assumption that reading disabilities represent normal variations in the acquisitional process represents a fundamental limitation of the model. Meeting this assumption for all readers is not likely because some reading disabilities probably reflect different types of disordered brain functioning that has yet to be specified (Rourke, 1975, 1978). However, it is not likely that either a traditional maturational lag theory (Satz *et al.*, 1978) or a cerebral dysfunction theory (Denckla, 1979) will provide an adequate conceptualization of the brain mechanisms that underlie reading disabilities. There is little support for traditional formulations of the maturational lag theory, especially in view of the absence of catching-up phenomenon. At the same time, the presence of developmental changes suggests that cerebral dysfunction theories making reference to adult neurological syndromes (e.g., aphasia) inadequately characterize the disabled reader. Indeed, the major value of the developmental model presented in this chapter is in showing that the possible types of disordered brain functioning should not be represented as a *deficit*, particularly if reference to an adult neurological model is made. In most children with learning problems, cerebral lesions and *hard* neurological signs are not apparent. In addition, neurological maturation continues in these children, evidenced in part by resolution of *soft* neurological signs (Satz & Fletcher, 1980) and by developmental changes in neuropsychological and cognitive tasks (Fletcher & Satz, 1980; Rourke, 1975, 1976). Finally, the time at which the disorder in brain function is induced may not coincide with the emergence of the reading problem, suggesting continued maturation and the possible development of compensatory mechanisms interacting between these two events. Summarily, neuropsychological models of reading disabilities based on the maturational lag theory or on an application of the traditional concept of deficit inadequately characterize the developing reader. Deficit models based on adult brain function may be particularly misleading because of the problem of developmental change.

These problems highlight one advantage of assuming that performance differences between disabled and nondisabled readers represent normal variations in the acquisition process. By studying disabled readers from a normal acquisition viewpoint, changes over time become a primary consideration. The similar sequence model, with its emphasis on rate, sequence, and degree of development, may provide a heuristic framework for studying developmental brain–behavior relationships in learning-disabled children. Understanding rate, sequence, and degree of development implies reference to normal acquisition, if only to specify cognitive skills that have not adequately developed. The nature of these breakdowns in the acquisitional process may help suggest brain mechanisms underlying reading failure.

Reference to several areas of research on the reading process, reading acquisition, and reading failure must be made in order to understand reading disabilities. Unfortunately, these areas of research tend to be treated independently. Research on the reading process usually employs fluent readers, whereas most reading acquisition research deals with normal children. Reading disability research is often vaguely conceptualized, relating neither to a model of the reading process nor to a model of reading acquisition.

The research on linguistic attributes in reading acquisition reviewed in this chapter may help to clarify the different trusts of these research areas. Most reading disability research deals only with *stimulus information* (i.e., performance differences as a function of the linguistic and visuospatial attributes embedded in a task). For example, performance differences on a syntactic comprehension test between disabled and nondisabled readers specifies only the nature of the linguistic attribute that disabled readers process less proficiently. Extrapolation to a theory of reading disabilities by invoking a *syntactic deficit* or more general *language deficit* (Vellutino, 1977) is a precarious inference. However, relating the disabled reader's difficulty processing syntactic information to another cognitive construct (e.g., short-term memory) provides a less precarious inference.

Models of the reading process commonly produce *process* statements that can be used to generate hypotheses about how stimulus attributes are processed. In relating stimuli and processes, it is critical to specify the role of the stimulus in the reading process and the nature of those strategies necessary to process the attribute. The work of Liberman and Shankweiler (1976) provides an example of this integration. Disabled readers clearly have difficulty with phonemic segments (stimulus attributes) that interfere with acoustic storage in short-term memory (process). Neither stimulus nor process statements explain *why* some children can and others cannot process the information. These kinds of statements require some mechanism within the child that mediates stimulus attributes and processes. In terms of reading acquisition, this statement must specify relationships between patterns of reading behavior and patterns on correlated measures, explaining why these sets of patterns occur in the same child. Neuropsychological research may help to specify these mechanisms, as an organismic theory of the child is implied. However, neuropsychological research on reading retardation has emphasized the presence of deficits that do not seem related to the reading process, suggesting that reading disabilities are more than disorders in reading (Rourke, 1975; Satz et al., 1978). This occurrence may be meaningless without reference to the reading process. It is also possible that these deficits are related in a currently unspecified way, in part because the tasks demonstrating them are also sensitive to reading-related skills (Doehring, 1978).

Nonetheless, neuropsychological models of the disabled reader provide examples of the types of theories necessary to explain why some children do not learn to read.

Research in these areas is constantly changing, with new theories suggesting different interpretations of previous research. However, this type of strategy has characterized aphasiological research, where cognitive and neuropsychological interests have long overlapped. Indeed, the development of more appropriate models of the developing reader may take a page from aphasiology. Aphasiological research proceeds by defining the nature of the linguistic attribute that can (or cannot) be processed. A hypothetical model of language processing is invoked to explain how the attribute is processed. Explaining why the person is aphasic requires an anatomical model of the brain and an information-processing model of language representations in the brain. Research in reading acquisition and reading failure may benefit from such an approach. Rourke (1978) and Satz and Morris (1980) summarized considerable evidence showing that there are a variety of forms of reading proficiency and reading failure. Relating performance differences between subtypes of reading ability to an information-processing model of the reader may lead to hypotheses about differences in CNS functioning among subtypes. These hypotheses could be evaluated with neuropsychological and electrophysiological techniques (Benton, 1978).

For reading achievement, these hypotheses should be based on developmental research on cognitive development and neurological maturation. Reading failure may well represent different types of cerebral dysfunction (Rourke, 1975). However, explanations on the basis of an adult model of brain function will be insufficient to incorporate the general phenomenon of developmental change. The model outlined in this chapter helps to illustrate why theories of reading disabilities based on unitary deficits are inadequate characterizations of disabled readers (e.g., Vellutino, 1977). Furthermore, comparison studies of good and poor reader groups composed of heterogeneously aged children are likely to distort research outcomes. More appropriate comparisons stem from comparisons over time, incorporating appropriate longitudinal and cross-sectional designs. Moreover, multivariate correlational methods will be necessary to demonstrate developmental phenomena. The continued reliance on simplistic analysis of variance methodology, inherent in the search for unitary deficits, is not likely to shed light on the mechanisms underlying reading failure (Doehring, 1978; Satz & Fletcher, 1980). Each of these closing points underlie the study of change (Wohlwill, 1973), inherent in the application of a developmental neuropsychological model to the problems of reading acquisition and reading failure.

References

Baron, J. Phonemic stage not necessary for reading. *Quarterly Journal of Experimental Psychology*, 1973, *25*, 241–246.

Benton, A. L. Dyslexia in relation to form perception and directional sense. In J. Money (Ed.), *Reading disability: Progress and research needs in dyslexia*. Baltimore, Md.: Johns Hopkins Press, 1962.

Benton, A. L. Some conclusions about dyslexia. In A. L. Benton & D. Pearl (Eds.), *Dyslexia: An appraisal of current knowledge*. New York: Oxford University Press, 1978.

Berger, N. S. Listening and reading skills. *Journal of Learning Disabilities*, 1978, *11*, 633–638.

Biemuller, A. The development of the use of graphic and contextual information in children learning to read. *Reading Research Quarterly*, 1970–1971, *6*, 75–96.

Bloom, L. Language development. In F. D. Horowitz (Ed.), *Review of child development research (Vol 4)*. Chicago: University of Chicago Press, 1975.

Bougere, M. B. Selected factors in oral language related to first-grade reading achievement. *Reading Research Quarterly*, 1969–1970, *5*, 31–38.

Bradshaw, J. L. Three interrelated problems in reading: A review. *Memory and Cognition*, 1975, *3*, 124–134.

Calfee, R., Lindamood, P., and Lindamood, C. Acoustic–phonetic skills and reading—Kindergarten through twelfth grade. *Journal of Educational Psychology*, 1973, *64*, 293.

Calfee, R., Venezky, R., and Chapman, R. *Pronunciation of synthetic words with predictable and unpredictable letter–sound correspondences*. Technical Report No. 71, Wisconsin Research and Development Center for Cognitive Learning, 1969.

Calvert, K. An investigation of the relationship between the syntactic maturity of oral language and reading comprehension scores. *Dissertation Abstracts International*, 1973, *33B*, 4838–4839.

Clay, M. M., & Imlach, R. H. Juncture, pitch, and stress as reading behavior variables. *Journal of Verbal Learning and Verbal Behavior*, 1971, *10*, 133–139.

Cromer, W. The difference model: A new explanation for some reading difficulties. *Journal of Educational Psychology*, 1970, *61*, 471–483.

Denckla, M. B. Childhood learning disabilities. In K. M. Heilman & E. Valenstein (Eds.), *Clinical Neuropsychology*. New York: Oxford University Press, 1979.

Doehring, D. G. Acquisition of rapid reading responses. *Monographs of the Society for Research in Child Development*, 1976, *41*, 1–54.

Doehring, D. G. Comprehension of printed sentences by children with reading disability. *Bulletin of the Psychonomic Society*, 1977, *10*, 350–352.

Doehring, D. G. The tangled web of behavioral research on developmental dyslexia. In A. L. Benton & D. Pearl (Eds.), *Dyslexia: An appraisal of current knowledge* New York: Oxford University Press, 1978.

Doehring, D. G. and Hoshko, I. M. A developmental study of the speed of comprehension of printed sentences. *Bulletin of the Psychonomic Society*, 1977, *9*, 311–313.

Dumas, M. R. An investigation of the relationship between reading disabilities and syntax and the temporal aspects of that relationship. *Dissertation Abstracts International,* 1976, *37A,* 3549.

Falk, J. W. A comparison of the comprehension of syntax in spoken language by poor and average prereaders in first grade and poor and average readers in second grade. *Dissertation Abstracts International,* 1977, 37A, 4921–4922.

Fennell, E., & Satz, P. A longitudinal test of the lag theory of developmental dsylexia. Paper presented at the Seventh Annual Meeting of the International Neuropsychological Society, New York, February, 1979.

Fischer, F. W., Liberman, I. Y., & Shankweiler, D. Reading reversals and developmental dyslexia: A further study. *Cortex,* 1978, *14,* 496–510.

Fletcher, J. M., & Satz, P. Unitary deficit hypotheses of reading disabilities: Has Vellutino led us astray? *Journal of Learning Disabilities,* 1979, *12,* 155–159. (a)

Fletcher, J. M., & Satz, P. Has Vellutino led us astray? A rejoinder to a reply. *Journal of Learning Disabilities,* 1979, *12,* 168–171. (b)

Fletcher, J. M., & Satz, P. Developmental changes in the neuropsychological correlates of reading achievement: A six-year longitudinal follow-up. *Journal of Clinical Neuropsychology,* 1980, *2,* in press.

Fletcher, J. M., Satz, P., & Scholes, R. J. Developmental changes in the linguistic performance correlates of reading achievement. *Brain and Language,* in press.

Fowler, C. A., Liberman, I. Y., & Shankweiler, D. Interpreting the error pattern in beginning reading. *Language and Speech,* 1977, *20,* 162–173.

Freston, C. W., & Drew, C. S. Verbal performance of learning disabled children as a function of input organization. *Journal of Learning Disabilities,* 1974, *7,* 424–425.

Fry, M. A., Johnson, C. S., & Muehl, S. Oral language production in relation to reading achievement among select second graders. In D. J. Bakker & P. Satz (Eds.), *Specific reading disability; Advances in theory and method.* Rotterdam: Rotterdam Univ. Press, 1970.

Gibson, E. J., & Levin, H. *The psychology of reading.* Cambridge, Massachusetts: MIT Press, 1975.

Golinkoff, R. M. A comparison of reading comprehension processes in good and poor readers. *Reading Research Quarterly,* 1975–1976, *11,* 623–659.

Golinkoff, R. M., & Rosinski, R. R. Decoding, semantic processing, and reading comprehension skill. *Child Development,* 1976, *47,* 252–258.

Guthrie, J. T. Reading comprehension and syntactic responses in good and poor readers. *Journal of Educational Psychology,* 1973, *65,* 294–299.

Guthrie, J. T., & Seifert, M. Letter–sound complexity in learning to identify words. *Journal of Educational Psychology,* 1977, *69,* 686–696.

Guthrie, J. T., & Tyler, S. J. Psycholinguistic processing in reading and listening among good and poor readers. *Journal of Reading Behavior,* 1975, *8,* 415–426.

Hagen, J. W., Jongeward, R. H., & Kail, R. V. Cognitive perspectives on the development of memory. In H. W. Reese (Ed.), *Advances in child development and behavior* (vol. 10). New York: Academic Press, 1975.

Harris, M. M. Second grade syntax attainment and reading achievement. *Dissertation Abstracts International* 1975, *35A,* 7635.

Helfgott, J. Phonemic segmentation and blending skills of kindergarten children: Implications for beginning reading acquisition. *Contempory Educational Psychology,* 1976, *1,* 157–169.

Hensley, B. The relationship of selected oral language, perceptual, demographic, and intellectual factors to the reading achievement of good, average, and poor first grade reading groups. *Southern Journal of Educational Research,* 1974, *8,* 258–271.

Isakson, R. L., & Miller, J. W. Sensitivity to syntactic and semantic cues in good and poor comprehenders. *Journal of Educational Psychology,* 1976, *68,* 787–792.

Katz, L., & Wicklund, D. A. Word scanning rate for good and poor readers. *Journal of Educational Psychology*, 1971, *62*, 138–140.

Katz, L., & Wicklund, D. A. Letter scanning rate for good and poor readers in grades 2 and 6. *Journal of Educational Psychology*, 1972, *63*, 363–367.

Kuntz, M. H. The relationship between written syntactic attainment and reader ability in seventh grade. *Dissertation Abstracts International*, 1975, *35A*, 2159.

LaBerge, D., & Samuels, S. J. Towards a theory of automatic information processing in reading. *Cognitive Psychology*, 1974, *6*, 293–323.

Lee, L. *Northwestern Syntax Screening Test.* Evanston, Illinois: Northwestern Univ. Press, 1971.

Lee, L., & Canter, S. Developmental sentence scoring: A clinical procedure for estimating syntactic development in children's spontaneous speech. *Journal of Speech and Hearing Disorders*, 1971, *36*, 315–337.

Liberman, I. Y., & Shankweiler, D. Speech, the alphabet, and teaching to read. In L. Resnick & P. Weaver (Eds.), *Theory and practice of early reading.* Hillsdale, New Jersey: Earlbaum, 1976.

Liberman, I. Y., Shankweiler, D., Fischer, F. W., & Carter, B. Explicit syllable recognition and phoneme segmentation in the young child. *Journal of Experimental Child Psychology*, 1974, *18*, 201–212.

Liberman, I. Y., Shankweiler, D., Liberman, A. M., Fowler, C., & Fischer, F. W. Phonetic segmentation and recoding in the beginning reader. In A. S. Reber & D. Scarborough (Eds.), *Reading: Theory and practice.* Hillsdale, New Jersey: Earlbaum, 1977.

Little, L. J. A study of the relationship between syntactic development and oral reading substitution miscues of average and disabled readers. *Dissertation Abstracts International*, 1975, *35A*, 5971.

Mahaffey, J. P. An investigation of the relationship between selected oral language and readiness factors to first-grade reading achievement. *Dissertation Abstracts International*, 1975, *36A*, 695.

Mark, L. *Phonetic recoding and reading difficulty in beginning readers.* Unpublished master's thesis, University of Connecticut, 1977.

Mason, M. Reader ability and letter search time: Effect of orthographic structure defined by single letter positional frequency. *Journal of Experimental Psychology*, 1975, *104*, 146–166.

Mason, M., Katz, L., & Wicklund, D. Immediate spatial order memory and item memory in sixth grade children as a function of reader ability. *Journal of Educational Psychology*, 1975, *67*, 610–616.

Meyer, D. E., Schvaneveldt, R. W., & Ruddy, M. G. Functions of graphemic and phonemic codes in visual word-recognition. *Memory and Cognition*, 1974, *2*, 309–321.

Oakan, R., Weiner, M., & Cromer, W. Identification, organization, and reading comprehension for good and poor readers. *Journal of Educational Psychology*, 1971, *62*, 71–78.

Pace, A. J., & Golinkoff, R. M. Relationship between word difficulty and access of single-word meanings by skilled and less skilled readers. *Journal of Educational Psychology*, 1976, *68*, 760–767.

Parker, T. B., Freston, C. W., & Drew, C. J. Comparison of verbal performance of normal and learning disabled children, *Journal of Learning Disabilities*, 1975, *8*, 53–60.

Paris, S., & Carter, A. Semantic and constructive aspects of sentence memory in children. *Developmental Psychology*, 1973, *9*, 109–113.

Perfetti, C. A. *Reading comprehension depends on language comprehension.* Paper presented at the Annual Meeting of the American Educational Research Association, San Francisco, 1977.

Perfetti, C. A., & Hogaboam, O. T. The relationship between single word decoding and reading comprehension skill. *Journal of Educational Psychology*, 1975, *67*, 461–469.

Rabinovitch, M. S., & Strassberg, R. Syntax and retention in good and poor readers. *The Canadian Psychologist*, 1968, *9*, 142–153.

Rayner, K. Developmental changes in word recognition strategies. *Journal of Educational Psychology*, 1976, *68*, 323–329.

Rayner, K., & Hagelberg, E. M. Word recognition cues for beginning and skilled readers. *Journal of Experimental Child Psychology*, 1975, *20*, 444–455.

Rayner, K., & Kaiser, J. S. Reading mutilated text. *Journal of Educational Psychology*, 1975, *67*, 301–306.

Ribovitch, J. K. First grade children's comprehension of selected oral language syntax and its relationship to reading comprehension. *Dissertation Abstracts International*, 1975, *36A*, 3391.

Rode, S. S. Development of phrase and clause boundary reading in children. *Reading Research Quarterly*, 1974–1975, *10*, 124–142.

Rosinski, R. R., Golinkoff, R. M., & Kukish, K. S. Automatic semantic processing in a picture–word interference task. *Child Development*, 1975, *46*, 247–253.

Rosinski, R. R., & Wheeler, K. E. Children's use of orthographic structure in word discrimination. *Psychonomic Science*, 1972, *26*, 97–98.

Rourke, B. P. Brain–behavior relationships in children with learning disabilities. *The American Psychologist*, 1975, *30*, 911–920.

Rourke, B. P. Reading retardation in children: Developmental lag or deficit. In R. Knights & D. J. Bakker (Eds.), *The neuropsychology of learning disorders: Theoretical approaches*. Baltimore: University Park Press, 1976.

Rourke, B. P. Reading, spelling, and arithmetical disabilities: A neuropsychological perspective. In H. Myklebust (Ed.), *Progress in learning disabilities* (vol. 4). New York: Grune & Stratton, 1978.

Rubenstein, H., Lewis, S. S., & Rubenstein, M. A. Evidence for phonemic recoding in visual word recognition. *Journal of Verbal Learning and Verbal Behavior*, 1971, *10*, 645–657.

Saffran, E. M., & Marin, O. S. M. Reading without phonology: Evidence from aphasia. *Quarterly Journal of Experimental Psychology*, 1977, *29*, 515–525.

Samuels, S. J., Begy, G., & Chen, C. Comparison of word recognition speed and strategies of less skilled and more highly skilled readers. *Reading Research Quarterly*, 1976–1977, *11*, 72–86.

Santa, C. M. Spelling patterns and the development of flexible word recognition strategies. *Reading Research Quarterly* 1976–1977, *12*, 125–144.

Satz, P., & Fletcher, J. M. Minimal brain dysfunction: An appraisal of research concepts and methods. In H. Rie & E. Rie (Eds.), *Handbook of minimal brain dysfunctions: A Critical View*. New York: Wiley, 1980.

Satz, P., Taylor, H. G., Friel, J., & Fletcher, J. M. Some developmental and predictive precursors of reading disabilities: A six year follow-up. In A. L. Benton & D. Pearl (Eds.), *Dyslexia: An appraisal of current knowledge*. New York and London: Oxford Univ. Press, 1978.

Sawyer, D. J. Intra-sentence grammatical constraints in readers' sampling of the visual display. *Journal of Educational Research*, 1976, *69*, 198–202.

Scholes, R. J. Syntactic and lexical aspects of sentence comprehension. In A. Caramazza & E. Zurif (Eds.), *The acquisition and breakdown of language*. Baltimore: John Hopkins Press, 1978.

Semel, E. S., & Wiig, E. H. Comprehension of syntactic structures and critical verbal elements by children with learning disabilities. *Journal of Learning Disabilities*, 1975, *8*, 46–58.

Shankweiler, D., & Liberman, I. Y. Misreading: A search for causes. In J. K. Kavanagh & I. G. Mattingly (Eds.), *Language by ear and by eye*. Cambridge, Massachusetts: MIT Press, 1972.

Shankweiler, D., & Liberman, I. Y. Exploring the relations between reading and speech. In R. M. Knights & D. J. Bakker (Eds.), *Neuropsychology of learning disorders: Theoretical approaches*. Baltimore: University Park Press, 1976.

Smith, F. *Understanding reading: A psycholinguistic analysis of reading and reading failure*. New York: Holt, 1971.

Steiner, R., Weiner, M., & Cromer, W. Comprehension training and identification for poor and good readers. *Journal of Educational Psychology*, 1971, *62*, 506–513.

Steinhauser, R., & Guthrie, J. T. Perceptual and lingusitic processing of letters and words by normal and disabled readers. *Journal of Reading Behavior*, 1977, *9*, 217–225.

Taylor, N. S. An investigation of selected grammatical and semantic structures and their relationship to reading achievement. *Dissertation Abstracts International*, 1977, *37A*, 4190.

Torgesen, J. K. Problems and prospects in the study of learning disabilities. In M. G. Hetherington (Ed.), *Review of child development research* (Vol. 5). Chicago: Univ. of Chicago Press, 1975.

Treiman, R. A. *Children's ability to segment speech into syllables and phonemes as related to their reading ability*. Unpublished manuscript, Department of Psychology, Yale University, 1977.

Underwood, B. J. Attributes of memory. *Psychological Review*, 1969, *76*, 559–577.

Vellutino, F. R. Alternative conceptualizations of dyslexia: Evidence in support of a verbal-deficit hypothesis. *Harvard Educational Review*, 1977, *44*, 334–354.

Vellutino, F. R., Smith, H., Steger, J., & Kaman, M. Reading disability: Age differences and the perceptual deficit hypothesis. *Child Development*, 1975, *46*, 487–493.

Venezky, R., & Johnson, D. Development of two letter–sound correspondences in grade one through grade three. *Journal of Educational Psychology*, 1973, *64*, 109–113.

Vogel, S. A. *Syntactic abilities in normal and dyslexic children*. Baltimore: University Park Press, 1975.

Waller, T. G. Children's recognition memory for written sentences: A comparison of good and poor readers. *Child Development*, 1976, *47*, 90–95.

Weber, R. M. First graders' use of grammatical context in reading. In H. Levin & J. P. Williams (Eds.), *Basic studies on reading*. New York: Basic Books, 1970.

Weinstein, R., & Rabinovitch, M. S. Sentence structure and retention in good and poor readers. *Journal of Educational Psychology*, 1971, *62*, 25–30.

Weitz, J. R., & Zigler, E. Cognitive development in retarded and nonretarded persons: Piagetian tests of the similar sequence hypothesis. *Psychological Bulletin*, 1979, *86*, 831–851.

Wiig, E. S. & Semel, F. H. *Language disabilities of school age children and adolescents*. Columbus, Ohio: Merrill, 1976.

Wisher, R. A. The effects of syntactic expectations during reading. *Journal of Educational Psychology*, 1976, *68*, 597–602.

Wohlwill, J. F. *The study of behavioral development*, New York: Academic Press, 1973.

Zifcak, M. *Phonological awareness and reading acquisition in first grade children*. Unpublished doctoral dissertation, University of Connecticut, 1976.

Zigler, E. Developmental versus difference theories of mental retardation and the problem of motivation. *American Journal of Mental Deficiency*, 1969, *73*, 536–556.

IV

READING
DISABILITIES

11

Alfonso Caramazza
Rita Sloan Berndt
John Hart

"AGRAMMATIC" READING[1]

The agrammatic speech of the Broca's aphasic is characterized by frequent omission of the grammatical morphemes of the language. Speech consists primarily of uninflected substantives—nouns, verbs, adjectives, and adverbs—uttered dysprosodically and articulated with difficulty. The general impression that these patients convey is that they have in mind precisely what they want to say, but have a great deal of difficulty saying it. Because the Broca patient's other language functions appear on clinical testing to be relatively intact, it is easy to understand why the "agrammatic" nature of their speech has been attributed to their effort to convey the largest share of information possible with the fewest number of "essential" words.

Recently, however, evidence has been accumulating that the problem that Broca's aphasics have with the grammatical function words (articles, auxiliary verbs, prepositions, and some pronouns) is not limited to their speech output. Zurif, Caramazza, and Myerson (1972) and Zurif, Green, Caramazza, and Goodenough (1976) have demonstrated that Broca's aphasics are impaired in their ability to perform metalinguistic judgments of sentence structure. Specifically, these patients present a faulty understanding of the organization of sentences that appears to be based on a failure to recognize the constituent-marking function of the grammatical morphemes. In addition, several

[1]The research reported here was supported by National Institute of Health Research Grant 16155 to Johns Hopkins University and National Institute of Health Research Grant 11408 to Boston University School of Medicine.

NEUROPSYCHOLOGICAL AND COGNITIVE
PROCESSES IN READING

studies have found a specific type of auditory comprehension deficit in Broca's aphasia that is apparent when the target sentence *requires* the patient to use a function word cue (or other syntactic means) to arrive at a correct interpretation (Blumstein, Statlender, Goodglass, & Biber, 1979; Caramazza & Zurif, 1976; Goodglass, Blumstein, Gleason, Hyde, Green, & Statlender, 1979; Heilman & Scholes, 1976; Schwartz, Saffran, & Marin, 1980).

The Broca patient's relative difficulty in producing grammatical morphemes in spontaneous speech is thus accompanied by a *receptive* agrammatism. That is, even when they require no expressive speech, tasks that rely on the grammatical morphemes appear to present problems to the Broca patient. We have attempted to account for this constellation of symptoms in Broca's aphasia by arguing that the patient's difficulties with function words are secondary to a deficit of syntactic processing abilities (Berndt & Caramazza, 1980). Focal damage to Broca's area comprises the patient's ability to perform syntactic analysis and thereby prevents effective syntactic interpretation of speech as well as the production of fully syntactic sentences. The function words and the bound grammatical morphemes, which serve a largely (if not entirely) syntactic function, are especially affected by disruption of the syntactic processing mechanism.

What are the implications of this hypothesis for the Broca patient's ability to read? With respect to comprehension of written sentences, the syntactic deficit hypothesis necessarily predicts a comprehension impairment similar to that found in the auditory modality. Comprehension should be faulty when the sentence *requires* syntactic analysis; that is, when it cannot be correctly interpreted simply by understanding the meanings of the major lexical items of the sentence. There is some evidence in support of this contention. Samuels and Benson (1979) report that a group of aphasic patients with anterior left hemisphere damage (which includes Broca's area) performed poorly on both auditory and visual administrations of two types of syntactically weighted tasks. Caramazza, Berndt, Basili, and Koller (in press) found that two Broca's aphasics (of different severity levels) produced a disproportionate number of errors to "syntactic" distractors in a sentence comprehension task regardless of whether it was administered aurally or visually. In addition, these two patients displayed a striking inability to construct syntactically acceptable sentences from sets of printed words. Both patients had great difficulty placing function words correctly in the sentences, and frequently produced bizarre combinations of one functor with another (e.g., article with auxiliary) or unacceptable juxtapositions of substantives and functors (e.g., noun followed by article). The limited data available suggest that there is no reason to believe that the patient's syntactic processing mechanism is selectively impaired such that reading comprehension is spared.

A related question is whether the Broca patient's ability to read words aloud will reflect this syntactic deficit. That is, it might be expected that words with an especially heavy syntactic weighting (the function words) will prove difficult to read aloud, just as they are more difficult for the Broca's aphasic to produce in spontaneous speech. However, if the patient is presented with lists of words, rather than sentences, it is difficult to see how a specifically syntactic deficit would interfere with his ability to read. The argument might be made that there is something faulty about the Broca patient's representation of function words as a lexical category. As these patients do not appear to be able to use function words efficiently in the performance of syntactic analysis in many types of tasks, it might be argued that the function word category is disrupted or is inaccessible. If this were the case, patients might be expected to have difficulty with the oral reading of a list of function words even though this task requires no syntactic analysis.

On the other hand, even if the lexical representation of function words could be shown to be faulty in Broca's aphasia, there might still be no reason to predict impaired oral reading performance. That is, a disruption of the function word lexicon should not prevent the patient from using grapheme-to-phoneme conversion rules (at least for orthographically "regular" words) to produce a verbal approximation of the word without contacting the lexicon (Coltheart, 1978). Although this method of reading aloud would not provide the patient with any "understanding" of the word being read, it would allow its successful articulation. As there is no reason to believe that these grapheme-to-phoneme conversion rules are disrupted in Broca's aphasia, the Broca patient should be able to read function words aloud without difficulty.

There is evidence, however, that at least some Broca's aphasics read agrammatically. Andreewsky and Seron (1975) report a case study of a French-speaking agrammatic patient who was unable to read unambiguous function words either in lists of words or in sentences. Similarly, Friederici and Schoenle (1980) tested an agrammatic patient who had great difficulty reading the function word members of homophone pairs (e.g., be) but could read quite well the substantive members of the pairs (e.g., bee). This patient was completely unable to read sentences. Despite these suggestive cases, it is not clear that agrammatic reading is a general characteristic of the Broca syndrome. Gardner and Zurif (1975) found that a group of 18 Broca's aphasics were not particularly impaired in their ability to read grammatical words. These patients read about 75% of function words correctly and performed slightly worse for abstract nouns and two categories of non-nouns.

The suggestion has been made that the occasional occurrence of agrammatic reading in Broca's aphasia is a reflection of the overlap of another (theoretically independent) symptom complex with the Broca syndrome (Schwartz, Saffran, & Marin, 1977). Some Broca patients (and other types of aphasic patients as well) present a reading disorder that has been called *deep* or *phonemic* dyslexia (Marshall & Newcombe, 1966, 1973; Shallice & Warrington, 1975). These patients cannot read function words orally and have difficulty in general reading abstract words. In addition, deep dyslexics find it very difficult to decode orthographically regular nonwords using grapheme-to-phoneme conversion rules (Patterson & Marcel, 1977). They have difficulty recognizing visually dissimilar rhyming words (*rough–cuff*), recognizing homophones (*where–wear*),and producing real words from homophonic spellings (*kween*) (Saffran & Marin, 1977). A cardinal feature of deep dyslexia is the production of semantic paralexias—reading errors that are semantically but not phonologically related to the target (Marshall & Newcombe, 1973).

This pattern of performance suggests that the deep dyslexic cannot transform graphemes to phonemes but, instead, accesses the lexicon directly from the grapheme without phonological recoding. This direct access route to the lexicon is presumably somewhat less constrained to particular lexical targets than is the phonological route, resulting in the occasional selection from the lexicon of incorrect but semantically related items. An important question within this framework that has not been resolved is why some words can trigger this direct access to the lexicon while other words cannot. That is, the argument is that concrete nouns and other substantives can be read because they can be accessed directly from the grapheme; abstract words (including function words) cannot be read because direct access is not possible and the grapheme-to-phoneme conversion system is not functioning. It has been suggested that there are different kinds of lexical representations for concrete and abstract words, with access to the abstract set available only through the phonological route (Shallice & Warrington, 1975). Several other bases have been suggested for this hypothesized dichotomy within the lexicon (Richardson, 1975; Schwartz et al., 1977), but as yet no compelling arguments have been offered to explain why this hypothesized division should exist. One suggestion has been made that the right hemisphere contributes in some way to the reading of the concrete words (Schwartz *et al.*, 1977), and there is some independent evidence that the right hemisphere has a limited capacity to read substantives (Ellis & Shepard, 1974; Hines, 1976).

Patients who present this deep dyslexic pattern of reading disorder will appear to read agrammatically when presented with lists of substantives and function words. However, their inability to read functors is part of a larger impairment of the ability to read abstract words in general and therefore may be unrelated to their agrammatic spontaneous speech, which we have argued results from a syntactic deficit. If further testing is not carried out to determine whether the other symptoms of deep dyslexia are present, it is impossible to know whether the agrammatic oral reading deficit is specific to the grammatical function words or is part of this larger problem with abstract words and grapheme-to-phoneme conversion. For example, the agrammatic reading performance of the patients reported by Andreewsky and Seron (1975) and by Friederici and Schoenle (1980), which is interpreted in both cases as a deficit limited to the grammatical function word class, might be a clue that these two patients are deep dyslexics. The relevant information for such a diagnosis (e.g., ability to read nonwords, production of semantic paralexias, etc.) is not available for these patients.

The incidence of overlap of the syndromes of Broca's aphasia and of deep dyslexia is not easy to estimate, as few studies of Broca patients include the types of tasks necessary to identify the reading disorder. Inspection of the 11 case reports of deep dyslexia in the literature[2] reveals that nine patients are described as producing agrammatic (or "telegraphic") spontaneous speech. In the two other cases, it was especially noted that spontaneous speech, though somewhat hesitant, was syntactically well formed. The neuroanatomic information that is available suggests that the cortical lesions of the agrammatic patients were not limited to the typical "Broca's area" infarct associated with agrammatism, but involved relatively extensive parietal and temporal areas of the left hemisphere.

The empirical evidence and arguments reviewed thus far do not allow a clear statement about the relationship between agrammatism as a central feature of Broca's aphasia and agrammatic oral reading. The major factor contributing to this uncertainty is the paucity of empirical evidence on the issue. We have recently tested a number of aphasic

---

[2]The studies of deep dyslexia on which this calculation is based are reported by Kapur and Perl (1978); Marshall and Newcombe (1973); Patterson and Marcel (1977); Saffran and Marin (1977); Saffran, Schwartz, and Marin (1976); Schwartz, Saffran, & Marin (1977); and Shallice and Warrington (1975).

patients with the explicit goal of providing an empirical data base to address directly the issue of oral agrammatic reading in Broca's aphasia. Four male patients classified as Broca's aphasics on the basis of the Boston Diagnostic Aphasia Examination (Goodglass & Kaplan, 1972) were tested. Two of these patients (B.D. & B.L.) had suffered a single left hemisphere cerebrovascular accident approximately 3–4 years prior to testing. CT scans were not available for these patients. A third patient (M.M.) was the victim of a gunshot wound approximately 3 years prior to testing, and CT scan revealed left hemisphere cortical damage to the frontal and temporal lobes. The fourth patient (H.B.) had suffered an aneurysm of the left internal carotid artery approximately 5 years prior to testing; CT scan revealed a large left frontal lobe lesion, a small deep lesion of the left superior temporal gyrus, and a small lesion of the frontal lobe of the right hemisphere. Mean age of the group was 46 years, with an average education level of 13 years.

To provide a control condition that would assure that the behaviors observed were associated with symptoms of Broca's aphasia rather than with language disturbance following any left hemisphere cerebral insult, we tested two aphasic patients who presented symptoms demonstrably different from those characterizing the Broca syndrome. Patient M.C. represents a clear case of the syndrome of conduction aphasia; patient V.O. had been classified as a Wernicke's aphasic immediately after onset, but, at the time of testing, his aphasic symptoms were limited to occasional word finding difficulties and frequent paraphasias in fluent spontaneous speech, with a mild comprehension impairment. These patients were 57 and 58 years old, respectively, and both were high school graduates. These patients were tested on their ability to read aloud single words (presented in isolation) and sentences of several different syntactic forms.

Reading Single Words

Patients were asked to read aloud a list of 175 words and 30 nonword letter strings. The word list was made up of 23 high frequency and 23 low frequency concrete nouns, 23 abstract nouns of medium frequency, 20 verbs, 20 adjectives, and 66 function words. The nonword list included 10 pseudohomophones (e.g., *trane*) and 20 pronounceable letter strings. The patients' responses were tape recorded for later transcription and analysis. In determining whether words were read correctly, we made allowances for the patients' articulatory difficulties. Thus, some responses were scored as correct even though

phonetically different from the target if the response produced conformed to the overall pattern of articulation errors for that patient.

The percentage of words read correctly by each patient is presented in Table 11.1. A simple comparison of the performance of the
Broca group with that of the two control patients indicates that the
Broca patients had considerably more difficulty reading function words
than reading nouns, whereas the control patients had little trouble with
either category. Thus, the results appear to support the view that
Broca's aphasics are agrammatic readers. However, there are obvious
factors that warrant a cautious approach to the interpretation of these
results. An inspection of patients' performance in each of the word
categories reveals important differences among the Broca patients both
in their relative ability to read function words and in their ability to
read abstract nouns and nonwords. The pattern of performance is a
complex one—a pattern that cannot be explained on the basis of existing hypotheses of the underlying disorder of Broca's aphasia.

It is apparent that the Broca patients as a group had a comparable
level of difficulty in reading nouns (73%), verbs (78%), and adjectives
(74%). Within the noun category, however, there were major differences between high frequency and low frequency concrete nouns and
between concrete and abstract nouns. A qualitatively similar pattern of
performance was obtained for the two fluent aphasics, suggesting that
the pattern of performance described for the Broca patients does not
depend on the disruption of the language processing mechanisms implicated in Broca's aphasia. Because performance in the reading of
function words does differ between groups, it might be assumed that
this difference is dependent on the language mechanisms affected in
the different types of aphasia. Furthermore, it appears that the Broca
patients as a group have more difficulty reading nonwords than do the
two fluent aphasics. This difference should also be interpreted
cautiously, however, as it could reflect no more than a difference in
severity of impairment: The reading performance of the fluent aphasics
was in general better than that of the Broca patients.

Consideration of individual subjects' performance reveals an even
more complicated situation. First, it is apparent that there are major
differences in performance among the Broca patients. The differences
are not merely at a quantitative level but reflect qualitative differences
in performance. One of the Broca patients (B.D.) had no apparent
difficulties reading function words aloud. It should be stressed, however, that this patient's ability to process the syntactic value of function
words is qualitatively similar to that of B.L., who had severe difficulty
reading function words aloud. We have previously reported that both

B.L. and B.D. had serious problems processing the syntactic value of function words as indicated by their relative inability to carry out a sentence anagram task (Caramazza et al., in press). Another important difference between B.D.'s reading performance and that of the other Broca patients concerns the ability to read nonwords. B.D. could read correctly 57% of the nonwords, whereas the other three Broca patients could read only 9% of the nonwords. B.D. also differed from the other three Broca patients in his superior ability to read abstract nouns (78% versus 46%), although M.M. may be more similar to B.D. than to the other two Broca patients in this regard.

Another qualitatively different pattern of performance among the Broca group is apparent in their relative ability to read nouns. Unlike the other three Broca patients, patient H.B. had considerable difficulty reading nouns, including high frequency concrete nouns. This is a critical difference in performance from other Broca-type patients and may indicate a different form of underlying impairment for this patient.

This pattern of results for the Broca patients suggests that there are important, qualitative differences in oral reading among patients of this type. It appears that there are three different patterns: the pattern exhibited by B.D., which is qualitatively similar to that of the fluent patients; the pattern found for patients B.L. and M.M., who have difficulty reading function words and nonwords; and the pattern exhibited by H.B., in which the patient has, in addition to problems with function words and nonwords, serious difficulty reading nouns. This heterogeneity in oral reading performance among the Broca patients undermines the attempt to provide a unitary account of the mechanisms responsible for agrammatic reading and the other symptoms associated with Broca's aphasia. There are, however, several factors that can be considered in an attempt to explain the observed differences in performance.

The most striking deviation in the data is the difference between H.B. and the other Broca patients. It is important to emphasize here that H.B. is the only patient with damage to the right hemisphere. It is not implausible to conclude, therefore, that the right hemisphere contributes importantly to the reading process. However, this conclusion must be tempered by the well-known result that unilateral insult to the right hemisphere (in left-dominant subjects) does not result in aphasia or alexia. Thus, the observed impairment for patient H.B. must result from a disorder to two reading mechanisms: one localized in the left hemisphere and one in the right hemisphere. In other words, the pattern of oral reading impairment in H.B. reflects the disruption of two reading mechanisms that can operate independently in unilaterally damaged patients.

The argument we are developing for H.B.'s performance can be further clarified by considering the differences in performance between patient B.D., on one hand, and patients B.L. and M.M., on the other. Without considering the types of reading errors made by B.L. and M.M., it would appear that their pattern of reading performance is qualitatively similar to that of the deep dyslexics—an inability to read function words, abstract nouns, and nonwords, with relatively preserved ability to read concrete nouns. Although patient M.M. is clearly a less severe case than is B.L., there is a qualitatively similar pattern to the performance of these two patients that conforms to the deep dyslexia pattern. It might be concluded, then, that these two patients manifest a disorder of the grapheme-to-phoneme correspondence system. Patient B.D., however, does not present any marked difficulty reading function words or nonwords and may thus be considered to have a normal grapheme-to-phoneme processing system. Extending this argument, it may be that H.B. has an impairment both to the grapheme-to-phoneme correspondence system and also to those mechanisms that are available to unilaterally damaged patients such as B.L. and M.M. that allow these patients to read some nouns. In that case, we might be able to infer something about the way in which deep dyslexics read without a grapheme-to-phoneme correspondence system.

This tentative explanation of the oral reading performance of the four patients allows the generation of predictions concerning the types of reading errors they should produce. Specifically, B.D. should not make semantic paralexic errors; B.L. and M.M. should make semantic paralexic errors (with B.L. presenting a large proportion of such errors commensurate with the severity of his impairment); H.B. should not make semantic errors if right hemisphere processes mediate reading performance in the deep dyslexics, but should make such errors if the basis for these errors is not related to right hemisphere functions. This last prediction is based on the hypothesis that deep dyslexics access semantic representations of the lexicon through a direct graphemic route possibly mediated by a right hemisphere process.

The types of errors produced by the four patients in the single word reading task are summarized in Table 11.2. It is apparent from even a cursory inspection of these data that there are qualitative differences in the types of errors produced by the four Broca patients. Specifically, the error analysis supports the distinctions made among the Broca patients on the basis of their correct reading of the various word types. Both B.L. and M.M. produced a substantial number of semantic paralexias (e.g., *Eskimo* → *snowman*) but this type of error was completely absent from the responses produced by the other two

TABLE 11.2
Classification of Errors—Single Word Reading[a]

	Broca patients				Control patients	
	B.D.	B.L.	M.M.	H.B.	V.O.	M.C.
Semantic errors (production of a semantically related word)	—	17	11	—	—	—
Visual errors (production of a word that deviates minimally from the target; includes errors that might be derivational or segmental errors)	13	48	48	45	58	96
Other (response bears no obvious relationship to target)	87	35	41	55	42	4

[a] Shown as percentage of total errors.

Broca patients (B.D. and H.B.) and from those produced by the conduction and Wernicke's aphasics.

The fact that patients B.L. and M.M. produced a substantial proportion of semantic paralexic errors, and the fact that these patients had marked difficulty reading function words, abstract nouns, and nonwords relative to other words, supports their classification as deep dyslexics. However, there are several features of their performance that are at variance with the favored explanation of deep dyslexia. First, although B.L. produced semantic paralexic errors to concrete nouns (e.g., *bible* → *pray*; *Eskimo* → *snowman*) he also produced such errors to abstract words and function words (e.g., *enter* → *in*; *both* → *you, me; very* → *many*). Furthermore, patient B.L. appeared to produce semantic paralexic errors to pseudohomophones (e.g., *kote* → *night, rain, wind; nale* → *hammer*). These types of errors produced in response to abstract nouns and especially to nonword pseudohomophones present difficulties for those hypotheses of deep dyslexia that assume that the semantic paralexic errors result from the patients' attempt to read by using a direct graphemic access route to semantic representations (Shallice & Warrington, 1975; Saffran & Marin, 1977). Quite clearly, this account of the basis of semantic paralexias cannot explain the semantic errors produced by B.L. in response to pseudohomophones. However, for present purposes, we will assume that the two Broca patients B.L. and M.M. may have an impairment in the grapheme-to-phoneme correspondence system that forces these patients to develop alternative systems to carry out the reading task.

Patient H.B. may also have an impairment at the level of grapheme-to-phoneme conversion as indicated by his inability to read abstract nouns, function words, and nonwords. However, this patient may additionally be unable to make use of the alternative route apparently available to B.L. and M.M. that permits them to read concrete nouns with a fair degree of success. As H.B. has bilateral damage and B.H. and M.M. have only left hemisphere damage, an inviting hypothesis is that the difference in abilities reveals processing mechanisms subserved by the right hemisphere. In other words, it could be argued that the alternative route available to patients B.L. and M.M. includes processes that are carried out by the intact right hemisphere.

Finally, the error analyses for the two fluent aphasics confirm our earlier suggestion that the Broca patient B.D. appears to be quite similar to these two patients both qualitatively and quantitatively. These three patients produced primarily errors that were classified as visual errors. Thus, both the error analysis and the analysis of correct oral reading performance as a function of word class support the conclusion that the reading performance of the Broca patients is sufficiently heterogeneous to cast doubt on the claim that Broca patients as a group are agrammatic readers.

Oral Reading of Sentences

The single word reading task was designed to assess patients' ability to process words of different form classes independently of their functional role in sentences. On the assumption that this task does not require the performance of syntactic analysis, we predicted that the Broca patients should perform adequately, as their impairment is presumed to be at the level of syntactic processing. As we have seen, however, several patients encountered problems reading single words of particular types, but there is no indication that this difficulty resulted from a syntactically based deficit. It is possible, however, that the oral reading of sentences will elicit more homogeneous performance from the Broca group as the disturbed ability to perform syntactic analysis would affect all patients' performance of this task.

Thirty-nine sentences were constructed of six different syntactic types, including indirect object and prepositional phrase constructions, passives, imperatives, WH questions and sentences with subordinate clauses. As there were no major differences in performance as a function of sentence type, the data were collapsed across sentences. Table 11.3 presents the number (and percentage) of errors the patients

TABLE 11.3
Number and Percentage of Error Types—Sentence Reading

	Broca patients				Control patients	
	B.D.	B.L.	M.M.	H.B.	V.O.	M.C.
Function word errors	9 (56%)	90 (63%)	30 (61%)	58 (57%)	8 (45%)	3 (42%)
Inflectional errors	4 (25%)	7 (5%)	8 (16%)	10 (10%)	6 (33%)	2 (29%)
Substantive errors	3 (19%)	45 (32%)	11 (23%)	34 (33%)	4 (22%)	2 (29%)

produced in the reading of substantives and function words, and in the production of grammatical inflections. Note that inflectional errors could be detected only if the patient read the word stem correctly, so the most severely impaired readers produced the smallest proportion of errors in this category.

Inspection of the total number of errors produced by the Broca patients in reading sentences shows that the three patients who performed most poorly reading single words again made the largest number of errors. Patients B.L., M.M. and H.B. read between 20 and 57% of the words in the sentences incorrectly. In contrast, the Broca patient B.D. and the conduction and Wernicke patients made very few errors in reading the sentences (between 3 and 7%). If we consider the distribution of errors by form class, it is clear that all patients produced more errors in reading function words than in reading nouns. Furthermore, the ratio of function word errors to substantive errors is roughly proportional to that obtained in the single word reading task. Because of the small number of errors produced by patients B.D., V.O., and M.C., however, it is difficult to draw firm conclusions about their reading performance other than that it is remarkably good considering their other aphasic symptoms. The other three patients, all Broca's aphasics, produced enough errors to allow a more detailed analysis of their reading performance.

The types of reading errors of the three types listed in Table 11.3 were further scored as to whether they involved an omission or addition of a word of a particular class, or the substitution of another word for the target. Table 11.4 shows the results of this breakdown for the function word errors produced by the four Broca patients.

There were considerably more substitution and addition errors (considered together) than there were omission errors. This result is surprising in that it deviates from the expected agrammatic pattern that

TABLE 11.4
Classification of Function Word Errors[a]—Sentence Reading

Error types	Broca patients			
	B.D.	B.L.	M.M.	H.B.
Omissions	1 (6%)	29 (20%)	7 (14%)	9 (9%)
Substitutions (within class)	5 (31%)	34 (24%)	8 (16%)	21 (21%)
Substitutions (out of class)	—	3 (2%)	—	18 (18%)
Additions	3 (19%)	23 (16%)	15 (31%)	10 (10%)

[a] Shown as number of errors and percentage of total errors.

involves simple omission of grammatical morphemes. A second unexpected result is that when patients produced the wrong word for a target function word (i.e., a substitution error) they most often produced another function word rather than a substantive.

It is worth noting (despite the small number of errors produced) that a breakdown of the inflectional errors produced by the Broca patients also shows a higher than expected proportion of addition and substitution errors. Of the 29 errors produced by the four patients, 15 were omission errors and the remaining 14 were additions or substitutions.

The incidence of production of additions and substitutions of function words and inflections in the reading of sentences is not easily accommodated within hypotheses of Broca's aphasia that were formulated to explain the pattern of omissions in patients' speech. That is, explanations of agrammatism stressing economy of effort (e.g., Lenneberg, 1973), the need for a salient (stressed) item to initiate speech (Goodglass, 1968) and the phonological simplification of utterances (Kean, 1978) cannot easily be modified to explain why patients add words or substitute incorrect words as often as they omit them when reading sentences.

The production of these types of errors in sentence reading is consistent with the view that Broca's aphasia results from a disruption of syntactic processing abilities. Clearly, the addition or substitution of function words and inflections must have resulted in syntactically anomalous sentences. If patients were unable to perform syntactic analyses on the sentences they read, or performed inadequate or incorrect syntactic analyses, they would not be aware of their ungrammatical productions. In addition, the large number of "within-class" function word substitutions suggests that these patients were aware of form class distinctions but may not have been sensitive to the syntactic value of these words. In other words, patients may have "known" that they should have been producing a function word but, because of an inability to carry out a syntactic analysis of the sentence, were unable to constrain production to a syntactically appropriate word.

The argument being advanced here is not that the Broca patients' syntactic deficit is the direct cause of the errors produced in reading sentences. As demonstrated in the single word reading task, three of the Broca patients produced significant reading errors even when no syntactic analysis was required by the task. We have argued that this reading impairment is not the result of their syntactic deficit, but involves an inability to convert graphemes to phonemes that is independent of their classification as Broca's aphasics. These three patients would be expected to have similar difficulty reading individual words when they are embedded in sentences. However, the Broca patients' syntactic deficit could play a role in determining the form of errors that will be produced as they struggle to read the words of the sentence. That is, production of syntactic anomalies that occur from misreading will not be monitored and thus prevented; incorrect function words and inflections will be added and substituted as a function of the patients' inability to read, without the normal constraints of syntactic structure. This analysis explains why patient B.D., who does not have difficulty reading words but who does suffer from a syntactic processing deficit, performed so well. B.D. could read the sentences adequately using a word-by-word strategy; on the few occasions of difficulty, he also produced function word substitutions and addition errors in violation of syntactic structure.

Performance of the Broca group on the sentence reading task supports the finding reported for the single word reading task that these patients do not form a homogeneous group with regard to their ability to read function words. In addition, when function word errors were produced by these patients, they involved addition and substitution errors as often as omissions. This finding provides further support for the argument that agrammatic oral reading is not a necessary symptom of Broca's aphasia.

What Is Agrammatic Reading?

In discussing the possibility that agrammatic reading may be a symptom associated with Broca's aphasia, we have drawn a distinction between *asyntactic* comprehension of written material and *agram-*

matic oral reading. Recent work has shown that Broca's aphasics present a pattern of comprehension of written material that takes the same asyntactic form as their auditory comprehension deficit. This pattern of performance reflects Broca patients' inability to carry out normal syntactic analyses of sentences independently of mode of input (Caramazza *et al.*, in press). Thus, if aggramatic reading is understood to mean asyntactic comprehension of written material, there would appear to be little doubt that Broca's aphasics are aggramatic readers.

The term *agrammatic reading*, has been used to describe an inability to read aloud the same items that are omitted in spontaneous speech (i.e., the grammatical morphemes, Schwartz *et al.*, 1977). If agrammatic reading is understood in this latter sense, it is not clear on what basis Broca's aphasics would be expected to present difficulties reading function words. In fact, none of the major hypotheses that have been offered to explain agrammatic speech predicts an impairment of the ability to read single function words. Nonetheless, independently of whether theories of the underlying disorder that determines Broca's aphasia predict difficulties in reading function words aloud, it is an empirical issue whether or not this symptom is associated with the syndrome of Broca's aphasia.

The evidence we have reviewed and the results we have reported on the reading of single words and sentences by Broca patients do not allow a clear resolution of the issue of whether oral agrammatic reading cooccurs with other symptoms that define Broca's aphasia. Two studies of single Broca patients (Andreewsky & Seron, 1975; Friederici & Schoenle, 1980) report patients who could not read function words. However, these authors do not report on their patients' ability to read other types of words, so it cannot be said that their reading deficit is restricted to an inability to read function words. In particular, there is no information available on whether these patients could read abstract nouns. In a larger study, it was found that, although Broca patients had more trouble reading function words than reading concrete nouns, they had even more difficulty reading abstract nouns than reading function words (Gardner & Zurif, 1975). Similarly, if we consider only the average performance of the four Broca patients we tested, they appeared to have more difficulty reading function words than reading concrete nouns. As a group, however, they also had severe difficulty reading abstract nouns. Thus, it could very well be the case that the patients studied by Andreewsky and Seron (1975) and by Friederici and Schoenle (1980) may have had as much difficulty reading abstract nouns as they had reading function words. On the basis of the available evidence, we cannot conclude that Broca's aphasics are agrammatic readers for single words. Not a single patient has been reported who could read abstract nouns but could not read function words. It appears, then, that a general oral reading impairment is correlated with Broca's aphasia, but that it is an independent symptom not related to the underlying syntactic disorder that characterizes Broca's aphasia.

On the basis of their oral reading performance and the types of reading errors they produce, we have suggested that patients B.L. and M.M. may be classified as deep dyslexics. The mechanism responsible for their poor oral reading is most likely a disorder of the grapheme-to-phoneme conversion system, which forces them to rely on alternative reading strategies (Marshall & Newcombe, 1973).

Several aspects of our patients' reading performance suggest the need for some modifications of existing explanations of deep dyslexia, however. A critical feature of the syndrome of deep dyslexia is the frequent production of semantic paralexias. It is argued that, as these patients cannot perform a grapheme-to-phoneme conversion of the written word, they must access a semantic representation directly from the graphemic representation. However, this access route to semantic representations is not an exact procedure and leads to the activation of a semantic network rather than to a single lexical representation. Thus, the patient is likely to produce an incorrect word from that semantic network (Saffran & Marin, 1977; Shallice & Warrington, 1975).

A close analysis of the pattern of semantic paralexic errors made by patients B.L. and M.M. undermines the view that these errors result from a direct access of the lexicon from the grapheme. As noted in the discussion of the single word reading task, patient B.L., in particular, produced semantic paralexic errors to pseudohomophones as well as to abstract words. If these types of errors are representative of errors produced by deep dyslexic patients in general, they suggest an alternative basis for the semantic paralexic errors. Specifically, it could be argued that deep dyslexic patients are carrying out some rudimentary grapheme-to-phoneme conversion operation, possibly through the mediation of right hemisphere processes, but that these analyses are imperfect and produce only a weak activation of the target lexical item. This alternative account is not incompatible with explanations that emphasize direct access of the lexicon from the graphemic representation; both types of processes could be at work.

The suggestion that the alternative reading strategies employed by deep dyslexics are mediated by right hemisphere processes (e.g., Schwartz et al., 1977) is given some support by the pattern of results we have reported for patient H.B. This patient appeared to have a deficit of the grapheme-to-phoneme conversion processes but in addition, perhaps because of damage to the right hemisphere, was unable to read concrete nouns. In other words, it is possible that this patient could not make use of the alternative reading route available to deep dyslexics with unilateral left hemisphere lesions. Interestingly, this patient failed to make any semantic paralexic errors, suggesting that the right hemisphere reading route may be responsible for such errors.

The co-occurrence of Broca's aphasia and deep dyslexia most likely reflects the neuroanatomical distribution of language processing mechanisms. That is, we assume that syntactic processing mechanisms (Broca's aphasia) and the grapheme-to-phoneme conversion system (deep dyslexia) may be neuroanatomically represented in spatially adjacent areas, increasing the likelihood that symptoms related to the disruption of these two systems will co-occur in a single patient. Thus, Broca's aphasia and deep dyslexia may show more than a modest correlation of co-occurrence. Importantly, however, these disorders can occur independently of each other, as we have shown in our results (patient B.D.), and as can be inferred from the published material on deep dyslexia showing that some such patients do not present agrammatism in their spontaneous speech.

Conclusion: Oral Reading in Broca's Aphasia

Our discussion of Broca patients' ability to read single words has emphasized the position that these patients are not agrammatic readers in the sense that would be the case if the mechanisms responsible for agrammatism in their spontaneous speech similarly compromised the capacity to read words. The syntactic impairment that we have argued is at the root of the Broca syndrome should not be expected to interfere with the oral reading of individual grammatical morphemes. We have uncovered no evidence that contradicts this expectation. All Broca patients who exhibited problems reading function words showed several additional symptoms indicating the presence of an independent reading disorder.

The results we have reported for the oral reading of sentences, however, indicate a pattern of impairment that may be related to the syntactic deficit. The types of errors produced in the sentence reading task cannot be explained as the result of a simple failure to apply grapheme-to-phoneme conversion rules. In addition to the difficulties some of the patients had reading function words, all of the Broca patients produced a type of error that would not result from a "low-level" disturbance in processing the individual lexical items (i.e., they added function words that were not part of the target sentence). This result is independent of problems reading individual words and should be explained on the basis of the mechanisms implicated in Broca's aphasia.

The theoretical framework we have developed for the underlying disorder of Broca's aphasia is based on the assumption that this syndrome is made up of two major symptoms—asyntactic comprehension and agrammatic speech production. Both of these symptoms reflect the patient's inability to carry out a normal syntactic analysis of sentences because of a disruption of the syntactic processing component of the language. We can now add a new symptom to the set that characterizes Broca's aphasia: *asyntactic oral reading*. The types of reading errors produced when the Broca patients attempted to read sentences reflect both the problems that some of them had reading certain types of words, and the unavailability of a syntactic frame that would limit the production of reading errors to grammatically acceptable constructions. Because the Broca patient fails to carry out a normal syntactic analysis of the sentence while reading, the errors produced are unlikely to be constrained by syntactic considerations.

As we have argued that the Broca patients' *omission* of function words in spontaneous speech and his *production* of function word additions and substitutions in oral reading both result from an inability to perform syntactic analyses, we must attempt to explain why the same deficit produces these two different patterns. We assume that because the reading task supplies the patient with written words as a model for production (however imperfectly processed), he is encouraged to produce something in response to each of the elements in the sentence. Furthermore, the large number of within-class function word substitutions suggests that patients recognize those items as a particular class but cannot always process them well enough to select the appropriate member of that class. It seems reasonable to conclude that the written words supply the patient with some minimal information about the target that is not available to him in spontaneous speech.

In summary, we have argued that Broca's aphasics demonstrate asyntactic comprehension of written materials. These patients do not have a selective disturbance of the ability to read single function words orally, although some Broca patients are also deep dyslexics. In this case, their reading impairment for single words is not restricted to the grammatical function words, but includes abstract nouns and nonwords. Finally, we have argued that Broca patients may read sentences asyntactically, reflecting their inability to carry out normal syntactic analysis of sentences.

Acknowledgments

We would like to thank A. G. Basili and J. J. Koller of the Department of Audiology and Speech Pathology, Fort Howard VA Medical Center, for their assistance with this research. We would especially like to thank our friend Edgar Zurif for his comments on the work reported here, for his spirited arguments that have helped us define more clearly our position, and for his perspicacity in catching a contradiction in an earlier draft of this paper.

References

Andreewsky, E., & Seron, X. Implicit processing of grammatical rules in a classical case of agrammatism. *Cortex*, 1975, *11*, 379–390.

Berndt, R., & Caramazza, A. A redefinition of the syndrome of Broca's aphasia: Implications for a neuropsychological model of language. *Applied Psycholinguistics*, 1980, *1*, 225–278.

Blumstein, S., Statlender, S., Goodglass, H., & Biber, C. *Comprehension strategies determining reference in aphasia: A study of reflexivization*. Paper presented at the Academy of Aphasia, San Diego, October 14–16, 1979.

Caramazza, A., Berndt, R. S., Basili, A. G., & Koller, J. J. Syntactic processing deficits in aphasia. *Cortex*, in press.

Caramazza, A., & Zurif, E. B. Dissociation of algorithmic and heuristic processes in language comprehension: Evidence from aphasia. *Brain and Language*, 1976, *3*, 572–582.

Coltheart, M. Lexical access in simple reading tasks. In G. Underwood (Ed.), *Strategies of information processing*. London: Academic Press, 1978.

Ellis, H. D., & Shepard, J. W. Recognition of abstract and concrete words presented in left and right visual fields. *Journal of Experimental Psychology*, 1974, *103*, 1035–1036.

Friederici, A. D., & Schoenle, P. W. Computational dissociation of two vocabulary types: Evidence from aphasia. *Neuropsychologia*, 1980, *18*, 11–20.

Gardner, H., & Zurif, E. 'Bee' but not 'be': Oral reading of single words in aphasia and alexia. *Neuropsychologia*, 1975, *13*, 181–190.

Goodglass, H. Studies on the grammar of aphasics. In S. Rosenberg & K. Joplin (Eds.), *Developments in applied psycholinguistics research*. New York: Macmillan, 1968.

Goodglass, H., Blumstein, S. E., Gleason, J. B., Hyde, M. R., Green, E., & Statlender, S. The effect of syntactic encoding on sentence comprehension in aphasia. *Brain and Language*, 1979, *7*, 201–209.

Goodglass, M., & Kaplan, E. *The Assessment of Aphasia and Related Disorders*. Philadelphia: Lea and Febiger, 1972.

Heilman, K. M., & Scholes, R. J. The nature of comprehension errors in Broca's, conduction, and Wernicke's aphasics. *Cortex*, 1976, *12*(3), 258–265.

Hines, D. Recognition of verbs, abstract nouns and concrete nouns from the left and right visual half-fields. *Neuropsychologia*, 1976, *14*, 211–216.

Kapur, N., & Perl, N. T. Recognition reading in paralexia. *Cortex*, 1978, *14*, 439–443.

Kean, M. L. The linguistic interpretation of aphasic syndromes. In E. Walker, (Ed.), *Explorations in the biology of language*. Montgomery, Vermont: Bradford Books, 1978.

Lenneberg, E. H. The neurology of language. *Daedalus*, 1973, *102*, 115–133.

Marshall, J. C., & Newcombe, F. Syntactic and semantic errors in paralexia. *Neuropsychologia*, 1966, *4*, 169–176.

Marshall, J. C., & Newcombe, F. Patterns of paralexia: A psycholinguistic approach. *Journal of Psycholinguistic Research*, 1973, *2*, 175–199.

Patterson, K. E., & Marcel, A. J. Aphasia, dyslexia, and the phonological coding of written words. *Quarterly Journal of Experimental Psychology*, 1977, *29*, 307–318.

Richardson, J. T. E. The effect of word imageability in acquired dyslexia. *Neuropsychologia*, 1975, *13*, 281–288.

Saffran, E. M., & Marin, O. S. Reading without phonology: evidence from aphasia. *Quarterly Journal of Experimental Psychology*, 1977, *29*, 515–525.

Saffran, E. M., Schwartz, M. F., & Marin, O. S. M. Semantic mechanisms in paralexia. *Brain and Language*, 1976, *3*, 255–265.

Samuels, J. A., & Benson, D. F. Some aspects of language comprehension in anterior aphasia. *Brain and Language*, 1979, *8*, 275–286.

Schwartz, M. F., Saffran, E. M., & Marin, O. S. M. *An analysis of agrammatic reading in aphasia.* Paper presented at the meeting of the International Neuropsychological Society, Santa Fe, New Mexico, February, 1977.

Schwartz, M. F., Saffran, E. M., & Marin, O. S. M. The word order problem in agrammatism: 1. Comprehension. *Brain and Language*, 1980, *10*, 249–262.

Shallice, T., & Warrington, E. K. Word recognition in a phonemic dyslexic patient. *Quarterly Journal of Experimental Psychology*, 1975, *27*, 187–199.

Zurif, E. B., Caramazza, A., & Myerson, R. Grammatical judgments of agrammatic aphasics. *Neuropsychologia*, 1972, *10*, 405–417.

Zurif, E. B., Green, E., Caramazza, A., & Goodenough, C. Grammatical intuitions of aphasic patients: Sensitivity to functors. *Cortex*, 1976, *12*, 183–186.

12

Francis J. Pirozzolo
Kathryn Lawson-Kerr

RECOVERY FROM ALEXIA:
Factors Influencing
Restoration of
Function after Focal
Cerebral Damage

Disturbances of complex cognitive functions have been the subject of numerous neuropsychological studies, and language disturbances have been among the most extensively studied of these disorders. The component processes of language disturbances have been described in detail, but relatively little is known about recovery of these functions. Many subject factors are presumed to affect prognosis, such as age, education, and premorbid intellectual status of the patient, but there is no consensus of opinion on the roles of these factors in the recovery process. This chapter reviews the general principles of recovery and the literature pertinent to the subject factors presumed to be involved in restitution of function. In addition, differential rates of recovery have been ascribed to the nature, locus, extent, and progression of the lesions. Ajax (1967) described a young patient with a left occipital arteriovenous malformation who did not improve to any significant degree after 2 years of intensive retraining in reading. By contrast, other investigators have noted considerable recovery of reading skills in patients with similar vascular lesions (Sroka, Solsi, & Bornstein, 1973) and after traumatic injury (Newcombe, Marshall, Carrivick, & Hiorns, 1975). Furthermore, it is possible that patients with alexia due to anterior lesions (see Benson, Chapter 3 this volume) may have an entirely different pattern of recovery than patients with central or posterior alexia. Longitudinal studies of aphasic and alexic readers are of critical importance in establishing the basic principles of prognosis and rehabilitation–remediation procedures. Unfortunately, there are very

NEUROPSYCHOLOGICAL AND COGNITIVE
PROCESSES IN READING

few qualitative or quantitative studies that compare the various factors involved in recovery. This chapter reviews the existing empirical literature pertaining to recovery. Data from these neuropsychological and neurolinguistic studies are analyzed, and a conceptual model for the processes involved in recovery of reading function is developed.

General Principles of Recovery of Function

The central nervous system (CNS) contains two types of cells, one dividing throughout life (glia) and the other nondividing (neurons). Because destroyed neurons do not regenerate, the functions that are served by these cells would be disrupted forever, were it not for the brain's ability to modify its activity and restore itself to working order.

During the acute stage immediately following the destruction of brain tissue, several processes interact to produce a clinical picture of disrupted function that is more extensive than that which can be directly related to the extent and locus of cell loss. Initially, some neurons undergo degenerative changes and die and are replaced by glial tissue, whereas other neurons become physiologically altered but do not die. These latter cells are held in a state of inactivity by the acute conditions that accompany the degenerative changes, namely the appearance of edema and alterations in the circulation of blood and cerebrospinal fluid (CSF).

Edema and Alterations in Blood Flow

The temporary loss of function can certainly be linked, in part, to edema. Edema is caused by increases in intracranial pressure and by chemical (e.g., blood) irritation of nervous tissue. Generally, edema is thought to resolve within two to three weeks after brain trauma. Exceptions to this rule include encephalopathic events that involve more than one acute phase (e.g., transient ischemic episodes).

Vascular adjustment plays an important role in recovery. The acute phase after CNS insult is characterized by a reflex diminution in blood flow to the perifocal region around the site of injury. Two other stages in recovery can be identified—the readjustment to the flow of blood to this region and a long-term adjustment in regional blood flow caused by increased demand for collateral circulation.

Diaschisis

Von Monakow (1911) used the term *diaschisis* to refer to the concept that certain functions could be disrupted by brain lesions that have occurred in distant areas of the brain. For reasons that were unclear to von Monakow at the time, lesions in one hemisphere were found to interfere with functions governed by the opposite but intact hemisphere. Subsequently, physiological studies employing electrophysiologic, regional cerebral blood flow, and metabolic methodologies have confirmed von Monakow's clinical findings. The effects of diaschisis were shown to exist not only in the short-term, posttraumatic stage, but to persist in some cases for many years.

More recent experiments of this phenomenon have shown that the pattern of cortical activity after a focal cerebral injury does indeed alter functions subserved by both proximal and remote cortical regions. Furthermore, it has been demonstrated that the functional disruption is related not only to the proximity of the lesion but also to the nature of the behavioral function (Thompson, 1977).

The final and perhaps most poorly understood physiological factor to be considered here involved in restoration of function is the role of acetylcholine in the production of "functional asynapsia." As discussed previously, certain cells that are not destroyed after cerebral insult are preserved in a state of physiological inactivity. Recent neurophysiological studies (reviewed by Luria, Naydin, Tsvetkova, & Venarskaya, 1969) suggest that this physiological inactivity is caused by temporary disturbances of synaptic conduction. The evidence for this mechanism is strongest for cholinergic synapses. Acetylcholinesterase, which catalyzes acetylcholine after it is diffused across the synaptic cleft, is believed to be increased in the perifocal brain region after insult. The administration of an anticholinesterase, which blocks acetyl cholinesterase and thus prevents the breakdown of acetylcholine, potentiates the action of acetylcholine at the postsynaptic cell membrane. Anticholinesterase therapy during the acute phase of cerebral injury can result in deblocking the activity of preserved yet inactive cells.

There are no conclusive data to support the widely held belief that functions that are lost after destruction of a certain brain region can be taken over by the intact, contralateral (homologous) or other distant brain region. Most evidence suggests that functional reorganization is related to collateral sprouting in adjacent neural tissue. Electron microscopic, electrophysiological, and behavioral data all support this claim. Glees and Cole (1950), for instance, studied the recovery of fine motor function (opposition of the thumb and forefinger) after ablation of sections of the motor cortex in monkeys. They observed that these animals could regain, within a few weeks, the use of their thumbs after extirpation of the thumb area of the motor cortex. After the initial period of recovery, the motor cortex was exposed and electrocorticographically mapped. Results showed that the new thumb area was adjacent to the old, ablated thumb region on the motor cortex. Subsequent lesions of this new zone resulted in the deficits seen after the first lesions, and recovery of function after the second extirpation was much slower than after the first.

Behavioral studies point to the same recovery process and perhaps provide a neuroanatomic basis for recovery. Numerous studies have shown that fibers grow around a lesion and make synaptic content with axon terminals of other cells. This reorganization mechanism seems to be plausible not only for higher functions, but for lower ones as well. Teitelbaum and Epstein (1962) produced the lateral hypothalamic syndrome in rats with bilateral lesions of this region. When these animals had recovered from aphagia and adipsia, second lesions were made in the area adjacent to the initial lesions. This subsequent destruction of the hypothalamic appetitive centers caused a reappearance of the lateral hypothalamic syndrome, suggesting that the plasticity may have been related to the reorganization of adjacent neural tissue.

Recovery from Aphasia

There have been a considerable number of studies of linguistic recovery after brain damage affecting regions of the central language system. Soldiers who had sustained penetrating missile wounds formed the subject population of many of the early studies of recovery patterns (Goldstein, 1948; Luria, 1966; Newcombe, 1969; Wepman, 1951). Fairly general agreement can be reached on several factors that influence recovery. Numerous studies have shown that the younger the patient at the time of injury, the faster the rate and the greater the extent of the eventual recovery. This principle is widely held, although there is now both animal and human experimental evidence suggesting that cautious interpretation of this rule is necessary. Recent evidence (Mahut & Zola, 1977; Schneider, 1979) shows that infant animals recover certain functions more slowly than older animals. Indeed, some studies of aphasia recovery have shown a lack of statistical significance between recovery and age (Culton, 1969; Sarno, Sarno, & Levita, 1971).

Another principle that has wide acceptance is the fact that the greatest improvement occurs during the spontaneous recovery period within the first 6 months after injury and, during this time, the fastest rate of recovery is seen during the first 3 months. Results of a study by Culton (1969) showed that the most significant spontaneous recovery occurs within 30 days of onset.

Several investigations of recovery from aphasia suggest a more rapid amelioration of expressive disorders, whereas other studies indicate that patients with receptive language disturbances show more rapid improvement. Butfield and Zangwill (1946) and Weisenburg and McBride (1935) were among the first to provide evidence that expressive disorders improve fastest. Similarly, Mohr (1973) suggests that motor aphasia often shows dramatically rapid recovery. Conversely, Vignolo (1964) found that the existence of expressive defects such as oral apraxia and dysarthria made for a poor prognosis. Basso, Faglioni, and Vignolo (1974), however, found no difference in recovery rates between Broca's and Wernicke's aphasics.

In one of the most extensive, well-controlled studies to date of recovery from aphasia, Kertesz and McCabe (1977) analyzed several of the aforementioned factors involved in recovery, including: the nature of language disorders, the etiology, time interval between aphasia onset and beginning of therapy, and age at onset. Results suggested that anomic aphasics had the most favorable prognosis, followed respectively by the transcortical, Wernicke's, conduction, and Broca's aphasics with global aphasics having the poorest recovery. In agreement with the results of Wepman (1951) and Luria (1970), traumatic aphasias showed better recovery than aphasias due to cerebrovascular accidents. No significant differences were found between speech-therapy-treated patients and untreated aphasics. The greatest recovery occurred for almost all subjects during the first 3 months postonset. Finally, the effect of age appeared to be one in which there was a strong negative correlation between age and recovery, suggesting that the younger the patient the better the recovery.

The first study to analyze treatment effects by using an untreated control group was published in 1964 by Vignolo. He found no statistically significant differences between the group that received language therapy and the group that was left untreated. Vignolo did conclude, however, that treatment was helpful in remediating large discrepancies between expressive and comprehension skills. Sarno et al. (1971) conducted a study of treatment effects and found similar results, that is, no difference in recovery rates between treated and untreated language disorders. This study is particularly important because attempts were made to eliminate the greatest proportion of spontaneous recovery by beginning the experimental treatment 3 months postonset.

In a follow-up study, Basso, Capitani, and Vignolo (1979) examined the influence of rehabilitation on certain language skills in 281 aphasic patients. Their conclusions were that formal language training (traditional stimulus–response language therapy) did significantly improve performance in all language modalities in many of their patients. In addition to these findings, they also found that age shows a weak correlation with language improvement during rehabilitation. In both spoken and written language, comprehension improved at a faster rate than expression. Although the evidence was less robust, oral language abilities (auditory comprehension and oral expression) seemed to improve more than written language abilities (reading and writing).

The efficacy of different types of language therapy has also been a topic of great concern to clinicians. A recent study involving several aphasia centers has tested the differences in recovery rates between patients who were treated with traditional, individual (stimulus–response) language therapy and patients who underwent group treatment (Wertz, Collins, Brookshire, Friden, Kurtzke, Pierce, & Weiss, 1978). Results showed that individual treatment was superior (although not overwhelmingly so) to group treatment. The largest differences were seen in writing ability, although significant differences in performance in verbal skill areas, and on the Porch Index of Communicative Ability (Porch, 1971) were seen. This study, however, has several limitations including no untreated group and no controls for certain subject variables, including such important factors as premorbid intelligence or education.

Recovery from Aphasia in Polyglots

Language representation in individuals who are multilingual may be different from that in individuals who learn only one language, and thus studies of recovery of language functions in polyglots may shed light on the structural and functional mechanisms involved in recovery. Two excellent reviews of cases of polyglot aphasia have been published recently (Albert & Obler, 1978; Paradis, 1977); and evidence strongly suggests that no single rule explains recovery of language functions in polyglot aphasics. Previously reported data were shown to be inconclusive in supporting either Pitres' rule or Ribot's rule. Briefly, Pitres' rule states that the language used most often before the onset of aphasia will be the one that recovers most rapidly. Ribot's rule states that the language learned first will recover most rapidly.

Albert and Obler (1978) analyzed 105 cases of polyglot aphasia that were reported in the literature. Factors analyzed by these authors included: personal factors (such as age, sex, education, and so on), language history (e.g., age of second language acquisition), neurological factors (lesion site and type), disturbances peculiar to polyglot aphasia (e.g., mixing) and other recovery variables.

Sex of the subject was found not to be a significant factor in the recovery pattern. Analysis of the age factor revealed an interesting interaction. The percentage of cases contradicting Pitres' rule increases with increasing age. That is, the younger patients tended to recover the most recent language first, whereas the older patients tended not to recover the most recently used language. The authors interpret this finding as attributed to declines in memory function that accompany normal aging. In a subsample of 47 patients, they found that, for 20 patients, restitution was parallel in all or both languages. Restitution in 25 patients followed Pitres' rule and restitution in 13 patients contradicted Pitres' rule. Polyglots were more likely to follow Pitres' rule than bilinguals.

The education factor was also found to be significant in that well-educated subjects tended to follow Pitres' rule. The rule of Ribot was not followed more often than chance. The rule of Pitres was followed more often than chance, especially for well-educated or multilingual aphasics. Albert and Obler have argued that their findings suggest that polyglots have more right hemisphere language representation than the monolingual population, and, thus, that the right hemisphere plays a prominent role in recovery.

Recovery from Alexia: Early Studies

In his excellent review of the pre-Broca history of the study of language disturbances, Benton (1964) presented evidence of several early references to alexia, the earliest of which was described in A.D. 30 by Valerius Maximus, who cited a case of selective loss of memory for letters with an absence of other language defects. The earliest reference to recovery of reading ability was given by Johann Schmidt in 1673. Schmidt presented two cases of alexia, only one of which recovered after special training. Two centuries later, Charcot (1877) discovered a strategy that was helpful in the retraining of reading in alexics. He described a patient who could read by tracing letters and words with his finger, thus providing a kinesthetic impression of the verbal information. Whereas the patient no longer had a "visual memory" for letters and words, the substitution of the tracing strategy provided an alternative sensory impression that enabled the patient to read.

Other early studies of alexia by Bastian (1898) and by Paterson and Bramwell (1905) showed no recovery of reading ability in alexic patients, whereas a study by Charcot (1889) showed slow but gradual recovery between 35 and 62 days postonset.

Franz (1918), in an intensive study of the rehabilitation of one aphasic alexic (secondary to neurosyphilis) found that object naming and color naming improved during the spontaneous recovery period, whereas single word reading did not.

Goldstein (1942) was among the first clinicians to conduct a thorough psychological investigation of patients' mental abilities in an attempt to characterize behavioral deficits. Once the cognitive disabilities were revealed, therapy proceeded using intact, compensatory skills. One case study he presented was of a patient with a visual agnosia who could not recognize letters by sight but could apprehend the meaning of words by touch. The strategy that the patient used was to trace letters one by one. Accompanying this were tracing movements of the eyes, although the patient was unaware of this strategy. He began scanning at the upper left, except with descending letters. Later in his rehabilitation, the patient was able to employ an analysis-by-synthesis or hypothesis testing approach (see Haber & Haber, Chapter 7 this volume), that is, he began to skip letters and words and was able to rely on the general appearance of a word and the context to abstract meaning.

In a second case study, Goldstein presented a patient who was unable to read words that he could not name in an object naming task. His strategy was to separate polysyllabic words into phonological segments, and once his pronunciation of the partial word aroused association of the correct sound sequence, the patient recognized the word. Goldstein hypothesized that this form of reading disability was not a visual disturbance, but an impairment in the structure of word ideation. The patient showed good recovery in a training program emphasizing that the variations in pronunciation do not alter the meaning of words. His progress could not be linked to spontaneous recovery, as 6 months passed since the beginning of therapy before progress was noted.

The Time Course of Recovery: Recent Studies

Many recent studies have charted recovery curves of various language skills in alexics. As Gardner, Denes, and Zurif (1975) have pointed out, reading is not well aligned with the recovery of other language abilities. The psycholinguistic components of reading are complex. Thus, difficulties in reading may arise from lesions involving many different parts of the brain. Many of the studies reviewed in what follows have attempted to determine the relative recovery of certain visual–verbal abilities (e.g., color naming, object naming, etc.), associated clinical findings (e.g., hemianopia), and reading ability.

Newcombe (1969) has followed the recovery of reading ability in several patients over many years. One subject, a highly intelligent classics scholar, sustained a left temperoparietal lesion resulting in aphasia and alexia. This patient, 1 year later, was able to read a page of print in a half-day and write only short notes. The subject's reading and writing, 4 years later, had improved to the point where he enrolled in a new university program, but he was still unable to translate Latin and Greek, a task that he had formerly performed well. A second subject had alexia in relative isolation during the acute phase of recovery from left posterior temperoparietal injury. Twenty years later, this patient's writing is intact, and he can read a narrative passage hesitatingly, but without gross errors, except for occasional alterations in suffixes or omission of the plural "s."

Kapur and Perl (1978) reported a case of aphasic alexia resulting from polycythemia vera with complete occlusion of the left middle cerebral artery. The patient had a right hemiparesis, aphasia, and alexia with no visual field impairment 6½ years after his cerebrovascular accident.

Wechsler (1972) reported a case of hemialexia, a selective inability to read in the left visual field. The patient had an arteriovenous malformation involving the medial aspect of the anterior inferior left occipital and adjacent cingulate areas. The reading disorder persisted for only 8 days with gradual clearing of visual recognition in the left visual field in the following order of restoration: object and color naming, letter and number recognition, and, finally, word recognition. A critical factor in this patient's recovery appears to have been partial sparing of splenial fibers, as hemialexia can be more persistent in patients who have undergone surgical division of the splenium (Trescher & Ford, 1937).

Similarly, Kurachi, Yamaguchi, Inasaka, and Torii (1979) have reported a case of alexia without agraphia in whom good recovery was achieved. These authors attributed the recovery to sparing of splenial–cuneate fibers. The patient, a 58-year-old Japanese teacher of German literature, suffered two separate cerebrovascular accidents (CVA) and two separate bouts of alexia without agraphia. The reading disability abated in 10 weeks after the first CVA and in 2 weeks after the second. Pathological examination revealed an old lesion in the posterior two-thirds of the fusiform and the whole lingual gyrus, but with preservation of the left cuneus and calcarine cortex. The inferior third of the splenium showed degenerative changes as did its occipital radiation and the tapetum. The authors argued that alexia clears when it involves the left splenial–lingual radiations, but that alexia persists when the splenial–cuneate system is involved. In the latter case, object naming and recognition are usually impaired to the same degree as is reading ability.

Wechsler, Weinstein, and Antin (1972) reported a case of alexia without agraphia in a 21-year-old patient who had undergone surgical removal of shrapnel from the left occipital lobe. The subject's reading disability resolved in 2 months time, apparently at the same rate as his word finding difficulty, but was unrelated to resolution of a dense right homonymous hemianopia, which persisted.

Gardner and Zurif (1975) studied reading and naming ability in patients with alexia with agraphia and in patients with alexia without agraphia. Their findings indicated that reading was relatively better than naming in most aphasics, suggesting that reading and naming are mediated by different mechanisms.

Aphasic alexics were impaired approximately to the same degree on naming and reading tasks. This pattern suggests that the underlying mechanisms may be the same for deficits in reading and naming in these patients. The pattern of reading deficit in alexics who did not have agraphia was different from that of aphasic alexics in that, if the words could be presented in another modality, the language disability would disappear.

Evidence suggests that individual patients may go through various distinct patterns of change during the course of recovery. Newcombe and Marshall (1973) and Newcombe et al. (1975) have described a pattern of spontaneous recovery of reading in a 41-year-old woman with a left occipital abscess. A month after surgery, the patient was totally alexic. She was noted to have, 2 months after the operation, "word-without-letter-blindness." She continued to improve over a 1-year period, although her alexia persisted. In addition, the pattern of change in her reading errors were recorded over a 3-month period. The authors classified reading errors into one of the following four categories: (a) failures of visual analysis (pat–pet); (b) vowel lengthening (met–meat); (c) failure of phoneme-to-grapheme transcoding (rig–ridge); and (d) combinations of a, b, and c (rib–ride). During the first month, the patient's errors were predominantly mixed. She also had difficulty with visual analysis and she tried to identify words by spelling out the letters. By the second month, her errors were primarily due to failures in visual analysis with a corresponding rise in vowel naming errors. She did not attempt identification of words by spelling. By the third month, there was a significant rise in errors due to faulty visual analysis and a sharp decrease in mixed and vowel naming errors. However, the proportion of grapheme–phoneme errors also increased during this period. This pattern of change in error type closely corresponds to a more sophisticated cognitive strategy, although errors of visual analysis may be a residual of faulty perceptual processing. The authors observed that, over a 2-year period, the patient had more difficulty with complex or irregular graphemes in words like *logic*, *porous*, and so on, than with visually confusing words.

These investigators examined the recovery of three patients and found that their progress could be characterized by a learning curve: $y = \alpha + \beta p^x$. α represents the asymptote, β the scaling constant, p the rate of learning, y the error score (in percentage) and x represents time. All three of the patients approached an asymptotic level of performance between approximately 5 months and 1 year. After 1 year, the quality of their reading errors may have changed, but there was little evidence of additional spontaneous recovery as measured by their performance on a reading test.

The pattern and degree of recovery has never been systematically studied in patients with anterior alexia; perhaps because the underlying linguistic disorder in anterior alexia has never been clearly elucidated (see Chapters 11 and 3 in this volume by Caramazza *et al.* and by Benson, respectively).

Summary

The studies discussed in the chapter again suggest that difficulties in reading can be the result of deficits at any of several levels of information processing during reading. Visual analysis, phonological recoding, and semantic identification are essential components in reading. Disturbances of any of these functions, and indeed at levels within each of these functions, may result in reading problems. Studies of fluent reading (cf. Chapters 7, 6, and 2 in this volume by Haber & Haber, Rayner, and Samuels & Eisenberg) provide a thorough information-processing analysis of skilled reading. The application of the theoretical models and the methodology employed in these studies would be of great utility in the study of reading impairment. Neuropsychologists and behavioral neurologists have taken the first step toward a better understanding of alexia through the identification of different forms of reading disability. The next important task is to determine, through a componential analysis, the exact nature of reading disturbances and to determine, through longitudinal studies, whether the impaired processes are subject to different recovery patterns, and, finally, whether these recovery patterns are related to specific subject variables, lesion variables, and treatment variables.

References

Ajax, E. T. Dyslexia without agraphia. *Archives of Neurology*, 1967, *17*, 645–652.

Albert, M., & Obler, L. *The bilingual brain: Neuropsychological and neurolinguistic aspects of bilingualism.* New York: Academic Press, 1978.

Basso, A., Capitani, E., & Vignolo, L. A. Influence of rehabilitation on language skills in aphasic patients. *Archives of Neurology*, 1979, *36*, 190–196.

Basso, A., Faglioni, P., & Vignolo, L. A. Etude controlee de la reeducation du langage dans l'aphasie: Comparison entre aphasiques traites et non-traites. *Revue Neurologique*, 1974, *131*, 607–614.

Bastian, H. C. *Aphasia and other speech defects.* London: H. K. Lewis, 1898.

Benton, A. L. Contributions to aphasia before Broca. *Cortex*, 1964, *1*, 314–327.

Butfield, E., & Zangwill, O. Re-education in aphasia: A review of 70 cases. *Journal of Neurology, Neurosurgery, and Psychiatry*, 1946, *9*, 75–79.

Charcot, J. M. Sur un cas de cedite verbale. In *Lecons sur les maladies du systeme nerveux* (Euvres completes de J. M. Charcot) (vol. 3). Paris: Delahaye and Lecrosnier, 1877.

Charcot, J. M. On a case of word-blindness. In *Clinical lectures of diseases of the nervous system* (vol. 3). London: The New Sydenham Society, 1889.

Culton, G. L. Spontaneous recovery from aphasia. *Journal of Speech and Hearing Research*, 1969, *12*, 825–832.

Franz, S. I. Studies in re-education: The aphasias. *Comparative Psychology*, 1918, *4*, 349–429.

Gardner, H., Denes, G., & Zurif, E. Critical reading at the sentence level in aphasia. *Cortex*, 1975, *11*, 60–72.

Gardner, H., & Zurif, E. Bee but not be: Oral reading of single words in aphasia and alexia. *Neuropsychologia*, 1975, *13*, 181–190.

Glees, P., & Cole, J. Recovery of skilled motor functions after small repeated lesions of the motor cortex in the Macaque. *Journal of Neurophysiology*, 1950, *13*, 137–148.

Goldstein, K. *After effects of brain injuries in war.* New York: Grune & Stratton, 1942.

Goldstein, K. *Language and language disturbances.* New York: Grune & Stratton, 1948.

Kapur, N., & Perl, N. T. Recognition reading (time course) related to disorder in paralexia. *Cortex*, 1978, *14*, 439–443.

Kertesz, A., & McCabe, P. Recovery patterns and prognosis in aphasia. *Brain*, 1977, *100*, 1–18.

Kurachi, M., Yamaguchi, N., Inasaka, T., & Torii, H. Recovery from alexia without agraphia: Report of an autopsy. *Cortex*, 1979, *15*, 297–312.

Luria, A. R. *Higher cortical functions in man.* New York: Basic Books, 1966.

Luria, A. R. *Traumatic aphasia.* The Hague: Mouton, 1970.

Luria, A. R., Naydin, V. L., Tsvetkova, L. S., & Vinarskaya, E. N. Restoration of higher cortical function following local brain damage. In P. Vinken & G. Bruyn (Eds.), *Handbook of clinical neurology* (vol. 3). Amsterdam: North Holland, 1969.

Mahut, H., & Zola, S. Ontogenetic time-table for the development of three functions in infant macaques and the effects of early hippocampal damage upon them. *Neuroscience Abstracts*, 1977, *3*, 428.

Mohr, J. P. Rapid amelioration of motor aphasia. *Archives of Neurology*, 1973, *28*, 77–82.

Newcombe, F. *Missile wounds of the brain.* New York and London: Oxford Univ. Press, 1969.

Newcombe, F., & Marshall, J. C. Stages in recovery from dyslexia following a left cerebral abscess. *Cortex*, 1973, *9*, 329–332.

Newcombe, F., Marshall, J. C., Carrivick, P. J., & Hiorns, R. W. Recovery curves in acquired dyslexia. *Journal of the Neurological Sciences*, 1975, *24*, 127–133.

Paradis, M. Bilingualism and aphasia. In H. A. Whitaker & H. A. Whitaker (Eds.), *Studies in neurolinguistics* (vol. 3). New York: Academic Press, 1977.

Paterson, J., & Bramwell, B. Two cases of word blindness. *Medical Press*, 1905, *13*, 507–508.

Porch, B. *Porch Index of Cummunicative Ability*. Palo Alto, California: Consulting Psychologists Press, 1971.

Sarno, M. T., & Levita, E. Natural course of recovery in severe aphasia. *Archives of Physical Medicine and Rehabilitation*, 1971, *52*, 175–186.

Sarno, J. E., Sarno, M. T., & Levita, E. Evaluating language improvement after completed stroke. *Archives of Physical Medicine and Rehabilitation*, 1971, *52*, 73–78.

Schneider, G. E. Is it really better to have your brain lesion early? A revision of the "Kennard principle." *Neuropsychologia*, 1979, *17*, 557–584.

Sroka, H., Solsi, P., & Bornstein, B. Alexia without agraphia: With complete recovery. *Confina Neurologica*, 1973, *35*, 167–176.

Teitelbaum, P., & Epstein, A. The lateral hypothalamic syndrome: Recovery of feeding and drinking after lateral hypothalamic lesions. *Psychological Review*, 1962, *69*, 74–90.

Thompson, F. J. Effects of acute cortical injury in the activation of the motor cortex in the cat. *Neuroscience Abstracts*, 1977, *3*, 280.

Trescher, J., & Ford, F. Colloid cyst of the third ventricle. Report of a case: Operative removal of the posterior half of the corpus callosum. *Archives of Neurology and Psychiatry*, 1937, *37*, 959–973.

Vignolo, L. A. Evolution of aphasia and language rehabilitation: A retrospective exploratory study. *Cortex*, 1964, *1*, 344–367.

Von Monakow, C. Localization of brain functions. *Zeitschrift fur Psychologie und Neurologie*, 1911, *17*, 185–200.

Wechsler, A. Transient left hemialexia: A clinical and angiographic study. *Neurology*, 1972, *22*, 628–633.

Wechsler, A., Weinstein, E. A., & Antin, S. P. Alexia without agraphia. *Bulletin of the Los Angeles Neurological Society*, 1972, *37*, 1–11.

Weisenburg, T., & McBride, K. *Aphasia: A clinical and psychological study*. New York: Commonwealth Fund, 1935.

Wepman, J. M. *Recovery from aphasia*. New York: Ronald Press, 1951.

Wertz, R. T., Collins, M. J., Brookshire, R., Friden, T., Kurtzke, J., Pierce, J., & Weiss, D. *The Veterans Administration cooperative study on aphasia*. Paper presented to the Academy of Aphasia, Chicago, 1978.

AUTHOR INDEX

Numbers in italics refer to the pages on which the complete references are listed.

SUBJECT INDEX

Language Arts

LANGUAGE ARTS
A Problem-Solving Approach

Sara W. Lundsteen
University of North Texas

1817

HARPER & ROW, PUBLISHERS, New York
Grand Rapids, Philadelphia, St. Louis, San Francisco,
London, Singapore, Sydney, Tokyo

Sponsoring Editor: Alan McClare
Project Editor: Carla Samodulski
Text Design Adaptation: Keithley and Associates, Inc.
Cover Design: Heather Ziegler
Cover Illustration/Photo: Sara Lundsteen
Text Art: Fineline Illustrations, Inc., Sara Lundsteen
Production Manager: Jeanie Berke
Production Assistant: Beth Maglione
Compositor: ComCom Division of Haddon Craftsmen, Inc.
Printer and Binder: R. R. Donnelley & Sons Company
Cover Printer: Lehigh Press

LANGUAGE ARTS: A Problem-Solving Approach

Library of Congress Cataloging-in-Publication Data
Lundsteen, Sara W.
  Language arts: a problem-solving approach/Sara W. Lundsteen.
    p.   cm.
  Bibliography: p.
  Includes index.
  ISBN 0-06-044094-5
  1. Language arts (Elementary) I. Title.
LB1576.L85   1989   88-32517
372.6—dc19   CIP

89 90 91 92 9 8 7 6 5 4 3 2 1

To the memory of my father, Professor H. Wynn Rickey
—a great scholar, teacher, and language lover.

To the full life and happiness of Natasha,
a young language lover.

Brief Contents

· ——— ·

Contents

·———·

PART 2
INTO PRINT   213

Preface

· ———— ·

"Enthusiasm is the electricity of life . . .
How do you get it?
You act enthusiastic until you make it a habit.
Enthusiasm is natural;
it is being alive,
taking the initiative,
seeing the importance of what you do,
giving it dignity and
making what you do important to yourself
and to others."

Gordon Parks

Language Arts: A Problem-Solving Approach is a complete and primary textbook for under-graduate and graduate college courses. Professors and those addressing in-service teachers will also find it useful. The text offers breadth and depth of coverage, a strong research base, attention to current curriculum issues, and a variety of fresh teaching suggestions. This is a "book for all seasons," a long-term investment for the student. Undergraduates can readily experience it on one level, but there is enough depth in it and its supplementary materials for graduate students to come back to it, a bit wiser, to profit on yet another level.

Students grow through creative problem solving. When teachers use a creative prob-lem-solving process in language arts instruction, the benefits are many: further integration, higher motivation, and an economical use of classroom time. Problems in this context are positive challenges, explored and profited from with satisfaction. During the process of solving problems with and through the language arts, children have the opportunity to pursue activities, interests, needs, and goals of their own choosing. In this way, they gain powerfully in integrated communication skills.

Teachers, too, grow through creative problem solving. Today's language arts teacher faces an interesting creative problem. The uses of language are many, cutting across all areas of the curriculum and needing a broad range of processes and skills. At the same time, children come to the classroom with a widening range of backgrounds, interests, attitudes, varieties of English, levels of preparation, and special needs—all demanding a tailoring of the language arts program. The teacher needs to be empowered to meet this challenge of addressing the why, who, what, where, and how of teaching each class member. *Language Arts: A Problem-Solving Approach* is designed to help preservice and in-service teachers solve this problem creatively.

The book has many desirable features. The style is designed to be interesting, inspira-tional, and readable. Many headings are questions. Visual materials appear throughout to clarify concepts. Some material is boxed for ready reference. Children's products are appropriately displayed.

Each chapter opens with an apt quote, the chapter table of contents, and a preview, often with questions to be answered during the reading. An opening scene with dialogue and characterization serves multiple purposes: to set the tone, preview important concepts, illustrate appropriate classroom practice, give examples for reference further along in the chapter, and help the reader visualize the methods of teaching suggested.

Each chapter also develops, where appropriate, answers to the why, who, where, what, and how of teaching. The *why* presents the rationale; the *who* inserts important developmental information; the *where* sections most often offer flexible room arrangements and management ideas for the physical and emotional climate; and the *what* sections review framework goals for the area. The reader is then genuinely ready for the *how* sections on teaching. Too often, mentioning *how* before exploring the other questions makes teaching seem like nothing more than a bag of tricks. The first chapter details the key themes, point of view, and organization of the whole language text.

An important feature is the activity book that supplements this text, *Choose Your Own Teaching and Learning Activities.* While designed to accompany the text chapter by chapter, it is also flexible. The user can move around and through it freely on the basis of need and interest. Activities are arranged in related clusters focusing on a certain topic. Each contains the rationale for its use, a description, and additional resource suggestions. The activity book serves as an applicative extension of the theories and implications presented in the text. A test bank is available in the instructor's manual, and appendixes to the instructor's manual offer further depth (e.g., "Help for a Teacher's Speaking Voice").

Taken as a whole, this text and its supplements will help teachers create a classroom environment that is joyful, creative, supportive, and challenging—one that will help students grow enthusiastically.

ACKNOWLEDGMENTS

Many thanks to everyone who helped, especially to contributing authors and area experts—Ann Robinson for authoring Chapter 8; Eileen Tway for Chapter 9; Gail Tompkins for Chapter 11; James Hoot for coauthoring Chapter 13; and Irene Rodriguez for her help with Chapter 14. I am grateful for their work, and I wish to point out that the responsibility for any mistakes is mine alone.

In addition, I am indebted to hundreds of students, teachers, colleagues, consultants, administrators, and children—too many to name individually but each one extremely important to this project. Special thanks to Pose Lamb, Eileen Tway (without whose encouragement yet another book would never have been attempted), Ernst Moerk, Karen Akhøj, Beverly Busching, Walter Loban, and Wes Earp, my supportive chairman at the University of North Texas, my new chair, Janet Black, as well as "supervisors" Burr and Meese. Very special thanks are due to Carol Mason Wolfe and my new and highly talented assistant, Cindie Aaen. Thanks to Carol's daughter, Natasha, who contributed many examples, and to Carol's husband Jon, who kept the computers working and created the poem *Fog* after reading Sandburg's poem. A very special thanks to Alex Lundsteen, without whose constant support none of those 11 other books would ever have been written. I need to invent a stronger word for "thank you" here.

I'd also like to thank the following people for their contributions: Blanch Chance, my art instructor, who offered advice on many of the illustrations; Judith Gilbert, Colorado Department of Education, for the annotated bibliography on textbook selection; Ann Dyson, University of California, Berkeley, for the saddened-teacher quote in Chapter 15; Pat Beck and class, Denton, Texas, Public Schools, for the inspiration for the opening scene of Chapter 13; Gail Lewis, for a language dialect example from North Carolina, traceable to Middle English, in Chapter 12; Helen Lodge, for language examples in Chapter 12; Jill Susson, a student at the University of California, Irvine, for collecting the "Indian" language example in Chapter 12; Dan Dolan, University of California, Riverside, for ideas for the opening scene in Chapter 12; Kathy Krebs, a kindergarten teacher and a student at the University of North Texas, for the word wall and garden shop center ideas used in Chapter 7; Brenda Whittine, a third-grade teacher and a student at the University of North Texas, for collecting Jason's "Crash in Our Trash" composition, Chapter 7; Warren Webster, who taught sixth grade in Goleta, California, for inspiring the opening scene for Chapter 1; Jim Miller, my dean at the University of North Texas, for the dean's wise words in Chapter 2; Velma Schmidt, for the turtle-lover anecdote in Chapter 2; Ralph Nichols, for the opening quote in Chapter 3 from his address presented at the first Annual Conference of the International Listening Association, Atlanta, Georgia, February 1980; Andra Penny, a kindergarten teacher in Denton, Texas, for the anecdote about the "shocker," Chapter 6; and Mary Cummings, a third-grade teacher in San Clemente, California, for inspiration for the opening scene in Chapter 6.

Finally, I'd like to express my appreciation to the following reviewers of this text for their long hours and invaluable help in suggesting ways to improve the book:

Ruth Beeker, Arizona State University

Howard Blake, Temple University

Ella Erway, Southern Connecticut State University

Sheila Fitzgerald, Michigan State University

Sherry Kragler, North Texas State University

Billie Jo Rieck, West Liberty State College

Leo Schell, Kansas State University

Mary Wilcox, formerly of Stanford Research Institute

Sara W. Lundsteen

Contributors

. ———— .

James Hoot
Early Childhood Research Center
Department of Learning and Instruction
University at Buffalo, State University of New York

Ann Robinson
College of Education
Teacher Education
University of Arkansas at Little Rock

Irene Rodriguez
College of Education
Department of Elementary, Reading, and Early Childhood Education
University of North Texas

Gail Tompkins
College of Education
Department of Instructional Leadership and Academic Curriculum
The University of Oklahoma

Eileen Tway
School of Education and Allied Professions
Department of Teacher Education
Miami University

PART 1

DEVELOPMENTAL BASES AND ORAL LANGUAGE

CHAPTER 1

Casting a Language Arts Net: Crucial Ideas for the New Teacher

"If we give people a fish, we feed them for a day. But if we teach them the **process** of fishing, we feed them for a lifetime."

Source unknown

INTRODUCTION

This chapter provides the organizational basis for the major themes and principles and the network of language arts concepts developed in this book. Here, we stress definitions of key terms and ideas—especially the unifying, motivating focus of creative problem solving (CPS).

Before reading another word, take a piece of paper and write your definition of *language arts,* off the top of your head. Now write what you think *teaching* language arts is. Tape these early definitions where you can easily retrieve them (perhaps to the back of this book) and look at them again when you have finished this text. Compare your definitions before and after. Concepts grow slowly, layer by layer, as one reads, thinks, discusses, and experiments.

Language Arts Defined

Some people would start their study of teaching language arts with a definition of *language,* diving for a dictionary. "The words, their pronunciation, and the methods of combining them used and understood by a considerable community and established by long usage." Then they might look for *language arts:* "The subjects (as reading, spelling, literature, composition, debate, dramatics) taught in elementary and secondary schools that aim at developing the learner's comprehension of written and oral language as well as his use of it for communication and expression" (to quote from *Webster's 3rd New International Dictionary*). As you will see, however, *the language arts are not restricted to the English language arts period, but permeate the whole school day and all curriculum areas.*

Briefly, the components of a comprehensive and integrated language arts curriculum include oral and written composition in subject areas; investigation of our linguistic systems; and responses to literature in all subject areas. Literature is a prime motivator in language arts learning. Its use in language arts creates closeness between teacher and child, child and child, self and the world of other lives, times, and places. Children's literature is frequently interrelated with other language arts areas throughout this book. The process of responding to it integrates many language arts.

The Teacher's Role Defined

The quality of instruction in language arts has advanced steadily in recent years. We've come a long way from too passive an approach to maturation, too many excuses for failure, too narrow a view of skills, too little regard for their integration in process, too much pressure, too little integration of the language arts, too little genuine use, and too little meaning.

In this book the functions of the language arts teacher include knowing the *why* (rationale), *who* (child), *what* (goals), and *where* (classroom climate), and letting all of these understandings flow into the *how* of teaching methods. One is rarely, if ever, ready for the how of teaching until one has attended to the why, who, what, and where. The organization of most chapters in this book reflects this idea. Another of the book's concepts is to avoid overteaching and instead to let children construct their own learning in large part. This idea is illustrated in the classroom scene to follow shortly.

In our definition of language arts we have included processes and skills of communication. But how do thinking and creative problem solving relate to the language arts? Is there any way of unifying and integrating all these areas for an economical use of time? Let's go directly to our opening scene to find out how an experienced teacher integrated CPS, children's literature, and language arts in his classroom.

OPENING SCENE: A Teacher and Class Communicate Using Literature and Problem Solving

The following classroom scene illustrates many of the ideas and ideals in this chapter, particularly those about teaching problem solving by guiding its process. The example is in large part taken from a classroom videotape recording of a sixth-grade problem-solving discussion about a piece of literature. The teacher of this class had previously spent much time helping the children learn how to solve problems creatively—how to do more than leap from an ill-defined problem to a surface solution. This scene illustrates how the teacher guided the process through five steps.

Step 1: Becoming Aware of a Problem

The teacher would read a cliff-hanging episode from a book to help the children *become aware of a problem* (a first step in a problem-solving process).

Using a discussion of unfinished episodes to stimulate thought, the teacher's overall design included the following:

1. A plan of probable questions to probe choice points of the CPS discussion. These questions were designed to elicit certain problem-solving responses while guiding the process.

2. Stimulating situations, frequently from high-quality literature for children, to get the process going.

3. Audio and/or video recorders to catch class discussion for later analysis.

In this particular instance, the teacher had selected the book *Crow Boy*, by Taro Yashima. The story began:

> On the first day of our village school in Japan there was a boy missing. He was found hidden away in the dark space underneath the schoolhouse. . . .

The boy in this story was a strange, shy, silent child. He was ignored or derided by his classmates, who named him Chibi, meaning "tiny boy." The teacher paused at selected points in this story to conduct a discussion about Chibi's problem.

Step 2: Gathering Information (Warm-up and Readiness)

TEACHER: Remember, in this discussion time I'm not looking for any one right answer. I am recording on the board any ideas you might have so that you can examine them.
From what I've read so far, what would you say about the boy they called Chibi? Let the thoughts race from your mind. What stood out for you?

The teacher's first open-ended question served to "warm up" the children and to bring out facts, conditions, feelings, and hunches about the problem in an unrestrained way. From the responses, the teacher could also get an idea of the children's boundaries: for example, recall of the story elements; interest, verbal fluency, and a subskill of accurate listening.

YOLANDA: The thing that stood out for me was he knows where the wild grapes grow.
PAUL: He can make interesting drawings. He knows and can make every call the crows make.
LOIS: Well, I would agree with what Paul said; but because Chibi can't get along with his friends, I think he tries to keep away and wants to . . . do it himself . . . by himself.
MARION: That's right, and the kids don't really appreciate him; it makes him feel kinda bad.
PAUL: Chibi seems like he's lonely and if people get to know him, they could like him better, because he had those talents of studying insects and . . . everything.

During this free exchange of ideas, the teacher wrote key words from each response on the board. He allowed many children to respond to the same question. A few (those with a less secure self-concept or an anxious style) tended to model their responses after those of other children. Children who were familiar with use of a problem-solving process helped the teacher move the discussion along to information that defined the problem situation. Some children supported ideas and some asked for clarification. Most did not stand in their own way. In this class, children had quickly learned that during such discussion *all answers, all responses, were respected and recognized by their teacher.*

Whenever a classroom situation called for one right answer, the teacher was direct with the children and informed them of the convergent task. When the situation was open (as in the present discussion), the teacher let the students know that, too.

Step 3: Pinpointing a Problem

Concluding that the children were ready, the teacher felt it was time to change focus, to advance or lift the discussion with another type of question. This question was designed to explore a direct definition of the main character's problem. This step in the classic problem-solving approach is frequently sought too soon. It is well to hold off until students get a chance to offer many ideas about facts, conditions, and smaller problems. The teacher avoided leaping prematurely to an abstract question (e.g., "what's the problem?") and continued with seeking and defining the problem.

TEACHER: To summarize, some of you have suggested that Chibi was in some kind of mess. More clearly, what would you say his problem was?

DAVID: Lonely.

KIM: Making friends.

FRED: A homeless child.

JAY: He lacks companionship: Well, that would be like Kim just said, "making friends," wouldn't it? [The teacher drew a line connecting the two recorded contributions.]

CARLOS: I think it might be his environment at home and he should change that if he can. Fred brought out the point that if he had brothers or sisters it would help him. Maybe so. But I don't think so. Maybe he does have them and they beat him down and say they're better than him; and maybe they get more rice than he does at dinner and first use of the shower. OK, well, maybe there wasn't a shower, but stuff like that.

TEACHER: Before we make more hypotheses and evaluate them, I believe some more people have things to say about the problem.

Here the teacher intended to control the *process,* not the content, and refocused on the problem and more divergent thinking. During a creative problem-solving discussion, it is acceptable to control the focus on the process but not on the ideas.

DAVID: Well, now I disagree with myself when I said his main problem is . . . I now disagree with saying that he was a lonely child, because I think that could be a smaller problem to a bigger one, like Jay said, "lacking companionship."

TEACHER: [Encouraging reasons] Why do you think he might be a lonely child?

DAVID: Well, he never had anyone to talk to. Well, maybe he had someone to talk to, but he didn't really have someone to maybe tell his problems to.

GAIL: I think making new friends, . . . the reason he can't make new friends is because he's shy. And I think that would be one of his subproblems.

Step 4: Finding Ideas (Hypotheses)

Encouraging divergence, the teacher then moved the process toward the making of hypotheses and the weighing of these alternatives.

TEACHER: If you think we've gotten out a good idea of Chibi's problem, let's go to what Carlos started to do. Let me now ask how you think Chibi might go about solving this problem that many of you agree on—lack of friends. Let your ideas flow freely. Remember to hold off criticizing alternatives until we've gotten most of the ideas out.

CARLOS: I think it could solve his . . . I think if maybe a new person that came into the school. . . . He could make friends with him, or her.

LOIS: He could get up enough courage to join in some different games or activities of the other children.

MARION: Show them how he feels; show the kids how he feels. Talk it over with them. And then he could get them to make friends.

PAUL: Go off alone and don't pay any attention to them.

LOIS: And a solution would come to him?

ANDREW: Some children just can't make friends and that's it; forget him.

MARION: You can't just do that, he might commit suicide or something! Then how would you feel?!

FRED: If the teacher liked him, maybe the teacher would take care of it.

ANDREW: I think the teacher might be hurting him by putting almost all of his work up and everything, and praising him so high, because people might begin not to like him . . . even more . . . because they think he's the teacher's pet; they'd think he's not really that good; he's just a big show-off.

PAUL: Back to Lois's idea of them becoming interested, well, I think, maybe out on the playground Chibi could tell some guy that he might want for a friend, "Let's see who can catch the biggest lizard," or something, and the guy he wanted for a friend wouldn't have as much practice as Chibi would, and Chibi would get the bigger one. And so Chibi could offer to tell him the rules he's found for catching big lizards. And while he's doing this, he could make friends.

Step 5: Gaining Acceptance for a Solution

The teacher's next move was to follow up on Paul's idea to seek transfer. That is, he asked if any of the children had ever tried Paul's way—getting others to share your interests so you could be friends—and how they tried it, or could try it.

After being stimulated by this part of the discussion, the children wrote their ideas of how to get their favorite solution accepted. Gaining acceptance, a fifth step, is a sometimes neglected part of the problem-solving process.

About the Scene

For further response to the experience, some children chose to write some dialogue with Chibi and the other characters, resolving the problem verbally. Others wrote a description of how the characters acted to make Chibi a happier child. Some of these scripts were dramatized in small groups. The teacher provided many options and choices. Thus, response to literature, oral and written composing, creative writing, listening, reading, speaking, tolerance for diverse ideas, critical thinking, and many other aspects of the language arts were integrated. The teacher also integrated the experience into their larger social studies unit on Asia.

By the end of the discussion just described, besides enjoying the literature, most of the children could identify with a problem and had experienced parts of a CPS process in some way. Children were learning to be persistent, to feel free to be original, to respect their feelings and those of others, to empathize, to think of reasons, and to harness critical thought productively to CPS. They were preparing for a demanding world that needs skilled, creative problem solvers.

This scene demonstrates how children can gain problem-solving concepts through discussion, in this case by using selections from children's literature. Of course, the teacher did not follow every story or episode with this kind of discussion, nor did he always go through every step suggested here. Moreover, he knew how to stop while the children were still interested.

Sometimes this teacher's questions highlighted other substeps, such as obtaining missing information, deciding on the type of problem, or looking for a major idea or principle in a problem situation. Sometimes the children responded through art or drama or just by silent appreciation. This teacher was alert, however, for opportunities to apply their growing problem-solving abilities and to contribute to their self-concepts as problem solvers.

Guiding creative problem solving in the language arts classroom may be easier said than done. In reality, teaching does not always obtain these results. Children do not always show keen insights or think creatively, quickly, and enthusiastically. Leading this kind of discussion is especially challenging for those who have not taught in this way before or for those in rural and urban areas with tired, hungry children. The teacher who furnished this scene felt unable to trust his students this much at first. He kept fishing for answers and cutting the children off. Acquiring the necessary strategies required time, observation of others, dissatisfaction with his old ways, persistent effort, and, finally, the reward of seeing positive changes in his students. For novice teachers, however, expert-teacher demonstrations can be inspiring. Striving toward such goals in one's own classroom makes it all seem worthwhile.

Many children, of course, have less command over their abilities to express themselves, think at an abstract level, or attend to task than the children in the scene. Chapter 14 offers some ideas on the special child. The methods used in our opening scene, however, have been adapted upward and downward, even to kindergarten level. At that level the teacher used puppet scenarios to gradually reveal information for the problem as the young children interacted (Lundsteen & Tarrow, 1981).

Under a teacher's subtle and expert guidance, CPS is a highly motivating, integrating, and economical focus for a language arts program. No computer can replace classroom interaction that is worthwhile, challenging, and stimulating to children. Each chapter in this book further develops aspects of CPS; for example, Chapter 6 covers discussion with an analysis of questioning, and Chapter 10 is about critical and creative thinking. Moreover, the activity/resource book that is a companion to this text also offers activities to promote CPS in your classroom.

PREVIEW OF SOME KEY THEMES IN THIS BOOK

Next, let's briefly preview and then further develop some key terms for this text: *process, integration, function, developmental know-how* and *positive self-concept, problem solving* (just touched upon), and *democracy.* We start with *process,* a crucial focus both for this chapter and for a successful language arts classroom.

Process

The first opening quote for this chapter said: "If we give people a fish, we feed them for a day. But if we teach them the *process* of fishing, we feed them for a lifetime." Process is another key idea in language arts teaching. A process is an integrated series of active mental—sometimes physical—behaviors moving an individual toward some goal or product. For example, the process of composing in writing is not just skill in putting in commas, but includes planning, translating, reviewing, and revising before final displaying (Chapter 8). And, as we saw in the opening scene, the process of CPS includes awareness of possible problems, gathering information, pinpointing a problem, and finding ideas that finally may make for an acceptable solution.

Listening, speaking, reading, and writing have underlying comprehending and composing processes that are essential and are therefore worth knowing, teaching, and evaluating. Point of view is often clarified and made memorable by creating analogies. We hope this one about fishing works to keep *process* in your mind.

Integration

As used in this book, the term *integration* refers to organizing language arts teaching to interrelate and unify subjects usually taught separately. We saw an example in the opening scene. More will be said about this term in the section on process and integration.

Function

In this book, *function* refers to a child's employment of language in a useful and meaningful way. That is, the child uses language not just because a workbook page says to, but to meet a real-world need—a classmate needs a get-well card, a field trip sponsor needs a thank-you letter, a daily journal needs an entry.

Developmental Know-how and Positive Self-concept

Another key theme running throughout this text is developmental know-how (stressed particularly in Chapter 2). Applying developmental know-how in the classroom includes understanding the importance of positive self-concept and the way it grows and can be enhanced though effective language arts teaching. Ideas about self-concept are developed in Chapter 14, on the special child, and in the Instructor's Manual. If child and teacher do not feel good about themselves, it almost does not matter much what else happens in school. Language arts growth (or any other growth) is seriously hampered.

Problem Solving

Although the term *problem solving* may have negative connotations, in this book, problem solving is something good, challenging, even joyful. You and your students will come to welcome its positive power in your teaching and learning. Briefly, problem solving in the classroom refers to the children's processes of deciding among the alternatives that will lead them to their goals.

Democracy

One might think of democracy as the Stars and Stripes, the Statue of Liberty, 1776, and the Fourth of July, but in this book it is a leadership style that takes others' needs into account in the language arts classroom. Participants, including the teacher, use CPS to meet the needs of all concerned. Everyone in the classroom participates in decision making and has options and choices when listening, speaking, reading, writing, delving into literature, or integrating these activities with any curriculum or life area. The English language arts classroom becomes a testing ground for the use of democratic principles in the child's larger and future worlds.

A FISHING NET: LANGUAGE ARTS PROCESSES AND SUBSKILLS

"Listening, speaking, reading, and writing are more like strands in a web than like four peas in a pod. You touch one strand of language experience and the whole thing vibrates and responds."

NCTE Committee on Curriculum Bulletins

We have used the fishing-process analogy to make one point. Now, let's move to another analogy using a fishnet. Each of the language arts with its processes and skills—listening, speaking, reading, and writing—might be visualized as located on the knots of a fishnet, as shown in Figure 1.1. In a textbook we can turn a spotlight on each knot in turn, but each language art is still interwoven with others. Pull up a knot (e.g., "listening") for focus in a classroom and the whole net moves, affecting all the other language arts knots. One weak or mishandled knot weakens the whole net.

As you read this book, you will find a spotlight turned on major knots of this net as relevant chapters unfold. Then an even finer network of ideas within each of these areas becomes apparent. In the final chapter you will again find a figure with a culminating language arts net. Finally, the language arts net can be part of other life networks.

Process and Integration

When a well-prepared teacher of language arts focuses on *process,* a natural and powerful *integration* occurs. Such a teacher knows that a composing process is part of all the language arts. Certainly we compose an oral "text" when speaking and a written "text" when writing. Most often we compose one or more texts in our heads before actually delivering them to an audience. We compose a text even when listening and reading, making the message our very own. A teacher can use the thread of a composing process to pull together much language-learning activity, just as it happens in life out of school.

For example, a young child's mother rises from the dinner table, saying, "I'm going to get changed now," as she is on her way to a meeting. Playful Dad, knowing full well what she means, puts his hand into his pocket and says, "Oh, you need some change. Here, I have some nickels and quarters for you." He composes a different text from the one intended. The five-year-old responds, "She didn't say *change;* she said *changed* with a *d* at the end." The child is able to compose both texts in her mind and so explain her father's "mistake" to him. Such a child will come to use this same composing process in writing and in reading. (You have just met Natasha, the subject of many examples in this book.)

This understanding of the child's involvement in a *composing process* in all of the language arts can be a powerful aid for a teacher. Teachers who have this basic, integrative,

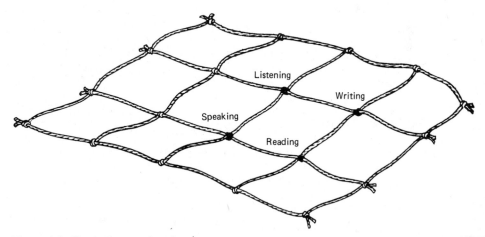

Figure 1.1 The language arts network.

and central key to curriculum need not be totally dependent on some state-adopted language text series. They know what the processes are, when a child shows strengths or needs help with them, and what alternatives are available.

Process as a Tool for Learning

A well-prepared teacher also knows that language arts processes can be tools for learning. For example, composing is a tool for learning. Have you ever realized that you did not really know what you thought about something until you clarified and organized your thoughts during the composing process of making a speech or creating a piece of writing? When children compose what they already know, take in new material, and then again compose what they have learned, they are more truly learning. Thus process is a tool to aid discovery in content areas such as science, social science, and literature.

A Process Continuum of Classroom Programs

Think of a process continuum of classroom programs as shown in Figure 1.2. Some programs have a heavy emphasis on process, and we could place them at one end of the continuum (as in the opening scene). Some have little emphasis on process and much on isolated skills of language arts (e.g., 15 minutes on handwriting pages, 15 minutes on vowels, and so on). We could place such programs at the other end of the continuum. In between, we could place other programs.

Some yearly programs could be placed according to the overall nature of the curriculum. Others could be so placed at certain times during the school year and with respect to certain language arts areas. (For example, one program would become very skill-oriented just before testing. Another might be very process-oriented with respect to written composition, but very fragmented with separate skills emphasis in almost all other language arts areas.)

In general, the more a program operates toward the process end of the continuum, the more meaningful and long-lasting will be the learning of the students. Of course, it may be necessary for a teacher to devote extra time to a child for coaching or polishing an isolated skill. But that would be the exception rather than the rule when the program usually operates at the process end of the continuum.

Some chapters in this book focus on a particular language arts area (e.g., listening, written composition) and then suggest ideas for integration toward the end of the chapter. In such chapters, the author has also surveyed state goals or frameworks with their related

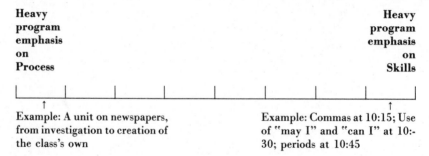

Heavy
program
emphasis
on
Process

Heavy
program
emphasis
on
Skills

Example: A unit on newspapers, from investigation to creation of the class's own

Example: Commas at 10:15; Use of "may I" and "can I" at 10:-30; periods at 10:45

Figure 1.2 Continuum for locating programs in the language arts.

objectives and essentials and has fashioned a brief curriculum framework with a process emphasis. You can use these guides in planning a unit of lessons for your classroom and as a comparison to whatever state and local frameworks you encounter.

REAL-LIFE FUNCTION

When a teacher focuses on real-life *function,* of the language arts processes, the child can construct long-lasting understandings. This is so because the child sees meaning and can transfer listening, speaking, reading, and writing skills to many new contexts. [Example: (child speaking) "I need to make a list of what we want to do for our classroom 'publishing company.' Then we can read it back."] Figure 1.3 on page 14 suggests uses of language as central, served by interactive language arts and backed up by comprehending and composing processes.

DEVELOPMENTAL KNOW-HOW

Teachers who understand and can apply *developmental know-how* appropriately are more likely to keep their invitations for children to use language at a reasonable developmental level and are more likely to individualize instruction appropriately. For example, sixth graders might handle almost every aspect of their classroom "publishing company"; first graders will need lots of help. Some children, because of developmental delays, may need to participate at first just by pushing the switch and keys that start the classroom computer printer. (Chapter 2 deals in depth with developmental know-how.)

THINKING AND PROBLEM SOLVING IN THE LANGUAGE ARTS

How does thinking relate to the language arts? Beneath processes and skills of communication (listening, speaking, reading, writing) lie processes and skills of thinking. Further, beneath a meaningful use of thinking lies an organizing process, *problem solving.* Figure 1.4 on page 15 depicts this idea. Language without thought can be useless and meaningless. Thinking not harnessed to something useful like problem solving can be a sterile exercise. A problem-solving focus needs to be central to a language arts program, not just peripheral or incidental. Problem solving is one of the prime uses of language (Brown, 1987; Goffin & Tull, 1985; Lundsteen, 1976).

When teacher and children use communication stimulated by creative problem solving (CPS), they are economically using a great number of thinking processes and skills (not a multitude of separated ones). Students then need little or no drill-type (or bottom-up) practice in basic mental skills, in attentiveness, or in atomized activity in six major processes of thinking: (1) perceptual, (2) associative, (3) inferential, (4) creative, (5) critical thinking, and (6) problem solving. These basic processes are usually integrated in a meaningful way when children use problem solving (Russell, 1956). Chapter 10 develops concepts about and applications of inferential, creative, and critical thinking in the classroom.

With a limited amount of time in the school day and massive expectations for covering "essential elements" in the curriculum for mastery of skills, an economical approach is a necessity. Many school districts now include a problem-solving emphasis (e.g., New York state and Dallas, Texas). An approach with a problem-solving focus tends to avoid the encyclopedia type of fragmentation typical of most language arts textbooks for children.

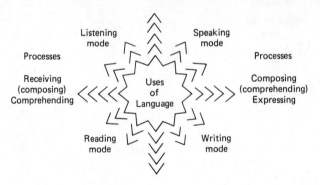

Sample Uses While Speaking/Listening—Writing/Reading

Self-expression
      Instrumental—use of language to solve own needs
      Personal—to express feelings (affective), uniqueness
      (Chapters 3, 4, 5, 8, 13)
Exposition
      Heuristic—to explore environment
      Informative—to convey information to others
      (Chapters 6, 7)
Literature
      Literary—to make language beautiful and memorable
      (Chapter 9, with reference throughout all chapters)
Persuasion
      Regulatory—use of language for controlling others
      (Chapter 10)
Other
      Interactional—use to interact with others—may cut across many categories
        (Chapters 3 through 10)
      Imaginative—use by child to create own world—may cut across categories; may go from
        self-expression to literary use of language
        (Chapters 3, 4, 9, 10, 13)
      Ritualistic—to exchange greetings or promote cordial social relations; to keep open lines
        of communication, of belonging; to establish procedural familiarity; to commemorate
        and satisfy ceremonial expectations
        (Chapters 3, 4, 14)

Figure 1.3 Central location of uses in the interactive language
arts processes.

Problem-solving concepts fit naturally with the challenge of learning the language arts.
Students can meet this challenge with confidence in their growing communication processes
and skills, and with a spirit of joyful adventure. By simply focusing on problem solving,
a prepared teacher can provide learning experiences integrating thought and language in
a motivating way that can remain throughout life.

    Teachers and their students use CPS in the language arts for everything from making
up their own instructional strategies for solving learning problems to using problem episodes
in literature to shed light on their own life choice points. Young creative solvers have
produced their own strategies for learning spelling and for authoring. (For example: "I try
seeing words nailed letter by letter to billboards." "When I write a story I sometimes get
it almost all planned in my mind first; then I write like crazy." "When my handwriting gets

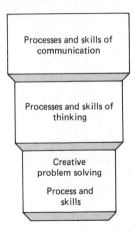

Figure 1.4 Relationship of communication and thinking to problem solving.

really bad, I slow myself down, breathe deep, hum, and 'ice skate' my pencil.'') Such children are taking hold of at least a corner of the learning problem, learning autonomy, and not just sitting back and saying, ''You just try to teach me.'' Consider three further examples: a nonreader, poetry makers, and literature explorers.

Examples

Second-Grade Nonreader A second grader who did not read, despite his teacher's best efforts, solved his problem by creating his own reading method. The teacher, who emphasized creative problem solving in the class, asked him how he thought he could learn to read. He decided to use *Charlotte's Web*, his favorite among the books that the teacher had read to the class, as his ''textbook.'' He copied words from the book, brought them to the teacher so that she could correct his reversals, then fixed the words with the aid of the biggest eraser in town. In this way he learned to read. The idea is not that copying words from a favorite book is a miracle cure for problems in learning to read, but when a child ''owns'' a challenge, problem solving can powerfully aid learning.

Poetry Makers A small group of sixth-grade students was concerned with a literary composition problem. While involved in an early-childhood cross-tutoring unit, they wanted to create poems about toys. These poems were to be used for choral presentation to kindergarten children. Here is a portion of one group's conversation.

MAX: I think a problem with our poem is that we need a refrain—to repeat. It might tie at least some of our ideas together.

VALENTINO: I'm open to that. Who's got some refrain lines we can try?

MARCIA: I don't think we need to do that. Those little kids are too young to know the difference.

MAX: Just because our audience is young doesn't mean we shouldn't offer them the best poetry we can write—as long as it's about things that interest them. That's why we chose toys. Would you want your little brother to get lousy poetry?

VALENTINO: How about. . . .

If the teacher had simply assigned these children a set task of writing a poem with no genuine function and no audience in mind, not even themselves, their response might have been less keen, integrative, and thoughtful. In working on their "own" problem these students were integrating listening, speaking, writing (the poetry), and eventually reading (the poetry to an intended audience). They used time economically, because many language processes and skills were interrelated within their one task.

Literature Explorers   A small group in a primary grade is discussing the picture book *And It Rained,* by Ellen Raskin (1969). The animals in the book try to deal with a persistent problem: Just after their tea party starts each day at four o'clock, it rains. The tea gets weak and the biscuits get soggy. The animals try out various solutions. The children read a couple of pages and then discuss the animals' solutions, critically analyzing them and concocting their own. As they read this book, the children are actively participating in the process of finding acceptable hypotheses. (They do not always do this with literature; sometimes they just enjoy the stories.)

The foregoing examples show that children get a progressively clearer hold on a meaningful problem based on both individual and group needs. They are aware of their progress. In a language arts program that takes advantage of challenges that children can "own," integrated growth takes off. Thus the core of the productive classroom is the individual student who is motivated to use communication for personally felt challenges.

Of course, a teacher cannot tuck everything in a successful classroom under the umbrella of problem solving. But an emphasis on problem solving is meaningful, motivational, and economical, and stimulates growth in communication and in thought of all kinds.

CREATIVE PROBLEM SOLVING IN THE LANGUAGE ARTS

Think back to a problem you've solved recently in a rather *unique* way, at least for you. Recall what steps you used to solve it and how you found the solution. Perhaps the problem was whether or not to be a teacher. Or perhaps you already have ideas of what creative problem solving is, and your problem is you want to get the children in your classroom to do more of it, better. Now it is time to clarify what we mean by *creative* problem solving: *Creative* problem solving in the classroom is a process of selecting alternatives that leads toward a goal the child desires and that results in a pattern of behavior that is *new,* at least to the child.

Problem solving is creative when it has a balance of outward exploring and inward evaluative thought while it moves deliberately toward a goal. Learning through problem solving is at its creative best when children find problems and answers that have *room for exploration,* or *unknowns.* Then the teacher and the students set out to explore together. For example, improvised drama in the classroom is productive because there is no one right answer, no one correct way to play out the ideas. (Drama is the subject of Chapter 5.)

Getzels (1964) long ago recommended that children in school be encouraged to meet the challenge of problems and answers that are full of unknowns. Problems with creative opportunity have unknowns at least for the child and sometimes even for the teacher. "Open" problems such as these stimulate children to be innovative. Much too often in school both child and teacher know what the problem is and what the one right answer is, and the result is a drill-like exercise. (For example, a child may know very well that periods go after sentences that aren't questions or exclamations, but is still given three workbook pages to do on the topic.)

If both teacher and child know both problem and answer, we see noncreative problem solving. Unfortunately we see a lot of it. The minute the child does not know the answer, however, there is room for divergent thinking—an important part of CPS. *Divergent* thought goes out in many directions to seek and explore.

Problem solving becomes even more creative when the child does not know what the problem is. Then problem *finding* is the challenge. The chances for creativity further increase when the teacher admits to not knowing the answer—or even exactly what the problem is—and remains willing to explore interactively with the child.

When Children Need Creative Problem Solving

Children do *not* need creative problem solving when they already know what to do and how and when to do it. Children *do* need creative problem solving when they:

1. Need to think about and experience new and unusual possibilities in varied ways.
2. Need to select alternatives.
3. Need to develop something new.
4. Need to respond to an opportunity, but don't know how.
5. Have a concern and don't know how to handle it (Isaksen & Treffinger, 1985).

In sum, we need to welcome unknowns, puzzlements, even "messes"; they are chances for growth.

A Trip up a River: An Analogy of a Problem-Solving Process

In tune with the earlier theme of process fishing and net casting, consider problem solving as a trip up a river. You will travel from the bottom delta upstream in a fishing boat looking for new grounds. This analogy illustrates five common steps in problem solving and many other real-world features. (See Figure 1.5.)

1. Becoming Aware of Potential Problems   In your small boat at sea you approach a delta. It is not clear if you've found more sea or the mouth of a wide, wide river. You are becoming aware of a potential problem with many unknowns that will allow you to deal with aspects of your journey creatively.

2. Gathering Information   Exploring the delta, you think you have found a river, so you go up some tributaries and double back. To check the depth, perhaps you examine formations at the banks or drop a line. Wind, stars, rapids, or habitation may furnish data. Although you do not appear to be making much progress in your journey, you are gathering information. *Too often we leap to a conclusion about what a problem is—and that isn't the problem at all.*

3. Pinpointing a Problem   Eventually, coming to a fork in the river, you pinpoint a problem. You use the information you have gained so far to choose one of the directions to take you to the fishing grounds you seek. You might, however, come back later and choose the other fork as another alternative.

When you choose a specified route, you are *converging,* narrowing down the possibilities. When you are wandering around and coming back, you are exploring, *diverging.* For a while you may seem to be going nowhere.

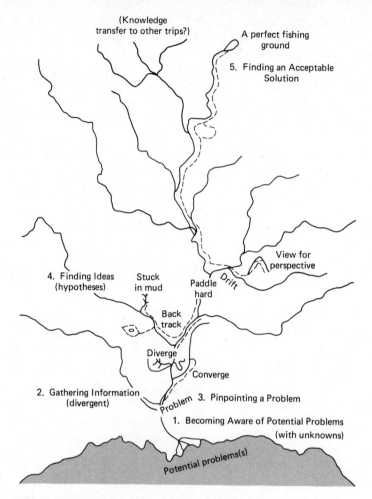

Figure 1.5 Problem solving as a trip up a river.

4. Finding Ideas (Hypotheses)   Then you choose yet another fork in the river (or course of action) and proceed. As you get closer and closer to the resolution you will finally adopt, the river gets more and more narrow. You may abandon your boat temporarily to seek a more abstract view, perhaps from the top of a mountain. From that vantage point you may be able to predict *consequences* of your choices and plan evaluations. Here is where a lot of problem solving breaks down; one doesn't consider the consequences. Just as there are many streams that form the sources of the river so are there many potential solutions.

In the real world, you do not always steer in a neat line toward your goal. You may backtrack at times. Sometimes, building on your past experience, you may start your journey somewhere along the river and not at the very mouth. Now and then you take side trips into towns and fields along the banks, as you take care of other related or unrelated concerns. Sometimes you seem to paddle along the same river route of a problem over and over, so many times that you and the river seem to cut a deep canyon in your life.

Sometimes you get stuck in the mud or caught in a storm; you can't seem to escape—

the whole thing becomes a *predicament.* Teachers of young children working with creative problem solving need to protect them from getting trapped in predicaments.

Sometimes it takes a lot of persistent, conscious attention and effort to paddle upstream. At other times you just let the boat drift with the currents or allow it to be pulled by other forces.

5. Finding an Acceptable Solution There is nothing more satisfying, invigorating, and self-fulfilling than finding a rich "fishing ground" full of acceptable solutions at the end of your problem-solving journey. Ideally the knowledge you have gained from your problem-solving journeys will *transfer* to future trips.

Here, then, are the important steps in a problem-solving process:

1. Becoming aware of potential problems.
2. Gathering information.
3. Pinpointing a problem.
4. Finding ideas (hypotheses).
5. Finding an acceptable solution.

These steps are not necessarily tight, straight, neat, even, sequential, or mutually exclusive in real life, as the river analogy points out. Our opening scene gave us a rather neat, tight demonstration of the use of CPS. In real life, the journey is not so smooth, but safe classroom experiences with CPS build children's confidence in solving life's more hazardous problems.

Problem Solving in a Classroom Context

Another aspect of using CPS is identifying *kinds* of problems. Approaches to problem solving often depend on context: When you know the type of problem a child is dealing with, you can match teaching methods to it. Table 1.1 shows some examples of problem areas.

An illustration pinpointing the social area is provided by a school (Patterson School in Long Beach, California) whose entire philosophy is built on the importance of creative problem solving. This school identified the following types of problems related to social interaction:

1. *Faulty environments.* Some shared social problems in school stem from faulty environments. If the teacher and class can alter the environment, the problem (sometimes called a "nonproblem problem") is solved swiftly. For example, if children in a reading group are constantly disturbed by the other students, the group can be moved to a quieter corner of the room.
2. *Breaking school or class rules or not following directions.* The trouble might again be a "nonproblem problem" that is related to clarity or information overload. For example, if children break a class rule (e.g., only so many people at a writing center), the teacher makes sure they are clear about the limits the class has set and tries to have as few rules as possible.
3. *Responsibility failure.* If children are acting irresponsibly, for example, not taking good care of the student stories in the class library, a discussion of feelings and responsibility may be in order.
4. *Interpersonal conflicts of needs.* If two children want the same book, the same pencil,

**Table 1.1   EXAMPLES OF PROBLEM AREAS AND CONTEXTS
THAT PERMEATE THE WHOLE SCHOOL DAY**

Social	Aesthetic
Speaking/listening	Literature
Observing	Observing
Usage	Composition: oral/written
Literature	Drama
Classroom/school environment	Art
Rules (breaking)	Music
Taking responsibility	Movement/dance
Following directions	
Interpersonal conflicts	
Racism/sexism	

Cognitive	Motor
Reading/writing/observing	Handwriting
Literature	Decision making for movement in drama
Physical science	Articulation
Biological science	Eye-movement decisions
Mathematics	Movement from activity to activity
Other academic areas	Nonverbal signaling
Composing/comprehending	

or whatever, the teacher does not rush in with judgments. A better approach is
to stand back and watch, use active listening, and, if necessary, help the children
with language of negotiation.

5. *Special problems of sexism or racism.* Special problems of sexism or racism may
require the use of probing questions that the teacher first models and that children
pick up and use. Children can become genuinely concerned about problems in this
social area, which are sometimes uncovered in response to children's literature.

Children can satisfy their genuine needs by communication and participation, with as
much autonomy as possible, in problem-solving processes in a wide range of areas. The idea
is to carefully consider the nature of the problem and match problem-solving strategies to
it.

Consider the sketch in Figure 1.6. The teacher in the upper portion, who is trying
to solve all the children's problems in the classroom, is stretched thin, frowning, and worn
out. The teacher in the lower portion, who is helping the children become autonomous
problem solvers, feels more content, is more energetic, and generally has happier students.

Notice that the representation of one child's face at the end is frowning (cross-
hatched). When problem solving is new to children, some feel particularly threatened by
the change, especially if they are accustomed to being overly dependent on adult dictator-
ship.

Genuine Problems

For problem solving to be creative, the problems must be genuine. Too often "problems"
are just tasks thrown at children (e.g., "Write three pages about your summer vacation").
This kind of teaching error can occur particularly with cognitive problems, but it can also
occur with what are meant to be aesthetic problems (e.g., "Make your poem just like this

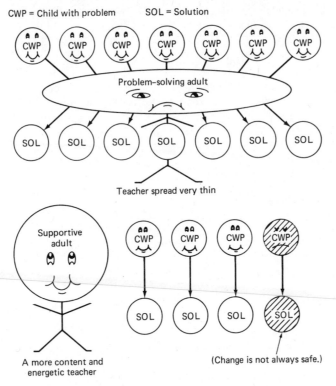

Figure 1.6   Problem solving in the classroom. (*Source*: Dr. Saundra Sperling.)

model, but change the first noun to one of these two words"). It is crucial that problems in the classroom reflect interests, goals, and concerns that are genuine from the child's point of view—not something a teacher or textbook has manufactured without reference to the child.

This point does not imply that the teacher can never set the stage for a challenge. A skilled teacher is able to motivate and facilitate so that a problem does become the child's. That is, the child understands the problem and has a desire to solve it. (Then the teacher is "teachin', not preachin'.") Thus, when we define creative problem solving, we refer to problems that children "own."

Deterrents to Creative Problem Solving

Too often something happens to children's solving power in school:

1. Children get poor opinions of themselves as creative solvers.
2. They are afraid to take risks.
3. They think that someone else must do most of the real solving, or they do not get opportunities.
4. Creative brainstorming gets snuffed out.
5. The ability to generate and select alternatives gets stifled; innovation in planning atrophies.

6. Problem solving becomes ritualized; the children already know what to do, and exactly how and precisely when to do it. The creative problem solver in the child is lost, and the artist-professional in the teacher is lost. This artist-professional encourages, probes, and lifts the child's creative ability.

Throughout the world, governments recognize the need for creative invention to keep up in international commerce and science, even in countries whose social systems do not encourage creative problem solving in most avenues. Theoretically, our democratic social system (committed to respect for the individual and participation of all) would encourage creative problem solving. What, then, can teachers do to remedy its lack in some children? The next section provides answers.

The Teacher's Guidance of Creative Problem Solving

In part, teachers can guide the use of problem solving in the language arts with five elements: (1) use of the language of problem solving; (2) freedom of response; (3) teacher avoidance of imposing predicaments; (4) teacher reassurance that it's all right to risk being wrong; and (5) guidance of the process, as we saw in the opening scene.

1. Use of the Language of Problem Solving   Using the language of problem solving does not mean simply knowing the meanings of terms such as *hypothesis, missing data,* and *search strategies.* The teacher must also understand the way children talk to themselves about problem solving and the way their positive self-concept is revealed in their words. (We deal with the language of problem solving in Chapter 2, and the opening scene at the beginning of this chapter illustrates children's use of it.)

2. Freedom of Choice   To guide children to appreciate the *freedom* (or open-endedness) of creative problem solving, teachers need to provide choices and options for children. To the extent possible, your language arts environment, your daily plan, and your curriculum need to involve children in decision making. Provision of choices and options is key to the popularity of some playground structures, to the choose-your-own-adventure books, and to successful leadership and teaching. Options and choices for open problem solving are powerful motivators, from the moment a mother holds out two toys for a baby to choose from to the time a child enters a learning center. Give your students options and choices.

For example, two children in a class wanted to use the same book. When one finally gave in, the teacher said, "Oh, I see you have decided to let her have it." Thus the teacher stressed the child's autonomy. A teacher's words about freedom of choice can help set up a mirror for children about their problem solving.

Furthermore, creative problem solving does not require that every problem have a neat and happy solution. One's choices and options in problem solving can include simply walking away from a stalemated conflict. For instance, when two kindergarten children became verbally abusive to a third, the latter simply terminated her part in the dramatic play by saying pleasantly, "Well, good-bye, I'm off to Hawaii," and she left the confrontation.

Choices may also include choosing to deal with a problem later, or even choosing someone else to help handle it. Especially with young children, participating in the *process* of problem solving is often much more important than the product or solution. Some people have a phobia about openness; they fear having to cope with ambiguity. Albert Einstein once said he thought it was good that human life had a natural limit so that it could be finished like a work of art. Young children have a long time to fashion that ultimate work of art; let them explore and enjoy the process.

Teachers can help children realize the power, responsibility, and choice they have in a situation. The children come to understand that they are not simply washed by the tides of fate, but can *choose* to act or react in certain ways. Chances are that the solution to a problem is already inside a child. Teachers and others can help the child bring the solution out, whether it is an interpretation of literature or an ending for a story.

3. Avoidance of Predicaments   Our analogy of a trip up a river mentioned getting stuck in the mud, or predicaments. Realizing that creative problem solving is nurtured in a free and open-ended environment, the guiding teacher takes care, however, that problems do not become overwhelming predicaments for young children. In a predicament—as opposed to a problem—the child lacks the freedom to leave a frustrating situation, or to leave a question unanswered, without serious consequences. If a child is simply not developmentally ready for formal group reading lessons, a teacher can think of other learning alternatives to get him or her out of a frustrating and embarrassing predicament. For example, such children might read their own environmental print, dictate their own material (language experience approach), benefit from one-on-one peer tutoring, and practice reading into a tape recorder before reading aloud to a group.

Sometimes it is wise for teachers to guide children to let go, step back, move out of a corner, and give themselves time and space to grow a little (as in the "Well, good-bye, I'm off to Hawaii" example). If the problem really belongs to the child, rather than to someone else, the child will have another chance at it.

4. Teacher's Reassurance that It's OK to Risk Being Wrong   Teachers can realize that there are two dimensions to saying, "It's all right to come to a wrong solution." One dimension is the long-range view of development: how young children use process creatively but come to qualitatively different conclusions from adults. (This aspect is discussed in Chapter 2.) The other dimension is the building of victory out of defeat.

Children can use initially inadequate solutions to *redefine their goals* and to find better solutions. After children have taken the risk, tried a solution, and found it wanting ("Hey that's not working, my story is confusing everyone!"), teachers can help them build upon and refine the first attempt. Thus this early attempt becomes a part of the problem-solving process rather than merely a failure. The key teaching idea here is not to let children be discouraged by inadequate solutions, but rather to use them as a part of the process of finding more successful ones, of "snatching victory from the jaws of defeat" (Klein & Weitzenfeld, 1978).

In sum, it is OK to take a risk, to be wrong, and to build from there. Remember the proverbial turtle, who makes progress only when it sticks its neck out. In order to be right a lot of the time, you've got to risk being wrong some of the time. (Consider Edison and his thousands of failures in trying to invent the electric light. He said he learned a lot—what *not* to try. Or consider the author of *Gone with the Wind*, who revised the first paragraph 50 times.)

It's also OK to put your problem down and rest a while. The chances are that no one is going to steal it from you, if it's really yours; and you can pick it up again when you're refreshed. (*Note:* See the activity book, Chapter 15, for an observation scale on problem solving and Chapter 1 and Chapter 5, Section 3, "Drama as Problem Solving," for related activities.)

DEMOCRACY AND THE LANGUAGE ARTS: A LARGER CONTEXT FOR PROBLEM SOLVING

The network (or fishnet) of the language arts mentioned earlier is part of other networks of life. The purposes and products of the language arts processes affect many audiences: the self, another person, a group, a larger audience, even the mass media. Not the least of the network areas that feels the impact of language is our cherished democracy.

In order to function truly, democracies need for their people, *all* their people, to be able to communicate effectively. Effective communication and creative problem solving for each individual are woven into the very fibers of a democratic network. Language arts teachers play a significant role as their guidance contributes to the functioning of democracies of the world. Teachers model democracy as they respect and enhance each child's autonomous and interactive communication development.

The new framework for the state of California emphasizes language arts for a democracy. For instance, some students learn and use language processes and related skills in a democratic way, thinking: "I count and you count; we can listen, speak, read, write, think together, and negotiate our differences; then we can all have chances to get our needs met, fairly and creatively, much of the time."

Here is a significant *use* of language revisited repeatedly throughout this text. Here is a service to humankind in which language arts teachers can take enormous pride. A quote from *Essentials of English,* published by the National Council of Teachers of English (NCTE) (1982), seems appropriate here:

The Responsibility of Teachers of English

The study of English offers varied opportunities for the individual to mature intellectually and emotionally. We believe in basic competency in English as a means by which the individual can acquire self-sufficiency and work independently in all disciplines. We believe further in challenges to both the analytical and creative capabilities of our students.

Toward accomplishing these aims, we as teachers of English hold ourselves responsible for

- helping all students become literate and capable of functioning in an increasingly complex society
- directing them to read and view materials appropriate to their abilities and interests
- encouraging them to exchange ideas, listen perceptively, and discuss vigorously
- urging them to write honestly in the spirit of open inquiry
- helping them expand their interests and reach their fullest potential through language

By contributing in these ways, we hope to expand the capacities of the human intellect and to preserve the tradition of free thought in a *democratic* society.

THE ORGANIZATION OF THIS BOOK

This book follows a developmental sequence in the following way. Part 1, "Developmental Bases and Oral Language," has six chapters. This first chapter, "Casting a Language Arts Net: Crucial Ideas for the New Teacher," previews crucial concepts and themes in the book, emphasizing creative problem solving. The second chapter, "Fields of Development—

Implications for Language Arts Teachers" discusses current ideas about developmental knowledge and how to apply it, and provides a thorough grounding in language development. Chapter 3, "Listening," singles out listening with perhaps the most thorough and unique treatment to date. The fourth chapter, "Talking/Speaking," relates listening to speaking with a fresh point of view and emphasizes new and creative forms of self-expression. Chapter 5, "Drama" adds drama to the reader's set of tools with a thorough developmental treatment; and the sixth chapter, "Discussion," does the same for discussion, with information on question asking and group management.

Part 2, "Into Print," begins by building bridges to reading and writing. Chapter 7, "Building Bridges to Reading and Writing with Informational Uses of Whole Language," emphasizes the composing process, language experience approach, whole language classrooms, and informative uses of language. Although Chapter 8, "Learning to Compose," is devoted to composition, the reader will find ideas about written composition throughout the text.

Chapter 9, "Children's Literature in the Language Arts," emphasizes how books for children can be incorporated into the language arts curriculum since literary uses of language are also important. Although selected children's books are featured in every chapter, this chapter provides a greater variety so that teachers can help children appreciate the art and craft of fine writing. Literature is presented as the verbal expression of human imagination and a primary means for cultural transmission.

Chapter 10, "Creative and Critical Thinking in Persuasive Uses of Language," moves from literary to persuasive uses of language by emphasizing the integration of higher-level thought in all the language arts. A discussion of critical thinking shows the reader how to judge the clarity, honesty, and scholarship of language by exploring its use of logic, organization, and style. (This presentation is supported further by the activity book.)

Chapter 11, "Spelling, Handwriting, and Other Writing Conventions," and Chapter 12, "Grammar and Usage: A Story of Controversies," illustrate how to teach spelling, handwriting, punctuation, standard usage, and other technical writing skills. In addition, Chapter 12 examines old and new controversies in grammar and usage, and offers concepts for analyzing the history, structure, and dynamic quality of the English language. New research findings and educational trends are considered and incorporated into suggestions for teaching, e.g., through patterned storybooks.

Part 3, "Resources," has three chapters. Chapter 13, "Creative Use of Computers, Textbooks, and Other Media," shows how to use computers and other emerging technologies in the classroom and other educational settings. The chapter emphasizes how nonprint and nonverbal media differ from print and verbal media, and stresses creative uses of the new technologies.

Chapter 14, "Children with Special Needs in the Language Arts," helps prepare the preservice teacher for work with the gifted, linguistically different, or other students with special needs. The chapter develops understanding and ways of adapting language arts instruction.

Chapter 15, "Evaluation and Assessment of Language Learners, Teachers, and Programs," distinguishes between evaluation and assessment, and advocates using informal assessment tools for describing students' progress in the language arts. The tools presented in this chapter and throughout the book can easily be used by almost any teacher. This chapter also explores uses and abuses of evaluative testing instruments and procedures, their limitations, and impact. The chapter concludes with a look at teacher assessment and evaluation. This final chapter also provides an epilogue which summarizes major themes and invites responses to suggested assignments from the first chapter.

Every chapter offers dramatic opening scenes to suggest models, illustrate, and enliven. Each chapter also offers ideas for integration (putting it all together) and reference to the related activity book. For activities related to this chapter see the matching Chapter 1 in *Choose Your Own Learning and Teaching Activities*. Filled with activities for your classroom, this book has a matching chapter for every chapter of this text. This resource will bring fun, enthusiasm, and excitement to your text reading, application, and daily planning.

A Final Task

As a final task in this chapter, try to visualize your new and rather empty classroom. Perhaps it simply contains a chalkboard, your desk, and some seats for students. Now, suppose you get a wonderful opportunity. If you can tell *why*, you can choose anything you want for your language arts classroom, and it is there, magically, free of charge to you. *How would you equip it?* Think about this question as you read this book, discuss the ideas, and apply your experiences. You may also get some ideas from the companion activity book.

The next chapter answers teachers' questions about developmental knowledge useful in teaching language arts, and offers a defense against inappropriate pressures.

SUMMARY

"There is no such thing as a problem without a gift for you in its hands. You see problems because you need their gifts."

Richard Bach

A strong and meaningful language arts network in all areas, especially if combined with a teaching style that emphasizes process, produces students who will create, revise, and strengthen networks of their own. Beneath the processes and skills of communication lie those of thinking, and beneath those are creative problem-solving processes that motivate students and integrate their learning. When the underlying process is stressed, skills fall far more effortlessly into place, and integration makes learning last. Furthermore, focusing on the genuine use of communication makes classroom tasks easier and more interesting for both teacher and students.

Successful teaching is based on helping children think. When applied with developmental know-how, this approach promotes the children's competence and enhances each child's self-concept. Its use in a democratic classroom, where all persons participate but each is autonomous, fosters growth in the language arts and in all areas. Finally, the successful classroom is infused with a spirit of excitement, fun, and creative discovery.

CHAPTER 2

Fields of Development—Implications for Language Arts Teachers

"Children are not setting out to acquire a group of linguistic rules; they're not trying to acquire grammar. What they're trying to do is learn how to communicate."

Catherine Snow (Nova, 1985)

INTRODUCTION

Fields of development include studies of thought and language. Studies in the language field include sentences (syntax), word meaning (semantics), and use (pragmatics). Our goal here is to build a bridge for the language arts teacher to these fields.

The chapter begins with an opening scene showing how ideas growing out of such scientific knowledge help classroom teachers to apply developmental know-how. Sound methodology growing out of developmental knowledge is the major focus of the opening scene and of this chapter.

The process of learning to communicate combines an interplay of innate language capabilities, the child's own thought processes, and the first educator's role as creator of a language-learning environment. With a fresh perspective on "readiness," we look for univer-sal patterns and individual differences in language development and literacy development (reading and writing). From your course(s) on reading methods you may think of readiness as referring to the following: visual, auditory, social, emotional, and mental growth sufficient to tolerate a beginning formal reading instruction with phonics and a group lesson format from a teacher's manual. This chapter develops some alternative ideas. It also distinguishes between literacy and literary development. (It assumes that you have had or will soon have an entire course on child development.)

There is a rift in the teaching profession between those who are steeped in ideas from fields of development and those who lack such a background. "You know," said one dean, "I like to have university students in my classes with a background in development. They are usually the ones who are keenly observant and care deeply about children. They have a long-range point of view, which incorporates understanding of self and others. They have explanatory, profound ideas that add to almost every contribution they make in class. They bring a developmental depth of understanding to any educational situation. I can't help thinking they're better teachers because of it."

A master teacher who had worked with many student teachers was asked, "What do you think the teacher preparation program should do before the trainee arrives in your classroom to teach language arts?" She thoughtfully replied, "I would wish that student teachers would arrive knowing something of development. Then when a child is having trouble learning, they know how to back up to an earlier developmental stage or way of knowing. Then they can help the child move forward successfully."

Because of its importance, you will find development mentioned in every chapter. But this one gives a start on important essentials for a language arts teacher to know. Now we visit a classroom where developmental methods are useful and put into practice. (Related references are gathered together at the end of the scene.)

OPENING SCENE: How Developmental Know-how Helps a Classroom Teacher

On the first day of class the kindergarten teacher, Lee Fisher, gave each child a booklet of blank paper saying, "This is your journal; you may write in it." One child spoke up for many, "But I don't know how to write!"

"That's OK," said the teacher, "just pretend to. If you think you don't know how to write, just pretend."

Once the children understood that scribble was OK, they took off. Since that day it has been the *children* who have requested help in labeling and in keeping a record of communications. Almost all the encounters with print have been initiated by the children.

The kindergarten teacher has just finished listening to Jason "rereading" one of his scribble stories during the daily drawing, "writing," and "reading" time, first thing in the morning. The teacher has checked the notes made two weeks ago about this same story and has found that Jason has "story-matched" his set of scribble to his specific message with good accuracy. That is, after a lapse of time he pretended to "read" it again, with good memory for it. The teacher had kept a transcription of what the scribbled story was supposed to be. (David's scribbles in Figure 2.1 are just about as long as the teacher's transcription turned out to be.)

When the teacher remarks, "I like your reading," Jason replies, "Oh, if you liked that one, then you'll love this one. I can 'read' it even better!" Jason has "written" a scribbled letter to the teacher, and his letter format does not look like his scribbled story format. Although they both know that Jason is not using language in a traditional sense, *they both think of him as a writer and as a reader.* He has a typical compulsion to communicate, and writing inevitably results in reading, which is a social experience most of the time. Through his writing Jason is also developing his oral language by "reading" what he writes.

Several years ago this teacher did not have much in the way of paper and pencil opportunities in the kindergarten classroom, much less individual notebooks for "natural writing diaries." Print usually referred to isolated letter practice. A workshop stimulated Lee to read about developing literacy, which prompted questions and more reading about this constructive process. Now print references in this classroom are almost always in the context of whole-language experiences. On the few occasions when children mention isolated alphabet letters, it is for spelling words in their messages. They *make* letters, but they *write* messages, differentiating terminology. (References at the end of the scene and in If You Want to Learn More in the reference section for this chapter give additional information about such ideas and classrooms that implement them.)

Emerging literacy level in this class varies. Some of the children are able to match a line of scribble to a complete thought, showing awareness of a sentence, with scribbles being horizontal and moving left to right. Some have spaces between their scribbles to represent spaces between words; a few use periods or slashes to separate them. Such inventions look odd to us, but are logical to a child. One child, Natasha, accustomed to a computer in the home, says the dots she makes between invented words are for the space bar. Some children leave conventional spaces between their scribbles so that each scribble matches a word. That is, the lengths of separated scribbles in the piece roughly match the length of each word. Others combine conventional letters with their scribbles. Some just use conventional random letters (see examples in Figure 2.1).

David's story-matching scribble

Karen's word-matching scribble

Michelle's scribble integration

Reinier's combination of scribble
and letters

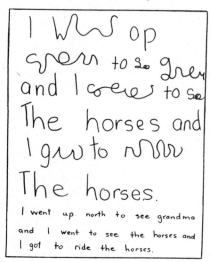

Figure 2.1 Scribble writings of various kinds and levels. (*Source:* Heald-Taylor, 1984, pp. 6 and 7.)

In their writing, some of the children who have command of some sound-letter relationships are combining letters, sound symbols, and scribbles (representing print). Initial consonant use is more common than final. A few are integrating actual words into their scribbles and one in this class is fully literate, using conventional print and mainly standard spelling to communicate.

Teresa, who is already reading, somehow finds one of those old preprimers and on reading some of the "Look, look, see, see, oh, oh" discourse wants to know what kind of child has written this book. Upon getting an answer to her question, she looks amazed and says incredulously, "You mean *adults* wrote this book!" (This child's lesson is not lost on our teacher.)

Another rather advanced child, Nathan, helps and inspires others, taking pride in being able to read or translate their invented spellings and serving as an additional teaching resource. Thus a whole range of emerging literacy has appeared in this class. The environment in this classroom, encouraging children upward, has spread them naturally even further apart in their literacy abilities. Yet at the same time the teacher's environment has encouraged a cohesive social unit.

Real-life function of literacy development is a theme in this classroom. Signs about the room are functional, not just labels. Examples are "Wet paint," "Do not remove," "Only 4 here," and "Sign up." The teacher knows that the *functions* of literacy are as much a part of learning to read and write as are the formal aspects (e.g., left to right, spaces between words).

Children in this class feel free to communicate not only what they know, but also how they feel. Functional use of language in a classroom needs to relate to development of the social and emotional side of children as well as growth in cognitive processes. One child in Lee Fisher's class, Joey, scrawls the word *bom* (bomb) on his picture of one falling earthward from a plane toward what appears to be his school. "Is a bomb going to drop on us?" he queries his teacher.

"What do you know about bombs, Joey?" responds the teacher, realizing the need to find out more about this child's ideas and concerns. This teacher will base further questions on what Joey says next, in order to respond with appropriate support, reassurance, and information. The teacher will work from the child's concern, not the concerns of adults, and will respond at the level at which this young child can use information.

"I think all planes carry bombs," continues Joey, "and I just heard one flying overhead, and I wonder if it will drop a bomb on our school."

"Airplanes that fly over our school do not carry bombs. They carry people. People like you and me." The teacher gives the child a hug. Joey crosses out the bomb in the picture and the word for it, and puts people looking out of the windows of the plane. Then he mouths "p-p-p-pee-e-e-p-l-l-l" and writes the letters *ppl* (people).

Once a child has as many as three consonants in a word with sound-letter correspondences meaningful to the child, the chances are high that the word is stable and the child will be able to read it back at a later time. A child who has around seven of these sound-letter correspondences is ready to take off in writing that most often both the child and others can read back. This intermediate achievement in writing is quite a breakthrough for the child. Not having to get it all perfect from the start increases freedom, initiative, and fluency—a long-lasting sense of ownership of the writing process.

Children are experimenting with emerging reading and writing strategies. Such opportunity is crucial to development of language arts processes and skills. "That's my name on the snack chart," says Nicholas, another child in Lee Fisher's room.

"No, that's mine," says Nathan.

"How do you know that's your name?"

"Cause it's got an A *here*" (points to the second letter). Nicholas has developed the reading strategy of focusing only on the first letter of a word; Nathan can go him one better. "And yours is a little bit longer," Nathan adds, finding the name in the unused pile and comparing. Nathan used one aspect of configuration (dimension of length). With two emerging reading strategies, first and second letter use, he showed double classification—to use a Piagetian term. (Some of Piaget's ideas are reviewed later in the section on universal patterns of development.)

Nicholas now takes his name card from Nathan and with his encouragement begins to copy it over and over, very carefully, letter by letter. He spends 15 to 20 minutes and several sheets of paper rewriting his name. The observant teacher quietly makes a note of this activity for Nicholas's file, remarking that this child is putting himself through a grueling practice. If a teacher had initiated it, it would have seemed inhumane. The teacher notes that this is a big step for Nicholas, who until now has shown little interest in printing words, though he has enjoyed scribbling. The teacher monitors this peer tutoring from a distance, not interfering, but encouraging the boys with smiles and nods.

Thus, in large part initiative comes from the children in this classroom. They come up with interesting ideas, problems, and questions. With a Piagetian perspective, the teacher can observe (and subtly encourage) as they put events into relationships and notice similarities and differences.

Lee Fisher realizes that young children are *actively* involved in the process of their literacy development, not just responding to a teacher or imitating. They are constructing solutions to written language puzzles. Through study, this teacher has come to the conclusion that others in the cited literature have come to rather recently: *It makes life harder for children if we try to teach them to read before we encourage them to write.* Language arts (listening/ speaking, reading, and writing) develop concurrently and interrelatedly.

Literacy development is a broader and more appropriate term for what is happening in this classroom than reading readiness. Lee Fisher believes that young children read and write their way to readiness. Children learn to read by reading functionally important material and they learn to write by writing. School is the continuation of literacy development, *not* the start of it.

In the book center of this room are varied items. In addition to picture books of good quality, there are homemade books, such as the environmental print folders. Amy and Jennifer are busy reading *The Cereal Book.* A caption to this series of stapled file folders reads: "Can you read the cereal book? Read it to a friend." Each page of the book has the front of a box of cereal that the children in this class have brought in. There are also a toothpaste book, a store book, and a soup book derived in a similar manner. Also, there are books about the children's experiences as a class, such as *Our Trip to the Zoo.* The children have made the illustrations; the captions have been written by the children themselves in some cases or have been dictated to the teacher.

The teacher knows that such materials can build developmentally on literacy that the children already have developed—their already extensive environmental print vocabulary. Moreover, such material can put into an understandable context later attention to sound/ letter symbol correspondence. *Meaningful contact with written language has started for almost all the children in the class long before their entering day.* Commercial logos, safety signs, and all manner of environmental captions have seen to this.

The teacher also knows that being read to plays a special role in literacy development. The class has quality story books and the "big books," which are enlarged versions of ones with predictable story patterns, old familiar favorites for a sense of confidence and control. The class also has quality literature for almost every content area.

Finally the class has another "reading" event the children look forward to. Each week three "authors of the week" pick six pieces of "writing" from their file folders, put them up on the board, "read" from them to a group, and then invite other children in the group to ask questions. Some of the children are bringing in what they have "written" at home. The children also enjoy the times of sustained, uninterrupted "reading" and "writing." During this time even the teacher and any volunteers (acting as models)—that is, *everybody* in the class—"reads" or "writes" for a period of time.

In summary, the children in Lee Fisher's classroom have a good grasp on what it is to read and write, and why they want to do these useful things. With a developmental perspective, this teacher is building instruction on what the children already know about oral language, reading, and writing, focusing on functional experience rather than on merely isolated skills, and easing them into literacy. Lee is encouraging the children's attempts at writing without undue concern for proper formation of letters or conventional spelling; is allowing active experimentation (e.g., periods between words); is encouraging independent reading and writing; and is providing opportunities for them to communicate what they know and how they feel.

Parents of the children in this class are aware of the developmental reasons for this total-language program. They have ideas to try at home (e.g., scribble writing, invented spelling, and environmental print reading). These parents realize that if early natural-language learning can occur slowly and meaningfully, instead of harshly and abruptly, then so can literacy learning, so can learning of the language arts in school.

(*Note:* Sources for this scene include Carlsson-Paige & Levin, 1985; Heald-Taylor, 1984; International Reading Association, 1986; Lamme, 1985; *Nova*, 1985; Palincsar, 1986; Texas Association for the Education of Young Children, n.d.; Vygotsky, 1978; Willert & Kamii, 1985; Wood, Bruner, & Ross, 1976.)

The next section considers questions often asked by pre- and in-service teachers about development.

QUESTIONS: IF I AM TO BE A LANGUAGE ARTS TEACHER K–8 . . .

Why Should I Know About Early Child Development?

One of the best things about Lee Fisher's teaching style is its contagion throughout that elementary school. Even the first-grade teacher down the hall is letting children scribble in class—an unheard-of practice a year ago in this school. Many teachers at varied grade levels are beginning to view error as developmental, and interesting, and indicative of growth. Many know better now when to back up and when a child on the brink of the next growth pattern needs nudging forward. Many now know how to observe evaluatively rather than just test, test, test with paper and pencil. They share developmental facts and research for parents and "significant others" in newsletters, meetings, and conferences. And they have copies of Elkind's book, *The Hurried Child,* for ammunition. For much of what they are now doing, they can give three developmental reasons and six research references.

These teachers feel professional, up-to-date, powerful, and creative. Observation leads them to believe they are helping children more effectively than ever before. Teachers who know about normal patterns of child development are alert to developmental delays needing attention. They can inform parents of the limitations of formal evaluations and standardized tests for children from kindergarten all the way through eighth grade. They know with greater assurance if the purposes and objectives of their language arts program are realistic in terms of what is known about children's language development. They know about different developmental learning styles and how to provide for them.

How Far Back in a Child's Life do I Need to Know About Development?

Children begin to learn to speak and listen, read and write very early in life. Any explanation of children's oral language that begins when they say their first words begins much too late. We need to go back earlier than that to understand what is going on. Similarly, to understand when children first begin to read and write, we do not want to begin when children get their first textbook in school, read the first word in their preprimer, mark their first readiness worksheet, or print their names in their best manuscript printing.

It is intriguing to know that babies apparently send out communication with their varied cry patterns, can segment a stream of sounds (*ta* versus *da*), form interactive patterns ("dances") with their mothers during feeding times, and intone in their babbling the sound patterns peculiar to the language in their environment. Though such prelinguistic phenomena are interesting and indicate that roots of communication begin at birth (and even before), we define language for the purpose of this text as follows: *Language is a set system of communication based on a specific set of rules that includes syntax, semantics, and pragmatics.*

Syntax refers to the grammatical rules that order the words in a sentence, for example, the rules that make statements different from questions. (For example, a 2-year-old asks "Daddy come?" when he hears a car pull into the driveway, and confirms "Daddy come," when he sees his father coming up the walk.)

Semantics refers to the rules that govern the links between words and what they mean. For example, a 2-year-old explaining what silly putty can do says "It getches" (knowing that it stretches). Linking the abstract word symbol *stretches* to its meaning, its domain, is an example of her grasping a part of a semantic system.

When a great deal of attention and context is attached to even a rather abstract and complicated word, children will surprise us with their grasp. Such was the case of the first graders who all knew the meaning of the word *confiscate*. (Their experience included a teacher adamant on not playing with toys sneaked in during ditto-sheet time.)

A further look at semantic learnings is revealed in Figure 2.2. It shows a map of a word or concept and its context of relations: concrete, sensory impressions; functional uses; and abstract relationships, products, and affective relationships.

Pragmatics refers to rules that govern the use of words in socially appropriate ways. When a 2-year-old says, "mo' juice pease" (being able to make a request using the word "please"), his language shows something about pragmatics—how to get things done with words in this world. Young children learn all these features of language (syntax, semantics, and pragmatics) simultaneously, and each is an enormous accomplishment.

A Child Comes to Your Classroom Bringing a Long Language-Learning History.
A 12-month-old may say "wow-wow-wow" (her first word) every time she sees a dog. By the time this child is 3 years old, she will be using language routinely, have a vocabulary of around 3000 words, know how to put words together into sentences, and use words to get things done. Investigators have uncovered some universal patterns or stages in such language development and also in literacy development, as well as some patterns of individual differences. Children do not go through these patterns at the same rate, nor with the same style. Knowing about normal patterns may alert you to developmental delays that warrant your attention. Understanding such early roots of language in your classroom gives you professional power.

What Universal Stages Can I Look for in Development of Language and Thought?

There is yet another important aspect to language learning: universal stages of cognitive development. The term *cognitive development* refers to a process of growth wherein a child acquires knowledge. By what private logic do children reach their conclusions—often reasonable to them, but illogical to us? Are there any common milestones? Any universal patterns?

In this section we cover language development milestones, cognitive development (including Piaget's stages), and some newer ideas about pattern abstraction in language acquisition. We also explore creative problem-solving characteristics at varied age levels,

Concept building is essential to meaningful communication. We are too often in a hurry to explain a term and go on to something we think more important. Actually, time spent in concept building is productive of many meaningful relationships. Below are some of the possibilities in the word *apple.* What is an *apple?*:

Sensory Impressions:

The first attributes a child will learn—concrete

Behaviors: reddens, softens, drips, drops
Qualities:
  Number: per tree, per acre, per season, per pound
  Amount: per pound, per recipe
  Texture: of skin, of flesh, of seed
  Flavor: of varieties
  Moisture: under varying conditions; in varieties; at stages of development
  Solidity: effect of touch, of dropping
  Size: to hold in one hand
  Shape: general; details
  Color: of varieties; at stages of development
  Sweetness: taste; aftertaste
  Acidity: degree of
  Odor: of varieties; at stages of development
  Sound: in eating; in dropping

The second attributes a child will learn—functional

Uses:
Food: in sauce, pie, and the like
  Housing: by insects
  Jelling: by humans
  Decoration: by humans
  Hunting: by robin looking for worm in apple
  Entertainment: bobbing for apples on Halloween
  History of human uses: evidence in early art
  Geography of human uses: cultivation and harvesting

Cognitive Relationships:

The third learning achievement of the child—abstract

Whole-part: tree-apple; apple-skin
Cause-effect: pollination-fruit
Sequence: seed-tree-blossom-fruit
Comparison-contrast: apple, pear
Subordination-coordination (awareness of hierarchies and parallelisms); appleness, kinds of apples; apples that ripen at same time

Cognitive Products:

Theories: An apple a day keeps the doctor away.   **Abstract**
Laws and principles: Sweetness is affected by rainfall.
Generalization: Apples are fruit, a form of food.
Summarization: Apples grown in the West are Gravensteins, and so on.
Definition: An apple is a tart, juicy fruit.
Classification: Apples, oranges, and bananas are fruit.
Procedure: Apples are grown, picked, sorted, boxed, and shipped.

Practical Extension of Cognitive Observations:

Example: the Gravenstein
Elaboration: description of various kinds of apples
Application: irrigation based upon principle that rainfall affects sweetness

Affective Relationships:

How we feel about apples.   **Connotations**

Linguistic Relationships:

We depend heavily on these in our teaching because they provide quick answers, but they are once removed from reality and less useful than the preceding relationships. Some are:
Pronunciation: [ap′ l]
Derivation: original form or meaning of word; changes in form or meaning of word, historically or regionally or in slang
Derivatives: plural—apples; compound—applesauce
Synonyms (word meaning the same or about the same)
Antonyms (word meaning the opposite)
Homonyms (word the same in sound)
Heteronyms (word the same in form but different in meaning)
Multiple meanings: apple as tree, fruit, design, color
Uses of word: as noun, as adjective
Application of word: an apple; an apple orchard; an apple-green dress

Figure 2.2   A map of a concept and its relations.

with implications of a common ground in language and thought development. Finally, this section concludes with the development of literary characteristics and story-making structure.

Language Development Milestones   Language development milestones can describe both receptive and expressive language in gross stages or even in monthly increments. One can label milestones with regard to grammar, sound, semantics, and pragmatics, or with respect to special skills such as spelling and written composition. Investigators conducting descriptive studies have looked at children and said, for example, "Here at seven months the child typically (and receptively) appears to listen to whole conversations between others; or he can vocalize (expressively) in sentence-like utterances without true words" (Bzoch & League, 1970). Thus they present typical behaviors. Table 2.1 presents one such classic list of language development milestones by Lenneberg.

Figure 2.3 represents one parent's careful observation of the emergence of a first word, a milestone usually recorded by parents. Ask your own parents for your language milestones and share them with someone. Try to capture language development episodes in the lives of young children. You could well develop language arts milestones for the grade you teach or would like to teach. Use careful observation and make notes from month to month, as in Figure 2.3 on page 38. You can verify whether or not your findings are typical in the subsequent years that you teach.

Three language stages (prelinguistic, protolinguistic, true linguistic)

One general way of looking at learning the language of others is in three stages: before language (prelinguistic), on the brink of language (protolinguistic), and true language (true linguistic). These stages (as is the case with those of Piaget addressed later) typically correspond to certain ages, but with great individual variation. While the order of language stages is stable, ages are approximate.

Three Language Development Stages

Prelinguistic
- Birth to 3 months (gurgle, coo)
- 3 to 12 months (babble)

Protolinguistic
- 12 months to 2 years (walk-talk)

True linguistic
- 2 to 6 years and beyond (progressive lengthening and complicating of sentences with embedding and subordination of phrases, and progressive refinement of social uses of language)

In the *prelinguistic stage* the child from birth to 3 months is often quieted by a familiar voice, making vowellike sounds similar to /e/ and /a/ while squealing or gurgling (called "cooing"). Then later the child may look at the speaker and respond by smiling, repeating a same syllable (e.g., /ma/, /da/, /di/), developing vocal signs of pleasure. At about 8 months, the child produces intonation patterns resembling, say, a question or an exclamation. This stage of language corresponds roughly to the early part of Piaget's first major stage of intellectual development, sensorimotor.

The *protolinguistic stage* finds the child of 12 to 20 months reacting to words and

Table 2.1 DEVELOPMENTAL MILESTONES IN LANGUAGE

At the completion of	Vocalization and language
12 weeks	Markedly less crying than at 8 weeks: when talked to and nodded at, smiles, followed by squealing-gurgling sounds usually called cooing, which is vowellike in character and pitch-modulated; sustains cooing for 15–20 seconds.
16 weeks	Responds to human sounds more definitely: turns head; eyes seem to search for speaker; occasionally some chuckling sounds.
20 weeks	The vowellike cooing sounds begin to be interspersed with more consonantal sounds; labial fricatives, spirants, and nasals are common; accoustically, all vocalizations are very different from the sounds of the mature language of the environment.
6 months	Cooing changing into babbling resembling one-syllable utterances; neither vowels nor consonants have very fixed recurrences; most common utterances sound somewhat like *ma, mu, da,* or *di.*
8 months	Reduplication (or more continuous repetitions) becomes frequent; intonation patterns become distinct; utterances can signal emphasis and emotions.
10 months	Vocalizations are mixed with sound—play such as gurgling or bubble-blowing; appears to wish to imitate sounds, but the imitations are never quite successful; beginning to differentiate between words heard by making differential adjustment.
12 months	Identical sound sequences are replicated with higher relative frequency of occurrence and words (*mamma* or *dad*) are emerging; definite signs of understanding some words and simple commands ("show me your eyes").
18 months	Has a definite repertoire of words—more than 3, but less than 50; still much babbling but now of several syllables with intricate intonation pattern; no attempt at communicating information and no frustration for not being understood; words may include items such as *thank you* or *come here,* but there is little ability to join any of the lexical items into spontaneous two-item phrases; understanding is progressing rapidly.
24 months	Vocabulary of more than 50 items (some children seem to be able to name everything in environment); begins spontaneously to join vocabulary items into two-word phrases; all phrases appear to be own creations; definite increase in communicative behavior and interest in language.
30 months	Fastest increase in vocabulary with many new additions every day; no babbling at all; utterances have communicative intent; frustrated if not understood by adults; utterances consist of at least two words, many have three or even five words; sentences and phrases have a characteristic child grammar, that is, they are rarely verbatim repetitions of an adult utterance; intelligibility is not very good yet, though there is great variation among children; seems to understand everything that is said to him.
3 years	Vocabulary of some 1000 words; about 80% of utterances are intelligible even to strangers; grammatical complexity of utterances is roughly that of colloquial adult language, although mistakes still occur.
4 years	Language is well established; deviations from the adult norm tend to be more in style than in grammar.

Source: Lenneberg (1966).

3/6/82 (where entries begin): 11 months

Makes noises that sound like conversation, imitates sounds, but does not say a word whose meaning I am sure of. Points at things and makes a "mmmm" sound (often quite loudly) when wants something.

(In week following, several entries indicate she was imitating sounds of coughs, of words, etc.)

3/15/82

Alexei said she imitated him by saying "Ow-ow" when he said "Bow-wow."

3/17/82

She points at things and says definitely "Aa-aa" or "ow-ow." The sound is somewhere between the 2; the tone is definite. I'm not sure if it means anything. She has done it in the last few days while pointing at a dog, while pointing (it seemed) at a boat, but when I looked carefully there was a small dog behind the fence behind the boat. Did she see it? I don't know.

She heard dogs barking outside this morning and said it (ow-ow) again, several times. . . .

Figure 2.3   Natasha's early language: notes from a notebook. (*Source:* Carol Mason Wolfe.)

sounds produced by people in the immediate interactive environment. A child moves from vocalizing in unison with adults, to imitation of adult sounds already in the child's repertoire, to echoing (after a pause) what the adult has said. Somewhere a breakthrough occurs in understanding that names stand for things and experiences in the world. Using an average stock of around 30 words, the child engages in imitative naming and one-word sentences and responds to simple commands (e.g., "Show me your eyes").

Ages 1.6 to 1.8 find the child using one-word sentences to cover many meanings. "Drink," might mean anything from "Bring me one," or "Look at it," to "I didn't like it, so I knocked it off the tray." Human infants apparently communicate complex underlying thoughts with their single-word utterances.

At the end of this protolinguistic stage, children give up this single-word approach upon making a dramatic discovery. They can combine words into two- or three-word sentences that reduce uncertainty ("Momma ju go," for *Mother's juice is gone.*) This protolinguistic stage, incidentally, corresponds roughly to the latter part of Piaget's sensorimotor stage.

The *true linguistic stage* at about 2 to 6 years of age finds the child rapidly increasing vocabulary. For example, at age 2 a child may have around 300 words. Some children this age will be naming all items in their environments. Joining of words into original sentences continues, observably leading to a rudimentary child grammar.

By age 6, the child has used most of the simple grammatical structures and sounds characteristic of the dialect in his or her environment. Spoken communication units are about six or seven words long. By age 4, children can generally share a connected account of some recent experience and carry out a sequence of two simple directions. By age 5, children hold conversations with others when context and language are familiar. Their language is usually easily understood. But, as thoughts forge ahead of performance, children may repeat words and phrases. Their competence outstrips their performance. Such repetitions may be mistakenly judged as stuttering (Lundsteen & Tarrow, 1981).

Table 2.2, a chart for stages in "written" composition and in spelling development, shows one way of looking at milestones of later early childhood. You can use such a chart to generally characterize individual children in your class. In addition, you can use the guidelines in Box 2.1 on pages 41 and 42 for fine-grained observation when planning and evaluating children's writing in a developmentally oriented way. A final list of milestones for the mastering of sound production is the classic Templin scale, shown in Table 2.3 on page 43. This type of scale alerts a teacher to possible developmental delays.

Writing Development Stages   During the past decade, several important ideas have grown out of research on children's writing development. Consider four of them.

1. *Young children widely exposed to print, drawing, and adult models often start writing with no formal instruction before they enter school.* Whether they are 3 or whether they are 6, a lot of what they "write" depends on their print-rich environment (Harste et al., 1984).

2. *Such children can tell the difference between their writing and their drawing by approximately age 3* (e.g., DeFord, 1980). They do this before they are able to produce letters or words that adults can recognize (e.g., Clay, 1980). Although this early writing may look like scribbling to an adult, symbols that children call writing have a linearity (strings), directionality, uniformity, flow, and rhythm. Moreover, such "writings" are interpreted as messages by the child, who attempts to read them back (e.g., Dyson, 1981).

3. *One may distinguish some early writing stages and a sequential development, although composition does not necessarily follow an orderly sequence.* Young children may move back and forth among stages depending on topic and motivation, and every child does not necessarily follow the same sequence.

Examples of stages are the following: (1) (beginning) scribble, the understanding that print "talks," and that symbols are necessary to write; (2) development of letterlike shapes; (3) grouped letters indicating word boundaries and some letter/sound correspondence; (4) writing of known, isolated words from memory and using more advanced letter/sound correspondences; (5) writing of simple sentence (or sentences) with control of thought and punctuation; (6) conventional stories, personal letters, and informational messages (e.g., DeFord, 1980).

Knowledge of all alphabet letters does not necessarily precede writing (words, sentences, stories). Language learning is interrelated rather than sequential but does reveal

Table 2.2 CHILDREN'S DEVELOPMENT IN COMPOSITION AND SPELLING

Composition stages	Invented spelling stages	Invented spelling stages
Precompositional 1 (Lamme/Green scale)	Precommunicative (Gentry, 1981)	
Scribbles		
Mock letters	Knowledge of alphabet, but no	
A few letters or numbers	knowledge of letter-sound	
A small string of letters or	correspondence; letters and	
numbers	numbers are used to randomly	
Precompositional 2	represent words	
Letters		
Mock letters read as words		
Repeated group of letters		
Incomplete alphabet or list of		
numerals		
One memorized or copied word		
Precompositional 3	Semiphonetic	First Stage (Paul, 1976)
Mock words in a long list (some	Most salient sound features are	First letter or phoneme used to
phonetic relationship to word)	represented in words (Srd =	represent a word (B = bird)
Message in invented spelling	sword, Matn = mountain)	Second Stage
Complete alphabet (alone or with	Mapping of each word	Ending and sometimes medial
any of above)	Letter = name strategy used	consonants are added (SN =
Word boundaries (spaces, dots,	frequently (U = you, R = are)	sun, MTR = monster, SRE =
lines, etc.) to separate words)		sorry)
Compositional 1	Phonetic	Third Stage
Simple message (I love you)	All surface sound features are	Short vowels are used;
List of ten or more words	represented in words; advanced	interchange of vowels formed
(phonetic or memorized spelling)	command of sound/letter	similarly in the mouth; variety in
Complete alphabet with over ten	correspondence (nis = nice,	use of vowels (het = hit, hul =
words	kampr = camper, pickshr =	hole, gud = good)
Compositional 2	picture, kak = cake)	Fourth Stage
Original message (complete	Word segmentation and space	Memorized sight words, (Chre =
thought)	orientation at end of stage	tree, slay = sleigh, skremed =
Message of two to four sentences	Transitional	screamed, Beth = beach)
List of short sentences	Many correct spelling patterns	
Short letter	are applied	
Compositional 3	Morphological and visual spelling	
Long story with plot (four or	strategies	
more sentences	Some memorized words (Howse	
Long letter that sticks to subject	E house, techre = teacher,	
	enrtoob = inner tube)	

Source: Green, C. (1985).

some "principles." Examples are: (1) the *recurring* principle shown by a child's repeated letters or words; (2) the *directional* principle shown by a child's starting at the left side of the paper as he or she scribbles; (3) the *abbreviation* principle shown by a child's letting one or two letters (usually consonants) represent a word (Clay, 1980).

    4. *Children's writing needs response within their social context of oral language and art.* For young children, writing is often embedded in speech and in the drawing of pictures and other use of media (Graves, 1975). Teachers can focus on and encourage children's embedded thought. (Chapters 8 and 11 give detail on evolving spelling strategies. Chapter 12 deals with later language learning, ages 5 to 12.)

BOX 2.1 Guidelines for Observing Kindergarteners' Writing

When observing (watching, listening to, talking to children about) their writing, you might consider the following questions:

The Message

1. Does the child believe that he's written a message? If so,
2. Does the child know what the message is? That is, can he read it? If so,
3. Did the child freely formulate his own message? Or, did the child simply copy something? Or, was the message confined to a small set of words which the child could easily spell?
4. How long was the message?
   —one word or a list of unrelated words
   —a phrase
   —a sentence
5. How does the child's written message relate to other graphics on the page?

The Encoding System

1. Can you read the child's message? If not,
2. Does there seem to be any system to how the child went from the formulated message to the print? For example, the child may have
   —put down a certain number of letters per object
   —rearranged the letters in his name
   —written a certain number of letters per syllable
3. If you can read the child's message, can you tell how the child encoded it?[a] For example, the child may have:
   —recalled the visual pattern (e.g., *COOW*, child intended to write *moo*)
   —based spelling on letter names (e.g., *PT*, which is read *Petie*)
   —requested spellings from peer or adult
   —based spelling on phonological analysis (e.g., *APL*, which is read *apple*)

The Written Product

1. How conventional are the child's written symbols? (Do they look like letters?)
2. Did the child follow the left-to-right directionality convention?
3. Is there any order to the way letters or words are arranged on the page? Or, does it appear that the child simply put letters where there was empty space?

Message Decoding

1. Does the child appear to have written without any particular intended message? If so,
2. Did the child attempt to decode the written message?
3. If so, how did the child go from text to talk? The child may have:

(Continued)

—engaged in apparent fantasy behavior
—requested that an adult read the unknown message (e.g., "What does this say?")
—based the decoding on the perceived text segments (i.e., matched a number of oral syllables to the perceived number of segments in text)
—used a letter-name strategy (i.e., "read" a word containing the name of a written letter, as reading "Debbie" for *PARA NB*)
—based decoding on visual recall of a word similar in appearance

Writing Purpose

1. *Why* did the child write? Possible reasons include:
   —simply to write; no clearly identifiable purpose exists beyond this (e.g., "I'm gonna' do it how my Mama does it.")
   —to create a message; the meaning of the message is unknown to the child (e.g., "Read this for me.")
   —to produce or to practice conventional symbols (e.g., the *ABC*'s, displayed written language) without concern for a referent
   —to detail or accurately represent a drawn object (e.g., the *S* on Superman's shirt)
   —to label objects or people
   —to make a particular type of written object (e.g., a book, a list, a letter) without concern for a particular referent
   —to organize and record information (e.g., to write a list of friends)
   —to investigate the relationship between oral and written language without concern for a particular referent (e.g., "If I do [add] this letter, what does it say?")
   —to express directly feelings or experiences of oneself or others (i.e., direct quotations, as in writing the talk of a drawn character), and
   —to communicate a particular message to a particular audience

[a]It may be that the child *is* using one of these methods, but you simply cannot read it. After asking the child to read the paper, you may be able to detect patterns in the child's encoding system.

Source: Genishi, C., & Dyson, A. H. (1984).

Elevator game   Here is a game you can play in order to go back to your earliest remembrances of your language development. Students have found this task helpful in taking on a young child's point of view, that is, experiencing what it is like to be a certain age. The task takes concentration. Sometimes it works best with a small group doing it and then sharing. To teach young children, you need to think as a young child would.

Pretend that you are on the top floor of a multistory building, with each floor representing a year in your life up to the present. You are standing on the top floor of your life, facing an ornate elevator. The elevator doors open. You step in and start to descend through the years of your life. Make your elevator stop at one of the early years. Get out and look around.

Table 2.3 ACQUISITION OF SOUND PRODUCTION: TEMPLIN SCALE[a]

Sound	Age	Sound	Age	
(m)	3	(r)	4	
(n)	3	(s)	4.5	
(ŋ)	3	(sh)	4.5	
(p)	3	(ch)	4.5	
(f)	3	(t)	6	
(h)	3	(th)	6	(voiceless)
(w)	3	(v)	6	
(y)	3.5	(l)	6	
(k)	4	(th)	7	(voiced)
(b)	4	(z)	7	
(d)	4	(zh)	7	
(g)	4	(j)	7	

[a] Age at which three-fourths of children mastered the sound.
Source: Templin, M. C. (1957).

What do you see? Smell? Feel? Hear? Who is talking? Are you? To anyone? Try to recreate an early language scene in you life. Now. . . .

When you have finished, the elevator doors open again; you enter and go back up the years of your life to your present age at the top floor. Step out of the elevator. As soon as you can, find someone with whom to share your early language experience. Perhaps your experience is indicative of a milestone of your own. This game can help you to get a bit more into the linguistic shoes of young children.

Cognitive Development Stages By way of definition, cognition in *cognitive develelopment* is an intellectual process by which knowledge is gained about perception or ideas (as opposed to emotional ways of knowing). The classic theories about development of thought are represented by Piaget (1955) and by Vygotsky (1978). The theory of Jean Piaget, a Swiss cognitive psychologist, holds that cognitive development precedes language. Babies have to reach a certain level of development before they can learn to say anything with meaning. The pacesetter in a child's language growth is cognitive growth. Children use language to express what they already know. Language is not the source of logic, but it is structured by logic. Vygotsky, a Russian psychologist whose brilliant career was cut short by an untimely death, investigated language and thought. Vygotsky's theory, in contrast with Piaget's, holds that babies began to talk, and that accomplishment also affects cognitive development. Do words come before thought? Yes, according to Vygotsky.

Babies begin to use certain words to express meanings just at the point where they are solving cognitive problems of great interest to them, such as the permanence of an object (e.g., a key is hidden under a cloth and a baby has to find it). It seems reasonable that both language *(gone!)* and thought are apparently developing simultaneously, at least during the earliest stages of language (Andrew Meltzoff on *Nova,* 1985).

Certainly a teacher of sixth grade will find children spouting off highly abstract language, sounding like college students, trying to impress each other. Upon questioning them, the teacher may find the concepts underlying their words to be shallow indeed. Language and thought are intricately and fascinatingly related. Do words help thought? *Language is an aid to thought, but not a guarantee of thought.*

Pattern abstraction   Just how do children learn language? A current belief is that language acquisition is basically a process of **pattern abstraction** performed by one's senses (Gibson, 1979). You do not need to teach a child what the pattern of a tree is if enough trees are standing around. The child will abstract the nonvarying pattern over the transformations of tree: large tree, small tree, holly tree, maple tree, young tree, old tree, and so on. Similarly, a child will abstract the patterns of syntax from clearly presented examples that also do not vary over transformations. (For example, noun-verb pattern: Natasha runs, mother runs, dog runs, daddy hops, etc.; noun-verb-object pattern: Natasha pets the bunny, mother pets the bunny, Natasha pets the dog, the dog bites the bunny, etc.) There are really not that many syntax patterns for a child to abstract (Moerk, 1986).

Piaget's ideas and stages   What use is Piaget's work to us? Although Piaget's main thrust was an inquiry into development of logical mathematical intelligence, let us review a Piagetian perspective of cognitive development for what it may be worth to a language arts teacher. Recall from your earlier courses that Piaget concerned himself with connections that children develop within themselves. See Box 2.2 for a diagram of Piagetian stages.

The framework shown in Box 2.2 shows that Piagetian stages in cognitive functioning are characteristic of certain approximate age groups; and in general, learners function differently in earlier and in later stages. Piaget describes early-stage children as using global unanalyzed relationships and as showing *un*awareness of conservation of substances, lack of ability to reverse operations, and lack of classification by more than one feature at a time.

Why still pay any attention to Piaget? More than any other psychologist he opened eyes to typical intellectual growth. His method was unique for his time. He arrived at his conclusions about four major stages of cognitive development by putting himself into the world of children to find out how they think. His finding that children learn best through their own discovery of how the world around them works still presents a valuable way of thinking about language arts education, though we can augment it with a point of view that includes social interaction.

Piaget believed that the principal goal of education is to create persons capable of doing new things rather than just repeating what others have done, persons capable of verifying rather than accepting just any idea that comes to them, persons who are creative, inventive, and discoverers. From the work of Piaget there are some important implications we can draw for language arts teaching. Let us review Piaget's stages. Note, however, that children do not pass between stages all at once. They construct these operations layer upon

---

BOX 2.2 Piaget's Basic Stages in the Development of Children's Thinking

Period	Stage	Title	Suggested Age of Beginning
EARLY	Stage 1	**Sensorimotor**	(birth onward) ⟶
CHILDHOOD	Stage 2	**Preoperational**	(about age 2 onward) ⟶
LATER	Stage 3	**Concrete Operations**	(about age 6 onward) ⟶
CHILDHOOD	Stage 4	**Formal Operations**	(age 11 onward) ⟶

layer, based largely on *their own understood actions on objects.* Transitions are gradual; boundaries are blurred.

Stage 1, sensorimotor: Children in this "body and senses" stage begin to distinguish themselves from outer reality, coordinating movements and repeating connective patterns. Some of these behaviors are related to language aspects. (For example, an 11-month-old points at things and makes a *m-m-m* sound.) These children begin to search for vanished objects, learn to use one thing to reach another, and begin to move beyond trial-and-error behaviors. Sensorimotor intelligence refers to gaining knowledge through real objects perceived through the five senses and coordinated with observable movements. Little children instruct themselves by personal sensory investigation. What they fail to perceive at first hand does not exist. They explore and sample life's bits and pieces close at hand. Sensorimotor experience at any age serves as an important base for further cognitive learning. New learning grows out of older learning.

Stage 2, preoperational: Children in the preoperational stage show a lot of egocentric thinking and ability to represent their world through language, dreams, and symbolic play. We can see the beginnings of symbolic representation. (A child puts two potato chips together for "wings" and says, "Butterfly.") We see gigantic leaps in the highly creative process of acquiring language. Yet children in this stage do not usually form very accurate concepts. (Examples: *Car* can refer to a wagon, bicycle, cart, truck, or train as well a car. *Chair* refers to lots of things you can sit on, but not one made of strings or one made of clear plastic, and a stool is also considered a chair.)

Children construct concepts slowly, assimilating and building experience upon experience. Concept development takes time and many contexts. Using word labels to accelerate the learning of abstract concepts without sufficient experience and maturation usually results in no learning of any lasting value.

A Piagetian task you can try with children to illustrate this point is the following. The task may show whether a child has mastered vocabulary without having mastered the underlying thought. Asking the following questions, use the word *sister* or *brother* as appropriate to the child who does have one.

> YOU: Do you have a sister?
> FEMALE CHILD: Yes.
> YOU: Does your sister have a sister?
> PREOPERATIONAL CHILD: No.

If you do get the "No" response, it is not just that the child is egocentric and cannot put herself in another's position. The difficulty may be that the child cannot think of *having* a sister (or brother) and *being* one at the same time, that is, being in two relationships at once.

For the preoperational-stage thinker, concepts and causes are based on appearances that are often misleading. (A child may think that the sun comes up because he pulled up the shade, or that her walking makes the clouds move.) With preoperational thought we note a private logic that is reasonable to these young children, unreasonable to us.

Preoperationals are also not usually guided by reversible thinking—for instance, the ability to follow a series of size transformations and then think back to when, say, the same piece of stretched-out clay was a round ball or when a stretched-out line of pennies in one row was spaced close together, like the apparently "shorter" row above it. (Donaldson, 1978, found better performance on this task when a naughty teddy bear came out of the drawer and spread apart the pennies.) A child without reversible thinking would not think of subtracting weights to reach a balance instead of just adding. In essence a child displaying such a stage would not think of going backward in time and reconstructing past events. Here may be one reason the flashback technique in literature is so difficult for young children. Even a 5-year-old might say, however, "I walked backward in my mind [to remember where I put it] (Bosma, 1986, p. 16)."

Stage 3, concrete-operational: We have a lot to say about this relevant stage. Most elementary school children operate at the concrete-operational level across most areas. Not all children will, however, and individuals may show varied profiles. Some may display this level in some academic areas (e.g., reading), but not in others (math or physical science). Recall that an *operation* is an organized mental action—for example, adding, subtracting, or conserving.

What can concrete-operational children do? They can understand the logic of classes and relations and can coordinate a progressive series. "This stick is bigger than this one and both are bigger than this smaller one." They can grasp part-whole relationships and use thought that is logical and reversible *with concrete things.* One young social science student showed this need for concreteness when he said, "Geography is polar bears at the top and penguins at the bottom." Concrete elements such as sensory impressions of a particular moment, or manipulable materials (e.g., blocks) help children use logical thought.

Children in the concrete-operational stage, however, are unlikely to do much thinking about thinking, unless it is socially very meaningful and well scaffolded. The child can, however, understand a more symbolic world with its rules and generalizations when the context is concrete: can be seen, touched, moved. These children are unlikely to think about theories as they reason from a hypothesis systematically to all its possible conclusions. That kind of ability comes in the next stage—formal operations. Concrete-operationals can, however, grasp almost any concrete sequence of actions or events all at once—an inning of a baseball game involving past, present, and future; stories and scripts encompassing not only the here and now but the history foreshadowing the future. They can describe a sequence of events without having to actually act them out.

Try this analogy: In a concrete-operational stage, thought processes are speeded up somewhat like a movie film, as compared with a slow succession of slides in preoperational thinking. Like a film being wound and rewound, concrete-operational thought can project itself forward in time and can reverse itself.

Stage 4, formal operations: The student in the stage of formal operations can manipulate knowledge systematically by means of abstract hypothetical propositions and has mastered "thinking about thinking." Such a student is capable of second-order removal from concrete reality to abstract relationships. A student using this way of knowing might be highly sensitive to motivations and relationships of well-rounded and complicated characters in fine literature crafted into plots with complex causes. Making such abstract connections can help to expand the student's thinking abilities.

Here is an example. Audra, age 12, had been reading the novel *Alas, Babylon* (an end-of-the-world type of story). As she read how one character gathered meat and then hoarded salt, Audra wondered why he wanted salt. Then she researched until she found out that the character would need salt to cure the meat, since there would be no electricity for refrigeration. She was intrigued by the characters trying to find different ways to survive in the face of a future holocaust. She had been thinking about the possibility of a nuclear war and about Russia. Partially in reaction to the book, she made some connections, saying, "I can't understand why Russia says the CIA killed Samantha Smith [as reported on a newcast]. . . . I guess they think they can control what people think by just telling them one side of the story" (thinking about thinking).

Implications for reading   To examine the relation of Piaget's developmental ideas to the teaching of the language arts, consider the area of reading and Piaget's stages of thought. When children in this stage begin formal reading instruction in school they will presumably be competent in *classifying* uppercase and lowercase letters, consonants and vowels, and word families *(bomb, bombardier, bombing)*. A child who is still in the preoperational stage of conceptual development cannot see that groups stay the same, for example, that an *A* is an *a* is an *A* across all sorts of insignificant variations in rendering it (conserving). By the term *conserving* we mean recognizing sameness despite change in appearance or shape. (A certain ball of clay is still the same mass and weight when rolled into a sausage.)

Consider these complexities in learning to read our language with reference to letters.

1. Each letter is like all other letters but also different.
2. Letters have an ordinal property—their position in the alphabet.
3. They have a cardinal property—their name (*A*, etc.)—shared with all typical variants in rendering the letter.
4. In addition to its name each letter also has sound (phonic properties in context).
5. And to complicate matters even more, a person can sound a single letter in more than one way, and can represent it with different letters *(a, ai, ay, ey)* with varying probabilities.

Thus, to understand phonics, children need to be in a stage in which they are able to perform logical operations on letters and sounds and to understand all possible combinations. You can see that just the concept "letter" is a complex logical product, and its construction and use require relational thinking. Further, a preoperational child who cannot use reversible thinking may be unsuccessful in converting letters to sounds by associating the sound that goes with the letter and the letter that goes with the sound.

A preoperational child, who is able to focus on *only one variable at a time,* will have difficulty in discriminating between, say, the words *wash* and *wish.* Preoperationals may be able to perceive the *whole* but not the *parts* at the same time. They may perceive the differences between the words, but not, at the same time, their similarities.

Preoperationals also cannot handle the transformations from one state to another with all their intervening causes. But in some formal early reading situations we expect preoperational children to (1) transform the sounds together into a word, (2) coordinate words into a meaningful sentence, and (3) relate sentence to sentence. Without the ability to hold all these relational aspects in mind at one time, the child is in trouble—especially in an unfamiliar context. (Chapter 8 has a section on ideas from Piaget and written composition.)

Language and literacy growth needs cognitive development. Developmentally appropriate literacy learning is natural, reality-based, socially supportive, and individualized. A look at developmental ideas reminds us to incorporate these and other supports from the child's past experiences into reading. These reading experiences need to be in tune with the child's growth, experience, and interests.

Implications for teaching language arts   Studying child cognitive development shows us that children at any age can be intensely, intrinsically curious and motivated to learn. They do not need bribes. They are impelled to regain their balance, or *equilibrium*, while thinking problematically. The teacher's job is to keep that curiosity alive and healthy.

In summary, one can stress the knower (which Piaget did); one can stress the language (as early linguists did, e.g., Chomsky, 1965); one can stress the interaction of the first two and the human contexts (e.g., Vygotsky, 1978). From an educational point of view, just stressing language, giving children language (e.g., drills) is like giving a bicycle to a child who cannot reach the pedals. Educators are often guilty of tossing out labels and assuming that learners have concepts and thought levels that they do not have. This is a fairly common fault of teaching at any level.

We also need to take into account the *gradualness* of a child's growth in understanding things that matter. A teacher who understands a child's probable way of thinking can offer language arts instruction in a way that makes the most sense to the child. These arguments offer a rationale that can be used with parents and administrators who push for developmentally inappropriate classroom activity.

Problem solving is a special case of cognitive development and another area needing descriptive stages. Let's take a closer look at its growth and relation to language since it is a central theme of this text.

Development of creative problem-solving stages and common ground in language development   Besides pattern abstraction, there is another common ground between the development of language and the development of thought. Common ground lies in children's ability to:

1. Find the predictable, as distinguished from the changing and irrelevant.
2. String together causes, effects, and relationships.
3. Plan (using a sense of the future) and make inferences (through a sense of the past).

These three elements feed into a common process of hypothesis testing for both language and thought. Hypothesis testing is a part of the total creative problem-solving process. It is this common process that we teachers can make it our business to promote. Thus we give assistance to development of language and to thought at the same time. All smaller mental and language abilities can feed into this larger unifying process for a productive and economical use of classroom time. Here we have a development rationale, for stressing problem solving.

Even at the very beginning of children's long push toward knowledge, they have some competence in comprehending, in imaginative kinds of thinking, and in hypothesis making. We find goal-oriented problem solving at 7 months of age when an infant shoves a blanket out of the way in order to get to a ball (using means A to get B); or crying deliberately (A) in order to get attention (B).

Preschool characteristics of problem solving   Although the major mental process of creative problem solving starts early in life, we find special characteristics related to the preoperational stage. For example, young children tend to solve problems by trying out all their hunches immediately, letting the consequences fall where they will. They usually cannot keep from acting at once; nor do they remain calm while they formulate hypotheses, think out solutions, and follow their ideas through to completion.

This lack of inhibition may be what makes the preschool child such a destructive experimenter in a household. This sometimes destructive play, however, permits children to explore combinations of things that they would never explore if they just kept to reasonable problem solving. Typically, they fail to vary their attempts and strategies for finding solutions systematically, and, of course, they lack information and experience for solving problems. Let's examine an example of problem solving as development continues.

Three-year-old turtle lover: By age 3, children may not be able to solve a great many problems on their own. They have, however, learned some tools and strategies for when they want to do something but initially are not certain what or how. Here is a perfect setting for creative problem solving. One 3-year-old wanted a turtle that was brought to a center (the most popular item of the day). Some larger children were playing with it. How he wanted it! As he stood watching, empty sand pail in hand, he made a connection; he made a plan. Edging in closer and closer with his pail, he waited until one of the older children tired of holding the turtle and let it drop. Our 3-year-old was ready with his pail to catch it, and triumphantly scooted away.

Some teachers have no idea that young children can do so much problem solving, and they do not give them much of a chance in class, either. Recall from Chapter 1 that children in classrooms may solve problems creatively in many contexts; for example: language, literature, science, and math (cognitive); art materials and drama (aesthetic); other people (social); or a situation involving many or all of these contexts. The context of problem solving is important throughout development, making the process easier for some children and more difficult for others.

Creative problem solving and language   Problem-solving behavior is often cued in words such as *because, although,* and *however* and expressions indicating thoughts such as *this is so, therefore . . .* and *if this is so, then this. . . .* Children are testing such hypothetical ideas long before the ages suggested for Piaget's stages of concrete and formal operations.

Verbal help can assist learners to formulate their goals, select hypotheses, uncover principles, and make plans—all part of problem solving. Enabling language can channel the direction of problem-solving activity more productively. Having useful words and phrases at command is an important building block of problem solving in young children. Early and later educators can help give children words to directly express feelings, social relationships, and the beginnings of negotiation strategy for social problem solving. Words can help children in clarifying problems, in considering alternate solutions, and in reaching compromises. For example, armed with the phrase *maybe because,* Natasha at age 5 could say: "She won't come over to play *maybe because* she doesn't like me any more; or *maybe because* she's sick, or *maybe because* I haven't called her. I'll call her!"

As middle school students and as adults we continue to learn to use language that helps us solve problems. For example: "I have described your needs, you say, to your satisfaction; and I have described my conflicting ones. Now let's see if we can figure out a way we can both get our needs met so no one loses." Language and problematic thought development go hand in hand.

In essence, to become effective general problem solvers, children must acquire masses of structurally organized knowledge that they can use creatively and communicatively in new, complex ways. Productive solutions come to a linguistically prepared mind that knows how to use effective attitudes and problem-solving procedures. Problem solving and language emerge often together, often bootstrapping each other. Teachers coming to the classroom well prepared in the developmental bases of the language arts program can be more helpful in the promotion of children's integrated language, thought, and problem solving.

We have one more area under the question on descriptive stages to keep in mind when teaching language arts—literary development. Consider it next.

Literary Development Stages   A distinction can be made between *literacy* development and *literary* development (Heath, 1985). Literacy development refers to functional writing and reading. Literary development refers to refinements in the written language system related to the art form called literature—both in responding to it and in producing it.

One form of this art is *storytelling* with its progressively developing story structures. Karen Blixen, in her book *Out of Africa,* reminds us of the human ability to tell stories (lost or pitifully dulled in the case of too many of us). Political leaders know the power to make a point and the communicative appeal of "that reminds me of a story. . . ." Retelling stories is part of the oral tradition, which is the first kind of literary development people knew.

Retelling stories   Children develop in the ability to retell stories with respect to response and production. Children reveal their growing understanding of the structure of narrative literature in their attempts to retell stories. Story retellings are part of language and cognitive growth.

Since analysis of retelling yields developmental information, they have spurred much current interest not only from researchers but also from school personnel. Genishi and Dyson (1984) analyzed some retellings by kindergarteners, second graders, and a sixth grader (Zidonis, n.d.). The varied ages differed in (1) the number of major events recalled, (2) the accuracy of the sequencing of events, and (3) the inclusion of logical links between events. Some parallels were found by the senior author of this book among children 3.5 to 5.6 years old in ability to interpret a wordless picture book (Lundsteen, 1985).

In addition, the retellings analyzed by Genishi and Dyson showed that the children differed in the nature of their language. These differences included fluency of the telling, complexity of the sentences used, precision of word choice, amount of story vocabulary maintained, and amount of needed teacher support.

The piece of literature used, the folktale "Salt," had been heard by the children only once. Let's look at some examples with three children in each group (Genishi & Dyson, 1984, pp. 207–208).

Kindergarten

TEACHER: Now, who would like to start telling the story? OK.
    JOHN: He had a big mustache grow and his mittens on the nose.
TEACHER: Right. But what happened first? Do you remember what happened first? Do you remember what happened first in the story? Joseph?
  JOSEPH: Ivan—um—his two brothers—uh—
    JOHN: Was going across the sea.

The dialogue continued in this vein, with the children having considerable difficulty retelling this unfamiliar tale. These young children did not provide motivation for the characters or any logic behind the actions. As is usual for young children, those actions recalled with teacher support were linked with a series of *ands.* The group did better with a highly familiar tale. Possibly, improvement occurred because they were not struggling in that case with memory, felt they "owned" the tale, and had had over time chances to put a richer, larger context with the story.

Second Grade

TOMMY: His father had had this boat and Ivan wanted . . . Ivan wanted a boat so he could go out and his father said if you went out you would get your head chopped off out in the sea and then Ivan was out there floatin' and—and—uh—what was the second brother's name?

TEACHER: Vasil.

TOMMY: Vaseline and . . .

TEACHER: Fodar.

TOMMY: Fodar was out there, too. And he—

GREGG: . . . wind come up. . . . And then the wind came and blew—

ROCKY: North and south . . . of Ivan . . . away and he landed on this dumb looking island, with this dumb looking giant.

TOMMY: And he found the salt and he told his men to throw all the wood and stuff out and then he loaded up the salt.

In contrast to the kindergarteners, the second graders started at the beginning and collectively remembered more major events. Still, they provided few details or explanations, and again linked events with many *ands*.

Sixth Grade

CHERYL: This merchant had three sons, Ivan, Versalas, and Fodiere. And their . . . the three brothers' father gave them a ship, but he didn't want to give Ivan one because he thought he was a fool playing the madeline so he saw how much Ivan wanted a ship so he gave a ship with a cheap, cheap cargo—beans and everything—and Ivan set out in the sea with his brothers. And they stayed for a day or two and he was blown off course to uh island of salt. And he took all the salt and put it on the ship and he went to an island and he sold it to the king (Zidonis, n.d.).

The sixth grader finally helps us grasp the nature of Ivan's cleverness and adventure. She provides necessary detail and explains the logic of the story—revealing it, in part, through the use of *but, because,* and *so,* rather than just using *and.* Needing no help from the teacher, Cheryl told the tale fluently, with her own sense of how a narrative should flow, supporting her retelling. A child (or any individual) who has moved into operating with Piaget's stage of formal operations in thinking could have an advantage. This ability is especially necessary if higher qualitative levels of thought are used in thinking about the characters' thinking.

Storytelling is a revealing window for the teacher to use in assessing language development of children. It appears that the younger the child, the more likely that only one chance to listen to the story is not enough.

Story structure development   It is interesting to see what Zidonis's examples reveal about children's growing sense of the structure of narrative, in relation to Applebee's (1978) developmental levels in story structure production. Figure 2.4 shows these stages.

As you can see from the diagrams and examples in Figure 2.4, narrative structures become more tightly controlled. They evolve from a heap of events, related only by closeness in time or space (diagrams 1 and 2); to unplanned-sequence stories that have a physical or psychological center, that is, a central character or theme (diagram 3); to unfocused (diagram 4); and then to focused chain stories (diagram 5), having a chaining of events in time or in cause-effect sequences later. But these cause-effect chained events (diagram 5) are not necessarily related to the central character or to endings that follow logically from the beginning. Finally, stories evolve to well-structured narratives in which events are linked

(*Text continues on page 54.*)

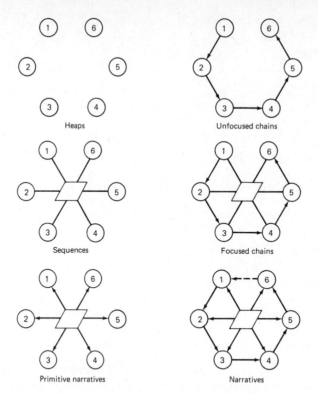

Heaps

Unfocused chains

Sequences

Focused chains

Primitive narratives

Narratives

1. *HEAP STORIES:* There is no inherent organization among the individual propositions—the organization comes from whatever happens to attract the child's attention. Such stories consist of labeling or describing activities. The sentences in such stories are generally simple declarative sentences, almost always in the present progressive tense.

Example:

The gorilla is climbing up the mountain. Snow's comin' up. And the people are down there and all the houses and all the trees. It's all black and it's all brown.

2. *SEQUENCES:* Sequences have simplistic macrostructures that involve a central character or setting. There is nothing that can be considered a story plot. Instead there is only a description of some activities that a character has done. The term *sequence* for this story structure is misleading because any apparent time sequence is not intentionally planned by the storyteller and one event does not follow temporally or causally from the preceding event.

Example:

A gorilla and robber were in the house. They were stealing things. They turned off the lights. They stoled all the food in the church and stoled the money and they stoled a bunch of things. And they were walking in the snow at night. They didn't see the gorilla.

3. *PRIMITIVE NARRATIVES:* A concrete core or center, object, or event has temporarily assumed some importance. Primitive narratives are developed by collecting around the center a set of complementary attributes or events. In primitive narratives, characters, objects, and events are put together because they have a similar function or because they complement a set such as good behavior and bad behaviors. Elements of the story follow logically from the attributes of the center. *The primitive narrative scheme represents the child's first use of inference in stories.*

Heaps

Sequences

Figure 2.4 The structure of children's stories. Arrows indicate complementary attributes; straight lines, shared attributes; parallelograms, centers; circles, incidents or elements. (*Source:* Applebee, 1978.)

Example:

> There was this gorilla and this town people. And the town people went
> to go see if they could catch the gorilla. And the gorilla says, "Oh, I'm lonely.
> Look at these people down there. I wish I could go meet them, so I won't be
> all alone any more." So the townspeople go, "Let's go get him. Let's put him
> up. Let's catch him as a hostage." Then the gorilla goes, "Oh, I wish those
> people would be nice to me. I wish they'd quit chasing me, trying to beat me
> up." So the townspeople and the gorilla get together and they live happily ever
> after. The end.

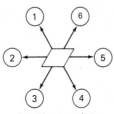

Primitive narratives

4. *UNFOCUSED CHAIN:* Children now perceive logical temporal or cause-effect relationships among events. Events are chained together. The unfocused chain stories, however, have no central theme or character. Each microstructure element shares an attribute with the next, but the attribute is consistently changing.

Example:

> Once upon a time there was a bee that said, "Buzz, buzz, buzz, buzz."
> The duck went "Quack, quack, quack." The sun went down, up down until it
> came back. There was a house which was the duck's house and they all went
> to his house to have supper. They ate hamburgers and drank their favorite
> punch. And then they all went out to take a little ride with a dog. Then they all
> went to the church to look around. They saw a ma married girl getting married.
> She was carrying a boy. The boy and girl went home. They date dinner. After
> dinner the baby came out.

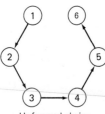

Unfocused chains

5. *FOCUSED CHAIN:* The child combines a central character with a true sequence of events. The child lacks complete awareness of understanding of reciprocal relationships between characters' attributes and events and the relationships between the events. As a result, the stories do not have strong plots because the events do not build on the attributes of the characters and do not result in growth of the characters' personality. The characters are not motivated to achieve a goal. The ending does not have to follow logically from the beginning.

Example:

> King Kong was on the top of the mountain at night. There was lots of
> snow all over. He was gonna throw rocks down on the town, and kill all the
> people. The people knew he was up there. They got fire to burn him up with,
> and they climbed up the mountain. King Kong threw rocks at them and ran
> down the other side of the mountain. The end.

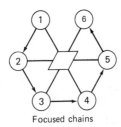

Focused chains

6. *TRUE NARRATIVE:* Narrative scheme stories have a central theme, character, and plot. The linking of events to the central character or theme is based on complementary attributes. Thus, the stories include the motivations behind the characters' actions as well as the sequences of events.

Example:

> Both mother and father dipladacus were afraid to leave the valley.
> Mother dipladacus was afraid of the great tyranosoras rex. So one day little
> dipladacus went to the rocks. He didn't have anything to do. Then he began
> to throw rocks at the mountain. Then the big tyranasoras rex heard him. He
> lumbered forward filled with rage. Little dip was frightened but he was brave.
> He knew what to do! He began to throw roots at tyranasoras rex. He had no
> more rocks. So he bagan to hit tyranasoras rex with trees. Tyranasoras rex fell
> into the water, and dip was saved.

Figure 2.4 *(Continued)*

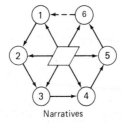

Narratives

structurally *both* to a common, central theme and to the events using close cause-effect and logical time relations (diagram 6).

Of course a top-stage story structure that a formal-operational student could produce could still be deadly dull, with little sensory texture, with trivial events and characters, satisfying to only a logician. A lower-stage story might have laudable sparks of creativity and intense personal fun and meaning for both its young creator and young audience.

Developing concepts about literature

To view literature as an ordered creation of the human imagination, to step back from literature and appreciate its wide array of attributes, is an ability that also develops gradually. Children may initially think that imaginative stories are events actually occurring long, long ago (Applebee, 1978).

Children may have trouble with figurative language, being very literal minded. Example (response to the line of poetry: "My love is like a red, red rose"): Child (puzzled)—"She pricks you?" Piaget might have explained a young child's inability to grasp metaphor as lack of decentering from self or lack of ability to think about thinking abstractly enough. A sociolinguist might reason that a child from an environment deprived of literary language uses up all his or her linguistic energy in simply making and using flat literal statements. Such a child has not yet mastered language to the extent of playing with it by using metaphors.

Another developmental example concerning metaphor is a response to Kay Starbird's poem "December Leaves," in which the poet describes fallen leaves as "cornflakes that fill the lawn's wide dish." First graders responded literally and with egocentrism: "[I don't like it because] Leaves can't make cornflakes"; "[I don't like it because] I have to rake leaves and I don't like them." Second graders apparently showed developing and more abstract evaluations based on poetry as a work of art: "I could see the leaves and snow in my mind"; "I liked the description of snow as sugar" (Fisher & Natarella, 1979).

On the other hand, a teacher will find individual differences in young children's grasp and use of metaphor. For example, Natasha, at kindergarten age (6.0), drew a picture and then wrote the following words in poem form, asking for spellings.

> Here are the children,
> sliding down the slide.
> They roll themselves in balls,
> pretending they are nuts
> falling from a tree.

In preferred programs, literacy and the literary use of language develop side by side. Look for literary development patterns in your students, both at their current status and in their development throughout the school year. Providing a literary environment in which to observe is, of course, a prerequisite.

What Is the Nature of Individual Differences in Development Among Child Language Learners?

We have talked about universal patterns and stages in language/thought acquisition and language learning, but we do not intend to exclude **individual differences.** Individual differences found in adult thought and sensitive, fluent language may have originated in early childhood years. Children differ in the time it takes them to move from, say, one-word to two-word sentences, to grasping difficult syntactic structures such as "Ted promised Jim to go." (Who will go?) They differ in the depth and variation of the word meanings they have acquired. This difference is especially significant in the elementary school, where this vocabulary-building aspect of language is still developing at full swing.

Children also differ in the ways they apply language rules, for example, how long they overgeneralize the rule for formation of the past tense with *ed* and ignore irregularities, resulting in such miscues as *cutted, goed,* and *feets.* They differ in the acquisition of the pragmatics and functions of language. Some of us are still not skilled in the use of language to console. If someone dies in a friend's family, we are at a loss as to what to say. Others have great skill in this area, sometimes having developed it quite early. These are individual differences.

One might think that there would be large cross-linguistic differences in the ways young children of differing nationalities acquire language. But studies seem to show similarities in basic "child grammar" across several dozens of different kinds of languages in very different societies (Slobin in *Nova,* 1985). These similarities indicate that young children overgeneralize the patterns they perceive in their distinct native languages. When this occurs they universally make creative errors based on their applications of a rule that is inappropriate in certain cases. For example, in Spanish nouns are considered to be masculine or feminine; the word *the* is *el* or *la,* accordingly. In addition, many feminine nouns end in the letter *a. The house* is therefore *la casa.* In the case of *the flower,* however, the Spanish word is *la flor.* Because they are used to the pattern of the two *a* sounds found in *la casa,* many children say *"la flora."* Investigators have found overgeneralization errors in almost every language they have studied.

At some point you will probably have children of differing nationalities bringing *linguistic* differences into your classroom. Although they may have had early acquisition processes in common, these children will have different problems in pronunciation and in recoding print to fit the natural syntax of their own language rather than that of English. They may even have different pragmatics for getting things they need and want via language. One teacher tells me a story of teaching in a foreign country. At home she was used to being able to say to her students, "Can you open your books to page 27?" The students would understand that it was an implied request to open their books to that page. The foreign students, however, would nod their heads and say "yes," indicating that they were capable of such a task, without taking any steps to complete it. (Such individual differences are addressed in Chapter 14 on special needs and in the activity book chapters corresponding to this chapter and Chapter 14.)

The range of individual differences makes pattern finding tricky and rigid ideas of stages outdated. Teachers need to rely heavily on careful classroom observation of how a *particular* child is developing. Each child is directing an orchestra of his or her very own. To have language is to have roots, symbolic and social. Experience with the media of art, music, and drama can feed into compositional experience, but individual children have different ways of using such symbolic material. One of the differences that shows some flexible patterns and is pertinent to the interests of the elementary teacher is *style.*

But now we move to an important question about another influence in language acquisition and later language arts development. This next question concerns you, the teacher, and the role of parents and caregivers in children's acquisition of language. The area has received much emphasis in recent developmental research. Mere exposure to adults talking is not enough for children to learn the rules systems of language—syntax, semantics, and pragmatics.

What Is the Later Role of Parents, Other Caregivers, and Teachers in Children's Language Acquisition and Literacy Development?

As a child, what kinds of interaction with other human beings do you need in order to get your language acquisition abilities going? As a child you really do not learn too well on the scraps of the language feast that is going on among adults around you. You need structured forms of *social interaction.* The mother who stimulates a baby during pauses in feeding may be the first guide in the rules for conversational turn-taking. Later, caregivers address the infant as if they were having a conversation. By asking the baby questions and commenting on sounds made, the caregivers ascribe intention to the child, showing they believe the baby intends to communicate *(intentionality).* By acting as if they were in a genuine conversation, the adults demonstrate for the baby the rules of conversational turn-taking.

For example, at 17 months on the way home from a visit, Natasha said at one point something like, "C-ca" and "bam-ba." The mother immediately responded to affirm that, yes, she had just played with the cats and a ball (during the visit). Natasha looked gratified. In a similar fashion a sixth-grade teacher may take a student's partially formulated hypothesis during a discussion about a character's motivation and ascribe intentionality to produce an even more insightful response than the student produced. The teacher affirms the competence that may not show up initially in the child's performance.

Young children receive a great deal of help in language development from routinized, predictable, socialized settings, such as the reading of storybooks with parents. Though some parents almost reach the point of exasperation from requests to "read it again," such socialized, interactive rereadings are important to a child's language growth. This idea sheds additional light on the problems young children encounter in retelling a story heard only once versus retelling from multiple chances to listen, interact, *assimilate,* and *accommodate* (to use the Piagetian terms).

Series of research tapings show that children grasp language used by the adult reader in a reading session, and then use it themselves in the next (rereading) session. It's almost as if a child gets to do a linguistic analysis of the story reading and feeds this into language acquisition systems. This can happen, of course, only if the routinized story reading recurs. Bruner (1983) calls these routinized, predictable, and socialized settings "formats." A format of reading aloud with a chance to respond is instructional not just for very young children, but at any age.

Scaffolding   Perhaps *scaffolding* is just a new term for something successful teachers have done for a long time. Just as a building going up has a scaffold to support its construction, so the adults operating in these formats provide a structured environment of social interaction, a framework, in order to facilitate the child's learning of language. Scaffolding has been described as a "process that enables a child or novice to solve a problem, carry out a task, or achieve a goal which would be beyond his unassisted efforts" (Wood, Bruner, & Ross, 1976, p. 90). In the present context a scaffold can be explanatory matter tending to confirm, validate, or bolster a child's language and thought. Recall the example of Natasha's "C-ca bam-ba" and the mother's confirming dialogue about the cat and the ball. As another example, a 14-month-old might say, "Wabbit," needing the help of an understanding adult to express the whole message intended by that one word. A mother might respond, "Yes, you have got a rabbit at home." The child then nods. Later, at age 3, the child will be able to say quite easily, "I've got a rabbit at home."

Teachers continue to use scaffolding techniques even with older children. In the following transcription, the reading teacher is trying to help the children understand something of what an aquanaut is before beginning a selection about aquanauts (Palincsar, 1986, pp. 86–87):

> [Note: T = teacher; S₁, ₂, ₃ = students.]
>
> T: Today's story is called "The Aquanauts." If I just said that the story is going to be about aquanauts, can you predict what you think . . .
>
> S1: What does it mean?
>
> T: Well, that's a good place to start. Has anyone heard the word aquanaut before? Have you heard of Aquaman, or aquarium? What do you think of when you hear aquarium?
>
> S2: A person.
>
> T: Who was Aquaman?
>
> S3: A person who helps people.
>
> T: How did he help people?
>
> S3: Underwater.
>
> T: Yes, he could help people underwater. Do you know what an aquarium is?
>
> S1: It's a fish tank.
>
> T: Do you hear any part of the word that is similar to what we are talking about?
>
> S1: No.
>
> T: Aquanauts, aquarium, Aquaman.
>
> S2: Aqua.
>
> T: Aqua is a word that means where Aquaman can live. Where the fish live, in the . . .
>
> S1: water.
>
> T: Aqua means water. So, aquanauts have something to do with the water. I wonder exactly what they are going to be.

A word of caution: Scaffolding can be used and misused. In trying to build a bridge between the child's mind with its limited understanding and the broader, more complex world that surrounds the child (whether in reality or in textbooks), the helping teacher can be said to be using scaffolding. On the other hand, too often one sees teachers fishing for one correct answer, using some techniques that superficially look like scaffolding but that are in effect discouraging to divergent, creative thought. Here is one example:

> TEACHER: Now what is the character's main problem? . . . Is it breaking the toy? Right! Now what should the character do? . . . Should he admit he did it? Right!

In this case the teacher is simply controlling the children's answers, not helping them deal with complexities. Guiding the process rather than giving the content is an approach that more often encourages genuine development (as in the opening scene).

Central to the notion of scaffolded instruction is Vygotsky's (1978) zone of *proximal development*. This term means the *distance between the actual developmental level (as determined by independent problem solving) and the level of potential development* (in other words, "can do" and "may do" behaviors). The child realizes potential through problem solving under adult or more capable peer guidance. The hallmark of scaffolded instruction is its interaction, its interplay, its dialogue between adult or teacher and learner in the joint completion of a task (as opposed to the child's being "talked at" or left to his or her own devices). The burning question becomes: How can teachers best aid learners in this zone of potential development, nudging them from one level to the next, and to independent application (Palincsar, 1986)?

The conscious or unconscious aim of scaffolded instruction is generalization to less structured contexts requiring less aid, and a gradual withdrawal of the scaffold. Here the metaphor of the scaffold becomes clearer because the helper uses it as an *adjustable* and *temporary* support for the child. (Activities for this chapter in the matching booklet carry this idea and other developmental teaching ideas further.)

Will you, as one teacher who was quoted at the beginning of this chapter suggested, "be able to understand what comes before, and back up to where a child having problems can be successful in the language arts"? Will you be able to *scaffold* and nudge this child forward when the child's previous experiences have led to the brink? If so, you will be truly counted among those who, in the words of the dean quoted earlier, "bring a developmental depth of understanding to any educational situation."

The next chapter deals with listening—the biggest but most neglected "fish" to catch in the language arts net. The structure of this chapter, repeated in other chapters, covers the why, who, where, what, and the how of teaching for listening competence.

SUMMARY

The process of learning to communicate combines the interplay of innate language capabilities, the child's own thought processes, and the guiding adults' roles as creators of a productive language-learning environment. Children learn language because they *desire to become effective communicators.* They do not set out to acquire a set of linguistic rules and grammar. They are motivated by the functions and pragmatics of language.

To foster children's love of language, teachers need to keep classroom instruction functional and make it joyful, memorable, and intriguing.

The following sound methodologies grow out of developmental ideas in relation to language arts teaching:

1. Literacy level in a class varies, even emerging literacy at the kindergarten level.
2. Real-life functions of literacy development are an important theme; the more realistic the use, the faster the growth.
3. Functional use of language in classrooms needs to attend to development of the social and emotional as well as cognitive processes.
4. Opportunity to experiment with emerging reading and writing strategies is important to development and can be a part of classroom activity.
5. A productive classroom environment promotes literacy development rather than just reading readiness, especially at beginning levels.

In regard to developmental knowledge, the following ideas stand out:

1. It is important to be well versed in child development from the standpoint of serving the child, parents, and the profession.
2. It is important to know the roots of development of syntax, semantics, and pragmatics of language and their interrelated universal patterns, both linguistic and cognitive. Theories offering stages give us explanatory power, descriptive milestones, and observational and planning strength. An important contribution of Piaget's classic work is emphasis on children's autonomy in self-construction of knowledge by action on responsive objects in their environment. Assimilating such experience, children learn from the inside out, slowly, with a genuine and lasting change in ways of knowing and viewing their world.
3. Children tend to hypercorrect, to overgeneralize their language principles. Such

developmental errors represent high, creative levels of cognitive functioning, not stupidity.

4. Children exhibit individual differences in language acquisition and development. Recognition of these differences keeps us from falling into traps of rigidly defined stages, especially in regard to growth in the language arts.

5. Caregivers and teachers play an important role in children's language acquisition, literacy development, and literary development. Teachers can build and remove scaffolds, assisting a child to function in a more creative style.

CHAPTER 3

Listening

"The most basic of all human needs is to understand and be understood.
. . . The best way to understand people is to listen to them."

Ralph G. Nichols

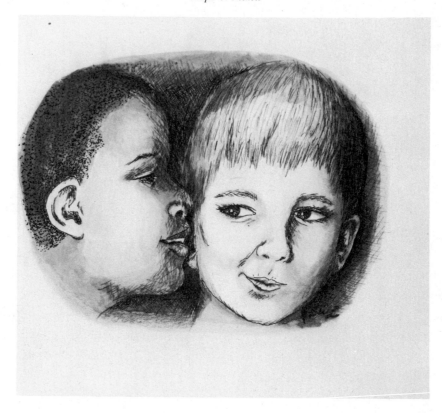

INTRODUCTION

You have an important role in developing the listening skills of children and your own competence as a listener. Most people who are learning to be teachers want to know first of all just how to teach a few activities. You are not ready for the *hows* of teaching, however, until you have grasped several prerequisite points: (1) a definition of successful listening, (2) a rationale of its importance, (3) the nature of child listeners, (4) an effective listening climate (both physical and emotional), and (5) goals that guide the selection of options for significant material for listening instruction. When you have answered questions about the *why, who, where,* and *what,* then you are far better prepared to move into the *how* of teaching listening. Answering such questions is an important part of creative problem solving during teaching.

Part of the recent importance of listening (the *why*) grows out of a federal law. On November 1, 1978, Congress passed Public Law 95-561, amending the Elementary and Secondary Education Act to include the addition of oral language—listening and speaking. This event stimulated great interest in the development of listening instruction and assessment, especially among members of federal and state departments of education. In order to stimulate progress, the U.S. government had appropriated grant money of over $25 million by 1981. Since states are receiving strong support for developing quality basic skills programs in listening, the movement has probably already spread to the school where you will teach. Legislation is only part of the importance of teaching listening; the *Why* section later in this chapter delves more deeply into this matter. One reason teachers like to teach it, however, is that it can simply be a lot of fun. So why not break into that vicious circle: "My teacher never listens." "My students never listen!" Instead, why not become the best listeners and teachers of listening around?

The illustrative classroom scene that follows sets the tone, reveals a teacher at work, and introduces some important concepts and strategies developed throughout the rest of the chapter. The teacher's behaviors preview some of the upcoming strategies about *how* to teach.

OPENING SCENE: Overview of the *Why, What, Who, Where,* and *How* of Teaching

Chris Anderson, the teacher, tapped a metal triangle and stepped into the center of a large yellow "spotlight" painted in the classroom floor. This action, saved for important occasions, did not happen often. Twenty-five pairs of fourth-grade eyes focused there, with one exception, Roderick. He was quickly nudged to attention by some classmates.

"Class," said the teacher, "I'd appreciate some time to share my recent experiences with you. I've just gotten back from a conference on listening. The governor of the state sent the conference a wire proclaiming it to be 'State Listening Week.' School people from all over the country were there. Can you guess why?"

"It's the year of the ear?" quipped Chung. All laughed.

"They want us to listen better in school?" suggested Karina anxiously.

"We're at war with nonlisteners?" grinned Roderick.

"Thank you for your ideas," said the teacher. "People said they came because although they had gotten the message that listening effectively is important, hardly anybody teaches it, or knows how to teach it. Now we have a national law that says listening is a basic skill that must be taught. I think that you are already successful listeners in school, but we can all improve, starting this week. I'm going to try to be a better listener, too."

"I'd like to have my parents come be with us," whispered Roderick, not too softly.

"It's about time somebody at school listened to me," thought Tim.

"I appreciate your ideas;" continued the teacher, "they can help us to get started on a listening unit. Chung, would you and your committee print us a sign for a corner of our room saying 'Year of the Ear,' " said the teacher, picking up on the children's ideas.

"And Karina, would you and a committee plan how to make our room a better place for listening, a better listening environment? Then we can, as you said, 'listen better in school.' Roderick, would you guide a committee to list with whom we are 'at war.' Who are the 'good guys' (whatever helps us be successful listeners)? Who are the 'bad guys' (whatever keeps us from being successful listeners)? Also plan how we can involve our parents," added the teacher, who hadn't missed his whisper.

"Can I help?" ventured Tim, who rarely volunteered for anything.

"Surely," smiled the teacher. "We're all going to plan together and have jobs in this 'Year of the Ear' unit. I'm open for ideas. Tomorrow at this time we will have a planning session, and work centers set up where committees will work."

"We missed you. What else did you do at the conference?" asked Chung.

"I'm going to show you. Someone demonstrated this listening lesson. See this paper bag? When I shake it, listen and tell what type of sound it might be," said the teacher, setting a lesson purpose and demonstrating.

"Jingling." "Ringing." "Rattling." "Metallic." (Various responses came.)

"Now, just to yourself, think what really might be in this bag." The teacher paused, then shook out the contents. "See, it happens to be filled with pennies." After putting them back, "Now listen again, but in a *new* way and think what it *reminds* you of when you hear it," said the teacher, setting a revised purpose, namely imaging.

"Grandpa's pants pocket." "Piggy banks." "Little jingle bells." "A rattlesnake." (Again various children responded.)

"Thank you for your ideas. Josephine, I'd like you to choose one of the ideas for us to work with to fashion a drama," the teacher said, using the strategy called *lifting,* in this case to a topic for an improvised scene.

"The rattlesnake," said Josephine.

"Where might it be?" asked the teacher, *focusing* and lifting to the setting. "Brainstorm a place."

"In the school yard," said Teddy.

"More ideas of where it might be," encouraged the teacher, using the strategy of *extending*.

"In our classroom."

"In the department store." The children brainstormed other ideas.

"Teddy, choose a place," said the teacher, focusing again.

"In the school yard."

"Then who discovers it?" said the teacher, lifting to the characters.

"A lady with a small child. The child discovers it."

"More ideas," said the teacher, extending.

"A unicorn finds it," offered Karina.

"A principal finds it. . . ."

We leave the scene here, but will pick up on it later in the chapter.

Analysis of the Scene

As mentioned earlier, this opening scene illustrates a number of points worth developing in this chapter. The teacher began by pointing out the government's interest in listening and will next ask the class to give their own reasons as to why listening is important in their lives, as uncovered in their logs or field notes. As their "year of the ear" progresses, such activity is likely to stimulate a more fully developed concept of just what is happening, of what listening is in their context, and of needed skills (part of the *what*). The class committee on effective and noneffective listeners may help both teacher and children to understand the nature of listeners in this classroom (the *who*). By interviewing one another, children can fashion cooperative profiles of how far along each is in effective listening development.

Recall that another committee was assigned that day to shed light on the environment in the classroom conducive to listening (the *where*). The children will find that this environment is both physical and emotional. The teacher brought back to the class the integrative activity using hidden sounds as stimulation for many of the language arts: listening/speaking (drama), writing (the script), and eventually reading the creations. Thus, Chris Anderson brought both material and teaching strategy (the *how*) into the class.

As already suggested, it can be premature to leap to specifics of the *how* without answers to the other questions firmly in mind and at least partially answered. In light of answers to such questions, Chris Anderson's teacher-talk was structured to produce effective student listening. After dealing with these organizing questions, the chapter offers some suggestions for integrating in class and then finishes with some ideas for assessment.

With some constraints, incidentally, the opening scene could take place with teacher adaptation at almost any grade level. Younger children can profit from committee work, too. Readiness at any age is individual and depends on previous experience. In essence, the point is to start with natural child needs occurring in the classroom and continue building your classroom listening experiences from such real events. Such is the most meaningful and motivating of instructional strategies. (See the companion activity book for many enjoyable how-to examples at other age levels, e.g., games, listening scavenger hunt, the good listener award.)

Figure 3.1 shows our major questions and their interaction. It also indicates that the teacher as role *model* plays an important part. The teacher attends to modeling and to these

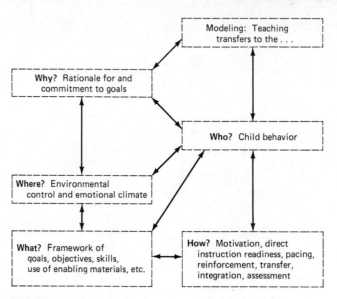

Figure 3.1 A framework for productive teaching behavior during listening instruction.

questions, and the children do too. The diagram suggests a sequence, but it is not mandatory. The *how* box, however, is placed last after the other questions have at least begun to be addressed.

The teacher in the opening scene will use many naturally occurring events in the classroom to teach listening, capitalizing on genuine communication needs rather than consistently using just the game or lesson approach with which the instruction began. Some useful natural events are likely to occur during the committee work planned for the next day. Children will probably encounter problems in listening to each other. The alert teacher can capitalize, for example, by encouraging creative problem solving about listening needs.

Next, consider definition. You will find successful listening has process, knowledge, and purpose.

WHAT IS LISTENING IN THE CLASSROOM?

Many of us think that listening is something children ought to do a lot more of. Teachers can accomplish such a goal, but not by the chiding that most of us were subjected to (and that usually failed to work). The teacher in the opening scene, for instance, never admonished the children to "listen." Most people have an oversimplified idea of what listening is. In fact, a definition of listening includes many important concepts; we deal with just a few here.

Process

First of all listening is a *process*. It is an *active* comprehension process that includes (1) receiving, (2) focusing, (3) attending, (4) discriminating, (5) assigning meaning, (6) monitoring, (7) remembering, and (8) responding to auditory messages. The children and teacher in the opening scene did all of these things as they listened *and* responded.

If we had actually been in that classroom, the chances are we would have noticed that listeners use many visual clues to guide their listening comprehension and responses. We have to "listen" with our eyes as well as our ears. The children were picking up visual cues from the teacher, cues that said. "It's OK; brainstorm; get out many ideas; there aren't going to be any 'bad' ideas." Body movements and stance inform listeners much of the time as they use this auditory comprehension process.

Knowledge, Attitudes, and Habits

Effective listening requires a learner's development of appropriate components: knowledge, attitudes, and habits. For example, the children brought their background knowledge to bear on the decision points in fashioning ideas for what was in the bag and for the rattlesnake drama. They brought attitudes and habits of attending when the teacher stepped into the spotlight. Much of successful listening consists of effective, reciprocal habits.

Purpose

People listen for a wide variety of purposes. Consider five of these. Sometimes the purpose is merely *ritual* (e.g., answering when the roll is called in school). Sometimes the purpose is to be *informed*. For example, in the opening scene the children listened to find out what could have caused the sound in the paper bag, and what the sound might remind them of *(imaging)*. Being informed can also help us solve problems. It can help us predict.

Sometimes we listen with the purpose of *feeling*. ("That made my ears happy!" said a kindergartener in response to a music box.) Sometimes our purpose is to listen critically when we are *being controlled*. For example, someone might try to influence us by saying, "Everyone else is doing it." We may wonder if the message sent is really for our own good and ask ourselves, "Who is 'everyone' and what's the cost?" (Critical thinking is stressed in Chapter 10.) Thus we have listening purposes with reference to the following:

Five Sample Listening Purposes
1. Ritual.
2. Being informed.
3. Imaging.
4. Feeling.
5. Being controlled.

Levels

We listen at many different communication levels, including the five that follow.

Communication Levels
1. Intrapersonal (within oneself).
2. Interpersonal (among people).
3. Group (three or more members).
4. Public (bounded groups, e.g., own class, other classes, school, scout group, parent group).
5. Media (TV, radio, audiotape, film, etc.).

Our opening scene can provide examples of these five communication levels. The teacher communicated at the *intrapersonal* level by deciding: "That's enough spotlight for me now; the children aren't getting to talk enough." At the *interpersonal* level, after the teacher invited dramatic improvisation, Josephine settled on a mother and child as discoverers of the snake, Karina furnished the child's dialogue, and Dorothy compatibly furnished the mother's dialogue. Creation of the snake dramatization also represented the *group* level of audience in operation. An example of the *public* level would be if the class presented its drama to another class or to parents. An example of the *media* level of audience would follow if the local cable TV station broadcast the drama.

Just as effective teachers see to it that their curriculum allows for a range of purposes, so do they provide for a wide variety of communication levels in which children can practice effective listening.

Another way of looking at levels is as (1) literal, (2) interpretive, (3) critical, and (4) creative. *Literal* listening to comprehend a message directly follows a communication line ("That is the sound of thunder"). The listener receives ideas and details accurately, adhering to the primary and explicit meaning. *Interpretive* listening goes beyond these lower levels to analyze ("And that means a storm is coming"). *Critical* listening employs a criterion for making a judgment ("Judging from the weather forecast and the appearance of those clouds this is going to be quite a storm"). *Creative* listening synthesizes many ideas to come up with a response that is unique, fluent, elaborated, perceptively visualized, and flexible. ("When I'm playful . . . I scratch my head with the lightning, and purr myself to sleep with the thunder. . . ."—Mark Twain.) It requires imagination to use what was heard to produce new ideas. (Chapter 10 details the critical and Chapter 13 deals with the creative uses of language.)

Developmental Aspects

The basic process of listening is in place quite early in children. (This process includes focusing, attending, discriminating, assigning meaning, monitoring, remembering, organizing, and evaluating.) Nonetheless, as children become more experienced they can make additional gains. They can gain from a more complex and abstract assortment of information, and process it with more competence, skill, and effectiveness. (The *who* section elaborates.)

For example, a kindergarten class might need to deal with just one task related to listening at a time, such as a group assignment of making a sign "Year of the Ear." On the other hand, an eighth-grade class might undertake all the projected tasks in the opening scene plus a documented history and a forecast of listening in the twenty-first century.

Listening and Hearing

Listening is *not* merely hearing. One can have perfectly healthy ears and yet not comprehend, say, an unfamiliar foreign language. It is in *comprehension* (and attendant responding) that we have the essence of classroom listening. We hear a lot that we do not, or do not care to, comprehend. Understanding during listening varies greatly. (Listening is compared to reading in the section on integration at the end of this chapter.)

In the final analysis, whatever you do in your classroom regarding listening provides an operational definition of what you and your children think listening is. *Listening is the way you and your children do it.* If upon being asked, "What is listening?" a child responds, "It's folding your hands and looking at the teacher," you have a fair idea of the operating definition in that classroom. In sum, listening is an active (often interactive), predominantly auditory comprehension process. It includes but is not limited to the following: hearing, receiving, focusing, attending, discriminating, assigning meaning and interpreting, monitoring, organizing, synthesizing, evaluating, remembering, and responding to messages. All these elements fit together in the process as shown in Figure 3.2. The net gathers the crucial concepts developed in this chapter.

A Listening Net

To begin fashioning a curriculum with a broader definition in your class, accumulate and arrange subconcepts related to listening. One device is to call up the analogy of the language arts fishnet presented in Chapter 1. Take the segment labeled *Listening* and surround it with

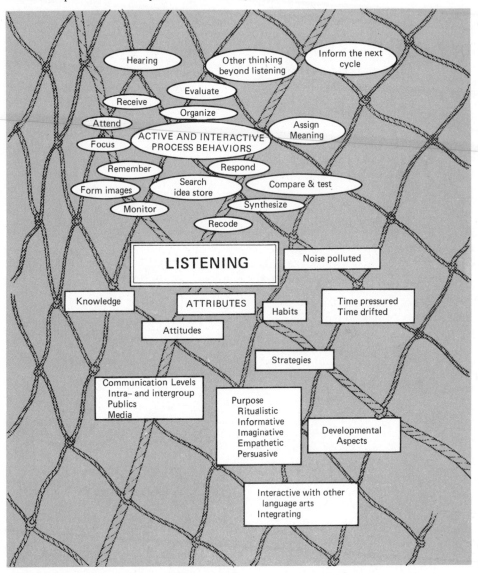

Figure 3.2 A network of listening concepts.

an even finer netting for its subconcepts. Cover up Figure 3.2 until you have had a try at "netting" some concepts about listening. Then compare your collection with Figure 3.2. The best learning experience, once you have glimpsed this model network, is to fashion your own network for this area and for others of the language arts.

WHY IS LISTENING INSTRUCTION IMPORTANT?

Optimally teacher and children work together through the question of why listening is important. They examine their real-life needs and experiences to discover the value of listening in other school subjects, in social and language development, and in problem solving.

Impact on Reading and Speaking

Remember that if one of the knots or strands of the language arts net is weak, it affects the function of the others. If a child cannot comprehend a message through listening, it is unlikely that he will comprehend that message through reading. Further, if a child cannot compose a text from a message presented to her ears, it is unlikely that she will be able to compose a text for herself using print symbols for that message. Because listening is a prerequisite for so many abilities, one may make the oversimplified statement: "Show me a child who is a remedial reader, and I'll show you a child who's a remedial listener."

Why does listening have a ceiling effect on the other language arts? For one thing, remember that listening vocabulary is typically the largest of the four vocabularies (listening, speaking, reading, and writing). Figure 3.3 illustrates with reference to typical elementary school children.

Getting Along in the Real World

Businesspeople recognize the importance of successful listening. Articles on oral communication appear frequently in business journals, and consultants in the area of listening earn substantial fees. Poor listening costs businesses dollars and loss of clients' goodwill when communication breaks down. "We listen!" and "It pays to listen!" are some common

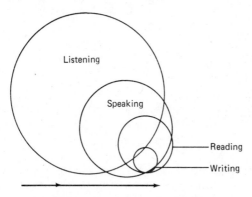

(Arrows suggest movement through time.)
Are all vocabularies basically dependent on listening?

Figure 3.3 Four overlapping vocabularies used in school.

business slogans. If we want children to succeed in the real world of work and living, it is well for us not to neglect this interrelated area—listening.

Impact on Social, Language/Thought, and Problem-Solving Development

Listening can bring about rich literate and literary language development and more positive social relations. A key to creative social problem solving is active listening. Just try plugging your ears for a day and see what happens. The impact of hearing loss can point to the harmful effects of depressed listening ability. Even mildly deaf children typically are retarded in language development. Respiratory diseases bring many temporary, undetected hearing losses in children. Even a brief hearing loss may cause a drop in self-esteem, a decrease in social relationships, and a feeling of loss of self-control.

Children cannot reach their fullest potential as thinkers and successful social (or cognitive) problem solvers if they are denied the best information their ears can bring. Listening is a subability of *problem solving*, an important part of the data gathering. A problem may be vague before discussion, but become more clear-cut after careful listening and focusing of questions. As several children contribute ideas, they can build on each others' hypotheses, use each other as sounding boards, and refine and evaluate their solutions. (A section of the activity book deals with the large amount of time spent in listening.)

WHO ARE THE LISTENERS IN YOUR CLASSROOM?

You may invest considerable time and effort preparing materials and planning instruction on listening only to find that, when the bell rings, the *wrong* listeners walk through your classroom door! They unexpectedly do not match your lesson plans or materials. What kinds of listeners were they before you and they met? What personal, social, and cultural baggage are they bringing as they step into your room? To find out about the listeners in a classroom, you can apply ideas learned from child development and anthropology to the thought levels, conceptual levels, style, and sociocultural differences of listeners in the classroom. (*Developmental know-how*, first introduced in Chapter 2, is found in the *Who* sections of most chapters.)

Levels of Thinking/Listening

Examine the maturity level of thinking that children display after listening. Know each one. A gifted kindergarten child from mainstream society may be relatively nonegocentric while listening and may process variables maturely, many at the same time. Ask if this child's listening diet at school is sufficiently challenging and varied.

A self-centered eighth grader from mainstream society might have great difficulty thinking about his reciprocal processes while listening and be highly egocentric in message sending and receiving. How might your listening program help the thought levels of this student?

An unlikely achiever (cultural minority, impoverished) in sixth grade may be capable of functioning successfully with almost any academic listening purpose and almost any level of audience. But suppose this student has a style showing strong internal locus of control and tunes in only rarely with *empathy* to others. Another of your impoverished students, however, may generally appear to have nonlistening habits, especially in a school setting. What do you do?

A second-grade child from a noise-laden environment may have impaired hearing and may receive so much negative emotional language in the home that only your most trust-creating yet most unique of listening environments can penetrate the learning blockage. In essence, by knowing how to improve individual listening skills and awareness you can open doors to a child's higher thought levels. But you can only plan your program effectively by *knowing each child.*

Level of Listening Concepts and Other Constraints

Recall that young listeners are prone to language overgeneralization (e.g., "I wetted the clay"). Some children will overgeneralize ideas as well, for example, that a speaker or a listener is totally responsible for the success of communication. Such children may not understand that communication is a two-way responsibility with both listener and speaker helping. In addition, young listeners may not be able to remember much at once and succumb to your information overload (too many instructions at one time). Also, your youngest learners may not be skilled in thinking about their own thinking, the metacognitive process that can assist much of their listening improvement.

The constraint of emotional control can also affect children's listening ability. Developmentally speaking, emotional control is easier for older children than for younger ones. To quiet yourself and listen carefully and effectively to someone who repulses you or threatens you in some way takes considerable self-discipline. Successful listeners, usually older ones, can understand the concept of control of bias while listening, and achieve it.

Young children, or children who operate at a less mature stage, tend to lack emotional control in handling physical and emotional distractions. Such children may confuse the auditory object with the auditory background; for example, they cannot tune out the distracting child next to them, or even the children in the next room ("They're playing games in there . . . what were you saying?").

Auditory and Other Styles

Some of your students may know their world primarily through their ears; that is, listening may be their predominant style. They may even be overly dependent on auditory modes of intake. Listening serves as a crucial advanced organizer for them. If they can listen to something and respond before attempting related reading and writing, their success rate is high. Many readers of this text would learn more if they could chat informally with the author about this chapter before reading it. Others would far rather see related slides or a film first (visual style). One of the reasons style was subtly integrated into the opening scene was to stress its impact on listening behavior. (Styles implied were rigid inhibited, undisciplined, acceptance anxious, and creative.) Try to observe and interpret the styles your children display. Sociocultural and linguistic differences affecting listening are discussed in Chapter 14 on the special child. An activity for interviewing children about their listening is found in Chapter 3 of the activity book.

In any case, the idea is to know your individual listeners and apply your developmental and cultural knowledge to each situation. It is unreasonable to expect peak listening from students of any age every minute of the day. Effective learning through listening is demanding work: Heart rate goes up and other physiological processes accelerate. People need to have chances to tune out and relax. Provide such a rhythm during the school day appropriate to the group and to individuals. (Such a teaching strategy is called *pacing.*) If you are able to answer questions about *who* your listeners are, you are well on your way to successful teaching, especially if you are also able to respond effectively to the next question, *where.*

WHERE DOES SUCCESSFUL CLASSROOM LISTENING TAKE PLACE?

In our opening scene the teacher asked Karina to guide a committee in planning how to make their room a better place for listening. On the overview chart in Figure 3.1 this area is mentioned as the *where.* The *where* of successful classroom listening refers to regulation of the physical and emotional climates in the classroom. Several aspects include seating, temperature, ventilation, and appropriate noise level for tasks. A teacher can make special provision for those handicapped in hearing (e.g., move them closer as suggested in Chapter 14). Teachers can inform administrators about flooring and ceiling materials that reduce noise, though these aspects may not be directly under teacher control. If we want children to meet state and local mandates regarding listening in school, we need to give them an enabling environment.

Teacher and Child Responsibility

Not only can teachers attend to physical environments themselves, but also they can guide children to assume such responsible behaviors. On their own, children can get up and move closer or to a less noisy place, or can offer to close a hall door or window in order to improve the listening setting. Teachers can reinforce such initiative with appreciation. Too many of us tend to tolerate the noise of poor environmental conditions. Too many assume it is someone else's responsibility to correct the problem.

Emotional Climate

Emotional climate is another important aspect of classroom listening. Effective teachers of listening model and create an environment, attitude, value, and feeling tone called *empathetic.* Ask yourself the questions in Box 3.1 on page 72.

We can find many areas for improvement when it comes to providing an optimal physical and emotional environment for listening. Karina's listening committee in the opening scene, for instance, might add many attractive features to the listening environment or center (e.g., a class mural of the "Road to Good Listening" with concepts discovered during the year, as illustrated in the activity book). But the most important part of the environment resides in the attitudes that the teacher and children will create, saying, "In this classroom, *this* is the way we listen to each other!"

To know about the *why, who,* and *where* is to be ready to consider questions about *what* to teach. This is the concern of the next section.

WHAT GOALS OF LISTENING INSTRUCTION ARE USEFUL?

The *what* of listening instruction refers to goals and their supporting processes, objectives, skills, related instructional content, and materials. This aspect of teaching is closely interwoven with the *how,* so the order of presentation here is somewhat arbitrary and sometimes

---

BOX 3.1 Emotional Environment Conducive to Listening Questionnaire

1. *Do I sometimes lean forward and say warmly, "Tell me about it," encouraging the child to unfold and expand, giving my undivided attention?*

When you listen simply and warmly to children, you "create" them. People define for us who we are by listening, talking with us, and looking in our direction while we speak.

2. *Do I listen to children without my mind pressing against theirs, without arguing or changing the subject?*

Someone once said, "Be not too much a teacher." In tune with that idea, a teacher would certainly avoid the practice of scolding a student and right then expecting him or her to listen at a high level of effectiveness. Under extreme stress all but the most automatic of comprehension processes are usually shut down or considerably hampered. Recall in the opening scene, during the brainstorming portions, that the teacher respected and thanked the children for offering ideas and did not judge them "good" or "bad" prematurely.

3. *Is the "environment" of my teaching voice relaxed, unhurried, nonthreatening, with appropriate and varied volume, pitch, and body language?*

When was the last time you studied yourself communicating on videotape or audiotape? (Recall that the teacher in our scene was recording.) Try it. If you do not like what you hear, you can change. Most of us can improve the way we project, modulate, and vary our voice.

4. *Do I limit my own "teacher talk" time, choosing my significant words with care and thus providing more opportunities for student communication?*

---

overlaps. This section covers a framework of goals for listening. Notice that major goal areas deal with process, purposes, and attitudes. These goals are major ports in the voyage of teaching listening.

A Framework of Goals

One of the state frameworks in tune with the ideas of this chapter is that of Maryland. An adapted version is given in Box 3.2.

Self-monitoring Techniques: An Example of a Goal Put into Action

As an example of a goal we consider the use of self-monitoring techniques to assess one's own listening effectiveness, subgoal 1.4 under goal 1 of the listening framework. Recently this aspect of the listening process has been researched extensively. The technical term is *metacognitive listening*—thinking about your thinking while you are listening, splitting your mental focus to correct and enhance meaning. Long ago, however, related productive (and less productive) listener patterns were pointed out (e.g., Nichols & Stevens, 1957). Combining these ideas, the teacher can help children become aware of patterns and guard against those unproductive ones when the occasion warrants.

BOX 3.2 Listening Framework

To communicate effectively, students need to be able to:

Goal 1: Be aware of and use stages of a listening **process** (e.g., task focus, discrimination, meaning getting, and monitoring).

Subgoals:

1.1. Focus on the listening task.

1.2. Discriminate among aural and related visual messages.

1.3. Assign meanings to the message received.

1.4. Use self-monitoring techniques to assess own listening effectiveness (illustrated in the next section).

Goal 2: Listen for a variety of **purposes.**

Subgoals:

2.1. Listen to comprehend the literal content of messages and recognize purpose of speakers (and self). (The activity book details lessons for this goal.)

2.2. Listen *empathetically* to help speakers clarify their thoughts and feelings.

2.3. Listen creatively and critically to synthesize and evaluate the validity of a message and the credibility of the sender. (See Chapters 10 and 13.)

2.4. Listen to solve problems (added item).

2.5. Listen for recreation and for aesthetic pleasure. (A bibliography of children's books with listening themes is at the end of this book in Chapter 3 references.)

Goal 3: Develop a lasting positive **attitude** toward listening.

Subgoals:

3.1. Develop a willingness to listen actively, openly, and responsibly.

3.2. Develop a curiosity about and interest in listening to a variety of topics and people.

3.3. Value the significant role of listening in human experiences. (Refer to the earlier section of this chapter on emotional climate. A later section on motivation expands these ideas.)

Note: Skills matching these goals and subgoals are found in Chapter 15 of the activity book.

Essential skills in monitoring communication include (1) realizing that problems can occur, (2) recognizing when they do, and (3) knowing how to remedy them (Revelle, Wellman, & Karabenick, 1985). With these skills in mind, let us examine listening patterns.

Patterns arise in what we might call leftover thinking space. Only a fraction of our thinking time is spent in physically hearing most messages, because thought is faster than most people's speech. How we use leftover thinking space significantly affects our success in understanding and using messages. The amount of leftover thinking space varies, but generally people can count on a usable amount, even as much as 90 percent. (See Figure 3.4.) With what do we fill this leftover space?

Four listener patterns are typical during use of leftover thinking space. These patterns show alternate ways of interacting with material. One of the patterns is effective for literal listening, and the other three are not. (You might say that some are skills and some are

THINKING SPACE

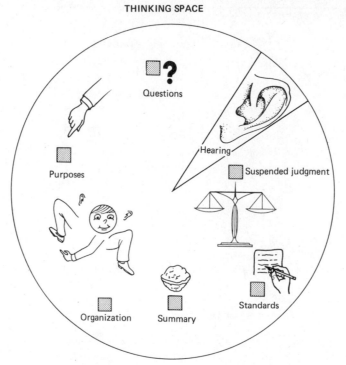

You normally use only about 10 percent of your thinking
space for hearing.

Figure 3.4 Leftover thinking space.

"antiskills".) To illustrate, first we need a message. Use the context of the rattlesnake drama
our opening scene children created. After we left the scene, Josephine chose the character
of a lady with a small child to be the one to find the snake, and volunteers filled the other
roles. Then the teacher said to Karina, who had volunteered, "What does the child say?"
Now, with this message and context in hand, consider the first pattern.

Pattern 1: Small Departures from the Communication Line   Let's suppose Karina
had taken small productive departures with her leftover thinking space. Let's say she
visualized a small child, maybe her baby brother, and then imagined what he might say in
response to seeing a snake for the first time. She would have made effective use of her
leftover thinking space. As a matter of fact she did when she said, "Mommie, look at the
short rubber hose; it's moving!" (A representation of pattern #1, small productive departures, is in the first part of Figure 3.5.)

Pattern 2: Tangent   But let's suppose, instead, that the moment someone said *"snake,"*
Karina's leftover thinking space became totally preoccupied with the terrible slithery creature. Suppose she went off on a tangent with her mind dwelling on her terror of snakes,
never to return to the communication line. Her pattern would probably look like the second
representation in Figure 3.5. She would probably never have even listened.

Pattern 3: Private Argument   Suppose that when a lady with a small child was decided
on as the finder of the snake, Karina had chosen to fill her thinking space with private

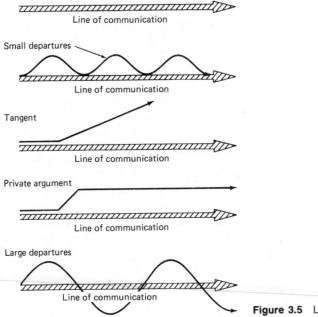

Figure 3.5 Listener patterns.

arguments. Let's say she really wanted a unicorn to be the chosen character for the improvised drama. "That could be much more fun," she could be arguing to herself. In fact, she could argue privately for the rest of the activity session, missing the fun, the class assignment, and the homework task.

Sound familiar? Sometimes this pattern is related to a distortion called *self-preoccupation.* Have you ever been introduced to people and then couldn't remember their names, perhaps because instead of listening you were thinking about the impression you were making? Sometimes people get wrapped up in their own parallel argument and never realize how close their position might be to that of their supposed antagonist. (This pattern, private argument, is the third shown in Figure 3.5.)

Pattern 4: Large Departures Suppose Karina had directed her attention fairly well to the line of communication but had let her mind play with images and wander too much (the fourth pattern in Figure 3.5). For example, she might have grasped some of the responses to the teacher's paper bag activity but then left the line of communication after "grandpa's pants pocket"; she may have followed the ideas for the locale of the drama but left the communication line after "the department store" was mentioned. The big gaps left by these large departures would prevent her from improvising or responding appropriately later.

Worries, enticing daydreams, or similar distractions have caused all of us to engage at times in this listening pattern, even when we were motivated and really wanted to listen. Sometimes the metacognitive strategy of telling ourselves that the very next words may completely change our lives helps even those of us who are most prone to wander. Up to a point, we can help children learn to quiet themselves and discipline their attention. They can visualize effectively to enhance the message with an appropriate amount of relevant, image-enriching experience during their leftover thinking.

Younger children might dramatize the first three patterns with puppets, after modeled examples. Older children might role-play all five contrasting patterns. (Chapter 5 of the activity book details role-play strategies.) The next section gives some further self-monitoring techniques and strategies (and offers a few teaching hints).

Metacognitive Listening Strategies

Take a look at some strategies you might help children choose from when they recognize that a listening problem has occurred. (Some of the ideas could relate to speakers as well as to listeners.) **Attention directing** may receive a boost with note taking, mainly to keep attention focused on the line of communication. Picking a focus also helps, for example: "I'm going to aim for the big ideas"; "I'm going to collect all the good anecdotes." In essence children tell themselves, "Get ready; get set; tune out all else; select a purpose; *listen.*"

Memory enhancing, a second strategy, is useful when the problem seems to be memory overload. Basics that help are imposing organization on the seemingly unorganized message, categorizing, labeling, and rehearsing. Applying the organization of the different speech patterns mentioned in Chapter 3 of the activity book may help. *Word signals* may help. Younger children can watch for word cues such as *first, second, third;* older children for *in contrast* and *as another example.* The use of an *advance organizer* (outline, web, study guide) helps a child with labels and categories—fewer concepts for the young child, more detail for the older one. Most of us *chunk* phone numbers saying, "dial 361 thirty-four, twenty-four" (instead of 3, 4, 2, 4). Many children unconsciously use the strategy of *rehearsal,* repeating under their breath over and over, for example, "Go to the office; ask Mrs. Lawrence for a pad of pink slips, a pair of scissors, and some tape. Go to the office . . ." and so on. Thus they try to assure that they will not forget a message.

Enhancing the communication, a third strategy, pertains to requests for clarity, active feedback, paraphrasing, and parasupports. Examples of parasupports are head nodding and phrases such as "Did you really!" and "Well!" Enabling words of active feedback might be, "Would this be an example of what you mean?" Words related to paraphrasing might be, "What I've learned so far is . . ."; "Is this what you're saying, that. . . ." Active feedback and summarizing can help memory, attention, and meaning during listening.

Enhancing the meaning, a fourth strategy, can be used positively in connection with the first listener pattern, small productive departures. Teachers can help children elaborate the message with appropriate mental images, referral to previous experience, and self-questioning. Examples: *"Metacognitive* . . . ah, like an overhead projector with one transparency laid over another, thought overlaying thought—I see" (elaborating with imagery). "He said, 'I *know* about you.' I wonder what he meant?" (self-questioning). *Teachers can structure their talk so that their students can listen better. Students can enhance meaning, too.*

As you can see, a number of strategies exist for assisting listening. Most children and adults could profit from becoming students of their metacognitive listening processes and applying appropriate strategies. Unfortunately, few if any strategies are typically at a sufficient level of awareness and conscious use by children (Tompkins, Friend, & Smith, 1987). On the other hand, even some 3- and 4-year-olds can realize ambiguities and puzzlements in communication and will rather directly seek to clear them up after monitoring a situation that is highly meaningful to them (Revelle, Wellman, & Karabenick, 1985).

The main point is to know your learners and help them with the following: (1) selection of appropriate *strategies,* (2) *monitoring* of the effectiveness of a selected listening strategy, and (3) *revision* of an ineffective listening strategy (or ineffective reading strategy, too, for that matter). Teachers can help children attend and alert themselves when the activity is not proceeding properly.

Teachers need to find appropriate places, however for instruction regarding strategies and not use the isolated practice of this split mental focus. That is, avoid seeking to clarify or summarize when neither is required. Instruction is not a matter of 15 minutes here and there with your metacognitive listening cap on; it is not a matter of a "quick fix." Instruction involves a sense of communication responsibility that teachers as models can seak to transfer to children's own use when it comes up naturally in the course of each day.

HOW CAN I TEACH LISTENING?

Now that you know something about the why, who, where, and what of teaching listening, you are more genuinely ready for the *how*. One parent said, "I'm wondering if teachers teach, or do they just assign work and send it home. It seems I'm having to do a lot of teaching at home!" How do teachers teach? And how do they get children to learn?

In a more "traditional" approach, listening practice (and supposedly learning) consists of the children listening to material that is read or spoken. The teacher follows this input with some kind of comprehension check for listening accuracy. This practice is similar to traditional reading comprehension exercises, but uses auditory channels. Some commercial materials have used this approach.

In teaching listening, however, as with any subject, genuine, long-lasting learning is an "inside" job on the part of the child. Teachers can do certain things that help, not hinder. Almost every chapter of this book brings a different dimension to the *how* of teaching, in part specifically related to the topic, but also of general interest, transferable, and usable in a wide variety of contexts.

This section describes how teachers can (1) motivate, working with internal needs of children; (2) use "direct instruction," including telling, tutoring, and probing discussion group; (3) employ a six-step strategy that includes readiness, pacing, reinforcing, and transfer seeking in real communication situations, and (4) integrate and assess listening.

Motivation

How can a teacher motivate crucial attitudes and habits related to the comprehending process? To motivate children, you work with, not against, their internal needs. (Such a teaching aim relates to goal 3 in the listening framework of Box 3.2, "Develop a lasting positive attitude toward listening.") The following section discusses and illustrates four of these needs: (1) self-competency, (2) modeling, (3) personal acceptance, and (4) peer status. If a child does not feel curiosity, a need to learn, a need to belong by learning, there is relatively little a teacher can do.

Four Needs of Children and How They Relate to Teaching Listening   You can refer to these four needs as internal "allies." Teachers can use them in almost any teaching/learning situation; you will find them referred to again in Chapter 8 on composition. Figure 3.6 displays them.

1. Self-competence: Children need to feel competent, from the "me-do-it" of the 3-year-old trying to tune in the radio, to the successful classroom debating of the middle school student. Children want and need to show self-competence and respect themselves for it. An inner tension appears to motivate this need for self-respect. (Perhaps it is the most "mature" of the allies, representing an important developmental goal.) Teachers can meet

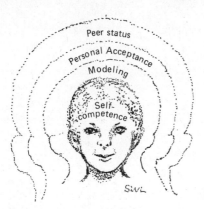

Figure 3.6 Four allies.

these needs by helping children gain assurance that they can indeed become highly skilled listeners.

By teaching them to use self-competence as a motivator, a teacher can help children construct concepts of thinking *before, during,* and *after* the listening situation starts. *Before:* Children can tune in to the context, predict what the speaker will say, gather background information about the speaker, and even find out how this speaker gets a feeling of importance. Such are the tools of the competent listener that each child can become.

During: Children can construct concepts of thinking while listening. They can make optimum use of leftover thinking space to visualize, to create relevant questions, to match up their own experiences, and to summarize. *After:* Finally, children can construct concepts of thinking after listening. At this time, they can do further relational thinking, apply the ideas gained, and evaluate them.

You can develop in your students the generalization that thinking before, during, and after listening can bring listening competence. There are several ways to achieve this goal: (1) Try to simply tell children, (2) model with them one-on-one (tutor), (3) discuss in small groups, or (4) use all three ways.

In essence, you can help children see that *they* have control. They create the real-life consequences when they competently facilitate a drama or a game by listening to context or directions. On the other hand, they can see that they may be responsible when they "mess up" because they failed to request clarity or to listen.

2. Modeling: Children need to find strong, competent adults with whom they can identify. They want to absorb their model's useful strengths and values into their own system and attitudes.

To use modeling as a motivator, teachers simply change the question "How can I get children to listen to me?" to "How can I strengthen the way I listen to children?" So much more is "caught" rather than "taught." Children suck up modeled behaviors like vacuum cleaners.

When you listen to children, their ideas begin to expand and bloom. When teachers and children listen to each other, an alternating current emerges that recharges both. After listening to yourself as an interactive, facilitative, responsible listener, keep a systematic chart showing to whom you have listened and who still needs a turn for this bit of quality time each week. Box 3.3 shows a sample form.

Be able to show the demanding, challenging listening material you as a model have selected from public television and community lecture offerings. Show how you prepare yourself for listening and how well you use your leftover thinking space. Model for your

Names	Mon.	Tues.	Wed.	Thurs.	Fri.
BOX 3.3 Children I *Really* Listened to This Week					
Liz	1				
Ted		1			
Ronny	1			1	
Clare					2

students the many strategies for remembering listened-to material. Model your techniques for creative response to and practical use of listening material. You will find that your enthusiasm is contagious.

In modeling, the teacher plays an active role using *appropriate context.* Again, the teacher does not clarify if nothing needs clarifying and does not summarize if there is nothing to summarize. In essence, teachers as models examine their own teaching habits and know how to give and get undivided attention and constructive feedback. (Nothing encourages inattention more than the habit of persistently repeating information.)

3. Personal acceptance: Children want to be respected, loved, forgiven, and accepted as they are at the moment. Most of us have a crucial need for at least one person in our lives to give us such unconditional, positive regard. People who stand out in our experience are the ones we have been bound to by affection and acceptance. It is usually through those who accept and love us that we have learned anything about life at all. Our learnings pass through a filter of our attachments. It is the loving, accepting teacher who makes a constructive impact on the listening habits and attitudes of children. Such acceptance is like the experience of a sports team playing on their *home court.* The fans cheer them wildly when they first walk out, and they tend to win. Even young children can grasp this idea and applaud each other.

One way you can demonstrate personal acceptance is to set up a *Creative Calendar* for a month in which, for example, one day is "Thank You for Listening Day." Children and teacher particularly note and praise this courtesy among themselves and exchange pictured awards. Another might be "Happy, Happy Sounds Day," when favorite poetry, music, bird calls, or literary passages are shared. Without restorative joy, we accomplish far less in school than we might. At the end of this book there is a bibliography of delightful children's books with listening themes that can be used in this activity. We can starve for beauty and joy just as we starve for food. Have students applaud each other often. We starve for applause, too.

The calendar might go on to include other areas such as "Smile Day," with warm, personal smiles seeking out those who need it most. Another day might be "Touch Day"; for each child unused to or displeased by being touched, there are twice as many who could really use a "laying on of hands." Invite the class to try communicating with a partner for a few minutes just by touching hands (e.g., "Hello"; "It's really OK"; "Good-bye."). Then have them speak with each other and compare. Touch is a form of personal acceptance that can work wonders and enhance listening. Other days related to personal acceptance might be "Listen to Problem Solve Day," a "Praise Day," and a "Forgiveness Day."

Too often our ears are closed because of bad habits of nonacceptance, prejudices about how the speaker looks, or the sound of the voice. A skilled listener takes a deep breath, relaxes, and overcomes such blocks to communication, listening effectively to the message. To accept personally is to open the door to listening.

4. Peer status: Children need to be liked by at least some of their classmates. The class members, with the teacher's guidance, can develop a positive and cooperative group spirit by cultivating the idea that "In *this* class, *this* is the way *we* listen!" Children can value the chance to walk in each other's shoes by anticipating each other's responses, questions, resistances, needs, and interests. Peers define an audience, and to have an audience is motivational.

Teachers can use this ally in many ways. Through class discussion (small and large groups), build a peer climate reflecting preparation, the seeking of accuracy, two-way responsibility, demand for meaning, fairness, patience, empathy, and respect. You model all of these. Through awareness-raising discussion encourage children to develop standards cooperatively for listening to discussion, for sharing written compositions, reports, joke sessions with analysis of humor, questioning strategies, analysis of propaganda. (Chapter 6 develops discussion strategies; Chapter 10 and the activity book, analysis of propaganda.)

Another peer-oriented activity is the game of *hitchhiking* on each other's ideas for a progressive, cooperatively built story. The children in the opening scene used this activity when they improvised a scene.

Another peer-oriented game is that of reflecting back each other's messages (*mirroring*). In this activity children make sure that the meaning is just as the speaker intended. An example occurs when children listen to a peer's story or argument ("I hear you say he entered through a tiny hole in the screen door!?").

Sociocultural aspects may have an impact on this peer status ally. Since listening is motivated in a sociological context, the need and motivation of peer status change with different groups. For instance, consider the variation in task of getting privileged peers to listen to each other when they have had a history of competing unmercifully. Or think about the task of working with minorities where there is a need for knowledge of and respect for a different culture. The task may involve a culture that might not normally choose to listen to women or that might scoff at children's ideas. The task of helping a single child from outside the majority culture win peer respect can be yet quite a different example. (Further details can be found in Chapter 14.)

These four allies, then, help the teacher motivate children's effective listening. But what should be done if none of them seems to be working? It is important that teachers know how to keep up even a faint glimmer of *hope* in children, hope for self-competence, for a suitable model, for acceptance, for peer status. Often if the other language arts processes and skills are in a woeful state, the child can make a successful start with effective and productive listening. Effective listening can fan flickers of hope into flames. Sets of listening tapes have given many a child some competence in the content areas of science, math, social studies, and literature. A productive part about these need-meeting "allies" is that they are equally motivating for the rest of the language arts (speaking, reading, and written composition). In fact, you can use these allies almost anywhere.

This kind of internal motivation meets natural growth needs regarding developmental tasks. All of these needs, when met, contribute to a child's sense of *belonging.* Without this sense, children give teachers and themselves much trouble. When students feel they belong, the chances are they will improve in listening. Employ these natural motivators and you can avoid using extrinsic bribes such as stars, tokens, gimmicks, nagging, commands, personal attacks, assertive discipline, and threats. These "allies" are natural reinforcers that increase the likelihood that related positive listening activity will occur again.

Direct Instruction

Several valuable teaching concepts related to direct instruction include the following: direct *telling* (generally used much too often), *tutorial* (one-on-one), and *probing group discussion*, sometimes called Socratic dialoguing. These concepts are useful in teaching any of the language arts.

Telling   It is understandable that teachers use direct telling as a way of teaching because it allows a teacher to reach a whole group at one time ("There is a difference between 'hearing' and 'listening'; this is what it is . . ."). It is rarely a successful method, however, for helping children attain lasting, meaningful concepts and generalizations.

Direct telling may be appropriate in conveying certain social warnings, conventions, or rituals; for example, "If you look at the speaker when you listen, you can get nonverbal clues that will help you get a fuller message." Even here, however, a discovery method could enhance long-term learning. Have the children experiment with not looking and with looking, and draw their own conclusions. While a discovery method takes longer, children are more likely to fit observations into their existing schemes about communication, with lasting results in learning.

Tutorial   One-on-one or tutorial methods are certainly useful in listening instruction. This method can work during individual conferences with children as you interview and diagnose for the child's listening attitudes, habits, and concepts. Every child can be a tutor or teacher by teaming up with a peer. ("Tim, you're going to need to really concentrate when you listen to this puzzler. . . .") Such "listening friends" take turns listening to each other and giving feedback as to what they heard or gained.

Probing Group Discussion   Probing group discussion includes dialoguing in the manner of the Greek teacher, Socrates. Through guided discussion the teacher (or guide) leads discoveries through probing of ideas. The guide might say, "Why do people think listening is important, or maybe they don't? Why?" Here we have interchange that prompts the leader's or teacher's next question, such as, "What's your opinion? . . . And you? . . . Do you agree? . . . Why? . . ."

Discussion groups, if well run, give the teacher an opportunity to have students participate in a democratic way to the best of their abilities. A teacher, or eventually a student leader, can ask students for their ideas, encourage exchange, and help students elaborate their thoughts. (More detail is found in Chapter 6 on discussion.)

In sum, you have choices of different teaching methods when you are directly engaged in instruction. In the long run simply telling and using admonitions are probably least effective. A teacher using any one of the direct teaching methods just presented may use teaching strategies involving readiness, pacing, reinforcement, and transfer. The topics of motivation and different modes of instruction lead into a six-step teaching procedure useful for organizing these principles of learning.

A Strategy for Teaching Listening

Consider a six-step procedure for teaching listening adapted from one school district (Dallas Independent). Summarizing much of the *how* of teaching, this strategy, given in Box 3.4, contains four key learning constructs. This school district tries to get teachers to use all of these steps in each lesson taught, and sometimes teachers can move appropriately through

---

BOX 3.4 A Six-Step Teaching Procedure

1. Find out *readiness* (what the pupils know about the intended learning).

2. Tell them the *objective*. (Let them in on what it is they are going to learn. In discovery-type learning, however, this step may come later, as the children themselves participate in finding the objective.)

3. *Demonstrate*. (Teach: tell, coach, or use a probing discussion. Avoid just telling too much; pace.)

4. Give appropriate guided *practice* (and confirmations).

5. Help them *apply* widely (transfer, integrate).

6. *Assess* at each step along the way; follow up (both teacher and children involved).

---

them all very quickly. Other times the six steps are best done in depth and spread out over an entire unit with much involvement of students as "teachers" themselves.

With such a procedure, teachers are not just assigning; they are teaching. Remember, however, that in a responsive environment much about listening is learned and self-constructed in a natural, autonomous, even playful and joyous way. Often the teacher sets up productive situations, simply models, and slips in a word about it to a needful student. Sometimes a "teachable moment" just appears and we need to be flexible and sensitive enough to take advantage of it. Teaching action is not just a threat but a message that helps bring the child's listening strengths to a level of awareness, a confirmation of individual success. In an area so important yet so neglected in our schools and homes, however, some direct teaching, as outlined in the six steps above, is also needed.

The basic concepts in these steps were used by the teacher in the opening scene. They include the following:

Principles

1. *Readiness*—preparing the students for new learning.
2. *Pacing*—directing the learning process appropriately through *focusing*, encouragement of wide participation *(extending)*, and *lifting* carefully to exploration of a progression of ideas.
3. *Reinforcement*—confirmations that give a sense of direction, and opportunities for appropriate practice and satisfaction ("Use it so you don't lose it").
4. *Transfer*—application of learning to other areas (including expectation, sufficient understanding, new instances, similarity finding, and assessment).

In practice, readiness, pacing, reinforcement, and transfer are interactive. The teacher moves from one to another of these focuses while leading a discussion or during many other kinds of lessons or units such as the one on listening found in Chapter 15 of the activity book.

Pacing is sometimes simply knowing when and how long to pause. Too often we set out at top speed and never give listeners a chance to respond. The three-blink strategy for waiting time illustrates a remedy. Pauses give time for children's thinking processes to operate and make the teacher's question time less than the student's answer time. To help

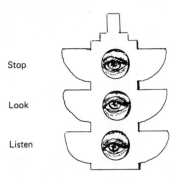

Figure 3.7   The three-blink strategy.

you to pause, simply blink your eyes three times before continuing. Slowing down for just three seconds has shown amazing results in tested classrooms. Chances are that you are processing much faster than your students because you come into the classroom with so much more background and experience. The three-blink strategy gives your children a chance to respond. Some children can profit from using it, too. (See Figure 3.7.)

The principle of *transfer* is related to the term *integration.* Integration is part of the economical and meaningful *how* of teaching. Once you have pulled up the knot in the language arts net called listening and brought it to a level of awareness, you need to lay it back down in context. You need to let listening's refurbished state add strength to the other parts of the language arts net—speaking, reading, and writing. You need to integrate this strengthened listening process with the other language processes. Plan and capitalize on activity that integrates and transfers the gains of successful listening know-how. The next section clarifies integration of listening.

Integration of Listening into the Curriculum

Ways of integrating range from narrow to broad. Three ways are listed below:

1. *Meaningful integration of subskills within each language mode.* For example, children holistically listen, speak, write, or read rather than merely practice fragments in some skill exercise (e.g., just listening for details).
2. *Various language arts integrated with each other.* For example, interactive listening and speaking in discussion are combined with writing; the class newsletter publishing activity in Chapter 8 of the activity book integrates all language arts.
3. *Various language arts integrated with other subjects in the elementary curriculum.* This third way is exemplified by the integration of listening and speaking. A teacher might ask the students how they have learned to clarify meaning when they are listening. After they respond, the teacher might say, "Now when you're *speaking* let's see if we can also check with your listeners to see if they have questions and are getting your meaning as we listen to our social studies reports." (You will find more about this kind of integration in Chapter 4.) Besides speaking, another important area for integrating with listening is reading.

Listening and Reading   When your students have learned something about the process of listening comprehension, immediately apply their learning to the context of reading comprehension. A teacher might say, "Could you use what you learned about spotting purpose and organization while listening when you're reading? How?" or, "We practiced forming pictures in our minds when listening; how could you use that when you're reading a new book?"

A word of caution: An attempt to integrate by turning a reading test into a listening test is not an accurate reflection of typical listening material and context. Although there is overlap in vocabularies, listening material is not necessarily the same as reading material (the written word). The spoken language is much more likely to be redundant, as we stutter, stammer, and try to find words to express our meanings. Spoken language tends to be incomplete, because the referents are in our heads and we are often too egocentric to remember that others cannot know exactly what we know. The language we listen to is often disorganized, as senders strive to shape spoken thoughts and sometimes do not know what they know until they have voiced it.

But as the teacher places listening material and reading material dealing with the same topic side by side in two different versions in the listening center, children grasp the interrelatedness of the comprehension process. They can also see that orally presented materials can be well organized and memorable. Such an integration can be fruitful. Try it.

Listening and Written Composition   Teachers can integrate written composition with enhanced listening. This productive integration comes about not just through a mutually interactive vocabulary and through listening to one's own drafts of compositions and those of others. The profit also comes from increased sensory awareness when writing, that is, employing the use of concrete auditory detail. Examples: "the harps of dry grasses"; "the crackle and scrape of crisp fallen leaves blowing across the concrete patio"; "the inquisitive wheeze of an opening drawer."

Listening and writing interconnected across the content areas integrate social studies, science, math, health, and other areas. (See activities in Chapter 7 of this text and in its companion activity book on listening to and giving reports, in Chapter 5 on drama, and in Chapter 13 on media.)

Listening Integrated into Problem Solving   As mentioned in Chapters 1 and 2, one of the most integrative forces in the curriculum is creative problem solving. When you focus on an appropriate problem of genuine interest to your children, an integration of many areas is highly likely to occur. Suppose the classroom problem or challenge is to have a Recipe and Food Fair to raise money for additions to the classroom library. Just think of the integrations this problem or challenge might bring! Children ask elders or neighbors for recipes that will be listened to, read, written, spoken about, and related to the math of measurement or the science of cooking.

Listening to get useful information is crucial to all steps in problem solving; and problem solving can pull in a wide array of language processes and content areas. (Again, the activity book gives additional illustrations of integrating listening, other curriculum areas, and problem solving.)

Assessment

A final part of the *how* of teaching concerns assessment, generally treated in Chapter 15 of this text. Let's examine some particulars of classroom assessment of listening. First consider diagnosis. An important part of dealing with readiness, diagnosis may take many

BOX 3.5 Diagnostic Checklist of Listening Skills

Goal	While listening each child can—	Date__(Enter I, P, or C) [List pairs of initials →]								
1.	1.1. Focus on listening task									
	1.2. Discriminate aural/visual relations									
	1.3. Assign meanings to message received 1.3.1. Grasp prerequisite vocabulary									
	1.4. Use self-monitoring techniques 1.4.1. Differentiate "hearing" and listening									
	1.4.3. Know how to clarify meaning									
	1.4.5. Evaluate listener patterns									
	1.4.8. Critique own note taking									
2.	2.1. Comprehend literal content re purposes 2.1.8. Construct a written outline									
	2.2. Empathize 2.2.2. Recognize how listener behavior affects a speaker									
	2.3. Synthesize creatively and evaluate critically re validity/credibility									
	2.4. Solve problems 2.4.8. List sources of assistance/resistance to problem solution									
	2.5. Take pleasure in the recreative/aesthetic aspects of material									
3.	3.1. Will to be active, open, responsible, curious, interested, and valuing 3.1.1. Construct benefit list									
	3.1.2. Prepare anticipatory questions									
	3.1.4. Control bias to extract meaning									
	3.1.6. Share in the instructional enterprise (why, who, where, what, and how)									

forms. (Listening evaluation as represented by standardized, norm-referenced tests is reviewed by the author in an issue of *Curriculum Review* [Lundsteen, 1984].)

Diagnosis   Diagnosis of listening is a strategy a teacher might use, having made certain that the learner is motivated and "warmed up." A prerequisite question, of course, is whether or not each child had passed a hearing test. After you have studied the *who* in your classroom, you are likely to have ideas as to appropriate motivation and to have diagnosed listening skill levels in your children. Diagnosis helps you provide worthwhile experiences for development of listening process and needed subskills. Examine the lists of skills that could be turned into a diagnostic questionnaire in Box 3.5 on page 85.

This diagnostic tool (Box 3.5) is related to the earlier framework of goals (Box 3.2). A teacher might pick and choose some of these skills to be objectives for a unit or thematic set of activities for the school year, thinking, "Is there something here in this list I've neglected?"

Evaluatively speaking, the skills in Box 3.5 might be more formally used to record children's progress, for example, initial start (I), progress (P), competence (C). A teacher might list children's initials across the top of a sheet of paper, number and indicate selected skills down the left side, then enter I, P, or C in the cell.

The checklist in Box 3.5 shows what one teacher might have pulled from a longer skills list in order to determine the readiness of a particular class. Such a list is found in Chapter 15 of the activity book. This teacher's checklist can serve you as an advance organizer for that longer, age-designated list. Most of these skills are not limited to the language art called listening, but play an important part in speaking, reading, writing, and observing and thinking in general. Teachers need to bring to a level of awareness the peculiar personal context, time pressure, tonal influence, and noise pollution that are part of listening. Finally, it is important to recognize that if children cannot listen using a skill, it is even less likely that they can read using it. Consequently, for readiness and diagnosis, start with listening.

Related items in the activity book involve children as assessors; in Chapter 15 on assessment are the following: a checklist of listening roadblocks, a self-report list keyed to unit objectives, and a "Road to Good Listening." This "road" is a device for tracking successes and recording listening concepts. At the end of this chapter is a questionnaire for teacher self-diagnosis. The reader can adapt it for student use.

Detailed ideas for assessment of integrated listening/speaking are found toward the end of the following chapter. Chapter 4 discusses the second largest "fish" in the language net—speaking.

SUMMARY

> The greatest compliment paid me was when one asked me what I thought and attended to my answer.
>
> *Henry David Thoreau*

This chapter has been designed to clarify some basic principles in teaching listening gleaned from theory, research, and experience. One of the important language arts goals for children is *use* of the language of others, including the ability to listen. Children cannot learn without listening, and teachers cannot teach without it.

Teachers are not ready for the (too often superficial) *hows* of teaching until they have defined *listening;* developed a rationale as to why it is important; studied the children served; prepared effective physical and emotional climates; and surveyed frameworks of goals, objectives, and related materials. When you have answered questions about the *why, who, where,* and *what,* then you are far better prepared to move into the *how* of teaching listening. Teaching is not just the use of one isolated activity, even if it is keyed to an objective mandated by the state. There is no "quick fix."

As for the *who,* it is wise to remember that both hearing (a prerequisite for listening) and comprehension vary among individuals even at birth. Both environment and native endowment affect children. The younger the children, the more interested they are in sharing their own free thoughts—in listening to themselves, really. This is not to say that listening to oneself is unimportant. But as children grow older, we would like to help them listen expertly both to themselves and to others.

Three goals provide a framework for teaching listening: (1) process, (2) purpose (including problem solving), and (3) attitude. Helping children understand the parts and sum of a communicative listening *process* is important. Since listening is an effective tool in going after meaning, it is also an important building block in one of the key *purposes,* creative problem solving. But without a constructive *attitude,* say, two-way responsibility for listening, it does not matter much what else you and your children know or do.

Remember to choose your goals, objectives, and enabling materials carefully and provide the best in language, music, and literature for listening material. If children are made to listen to mindless trivia that provide few opportunities for setting their own purposes, optimal development is unlikely.

To *motivate* children to learn about listening, teachers can align themselves with four needs that are within each child: self-competency, modeling, personal acceptance, and peer status. These "allies" are, of course, useful in all language arts teaching—in almost all teaching. They help children achieve a sense of belonging in the classroom and prepare them to learn about listening to themselves and others.

Three forms of direct instruction are: (1) telling (used too much and too often in the form of admonitions); (2) tutorial (one-on-one coaching); and (3) probing group discussion, in tune with child autonomy, creativity, and long-lasting learning.

A six-step teaching strategy includes four key constructs: (1) readiness (including diagnosis), (2) pacing (including concept attainment steps for teaching), (3) reinforcement, and 4) transfer of learning about listening. Pacing (focusing, extending, and lifting thought) includes sufficient child-response time, which the teacher can provide by using a "three-blink" strategy. Remember that in tune with the idea of transfer, a teacher seeks to transfer responsibility for the listening/teaching/learning enterprise to the children as rapidly as possible. The teacher then only comes back as an authority figure in rather extreme cases. Such teaching methods can help make children aware of process goals for their own productive listening strategies (metacognitive self-monitoring). Children become students of their own processes. The teacher helps them gain a kind of internal split mental focus that helps successful listeners concentrate on and monitor their own comprehension.

One of the most important aspects of teaching listening is to integrate it with problem-solving processes, all the other language arts, and school content areas. One of the best ways to begin to plan for integration is to create a listening unit.

Teacher assessment of listening includes diagnosis with use of a checklist. Children can assess themselves using suggested items in the activity book. At the end of this chapter is a self-diagnosis questionnaire for prospective teachers that is adaptable for older-student use.

Finally, the third attitudinal goal from the suggested framework, the "significant role of listening in human experience," is based on the belief that an effective listener will be more fulfilled in school and in life than will an ineffective one. Your attentive empathy as you listen to another can cause that person to do the same to someone else and so on, possibly around the world and into the future—the ripple effect of a big fish surfacing in a pond.

APPENDIX 3A A Questionnaire on Listening for Prospective Teachers

PERSONAL

1. To what do I like to listen?
2. Here is a recent occasion when I was a good listener. (Why?)
3. Here is a recent occasion when I was not an effective listener. (Why?)
4. Here is a recent occasion when someone listened gratifyingly to me; when someone did not. (Why?)
5. Have I had instruction in listening in the past? (What?)

DEFINITION

1. Can I give some parts in a listening comprehension process? (What?)
2. Can I define listening? (How?)

WHY (RATIONALE)

1. Why is listening important in my life?
2. Why is it important in the life of children?

WHO (CLIENTELE)

1. Do children of the age level I am planning to teach or am teaching show any of the following: ☐ hearing deficits, ☐ well-developed memory, ☐ retrieval strategies, ☐ attention strategies, ☐ ability to think about thinking (metacognition), ☐ emotional control, ☐ concrete-operational or even formal-operational thinking levels (Piaget), ☐ strong or weak peer orientation, ☐ cultural or linguistic differences impacting on listening, ☐ mental ability extremes?
2. With respect to individual learners, do I have the ability to: ☐ diagnose, ☐ select, ☐ and assess an appropriate sequence of competencies, skills, and effectively completed tasks?

WHERE (SOCIAL, EMOTIONAL, AND PHYSICAL CLIMATES)

1. Do I realize the importance of guiding children to take part in responsibility for an advantageous room environment? Do we attend to both physical and emotional aspects? Physical: ☐ temperature, ☐ ventilation, ☐ noise level, ☐ seating arrangements. Emotional: ☐ mutual respect, ☐ warmth, ☐ openness.
2. Is the "environment" of my voice: ☐ relaxed; ☐ unhurried; ☐ non-

threatening; ☐ well projected; ☐ supported with appropriate and varied volume, pitch, mood, melody, and body language?

3. Do I monitor my "talk time," avoiding the climate of a dictatorial monopolizer?
4. Have I witnessed myself and my communicative climate recently on videotape or audiotape?
5. Do I know how to show a child who speaks to me my undivided, empathetic attention? (That is, do I stop whatever I'm doing, lean forward, and look directly into the child's eyes, being easy to talk to?)

WHAT (GOALS AND MATERIALS)

1. Do I know what goals, skills, curriculum, and assessment my State Department of Education recommends for the levels I plan to teach?
2. Can I select and develop listening materials at appropriate levels of difficulty and for appropriate purposes?
3. Do I know what is entailed in determining a speaker's purpose?
4. Do I understand what is entailed in a listening comprehension process?
5. Do I understand and help children know the role of listening in problem solving?
6. Do I know resources for beautiful, memorable listening materials?
7. Do I have some ideas for setting up a listening center?
8. Do I know some unproductive and some productive listener patterns and metacognitive strategies to help children cope with distortions?
9. Have I started collecting ideas for a listening unit? (See the accompanying activity book, Chapters 3 and 15.)

HOW (TEACHING STEPS AND STRATEGIES)

Motivation

1. Do I know how to motivate children's listening, and their learning about listening, in constructive and developmentally appropriate ways?
2. Do I know who my "allies" within each child are, and how to employ them?

Readiness

1. Do I know how to watch children for verbal and nonverbal hints as to the boundaries of each learner's competence, skill, and effective performance?
2. Do I know how to use challenging vocabulary and sentence structure to help children reach ahead of their boundaries?
3. Do I know how to focus for listening purposes by providing advance organizers, "maps," and study guides that provide students with a sense of direction?

Pacing

1. Can I use pacing and inductive strategies to help children attain listening concepts?
2. Can I avoid needless repetition of my instructions (which encourages careless listening), and avoid presentation of too much listening material at one time?
3. Can I use provocative words concisely and then wait for student responses, respecting silences? (Do I know how to use the three-blink strategy?)
4. Can I use open-ended questioning techniques that extend comprehension from lower level facts and conditions to higher cognitive levels, e.g., to progressive parts in a problem-solving process?

Reinforcement

1. Can I help children achieve a sense of direction, using confirmations that strengthen desired behaviors?

Transfer and Integration

1. Do my children and I know how to say what we think we heard a person say, for purposes of clarification?
2. Can I encourage children to expect meaning from vocabulary and discourse heard, in preparation for further use (listening as a tool for learning)?
3. Can I help children transfer and integrate listening by: ☐ developing an expectancy for transfer; ☐ using meaningful, reinforced learning; ☐ discriminating similar aspects in two listening contexts; ☐ and providing new occasions for transfer?

Your Own Reinforcement, Transfer, and Integration

1. If I want to learn more, do I know three places I could look?
2. Have I started my "Listening Journal?"
3. Do I have some ideas collected for involving parents?
4. Other—my own ideas.

CHAPTER 4

Talking/Speaking

"Language learners need contexts with something to say, a deep desire to say it, and someone to whom they genuinely want to say it. The awesome importance of oral language as a base for success with literacy is crystal clear."

Walter Loban

INTRODUCTION

If listening is the biggest fish to be caught in the language arts net, because studies show we spend the most time doing it, the second largest "fish" in the language arts net is talking/speaking—the subject of this chapter. Goals encompass well-motivated, self-expressive uses of an interactive speaking process. This process works for a variety of aims and forms. Forms presented in depth are: show and tell and conversation (in ways you have probably never thought of them before); children's story telling; and anecdote telling. (Chapter 5 goes on to develop the oral form of drama, and Chapter 6 the form called discussion. Chapter 7 builds a bridge from this strong oral foundation over into print forms with emphasis on expository use.)

From the beginning of this chapter, sections solidly build toward the *how* of teaching oral language, culminating with a reemphasizing of the importance of integration across all the language arts and the total curriculum. Talking and listening are considered as interactive aspects of discourse, far more complex than isolated aspects such as sound system, oral vocabulary, grammar, and sentence sending and receiving. We see such integrations in our opening scene. Last in the chapter come some new and needed ways of assessing talking/speaking.

Teachers' Roles

Teachers have two overall roles to play in developing children's talking and speaking that are highly important, and different. Guided growth includes (1) learning *to* talk and (2) learning *through* talk. That is, part of teaching is to see to it that talk promotes growth in and of itself *and* is also a tool for learning.

When oral language is a tool for learning, teachers ask these questions: (1) Are my children stressing purposeful talking as a means of coming to an understanding? (2) Are demands being made on my children's oral language by the nature of a **problem** (or questions), and the process of arriving at solutions? (The opening scene illustrates.) (3) Are my children grasping more and more ambitious ways of using language? It is not enough for students to imitate the patterns of a teacher's language as though these forms were models to be copied, as in some second language drills. Students need to try out language in reciprocal exchanges, in classroom talk, and in dialogue with their teachers and peers. Children may be grappling with a problem that has come up naturally. In the process of defining the problem and attempting solutions, they may well need to experiment with more advanced forms of language. For instance, students might be developing lines of arguments as to why they are not speaking in a racist way; or someone else is, and they challenge overgeneralizations (as in our opening scene). The teacher's overall role, then, is to provide chances for such meaningful talk to happen (Dillon & Pinnell, 1986).

Speaker, Use, and Context

An overview of a teacher's goals and teaching method needs to consider the following three sets of factors bearing on oral communication:

1. *Speakers/talkers:* the students, with their personal experiences, language abilities, cognitive abilities, and attitudes. This factor considers the *who*, with language development outward from the child's own experience.
2. *Uses:* the kinds and uses of talk (the *what*). Examples of uses are naming, proposing, describing, classifying, summarizing, explaining, inquiring, exploring, narrating, presenting and discussing a point of view, persuading, and especially problem solving. Through such purposeful use your students can construct meaning that is real, not contrived.
3. *Context:* situations that promote genuine, meaningful exchange (part of the *where*). Examples are: setting, "climate," subject, audience—all related to purpose. It is essential to avoid blatantly artificial or contrived contexts, such as each child making a little ritualistic speech about "my favorite vacation," with nobody caring or listening. Again, stress throughout is on activities that evolve from *students'* experiences and interests—with process as important as end product, and affective learning as important as cognitive.

The illustrative classroom scene that follows sets the tone, introduces some important concepts and strategies developed further in this chapter, and previews some of the *hows* of encouraging children's development of talking and speaking. It is as talkers, questioners, arguers, gossips, and chatterboxes that children do much of their most important learning.

OPENING SCENE: Show and Tell

The teacher, Robin Sidney, noticing how first-grade students cared about their clothes, asked the class toward the end of the school year to bring or wear their favorite outfits and tell what they liked about them.

The teacher prepared the children the day before. "Bring one piece of clothing. Bring what is special to you. What could we ask the 'bringer'?"

NICK: Tell how you got it.
MEI LEE: Why you like it.

The teacher summarized a written chart of the children's questions for them, adding "We'll listen to each other. Then we can ask more questions. We'll know more." The next day the teacher gathered five of the children on the rug and motioned to Natasha to start, with her green dress.

MEI LEE: Why do you like your green dress, Natasha?

NATASHA: Because I got to wear it last Christmas . . . at godmother's house. She took a lot of pictures of me. And here's a photo of me wearing it . . . and holding the doll she gave me. And she wrote a book about the doll. Just for me. Here's the book. [Children look.]

TEACHER: Any other questions?

MEI LEE: Was the dress bought new for you? Or did you get it handed down?

NATASHA: It was new for *me*. My momma found it at a garage sale. And I think I look like Alice in Wonderland in it.

JERAMY: Who's Alice in Wonderland? . . . I think I saw something on TV . . .

MEI LEE: It's a book. I'll bring it . . .

JERAMY: I brought my cowboy boots. My uncle from Wyoming. . . . He just gave them to me. They're my favorite thing in clothes. And I'm never going to give them away.

NATASHA: I have a question. [Looks at teacher.]

TEACHER: Go ahead.

NATASHA: I think your feet will grow too big for them. Will you keep them . . . when you can't wear them?

JERAMY: Yes. Always.

EDWARD: Sneakers go with boots—can I be next?

JERAMY: Why do sneakers go with boots?

EDWARD: They're both for feet.

FREDRIKA: Pardon me, but pinafores go with Natasha's dress. So I'm next. OK? I won't take long.

EDWARD: OK.

FREDRIKA: I brought my pinafore. It has a rising sun, mountains, and sea. They're appli—appli—appli . . .

TEACHER: Appliqued?

FREDRIKA: Yes, appliqued on it. My grandmother brought it to me . . . last summer . . . from Denmark. I think it's the beautifulest thing I have.

EDWARD: How do you know the sun on it is rising? It might be setting. [Fredrika laughs.]

JERAMY: What's *appliqued* mean?

FREDRIKA: You take some material. You make a shape. And you fold it under all the way around. And stitch on top of the other material. See . . . appli . . . appliqued. [Triumphantly.]

MEI LEE: Where's Denmark? In Texas?

FREDRIKA: **No,** it's far, far away . . . I don't know.

TEACHER: Anyone have any idea, any idea how we could find out?

EDWARD: Ask her grandmother.

NATASHA: Look at a globe of the world. [Looks at Mei Lee.] *I'll* bring one.

EDWARD: Please, now my sneakers, please! They're real Adidas, like my dad's. Look at those soles. When you put weight on it they spread out and *grip*.

FREDRIKA: What are they good for?

EDWARD: For running, for playing ball, . . . for climbing trees—for everything!

FREDRIKA: Could they grip slippery stones . . . when you . . . cross a little stream?

EDWARD: Everything!

NATASHA: Could you . . . eat ice cream out of them?

EDWARD: Only chocolate. [They both laugh with great glee.]

MEI LEE: I brought these silky pajamas with a dragon embru . . . embroi . . .

TEACHER: Embroidered?

MEI LEE: Embroider—dered on the back. They're from Chinatown. My aunt . . . brought them to me. [Silence while the children finger the embroidery.]

FREDRIKA: It's not the same as appliqued . . . embro . . .

MEI LEE: Embroidery. You use lots of needles and threads.

TEACHER: Do you feel like any story book character when you wear these?

MEI LEE: I once saw a dragaon lady spy on TV. I think about that.

JERAMY: I'm surprised.

MEI LEE: How?

JERAMY: You should know. My father says Chinese . . . just aren't . . . just aren't spies and dragon ladies.

NATASHA: Maybe because . . . Maybe Mei Lee said it because she thought, we thought . . . Mei Lee you thought we'd think you would say it.

MEI LEE: No . . . maybe . . .

FREDRIKA: If Mei Lee wants to be a dragon lady spy, it's OK. It's OK to pretend.

MEI LEE: I like dragaons . . . dragons.

JERAMY: Can we pretend to be . . . anything we want to?

TEACHER: Here's a poem. It's called "Any Me I Want to Be," by Karla Kushkin. [Shares poem from book at hand. Children talk about it.] And here's a story book, *The House of Seven Fathers*, and the main character, a little Chinese girl, wears something like you have, Mei Lee, every day, not just for bedtime. [Children look at pictures.] I'll read it later.

TEACHER: What have we learned so far from talking about our favorite clothes? [Talking to learn.]

NATASHA: Everybody likes . . . likes . . . something different.

JERAMY: I learned a new word—*embroidery*.

FREDRIKA: Favorite clothes are a part of me . . . a beautiful part.

MEI LEE: These clothes remind us . . .

TEACHER: Remind us? [She waits patiently.]

MEI LEE: . . . of happy times.

TEACHER: I'm writing down the things you say you've learned. I'll make a copy for you. Then you can add thoughts of your very own.

Analysis of the Scene

Consider the factors of context, use or kinds of speaking, the speakers, and the teacher's roles.

Context   The teacher had prepared the children, limiting the number because usually with a group larger than five, someone does not participate in the interaction. A first concern was creating a safe emotional climate necessary for fluency. The setting was cozy, on the rug, and informal. The teacher and the children were prepared but also flexible and open. To encourage interaction, the children were seated in a tight little circle, with the teacher close by, but just outside the circle and moving behind whichever child was sharing an item.

Uses   We saw many kinds and uses of talk. We saw the children using language to grapple with and reorder their experience with the clothing in a new way. We saw reciprocal exchanges among the children, dialogue with the teacher, and peers, the negotiation of turns. Children drew upon the familiar to make generalizations (e.g., "Everybody likes something different"). We saw emphasis on purposeful talking as a means of coming to understandings (appliques versus embroidery, clothing preferences as a part of individual differences). We saw naming, describing, classifying (boots and sneakers are "both for feet"). We saw presentation and discussion of points of view regarding stereotypes (though the children in referring to the Chinese did not use this term).

The Young Talkers   In regard to the young speakers, we saw that this oral work grew out of child interests. We found the hesitancies, pauses, emphases, false starts, redundancies typical of almost all speech. Listeners usually edit (or ignore) many such freckles and moles on the face of spoken language. Pauses, false starts, and repetitions often give clues to planning processes, patterns of thought, and structuring in children's speech. The display of the children's language just given does not include all such features. Neither does it include the complex characteristics of a detailed transcription, in order to keep their messages fast moving and easy to interpret.

The scene revealed many other language aspects of the young talkers. We saw children adding to their vocabularies and pronunciations *(appliqued, embroidery, dragon)*. We saw them **solve a problem** and support each other ("If Mei Lee wants to be a dragon lady spy, it's OK"); bail each other out; and negotiate the direction of their talk ("I won't take long") and their understanding of reality ("I'm surprised!"). We saw some rather amazing insights ("Favorite clothes are a part of me . . . a beautiful part"). Talk gives children resources for thinking and learning, for self-prompting, and for intellectual adventure.

Teacher Roles   We saw a teacher playing a relatively nonobtrusive role ("Anyone have any idea . . . how we could we find out?"). We saw a teacher who had worked with the children to get *them* to ask questions. We saw a flexible teacher able to pick up on interests and *integrate,* relating to the other language arts of writing and reading of children's literature.

Your classroom needs to be a place where students enrich their oral resources. In this class children explored ideas partly intuited, partly grasped, but not yet fully articulated. It is through the enormous variety of dialogue with others that we gather together the linguistic resources to dialogue in our heads. *To restrict the nature and quality of that dialogue for children is to restrict their thinking.* Your simply providing opportunity for children to talk freely and informally about whatever interests them is of great value. But your curriculum needs to also develop children's ability to use oral language as a tool for learning.

After a section dealing with definitions, this chapter will continue the format in this book of answering questions about the *why, who, what, where,* and *how* of teaching and learning the language art of talking/speaking.

DEFINITIONS

If you are already clear on the terms *speaking, oral language, talking, conversing,* and *oracy,* you can skip this section. If not, continue here. *Speak,* a general term of wide application, differs in its sometimes weighty formality from *talk. Speak* refers to something formalized and noninteractive, such as oral reports before the entire class and speaking pattern drills, in fact all such artificial practice.

Talk in general suggests less formality and more interaction. We might visualize pairs and small groups caught up in constructing a project or solving a problem, wondering, challenging, discovering, or making meaning—with or without a teacher. Talk is purposeful. Children use it as a means of doing things and getting things done in collaboration with others. Accordingly, talk serves many varying functions with different skills and kinds of language organization. *Converse* may imply interchange of opinions. *Oral language* in school often relates back to the term *speak*.

Finally, *oracy* is a term coined by analogy with *literacy* to refer to the ability to communicate effectively in the spoken (as opposed to the written) mode. In their program, children need to experience varied contexts for meaningful tasks of talking, speaking, and conversing to reach oracy.

The diagram in Figure 4.1 shows a network of concepts for talking/speaking components in this chapter. Note that the *why, who, what, where,* and *how,* and their related subconcepts move outward as the network spreads. You can use this diagram as a springboard for creating your own network for this chapter and your teaching.

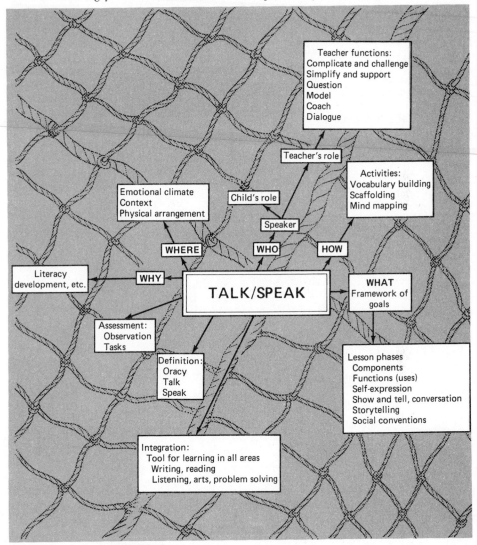

Figure 4.1 A network of speaking concepts.

WHY IS TALKING IN SCHOOL IMPORTANT?

"For human beings, not to speak is to die."

Pablo Neruda

"Give me some specific reasons why I need to plan for children's spoken language in my classroom. Don't they talk enough?"

All children talk. Why should teachers give a moment's concern? Educators could say that children's talk is there, so all teachers have to do is draw upon it, but they don't, not now. They are asking new questions with new answers. Curricula need to promote both talking and speaking in their own right and as tools for learning. Reasons for this need are many and include (1) the sheer importance of fostering competent talkers, (2) the impact of oral language development on thinking and problem solving, (3) the influence on literacy (reading and writing), and (4) the positive self-concept of the student as a person. We have addressed the first reason in the overview and the second in Chapters 1, 2, and 3. We will come back to the first reason at the end of this section. Examine the third reason now.

Oral Language Activities as a Basis for Literacy Development

Talking/speaking activities are important because oral language is the basis for literacy development. For most children, the basic vocabulary that they understand and speak is their only vocabulary; they have no other base on which to build comprehension skills in reading and skills of expression in writing.

Reading   Children who have little or no oracy may learn to read, but it is unlikely. Children talk their way into reading. When they have the sound patterns of their language ringing in their ears and shaped on their lips, reading instruction can begin. When they read, children are not likely to understand language that is much more mature, involved, or atypical than what they use in speaking (and listening).

Consider a reading instructional strategy that uses an oral cushion. The teacher builds a framework around the reading by talking about the selection before the child reads it (not just introducing a list of vocabulary words). Teacher and child converse about the book, looking at its pictures, predicting what might happen, and predicting language that the author might use—all before approaching the print. Such a strategy helps children take on a text because it is linked to their oral language.

Writing   Oral language is basic to writing; both draw on past experience of organizing speech in appropriate sequences, choosing words, and using language patterns. If a child's written composition is a disaster, the teacher would do well to consider offering help on oral language. Usually children will not write better than they talk. Whether the aim is effective reading or effective writing, the factor of spoken language generally sets the child's ceiling of performance. Once into the writing process, at many points children find it helpful to talk over their ideas with others, to have conferencing. Or at the beginning of writing a piece, children might talk to each other while formulating what they will write.

Oral language activities facilitate the development of literacy at the beginning stages and all along the way. Early on, children need a cushion of oral language around every attempt made to get messages from a text and in order to communicate a written text. Talking like a book is part of moving into literacy. Sorting out the differences between oral and written language, children try out different kinds of texts, borrowing freely, for example, from Bill Martin's *Brown Bear*, from Pat Hutchin's *Good Night Owl*, and other literature with memorable, patterned speech. If children do not have a wide oral reservoir, they may understand their tasks in school as producing a very narrow kind of language.

Consider the following example from Nelcine's second-grade writing:

Find three green leaves.
Find two tan tops.
Find four funny tops. . . .

And so on for 18 more lines of this sort of thing; Nelcine toiled dutifully during the entire writing period. It was not that Nelcine was unable to produce something more lifelike and creative. But because of her oral classroom experiences, she thought this was the way one was supposed to approach writing. Her teacher had been using a phonics oriented method of reading instruction, with emphasis on vowel and initial consonant patterns in simplified formats.

It is a mistake, however, to think that the main value of oral language activity is just to promote the literary, informational, and linguistic background for development and enhancement of reading and writing. Consider next social and personal development—the fourth reason.

Social and Personal Importance

Talk is our way of negotiating meaning with others, in social relationships and in the workplace. A certain level of literacy is essential, but the business of life is conducted through human oral interaction. Being spontaneous and fluent in the use of language gives a child a positive self-image. Being awkward causes social distress.

Eventually the orally inept child shrinks from contact with others or becomes an aggressive bully relying on physical prowess to enhance self-image. Since inadequate speech may be a factor in a warped social adjustment, the teacher's first job is to help the child who has this problem feel welcome, accepted, and at home. Then the teacher can set about getting the child involved with climbing the first rung of a ladder of language progress.

As an example, consider the case of one preschool child from a home where elders demanded that he speak two languages and where they appeared unsatisfied with his performance in either language. He would open his mouth to speak when in confrontation with other children, but nothing would come out. Then he would bite hard enough to draw blood, thus earning a formidable reputation.

Talk, then, is an important vehicle children use to get what they need for physical and mental survival. Talk is children's main tool for establishing and maintaining human contact, and for exploring and finding a place in their emotional environment.

The Learning of Language Itself

Now let's return to our first reason for importance. Children learn language through use. Talking and speaking activities are essential because through them children learn how to use oral language in varied contexts and with varied individuals. Children learn language itself through many uses: thinking aloud, interviewing, greeting, instructing, disagreeing, imagining the creation of new worlds, using metaphor, taking turns in conversation, signaling intentions, summarizing, exploring implications, timing responses appropriately, and assessing in context appropriate ways of talking. To develop their oral language prowess, children need to talk a lot.

Learning Through Talk

Given that talk is developing nicely, a most compelling reason for importance is the growing awareness that children *learn* academic school subjects through talk. Children can use oral language to organize experience in a new way. For example, explaining a new math process to another child aids the explainer's understanding. By talking, children can make explicit to themselves what they think they see in a science observation. Children will read with comprehension about a social studies concept such as interdependence when they have thoroughly discussed the facts, conditions, and relationships among concepts leading to this more global concept. The usual reading of narratives does not prepare children for expository texts; discussion helps.

You, yourself, are unlikely to come to a position from all your reading—for example, on discipline—until you have talked it over and out with yourself and others. The experience of expressing and shaping ideas through talk, and of collaborating to discuss problems or topics, helps children develop a critical and exploratory attitude toward knowledge. Talk can be the most powerful learning resource that children have at their disposal.

In essence, then, talk is directly related to the later development of skills—reading, writing, and the learning process itself. Because of all these reasons, talk deserves continuous and focused emphasis in your classroom. Such considerations about importance put into perspective the activities to follow in this chapter that suggest uses of talk in the classroom.

The Error of the Silent Classroom

Unfortunately, the guiding words in some schools appear to be "shut up." Teachers may consider talking to be simply bad behavior. Some teachers (nudged by tradition, administration, or other factors) appear to consider it their job to be the silencers and subduers of small children. ("Don't talk! We're learning language.") While children are taught to listen passively, to mimic, and to answer factual questions in such classrooms, they are seldom given the opportunity for self-expression. Unfortunately, oral expression may be becoming more limited as modern classrooms become more and more mechanized and test-score oriented.

What goes on in the silent classroom? Talk about the "real" world? Is there intellectually honest academic and scientific discipline and method? Is talk harnessed for learning purposes? Is there talk about relevant feelings, hopes, interests, doubts, fears, and challenges? Are there chances to develop the full range of oral capabilities? Usually the silent classroom is a world all its own, where children are cheated of their first mighty steps. If attention is given to children's speech in such classrooms, it may be directed to the mechanics of posture, articulation, and "bad habits." Teachers need to be more interested in *what* children say than how they say it.

Maintaining silence, then, is not an appropriate role for the teacher. The first duty of the teacher is to free the child to communicate. Until children talk freely, the teacher can diagnose nothing of their language attainment and can know nothing of where to help them help themselves. Since the entire curriculum is a language program, the teacher's job is to make talking in school legal and provide an educational payoff. Since oral language is the child's greatest show, it is the teacher's responsibility to allow the show to go on.

WHO ARE YOUR TALKERS/SPEAKERS?

This section examines talking/speaking from the perspective of the child (the *who* in your classroom). When young children make sense of their environment by means of speech, they sometimes chatter away in monologue, uninterested in interacting with listeners. When children enter school they are still using this way of knowing things by talking about them. To close down these children's mouths may be to close down their minds. First consider a developmental look targeted to this language arts area.

What Can We Learn from Mothers as Language Teachers?

We can learn by applying a page from developmental research on mothers fostering talk in their young children (Edelsky, 1978; Nelson, 1985). First, facilitating mothers use a context of whole language, not partitioning or sequencing artificially (i.e., not this objective for 15 minutes and the next objective for the next 15 minutes). Second, they interact, have dialogues with their young language learner, one-on-one. (Classrooms can be set up in this way, too.) In their dialogue mothers produce a simplified model that is slightly more advanced than a child's discourse. Third, they go for the ideas rather than correct forms of language. (A teacher can stress ideas too, instead of harping on usage.) If they correct, mothers do it subtly, with expansion and definition, all in context.

Fourth, these mothers talk about things their child can actually see or is presently attending to. (Teachers can stimulate language with objects that children care about or intriguing people, and incorporate first-hand trips related to projects vital to children, as in the *where* section of this chapter. Teachers can notice what children focus on and build language learning thereon.) Fifth, such mothers expect their children to succeed and take enormous delight in their progress. A teacher and a class can have a climate in which participants get genuinely excited about progress and successes in oral language development. ("Didn't we have a great conversation!")

Natural Hesitancy and Unnaturally Quiet Children

It is a courageous act of faith for most young children to address an adult they do not know. To do this across the silence of 25 other children magnifies the ordeal. Add to that the fear of rejection and the formidable picture is complete. Here we have natural hesitancy.

People vary extensively in the amount that they talk with others, and even the most verbose of us are quiet and reticent about speaking at times. But you will encounter some children in your class who rather typically think they can gain more and lose less by remaining silent. We need to become more aware of the different kinds of quiet children (and teachers) and some general ways of encouraging them to talk with others (McCroskey, 1977). Chapters 5 and 6 offer many suggestions.

Next we address a framework of goals for your program to enhance talking and speaking. What does one do with such a framework? It guides the provision of a physical and emotional classroom climate and gives the broad outline for the *how* of teaching strategy and classroom activities.

WHAT FRAMEWORK OF GOALS IS USEFUL TO THE TALKING/SPEAKING CURRICULUM?

This section concerns a framework of goals, culled from many sources. Speaking and listening are not two sets of separate skills, but are *interactive* aspects of discourse far more complex than oral vocabulary, sentence expression, or sentence comprehension. Skilled oral language use is not the result of performing a series of discrete skills in sequence; it is a synchronized *process* with information from many different resources used simultaneously. For our own mental networks or maps we need to analyze component skills, but successful oral language use is a unified act. The subskills flow together in a smooth performance. The oral language user coordinates knowledge about topic, strategies, and the forms of language. One can master component skills in isolation and not be able to talk and speak well (i.e., construct and express meaning in an independent and flexible manner). Students need to unify the *when, why,* and *how* of talking/speaking.

Consider an illustrative analogy: To become proficient at golf, the player needs to learn how to select the appropriate club, depending upon the terrain and the distance. Similarly, to become proficient at expressing and constructing meaning, the speaker needs to learn how to employ skills differently, depending on context, purpose, and message. The most skilled speakers are those who can rapidly and confidently tailor their abilities to the demands of each situation. Their behavior is active, interactive, constructive, fluent, strategic, motivated, and synchronized.

One of the most important requirements of successful oral communication is the goal of appropriate *use* of language for different purposes. Telling a story, for instance, makes different demands on speakers' language resources from giving instructions or arguing a point of view in a discussion. *It would be well for teachers to know what kinds of language resources and skills go into a child's successful carrying out of different kinds of oral communication uses at varied ages.*

A Framework of Goals

With that overview, Box 4.1 gives a suggested framework of goals and subgoals for the language art of speaking, all within the developmental competences that are reasonable and appropriate to the child. The three major goals deal with (1) process, (2) purpose (or uses), and (3) attitude (or valuing).

This framework offers options for you to consider and select from in planning your yearly program. Generally, details for the subgoals are presented from an easier to a

---

BOX 4.1 Framework of Goals for Speaking

Goal 1: Understand and use stages of an interactive speaking *process.* Its subgoals deal with context, repertoire, student-constructed meaning, monitored strategies, and synchronization of all parts, including assessment.

Goal 2: Talk/speak for a variety of specific *purposes* and their forms. These include getting things done with self-expressions, instruction/direction, and persuasion. Also included are sharing feelings and views of self and others, informing, using social conventions, and imagining for artistic purposes.

Goal 3: Develop a lasting positive *attitude* toward talking/speaking. Subgoals include satisfaction, curiosity, choice, and recognition of the power of speech and its role in the creation and perpetuation of culture.

more difficult level. You have, therefore, a rough suggestion of use for younger to older children, lower grade levels to upper ones. The *how* section illustrates these goals and subgoals with in-depth examples of objectives and activities based on oral *forms* growing out of common or artistic uses. (See Appendix 4B at the end of this chapter for an elaboration of these goals with details for subgoals.)

WHERE CAN SPEAKING TAKE PLACE?

This section emphasizes aspects of the context. As was mentioned in Chapter 3, part of the context is the emotional climate the teacher creates. The way a teacher can develop a communication-nurturing climate is simple: Reinforce students for communicating with others, instead of punishing them.

This section focuses on aspects of the classroom environment for oral language development such as diagrams and floor plans for enhancement of talking and speaking. An environment that promotes interaction is conducive to a slow building of conceptual and social relationships, especially when designed by teachers who listen to children talk.

Room Arrangements and Materials

Space influences human behavior, including verbal behavior. Organized well, it creates an aesthetic environment conducive to language growth. Quiet areas need to be separated from ones needing a higher volume. (You may need to have the library area away from records.) Children appreciate one quiet nook so they can retreat from the group at times.

Not long after the ink is dry on your teaching contract, you will want to visit your classroom and begin the process of arranging the physical environment. This section may help you visualize an arrangement you want. Try to visualize what you wish to have ready to greet your language learners and parents on that first day of class by designing a floor plan. The level of your children will help you decide. (See the section on centers in Chapter 3 of the activity book.)

Of course, even with all your planning, you may find your physical arrangements are not working out. Rearrange, with the help of the children. You will be surprised at how they can help solve your problems and come up with fine ideas. In fact, save some part of the room for them to talk about and plan.

If you are conducting a conference or evaluating the oral language of an individual, a pair, or a small group, you need a location with minimal distractions. The conference location is usually in your classroom so you can keep an eye on the rest of the class while you confer (one of those feats of magic that teachers must learn to do). There are times when children need and want to work separately, and movable small tables can accommodate this need. You will find classroom plans arranged for flexible grouping and learning centers in Figures 4.2 and 4.3 Note the "softness/hardness" features. Softness comes through the presence of objects responsive to one's touch, for example, rags, pillows, couches, finger paint, clay, curtains, plants. Figures 4.2, 4.3, and 4.4 on pages 104, 105, and 106, respectively, show sample room plans for varied ages. Discuss them.

"How can my classroom be arranged to encourage language use and dialogue?"

In order to implement productive dialogue and group talk, the teacher may arrange the class into a series of small discussion groups. Some teachers are able to bring additional trained

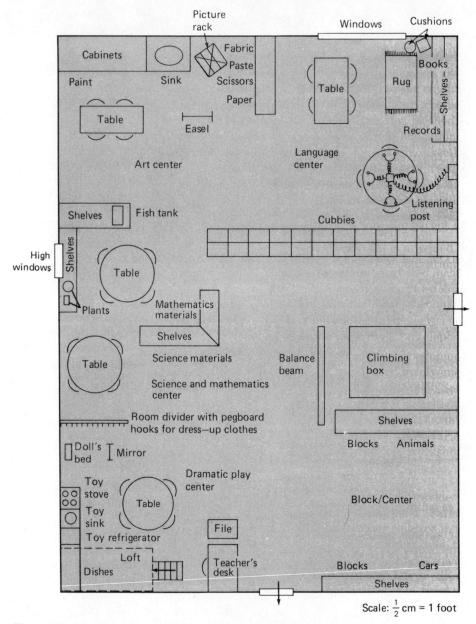

Figure 4.2 A sample room environment encouraging talking/speaking for young children. (*Source:* Schickendanz et al., 1983.)

people into the classroom for this purpose (high school students, college students, volunteers young and old, and aides). They stimulate talk in small groups so that the situation is not always the teacher with 27 or more children. The diagram in Figure 4.5 on page 107 suggests how such a classroom might look in action.

The principal instructor or teacher moves from discussion center to discussion center (set up bit by bit during the school year). Aides or student leaders in this opened-up classroom are positioned as needed. Children with a richer language repertoire and ease can

Figure 4.3 Arrangement of space in a kindergarten-primary room, encouraging talking/speaking. (*Source:* Lundsteen & Tarrow, 1981.)

help any less fluent or non-English-speaking children in such a classroom environment. Some teachers in traditional upper grades negotiate to turn in children's desks for a series of round tables, which facilitate talk and group discussion.

In essence, then, a positive communication environment is enhanced by the arrangement of the physical layout. Such an arrangement is flexible, comfortable, and permits maximum interaction based on the purpose of the specific activity. Seating arrangements that allow for eye contact for most large- and small-group discussions are desirable. A horseshoe or semicircular arrangement of the audience with the speaker positioned at the end allows greater interaction than seating in rows. Informal arrangements such as sitting on the floor add a positive dimension to certain activities. (Start making a list of people who can help you with your room environment.)

"What materials are stimulating?"

So you have your room arranged—what materials will you put in this facilitative environment? You can help talk sessions with a chalkboard, bulletin boards, easels, display charts, artwork, graphs, illustrations, slides, and audiotapes or videotapes. Materials at the talking/speaking center might include items in Box 4.2 on page 108.

Students can add to these materials. Materials relevant to school *content* areas are

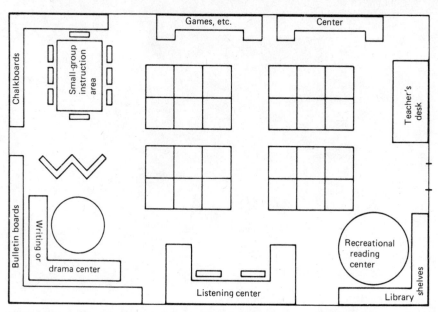

Figure 4.4 A classroom arrangement for flexible grouping, upper elementary, encouraging talking/speaking. (*Source:* Norton, 1985.)

appropriate to this talking/speaking/listening center. Here, again, children learn *to* speak and *through* speech. Have a classroom in which children will become aware of their talk and speech, not out of embarrassment, but because of and through the natural opportunities that curiosity and challenges provide. They will make efforts to enrich and change their language, not out of obedience to direction, but out of their own desire to make of it a more effective and useful communication tool. Language is a child's means of survival. Accept the language the child brings to school and enrich it with an enabling and interactive environment.

HOW CAN I TEACH TALKING/SPEAKING?

"What instructional activities seem most productive in the development of children's language?"

From the beginning this chapter has been solidly building toward the how of teaching that language art called talking/speaking. Not much remains because the other questions feed so importantly into this one.

Preview

When it comes to the *how* of teaching oral language three self-questions for teachers are useful: (1) What am I doing? (2) Why am I doing it? and (3) How can I do it better? Doing it better may mean forgetting all of that "frontal teaching" of the past and playing more the role of a dialoguer and a coach. The *how to* of teaching oral language includes modeling and being a learner yourself. It includes learning from your children as you listen to and watch them carefully. *How to* also means inspiring children to talk. It is selecting an activity that is integrative, that unifies listening, speaking, reading, writing, and children's literature.

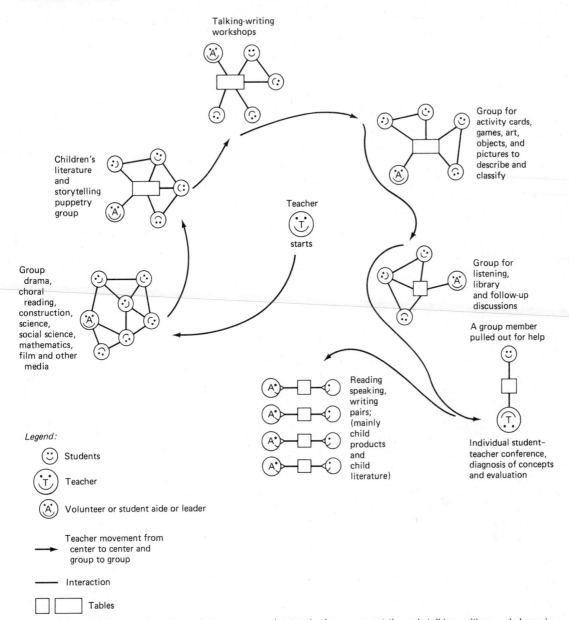

Figure 4.5 A bird's eye view of people in groups and a teacher's movement through talking-writing workshops in a classroom designed to promote talking.

Finally, as in the opening scene, it is believing in children's ownership of their own learning and use of oral language. Understanding how to teach also means knowing procedures for many interesting *forms* of oral language, such as: (1) show and tell, (2) conversation, (3) choral speaking, (4) story telling. Each is treated in depth to give through understanding for immediate trial.

What are some steps in using an oral expression form? First, you familiarize yourself

---

BOX 4.2 Materials for the Talking/Speaking Environment

- Tapes of poems.
- Tongue twisters.
- File of jokes, riddles, student-written anecdotes for sharing and resharing.
- Pictures, scribbles, experiment construction ideas, objects, puppets for conversation starters.
- Tapes of peer-composed introductions to classroom visitors, or famous people. (Groups guess the identities of the people.)
- Tapes describing a place familiar to the students through field trips, personal experience, social studies, or literature. (Groups identify the place described.)
- Pictures (some taken by or brought in by students) to arrange in order and then make up a story together.
- Tapes of a process (e.g., how a spider builds a web) and cue pictures for telling the process (already listened to) to someone who hasn't heard it, who then tells it to someone else. (Children can record and self-check with the original tape.)
- Equipment for recording all of the above so that the students and teacher may listen later to the results and progress of the talking at this center.

---

and the children with the form, trying it out (e.g., choral speech). Second, you and the children talk about what happened when you used the form. Third, you and the children try the form again with focus not on the form but on the content, understandings, learnings, and appreciations gained. You introduce the form and its skills, review and reinforce as necessary, and then refine.

The format of the *how-to* activities in this section is roughly as follows:

1. Definition of the form.
2. Teacher and child roles.
3. Specific objectives (tied into the larger framework given in Appendix 4B at the end of this chapter).
4. Values or advantages of the form.
5. Planning and procedures.
6. Description of a main activity.
7. Assessment of the activity.

You can see that each example treated comprehensively is not isolated, not cutesy, not a hit-and-run time filler. Begin with the form called "show and tell" commonly found in the preschool and early grades. You're in for some surprises.

Show and Tell

Show and tell has a long history in classrooms. A college student, on previewing this book, said, "I was happy to see a section on show and tell. I hope that many teachers-to-be read it because I remember how lots of my teachers made a waste of this useful activity."

Show and tell, sharing (or bring and brag, as it is sometimes called), can employ different procedures and call forth many uses of language. In its *unfortunate* forms the activity can easily degenerate into a senseless ritual while the teacher, obviously anxious to get it over with, catches up on some clerical work. The children take turns marching to the front of the room and speaking, mainly ignored by the other listless children. Members of the student audience may tolerate "sharers" only because they are awaiting their turn to stride to the front and continue the ritual. Some teachers see the only advantage in show and tell as this: "Children get to tell once and for all what they might otherwise whisper to 40 different children all day long."

Some teachers, labeled the tea-for-two type, form duets with each child. But then the teacher, as nervous hostess, asks all the questions, makes all the remarks, and gets all the language experience. This sort of show and tell, often is not particularly interesting to children and causes management problems for the teacher. Only about one-third of the children observed in one study were attending in an appropriate manner (McAfee, 1985).

Handled, however, with a little more thoughtfulness and planning, as did the teacher in the opening scene to this chapter, this oral reporting activity can provide valuable opportunities for varied language use: self-expression, exposition, description, classification, explanation, heuristics, imagining, entertaining, use of social conventions, interactive communication, and even creative problem solving.

Roles   The teacher's role is mainly as observer/provider, planner/supporter, and sometimes seeker, negotiator, and reflector. Teacher roles may vary depending on the context; the teacher may be highly active until the children can take over enabling roles. Sometimes the teacher simplifies and supports; sometimes the teacher complicates and challenges.

The idea is for the teacher not to create a testing situation with questions, but rather to *follow the child's lead,* sometimes just nodding and giving nonverbal support. Questions and responses are more collaborative replies than assessments. A teacher receives students' most interesting ideas when responding as a curious human being, asking about something he or she really wants to know. Often *one* really thoughtful question is enough. (For example: "What did you think of the writing in the two versions of the same story?") The teacher is not searching for right answers, but for genuine expression. Effective teaching is related to how teachers see their students as learners and how students see their own roles.

The teacher's first concern, besides giving undivided attention to what is going on, may be with a shy new child who may "show" the shared object only to the teacher at first. Then when the child progresses with a few words just to the teacher, the teacher, in turn, can encourage the child to repeat to a larger group. During show and tell there is opportunity for the teacher to model attentive, nurturing listening along with interactive questioning behavior, and encourage children to imitate the model. Then the teacher becomes unobtrusive as quickly as possible. The teacher as curiosity arouser can help children and their audiences to formulate questions (as did the teacher in the opening scene). Questions help children extend the topics.

The children's roles may be those of initiator/communicator/participant, seeker, negotiator, and critic. Children are questing to say something in their own voices, in voices that ring true to both the speaker and the listener. They quest to say and think what they had never said and thought before. Their role is to express fresh perceptions grounded in their developing sense of self. As meaning makers, their role is to express what most matters to them.

Specific Objectives and Advantages   Show and tell activity can have many objectives and advantages. Consider the eight listed in Box 4.3.

BOX 4.3 Objectives and Advantages of Show and Tell

1. *Bridging the gap between home and school.* Sharing can help span the distance between school and home. It can bring, for example, the cultural aspects of food, holidays, pleasureful pastimes, gift giving, and the arts from the home environment into the classroom.

2. *Going beyond monologue to communicating with an audience.* In developmental terms, show and tell rises above prattling monologue because the child's audience is usually unfamiliar with the object he or she has to display. The new photo, the beloved turtle, the book (or whatever was brought) serves as a focus to which the child can direct his or her attention. While the object is looked at and manipulated, it gives some organization to the child's exposition or personal narrative.

3. *Continuity.* Out of such behavior comes continuity and elaboration: the past (e.g., stories about how the child got the shown object and what he or she does with it); explanation of information; possibly evaluation; expression of related feelings; and anecdotes that narrate a bit of autobiography.

4. *Elaboration.* Moreover, as children turn the object in their hands, they are prompted to give description, classification, and exposition of characteristics.

5. *Increase in organization.* Organization also occurs when children, aware of their interacting audience, may find they need to structure by mentioning some things first so that later events make sense.

6. *Developing vocabulary.* Besides encouraging awareness of audience response, the teacher can also be alert for opportunity to help children develop vocabulary. The teacher transfers this expectation to the children (as we saw in the opening scene). The teacher helps the child attach labels and note multiple meanings and needs for qualifying.

7. *Language awareness.* The teacher and children can point out interesting sounds, intonations, stress patterns, elaboration, effective language, contrasts, similarities, if-then deductions, wonderings, predictions, alternatives, and clues suggesting challenging problems for solving.

8. *Contrasting varied uses of language.* The teacher and class can be alert to interrelations of language uses. If a child has treated a topic in an expository manner, the teacher might invite contrast with a poetic or dramatic treatment of the same thing. For example, if a child tells about a new swing, the teacher might ask if any one knows any poems about swinging or other pieces of literature in which a swing figures. A child might recall Stevenson's poem "The Swing" or Mary Ann Hoberman's "Hello and Good-bye."

A word of caution is appropriate here. Concentration on trying to change the young child's language usage at this point is unsound. *To respond freely, students need to feel that their language is acceptable.* The idea is to *extend* utterances. The teacher can model clear pronunciation, enunciation, and interesting and appropriate intonation, rather than continually correcting children's surface language features.

Planning and Procedures   Recall from Chapter 3 that in the opening scene the teacher had taped a bright yellow paper "spotlight" to the classroom floor. This device or a series of them spaced around the room for simultaneous sharing groups might create an encouraging space. Maintaining eye contact, scanning the group, and varying pace and mode of presentation can aid in keeping the group's attention (McAfee, 1985). Stop the sessions while the children are still interested.

To stimulate interaction, teachers might select themes such as asking all to bring (1) something made or grown themselves, (2) something with a history, (3) something funny, (4) dolls or animal toys to be worked into a character sketch, (5) something they can make work or move, and (6) something they can classify doubly (blue and made of paper). Recall the way the teacher planned and organized the activity in the opening scene to this chapter.

Main Activity   One teacher had a "Bring Your Grandparents to Share Day" (or other "grand" or even "great grand" relative or friend). Some "grand" visitors told of days gone by (of a fire engine with clanging bells pulled by a team of six black horses), some brought photos or artifacts, some shared songs of their youth. The guests had been coached by the teacher to involve the child who invited them and the other children in the class. One helped the children make hand-made ice cream.

In one 4-year-old class during circle time the children were to bring from home things that started with the letter *M*. The teacher, having gathered the items all on a tray, intended to integrate a reading skills concept with oral language. The children came forward to pick up their items and share them with the group. When it was David's turn, he bounced up and retrieved a brown paper bag, laying some newspaper on the floor. Certainly no *M* items were visible yet. Then things began to come out of his paper bag: a jar of water, a spoon, a bowl, a small container with dirt in it. The children, mystified, craned their necks forward. But David said nothing. He had captured the attention of his audience. Then he poured the dirt in the bowl, added water, and stirred. Every eye was riveted on what he was doing. The expressions changed from puzzlement to glee as they chorused, "Mud! Mud!"

Here perhaps we could also see the beginning of *showing* versus just *telling* that becomes so important later in vivid written composition. (For example, writing or speaking that just *tells* might say, "The cat was shy." One might more descriptively write, "The cat turns her head, rises, quivers, and goes under the couch, finally coming out with dust on her whiskers.")

Productive sharing also grows naturally from the ongoing work of the class. A room where not all children are engaged in working on the same task prompts sharing (e.g., their writings, books read, and projects). Sharing can cut across content areas and also across grades, as a fifth grader shares books read with a fourth grader in cross-grade reading partners. If children keep learning logs for content areas, these are fuel for sharing times. When sustained silent reading or writing times have ended, teachers and children can move to sharing-time groups. Thus they develop ownership about the content of their reading and writing as an aspect of the main sharing activity.

Assessment   Teachers can help children formulate standards for their show and tell sessions. The students can apply these criteria before, during, and after, as they evolve them. Older children, especially as their show and tell moves into "news," can formulate and apply standards such as the following five:

Our Standards for Reporting

1. Think before you talk.
   Why do I want to say anything?
   What do I want to say about it?
2. Consider your audience.
   What do I know about my audience?
   What do they already know about my topic?
3. Test run your reporting.
   Can I get someone to listen beforehand?
   What questions do they raise that I've overlooked?
4. Make it two-way.
   Did *my* questions encourage my audience to offer their own thoughts and feelings?
5. Think about whether there is any way your listeners can follow up on your topic?
   Does my audience know now how to find out more?
   What can they do with what I talked about? When and how can they go further?

Such sharing can continue to grow and be used throughout the school years and on into adult life, as can the next activity, conversation.

Conversation

Some educators classify conversation as a simple activity. Actually the art of conversation can be highly complex, requiring considerable skill. But a teacher can start in a more simple way with young children. Upper elementary teachers can still be refining this use of oral language, and individuals can work on the art of it for the rest of their lives. Whether or not conversation is dying out as a result of passive TV viewing is debatable, but conversation still appears to lead as a highly common oral language activity. It is often a prelude to even more serious business. Provide lots of opportunity for academic, content-related conversations to happen naturally in the classroom during the course of the day, and also plan special occasions for its use.

Definition   A social ability, **conversation** is an informal oral exchange of opinions, sentiments, observations, and ideas on topics of common interest. It usually takes the form of a chaining of topics, rather than focusing on one topic, as is true in certain forms of discussion. A satisfying conversation is something like a tennis match, in that the subject of conversation is lobbed back and forth, with all players participating. It is not like being a spectator at a backboard practice where one person keeps hitting the ball while others simply stand by.

Nor is the art of conversation simply having the patience to wait to speak until the other has finished—a series of unrelated disconnected items, each pent-up piece tenderly saved and eagerly released as pauses develop. Conversation is the art of group development and exploration of an idea or a series of ideas. In this art one does not seek to place ideas before the others, as a merchant displaying wares. Instead one tries to explore the other minds to see what they have to offer, coaxing and challenging, revealing ones' own mind during the process, but only as a by-product. *There* is the art to continue to grow toward!

Roles   The teacher's role is mainly as observer/provider (planner/assessor), and sometimes as seeker, negotiator, and reflector. Seekers are not afraid to explore. As seekers, teachers might model questions to draw out the other members of a conversation group. A reflector causes the students to ponder their ideas. The teacher is not a crucial element of the group, but might circulate from conversation to conversation or monitor from afar, and assist in assessment.

The child's role would be as participant/initiator/communicator, and, it is hoped, seeker, negotiator, and critic. Negotiators seek cooperative decisions. Initiators affect the course of the conversation with new ideas. Communicators interact with each other in the conversational group. Participants involve their intellect, feelings, and imagination in the conversation. Critics make assessments using a growing set of standards developed by reflection on their own and group experience.

You probably have noticed that the key child role in almost all the activities in this book is that of active agent, moving from unconscious to conscious awareness of form and feature in their speaking (or listening, reading, or writing). Children show ownership, self-initiation, and self-assessment. (For example, a child says, "I need to change this title," and goes about changing it.) They serve as models for one another, influencing others to try and stimulating interest. They are making choices, experimenting, and taking risks. They talk about the communication process and live it. They abstract their own strategies and develop new strategies. *Children are creators of meaning.*

Specific Objectives   Conversation can relate to many goals, especially the second goal of purpose, e.g., sharing and exploring the feelings and views of self and others. Conversations also have value from strengthening children's self-concept and as a tool for conceptual learning in academic content areas such as literature, social studies, and science. Children develop the ability to present ideas in logical order, to fit the conversation to the occasion, and to change topics appropriately. See Box 4.4 on page 114.

Planning and Procedures   In preparing the conversational space the teacher might set chairs for two to five children. Truck tires covered with plush material could also be used for seating. At chat times children would sit around the rim. One such tire could be kept in the room all year as a chat center related to ongoing activities.

Introduction or Reinforcement of Control "Signals"   Children may need help in knowing how to get things done in a conversation. Box 4.5 on page 114 lists needed expertise. A teacher might start with the first three and add the others gradually as the need arises, or take just one at a time. A teacher might give the children a signal for stopping and coming to a "debriefing" session with the teacher.

Warm-up Activity   A teacher could start a conversational group off with a warm-up activity such as a round-robin starting, "I felt good today when . . ." or use a clapping-finger-snapping chant round-robin such as, "My name is _____ and I like _____." (Example: Clap, clap, snap, snap—"My name is Sara and I like ice cream.")

Main Activities and Topics   Much of the time children will be able to come up with their own conversational ideas, but you might brainstorm a list as a group or use a mystery bag with objects. The topics might deal with those in Box 4.6 on page 115.

Once children get started they will have their "antennas" out all the time for conversational ideas. The teacher can interview children to help them discover their own topics.

BOX 4.4 Some Specific Objectives

Effective student conversationalists are able to:

- Follow the line of communication, commenting and asking questions.
- See the relationship between the major topics and ideas being discussed and specific information they can contribute.
- Move the conversation forward by summing up or asking "What if . . ." questions.
- Change the topic of conversation by:
  —Using a remark formerly made as a means of presenting a new idea related to that remark
  —Bringing in illustrations or comparisons that refer to the topic but also introduce a new one
  —Addressing a question of general interest to the group or a qualified member
  —Tactfully suggesting postponement or conceding an argument
- Contribute courteously. (Examples: "I don't think I agree with that idea; let me tell you why." When two children start at the same time: "Please finish what you were saying," "Please wait until I finish," or "Excuse me."
- Offer a proposition and/or modify, qualify, restate, test, approach freshly, and perhaps discard it.
- Know how to get interesting material for conversation.

BOX 4.5 Control "Signals"

- How to get a turn.
- How and when to interrupt the person talking.
- What to do when participants begin to talk at the same time.
- How to disagree with a person's idea.
- How not to monopolize but to encourage others.
- How to include all members of the group in one's remarks.
- How to monitor volume of voice.
- How to avoid a futile argument.
- How to be considerate of a child entering the group after the conversation has started.
- How to change the topic of conversation.
- How to introduce an outsider and follow up with a conversational lead.

BOX 4.6 Conversational Ideas

- Themselves; or close others:
  —What they have done
  —What they would like to do
  —Likes and dislikes
  —Hobbies
  —Pets
  —Animal rights
  —Neighborhood
  —Community
  —"People I love, people I love,/what can I do that is special for you?"
- Observing and reporting on media or objects:
  —things heard, seen, or read; new books (in the library, or written); stories heard; current news; reports on out-of-school conversations
- School context: content subjects (content area readings and writings, e.g., "What do we already know about . . . ?"; "What did we learn about . . . ?"); their own writings, self-selected readings, and storytelling from wordless picture books

---

Children can do this, too, just as they help each other come up with ideas of what to write about.

Assessment   If a conversation bogs down into a long silence, the teacher might share a secret technique which is the subject of a poem by Rudyard Kipling:

> I had six honest serving men—
> They taught me all I knew:
> Their names were Where and What and When
> And Why and How and Who.

The secret is nothing more than teaching the children the knack of asking open-ended questions. You might call it the **Six *W*s + *H & I* Technique.** Children simply begin their questions with *where, what, when, why, which,* or *who.* These are the six *W*s. Add *H* and *I* for the words *how* and *if,* and you have it—Six *W*s + *H & I.* When children begin their questions with these words, the children with whom they are speaking cannot simply answer *yes* or *no.* TV interviewers learn this secret. The device leads to more thorough answers. The questions are conversation starters.

For example, if a questioner asks, "Did you go on a vacation trip this summer?" a child can simply answer "yes" or "no," thus ending the conversation. The question *"What* did you do about a vacation last summer?" might get a more complete response, however. If it turns out the child took a vacation trip, the questioner might next ask, *"Why* did you pick that place?" Some open-ended questions that draw out conversations are: *"How* did you happen to . . ."; *"When* did you first decide . . ."; *"Which* would you recommend . . ."; *"If* you had your choice . . ."; *"How* would you like. . . ."

BOX 4.7 Debriefing Questions After Conversation

- How did our conversation begin? (Who talked first? What did they say?)
- How many different topics did our group talk about?
- How many of us were participants? Initiators? Any negotiators? Seekers?
- How was courtesy shown in our group?
- What *W H & I* questions did you ask? (You may need to replay the taped conversation for this item.)

After a conversation the teacher might lead a debriefing session with the conversationalists, asking such questions as those in Box 4.7.

Occasionally you might tape record or videotape the conversation to aid assessment. Children can have individual file folders, "oral language files" in which to put logs and tapes. Taped samples can serve as a stimulus to writing or dictation. (A small ziplock plastic bag stapled to the file holds tapes.)

The chances are that, as increasingly adept conversationalists, your students are going to be even more interesting to know. I used to look forward to enjoying lunchtime conversations with members of my fifth-grade class. We talked about books, travels, observations on propaganda devices, amusing anecdotes, and their individual "research" projects. When we returned to the classroom we were all the better for it as ideas enriched the academic work.

Storytelling by Children

Invitation

If you are a dreamer, come in
If you are a dreamer, a wisher, a "liar,"
A hope-er, a pray-er, a magic bean buyer . . .
If you're a pretender, come sit by my fire
For we have some flax-golden tales to spin.
Come in!
Come in!

                                            Shel Silverstein

Another valuable instructional activity for oral language development is the dramatic form of expression called *storytelling* by children. In it the teller gives consideration to both content and means of communication. It is usually initiated by an adult in the school context and elicited from children as soon as possible. Again the focus is on speaking, though storytellers incorporate some movement, gesture, and considerable eye contact involving the audience. For centuries people communicated mainly by word of mouth. A storyteller, transmitting what was received, returned to new life what was entrusted. Thus the storyteller, enjoying much prestige, carried culture from one place to another producing literature in the oral tradition. Told again and again, classic tales became hewn and polished like diamonds. Ask your students why *they* think stories have been told for so many centuries.

Definition   The relating of a narrative that may or may not be original is **storytelling.** The story is re-created as if it were **spontaneously** happening. ("Once there was an old seller of caps who went through the streets calling, 'Caps for sale, caps for sale!' ") Storytelling deals with such dimensions as character, language, and situation. An act of sharing, it gives life to words by using expression, sound, pacing, moments of silence, and even a bit of clowning. It requires that the telling explain the setting, appearance of characters, motives, actions, and sequence of events clearly and colorfully while sustaining a monologue.

Some Values   Stories represent the essential units of our lives, offering the magical imperatives of "so it began" and "so it came to an end." A story encompasses us, justifies our stay, and prepares our leaving. Another value is that storytelling helps children become familiar with story language (vocabulary, syntax) and story structure. These aspects help them listen to and read stories themselves with greater facility and enjoyment. Storytelling introduces children to *archetype plots* and themes that run through all literature that they can use later in their own writing. (Example of such plots are the journey, the overcoming of a monster, or the quest.) Children get actively involved with literature; it gives them yet another avenue of response. Storytelling helps them organize their thoughts, think predictively, and become confident, poised speakers.

By giving a sense of story, storytelling lays a foundation for composing in writing. It is apparently common in the background of famous creative writers. Pearl Buck received family history and culture preserved through stories while growing up in China. In addition, her Chinese nurse told her Asian fairy tales (Fairweather, 1986). You will discover your own advantages. (For a review of research on the values of story telling see Morrow, 1985.)

Roles   Roles played by the teacher include model and provider. Sometimes the teacher plays the role of story structure exposer and guider of reflection. Roles played by the child include performer, communicator, responder, reflector, and critic. Children may also be gatherers of storytelling material. All of us are potential storytellers. We've been doing something like storytelling since we first learned to talk. If a teacher starts, "When I was about your age," then the chances are that a story is in the making. All of us have experienced the role of enjoyer.

Specific Objectives   Besides general speaking skills mentioned under previous activities, children as storytellers also can:

- Develop and extend the ability to recall, construct, organize, and logically sequence events.
- Develop an awareness and understanding of differentiation of character within the story, relating character to events and central ideas.
- Establish eye contact and audience involvement.
- Develop an ear for and a use of dramatic language. (What colors are for the artist, words are for the storyteller—"a wavering leaf-shadow of a breeze combing the grasses.")
- Apply storytelling skills to other areas of study (e.g., reading comprehension, social studies, and "stories" about spelling word origins, the origins of math concepts and conventions, and the lives of famous scientists and writers).

Planning, Procedures, and Activity

Material   First the storyteller finds suitable material. Suggested criteria are given in Box 4.8.

For the daily telling (or reading) of tales you might first select from world folktales. (A list is given in the references for this chapter.) Ask students to bring in tales of their own choosing. Find tales from your immediate region and from the cultures represented locally. You might have a balance of traditional and contemporary literature. Thinking agewise, preschool through kindergarten might start with familiar ones, such as "Three Little Pigs"; grades 1 through 3 might start with "Hansel and Gretel"; and grades 4 through 6 might start with more complex myths, legends, and tall tales such as "Pecos Bill."

More lengthy children's books can be "told *from.*" (That is, just enough is told from the beginning to whet the appetite to read the rest of it.) When children want to furnish their own material for storytelling, sometimes a frame is helpful. Children complete it in their own ways. See the following one structured on the theme of "the quest."

A Storytelling Frame

Once upon a time there were three (or whatever) _____.

They wanted some _____.

So they went to _____.

But in their way was _____.

So they _____.

Wordless books as stimulus material   One of the best ways to promote children's inferential speaking and story telling is through the use of textless picture books that

---

BOX 4.8 Criteria for Storytelling Material

A good "storytelling story":

1. Stimulates the imagination of the listeners.

2. Fits their interests.

3. Is closely knit and is appropriate in length for the listeners.

4. Includes characters and events with which the listeners can identify.

5. Usually includes characters who speak dialogue.

6. Includes the use of conventions such as repetition, rhythm, alliteration, and some rhyme.

7. Includes structures of a quick beginning, a simple plot, sufficient conflict to create action, a definite climax, and a quick, satisfying ending.

8. Appeals to motivational aspects of emotions, humor, love of adventure, desire for courage, compassion, joy, and imagination.

tell a story without words. Children tell their "own" stories by interpreting the pictures. Some are short and easy; others are long, complex, and sophisticated *(The Silver Pony)*. If illustrations are explicitly detailed, children can not only supply basic plot (with a clear beginning, consistent characters, logical actions leading to a climax, and a conclusion), but also infer feelings, motivations, and colorful detail.

You might model by telling a story from a wordless book to a small group. Then, with another book, ask, "What's happening here?" as you turn the pages. Pairs of children can each have a different wordless book to tell to each other, thus giving the fledgling storytellers a structured approach.

When several children (separately) audiotape their renditions of the story as they infer it from the book, sharing provides valuable listening/speaking/thinking comparisons. Each rendition will be individual, with its own insights and oral-literary tradition. Related activities of transcribing (writing), reading transcriptions, and art are happy by-products.

Many children who thought they could not tell a story or that they did not like books have bridged the gap by using wordless picture books. They learn how elements of story interconnect and build. Some of my old favorites are listed with the references for this chapter. Ask your librarian for other newer ones as they continually appear.

Story Preparation   Teachers as models (and later children) prepare the story by becoming familiar with the elements in Box 4.9.

How Teachers as Models *Tell* the Story

1. Planning a very brief introduction relating the story to the audience.
2. Relating the incidents in the intended sequence while building to a climax. (Again, do not memorize; be spontaneous, as if it's something that is just happening. You can hold a series of pictures—scenic units—in your mind instead.)
3. Making the characters come alive by varying voice, gesture, or posture.
4. Creating a mood (e.g., awed, mysterious, scary, sad, mischievous).
5. Using interesting speech patterns (e.g., varying volume, pitch, rate, tone, quality, and pauses; finding just the right voice for the old witch).
6. Using verbal, mechanical, or musical sounds to accompany the telling when appropriate (e.g., a soft clucking for the little red hen, a sharp clap when the frog turns into a prince, a bit of tune as the ugly duckling goes on his lonely way).

BOX 4.9 Elements to Account for in Storytelling Preparation

- *Plot.* Be able to outline it and visualize the related sequence of events. (Children might make simple outlines of units of conflict or pictured action, called scenic units.)

- *Setting.* Perhaps draw a rough map of all the places or settings mentioned in some stories.

- *Characters.* Be able to understand and project them.

- *Flavor of the language.* Memorize *only* repeated phrases, chants, or songs for the story. Use a rich vocabulary as you enjoy the language and its patterns. Plan to use repeated interesting phrases to enliven. (For example, from *Rumpelstilskin,* "And so she sat and so she spun and so she wondered what she had begun!")

7. Using gesture, facial expression, and other nonverbal aspects to reinforce the message. (Eye contact is important!)
8. Sometimes employing visual aids and props to enhance the telling (e.g., a flannel board, finger puppets, a crown, a peasant's scarf).
9. Using timing—recognizing moments calling for slow, leisurely telling, hurrying the tempo when the action is strong, pausing before a moment of awe.
10. Remembering the motto: "Enthusiasm has'm."

Some General Procedural Thoughts   Some general procedural ideas are the following:

• Practice well before modeling story telling for your children. (Doing it in front of a mirror helps.) Read the story first for the series of mind pictures or scenic units of conflict; then read a second time for the flavor of the language.
• Establish routines of warm-ups and signals. A warm-up might entail listening intently to short "stories" entirely conveyed by a series of sounds. (On tape children hear a thud of a hurled newspaper, a door opens, the newspaper scrapes the stone porch as it is picked up, the door closes, and children guess what happened.) A signal to get the children to listen attentively might be that all in the story-telling circle (say five or six) hold hands briefly and then fold them in their laps; thereupon the teller immediately begins.
• After the story, allow time for reflection, responding, and problem solving.

Response Options   There can be many reflective response options. Use a tape recorder to aid assessment of the telling in class. After "Cinderella" your group reflection might focus (with older children) on translating her *problem* to modern days. "What do you do when a stepmother is really mean to you? How do you let your dad know?" Capsulize the tale by writing a verse about it, as did the French storyteller Perrault for his version of "Cinderella" and his other tales. Consider why this tale type is universal and is still told in some form in places such as Finland, Germany, Haiti, and China. Are there any implications for global understanding? Look for references to the tale in present-day media or conversation ("It's a Cinderella story"; "I'm going to turn into a pumpkin then"). Look at how varied artists have chosen to illustrate the same tale and the elements stressed. Give the students time to simply reflect.

Instructional Sequence   An instructional sequence for the year (or a unit for older children) might include items in Box 4.10.

Assessment of Storytelling   Criteria for assessment of performance might include appropriateness of materials, voice technique, and characterizations; continuing eye contact; sensitivity to audience; appropriate language; artful presentation—with capturing beginning, logical development, distinct characterizations, expressive dialogue, mood, built-to climax, and closure (Alberta, 1985).

Story retelling also serves as a way to analyze children's growth process in language and response to literature (though the activity may be limited as to context and responsive language). Special linguistic properties to assess include children's story vocabulary and syntax (e.g., "once upon a time," " 'scoundrel!' said he," and "lived happily ever after"). From regularly collected tape recordings of children's retellings, teachers can document children's growth using Box 4.11 on page 122.

BOX 4.10 An Instructional Sequence for Incorporating Storytelling into the Yearly Curriculum

1. Teacher models telling a story.

2. As teacher tells a story, children echo recurring phrases or accompany with sound effects.

3. Teacher helps children through retelling of highly familiar stories. Subtle teacher-offered prompts can relate to story structures of setting (time, place, characters), events causing the main character(s) to face a problem, plot episodes, and resolution. Teacher guides reflection afterward.

4. Children tell stories just heard for the first time or create one from personal experience.

5. Teacher provides beginning of a story and children make up the rest with a partner.

6. Children tell familiar stories to each other.

7. Children make up their own story and share with a partner.

8. Partners collaborate to make up one story, perhaps stimulated by selected music or picture cards.

9. Children share these stories with yet other partners.

10. Children volunteer to share stories with a whole group, varying audiences, taping and relistening reflectively.

11. Through ongoing reflection, children abstract elements of the art of a satisfying story, the art of story telling, and story-telling techniques. (Recall that Chapter 2 gave stages in the development of story telling.)

Note that regarding sequence step 3 on children's retellings, A **flannelboard** can help children to get back to the beginning of the story and hang on to characters, events, and crucial details in both time and causal sequence. Number each piece on the back, lay the pieces face down, and remove each piece when it is no longer needed so as to avoid confusing clutter on the board.

For older children the teacher can adapt the list, "How Teachers as Models *Tell* the Story" found on page 119. Also, ask students what makes a good story and a good storyteller. Post an ongoing list of elements *they* choose (animals that talk, dialogue, funny characters, exciting happenings, magic, words that really "show"). Student storytellers can assess their own experience with the help of a reaction form, such as the one below, containing a place for their name, date, context, story told, and what was learned from the experience:

Self-Assessment for Storytellers

Name: Context: Date:

Story told:
   I learned that _____

BOX 4.11 Items for Teacher's Assessment of Children's Storytelling

- Sense of story (recall Chapter 2 section)
- Fluency
- Precise descriptive words
- Complexity of language, including vocabulary, and syntax
- Reasonableness of sequence and linking of events
- Nonverbal enhancements

As storytellers your students are applying important integrated language arts processes and skills. But the biggest bonus is joy in the magic of weaving a tale. Storytelling is like old silver that increases in beauty each time you polish it (Ross, 1980). Enrich a life; tell a story. Start telling stories today! (*Note:* The appendix to Chapter 4 of the activity book has an extended section on choral speech that can be a delight for you and your students. The activity book also presents forms related to word play, finger play, dialect, vocabulary development, role play, interviews, panels, debate, questioning, persuasion, and more. Subsequent chapters in this book deal with the forms of drama, discussion, expository oral and written language, and persuasion.)

Integration of Talking/Speaking into the Curriculum

Recall that *integrating language arts means providing natural learning situations in which children develop speaking, listening, reading, and writing together for real purposes and real audiences.* Also recall from Chapter 3 that you can consider integration in three ways: (1) learning each of the language arts in terms of the others (such as reading and discussing a written draft with peers); (2) considering each language mode of speaking, listening, and so on as an integrated whole, not a set of isolated, minute parts; and (3) developing language while learning other content areas (e.g., social studies, science, math, literature—with task/topic-related conversations). Although the activities in the *how* section have offered concrete examples of the three types of integration, reconsider types one and three, to follow.

Learning Each of the Language Arts in Terms of the Others   *Listening* and *speaking* are considered as reciprocal and integrated aspects of students' oral communication ability. Although listening and speaking have been assessed independently of one another, listening is rarely done by itself for the private acquiring of knowledge. Far more often children listen in order to speak appropriately. With a copy of, say, *Where the Wild Things Are* in front of them, they talk about what they would need to turn the story into a puppet play and collaborate on who will make what. Speaking may well be assessed in conjunction with listening (as we see in the section on assessment found on page 123.

Oral and *written* modes are also considered as reciprocal and integrated aspects of students' overall communicative ability. We have seen in this chapter's activities that written material and spoken language activities often interact with one another (e.g., reading to find stories to retell).

Written composition furnishes further examples. Children talk in order to plan for writing; they read and then relate what they have found out or thought; they take notes to report back to others. *Speaking may well be assessed in conjunction with coordinated use of writing and reading.* The first day of first grade the teacher said, "I've written a letter to each of you. What would I say in a letter to you?" And the children talked about it. "Write *me* a letter," continued the teacher. "What might you say to me?" And they talked about that. As another example, an older child listened to the story *House Without a Christmas Tree*, noting that the book had a prologue. After talking about it, the child went back to a story he was writing and added a prologue to it. Tapes in a child's oral language file serve as ideas for writing. Children's puppets tell part of a story. Children talk about the story and then write their own ending.

Developing Language While Learning Other Content Areas   Finally, oral communication is relevant across the total curriculum. We have seen in this chapter that opportunities for collaborative and exploratory talk are not restricted to the language arts lesson. Integration can span all areas, such as literature, social studies, and health.

For example, children discuss and report on a science lesson or use collaborative talk to plan an environmental studies project; they tell the significance of major historical celebrations in the community; they listen to music that tells a story and recall and describe events in the story; they talk about line, color, shape, and texture as they mold clay. Finger puppets that children have made sit on little stands in the library center with a sign saying, "Let me read a science book with you." The child puts a puppet on a finger and reads aloud to it (or the "puppet" "reads" to another child). Or a child reads during silent sustained reading time while investigating questions in social studies; she creates a short dialogue with a puppet to explain what she discovered to a peer. A child can have her self-constructed puppet make asides to the audience while she is retelling a story from the realm of literature. (You will find more about puppets in Chapter 5 and in the activity book.)

Talking is a social activity that is purposeful, varied, and integrated with other modes of communication. Talking uses many varied goals and is responsive to the changing requirements of diverse others present in interactional encounters. It is in this context that talking/speaking needs to be assessed—the topic of the next section.

Assessment of Talking/Speaking

Assessment has been a part of almost every activity suggested in this chapter. This section is organized by question and answer.

"Who are effective speakers?"

Effective speakers are people who are successful, clear, sincere, persistent, flexible, and direct in communicating with others. This is a standard you use in assessment. In the case of request making, effective child speakers are ones who receive responses when they produce requests (Wilkinson, 1984). A teacher, volunteer, or video camera can observe and record such successes.

"Why assess?"

The spontaneous, natural onset of talking and listening in the normal development of the child has led some educators simply to expect growth in language through normal, everyday experiences without special assessment and teaching. Without denying the significance of children's already acquired powers, we now see that classroom teachers do need to be involved. What we teachers think (or hope) we are doing is what we try to assess. We assess in order to teach better and to see if and how we can help children.

"Can I just rely on standardized, objective tests?"

Teachers' assessments by naturalistic observations operate inseparably in the teaching process, but scores from formal, standardized measures may remain just that. Some teachers need to get away from judgments based solely on grade-level expectations. Instead, they need to know if each child is achieving both affective and cognitive language growth. They collect samples of speech structures and vocabulary; they also assess attitudes and values implicit in the child's use of that language. Standardized tests cannot tap these (Ylisto, 1984).

Instead, assess in as natural a situation as possible in order to get a truer view of what children are actually able to do. Formal test situations often do not give a realistic portrayal of children's speaking abilities. Put children at their ease and encourage them to talk spontaneously. It helps if the assessment situation is stimulating and fun to take part in.

"What can I do with information gleaned from naturalistic observation?"

Knowledge of results of our teaching can further direct our methods of record keeping and its use. (Do we place this item in the child's folder? Do we use it in a parent conference? Does it help us decide on the next activity?) In assessing, the teacher needs to recognize that differences in language use result from differences in experience and social environment. *Differences are not deficiencies.* High ability to communicate does lead to speaker/listener self-confidence, affecting almost all areas of life. Low ability needs immediate help or it means unfulfillment. Talking and listening are mutually supportive, both prompted by a search for meaning. If we teachers own these points of view, it makes a difference in how we use information gleaned from our assessments; we then teach better.

"If I'm planning assessment what does it need to reflect?"

Assessment needs to reflect (1) the variety and complexity of spoken language; (2) both the production and interpretation of sustained talk; and (3) a normal, integrated, and communicative sequence of activities. First of all, a global impression of the quality of the performance is needed, then each activity needs to be analyzed in more detail. In an optimal assessment situation, speakers have information that listeners do not have; there is then a need for authentic communication. The examiner needs to be as unobtrusive as possible. (MacLure & Hargreaves, 1986).

"So just what can I try?"

Try using friendship pairs and groups formed by combining pairs for natural audiences during assessment. Use recording for subsequent analysis. Give an on-the-spot, overall assessment too. Use multiple assessments. In any *analytic* scoring, try to provide insights into the extent to which specific features of talk contribute to your overall ratings.

"What categories might I use for marking?"

Categories in your general analytic marking scheme might be the following:

Categories for a General Assessment Scheme
1. The overall **organization** of the child's talk
2. The ideas and elements of **meaning** in the oral performance
3. The **sentence structures** (or grammar)
4. The **vocabulary**
5. Nonverbal aspects of the child's communication

Special forms of oral language use vary in specific characteristics to be noted. For instance, for category 1, storytelling requires a different kind of organization from scientific reporting; this organization in turn differs from that of describing or from anecdote telling. Imaginative use of words and phrases may be important for adept storytelling but not required for giving clear instructions or conducting a scientific experiment. (Indeed they would probably be inappropriate.) Using such categories and criteria, teachers can also see what specific qualities distinguish the less from the more successful spoken attempts.

"Can you give me a concrete classroom example?"

Anecdote-telling Assessment Task   A teacher can determine much in the way of pre- and post-assessment by observing any of the activities described in this or other chapters. Consider, however, this example: a recorded telling of an anecdote to a friend in class. First, students would have listened to another child on tape tell anecdotes and would have reviewed this form. Each in the pair gets a turn. This task, relatively informal, allows children to speak from their own experience (a self-expressive form of discourse). Specifically, this task requires the pair not only to (1) depict events in the past, but (2) convey a perspective or point of view about these events and (3) make these interesting to a listener. The accomplished teller of anecdotes (4) alerts listeners to the speaker's perspective (tongue in cheek?) and the response expected (amusement? skepticism?).

"What specific criteria can I use for this anecdote task?"

Criteria follow that deal with organization, language, grammar, and performance features. **Organization** includes an opening component, telling the listener where and when the events to be related took place (context). After a clear account of the events (what happened and when), the anecdote concludes with a closing that sums up the point of the anecdote and indicates that it has reached its end. Less successful anecdotes leave the listener uncertain about the point and the response expected, and stop in mid-air with no punch line or satisfying conclusion.

A bonus regarding criteria can be **language** and vocabulary that "show" the listener with well-selected wording. This wording might be appropriately colloquial.

Complex **grammatical structure** other than past tense is not a necessary criterion in anecdote telling. *Ands* and *buts* will do nicely. Adverbial clauses of time and consequence are not necessarily required (e.g., "When we got there, we found . . ."). Again, the teacher evaluates appropriate use of language within the demands of the particular task; tasks also need to be lifelike and interesting.

For anecdote telling, a high level of performance may involve the following nonverbal criteria: stressing certain words for emphasis or contrast, pausing at appropriate points, orienting to the listener, and avoiding undue hesitation or self-correction. These aspects are particularly important in anecdote telling (MacLure & Hargreaves, 1986).

"What would a form or checklist for this kind of assessment look like?"

Forms and Checklists   To maintain informal records the teacher can use a form such as the following:

Form for Oral Language Assessment

Child's name _____   Date _____

Time of day _____   Activity or child's purpose _____

Setting _____

Others in group _____

Tape _____ counter # _____

Global impression _____

Analytical markings:
   —overall organization _____

   —key ideas and elements of meaning _____

   —grammatical structures _____

   —vocabulary _____

   —nonverbal or performance features _____

   —aspects special to this task or intent _____

   —key, illustrative samples of language _____

The activity book contains an example of a child's well-told anecdote.

"What are some other informal assessment devices I can use?"

Figure 4.6 is another sample assessment form, a checklist that you can adapt to the items you select from the framework of goals given in Appendix 4B. Note that the checklist in Figure 4.6 includes the following: both informal and formal situations, what, with whom, in what context, attitudes, and speech factors.

Finally, see Appendix 4A for a questionnaire for teachers constructed for oral language appraisal in the classroom. It asks you about your procedures; the child's process; uses, including problem solving; attitude; linguistic aspects; and your modeling, and your own ideas about what is worth assessing.

The next chapter, on drama, promises your classroom a self-expressive avenue so motivating of learning, so growth producing, that your students remember you gratefully for the rest of their lives.

In each of the following situations:	Situations						
	Informal Interactions to Formal interactions						
	With peers	With teachers	With other adults in school settings	In drama, role-playing activities	In small-group activities	In sharing time	In large-group activities
Does the child willingly participate orally?							
Does the child listen attentively to others?							
Are the child's contributions							
—relevant to the topic?							
—responsive to others?							
Does the child ask questions or request assistance?							
Does the child speak fluently, with apparent ease?							
Does the child speak audibly? Too loudly?							
Does the child use nonstandard forms?							
Does the child demonstrate an ability to change language style (word choice, pronunciations), particularly in role-playing activities?							

Figure 4.6   Checklist for observing children's use of oral language. (*Source:* Genishi & Dyson, 1984.)

SUMMARY

"If language is the clothing of life, no child should be sent naked into the world."

Daniel Fader

Your role as a teacher of oral language is to help children not only learn more ambitious ways *to* talk, but also *through* talk. Talking is a powerful tool for learning. Teachers and children can talk to each other daily about important issues. Talking/speaking is an entity that is integrated in terms of the other language arts and in the context of other academic areas.

Distinctions can be made among some common uses of words such as *talking, speaking, oral language, conversing,* and *oracy.* Purposeful, informal talking is as important as more formal modes. As illustrated in the opening scene, the expression of meaning occurs with an interaction among the language user, the message, and the context. The children in the opening scene used language in a social context rather than in an artificial one; they were not just trying to read the teacher's mind.

A strong case can be made against the silent classroom. Talking in the class encourages literacy development, social and emotional growth, and concept development for all content areas. Of course, it is of great importance to the increasingly varied and refined learning of oral language itself. Interactive child talk and plenty of it is crucial to education. This chapter furnishes the teacher with a resource for communicating with parents, administrators, and significant others.

From a developmental standpoint, teachers can adapt the methods of mothers who successfully "teach" their children informally. Teachers can also help students progress from egocentric to nonegocentric processes of oral communication and encourage them to overcome their natural hesitancy.

A framework of goals for the oral language program stresses (1) process, (2) purpose, and (3) attitude. To meet the process goal, students need to understand where (context), in what ways, with what meanings, and strategy (including self-assessment); then they bring together all of these parts. Thus successful speaking is a synchronized process using information from many different resources simultaneously. It is not the result of performing a series of discrete skills in sequence. Proficient strategy shows awareness of skills and resources needed to perform an oral task effectively. Proficient users differentiate strategies depending on the topic and purposes of the task. But without the motivational, attitudinal, and valuing dimension, little lasting learning occurs. Language learners need contexts providing something to say, a deep desire to say it, and someone to whom they really want to say it. Skilled oral language users are motivated and have confidence in their abilities to speak.

The successful classroom environment includes resource people with stimulating objects and enabling room arrangements to encourage productive talk and dialogue. Teachers can create an encouraging emotional climate by listening intently and expanding the language the student uses in a meaningful context, without imposing stifling correction. An enabling climate accepts the language the child brings to school and enriches it, for it is the child's means of survival.

The teaching role ("how") includes dialogue and coaching, providing and seeking, but also simply the role of a sincere, curious human who genuinely wants to talk with children. A key teaching role is believing in children's ownership of their learning through oral language use. Productive teaching also means knowing how to make various oral language *forms* familiar, try them out, talk them over, and try them again with reflection. Examples of these forms include conversation, show and tell, and story telling. Whatever the academic program, unit of study, or content activity, provide time and motivation for children to formulate and orally share their ideas with others.

Assessment of talking/speaking is best embedded in integrated language arts, such as natural tasks and situations calling for interactive communication. As illustrated in the section on anecdote telling, when students know that what they say will be heard, teachers most often observe them listening actively and respectfully and speaking often and confidently.

The overall goal of the language arts program is to give children the opportunity to experience themselves as thinking, communicating human beings. Learning this is a lifelong process. Our goals need to be long-range. Such learning is a *creative problem* you can continue to enjoy solving as you interact with children. First learn to know them, then orchestrate their classroom environment, and you are a long way toward helping children learn to communicate.

APPENDIX 4A   A Questionnaire for Prospective Teachers on Talking/Speaking: An Observational Tool (for Child and Self)

I. Procedures
  1. Do you have a system for jotting down observations immediately?
  2. Do you tape children's talk in both formal and informal situations?

II. Process
  3. In what ways does the child initiate conversation? Does the child speak only to one person or to a group?
  4. Does the child speak interactively or in a monologue or to give commands?
  5. What evidence does a given child display of tailoring speech for the intended listener?
  6. Have you noted facial expression, gestures, and other nonverbal responses that a child's talk elicits?

III. Use
  7. Do you observe children's *use* of language? Which of the categories of the framework of goals in Appendix 4B do the uses fit?
  8. Does a selected child use language to solve problems? If so, what steps of the problem-solving process are employed? Does the child make hypotheses?

IV. Attitude
  9. Has the child's use of language revealed an identifiable style?
  10. Is the child curious about language? For example, does the child ask about new words in the environment? (Collect instances.)
  11. Does the child use humor in language? (Collect instances.)

V. Linguistic Aspects
  12. What kinds of language structures does the child's recorded talk reveal (e.g., simple, compound, and complex sentences; further information is in the chapter on grammar and usage)?
  13. In what ways does the child ask questions? Does the child use the 6 *W*s and *H* & *I* questions (see p. 115)?
  14. In what ways does the child organize language? (Look for use of the organization of varied forms, e.g., of logical sequences of time, of cause-effect, of contrast.)
  15. What styles are in the child's repertory that you can observe (such as varied colloquial, literary, formal scientific, or humorous means of expression)?

VI. Personal
  16. Do you detect any effect of children modeling after your speaking voice and language?
  17. Other question(s) you think of.

APPENDIX 4B Speaking Framework of Goals and Subgoals*

To talk and speak effectively students need to:

Goal 1: *Understand and use stages of an interactive speaking* ***process.*** (Includes preparing and presenting speech; receiving and giving feedback)

Subgoals:

1.1. Identify and use context and background knowledge.
- Determining purpose appropriate to the oral language task
  Approached formally or informally; with one register or another; with one language form or another (e.g., literary, expository, self-expressive, or persuasive aims of spoken language)

1.2. Explore repertoire for the task, selecting criteria for making flexible choices.

1.3. Express fluently the meaning constructed.

1.4. Operate flexibly and effectively in a strategic manner.
- Monitoring and selecting strategy while being interactive with listeners' needs (e.g., attending to body language, intonation, pause, gesture; topic; and purpose)

1.5. Synchronize, independently tailoring a fluent and effective message while attending to parts of the process and demands of the situation—meaningful unity of *why, when,* and *how.*
- Noting cues or attributes of the audience, the context, topic, strategy, and forms of language, including appropriate usage, vocabulary
- Avoiding undue hesitancies and self-corrections

1.6. Assess orally for effectiveness of the exchange of meanings and accomplishment of purpose
- Recycling to parts of the above process as needed

Goal 2: *Talk/speak for a variety of specific* ***purposes*** *and their forms* (enlarging repertoire of communication acts). Examples are the following: informal to formal, small to larger groups and varied audiences, different communication forms (e.g., conversation, public speaking), and different speaking styles (e.g., impromptu, artistic reading—adapting content and formality level).

Subgoals:

2.1. Talk/speak to get things done.
- *Using self-expression* regarding control functions, instrumental use, satisfying material needs, regulatory use ("I want . . ."; "Do as I tell you . . .") (e.g., offering, commanding, threatening, warning, prohibiting, suggesting, formulating, permitting, intending, contracting
- *Restating, rehearsing,* and *reciting* in order to aid memory
- *Instructing/directing* (e.g., teaching partner how to play a board game or giving directions for a science experiment)
- *Persuading* influencing others to bring about some action or change (Chapter 10)

2.2. Share and explore the feelings and views of self and others.
- Using self-expression of feelings: personal ("Here I come . . ."), interactional ("you and me . . ."), exclamation, expression of state or attitude, approval, disapproval, commiseration, apology

2.3. Inform.
- Using exposition, representation ("I've got something to tell you . . ."), message, proposition or statement, information

Sources: California State Department of Education (1986); Fox & Allen (1983); Halliday (1976); Lundsteen (1976); MacLure & Hargreaves (1986); National Council of Teachers of English (1983); New York State Education Department (1984); Texas Education Agency (1984); Wells, (1975); Wolvin et al. (1985); and Wood (1977).

- Giving and interpreting information—relaying information (e.g., how a spider builds its web as heard first on tape); conveying information based on personal knowledge (e.g., an account of an occupation); conveying information based on observation (e.g., effects observed in an experiment); summarizing and conveying information from notes and pictures (e.g., extracting facts about crops to be grown); reporting the outcome of a collaborative project (e.g., steps taken and hypotheses developed during experiment)
- Describing/specifying (e.g., describing pictures for partner to identify, for comparison and information)
- Clarifying ideas by thinking aloud; semantic mapping (Chapter 7); questioning to acquire information; narrating for others an event or series of events (e.g., "show and tell," sharing, or "reporting," using visual aids, or perpetuating—"How it was")
- Questioning (e.g., yes-no question, content question, why questions, label question)
- Affirming, denying, or rejecting information
- Giving directions
- Explaining a process
- Using *heuristic* expression ("I'd like to know why . . ."; "What's the problem here?") seeking and testing knowledge; presenting arguments in an orderly and convincing way; evaluating evidence; speculating about possible alternatives; hypothesizing and justifying an argument
- Using discussions, panels, committees, and group problem solving; clarifying, qualifying and extending ideas

2.4 Use social conventions of speaking (how it must be done in our group or society).
- Exhibiting socially appropriate speech, ritualizing function, authoritative/contractual (examples: how to interrupt, add to a conversation, request help, make greetings, make farewells, take turns, request, repeat, introduce, welcome, acknowledge, challenge ideas of others)

2.5 Use the imagining function for artistic purposes. Literary, aesthetic, oral tradition of using language in a memorable, beautiful, entertaining and well-crafted way.
- Choosing *form* (e.g., word play, retelling a story, telling a personal anecdote, summarizing the plot of a book, constructing a story, choral reading, role-playing, puppetry, drama, reader's theatre); and using vocabulary and syntax appropriate to the form
- Interpreting literature written by others and self, creating a mood and varying tone (creating new worlds, "Let's pretend . . .")
- Entertaining and diverting (e.g., with puns, jokes, tongue twisters, and riddles)

Goal 3: *Develop a lasting, positive* **attitude** *toward talking/speaking.* (Becoming motivated for personal, social, academic, pragmatic, and professional reasons)
Subgoals:
3.1. Experience the satisfaction of talking/speaking and being understood.
3.2. Develop a curiosity about and interest in the talking/speaking process.
3.3. Choose talking/speaking not only as a means of communicating with others, but also as a means of learning, self-expression, and an aesthetic option.
3.4. Recognize the power of speech to get things done, to express self, to inform, to change attitude and behavior, to entertain, and to spark imagination.
3.5. Appreciate the significant role of oral expression in the creation and perpetuation of culture.

CHAPTER 5.

Drama

"Education is concerned with individuals; drama is concerned with the individuality of individuals.
Ultimately, theatre may always remain the concern of the few—*drama* will . . . become a way of teaching and a way of learning for everyone.
The most important . . . factor in the use of drama [in] . . . education is the *teacher.*"

Brian Way (italics added).

"What I had thought might be a chapter on performing was instead a chapter on growth and ways of learning that even a shy student would enjoy."

Cindie Aaen, a student

INTRODUCTION

Drama in the language arts classroom is renewing, refreshing, and revitalizing. The overall goal of drama, both as an art form and as a medium for learning and teaching, is to foster a positive self-concept in students that enhances communication. Informal drama in schools promotes children's self-image while it encourages them to explore life by assuming roles and acquiring drama skills. First, imaginative exploration sets up a dramatic situation, which children act out. They then communicate within that situation and reflect on consequences. Children's reflections on drama provide them knowledge for self-development.

Briefly, the goals of drama in the language arts curriculum are that students:

- acquire knowledge about themselves and others, stemming from reflections on dramatic play
- develop competency in communication skills through drama
- appreciate drama as an art form

Although some teachers effectively use drama as a teaching tool, providing a medium for integrated language arts learning, others have fears about using drama. This chapter is designed to put such fears to rest and to help you start where you'll feel comfortable. Using drama will help you move beyond safe but boring methods of instruction. The chapter provides a rationale, presents a sequential development of skills that clarifies the child's and the teacher's roles, and gives some appropriate resources. But major emphasis is on giving you a powerful teaching tool while allaying your fears.

Children are a joyful, cooperative resource in drama. They build on the richness of their imaginations and their natural willingness to accept the magic of drama that is found in well-loved stories, poems, historic tales, and their own experience. Children's minds are something like small lanterns, probing the surrounding darkness of ignorance and illuminating what intrigues them and what fits with the sometimes tiny circle of their knowns. Drama can help children increase their circles of enlightened human experience. Children are motivated by what they have struggled to express in drama, and such motivation enables learning that adds to their brightened world.

What Is Drama About?

To define briefly, drama is joyful learning through action, reflection, personal and vicarious experience, cooperation, presentation, and reflective discussion. Drama belongs in the classroom, not just the theater. It involves children in working together within the framework of a situation to build their own story, so that they can discover why people behave the way they do, and then can reflect on their own behavior. Drama encourages affective development and divergent, creative thinking in all the language arts. Finally, drama acts as both a microscope and a prism. Just as a microscope focuses on a small aspect of an organism and enlarges it, so can drama. Just as a prism separates a beam of light into a spectrum of colors, so can drama as it helps children see a whole spectrum of the physical and emotional aspects of life.

When Do I Have the Time?

You have time for drama activities because they are already included in language arts, social studies, science, and other areas. As a teaching tool, drama integrates well with the rest of the school curriculum. Further, you are not wasting the time of many for the benefit of a few, because every child in your class is usually working on drama *at the same time,* not just observing. You can orchestrate the drama time this way because you are more intent on *process* than on performance and product.

Why Is Drama a Useful Tool for the Teacher?

Oral verbal ability is the cornerstone for building all the language arts skills, and drama encourages talk that is both meaningful and educational for children. Drama also is a highly productive tool for developing knowledge, self-enhancement, and recognition of others. These are some of the reasons, along with the integrative effect and power of drama as a tool for learning, that prompt the inclusion of drama in the language arts curriculum, and that induce states such as Texas to declare drama an essential curriculum element and require the teaching of it. Let's briefly elaborate on each reason. (Advantages that result from the integration of drama are detailed toward the end of the chapter.)

Oral Verbal Ability   Drama helps children become proficient talkers and improves their spontaneous oral composition abilities. Even when very young children engage in dramatic play, they are required to present themselves to the other participating children. In their dramatic roles, they have to be aware of others' desires as they engage in what needs to be informative and comprehensible dialogue (Verriour, 1986). With impromptu invention, children get practice in thinking on their feet and expressing themselves fearlessly. Such expression forms the roots of leadership and organizational ability. With drama, children have a chance to achieve a genuine goal of language instruction: not just fluent talk, but speech that exhibits depth of perception, clarity of observation, and eloquence of expression. A child participating in drama is challenged to develop clear focus, produce apt responses with melody and rhythm, exhibit more sensitive attitudes, use appropriate and affective phrasing and precise vocabulary, handle multiple meanings, and employ convincing argument.

Self-Enhancement and Recognition of Other   Since a child thinks "my language is me," drama can enhance the self-image of the language user. Going beyond the *me* by improvising dialogue for a variety of persons, drama also shows children that different people speak in varied ways, using different body language with varied results. Such a broadened understanding is a valuable language arts learning goal. Emotionally therapeutic, drama is also important because it can be a positive and negative energy release that is socially acceptable. For example, puppets can help children express emotions otherwise frowned upon or frightening. Through a puppet, a child can evoke a monster that appeared in a nightmare last night, and treat it just as it deserves. Thus, drama provides an avenue for safely trying out many kinds of decisions. A child with emotional equilibrium contributing to self-esteem is ready for learning language arts.

Is the central concern in your region a call for "back to the basics"? What is basic? Drama is basic. Your rationale for using drama has many aspects; the preceding reasons are just a few instances. You and your students will discover others.

How Do I Begin?

You begin where it feels most comfortable, providing children opportunities for experience in the use of body and voice, creative drama, and aesthetic growth. You plan lessons compatible with your own teaching style, considering class size, space, time, and control needed for your lesson objectives. You select from ideas in this chapter and the related activity book, from the children, and from other suggested resources.

This chapter invites you to explore the *why, who, where, what,* and *how* of teaching drama. Most of these organizing categories are touched on in the following opening scene.

OPENING SCENE: A Dramatic Response to Literature

Chris Anderson shook a ribbon-bedecked tambourine, finishing with three clattery thumps—the signal for drama time. Well practiced, the children quickly pushed back the fourth-grade classroom furniture to the outermost limits and gathered in a circle near the teacher's spotlight, which was painted on the floor. The teacher in the spotlight began with the customary warm-up for drama, this time asking students to shake out parts of their bodies, soliciting from the class suggestions of what part to shake next, with tambourine accompaniment.

At four thumps on the tambourine, growing increasingly softer, and with the ensuing silent concentration from the children, the teacher gave a brief one-person demonstration of readers' theater, using the book *Sam,* by Ann Herbert Scott. The teacher did not conclude the story, but stopped at its climax. Readers' theater—or book-in-hand drama—is usually characterized by the following: The teacher first scripts the book, omitting the *he saids* and *she saids.* Then, sitting on a stool and using a music stand to hold the book, the teacher focuses on a point just beyond the audience while in the role of narrator, and changes voice and uses head movements to indicate different characters. (Note: Readers' theater usually offers many roles, with each child reading a different one.)

Thus, as the teacher read, the class experienced Sam's repeated frustration as, in turn, mother, brother, sister, and finally daddy rejected his overtures to play and sent him to someone else. Then they experienced Sam's bursting into tears when being sent by daddy full circle back to his mother.

At this climactic stopping place, the teacher asked the children to close their eyes and image Sam and his trials of the day. They were to think of the things about Sam that stood out for them. Then at a soft, almost whispering, shivering of the tambourine, children arose slowly and found their own play space, a space where they could stretch out their arms and move around slowly without touching anyone. With *side coaching,* the teacher suggested to the children, "Be Sam, playing on his own as in the opening illustration of the book." The children's physical movement continued for about 15 seconds. At a shake of the tambourine and one thump, all the children froze in the form of an action tableau, a stationary pose communicating an idea or part of a story.

Next the teacher numbered the class off, 1, 2, 1, 2. Ones were to play the role of the mother, twos were to play the role of Sam. Pairs sat down and for three minutes discussed the two characters, the setting, the actions, the way Sam may have picked up the knife, its weight, the ways the mother might have shown displeasure. At the tambourine signal, the teacher read the scene and the pairs pantomimed the action at the same time.

At another tambourine signal, the pairs switched roles and the teacher read the script again, inviting an additional enactment. The teacher had the children give each scene a title, and class scribes listed them on a transparency. The teacher repeated the procedure, beginning with the 15-second warm-up and tableau, through all of the scenes until the preclimax one with the daddy. At this time the teacher invited all the children to make up their own dialogue between father and son as Sam pantomimed pushing down the keys of the typewriter, triggering his father's irritation. ("Sammy, stop that! Typewriters are not for banging on. It would cost me a lot of money to fix it. Go find Mama!")

Again, the tambourine signal brought quiet and led the children from their paired dramatizations back to the circle for reflection and assessment. Different volunteer pairs shared before the entire group each of the tableaux for the listed scenes in order, re-creating the whole story up to the climax, like a series of camera shots.

Next, during reflective group discussion, the teacher and children commented on the freezes held in the tableaux, the pantomime of the father turning pages in his newspaper, and the convincing crying of Sam at the climax. They discussed the different interpretations, drawing on personal, related experiences.

Next the teacher asked what the children thought Sam's main problem was, as illustrated by all the little episodes of conflict they had observed. The many main problem statements were accepted by the teacher and recorded on a transparency, where they could be read, remembered, and reflected upon by all. ("His problem is he's lonely." "He thinks no one loves him." "He needs someone to play with—his own age.")

Since interest was still high, the teacher asked the students to pick a problem and think of solutions. Pairs were numbered off, 1, 2, 1, 2, and then shared their ideas orally with each other. ("Get him a dog." "Learn how not to mess up." "Go to a preschool." "Find some neighbor friends." "Get a new family.") The teacher and a volunteer improvised on one of the solutions ("Get him a dog"), creating dialogue.

The lesson concluded with some deep, relaxing breathing to tambourine whispers. This signal helped the children settle down. Then they were ready for a group critique of the day's work and a few plans for what they might do next. The following dialogue is from their discussion.

> TEACHER: Was the *enactment* of the story, *Sam,* satisfying to you? What are your reactions?
> KARINA: Yes, I could follow the story fine when we had all our tableaux. (Others nod in agreement.)
> TIM: We really froze in the tableau . . . and held our eyes right where they should be. . . .
> CHUNG: I liked the tableau best from the last scene, when the family all comes when Sam

cries. In space . . . some of us were high in our positions, some middle, and some low in the scene. I liked the way Sam . . . held his body. (Others nod and murmur in agreement.)

RODERICK: I liked the beginning, lots of cartwheels and headstands, and the ending scene. . . . They were the best.

TEACHER: What did you think about the *characterizations?*

KARINA: I could really tell who was Sam in Chung's group . . . and he really looked sad!

CHUNG: I thought almost all of us really made each character . . . different. You could tell who we were supposed to be.

TEACHER: [Encouraged by Tim's earlier and unusual response.] Tim, I can see by your face that you are having some more thoughts about this. Would you share your ideas with us?

TIM: [Shakes head.]

TEACHER: You're a keen observer, Tim. I'll come back to you later.

JOSEPHINE: I liked the way the father moved, but I think his voice . . . it could be deeper next time.

TEACHER: Was there anything else you noticed about the *dialogue?*

TEDDY: I liked the dialogue in the last scene . . . the one you and Roderick just did. You talked about solving Sam's problem by getting him a puppy; it sounded real.

KARINA: I know just how Sam felt. I know just how my little sister feels . . . sometimes; now I know some words to help her.

The teacher ended the activity with a shake and slap on the thigh of the tambourine. At this signal, the class went into their usual routine of quickly moving the furniture back, and, refreshed and renewed, they entered into the next portion of their daily schedule.

Some ideas generated just before the end and during future drama sessions included the following: working further in voice characterization by listening to and collecting voices on tape; pantomiming solutions; writing a description of their drama experiences for the day (adding to journals); transferring and writing about their *own* experiences when they felt left out, like Sam; finishing reading copies of the story themselves to see what the author did; working at a puppet-making center and choosing from among many techniques—finger puppets, paper bag or plate puppets, stick puppets—in order to render the story in this medium; and preparing for a readers' theater group that might tour the lower grades and library if the *children themselves* wanted to. Other activities the teacher suggested were looking for more stories related to the theme of *Sam* for possible scripting or tableaux. The last book they had adapted for drama was *The Friendly Wolf,* by the Gobles; it had led right into their social studies unit on life and lore of the early plains Indians.

Analysis of the Scene

First of all, portions of this drama lesson are typical: (1) the routines for making space and attending to safety, (2) the warm-up, (3) the imaging, (4) the individual work, (5) the group work, (6) the calming down with relaxation and reflecting, and (7) the follow-ups or variations. Second, this opening scene could have occurred, with some adaptation, at any number of age levels. Third, the integration of listening, speaking, reading, and writing was apparent in the activities.

The teacher, displaying a number of techniques, sometimes used modeling to introduce new activities and used side coaching to stimulate, encourage, and reinforce. We saw the use of pantomime, tableaux, pair planning, simultaneous playing, improvisation of dialogue, a bit of the strategy of readers' theater, reflective group discussion, and *problem solving*. We saw the teacher guiding reflective assessment with focus questions on the enactments and tableaux, characterization, and dialogue. Finally, we saw children gaining understanding of themselves and others. Thus we saw drama functioning as both a microscope and a prism.

DEFINITIONS

Children's drama lessons fall somewhere between two extremes of play and theater. Young children's play tends to be spontaneous, with relatively little structure or adult guidance. At the other extreme, children's theater characteristically relies on the structure of a ready-made script that leaves little room for student initiative. Children's drama sessions, providing some adult stimulation, guidance, and direction, capitalize on the strengths, creativity, and autonomy that children bring to the experience. The creative yet educationally appropriate forms to be stressed and discussed here are: *structured dramatic play; movement* (dramatic movement, mime); and *movement with speaking* (creative drama, puppetry, readers' theater, play making, and group drama). See Figure 5.1. (If you are already familiar with these terms, skip ahead.)

Dramatic Play

Dramatic play, usually initiated by the child, is a common experience during the preschool years. (See the beginning of the continuum in Figure 5.1.) This make-believe activity of young children is spontaneous and plotless, needs no audience, and has no set sequence.

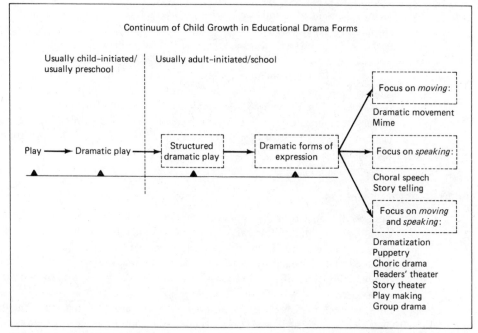

Figure 5.1 Continuum of child growth in educational drama forms. (*Source:* Alberta, 1985.)

In this process children take on the feelings, attitudes, and actions of a person or thing. While using themselves as symbols, children develop physical, emotional, and intellectual identification with a fictitious situation (Alberta, 1985). Children assuming the role of a person, animal, or thing may shift instantly, according to impulse. For example, young children can play getting off to work by using an easel (to mark off a corner of the room), breakfast utensils, and an adult's jacket, briefcase, and "car keys." All these items may instantly turn into the setting for a diner on a highway. Young children's natural inclination to use drama as a way of knowing is the root of the planned program in creative drama coming later in school. In dramatic play the child's role is usually *initiator/participator* and the adult's role is *observer/provider*.

Children's Theater

At the other end of the continuum, children's theater is product-oriented. Performances are for the entertainment of others, placing constraints and pressures on children. In children's theater, students act out and are locked into the lines of a script, complete with staging and acting directions, over which they have had no control. As it does not serve developmental and educational needs of many and is not a tool for curriculum learning, children's theater is not the concern of this chapter. The child's role in children's theater is mainly *memorizer/enacter* and the adult's role is *director*.

Structured Dramatic Play

Structured dramatic play, next in line on the continuum, encompasses a range of introductory drama games, exercises, and activities that prepare the child imaginatively and behaviorally for participation in further drama forms. Through structured dramatic-play activity, children learn to follow directions and work productively on a focus, both as individuals and as cooperative members of a group. A focus can be on the physical (body and voice), on an emotion (its exploration, control, and expression), and on the intellectual (imagination, concentration, intuition/divergence/convergence). The teacher in the role of planner/guider may use techniques of improvisation, group play in which all children work simultaneously, role-playings, side coaching, and tableaux. Tableaux refers to the creation of individual, pair, or group stationary poses communicating an idea, emotion, or part of a story. Side coaching is done by an observant and verbal bystander. All of these features were illustrated in the opening scene, and further examples are found in the *how* section of this chapter. Since structured dramatic-play activities are essential starting points for drama experiences with any school-age group, teachers develop, review, and reinforce such skills on a continuing basis at all levels. The child's role is usually *participant/responder* and the adult's role is *guider/planner*.

Dramatic Forms of Expression

Dramatic forms of expression include those with a focus on moving (dramatic movement, pantomime) and those with a focus on moving *and* speaking (dramatization, puppetry, readers' theater, play making, and group drama). The child's role in each of the dramatic forms becomes *participant/communicator/evaluator* and the adult's role becomes *instructor/evaluator*. (A form with a focus on speaking—story telling—was discussed in Chapter 4; choral speech is covered in the activity book.)

Focus on Movement   Dramatic movement, a form of physical communication coordinating mind, body, and imagination, provides for exploration and expression of inner feelings and reaction to sensory experience. For example, in one introductory lesson children learn about personal space (as far out as your arms can reach without moving your feet). They also learn about general space (shared by pairs, small groups, and the whole group). In the opening scene we saw a focus on dramatic movement when the children "became" Sam playing by himself at the beginning of the story.

Pantomime, a silent art form, uses the body as an instrument of communication to translate observations of humans into movement and gesture. Thus it is an expression of doing, feeling, and reacting without words. As an art form, it requires great concentrated effort and is not perfected at the elementary school level. Children pantomiming spontaneously, however, become increasingly adept at telling a simple story by this means.

Pantomime might start with a simple prop and one action and develop into whole scenes; it may start with one child and end up with the whole group interacting (Lundsteen, 1976). Examples might be animal mime; occupational mime; the noting of weight, texture, and resistance of objects; and character mime (physical characteristics and ways of nonverbal communication).

Focus on Moving and Speaking   Forms in this category include dramatization, puppetry, readers' theater, play making, and group drama.

Dramatization (listed in the last column in Figure 5.1) is an activity wherein teachers guide children to improvise an informal drama from a story or poem. Children create scenes with improvised dialogue and action. We had an example in the opening scene using the book *Sam*. Dramatization, sometimes called creative drama, is a more mature, leader-structured, group-centered form of spontaneous dramatic play. Dramatization, like dramatic play, is oriented to process, not performance. The emphasis is on drama as a communication skill rather than an art form. Dramatization stresses improvisation where children work together within a framework (say of a poem or a teacher's beginning) to build their own story. There is no absolute "right" or "wrong" response. Sometimes also referred to as informal classroom drama, this mode has students inventing and enacting spontaneously generated dramatic situations for themselves rather than for an outside audience. They perform a dual role of composing and enacting their parts as the drama progresses, unrehearsed, for the benefit of the participants. The teacher sets the framework and leads this guided discovery (NCTE/CTA, 1983; Agency for Instructional Television, N.D.).

In essence, then, dramatization is a teacher-led group experience with children enacting events. These events may be extended from children's literature or their own lives as students take on the roles of the characters. The events form a *plot* that builds toward a *climax*. But the enactment is improvised—without script or memorized lines—and is not played the same way twice. The absence of prewriting, memorizing, and formal audience is an important and deliberate distinction to be desired. In dramatization, the mainstay of the elementary drama program, the authors, players, and audience are one (Lundsteen, 1976).

Puppetry is an art form in which a child can give an inanimate object the appearance of life by manipulating it. Children can apply previously learned skills of movement, dialogue, story enactment, and characterization to this form. Then they can transfer its highly motivating use to many other subject areas. For example, children can read to a puppet; let it reflect home talk, school talk, and book talk; let it act out math problems;

costume a puppet for a social studies unit; and let it "guard" and report on observations concerning a science experiment.

Readers' theater is a form of oral interpretation that presents a group of readers performing works of literature using voice and gesture. Though "book-in-hand theater" is not as creative perhaps as improvisation in dramatization and in group drama, teachers can involve children in finding, scripting, and planning the performance. (Seven steps to readers' theater are given later in this chapter.)

Play making tends to be developed by one or a few children acting as playwrights, struggling and composing, using elements of a play. Building on the earlier dramatic forms, play making allows students to originate, shape, and communicate a dramatic story. A variety of sources to stimulate this play construction might be news articles, photos, a "composting" of literature, videotapes, songs, history and other content area readings, and (most importantly) children's own experience. Students decide on a situation, cast, and initial setting; explore, select, and sequence episodes; and refine the play. They do this in terms of theatrical elements such as theme, conflict, mood, darkness/light, movement/stillness, sound/silence, and props. Presentation can be, again, in groups, not for the whole class.

Group drama involves the children as a group taking *roles,* trying to step into someone else's shoes. The group-played roles drive the activity. The group interaction practically takes on a life of its own as the members of the group respond to each other. Group drama, then, is an activity in which student autonomy and decision making are highly prominent. Building on all previous drama learning, the teacher guides the class in coopera-tive building of a drama from scratch. The emphasis is on creating the drama from the *inside out,* for understanding more than for presentation. Steps are as follows: (1) planning, (2) building belief, (3) empowering students in decision making, (4) creating tension and conflict, (5) speaking in role, (6) reflecting on the meaning of the topic to oneself, (7) gaining insight, and (8) logging the experience (Alberta, 1985).

Thus *drama* is a factor in education, and *theater* is a sophisticated art form to be appreciated. Drama in the classroom is concerned with the logical behavior of humans; theater concerns the rearrangement of that behavior for an illusion of logic on a stage, with its illogical conventions. Theater is largely concerned with communication between actors and an audience; drama is largely concerned with experience of and by the participants. Any child can do drama since development, not performance, is the aim (Way, 1967). Drama is informal, appropriate for the classroom, and process-oriented; children's theater is far more product-oriented.

With drama and many of its forms defined, the next task is to look at a developmental reminder.

WHO ARE THE STUDENTS IN DRAMA?

Dramatic growth parallels the natural development of the students as they grow in their use of imagination and aesthetic appreciation. Figure 5.1, presented earlier, indicates that drama originates in home play. From those beginnings, children characteristically develop capabili-ties for drama in many ways as they move outward from self to the larger world. This section explains developmentally appropriate experiences for younger to older, more experienced children. A final aspect deals briefly with the functions a child displays as a member of a group.

Developmental Capabilities

The following are categories and examples of developing capabilities used in drama:

Physical   Children characteristically grow in the following physical capabilities important to drama: gross and fine motor development, sensory awareness (which may later become dulled), selective use of senses, sound production, and use of the voice as an instrument.

Intellectual and Linguistic   Children characteristically grow in the following *intellectual* capabilities: concentration span (highly crucial in drama learning), spontaneous response, sustaining of focus and role, use of imagination, distinction between fiction and reality, planning in problem solving, expressive language, and aesthetic appreciation. Expressive *language* development relates to capability in sensing what to say during drama time and how to say it so as to enhance action. Young children in early stages of drama may not feel any need for language. They may make plans for playing out an episode, yet do it without talking, except for possible sound effects. Children come to feel a need for language to support and carry an enacted plot along. Through drama, children develop an ear for powerful language.

Emotional   Children characteristically grow in emotional capabilities, such as control of extremes of reaction, expression, and empathy. Many of these factors may become dulled, repressed, almost snuffed out as age increases. The younger the children, usually the more they need emotional security and order to offset any fears during drama instruction. The older the children, the more we may need to rekindle emotional sensitivity and expression.

Social   Children characteristically grow in such social capabilities as enjoyment of interactive, imaginative play. Children move toward more finely negotiated drama work with others and deeper exploration of age, cultural, and occupational roles. Be alert to overuse of stereotyping of sexes and of the elderly, and the danger of ethnic insult (Alberta, 1985). Achievement-oriented, the 6- to 11-year-old usually likes to produce and takes pleasure in work. Anxieties characteristic of this period are eased through play presentation ("I am not alone. . . . There is a group of us . . . a drama group"). Knowing where each child is in regard to these growth areas gives implications for appropriate and effective drama teaching. Table 5.1 is a portion of a sample chart doing just that.

Circles of Progressive Experience

The child moves into drama learning through circles of progressive drama experience affected by physical, intellectual, and emotional growth. Recall the earlier analogy of the child's mind being like a small lantern casting a small circle of light. The learning of drama needs to start with this first small circle, representing the discovery of one's *own resources*. After this discovery comes an outward release and a progressive mastery of these resources. *Self* becomes the displayed character.

At a later age and stage, as the light from the child's "lantern" grows larger, experience includes another circle—*discovery and exploration of one's environment.* For example, place ultimately becomes the "setting." In that environment the child begins to see and grow sensitive to other people.

In the next circle, at a still later age, the child needs and uses the *enrichment of other*

Table 5.1 SOME CHARACTERISTICS OF CHILD DEVELOPMENT IN DRAMA

Characteristics (the child)	Implications for drama (the teacher)	Examples of dramatic activity
Grades K–2 (ages 5–8)		
Physical		
Is very active; is usually in control of gross motor and developing fine motor skills	Provides space and time for intense physical activity alternately with quiet, relaxed moments	Children move freely about the room, exploring Levels, i.e., high/low Space, i.e., small/large Time, i.e., fast/slow then relax on the floor
Is developing sensory awareness	Introduces many and varied sensory experiences	Children listen for three distinct sounds outside
Is able to produce most of the sounds	Provides opportunities to explore alternative sounds	Teacher tells story, children supply sounds
Intellectual		
Has a short concentration span	Provides short, varied activities using repetition and ritual	Children act out the physical movements of characters in a story; discuss; then act out the story
Responds spontaneously	Allows opportunity for spontaneous acting out, as well as reflection on what was done	Without planning, children act out a situation, then discuss the dramatized character's feelings as related to self
May still have some difficulty distinguishing between fiction and reality	Gives opportunities for both exploration of real world and imaginative play	Children act out sequence of events or problems anticipated on a field trip or dramatize a fairy tale
Has an adequate vocabulary to get along in world but limited for expression of feeling and thought	Builds confidence in speaking and provides experiences so that there is a reason to communicate orally	Children discuss drama experiences with a partner first, then share in the larger group
Emotional		
Leaves self open to a variety of emotional responses; expresses emotions readily; given to extremes in emotional reaction; responds to rhythm	Provides understanding and vicarious experiences for experiencing strong feelings	Children dramatize fairy tales or nursery rhymes as they are recited or other situations where strong feelings are expressed
Becomes aware of personal feelings and begins to recognize the attitudes of others (sensitivity developing)	Leads students into conscious reflection of their personal responses and recognition of the signs that tell about others' feelings	Teacher assists students in making connections between their acting out and their everyday responses through questioning—"Have you felt as angry as the . . . ? What did you do?"
Needs security and order to offset real fears	Sets up routines and provides much guidance and positive reinforcement	When students enter drama time they move desks aside, sit on floor, close eyes, and wait for teacher

Table 5.1 (*Continued*)

Characteristics (the child)	Implications for drama (the teacher)	Examples of dramatic activity
Social		
Is preoccupied with individual play, "I" stage; becomes increasingly able to work with others	Works with entire class as a group or groups within the personal world they are experiencing Avoids having formal audiences	Students all experience being parents (attending to chores) before they break into parent/child pairs and act out scene at home
Explores roles, i.e., male/female, occupational	Provides physical activities in a variety of role experiences	Students mime activities pertaining to a particular occupation
Enjoys imaginative play, fantasy	Encourages input from class for dramatic ideas	Teacher and students develop a story to act out
Learns behavior appropriate to the social situation	Provides a wide variety of social contexts for dramatic experiences	Students role-play royalty one day and servants the next
	Grades 3–4 (ages 8–10)	
Physical		
Action becomes controlled; has developed finer and finer motor skills	Provides activities that involve isolated body parts	Through mime, children demonstrate the use of imagined objects
Continues developing sensory awareness	Provides students opportunities to use sense experiences to enhance their drama work	Students create a sound story
Is discovering the voice as an instrument	Provides exercises for students to practice control of vocal production	Children orally read poem using light/dark group voices (antiphonal)
Intellectual		
Is able to concentrate for longer periods of time	Allows more time for a given activity	Teacher presents open-ended story; in groups students create original ending
Starts more and more conscious planning	Develops longer, more involved activities; allows more independence	Students may dramatize a story one day and work out an alternative ending on the following day
Starts utilizing more and more realism	Encourages exploration of man-made disasters, natural disasters, travel, humor	In a group drama, students explore the problems of a pioneer settlement
Language shows a marked development; can reason more abstractly	Continues to encourage sharing of ideas verbally and consideration of alternatives	Group in circle tells cumulative story

Source: Adapted from Alberta, 1985.

influences and *resources*. Examples are: the story becoming a studied "plot"; addition of the taught concept of "conflict"; and the inclusion of props, scenery, and costume, all creating "spectacle." The child gets to such enrichment through the use of developmental capabilities (e.g., physical, intellectual, linguistic, social/emotional).

    Figure 5.2 shows these ideas in the form of outwardly expanding circles, with the child in the center and the developmental abilities arranged around the outer circle. The dotted lines represent the absence of any hard and definite division in this outward movement. In fact, a more accurate representation may not be neat circles but a wavering in and out as some areas of development excel and others lag behind in each individual. All of these ideas

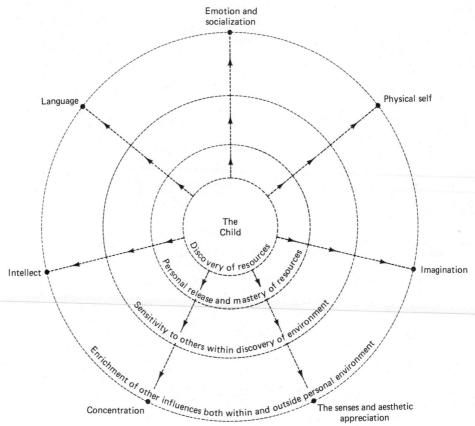

Figure 5.2 Progressive circles of a drama-learning experience facilitated by areas of development. (*Source:* Way, 1967.)

not only give the teacher a framework for thinking about each child, but also provide a rationale as to where to start drama instruction and where to go next.

Concentration and Audience

Perhaps the key developmental capability in Figure 5.2 is intellectual *concentration.* The more complete the concentration, the higher the quality of individual effort in drama. (See the children in Figure 5.3. One child is trying to mimic the movement of the other.)

One major factor interfering with concentration is *audience.* The moment a child has an audience watching, concentration gets divided. For this reason drama instruction protects the children from audiences until they are ready to avoid the distraction of being watched.

Function of the Child in Drama

Some of the child's functions in drama might be labeled the following: (1) communicator, (2) critic, (3) participant, (4) signaler, (5) negotiator, (6) initiator, and (7) seeker. Figure 5.4 shows these functions or roles. Some of them may develop earlier in a child's life than others.

Figure 5.3 Concentration in mirroring activity.

The figure also shows that the child is both the learner and the teacher in the dramatic enterprise, responding and modifying behavior in all of these various ways. Again, the dotted lines indicate that there are no hard, definite categories; that is, a child may be using several of these functions almost simultaneously during a class drama session. Moreover, there can be internal differences as to which roles a child plays in a day.

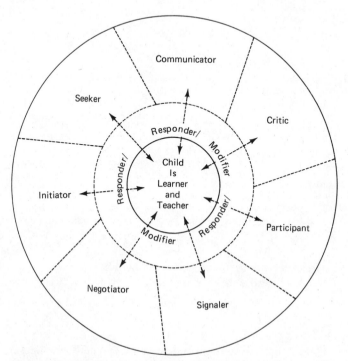

Figure 5.4 Some functions of the child in the drama session. (*Source:* Alberta, 1985.)

WHAT PROCESSES, GOALS, AND MATERIALS ARE USEFUL
TO DRAMA INSTRUCTION?

This section briefly mentions five goals of classroom drama. Without a strong grasp of goals, the classroom flounders.

1. *Self-discovery* of positive inner resources
2. A *way of knowing* becoming a tool of learning
3. *Sensitivity* to and *communication* with *others*
4. *Forms* of drama as a content area
5. Positive *attitude* leading to aesthetic appreciation

The *process* of drama, a key part of a framework of goals, gives form and meaning to experience through enactment, an important way of knowing. This framework moves from uncovering one's own resources to a process way of knowing, to a sensitivity to others in the drama environment, to a study of drama and its forms as a subject in its own right. These goals contribute to a positive attitude toward drama, paving the way for aesthetic appreciation of dramatic art. Thus the goals are developmental and reflect the earlier considerations of the *who* (Figure 5.2).

The framework detailed in Appendix 5A states these goals and gives some subgoals and objectives. No inflexible linear sequence is intended for teaching. Some children can integrate and touch on all goals almost at once and at any age. Prepared with goals, we can next consider the classroom environment.

WHERE CAN DRAMA TAKE PLACE?

In our opening scene, drama instruction was taking place right in the *classroom.* With our definition of drama and a developmental perspective for children in mind, there is only one *wrong* place for drama—a formal theater setting. Avoid a conventional picture-frame stage raised up at one end of a large room (Way, 1967). The best location for drama is one that is in tune with the children's natural development and is well signaled, well spaced, and protected. There the children can explore, discover, and master their own resources.

As shown in the opening scene, you may need to establish a routine and signals with the children for a quick and efficient clearing of needed space, often entailing pushing back of desks and chairs. (This aspect is also part of the *how* of teaching drama.) In some cases you will need to establish safe physical boundaries and guidelines as to where children can work at drama. Some find starting right at their desks comforting and nonthreatening; space-clearing signals can be added later.

Introduce and reinforce consistent control signals for beginning and ending activities (as the teacher in the opening scene did). Avoid getting too theatrical about these control signals, thus making students become self-conscious. (For example, avoid announcing "Curtain up!" or "Give the actors a hand.") Remember, at the beginning of drama instruction in your classroom, the teacher is totally in control. Responsibilities are delegated to students as they are ready for them. Such control does not mean, however, that the teacher is going to tell children exactly how to enact.

What kind of space is needed? Imaginatively speaking, what is needed is a space "where anything can happen" (Way, 1967). Moreover, a place is needed where all class members can be working at the same time, in one large or a few small groups, each group finding its own space. A space is needed where children can develop and maintain concentration. Though you need free space, remember that young children may be afraid of too vast a location. Use desks and furniture in the classroom by working under and over them to create differing levels of space and recesses. Children may assume roles of very small children or animals exploring their classroom for the first time. Suggest that the children explore for the following:

1. Safety (Where are the danger spots?)
2. Structure
3. Texture (What did their hands feel? What did they discover?)
4. Hiding places

What about the audience and protection from its pressures? It is more important for children to solve problems of cramped conditions creatively than to force them to have audiences before they are ready. Keep discussion and exchanges as close together in space as possible so that there is no problem about being heard from distant parts of the classroom. When the class develops to the point of sharing small-group work, again, avoid any conventional theater stage playing area. For example, let the sharing area be in the *center* of the room, so children can avoid playing self-consciously outward in one direction. Move swiftly and informally from one sharing group to the next. Listeners can sit naturally in any part of the room in which they were working. Finally, protect children from visitors until concentration is so strong that it cannot be readily undermined (Way, 1967). Instruct any necessary visitors in the climate and philosophy of educational classroom drama.

HOW CAN I TEACH DRAMA?

Now that you know about the *why, who, what,* and *where* of teaching drama, you are ready for the *how.* Recall the first quote of the beginning of this chapter: "The most important single factor in the use of drama as a genuine part of education is the *teacher.*" Unless you know your individual students, you are less likely to be successful in teaching drama. The form of drama that your children will be ready for and your functions depend on the maturity level of the child. Keeping the knowing of the learners in mind is the first task; preparing the drama space (including control signals) is the second. Now look at some of the general functions of the teacher in drama. How does the teacher behave?

Functions of the Teacher in Drama

Both teacher and child fulfill differing roles before, within, and following learning experiences, with interactive effects. Figure 5.5 presents functions the teacher displays when planning for and using drama. Knowing these roles, a teacher can more effectively understand, choose, and use them.

Teaching functions are labeled: (1) reflector, (2) observer, (3) assessor, (4) signaler, (5) negotiator, (6) strategist, and (7) seeker (Alberta, 1985). Comparing Figures 5.4 and 5.5, you will see that signaler and negotiator roles appear for both teacher and children. Note also that while the child is first the learner and then the teacher, the teacher is first the teacher and then the learner. Additionally, during the drama session, while the child responds then modifies, the teacher plans then assesses. Both recycle over and over. Again, the dotted lines indicate there are no hard, definite categories; a teacher may be using several

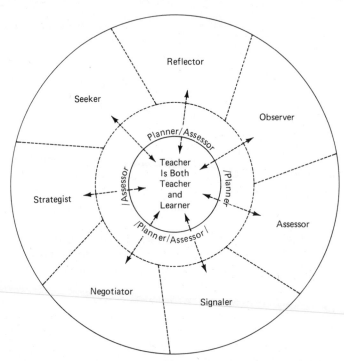

Figure 5.5 Some functions of the teacher in the drama session.
(*Source:* Alberta, 1985.)

of the functions during a drama session almost simultaneously. Some of these roles will be much more comfortable for you than others. Start with a role that fits your style and grow into others gradually. The list in Appendix 5B explains teaching functions and uses examples from the opening scene for this chapter.

Fears   Fears plague the functioning of some teachers. Some teachers are afraid to enter into the dramatization with older children, afraid of losing the children's respect, appearing ridiculous, or simply not being creative enough. Pretending is natural for most children of any age. Expect them to become involved and they will. For example: A teacher stoops down, picks up a child's dropped pencil, and not only puts it on his desk but says to the pencil, "My, you had a nasty fall; how was it down there? Not too dusty I hope. You'll soon be feeling better once Ted holds you again." The teacher winks at the student and walks on, while the student grins, picks up the pencil, and pats it. Such a teacher is really appreciated, not disrespected.

As for not being creative, we are all far more creative than we may give ourselves credit for being. We were born creative problem solvers with a high potential for imagination. Some of our wheels of creativity may need a little "oiling" by suggestions and a bit of use, but we can get them going again. Enter into drama and you will find new energy, new sensitivity, and a loss of fear.

Some of the role characteristics of a successful drama teacher are flexibility, ability to listen, ability to ask stimulating questions, and commitment (Stewig, 1983). These characteristics thread through all of the mentioned functions of reflector, observer, assessor, signaler, negotiator, strategist, and seeker. You might boil all teaching functions down to two: (1) discovering what children already want to do in a drama context and letting them do it; (2) helping them discover new things to do while being encouraging (Way, 1967).

Program Planning

This section on program planning for the teaching of drama considers materials and a center to house them. It also considers planning steps to apply to drama forms.

Materials   Varied materials help the implementation of the goals and provide ideas to spark the drama sessions in your classroom (the "how"). Choose open-ended materials appealing to the children's senses and giving the students chances to create their own individual responses. The teacher has a flexible plan with respect to the material, but not a specific "chunk" that must be covered in a given span of time. For example, the teacher in the opening scene of this chapter used a part of a story, *Sam*.

Or, you might use *sensory* materials found in the environment. Using, for example, the surface textures of corrugated cardboard, of a mushroom, of a shingled roof, or the gripping surface of a new truck tire, you can have children interpret textures through movement. Sense of smell prompted by a collection (mint, burned rubber, burned wood, perfume, soap) may serve as a stimulus to pantomime, or to create impromptu scenes built around an imagined character's reaction to the smell. The sensory imaging of taste can start a pantomime or scene. You might have the students imagine going out into a garden and finding a beautiful lemon tree, picking a fruit, scratching it open, and letting a drop fall on their tongues. (You don't need a real drop of lemon for children to react to this one!)

You might also use a *pictorial* kind of material: a provocative magazine picture or a work of art, such as a painting or sculpture, that seems to tell a story. Social studies kits and materials for all levels may include posters of people in social action.

Or you might use *concrete objects*, such as masks, created by the children or lent. Children can mimic or improvise the suggested character and facial expressions. With skilled questioning, the children themselves can give you a choice of topic, plot, character, mood, and conflict (Stewig, 1983).

Thus the sources of materials are many. Whether you use one or the other does not matter. Many can develop children's concepts of characterization or mood. You and the teacher next door can both help children attain goals of drama working from quite different materials. (See the activity book for an annotated list of children's books that lend themselves to instruction for an enactive way of knowing.)

Drama in Centers   Why not have a learning center in your classroom to house stimulating materials for drama? Classrooms for young children have long had their drama centers. Usually the space is filled with a collection of costumes, hats, and characterization props (a pretend sword, a wand, a fire fighter's "ax"). Sometimes kits are stored for thematic play (e.g., hospital, post office, grocery store). Often a corner is set up for "housekeeping" and such associated dramatic play, usually not structured by the teacher. Why not borrow and adapt it for older students?

Children can come to your classroom drama center in their free time to work further on projects started in the class drama session, or in conjunction with drama in other curriculum areas. An earphone set(s) could enable students to listen to drama associated with social studies, history, and cultures around the world. Such materials can be commercial or student-made.

A playwright's section can be part of a creative writing center where students come to draw inspiration, start a script, try it out, or polish dialogue. This area can house blank "script" booklets to write in, a typewriter, and a computer with a word-processing program. Children can work individually, with partners, or in small task groups. Alternatively, the drama center could be not part of, but near, the creative writing center. (One would need to take into account the distractions the drama center could cause for those trying to concentrate on writing.)

As you rotate activities, keep your puppet collection and puppet-making materials at this center (marionettes for older students). At other times, art materials for making head-dresses or props may be part of the center. Keep your readers' theater materials organized here and a reference section of likely books to adapt for this dramatic form. Keep shadow play-making materials here.

For the goal of appreciation, keep recordings of famous actors and groups rendering drama, videotapes of TV drama, and public-radio taped drama. Keep books on the history of drama and (for older children in cities) local and national play reviews, and student reviews and recommendations. Needless to say, these materials should not all be taken out at once! (The section of this chapter on integration gives further ideas for drama across the curriculum, in varied subject centers.)

Four steps to program planning   Recall that in Figure 5.1, the continuum of child growth in drama had a basis in child-initiated, preschool forms of play and dramatic play. This figure contained dramatic forms you can use for your program. (Boxes representing forms of drama progressed toward the right side.) There are four steps to program planning using these forms: (1) starting, (2) deciding on the dramatic forms that will make up your program, (3) developing unit plans, and (4) developing session plans for the unit. (Teachers can adapt such steps in many areas besides drama, for example, listening and composition instruction.) Let's now consider each step in turn.

Starting   The elementary school teacher would probably start with the form of structured drama (including some time with relaxation, physical, mental, and emotional warm-ups). Structured dramatic-play experiences prepare the child imaginatively for partici-pation in drama. You can establish controls and expectations so that children can function productively in active learning. The younger and less experienced the students, the more time they will need in this form. Also you can use this form as a review for experienced students (Alberta, 1985).

If you need to be extra "safe," begin with activities in which children can remain seated at their desks. For example, students help you by furnishing sounds of the wind in a story. Invite students to help develop a signaling device to represent volume, as on a TV or radio dial. For example, a stick with white tip pointing down equals no wind sound at all; pointing straight up equals loudest sound. Try out the signal. Later add motion to the wind sound (Way, 1967). While the child's role in starting is *participant/responder*, the teacher's role is *guider/planner*. Although you are much in control at first, eventually students will learn to be responsible for every aspect of the drama session.

Deciding on dramatic forms   Identify areas of comfort and interest for you and your students as you go into exploration and study of a dramatic form of choice. Aim for balance, and during the year select from at least one form in the areas of (1) moving, (2) speaking, and (3) moving/speaking (see Figure 5.1.).

It is usually not feasible to try to cover all forms in one year. For example, grades

1 and 2 might start with structured dramatic play, go to dramatic movement, then to story telling, and then to dramatization. Grades 5 and 6 might start also with structured dramatic play, go to mime, to story telling, to dramatization, and to group drama. Time is flexible, but, assuming accumulations of one hour a week, use of each form might last from six weeks to three months.

Developing Unit Plans   Choose your goals and objectives from the framework in Appendix 5A and, with the help of this chapter and its corresponding pages in the activity book, make your own framework plan and determine how you will work to achieve it. (Remember your goals rarely, if ever, include polished performances. After a few sessions resist the strong temptation to "put on a play.") Since your assessment function is ongoing, you determine what comes next by what you and the children have achieved. *Be flexible.*

Many times your activities will develop skills in more than one dramatic form. Thus you integrate forms. For example, students explore a poem through dramatic movement before doing dramatic improvisations based on it and before going into group drama that has taken off from it. For instance, a class uses the poem "Behind the Waterfall," by W. Welles. They image it, enacting movements of going through the falls, improvising what they find on the other side, and preparing as a group for first, second, and third explorations as the teacher helps them discover new things to enact.

Developing session plans   Examine sample drama sessions in this chapter and in the activity book, keeping your own students, your preferred teaching style, and goals in mind. Evaluate your sessions with the children to gain future direction. Again, *be flexible.* Be willing to give up a plan and follow up on something more promising.

Each session typically includes the following parts listed below.

Parts to a Drama Session Plan
1. Preparation and warm-up (one-fourth to one-third of the session time)
2. Main activity for the session (one-third to one-half of the session time)
3. Reflective activity and transition (one-fourth to one-third of the session time)

An example of number 2, the main activity, might be creating tableaux or frozen statues of characters in literature, as was done in the opening scene. Try not to be in a hurry to go on to the next session part, however, in order to stick to a schedule.

Examples follow shortly, illustrating some of the features of program planning and procedures for some of the forms, beginning with starting and warm-up. You might start almost any session with something as simple as pretending to wake up and stretch. Some of our most creative moments come at that relaxed, receptive time. You will be amply rewarded if you even plan a few minutes of drama to use with some children within the next day or so. Remember, however, you are entering a long-term creative dramatics and *problem-solving* experience.

Structured Dramatic Play: Warm-up Activities for Relaxation and Imagination

Begin with warm-up and relaxation activities to pave the way for using the senses to stimulate imagination. Relaxation activities are part of every session because they calm the children and help them concentrate and reflect. They are also used at the end of a session.

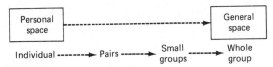

Figure 5.6   Movement continuum.

In structured dramatic play you are seeking physical relaxation, sensory awareness, and body and voice as instruments of expression. You are focusing on intellectual concentration, imagination, and trusting of intuitive response. You are encouraging children in emotional exploration, control, and expression.

Physical warm-up progresses from individual movement in personal space to pairs, small groups, and the whole group in general space. Begin with the children working in their own personal spaces, interacting occasionally. Progress to the use of larger space and sharing it cooperatively. Physical movement ranges from simple rhythmic activities to the complex communication of feelings, ideas, and characterization. (See Figure 5.6.)

Simple verbal suggestions can stimulate one or more of the focuses of structured dramatic play. For example, for a relaxation activity you might say: "I am the sun and you are all snowmen or snowwomen. I am going to melt you slowly. First I shine on your head. Let it relax. Then your neck, shoulders, [arms, fingers, back, legs, etc.]. Now you are almost a puddle." Or have them pretend they are rag dolls and sawdust leaks out of parts of the doll (Agency for Instructional Television, N.D.). Or you can simply have the children lie down, close their eyes, and tense and relax various parts of the body, perhaps to soothing music. Eight activities for structured dramatic play are found in Box 5.1.

Imagination   Imagination, upon which all the structured dramatic-play activities in Box 5.1 are focused, is a three-part process:

1. Get the image.
2. Do imagery, which involves retrieving feelings based on the senses and manipulating them.
3. Imagine, making the connection between images and manipulated uses.

If you are not getting results, return to the first part, image getting.

Individual processes for imagination vary. Some children may respond, get the image, retrieve, and make a connection to action immediately. Others do a slow fade from the outside inward. Costumes, props, and concrete objects help them a lot. Still others imagine and connect to action from the inside out, maybe from inside the spine and out or from the top of the head or tips of the fingers to the toes (Rosenberg, 1985).

A word of caution. Warm-ups and starters do not need to be merely bizarre. As in the case of written composition, go for the genuine experience, not just the cute. Sometimes, though, the overcontrolled individual needs to try bizarre, unreal extremes of imagination to get the creative imagination that was once flowing so naturally going again.

Summary of Structured Dramatic Play and Warm-up Activities   It may seem that this chapter has spent a great deal of time on warm-up activities. But they are needed. Avoid the mistake of trying to omit the step of tuning children into sensory experience—the here and now of imagining and manipulating objects. There are three transformations into dramatic forms: (1) person gets into character, (2) story becomes plot, and (3) place becomes

BOX 5.1 Some Activities for Structural Dramatic Play

"I Am the Master" The game of "I am the master and you are all—" (whatever I choose you to be: cats, seeds growing, circus parade animals) is a further example of warm-up movement that relaxes and also stimulates the imagination. It can be the main activity of the session, with children taking turns as master, if it fits the specific objective. Each session culminates with a reflecting and evaluating activity.

Example of reflecting: According to previously settled routine, the teacher has the children return to the circle and guides a discussion related to the preceding main activity ("I am the master"). The teacher encourages participation through questioning and seeking out children's discoveries. Sample questions follow:

- *Physical:* Did we use our bodies in controlled and creative ways? How did our bodies communicate?

- *Intellectual:* Could you hold to the idea of the master during his or her whole turn? (Concentration, sustained focus.) What details did you notice when we were all elephants? Did you notice something about size, shape, weight, ways to move? (Attention to category and detail.)

- *Social:* Did we cooperate with our master? Did we respond appropriately to signals?

- *Integrative:* Did you have a beginning, a middle, and an end to your enactment? (Realizing form of a drama experience, speaking/listening skills.)

- *Role-playing:* How did we act like a master? Could we switch enactments easily? Could we concentrate on the new role? (Consistency, flexibility, spontaneity.)

Review the ingredients for a session. You need to plan for (1) space and positioning of children, (2) control signals (practice them first), (3) a warm-up activity, (4) a relaxation activity, (5) a main activity keyed to the session objective(s), and (6) a reflecting and assessment activity (questions you will use). Now consider another activity.

Movement Vocabulary Movement-enriching vocabulary serves both structured dramatic play and the language arts. As a further example for encouraging physical warm-up, have the children help you make a list of movement words and categorize them. Some may be done in place: *bob, collapse, lunge, revolve, sink, rise, sway, rock, shake.* Some may be done moving from place to place: *creep, stalk, trudge, strut, hobble, slink, march.* Other words may be categorized as *leg and foot* movements: *tiptoe, skip, kick,* and *step.*

Some ideas for getting children moving through space once they have generated vocabulary include the use of a tambourine (as in the opening scene) or a drum to establish various rhythms and moods. (Concepts of respecting the space of others are prerequisite here.) Children move alone, then in pairs, then in large groups, freezing on cue into any shape they can think of (tableau). Then they discuss what or who the shape was, how they communicated through space, and the consequences of their dramatic decisions. Or, as they move they might image their bare feet on warm sand, hot sand, soft grass, pebbles, or rocks. All of the preceding make good warm-up activities.

Some other vocabulary children could generate suggesting movements may be categorized as *arm and hand* movements: *dig, pull, grope, box.* Some elements with hands alone might be: *clench, open, wring, scratch, pick, knead, point, flick,* and *cut with pretend scissors.*

Vocabulary for *facial* movements might include *smile, chew, wink, pout, wrinkle nose in disgust, squint, brows lowered and drawn together, tightened lower eyelids and pressed lips in anger,* and *lifting of eyebrows and dropping corners of mouth in fear.* Talk about what the children chose to do and let them know it is all right to have and show emotions. They can, for example, show anger with their shoulders and backs, and joy or depression with their feet. Children can discuss feelings accompanying the following: seeing something scary, going out to buy a present, not getting a present they wanted, or losing something. Pairs in parallel play can role-play and improvise on each of these emotional situations.

Forest Animal Pretending to see and sense animals is another structured play activity combining many skills (best based on actual experience). In this activity you are inviting the children to use *improvisation,* a spontaneous response to any situation. This activity also employs *parallel play*—all class members work simultaneously. You can pretend and image with children that as they are in the forest, raking their hands through the leaves, they find a tiny animal. "The animal lets you gently, ever so gently, pick it up. Hold it in your hands. Gently show it to your neighbor." Later reflect on and discuss this experience. Bring out children's discoveries, and show that you could have a *beginning,* a *middle,* and an *end* to this enactment. Keep the discussion on the action, not on the child portraying it.

If you think you are not going to get boys to do any of this "drama stuff," you're wrong. Even big, macho high school boys will concentrate fully on the pretend animal they have uncovered in the leaves of a forest. Children will enter into your suggestions unless, of course, they have no background of forests or tiny animals (or no concentration). You may have to provide a real field trip or film experience to build on.

Noodle Game Pretending about noodles after some are served in class is a further example of structured dramatic play emphasizing sensory recall and imagination. You can guide the children by saying: "You are a hard, stiff, uncooked noodle. See it, feel it, be it. Now you are in a watery substance; first it's cold; now it's getting warmer and warmer. You're being cooked, getting softer and softer as you bubble around in the water. Now you are being lifted up and then plopped on a plate." Children can join with other "noodles" in structured dramatic play leading to a focus on dramatic movement.

Hair Care Enacting care of the hair is a more realistic activity for structured dramatic play. Invite children to image someone rolling up their hair. Recall and visualize specific details. Now use those images to pantomime the rolling-up motions. Next imagine undoing the hair and again use those images to move as if undoing hair in the same sequence, having had a compressed rehearsal in the mind. Assign observation beforehand for better results with dramatic movement activities.

Help children to concentrate on real rather than audience-oriented, theatrical, exaggerated, or stereotyped responses. Be patient and give encouragement. Again, focus on discoveries that children are making through these beginning steps in the dramatic process.

(Continued)

Concrete Objects Concrete objects are another way to start. Have some pieces of yarn. Put a piece on you. Pretend the yarn is a worm. React. (Best done after experiencing real worms.)

Or, have a photograph. Go into the photograph. Go above it. Go below it in your imagination. Pretend it is a "still" from a film. Imagine that the film is running in slow motion backward for 10 seconds. Reproduce this movement. Then, in slow motion, run the film ahead for 20 seconds. Reproduce this movement sequence. Create a tableau for the opening, for the photo itself, and for the last still of the imagined continuation.

Pass around an empty box and invite children, in turn, to open it, pantomiming to others what they supposedly took out and put back. (Maybe it's an orange and a child pretends to peel it and eat it. Again, the activity is best done after observed experience with an orange.)

Give each child a piece of food (e.g., raisin, marshmallow, pretzel). Say, "See your food as if you were seeing it for the very first time as a little child. Say to your partner what you see. Feel it with your fingers. Say to your partner what you feel. Taste your food. Sweet, tart, spicy, salty? Say to your partner what it tastes like. Is there some sound your food might make? Smell it; what's it made of? Talk further about it to your partner." Remember that in using objects you are helping children discover new, enactive things to do with them. And you are being encouraging.

Emotions Pictures Emotions need exploring, controlling, and expressing in structured dramatic play. Again, use verbal suggestion or objects. Have a set of pictures showing emotions (children laughing, crying). Go from individuals, to pairs, to groups imaging the situation that might have produced the emotions in the pictures. Later they can enact these scenes and freeze-frame (as did the children in the opening scene) when they arrive at the point of action shown in the picture (tableau). They can go beyond the picture and imagine and enact what might happen next. Here we can see that these warm-up and starter activities in structured dramatic play are serving as prerequisites and preparation for forms of movement, pantomime, and dramatization.

Mirroring Mirroring is another starter excellent for developing concentration and observation (prerequisite for pantomime). After observation in a real mirror, two children face one another. One is the mirror and the other initiates all the movements. The player who is the mirror reflects the other player's movements and facial expressions. (The children in Figure 5.3 are engaged in mirroring.)

Again, the best sources of ideas are *the children themselves,* if encouraged and given the chance. Your function is to elicit as many ideas as possible, helping children choose which ones to use as starters. From their brainstormed ideas you help them discover what they want to do and help them implement it. You and your students will develop a dramatic sensibility; they will be alert for things to dramatize in the real world and in reading material. Soon they won't be listening *to* drama, but *for* drama. Children need time, encouragement, and practice in exploring their *own resources*—the "stuff" from which drama is created. (See the activity book for additional starter activities.)

setting with added conflict and created spectacle. All of these transformations come after a firm grounding in starters that help children discover characteristics of themselves, find and enact stories, and explore and discover environments. Only after the children grasp character, plot, and setting can they master *forms* of drama.

Figure 5.7 on page 158 shows skills to be developed in structured dramatic play and definitions of each. These skills are essential. No matter what the age, students need these skills before proceeding to other dramatic forms. Although most sessions develop several skills, each skill needs to be the focus of at least one session during the unit on structured dramatic play.

Techniques to be taught to the children for the unit include the following: improvisation, parallel play, role play, characterization, side coaching, and tableaux. All of them have been illustrated in the opening scene and in the activities for unit sessions above.

Two *Forms* of Dramatic Expression

This section samples two of the dramatic forms of expression that structured dramatic play prepares the child for: puppetry and readers' theater. (The activity book provides ideas for other dramatic activity.)

Puppetry   Before beginning a puppetry unit the teacher may have more success if the children have worked through a unit on structured dramatic play with ample focus on dramatic movement (presented in the preceding section) and through a unit on story telling (covered in Chapter 4). Again, remember you are making a long-term commitment. A teacher who has young students create a puppet during one lesson and produce a puppet play the next can expect a low level of manipulation. Some specific skills for the puppetry unit follow in Box 5.2 on page 159.

Introducing the Puppetry Unit   The teacher employs a personal collection of various puppets. There might be a stick, paper bag, finger, tennis ball (with a slit cut in the ball for a mouth and features drawn around it). Employment includes the puppet telling a story, reading to the children, or talking to the children. Further teaching strategies for introducing the puppetry unit may include the following:

1. The teacher uses pictures and films relating to puppets.
2. The teacher invites a local artist to discuss the history of puppetry and present a play. Such introductions can motivate construction.
3. Introductory warm-ups can include one child pretending to move another child as a puppet and consequently exploring the body awareness of standing, walking, and sitting. Then this pair relates to yet another pair through movement and voice.

Construction   Children's construction of puppets occupies a portion of the unit. Have the children create their own, *avoiding premade or patterned puppets*. Again, stimulated children can come up with many imaginative ideas. Most can construct a simple age-appropriate puppet within 30 minutes. Children take pride in their creations and learn to respect puppetry as an art form. (Avoid frustrating the children, e.g., asking kindergarteners to create complex marionettes.)

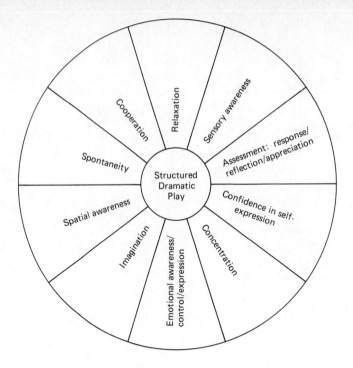

Concentration

Developing the ability to focus on a given task for a given time.

Confidence in self-expression

Discovering one's own resources and building upon positive experiences in order to communicate successfully with others.

Cooperation

Developing the desire and the awareness of the need to work responsibly with others in order to accomplish a shared task.

Emotional awareness/control/expression

Developing a bank of personal experiences and understandings of feelings which enable one to understand oneself and to empathize with others.

Assessment: response/reflection/appreciation

Developing the ability to assess one's own work and the work of others to contribute to one's own growth and the growth of others.

Imagination

Creating mental images of what has never been actually experienced or creating new images based on previous experiences.

Relaxation

Developing the ability to relax physically, emotionally, and mentally.

Sensory awareness

Exploring the senses in order to develop them and heighten the reality of imagined situations and experiences.

Spatial awareness

Learning to move and work safely within the space provided and to share that space with others in a generous and responsible manner.

Spontaneity

Activating an idea or responding to an idea without apparent premeditation—the basis for improvised activities.

Figure 5.7 Skills to be developed in structured dramatic play. (*Source:* Alberta, 1985.)

BOX 5.2 Some Specific Student Skills for the Puppet Unit

- Become aware of the puppet as a communicative medium by:
  moving as a puppet
  moving another as a puppet
  constructing a simple puppet
- Apply skills of moving to puppetry by:
  experimenting with puppet manipulation
  exploring and creating various environments the child can move the puppet through
- Apply skills of speaking to puppetry by:
  communicating through the puppet as extension of oneself
  responding to another puppet, creating dialogue
- Apply dramatization skills to puppetry by:
  creating a character for a puppet (name, age, abode, preferences, dislikes, voice)
  creating an environment in which the puppet character will react
  expressing feelings as a puppet
  working with others to create a puppet story
- Apply the skills of puppetry for use in other subject areas

---

Start with simple puppets. The following are some examples:

Stick (simple drawing on cardboard cut out and taped to a stick)

Paper bag (put hand in bag; bottom of bag is face and top lip, where bag naturally folds can be jaws, and bottom lip can be drawn where folded bottom meets bag)

Sock (features put on with marking pens or glued felt)

"Found" or analogy puppets (discarded phone receiver, dish mop, egg beater, spoon

Paper plate puppets (fold over for mouth)

Stocking stretched over a Slinky with decorated Styrofoam head attached

Cardboard tube puppet with Ping-Pong ball for head

"Instant" puppet (clench fist, tucking thumb under; with a red marking pen fashion a mouth around where the thumb is tucked in; a slight movement of thumb joint moves the "mouth"; see Figure 5.8; also see the activity book)

Then go to more complex puppets: for example, head molded of mixture of sawdust, flour, and salt or papier-mâché with button or bead eyes, feathers, yarn hair. To vary your puppets, apply basic principles of creative production presented in Box 5.3. Once you "own" these principles you have great power for inventing on your own.

Manipulation   Manipulation of puppets occupies another portion of your unit. Have the children create a *history* and *character* for their puppet: name, age, where it lives, what it likes to eat, favorite games, problems, friends, enemies, needs, wants.

Figure 5.8   Fists as puppets.

The teacher can help bring out the character of each puppet by conversing with it. Explore a variety of voices for the puppet to find one that fits and one that contrasts with other puppet voices. Have children project their voices. (See the section on choral speech in the activity book.) More manipulation ideas follow: Some sock puppets or puppets with open-and-close mouths are flexible enough so that mouth corners can be turned up or down to depict mood or emotion. Some can let little finger and thumb be the hands while index finger nods or shakes the head. Some can bow. Most can sway or bob up and down. Some can be made to stand, walk, and sit. In pair or group work, puppets not talking are usually still so as not to distract. You can side coach, suggesting movements and encouraging interaction. (More ideas are in the activity book.)

Setting   The setting can be any place, any time. No stage is required. Some shy children may like to hide behind a table on its side, a shipping box, or a curtain suspended with a spring-type extension rod in a doorway. Some shy ones like to hide behind simple masks to practice expressing a feeling (e.g., a paper bag decorated with colored construction paper and paint). Puppets can come out of large apron pockets, a cloak with slits, or simply

---

BOX 5.3 Some Basic Principles of Creative Production with Examples for Puppet Variation

1. Change *size* (a very small puppet can fit on a finger; a large one can require a team of students to work it).

2. Add *sensory* components (smells like cinnamon, has own music theme, glitters, feels velvety).

3. *Multiply* it (a whole family or brood of puppets).

4. *Subtract* (a bare geometric shape for a puppet; a shadow).

5. *Reverse* it (upside-down paper cup with head attached becomes puppet; puppet turned inside out becomes yet another; front side and back are different puppets).

6. Give it *other uses* (not only a puppet but a reading or writing partner, monitor, science observer, math introducer, class host or welcomer; also can be used as a pot holder, a cushion, or a purse).

enter and exit from behind one's back. Setting can be the following: an old sweater to explore, a collection of leaves, twigs and small branches, the library book display table, racks and shelves, building blocks or discarded odd pieces of wood, or scenery painted on a roll of paper unrolled and rolled up between two sticks inserted in a windowed box.

Scripting   Scripting a puppet play is optimally attacked after the children have worked through a unit on play making (and achieved a grasp of beginning, conflict, middle, and end). You might have two (well-characterized) puppets meet for the first time with the teacher interviewing them to help the improvisation. Other ideas follow.

Three puppets in a setting might meet with a *problem* (e.g., one of them wants to join in the play of the other two and they do not want the intruder; two of them have played with and broken the toy of a third; they are all lost; two have lost a third). The play might end with the solution or just the generation of ideas and possible solutions and the announcing that the puppets will go off and try them out.

Or two or three puppets may meet and simply explore a setting, streaming out their thoughts about it. Two puppets flash back to their earliest remembrances. Two puppets say what they think about each other and then reveal what they *really* think about each other (older students). Activity can be parallel with small groups operating at the same time. Original puppet scripts can take off from or elaborate upon well-known tales and archetypal plots or *motifs*: the journey, the confrontation with a monster, worthy child in search of a home. (The activity book gives an additional example [script included]—a drama session with "puppet" being the child's two index fingers, and the setting being a "sweater island.")

Readers' Theater   Readers' theater is a form of oral interpretation in which a group of readers performs literature using voice and gesture (Alberta, 1985, p. 130.) Its objective is to bring literature to life in the minds of the listeners. Needed background includes drama forms of choral speaking and/or story telling and dramatization.

Advantages for classroom use are many. One is that there is no stigma of high, middle, or low groups in reading. The teacher can start with easy pattern books of high quality (e.g., Hutchins's *Goodnight Owl*), where language has a predictable, catchy pattern that aides readers greatly. If you attack challenging pieces, children can get an inner ear for a more complex style. Children can view shorter works as a whole, getting the tone and nuances of meaning enhanced by gesture. Teacher and children can avoid reading as private suffering and public humiliation. Most children do not mind this kind of reading practice; in fact some will practice all day if you let them. Readers' theater is valuable because it promotes concentration, activates speech, is a "friendly" learning instrument for reading, develops discussion skills, and provides worthwhile vicarious experience.

The student objectives for the dramatic form of readers' theater parallel those of speaking in general, with the addition of interpretative skills. The following are examples: fully communicating the meaning of a piece of literature by expressing mood; exploring natural rhythms; phrasing for meaning; coloring individual words; and developing skills of presentation using face, voice, and body. A further speech objective is to develop use of vocal characterization, pitch, pace, and projection. Older children can add the learning of scripting techniques.

For background, children have typically had previous experience with choral speech, and their speaking skills are operating well. They have had experience with dramatizing stories and scenes from stories, sharing with other groups. You could introduce the unit as did the teacher in the opening scene of this chapter, with a demonstration yourself. Or other options may be available to you: an older performing group, a local professional group, a TV special.

Seven Steps   The following seven steps make readers' theater in the classroom easy. They amplify selecting, rehearsing, and staging.

1. *Selection of material.* Box 5.4 shows some criteria for selection.

2. *Adaptation and development of the script.* Rewrite, omitting the *he saids, she saids.* You might use yellow highlight and cover up unwanted print with a black marker. You may need to retype it. Determine how many readers you will need and how they can be positioned for the reading. A very short part might be deleted or combined with another. Or one child might take several short parts, entering and exiting with some minimal prop to indicate character change. Characters might read their own narration rather than having a narrator. (It may work well for you to have about five readers.) In longer selections condense and tighten the action and plot, reducing the piece to a manageable length while retaining all the essential action and characters.

Make copies of the script and color code it for the character, putting it in a matching-color file folder. (Children like to decorate these character-part file folders.) When the child with the orange file folder sees orange underlining, he or she knows when to read. Simple props that go with the part can also go into the file. Examples of these props might be a handkerchief for crying into, a paper crown, and a character name tag.

3. *Silent preparation.* The teacher might read the script first from the copy with all the color coding for each part. Then all simply enjoy the script by themselves.

4. *Study of the character and sorting out of its traits.* Group discussion is advantageous here. This is a place to develop concepts of setting, mood, conflict, and climax.

5. *Practice.* This is a practice that children usually relish. They can engage in role change, changes in voice, changes in setting. They can practice with the narrator. When casting the drama, children can try out all the characters of the story (more practice). They can work on oral interpretation. They can explore voice quality: a grandmother's voice, a witch's voice, a giant's voice. They can videotape or audiotape, play back, read along, and listen with or without headsets.

They can practice incorporating simple props. (Don't let props interfere with the

---

BOX 5.4 Criteria for Choosing Readers' Theater Material

- The quality of the piece ensures that the time is well spent.
- It has sufficient interesting and appealing dialogue in addition to the narrative.
- The language is rich, rhythmic, and colorful, with suitable vocabulary and student appeal.
- The story line has conflict and suspense with a beginning, middle, and end.
- The piece is sufficiently easy to read.
- The script is not too long for the age group. (Eight pages, for example, is typically sufficient for fifth graders.)
- You have considered the audience for which the children will perform the piece (small groups, total class, other).

continuity of the drama.) You might practice with tapes for mood music, or for beginning and end of the drama.

6. *Dress rehearsal.* Children can stand or sit (e.g., on tall stools). They can use music stands for their scripts during this final practice.

7. *Actual performance.* It may work well for you to have about five groups with five readers in each group. If the children are interested, groups can "go on tour" to lower grades or to the library. They can videotape the performance for themselves and for the library (adapted from Loch, 1985; and Alberta, 1985).

Chapter 9, on children's literature, offers many *resources.* As mentioned, predictable pattern books are suitable for younger children (Chapter 12). For older children you can use a book such as *Young Girls Don't Slay Dragons,* but any age enjoys doing *Horton Hatches an Egg.* The activity book gives more ideas (Chapter 9, Section 2, Part 3, "Performing Fiction"). You can select and script incidents from longer books. A collection of scripts ready for readers' theater can be one of your best teaching aids for language arts.

Integration of Drama into the Curriculum

You can teach drama as a separate subject or integrate it with other language arts or subject areas. For economy and meaningfulness, integrate it wherever possible. Drama can be integrated with listening, speaking, reading, and written composition; with problem solving and other thought processes; and with literature, social studies, science, and even math. As a tool for learning and an enactive way of knowing, drama across the curriculum not only sparks student interest in studying content areas but gives children an opportunity to show an audience what they know (Bruner, 1973). Almost any broad unit has room for drama. The following are some steps to integration (adapted from Alberta, 1985).

Match Objectives   Start with seeking a match of elements for the integration. Be familiar with the goals, objectives, processes, and skills of the areas to be integrated, and look for similarities. Drama can be a tool for learning in another subject area. Ask yourself whether it is an appropriate means for teaching language arts, social studies, health, music. For example, since what makes language effective in drama is similar to what makes language effective in written composition, integration enhances both forms of expression. Criteria for effective language in an improvised drama are similar to those in composition: achieved purpose and effect, consistent role, appropriate elaboration, relevant use, coherence, and precisely chosen words.

Ask this question: Does the study entail an understanding of human experiences in particular circumstances, the exploration of attitudes and opinions, or the representation of abstract concepts in concrete form? If so, then drama will be an appropriate teaching/learning strategy (O'Neill & Lambert, 1982). An example might be integrating the dramatic form of role play with social studies so that students can better realize conflicting points of view between the natives who want to keep their homelands and the entrepreneurs who want to build an energy-generating dam that would flood the lands. An example associated with science study is enacting through dramatic movement the metamorphosis of a monarch butterfly. Thus an abstract concept is brought to life. (See the end of Chapter 5 in the activity book for methods of role play.)

Choose an Appropriate Dramatic Form   Identify the dramatic *form* that will be most appropriate. Ask yourself what techniques (role play, dramatization of literature, oral speaking) are already inherent in the subject to be integrated with drama. Drama may be integrated with the skills you are trying to teach in language arts. For example, when students dramatize stories, they are being reinforced in sequencing skills in composition and reading. Ask yourself how much experience you and your students have with drama. If the answer is little, start with structured dramatic play. (Avoid getting in over your head with advanced dramatic forms.)

Ask yourself how much of an investment you are willing to make in learning about and planning the drama experience and in using class time and resources. If the answer is "not much," then avoid long, involved projects using advanced dramatic forms. Again, simple structured dramatic play may help integrate objectives. For example, literature stimulates creative movement and children continue by creating tableaux of characters and scenes from that literature. They might start with the "all asleep" scene ("not a creature was stirring") from " 'Twas the Night Before Christmas."

Drama is integrated with social studies using the form of *group drama*. That is, students create an imaginary society in order to build understanding about how community members need each other. To start, hold up a blank piece of paper and say: "This is all we know so far about the Xs in X land. Do you want to go there and find out more? What can we do next?" Group drama can be started anytime as far as the children are concerned, but this form is demanding as to the roles the teacher plays.

Get Familiar with the "Drama Way of Working"   At first plan five to ten sessions to get familiar with drama before proceeding to the planned integration. For example, after a brief unit on drama, drama is integrated with social studies. In this integration, students use role play in interviews as a way to explore people in the past and gather information. Children can interview actual representatives in a studied culture. Then they take on roles themselves in order to be interviewed.

When ready for a greater drama challenge, children construct a play about a society they have studied, incorporating what they have learned (a conscious simulation of a real situation). The study of a civilization through group drama creates a genuine need to integrate writing by doing the following: "recording" its "history," keeping ongoing journals, and imagining the uncovering of writings necessary to the functioning of this community.

For example, in studying the westward movement a child first engages in belief-building activities. Then, in the role of wagon master, a child makes a list of needed supplies for the long wagon trek west: 10 barrels of beans, 1 barrel of sugar, 10 barrels of meal, 3 barrels of coffee, 30 rounds of ammunition, and so on. Children might map the storage area of their wagon on the classroom floor to get a feel for what might be stored where. A page from the wagon master's journal might begin:

> April 30, 1840. Twenty wagons will start tomorrow morning from our place in St. Louis, a larger group than I like to manage. Military discipline will be an absolute necessity if we're to have any chance of survival. We should make 15 miles the first day and daily thereafter—barring any wagon breakdowns.

Besides letting students thrill to a moment in history in an imagined swirl of wagon train dust, drama may be used in this case to show what the children know about the westward movement.

The teacher takes the children on a journey of learning, posing challenges and pressing for discovery and connections. History is full of interesting journeys just waiting for children to dramatize them—settling new lands, getting out of entrapments, working out what happens between those with power and those without power. (See "Literature as Journey" in Chapter 9 of the activity book.)

Problem Solving Integrated with Drama   Both dramatic improvisation and written composition depend on thinking processes. Children solve problems in drama as they do in composition and in the real world. The language of drama makes children's problem solving visible. While reflecting in groups on what they have spoken in dialogue (or written), children have a chance to recall effects themselves and have their actions reflected by others.

The teacher plays an important role in the integration of creative problem solving and drama with skillful questions (as did the teacher in the opening scene). Examples: "In what other ways might Sam and his family solve Sam's loneliness problem?" "Is it just Sam's problem or is it also a family problem, and why?"

The integration of drama and problem solving may appear in many contexts. Drama challenges may be motoric in nature. For example, a teacher may say: "Image a spider with a lacy web. In what ways might you move? Try one. What if a bird comes looking for a spidery meal?" Or the problem might be vocal: "In what ways might you create the sound of the wizard's voice?" Or the challenge/problem might be in the context of creating an original play script. Choose literature with cliff-hanging episodes or crisis points. Anything from "Old Mother Hubbard" to *Call It Courage* will invite children to start problem solving, stimulated by your questions.

Integration of Drama and Oral Language   It goes without saying that drama stimulates speech, giving children a valid reason to talk. Similarly, drama provides many opportunities for purposeful listening as children make decisions about their enactments, turn taking, and making sense. Children get chances to improvise speech before others and to listen to others while reenacting favorite stories ("The Billy Goats Gruff"), role-playing varied situations (*Sam* in the opening scene), and using puppets. Often the maturity of the language evoked in drama astonishes teachers. When this language is taken to paper, the quality of children's writing also leaps upward (Wagner, 1983).

Integration of Drama and Written Language   Perhaps the most obvious integration of drama and reading is in regard to comprehension processes. Drama's improvement of children's background of experience, vocabulary, and language in general makes for a greater understanding and enlivening of the printed page. Dramatic activities help children grasp *story structures* and features contributing to comprehension; for example, such activity helps children appreciate the concepts of beginning, middle, end, character, motive, and conflicting forces that complicate plot. When drama helps children see beneath the surface of a text, it deepens their comprehension. Because a child attempts to explore how a character would behave in a scene, a child is likely to discover *deep structure* in a story. Children will *read* avidly and purposefully the background materials needed to create a group drama.

Drama may serve as a bank of experiences for *written composition.* Students may write about drama, describing their own experiences with it. Or, they may use drama as a readiness activity for written composition; for example, children might pantomime opening a package and then write about what they wish might really be inside it.

Drama can feed writing by *slowing down* the writer and encouraging him or her to look carefully and note movement, gesture, voice, object, and character detail—the hows and whys of portrayal, the flavor of dialogue. All of these observations can add richness as the writer continues to work. With drama children can stop to explore all aspects of an experience. Group drama is a form of composition, just as narrative is. Group drama may be done with older children, with the advantage of quick changes and instant feedback from the other players. Since drama fleshes out narrative and narrative summarizes drama, children can improvise dramas for narratives and make narrative summaries of improvised dramas. Thus they grasp an important integration. A delightful and far-reaching example entitled "The Birds" is found in the activity book. Beginning as a mural or art integration, this drama takes the children through all of the language arts.

Finally, remember the integration inherent in drama of reacting to and talking about *literature.* Through drama a child can examine a product of literature closely and with satisfying response. An example of a response might be having characters with something in common from different books meeting in improvised drama (Dorothy just back from Oz meets Alice just back from Wonderland). Another response might be story theater. Children pantomime actions as a narrator reads the story aloud. For example, as the narrator reads, "Once a widowed man with a lovely daughter married a woman with two ugly daughters," the characters appear, bow, and then proceed to pantomime doing things about the house. As the narrator goes on: "The stepmother and stepsisters became cruel to the lovely daughter and called her Cinderella," the characters pantomime ordering poor Cinderella around, and so on.

Assessment

How can you measure children's ability to express themselves through an artistic medium or growth in spontaneous oral composition? Assessment of drama includes a rationale, a reference to goals with matching questions, and an exploration of a variety of ways.

Why Assess?   We assess our programs in drama to check up on the implementation of the following goals: (1) self-discovery of positive inner resources, (2) a way of knowing that is a tool for learning, (3) sensitivity to others (interpersonal skills), (4) skills in dramatic art forms, and (5) a positive attitude with aesthetic appreciation. Another reason we assess is to have a formative tool for guiding and improving what we do with drama. Assessment gives teachers a means to communicate attainment to others (e.g., students, parents, administrators). A final reason is to encourage self-assessment. Self-assessment includes the child and the teacher during and after drama work. You can simply take each of the goals and subgoals in your drama framework *and turn them into questions.* (See Appendix 5A.)

Methods of Assessment   Methods of assessment include (1) observing the children and recording observations, (2) keeping and assessing artifact records, and (3) reflecting (adapted from Alberta, 1985).

The teacher can *observe* the children's responses during and after the drama experience, their verbal contributions, and interaction between the children. The teacher could do this by keeping an anecdotal record on children or by developing and using a checklist ("Which children are successful in capturing an idea and conveying it?" "Who grasps and displays concepts of mood, plot, characterization, and conflict?").

Artifactual records are simply items in the categories of children's drama related to written work, art, responses or motivation of reading, audiotapes or videotapes, and the like. Written artifactual records might include drama journals, diaries in and out of role, letters, and poems. Artwork might be depictions, masks, puppets, scenery. Reading products might be reports, booklets, and other information-gathering efforts relevant to the drama. The teacher could develop a cumulative file or portfolio of each child's artifactual work or keep a record book or chart. The teacher can keep notes following each drama session in order to record successes and variations for the future.

Opportunities to *reflect* can occur before, during, or after a drama experience. Discussions suggested throughout this chapter can focus on various goals and objectives as children participate ("What could we do next time with our arms to make them seem more like birds' wings in flight?"). The focus may be on what has been accomplished and what remains to be accomplished ("What did we do that was particularly effective?" "What do we need to work on next time?"). The tone is, "We assess together how it went, giving ourselves a goal for next time." Finally, another reflective opportunity can occur during scheduled individual interviews or conferences with children. These exchanges could be combined with the reading/writing/listening conference in an integrated way.

We have seen that reflective discussion has been an important part of the drama session. The next chapter, "Discussion," shows you how to further some essential skills used in integrating drama and all language arts.

SUMMARY

Drama in the language arts program provides opportunities for all children, as well as the flexible teacher, to participate. It is first a process of great use and interest to children. Teachers employ this process in order to bring out creative, enactive, and even artistic responses from children. Emphasis is on the growth of the student, not the finished product. With drama, there are no absolute right or wrong responses.

Drama promotes self-development, teamwork, problem solving, and communication. Children grow in vocabulary, in nonverbal language, and in extracting drama's value as a way of knowing. There are no limits to the amount of language growth possible by using drama if the teacher is as willing as the children. Most dramatic activity can be effective in integrating the language arts and many other academic areas.

Who your students are in regard to drama has developmental ramifications. Circles of progressive drama experience interact with growth areas: physical, intellectual and linguistic, emotional, and social. Children play different roles during the drama experience and so do teachers. Students need time and practice to explore their own resources for creating drama.

Deciding *what* process, goals, and materials will be useful is a prime function of the teacher as gatherer and organizer. This chapter suggested a drama framework on which to hang a program and suggested materials to provision centers.

Where drama takes place can be highly flexible. Climate can be both physical and emotional in tone. Routines learned become automatically helpful. All that is really needed is a safe space and imagination. Drama requires an emotional climate that is flexible, not authoritarian, and secure, not judgmental.

How one teaches drama depends in large part on answers to the *why, who, what,* and *where. How* includes starting, deciding on the form, planning a unit, and developing sessions. Prerequisites are structured dramatic play with appropriate teaching techniques (e.g., "side coaching"), and sessions for relaxation, movement, imagination, the senses, emotions, improvisation, and characterization. The teacher leads a "workshop" where all can participate in planning, then playing, then reflecting and assessing—recycling over and over. Children can come to see the pattern that after establishment of a believable environment for drama, then some conflict may happen, with the building and releasing of tension.

Detailed in this chapter were dramatic forms of puppetry and readers' theater. Find your own style and favorite forms, as each person works differently. You do not have to be an expert to try drama in your classroom. Start with simple structured dramatic play sessions and build up to forms.

Integration of drama depends on a match of objectives, choice of form, and grasp of drama process or ways of working. Problem solving, listening, speaking, reading, and written composition are all grist for the integration mill. (So are the content areas of literature, science, math, and social studies.) The pretend world is a protected and valued place. It gives students a unique opportunity to experiment with solving problems important to them, putting to test things they know, focusing and clarifying ideas and information.

APPENDIX 5A   Drama Framework

To participate productively in drama, students need to show growth in and be able to:

GOAL 1: Use drama as a means of **self**-discovery of positive inner resources.
SUBGOALS:
1.1. Develop a positive self-understanding and self-concept; appreciate one's own uniqueness in regard to body, voice, and emotions through abilities to concentrate, discover, control, recall, and expressively use:
    1.1.1. Relaxation. Develop techniques for physical and emotional relaxation before enactment to prepare for focus and after focus.
    1.1.2. Body and voice.
        1.1.2.1. Develop a sensory awareness of body and voice as tools of internal communication, instruments of expression to oneself.
        1.1.2.2. Develop body awareness and spatial perception, using rhythmic and imitative movement (both large and small), sensory awareness, and pantomime.
    1.1.3. Emotional experiences.
        1.1.3.1. Imitate sounds and movements conveying emotions.
        1.1.3.2. Create sounds and movements conveying emotions.
1.2. Develop a positive self-concept regarding ability to use intellectual experience in drama.
    1.2.1. Develop sensory awareness, recalling and using own sensory experience.
    1.2.2. Sharpen internal observations of people, of situations, and of the drama environment.
    1.2.3. Respond internally to presented stimuli that are concrete, pictorial, and symbolic (e.g., objects, music, pictures, and literature).
    1.2.4. Recognize and learn to trust intuitive and spontaneous responses, activating an idea without apparent premeditation (the basis for improvised activities).
    1.2.5. Create mental images of what has never been actually experienced; make images drawn from past experience. (Imaginative and creative thought; divergent before convergent thought.)

GOAL 2: Use drama as an enactive **way of knowing,** so this way becomes a tool for learning language arts and other academic content areas.

SUBGOALS:

2.1. Give form, shape, and meaning to ideas and experience, to more and more abstract concepts through the enactment process. (Express concepts to oneself using interpretive movement.)

2.2. Integrate drama and language arts, social studies, and science by using drama as a motivating, enactive, and introductory activity.

2.3. Integrate body, voice, language, and emotional state to interpret literature dramatically and enhance understanding of story.

GOAL 3: Develop sensitivity to **others** within drama environment.

SUBGOALS:

3.1. Experience feeling of reflected success and acceptance.

3.2. Develop respect for others—their rights, ideas, and differences.

3.3. Learn to share space with others in a generous and responsible manner.

3.4. Develop competency in communication skills, increasing fluency in oral language, expanding vocabulary and precision in conveying information, feelings, and moods to others. (Spontaneous oral composition.)

    3.4.1. Be aware of others' desires when engaging in informative and comprehensible dialogue.

    3.4.2. Be able to express apt responses extemporaneously, fluently, and fearlessly.

    3.4.3. Acquire multiple meanings and functions, melody, and rhythm.

    3.4.4. Demonstrate speech exhibiting depth of perception, clarity of observation, clear focus, eloquence of expression, sensitive attitude, and convincing argument.

    3.4.5. Improvise dialogue for a variety of persons speaking in varied ways with different body language.

3.5. Develop the confidence and ability to discuss, share, make choices, test, and reflect on drama experiences with others.

3.6. Develop the desire and the awareness of the need to work responsibly with others in order to accomplish a shared drama task.

3.7. Develop belief in, identification with, and commitment to roles for oneself and others.

GOAL 4: Understand and use **forms** of drama and their techniques for a variety of purposes.

SUBGOALS:

4.1. Develop an awareness of a variety of dramatic forms of expression (e.g., structured dramatic play, dramatic movement, mime, dramatization, puppetry, readers' theater).

    4.1.1. Engage in creative drama moving from limited-action stories and poems, to literary selections, to original stories.

    4.1.2. Grow to use forms such as structured dramatic play, dramatic movement, shadow play, pantomime, improvisation, puppetry, characterization in readers' theater, play making, and group drama (situation role-playing with group-centered planning for drama).

4.2. Develop an awareness and use of a variety of techniques appropriate to varied dramatic forms, building from simple to more complex and demanding ones. (Forms were shown in Figure 5.1.)

GOAL 5: Develop a lasting positive **attitude** and aesthetic appreciation of drama and theatrical events as art forms.

SUBGOALS:

5.1. Develop an awareness of and respect for potential excellence in the drama work of oneself and others.

5.2. Experience enrichment from drama, both within and outside personal environment.

5.3. Explore the use of dramatic symbols and theater conventions.

5.4. Develop a capacity to analyze, evaluate aesthetically, and synthesize ideas and experience regarding drama.

5.5. Appreciate the variety of dramatic forms of expression.

5.5.1. View theatrical events emphasizing varied player-audience etiquette.

5.5.2. Recognize similarities and differences between TV, film, live theater, and other forms of drama.

[Sources include: Texas Education Agency, 1984; Way, 1967; Alberta, 1985.]

APPENDIX 5B   Some Functions of the Teacher in the Drama Session

Use: These definitions, illustrated by examples based on the opening scene, can serve as a review for your role in drama sessions and as items to select for a self-assessment checklist.

1. The **reflector** function is fulfilled when the teacher prompts children to ponder their dramatic actions. For example, at one point the opening-scene teacher said, "I wonder why Sam keeps getting the same result each time he approaches another family member seeking play? What do you think is really going on?" This function uses your ability to ask thought-provoking questions. (A prerequisite is careful listening).

2. The **observer** watches and listens in order to facilitate the drama's progress. For example, the teacher in the opening scene walked around from pair to pair listening and making notes as children planned scene enactments from *Sam.* The teacher did the same thing during the paired-for-practice dialogue between the characters of the father and Sam.

3. The **assessor** makes decisions and guides the children to do constructive critical thinking linked to problem solving. "Let's make a list of all the things you liked about today's enactments." (Pause.) "What things can we do to make our improvisations even better tomorrow?"

4. The **signaler** gives cues indicating changed setting status, a switch in the nature of the environment, or a change in the character the teacher is playing. Signalers can make such cues with words, gestures, facial expressions, or props. (The opening-scene teacher, playing out a suggested solution to Sam's problem with a student, said, "Look, Sam, let's go into the kitchen and talk." Taking a few steps, the teacher settled on a stool next to Sam, signaling change of setting. "Cookie?" The teacher took a pretend cookie out of a pretend cookie jar, offered one to Sam, and they pretended to munch.

5. In the **negotiator** function the teacher endows the students with the power to make cooperative decisions. "Which one of the brainstormed solutions to Sam's problem shall we play out next and how shall we organize enactment?"

6. In the **strategist** function the teacher searches for the most effective plan to meet the needs and goals of the class through the progress of the enactment. Teacher to self: "I think we'd better switch to puppets for a while so the shy ones will participate more and won't feel so self-conscious."

7. In the **seeker** function the teacher is open to alternative ideas, methods, sources, and inspirations. "What do you think is the character's main problem? . . . What other dramatic forms could we use with this material? We've played out the decision to get Sam a dog. What scene might follow next? Who might be where and what might happen?" A prerequisite to being a seeker is commitment, being convinced of the value of creative drama for children.

CHAPTER 6

Discussion

"Why didn't they tell me in teacher training that children learn by
discussing and working together?!"

Third-grade teacher, trying discussion groups at learning centers for the first time (Cohen, 1986)

INTRODUCTION

Have you noticed that you learn more about ideas when you discuss, explain, and argue about them with others than when you read a book or listen to a lecture? Group discussion can be an effective technique in your classroom for concept learning across the curriculum, for creative problem solving, and for increasing oral language proficiency. An effective technique for certain intellectual and social learning goals, it can increase trust and friendliness, transferring to many student and ultimately adult work situations. Properly planned for, group work can not only keep students involved with their tasks, but also help the teacher meet a wide range of student academic skills. The purpose, then, of this chapter is to help you understand the teacher's role in using discussion as a tool for children's learning, discovery, and growth in communication.

The chapter deals with problems that might occur during your class discussions. It suggests how to work with nonparticipation, monopolizing, and other roles that block communication and cripple discussion. It presents suggestions for the teacher who is concerned about disorder in small-group discussion (or any time). In addition, the chapter covers various modes of discussions related to creative problem solving and shows how to use them. Other topics explored include dos and don'ts of questioning, "mapping" a question series, fostering cooperation, planning for group work, delegating authority to students, the multi-ability approach, and assessing discussion.

Discussion builds upon the foundation of self-expression, fitting mainly into the portion of expository talk called *exploratory discourse.* Some students who usually do anything but what teachers ask them to do become actively involved with school work, held there by the action of the discussion group.

Why Is Discussion a Useful Tool for the Teacher?

In the past, language arts programs were concerned almost solely with learning to read and write. Earlier chapters in this book have stressed that oral language is just as important. Discussion, an oral language form, can be a key learning, motivating, and thinking activity in any curriculum area. Kindergarten children as well as older ones can grasp the functions of group discussion and understand what it is and what it is not.

There are many reasons, both conceptual and social, for including discussion in your classroom program. Conceptually speaking, through discussion children autonomously learn academic ideas and principles for long-term use and transfer. Socially, they learn to trust, voice opinions, question in a friendly way, negotiate, be assertive and less aggressive, clarify their thinking, and perform many other functions important to a democracy. When members of a group engage in *cooperative* discussion tasks, they are more likely to form friendly ties and to influence each other than when the task stimulates graded competition (Deutsch, 1968). Many of life's important activities require discussion skills. For example, from participating in discussion groups we learn how to manage, coordinate, empathize, teach, learn, research, direct, supervise, write, draw, build, assess, count, and calculate (Cohen, 1986). Children who discuss favorite selections from literature expand their own understanding and motivate classmates to read. You will see in this chapter that discussion is one of your prime teaching tools.

The following is an anonymous "testimonial" from a university student:

> When I was in school we seldom had discussions. On the rare occasions when we had a semblance of one, it was no fun for anyone but the teacher and the one or two "talkers" in the class. I don't think any of my teachers ever realized how discussion operates. As it is, only toward the end of college am I finally forced to speak enough so that I'm gaining some sort of confidence while doing it. I can see how important more help, earlier, would have been. I want to make discussion a more valuable experience for my children than it has been for me.

The following opening scene illustrates most of the types of discussion groups in action and some of the roles and skills. We have all experienced discussion, so instead of detailed analysis, let's see how a productive one works naturally. Later examples show more academically oriented discussions, but in this scene we will see a teacher who is a subtle catalyst rather than an answer provider.

OPENING SCENE: The Broken Tree

A small *buzz session* took place before M. Cummings's third-grade class started in the morning. Children rapidly joined this free exchange of ideas. The following is a sample of the discussion:

> RICKEY: I can't believe someone would do such a thing!
> GYNNE: They must have been feeling awful mad . . . or nuts!
> LINDA: Do you think it was some high school kids? . . . On drugs?
> JOEY: None of us would do anything like that.
> GYNNE: My big brother's in high school . . . he'd never do anything like that.

Some of the children had noticed that over the weekend a little tree on their playground had been ruthlessly hacked in two. Since the children appeared interested and concerned, the teacher let those who had seen it draw a diagram on the board. When opening formalities were over, the teacher took the class out to the playground, where they formed a circle on the grass around the broken tree.

> TEACHER: Would someone else like to say how they feel?

After children had expressed their feelings over the death of the tree (with some moments of silent thought), they proceeded to *brainstorm* about what they might do.

GYNNE: I don't want to sit here feeling sad. I want to do something about it.

RONNY: They probably used an ax. But we don't seem to find any other clues. So there's maybe not much we can do.

ZONYA: Why, why would anyone do such a thing? It was on its way to giving us shade. We really needed it!

LINDA: We could have small groups go to the other classes . . . and we'd tell them how we feel about it.

TEACHER: Would someone like to respond to Linda's idea?

RICKEY: Look, I think Linda's idea is a good one. And maybe they know something we don't know. But we seem to agree that we want another tree here. So why couldn't we just plant another one?

TEACHER: Linda, you looked as if you wanted to say something to Rickey about his idea, but then stopped.

LINDA: Well, I was wondering how we'd know a good tree . . . and how would we dig such a big hole? But I didn't want to cut his idea off.

Occasionally a child would move into the *Socratic* role and *probe* as to why someone would do such a thing. The group then progressed into a *creative problem-solving* session to plan and to elaborate on the favorite hypothesis or remedy. By group consensus, the children decided on the following procedure: They would wage a consciousness-raising campaign, gather more information, and then collect money to buy another tree.

MARY: We'll need to find out if the principal will let us plant another tree; that would be first, wouldn't it?

JOEY: We'll need to find out who we can collect money from.

SUSIE: But before that, like Linda said, we need to find out about trees . . . a good fast-growing one . . . and how much it'd cost.

TEACHER: I see you're thinking about missing information we need to collect.

The children went through some problem-solving steps to decide, for example, what they still needed to find out, what sequence of steps they would take, how they would know if they got a good tree. By the end of the school day, unified by a total group concern, the children had formed task groups composed of four or five members each. Groups ironed out who would do what. Thus they began to carry out plans generated in that creative problem-solving session around the tree. This was a group used to such functioning in planning for social studies units and writing workshops. When a natural, teachable moment such as this one loomed, teacher and children were ready for it and their skills transferred.

Some of the *task-oriented* group activities that the children carried out were the following: They made and decorated cans for each room in the school in order to collect money for replacing the dead tree. Still later, one group designed and constructed written invitations to others to come watch the new tree planting. Later individuals, tutorial two-somes, and one group of five wrote stories about the event, which they read to one another and to other classes. Another group planned contact with the local newspaper.

Analysis of the Scene

Although there are differences between creative problem-solving discussion and other types in this scene, the many modes of discussion fed into and complemented problem solving in a productive way. In one day's time this class experienced buzz session, brainstorming, task, probing modes of discussion, and creative problem solving. At the start of the school year the teacher would not have dreamed that these children would come up with so many feasible and creative ideas, cooperate so well, help each other, and rely on each other's abilities.

If a group has a genuine and challenging problem in any content or real-life area, they are more likely during group work to face and overcome disruptive elements of misunderstanding, frustration, jockeying for status, and ambiguity. The teacher also knew that students work together better if they can explain how they feel—even if they are very upset. An important element of the creative problem-solving discussion is helping children to be aware of skills in this group process as they work together over time. Too often teachers squelch such natural productive opportunities to get on with the scheduled prescribed curriculum in the textbooks.

DEFINITIONS

Discussion is an experience in group thinking. Ideally, everyone contributes and each member learns from the others. Discussants put forth multiple points of view and are willing to change their minds; they interact with one another as well as with the teacher; and this interaction exceeds two- or three-word units common to recitation lessons (Alvermann, Dillon, & O'Brien, 1987). Taking several forms, it is more focused and structured than conversation (Chapter 4). Discussion is a rule-governed activity and serious business. Among the seven forms of discussion to be presented in this chapter are those just illustrated in the opening scene. Figure 6.1 on page 176 shows them in overview. First consider the form called creative problem solving, a central focus of this text.

Creative Problem-Solving Discussion

A creative problem-solving (CPS) discussion might be thought of as a central portion of an outwardly spiraling shell in relation to other types of discussion (i.e., tutorial, buzz session, brainstorming, task, inquiry, and Socratic). (See Figure 6.2 on page 177.) Many of the characteristics of these other types are found in, or are supportive of, problem-solving discussions. A CPS discussion probably uses the greatest number of skills combined with the highest degree of creativity. This combination comes about mainly because of the type of problem a CPS discussion demands.

Types of Problems for CPS Discussion   The more unknowns in a problem, the greater the chance for creativity. What is needed is a problem with no clear-cut right or wrong answer, as was the case for the children in our opening scene. Openness of inquiry is a difficult concept, however, for those who have grown up learning that there is one right way to behave, speak, and do things.

If right and wrong are relative to the values and characteristics of different cultures, then there are more than two sides to an issue. That is, each person is entitled to an opinion influenced by various past experiences. This point of view from social science and the humanities gives backing to the CPS type of discussion.

In any case, the CPS discussion needs no one best solution. As we learned in Chapter 1, the process is what is important. The problem may have a range of more plausible, satisfactory, workable solutions from various points of view. But no one right answer. The common compulsion for closure, referred to as *lysophobia*, means that everything must be tied up in a neat little package. We need to remind ourselves that we can rarely if ever know

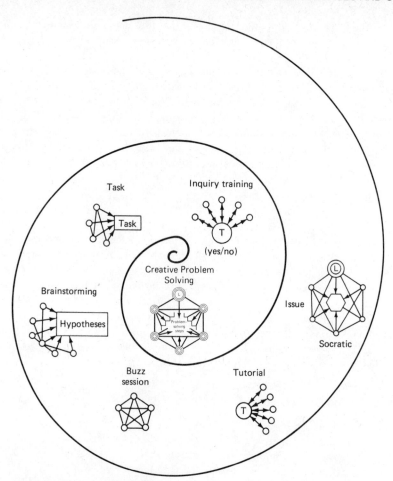

Figure 6.1 Seven types of discussion.

all; we can only abstract a limited amount. To say that a group must come to a consensus is in this sense invalid. Human situations go on and on, and participants learn unceasingly from them.

In a CPS discussion participants take into account feelings of sympathy and empathy, not just internal and external logic and validity. ("Could you see it from her point of view?" "Did your feelings change?") At the same time one learning to be a leader or facilitator in CPS discussions is encouraged to use a sense of humor and a light touch to avoid the grim, demanding, competitive manner characteristic of some Socratic or probing discussions. Also the leader may use a permissive silence in order to give participants time to become aware of the nonverbal aspects of what is going on.

Problems for the CPS discussion need to be complex enough to make worthwhile the use of four areas: (1) problem area, (2) hypothesis or solution finding, (3) planned procedure, and (4) planned assessment. Steps detailed in Chapter 1 may be revisited: becoming aware of potential problems, gathering information, pinpointing a problem, finding ideas, and finding an acceptable solution. We saw some of these steps being used in the opening scene.

Although discussion participants use a planned progression reflected in these steps,

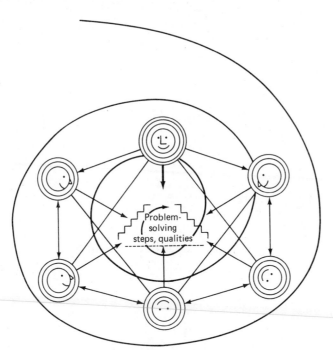

Figure 6.2 Creative problem-solving discussion.

certainly some circling back, almost simultaneous attention, and leaping ahead go on. The ordering of steps may serve as an instructional sequence, converging on the main problem after a great deal of preliminary thinking and interaction.

Some Suggested Procedures Thus, in a CPS discussion the step *not* to begin with is a definitive statement of the main problem. Tossing it out like a stone at the beginning of the discussion may require too much of a conceptual leap for children, bringing about empty verbalization and overgeneralization. If you use a more inductive approach to the problem, children are less likely to be overwhelmed by abstractness.

Other procedures associated with these steps are clarifying key terms associated with the problem, discriminating smaller problems making up a larger problem, dealing with missing information (as illustrated in the opening scene), developing search strategies for it, and assigning the problem to a type or class of problems (seeing the "forest" rather than an isolated "tree").

Diagramming a CPS Discussion Figure 6.2 displays several characteristics of the CPS discussion (Lundsteen, 1976). First, the multiple circles for the participants indicate the many interactive roles the participants play. Second, the person assuming the facilitative or leadership function *(L)* helps to guide the group and the thinking process as participants play their roles. This thinking process, which can evoke many positive feelings, incorporates problem-solving steps just mentioned. The leader may be the teacher initially and later on a prepared student.

Third, the "staircase" in the center suggests the use of some sequential problem-solving steps. Fourth, spaces left open indicate open-endedness. And fifth, the spiraling form overlying the whole suggests the ever-widening effects of engaging in a CPS discussion, a movement to and from other forms of discussion and throughout all areas of the curriculum, and life.

Starters   Besides the opening scene about the broken tree, topics abound in the course of ongoing classroom and curriculum activity. As for literature, recall the opening scene in Chapter 1 where the children were discussing the book *Crow Boy*. The activity book suggests adaptable literature. Some other topics are the following:

> *Science*—why doesn't the water run out of an overturned glass jar just covered with wire screen?
>
> *Health science*—why does a puppet collapse when you let it drop, while we can stand up stiff or move at will?
>
> *Written conventions*—how do we choose whether to put a comma after a salutation to a letter, or is the colon now the mark for any kind of letter?
>
> *Social science*—how can we establish workable standards for care of the classroom?

After formulating a problem, children can work in small groups to solve smaller parts of that problem. Guide questions may be: (1) What do we know about this problem part? (2) What information is relevant to the problem? (3) What data do we need to construct a solution(s)? (4) What are some solutions? (5) Which ones might work (based on what we know or can find out)? The total group then gathers to observe the many ways one problem part is thought about. The class as a whole selects, combines, or decides to continue the search for problem information. When a new problem part is identified the cycle begins again (Maier, 1963).

CPS and Other Modes of Discussion   Recall that CPS discussion might be thought of as the central part of a spiral shell in relation to most other discussion types. Consider contrasts as well as similarities. Although you will find differences between CPS discussion and other types, the many modes can feed into and complement CPS in a productive way.

Buzz Session

Buzz sessions are casual, free, and uninhibited rap sessions on any topic of great interest to the group. During the buzz session, participants can express important feelings and values that they can later carry over into more structured CPS discussions. Once the group starts, teacher involvement is negligible. A purpose and value of this kind of group is to have small, realistic audiences for children's attempts at self-expression, exposition, and interaction. This mode gives them a chance to share themselves with others.

This type of discussion can serve many constructive purposes, for example, the exchange of jump-rope rhymes, jokes, songs, or poetry. The session may, however, simply be an exchange of ignorance, prejudice, put-downs, and aimless random talk lacking in turn taking, reasons, and different ideas. Although a buzz session can be just a means to get to know each other, to get to know feelings and experiences, it can also be an important step in preparation for other, more complex types of discussion (e.g., a first step in developing brainstorming).

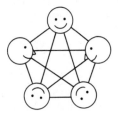

Figure 6.3 Buzz session.

The buzz session may provide a time when a teacher can observe and learn much about the children's thought processes, needs, status, and interests. For example, the opening-scene teacher might learn that Ronny needs more background in how to approach a newspaper editor, that Gynne has some trouble with listening skills, and that Rickey shows skill in synthesizing ideas that could be useful to many groups. Finally, the session may be a chance for teachers to share themselves as human beings.

Starters Besides all of the natural opportunities, the following are some possible starter or demonstration topics:

> Times we want to remember—times we want to forget.
>
> We wish friends wouldn't—we wish friends would.
>
> Who am I?
>
> What is power and how do you get it?
>
> How I feel about this school.
>
> What is the best program on TV and why?
>
> Masks, false faces, and makeup.
>
> If you could be anywhere, where would you choose and why?
>
> Money and. . . .
>
> How we think college students (or any other older or highly different group) spend their time.

In the diagram of the buzz session shown in Figure 6.3, the lines represent interactive, multiway communication in which each participant interacts with every other one. Note that a leader *(L)* (or teacher) is not necessarily present.

Brainstorming

The uninhibited making of hypotheses in brainstorming represents a portion of the creative problem-solving process. These two discussion modes differ in that brainstorming does not include an evaluation step. A brainstorming session, separating invention from decision making, is designed to produce as many ideas as possible to solve the problem at hand. Brainstorming is free and uninhibited, like a buzz session. Here the fluency, confidence, and respect for others' feelings can carry over to other discussion types.

Inventing new ideas requires one to think about things not readily in one's mind. Accordingly, a facilitator does the following: keeps the purpose before the group; makes sure everyone gets a turn; enforces any ground rules; may stimulate by asking creative questions;

and sees that the group comes up with a long list of ideas that approach the question from every conceivable angle (Figure 6.4).

Suggested Procedures   Seat the participants in a semicircle facing the written problem. Record the ideas in full view to give a sense of collective achievement, to reduce the tendency to repeat, and to help stimulate other ideas. Make sure a chalkboard, transparency, or tape is available for the quick recording of ideas. Participants might be seated around a table. Some children need something in front of them during intense interaction so that they do not feel quite so exposed. Note in Figure 6.4 that the teacher is not necessarily present. With young children, you may act as a recorder, having already prepared the group with the rules for this brainstorming. You or your student facilitator may need to remind participants of the rules. Given a congenial setting, an experienced facilitator, and a purpose in mind, the discussion can follow the typical rules shown in Box 6.1. These rules can be tailored to fit individual needs and resources.

The sixth rule outlaws negative criticism of any kind. Adverse judgment of ideas is held off until later, when all ideas have been entered and reviewed. There is no attempt during the process to sort out the most promising solutions from the good, bad, unrealistic, or unworkable ones. If even those wild ideas that lie well outside the realm of the possible are encouraged, the group may generate other options that *are* possible and that no one would have considered.

After brainstorming, the participants can form a task group and concentrate on the most promising ideas, nominating ideas worth developing further, inventing improvements on promising ideas, relaxing the no-criticism rule. Members can preface constructive criticism with: "What I like best about that idea is . . ."; "Might it be better if . . . ?" The group can develop a time line for deciding which of the selected and improved ideas (possibly two at a time) to advance and how. Children may be typically unaware that ultimately coming to a collective decision involves some procedural discussion about how and when the group will narrow down to a decision (Fisher & Ury, 1981).

Figure 6.4 depicts not only the free-flowing interaction of brainstorming, but also the major centering on the generation of ideas (hypotheses). The key to wise decision making lies in selecting from a great number and variety of options. One might try to look through the eyes of different experts during the brainstorming.

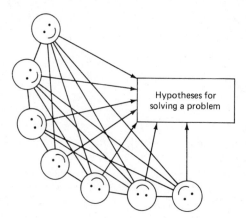

Figure 6.4   Brainstorming session.

BOX 6.1 Brainstorming Rules

1. *Composition:* The group needs to be large enough to include a composite of heterogeneous skills that are relevant to the problem area. The size is *just* large enough to contain individuals with the kinds of competencies needed. (If the group is larger than five elementary-age children, it is likely that someone will not contribute.)

2. *Shooting high and wide:* The group welcomes wild, "way-out" ideas; none are excluded; no one feels foolish.

3. *Quantity:* The group seeks, stresses, and desires quantity. The group works quickly.

4. *Hitchhiking:* Group members seek to hitchhike on others' ideas, to combine ideas. One idea should stimulate another, like a string of firecrackers setting off one another.

5. *Last push:* The group pushes hard for one last stretch of ideas; sometimes the breakthrough comes in that last persistent push.

6. *No negatives:* Invent first, decide later.

Starters   Brainstorming discussions can grow out of statements like these:

"We've got all this leftover velvet material. What could we do with it?"

"We can't go to the zoo today. What could we do instead?"

"Pretend we're shipwrecked—here's a box of objects [egg-slicer, pantyhose, etc.] washed up on the beach. What might we use them for?"

"What easily available materials can we use to change our room these last few weeks?" (For this idea a matrix can be formed of materials—paper, fabric, paint—and common components in the classroom that might be altered with them. Common components might be desks, walls, windows.)

(See Chapter 8 for a description of how brainstorming may be used as a prewriting activity. Also see the activity book.)

Tutorial Session

Tutorial discussions may provide basic information and practice for skills that are used later in creative problem solving, although tutorials differ vastly in amount of interaction and probably in complexity. The most simple diagram of a tutorial session would show a two-circle display—one for the tutor, one for the student being tutored—with some dialogue as the two center on the task. But with a larger group the tutor typically does most of the talking, as shown in Figure 6.5. Skilled tutors are adept at drawing out the tutee so that the balance of talk is altered.

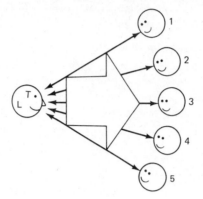

Figure 6.5 Tutorial session.

Task Group Discussion

In the task group, the development of procedural steps is clearly related to creative problem solving. But, in contrast, the task group problem may have a right answer, and the group may be on a schedule. (The task, however, needs to require more thinking than learning to memorize or apply a rule.) If the problem is narrowed so that it requires a solution that is a finished product, the task group may employ few of the kinds of steps and leadership roles found in creative problem solving. Since each group member may have his or her own assignment, coordination and interactive communication may occur mainly at the beginning planning session and at the end of the work period—quite different from the CPS discussion.

The task group usually has a clearly defined and understood job to do. A child will think: "What we decide will affect me. Why? Because I am going to have to do something if we decide to do this instead of that." Although the structure varies, the components are usually the following:

Components of Task Group Discussion
1. *Task definition:* A clearly defined and understood task
2. *Assignment:* Clearly defined individual roles and assignments
3. *Resources:* Necessary resources (e.g., books); optimally, willingness to help each other, to serve as resources
4. *Time schedule:* A schedule and close supervision of progress among peers or by a student facilitator, within a limited amount of time
5. *Report:* A final reporting to a larger group on the product

Figure 6.6 represents the major focus on a task. It shows some interaction and indicates that the teacher is present in the room, but generally apart from the work and the interaction. The group needs to have the resources to complete the task successfully. These resources include thinking skills, vocabulary, relevant information, social skills, and properly prepared task instructions.

Suggested Procedures   All this use of skills and resources is unlikely to happen by magic. Teachers lay groundwork through careful planning. Groundwork includes learning to be responsive to the needs of the group and its members, including their specific cooperative behaviors, and using norms for equal participation. Groups may use any number of ways to record or keep track of the various things they will need to do in order to

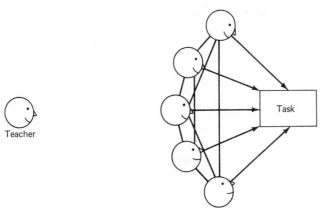

Figure 6.6 Task group discussion.

accomplish a task. Figure 6.7 on page 184 is a sample form for a group of about five children to note their plan of action and specify who is responsible for what.

   If teachers require each task group member to turn out a product or a piece of the final product demonstrating understanding, but with use of resources of the group, motivated students with undeveloped academic skills will demand assistance and explanation. For the advanced students, the act of explaining to others solidifies their own learning. When they are able to use each other as resources, even slow readers, writers, and computers can encounter more challenging conceptual material.

   Table 6.1 on page 185 gives student behaviors required for task groups in learning centers and in task discussions.

Starters   Task groups exist in many forms in the school. In social studies projects, committees may be found to focus on the making of murals, plays, scripts, or dioramas. A group might have the task of building a tent, planning a nutritious meal, eating it, and cleaning up. Advisory groups for written composition are sometimes task-oriented—committed to help each other with a proposed or written piece. Further examples of group tasks might be solving a difficult word problem in math, discovering what makes a battery in a lantern work, interpreting a passage in a book, understanding plant germination behavior, role-playing some event in regional history, creating a pantomime or charade to illustrate an idea, and creating a three-minute conversation using new words in a foreign language. All of these are conceptual tasks.

Inquiry-Training Group

   Inquiry learning is a process of acquiring knowledge whereby the children ask questions and the teacher answers yes or no. Closed inquiry-training discussions differ from creative problem-solving ones on at least two counts: (1) the direction of thinking (convergent-divergent) and (2) the formulation of questions by the leaders. Both are elaborated below.

Direction of Thinking   In creative problem solving, students do not need to converge toward one correct response. Participants value multiple alternatives. In closed inquiry there is immediately one right answer and the teacher usually "fishes" for it.

Name _____

Project _____

Date _____

GROUP PROJECT
PLAN OF ACTION*

Things we will do (in order):

1. _____
2. _____
3. _____
4. _____
5. _____

Things we will bring from home (materials needed):

1. _____
2. _____
3. _____
4. _____
5. _____

Things we need to find out more about (topics/subtopics for research):

1. _____
2. _____
3. _____
4. _____
5. _____

*After you have completed this page, go back and put the name of a group member by each item number. A group member's name may appear more than once. It will be the group member's responsibility to do each job his or her name appears by.

Figure 6.7   Group project plan of action. (*Source:* D. Jim Laney, University of North Texas)

Questions   In a CPS type of discussion, questioning is not designed for yes/no answers from an all-knowing source. Questions are more open ended. They are designed to provoke certain steps in the process and with respect to divergent thought. In closed inquiry, the yes/no response from the leader serves as a responsive environment for the learner. In the following example the teacher has a bimetallic strip that is bending upward when held over a burner:

> CHILD: Is it made of wood?
> TEACHER: No. Ask me another question.

This kind of dialogue goes on as children become skilled in systematically forming hypotheses. Figure 6.8 depicts this type of discussion.

Socratic or Probing Discussion

Finally, the CPS discussion differs from the Socratic one, especially in process. Problem solving is, as mentioned, concerned with steps leading to a goal and procedures for solving

Table 6.1   STUDENT BEHAVIORS REQUIRED FOR TASK GROUPS IN LEARNING CENTERS AND DISCUSSION GROUPS

Learning centers	Discussion groups
Asking questions	Asking for others' opinions
Listening	Listening
Helping others	Reflecting on what has been said
Helping students do things for themselves	Being concise
Showing others how to do things	Giving reasons for ideas
Explaining by telling how and why	Allowing everyone to contribute
Finding out what others think	Pulling ideas together
Making up his or her own mind	Finding out if group is ready to make decision

Source: Cohen (1986).

the problem. The Socratic-style leader (named for the classic Greek teacher, Socrates) tries to stir participants from their complacency. The leader in the Socratic type of discussion provokes participants to explore the sides of an issue. Such leaders probe critically in the manner of a devil's advocate. The leader in the CPS discussion, however, avoids pointed, critical probings. Criticism (even implied by a question) can be taken personally by children and may promote defensiveness that blocks communication. The CPS leader treads more carefully than the Socratic one. Some assessment, decision making, and convergent thinking, however, take place as CPS participants progress from step to step in problem solving after each divergent phase.

Even preschool teachers can use this probing-discussion strategy to react to problems of sexism and racism. For example, a group of boys in the wheel toy area were refusing to allow any girls in, saying, "Girls can't play here!" The teacher began to probe: "Oh, why not? Doesn't your mommy drive a car?"

Probing can be an important strategy for subject mastery discussions. Teachers need probes to encourage students to go beyond initial, sometimes superficial, responses. Below are some examples of probes from a seventh-grade social studies discussion of events leading up to the Civil War read first in their textbook (Alvermann, Dillon, & O'Brien, 1987):

Probes can seek to *clarify:* "But why was the book *Uncle Tom's Cabin* so important?"

Probes can seek to *justify:* "You say the book was fictional; what evidence is there in your textbook that makes you think it was?"

Probes can *refocus* on key concepts: "So if the book was only fictional, why was it so important?"

Teacher
acting as
responsive
environment
(yes/no)

Figure 6.8   Inquiry-training discussion.

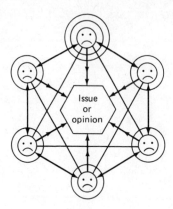

Figure 6.9 Probing-role, Socratic discussion.

Probes can seek greater student-to-student *interaction:* "Each turn to a neighbor and ask one another, 'Why does the teacher think *Uncle Tom's Cabin* was so important?' "

Figure 6.9 depicts the multistrategy, interactive, rather grim-faced probing of an issue or opinion.

In summary, the seven types of discussion we have examined were depicted in Figure 6.1. They often grow out of, feed into, or complement the central one, creative problem solving.

WHO ARE THE PARTICIPANTS IN CLASSROOM DISCUSSION?

One of the most important considerations is the roles that participants play during discussion. Think back to the roles you have noticed yourself.

Roles in Classroom Discussion

After a classroom discussion, a teacher can ask children to tell behaviors that the different participants showed. Then the children can try to group these behaviors and give them labels, such as "all those that clear up ideas," "all those that get things started," "all those that help other people." Box 6.2 gives a partial list of roles that other students and teachers have spotted. Some especially valuable for children have been placed first and starred. You can probably think of others or of different terms you would prefer.

Some of these roles are excellent aids to communication; some tend to cripple it. For example, the *facilitator's* role may include the following:

1. Seeing to it that the job gets done (that the group makes clear decisions in the time allotted)
2. Ensuring that everyone participates
3. Making certain that the group does not ride over the feelings of individual members
4. Representing the group in asking for teacher help when group resources are exhausted

---

BOX 6.2 Some Roles Taken During Discussion

Facilitator ★	Comparer	Teacher
Clarifier ★	Expert	Goal definer
Summarizer ★	Problem typer	Definer
Evaluator ★	Labeler	Dissenter
Harmonizer ★	Translator	Encourager
Resource ★	Monopolizer	Noncontributor
Recorder ★	Data seeker	Appreciator
Spokesperson ★	Observer	Compromiser
Active listener	Hypothesizer	Example giver
Arranger of physical	Compromiser	Initiator
conditions	Summarizer	Rule reminder

Everyone understands that the facilitator does not control the decisions or the content of the discussion.

A *resource* student may have directly relevant academic skills for the task (e.g., may be a good reader who responds well to uncertainty). The *harmonizer* eases any interpersonal conflicts that arise and is attentive to the feelings of individual members. The *spokesperson* addresses the class as a whole on behalf of the group or is a representative to a class coordinating committee. You can classify roles you uncover in various ways, including those showing the following:

- Functions related to tasks
- Functions maintaining group processes
- Hindrances

Consider next the hindrance roles, roles that are unproductive for the group.

Roles that Block Communication

Assessment of discussion roles and skills that children already have is a first step in knowing who your discussants are. The teacher can anticipate problems that may arise in organizing instruction and in using discussion by looking at and trying to uncover the reasons for roles that block classroom communication. Consider five roles that may halt interchange of ideas in your class: (1) the nonparticipant, (2) the monopolizer (or chronic interrupter), (3) the off-the-tracker, (4) the scapegoat maker, and (5) the shocker.

The Nonparticipant   What can teachers do about their timid nonparticipants in discussion? Perhaps the first step is assessment, to try to find the reasons. Does the child's behavior stem from timid patterns brought from home? Fear of exposure? A preference for daydreaming? Is this a child who makes few contributions, but when made they are highly valuable? Or is this a child in a dangerous state who has given up trying?

What to do   After helping such children take some responsibility for their problem, teachers can guide them to *pinpoint* for themselves their nonparticipating behavior and *chart* their own progress. Help them participate by preparing them beforehand for the discussion whenever possible, tuning up their special abilities and role.

Forewarning helps. That is, perhaps teachers need to reverse the usual procedure of always asking the question first and then mentioning a pupil's name. Forewarned of expected response, the timid child has some extra time to think. Give him or her plenty of time, extending and rephrasing the question if necessary.

A *supportive social climate* helps to motivate such a student. Try the child in small groups with others who do or who will agree to play supportive, respectful roles. Failure to treat individuals with respect blocks communication. If asked about nonparticipation, the timid child may say that another child already said what he or she was going to contribute. In this case, the teacher or facilitator can say:

"Please explain why you agree with Susan's comment."

The reason for agreement may even turn out to be unique, and a contribution of new information to be confirmed.

Even the slowest and most inarticulate child can learn to discuss, unless unmotivated or unless the topic is too difficult. A teacher who can weld the class into a constructive unit with basic group solidarity has most of the battle won. ("We take care of each other.") If the nonparticipants know clearly what they have done that is successful and what still needs to be improved, the situation gets better.

Motivation is crucial. Actually the first objective is to get nonparticipating children to like or want to communicate in a discussion group, to feel that it is not only their right but their duty to have a defensible opinion. The problem of the nonparticipant may be deeply rooted in feelings of social and performance inferiority. If some children always know less about all group discussion tasks and topics, then they come to have such a low opinion of their skills and potential success that they will not participate. But nothing succeeds like success, even a series of very small ones.

Coaching is one device that a teacher can use. You can coach a child who says "I can't do it" to the point of genuine competence in a given area (e.g., animal care, a foreign culture, operation of a machine, handling a set of guide questions or prompts for responding to a storyteller—I learned . . . ; I liked . . . ; I'd like to know. . . .). Then place such a child in the role of "expert." Rotate this coached role of expert so that all the children get a chance to play it at some time and thus to assert themselves.

Certain procedures can help the nonparticipants. When shy children withdraw and more aggressive children take over, the teacher can instruct children to do several things. Consider three of them.

• First, the discussion leader could ask the group to say nothing at all for a minute while they take time to just think. They might think about the most important thing the group could accomplish in the next few minutes. In the case of older children the leader could ask everyone to write down a brief note about thoughts during this time. The leader could then call on children who have not contributed earlier, saying "Can you help us?" With their notes at hand, shy ones may get over their fear or hesitancy.

• A second procedural way to reduce takeover by monopolizers, but still allay their fear that they will not get a chance, is to have the leader say:

"The next five minutes are for those who haven't had a chance yet. Those of you who want to speak, I'll write your initials here so you'll get a turn later."

As the withdrawn children are then encouraged to contribute, the aggressive children, reassured that they will get a chance, can listen more attentively to what others have to say.

• Summarizing several times is a third procedure designed to draw in the nonparticipant. For example, say:

"Alex, will you tell what we've said so far?"
"Beth, will you state what we think we know about spiders?"
"Tim, will you restate our agreement about kickball?"

Such contributions will help the group become clear on what has been accomplished and what may lie ahead.

The Monopolizer   A monopolizer is one who jumps right into the middle of others' sentences with both feet (if indeed anyone gets a chance for even a sentence when the monopolizer is around). The monopolizer appears to sit in one place with mouth open, tongue wagging, eyes shut, and fingers in ears. Is this student just too immature to work in a group? Probably not; adults also can exhibit problems of dominance, struggling over leadership and participating unequally.

What to do   Since this role blocks the communication of others, it is urgent for the teacher to intervene. First be certain that students have grasped the rules for working in a group. When teachers hear students reminding others of how they need to behave, they know that the children have internalized the norms introduced and kept before them on charts such as that shown below.

Discussion: What We Remember

- Everybody gets a turn.
- Bring out many different ideas.
- Listen to each other and think about it.
- Give reasons.
- Help each other. (But don't just do it for them—help them do it themselves.)
- Ask for others' opinions.

With internalized norms, much of the work that teachers do will be taken care of by the students for themselves. That is, the group makes certain everyone understands what to do, the group keeps members on task, and group members assist one another.

Having set up specific group roles, the teacher can encourage the aggressive monopolizer to try the role of the *recorder,* who gets to summarize the proceedings of the discussion periodically, and the *spokesperson,* who gets to report the group findings to an outside group. This reporting role represents a delayed but a definite hearing. Once monopolizing children see themselves as others see them, as precipitating a group problem and hindering group

effectiveness, they tend to change their egocentric disregard and to try other, more cooperative roles.

Intimate grouping and *skilled questioning* can help. Students who are simply talkative
and enjoy impressing a large class may feel differently in a small-sized, intimate group
involved in enhancing cooperative skills. Excessively verbal children can learn to channel
their valuable fluency so that it makes a greater impact and helps others. Also, the teacher
can guide such children to sharpen their skills in listening for interpersonal insights that
are more valuable than their pouring forth on every point. During a discussion the teacher
might ask aggressive or monopolizing children questions or offer suggestions such as these
from time to time:

> *"What do you think was helpful (or interesting) about so and so's idea?"*
>
> *"Ask her a question to see what she means."*
>
> *"How could our words show that we respect other speakers, even if we don't agree with them?"*

Courtesy acquisition is another factor in improvement related to the preceding questions. Frequently the aggressive, monopolizing child especially needs help with the language
and attitude of courtesy. The teacher might say:

> *"What words can we use when we have interrupted?"*
>
> *"How could we say that in a more kindly way?"*
>
> *"How could you say it differently so that you leave out people's names?"*

It takes more linguistic energy to be polite, to say, "Excuse me, yesterday I read in [gives
reference] that the fact was . . . instead. So I wonder what reference you used," instead of
"You're wrong!" or "That's a lie."

Peer control, modeling, and *role-playing* can help, too. Along with the teacher giving
the monopolizer suggestions for alternative actions, the group itself will usually handle the
consistently impulsive, overanxious interrupter or chronic arguer. They can do this in the
nonpunitive, restraining, yet pleasantly helpful way that the teacher models. Role play may
also help (see the activity book). The basic idea is that the teacher and the group value the
talkative child's contribution but want to include others.

Pinpointing and charting can also help. Monopolizers can pinpoint their monopolizing
behavior at its base level (usual level of frequency), then, with the teacher's guidance, chart
their daily progress in restraining and redirecting themselves. Charting will usually bring
behavior to a tolerable level quickly if the children see the behavior as something they want
to improve. Children who see their weekly number of interruptions decrease from 50 to 30
to 10 are motivated by their feeling that it is *their* problem, *their* responsibility, *their*
progress, and *their* success.

Valuing differences is another acquisition that helps children who tend to play the
monopolizing role (and the nonparticipant role too). As mentioned, learning to disagree with
courtesy and respect is particularly difficult for this type of child. The teacher might say to
such a child:

"You don't have to agree completely. Just listen to see if there isn't a bit of the other person's idea you might want to explore or to borrow."

Then have the child's group play the following game for a while. The idea is to find something in the last speaker's message that they can agree with, or at least that they find interesting or worth exploring, *before* they can state their own disagreement.

Too often a person leaps to disagree and tenaciously clings to this position before seeing what the areas of disagreement are. Thus, a major task of the teacher is helping children (especially the monopolizing kind of child) to learn that differences are valuable, that unanimous views can be dangerous, and that one can still value a person even when strongly disagreeing with that person's views. The teacher can help make it easier for the child to accept views that are well supported by pointing out that such open-minded behavior is a mark of maturity in a discussion.

When a teacher and class have internalized the norm or motto that *everyone will be good at something, but no one will be good at everything,* the philosophy of the multiability classroom can help with negative role problems. The **multiability** strategy convinces students that many different abilities will be necessary for successful group performance. Again, students know that many different skills will be needed and that each person in the group will be competent in at least one (Tammivaara, 1982; Rosenholtz, 1985).

For example, one group member might be good at understanding why a character in a story behaved the way she did; another might be good at going over the text with much care to glean more clues about it; another might be good at finding a way to phrase the group's answer about main character motive; and yet another might be good at dramatizing it as a report to the total group (Cohen, 1986). As a teacher you can set up multiability tasks that deter the monopolizer and encourage the nonparticipant. (The activity book for Chapter 10 has a multiability activity called "advertising designer"; Chapter 14 deals further with the advantageous strategy of multiability grouping and the bilingual, low-lingual, and low-status child.)

The Off-the-Tracker   What about the child who typically appears to be getting off the track during a discussion? Much depends on the type of discussion and on its goal. Repetitions, irrelevancies, and comments on points and questions made much earlier are a part of most normal discussions. Oral speech and its ideas do not come in a linear way with paradelike precision. Severe control blocks creativity and spontaneity.

There are several reasons why children make apparently irrelevant statements. Their private planning may have been triggered by a few words that caused them to leave the stream of discourse (Chapter 3). Also, a child with a good idea to present may be afraid of forgetting what it is before having had a chance to give it. Efforts to hang on to an idea can so occupy children that they lose the trend of the discussion. They may even fail to realize that they agree with what someone else has just said.

What to do   Keeping a pad of paper and pencil handy for quick jotting or drawing cues can help the child get back to the main trend of the discussion. Note taking or picture cuing may help the chronic interrupter and the timid child, too. If an off-the-tracker consistently creates an outstanding problem, provide the kinds of discussion in which wild brainstorming is appropriate and in which, by contrast, a clearly detailed task creates discipline. The teacher or group facilitator can ask questions and make statements such as these:

"Does this idea help us with our task?"

"What has this idea to do with the earlier one?"

"Can you help us relate what you're saying now to an earlier idea perhaps?"

Again, such verbally straying children can chart their own progress. They can tell better than anyone whether they are trying to stay on task.

The Scapegoat Makers and Their Victim   What if one of the members is treated as a scapegoat, ridiculed by the others? What can be done? Again, the teacher or student facilitator can model a demonstration of support and appreciation that clearly indicates the right of every contribution, especially minority opinion, to be heard. Clever facilitators can find something of value to the group in almost anyone's comment. They can take the simplest, most inane comment and somehow give it face-saving dignity and importance to the task. Facilitators can model the desire to see a situation corrected rather than an offender punished. They can help the group take care of problems immediately in order to clear the air, maintaining a healthy emotional climate so that grudges do not build. Role play using fictitious names, masks, and puppets helps.

The Shocker   The obvious response to the intentional shocker is not to be shocked. Nonreinforcement usually will extinguish behavior while you are searching for and developing more desirable behaviors for the child to engage in. Ignore the behavior, taking others into your confidence, if necessary. If shockers fail to provoke that horrified reaction so delicious to them, they'll forget this tactic.

For example, on an observational walk in which a kindergarten class was out looking for signs of spring, one young observer gleefully announced to the world, "Look on this leaf—bird do-do!!!" The effect on the rest of the youngsters was so gratifying it seemed he would repeat it to the world at every possible chance. The teacher responded quietly, "Yes, it is bird do-do; just one of the signs of spring. Now let's go on and look for others." A district teacher-evaluator, who had accompanied the class, commented later on the teacher's cool way of handling the would-be "shocker."

WHAT FRAMEWORK OF GOALS FITS DISCUSSION?

Recall that goals grow out of needed attention to processes, purposes, and attitudes of learners. *Processes* of group discussion are interactive and cooperative. They integrate most thinking and communicative processes. *Purposes* of group discussion span a wide range of problems, tasks, and conceptual understandings. *Attitudes* range from simple pleasures in self-expression to commitment to deep democratic values. One motivational goal is to develop an identity in relation to others. Thus frameworks in earlier and subsequent chapters are related to discussion regarding process, purpose, and attitude.

Table 6.2 on pages 194 and 195 shows a sample of communicative purposes in relation to assessment tasks. Teachers can use this table for planning and assessment tasks for the yearly curriculum and for related daily lesson planning.

WHERE DOES DISCUSSION TAKE PLACE?

In spite of being clear about rationale goals, objectives, and knowing how to handle problem children, some teachers might be discouraged from organizing small-group discussion because they feel they have an inappropriate physical room arrangement. But if determined teachers in classrooms with 48 seats (screwed inexorably to the floor) can block them into eight groups and find success, those of us with fewer students ought to be able to organize small-group settings in our classrooms. During brief discussions, two to a seat is not too uncomfortable; extra stools help. There may be a multipurpose or media room you can borrow. One teacher created the class newspaper—the *Bookland Blabber*—with small groups working on the floor in the hall outside the classroom.

Even if your furniture is readily movable, try sitting on small carpet squares, cushions, or wrapping paper on the floor. Discussion groups will need space and sufficient freedom from the noise of others in order to hear themselves talk. Discussion groups have less space demands than task groups working with materials. Most discussion groups preferably sit in a circle so that everyone can see and hear everyone else; otherwise there may be little interaction between those who have to twist around to see each other. Place the groups as far apart as your room will permit, leaving space for you to circulate freely between groups. You might map out your classroom arrangement with the children.

Plan space for groups who work with pretested manipulative or written materials so that they have room to lay out tasks and keep materials from tumbling off the table and being jostled. The advantage of common task cards is in bringing the group immediately together in sharing understanding of the instructions.

Getting 35 children into and out of groups does require some of the following provisions: careful and detailed preplanning, prearranged signals, and a breaking down of the task into small practicable parts concerning the participants, the location, and the activities. The rewards in the growth of oral communication and learning are great enough that it is well worth the trouble.

If setting up work stations with instructions and materials sounds to you like too much for one typical busy teacher, you're right. Teachers can train students to do the work of setting up task-group stations, moving furniture, and setting out materials needed. Lists or pictures (for nonreaders) on laminated task cards guide the students. Students set up and clean up.

HOW DOES A TEACHER USE AND HANDLE DISCUSSION?

As usual, by the time we have answered questions about the why, who, what, and where, the road is well paved to the how of teaching. This section considers mainly the roles teachers play, some specifics about handling disorder—a prime concern of many—and last, but definitely not least, questioning strategies.

The Teacher's Role

In group discussion and task work the teacher's role includes the functions shown in Box 6.3 on page 196.

Teachers do *not* directly supervise students when group work actually starts, and they do *not* ensure that students do their work exactly as directed. Nor do teachers watch for and immediately correct every mistake. Instead teachers delegate authority to students in charge of seeing that members get needed help and that group jobs get completed. When the task groups start, the teacher *lets go* and allows the groups to talk and do their work using provided instructions. In preparation for group work with objectives and criteria for evaluation, and in the debriefing or wrap-up afterward, teachers supervise directly.

Table 6.2   **COMMUNICATIVE PURPOSES IN RELATION TO DISCUSSION TASKS**

General purpose	Specific purpose		Task	Audience/partner
Discussing	Collaborative: hypothesizing	(L)[a]	Discussing possible explanations for effects observed during science experiment	F[b]
	Collaborative: decision making and evaluation of evidence	(L)	Pooling information to decide which crop should be planted on an imaginary island	F
			Deciding which "suspect" committed crime in "whodunit" game	F/PP[c]
	Collaborative: story construction	(L)	Sequencing pictures to make a story	F
	Persuasive/argumentative	(L)	Justifying point of view in discussion about occupations	F
Instructing/directing [task group]	Giving instructions		Teaching partner how to play a board game	F
			Giving directions for carrying out a science experiment	F
			Following directions in a science experiment	F
Giving and interpreting information [task group]	Relaying information	(L)	Giving an account of how a spider builds its web (listened to on tape)	PP
	Conveying information: based on personal knowledge		Giving an account of an occupation	F/A
	Conveying information: based on observation		Giving an account of effects observed in a science experiment	F/A

What is the secret of effective management of such complex instruction? In general, students work well when they do the following: (1) have a clearly defined task, (2) take responsibility for their own and others' behavior, and (3) receive advance preparation. Teachers need to avoid hovering and looking as though they were a potential member of the group. If students see a teacher hovering nearby, they will stop relying on themselves and their group. They will stop talking and look to the teacher. Observe carefully and listen to the discussion from a discreet distance.

A fine line exists between direct supervision and the supportive role. Teachers can ask key questions at a critical moment to stimulate a group to rise to a higher level. Teachers can help reinforce rules and roles when necessary. For example, if a group has gotten stuck and frustration is rising, the teacher raises a few open-ended questions to get the students going—and then leaves. Or, if a group has finished its task very quickly, the teacher asks them an application-type question to get them thinking about another situation—and walks away.

Table 6.2 (*Continued*)

General purpose	Specific purpose		Task	Audience/partner
	Summarizing and conveying information: from notes and pictures		Extracting facts about crops to be grown on an imaginary island	F
	Reporting the outcome of a collaborative task		Recounting (from notes taken) the particulars of a "suspect" invented by pupils during a "whodunit" game	PP/A
			Recounting steps taken and hypotheses developed during a science experiment	PP
Narrating [task group]	Retelling a story	(L)	After listening to story recorded on tape	PP
	Telling a personal anecdote		After listening to anecdotes by other 11-year-olds, recorded on tape	F/A
	Constructing a story		Based on sequencing 4 pictures in collaboration with partner	PP/A
	Summarizing the plot of a book		Telling about a favorite book	F/A
Describing/specifying [task group]				
	Describing pictures: for comparison and information		Taking turns with partner to describe pictures on a related theme	F

[a]L indicates a substantial listening component.
[b]F = pupil's friend.
[c]PP = other pupils.
[d]A = assessor.
Source: Adapted from MacClure & Hargreaves, 1986.

Early on when a teacher participates in discussion groups, it is mainly to model and guide process, not to provide content. In fact, when teachers are skillful at developing abilities, eventually they eliminate most of the need for their guidance in a discussion. There are, of course, times when they disseminate information in the classroom. But if teachers need compulsively to be needed and to dominate, then open-ended discussion activity is not for them—unfortunately for the growth of the children.

In sum, teachers can play four roles, which they may move into and out of for varied reasons. Teachers concentrate on the last role. (1) The instructor role places teachers in a telling or clarifying position. Overuse resembles a lecture. (2) The participant role shows a teacher as a group member, sharing information and freely expressing opinions, perhaps modeling varied ways of responding, reacting to issues or other points of view, and applying critical and creative thinking. The participant role, however, may rob students of credibility. (3) The consultant role has the teacher serving as an advisor moving from group to group on request. However, students need to use this resource only after all other resources have

---

BOX 6.3 Role of the Teacher in Discussion

1. Set up directions.
2. Assign students to groups so that there is a good mix of needed abilities.
3. Help students internalize group work rules.
4. Train students to use them for cooperation (all participate and help).
5. Delegate authority to students playing special roles (e.g., facilitators).
6. Hold groups accountable for any products and much of the process of their endeavors.

---

been exhausted. (4) The nondirective teaching role promotes children's autonomous thinking. Placing trained responsibility on the students for group-centered leadership and discussion, this teacher role is the least intrusive (Alvermann, Dillon, & O'Brien, 1987).

A teacher taking a nondirective, neutral role does not offer opinions, ask questions, or confirm responses. Students' questions are redirected to other students in the group. Use of such a role is an ultimate goal and is possible because of transferred model behaviors.

A teacher may have developed skillful questioning strategies, management procedures, and assessment techniques, but none of these is worth much in a vacuum without dynamic classroom discussion. Box 6.4 presents some specific criteria for topics or content that a teacher can use to stimulate discussion.

Help children to become note takers and collectors of information (as suggested in

---

BOX 6.4 Criteria for Topic Selection

1. *Class needs and interests.* Class needs and interests are a cornerstone for selecting the content for discussion. Productive topics are also the ones that grow out of what the children think they know and feel. These topics are the ones that ease them into the realities of the external world.

2. *Teacher observation.* In general, successful topics are those that the teacher derives by careful observation of the group and diagnoses as belonging in a map of skills and concepts that the children need.

3. *Assertion or question making.* Select topics you can put into a sentence with a verb implying action—as either an assertion or a question.

4. *Alternative views.* A topic for discussion needs to be able to accommodate honest differences of opinion, rights and wrongs, and relative merits of causes or solutions (e.g., which of two field trips?). Openness for alternatives is important.

5. *Available information.* No matter what the topic, however, the quality of opinion depends on the amount and accuracy of the information held by those discussing (content). Children cannot easily discuss the relative merits of a TV show that only one child in the group has actually seen.

Chapters 4 and 7). One mark of successful discussion participants is their awareness of the potential value of almost all experience (theirs and others') as material for discourse. If children continually collect an ample store, they will be convinced that they have something worthwhile to contribute to a discussion group. (See Figure 6.13 on page 208 for a partial list of skills involved in discussion.) Examples of sample topics follow:

Sample Discussion Topics

- Drugs: What do we need to learn about them?
- What does a president do?
- What good are rules? What is a law and why was it made? What are customs and why do we follow them?
- What is a group? Do the members have the same goal? Do they depend on each other? Is this a group? Why or why not? When does concern with groups go too far and the individual lose out? (Many more ideas for topics are in the activity book.)

What to Do About Disorder

Some teachers fear having several discussion groups going on simultaneously because signals might not work and there might be some loss of classroom control. When and if general disruption does occur and the supposedly prepared groups cannot handle it themselves, let natural consequences of limit setting and postponement operate immediately. For example, a teacher might say:

"The noise level from discussion in this classroom is too high. Since we cannot seem to lower it, for the sake of the class next to us we will have to postpone our discussions until they have left the room, or until we can discuss more quietly."

Your group will help in establishing and maintaining limits for the behavior of its members if this responsibility extends reliably and reasonably to all areas of classroom experience. However, this group valuing of constructive behavior is not a trick pulled out of the bag to meet some crisis or to be played with superficially. This attitude evolves with struggle and testing through problem situations that have been met and overcome. Each success sows the seeds of the next success.

The teacher trusts the children and gives them freedom for action. The children try, then succeed, then dare to try again. Progress depends on two factors: (1) the confidence that any errors will not be fatal, and (2) the confidence to let children make some wrong choices, for they learn from those, too.

The Class Versus the Teacher Sometimes a classroom suffers from the "versus" disease—the children versus the teacher. The teacher then asks, "Who knows more, you or I?" and wisely continues:

"I with my experience and training?

You with your feelings, knowledge of where you are, and your understanding of your friends?

All of us together?"

In a class that answers "all of us together," the interactive rapport shows clearly in the classroom discussions.

Duties Before Rights   The gradual development of an autonomous, responsible, and cooperative climate is essential. But another factor emerges: the acceptance, by all concerned, not only of rights but also of responsibilities. We cannot have rights until we can or will fulfill duties. This balance is a natural consequence that can operate instructively in your classroom.

For example, the person who drives a car cannot have the rights of a driver (to go anywhere) without fulfilling the duties of a driver (staying on the correct side of the road, respecting the rights of other drivers, and so on). So it is with your children: They cannot have the right to engage in small-group discussion if they cannot fulfill the roles involved in discussion. It is the old principle that you get out of something what you put into it. The teacher's idea in the classroom, however, is not denial of rights but postponement for another considered trial, when the class is ready to fulfill its duties in productive discussion.

Rewards for the Teacher   Is the patience needed for trial and retrial worth it? To enhance the growth of children's language and thought, nothing works better than a vital exchange of constructive leadership roles in a group. It is here that children shape fuller statements as they build on what others say. These thinking-expressing-solving groups serve at least as much to develop total language progress as do reading groups.

Some Practical Considerations and Criteria   It helps to review steps of group work, shown in Box 6.5, before proceeding to some highly specific suggestions. Assessment is discussed in the next section. If your design of steps works, preparation is largely already completed for next year's class (Cohen, 1986). The productive task for a group includes

---

BOX 6.5 Steps in Group Work

1. Decide how your children will work together.
   - Creative problem solving?
   - Task group?
   - Brainstorm?
   - Long-term investigation?
2. Be sure that your children have some cooperative skills.
3. Find tasks with discussions your children need to perform.
4. Lay the groundwork with great care, including consideration of:
   - How to compose groups
   - What instructions and materials to prepare in advance
   - How the children will help you physically arrange the room
   - How and when you will assign students to groups.
5. Plan assessment.

multiple ways of knowing (multimedia, sight, sound, touch, reading, and writing). A teacher's general orientation might be a set of written, pretested instructions, descriptions of cooperative behaviors needed, and special roles. Have the group discuss and clarify what the written instructions say. General criteria for tasks include the following:

Criteria for Discussion Tasks

- They have more than one answer or way to solve a problem; sufficient complexity.
- They are interesting and challenging to the group.
- They allow different children to make varied contributions (multiple abilities) and show a variety of behaviors.

Selection of Group Size and Composition   The size of the discussion group depends on the following sampling of points: the type of discussion, the shyness of students, the number and kinds of skills inherent in the members and needed for success, the use of uneven numbers to discourage ganging up, and the leadership skill in allowing a hearing for a minority viewpoint. Experiment; try groups of five. Try a total group discussion, then follow up with small-group work, with special attention to favorable location of any nonparticipants.

In order to compose groups, you might put the name of each student on a card. After deciding how many groups of five or more members you will have, put a reliable resource student in each group. Pair your problematic students with resource students, then assign the others. Be on the lookout for new resource students. Ultimately each student can probably qualify as some kind of resource. A balanced, heterogeneous group seems to be best.

Once you have formed groups, you need to decide whether to keep the membership the same or to switch students around. Try it out. You can weigh the advantage of consistent groups who learn well to trust and work together with chances for variation in which you might shuffle the remaining student cards like a deck. If, however, groups are to become a keeping place for values, a place of mutual respect, they need some continuity and tradition. See Figure 6.10 on page 200.

Frequency and Allotted Time   If group effects are to be cumulative, discussion needs to occur regularly. Children cannot learn to discuss without discussing. If the skills of this week are to progress from those of the last, practice needs to be continued.

How much time per discussion? A general rule is to stop while participants are still interested. Closure in a creative problem-solving discussion is of secondary importance if the goal is improved process. Experiment. Allow too little time rather than too much. Let the children conclude the formal class discussion with questions and issues still churning in their minds. Let the discussion spill over into the playground and lunchroom. Exploratory discourse uncovers and discovers rather than covers.

Guiding by Questioning

This important section deals with how teachers phrase questions to match various purposes of discussion. It also traces the pacing and sequencing of questions and shows how to avoid asking too many of them. We need to ask ourselves the purpose of our questions, as they

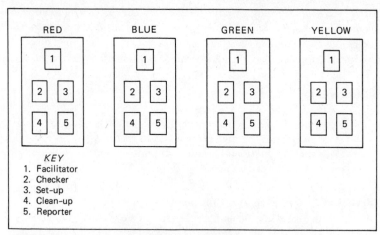

Figure 6.10   Chart showing group and role assignments (add students' names). (*Source:* Adapted from Cohen, 1986, p. 64.)

can be one of the basic language units underlying discussion and most of classroom instruction. We need to refine what we ask, how we ask, and what we do with responses to further motivate children's thinking.

The phrasing of questions depends partly on the developmental level of the "who." One rule of thumb, especially when working with younger children, is to determine the child's age. Then keep the length of the questions *no longer than the child's age, plus one.* That is, if the child addressed is 4 years old, the question contains no more than five words. This guideline helps the teacher avoid overloading the child with information. Consider some other cautions given in Box 6.6.

BOX 6.6 Teacher Behaviors to Avoid During Discussion

During discussion beware of:

1. *Consistent answering of one's own questions.* (If it is important that children know the teacher's thinking, simply tell rather than ask.) Give time to allow the interchange to swell, trail off, even fall silent.

2. *Interruption of a child's responses.* Interruption, besides showing lack of respect for the child, can cause the discussion to stray from a line of communication. Another kind of interruption is the breaking of eye contact, of restlessly moving away. Convey calmness and an unhurried atmosphere. To indicate the need for some thoughtful deliberation before answering, give the child time.

3. *Too much dependence on a stimulus/response model.* In this behavior the teacher provides the question, a mere measure of retention, and the pupil reacts with an answer, passively and with intellectual dependence. Students need to construct their own inquiry and their own questions for exploration.

4. *Too many questions at once.* Avoid causing information overload by a rapid-fire series of questions.

One of the simplest things a teacher can do to decrease the amount of teacher talk and increase the amount of student talk during discussion is to stop asking so many rapid-fire questions. Instead, the teacher can: (1) make a statement and wait for or encourage students to elaborate on it; (2) reflect what a student just said; (3) guess the student's state of mind to get student analysis or challenge of the guess; (4) encourage the students to ask a question of the teacher, the text, or one another; (5) maintain a deliberate silence of three seconds or longer to encourage appreciative reflection or a change of pace (Dillon, 1984).

Teachers and children play several roles during the questioning process when they react relevantly. Among these roles are recording, reinforcing, clarifying, and challenging or lifting. Consider each in turn.

Responses to Questions

1. *Function as a Nondirective Recorder.* Recording means writing the response for all participants to see, suspending judgment, simply absorbing the literal message. The recorder's mind can be busily at work analyzing what is happening and planning ahead, but the recorder does not respond overtly. The children expect no leader response, realizing that they are to act autonomously. Possibly the teacher as recorder is replanning the development of the discussion process in light of student response. Establish a classroom climate where recording parts of responses is not a threat. (The three leader reactions that follow are directive.)

2. *Accept with Positive Reinforcement.* Especially in the beginning, children may need some thoughtful praise and approval to reassure them that they are on a productive track, behaving successfully. Avoid overdoing praise; you may embarrass or alienate children, or make the praise impossible to live up to. Later, the natural consequences of productivity, self-satisfaction, learning, and peer group response can act as the major reinforcers.

3. *Seek to Clarify Answers.* Teachers or students may need to have the one who answers the questions rephrase, elaborate, and support responses. As in the opening scene in Chapter 3, the teacher or student may *extend,* seeking additional responses to the same question; or *refocus* for a group member who is wandering helplessly in a verbal maze, apparently straying from the task; or *backtrack* to an earlier, easier level. Sometimes it is the question itself that needs clarifying or rephrasing.

4. *Challenge the Answer.* The teacher or student may disagree, correct, disapprove, modify, or encourage interaction in response to an answer. For instance, say, "No, I don't think so; here's why," rather than "No, you're wrong!" Or, say, "How does your comment relate to Mary's?" to encourage the two to compare and interact. Avoid questions with fixed right answers in the first place. Instead, explore options and values, weigh opinions. In the discussion as early as Chapter 1, we saw students challenging themselves in this way.

Teachers and even students may challenge in order to lift the responder with a question to a higher, more complex, more abstract level of thought. Such a question may probe not only the content under consideration and the student's experience, but the experience of others and the realities of the outside world. For example, a teacher might ask, "When might it be more right to go against social rules of your peers?" The teacher may not reject answers but "hitchhike" on them in order to ease the next responses upward to a more complex level.

Teachers and students can incorporate these four reactions along with sample questions to follow into a checklist to use during taped discussion time. Remember this additional caution, however: If the teacher sits with the children as part of a discussion group, the members may immediately begin to defer to the teacher's authority. If this happens, teachers can pass the questions back to the group or to another child and/or open up another question. But, as rapidly as possible, teachers need to move out of the group so that the children get a chance to ask questions and interact. Remember that for some children, teachers' questions become not an opportunity to explore but a source of great tension and anxiety.

The way teachers react to children's responses is in large part a result of the questions they ask the students in the first place. A question may be phrased in a particular way to produce a desired change of behavior in a student. Purposes behind a teacher's questions may be to get the student ready or motivated, to reinforce learning, to help with transfer of an idea, and to bring out facts, inferences, applications, or principles. Questions are not ends in themselves, and what you ask is usually what you get. Set the question level low and convergent, and you'll get a single low-level response (Teacher: "What color was the dress in the story?" Child: "Blue").

If you focus your question just on content, or just on personal experience, or just on the experience of others in the outside world, the response will be just at that particular level. For older children, all these areas can be combined in a question. This broader focus promotes more varied and solidly based abstract thought. Young children may need to build up to an outside-world point of view because they keep backtracking to the egocentric focus. But part of a group's criteria for evaluating discussion could be touching on all three of these levels—content, oneself, and the outside world. (Also see the activity book, Section 3 for this chapter, "Building Question Skills for Better Class Discussions.")

Process and Content Maps for Discussions   Sets of question functions might be called process *maps* for a discussion. The teacher or facilitator may also keep in mind maps of content areas. Such maps help focus a discussion by keeping it from rambling pointlessly over too broad a content area.

For example, in a third-grade social studies unit on rules, group discussions of rules might range over the following areas: (1) maintaining order in your school and home, and those of others; (2) safety and health (e.g., "Look at this picture—would you ride your bike here?" "What provisions does our community make for bike safety?"); and (3) government resolutions of conflicts among people (e.g., "How is our state handling school integration and busing?").

The possibilities of areas to treat are vast. Teachers and facilitators needing content and process maps may also need to decide what part of the maps to use at a certain time. To illustrate, the map in Figure 6.11 shows a fanning out or web of the hypotheses children made in response to the question: "What will happen to the way of life in the desert if sufficient water is available?" (Taba, Levine, & Freeman, 1964). Showing the application of social studies learning, each curved line represents a leap in prediction from the original condition (at the bottom). The vertical lines represent the areas of prediction. The figure is a map of the ways in which bits of information provided by one child in the group lead to further predictions by third graders interacting.

This type of discussion demands much of the teacher or facilitator. In most discussions these leaps of predictions and their verification are not ordered so neatly. The group can easily lose focus unless the facilitator and group have a process map in mind and some idea of content possibilities. In the map given, one can see the group's movement from more concrete ideas at the bottom (e.g., trees) to more abstract ideas at the top (e.g., houses, building, and trading). Groups are not expected to direct all discussions according to maps

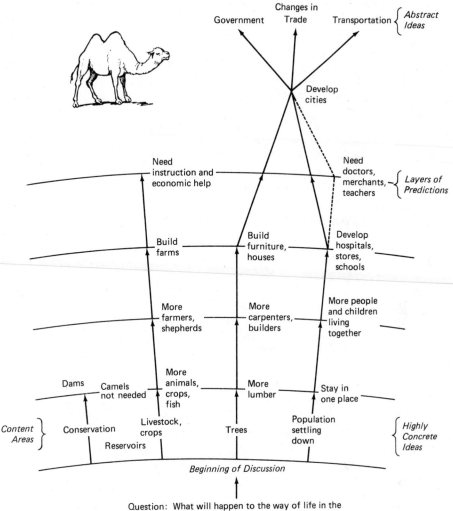

End of Discussion

Government | Changes in Trade | Transportation { *Abstract Ideas*

Develop cities

Need instruction and economic help — — — Need doctors, merchants, teachers } *Layers of Predictions*

Build farms — — Build furniture, houses — Develop hospitals, stores, schools

More farmers, shepherds — More carpenters, builders — More people and children living together

More animals, crops, fish | More lumber | Stay in one place

Dams   Camels not needed

Content Areas } Conservation   Livestock, crops   Trees   Population settling down } *Highly Concrete Ideas*

Reservoirs

Beginning of Discussion

Question: What will happen to the way of life in the desert if sufficient water is available?

Figure 6.11 Water comes to the desert. (*Source:* Taba, Levine, & Freeman, 1964.)

such as the one in Figure 6.11, but such maps can be a useful tool for reaching high levels of thinking. A map may be steps in a problem-solving process or areas of predictions regarding social studies or science.

A Questioning Circle The areas, or circles, in the following format for developing instructional questions are not necessarily sequential but may overlap (Christenbury & Kelly, 1983). The three circles below are suitable for use through middle school and beyond:

1. Content (or the matter)
2. Self (or personal reality)
3. World (or external reality)

The first circle, *content,* represents the subject of discussion (e.g., a book, a composition, dialect differences). The second circle, *self,* represents the student's experiences, ideas, and values. The third circle, *world,* is the experience, history, and ideas of other people and cultures—the external reality. While each circle represents a different domain of thinking, the circles of knowledge typically overlap as shown in Figure 6.12. In the one area in the center where all three circles intersect lies the unity of the subject or content being explored. Here the content, the student's experience, and the world come together. Here are likely to be the richest and the highest-order questions and responses with the deepest consideration.

Thus an instructional goal would be that the teacher and group include not only questions in the three separate circles (content, self, and world) but also questions combining two or even all three for mutual enrichment. Students may wish to move back and forth among the circles and their intersections, returning flexibly again and again to the richest questions. Some examples follow.

1. In a discussion of literature, the content would be the story or text, the self would be the reader, and the world would be other related literature and real-life events.
2. In a discussion of language study, the content would be the concept under study (e.g., dialect), the self would be the student speaker (writer or reader) of language, and the world might be the language (dialect) as used outside the student's own environment.
3. In a discussion of composition, the content could become the subject of the proposed piece or draft of the written composition, the self would be the student writer, and the world would be the intended audience.

Let's consider an example from children's literature—*The Buffalo Woman,* by Paul Goble (with beautiful illustrations widening our vision). First comes a story summary, then some questions.

Summary of legend: A young hunter who is thankful and kindhearted is given a gift

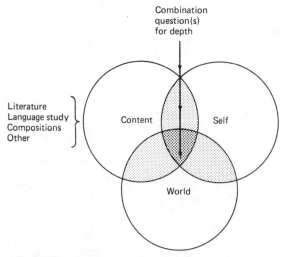

Figure 6.12 Questioning circles. (*Source:* Christenbury & Kelly, 1983.)

from the Buffalo Nation of a beautiful, transformed woman. The hunter and his buffalo wife love each other and their son. The Indian relatives, however, cruelly reject the mother and child; so they flee and rejoin the Buffalo Nation in animal form. The young hunter pursues his family and manages to prove his love for his wife and child to the Buffalo Nation, and so joins them in animal form.

The following are some sample questions from each circle based on the above story. They cover content, self, world, and the intersection of all three.

> *The content:* What did the relatives say when they tried to get rid of the Buffalo-woman wife? Why was the Buffalo Nation angry?

> *The self:* How would you handle it if relatives treated you as they treated the woman and her child?

> *The world:* Why did Indian tribes tell such stories as *The Buffalo Woman?*

> *Intersection of all three:* Are there any stories told in your family that strengthen bonds of kinship, roots, and seem to explain life's relations? (Such as this story's telling of the kinship between man and animal, and the transfiguring power of love.)

Other Integrations Through Discussion Across the Curriculum

A wise selection of discussion content promotes unity in the total curriculum. One integration is between discussion and reading. Children do not need to depend solely on direct experience for their discussion content, but can read for topic ideas and supporting material. It is hoped that children will not feel compelled to go to an encyclopedia and then regurgitate a pale, confused, and poorly digested imitation of the original writing. This misfortune is unlikely if children are secure and value their own autonomy and experience in discussion.

A listen-read-discuss (LRD) strategy is designed to help students assimilate key concepts found in their regularly assigned content area texts (Manzo & Casale, 1985). During the discussion step teachers encourage students to clarify/elaborate the same text experienced through teacher lecture and initial reading. Thus slower learners get to use three of their four senses. Students compare their understanding of the overview lecture with the text, noting concepts that are difficult to understand. Discussion not only clarifies basic meanings but includes the raising of unanswered questions. Teacher discussion questions include the following:

> *"What did you understand best (from what you heard and read)?"*
> *"What did you understand least?"*
> *"What do you still want to know or think about?"*

The reading-discussion relationship links up with writing to form another integration: Discussion stimulates reading; reading uncovers ideas for discussion, and in turn can stimulate writing. Discussion on improving the environment becomes an editorial for the school or class newspaper, which prompts reading of related articles in magazines. For economy of time as well, find problems for discussion in math, social studies, science, literature, music, and language history. (Also see the activity book sections "Discussions of Class Work," "Book Talks," and Section 1, Part 4, "Organizing a Book Club.")

In essence, then, the *how* of teaching discussion involves and includes the children in: cooperative planning, learning, and—the next topic—assessing.

Assessment

Some teachers do not want to spend time on discussion because they think there is no way to assess it or the individual children participating in it. It is well to separate the issue of learning from simply giving grades to individuals. Assessment procedures for learning are important from the beginning to the end.

In the beginning the teacher may need a rough assessment of the levels of fluency in the class in order to plan for composition of the small groups. Groups and members need to have some way of finding out if they are progressing in solving problems and gaining skills. They need to know how they measure up to some sort of criteria and how they can improve both process and product. These aspects relate to learning apart from grading.

Initial Fluency Checks   Besides observation, a way to find out about fluency is to ask the children. Request them to mark a picture or check one of these two statements as more nearly describing them:

Name _____   Date _____
[ ]   I talk a lot.
[ ]   I almost never talk.
Comments or drawing

Or, for a bit more refinement with older children, use a continuum they can mark with an *x*.

/_____/_____/_____/_____/_____/_____/

I never talk   I talk a lot

Assessment Through Children as Observers   Next, conduct brief discussions using almost any one of the seven types described in the definition section of this chapter. But place the talkers in the middle in a circle to discuss and the avowed nontalkers around them in an outside circle to participate as silent but involved observers. Then, have the two groups switch places. Have the prepared nontalkers in the center do the reporting on what they just saw, while the talkers sit in the outside circle as involved but silent observers, soon reporting. This rotating kind of activity, sometimes called the *fishbowl game,* can be stimulating for the child who would otherwise participate very little.

This game is useful when children are at the stage of developing assessment skills as observers. Their assessment may be a simple keeping track of who speaks to whom. Or it may be a more elaborate look at who initiates, who agrees, who makes positive contributions, and other dimensions such as the following (where abbreviations are given for speedier noting):

Observers' Assessment of Group Discussion

1. Clear—confused (cl—cn)

2. Related—unrelated (rl—unrl)

3. Trust—distrust (tr—dstr)

4. Helping—unhelping (hl—unhl)

Observers can also keep track of the following elements, adding them later to a checklist:

- Participation
- Processes such as problem solving
- Roles used
- Interactions
- Types of discussion
- Group member relations
- Facilitator-member relations—or whatever the group decides it wants to include on its checklist

For example, maybe the group decides to work on getting out lots of ideas from everyone, or giving reasons. An observer (who takes no part in the discussion) keeps track of these, even adding to a week-by-week chart. Children need to understand that the observer does not tear down participants, but mainly points out behaviors that helped the discussion.

Children as observers can assess two basics: ideas and processes. As process improves, ideas become of more concern. In all the types of discussion suggested in this chapter, assessment is probably best accomplished by having students take an active part in developing their own standards, making sure they are legitimate, applying them with constructive criticism, and then discussing their application. They can then revise their standards if necessary. Next, children can turn these group standards into personal rating scales. Thus an important component in assessment is child involvement and autonomy. Children can tape samples, older ones can transcribe samples, and (using the abbreviations above) code their behaviors during discussion.

To ready children for such assessment responsibilities, the teacher might ask questions such as the following:

Teachers' Assessment Questions

"What ideas did members bring out today not thought of before?"

"How can we find out if this idea is better than that one?"

"How far did your group get on its project by working together?"

"How do we still need to improve? What objectives can we set for ourselves in order to make our discussion better?"

Student Self-Assessment   Students can make entries in their own personal discussion logs, incorporate them into listening logs, or have a section in their writing journal. Included might be a personal chart with some items from the comprehensive one in Figure 6.13, indicating each role taken, type of discussion, and skill practiced. Children can infer operation of general goals (such as fair-mindedness and open-mindedness) from specific behaviors and words caught by the tape recorder. Examples might be: "You haven't had a turn; go ahead of me"; or "Tell us more why you think so" (drawing others out).

STUDENT SELF-ASSESSMENT CHART

Name _____ Date _____

1. The type of discussion we were using was:

    _____ Tutorial

    _____ Buzz session

    _____ Brainstorming

    _____ Task

    _____ Inquiry training

    _____ Socratic

    _____ Creative problem solving

2. The role(s) I tried to play was:

    _____ Facilitator

    _____ Clarifier

    _____ Checker

    _____ Summarizer

    _____ Assessor

    _____ Harmonizer

    _____ Resource

    _____ Recorder

    _____ Spokesperson or reporter

    _____ Setup and/or cleanup

    _____ Other:

3. The skills I tried to use or improve were:

    Language—

    _____ Listening

    _____ Asking questions

    _____ Being concise

    _____ Describing

    _____ Explaining by telling how or why

    _____ Summarizing

    _____ Other:

    Group Process—

    _____ Focusing the attention of the group

    _____ Extending—allowing everyone to contribute; asking others their opinions

    _____ Pooling information

    _____ Making relevant contributions

    _____ Fostering the work of the group through its phases toward a goal

    _____ Finding out if the group is ready to make a decision

    _____ Participating in the decision making of the group

    _____ Specifying a plan of action, where appropriate

Figure 6.13 Student self-assessment chart.

_____ Appropriately assessing the work of the group

_____ Other:

Thinking—

_____ Reflecting on that has been said

_____ Putting ideas together

_____ Hypothesizing (coming up with possible explanations or solutions)

_____ Giving reasons for ideas

_____ Assessing evidence

_____ Making my own decision about the topic and presenting it

_____ Other:

4. Ideas I offered were:

Figure 6.13   *(Continued)*

Group or Individual Product   Some task groups have built-in assessment of their product. If the task group is trying to construct a smoking volcano and it doesn't work, they can go back and review their group task card, use each other as resources, learn from their mistakes, and try some other strategies. If the group is working on bar graphing or critiquing paragraphs, let the group work become individualized with each member completing his or her *own* bar graph or corrected paragraph for you to check. In other words, the group members use one another as resources in solving the problem, but then each child prepares an individual product. This method firms up what the students have learned and provides the teacher with an individual progress check.

Debriefing   Coming together at the end of small-group discussion for reflection as a whole group is another way of assessing. Members can reflect on progress in cooperative behaviors featured in the preparations and on any products. They can point out specific areas where the groups did well and where they might improve. Some sample question areas for debriefing are given in Box 6.7 on page 210.

Debriefing and knowing the results of group products is preferable to grading them (Cohen, 1986). Group learning is intrinsically rewarding and does not need grades to be motivational. Teachers can meet their responsibilities for giving grades by incorporating some individual products that could grow out of group discussion, and even by designing tests of basic concepts the group work was designed to develop. Examples of individual products are bar graphing, paragraph constructions, types of listening and reading comprehension for varied purposes. (The instructor's manual contains a section on research on questioning.) Well-designed "groupwork can produce major gains on even standardized achievement tests" (Cohen, 1986, p. 71).

When children learn to use discussion or solve problems important to them in school, then competency in language and thought coalesces. Children succeed, schooling succeeds, and consequently, our society succeeds. In this chapter, we saw expository use of language playing an important part in classroom discussions. The next chapter continues our quest for learning and teaching languages arts by building a bridge between oral and written language, and by stressing often neglected expository uses.

BOX 6.7 Areas for Debriefing After Discussion

Praise

- What were the strengths of this discussion?
  —Handling of events?
  —Facilitator's behavior?
  —Resource person's work?

Clearing things up

- What needed clearing up?
  —Things not understood?
  —More information needed?
  —Puzzling actions?

New leads

- New possibilities?

- New techniques?

- New ideas triggered?

Constructive criticism and solutions

- How might the discussion have been even better?

- What might have happened more frequently? Less?

SUMMARY

"Oh, I'll come back when you're teaching."

*(Well-intentioned but uneducated principal, upon entering a classroom
during well-designed group work)*

Unfortunately, the above quote shows a common lack of knowledge about the value of group discussion in the language arts (or any area). It is up to teachers to educate their administrators and significant others as to the rationale for what they believe in and are so professionally, scientifically, and artistically implementing.

This chapter described types of discussion (buzz session, brainstorming, tutorial, task group, inquiry-training, and Socratic probes), comparing and contrasting them with the creative problem-solving (CPS) type. Other sections of the chapter gave different contexts for discussion.

The *why* section gave you some ammunition for justifying these important teaching/ learning strategies. The *who* section detailed what to do about problem roles such as the nonparticipant and the monopolizer. *What* you use as guiding goals affects the process, purpose, attitude toward, and content of discussion. *Where* discussion takes place (the environment) also affects the quality of discussion.

How you handle the many types of discussion depends on your perception not only of productive student roles but also of the teacher's role. Careful preparation and planning are essential. The teacher steps back and delegates authority and autonomy to students during group work time. Such actions create success in the spirit and long-range achievement of democratic and scholarly learnings.

To get the most out of discussion, teachers and students need skill in using questions. This chapter explored content/process maps and categories of questions, including the intersecting circles of content, self, and world. Questions can bring these facets together for the deepest consideration of literature, language, and composition. *Integration* was illustrated using several examples of discussion activities.

Assessment has a place from beginning to end in discussion. It is important from the first initial fluency checks on the projected group participants (for the sake of optimal group composition) to ongoing student and teacher assessment while groups are in action. Assessment extends to debriefings after sessions, to final group products, and to offshoots of individual products. Process assessment is highly important.

Stressing objective criteria, teachers need to separate concepts of learning from district requirements for grading. Teachers need to meet unavoidable mandates in ways that do not destroy cooperative climates and children's positive self-concepts. Of great importance is self-assessment, supplemented by pupil-teacher conferences.

Not every group discussion is successful every time, and not all learning outcomes are best accomplished by discussion, important as it is. Both peers and the teacher can assess results of both process and product. Children may need to realize that they have had many small successes before undertaking highly complex discussion tasks.

PART 2

INTO PRINT

CHAPTER 7

Building Bridges to Reading and Writing with Informational Uses of Whole Language

"In their curriculum planning whole language teachers create opportunities for pupils to use language in authentic, richly contextualized, functional ways."

Kenneth S. Goodman

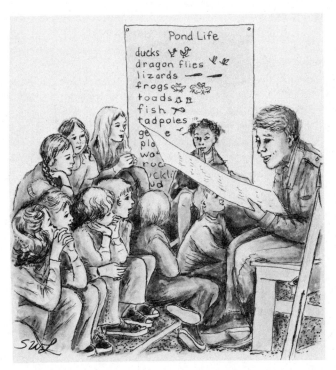

The purpose of this chapter on whole language is threefold: (1) to illustrate the bridges between comprehension and composition; (2) to highlight exposition—a neglected use of language; (3) and to exemplify one way a teacher can build such bridges to reading and written composition using a whole-language activity. An example is the language experience approach (LEA) in its broadest meaning. Used as a beginning (and remedial) reading methodology, LEA also serves as a bridge to composition in general. You will find material to help you add this and other valuable techniques to your repertory.

Children's success in being informative and objective in their language, an emphasis of this chapter, grows out of their competence in self-expression—an emphasis in earlier chapters. First described is a rationale and matching classroom activities through an opening scene. The scene emphasizes that comprehension and composition are two sides of the same basic process of communication. The opening scene in Chapter 2 foreshadowed such a whole language approach.

With these ideas in mind, it is well to revisit the reasons for placement of chapters in this book thus far, and in this second part, "Into Print." Part 1 of this book focused mainly on the overall bases of problem solving (Chapter 1), development (Chapter 2), and self-expressive use of oral language (Chapters 3, 4, 5, and 6). Part 2 contains the following: it begins with this bridge-building chapter stressing the informational use of both oral and written whole language; next comes written composition with a multitude of language uses (Chapter 8); then come the literary (Chapter 9) and the persuasive (Chapter 10) uses of language; and finally Chapters 11 and 12 cover the craft, conventions, and skills in composing—after a thorough orientation to broad language uses.

Of course a user can move around this book freely, skipping ahead to composition (Chapter 8) and returning to this chapter's more complex sections on exposition later. But the foregoing ideas explain the present ordering of the chapters in this part. Focusing on the communication of information, this chapter again offers definitions and answers to questions about the *why, who, where, what,* and *how* of bridging into print.

INTRODUCTION

An understanding of the relationship between comprehension and composition can help teachers plan activities that build bridges from oral to written uses of whole language. Figure 7.1 helps to define these relationships and their factors. As the diagram suggests, comprehension, in the first circle, and composition, in the adjoining circle, interact. They do this with common language and thought.

Comprehension Related to Composition

In comprehension the reader or listener starts the process by searching for meaning. That individual uses language knowns and content of text to interact with senders, reconstructing messages in a personally meaningful way. Factors that join comprehension and composition include the following (adapted from Indrisano, 1984):

1. Purpose (with *reasons* for reading in comprehension; *intent* for writing in composition)
2. Content (with knowledge prior to the presentation for comprehension; world knowledge prior to composition)
3. Organization (with a network of ideas about the text topic in comprehension; a sense of structure and audience for composition)
4. Language (with *receptive* vocabulary, not in isolation, for comprehension; *expressive* vocabulary, again networked, for composition)
5. Creativity (with *imagery* helping comprehension; *imagination* fueling composition [see Table 7.1])

Consider each of the above five factors showing up in reading and writing or in comprehending and composing. Conscious **purpose** is required in both effective comprehending and composing. A decision sets the process in motion and provides a prompting

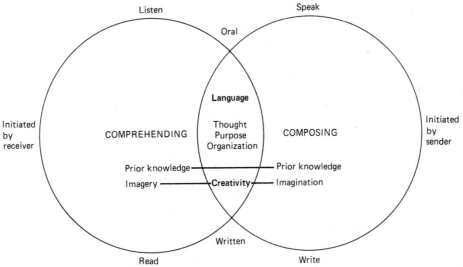

Figure 7.1 Comprehension related to composition. (*Source:* Indrisano, 1984.)

Table 7.1 COMPARATIVE RELATIONS FOR COMPREHENSION AND COMPOSITION: FIVE FACTORS

Factor	Comprehension	Composition
Purpose	Reasons for *reading*	Intent for *writing*
Content	Knowledge prior to presented material	Knowledge prior to writing
Organization	Networking of ideas about topic Listener/reader text	Structure re: audience/message
Language	Receptive vocabulary in a network	Expressive vocabulary in a network
Creativity	Imagery	Imagination

Source: Adapted from Indrisano, 1984, p. 3.

context for decisions that follow. For instance, a student reader might decide to scan another class newspaper for usable formats, rather than reading word by word from beginning to end. A writer with an informative purpose may decide to use a news story format rather than the format of a persuasive editorial.

A K–1 classroom teacher, for example, builds a bridge with the following related activity: selects a topic within a current reading, social studies, or science unit; chooses two short books—one a story (say, *The Little Auto*), the other with informational content (say, *Cars and How They Go*); discusses with the children reasons for reading for enjoyment and reasons for reading especially for information; has the children identify the reason for reading each book; and finally reads each book aloud and then asks the children to take turns as composers retelling the story or paraphrasing the information (adapted from Indrisano, 1984).

Content of prior knowledge of the world helps both comprehenders and composers. As you read this section, you are aided by your prior knowledge of comprehending and composing, and your observations of teaching and children. In writing this section I depend on your bringing that knowledge and experience to the printed word. Printed symbols are in themselves meaningless without our common language, experience, and information to give meaningful content. Once they have determined a purpose, children who are crossing the bridge into reading and writing can use a title to call up a network of prior ideas bearing on comprehension. (This network is called a *schema.*) Effective composers try to consider their comprehenders' prior knowledge when choosing content.

For example, a grade 4–6 classroom teacher uses a series of lessons to build a bridge with the following sort of activity (adapted from Indrisano, 1984). First the teacher instructs the students to ask the following questions before they *read:*

- What topic did the author write about?
- What do I already know about it?
- What questions do I want the author to answer?

The teacher includes such questions in introductory discussions of informative text until the students are proficient with them, and also uses them to introduce independent study activities. Then the teacher helps the students use somewhat similar questions in preparation for *composition:*

- What do I want to write about?
- What will the reader want to know or what does the reader already know?

- What do I already know?
- What information will I need before I write?

Organization is related to the previous activity on content. Grasping various structures of content helps children comprehend similarly organized text. Later in this chapter we will examine the organization of expository texts that children might be helped to make their own in the same way that we examined story structures for literary use of language in Chapter 2.

Language, an important factor in comprehension and composition, emerges as a common vocabulary. There needs to be an appropriate match between the receptive vocabulary of the reader and the expressive vocabulary of the writer of the text. Children need to have the word within their network of vocabulary revolving around the concept, rather than in isolation. One student thoroughly confused by her science book thought *culture* meant only that part of her network including music, art, theater—but not a medical network including bacteria or tissue cultivated in a medium to promote its growth for diagnosis of soreness, irritation, or fever. Networks of language meanings are better represented by a thesaurus than a dictionary (Indrisano, 1984).

What can a teacher do? Semantic maps, discussed and diagrammed later in this chapter, are useful in comprehending and composing stories and give a helpful boost for reading and writing expository content. Young children can create a thesaurus of words with pictures and illustrative sentences related to categorized topics of reading and content units. For example, with categories of "Pets" and "Work," children can see that a given meaning changes when the word *fish* is moved from one category to another (Indrisano, 1984).

Creativity shows up as a common factor in both comprehending and composing as imagery and imagination. Finally, it is the imagery of the reader (or listener) that fashions language into a story or other piece. It is in the imagination of the writer that language becomes an artful tale or a gripping exposition.

For illustration, a grade 4–6 teacher and class cooperatively select a theme that lends itself to creative expression (e.g., animals, the night, an author). Students locate the theme in a variety of genres: expository piece, essay, story poem, play, painting, sculpture, music. Teacher and class discuss the similarities and differences in the images they "see" as they read, view, and listen to the various modes of presentation. Next children select from aspects of this theme and compose a series of written works in a variety of genres and artistic media (Moss, 1984). Such creativity can turn into strong personal interests associated with intense comprehending and composing that change the lives of individuals.

Focus on these bridge-building processes of comprehending and composing integrates teaching of all the language arts. The theme of comprehending/composing, of new light on the relationship of reading and writing, underlies the rest of this chapter. Comprehending/composing pervades the opening scene. Later it is included in the rationale and definitions for the use of language called exposition. The chapter gradually moves into a thorough explanation of a teaching example, a key bridge builder for comprehending/composing—the *language experience approach* (LEA).

The opening scene to follow illustrates many constructs of this chapter through an interview, originating in conversational activity, detailed in Chapter 4. Interviewing, a respected tool of researchers, is also practiced for public service by TV newscasters. When children own this strategy for the informational use of language, interviewing can be highly motivating. While interviewing, children both comprehend and compose.

OPENING SCENE: Relating Composing and Comprehending Processes
While Interviewing an Officer

Twenty-five first graders formed a semicircle inside the doorway of their classroom, stretching on tiptoe to see what was happening. The handlebars on the giant 900-pound motorcycle facing them spanned 36 inches; but their classroom doorway was only 33 inches wide. Officer Huggins dangled his shiny helmet from his left hand and balanced his vehicle with his right as he studied the problem (Haley-James, 1980).

"How tall is it?"

"How fast can you make it go?"

"Why does it help you more than a car would in your job as a policeman?"

"Did you ever have an accident on it?"

"If you tilted the handlebars, could you get it in?"

The questions came thick and fast to this fourth guest in a series of visitors invited by the first graders. (Other guests had been a children's book author, a newspaper editor, a nurse, a pilot, a state representative, and a botanist.) It was an hour before the teacher could finally shake the interviewers loose from their interviewee.

How did the children get to be such adept and avid interviewers? First, they had had a practice interview with the teacher, who showed them an object related to a personal interest in collecting exotic musical instruments. The teacher gave the children only as much information as they asked for. If they asked yes-no questions, they got yes-no answers. (Recall Chapter 4—the six *W*'s + *H&I* kinds of questions.) After the initial interview the teacher asked the children what questions produced the most information and listed them.

Then, with a genuine *purpose* for composing, the children paired off to interview each other and review their questions. The children tried to move from "Easy-to-see" or obvious questions to thoughtful questions dealing with reasons, feelings, and conjecture ("What-would-happen if?"; "Did you ever?"). After a pair had worked over their questions, they met with another pair to share and revise.

Next the teacher surveyed the children's interests and their *prior knowledge* and, thus informed, arranged for phoning and corresponding with guests, and then for the interviews. The guests reflected the children's preferences. After the children had interviewed a guest and written it up, the teacher used their oral and written products to find out what skills to teach them in order to help them clarify their meanings. Spelling, punctuation, other conventions, and standard usage grew from the children's reworking of their own valued expository language. The teacher provided genuine audiences for the children's written responses to the interviews. Thus we see how such activity helped build bridges from oral language to reading and writing.

In large part the children were *first* speakers (composers), then listeners (comprehenders) in the interview situation, then writers (composers) about it, and *finally* readers (comprehenders again). This sequence was a vast improvement over the usual one of listening to the teacher first and then speaking; reading and then perhaps writing. When children asked questions to obtain information, they *had* to listen for cues in the answer that would lead them to come up with more questions. Because the children wrote to be read, they wanted to write. Responses to the first interview were only a few sentences, but the number grew by leaps and bounds for subsequent ones (Haley-James, 1980). Thus both sides of a bridging process (composing/comprehending) were harnessed to promote writing and reading.

We saw in this scene another example of an ongoing program that assists growth in informational use of language. The children were involved in honing their skills as *comprehenders* of information. Some of these skills were: grasping important points and crucial details through asking questions; making rough notes, or pictures; making simple concept maps (explained later in this chapter); drawing their own conclusions to answers; and making their own summaries.

As *composers* of information they did the following: selected the guest; narrowed what they would report; located more information if they needed it after the speaker left; and fit the information from books and other sources to their peer audience. Moreover, they used language for exploration and for information. In the case of the visiting botanist, they used language for scientific purposes as they created their own plant experiments to report. (These informative, exploratory, and scientific uses of exposition are detailed later in this chapter.)

Children in this class were beginning to grasp the logic of exposition in the following ways: its identifications and definitions ("How tall is it?"); its comparisons ("How does it help you more than a car would?"); its cause-effect relations ("How fast can you make it go?"); its problems, hypotheses, evidence, and solution ("If you tilt the handlebars, could you get it in?"). Figure 7.5, presented later in this chapter on page 235, summarizes these and other features of expository communication.

Finally, the teacher in this scene followed up more systematically with the language experience approach to reading. The interviewing activity described paved the way for the basics of this method. Let's listen in on our teacher and Timothy at work with LEA.

TEACHER: Timothy, would you like to have a turn? Would you dictate part of your response to having interviewed our guest, Officer Huggins? [The teacher settles down with him.]

TIMOTHY: I was standing right by the door. [Pauses.]

TEACHER: [Writing what he says.] This goes right along with your picture, doesn't it? [Rereads the dictation, sliding hand under it.] "I was standing right by the door." You want to reread it with me? [They do.]

TIMOTHY: I've got more. [Continuing.] I think he was surprised when the motorcycle wouldn't go through the door. He took off his cap and kinda scratched his head. [Teacher continues writing to the end; then they reread it together and place it in Timothy's file for further use.]

Analysis of this Whole Language Scene

Many activities found in this classroom could be labeled *whole language*—uninterrupted time for reading/writing, journals, literature study, author's circle, and language experience approach (LEA). These activities are all loose organizational devices allowing each child to start in terms of his or her own experience and build from there. Later sections detail the LEA approach further and give a rationale for making use of expository language with it. Note that when Timothy dictated his LEA story he used an expository organization, noting his relationship to the topic at the beginning ("I was standing right by the door"), and indicating a further relationship by giving his opinion and a reason in his last two sentences. The teacher will call these expository strengths to his attention when he reads his piece to a small audience.

From the interview discourse with the guests, children gradually became familiar with expository organizations—the nurse dealing largely with cause and effect; the state representative with opinion and reason; the newspaper editor with most important and least important features of a story; and the pilot with problem and solution.

The children in this scene certainly expanded the relationship between comprehension and composition called language vocabulary, both receptive and expressive (recall Table 7.1). They did this as they furthered their ownership of words in a related network of meanings—for example, *policemen, helmet, handlebar, motorcycle, accidents, streets, speeding, carelessness, laws, fairness, safety, public protector, justice* (recall again the factors in Table 7.1 on page 218).

Preliminary "research" and question making was intertwined with *creativity* as children called on prior knowledge to help with imagery before the guest arrived. Comprehending, they then reworked the experience with imagination as they composed using picture, expository piece, or even finally a literary piece, a poem such as the one later dictated and reworked by Timothy:

> Policeman
> Your "reindeer" has silver-horned handlebars.
> Your journeys follow our streets and alley ways.
> Your gifts are protection, fairness, and safety.
> Our Friend

You can probably tell from the opening scene that the teacher did a great deal of planning: logistics, public relations, preparation of the children, gathering of related materials, and follow-up. Whether the goal is developing children's composing/comprehending and building a bridge to literacy with informational use or any other use, careful planning is essential. It bears repeating that the language arts of listening, speaking, reading, and writing were integrated in this scene along with content areas. Finally, environmental surroundings (the *where*) were brought into this classroom. The community needs to be tied closely to school, if our goal is informative communication in a democracy.

Next examine a rationale and definition for expositional use of language. We saw in Chapter 6 that the informative use of language can play an important part in classroom discussion. Also recall that exposition was advocated as a viable use of content from which children can compose and comprehend their way into literacy.

RATIONALE FOR EXPOSITION IN THE LANGUAGE ARTS CURRICULUM

What kinds of informational communication have you experienced lately? Presenting information read in class? Reading information to prepare for tomorrow's class work? Did your schooling prepare you for handling such tasks? Will you be able to help children? Informative communication is important in their lives, too.

Informative communication makes up the bulk of our handling of daily affairs. It makes sense for a child to deal with informative content first orally as a basis for successful reading and writing of it. Many language arts programs, however, are overbalanced on the personal-account or story type of discourse. No matter how valuable stories are, they represent only a part of the real world of language use. (Basal reading materials are getting better—slightly better—about reflecting the natural proportion of informative use of language in our lives.) If teachers confine the writing program (Chapter 8) solely to imaginative self-expression and narrative literature, they restrict experiences needed for human success. Nonfictional writing has a place in the curriculum just as much as fantasy does. This chapter helps you prepare to balance your reading/writing program with yet another important language use—expository reading and writing. To teach children to compose in the varied patterns of exposition is to teach them to comprehend and think in these patterns.

When building bridges to the craft of writing (Chapter 11), a teacher is often well advised to use children's expository material. That is, use their informational work rather than their personal, imaginative stories for teaching editing skills of spelling, punctuation, and usage. In the opening scene and toward the end of this chapter, we have examples of a teacher encouraging children's dictations from experience with expository materials and then judiciously using this child-produced information for craft development.

Children need to cope with many forms of and many audiences for expository discourse. Although even very young children seem able to grasp the structure of narrative text (stories), they seem to have less grasp of expository text structure. Studies further suggest that children of almost all ages, including high school, have trouble comprehending (much less composing) the structures of expository prose (McGee, 1982; Meyer, Brandt, & Bluth, 1980; Taylor, 1980).

The reason for the problem may lie in children's lack of experience. Even some elementary social studies texts, which one would consider a source of expository prose, present information in a pseudonarrative form (Pearson et al., 1981). But an important part of any rationale must stem from a careful look at the nature of children themselves, the emphasis of the next section.

WHO ARE THE CHILDREN LEARNING TO USE INFORMATIONAL LANGUAGE?

Informative language use in a language arts program is linked to children's natural curiosity about the world (Chapter 2). The early school years are a time when children naturally seek out informational activity to cut their intellectual teeth on. If they are not provided informational material then, children may move past the time for natural motivation for such learning. One set of informational books for the very youngest (aged 3–6) is *The Four Elements: Fire, Earth, Water, and Air*, with simple expository text and unforgettably beautiful illustrations by Parramon (1985). At the other end of our age spectrum, Chapter 8 shows a detailed science report in an upper-grade child's journal. Children's natural curiosity and need for self-competency and communication at any age are their internal allies. With this internal help, children can happily learn and practice the difficult language crafts needed for some exposition.

DEFINITIONS

Children's informational use has several distinguishing features, as might be inferred from our opening scene. In contrast with self-expression, the emphasis is on instruction, on reality, on communicating, and on transacting "business" with the message receiver. Also somewhat in contrast with self-expression, informative communication often tends to involve cooperation, working together to acquire information of importance to all in the transaction. Called "language to get things done," it shares known facts and conditions. Facts may be historical, observed (as in the opening scene), or derived from experiments. (A reader who already has clear definitions for aspects of informative discourse can skip ahead to the next section.)

Exposition is public, not private, and seeks a wider audience with precise, explicit meanings (in the opening scene the wider audience was the class and guest). In your classroom, children give descriptions, explanations, sequences, and instructions about people, places, experiences, and pets ("Here is how to set up an aquarium"). Children dictate titles, letters, observations, and labels ("Dinosaur Cave," so others will know and won't move their cave made of blocks). They make plans, teach each other games, formulate standards, solve problems, and hold informative discussions. They record, report, speculate, and even theorize ("All thin, flat things float, if you put them down carefully on the water"). Children use this workday language as they deliver and unlock straightforward prose meanings. Sources of information children use in your classroom are encyclopedia entries, maps, charts, graphs, globes, posters, radio and TV news and documentaries, dictionaries, and instructional computer programs. When thought of in this way, informative communication is recognizable as a key part of life and school curriculum.

It is often difficult to determine the precise purpose of a speaker or writer. To make the task easier, you can classify as informative communication any message thought to have informative value by any person in the communication transaction. Children giving reports, announcements, or book reviews may have some other intents, but if someone takes their discourse as informational (not mainly persuasive or entertaining), we will call it just that. Predominantly this textbook is informative in intent, but at times the intention is to be persuasive, self-expressive, and even literary.

The *process* in exposition involves one or more composers providing directions, explanations, and other information to comprehenders. These listeners, readers, or viewers image, connect with prior experience, note sequence, or grasp key features of the exposition.

Children can grow in informative communication skills *across the curriculum* as they encounter content areas such as science, math, social studies, and literature. For example, a productive integration occurs when you provide fine children's books with informative intent [e.g., *Jupiter* (Simon, 1985), *Mushrooms* (Selsan, 1986), and *Volcano* (Lauber, 1986)]. The social side of informative communication promotes such learning as children work cooperatively to choose topics, get information, record it, share and revise drafts, and prepare for "publication" or oral display.

There are three major types of informational use: (1) *Exploratory,* which asks; (2) *Informative,* which answers; and (3) *Scientific,* which tests and rejects. The last two tend, at least in substantial part, toward convergent thinking, that is, thought that retains the known and deals with facts. They tend toward the predetermined, conserving what is. Consider each of the three in turn.

Exploratory Language Use

More frequently oral than written, the exploratory use of language does not deal so much with known facts and conditions as with analogies and models. It has a shifting of personal perspectives and positions. It exposes something and explains a certain point of view. Besides conversations (Chapter 4) and discussions (Chapter 6), some classroom examples are work conferences, interviews, round table, panel discussions, and role play (detailed in the activity book, Chapter 5).

Informative Language Use

Informative language comes from facts and conditions that the child wants to present or receive. Journalistic reporting illustrates distinguishing standards of comprehensiveness of coverage and newness or surprise value. Children use informative language in giving news and weather reports in class, in reading encyclopedias, and in sending away for free social studies materials.

Scientific Language Use

In the scientific type of informative language, the message is usually accompanied by the following characteristics: experimental evidence ("proofs"), careful description, grouping, classifying, and carefully laid out assumptions. Examples are reports of hypothesis-testing studies, taxonomies, and historical analyses using original documents. Scientific language avoids emotional statements and intentional humor, while it packs much information into a brief space (see Figure 7.2). The standard expected for the use of evidence is high—*not* like the cartoon in Figure 7.3 on page 228.

WHAT INSTRUCTIONAL CONTENT, STRUCTURE, AND GOALS FOR INFORMATIVE LANGUAGE CAN A TEACHER USE?

Informational language use and study revolve around three focal areas: (1) organization, (2) style, and (3) logic. Since these elements are basic to the *how* of teaching informative language, consider each in turn.

Organization of Informational Language

The organization of information usually depends on the point being examined. For example, chronological order may be important for historical exposition when children get grandparents to share early photos and letters. Science may have hierarchies or treelike classifying structures. Social science may have a big idea or construct as the hub of a wheel, with spokes leading out to related ideas. The humanities may have big ideas or themes that are not necessarily related to each other. Progression by topics remains important to some types of content. Recall that a child may use both historical and chronological order in show and tell (detailed in Chapter 4).

Description   Message senders may organize an informative description according to space and topic in order to help the receiver visualize. Senders keep the description factually correct while including as complete a rendition of significant features as possible. ("My new doll came in a velvet-lined box; her hair is auburn under her yellow bonnet; she has a pinafore over her long flowered dress.")

Directions   In direction giving, the composer generally organizes ideas in the order in which they happen—a step-by-step sequence. Composers help their comprehenders by partitioning the directions into manageable chunks. ("First lay out all the following cooking materials you'll need, then. . . .")

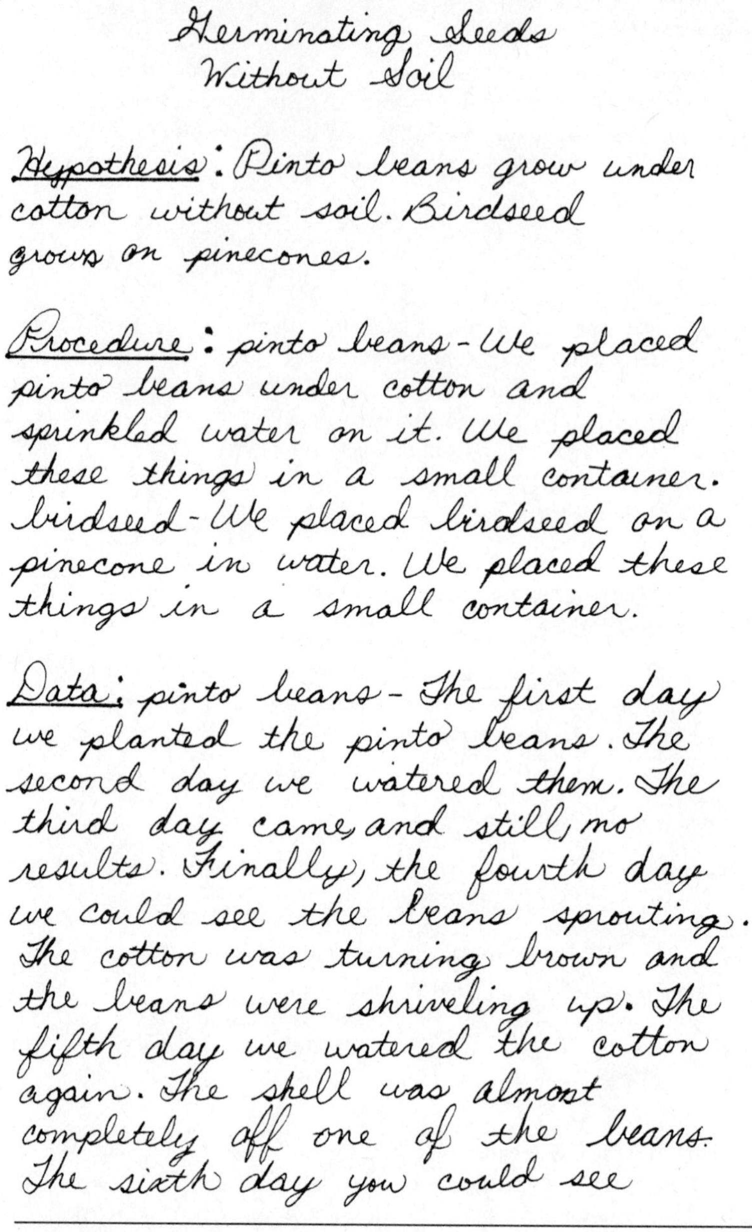

*Germinating Seeds
Without Soil*

Hypothesis: Pinto beans grow under cotton without soil. Birdseed grows on pinecones.

Procedure: pinto beans - We placed pinto beans under cotton and sprinkled water on it. We placed these things in a small container. birdseed - We placed birdseed on a pinecone in water. We placed these things in a small container.

Data: pinto beans - The first day we planted the pinto beans. The second day we watered them. The third day came and still no results. Finally, the fourth day we could see the beans sprouting. The cotton was turning brown and the beans were shriveling up. The fifth day we watered the cotton again. The shell was almost completely off one of the beans. The sixth day you could see

---

Figure 7.2 Sixth-grade report on seed sprouting.

Explanation Composers organize explanations to clarify or amplify. They identify what exists and reveal its importance, or how or why it works. Explanations are often organized by employing definitions, examples, comparison/contrast, descriptions, and statistics that show size. ("First a spider builds its web by a single horizontal thread from one support to another. Then midway in the cross line, it spins another thread down to a third support before adding more reinforcing spokes. Then. . . .")

little roots coming out. The seventh day it seemed that the beans were almost fully grown. birdseed — The first day we planted the birdseed on the pinecone. The second day we couldn't see anything, so we waited til the third and fourth day — no results. On the fifth day we could see that the birdseed turned the pinecone into a different color. From the sixth day and on, nothing has happened since.

<u>Conclusion</u>: Pinto beans will grow under cotton without soil. Birdseed will not grow on pinecones, but it will change the color of the pinecone.

Tracy, Grade 6

Tracy, 6th grade

Figure 7.2 *(Continued)*

Scientific Use To someone using scientific language, an organization by problem, method, results, and conclusion may be important. A third-grade group wrote: "We couldn't get the marigolds in our class window box to bloom" (problem). "We tried putting them more in the sun" (method). "They bloomed" (results). "We think marigolds need a lot of sun" (conclusion). Sometimes the structure follows problem-solving steps with evaluation deliber-

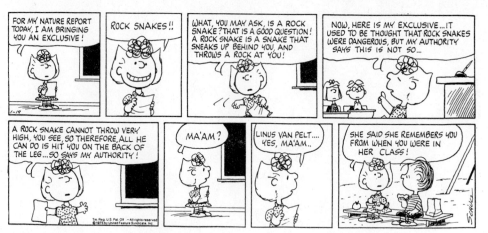

Figure 7.3 On evidence in scientific discourse. Reprinted with permission of UFS, Inc.

ately held in abeyance until the language user has generated as much information as necessary. (Recall the brainstorming discussion in Chapter 6.)

Journalistic Use Of most importance to journalistic use is the *who-what-when-where-how* type of organization (detailed in Chapter 4). The inverted pyramid of information, also important, has the most newsworthy items first. Objective flashbacks and leaps into the future may be the common organization of exploratory discourse and editorializing. (The accompanying activity book has a section on the newspaper.)

Organizational Features and Patterns Well-organized informational language is easy for the receiver to grasp because it has:

- Overviews
- Carefully planned structures
- Headings
- Internal summaries
- Strong indications of transitions
- Relationships between parts
- Final summary
- Study guide
- Outlines
- Follow-up questions

Teachers' well-chosen or carefully crafted information provides a model for children's own expository productions.

Six organizational patterns common to informational language are given in Box 7.1. Knowledge of these organizational patterns can prove useful in many phases of learning and teaching.

> ### BOX 7.1 Six Organizational Patterns of Informative Use of Language
>
> 1. *Chronological pattern.* Arranging events according to order of occurrence.
> 2. *Spatial pattern.* Arranging ideas in terms of physical relations.
> 3. *Topical pattern.* Arranging ideas according to natural divisions of the question or content.
> 4. *Causal pattern.* Considering cause and then effects, or considering effects and then trying to ferret out causes.
> 5. *Problem-solving pattern.* Uncovering problems and solutions.
> 6. *Comparison-contrast pattern.* Considering similarities and differences among, e.g., concepts, events, objects, problems, books.

Style in Informational Language

Compared with self-expressive language, informational language is more precise about meaning. The language user tends to use nouns instead of pronouns, to finish sentences, and to be appropriately tentative and conditional. ("The reason Joan's seeds did not sprout when she placed them in the pine cone *might* be that Joan did not keep them moist enough.")

This does not mean that the style is dull and pedantic. Informative speaking and writing without any creativity becomes wooden and dreary. Many informational books for children are both accurate and highly readable. Children can model after such a style. The utilitarian and artistic phases of speaking and writing are not necessarily opposed to each other. The following is a small sample of interestingly written exposition:

> *The Story of English* is an extraordinary tale of a language that came from nowhere to affect the world. Two thousand years ago English was confined to a handful of savage and now-forgotten tribes on the shores of northwest Europe. Today, in some form or another, it is spoken by perhaps a billion people around the world. . . . Why do people of Newfoundland speak English with an Irish brogue? What do Australians have in common with Cockneys? . . . (McCrum, Cran, & MacNeil, 1986)

A teacher performs a balancing act promoting both the reality of the utilitarian and the personal creative freedom of the artistic. Informational speaking and writing (the utilitarian) can be almost as vigorous, vivid, and full of sensation as artistic composition. It can invite the listener and reader to participate almost as much. Above all, however, this kind of communication is *accurate* and *honest.* Teachers need to develop this idea with children. Sometimes informational preparation furnishes a base from which imaginative composition takes off. Science fiction that is well grounded in outer-space study is one example.

Another idea involves the following *activity:* Have the children collect pictures of hats from various places and cultures found in social studies, then let the students craft stories that each hat could tell (you might use coins from different countries instead of hats).

The grammar, sentence structure, or syntax of exposition tends to de-emphasize the personal. That is, the third person is used frequently, the first person less frequently.

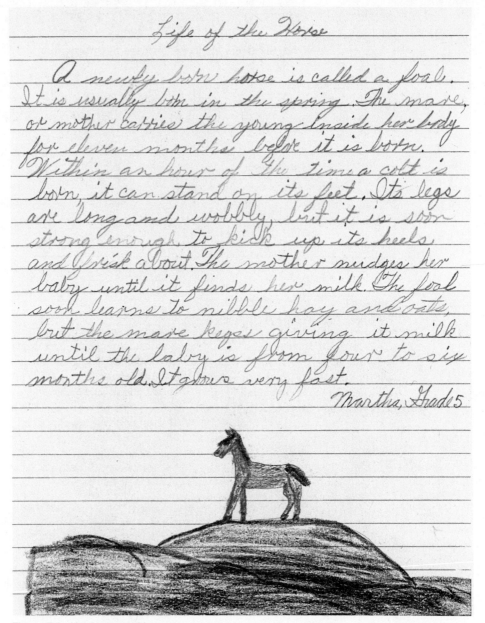

Figure 7.4 Horse compositions.

Sentences tend to be in the normal order, but exclamatory (!) and imperative patterns ("Do it!") are generally absent. Dialect is usually standard and formal, especially for scientific speaking and writing (*not* "Well, here's the way it's gotta be . . ."). Style in some informational and scientific writing may be terse, with a high density of complex concepts.

Finally, in exploratory language, sentence forms are often both questioning and conditional. For example, consider a kindergarten conversation in response to a question on what makes the birds fly: "Could it be . . . the wind pushes the birds and makes them

What a Horse Should Eat and What He Likes

Horses should eat mostly green foods. It must have water in the stall at all times. Both heavy and light horses should be fed well. Hay, oats, corn, bran, cottonseed meal, and cornstalks are good for horses. Horses are fond of apples, carrots, turnips, sugar, and molasses. A cake of salt should be kept in the stall too.

Martha, Grade 5

Figure 7.4 (*Continued*)

fly faster?" Some questions check on other questions, and the communicator uses if-then and either-or kinds of constructions: "If the wind pushes the birds to make them fly faster, then they sure must have been speeding around yesterday with all that high wind."

Logic in Informational Language

The three types of exposition—exploratory, informative, and scientific—have a progressively rigorous logic. The logic in exposition may be deductive or inductive (as detailed in

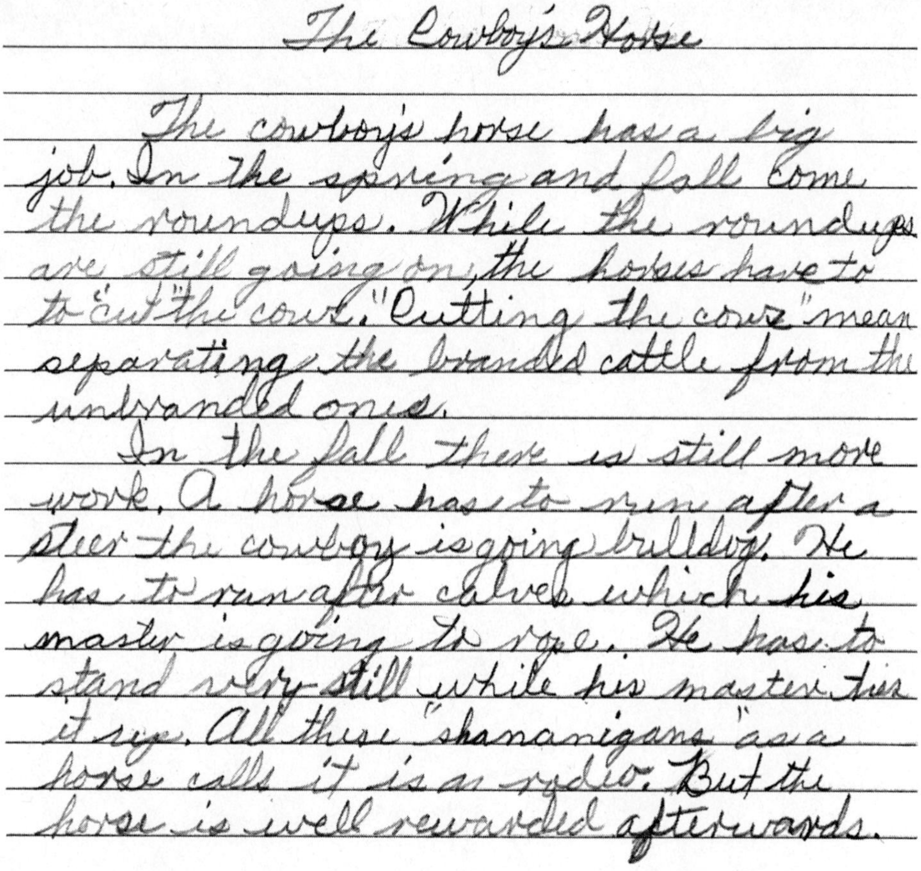

The Cowboy's Horse

The cowboy's horse has a big job. In the spring and fall come the roundups. While the roundups are still going on, the horses have to to "cut the cows." "Cutting the cows" mean separating the branded cattle from the unbranded ones.

In the fall there is still more work. A horse has to run after a steer the cowboy is going bulldog. He has to run after calves which his master is going to rope. He has to stand very still while his master ties it up. All these "shananigans" as a horse calls it is a rodeo. But the horse is well rewarded afterwards.

Figure 7.4 *(Continued)*

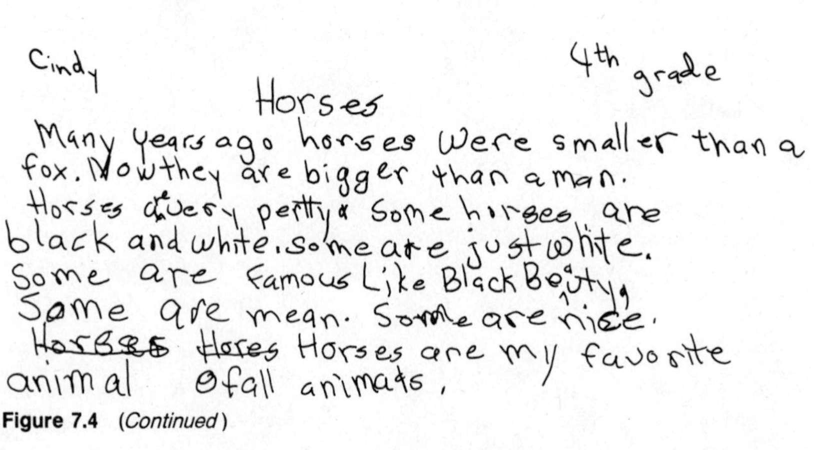

Cindy   4th grade

Horses

Many years ago horses were smaller than a fox. Now they are bigger than a man. Horses are very pretty. Some horses are black and white. Some are just white. Some are famous like Black Beauty. Some are mean. Some are nice. Horses Horses Horses are my favorite animal of all animals.

Figure 7.4 *(Continued)*

Chapter 10). Briefly, *deductive* logic goes from broad generalization to particulars; for example: "All major differences among people are cultural, not biological. Juan is culturally different from John, and therefore not biologically different."

Or the logic in exposition may be *inductive*, going from particulars to generalization. For example, if a visitor to school W sees around 80 percent boys in five classrooms, he or she may induce that this school has a larger number of boys than girls. It would be poor logic, however, to deduce that *all* schools have more boys than girls and thus so do schools X, Y, and Z. Scientific discourse is particularly careful about logic. (Suggested activities in Chapter 10 and in the activity book support this idea.)

Content in Exposition

A child needs intriguing experiences about which to be informative. Children learn appropriate organization, style, and logic for the informational use of language when they have ingredients from social studies, science, math, and language history that are important and appropriate to communicate about. For example, one third-grade teacher invited her children to research an underground animal to find something (not everything!) they would like to learn about that animal. The students shared books and helped each other take notes and categorize them.

We have a wealth of appealing, high-quality informational books for children. Children can "prowl" for ideas. Consider, for example, Kohn's (1970) colorful book *Chipmunks*, which translates scientific information into simple, direct prose ideal for young children's visualization of concepts. The informational compositions in Figure 7.4 on pages 230, 231, and 232 came from prowling for information about horses.

Appropriate Goals and Objectives

Emerging from the foregoing content, goals for informational language can include (1) use of the *process* of practical, honest, increasingly scientific language with discipline and rigor in organization, logic, and appropriate style; (2) facility in employing a multitude of informational *uses* of language, detailed in this chapter; (3) development of direct, honest, and scholarly *attitudes* about expository language. Many messages in life have informative value. Children can come to appreciate the richness of the information that surrounds them. They can value listening, speaking, reading, and writing to learn.

As initiators of informational language, children generally need several skills that may find their way into framework objectives, sometimes called study skills. Some examples are given in Box 7.2 (these examples tie in with Figure 7.1 on page 217).

Figure 7.5 on page 235 is a curriculum checklist for more advanced constructs in expository communication. Use it as a partial framework for upper-grade skills and for assessment. Fortunately, with National Writing Projects stressing composition across the curriculum, no single teacher has to do it all. Yet it is well to have a sense of the range. When use of communication is purposeful, relevant, and meaningful, many expositional skills develop naturally. Typically there are few (if any) isolated exercises or drills needed. Helpful is a well-arranged classroom—the topic of the next section.

WHERE DOES INFORMATIONAL LANGUAGE DEVELOPMENT TAKE PLACE?

The classroom in the opening scene was well stocked with materials for developing and displaying informational uses of language; for example, the classroom library was filled with

---

BOX 7.2 Informational Language Skills

Some Skills for Comprehenders of Information

- Given purpose and reasons, grasp important points and crucial details
- Using any prior knowledge of the content, network the concepts and/or the vocabulary
- Figure out the organization, make notes, construct concept maps or webs, or outlines
- Work personal imagery associated with the concepts and prior experience or information
- Draw own conclusions, applying criteria for logic and organization of exposition
- Make own summary
- Verify by asking and answering questions

Some Skills for Composers of Information

- Given purpose and intent, select informational topic from content to share
- Keeping a selected organizational structure, audience, and message in mind, narrow appropriately
- Locate needed information—listening and reading to learn and share
  —library skills
  —note taking
- Use vocabulary networks or thesaurus to better fit the information to the intent and the audience
- Reorganize it with imagination, applying criteria for organization, logic, and style of exposition
- Draw conclusions
- Summarize it
- Seek and handle feedback

---

interesting material relevant to the guests. Topics were nature, people, places, and how-to books. In addition, encyclopedias, atlases, almanacs, books of quotations, audiotapes and videotapes and films were available in the school library and media center. Other useful features and materials are the following: felt board, computers, menus, magazines, coupons, sales receipts, telephone books, TV guides, catalogues, newspapers, photos, categorized picture files, instructional pamphlets, junk mail, road maps, cookbooks—almost anything with informational, auditory, or visual material.

A question to ask yourself about the environment is this: *Do my students have an opportunity to "research" topics of interest and relate their findings to their own questions and observations?* Having explored a rationale, definitions, and the *who, what,* and *where* of expository discourse in the classroom, we are now already well into the *how* of teaching—the next topic.

**PICKING OUT AND USING INFORMATIONAL ELEMENTS
IN
EXPOSITORY TEXT**

Identification

_____ Introductory statements

_____ Definition of terms

Classification

_____ Inclusion

_____ Exclusion

Comparison and contrast

_____ Analogy and illustration

_____ Details relating to principles

Relationships

_____ Cause and effect

_____ Opinion and reason

_____ Problem and solution

_____ Hypothesis and evidence

_____ Least important and most important

_____ Subordinate and coordinate

_____ Question and answer

_____ Conclusion and proof

_____ General to specific

Figure 7.5 Curriculum checklist for expository communication.

HOW DO YOU TEACH INFORMATIONAL COMMUNICATION?

In this section we further explore classroom use of the language arts in informational communication. Some of the areas covered in helping children listen, read, and write to _learn_ are the following: (1) mapping, (2) helping children begin and end informative discourse, (3) developing an ongoing and well-assessed program that generates cumulative enthusiasm. Such a program is grounded in whole language (specifically language experience approaches). Box 7.3 on page 236 gives an overview.

It is common knowledge that to retain information one needs to use it. The point is to make the content one's own—to "own" it. _Previewing_, the first item in Box 7.3 helps avoid the reaction "I have no idea what this is all about."

Mapping to Learn

Another of the study skills in Box 7.3 is mapping. Sometimes it is called webbing, networking, and a host of other terms. Mapping is a visual means of portraying and analyzing a subject and its related topics and subtopics. It is feasible even for primary students. Figure 7.6 on page 237 is a sample map about mapping.

BOX 7.3 Guidance for Using Language to Learn

- Previewing
  - ☐ Skimming
  - ☐ Predicting
  - ☐ Checking glossary and index
  - ☐ Providing advance organizers—"maps" of what is already known, study guides, the ordering of the topics (preliminary analysis of content)
  - ☐ Looking at introductions, summaries
  - ☐ Discussing importance, uses now and future, prior experience ("I already know this.")
  - ☐ Relating new, complex concepts to prior experience
  - ☐ Turning headings into questions, or posing questions from the oral preview

- Identifying and absorbing the content in developmentally appropriate, meaningful chunks of it; noting the strong transitions and relations (written and oral, e.g., *first, second, in contrast to*); internal summarizing along the way

- After intake of content
  - ☐ Reviewing with a peer, summarizing, relating to and updating content maps of what they already know, questioning (Chapter 6), seeking feedback, predicting what might be next, comparing notes or dialogue journals *(writing to learn)*
  - ☐ Translating to other media (e.g., drama, art, writing, movement
  - ☐ Transferring the content to other uses
  - ☐ Undertaking independent research on the content to share later orally on a panel *(speaking to learn)*

How might your students use mapping? One use is for previewing, indicated on the guidance checklist in Box 7.3. For example, children construct a map of an upcoming field trip to a bakery and brainstorm for the map where they might go and what they might see and learn. Then, analyzing the content after the trip, they revise and update their map. Thus mapping is a useful tool both in composing and in comprehending. (Maps or networks of language arts areas are displayed in Chapters 3, 4, 8, 10, and other chapters in this book.)

Figure 7.7 on pages 237–240 gives an example of a first-grade activity including pre- and postreading, vocabulary building, and writing while mapping information on sea otters. Given are objectives, day 1, 2, and 3 procedures, before and after maps, and comments. (Also see Figure 7.8, p. 240.) The map (or web) in Figure 7.9 on page 241 started with an element in nature, *rain*, and radiated to exploratory, informational, scientific, and poetic material found in books, poems, and songs. A quarterly publication called *The WEB: Wonderfully Exciting Books* (Ohio State University, 1987) provides webs on different themes and/or books to aid teachers who use literature-based reading programs.

One more map, Figure 7.10 on page 242, shows informative use of language for the classroom teacher, as detailed in this chapter. It would mean more to you if you had constructed or at least added to it yourself. The same idea applies to children.

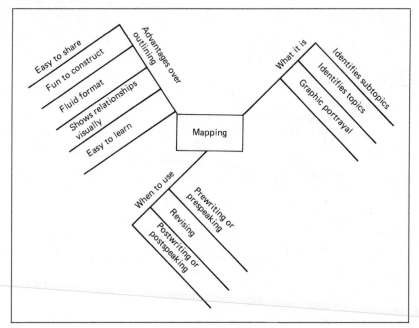

Figure 7.6 A map on the subject of mapping. (*Source:* Allen, Brown, & Yatvin, 1986.)

A PRE- AND POSTREADING VOCABULARY-BUILDING AND WRITING ACTIVITY: GRADE 1

(a) In this application, semantic mapping is used with 15 first graders near the end of the school year. Students read a story in their basal series that relates to a science topic being studied and then organize the information from the story onto a semantic map. The students use the map to help them write a short report of several sentences. Mapping is done prior to and after students read the passage and again after students have done independent reading from resource books and viewed a filmstrip. Students, who have been studying wildlife creatures, research the topic *sea otters* and write reports for their wildlife folders. (See Figures 7.7b and c.)

Objectives

The semantic mapping process is used to meet the following objectives:

- Assess students' knowledge of sea otters.
- Share prior knowledge of sea otters with peers.
- Learn new vocabulary related to sea otters.
- Organize and structure the information about sea otters.

Figure 7.7 Mapping information on sea otters. (a) Explanations of maps; (b) and (c) semantic maps. (*Source:* Heimlich & Pittelman, 1986.)

Procedure

Day 1

1. Place a picture of sea otters on the chalkboard. Then print the words *sea otters* below the picture and draw a circle around the words.
2. Ask the students to think about sea otters and to share as many words as they can that relate to the topic.
3. Discuss and record on the map information and words that the students suggest. Write this information on the chalkboard in clusters (categories) using white chalk.
4. As necessary, add and define key vocabulary words important to story comprehension (words that had been suggested by the basal series). Write these words on the map with blue chalk.
5. Discuss each of the clusters or categories of words and determine appropriate labels or headings. Add these to the map.
6. Have the students read the story by following the procedure suggested in the teacher's manual.
7. After the students have finished reading the story, ask them to suggest new information that can be added to the map. Write this information on the map using green chalk. (See Figure 7.7b.)

Day 2

1. Review the information about sea otters on the semantic map. Ask the students what else they would like to know about sea otters.
2. Give the students resource books to read for additional information about sea otters. Have the students write down important information they learn from reading these books.
3. Have the students use their notes during a discussion period in which they share the information about sea otters gained through their independent reading. Add new information to the map using red chalk.

Day 3

1. Briefly review the categories on the semantic map.
2. Tell the students that you are going to show them a filmstrip about sea otters and they should look for information to add to the categories on the semantic map.
3. Show the filmstrip.
4. Discuss the information from the filmstrip. Add this new information to the map using yellow chalk. (See Figure 7.7c.)
5. Direct each student to select three to five facts about sea otters from the map. Have students use these facts to write complete sentences. These will form their reports about the sea otter.
6. Have the students illustrate their reports.
7. Let each student read his or her completed report and share the accompanying illustration with the entire class. Place these reports in the students' wildlife folders.

Comments

This activity illustrates how semantic mapping can be used in the primary grades to integrate science, reading, and writing. Using a picture above the written topic label is an effective

Figure 7.7 *(Continued)*

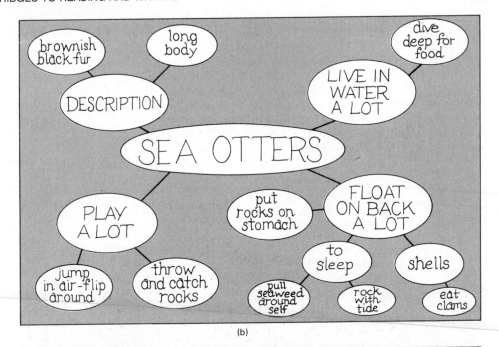

(b)

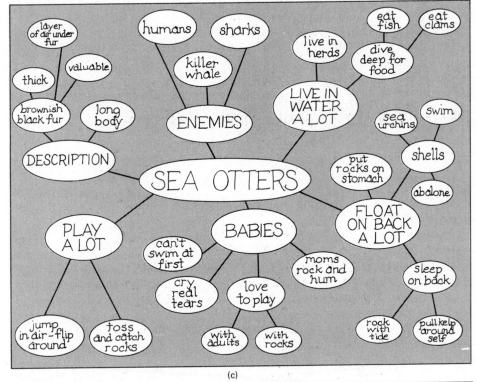

(c)

Figure 7.7 (*Continued*)

technique for use with primary students as it stimulates the children's thoughts and gets the brainstorming procedure off to a quick start. The mapping experience was not only motivational but it also gave the first graders the opportunity to share new and known vocabulary, to read for new facts and ideas, and to see how information can be organized. The completed map helped them with their report writing by serving as a guide in information selection, as a springboard for ideas, and as a spelling guide for writing their sentences.

The map itself provided the students with a graphic picture of the "territory they had traveled," showing what they already knew, prior knowledge (written in white chalk); what they learned in reading their basal text (green chalk); what they learned from their independent reading (red chalk); and the information from viewing the filmstrip (yellow chalk). At each stage of the map's development, students could refine as well as add to the existing map. While the maps reproduced here in black and white do not show the effect of the use of different colors of chalk, the additions to the map can be seen by comparing the initial map (Figure 7.7b) with the completed map (Figure 7.7c).

Figure 7.7   *(Continued)*

Grades 4–6

1. In addition to using semantic mapping for comprehending and composing stories, the technique can be used to aid reading and writing of expository content. An example of a map used to help pupils comprehend and interrelate the vocabulary of a selection on the ocean follows.

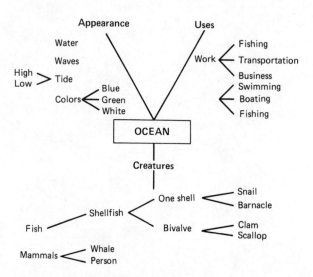

2. Have pupils use the semantic map to compose an outline of the content of the selection using the topic as the title, the subheads as the headings, the entries as subheadings, and the related ideas as details.
3. The pupils may use the outline to re-create the content of the selection.
4. Once the technique has been mastered, pupils may use it to prepare for outlining and for expository writing in both social studies and science.

Figure 7.8   Ocean web. (*Source:* Indrisano, 1984.)

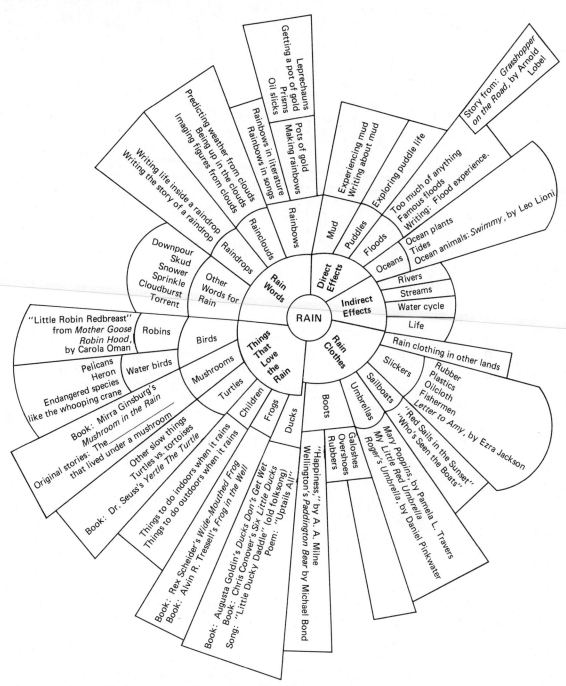

Figure 7.9 Rain web. (*Source:* Hurst, Healy, Witherell, & Alouise, 1983.)

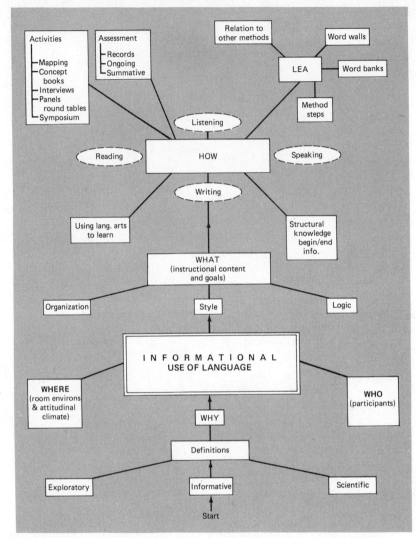

Figure 7.10 Map of informative use of language as explicated in this chapter.

How the Teacher Can Help Children Begin and End Informative Communication

Maps help many children with organizing the midportions of their informational pieces. But many children (and adults) become frustrated when composing a beginning and an ending. You can help them offer more than "It's about a boat trip" or "The End." You can call attention to the options given in Box 7.4 (Allen, Brown, & Yatvin, 1986). Figure 7.11 on page 244 maps beginning and ending in an informative piece in a directional format.

BOX 7.4 Beginning and Ending an Informational Piece

Beginning

- Reveal the topic or purpose. (A fifth-grade child gives us a set of examples in an informative anecdote: "My first ferry crossing. . . . ")
- Spark attention. ("I was really excited. . . . ")
- Provide background information needed (context). ("It was last year, summer holiday . . . to Catalina Island. . . . ")
- Stress the importance of your purpose. ("I'd never been even for just a little boat trip. . . . ")
- Note your special relationship to the topic. ("So it was really big in my life. . . . ")
- Provide a preview of the body of the message. ("I'm going to tell you what I could see, how rough it was coming back, and what my folks made us do. . . .")

Ending

- Draw together the ideas explored or presented.
  —Summarize.
  —Give an apt quotation. ("So we said, 'It wasn't fair to keep us inside when all the big waves were spashing up on the boat sides. . . .' ")
  —Suggest to the audience applications of your information. ("If you go to Catalina, get your folks to agree to let you stay up on deck, even if it's a bit rough.")
  —Indicate personal intent, if appropriate. ("That's what I'm going to do next time.")
  —Refer back to the beginning of the information, suggesting that the "circle" of the message is complete. ("That trip was still a really big thing in my life.")

Activities to Illustrate the Teaching of Informational Language Use

The activities in Box 7.5 on pages 245–246 grow out of those for Chapter 6 on discussion. They also serve as tools for content learning and as bridges into writing and reading. You will find whole language procedures such as self-sharing, concept books, and language experience approaches. The activities answer in part the following student teacher questions:

> *"How can I help children listen/speak and read/write to* **learn?"**

> *"How can I develop an ongoing program that generates cumulative enthusiasm and is not just "excess baggage" of minor, isolated activity, but is activity I would feel good about doing myself?"*

We next examine the details of that unsurpassed method for building bridges to literacy—the language experience approach. (The topic is developed by presenting typical questions and answers.)

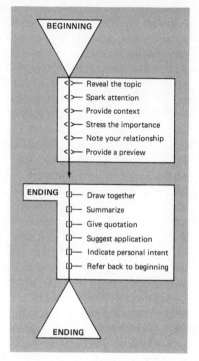

Figure 7.11 Map for beginning and ending an informational piece.

BRIDGING WITH THE LANGUAGE EXPERIENCE APPROACH (LEA)

One of the best ways to help children bridge into reading and writing is the language experience approach (LEA), part of the whole-language activity illustrated in the opening scene. One of the best ways to ease into growth in *informational* use of language is also LEA. Since LEA is so integrating and applies to a wide range of ages, including remedial cases, it is worth substantial consideration. Originally formulated by Dorris M. Lee in the 1950s, it was then popularized and is finally well recognized in textbooks and teacher education.

What distinguishes LEA is that it uses the child's *own* language as the teaching medium. The material collected from the child usually consists of language units larger than words, though a dictated caption for a picture might just say "cats," or later, "The Anatomy of Cats."

It bears repeating that the language experience approach can make a significant contribution to children's literacy development at many age levels, not just at the beginning. Children are free from the demeaning fear of using "incorrect" language. They can see a large portion of their speech sounds written by adults. If the message is expository and must immediately communicate with an audience, children have an additional boost.

Using the LEA method is more challenging than simply following the dictates of a basal reader. For this reason, you will not find every teacher using it. But once a teacher has used LEA and seen the meaningful ease of learning and the motivation stimulated in children, this valuable addition to any teaching repertory is usually around to stay. Use it in conjunction with other more "teacher-proof" materials (such as basals) if you must, *but use it*. Most research studies on LEA demonstrate that such methods are as effective as basal-reader approaches and even have special advantages (Hall, 1978).

BOX 7.5 Activities for Teaching Informational Language Use

Sharing by the Teacher (Personalizing an Informational Communication Process). Use a bulletin board to share your own informational writing with your students. Take pictures of yourself at each stage. Having gathered information, write a first draft for your selected task (e.g., applying for a summer workshop, a proposal to be on a professional program, a vacation plan). Read it to someone else. Remember to include a picture representing the revision, final typing, and mailing. Post your pictures with descriptive labels, especially for the prewriting, writing, revision, final editing, and display stages (detailed in Chapter 8). After sharing your experience via the bulletin board, do the same for your students with their informational tasks in, say, writing away for something. Also take progressive pictures of the children's work stages and post these (adapted from Jacobson, 1987).

Concept Books Consider a unit or units employing concept books. One category of books that Tomie de Paola (a favorite author-illustrator) has written are concept books that teach children facts in storylike form. A teacher can use five of his books as models for writing about "real" things. Children can compare and contrast his books with state and district adopted student textbooks, and with the styles of authors Gail Gibbons and Donald Crews, who also write and illustrate concept books. Working in pairs or small task groups, children check the facts in the concept story books with several sources, discussing and charting findings.

Children can write their own concept books related to topics they are studying (e.g., in math, science, social studies, health, and computers). They can work on these individually or in small groups. They might consider modeling after the style of de Paola or using some other style. Have them use the map in Figure 7.11 for beginnings and endings. Then select a developmental pattern—compare/contrast, sequence, topical, problem/solution—as listed in Figure 7.5. Recall the idea of writing to learn: that writing greatly helps one to make sense of what one finds out. Putting information in written format helps students make many connections (adapted from Chambers, 1987). Also see the activity book that goes with this text (Chapter 9 for literature). See books and extension ideas for activities depicting journeys, especially those rooted in historical or current fact. For these, children could prepare a travel lecture, a newsletter, a bulletin board, a sequential mural, or a time line.

Mathematical concepts in children's literature are another source for unit activity to promote growth in the informational use of language. The teacher and children make sure that the math content is accurate. Another criterion is aesthetic pleasure: children can understand and use math content with application to life experiences and appreciation of its patterns and beauty (Young, 1985).

Seuss's *500 Hats* (Geisel, 1938) can spark interest in the mathematical idea of addition and multiplication. *Gator Pie* (Matthews, 1979) introduces children to the inverse relationship of the number of pieces a whole must be cut into and the resulting size of a fraction. This idea is presented through a pair of alligators as they attempt to cut a chocolate pie into equal pieces for

(Continued)

everyone. A model for subtraction might be Matthews's *The Great Take-Away;* for multiplication, Anno's *Anno's Mysterious Multiplying Jar.*

Children can describe numbers and shapes in a *feely box* that replicates the numbers and shapes from a story. (A feely box or bag is one in which interesting objects are placed and into which children can insert their hands to feel the objects without looking, to gain alternate perceptual impressions. Chapter 8 has more on using the feely box to stimulate writing.) For this activity one might use counting stories, such as Carle's *The Very Hungry Caterpillar* or Seingobosc's *Jeanne-Marie Counts Her Sheep.* Children can work out their own stories based on these models, e.g., first on a flannel board before writing and illustrating them. They can write reviews on books (including their own) for the class newspaper or make their reviews oral with a prop in the form of a mobile. (Activity adapted from Young, 1985).

Applying the method especially to expository language competence, this section takes you through five steps and five days for a concrete though optional start with LEA. It also answers many common questions and finishes with some words on public relations.

Basic Ideas in LEA

The basic idea in the language experience approach, as illustrated briefly in the opening scene, is simple and fourfold:

LEA Basics
1. Children have something they want to say.
2. One child at a time says it to you.
3. You write it down in dictation from the child with the child watching.
4. You and the child read it back.

The chances are that because the text, coming from the child's experience, is so meaningful, ego-motivated, and natural to the child, the child will learn to read that text and subsequent ones more easily. (There are variations on the number of children cooperatively dictating and who takes the dictation, described later). The words the child recognizes are later transferred to a personal word bank that serves for review and as a source of words for the child to use in independent writing. The child and teacher can later spend a brief amount of time analyzing the produced language in order to develop comprehension and skills in word attack (ways of learning to identify and pronounce words when reading).

These ideas are the key to the LEA method. To explore the rationale of the LEA approach in terms of concepts for the child and for the teacher, we turn to the following questions and answers.

"What are LEA concepts for *children?*"

The language experience approach has a certain "credo." Box 7.6 on page 247 is one version. It indicates that LEA can produce a pattern of thinking about reading that is grasped

---

BOX 7.6 LEA Credo

- What I can *think* about I can *talk* about.
- What I can say can be *written.*
- What has been *written* in my language can be *read.*
- What other people have written I can read because:
  They use many of the *same* words and sentence patterns I do
  They say some of the same things but in *different ways.* (Allen, 1976)

---

by each student. For diagnosis and assessment, a teacher can use these concepts as a checklist for a child's LEA file.

Allen (1976) adds other concepts that children gain from this LEA method:

- As I talk and write, I use some words over and over, and some not so often *(recurring words).*
- As I talk and write, I use some words and clusters of words to express my meanings *(meaning symbolization).*
- As I write to represent the sounds I make through speech, I use the same symbols (letters) over and over *(recurring letter symbols).*
- Each letter of the alphabet stands for one or more sounds that I make when I talk *(sound-letter correspondence).*
- And, as I read, I add from my experience to what an author has written, if I am to get full meaning and pleasure from print *(bringing prior experience to bear).*

"What are some LEA concepts for *teachers?*"

The concepts for teachers strengthen the rationale for using this method. They also help to justify it to parents, principals, and school boards.

- The *basis* of children's oral and written expression is their sensitivity to their *own environmental experience.*
- Freedom in language self-expression leads to *self-confidence* in all uses of language, including spelling, punctuation, and manipulation of grammatical structures. (Chapter 1 stressed the importance of self-concept.)
- If a literacy program is based on children's personal language patterns and vocabulary, children will experience a *natural flow* of language production and a high degree of *independence* in writing and reading. (Another bonus is counteraction of boredom from irrelevant stories and contexts with severely limited vocabulary.)
- To get to the processes through which children's language matures, it takes many productive, sensory activities that get children to *interact* and *use* language. (Adapted from Allen, 1976)

"Why is it strongly recommended that I take down the child's *exact* language?"

With the exception of spelling, the teacher generally does not control the child's language in any way during LEA dictation. If the child says "done went," the teacher writes "done went." Why? Children tend to read their material as they have dictated it rather than as a teacher might have edited it. If the teacher edits usage, grammar, and content at this point, the link between print and speech may be broken. Breaking the link may cause children more difficulty in developing vocabulary and concepts of reading for comprehension and genuine communication. Children may become less willing to give ideas. They may become anxious for acceptance and think the whole process revolves around pleasing adults in power. They no longer own their material. Self-motivation disappears.

In certain circumstances the point may be arguable, but the rationale and evidence are strong. As public servants we need to attend to the goals of our clientele of parents. But if teachers cannot negotiate with and educate parents, teachers need to move and serve another clientele whose hopes and dreams for their children are more compatible with the teachers' knowledge and ideals.

"What do I need to know about a child before embarking on LEA?"

Make some assessment of the child's interests, background experiences, and language production before using this approach. Abilities for language production will bear, in part, on the child's ability to symbolize experiences with language, to make up stories, and to repeat observations. Knowing about a child's concepts of print and language will guide what you will make explicit during the dictation interaction (e.g., whether you slide your hand under words as you reread left to right to show directionality).

Knowing about the child's interests gives the teacher clues to the child's perceptual sensitivity and gives hints for providing further usable experience in school. It may be wise to see if the child is in (or is in transition toward) a concrete-operational level (Chapter 2). If so, it is more developmentally appropriate to move from the child's dictated story to any word attack skills demanding more than one-to-one correspondence (i.e., more than one letter standing for a sound).

"Who does LEA with whom?"

The *who* in LEA may be a teacher; or, to ease the burden of taking dictation, you can train volunteers (including parents), aides, or cross-age tutors (older students) to help. You can even set up a tape recorder: Children push the controls themselves and someone transcribes portions later. Do at least some portions while the child watches the actual process. Your interaction with the child makes for some important on-the-spot learning.

The *who* may be an individual child, a small group with a common interest, or the whole group (especially in initial modeling sessions and for special occasions). Groups usually work with large recording charts and then also with small personal copies on which to underline mastered vocabulary to go into personal word banks. An example of a group-dictated chart might be "What We've Learned About the Peanut," stimulated by a multitude of classroom activities.

"Where does the child find stimulation and ideas for dictated stories?"

Children may find stimulation for their dictation from their own lives and families (a wedding, an outing) and even from school itself ("Mrs. Penny was scared of the dark when she was little!"). Kindergarteners and first graders generally have little difficulty in finding things they would like to dictate about once the creativity becomes contagious. The most fluent pieces dictated are often exposition about real events. If a child is still reluctant, try taking turns: You come up with an idea, then the child comes up with one, and so on. Dictated material stressing the expository use of language can come from field trips, such as an aquarium visit, or an analysis of the weather. Children also get inspiration from the following audiovisual materials:

Their own paintings made into a slide sequence begging for a story

Friends

Adventures

Categories (e.g., toys, transportation, color, shape, motion, sound, size, texture)

Popping corn

What happens on the playground

Original or adapted songs

How yesterday is different from today (or tomorrow)

Books they listen to or "read" themselves and with patterns they can model after, e.g., "a web is a house for a spider," "a frame is a house for a picture; a shell is a house for a snail (Hoberman, 1978).

"What are some basic steps I would go through in using LEA?"

A prerequisite to the steps that children take could well be teacher planning and selection of appropriate learning experiences in content areas. Examples might include science experiments, a visit to the custodian's quarters, making butter, or response to factual material read orally by the teacher. A productive use of LEA can be with a group after a planned learning experience in a content area.

Step 1: Child experiences. Encourage the child to share ideas and experiences. (Stimulate expression in as many forms as possible: observation, experimentation, painting, dramatic play, singing, building, discussion. These forms of symbolization precede and lead into print symbolization, as stressed in Chapter 8.)

Step 2: Child talks. Help the child clarify and summarize the ideas and experiences. The child associates his or her own words with these expressions. Avoid rushing into dictation too soon; give time for discussion with the child. All of the language arts are important in LEA, and process is more important than product.

Step 3: Child dictates. Record the child's self-directed language. Dictation can be both individual and collective for group-composed chart stories. For recording you can use a sentence strip, regular note paper, a booklet, a chalkboard, a chart, or whatever. (Teacher: "How might we begin? Tell me what to write.")

Step 4: Child reads along. Ask the child to share his or her own written ideas by reading them back. (And the child can read them back to someone else, then someone else, etc., for more practice than you would ever believe!) In addition, there are advantages to having children illustrate before dictation: Their art symbols will feed into the oral language and print symbols, making production and retention of the words more likely. (Timothy, in the opening scene, drew the policeman before dictating.) Or the child can illustrate after dictation, or do both.

Step 5: Child abstracts language. Design skill development and extension activities based on the child's piece, especially exposition—if the child is ready for this kind of work. (Avoid overdoing the skill development aspects.)

The following dictated piece is both narrative and informational.

A Crash in Our Trash

Last night something woke me up. I heard a noise. It went c-r-a-a-s-sh. I looked out the window. A wild animal was digging in the trash can. What was it? It was a raccoon.

Jason, Grade 1

"Can I use LEA to teach word analysis skills?"

One of the many advantages of the LEA approach is that using material produced by the students reduces the comprehension load when the teacher introduces them to word recognition skills. Sample word recognition skills are the following: *rhyming* of patterns of repeated sounds; *blending* of sounds of certain letter combinations; *sight vocabulary*, especially structure words like *of*; and *form-class vocabulary*, that is, naming, doing, and describing words or nouns, verbs, and modifiers (adapted from Allen, 1976). Children gain and can discuss language concepts such as letters, words, sentences, and spelling. Remember the admonition, however, "nothing in excess."

"How does the word bank work?"

Every word that a child marks as known during the rereading is printed on a slip or card and placed in the child's personal word bank. The following containers are used for keeping personal word banks: a file folder, a milk carton laid on its side with a lid cut, a child's shoe box, a recipe-card box, a plastic baggie, cards on a metal ring, or a notebook with a page for each letter of the alphabet. Students can add some favorite "key" words or room labels to their banks that are not in a dictated story. Word banks can provide a record of the reading vocabulary of individual children.

Children can review their words (later alphabetized, first roughly with alphabet dividers, perhaps), match words to duplicated copies of group stories and to individual stories, and use their words to develop reading concepts and to review letter names. They can use their materials for visual memory (holding up a personal word card, covering it, then finding it in their story).

They use their words in many other ways: for independent writing, visual and auditory discrimination, phonic analysis (e.g., all words that begin with the *b* sound), word patterns (e.g., *had, sad, mad, bad*), and final phonograms (n*ight*, f*ight*). They can use their material for context analysis (blocking out words, predicting what word fits, and giving clues used). They can use their own material for the comprehension skill of locating significant detail. (Teacher: "Who can show on our chart what Frank informed us about octopus ink?") Teachers who use LEA find those teachable moments for skills in the materials that children produce. Again, the students' expository material is more appropriate than their personal narratives for such a purpose.

In addition to private word banks, you could have **word walls** (taped butcher paper), where categories of words useful to independent writing are collected and kept for the total class. Holiday words, color words, sound words, feeling words, and classmates' names are common. (The opening illustration for this chapter showed one on pond life.) For example, a word wall stressing informational language might contain vocabulary for a garden shop, with names of flower seeds printed next to pictures of the mature flowers. Using language from this "wall," children design their own seed packets with instructions on planting depth, amount of sunlight, spacing, and days to germination.

"What kinds of records do I keep and how do I assess?"

Box 7.7 lists some records the child's file can contain.

Each week or so you could check children on their concepts and select activities appropriate for three major areas: (1) *use* of language (including informational), (2) *study* of language (including word attack and even expository structures), and (3) use of the communication of *others* (books and other materials that find their way into and enrich the child's own pieces). An important general resource is Goodman, Goodman, and Hood, 1989.

BOX 7.7 Possible Contents of Child's LEA File

1. Stories dictated by the child; observations and anecdotes.

2. Books and other materials read to or by the child (including child-selected ones).

3. A checklist based on the language concepts gained (listed earlier).

4. The child's word bank, serving as a record of words known.

5. The child's own writings (writing is emphasized early with the language experience approach.)

6. Tests and specific suggestions for help needed. (Any progress checks that are applied to basals can be applied to LEA. LEA users usually do as well as basal users on phonics skills—without all the boring practice with someone else's language.)

"How does LEA relate to independent writing?"

Writing may relate to the time spent discussing ideas, with a view to summarizing in written form. If children want to write when they are not yet fluent writers, they need to be able to summarize important thoughts in a few words. With LEA, summarizing skills do not wait until fifth or sixth grade. Group work in summarizing keeps some highly talkative children from running on and on pointlessly. Summarizing is an important skill in the informational use of language.

Moreover, the LEA teacher keeps at least one writing project going that features *children as authors* (class, group, or individual). The materials produced by the children are highly valued, celebrated, and displayed (e.g., framed, laminated, ring bound, stapled, tied, paperbound, and cloth bound). For example, Timothy's poem in the opening scene was featured in the class book, *Why Not Have "Christmas" All Year Round?*

Child writing in LEA is not only individual but also can involve the *total class* in an in-depth response to a topic. After the students dictate, perhaps having made a conceptual map (sea otters), the teacher and class members probe to sharpen their constructions in their "first draft." The group reads the piece recorded on the chart for needed re-expression, thus developing concepts of **revision.** "Have we written everything we need to about sea otters? In the way we wanted to?" The teacher and children can use carets (ˆ) for insertions, balloons and arrows, and deletion marks to make changes. The group may institute a second or even a third draft. A simple word-processing program for the computer may assist the LEA group in its written endeavor. (See the opening scene of Chapter 13 of this book, which includes an example from second grade.)

"How does LEA relate to independent reading?"

Other reading materials such as easy-to-read, high-interest, low-vocabulary books are accessible to LEA students from low racks around the room. Included are interesting materials that build literary, academic, and expository language that is not always found in the home. Chapter 12 presents a categorized list of predictable pattern books for young readers. In full circle, then, LEA children have chances to add to the written ideas of others with their own compositions. (Examples: their own "What to Know Before You Grow" garden booklets, their own noun and verb substitutions for "Brown bear, brown bear what do you see . . ."; their own fables taking off from others read.)

"What might be a five-day sequence for LEA?"

The following reveals five days at the beginning of a LEA unit. The intent is not to imply, however, that LEA can only be used in a five-day-long instructional unit. The opening scene, for example, showed a much more informal use.

Day 1: Getting started. Example: A sea unit is initiated with a visit to an aquarium (or filmed media). Class discussion ends with listing of the children's shared information on a board or chart.

Day 2: Brief review; pictures; dictation or writing options. The day begins with a memory refresher of the children's first-day discussion. Students begin to draw pictures of their ideas of sea creatures. Dictation, private or invented writing, and, in the case of some children, their own standard writing begins after the symbolization in drawing starts to develop. Children's dictation or writing may be on the inside of two paper plates stapled and cut to resemble a scallop shell, or on manuscript paper, or in a booklet. Box 7.8 shows some print options.

The writing done, the teacher and child reread the story. (If the child's independent writing is private or highly nonstandard, the teacher may need to make some notes in order to be able to recall meanings later.)

Day 3: Rereading 1. Each student reads his or her piece as independently as possible to the teacher. Known words are lightly underlined.

Day 4: Rereading 2. Each child rereads his or her piece to the teacher. The teacher *again* lightly underlines known words (and pronounces unknown words as necessary). At this point, some words may have one, two, or no lines under them. (For lengthy pieces, you may have to be selective in the rereading.) Children can also reread to a puppet, an imaginary friend or book character, the classroom pet, volunteers, and in groups. Recall that if the piece was produced by a group, each member may get a duplicated copy for underlining known words. The teacher checks and makes a word card (or checks the child-made one).

Day 5: Skill development. Children put their words into a word bank. Each word underlined twice in the story is copied for the bank (and checked). Words in the bank may be used for further review, writing, matching, game, and word attack activities if individually appropriate (adapted from Mallon & Berglund, 1984).

Days 4 and 5 may be combined. You might incorporate LEA into your basal reading program, using LEA every third week with one of your three reading groups while the others do work associated with the basal reading series. Try to network with other student teachers and teachers using LEA for support. But remember that each LEA use is somewhat unique

---

BOX 7.8 Some Print Options for LEA

1. The student dictates to the teacher. (Remember, with few if any exceptions, what the student says is exactly what the teacher writes.)

2. The student dictates to the teacher and then copies the dictation.

3. The student writes using scribbling, "private"-writing, inventing, or advanced-stand-ard-writing.

4. The student writes part in standard form and dictates part.

to the classroom and teacher. Adapt the LEA method to your own teaching strengths and style, and make it your own.

"What do the other students do while the teacher is with one child or a small group?"

The other students might be involved in a variety of activities such as the following examples (note that ditto sheets are **not** mentioned): continue working on their sea illustrations; read their stories to a partner, a tape, or a volunteer; look at informational books about the sea in that center; work at another center; work on other sea unit activities or other projects; or put one of their stories to song (singing it softly into a tape recorder).

"What are some options in reading the child's material?"

Children may get to read their materials in several different ways each time. Some teachers read the story as they write it, offering speech echoing for each word. Some wait for a phrase or sentence and then read it back, as did the teacher in the opening scene. Some do both, and then read the entire story. In any case, the teacher reads the story before asking children to read it. Then the teacher asks the children to read in unison. Next the teacher calls on children to read parts, helping. It is crucial that the reading experience be enjoyable and successful (May, 1982).

"How can LEA assist growth in informational language use?"

One teacher used an LEA method with first-grade children to develop a text with a compare/contrast organization. The children had previously made little or no use of this expository pattern (adapted, Kinney, 1985). Box 7.9 presents the teacher's five-day plans.

If first-grade children can learn to compose and comprehend such exposition structures, it seems likely that the rest of the elementary grades can, too. Two precautions: Do not violate the spirit of the LEA method by forcing children to dictate about objects in which they have no interest or experience, and do not use too many total-group sessions in which it is highly unlikely that all children are interested and attentive. Teachers of upper grades use experience *journals* and charts for personalizing content areas. One fourth-grade class made an experience chart listing steps in a science experiment for conducting sound (scientific organization). The chart was used by other groups to "replicate" the study (May, 1982).

"How can I combine LEA and a basal approach when I first start teaching?"

Besides using LEA once every three weeks for one of your three basal reading groups, consider these other ideas. Provide many chances for children to express themselves creatively in discussion, in drama, and in writing in order to make the basal program better. If you are teaching first grade, use LEA during the first half of the school year and then gradually switch to a basal program using your informal reading inventories and placement tests from the basal. Or from the first, use the basal program for skill development and LEA for development of concepts such as "reading as communication." Use LEA material to supplement basal stories. Let word banks include both basal and experiential material.

"How can I handle public relations and LEA?"

Carefully explain your instruction rationale at the beginning of the school year in meetings with parents. You can follow up with a newsletter. Have children take home copies of standard-language material produced (until parents thoroughly understand your program

BOX 7.9 A Five-Day Expository Lesson Sequence

Day 1: On day one of a five-day lesson sequence, children selected types of tree leaves collected on a field trip (e.g., a magnolia leaf and a mimosa leaf) to be compared and contrasted. The teacher led a group discussion on how the selected leaves were alike and different. After the discussion, the class made a list of likenesses and differences.

Day 2: The children dictated a group expository piece to the teacher using their earlier list for guidance. The teacher controlled the structure of the story by asking students to dictate first how the leaves were alike, then how they differed. The teacher reminded the students that when they told about one object, they needed to tell about the other: "An elm leaf looks oblong, but a holly leaf looks and feels sharp-pointed," for example. The children then practiced reading their story.

Days 3 and 4: These were practice days. In addition to typical LEA activities such as underlining known words and placing them in word banks, children practiced understanding the contrastive structure of their informational piece. They matched one contrastive part with another (e.g., "elm leaf looks oblong" was matched with "a holly leaf . . . sharp-pointed").

Day 5: Each student rearranged a scrambled version of his or her piece in contrastive order. On later testing for recall of a contrastive structure in a piece, significantly fewer children recalled mere random details. They phrased their recall in a way that mirrored the passage structure. All the students increased in ability to use text structure, thus improving their comprehension of pieces with this contrastive pattern. (Again, LEA can be used almost any time and does not require such a structured five-day plan.) Other content-oriented examples for contrast might be the making of varied soups, and comparing what magnets do and do not attract.

rationale). Show parents the materials the child can read, tapes, word bank, retention results, list of LEA child concepts gained, your observations, and any mastered concepts and skills, including uses of expositional language. Displaying a variety of uses gets around such parental criticisms as: "They're just memorizing little made-up stories, not reading." Prepare the children to tell their parents what they have accomplished and learned, and how they feel about being an author, reader, and researcher.

Some Conclusions about LEA   In essence, with LEA, children acquire basic skills while employing their own experience and language that they understand and use. Motivating students to want to read, LEA demonstrates the many connections between spoken and written language. LEA emphasizes that reading is a highly meaningful process and that authors and readers are truly communicators. Writing and reading about something children have actually experienced usually ensures that the concepts are within their grasp. Using a student's own language encourages acquisition of reading vocabulary, print comprehension, and integration of all the language arts. LEA students read not only their own narrative and expository material and the material of peers, but adult authors as well. In later grades teacher and children cooperatively create materials as records of information they are learning. These they read again and again as needed. Since the children have written the material, their interest and motivation are usually high. A final advantage of LEA is that it promotes such closeness between teacher and student, and can influence children throughout their school lives in the way they relate to instructors.

Let's answer another prospective teacher's question:

"If I give my students freedom in communication, will they discover various types of discourse for themselves (e.g., description, exposition, narration, and argumentation)?"

By "freedom in communication" the questioner means activity such as LEA and whole language approaches stimulating writing, reading, and oral language. An answer is, "It all depends." It depends in large part on a teacher's orchestrated classroom environment. Such an environment makes many uses of language attractive, is resource laden, and is intrinsically rewarding.

Now that you are ready to build bridges with LEA, we answer one more important question that teacher trainees ask: "How can I assess children's *informational use* of language?"

Assessment

The motivational assessment methods given in this section relate to the real life of children and to their genuine concerns. The aim of the assessments is to be nonthreatening, personal, and uplifting. The Assessment of Performance Unit (APU) in England, Wales, and Northern Ireland has carried out surveys of children's language performance in English since 1979 (ages 11 and 15). The action was in response to the Bullock Committee recommendation for the development of new methods of evaluating language performance. Indications were needed about children's ability to use language effectively to meet demands in school and in daily life in different circumstances (Gorman, 1986).

Materials, Content Areas, and Levels of Complexity   APU's assessment of informational *reading* included works of reference, charts, diagrams, tables, and maps. The British primary level, for example, had a booklet on whales, giving facts and types. In the booklet, children were gradually exposed to information of greater detail and complexity. A number of questions toward the end of the assessment booklet required children to integrate information from different sections. Everyday kinds of reading material included magazines, newspapers, classified ads, forms, instructions, notices, and listings. One item was a travel brochure, map, and reservation form. Questions set in a family context required meeting different members' needs and interests. Students had to not only extract information from the booklet but also determine its relevance and usefulness to family members. The test questions asked differed on the following: (1) focus (assertion, implication, presupposition); (2) scope (very little material to respond to or a lot); and (3) strategies (careful word-by-word reading or scanning). These assessment materials are not all that different from what you could use in your own classroom.

Types of Response   Types of response included the following: completing forms, filling in tables, labeling diagrams, making notes, and preparing a summary. The surveys showed that in *reading* works of reference, some pupils found it difficult to locate the information they needed. Location may require understanding of both the general structure of the reference work and the relative importance of its ideas. Some children lacked concepts and vocabulary used in the reference (Gorman, 1986). You could check to see if your children have this problem. Informational *writing* response examples were the following: description of memorable person or animal, comparative description of insects/moths, pictures, games, the sequencing of spider web making, a scientific experiment to describe and do, and a problem-solving piece on processing data to select and grow appropriate plants (found in the activity book, Chapter 6, Section 1). Other informational examples follow in Table 7.2. The table displays some of the range of activities introduced into the surveys.

The Scoring Process   There are two stages of assessment in APU writing (and speaking) assessment. One is *holistic* scoring, an overall impression on a scale of 1 to 7, including a task-specific checklist. The other, *analytic* scoring, has the following five components: (1) content (related to instructions, audience, and appropriate source material); (2) organization (e.g., sequencing, diagrams for an experiment); (3) knowledge of stylistic conventions (appropriate to task, e.g., in business letter writing); (4) knowledge of task-appropriate grammatical

Table 7.2 EXAMPLES OF WRITING TASKS USED IN APU ASSESSMENT

General purpose	Informational use
To describe/observe	Description of a memorable person or animal (11, 15)[a] Comparative description of insects/moths (11, 15) Description of a picture (11) Description of a game (11)
To record/report	Eyewitness account of a series of events (11, 15) An account of something learned (11, 15) A report based on source material (15)
To plan/speculate	Planning an experiment (11, 15) Giving an account of an activity to be undertaken (11, 15) Planning a room design (11)
To instruct/direct	Notes for a household manual giving directions (15) A poster announcing an event (11) An account of a skill (11, 15)
To evaluate/review evidence	Review of evidence relating to the age of retirement (15) Review of book/TV program (11) Review of arguments relating to legal ages (15)
To correspond/request	Personal letter (11) Letter of application for a job (15) Letter of request (11)
To explain/reflect	Explanation and justification of a rule or regulation (11, 15) Explanation of attitudes toward subject areas (15) Explanation of reasons for selecting an experimental design (11, 15) Explanation of reasons for liking a game (11)
To reason	Analysis of the accuracy of deductions (15) Analysis of the validity of generalizations (15)
To edit	Editing a written account (11, 15)

[a]The age groups completing the tasks are given in parentheses, but tasks could easily be adapted to younger age groups.
Source: Gorman (1986), pp. 15, 16.

conventions; and (5) spelling conventions. You could use such a scoring process with your students.

How did these tasks look? Figure 7.12 is a page that shows some primary oracy tasks from APU and reflects the informational use of language. Pictured are cooperatively attacked tasks involving an informational piece concerning the sequencing of a spider making its web and a scientific experiment to describe and do.

Handling of the Cooperative Testing Situation   For assessment of listening and speaking, APU uses friendship pairs or small friendship groups seated around a table. The assessor's role is to establish the context for talk and to record it, but not to direct or control it. For example, a science experiment task involves dropping "marbles" of various materials onto a curved track to observe movement. For this task, a friendship pair sequences instructions in carrying out the experiment. The task sequence includes (1) describing observations, (2) reporting to a second pair, and (3) hypothesizing about reasons. You could find an appropriate science "experiment" for such observation of your own pairs.

These ideas give a sense of what a group that has spent a lot of time and money on evaluation has come up with for testing informational use of language. The intent is to give some ideas of what a teacher can look for while assessing in the classroom in a natural way. APU has tried hard to make the tasks interesting to children, nonthreatening, and as natural

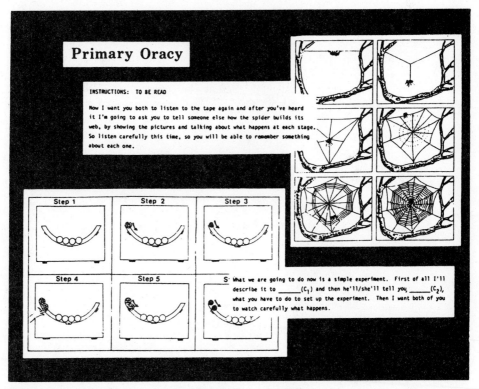

Figure 7.12   Informational oral tasks. (*Source:* Gorman, 1986)

and true-to-life as possible. It seems we have some lessons to learn from our British friends when it comes to testing in the schools.

Your Classroom Assessments   Earlier sections of this chapter gave you several assessment helps, including checklists of skills for both senders and receivers of information, a list for advanced students (Figure 7.5, p. 235), and the chart in Box 7.3, which can also be a checklist. For a check on children's informational vocabulary, examine their LEA word banks. Also see other assessment ideas in the record-keeping portion of the earlier LEA section. To provide a picture of each student's growth and development, consider keeping folders containing students' informational products (along with other language arts products). Such assessment is continuous and guides your instructional decisions. Such procedures also encourage students' self-assessment—the most important assessment of all.

Building on the bridge created in this chapter, the next chapter addresses written composition in detail. Written composition has been no stranger to us in past chapters; but the next one puts it all together.

SUMMARY

"Comprehension and composition are two sides of the same basic process of communication whereby the senders and receivers of a message interact through a common language."

Roselmina Indrisano

Teachers have long sensed intuitively that whole language processes of writing and reading are related. Now we have evidence clarifying the relationship between composing and comprehending. Both are processes using common language and thought as a medium of communication and both share similar experiences. Besides linguistic, cognitive, and organizational factors, comprehending and composing share human purposes and creativity.

With the help of a teacher who believes in children as capable and resourceful learners, classroom curriculum optimally integrates language use with thinking development and the growth of useful knowledge. It is important to provide informational use in your language arts program because of its large function in our lives, its neglect in many basal texts, and its usefulness in serving the craft of writing and speaking (usage, spelling, punctuation, appropriate forms and formats). It makes sense for children to deal with informative content orally as a basis for advanced reading and writing of it. To teach children to compose in varied informational patterns is to teach them to think in these patterns. Children need help with expository text structures as these structures are unfamiliar and difficult for some.

Three types of exposition are *exploratory* use, *informative* use, and *scientific* use. Emphasis in informative language is on instruction, reality, communication, and "business" transactions. Exposition is any message thought to have informative value by any person in the communicative transaction. A teacher guards the reality of the utilitarian and protects the personal freedom of the artistic. Above all, informational language is logical, accurate, and honest.

The choice of instructional goals and content revolves around a consideration of three components of informational language: its organization, style, and logic. A wealth of fine books for children addresses informational uses of language illustrating these components.

With an enabling environment enhanced by well-selected resources, both in the classroom and nearby, children can appreciate the richness of information that surrounds them. They can value listening, viewing, and reading/writing to *learn*. A prime point is whether children have the opportunity to research topics related to their own questions. Children have an internal ally for such questioning in the form of a natural curiosity about the world. Coupled with other internal allies—a push for self-competency and a desire to communicate—they can practice difficult language crafts with great intensity and glee. Children make sense of their world by moving from symbols in their art to more abstract symbols, organizations, and logic in language designed to inform.

The *teaching* of informational uses of language involves the following: the reading of well-written informational pieces to children; employment of strategies such as mapping and language experience approaches (LEA); children's writing of their own informational pieces, with help on organization, style, and logic; and children's reading of expository materials they have selected (both student and professional authors). You also teach by helping children select projects and tasks in larger units of study that integrate all of these methods. Integration of comprehension and composing, helped by both LEA and the informational use of whole language, builds bridges to important skills in reading and writing.

Assessment includes helping children learn techniques of confirmation of information and of self-correction. The Assessment Performance Unit (APU) gives many examples of carefully planned testing of informational use in all the language arts. This chapter provides you with options and choices of checklists. LEA record keeping offers continuous assessment that guides instructional decisions appropriate to exposition. Student self-assessment of whole language is an ultimate goal.

CHAPTER 8

Learning to Compose

by Ann Robinson

"Composing requires an orchestration of experience. There are different ways to say things, and all are worthy of investigation."

NCTE Committee on Curriculum Bulletins

INTRODUCTION

Why has writing become a top priority in classrooms? Educators, business leaders, and politicians all stress the importance of written communication. Pragmatists remind us that the ability to write is crucial in many professions. Success at getting and maintaining a job may depend on one's writing skills. Educators are well aware of the value of writing as a way of learning (Applebee, 1984; Emig, 1977; Mayer & Lester, 1983). Writing to learn helps students to organize their thoughts and to reason about complex issues. In addition, professional authors remind us of the importance of the aesthetics of writing (Gardner, 1984; Zinsser, 1980). Writing to express oneself or to indulge one's fascination for words is an important experience, too. Thus, we can say that writing is a tool for getting along in the world. By writing, we reach out to others to communicate with them over time and distance. We also reach inward to ourselves to record and examine our thoughts and feelings. Written communication, then, is a powerful and important force that children need to use and master.

Every chapter in this book thus far has fed into this chapter in many ways, as we shall see. In Chapter 7, we discussed bridges from oral to written language that teachers can build with LEA, so that comprehending and composing find their reciprocal strengths. This chapter aims to help illuminate the nature of the writing process related to the particular characteristics of the developing child writer. Understanding the child as author is a prerequisite for learning the *hows* of teaching writing. This chapter includes a description of a composing process, a summary of the developmental characteristics of child writers, guidelines for organizing a writing classroom, suggestions for instructional strategies, a discussion of the kinds of writing engaged in by elementary children, a brief discussion of computers in the writing curriculum, and guidelines for assessing writing growth.

The following scene of child writers at work in the elementary classroom is designed to illustrate some important concepts about learning and teaching writing developed in this chapter on composing.

OPENING SCENE: Writing in a Third-Grade Classroom

Terry Rivera, the teacher, listened intensely as two third-grade writers presented their piece. Sitting forward together, Mike and Jason began to share their coauthored directions for constructing a device for projecting constellations. Jason read fluently and in a businesslike tone while Mike hung over his coauthor's shoulder. The written directions were accompanied by an intricate and extensively labeled diagram that Mike fluttered around the circle of seated children.

Questions came quickly from the audience.

"How did you decide which constellations to do?" quizzed Maggie, who was very interested in astronomy.

"Did you number the 'how-to' steps before or after you built one of these things?" Tim wanted to know, because he had been struggling with a piece explaining guidelines for organizing a classroom play.

"Mike," the teacher asked, "how did you and Jason choose this topic?"

The group talked a little longer about what Jason and Mike had written and how they had gone about it. Then the teacher disbanded the audience circle.

Maggie and her writing buddy, Susan, headed for the microcomputer on the cart in the back of the room.

Tim sat at his desk and worried over the play piece in his folder.

The teacher invited six children, including Mike, to join a group at the round table. "Leave your folders, folks. We're going to work together for a few minutes on *to, too,* and *two.*"

Jason and the rest of the class scuttled back to their desks and picked up where they had left off the day before. Jason and Mike's constellation piece was almost finished, so Jason shuffled through his papers and found an idea for a story he had started earlier.

Other children were writing and drawing to get ideas or to illustrate publishable works. Some talked quietly with a friend to ask about spelling a word, where to put punctuation marks, or which details to include, which to leave out.

Tim stared at the page.

After a few minutes, the teacher moved from the group working on skills to sit near him.

"How's it going, Tim?"

"Terrible. I can't think of anything else to say."

"Well, let's see. Why don't you read to me what you've got so far. Maybe I can think of some questions to ask and you can dictate the answers."

While Tim and the teacher talked, Maggie and Susan burst into laughter at the computer.

"We've got some good stuff here," chuckled Maggie. "I can't wait to print out. Susan, let's work this one up for publication."

At his desk Jason stopped writing to reread his story. He made a few changes, crossed out words, and drew arrows to change the sentence order rather than erasing. Jason is an accomplished child author. He revises his pieces, takes his audience into account, writes for many purposes, and enjoys the feeling of getting it down on paper.

Terry Rivera moved away from Tim and stepped toward the communication center, a Rube Goldberg collection of letter boxes, message boards, and a tape recorder. Terry checked the teacher letter box to see if anyone had left a note requiring an answer. Inside was a colorful card with an original poem. The teacher looked at the clock to see how much writing time was left and settled into a chair to write a thank you note to Susan, the poem's author.

For the next few minutes, teacher and children wrote.

Analysis of the Scene

The scene in Terry Rivera's classroom illustrates a number of important concepts about children and their writing today. First, it emphasizes the problem-solving aspects of the composing process. The children questioning Jason and Mike wanted to know how the two partners made decisions about their piece. How did they come up with the idea, decide which constellations to use, and organize their directions so others could understand?

Second, the scene illustrates the variable nature of child writers. Some, like Jason, are advanced revisers; others, like Mike, rely on pictures and labels to communicate. Others, like Tim, hit temporary blocks, for which we saw the teacher offer help. And some, like Maggie and Susan, are fluent, goal-directed, and enthusiastic authors.

Finally, the scene illustrates some ways in which the elementary classroom can be organized to promote writing. The teacher is active in the roles of advisor, audience, and model. The students have time and places like the communication center in which to write. The many purposes for writing are evident: Children sometimes write to learn, to tell others, to enjoy creating something new. These concepts and other related ideas are explored in more depth later in the chapter. We can begin, for example, with the importance of the teacher's role.

WHY IS THE TEACHER'S ROLE CRUCIAL?

Although writing is an important activity, many children and adults do not like to write, finding it mentally and physically difficult. There are many possible reasons for the dislike, but a few seem worth mentioning here. First, if young children have not had many prior experiences with the printed word, they may not grasp the purpose for writing. Engaging in a writing activity simply because the teacher says so or assigns a specific writing task, as in the old days, may seem senseless to the child. Second, children may have developmental and skill limitations to overcome. Holding a pencil tires youngsters, and while they may have something exciting to say, their hands may go too slowly and fatigue too quickly for the important thought to be written down. Children may lack the spelling vocabulary (lexicon) they need in order to write.

Although young children are comfortable scribbling and inventing spellings, older children quickly learn that correct spelling is important, particularly to the teacher. Children may worry about misspelled words and mechanical errors; consequently, writing becomes a risky business. Finally, children may not like to write because they do not feel their writing will be valued. Putting words on paper leaves a highly visible trail of what children think or feel; writing is an extension of children themselves. If children do not feel good about themselves, if they are afraid of rejection from their teacher and peers, they may be afraid to expose themselves to others. Feelings of uncertainty and vulnerability may lead children to dislike writing.

The teacher is the crucial agent in overcoming a child's uneasiness about writing or in sustaining the enthusiasm of confident child authors. The attitudes we have about writing and about the child, the classroom environment we create, and the model we provide all influence children as they become writers.

WHAT IS THE CREATIVE PROBLEM-SOLVING APPROACH TO WRITING?

"Creative problem solving (CPS) refers to the process of selecting alternatives that lead toward a goal the child desires and results in a pattern that is new, at least to the child" (Lundsteen, 1976). It is a juxtaposition of fanciful imagination, novel insights, and emotional response with logical reasoning and goal-oriented behavior (as was suggested in Chapter 2). Successful writing experiences for children involve both the playful and fantastic as well as the more deliberate activities of planning, organizing, and verification in CPS. Writing is not a mechanical, mundane task. It is a complex set of behaviors that involves many components of the creative problem-solving process. As children make decisions at choice points all along the way of the writing process, they are engaging in creative problem solving (Lundsteen, 1976).

Many of the suggestions that follow will specifically address components of problem solving as they relate to the writing process, but there are two important ideas about children's writing that help us focus on the problem-solving approach. First, consider children's writing as a *whole.* It is the product of many complex cognitive, affective, and psychomotor behaviors. When children compose, they think, they feel, and they manipulate a pencil or a microcomputer keyboard. A child absorbed in a writing task brings many skills, talents, and abilities to bear on the work. Therefore, teachers analyzing the child's written product or writing behavior need to consider it in context. The child's overall message is what is important. Harping on the conventions of mechanics, spelling, or neatness in early drafts prevents the teacher from keeping the big picture in mind and may unnecessarily frustrate the child. Neither the narrow viewpoint of the teacher nor the frustration of the child will contribute to successful creative problem solving. A related question of some in guidance is "Should I concentrate on the paragraph?" The foregoing discussion would indicate the answer is no. Just as a sentence is part of a whole composition, a paragraph is part of a child's total intent or composition. Of course, teachers use a paragraph unit to teach some concepts of writing. But, as suggested earlier, teachers need to encourage written composition that is long enough to fulfill the child author's intent and to solve his or her problem.

Second, we need to respect the *task* of writing. Children frequently find writing a challenge because it *is* difficult. Reflect for a moment on your own experiences as a writer. Think of the preparation and procrastination that generally go into your written class assignments or papers. You may shuffle your notes, cast about for a good topic, doodle around for a beginning, and push away from the desk a number of times before you really get rolling. When you've finished writing, you may feel proud, relieved, or embarrassed that you hadn't got to work sooner, but one thing is generally true about writing: You knew you were doing something that took effort and imagination. As children develop into writers, they face the same concerns, difficulties, and feelings of accomplishment as adults do.

In tune with the networks presented in earlier chapters, Figure 8.1 lays out the concepts in this chapter concerning written composition. This overview of related concepts highlights the interactive composing process. It is not merely linear but nourishes all parts in continual interchange. This network also shows other chapters that have fed into this chapter or will do so. Examples are Chapters 7 (sections on written exposition), 9 (literature), 10 (sections on writing persuasion), 11 (spelling, punctuation, handwriting), 12 (grammar and usage), 13 (media, including computers), and 15 (assessment). Note that *creative problem solving* is joined to every major cluster radiating from written composition. The major concepts radiating clusters in this chapter are the composing process, developmental charac-

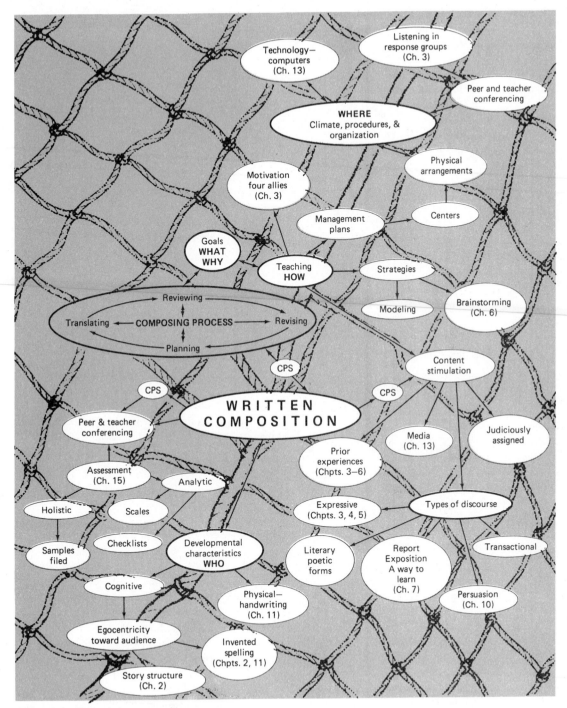

Figure 8.1 Network for composition.

teristics, teaching, and types of written discourse. (A later section explores the relation of CPS and the composing process, and the activity book gives further ideas; also see Figure 8.16 on assessing problem solution in writing.)

WHAT IS A COMPOSING PROCESS?

Educators interested in children's composition live in exciting times. During the last 20 years, even the last 10 years, researchers and teachers have changed the ways we look at writing and the methods we use in the classroom. In the early seventies, Emig (1971) published a very influential work that initiated new directions for us. She reasoned that in order to understand students who were writing in the classroom, she ought to be watching them at work rather than simply looking at their papers once they had finished. Her method was radically at odds with traditional research and pedagogy. Most researchers and teachers left children to themselves as they wrote and reacted to what was written after the fact. Emig's attention to writing as it was taking place rather than the finished product of writing has led to a number of important insights about how students write and what we can do to help them write their best.

One of the most important insights we now have about the composing process is that it "does not move in a straight line from conception to completion" (Humes, 1983). That is, we do not plan everything we have to say, then put it down on paper, and finally go over it to edit, recopy, and turn it in to the teacher. Instead, writing is recursive; it goes back and forth. We plan a little, put words on paper, stop to plan what we want to say next, go back and change a sentence, or change our minds altogether.

In order to describe such a complex activity, recent researchers have formulated cognitive-process theories of writing (Flower & Hayes, 1981). The process theories describe several components or subprocesses of the writing activity in order to clarify what is actually going on in our minds as we write. For purposes of discussion in this chapter, we will examine the composing process under four headings: planning, translating, reviewing, and revising (Humes, 1983). We are treating revision separately because it is during this important subprocess that the teacher has a particular opportunity to be especially helpful or, conversely, especially detrimental to the child writer.

Planning (and Prewriting)

Planning is thinking that goes on throughout the composing process. Planning involves generating ideas, organizing content, and setting goals (Flower & Hayes, 1981). In other words, writers ask themselves or one another what they are going to say and how they are going to go about saying it. In the opening scene, we gave an example of Susan and Maggie planning by collaboration. Jason, on the other hand, was generating ideas for the beginning of his new story by himself. Generating ideas means getting information to write about, and that information can come from prior experiences, outside references, the writer's own mind, or, most likely, a combination of all these sources. Next, organizing means putting content or ideas in order. Organizing can mean arranging content so that writing has structure, and it can also mean removing ideas if there is too much content. One interesting finding with implications for teaching is that organizing content *infrequently* involves formal outlines (Emig, 1971; Stallard, 1974). Writers seem to be able to plan effectively without detailed, written outlines dividing content into roman numerals and letters. Good news for students who struggle with formal outlines! (Chapter 7 gave alternatives with more informal mapping on networking in order to organize an area.)

Finally, the subprocess of planning also involves setting goals or purposes. The writer's intent was compared to the reader's purpose in Chapter 7. Writers have two kinds of goals: content and process (Flower & Hayes, 1981). In setting content goals, writers ask themselves what they want or need to write about. For example, a child writing a story may think to herself, "I'll talk about the scary old mansion in my Halloween story." Writers also have process goals that help keep them on track. For example, halfway through writing a story, a child may stop writing and say to himself, "I forgot what color the door is. I'd better go back and read the first part to find out." (Later in the chapter we will consider how teachers can help children plan.)

Translating (and Drafting)

Translating refers to putting thoughts down on paper. Sometimes the terms *writing* or *transcribing* are used to identify this component of the composing process. Although putting words down on a page may sound simple enough, translating is actually a highly complex activity. It includes handwriting, conventions such as spelling and punctuation, word choice, sentence order, organization, and author purpose, to mention a few. Many of these tasks have become automatic for experienced writers (Scardamalia, 1981). For children whose handwriting and spelling, for example, are not automatic, the demands of writing are monumental and translating becomes a struggle with the empty page. Automaticity is as important in translation as it is in reading fluency.

Reviewing

Reviewing is rereading what is written in order to determine if it says what one intended. Like Jason in the opening scene, writers review for many reasons: for example, to decide what needs to be revised and finally to proofread (Pianko, 1979). They review to remind themselves what is already written, to decide whether to stop or to go on writing. Virtually all writers review, even young children (Graves & Murray, 1980). However, young writers are less likely to review for meaning and clarity of their writing to the audience and are more likely to review for conventions such as spelling (Nold, 1981).

Revising

Not all writing researchers agree on the definition of revising, but those in the majority define revising as changing a text that is already written down. Revising includes major changes in organization and content and also editing changes in spelling and punctuation (Humes, 1983). Others take a looser position and maintain that even activities like selecting one topic and discarding others is a form of revision early in the process (Graves & Murray, 1980). One important idea to keep in mind is that revision is *not* a one-time process that occurs after the writing is fully completed (Nold, 1981). Writers revise constantly as they work. As did Jason in the opening scene, they change initial drafts as they go, crossing out words, changing sentence order, adding details.

Of particular interest to prospective teachers is the finding that there are developmental differences in the ability to revise, as detailed later in this chapter. Young children, unskilled and skilled students, and expert writers all revise differently (Bridwell, 1980;

Faigley and Witte, 1981; Stallard, 1974). In general, the trend is for more experienced writers to revise globally, that is, to pay attention to the overall meaning and the impact they want their writing to have. In other words, older and more experienced writers revise their work to take their audience into account (Sommers, 1980).

In contrast, children do not automatically and immediately revise. Children are reluctant to mar a page of writing with any revisions or changes (Calkins, in Gentry, 1980). They see the first draft as a final product. Only after they come to view their drafts as temporary works in progress will children attempt to revise. Maggie and Susan, for example, agreed that the current draft of their collaboration in the opening scene needed to be "worked up" further for *publication*. Understanding the revising behaviors of children is important to the teacher. By observing children as they write, we can note their revising strategies and have a better chance at matching our instruction to their needs. *Editing*, as distinguished from revising, includes proofreading for mechanical errors. (Later in the chapter we'll consider how teachers, especially in writing conferences, can help children to translate experiences, review, and revise.)

The Relationship Between Problem Solving and the Composing Process

Once we recognize that the composing process is a complicated intellectual undertaking, the relationship between writing and creative problem solving is more understandable. Writers need to be both creative enough to generate ideas and goal directed enough to organize those ideas into meaningful text. The view of writing as problem solving is at the heart of the cognitive-process theories of composing. Child writers face a problem when they generate exciting ideas to communicate but have yet to complete a piece of writing that captures their excitement. They use their creativity and knowledgeability to solve the problem of producing interesting text.

Often writers and writing researchers refer to the *rhetorical problem*. Broadly, the rhetorical problem refers to the elements of the problem the writer has to take into account when composing. Flower and Hayes (1980) separate the rhetorical problem into two major units: the rhetorical situation and the writer's own goals. The *rhetorical situation* involves the assignment the teacher gives the students or the tasks they set for themselves ("Write a story using yourself as one of the characters"). The rhetorical situation also involves the audience ("We can read some of these stories aloud during class story time").

The second major part of the rhetorical problem, the *writer's goals*, can be divided into four areas to which writers must pay attention: the reader, the persona, the meaning, and the text. The *reader* is the person or persons the writer wants to affect. Problem: "I want my story to scare my friends!" The *persona* refers to the voice a writer wants to create. Persona is usually affected by the kinds of words a writer uses to set the tone and may be funny, sarcastic, earnest, happy, or any number of other attitudes. For example, one child may write a sentimental poem about Christmas at grandmother's house; another child may poke fun at Santa Claus in a humorous limerick. The *meaning* refers to the writer's ideas about the topic, in other words, the content. And finally, writers must attend to the *text*. They must decide how to organize, when to add an example, and when to stop.

Clearly the global rhetorical problem, to produce an effective piece of writing, is quite complex. In order to solve the problem successfully, that is, in order for the writer to write what he or she wants and to have it affect the reader in the desired way, the writer needs to break the global problem into manageable segments and be creative, imaginative, thoughtful, and disciplined. Such are the marks of a productive problem solver. (The opening scene in Chapter 10 displays the writing process of one child, Naomi, from planning to publication. Figure 8.6, on page 279 of this chapter, contrasts process writing and traditional writing instruction.)

WHO ARE THE WRITERS IN YOUR CLASSROOM?

During deliberations on problem and process it is important to keep in mind that we are interested in these as they relate to children. Most of the studies we have about writing are based on adult behaviors and on examples of mature writing, although there are a few exceptions (Harste, Woodward, & Burke, 1984). We know from studies in child development that children are not miniature adults; they think and communicate differently than adults. Thus, if we want to understand children as they write and teach them in a helpful way, we can take a developmental approach to composition.

Two areas of child development having importance for children's composing are cognitive development and language development. In fact, the two are closely related and together have tremendous impact on a child's writing. First, consider the impact of cognitive developmental level and its relationship to writing performance.

A primary function of writing is to communicate to other people. This written communication may take the form of writing a letter to a parent or neighbor, writing an assignment for the teacher, perhaps writing an original story for a friend who is home with a cold, or as Susan did, writing an original poem for her teacher in the opening scene. In any event, children often write for an audience. Audience awareness is an important part of effective written communication. Writers need to keep in mind what the audience has to know in order to make their message interesting and important to the reader.

Yet Piaget has observed that children are *egocentric* at certain developmental levels (Inhelder & Piaget, 1958). They do not take the perspective of another person and therefore many of their messages are incomplete (Flavell et al., 1968). They do not give their audience enough information and, furthermore, are unable to discern when it is lacking. The child's developing sense of audience is an important aspect in the child's growth as a writer (Britton et al., 1975). As teachers, it is well for us to remember that compositions that are confusing to adults may be the result of a child's egocentricity, a perfectly normal developmental characteristic.

As mentioned in Chapter 2, another cognitive developmental characteristic is the ability to keep in mind several ideas at once. This ability to coordinate more than one idea may well account for some of the advances we see in children's writing. For example, children who are able to move from loosely connected writing (not well focused) to tightly connected writing (all ideas related to the main point) do so because they are able to coordinate an increasing number of ideas (Scardamalia, 1981). Recall the section on story structure and its development in children in Chapter 2. The ability to keep several variables in mind at once is, again, a developmental characteristic that will influence the child as writer.

In addition to cognitive level, the linguistic development of the child will have an impact on the child's writing. Much of the work on the linguistic maturity of children has measured quantity (number of words, phrases, sentences), variety (number of different words, parts of speech, sentences), and complexity, including the degree and type of complex and compound sentences (Wilkensen et al., 1980). It is not surprising that the more words a child knows and the more facility with sentence order a child has, the more likely the child will use them in writing.

One particularly interesting aspect of language development having implications for children's writing is the use of *invented spelling* mentioned in Chapter 2. Recall that as young children begin to write (in contrast to scribbling), they tend to represent words with single letters or a few letters that represent the sounds they hear (Read, 1980). The development of invented spelling is fairly standard (Sowers, 1980). First, children spell the word with the letter that represents the first sound (e.g., *p* for purred). Next, they add letters that stand for the other sounds (e.g., *prd* for purred). Then they fill in vowel sounds (e.g., *purd* for purred). Finally, they learn the conventional spelling. (Chapter 11 gives children's examples.) The importance of invented spelling is that it "gives young writers early power over words. Professional writers don't worry about correct spelling on their first drafts, and neither do inventive spellers. They want precise and lively words to tell their stories," not just easy ones they already know how to spell (Sowers, 1980). Early writing by children will be sprinkled with invented spelling (Chapters 2 and 11). It gives them freedom to be fluent and is best viewed as a developmental characteristic, not an opportunity for teachers to correct spelling prematurely. This is probably a major new idea for some teachers. (Chapter 11 discusses physical development of handwriting.)

HOW CAN A TEACHER HELP CHILDREN LEARN TO WRITE?

Although writing is an enormously complex task, children do write, and many, like those in Terry Rivera's class, enjoy themselves. As prospective teachers of writing, you need to keep in mind the nature of the composing process and the nature of the developing child. Such a task will not be easy. In fact, you will have to use all of your creative problem-solving abilities to be effective in helping children write. The framework of goals in Box 8.1 (adapted from the NCTE Essentials of English and the Maryland State Framework for the Language Arts) can guide instructional practices. Goals will be discussed in various ways in the rest of the chapter.

Teaching Writing

Two very important ideas undergird the suggestions for pedagogy made in the rest of this chapter. First, *teach* writing, don't simply assign it. Second, don't simply teach writing, *model* it. In the past it had been standard elementary classroom practice to have children write in response to some stimulus, perhaps a picture or a story starter—a cliff-hanging first sentence which the child uses to begin his or her composition. Generally, most teachers talked a bit with their students about the assignment. Perhaps they led the class in a brainstorming session and put important ideas or difficult words on the board. Then all the children were told to begin writing; some time limits may have been set ("Let's write for twenty minutes"). Finally, children were admonished to use their best handwriting and spelling. At this point, many teachers were quick to use these quiet classroom minutes to grade papers or organize the next lesson. *They were missing the opportunity to help children learn to write.*

While children are busy at the tasks of individually self-selected writing, it makes sense for the teacher to observe them and to check individual progress through conferences, as Terry Rivera did with Tim. Unfortunately, we are much more likely to respond to the child by grading the paper or by putting red-ink comments on it after it has been handed in and is no longer immediate for the child. If a child does poorly, we are more likely to complain about his or her skill level rather than to determine the child's developmental level

---

BOX 8.1 Framework for Written Composition

Child authors need to:

Goal 1: UNDERSTAND AND USE A WRITING PROCESS
Subgoals:
1.1 Generate ideas for writing.
1.2 Select and arrange ideas.
1.3 Select the modes appropriate to the audience and purpose, having planned, translated, and reviewed.
1.4 Revise the writing by adding, substituting, deleting, and rearranging content receiving responses.
1.5 Assess, edit, and celebrate the writing.
Goal 2: WRITE FOR A VARIETY OF PURPOSES
Subgoals:
2.1 Develop a talent for creative, imaginative, even poetic expression.
2.2 Communicate personal information and values.
2.3 Recognize writing as a way to learn.
2.4 Learn the valid techniques of writing to appeal to and to persuade others (discussed in Chapter 10).
Goal 3: VALUE WRITING FOR PERSONAL AND SOCIAL REASONS
Subgoals:
3.1 Experience the satisfaction of writing clearly and honestly.
3.2 Choose writing as a means of communication and self-expression.
3.3 Appreciate the influence of writing on society and its individuals.

---

and start at that point. By simply assigning writing, we expect children to do it the way we want them to. What an unfair and hidden expectation!

Contrast these implicit rules we have for children's writing performance with the way we teach skills in another symbol system, mathematics. Imagine a fourth-grade class beginning a unit on fractions. Children may be given the concepts verbally and then allowed to manipulate Cuisenaire rods or pie shapes. Then they may have the opportunity to do practice problems on the board. Finally, they work assigned problems in class so they may check answers and consult with the teacher. Such structured assistance in mathematics class is a far cry from "Write a story using your best handwriting." True, the analogy between writing and learning arithmetic skills breaks down when one realizes that writing is more open ended than practicing fractions. Checking for right answers is far less likely during writing time than during arithmetic drill. However, the opportunity to consult with the teacher for individual help is certainly relevant to both. To recap, the motto is—Teach writing; avoid mere assignment.

Modeling Writing

This brings us to our next general guideline: Don't simply teach writing, *model* it. Teachers as well as children need to write. Many of the national writing projects designed to help teachers become better teachers of writing, such as the Bay Area Writing Project, are guided by the principle that teachers need opportunities to write "on the job" (Goldberg, 1984). In order to help children do their best writing, we as teachers need to spend time defining our own rhetorical problems and solving them creatively through writing. Giving children advice about their writing is much easier but has less credibility than engaging in the composing process along with them. If we, like Terry Rivera, write when children write in the classroom, our writing serves two purposes. First, it increases our respect for the task; writing is a challenging business. Second, we serve as visible models to children. They see us write for real audiences, revise our work, struggle to select a topic, or be struck with a great idea ("Aha!"). Show them your own revised copy with words blocked out and sentences rearranged. Allow them to see that you, as most writers, revise. Such deliberate modeling has far more pedagogical possibilities than pleas for neat papers.

How might we go about serving as writing models for children? Here are two suggestions for modeling in the classroom. Use silent sustained writing in much the same way that silent sustained reading has been used by schools (Burns & Broman, 1983). At some point during the day, children and teachers quietly write together. Ongoing pieces of work such as journals or extended stories are best because children sense the continuity of their efforts from one day to the next. To stay on top of the situation, begin after your students start, and end before they do. Share your journal entries, expose your process.

Another form of the teacher as writing model is recommended by Graves (1983). His comprehensive recommendations for school writing programs include the teacher's writing uninterrupted by students for five minutes before circulating around the room or conferencing individually with children. The initial five-minute period allows children to get going on their own and does not encourage their many questions, which are best answered by themselves. The writing done by the teacher can take many forms: writing a memo to parents, experimenting with a personal anecdote, or, as in Terry Rivera's case, writing a response to Susan's message. In order to make this system work, the classroom has to be set up so children can get their own paper and pencils, and the teacher has to be consistently firm about *no* interruptions during the first few minutes. Children need to see the adult writer model at work. They will enjoy hearing your words, just as you enjoy hearing theirs. Teachers can no longer afford to just follow a do-as-I-say program; now they need a do-as-I-do program. (See the activity book for further ideas and for a list of *don't*s that were unfortunately common practice in the past.)

Finding What to Write About

Inevitably teachers will face the problem of children who are frustrated before they have a word down on the page. "I don't know what to write about," a child complains. "I don't have anything to say," choruses another, like Tim struggling with his play piece in the opening scene. There are several things a teacher can do to help children overcome the problem of having nothing to write.

One obvious avenue is, of course, to give children plenty of *observational experiences* so they will have something to write about. Nature walks, a story read aloud, field trips, show and tell are all viable alternatives. For young children particularly, concept building is important. Naming and classifying concrete objects such as toys, animals, or modes of transportation are suitable activities. However, these are very general experiences that may or may not involve writing. There are more specific prewriting activities to help some children compose.

As mentioned in Chapter 7, a young child can draw a picture and explain it, and then the teacher can help to put the spoken words into writing. You can ask guiding questions while writing down the child's words. Then you can ask the child to copy his or her own words. You can encourage the older student to speak into a tape recorder while you ask some key questions about his or her topic. The student then listens to the tape and uses it to help with the writing. Encourage students to maintain a "topics" wall (or graffiti board) to serve as motivation for personal writing and writing in other curriculum areas. Topics mostly contributed by children can be suggested by posters, headlines, pictures, small objects, provocative questions, striking quotations, bits of poetry, and cartoons. One week "injuries" was a hot topic. Have the children add to and change the display often. Allow the students freedom to choose from all the suggested topics. (Chapter 5 offered ways to motivate and integrate drama with writing, and the activity book chapter corresponding with this one has further suggestions in Part 1.)

Additionally, there are several types of brainstorming activities that can assist story writing. Recall from Chapter 6 that generally brainstorming is a creative problem-solving technique for producing lots of ideas about a certain topic (Osborn, 1953). When the brainstorming session begins, remind children of the rules:

Brainstorming Rules
1. Accept all ideas initially. Criticism or evaluation comes later.
2. Encourage "way-out" ideas.
3. Encourage children to suggest as many ideas as possible. Quantity of ideas is important.
4. Encourage children to build on one another's ideas. When they work together in a class warm-up, children "hitchhike," or get ideas from one another and embellish them.

Such creative problem-solving components as brainstorming in pre-writing planning help children release the flow of ideas, provide some structure, yet permit them choices.

A creative problem-solving strategy labeled *morphological synthesis* in the literature on creativity is useful in helping children put ideas for stories together in new and unusual ways. The strategy (promoting the *aha!* rather than the *ho-hum*) requires students to brainstorm ideas in several categories. When used for story writing, the categories parallel the story elements such as character, setting, plot. Children brainstorm a list of as many *people* as they can: an old Indian chief, a woman astronaut, and a talking raccoon, for example. Then they brainstorm *places:* a swamp, an asteroid, New York City. Finally, children suggest the *problem:* lost in the city, chased by a moose, late for a music lesson. Children randomly or intuitively select one idea from each category, put them together, and begin their creative potboiler. The children select the ideas by closing their eyes and dropping a pencil or pointing a finger in order to come up with unique combinations they may not have considered. The activity in Figure 8.2 is an example suitable for primary children. Figure 8.3 gives an example evolved by a second-grade child, Kimberly, selecting a character (a leprechaun), a place (the bright land), and an action (dancing).

There are other, more structured, means of helping children find a topic: One is simply to assign them. However, teacher-assigned topics are risky because some students may not be interested in the topic. Research indicates that topic assignment does not necessarily make for better student writing (Carlson, 1963). If the teacher does decide to assign topics, they need to be broad enough not to constrain the child, be *within the child's experience,*

Name _____ Date _____

20 Spin a story (b)

Write the names of three jobs, three machines, and
three actions. Be sure to put them in the correct box.
With the help of a spinner, choose one idea from each
box and write a story.

Jobs	Machines	Actions
1. _____	1. _____	1. _____
2. _____	2. _____	2. _____
3. _____	3. _____	3. _____

Figure 8.2 Story generator. (*Source:* Renzulli, J. S., et al. (1976), *New
Directions in Creativity.*)

The Super Leprechaun
Hi I am Kimberly

Kevin and I will dance in
the bright land and will see
the leprechaun. Kevin is very
very handsome. Oh, Kevin saw
is the leprechaun in the house.
He is very very powerful. There
are the very cute fairies.

Figure 8.3 Kimberly's leprechaun story. (*Source:* Carolyn Curfman.)

and used sparingly. See Figure 8.4 for a list of possible topics found in the professional literature.

Two other kinds of topic assignments are *composition frameworks* and *story starters*. Composition frameworks provide settings from which children develop a title and a piece of writing (Petty & Jensen, 1980). Related to composition frameworks are story starters. Generally, teachers give children exciting or provocative first sentences and tell them to complete the story themselves. For example, a first-grade teacher might write on the board, "I was ready to step off the curb when I looked up and saw . . ." Children can let their imaginations furnish them with any number of realistic and/or emotionally meaningful experiences. Encourage your students to tell you about the writing and how they will rework their own or imagined experience. See Figure 8.4 for examples of composition frameworks and story starters. (Also see the activity book, Chapter 8, Part 3: "Stem Gems.")

TOPICS

The following topics are examples of those frequently found in the literature:

Things I like most (or least)

How I got surprised

Sometimes I wonder about . . .

My life as my tennis shoe (or any other personally valued object)

If I could telephone anyone, I'd call . . . and talk about . . .

Advantages and disadvantages of being a 10-year-old

FRAMEWORKS

1. You are a member of that arctic exploration team we studied. Write about your most exciting discovery.
2. You are a gallon of milk from your refrigerator. What's it like to watch as dinner is being made?
3. You have just received an invitation to participate in a community play. What are you going to do?

STORY STARTERS

Primary

I opened my closet door and out crawled a _____ .
On the way home from school yesterday, we heard a _____ .
Up, up, up we went on a ferris wheel and we saw _____ .

Intermediate

When I heard the doorbell ring, I opened the front door and found a basket. Whatever it was, it was moving and making noises, so I _____ .

The door slammed. The rocking chair was rocking, but no one was in the empty room. I turned around and _____ .

Figure 8.4 Topics, frameworks, and starters.

Cautions About Topic Assignment   For the beginning teacher of writing, specific writing assignments are tempting. Story starters can be clever; topics and frameworks can produce a nice array of children's work for a parents' night bulletin board. Title topics, composition frameworks, and story starters have been widely used in the past; *however, they should be used only occasionally and with discretion.* Many of these topic "aids" have been included in writing activity books and reproducibles. In an attempt to foster creativity, some topic activities have become so fanciful as to be bizarre. Such activities tend to elicit gimmicky writing from children. To help children develop the ability to find a topic, look to the child writers themselves rather than rely solely on external aids. By providing students with ready-made topics, we are robbing children of the opportunity to make important decisions about their own writing and hindering them from developing thoughtful, independent writing habits. Release the writing process into the hands of the children by letting them choose their own topics (Graves, 1983).

Several means of helping teachers organize for the "release" are possible. First, look to students' interests and experiences for topic ideas. Keep a rough chart listing each child's name, with notes about special interests next to each name. If a child stoutly maintains he or she has nothing to say, the teacher can ask about one of the child's interests. Perhaps both can uncover one there. Second, children pick up ideas from each other. Children who agree to it may have their writing displayed, published, or read aloud in response groups or at sharing time, as did Jason and Mike. Children can interview one another to find their topics as well. Also use teacher modeling as an effective means of helping children choose a topic. ("Here is my list of topics I want to write about. I keep it here inside my writing folder.") Children also need to see adults struggle with topic selection and refinement. Box 8.2 lists steps in selecting a topic (Graves, 1983).

Generate four topics to expand the child's thinking. Asking the child to come up with one topic initially may cause frustration, paralysis, and no topic selection at all. Keep topic selection in perspective. At any one time probably only five or six children will be writing on a motivating topic. Others will be engaged in fairly pedestrian writing that is less than their best. Such cycles of performance are normal. Young children seem to have fewer difficulties with topic choice. Older children who have become dependent on teacher-assigned topics and more accustomed to the conventions of writing are more likely to have difficulty (Graves, 1983).

BOX 8.2 Topic Selection Strategy

1. Pass out paper for writing *and* some scrap paper children can use for jotting down topic ideas.

2. Take some paper yourself and number from one to four.

3. Write down two topics and talk briefly about each one. Give the children some background about your interest in the topic and how you selected the topic.

4. Do the same for the next two topics.

5. Select one topic and tell the children what you hope to find out by writing about it.

6. Write.

In essence, teachers can address the important task of helping children select a topic by outside stimulation. Rich prior experiences, specific creative problem-solving techniques, and a few assigned topics may help them decide what to write about. *Ultimately, however, the children's own interests and knowledge are the source of topics that will engage their thinking and imagination.* Tap into genuine and impelling reasons to write.

WHAT KINDS OF WRITING DO CHILDREN PRODUCE?

Types of writing are sometimes called modes of discourse. Most of us remember narration, description, exposition, and argumentation from our English classes. These terms were used to identify writing that told a story, described something, explained something, or tried to persuade. The terms used to describe the four modes of discourse are generally attributed to a nineteenth-century logician and educator, Alexander Bain (Connors, 1981). They were the most widely used classifications for classroom instruction for several decades. However, after 1950, the modes of discourse fell into disfavor among process enthusiasts and started to disappear from texts. Most writing researchers felt that narration, description, exposition, and persuasion may have classified the types of writing *products,* but they did very little to address a writing *process.*

Other classifications of discourse are more theoretically sound and more useful in the classroom. We will mention one of the more influential and widely accepted, and we will give examples of activities that will elicit various types of writing.

Britton and others (1975) devised a set of categories that classified writing according to its predominant function. Britton identified three kinds of writing: *expressive, transactional,* and *poetic.* Each will be briefly defined, and several example activities for products for each are included.

Expressive Writing

The first of Britton's categories, *expressive,* refers to such writing as letters and diary entries. Certainly, both are very suitable writing experiences for children. (Chapter 4 referred to expressive language in its oral form.) Letter writing is valuable and enjoyable for elementary children and something primary-age children will initiate on their own (Collerson, 1983). In the opening scene of this chapter, the communication center, with individual letter boxes for everyone, suggests one means of encouraging expressive writing in the classroom. Children learn that their messages can have real audiences and can be a medium for expressing what they think and feel.

Most classroom letter writing begins with short, personal notes to people the children actually know. Letters to family members, class pen pals, class visitors, or community members are within the experience of young children. Older children can write to a more abstract audience as well. They may want to write a fan letter to a sports figure, a politician, or a children's author. In addition, children in the intermediate and middle-school grades may want to write to businesses or governmental agencies for information and pamphlets. And, of course, letters to imaginative personages such as the Easter bunny or E. T. allow children to daydream and to express their wishes.

One example of imaginative letter writing took the form of a problem-solving activity based on Tommie di Paola's illustrated book of Mother Goose rhymes. After reading the rhymes, children selected a Mother Goose character with a problem and wrote a letter suggesting solutions. Since Mother Goose characters face problems ranging from opportunistic spiders to lost sheep, the activity provided rich possibilities for clever "advice" letters from youthful problem solvers (see Figure 8.5).

Letter writing is also often used to teach certain conventions such as abbreviations or addresses. Certainly, there is a place for this kind of activity. However, once the letter becomes an exercise in learning conventions, it is no longer considered expressive in Britton's scheme. Expressive writing is very personal; the writer and the reader share the context.

Diary or personal journal entries are also examples of expressive writing. The daily journal is often a successful medium for the silent sustained writing mentioned earlier. Young children in kindergarten and first grade will write and draw on simple unlined-paper journals that have been stapled together by the teacher. Older children may enjoy keeping their thoughts in a spiral notebook. Children often like to share their journal entries, but do not require a child to share diary or journal writing if it is private (one of the *don'ts*). Journals are also an excellent means of getting children involved in long-term writing projects. For example, a resource room teacher working with a group of academically able sixth graders reading Arthurian legends had the students keep journals about their experiences with medieval culture. Their multidisciplinary studies led them to write about chivalry,

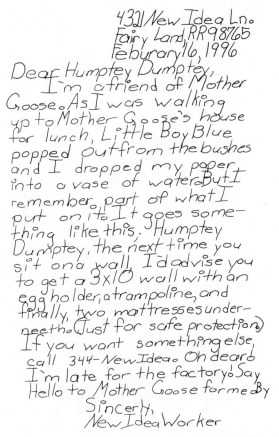

Figure 8.5   A child's letter to Humpty Dumpty. (*Source:* Carlyle School, Plano, Texas.)

heraldry, and sorcery. They also learned that *journal* comes from French and means daily *(jour)* thoughts. Expressive writing, both letter and journal, is immediate and personal. As such it will help the child find his or her own voice as a writer.

Transactional Writing

The second of Britton's categories is *transactional* writing. Much of the writing done in schools falls into this discourse type. Transactional writing for getting things done involves *informative* and *persuasive* writing. (Chapters 7 and 10 address both oral and written modes of these categories.) Examples of informative writing are Jason and Mike's explanation of building the astronomy projector or Tim's guide for organizing a classroom play in the opening scene. Younger children also write simpler nonnarrative pieces such as lists or "catalogues" of facts they know (Newkirk, 1987).

Certain kinds of *description* are also considered transactional. To sharpen their powers of observation, young children can be given feely boxes that contain objects with interesting textures. With the aid of the teacher in extending their vocabulary, they can use descriptive words to write about the objects—lumpy, rough, smooth, nubby, slick. For young children sensory experiences are effective prewriting activities. Interesting shapes and colors of seashells, for instance, encourage attentive visual observation and description. Calling attention to sounds and their written representation encourages children to use interesting inventions like *row-r-r-r* for a racing car engine. Mike's opening-scene diagram included sounds as well as labeled parts.

Britton is also interested in the kind of writing that reflects the child's ability to think abstractly. This kind of writing is often found in *report writing.* Young children tend to record concrete information about a topic. As children progressively generalize, speculate, and theorize, their report writing can become surprisingly rich in imaginative explanations across the curriculum. For example, a second grader's science hypothesis about prisms and subsequent test of it in Figure 8.6 are uncannily correct.

PAUL'S KNOW-IT-ALL VOL. I

p. 1 Mar. 9

A prism is a thick (mostly) piece of glass that puts the colors of the sunlight visible to the human eye. The average colors a prism reveals are: red, yellow, bluish green, and purple. Steve and I proved that the world moves. (See pg. 2.)

p. 2 Mar. 9

Steve and I proved that the earth moves. How we discovered it:

Discovery No. 1 we put the prism on the desk in the sunlight and it projected a rectangle spectrum on the ceiling. While we were talking and recording the colors in the spectrum (See page 1) we noticed a change in the spectrum. It wasn't a rectangle any more! It was smaller than last time we looked. It was a very thin rectangle! We couldn't figure out why it had changed shape. We moved everything we could out of the way . . . nothing happened. Then I said, "The sun moved!" But then I remembered the sun couldn't move and Mrs. Mosher said, "No" "The sun can't move," so we knew that the earth had moved.

Figure 8.6 A child's journal entry on prisms. (*Source:* Bissex, 1980.)

Report writing varies in its formality. Paul (see Figure 8.6) was essentially writing informal, informative reports in his journal over a long period of time. However, most report writing is done on a specific topic related to one of the content areas such as social studies or science. Formal reports are usually short-term, single writing assignments such as the one in Figure 8.7. (The activity book for Chapter 7 has additional related activities.)

These delightful examples of children's report writing belie the effort that goes into transactional writing. Children must keep information in mind, organize it, and discard extraneous material, not to mention attending to the difficulties of conventions.

There are many prerequisite skills for report writing, particularly if it is more formal. Although children do not generally write formal reports until they reach the intermediate grades, there are activities for primary grades, too. Informative writing quite often depends

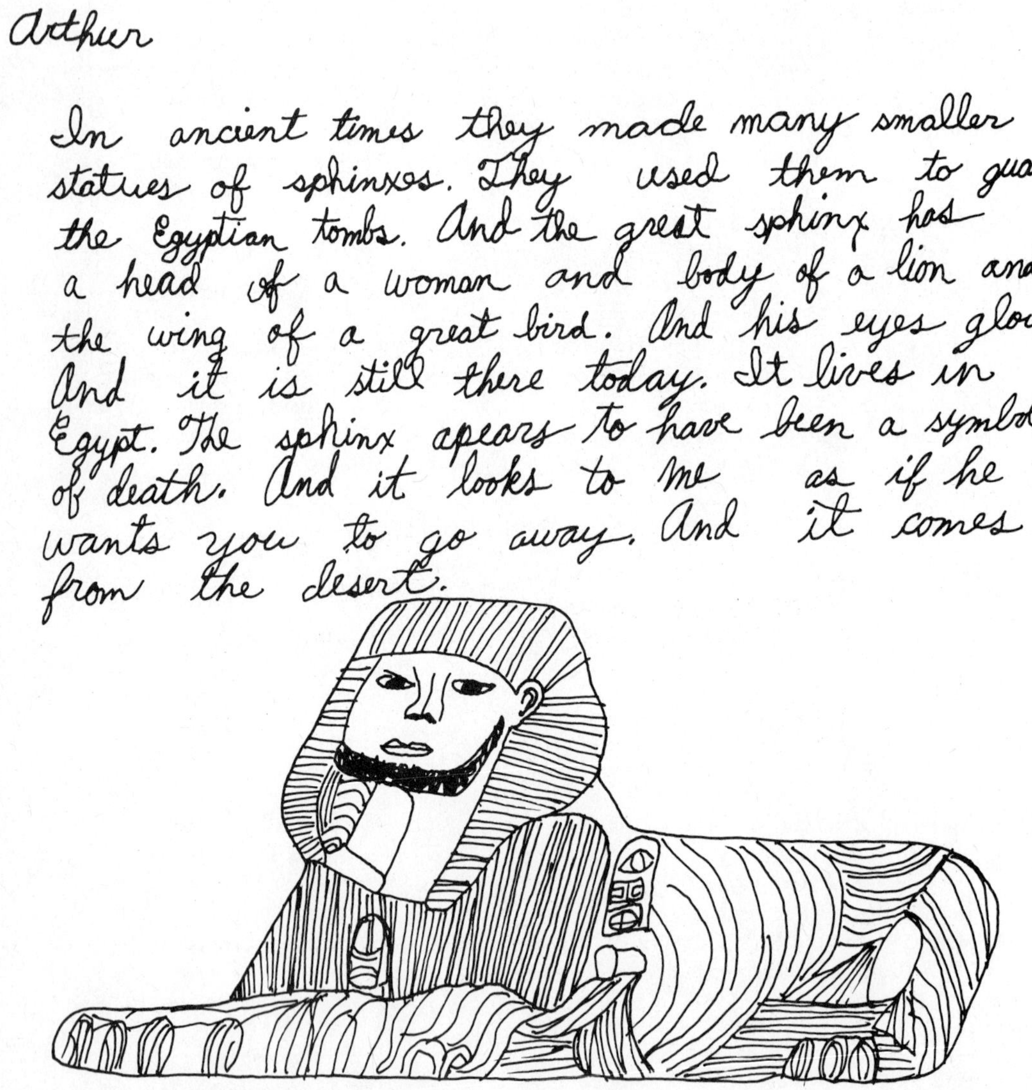

Arthur

In ancient times they made many smaller statues of sphinxes. They used them to guard the Egyptian tombs. And the great sphinx has a head of a woman and body of a lion and the wing of a great bird. And his eyes glow. And it is still there today. It lives in Egypt. The sphinx apears to have been a symbol of death. And it looks to me as if he wants you to go away. And it comes from the desert.

Figure 8.7 A child's report on the Sphinx.

on secondary sources such as reference books and other library materials. Many teachers are disappointed with their primary students' first attempts at writing reports because reporting becomes copying directly from the encyclopedia. However, *if children are given opportunities to manipulate material and make it their own before they write, copying is much less likely.* One ingenious teacher has her second graders begin informative report writing with the encyclopedia activity given in Box 8.3.

Global topics such as dogs, elephants, playground equipment, or airplanes are reasonable subjects for primary report writers. In fact, child writers in kindergarten and first grade often write *attribute books* (Calkins, 1986). These are collections of loosely related ideas that look similar to children's reports. The records often contain intriguing information, and young children have a way of personalizing their writing. A report on dogs usually contains a line or two about the family pet. (See Figure 8.8 for an example on frogs.)

For children in the intermediate grades and middle school, formal report writing is more focused. One kind of activity that helps children focus their report writing is to ask them to frame their reports as *questions.* A young child might write a report on dogs; an older child might write a report to answer the question "How did dogs help early humans?" Additional examples follow.

Topic Focus Through Questions
1. *Medical discoveries* becomes *What medical discovery might be made in the next 25 years?*
2. *Movies* becomes *Who decides what movies are made and how do they decide?*
3. *Dinosaurs* becomes *What were some differences between carnivorous and herbivorous dinosaurs?*

Teachers can model thinking of (1) questions, (2) global answers, and (3) supportive details before inviting child authors to do the same (or to "think, pair, and share").

BOX 8.3 Encyclopedia Activity: Organizing Information

1. Give each child a blank 3 × 5 index card. Ask the children to write their topic at the top of the card. The first time you use this activity, you may want to model and assign a group of optional topics for beginners.

2. Each child gets an encyclopedia and reads the entry on the topic listed on the index card.

3. After putting the encyclopedia away, the child writes one thing he or she remembers about the topic on the index card.

4. Repeat the procedure at least twice so the child reads an entry in more than one source.

5. When the child has three cards with information, have the child lay them out on the desk so all three can be seen at once.

6. Using these paraphrased notes, the child can write the report, in this case a single, short paragraph.

Figure 8.8 Example from a kindergarten child's attribute book.

In addition to informative writing such as how-tos, descriptions, and reports, transactional writing is also used for *persuasive* purposes (detailed in Chapter 10). This type of writing is most like the argumentative mode. Children write to persuade their reader to agree with them or to act. A letter written to influence a politician's vote or to make a case for extended recess is persuasive. For older children these persuasive letters may develop into editorials and debates. One form of transactional writing suitable for elementary school children is creating advertisements for real or imaginary products. The children can write scripts for radio or television spots or ad copy for the newspaper. For example, ask the children to imagine items in their closet or basement that they might want to sell at a garage sale, then let them write ad copy for one of these items. Depending on the age and sophistication of the children, the teacher may want to point out characteristics of effective ads: a grabber to catch the buyer's attention, unique features of the item, a means for locating the seller, such as an address or telephone number. Writing ads is one way of offering children the opportunity for transactional writing. (See Chapter 10 on use of persuasive language and its activity book chapter for additional activities.)

In summary, the type of writing classified as transactional includes many kinds suitable for elementary school children. Using their senses, they can produce descriptive writing. They can write reports to inform and explain. They can persuade us in many ways, for example, with original advertisements.

Writing As a Way to Learn Across the Curriculum   One final observation about transactional writing in the classroom: Currently, writing researchers are interested in the relationship between writing and learning (Applebee, 1984). They speculate that when children take information and make it their own by manipulating it and writing down what they think, writing can become a powerful learning tool. The idea is intuitively appealing, although classroom studies of writing as a means of learning are few (Langer, 1984; Tierney, 1981; Weiss & Walters, 1980). If children are actively engaged in writing about a topic, rather than passively receiving information, the very act of writing may increase their understanding.

Learning logs are one means of giving students the opportunity to use writing as a way to learn content in science, math, and literature (Calkins, 1986). Logs may be spiral or loose-leaf notebooks or folders. Students jot down notes, possible questions, sketches, or topic maps. These informal, informational writings may in turn become the basis for more extended transactional pieces. Thus, teachers who encourage report writing based on original data or on multiple secondary references, or who offer occasions for persuasive writing about real concerns, provide students with the opportunity to analyze and synthesize information in a new way for themselves. Children discover what they know by writing it down.

Poetic Writing

Britton's final discourse category is *poetic.* Writing is used as an art medium, and it exists for its own sake, not necessarily to inform or persuade the reader. Poetic writing is closely tied to beautiful language, imagery, and emotion. Examples of poetic writing include poems and songs, plays, novels, and some stories. (Chapter 9 develops additional ideas on this use of language.)

Children's Stories   Stories are, of course, a frequent writing medium for children. Young children often have a well-developed idea of what a story should be (Applebee, 1978). Presented and diagrammed in Chapter 2, *story structure* is called a *story grammar* and includes, among other things, a setting, an event and a response (Mandler & Johnson, 1977). In organization, children's stories are often surprisingly like stories written by adults. The composition framework (Box 8.1) and story starter suggestions earlier in the chapter are, of course, prewriting activities for story writing. The earlier story generator (Figure 8.2) is a motivating means to address characters, plot, and setting. Teachers with current know-how, however, encourage children to write action stories drawn from their own experience. The child's story in Figure 8.9 blends both the real and the imaginary. Third-grade students wrote true-to-life books about something that had happened in their family recently. Mike's big yellow cat, Butterscotch, frequently got into fights, and Mike used those exploits as his material. Mike's story began as "The Life of Butterscotch." Later, he retitled the piece "Jeff the Cat" and transformed the cat fight into a boxing match with a dog. We see crossed-out evidence of some of his prewriting planning in this figure.

For children in the primary grades, story writing is a time for free expression. As children become less egocentric, the characters they write about become more separate from themselves. They may move from single to multiple events and increase their use of dialogue (Fisher & Terry, 1977).

Two kinds of activities that foster growth in story writing are those that help children create interesting characters for their stories and those that help children learn to write dialogue. Both kinds are built on observation. Teachers can give children a character profile

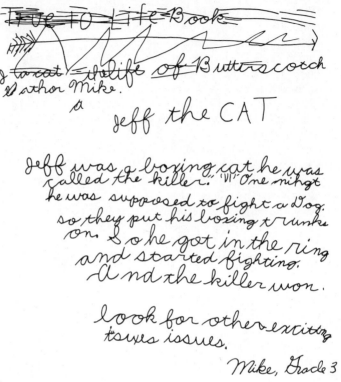

Figure 8.9 A child's story.

and ask them to observe one or more persons and check off adjectives that describe physical characteristics such as hair color, dress, or speech patterns. Older children can include mannerisms and personality traits as well.

Sensitizing children to the possibilities of using dialogue in their stories is also an observational activity. A published writer teaching children in a special summer class asked her students to listen carefully to conversation during family meal times. The next day children tried to re-create what they heard from memory. The writer explained that she wanted them to develop an ear for the way people talk and to use dialogue in their stories. Dialogue gives the reader a lively picture of the characters and puts the action of the story in the here and now. Although dialogue is a fairly sophisticated literary tool, young children also sprinkle their writing with direct quotes. While speaking displayed in the writing of young children is usually a monologue with one speaker rather than two, encourage these efforts as well (Temple, Nathan, & Burris, 1982).

Children's Poetry   In addition to story writing, poetic writing includes poems. Generally children like to write poetry; rhyme and rhythm are appealing to them (Fisher & Natarella, 1982). However, in order for children to be successful at writing poetry, they need to hear and see it. Read it to them; toss it into your daily curriculum, like spices in a good meal; have it available in varied media. Teachers can display poetry visually around the room and can make judicious use of the overhead projector to share poems. *Most of the preparation for poetry writing is poetry reading.*   The teacher can provide a rich selection of poems to be read aloud to the class. Almost all children, including boys, tend to enjoy humorous, familiar poems with rhythm and rhyme (Terry, 1974). Allow children opportunities to write free verse, concrete poetry, invented unrhymed forms, and simple rhymed forms. (See the activity book, Chapter 8, Section 3 on writing poetry, and Chapter 9, "Read Aloud Poems.")

Color and sense poems for beginners   Examples of *free verse* poems that are successful for beginners are *color poems* ("Red is . . .") and *sense poems* ("I hear . . ."). Color and sense poems encourage children to observe closely and to use imagery in their writing. In addition, the *use of the single color and repetition gives the poem focus.* Such poems are particularly suitable for young children because there is no need to be constrained by the search for a rhyming word or a particular poetry form. Child authors can concentrate on the ideas and emotions expressed and not sacrifice meaning for structure.

Color and sense poems also work well as collaborative efforts. After children select a color or a sense, the teacher can place the selection on an overhead or a flip chart and record the responses volunteered by members of the class. The result is a group poem of several lines, for example:

Listening in the Lunchroom, I Hear . . .

spoons clinking
lots of laughing
Mrs. Yoo's voice
the sound of big dishwashers
crash! Somebody dropped a tray
too much noise!

Concrete poetry   Generally, we think of an image as a picture painted with words. In *concrete* poetry, children use words to outline a visual picture of the idea expressed in the poem. Concrete poems that depict motion are particularly effective. For example, the poem in Figure 8.10 visually communicates the feeling of a common childhood experience— jumping rope. Concrete poetry is one of the easiest kinds of poetry for students to write because children are familiar with pictures and drawing. The visual nature of concrete poetry is an appealing form for them.

Invented unrhymed poems   In addition, there are several kinds of *invented* unrhymed poems that allow children to experiment with patterns and to create something that looks like a poem. *Cinquain* and *diamante* are two of the most widely used. The cinquain is a five-line poem: line 1 is the name of someone or something; line 2, two words that describe; line 3, three *-ing* words that show action; line 4, four words that show feeling; line 5, one word that repeats or suggests the word in line 1 or is a synonym for it. The following poem, "Desert Hiking," is an example of a cinquain.

Scrub brush
Stubborn, windbent
Scratching, tearing, tangling
I like hiking through
Scrub brush

Another type of invented form, the diamante, requires children to manipulate antonyms. Invented by Tiedt (1978), this seven-line poem begins very much like the cinquain.

Figure 8.10   A child's concrete poem, by Elizabeth, grade 4.

However, the diamante involves contrast between the first line subject of the poem and its antonym ending. To introduce the form, the following procedure is recommended:

1. Children brainstorm a list of several nouns that might be used as the subject of a poem.
2. Children select one of the suggested topics and list a number of antonyms for the subject. For example: storm—*calm, sun, sunshine, good weather.*
3. Children complete the first three lines of the poem spaced to form the top half of a diamond.

   1 word: subject noun
   2 words: adjectives
   3 words: *-ing* words

Storm
Willful, wild
Blowing, moaning, raining

4. Ask children to select an antonym for storm and place it in the last line position. Complete lines 6 and 5 working backward from line 7.

Warming, touching, cheering
Bright, friendly
Sunshine

5. The diamante is now complete except for line 4, which requires children to use contrast. They think of four nouns. Two nouns relate to the subject noun in line 1; two relate to the antonym in line 7. The finished poem is arranged in a diamond shape.

Storm
Willful, wild
Blowing, moaning, raining
Gale, wind, calm, sunlight
Warming, touching, cheering
Bright, friendly
Sunshine

Rhymed forms Children can also compose simple *rhymed* forms, including *jingles* and *limericks.* Figure 8.11 is an example of a third grade child's simple rhyming. An easy rhymed form for beginners is the *clerihew,* a four-line poem invented by mystery writer E. C. Bentley. Line 1 is someone's name; line 2 rhymes with 1; lines 3 and 4 also rhyme. One way to use the clerihew is to have class members write them about one another. Original clerihews can be arranged on a bulletin board next to a picture of the child who is the subject of the poem. The following is a suggested sequence for introducing clerihews in the classroom.

1. Ask children to brainstorm the names of famous people. Encourage them to consider famous figures in history, current sports stars, musicians, or characters from children's books. For example:

   Amelia Earhart
   Babe Ruth
   Michael Jackson
   Stuart Little

2. Ask children to select a name for which they can list a number of rhyming words. If the last names of famous people are difficult to rhyme (and many are), suggest to the children they list words that rhyme (or nearly rhyme) with the first names,

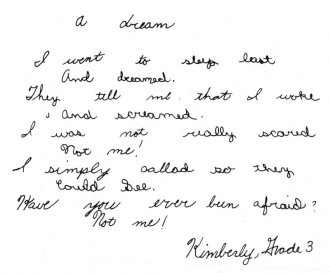

Figure 8.11 A child's simple rhymed poem. (*Source:* Collected by Carolyn Curfman.)

too. Children enjoy writing clerihews with a coauthor. Collaboration may increase the number of rhyming words children generate.

3. When they have a list of rhyming words, children may write out the person's name as the first line of their clerihew. For example, *Charlie Brown* or *Brown, Charlie* if the last name is difficult to rhyme and can be inverted.

4. Ask them to complete their humorous idea on the next line so that it rhymes with the name. For example:

> Brown, Charlie
> He'll worry

5. Finally, children can write lines 3 and 4, which should also rhyme. The complete clerihew is a set of two couplets.

> Brown, Charlie
> He'll worry.
> Baseball season
> Is the reason.

Forms versus poetic child thought   Poetry writing, like story writing and other forms of poetic writing, is essentially an opportunity to be imaginative. One important concept underlies the effective use of poetry in the writing classroom. Child authors need opportunities to experiment freely with language. *It would be a misuse of poetry writing to insist that young children accurately rhyme lines or reproduce stanza forms at the expense of the thought expressed.* When Terry Rivera wrote to Susan about her poem in the opening scene, the response focused on the idea expressed, the creative use of words, and the thoughtfulness of the child's gift, not on the accurate reproduction of cinquain form. Poetic writing involves creating for its own sake. We expect children's poetic writing to be fanciful, humorous, and serendipitously sprinkled with images. An eight-year-old French boy's poem, shown in Figure 8.12, illustrates some of these features.

Conclusions

In essence, children do many kinds of writing. They express, describe, inform, persuade, and create beautiful language objects. Any type of writing at any level is preferable to no writing at all. Rather than rely on workbooks or ditto sheets that require circling, underlining, and crossing out, provide children with the opportunity to write messages of their own. (See the activity book, Chapter 9, for connections between literature and writing.)

WHERE DOES COMPOSITION TAKE PLACE?

Organization of the classroom involves the emotional climate, the physical arrangement of furniture and materials, and the managerial concerns of record keeping, conferencing, and publishing children's work.

Emotional Climate

We have alluded to a number of issues that contribute to a classroom atmosphere that encourages writing. Chapter 3 discussed four allies that teachers can also use to increase a child's motivation to write: self-competency, modeling, personal acceptance, and peer status. We have already discussed self-competency and modeling as they relate to writing

L'Automne et la pluie

Les feuilles tombent doucement
Avant de s'amonceler en un épais tapis.
Là s'étend un paysage merveilleux.
Il est vêtu d'arbres qui se couchent dans la bise,
Et semblent saluer le soleil brillant.
Tout à coup le soleil se cache!
Les nuages arrivent, il pleut très fort!!
Le vent siffle, siffle, et les animaux sont effrayés.
Et moi, au coin du feu, je me réchauffe tranquillement.

[Translation below]
Autumn and the Rain

The leaves are falling softly
Before piling up in a thick carpet.
There is spread out a marvelous landscape.
It is clothed with trees which have gone to sleep in the north wind.
And seem to greet the dazzling sun.
All of a sudden, the sun hides itself!
The clouds arrive, it's raining very hard!!
The wind hisses, hisses, and the animals are frightened.
And I, by the corner of the fire, I am warming myself contentedly.

Michael Ringenbach
Bordeaux, France
8½ years old

Figure 8.12 A French boy's poem and its translation. (*Translator:* H. W. Rickey.)

at length. Children's sense of self emerges when they are given control over their own writing, when they have opportunities to find their own voice. The image of teachers as writing models has been a theme throughout the chapter.

Personal acceptance and peer status, however, are also powerful allies. Children want to be accepted as they are. When teachers fail to appreciate writing by marking up the paper unnecessarily, children feel rejected. If, however, the teacher accepts the child's writing, looks for its successes, and secures an audience for the child writer, what a positive influence the teacher has on the child's growth! Sensitive teachers look for avenues for publication, both formal and informal. There are several children's magazines that accept original work, but books "published," bound in class, and added to the classroom library are appreciated as well. Several ideas for classroom publishing are presented in Box 8.4. (Also see the activity book, Chapter 7, on writing a class newspaper.)

Finally, children find an ally in each other. Because peer status is important, encourage children to value writing in general and one another's writing in particular. If children have an opportunity to share with an audience as did Jason and Mike, with a collaborator as did Maggie and Susan, or with the teacher as did Tom, they may find that writing is not necessarily a lonely business. (There is a later section on peer conferences.) The teacher

---

BOX 8.4 Classroom Publishing Ideas

1. Write for children in lower grades (sixth graders write for fourth graders, fourth graders write for second graders).

2. Write letters, poems, or stories for school staff (teachers, principal, secretaries, cooks, custodian).

3. Publish a classroom or school newspaper or literary journal. These can be placed in the offices of doctors, dentists, or businesses in the community.

4. Write and publish books for a classroom or school library.

5. Write letters to community members, city officials, and civic organizations.

6. Display children's writing in the school display case, in community shop windows, or in the public library.

---

wishing to establish a positive classroom climate for writing can use the "allies" to set the tone for successful writing experiences.

Physical Arrangements

In addition to the emotional support of the classroom, children benefit from some simple physical arrangements. For young children, the availability of paper and pencils during writing time is important. When a teacher is busy with a conference or involved in silent sustained writing, children need to be able to replenish their own supplies. Older children will probably want access to dictionaries as well. If access to materials and references is controlled by the teacher, interruptions are inevitable. Place materials so children can get them independently.

Another physical arrangement that encourages writing is the use of a writing corner or center as in Terry Rivera's room. Children who want to write during spare moments of the day benefit from having a quiet place in the classroom devoted to writing. The corner can be as simple as a desk separated from the rest or as elaborate as any learning center complete with activities and artwork. One creative second-grade teacher made a popular writing center by bringing an old typewriter from home and putting a letter box on a nearby shelf. Children liked to hunt and peck messages to the teacher and to one another.

HOW CAN THE WRITING CLASSROOM BE ORGANIZED?

Perhaps one of the most difficult tasks a teacher has in organizing the classroom for writing is developing a managerial plan. The plan should include a means for keeping track of children's progress, a framework for individual and group conferences, a schedule for writing groups, and student writing folders. The best means for keeping track of children's progress is to keep a *writing folder* for each child. Usually children keep their work in the folder and return it to a central file each day. By having the children date each entry (keeping the most recent work on top), the teacher retains a visible record of growth. Teachers, students, and their parents can review the first writings and contrast them with later ones.

When folders become too full for children to handle, early papers can be removed and retained in another file for the teacher. You can pass on a writing sample from the folder to the student's next teacher.

The simplest *record-keeping* systems are best; teachers are too busy for elaborate schemes. Individual folders may contain four lists for both teacher and child: (1) a list of the titles the child has completed with the date each was finished, (2) a list of new ideas the child might use next, (3) a list of writing skills the child can use, and (4) a list of topics about which the child is knowledgeable (Graves, 1983). Transparent sheet protectors can preserve often-used items, such as editing lists, lists of topics or new ideas, and a list of writing accomplished (with date begun, title, and date finished).

Teachers may also want to keep a class checklist that shows at a glance when each child last had a conference, what skills are needed, and when work was shared with the class. Other more elaborate records are certainly possible, but for the teacher implementing a writing program for the first time, too many records can be intimidating.

Conferences: Teacher with Child

It is clear that the writing *conference* is an essential part of writing instruction. Where do you find time with 30 other children in your class? Schedule conferences while the rest are doing independent reading, writing, or other assigned work. Use trained volunteers, aides, older students, and as we discuss later, peers. As with individualized reading conferences (and the two might be combined), there are several reasons for an individual writing conference. Ideally, a child will be ready to share a work in progress or one just completed, but conferences may be used to help children find their topic or to teach a skill. The key to a successful conference is to get the child to do the leading. Begin the conference with a general question like "How's the writing going?" or "What are you working on now?" Let the child talk about what he or she is writing and respond initially by asking questions about the content of the piece. The teacher listens, reflects, understands, celebrates, and extends what the child has done.

With experience, a teacher and child can cover a great deal in a two- to five-minute conference. Conferences need not be that long to be productive. Make every moment count with specific comments on the content of the writing. Start with something positive. Your kind words make children feel comfortable. You might ask the following questions:

Some Questions for Your Conference
1. What part do you like best?
2. What part was most difficult?
3. Does your writing say . . . ? (Here you restate and give or guess the intent.)
4. Can you tell me more about . . . ? (Here you ask the child about an underdeveloped part.)
5. What part will you work on next?

Conferences are also excellent vehicles for helping children with fluency and revision problems. Sometimes children cannot write fast enough to keep pace with their ideas. Young children in particular do not have the motor development or the facility with spelling to write quickly. To avoid frustrating the eager young writer, teachers can take *dictation*, a topic developed extensively in the Chapter 7 sections on LEA. The child dictates the story; the teacher becomes the secretary. Children can see their work in print without having to wait for their muscles to match their imaginations. Writing that is partly scribbled and partly invented spelling is another option for the young child, as elaborated in Chapter 2.

As mentioned, dictation is also an important tool for the older child who has developed writing apprehension or who is suffering from a temporary block, as was Tim's case. Thus, during the conference, the teacher, like Terry Rivera, can offer to take dictation. Talking through the topic may reduce anxiety and temporarily removes the worries about spelling and mechanical errors from the child's mind. Fluency may return.

Revision can also be encouraged through conferences. As was mentioned earlier, children are often reluctant to revise. Encouragement and the right question from the teacher may trigger revision. Calkins (in Gentry, 1980) observed four kinds of children's revising behaviors and developed suggestions that she believes help children to move toward more sophisticated strategies. For example, one kind of child reviser does not reread what he or she has written. The teacher asks the child to point out a favorite part or asks the child to revise in other media. For instance, if the piece is accompanied by a picture, the teacher can encourage the child to add details or to draw another picture depicting what will happen next.

A more advanced (stage-two) reviser will reread and make small changes. This child is likely to erase rather than cross out and will probably add material at the end rather than insert it into the text. The teacher can help this reviser by questioning the child about the content of his or her piece. By focusing on content, the teacher may be able to encourage the child to do more than tidy up the page. For example, one study found that asking content questions increased the intellectual complexity of children's written explanations (Robinson & Feldhusen, 1984).

Calkins's third kind of reviser independently recopies his or her paper. This is an advance over the child who corrects the original because now there are at least two drafts, and handwriting and spelling corrections can be accomplished later in the revising process. The child can concentrate on content and word choice initially and leave the cleanup changes to a subsequent draft. The teacher can help a third-stage reviser by demonstrating ways to use the draft. For example, teaching children how to use carets ($\wedge$), asterisks, or arrows to insert material is helpful. Young writers may find it comfortable to cut their text with scissors, rearrange the order of the sentences, or make room for another section (or use a word processor).

According to Calkins, the most sophisticated child revisers in stage four begin to see second drafts as a second try rather than a copy of the first. She notes that the child may ignore the first draft and do the second one independently of the first. The teacher can help these children by calling attention to the first draft as a way of learning about the piece. Asking questions about what could be cut, saved, or changed is helpful. Again, as is consistent with the writing process approach, the teacher can direct the child's attention first to content and organization, later to word choice, precision, and mechanics.

The preceding review of Calkins's observations and suggestions about revision illustrates the importance of classroom organization. In a classroom of 30, children will demonstrate all levels of revising behavior; therefore, teachers need to organize their time so that individual attention is possible, as it was in Terry Rivera's class.

Peer Conferencing

Chapter 6, on discussion, had much to say about organizing peer conferencing across the curriculum. Prospective teachers want to know: What is peer conferencing for writing, why

---

BOX 8.5 Some Rules We Made for Our Writing Conferences

1. Every person takes a turn at reading his or her composition aloud.

2. Everyone else *listens.*

3. The author reads twice.
   —peers listen
   —peers listen and make notes on response forms

4. Each listener writes what he or she liked best.

5. Each listener writes what he or she would like to know more about or makes a constructive suggestion.

6. The author collects the peer response sheets and may or may not use the comments when making revisions.

---

should I bother, and how do I organize it? Peer conference groups encourage children to take their writing seriously; you can build group valuing of writing. The writing conference group becomes a genuine audience and inspires changes and revision. As a result, you will receive pieces that have already gone through one revision. Ultimately, you relieve yourself of much work as students confer and help each other.

For organizing the peer conference group, refer to many suggestions in Chapter 6, including selecting students who work well together. Building on your knowledge from Chapter 6, start with pairs first. When two children have had practice, introduce a third. Include a variety of performance strengths. Remember from Chapter 6 that all have something to contribute in the multiability group. Explain that the purpose is to improve each member's abilities to read, write, speak, listen, and think. A prime purpose is to be supportive and help each writer. Finally, the purpose is to produce specific suggestions he or she might want to consider for revision, but the story belongs to the storyteller, who has the last say.

Structure for the peer conference emerges from your modeling for the class and from observing rules such as those in Box 8.5. Students can also adapt the teacher's questions suggested in the list given earlier, "Some Questions for Your Conference." You can see from items 2 and 3 in that list that preparation, with ideas in Chapter 3 on listening, plays an important part.

Writing Schedules

How often do students need to write? Preferably every day. A schedule, a predictable structure, may help. For example, beginning teachers can reasonably expect elementary school children to write for at least 20 minutes a day. If they adopt the process approach, they might begin by writing silently with the children for 5 minutes, then circulate to assist children who have questions or difficulties for 5 minutes, then schedule individual conferences for 10 minutes. This 20-minute writing period can be followed by sharing time. Twenty minutes is a manageable block of time for the beginning teacher. However, as children become more independent and the teacher more experienced, the writing time can be

Box 8.6 Some Ways Process Writing and Traditional Writing Instruction May Differ

Process Writing	Traditional Writing
1. *Prewriting/rehearsing/planning.* Topics are selected and/or made more specific by cooperation between teacher and students (authors). Autonomous decisions about goals, audience, form, tone, mood, and the organization of ideas to be used may take place at this time. The author is the prime decision maker with the teacher being the facilitator, prober, and supporter of those decisions.	1. Writing topic is assigned by teacher. This assignment may specifically tell students the audience to address, forms to use, how long it should be, and other parameters. The student rarely is referred to as an author.
2. *Writing draft (or translation of child's experience).* Positive receiving by teacher of rough content written. Invented spelling understood.	2. Writing first copy. Possible comments by teacher usually noting mistakes or what might be "wrong."
3. *Response groups.* Talk about writing content with peers and teacher; review it for meaning.	3. Unusual to talk about writing with any peer.
4. *Revise content.* Response groups may reoccur. Author makes decisions about content changes. May be ongoing for extended period of time.	4. May rewrite ideas once to please teacher.

extended and the scope of instruction expanded to include additional skills teaching, as in Terry Rivera's small-group instruction in usage.

In any event, one factor in organizing the classroom for writing is to schedule specific time for this important activity (Tway, 1984)—and to schedule it regularly, as a whole block of days (Calkins, 1986). The current recommendation is for an ongoing writing workshop rather than for any one-day assigned compositions. *Day 1* of the weekly workshop may encourage prewriting and planning activities; *Day 2* highlights continuation of drafting; *Day 3* includes response groups; *Day 4* continues revision; and *Day 5* features celebrations of children's writing. But any day can include any and all of the process activities as experienced individual children need to engage in them. The activity book, Chapter 8, shows a process wheel that each individual writer can display. Then the teacher can know the part of the writing process each child, pair, or group is currently addressing. Box 8.6 synthesizes much that has been explained in this chapter. The reader can study it carefully and add to or modify it.

Scheduling, record keeping, conferencing, and making materials and space accessible as well as establishing a supportive emotional environment are all a part of organizing the

5. *Edit and proofread.* Done according to purpose and audience, usually late in the process.

5. Edit and proofread all material and do this quite early in the process. This often is the only reason for the rewriting step above.

6. *Prepare for publication or presentation to others.* May or may not be selected as a writing to bring to this point; not all writing need be brought to *publication.*

6. May recopy in ink for neatness, margins.

7. *Assessment.* Ongoing assessment may be from self, peers, and teacher. Author learns how to improve the writing through assessment, and the teacher uses it to plan future instruction. Primarily content but also mechanics will be assessed. Students keep cumulative files. Students consider themselves growing authors.

7. Evaluation will be done by teacher. A letter grade will most likely be assigned the paper. Comments may be written on the paper. The majority of comments highlight what the student did wrong. Comments may or may not be helpful for future writings the student will do. Grammar, spelling, and punctuation areas frequently are circled in red ink throughout the paper.

8. *Celebration.* Writing is celebrated in the classroom with many varied options and choices. Authors discuss or read and comment on their writings with each other.

8. The best (neatest and most correct) writing may occasionally be posted, but rarely will there be celebrations of writing completed where students talk to each other and express how they feel. Usually graded writing is put in trash.

SOURCE: (Adapted from) Frederick County Board of Education (1988). *The Writing Process and Suggested Topics and Activities* (K-6). Frederick, MD.

classroom for writing. Another feature that is increasingly becoming a part of the writing environment is the computer center with its printer and word-processing software. Mentioned in Chapter 9 and explored in depth in Chapter 13, consideration of computers is also highly appropriate here.

Computers in the Classroom Writing Environment

The impact of computers on educational practice appears at all grade levels and in all subject areas as part of the climate. Composing is no exception: Microcomputers have engaged the attention of students, teachers, and researchers. With the availability of microcomputers for classroom instruction, children are able to compose at the computer keyboard with word-processing programs, construct stories with branching programs, and send messages electronically to other child writers.

Current research indicates two areas of the composing process most likely to be affected: invention and revision. **Invention** is that part of the composing process sometimes referred to as *planning:* Invention means coming up with ideas and deciding what to do with them. At this point, most invention programs have been written for and used with older and adult students. According to Rodrigues and Rodrigues (1984), invention programs can (1) help students produce an outline, (2) question students to help them develop a topic, and (3) provide students with open-ended inquiry for idea generation.

The program developed by Rodrigues and Rodrigues uses a creative problem-solving technique, synectics, to stimulate student thinking. Students select a picture from a packet and type in a list of what they see; then the computer asks them to make a connection between each listed item and the topic on which they are writing. Like the morphological synthesis strategy in the earlier section on generating topics, the synectics program forces the student to see things in an unusual way. The intention is to help them break out of rigid thinking. Although data is yet to be reported on the effects this invention software or any other has on the quality of children's writing, it seems likely that most teachers will need to be computer literate in the composition classroom.

The second area computer use is likely to affect is children's **revision** processes. There are programs that help students make editing changes in spelling and mechanics. However, word-processing software also makes larger revisions easier. Text can be moved, inserted, and deleted. Such tasks are much easier with a word processor than a pencil! Children no longer have to mar a page of hard-wrought written discourse.

Although current research is scarce at present, it is logically appealing that children would be more likely to edit and revise their work if they did so on the computer (Daiute, 1984). A series of case studies reported that first graders using a simple word-processing program tended to reread their writing from the previous day as it was loaded on the screen (Phenix & Hanna, 1984). They spent longer periods of time writing, and their transcribing skills improved because it was easy to put spaces between the words.

The relationship, however, between computer use and the *quality* of writing children produce is far from simple. It is likely that the child's knowledge of the keyboard, skill as a collaborative writer, the kinds of word-processing software used, and the way it is integrated into the writing classroom will affect the outcome. Computers are important tools for writing. As teachers and researchers continue to use them in schools, we will increase our understanding of the conditions under which they are most successful. (Chapter 9 discusses the Bank Street Programs and software regarding children's literature; Chapter 13 gives a detailed exploration relevant to the language arts; the activity book, Chapter 8, Section 4, has activities regarding computers.)

ASSESSMENT

Assessment of written composition is touched on in many places in this book. For example, Chapter 7 gave suggestions for assessing written composition integrated with reading, speaking, and listening using informative discourse. Chapter 15 deals with general principles. In this chapter, Box 8.1 offered parameters that could be a checklist for a program, and the section on conferences offered still other ideas. For example, students can reread all of their pieces in their files and rank them, with the best on top.

Measuring growth in children's written composition, however, is a sticky issue. Increased pressures for accountability sometimes result in inappropriate measures and unrealistic expectations. It is important to chart the growth in written language development over time, but generally speaking, severe evaluations of perceived shortcomings in children's writing are not helpful. In the elementary grades, assessment of children's writing needs to be developmental and formative in nature. In the traditional approach, what passed for assessment was red ink. Often assessment has been confused with revising or with grading.

Writing assessment can be exactly that: *writing*. Teacher-assigned language drills or editorial tasks will not adequately represent children's ability to produce coherent discourse. *Holistic* evaluation—that is, marking a student paper on its overall merit—is useful for making comparisons among a group of children or for evaluating the effectiveness of the writing curriculum. However, it gives the teacher little guidance for the individual child's further development. For the beginning classroom teacher, the most immediate use of assessment is instructional: assisting the children and monitoring their progress.

In a landmark study of writing assessment, Diederich (1974) found that people were most likely to be affected by the quality of ideas and organization of the writing. Other factors that influenced assessment were word choice, spelling, punctuation, and "style."

Teachers seeking some kind of guidance in what to look for in children's writing often turn to *scales* or *checklists*. Applying a scale sensitizes the teacher. A scale generally gives guidelines and accompanying examples that teachers can use as a reference in assessing a child's writing. Comparing a child's sample with the examples in scales permits the teacher to make a general assessment. For example, a teacher can judge whether a child is very effective in organizing his or her writing; improved but inconsistent in organization; or poorly organized and sequenced. Scales are frequently divided into subscales that parallel Diederich's (1974) factors, and thus a teacher can assess content and organization separately from word choice and mechanics.

Although it is possible to apply the scale to each child's writing sample, a more practical classroom application of the scale is as a reference for planning further instruction for a single child or a group of children. For example, a teacher who observes that several children have difficulty in organizing their pieces may wish to introduce the use of sequence words such as *first, next,* and *finally.*

In addition to the scales, which can serve as general guidelines, teachers may also use *checklists* to assess a child's writing. Generally, a writing checklist is a list of several skills or details a teacher may want to look for in the piece. If the teacher is assessing stories, the checklist may probably include items such as the following:

A Story Feature Checklist

Is there a title?

Does the story include dialogue?

Do the characters have names?

Does the story take place in a particular time or location?

Do the events connect?

Children who read can apply the checklist themselves to their own pieces, or two friends can use a checklist together to go over one another's writing. Scales and checklists are often very similar. The difference is that scales are generally accompanied by model samples of actual writing by children; checklists are not.

Plans for the assessment of children's writing need to include *variety* (Klein, 1985). Sometimes the overall impact of the child's piece or the child's general level of development may be assessed. At other times, the teacher may want to assess for particular skills, though mechanics are of secondary importance to content. In either case, the most useful practice to adopt is *gathering examples of the child's writing over time.* The samples, which can be an outgrowth of the classroom writing program, are dated and kept in individual folders. At a glance through the folder, the teacher can see documented evidence of a child's progress or lack of it.

To summarize, in assessing the child's growth in composition, teachers will find their efforts more rewarding if they keep the child's level of development in mind, and use errors in the child's writing as information about what to do next for that particular child. In other words, *the elementary teacher assesses writing for instructional purposes.* (Discussion of the National Assessment of Educational Progress (NAEP) is found in Chapters 10 and 15.)

Examples

The following examples give further illustrations for assessment of written composition. They include checklists and analytic scales, and also a scoring guide on effectiveness in problem solution designed by the California Assessment Program (CAP), eighth-grade level. Criteria are given for a one- to six-point scale.

Writing Process Assessment   The first example of writing assessment, Figure 8.13, focuses on the writing process. With an integrated method such as this, examination is not limited to a few isolated aspects. As one can see, it covers major process areas.

Partial Checklist for Analyzing the Classroom Writing Situation   The checklist in Figure 8.14 (p. 300) is another example of informal classroom assessment, this time with respect to the climate for composition. This checklist is useful for checking the larger context in your classroom.

Analytic Scale for Composition Evaluation   Figure 8.15 (p. 301) shows use of analytic analysis of composition. The sample is a third-grade composition rated highly according to a scale devised by the Grosse Point, Michigan, public school system. As you examine the figure, *hunt for successes* in this composition. See how many you can find on your own. Then turn this textbook upside down to see the analytic criteria, 17 points, that the judges felt this composition met.

Problem-Solving Writing Task   The problem-solving writing task incorporates the use of language to solve problems with an analytically scored task. The example in Figure 8.16 (pp. 302–303) is a draft from the California Writing Assessment Project, which also offers teachers a sample composition for each value on the scale.

The next chapter addresses literary use of language, a prime inspirer of children's written composition. It presents that highly motivating resource called upon in all the chapters of this book—Children's Literature.

Integrated Evaluation Checklist

Student _____ Date _____

Prewriting

Can the student identify the specific audience to whom he or she will write?

Does this awareness affect the choices the student makes as he or she writes?

Can the student identify the purpose of the writing activity?

Does the student vary the register according to the purpose?

Does the student write on a topic that grows out of his or her own experience?

Does the student engage in rehearsal activities before writing?

Drafting

Does the student write rough drafts?

Does the student place a greater emphasis on content than on mechanics in the rough drafts?

Revising

Does the student share his or her writing in conferences?

Does the student participate in discussions about classmates' writing?

In revising, does the student make changes to reflect the reactions and comments of both teacher and classmates?

Between first and final drafts, does the student make substantive or only minor changes?

Editing

Does the student proofread his or her own papers?

Does the student help proofread classmates' papers?

Does the student increasingly identify his or her mechanical errors?

Publishing

Does the student publish his or her writing in an appropriate form?

Does the student share this finished writing with an appropriate audience?

Figure 8.13 Writing process assessment. (*Source:* McKenzie & Tompkins, 1984.)

A Partial Checklist for Analyzing the Classroom Writing Situation

A. Quantitative assessment of time and resources available, amount of pupil writing, and types of writing

      1. Time available for pupil writing

          _____ What amount of time is available?

          _____ What amount of this available time does the student actually spend in writing?

          _____ How else does the student spend his or her available time?

      2. Availability of resources

          _____ Do the children have access to a physical environment conducive to writing?

          _____ Where do the children do most of their writing?

          _____ Do the children have access to materials, human reaction and encouragement, enactive opportunities, writer's (or editorial) aids, publishing opportunities?

          _____ Do they avail themselves of these facilities?

          _____ How much writing do the students produce?

          _____ What types of writing do they do?

B. Assessment of attitudes about writing

          _____ Is willing to write

          _____ Occasionally shows a preference for writing

          _____ Seeks out additional writing activity

C. Assessment of motives for writing (consensus of reasons)

          _____ Habit, compulsion, or assigned and required automatic, ritualistic writing (such as name and heading) done without real meaning or awareness; or externally required, such as assigned in school, forms

          _____ Status or prestige among peers or with teacher as model

          _____ Diversion and escape, pleasant feedback, communication and emotion as incentive and as reinforcer

          _____ Self-explanation, to discover what one thinks, self-competency

          _____ Reinforcement and reassurance to affirm one's own values, sense of right or wrong, personal acceptance, or resolution of paradoxes

          _____ Production of a total commitment in the search for truths or literary pleasures

Figure 8.14 Analysis of classroom writing situations. *Note:* This assessment asks *not* how well the child has done, but about what he or she has done and the resources available, the attitudes, and the motivation. (*Source:* Lundsteen, 1976.)

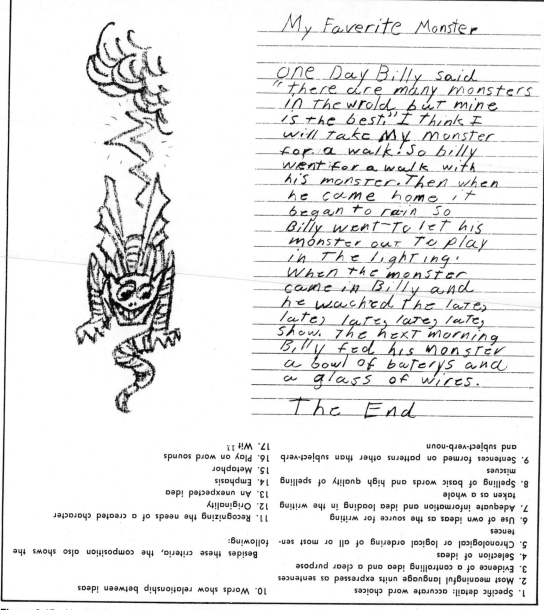

My Faverite Monster

One Day Billy said "there are many monsters in the wrold, but mine is the best." I think I will take My Monster for a walk! So billy went for a walk with his monster. Then when he came home, it began to rain So Billy went To let his monster out To play in The lighting. When the monster came in Billy and he wached the late, late, late, late, late, show. The next morning Billy fed his monster a bowl of buterys and a glass of wires.

The End

Besides these criteria, the composition also shows the following:

1. Specific detail: accurate word choices
2. Most meaningful language units expressed as sentences
3. Evidence of a controlling idea and a clear purpose
4. Selection of ideas
5. Chronological or logical ordering of all or most sentences
6. Use of own ideas as the source for writing
7. Adequate information and idea loading in the writing taken as a whole
8. Spelling of basic words and high quality of spelling miscues
9. Sentences formed on patterns other than subject-verb and subject-verb-noun
10. Words show relationship between ideas
11. Recognizing the needs of a created character
12. Originality
13. An unexpected idea
14. Emphasis
15. Metaphor
16. Play on word sounds
17. Wit

Figure 8.15 Hunting for successes in a third-grade composition, using an analytic scale for composition evaluation. (*Source:* The Grosse Pointe Public School System.)

Rhetorical Effectiveness Scoring Guide
for Problem Solution

Prompts for problem solution require writers to convince specific readers of the seriousness of a problem and the feasibility of a solution (or solutions) for the problem. This requirement makes problem solution essentially argumentative or persuasive. It is a complex type of writing involving potentially several diverse writing strategies—definition, description, anecdote, causes or results, examples, statistics—but its central strategy is argument. Though it is complex and challenging for students in grade 8, it has the great advantage of enabling them to rely on personal experience for content: All of the prompts invite students to propose a solution for a community, school, or personal problem. Because problem solution can rely on personal experience and information, it provides grade 8 students an accessible introduction to serious argumentative writing.

Writers maintain focus by identifying or defining a problem and asserting a solution to it. This identification and assertion provide the twin theses of problem solution essays. The writer's attitude toward the problem and solution, along with the writer's continual awareness of readers' needs, helps maintain focus. Writers organize problem solution essays by presenting the problem coherently, describing the solution clearly, and then shrewdly sequencing reasons for readers to support the solutions. For these reasons to be convincing, writers must support them with careful arguments.

Summary of Score Points
for Problem Solution

Score Point	Criteria
6	**EXCEPTIONAL ACHIEVEMENT** **Readers:** Aware of readers throughout the essay. Makes a genuine attempt to accommodate readers' concerns or objections. **Problem:** Presents problem fully with respect to readers. **Solution:** Offers one or more solutions to problem. At least one solution is fully developed and convincingly argued.
5	**COMMENDABLE ACHIEVEMENT** **Readers:** Reflects readers' concerns but may not have the continual focus on readers of a 6. **Problem:** Deals with the problem with respect to readers. **Solution:** Offers at least one relevant, well-argued solution to the problem.
4	**ADEQUATE ACHIEVEMENT** **Readers:** Readers may be mentioned at beginning but may not be referred to again until conclusion. **Problem:** Will at least briefly discuss the problem. **Solution:** Will offer at least one moderately developed, logical solution. Solutions are relevant to the problem.

Figure 8.16 Problem-solving writing task. (*Source:* California Assessment Program.)

3   SOME EVIDENCE OF ACHIEVEMENT
Readers: Readers may be mentioned but seldom accommodated.
Problem: Identifies a problem.
Solution: Offers at least one relevant solution. A solution may be minimally developed, or writer may list solutions without developing any. Weak argument. May seem perfunctory, flat, hurried.

2   LITTLE EVIDENCE OF ACHIEVEMENT
Readers: May not address readers, but will seem appropriate for designated readers.
Problem: Only mentions or implies a problem.
Solution: Only lists solutions without developing any. Solution will seem relevant to problem. Little or no argument.

1   MINIMAL EVIDENCE OF ACHIEVEMENT
On topic
Readers: Little or no sense of readers.
Problem: Problem may be difficult to identify.
Solution: May not offer a solution. Solutions offered may not seem relevant to problem. Solutions not developed. Brief. May be illogical or incoherent.
Reminder: Unusual papers that develop a topic in unexpected ways should be referred to the table leader.

Figure 8.16 *(Continued)*

SUMMARY

Teachers of written composition need an understanding of the composing process; children's developmental characteristics; the goals and types of written discourse; modeling, strategies, stimulation, and motivation; the classroom environment, including new technology; and assessment. Much of the activity in the classroom is related optimally to creative problem solving.

The ways we select to teach children in the writing classroom are affected by our understanding of child authors. If we are knowledgeable about the nature of the composing process, the characteristics and needs of our students, and instructional strategies that are informed by research, we are better equipped to manage student learning and integrate emerging technologies into the composing classroom.

In recent years there has been a *change in the way we look at composing.* The stereotype of the grim teacher joylessly supervising silent children printing neat lines of adultlike text on a page has given way to the idea that composing is a lively activity for both teacher and child.

Children are capable communicators. They can devise messages of their own for an audience of their choosing. Teachers are active models, advisers, collaborators, and advocates for child writers. Writing in the elementary schools is not limited to neat transcribing of "canned" holiday stories, one to a child. Children write many kinds of messages, much earlier than we often suppose, and frequently with an interacting partner. Composing includes the following examples: A very young writer dictating to the teacher, a group collaboration on a poem, third-grade writers coauthoring a report, and a first grader using a word processor. In all these examples children learn to compose while their teachers organize the resources, secure the time, teach, and encourage the child writers in the classroom.

CHAPTER 9

Children's Literature in the Language Arts

by Eileen Tway

"There is no frigate like a book to take us lands away.
Nor any coursers like a page of prancing poetry."

Emily Dickinson

INTRODUCTION

Children's literature is a very special kind of communication: It is reading at its best, writing at its finest, and a transaction between reader and writer. In constructing meaning from literature, children are exposed to creative problem solving that will lead to a command of the language. Children's literature belongs at the heart of the language arts program. It provides almost unlimited resources for reading, writing, oral response, language models, coping strategies that can lead to understanding both self and others, and language enjoyment.

Earlier chapters in this book have concentrated on self-expressive and expository uses of language. This one stresses *literary* use. This chapter will show theory, research, and practical classroom examples of how literature is central to the language arts and integrates all areas of study. The following opening scene previews many ideas related to the centrality of children's literature.

OPENING SCENE: Talking and Writing About *Call It Courage*

It is discussion time in the third-grade language arts classroom in Kenwood School. The building is an old one; the classroom has the original black chalkboard and dark wood paneling, but it is made bright by the children's work and the open-weave orange drapes at the windows. The desks are individual, flat-top wooden tables that can be arranged to make bigger tables for work groups; but now they are in a semicircle for story time and discussion.

The teacher, Ms. Tolle, has just finished reading aloud the ending to the story *Call It Courage,* by Armstrong Sperry. The teacher and the class are sharing their reflections and feelings about the story. It is about a boy of long ago and far away, but it is a new story to the children, one that reaches across time, space, and age levels in its universal appeal. It deals with cowardice and courage, and the struggle to survive. Upon request, the teacher rereads a dramatic passage from near the end of the story. The main character, Mafatu, is trying to reach home but is adrift in his canoe with his dog, Uri. Followed by sharks, he calls out to the sea in a voice thick and hoarse with rage.

"Moana, you Sea God! You destroyed my mother. Always you have tried to destroy me. Fear of you has haunted my sleep. Fear of you turned my people against me. But now I no longer fear you, Sea!" His voice rose to a wild note. He sprang to his feet, flung back his head, spread wide his arms in defiance. "Do you hear me, Moana? I am not afraid of you! Destroy me—but I laugh at you. Do you hear? *I laugh!*"

His voice, cracked but triumphant, shattered the dead air. He sank back on his haunches, shaking with spasms of ragged laughter. It racked his body, left him spent and gasping on the floor of the canoe. Uri, whimpering softly, crept to his master's side."

The principal, Mr. Newsome, who has come by, joins the discussion because *Call It Courage* is one of his favorite books.

"But wasn't it a fine moment when Mafatu comes home again, wearing his hero trophies?" Mr. Newsome comments about the ending.

"What happened to Mafatu when he fell at his father's feet?" Mary asks.

"I hope he died," Fred says quickly.

Ms. Tolle reacts in surprise, "Fred, didn't you like Mafatu?"

"Oh, I liked him okay, but I get tired of always being able to predict what's going to happen. Just once I'd like for the hero to die."

"I like it better when I can predict," Josh announces. "It gives me a good feeling to be able to figure things out."

"Could we write a story of what we think happened after Mafatu got home—a kind of like a sequel, maybe?" Sara wonders.

"That's a good idea. Some of you may want to work on that during your work-study period," Ms. Tolle says.

"I'd like to do a review of the book for *Book Notes,*" Fred offers.

"Good, and I'll critique your review," someone else volunteers.

After a few more minutes of talk about *Call It Courage,* the children arrange their desks into bigger tables for their work-study period, a block of time in each school day for the children to use as they choose or need. This time is carefully preserved and cherished because it allows for ongoing projects or for self-selection of work in areas of most interest or need.

As today's work-study period gets under way, Fred consults with the student editors of *Book Notes,* the class book review magazine, about his plans for the review of *Call It Courage.* Sara, who earlier had done a review of *The Hundred Dresses,* by Eleanor Estes, tells Fred that her book's ending was not predictable, but more like real life. One of the editors adds that Katherine Paterson's *Bridge to Terabithia* has one of the main characters die. "You ought to read that, Fred."

Mary and Sara start to collaborate on a sequel to *Call It Courage.* Richard asks Ms. Tolle if she knows another book as good as *Call It Courage.* She suggests a book with a much later copyright date, *The Summer I Was Lost* (also called *Terror on the Mountain*). Soon the class is humming with literature-related activities: reading, writing, working on the book review magazine, and so on.

Analysis of the Scene

In this classroom, the arts of language—listening, speaking, reading, and writing—are being practiced in real situations with content that is appropriate and interesting to children: children's literature. The situations are real because both children and adults can relate to the human problems presented in a story, and they are listening, discussing, writing, and reading because they care about the problems and solutions. Language arts activities grow naturally from involvement with literature. This chapter will discuss *what* children's literature is, *why* it is so important as content in the language arts program, and *how* the teacher can integrate its use to the benefit of all in the language arts.

WHAT IS CHILDREN'S LITERATURE?

> "A child's book is a book a child is reading."
>
> *Charlotte Huck*

Literature gives us a verbal expression of human imagination and a primary means for cultural transmission. But what can it mean in particular for your students?

Literature for Children

Literature as a form of communication is a major resource in a language arts program. "Literature—appearing in oral, written, and enacted forms—communicates feelings, interpretations, and visions of human life" (Lundsteen, 1976). Its written form, especially, gives the kind of permanence that permits contemplation of its language, invites returning to it again and again, and serves as a ready model for language use at its best. Literature for children is any literature that appeals to the young reader. Children have always usurped stories, short or long, that they liked, and made them their own, no matter the first intended audience. Consider *Robinson Crusoe, Grimms' Tales,* or *Love Story.* Today's books designated as children's books often deal with mature, sophisticated issues, and the line continues to be blurred between adult and children's literature, even though there is now a distinct body of literature for children.

Children deserve the same fine writing in their literature as that found in any other kind of literature. Walter de la Mare (1960) once said that only the rarest kind of best is good enough for children. Certainly, literature for children should not differ in quality from literature for adults. Such an understanding of children's literature is important in selecting books for the language arts classroom. However, both adults and children sometimes read material of only moderate quality and find something in the content that reaches them, makes them think, or has a powerful influence on their lives. When a marginal book sparks such a response, it is a case of quality of content, if not style, for the individual reader. This kind of quality will also be a consideration in balanced book selection for the classroom.

Differences in kind of topic or content rather than differences in quality, however, are what distinguish children's from adult literature: "The content of children's literature is limited by the experience and understanding of *who* children are" (Huck, 1979). A bright 7-year-old who could understand vocabulary far beyond her years was frustrated when a story she heard ended with a play on words. It was a simple story from oral folklore about three little rabbits, Fut, Fut-Fut, and Fut-Fut-Fut. Fut went out to explore and was never heard from again. The other two thought something had happened to Fut, but Fut-Fut finally got brave and decided to go out to explore, too. Fut-Fut-Fut cried out, "Oh, please don't go. We already have one Fut in the grave." The child did not understand the pun, for she had never heard the expression "one foot in the grave." For her, the story was ruined. It did not end properly, and she said, "I do not like stories without periods." No matter how fine or challenging, or even simple and concise, children's literature must appeal to the interests and experience of its audience.

Literature for children, especially *fiction,* is largely about children and their lives, adventures, problems, and solutions. Sometimes, in fact often, animals are the main characters, and in fantasy stories, these animals are personified to give them human characteristics so that in these stories, too, youngsters are reading about human concerns. A look at recent award-winning books will show stories of *childhood concerns.* For example, Beverly Cleary's *Ramona Quimby, Age 8* (Newbery Honor Book, 1983) is about a little girl whose problems are delightfully recognizable to almost any reader. *Dicey's Song,* by Cynthia Voigt (Newbery Award Book, 1983) is about adventure and hardship for children struggling on their own. In the realm of fantasy, animals deal with solving some very humanlike problems in books like William Steig's *Doctor De Soto* (Newbery Honor Book, 1983) in which a mouse dentist outwits a scheming villain-customer, and Grimms' *The Bremen Town Musicians* (Parents' Choice Award, 1980), the classic story in which animal musicians work together to survive.

In *informational books,* animals are again popular, with stories about animals in their natural habitats, animal habits, and animal families all holding great interest for young children. Other topics that appeal are machines; how things work; curiosities or little-known facts about history; children in other lands; lives of famous people, such as sports or television figures; and curiosities of the natural world. Currently, there is a wealth of interesting and clearly written informational books available for children. Again, recent award-winning books provide examples: Jean Fritz's *Homesick: My Own Story* (Newbery Honor Book, 1983), an autobiography of a well-loved author of children's books, and *Truck,* by Donald Crews (Caldecott Honor Book, 1981). This is a beautifully illustrated picture book about a truck for young readers. (Recall additional ideas on informational books from Chapter 7. Other ideas can be found in the corresponding chapter of the activity book.)

Poetry is taking its rightful place as a substantial body of literature for children, especially since the National Council of Teachers of English (NCTE) created a national poetry award in 1977 to honor a living poet for excellence in poetry for children. Since then the works of winning poets have had the award seal affixed to their covers, calling attention to the importance of poetry in the lives of children. Poetry is the essence of *problem solving* in language, with its precise use of language and rhythms to convey feeling. The fact that poetry can be about any topic or experience in life makes it as universal as any other kind of literature in its appeal. Teachers need only to share some of the recent works of award-winning poets to assure children of this appeal. For example, Karla Kuskin's *Dogs and Dragons, Trees and Dreams* (1980) and Myra Cohn Livingston's *O Sliver of Liver* (1979) contain a variety of poems about daily life, human relationships, and emotions.

The elements of daily concerns, feelings, curiosities, and the like make literature prime content for the language arts curriculum. First, it is the stuff of good reading, the kind of reading that children want to read. Wendell Johnson (1962) has said that one cannot read reading, one has to read something. In the case of children, that something is literature about other children; the natural world; adventures, both real and fantastic; and coping or problem solving. Next, literature provides excellent material for springing into all kinds of oral language, from discussion to dramatics. Finally, and just as important as the other points, literature provides both model and springboard for written language experience, whether the writer attempts to write a critique or to write in a new way based on something noted in reading literature.

Good Children's Literature

As mentioned, the benefits of literature in children's lives are many. First of all comes enjoyment: Literature entertains, informs, and satisfies. Good literature in the language arts program provides children a model of beautiful or interesting language, stretches their imagination, and extends their experience. A good book for a child is one in which the child lives for awhile and finds meaning for his or her own life. Rebecca Lukens (1983) writes that by placing the relevant episodes into coherent sequence, literature gives order and form to experience, and shows life's unity or meaning.

To put order and form into experience, however, literature must have *quality* of order and form itself. In fiction, quality means that *characters* are well developed, that *plot* is skillfully structured, and that the *setting* puts the reader into the story through well-chosen details and appeals to senses, as in the book used in the opening scene. In factual writing, quality means that facts are accurate, that the material is interesting and well organized, and that the author writes with an authentic voice.

Beyond quality of presentation and style, other criteria to look for in books to use with children include those that have to do with the appropriateness and fairness, or honesty, of content. In editing the booklist *Reading Ladders for Human Relations* (Tway, 1981), a National Council of Teachers of English committee used the criteria listed in Box 9.1 on page 310 to select books that would promote understanding.

In seeking books of quality, teachers have many selection aids available, including human resources. Librarians are excellent sources of recommendations, especially for the latest in good books. Librarians read widely to keep up with current literature. Sometimes librarians and teachers form local reading roundtable groups to share book talks and exchange ideas. The Chicago Children's Reading Roundtable, for example, includes authors, teachers, librarians, and professors of children's literature in its roster of membership.

If a college or university is nearby and offers conferences on children's literature, teachers can often find programs or exhibits about children's books to attend. Or if a professional organization, such as the International Reading Association, has a conference in the area, exhibits of recent books and materials are usually presented. These resources in the community, including libraries and their children's librarians, are among the most important and useful aids to book selection.

Other aids are found in professional journals. *Language Arts,* the elementary journal of the National Council of Teachers of English, regularly contains a book review column. *The Reading Teacher,* the elementary journal of the International Reading Association, also carries book reviews. A magazine devoted mainly to children's book reviews is *The Horn Book.* For classroom-tested ideas, *The Web,* a magazine put out by The Ohio State University College of Education, offers reviews of books that have been used successfully throughout the curriculum.

Another resource for book selection is the booklist, an annotated bibliography of books reviewed by professional people who are knowledgeable about children's books. The National Council of Teachers of English publishes periodically a general elementary booklist, *Adventuring with Books.* Other booklists published by NCTE include *Reading Ladders,* mentioned above, and *Your Reading,* a booklist for junior high and middle school students. An example of a specialized booklist is *UNESCO's Bibliography of Books for Handicapped Children.* (See also the activity book, especially the lists in Chapter 14.)

Professional books about children's literature also contain lists of selected books for various purposes. Nancy Larrick's *A Parent's Guide to Children's Reading* (1975) is one of

---

BOX 9.1 Book Selection Criteria

1. Books that contain the essentials of all good literature; for fiction, well-developed plot, characterization, setting, theme, and style; for nonfiction, clear, logical writing and accurate information; for poetry, lyrical beauty of language or poetic statement of truth.

2. Books that are positive and fair in their presentation of all people, both in text and illustration, and that belittle no people either through condescension, deprecatory statements, or ridicule.

3. Books that are natural and convincing instead of those that are contrived and suggest superficial treatment in solving the difficult problems human beings face.

4. Books in which the illustrations supplement the text in adding content or contributing to the mood.

5. Books that prevent the carrying forward of old prejudices and stereotypes into the new generation.

6. Books that recognize minority groups' participation in and contribution to the history and culture of our country.

7. Books that can help each reader to a realization of identity, an appreciation of individuality, and a respect for heritage.

8. Books that contain subject matter appropriate to the age levels given.

9. Books that show women in active, interesting roles rather than stereotypic ones; books that avoid sex role stereotyping in general.

10. Books that contain an honest and authentic portrayal of the human condition, including different stages in the life cycle, different life-styles, and life in different cultures.

---

the best for both parents and teachers. For teachers of preschool youngsters or teachers who want to work with parents, *Raising Readers,* edited by Linda Lamme (1980), is one of the most helpful sources of book ideas. To choose books to read aloud, Jim Trelease's *The Read-Aloud Handbook* (1982) is an excellent reference to use. Finally, a general textbook on children's literature, such as Bernice Cullinan's *Literature and the Child* (1981), can help with understanding what makes a book "good."

It is the teacher's challenge to find the best possible selection of books for the classroom, one that calls for creative problem solving. All of the aids to selection discussed above—human resources such as the neighborhood librarian, book review magazines, book exhibits, and professional reference books—will help the teacher meet the challenge. Finally, simply by reading children's literature, especially the titles mentioned in this chapter, the reader will get a feel for what is fresh and original compared to what is trite and boring.

Value of Children's Literature in the Language Arts Class

Why include literature in the language arts? Literature is important in its own right as literary art to be appreciated and enjoyed. It is also "one of the greatest sources of nourishment for developing minds and imaginations," according to Glenna Davis Sloan (1984). As a child reads a good book, that child is able to enter into the pages, to step into another role, another person's thoughts, another time, another place. Literature in its broadest sense is the *what* of reading and is a vital part of a balanced reading program. The *how* of reading will not suffice. Children who are involved in reading something interesting or important to their lives will learn to read, not just how to read.

Oral Language Development   Reading a variety of books will *extend and enrich vocabulary* and broaden units of discourse. Children find challenging new words to add to their speaking and reading vocabularies. In reading Konigsburg's *Father's Arcane Daughter,* for example, a child will discover what *arcane* means and usually find it an interesting word to possess. Most books are bound to offer new words to add to a reader's vocabulary. The more a child reads, the more the vocabulary grows.

Many books offer *plays on words* or other kinds of fun with words. Peggy Parish's *Amelia Bedelia* stories have delighted children for a number of years with the humor of taking common expressions too literally. When Amelia Bedelia is asked to draw the drapes, she draws a picture of them, a misunderstanding that amuses young readers and is typical of the language fun of all the books in the series.

Books of puns, tongue twisters, funny homonyms, word histories, language bloopers, and the like are readily available today. Books for children of the 1980s include *Wally the Wordworm* (Fadiman, 1983), *How to Make an Elephant Float* (Hopkins, 1983), *Ohm on the Range* (Keller, 1982), and *Words with Wrinkled Knees* (Esbensen, 1986). Our language provides almost unlimited opportunities for playful exploration with words, and literature for children includes books to spur this kind of exploration.

The rhythm and rhyme of a book like *Jamberry* (Degen, 1983) provide examples for children to experiment with in their own language use. When a bear and a child pick berries together, the rhyme scheme includes the words *finger and pawberry* to rhyme with the kind of berry being picked. *Jamberry* is full of clever word usage. For older children, the beautiful language and vivid imagery of Natalie Babbitt's *Tuck Everlasting* provide a model of excellence. "Blank white dawns and sunsets smeared with too much color" puts the reader right into an August setting (Babbitt, 1975).

As children read or listen to a book like *Jamberry* or *Tuck Everlasting,* they often want to respond orally. To *Jamberry,* they can respond by joining in the chanting or creating their own funny rhymes. To *Tuck Everlasting,* they can respond with questions or discussion comments. *Tuck* is about a fountain of youth and the awesome possibilities it presents for life everlasting. The problems and pitfalls of living forever are presented. Provocative discussion of what each person would choose, to drink of the fountain or not, grows out of this book. Here is an example of a book that stimulates oral *problem solving*—discussing and attempting to resolve the issues involved.

In addition to listening and discussing, oral activities motivated by literature include acting out or role-playing favorite stories or parts of books, using the tape recorder to experiment with oral expression, and giving informal book talks to let others know about exciting discoveries. Informal talking with classmates or the teacher about books is another worthwhile oral response to literature. Book conferences between student and teacher can be satisfying and can help a teacher monitor student progress.

Written Language Development   As children compose oral responses to literature, they are developing the fluency in composition that will help them in their *written responses* to literature. *Reporting* about books in writing will follow the same protocol and purposes as reporting orally. Written reports about books may be somewhat more formal and organized than spontaneous talks about books, but they serve the same purpose: to entice the reader, to interest someone in the book, to share concerns about the book, or to convey insights and emotions gained from the reading experience.

Reports are only one kind of written response to literature. Children can respond imaginatively by creating their own stories, poems, plays, or whatever kind of literature evolves from a stimulating experience with someone else's writing. Commercially available books of other children's writings, such as Nancy Larrick's *I Heard a Scream in the Street,* also invite children to try their own writing.

Writing letters to authors is one of the best motivational activities for both writing and reading in the elementary classroom. Most current authors of children's books respond to personal mail (but not to letters copied by an entire class) by post card, letter, or flyer put out by the publisher. Sometimes authors send pictures or other promotional material. Beverly Cleary's *Dear Mr. Henshaw* (Figure 9.1) is a fictional example of a boy who learned more about himself and about writing through his letters to a favorite author. While a correspondence does not usually develop, the one-time answer to a letter is a special event that can spark further interest in reading the author's works.

Beyond reporting, composing stories or poems, and letter writing, students can write personal responses in the form of critical reviews of books to share in class, in school newspapers, or on bulletin boards. As an example of good writing, literature provides all kinds of stimuli for the written language arts. Literature contributes to writing by providing

Figure 9.1 The cover of *Dear Mr. Henshaw,* by Beverly Cleary.

insights into the way stories and exposition are structured so that future writing is improved. For example, a child can note the way a writer in his or her selected book is getting the reader involved and eager to read on.

To sum up, literature, by enabling the child to lead many lives vicariously, becomes a vehicle for the playful exploration of words and ideas, for stimulating the imagination, and for the serious examination of the human condition. The books to promote these communicational pursuits belong in a language arts classroom. Fortunately, such books are easily available at libraries, where many books may be loaned to a teacher at one time. At the same time, teachers can work with school libraries to build up the collection there.

HOW CHILDREN'S LITERATURE FITS INTO THE CURRICULUM

"No resource for teaching the language arts . . . can compare with a collection
of excellent library books"

Betty Coody and David Nelson

Using Children's Literature in the Language Arts Classroom

This section offers literature-related activities for each of the language arts at three levels: preprimary, primary, and postprimary. Many examples suggest how literature can contribute to language arts curriculum. The reader is urged to secure copies of the suggested books to share and analyze with colleagues, and to try out in the classroom for language arts enhancement among varied age groupings.

The reader will find ample suggestions for starting a *personal card file of children's books* that can enhance each language art, and will find that some books remain fresh and useful at almost any age level and for any language art year after year.

Literature and *Speaking* Activities: *Preprimary* In the home, in the nursery school, and in the kindergarten, literature is one of the finest resources for extending language experience. As the parent or teacher reads to children from the best that children's literature has to offer, vocabulary is enriched, concepts are developed, and universal human concerns are shared. In turn, children try out the new words in their speaking or story telling, talk about new concepts as they respond to what they are hearing, and act out their feelings or concerns through role-playing, skits, and other forms of dramatization. Cullinan and others (1974) found that children who are read to and who are encouraged to respond to what they hear do better in later language learning in school than children who do not have such experiences.

For vocabulary development at this age level, any good book will serve. *A, B, C Say with Me,* by Karen Gundersheimer, is an example of an appropriate book for this purpose. It is a tiny alphabet book, just right for small hands to hold for further enjoyment after an adult has shared the book. Its brightly colored pictures are about everyday objects, but the captions are all verbs, wonderful action words to invite child response. A tiny person is shown acting out the words for each picture. For *N* and *Nuts,* the little person is shown *nibbling.*

For concept development, picture books with everyday objects and captions are good to use. Janet Wolf's *Her Book* is about the simple, everyday pleasures and experiences of a very little girl. For older preschoolers and beginning primaries, a book such as Tana

Hoban's *Push-Pull, Empty-Full,* with its black-and-white photographs illustrating opposites in a simple but effective way, aids language and concept development.

John Burningham's *The Baby* is the ultimate in simplicity, but it gets to the heart of a very real concern for preschoolers: the advent of a new baby in their home. Burningham has two masterful lines in his book. After telling about everyday things such as baby carriage rides and the baby's bath, the older child says, "Sometimes I like the baby. Sometimes I don't." These lines about mixed feelings will reassure children who also may have mixed feelings about younger siblings. Children may want to talk about their own feelings or act out similar situations. When children are reassured or learn how others adjust to problems through stories, it is a form of *problem solving* for them. Their problems and concerns may not loom so large when they see them in perspective and can talk about them.

Literature and *Speaking* Activities: *Primary*   Oral language development, continuing to grow at a rapid pace in the primary grades, provides the background, reinforcement, and support for strong, written language experiences. The same kinds of activities that were helpful in the preschool years continue to be important: activities that promote vocabulary development, concept development, and oral response.

A sense of story is basic to successful experiences in *storytelling,* listening to stories, writing, and reading. The opportunity to retell stories helps develop this sense and is a natural way for children to internalize the structure of a story. John S. Mayher and his coauthors (1983) say that a sense of story helps children with understanding, order, and the ability to look ahead in a story. Such understandings and abilities are essential in the language arts. (Recall information from Chapter 2 regarding children's development of story structure.)

After hearing the traditional tale of "Goldilocks and the Three Bears," children will enjoy comparing and contrasting the story with Brinton Turkle's *Deep in the Forest,* in which the roles of bears and people are switched and a little bear invades a "people's house." Possible activities include retelling the traditional tale and telling a story to go with the pictures in Turkle's wordless book. Either story could be dramatized. Another possibility is puppetry. Commercial puppets or puppets made by children inspire much oral activity. Even shy or speech-handicapped children relax and do very well when the puppet does their talking for them.

Other wordless books that will promote oral telling, retelling, discussing, or acting out include *Look What I Can Do,* by José Aruego; *Paddy Goes Traveling,* by John S. Goodall; *Frog Goes to Dinner,* by Mercer Mayer; *Noah's Ark,* by Peter Spier; *The Other Bone,* by Ed Young; and *Up a Tree,* also by Ed Young.

Picture books such as *When the Sky Is Like Lace,* by Elinor Lander Horwitz, or Crescent Dragonwagon's *Will It Be Okay?* deal beautifully with feelings in both language and pictures. Barbara Cooney illustrates with dreamlike pictures the story of a bimulous night in *When the Sky Is Like Lace.* Children have an intriguing *coined* word, *bimulous,* to discuss and describe after hearing this book read aloud. Ben Shecter's pictures show sensitively a parent's reassurances to a child in *Will It Be Okay?*

Picture books are especially useful for promoting oral response, since they are short and easily read in one class period, with time left over for discussion, acting out, or whatever. Any book, however, can provoke enlightening discussion or drama. Productive occasions of response to literature are those that come spontaneously after a child has read a moving book.

Literature and *Speaking* Activities: *Postprimary/Middle School*   Provision for oral language activities is still important in the upper grades, though much time and effort will be going into written work. Oral language development and written language development are complementary and reciprocal processes according to recent research (Tierney & Pearson, 1983). Students will do better with written communication skills as they continue to improve their oral skills. Children's literature as written communication has an impressive influence on speaking. As in earlier years, literature continues in the upper grades to be a source for new vocabulary, it gives topics for discussion, and its sharing leads to important reporting skills. As mentioned, children's literature currently abounds with books about words themselves, with books that are provocative in topic and beg to be discussed, and with books that children want to recommend to others.

Ann E. Weiss's *What's That You Said? How Words Change* is an easy Let-Me-Read book that will help late primary and early intermediate students understand the history of some common words and expressions and show how words change. *In a Pickle and Other Funny Idioms,* by Marvin Terban, is a picture book with explanations of familiar idioms. These expressions will find their way into children's language and may become topics for discussion at home or at school. *The Celery Stalks at Midnight,* by James Howe, an animal story, is hilarious with plays on words that late primary and intermediate-age schoolchildren will enjoy.

For older students, *Tom's Midnight Garden,* by Philippa Pearce, is illustrative of a book that will last in its readers' hearts and minds long after the reading is finished. Well crafted from the standpoint of *plot,* it is the kind of book to mull over and to recommend to friends. The hero, Tom, lonely and inactive as a guest of his unremarkable aunt and uncle, finds adventure in a midnight world that exists in another time. The skillful interweaving of episodes from that other time with Tom's present life makes this book one to remember and one that will make a provocative subject for a book talk. Rush to the library for a copy!

For adolescents, a contemporary book, Toecky Jones's *Skindeep,* will provoke thoughtful discussion about the problems today in South Africa. It is a love story, a political story, and a story of racial problems. Students will find a number of very real *problems* to address and this will stimulate discussion of possible solutions.

> "The tiniest sound in the whole world is the sound of smoke drifting out of chimneys on a snowy night, the grey ghostlike figure vanishing into the vacuum of space. Could there be a tinier sound?"
>
> *Elizabeth H. Meehan*

Literature and *Listening* Activities: *Preprimary*   The preschool years are a wonderful time for listening to the magic found in books: the mesmerizing stories; the sometimes playful, sometimes awesome sounds of words; the rhythms of language. For the baby or toddler, almost any rhythmic language holds fascination, but books exist that are especially appropriate for preschool children at different ages and stages. For the youngest, a book such as Beatrice Schenk de Regniers's *Going for a Walk* offers the sights and sounds of the experience of a walk in the country. The sounds of the different creatures met on the walk are given: birds cheep, dogs go bow-wow, and so on. For most small children, an everyday experience like falling asleep is a happening at which to marvel. *Tonight's the Night,* by Jim Aylesworth, is the story of a little boy who wants to stay awake long enough to find out what it feels like to fall asleep. What he finds or learns instead is what the night sounds are like around his house: footsteps on the stairs, the ticking of his clock, and so on. Listening to this book can encourage children to be more aware of the sounds in their own environment.

Hippo Thunder, by Susan Sussman, is about listening to thunder and counting off the time between lightning and the resulting thunder by saying, "one hippopotamus, two hippopotamus," and so on. It is a wonderful counting book for listening, saying, and learning. Books of poetry are also important to the listening life of young children. Here, the rhythms and joys of language are quite apparent. A good example is Lee Bennett Hopkins's collection of poems in *Morning, Noon, and Nighttime, Too,* which takes the listener through a day of amazing and amusing sounds.

Literature and *Listening* Activities: *Primary*   There are many books for primary school children that focus on listening itself. *Nobody Listens to Andrew,* by Elizabeth Guilfoile, has been a favorite with children for over two decades. Children who sometimes feel lost in large families or large classrooms can relate to Andrew's predicament, in which busy people pay no attention to him, even when he says there is a bear in his bedroom. The story is done sensitively and with gentle humor, and perhaps its message about listening to others is more for adults than for children. Yet Andrew is beloved by children who understand his problem. Benjamin Elkin's *The Loudest Noise in the World* points up, in a delightfully fantastic way, the need to be quiet once in a while and to listen to the sounds of nature.

Long-time favorite Dr. Seuss's *Horton Hears a Who* shows the importance of listening to others, no matter how small or seemingly insignificant they are. This book stands as a good story in its own right, of course, but there is an element of listening that will not be missed by children. The story of Horton is just one example of many. The choices of books to read to a class for listening enjoyment are almost legion. Asking children to listen for certain things before reading a story to them will help them direct their listening better.

Literature and *Listening* Activities: *Postprimary/Middle School*   It is never too late nor are children ever too old for reading aloud in the classroom. Even picture books have their place in the upper grades. They are short, often great fun, and can provoke critical thinking on a sophisticated level. Moreover, the kinds of critical listening skills that are developed in this way carry over into critical reading: grasping the main idea, recognizing the supporting details, identifying the language of persuasion, and so on.

Good read-aloud books for rich listening experiences include the following. *The Search for Delicious,* by Natalie Babbitt, is a fantasy based on word play and represents the English language at its rollicking best. In *The Twenty-One Balloons,* by William Pene du Bois, a retired teacher attempts to sail by balloon across the Pacific in 1883. Sophisticated language, delightful humor, and adventure make a fine listening experience. In *Where the Red Fern Grows,* by Wilson Rawls, the love of a boy for his hound dogs and their story as they hunt together give the listener an emotional experience and a new appreciation for the close relationship between an owner and good hunting dogs. Robert C. O'Brien's *Mrs. Frisby and the Rats of NIMH,* a science fiction story in which laboratory rats become superintelligent, is a fascinating tale of growing intelligence and suspense. *The Enormous Egg,* by Oliver Butterworth, is a rare story in which a boy cares for an oversized egg on his parents' farm, only to discover that the egg does not contain a chicken at all. It is a prehistoric triceratops. This is a fast-paced story of what happens when a dinosaur is found in the mid-twentieth century. The attempts by many people and agencies to exploit the boy and his "pet" make good material for honing critical listening skills. For humorous listening, *The 18th Emergency,* by Betsy Byars, has few peers. Even though its subject is one of fear of a bully and reaches close to the lives of many children, Betsy Byars has a way of helping us laugh at ourselves and the absurdities of life. Shel Silverstein's *Where the Sidewalk Ends*, a book of poetry meant for sharing aloud, will encourage students of any age to listen to poetry and more poetry. *Amy's Eyes*, by Richard Kennedy, a remarkable fantasy, and *My Life in the 7th Grade*, by Mark Geller, a humorous first-person account of seventh-grade problems and predicaments, are two books for older adolescents in middle school.

Books, stories, or excerpts from them can be taped for another kind of listening experience. Taping can solve the problem of a less than skillful reader who wants to know a story that more avid readers in the class are discussing. A student can listen to the tape at his or her convenience for still a different literature experience. These stories or parts of stories can be taped by teachers, aides, student volunteers, parents, or interested community members. A file of such tapes is a fine addition to the listening center of the classroom. (Also see the categorized list of children's books with a listening theme found in the references for Chapter 3 at the end of this book.)

> Children learn to read by reading "books that will become tattered and grimy from use . . . that will make them weep . . . that will rack them with hearty laughter . . . that give them gooseflesh and glimpses of glory."
>
> *Robert Lawson*

Literature and *Reading* Activities: *Preprimary*   Reading books to children is one of the best ways to interest them in reading books for themselves. Children who are read to often pick up a book and point out words they recognize, or pretend to read by reciting the story of the book as they remember it. Some books have only a few words and big, bold manuscript letters that make it easy for the young child to identify words on the page. As parents, grandparents, babysitters, or preschool teachers read to preschool children, they are sharing more than the book's content; they are using a book to communicate their enjoyment of books, their respect for books, the way in which they should be handled, and the conventions of reading our language, such as left-to-right progression and reading from top to bottom.

A simple book for early "readers" and one that has few words and big print is John Stadler's *Hooray for Snail!* Preschoolers who want lots of action will like this baseball story. Besides story books, there are picture books with captions that belong in every young child's experience. Perhaps the most popular of these books with captions is the alphabet book. Most ABC books have the potential to aid young readers because they bring greater familiarity with the letters of the alphabet in an enjoyable way. An ABC book that is especially suited for the almost-reader is *ABC Cat*, by Nancy Jewell. Alphabet books offer more than just experience with letters. The rhymes and alliteration of this book and others help children with predicting and comprehending. (See related sections in the activity book.)

Just-Beginning-to-Read books (Follett) and Early I-Can-Read books (Harper & Row) are interesting for preschoolers as well as for beginning primary school children. *Little Chick's Breakfast*, by Mary DeBall Kwitz, is an Early I-Can-Read book designed to get young children interested in reading on their own. Such easy books with few words enable children to have successful reading experiences to build on as they continue to grow in understanding and ability.

Literature and *Reading* Activities: *Primary*   A wealth of literature exists today to entice the primary school child into reading. From bright, new versions of familiar nursery tales to cumulative tales with predictable repetition, and from easy-to-read books on all kinds of subjects to more substantial books with content that appeals to young readers, primary libraries can be full of books that enable young children to read.

Cumulative tales such as Audrey Wood's beautifully illustrated *The Napping House*, with its repetition and predictability, help children know what's coming and thus help them read whole books early on. A simple nursery rhyme retold in a special picture book, such as *The Key to the Kingdom*, by Betsy and Guilio Maestro, is also predictable and easy to read for beginners.

Some books, like *Signs*, by Ron and Nancy Goor, illustrate the *reading that is all around us* in the form of signs, reading that adults may take for granted. The Goors use photographs of actual signs and brief, simple explanations to show how prominent this kind of reading is in our lives. Many easy-to-read books, *Signs* included, are interesting and inviting in spite of limited vocabulary. Some are even award winners for their content and use of language. (See *Frog and Toad Together*, by Arnold Lobel, for example.)

From I-Can-Read books about *Little Bear* by Else Holmelund Minarik in the 1950s, to Let's-Read-and-Find-Out science books of the 1980s, *easy-to-read books* have proliferated until today's primary school children have many books on which to begin. A Let's-Read-and-Find-Out science book by Franklyn M. Branley about the possibilities of life in outer space, *Is There Life in Outer Space?*, uses both colored artwork and black-and-white photographs to illustrate the factual discussion of the book's question. As children successfully decode and comprehend such books, they are undertaking one of life's greatest satisfactions in problem solving: reading for meaning.

For older primary children, interesting *informational* books and books of realistic fiction, fantasy, and poetry provide important reading material. Children can even read about how a book is made in *The Puzzle of Books*, by Michael Kehoe. Interests and concerns that are a part of school life are found in many books of realistic fiction, such as Beverly Cleary's *Ramona Quimby, Age 8*, while some books are humorous spoofs on problems and may help children put their own problems in better perspective. A spoof on reading in school, *The Problem with Pulcifer*, by Florence Parry Heide, is a picture book that takes a sophisticated reader of any age. However, it does not take a sophisticated reader to enjoy poetry, especially the increasing number of books of poetry for young children. *Circus! Circus!*, edited by Lee Bennett Hopkins, is one of the many short, interesting books of poetry for children today. The short, rhythmic lines and the rhyme patterns of the verses make it easy for children to read.

Literature and *Reading* Activities: *Postprimary/Middle School*   The world of children's literature awaits the postprimary reader. Now the student will be able to read widely among the thousands of children's books in print and, with experience and guidance, to read with growing discrimination. For those students at this level who are not yet ready to read widely, at least in books of substantial size and content, some of the easy-to-read books will appeal. These books, although short, will offer an opportunity to build fluency as the student reads several of them. Syd Hoff's boldly humorous works and cartoons will appeal to the postprimary reader, for example. Hoff's titles include *Sammy the Seal, Stanley, Danny and the Dinosaur*, and *Grizzwold*. Students can also get into reading by writing and creating their own books about their own interests and concerns, from motorcycles to moon trips.

Clyde Robert Bulla's books are good bridging books to take students from slim, easy-to-read books to the more substantial volumes that make up most of a library's collection. Bulla's books are not so thick, still have some illustrations, and have an interesting story line. Bulla is a versatile author and has written all kinds of books, from historical "novels" to contemporary books such as *Shoeshine Girl,* showing a very independent female character.

When students "graduate" into the rest of literature for children and young adults, the pickings are excellent indeed. Young *problem solvers* will identify with Anastasia's concerns in Lois Lowry's *Anastasia Krupnik* and may be induced to keep a notebook, writing the way Anastasia does to weigh the pros and cons of her concerns. Students will gain insights from the courage and strengths shown by a black family in *Roll of Thunder, Hear My Cry,* by Mildred Taylor. In a book like *Freaky Friday,* by Mary Rodgers, readers will step into two other roles for a while as they follow the adventures of Annabel, who has turned into her mother for the day. In *My Brother Sam Is Dead,* by James and Christopher Collier, students will be exposed to some difficult questions about war and peace. Such reading extends into all areas of the curriculum and can be a springboard to all kinds of activities, from discussion to journal writing.

> Since writing serves as an effective response to literature, fledgling readers, who write as they read, learn "how professional writers use language to create mood and images."
>
> *Betty Coody and David Nelson*

Literature and *Writing* Activities: *Preprimary*   Oral composition becomes the first written composition when adults write down faithfully what a child says (see Chapter 7). One way to encourage oral composition, of course, is through talking about or retelling stories. Traditional stories in old or new versions lend themselves to retelling, for they are essentially oral stories. Hans Christian Andersen's *The Emperor's New Clothes* or the Grimm brothers' *Mother Holle* are fun for children to try.

Preschool children often write on their own, especially if they have been surrounded by the print of books, magazines, signs, and notes. *Scribbling* becomes the child's own first writing when it is intended to show meaning through graphics. (See Clay, 1975.) Scribbles become more and more sophisticated and begin to resemble English writing as the child experiments and grows. Finally, using invented spelling, the child can write material that is often readable to others. All of this can happen in the preschool years when children are in a print environment and surrounded by other people's writing, including good literature.

Several books seem especially conducive to promoting writing activities for young children. *Elly the Elephant,* by Norma Simon, a story of a beloved toy elephant, is one in which the author encourages children to tell stories about their own special toy friend so that grown-ups can write down the stories for the children to keep. Janet Wolf's *Her Book* uses text that appears hand printed, not machine printed, for its captions about everyday things in a child's life. Children can be encouraged to make or dictate captions for their own drawings of familiar things and then collect these drawings and captions into similar personal books. Jack Kent's *The Scribble Monster* is a wordless book and not a model of writing, but as a picture book about scribbling, it invites children to tell the story and to furnish their own words for the book. For kindergarten and primary students, *Harold and the Purple Crayon,* by Crockett Johnson, suggests ways of turning drawings into stories. All of these books and more serve as springboards to turn literature experience into writing experience.

Literature and *Writing* Activities: *Primary*   Literature provides model, inspiration, and invitation to write. A picture book like *Swimmy,* by Leo Lionni, has few words, but because these words are used well, they offer a model of fine writing. In describing the length of an eel's tail, Lionni writes about "an eel whose tail was almost too far away to remember." How much more effective that description is than saying, "an eel with a very long tail." Other books, such as wordless books or books with few words, invite children to provide the story, to go on beyond the ending, or to make a similar story. Still others have something in them about writing.

Jim Arnosky has created two unique books to encourage early writing attempts, one in manuscript and the other in cursive writing. In *Mouse Numbers and Letters,* a mouse character has a wondrous adventure that is told first in counting book form, and then in alphabet book form. In this part, Mouse constructs manuscript capitals with twigs and branches until he makes a *Z* and falls asleep: *ZZZZ.* Children will enjoy taking Mouse through more adventures and creating word captions with twig letters. In *Mouse Writing,* Mouse and a friend make cursive letters by ice skating. One mouse makes the capital letters and the other, smaller mouse makes the lowercase letters. Writing a story of Mouse's further escapades will lead naturally from such a humorous book on writing.

Some books show characters who like to write or who write to achieve what they want. Peter, in *A Letter to Amy,* by Ezra Jack Keats, writes to invite Amy to his party. Kerby, in *The Limerick Trick,* by Scott Corbett, finds that writing well takes real effort. A story does not have to have a character who writes, however, to suggest ideas for writing. Another book by Ezra Jack Keats, *Dreams,* ends with Roberto, the main character, asleep and dreaming, but readers are not told what Roberto is dreaming or what happened to his paper mouse that fell off the window sill during the night. Children have their own ideas about what happened and can talk about them in response to the story, or write down their ideas in a sequel to the story. Many other stories will also trigger such responses.

Writing in different forms, such as myths, legends, or tall tales, follows experience with the various forms. A teacher who reads several of one kind of story, perhaps a series of myths, can encourage children to try this kind of story in their own writing. Literature, someone's writing, is a natural resource for promoting more writing in the language arts classroom.

Literature and *Writing: Postprimary/Middle School* When children have been freed to write, they soon find that they want new frontiers to explore, new ideas to try. Literature can provide all kinds of ideas and inspiration for fluent writers. Areas to explore include the structure of a story, poem, or other kind of writing; characterization; setting; point of view; and literary devices, such as simile and metaphor.

Use of frameworks Framework stories, haiku verse, and many other forms offer different structures that children may want to try (see Chapter 8). A picture book example of a framework story is *Tico and the Golden Wings,* by Leo Lionni. *Tico* starts out with the narrator saying, "Many years ago I knew a little bird whose name was Tico. . . . Once Tico told me this story about himself." From there, the story is told in the first person, as though the bird is telling it. "A little bird told me" makes an excellent opening or framework for a series of stories by one writer or several in a class. Children's versions of *The Arabian Nights* are another potential stimulus for a series of class stories. Cumulative tales or verses like "The House That Jack Built" make good models for humorous class or personal stories. Haiku is a difficult but popular form for children to try. Its 3 lines and 17 syllables give it a brevity and forced succinctness that help children streamline writing and work on precise word choice. Several examples can be found in children's literature. Harry Behn's translations of oriental poetry, *Cricket Songs* and *More Cricket Songs,* are two of the best known.

The possibilities for modeling or using a framework are as many as there are children's books worth admiring. In a classroom rich with books, there will be no shortage of writing ideas. They are *there* for the taking, if teachers will point the way and encourage children to experiment.

Characterization   *Characters* are the mainstay of a good story, and a master storyteller will reveal what a character is like through several methods: through what the character says, does, thinks, and so on. An author does not just tell what a character is like, but *shows* the reader. In *Anastasia Krupnik,* Lois Lowry lets the reader know about the 9-year-old Anastasia through the girl's thoughts, her interactions with her family, her reactions to school, and her notes in her notebook. The reader laughs with Anastasia, suffers with her, and grows to love her as a friend. In most good stories, a character grows and learns; there is character development. Recall the growth in courage of Mafatu from the excerpt of the story presented in the opening scene. In *The Great Gilly Hopkins,* by Katherine Paterson, Gilly is a foster child passed from home to home, living by her wits and thinking only of herself to survive; but she finds a home where there is love, and in learning to love others, she grows enough to find inner strength that is no longer quite so selfish. Stories in which characters show development help young writers learn to develop their own story characters more fully.

Setting   Amateur writers often neglect *setting.* They fail to account for where the story takes place. Sharing books like *The Little House* series, by Laura Ingalls Wilder, or *Tuck Everlasting,* by Natalie Babbitt, will give young writers a firsthand look at how some of the best writers make a reader feel *there* in the story itself. As mentioned earlier in this chapter, a reader feels the heat of August in Babbitt's prologue when she writes of "blank, white dawns and glaring noons. . . ." Appeals to senses help writers give a you-are-there feeling. Authors use appeals to more than one sense to show how it is.

Point of view   *Point of view* is not as tricky for the intermediate-age writer as it was in the earlier years. An older elementary school student can usually keep a consistent point of view, unlike the beginning writer who often changes from first person to third person and back again. Now, in the upper grades, a writer is ready to experiment with different points of view and different effects. Now is the time to bring out the folk and fairy tales again and to try rewriting, e.g., "The Three Billy Goats Gruff"—from the troll's point of view. For another kind of switch, some stories are told by two different characters, taking turns, each telling the story from his or her own perspective. *Pigman,* by Paul Zindel, is a book that middle school children enjoy and one that illustrates how a story can be told by alternating points of view.

Simile and metaphor   Natalie Babbitt's *Tuck Everlasting* is a fine example of good writing in more ways than one. In the prologue, Babbitt makes use of *simile* and *metaphor* in a memorable way. She compares her story to a wheel that must have a hub. She talks of fixed points that are best left undisturbed and compares the *hub of the ferris wheel to the sun as the hub of the wheeling calendar.* If the hub is disturbed, she warns, nothing holds together, and she implies that there is a hub that is threatened in the story to come. In this way, Babbitt's whole book is based on a metaphor. Other examples exist on a smaller scale in most well-written books. One succinct example is Betsy Byars's line in *After the Goat Man:* "Then he snaked his way back and forth across the highway. . . ." Byars shows in just one word, *snaked,* how a boy on a bicycle weaves across the road. In another line in the same book, Byars describes an old man as a neighbor boy sees him: "His eyes were pieces of iron." Pointing out implied comparisons such as those in Byars's book will give children more understanding of comparisons and word choices that authors use to make their writing more interesting.

   Factual accounts   Setting, characterization, and point of view are all elements of fiction, but literature-as-model is not limited to fiction. Well-told *factual* stories or accounts also help young writers know that any kind of writing can be well done (see Chapter 7). Factual material written with style and verve can be found and shared in the language arts and other subject area classes. Marcia Keegan tells a dramatic story in *The Taos Indians and Their Sacred Blue Lake.* Robert Lipsyte shows crisp reporting from a human interest angle in *Assignment: Sports.* Margaret Hope Bacon writes interesting biography in *I Speak for My Slave Sister: The Life of Abby Kelley Foster.* These are only a few examples of the many excellent books available today about the lives of famous people, noteworthy events, human struggles, sports, science, music, art, and on and on. (See Chapter 7 and the activity book on expository writing.) Stephen Judy asks in *Explorations in the Teaching of Secondary English* (1975), "Must they always write essays?" The answer is obviously no; students who read widely will have experience with all kinds of writing and can be encouraged to experiment in their own writing.

   As teachers and students of all ages work together to build a literate classroom environment where people care about and share books, they are doing some of the best cooperative learning and problem solving to find the most appropriate, interesting, and finest stories of all. In the next section, such personal book selection for the student will be addressed.

CREATIVE PROBLEM SOLVING: PERSONAL READING FOR THE STUDENT

Literature and Self-Concept

Through literature can come recognition that it is all right to be oneself, while at the same time discovering that one is not so very different from many others. This recognition of common concerns about self is important to the child. Today's world offers many challenges, and children are called upon to face them, cope with them, and do some creative problem solving about them. To do these things or to feel that they *can* do them, children need resources from which to draw. Books are among their chief resources, for it is in books that children gain "a better understanding of their world and the potential for individual growth in the face of . . . challenges" (Winkeljohann & Gallant, 1981). Books can provide solace that one is not alone in one's problems and examples of solutions to personal concerns that reaffirm the importance of the growing self.

   Only as a person gains self-acceptance can he or she truly accept others. "Acceptance . . . is the beginning of a positive self-image—and the path to maturity" (Winkeljohann & Gallant). It takes a positive self-image to enable a child to tackle creatively the problems of modern living. For example, in the book *Ramona the Brave,* by Beverly Cleary, Ramona Quimby is a character with whom many children identify, a plucky character who discovers new strengths in herself when she needs to do so. Matt in *The Sign of the Beaver,* by Elizabeth George Speare, learns to be self-reliant when circumstances force him to be on his own for a while in his family's wilderness home. In books such as these children will find role models for the search for personal strengths.

Literature and Identification

Through literature children can come to recognize universal experiences—the experiences shared by much of humanity: getting along with family members, making friends, facing loss of friends or loved ones, and developing courage (as in the story excerpted in the opening scene). Children can identify, for example, with the feelings expressed by Peter in *Tales of a Fourth Grade Nothing,* by Judy Blume, when he tries to cope with a little brother. Or, for another example, children can relate to Emma in Louise Fitzhugh's *Nobody's Family Is Going to Change* when she strives for individuality in a strong-minded family. Everyone, young and old alike, relates to Wilbur in E. B. White's *Charlotte's Web,* first for his yearning for survival and then his mourning for his friend, Charlotte.

Along with the recognition of similarities between ourselves and others is the companion appreciation for differences. A classroom with literature reflecting our country's multicultural heritage will be a place where children of different backgrounds can find identification with their heritage and with others through books—and also learn to appreciate vast individual differences.

All children can appreciate the cultural heritage collected in Dorothy Strickland's *Listen, Children,* an anthology of black literature for children. In her introduction, Strickland says, "This book is for *all* children." She confirms that it is a collection of stories for children who are learning about their heritage, but she also says that it is a book for all children learning to value themselves. She states, "In the process of growing up, understanding yourself comes with reaching out to broaden your understanding of others" (Strickland, 1982).

In reaching out, children in general can read about Jewish children's heritage, among others that have contributed to our country's growth. Children can find a factual account, such as a book about Hanukkah, *The Hanukkah Book,* by Marilyn Burns, or they can read a book of fiction about a Jewish child's experiences, such as *There's No Such Thing as a Chanukah Bush, Sandy Goldstein,* by Susan Sussman.

More and more books that recognize children with a Spanish-speaking heritage are available in our country today. One example, *Idalia's Project ABC* by Idalia Rosario, is an alphabet book based on the urban experience and is printed in both English and Spanish. Other books about Native American, Japanese-American, Korean, Vietnamese, and other cultures that exist across our country can now be found. (Others are listed in Chapter 14 and in the corresponding chapter of the activity book.) Since the language arts are communication arts, the more books there are in the classroom to help children better understand themselves and others while communicating, the better the language arts program will be.

Literature for Understanding and Other Curricular Areas

Literature gives children a chance to try on other roles, to live in someone else's shoes for awhile. History or historical fiction can enable children to experience vicariously what life was like in times past. For example, *The Long Way to a New Land,* by Joan Landin, is an I-Can-Read history book about children in an immigrant family coming to America in the 1860s. Clyde Robert Bulla's *A Lion to Guard Us,* a book for the middle reader in grades 3 or 4, tells of children coming to America to find their father in the new colony of Jamestown in Virginia. These books help children appreciate why and how people came to America to search for freedom and a better life. *The Sign of the Beaver,* by Elizabeth George Speare, helps older readers in grades 5 and 6 and up understand some of the trials and hardships of the early settlers of our country.

Contemporary books of fact or fiction let children experience for a little while, through identifying with characters or real people, the problems that some children face today, such as coping with illness or a different family structure. In *The Boy Who Wanted a Family,* by Shirley Gordon, a little boy hopes to be adopted into a regular family, but when a single mother adopts him, he adjusts to his new family situation. Many contemporary books deal with different family structures, the divorce of parents, and various family life-styles. A delightful story of an extended family is found in Eleanor Clymer's *The Getaway Car,* which has humor and mystery along with human concerns about aging, the balancing of work and fun, and family relationships. For a more sobering fictional account of different generations coping with life's difficulties, Sue Ellen Bridgers's poignant *Notes for Another Life* is a book that will give older children of grades 6 and up a look at what it means to cope with parents who seem to be abandoning family responsibilities.

Many books are about problems that most children do not face, but such books help all children toward better understanding of the human condition. *Sally Can't See,* by Palle Petersen, is a factual account of a 12-year-old girl who is blind. The book shows in picture book format that the girl is like everyone else; she just "sees" in different ways. *Hang Tough, Paul Mather,* by Alfred Slote, is a realistic portrayal of a boy's struggle with leukemia. Readers will admire Paul's courage and determination.

Books of faraway places or even little-known nearby places expand children's horizons and knowledge. Mitsumasa Anno, an artist, creates picture books for all ages, using famous places as backgrounds for his scenes. Some scenes show details from paintings or characters from children's literature, but the settings are real places. *Anno's Journey* is based on Anno's travels through Europe. *Anno's Britain* and *Anno's Italy* are about specific countries. Books about regions, countries, continents, and so on transport children by the well-known armchair travel route to many places within a very short time. From Margaret Ronan's *All About Our 50 States* to Miriam Schlein's *Antarctica: The Great White Continent,* these books of history and geography offer a smorgasbord of information for satisfying children's curiosity about the world. Such reading relates naturally to language arts and social studies.

Literature and the Future

Children today will be the leaders and working adults of the twenty-first century. Books that look to the future can help prepare children to enter the next century as caring, coping people. *What Can She Be? A Scientist,* by Gloria and Esther Goldreich, with photographs by Sheldon Horowitz, is a picture book showing new careers for women in science, specifically genetics, but also microbiology and botany. *Space Age,* by Reginald Turnill, is a book on the edge of tomorrow, dealing with space travel and exploration. Jane Werner Watson's *Living Together in Tomorrow's World* makes the point that the quality of life in tomorrow's world depends upon the preparations people make in today's world.

Strange as it may seem, one way in which teachers can help children make preparations for future living is through sharing fantasy or science fiction with them. Such fiction frequently offers a look at "worlds as they should be," a term coined by Mary Lou Colbath (1971). Living in any time or place requires good human relations; living together and coping with the complex world of the future will demand almost utopian conditions if there is to be improved quality of life. Thinking about conditions for *creative problem solving* and for optimum human relations can be enhanced by reading about worlds such as Narnia in C. S. Lewis's *The Lion, the Witch, and the Wardrobe,* and Prydain in *The Book of Three,* by Lloyd Alexander. Such reading can lead to rich discussion and to writing about children's own versions of "worlds as they should be." Whether it involves reading, listening, discussing, or writing about concerns in modern living, literature provides insight that can lead to personal learning and problem solving.

HOW CHILDREN'S LITERATURE TIES THE LANGUAGE ARTS TOGETHER: THE PROBLEM-SOLVING CLASSROOM

> . . . But out of doors the fog twisted about the cottages like slow-motion smoke. It dulled the rusty scraping of the beach grass. It muffled the chattery talk of the low tide waves. And it hung wet and dripping, from the bathing suits and towels on the clothesline.
>
> *Alvin Tresselt,* Hide and Seek Fog

The language arts involve many discrete skills, but communication is not achieved one discrete skill at a time; it is achieved by an orchestration of many skills, as the author of the descriptive quote above displays. Concentrating too hard on one skill at a time will result in slow motion and awkwardness or even a breakdown in communication, as it would for swimming, bicycling, or any other human activity. People learning to swim or ride may find reading about rules or listening to lectures on the activity helpful, but they get into the water or on the bicycle and try it out before they can truly *do* the activity. In the language arts of listening, speaking, writing, and reading, people must also be active doers to learn. Practicing the language arts effectively means interrelating many skills. For example, writing a note involves thinking about what one wants to say; forming the graphics that are needed to convey the message; using appropriate conventions such as commas and periods to aid meaning; reading the note to check intended meaning; and perhaps rewriting or adding a part. All these activities overlap during the process; using the language arts requires putting it all together.

Literature is one of the best resources for unifying the language arts in a classroom. It is someone's purposeful writing; it involves purposeful reading; it promotes discussion; and it provides substantial listening opportunities. Children's literature and their own compositions are the major content of the language arts program (Lundsteen, 1976). Literature, by serving as a springboard for children's writing, provides them with a variety of forms that, in turn, reveal their previous exposure to literature through the use of vocabulary, pattern, and content. In *assessing* children's responses to books we can look both at the way literature has influenced their own writing and at their written and oral responses to books. With consideration of an integrative classroom environment, it is as easy to identify a class in which literature is an integral part of the language arts curriculum as it is to recognize a home where books are loved and valued (Huck, 1976).

Unifying Projects in Language Arts

A literature project can ensure the integrative use of time, since the project involves all the language arts and builds on their interrelationships. The following list of suggested projects is by no means inclusive. (Also see the activity book, Chapter 8.)

Literature Projects to Unify the Language Arts

1. *A unit on mythology:* Read many myths to the class, place other collections of myths in the class library for independent reading, discuss characteristics of myths, and encourage the students to write their own.

2. *Poetry and writing:* Share several anthologies of poetry in the classroom, first general anthologies and then specialized collections of different poetic forms. Next, let everyone try writing in different forms, such as haiku, limerick, cinquain, and particularly blank verse.

3. *Writing about characters:* As a change from using reports to share class reading choices, have a favorite-character project. Ask students to write about their favorite characters, then dress up as the favorite characters and tell about their choices; encourage a follow-up project of writing about what the characters will do after the ending of the books.

4. *Class sequel project:* If a favorite book of a class has no sequel, suggest that the children create one. Encourage children to write to the publishing company of the original book to get permission to use the characters' names in their sequel. Make the sequel a class project, involving team writing, discussing, sharing, and so on.

5. *ABC book project:* For children of any age, reading current ABC books can lead to writing all kinds of creative alphabet books.

6. *Bookmaking projects of all kinds:* To encourage writing to read, provide for different ways to bind or put stories into books for personal keepsakes or class and school libraries. Class books or anthologies of children's own writings can be bound together by sewing, stapling, or tying yarn through punched holes, using cloth-covered cardboard or construction paper covers. The same kinds of bindings can be used for individually made books of students' own writings. Small books for small hands are easily made. (See the activity book, Chapter 1.) Shape books are another enjoyable way to share personal writing. Stories about special topics, such as fish or rockets, can be bound between covers shaped in the form of the topic. See commercial books bound in different sizes and shapes for ideas.

7. *Class magazines:* Collect children's stories, poems, and reviews and put them together in a general class magazine, using ditto or offset to reproduce it for other classes or parents. An aide or parent volunteers can help with typing and reproducing. Encourage children to take over responsibility for the magazine. Set the stage for children to think of creating their own magazines by introducing them to commercial magazines or magazines created by other children (e.g., *The McGuffey Writer*).

8. *Class publishing company:* Visit or read about a publishing company. Encourage a group of interested children to form a class publishing company to publish books, magazines, or newspapers for the class. Challenge gifted children to publish for other classes, too.

Keeping Up to Date in Children's Literature

Once you have finished a course in children's literature, and have cooperatively investigated a sizable number of books suggested in this chapter, how do you keep up to date? How do you add to your card file? How do you continue to enrich your language arts, other curricular areas, and your daily reading to children with those newfound and effective motivators? The following list of references should help keep you abreast of what is recent and good in children's books. Other references in this section that will help to expand your knowledge include films, computer software, and a network of professional organizations.

Professional Books and References   In addition to the books already mentioned in this chapter, these selections are recommended:

May, Jill P. (1983). *Children and Their Literature: A Reading Book.*

Moss, Joy. (1984). *Focus Units in Literature.*

Rees, David. (1984). *Painted Desert, Green Shade: Essays on Contemporary Writers of Fiction for Children and Young Adults.*

Sims, Rudine. (1982). *Shadow and Substance: Afro-American Experience in Contemporary Children's Fiction.*

Sloan, Glenna Davis. (1984). *The Child as Critic: Teaching Literature in the Elementary School,* 2nd ed.

Townsend, John Rowe. (1979). *A Sounding of Storytellers.*

Booklists   Booklists provide an annotated bibliography of books reviewed by librarians or other professionals whose interest is children's literature. The annotations help with selection, as mentioned earlier in this chapter. A few booklists not mentioned earlier are given below:

Dryer, Sharon S., ed. (1977, 1981). *The Bookfinder.*

Gillespie, John T. (1985). *The Elementary School Paperback Collection.*

Lima, Carolyn W. (1986). *A to Zoo: Subject Access to Children's Picture Books,* 2nd ed.

Monson, Dianne. (1985). *Adventuring with Books.*

Films   Films about children's literature are available for enjoyment, college courses, in-service programs, and so on. The following are recommended:

Weston Woods. *The Lively Art of Picture Books.* Although dated now, the film presents picture books that are modern classics and still deserve consideration.

Weston Woods and the Dayton and Montgomery County (Ohio) Public Library. *What's a Good Book?*

Weston Woods. *Randolph Caldecott: The Man Behind the Medal.* (Filmstrip and cassette.)

Computer Software

Compupoem: A Computer-Assisted Writing Activity. Developed by Stephen Marcus, University of California, Santa Barbara. Designed for use in grades 4–16, *Compupoem* encourages initial poetry experimentation and can lead to a closer look at what other poets do.

Sunburst *Communications Computer Programs* to accompany Newbery Award–winning books. Pleasantville, New York. These programs extend experience with the best literature for young people.

Word Processing Software: *The Bank Street Writer.* Scholastic, Jefferson City, Missouri. Word processing helps children create their own literature.

Also related to literature and writing are integrated software programs such as *Quill* (D. C. Heath) and *AppleWorks* (Apple Computer), which provide the user with prompts (starters or formats) for carrying out a given writing task. When writing a book report, for example, *Quill*'s "Planner" program might ask students for the name of the book, some of the characters, the type of book, and whether they liked it. These prompts may be useful for hesitant writers.

Professional Organizations   Joining one or more professional organizations can help a teacher keep up in all areas of the curriculum. To keep up with children's literature, the following organizations are recommended:

Chicago Children's Reading Roundtable. Chicago, Illinois.

Children's Literature Assembly of the National Council of Teachers of English. 1111 Kenyon Rd., Urbana, Illinois 61801.

Children's Literature Association. West Lafeyette, Indiana (headquarters).

International Reading Association. (This organization also has state and local councils.) 800 Barksdale Rd., Newark, Delaware 19714.

The National Council of Teachers of English, 1111 Kenyon Rd., Urbana, Illinois 61801, and its state and local affiliates.

The next chapter on critical and creative thinking relates to the problem-solving theme of this chapter but stresses the judging aspects of it. A rich background in creative and critical thinking about literature provides a suitable bridge to critical thinking as applied to all the language arts in daily living. This book has now examined the following large categories of language use: self-expression, exposition, and, with this chapter, literature. The next chapter helps the teacher to enhance understanding and use of persuasive language.

SUMMARY

With reading at its best and writing at its finest, children's literature is a special kind of communication. It provides almost unlimited resources for reading, writing, oral response, language models, coping strategies, and language enjoyment. Every chapter in this book taps into this resource. In constructing meaning from literature, children are exposed to creative problem solving that will lead to a command of the language.

Reading to construct meaning, to seek answers to questions, to find coping strategies for living, and to share common bonds with others is reading that represents problem solving germane to present-day living and communicating. Thus, children's literature belongs at the heart of the language arts program.

CHAPTER 10

Creative and Critical Thinking in Persuasive Uses of Language

"The fatal tendency of mankind to leave off thinking about a thing when it is no longer doubtful is the cause of half their errors."

John Stuart Mill

The human mind, 12 billion or so cells operating on a self-generating electrical current, still stumps the world's best scientists. It is so priceless that all the money in the world could not put one together. Each child in your classroom has one free, as standard equipment at birth. What contribution will you make to its growth, development, and use? One idea: *teachers can help children learn that there are degrees of honesty, quality, and depth of scholarship in the language they send and receive.*

INTRODUCTION

Topics in this chapter stress two functions of language: persuasive and creative. The look at persuasion includes thoughts on critical thinking, self-defense, and ethical responsibility. Briefly, persuasive language requires creative thought in its formulation and critical thought in its analysis. The person trying to persuade needs to be creative in figuring out how to influence someone else. The person receiving the persuasive message needs to be critical in order to see if the message is accurate and in his or her best interests.

You and your students can learn (in the rich environment you create for thinking) that verbal and visual languages are powerful influences upon human thinking and behavior (National Council of Teachers of English, 1986b). The most common use of language is probably persuasion. It creeps up on us over the airwaves and from the political platform, the pulpit, and the press. By examining various relationships between verbal and visual languages, you and your class can learn together how to distinguish among persuasive purposes of language.

With the knowledge you gain you can help your students recognize differences among some important aspects of persuasive language: fact, fiction, opinion, propaganda, valid and invalid arguments, inferences, and assumptions. This chapter provides you with ways to help children learn about the logic, style, and organization of language designed to be persuasive. You will find that a major theme of this chapter, often repeated, is that teachers can help children learn that there are degrees of honesty, quality, creativity, and depth of scholarship in the language they receive and send. In showing what persuasion is and how it works, this chapter gives methods of helping children cope with it intelligently. The chapter suggests critical-thinking strategies that will enable children to filter out "polluted" language from educational and informational messages. By way of preview, examine a few typical questions and answers in the headings that follow.

"How is the teaching of thinking related to language arts instruction?"

The teaching of creative, logical, and critical thinking is close to the core of effective English instruction (National Council of Teachers of English, 1982). Language use and higher-order thinking skills are closely linked. Language is an important way of developing meanings through the intricate use of inquiring, organizing, realizing, discovering, and interpreting. Language as a way of thinking and learning is an essential element in every school content area and a way of ensuring that thinking skills can be taught effectively. *Writing is visible thinking.* In sum, to participate in our democratic society, individuals need to listen, speak, read, and write critically and creatively (California State Department of Education, 1987).

More specifically, inclusion of critical thinking about persuasive discourse in the language arts curriculum puts other uses of language into a clearer perspective and sharpens integrity. If a work of literature does not seem to hang together well, the problem may lie in the author's overstriving to persuade the reader. Students may learn to see self-expressive language as really sometimes self-persuasion or rationalization ("I can't do well in school because life is just against me—so why try"). Finally, children can learn to distinguish the careful use of facts and probability in exposition and scientific language from the careless or intentional misuse of these in some persuasive language.

"Can I really teach thinking?"

Some consider teaching creative and critical thinking to be rather like trying to nail jelly to the wall. Apparently psychologists rarely agree on what constitutes higher levels of thinking, and no one has developed a generally compelling taxonomy of thinking skills for use in educational programs (Suhor, 1984). (Appendix 10A provides a framework of goals and objectives created especially for this chapter.) Researchers dispute vigorously over claims for the effectiveness of various approaches. Bewildered, some teachers ask: "Can I teach thinking as a separate skill? As part of each subject area? In an integrated way? Does the language arts teacher have a special role in the teaching of thinking? How does a concept such as writing across the curriculum relate to teaching thinking? Am I a critical thinker and reader and do I display my processes to children?

By the end of this chapter, these and other questions will be explored and the task of teaching will seem more approachable. You will be able to help students realize that how to think is different from what to think.

"Why is teaching thinking important?"

There are many reasons in a rationale incorporating creative and critical thinking processes in any classroom language activity. Consider a few further justifications useful in talks with parents and administrators: responding to needs assessments, teaching children to protect themselves from pressures toward undesirable conformity, avoiding the consequences of waiting until it is too late, and helping children reach their highest potential.

Needs Assessments Revelations   Recent national tests, studies, and surveys indicate that students are not demonstrating competence in using higher mental processes. The National Assessment of Educational Progress (NAEP) has reported that scores on test items requiring students to reason, understand, and apply knowledge declined in the late 1970s and early 1980s (National Assessment of Educational Progress, 1981b). When students ranging in age from 9 to 17 were given a passage of literature to read and react to, they had difficulty in thinking elaboratively or giving any but the most superficial reasons for their interpretations (National Assessment of Educational Progress, 1981a, 1986). Similar findings were reported in England when a substantial group of 11-year-olds were noted as having problems with evaluating evidence, speculating about possible alternatives, hypothesizing, and justifying an argument or point of view in discussion (MacLure & Hargreaves, 1986). The National Commission on Excellence in Education (1983) has also suggested that students have a low command of various reasoning abilities, such as drawing inferences and solving problems.

Why do we seem to have so many "mindless" classrooms? Analysts speculate that a contributing factor is that information and academic skills have been taught without enough emphasis on their meanings and clear, communicative use (NAEP, 1981b). A further speculation is that teachers have been so busy teaching children to pass minimum competency tests that they have stopped devoting time to writing, reading, and discussion that develop thinking ability.

Self-Protection from Pressures Toward Undesirable Conformity   Another important reason for the study of critical thinking and persuasion is self-protection against unethical or unwise pressures. The constant chants of advertising move individuals to buy what is produced, not what they need. Persuasion itself can be relatively neutral; much depends on the context, on the user, and on the ignorance of the receiver. The dramatic range of uses of persuasion—from enslavement to peacemaking—justifies its study. Incessant messages from mass media tend to produce not individuality but conformity in children. TV is like a giant cookie cutter, patterning minds. Tyrannies begin in the uncritical acceptance of ideas.

Postponement and Irretrievable Loss   Furthermore, it seems that if we wait it may be too late. If we wait until middle school, high school, college, or graduate school, we close the proverbial barn door with instruction that comes too late for changing bad habits, biases, and missed opportunities. As early as the 1950s, researchers saw young children's biases develop a resistance that no typical instruction could shake loose (Traeger & Yarrow, 1952). The easily persuaded young need encouragement to think and rethink for themselves, to weigh values foisted upon them, especially by peers. "Wait—too late" capsulizes a prime reason for bringing such study into the elementary school curriculum.

Helping Children Reach Their Highest Potential   The way in which well-educated people use language productively is closely related to higher-order thinking processes. Increasingly, attractive and rewarding jobs will require thinking skills such as problem identification and analysis. To participate effectively in our democratic society, people need to express and comprehend ideas creatively and critically. While recall and recognition may be necessary as *bases* for higher-order thinking, your students need to use language in much more critical and creative ways (California State Department of Education, 1987).

Children do not automatically acquire critical-thinking skills as a matter of natural growth. Nor does the critical process or creative process necessarily accompany high mental ability, general reading, or listening scores (Lundsteen, 1969; Saadeh, 1969). Students too often find that all their creative problem solving is for naught, because they have been unable to persuade the right people of the feasible desirability of their solutions (Sternberg, 1985). As children develop in their use of persuasive discourse, education can guide their growth in integrity and honesty in language use rather than leave these to chance.

Finally, creative expression and discovery can help every child enjoy a richer, happier life. Joy comes from recognizing and developing such abilities within, not from just imitating. The world is beginning to realize that few if any solutions to its problems become permanent and that it needs people capable of productive thinking.

OPENING SCENE: Creative Planning and Critiquing While Naomi Writes

It's 12:45 and the fifth-grade students in Jamie Lee's room are just returning from lunch. Bernice, having selected the poem of the day, seats herself on a high stool and to a quiet group begins to read Langston Hughes's self-expressive poem (1959).

> To fling my arms wide
> in the face of the sun,
> Dance! Whirl! Twirl!
> Til the quick day is done.
> Rest at pale evening . . .
> A tall, slim tree . . .
> Night coming tenderly
> Black like me.

NAOMI: Say it again, Bernice. [Bernice does so.] Langston Hughes is black? [Bernice answers yes.] Black like me . . . I feel a poem coming on [Naomi dives for a piece of paper.]

The other children pull out books from their desks, from the shelves, from the recreation project area (where some new books had been dropped off and introduced by the school librarian); and they begin the school-wide 20 minutes of sustained silent reading.

A peaceful silence settles over the room as teacher and children become absorbed in their books. Naomi has borrowed the Langston Hughes poem from Bernice and reads again and again. Soon she starts her own poem, but then stops and compares the Hughes poem with a verse she has already collected by Chetin (1970):

> Black is the sky of a jungle night,
> Leopard spot and zebra stripe,
> Black is the color of a storm at sea,
> Eye of a lover, belly of a bee.
> And you are beautiful, too, my son,
> And you are beautiful, too!

At a signal, the soft flutter of turning pages melds into the beehive of children talking to their sharing partners, as pairs or small groups communicate about their books with one another. Some read a "good part" aloud and invite the teacher to experience it too. Some try a partner who has already read their same selected book:

HORACE: That story began just like mine!

JOEL: You mean the one you wrote yesterday? You hadn't read this one first?

HORACE: No. I guess it's a pretty common beginning.

JOEL: I've read that story and I think the author prepared me better for his ending than you did with your story, at least the draft of yours I read.

HORACE: Wha-d-ya mean?

JOEL: Let's talk about how you both got your stories going at the beginning. A boy sets off to find his sister, who has run away. Right?

HORACE: Right.

JOEL: In your story the boy goes off with his hero, Great Gregory-Gets-Em, and they have all these adventures. Right?

HORACE: Right.

JOEL: But at the end, we still don't know what has happened to the sister. The author of the other story told me—told how the sister was found and rescued.

HORACE: I get it. I'll rewrite to show how she was found. And I think I'll switch to first person this time. That'll make the story more interesting.

JOEL: How many drafts of that story are you going to write?

HORACE: I don't know. Maybe four. Picasso reworked his sketches and writers rework their drafts.

JOEL: And analogies have to match up to be good evidence. Putting Picasso and writers and *you* together . . . ?

HORACE: And why not?

When time for sharing with partners is over, the children retrieve their reading workshop logs. In these they note such things as when they began a book, when they finished it, what stood out for them, what pleasures it gave them, what difficulties they wanted help with, and what options they selected for responding. These children are on their way inside the writing they have read.

Naomi, the poem writer, goes over to the teacher.

NAOMI: What's the name of the wildflowers I picked and brought you, the ones with the yellow petals and the black center?

TEACHER: I think I know, but where could we check for sure? [Looks toward the pile of books on the round committee table.]

NAOMI: That book about plants that grow here. [Opens it.] Here's the section on flowers and here *it is*, "cone flower." Wait . . . what's the date of this book? Five years ago. . . . I don't think names of flowers would change that fast, do you?

TEACHER: No.

NAOMI: It's my mamma's favorite flower. . . . I think I know *why* now!

TEACHER: I wonder why they call it a cone flower.

NAOMI: Look . . . 'cause its center is shaped up like a cone, an upside-down, black ice cream cone, I bet. I think I've heard it called black-eyed Susan, but I don't think that would fit in my poem.

One of the reading options alluded to earlier is group involvement in committee work related to the proposed recreation area near the school. A city council member had invited nearby schools to become involved, and the teacher and the class had decidedly done so. They started with a survey of families in the area and interviews. They had discussed different ideas at the roundtable and before the total class. In the beginning they had been focusing on what they wanted for themselves; but working on the survey had broadened their outlook to include what would be good for very young children and old people.

The current committee sits at the roundtable with a schedule of meeting times and a stack of books. There are also pictures, pamphlets, drafts of position statements and letters (one just pulled from the computer printer), diagrams, minutes of meetings, letters asking for information, and letters trying to persuade others to become involved in the decision making. The teacher has given careful attention to creating a productive environment for thinking. In this classroom listening, speaking, reading, writing, and *thinking* are all integrated. Some of the queries and materials deal with different kinds and philosophies of adventure play areas for young children, safety considerations, beautification, Oriental gardens (reflecting the Asian culture of a sizable segment of this community), and a vegetable patch to be tended by neighboring schools. The students have organized much of the material in an open box with labeled hanging files.

The teacher, having worked thoroughly with the children at the beginning of the year, is now unobtrusively in the background during the meeting taking notes on the problem solving, mainly related to acceptance-finding practicalities. The dialogue illustrates some persuasive discourse and thinking in action.

CHRISTOPHER: We need to get the other grades interested in this play area; we can't do it all ourselves.

JENNIFER: We could set up an information table in the lunchroom . . .

CHRISTOPHER: And invite kids to come by and browse after they've eaten.

TED: No, they'd be in too much of a hurry to get outside and play. We could go directly to each room. [The teacher makes a note to talk with the children about getting teacher approval.]

JENNIFER: One of us could tell about the recreation project . . . and how we've been invited to give ideas . . . and the other could answer questions.

TED: I'd like it better if there were two to persuade and two to handle questions. We could take a few of our books along . . . and we could lend them if they wanted to learn more.

CLARISE: Pick the books with the most recent publication dates and the authors we looked up in *Who's Who.*

ANDREW: I don't know why we're going to take the trouble with the young ones in kindergarten and first grade. I can tell you what they are going to want—swings, swings, swings.

CLARISE: How do you know that?

ANDREW: Well, I have a little sister in kindergarten. And that's all she ever wants to do on the playground. Young children are just "swingers."

CHRISTOPHER: You mean it looks that way to you.

CLARISE: That's just one little kid. We can't say the whole class is like that, just because your little sister is.

TED: That's right . . . but . . . that's all my little brother wants to do, too.

JENNIFER: We can see swings used a lot.

CLARISE: Maybe. . . .

JENNIFER: When we interviewed our P.E. teacher, she said that children need things that develop different muscles.

CHRISTOPHER: And they need things that give kids a chance to make decisions.

ANDREW: How? I forget.

JENNIFER: Like getting down from a bridge by steps, or a rope ladder, or a slide—

CHRISTOPHER: Or a pole. Remember?

ANDREW: Humm . . . you're persuading me. . . .

Meanwhile, after many revisions and with a great look of satisfaction on her face, Naomi puts her inspired poem in her writing folder. Here it is.

Naomi's Poem

I prance and twirl on the asphalt,
Gathered jet-coned flowers dancing with me,
Buzzing round and round a leafless tree,
Like dark belly of a bee
Til the day is done
All black
like me.

The class now moves to a total group reflection, assessment, and planning mode before preparing to end the school day.

Analysis of the Scene

This scene illustrated a number of points to be developed later in this chapter. The teacher and class had gone through much preparation and learning to get to the *whole-language* approach, the self-owning of language and thought, and the cooperative roles displayed. In this scene we saw risk taking in thinking and the creative reading and writing process in action.

As Horace, with Joel's help, compared his story to one they had both read, the boys' dialogue showed evidence of varied modes of thinking and classroom study of analogies. Horace thought about how authors wrote and selected narrative voice ("I think I'll switch to first person"). Both considered how authors developed and concluded their books ("the author prepared me better for his ending than you did with your story").

In this scene integrated children's literature played an important part in stimulating both creative and critical thought. The children used books that helped them grow up and helped them love books; they browsed, chatted, and were selective. All of this integrative and long-term activity was conducive to creative and critical thought.

The children saw their teacher thinking in the classroom, asking questions ("I wonder why they call it a cone flower"). The children revealed creative and critical thinking stimulated by many options and choices in responding to books.

The scene showed children engaged in meaningful, creative problem solving that brought the outside world into the classroom. The classroom itself provided a climate for inquiry and rich resources for finding solutions. The committee gathered data from reading material to use in solving problems about the new recreation area. The children used taught ideas about the credibility and validity of authors and their works ("Pick the books with the most recent publication dates and the authors we looked up in *Who's Who*"). Children were engaged in *direct* persuasion ("Tell about the project") and *less* direct but still valid persuasion ("We could set up an information table"). They were wary of overgeneralization and sifted evidence ("That's just one little kid"). They were on their way to learning that there are degrees of honesty, quality, and depth of scholarship in language received and sent.

Finally the scene showed Naomi's creative synthesis of two verses with her own experience as she reworked the theme that black is beautiful. During that afternoon Naomi put her poem through much critical revision, thinking about every aspect of it as she worked on it. (A later section on integration details her composing processes.)

Thus, in this classroom scene we saw writing as visible thinking, an integrated language arts program, and creative problem solving combined with critical thought stimulated by a well-prepared environment. We saw listening, speaking, reading, and writing processes used as rational actions relating (1) purposes, (2) materials, and (3) circumstances. Finally we saw a teacher who (having set the scene) got out of the children's way and encouraged them to think.

DEFINITIONS

The opening portions of this chapter have given some idea of the nature of creative and critical thinking. This section seeks to clarify and contrast these processes and their components. (Extended definitions are in the glossary in the instructor's manual.)

Critical thinking is characterized by its highly conscious and judgmental aspect. Its actions and conclusions are drawn in terms of specified internal and external criteria that are as objectively derived as possible. It is not thoughtless and biased. **Critical listening,** using the auditory language mode, is much like critical reading, another receptive process. Critical listening, however, requires a special awareness of time pressures, media, and live personal contexts.

Both critical and **creative thinking** are well used when harnessed to the solving of a genuine and significant problem a child appreciates. The creative use of language is aided by qualities of fluency, flexibility, originality, elaboration, perception, and imagination linked to curiosity. Reading can be a creative thinking process when readers use previous knowledge to make enriched meanings. Self-monitoring of process and habits can enhance both creative and critical thinking in all the language arts, including reading (see Chapter 3). A final section in Chapter 13 elaborates the creative process.

The Persuasive Use of Language

Persuasive communication attempts to influence or control beliefs or behaviors. You find it in traditional forms and in political cartoons, banners, buttons, bumper stickers, songs, literature, and painting. Even young children have been known to write hints to godparents for gifts or tape persuasive notes on their mailboxes (as shown in Figure 10.1).

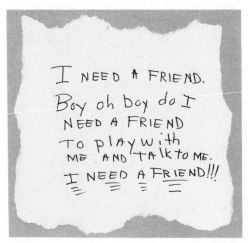

Figure 10.1 A 7-year-old child's persuasive note.

Higher-minded and Lower-minded Persuasion   Persuasion can be higher-minded and lower-minded. With respect to lower-minded, when the person making a persuasive effort believes the goal to be of advantage to the self (but not to the audience), that person is a deliberate propagandist. But persuasion need not be villainous, need not be an insincere attempt to fool the audience. Among the generally constructive or higher-minded instances of persuasive discourse in our lives (with valid, rational evidence) are the following: smoking prevention billboards, safety slogans, and educational rationales for the importance of thinking.

Sinister distortion is not essential to propaganda. In our democracy we live in a multiplicity of competing propagandas and persuasions. We can exercise informed autonomy in selection. As both an overview and an example, Table 10.1 below shows some propaganda techniques side by side with some related legitimate persuasive devices.

Persuasive strategies   Briefly, "lower-minded" persuasion may use nonlogical strategies, such as classic propaganda devices and sheer power; "higher-minded" persuasive strategies may use valid reasons and evidence. Strategies may also hinge on whether the audience to persuade is familiar or unfamiliar to the persuader, and whether the task of persuading is going to be relatively easy or difficult. A combination of an unknown audience and a difficult persuasion task usually brings the greatest challenge for the persuader and demands more knowledge of strategy.

Borrowings from Other Language Categories   The persuasive aim borrows many of its aspects from other broad classifications of language use: (1) The emotional aspects may

Table 10.1   COMPARISON OF LOWER-MINDED AND HIGHER-MINDED PERSUASION

Propaganda techniques	Persuasive devices
1. Testimonial—a prominent person recommends an action or provides an endorsement for a product or service	1. Authoritative opinion expressed by someone in a position to know either because of research or personal or professional service
2. Claiming a cause-effect relationship where none exists	2. Showing a legitimate cause-effect relationship
3. Bandwagon—suggesting taking an action because others are taking it	3. Suggesting an action because your own decision-making process indicates that it is the right, just, or appropriate thing to do
4. Glittering generality—using language deceptively or in such a way as to mask the intention; thus, the generalization only has the appearance of truth	4. Presenting a generalization drawn from several independent and reliable sources
5. Plain folks—making reference to nonexistent bonds of ordinary or common relationship	5. Making reference to human bonds that are legitimate, universal, and clearly related to the topic
6. Card stacking—omitting important facts	6. Presenting all of the arguments in support of one side of an issue with regard for moral and ethical use of evidence (including acknowledgment that other sides may exist)
7. Encouraging action out of unreasonable guilt or fear	7. Encouraging an action based on personal and social responsibility

Source: VanCamp, 1987.

come from language for self-expressive use; (2) the (pseudo-) scientific jargon is corrupted from exposition; and (3) the style of rhythmic repetitions, figures of speech, and the connotative use of words comes from the literary use. For example, a politician poetically calls constituents with low incomes "withered leaves of industrial enterprise."

Audience Focus   Whatever the audience, the persuasive aim of language focuses on it in dead earnest. The aim is primarily to get the decoder (listener, reader, or viewer) to perform a specific action, to react with a given emotion, or to uphold a certain conviction. The aim is not merely self-expressive, informational, or solely artistic. At times a persuader may be trying to inspire those who are already convinced but who fail to act on their convictions. But more often the audience has an opinion different from the sender.

Grammatical imperatives   One of the attributes of persuasion is appeal with direct and indirect imperatives. Sir Winston Churchill, in his speech on Dunkirk (House of Commons, June 4, 1940), gave us a classic example of direct imperative:

> We shall fight on the beaches. We shall fight on the landing grounds; we shall fight in the fields and in the streets. We shall never surrender!

Four years earlier in a radio broadcast, the Nazi Hermann Goering gave German people a classic example of a more indirect imperative:

> Guns will make us powerful; butter will only make us fat.

A combined direct and indirect imperative occurs when a youngster says to another: "Come on, do it; everyone else is doing it."

Image   Finally, the authors of persuasive discourse are interested in their image—the truth or myth of their expertise, common sense, goodwill, and trustworthiness. The cynical propagandist knows that genuine sincerity is not important; but the audience's belief that the message is sincere is crucial. To create a positive image, a company plays up its dignified support of the arts or popular approach to ecology. Two illustrative and related strategies are the propagandist's use of the "testimonial" and its transfer from a desirable image to ourselves (e.g., a famous athlete advocates a certain bug killer, so we go buy it).

Propaganda and Teachers   As educational persuaders, teachers believe they are acting in the best interests of the child. Where teachers repeatedly prove to be caring, well informed, and unselfish, the child will not identify persuasive efforts as negatively propagandistic. The children will feel that the teacher's interests are identical with their own, but better advised. However, it is also true that teachers and parents occasionally try to persuade a child to do something solely for the adults' advantage. And we teachers are proved wrong in our information from time to time.

Children come to regard us as often reliable but occasionally self-servingly propagandistic. And their task becomes to discover when we are making lower-minded propaganda (Brown, 1958). The basic questions asked are these: "Is this person trying to get me to do or believe something? What? Is it in my best interests?" According to Roger Brown (1958), from the moment a caretaker or parent pokes a spoon of spinach in a baby's mouth and says, "Um, um, oh so good," a propaganda analyst is born.

WHO ARE YOUR YOUNG THINKERS?

We turn our attention now to what fields of development have to tell us about the potential thinkers in your classroom. Topics include underestimation of children and the issue of mind ownership.

Developmental Aspects

Children who want to be persuasive become more and more adept at fashioning their messages to fit their intended audience, and finally develop some audience-specific strategies (Delia, Kline, & Burleson, 1979). Young children soon perceive that parents and teachers are in positions of greater power, and therefore youngsters sometimes use disagreeable means, such as whining and persistent begging, to get their way. When children want to do something for which permission is somewhat unlikely, boys are more likely than girls to go ahead and do it without trying to persuade the parent or teacher to give permission. According to Cowan and colleagues (1984, 1987), children are accorded less power in their relationships with adults and girls are accorded less power than boys. Their attempts at influencing often reflect a position of less power. When children are dealing with same-sex peers, however, they are more likely to be in a position of more equal power and can use techniques, such as bargaining and giving important reasons, to try to persuade an equal. It is the job of teachers to help children develop the ability to use these more socially appropriate means of persuading others: to use their cognitive development and mastery of language to persuade rather than to harass, bully, or ignore the wishes of others.

If one overgeneralizes about Piaget's age-stage work, one might conclude that young children cannot think critically and that, consequently, a teacher who tries to teach thinking is wasting time. A contrary view is that although background knowledge may be missing for some contexts, young children's processes of critical and creative thought are certainly in place early on. Consider some examples.

Examples of Early Critical Thought   Tonya (age 3.5) listened intently as her mother and she were visiting the woman next door, who complained she had locked herself out of her house.

"How did you get in?" queried Tonya of the ample-sized woman.

"I let myself in through that little hole," the woman replied, indicating a small opening in the back screen door near the latch.

"That little hole!" replied Tonya, extreme skepticism showing all over her face. The knowledge background of sticking something through a small opening near a latch to lift it up was missing, but the critical process of applying a matching-size criterion was clearly there.

Timothy, age 3.6, was being read "The Three Little Pigs." Upon hearing the part where the third pig gets to the apple tree before the wolf, climbs it, and picks all the juicy apples, Timothy pointed to the picture of the pig up in the tree. He said, "If I had feets like that, I couldn't pick the apples, and I couldn't climb the tree." Again, the critical process was there and working.

Karen, age 4.3, was being read a new folktale at bedtime. According to the story, someone had been stealing corn from the family field at night. The oldest brother was sent to watch the field at night, but fell asleep; the same thing happened to the second brother. At this point Karen suggested, "Why didn't they use an owl? Owls stay awake all night long and sleep during the day." Here, again, we have the creative process and application of background information for some problem solving.

At age 5.2 Jon commented one evening, "That's not really true; you have to learn it." Mystified, his mother questioned him and discovered that Jon had been watching some cereal commercial on TV that morning. Jon explained, "When you eat cereal, that doesn't make you a good surfer; you have to learn how to do it." When his mother began to write this happening down, Jon wanted to know what she was doing. Upon learning he then added, "And Oreo cookies don't make you unafraid, either."

With all due respect to the significant work of Piaget, the critical process is apparently intact early on in the lives of children, with wide variation from experience, environment, interaction with adults—all aspects of context. The children in these examples were all actively constructing their own knowledge and using a critical and creative process.

Thinking big about the little   We do not want to hurry and rush children, but we do not want to underestimate them, either. The work of the teacher is to select appropriate goals, content, and experiences to encourage productive growth. We want to *think big* about even young children when setting goals and planning learning activities. We do not want to think small about children, lacking respect for what they can do and doling them only tiny fragments of learning. We are thinking big when we value them where they are, use long-range planning, work for long-term results with integrated language use, and help them stretch to their fullest potential.

Implications for a Genuine Developmental Orientation   When teachers present, for example, the differences between fact and opinion, they move from the more obvious to the more subtle differences in context. They do this taking into account individual abilities. They teach individual children at their growing edge of learning, at the cutting edge of their own level of development. Reflecting genuine developmental constraints, their instruction needs to be kept not only in context but also ongoing, rather than pursued with intensity for a limited set of lessons or a unit.

In light of the foregoing explications a controversial issue emerges. (See Box 10.1.) Find someone with whom to discuss it.

BOX 10.1 A Discussion Issue: Mind Ownership

You may find some parents and some teachers who do not share your enthusiasm for developing children as independent, creative, and critical thinkers. Some parents may be fearful that they will lose the maturing minds of their children. Literacy, literary learning, and thinking can be threatening. Some parents may fear that teachers are snoopers or agitators. Accordingly, some teachers may drag their feet in giving children control over their language and thought. But if student writers (and speakers) do not feel that they control the content and the thought, "they don't want to write" (Moffett, 1986). And they don't want to talk. (And they don't want to do much of anything important in the language arts.)

WHAT GOALS ARE USEFUL TO AN INSTRUCTIONAL FRAMEWORK FOR TEACHING THINKING?

To put an instructional framework in context, we need to recall relevant ideas from earlier frameworks presented for the language arts of listening, speaking, and writing. Our goals usually fall into a pattern of, first, process; then, purpose or use; and last, attitude. A framework for thinking is no different.

The major points of this chapter's framework of goals for creative and critical thinking will provide some organization for your curriculum decisions. These emphases are spotting purpose (getting to the heart of a persuasive claim) and using evidence (making and acting on a well-founded judgment). See Box 10.2 on page 344. (The complete version in Appendix 10A offers greater detail for study and use for the year's curriculum.) Once goals are established the next step is to implement them in a program, thus entailing more decisions.

WHERE DO CHILDREN GAIN CONTEXT FOR THINKING?

"If two people agree on everything, only one person is doing the thinking."

Sam Rayburn

This section does not stress the physical and emotional classroom climates for critical thinking, important as they might be. Those aspects have been implied in the opening scene and dealt with amply in other chapters. What is stressed here is **context:** the *where* of the thinkers' own multiple situations.

Message Contexts

A big communicative mistake is ignoring the context(s) of a message. One propagandist trick is to quote someone out of context or only partially quote. Significant messages where our critical thinking is most crucial have complicated, complex, and multiple points of view. For example, what do we think and do when *we* have been wrong as opposed to when a president is likely to have been wrong? Our interpretations are determined in part by personal aspects, content, and larger and larger world contexts. (Chapter 6 on discussion stressed these in question asking.) It helps the student to be well informed regarding the content area in question *and* the larger-world contexts—for example, perceived school, city, region.

Communicator Purposes and Contextual Bias   The contexts of purposes are important. All speakers have biases, coming from sources such as home rearing, broader culture, education, religion, job, and self-generated interests. All these contexts act to bias the messages we send and receive and affect our open and hidden purposes. Students can look for potential sources of bias in messages, from Brown's spinach propagandist to political candidates' orations.

Human Contexts and Meaning   Words mean different things to different people based on their past experiences—their contexts. Whether the first connection that pops into your mind at the word *pig* is a dictionary classification in the animal kingdom, an obese or gluttonous person, a cartoon or literary character, a type of iron, or something else depends in large part on your contexts (and your broadness and depth of vocabulary meanings—how

---

**BOX 10.2 Brief Framework for Critical and Creative Thinking for
the Language Arts***

To think critically students need to:

Goal 1: Be Aware of, Integrate, and Use Stages of Critical Thinking Processes in All
the Language Arts.

Subgoals: Students need to understand, engage in, and monitor the:

1.1. Critical process (evaluative use of leftover thinking space). Includes intake, purpose
spotting, construction and application of standards, skill in applying evidence,
judgment, and action taking. (*Note:* See assessment section for detail, or the entire
framework in Appendix 10A.)

Goal 2: Think Critically for a Variety of Purposes.

Subgoals:

2.1. Appreciate critical purposes in the context of the language arts used in listening,
speaking, reading, writing, and their forms across the curriculum. (Includes analysis
and response to persuasive logic, style, and organization, contrasting their use in
other purposes of language use.)

Goal 3: Develop a Lasting, Positive Attitude Toward the Value of Creative and Critical
Thinking and Responsible Use of Persuasive Speech.

Subgoals:

3.1. Develop a willingness to think creatively and critically.

3.2. Use persuasive language logically, ethically, and with responsibility.

3.3. Establish personal standards independent of peer influence.

3.4. Develop a judicious attitude of careful analysis and judgment for self-protection
(realize that there are degrees of honesty, quality, and depth of scholarship in
language received and sent).

3.5. Be open to many different perceptions of the world.

**Checklists based on the expanded framework are in the assessment section at the end of this chapter,
in Chapter 13 on media, and in the total framework in Appendix 10A.*

Sources: California State Department of Education (1987), New York State Department of Education (1984), Wolvin
& Coakley (1985); Lundsteen (1969, 1976, 1986). Illustrative examples for this framework are found in the section on
how to teach.

---

well informed you are). *Meanings are not in the common word, but in the person using it.*
Meanings are not context-free.

Differences in Interpersonal Contexts   Many of our problems in communication arise
because we forget for the moment that individual experiences (contexts) are *not identical.*
We establish communication best by discovering what is common in the succession of our
experiences, while holding in mind that we may differ in our view of any single experience.
Even a dictionary does not tell us what common words "mean." A dictionary is a history
of how a word has been used most frequently in some contexts and at different times. It
indicates various areas of meaning. Instead of saying, "What does it mean?" a better
question in terms of understanding each other is "What do *you* mean?" (*your* contexts).
Specificity is important. Assuming that everyone knows what you are talking about and

---

BOX 10.3 An Activity on Meaning and Contexts

In a relevant and appropriate context, ask students in your class to write (or tell) first-in-mind meanings for common words that come up naturally in class, such as *pig, lead,* or *check.* You and they will find wide differences among class members' meanings. You can discuss how past experiences might have influenced the selected *connotations* and the possible effect of experience on them as critical thinkers.

---

assuming that you know what others are talking about (without asking questions to make sure) are two common causes of erroneous thinking. (Recall in the opening scene that the variation in context led to the challenged assumption that all young children want or ought to swing.) Communication and thought about real-world problems are deeply embedded in multiple contexts. Multiple contexts are like the layers of an onion. Layers might be the child, the class, the region, the nation, and the world. This section features some illustrative activities such as the one in Box 10.3.

Communicator Credibility and Context   Our act of determining speaker *credibility* is influenced by contexts—ours and the speaker's or author's. Depending on your contexts, you will select as credible those persons who have qualities such as the following: competence in the area under discussion, positive character, positive goals, enthusiasm, likability, and closeness or proximity to your cultural group. How you rank these standards will depend on your contexts, as shown in the illustrative activity in Box 10.4 on page 346.

In essence, real-life communication contexts are complex, multiple, and flowing. What begins for us in any communication situation is our awareness that something is going on. Otherwise experiences rarely if ever just begin, because there was something that preceded them. Our story never really ends, either. Something more will happen. There is always more to start with than we can take into account; there is more to say than we can possibly say; more to end with than we can imagine. We need to take this idea about context into account when we think critically and when we *teach* critical thinking to students in our classroom— the next topic. Since earlier chapters have stressed creative thinking, as will Chapter 13, the following section focuses largely on how to teach critical thinking (without forgetting its place in creative problem solving).

HOW DO I TEACH CRITICAL THINKING?

> "Students can learn that *how* to think is different from
> *what* to think."
> *NCTE, 1982*

Basic teaching stances grow out of your definitions and rationale; skills grow out of your framework of goals; teaching strategies grow out of a combination of these plus developmental and psychological know-how, as you structure a learning environment that is both enriching and psychologically safe. Be reminded, especially when considering this area, that teaching is complex, demanding, and uniquely human. Recall that the relation-

---

BOX 10.4 Activity on Personal Credibility and Contexts

Consider speakers, their credibility, personal biases in thinking critically about them, and contexts.

1. Employing relevance to content area study that is ongoing, you can ask your students to help you gather a list of people in the entertainment, sports, political, literary, historical, and their own personal worlds.

2. Next ask the students to rate them on a scale of 10 as highly favorable, to neutral, to unfavorable.

3. Then generate a list of topics.

4. Next ask the students to indicate on which of the topics (if any) they would think of the people as believable sources of information.

5. Discuss in what way their favorable bias toward the persons might affect their willingness to accept them as a credible source for an area (even when they know there is little or no evidence that they would be experts). Include current TV ads using testimonials of popular people in your interaction, and include the idea of *contexts* in your discussion.

---

ships of critical thinking and communication suggest the language arts as an appropriate place for such instruction. The language arts teacher realizes that children's communication is a rational process using interdependent purposes, materials, and contexts.

By way of overview, Figure 10.2 gives a schematic diagram of the higher mental processes of creative and critical thinking. It shows their overlap and integration in the process of creative problem solving as used in this chapter. It also includes some major constructs in this chapter as we have moved through definitions, rationale, who, what, where, and how. Dotted lines for the circles indicate that there are no hard, fast lines between areas. Use (and add to) this chart as an organizer for this chapter, as a check on the comprehensiveness of your own curriculum for teaching thinking, and as a framework when using the series of connected activities in the activity book.

This section could give lessons to teach (as in the activity book), or learning experiences to present or arrange. This section could stress five steps to teaching critical thinking as shown in Box 10.5 on page 347 (adapted from Cooke & Haipt, 1986). This section could (and in Box 10.5 does) offer such an instructional organization. But of far more importance for the teaching of critical thought is the basic stance and principles of the teacher, and the knowledge of possible instructional inclusions, coupled with ability to integrate and to assess students' application of criteria. These topics are addressed in the remainder of this chapter.

Basic Instructional Stance

Instructional stance with regard to critical thinking includes a position on issues such as (1) the isolated lesson versus integrated instruction and (2) other basic ideas about instruction concerning persuasive language. Consider each in turn.

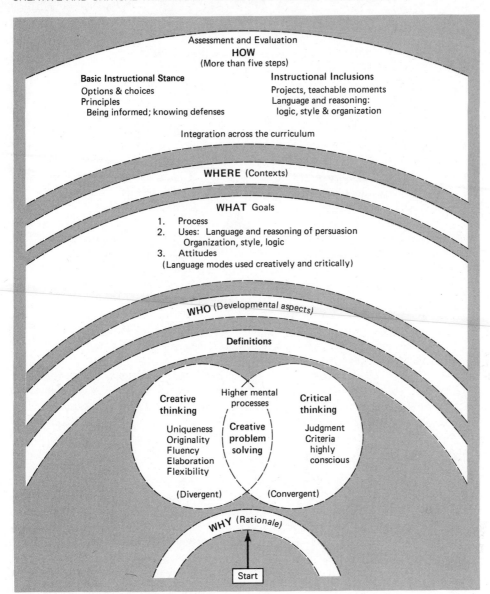

Figure 10.2   Creative and critical thinking.

**BOX 10.5 Five Steps to Teaching Critical and
Creative Thinking in the Language Arts**

Step 1. *Oral approach.* The teacher provides for the *oral reading* of segments from literature prompted by the following: open-ended questions (Chapter 6); discussion of artistic illustrations; student identification with story characters, themes, and their relationships to personal life experiences—*keeping identifiable criteria in mind.* (Almost any of the books for children in the previous chapters could be selected.)

Step 2. *Imaging.* The teacher guides students through *imaging* and experiencing with all senses, thus bringing to life the book's major themes and relevant social concepts—again, with identifiable criteria in mind.

Step 3. *Response projects.* The teacher provides options and choices of *response projects.* These focus on art activities that are representative of the emotions. They are self-expressive and use identifiable criteria. The arts are valued for their impact on cognitive and personal development. Such artistic projects involve whole-brain images, feelings, thoughts, and kinesthetic activity. This step encourages right- and left-brain interaction and growth.

Step 4. *Discussion.* The teacher guides tutorial, pair, small-group, and total group *discussion* of process and product in response to literature, in order to obtain communication of personal thoughts, feelings, and well-reasoned judgments (as in many of the opening scenes in this book).

Step 5. *Assessment.* Although application of criteria is ongoing throughout all the preceding steps and the entire learning experience, the teacher guides *assessment* of the literature-based activity again with questioning at the concluding time of reflection (Chapters 5, 6).

Isolated Lesson versus Integrated Instruction   There are two major camps at present: (1) those who want isolated lessons in thinking (context-free) and (2) those who want to integrate thinking instruction as part of the teaching of school content areas. Some programs for the development of creative and critical thinking start with and emphasize large processes, purposes, attitudes, and their real-world, functional use in children's lives. Other programs try to build up creative and critical thought from isolated skills, like Tinkertoys. From the "skills point of view," for example, the implemented framework might call for many isolated lessons on similarities and many lessons on differences *before* any lessons combining their use in analogy. Such an isolated, mechanistic program forgets that first the child needs a genuine and important reason to use analogy. Such programs may try to justify the isolated-skill approach under the guise of saying it is developmental. But we know that natural development is firmly rooted in children's genuine use of and need for thoughtful communication—the big, whole picture (Chapter 2).

Although the teacher in the opening scene spent much time at the beginning of the year building group skills (Chapter 6), the teacher was developing thought mainly with large projects, such as the students' involvement with the new park (social studies), their extended writing workshops, extended responses to literature, and other content areas across the curriculum. Rarely if ever did the class use isolated, gimmicky activities unrelated to larger purposes and projects. This practice was part of the teacher's larger instructional stance related to implementation of goals. One commentator on the isolated-lesson approach said he grew increasingly disturbed by the lack of correspondence between what is required for critical thinking in adulthood and what is being taught in school programs (Sternberg, 1985).

In the isolated-lesson approach, the problems given to students are not only unrealistic but also do little to teach children to solve significant problems of life. ("If your pet, a 50-pound alligator, had a fever, would you put him in the ice box? Why or why not?") While this question may liven up a class for a few moments, it is not nearly as worthwhile as genuine problems that can turn up in children's conversations, arguments, discussions, commercials, newspapers, sales pitches, political speeches, and classroom projects such as the one in the opening scene. Teachers can make greater use of teachable moments with genuine problems than with artificially contrived ones. Teachers can be committed to teach integratively and realistically, and to grab the important, context-laden events in children's daily living, using them for instruction. Most of the opening scenes in this book have illustrated this point about integrative, whole-language teaching.

Basic Position   Basic ideas for teaching critical thinking include strategy about (1) giving options and choices, (2) principles, and (3) instructional inclusions. Inclusions encompass the nature of persuasive language and reasoning—its logic, style, and organization. Consider each in turn.

Options and choices   Teachers are engaged in systematically weaning students from their control so that the children can think and act for themselves, taking their place in the real world. Thus, how to develop children's thinking includes the key instructional strategy of providing options and choices. As part of such a strategy teachers can encourage opportunities for playing with divergent ideas and putting them together in new ways (combinatory play). The teacher's *sentence stems* can reflect these options and choices. For example, instead of saying "I want you to . . ." (do or think thus and so), which limits the chance for child response, choose other sentence stems in your teaching. The teacher in the opening scene used "I wonder why. . . ." Some of these more open stems (question stems) are given in Box 10.6.

In other words, the idea is to have teacher-student and student-student interaction in

---

BOX 10.6 Encouraging Options with Sentence Stems

"Can you find some ways . . ."

"Can you try (e.g., to think) another way . . ."

"Can you show us many possible ways . . ."

"In what ways might you . . ."

"Can you find anything else . . ."

"I wonder why . . ."

"What might you try next time . . ."

"What might happen if you . . ."

a format that encourages divergent and autonomous thinking ("What are some things that make a bird a bird?") Such an open-ended strategy is part of a larger instructional stance.

Principles   Consider the next four teaching principles. They relate both to instructional stance and inclusions.

1. *Persuasion competition.* Teachers need to help children be aware that they do not live in a place where there is a persuasion monopoly backed by force. They can help children know that they live in a *persuasion competition* where it is up to them to gather information and make the most appropriate judgments. While propaganda is concerned with influencing what people think, education is even more concerned with how people think.

2. *Honesty.* Again, teachers can help children learn that there are degrees of *honesty,* quality, and depth of scholarship in the language they receive and send. Here we have critical thinking as part of the communication process—examining the effectiveness and ethics of oneself and others as communicators. If teachers build their instruction just around that one idea, they will have made an important contribution to the growth of their students during the school year. Teachers need to take care that children are not somehow encouraged to distort truth themselves, but that they act as analysts and judges of distortion during classroom activity about ads and propaganda. In any role-playing of a falsifying ad person, discussion needs to emphasize an ethical stance.

3. *Being well informed.* Teachers help children see that when they are *well informed,* persuasion usually succeeds only when it is to their advantage. But young children may not be well informed. They may not realize that although some advertisers have some concern for public welfare, they have more concern for company profits. Young children, unlike young Jon in the earlier developmental example, may not know an ad form when they see one. They may not realize that the aim of ads is usually not to benefit them and sometimes not to be straightforward.

    The best protection is to quit being ignorant, and to be aware that persuasion is continually, consciously, and unconsciously being used and absorbed. Although basically it is important to trust people, it is wise to remain judicious, and to be careful of what verbal actions we condone—including our own. Communicators need to ask important questions of themselves: "With my language, how have I been treating the people I know? With respect? As ends in themselves? Or with disrespect, as just means to my own ends?"

4. *Being gentle.* A final teaching principle is that critical thinking in the classroom needs to be not only tough-minded but also *tender-hearted.* For instance, it was important that Joel and Horace in the opening scene were good friends and could criticize each other's writing productively rather than destructively. The language of critical thinking in the classroom is not meant to become predatory.

    With such principles in mind, the next aspect to consider in teaching critical thinking is your instructional inclusions for your program.

Instructional Inclusions

Box 10.7 provides a brief overview of some instructional inclusions for critical thinking about persuasion. The list focuses on (1) the *communicators* (including teacher-student and peer interaction), (2) the *language* (including its organization and style), and (3) the *reasoning*

BOX 10.7 Brief List of Some Instructional Inclusions

Communicators

- Ethics, integrity, straightforwardness, and honesty (attitude)
- Self-protection and protection of the rights of others (recognizing doublespeak, defensive strategies)
- Realities and contextual ways of knowing (some general semantics from the *where* section)
- Being well informed (knowledge)

Language

- Style and organization of persuasion
- Lots of student-selected projects, demanding creative and critical thought (skill in applying the above inclusions and taking action)

Reasoning

- Analysis as a prelude to selecting a standard or criterion and judging, e.g., evaluating the amount and quality of materials supporting a proposal (*process* of evaluation)
- Relations to creative problem solving
- Inference making
- Logic

(or logic that is part of the other two). Some items relate to the four teaching principles presented earlier.

Note that the projects mentioned under language in Box 10.7 use active strategies including the following: questioning each other with criteria in mind, dialogue, role-playing, dramatization, and discussion for genuine concept attainment (i.e., multiple avenues of learning). Teachers design a few carefully formulated questions to stimulate critical and creative thinking. Now consider the reasoning of inference making. Such an instructional inclusion encourages critical thinking and provides a *basic building block* for analyzing logic.

The Language Uses of Facts and Inference   When we use language, we sometimes make mountains of inference out of molehills of fact. The term *inference,* often mentioned in connection with critical thought, refers in part to the analysis of the logical unity of a message. Briefly, in using inference you attempt to understand what the speaker or author has left unsaid or expressed only through implication. In order to unify, inferencing takes leaps from what is stated literally to what may be actually intended. Recall how Naomi in the opening scene inferred about the black-eyed Susan. "It's my mamma's favorite flower . . . I think I know *why* now!" Inferences grow from a listener's or reader's background and intuitive prediction, usually from putting several clues together. Before continuing, play the game in Figure 10.3 on page 352. You can also use it with your students.

To most of us this is a pretty familiar scene, so familiar that we may tend to feel that we see more in it than is there for us to see. Try answering the questions below and see how you come out.

Which of the following statements are true, false, or cannot be answered at all?

	(T)	(F)	(?)
1. The Jones family owns a TV set.	( )	( )	( )
2. Johnny is doing his homework while he watches TV.	( )	( )	( )
3. Johnny's father is a stockholder.	( )	( )	( )
4. The screen is showing a scene from a western.	( )	( )	( )
5. Mrs. Jones is knitting a sweater.	( )	( )	( )
6. Mr. Jones is a cigar smoker.	( )	( )	( )
7. There are three people in the room.	( )	( )	( )
8. The Jones family subscribes to *Time, Life,* and *Fortune.*	( )	( )	( )
9. The Jones family consists of Mr. Jones, Mrs. Jones, and Johnny.	( )	( )	( )
10. They have a cat for a pet.	( )	( )	( )
11. They are watching an evening television show.	( )	( )	( )

Figure 10.3 Facts or inferences? (*Source:* Kaiser Aluminum & Chemical Corporation.)

None of the statements on page 352 can be said to be true from what you actually saw in the picture.

1. You do not know that the set is owned by them; it could be borrowed, or a demonstration set.

2. You do not know whether Johnny is doing homework or not; all you can see is that he has a book in front of him.

3. You do not know that Johnny's father is a stockholder; you only know he is looking at the stock market report. Matter of fact, you don't know he is Johnny's father, either. He may be an uncle or friend just visiting in the house.

4. You do not know that it is a western. It could be a commercial or a foreign-made movie, or almost anything.

5. You do not know that it is Mrs. Jones, and you cannot tell what she is knitting.

6. You do not know that Mr. Jones (if, indeed, that is Mr. Jones) actually smokes cigars. You only can see that there is a cigar on the ashtray. Perhaps someone else left it there.

7. You do not know how many people might be in the room; you can only see that there are three people in the part of the room shown in the picture.

8. You do not know what magazines they subscribe to. The ones on the table may have been purchased at a newsstand or loaned by a friend.

9. You do not know if this *is* the Jones family; nor can you tell if there are other members of the family who are not present.

10. It could be a neighbor's cat, making itself at home.

11. You cannot tell if it is evening or not; only that the lights are on. Perhaps it is midday and the shades have been drawn.

Figure 10.3 *(Continued)*

To most of us this is a rather familiar scene, so familiar that we may tend to feel that we see more in it than is there for us to see. How did you come out?

Chances are you felt that some of the statements about the people in the picture were true. You may have even considered some to be facts. Instead they are labeled inferences here. A "fact" for you is something you personally experienced or tested—touched, heard, tasted, smelled, saw; the rest is an "inference." If we are conscious of the difference between facts and inferences, we are less likely to have communication and logic difficulties. Facts can be tested. Facts change with time. The statement that New York City has a population of 10,000, of 200,000, of 7,891,000 were facts *at the time* somebody counted.

Another way to think about inferences is that they indicate higher or lower probabilities. The inference that night follows day has a high probability because of the wide observation of past performance. We can build a whole crazy quilt of inference built upon inference, attributing motives on top of generalizations as in some comic plots in literature

---

BOX 10.8 Question Criteria for Inference

1. *Who* said so? (Don't rely blindly on "them," or a gang leader, or anyone indefinite.)

2. *What* was said? (Not what persons say they "think" someone says—who also thought someone said. Third-hand information is probably wrong; forget it.)

3. What did the person *mean*? (Ask if he or she is present; tell the message back. If not, ask *yourself* the question. Then at least you can realize that they may not mean what you think they mean.)

4. *How* did the person know? (What are the sources of information—expertise, observation, experience, experimentation, or intuition?)

5. *When* did the person say it? (Five years ago? Fifty? When sick? Often we find ourselves disagreeing when one of us saw something at one time and the other at another time.)

6. *Why* did the person say it? (I'm not sure; let's find out.)

---

and other media intrigues ("I thought that he thought that I thought that he thought that I thought . . ."). These ideas about inferences are an important part of the foundation of your teaching program for thinking. (The activity book elaborates.)

Question checklist for inference making   Box 10.8 gives a handy checklist of questions, a check on inductive inference. Perhaps it will work as well for you as for your students. Develop such a checklist with your class.

To move yet further into instructional inclusions, we consider next in detail that the persuasive aim of language has the following three characteristics: (1) logic, (2) style, and (3) organization. We examine each of these in turn.

Teaching About Persuasive Language and Reasoning: Its Logic, Style, and Organization.

We would hope that an honest, knowledgeable persuader would use well-founded, clear logic, style, and organization. But it is well to understand what more frequently happens, both unintentionally and intentionally. Consider logic first.

LOGIC of Persuasion   The "logic" of persuasive language is simply to present ideas in a fashion that the receiver will be likely to accept. Two traditional forms of thinking may be considered to be logical: deductive and inductive. In *deductive* logic, recall that one goes from the general to the particular. A statement is made about all the members of a set, a particular case is shown to be a member of that set, and so the general statement applies to that particular case. The classic example, of course, goes something like this:

All persons are mortal. (General statement about a group—persons.)

Leslie Jones is a person. (A particular case belongs to that group.)

Therefore, Leslie Jones is mortal. (A logical, deductive conclusion.)

Classically, arguments consist of a *true* proposition (or evidence) and *valid* relationships between all the evidence presented and all the conclusions reached.

In *inductive* logic, one goes from the particular(s) to the general. For example, you have observed the sun rising every particular morning since you can remember, and so have your family, friends, and neighbors—and astronomers. You have justifiable, inductive reason to expect that it will rise tomorrow morning as well.

The logic found in deductive and inductive reasoning can be misused, however, by implying that the criteria for making logical conclusions have been met, when in fact they have not. Two kinds of seeming logic commonly appear in persuasion: (1) *example* (often a single one, a misuse of inductive logic); and (2) *incomplete argument* (a misuse of deductive logic). That is, *induction* in persuasive discourse is too often reduced to an isolated or even a fictional example. *Deduction* in persuasive discourse is too often reduced to incomplete patterns of reasoning from dubious reasons or general statements. Study reveals a difference between the logic of an ethical and well-trained scientist and that of an unscrupulous propagandist. Consider incomplete argument first since it occurs foremost in the language of misleading persuasion.

Incomplete argument   Aristotle, an ancient Greek philosopher, claimed that in order for a conclusion or argument to be worthwhile, it had to have valid, supporting reasons. In the incomplete argument, persuaders, who may not bother giving any supporting facts, leave reasons vague, unstated, only barely probable. Example: "Every child needs one of these cute little Huggy Buggy stuffed animals." But why? If one uses the example of deductive logic above about all people being mortal, we could set up a series of arguments for that example, as follows:

Every child needs every kind of stuffed animal.

Huggy Buggy is a stuffed animal.

Therefore, every child needs one of these cute little stuffed animals called the Huggy Buggy.

Stated in this manner, it does not take long for one to figure out that the original statement is ludicrous and that the conclusion is one we do not need to take seriously.

One of the ways you can help students to identify an incomplete argument is that one could just as easily claim the opposite. "Absence makes the heart grow fonder" can be turned around with "Out of sight, out of mind." Students in your class can collect many of these contradictory arguments or practical maxims. ("He who hesitates . . . ; Look before you . . .")

Deductive reasoning, when based on reliable, carefully stated facts, can lead to logical conclusions that are of the highest quality. But some intentional propagandists do not let lack of facts hold them back. If they do not have any needed facts to support their ideas, then they simply make them up, especially if a check on them is difficult. When facts have been minimized, concealed, or fabricated, or selected ones have been magnified out of proportion, the result is a lack of comprehensiveness (e.g., "War is peace"). The Institute of Propaganda Analysis has referred to deliberate use and emphasis of only selective evidence as card stacking or half-truth. Comprehensiveness is an important criterion of expository discourse and honest journalistic reporting (Kinneavy, 1971).

In fact, one of the prime reasons that the statements in some persuasive arguments are incomplete is that the persuaders know they might fail to stand up under close scrutiny.

Thus they avoid calling attention to their lack of logic and evidence. This incompleteness gives an opportunity for defense of the indefensible. Such deduction can be reduced to invalid, incomplete patterns of reasoning from dubious premises.

Single example   Now we move from deductive logic and persuasive language use to induction, making a generalization from many instances. For the inductive side of logic we find many persuaders (including advertisers) using the single example to substitute for a representative sample. Persuaders may even try to suggest that the single example is equated with the total population. (Examples: *All Indians walk in single file . . . at least the one I saw did.* Or, based on the opening scene, *My little sister just wants to swing—so do all young children.*) Single example is a watered-down form of inductive thinking sometimes used in persuasion with overgeneralization of its application. By overgeneralization is meant the implication that if it is true for one person in one instance, it must be true for all people at all times. (This overgeneralization could lead to a discussion of stereotyping. See the activity book for a lesson that goes with this aspect of thought.)

Whether the example the persuader offers is fictitious or supposedly a testimony from a real person appears to matter little. Nor does it bother the advertiser to suggest that you generalize from a sample size of one (or ten, in the phrase *one out of ten*). We take vivid examples to our hearts easily and endow them with the dignity of logic. People "buy" the single advertising example of the cavity-free family, the mother with a whiter wash without pollutants, and the child demonstrating the remarkable strength and operational power of an actually quite flimsy toy. (Recall once again from the opening scene the child using his sister's preference for swings as evidence—and being checked on his sample size by a peer.)

In sum, induction in persuasive discourse is often reduced to isolated or even fictional examples. The *standard* for logic that builds from particulars to a general idea (inductive) is both probability and plausibility. Young children have difficulty in grasping the concept that generalizations are only probable. They have difficulty in thinking only tentatively about generalizations. *They need teacher guidance.*

Of course, we run into situations when any kind of formal logic is of little use—when facts are simply not available to us, when we have to begin with a value judgment. Sometimes in addition to standards of probability and plausibility, organized thinking has to depend on gradations or rating scales. Then, too, thinking during any of the language uses is unlikely to be purely deductive or inductive but rather a combination.

For instance, using language for literary purposes, we may identify the theme of a story through finding relationships between key episodes or examples (inductive logic). An example might be Shirley Gordon's *The Boy Who Wanted a Family* (Chapter 9), with its theme of adjusting to a different family structure. We also may test the "truth" of the theme against our own generalizations about life (deductive logic). As our children evaluate a piece of persuasion, they use the same thought processes. That is, they *induce* as they note clues about the persuasive piece (its logic, style, and organization); and they *deduce* as they test the action the persuader wants against the realities that they already hold. For example, a group might discuss what authors want them to do or believe and whether or not they can accept such ideas. Examples of authors might be Zolotow, of *William's Doll,* or Lifton, of *Return to Hiroshima.* Such thought processes are crucial to a child's progress in creative problem solving.

Seven propaganda devices and their faulty logic   To continue our examination, most of the seven original propaganda devices first described by the Institute of Propaganda Analysis reveal errors in (or bypassing of) inductive and deductive logic. In Box 10.9

BOX 10.9 Seven Common Propaganda Devices and Their Faulty Reasoning

1. *Name calling:* attaching unfavorable labels to a person, object, event, or cause to bring about rejection.

The name caller avoids discussing the facts or presenting a full deductive or inductive argument for examination (*chicken, flakey, activist, racist,* etc.). Name-calling words are often "snarl" words as opposed to "purr" words.

2. *Glittering generalities:* vague phrases that promise much, that prompt automatic approval ("Ours is always the best"; "This candidate is a strong proponent of justice"; "All students who pass study hard").

The reasoning stays general and never spells out the specific. The user of this device wants you to make that leap yourself. The generalization is unlikely to be universally true. An implied specific instance may not be a valid one, may not really belong in the broad, general class indicated.

3. *Transfer/testimonial: transfer* refers to associating a set of symbols or positive qualities with a purpose for which they were not intended (such as associating the Statue of Liberty with a product—you are being patriotic in using that brand). A psychological appeal is used to gain an emotional response. *Testimonials* refer to getting some prominent person with a good image to endorse the idea or product, whether or not he/she is qualified as expert in that field.

The inductive reasoning is based on too few examples. The propagandist hopes that you will think that the positive image of the testifier will rub off on you (transfer) if you do what is advocated.

4. *Red herring across the trail:* bringing in information irrelevant to the topic, not necessarily following the topic, often in order to cloud, ignore, or duck the issue.

This device violates relational validity in thinking. ("Buy our [inferior] soap and get free panty hose.") For example, one candidate who is attacked for not keeping promises simply switches the topic to alleging the opponent's falsification of a tax return, attacking the person rather than the content of issues, proposals, and political record. (The red herring refers to a tactic of an Eskimo sled driver for keeping a pack of wolves from catching him. He threw out a piece of fish to his rear from time to time and so gave his dog team opportunity to reach the village.)

5. *Plain folks:* pretending to be one of the group, trying to establish identification with the audience, adopting their language, dress, and behavior. "I am a good, ordinary person, just like you, 'down home,' and this (somehow magically) qualifies me. You can vote safely for me." Again, valid premises and relational thinking may be faulty.

6. *Bandwagon:* using language to create the impression of universal approval (ignoring individuality and the rights of a minority). Some people may claim that "everyone is doing it" (so you should, too). "All your friends are . . . "; "Millions can't be wrong." (The word *bandwagon* comes from the idea that small towns sometimes were entertained by a band riding in a wagon large enough for some people to scramble on for a wonderful free ride.) This trick is hard for many children to resist when pressured by peers.

(Continued)

Again, when the complete argument is exposed, as was done in the Huggy Buggy example, reason and alternative facts can take over. Also, the question checklist for inference, given in Box 10.8, can help children deal with this device.

7. *Card stacking:* presenting only the parts of the facts that favor one side (half-truth; out of context). Tricks of manipulating by withholding, ignoring, and over- or underemphasizing evidence are often used in card stacking.

A half-truth deliberately suppresses basic parts or sides of the argument that the propagandist knows about. Some of your young tattlers in school will use this one. (Example: Salesman to farmer, "This bucket has never leaked a drop!" [But, of course, it has never been used.])

they are gathered with brief explanations and notes on their logic. Teachers can provide examples and nonexamples to elicit significant attributes of each propaganda device. Then children can collect, analyze, and judge their own examples.

Analyzing propaganda examples is not enough; children need also to *apply criteria for evaluating the propaganda* in its context. It seems important to guide children to be aware of propaganda devices, especially the "bandwagon" one, so that they can listen, view, and read critically when exposed to them. Since freedom of speech in our democracy ensures equal rights to both honest and dishonest speakers, our children need to become effective critical thinkers in order to protect themselves and control their own minds.

Figure 10.4 shows a wheel of these devices with *repetition* as the strengthening hub of propaganda. Effective propaganda may not bring about a change in desired behavior on the basis of one persuasive message. Propagandists often need a series of messages to accomplish the task of influencing. Thus, some persuasive efforts take the form of a campaign with repetition a key ingredient.

Figure 10.4   Seven propaganda devices.

See the activity book for activities related to induction, notably "The Blind Men and the Elephant" and "The Rumor Clinic". Also see the activities on stereotyping, assumptions, analogy, tests of cause-effect statements, faulty arguments, debating, and inference diagramming. Having considered logic, next we consider style.

STYLE of Persuasion   The language of persuasion needs to be extraordinary enough to arouse attention and interest, but at the same time the style has to seem natural to the audience. Modern advertisers appear to try almost any technique to get attention. But then they must lead this attention to the product they are selling. Persuaders may choose words to make listeners hear things not said, accept as thoughts things only implied, believe things only suggested, and transform nondifferences into significant ones. (Is X's computer screen really that much better?) They may use trick words such as *free, new, miracle, bargain, fortified,* and *exclusive.*

Generally speaking, the persuasive style relies heavily on appeal to the person addressed and on emotional biases to achieve an appearance of trustworthiness and knowledge. Thus one feature of persuasive style appears to be the attempt to adapt the dialect of the message to the context of the audience. This adaptation to context means appropriate stylistic use of cultural conventions. Examples are: space distances between speaker and listener, bodily contacts, gesture, posture, rhythm in repetitions, and parallel language structures.

Dialect adaptation   Adaptation of dialects may relate to the propaganda device labeled *plain folks* in Box 10.9. It is a method often used by politicians who, by speaking in a particular dialect, refer to their humble origins. They hope that the audience will accept the politician's plain-folks background as qualification for the office. ("This candidate will work just as hard for his paycheck as you do for yours!") One fifth-grade class discovered and labeled the apparent opposite of the plain folks: *better folks,*—a device with snob appeal. (Dialect is discussed further in Chapters 12 and 14.)

We see, then, an adaptation of style to context and culture. The immediacy of persuasive style with its personal appeal and emotional biases usually means that persuaders must be so much of their particular time and place that their messages are soon dated. This kind of discourse is unlikely to endure in the same way as does the less immediate language of classic literature. Since language changes (Chapter 12), the most successful methods of propagandizing change, too. Scientists are also tied to the time and place of their data and current statistical techniques.

Repetition   Repetition may also be seen as a form of style in persuasion. A brand name, for example, is frequently mentioned along with a depiction of the buying act, *over and over and over.* This style is especially true in competition where all sources are equally favored (or equally untrustworthy), and the audience is probably going to buy a brand of the type of product, such as toothpaste, one way or another.

Symbolism in persuasion   Persuaders may use changing and current symbols and myths of the target culture. These objects and beliefs are usually related to important cultural institutions, such as the family, religion, and politics. Symbols may take the form of flags, anthems, group heroes, and supposed scientific findings. Most cultures have these authority-laden beliefs (sometimes inconsistent and changing). Each child absorbs these symbols and myths unconsciously. Lenin, Hitler, Roosevelt, and Reagan all had a clear view of the contemporary myths of their respective countries. Examples deal with the vagaries of *good, love, the value of hard work,* the jargon of *isms,* and elaborate or euphemistic scientific words.

In persuasion, these symbols dear to our hearts are used purposefully to rouse our emotions. Draping an American flag over a car, for example, stirs patriotic feelings in the viewer, who links these feelings to the car being promoted. Suddenly buying that brand of car becomes a patriotic thing to do! Teachers can guide children to look for and collect such use of symbols.

Humor in persuasion   Another twist in persuasive style is use of words to get the audience to laugh. The persuader's humor is not there just for fun, as is the case with much literature. Persuasive language uses more humor, plays on words, satire, and amusing surprise than expository language. Persuaders know that laughter is a vital need of people. An example is a political candidate's collection of "one liners."

Figurative language in persuasion   Another aspect of persuasive style is the use of imagery (simile, metaphor, analogy) to make communication more concrete. Persuaders dare not leave their messages totally to vague abstractions, or they lose their audience. One major use of figurative language in persuasion is the *euphemism.* When clever persuaders know the target's contexts (and the limitations of their information), they can tailor words and use euphemisms that sound better but are often not as accurate as more straightforward words.

Examples of political euphemisms are "revenue enhancement" for *taxes,* "air support" for *bombing,* and "arbitrary deprivation of life" for *killing. Spies* are "intelligence specialists" or "covert human collection sources." A U.S. Air Force cruise missile merely "impacted the ground prematurely" when it *crashed.* The head of an organization of high school football coaches was quoted as saying that players "are not *failing;* they're deficient at a grading period" (National Council of Teachers of English, 1986a). These examples represent too many words supported by too little valid thought. **Doublespeak,** as it is sometimes called, with its pomposity in language, may make the bad seem good, or at least tolerable, and the ordinary sound better. Doublespeak may avoid responsibility, conceal, cover lack of information, or try to prevent thought. *Teachers can encourage older children to collect these stylistic forms of propaganda,* noting (to repeat) the degree of honesty, quality, and depth of scholarship in the language sent their way.

Hyperbole is another device. It uses exaggeration of a statement (e.g., "to wait an eternity"). Persuaders may exaggerate a statement to get their way, or make the conflicting idea seem unworthy. For example, when one child in the group suggests lowering the cost of the pencils they are selling in the class store, a second child in opposition says, "That's giving 'em away!" This device can block objective examination of an idea by its exaggeration toward the ridiculous. It does not extend thought but limits it.

Paradox in persuasion   Another language device found in literature is contradiction (paradox, antithesis, or saying the opposite of what you mean). In persuasion, an advertiser may paradoxically use a "humble" approach, admitting that the product is not the most popular—yet. An ironical example from a child: "Me scared? Naw, I always like to wear goosebumps."

In general all of these stylistic devices represent nonliteral language designed to achieve impressiveness or concreteness in an influential way. Box 10.10 suggests a related classroom activity regarding the aspect of style.

BOX 10.10 Advertising Style and Persuasion

If your school is having a garage sale, for a taste of style and persuasion, ask children to list objects to sell. Next, generate with them a list of pleasing or rousing actions. Match them up to see if they arouse attention. Examples:

Item	Action
bicycle	waltz
tires	begging
shoe polish	wink
toy	cuddle

"This bicycle will waltz you down the street."

"Listen to your bicycle grumbling down the road begging for these 'new' tires."

"With this can of shoe polish, your shoes will wink at others as you walk."

"This toy monster will cuddle you to sleep and scare away your nightmares."

Children can playfully add other stylistic features described in this section to get a feel for recognizing the language style of advertising. This activity can be part of a larger one in the activity book where children play roles in an advertising company.

Manipulation of grammar in persuasion   The grammar of persuasion influences language. The following examples represent a few variations: One is the use of the superlative *(greatest, most terrific)*. Another is the intruding pronoun *you* or the bond of the pronoun *we*. A persuader may use the first person *(I)* when trying to establish his or her good intentions or intimacy. Persuaders often use the imperative sentence structure: "Vote for so and so"; "Stop eating cholesterol"; "Be mine." Another grammatical feature is a persuader's use of *subordination.* Examples are subordination of facts not fitting the persuader's intent, thus changing the emphasis, and subordination of facts to highlight irrelevant or mythical differences instead.

***The presumption and danger of using* is**   Behind the unqualified use of the verb *is* lurk a number of assumptions. All the following statements have one thing in common—the use of the verb *is.*

"It is good . . ."

"He is lazy . . ."

"This is a book . . ."

Such use implies that we are describing something "out there" that has a certain quality—*goodness, laziness,* or *bookishness*—existing independent of our personal experience of it. The next assumption is that the receiver of the message must agree, because obviously it *is* what it is! But what we, the message senders, are really describing represents an internal experience that may have existence only for us.

A remedy includes using and encouraging our students to employ qualified and more tentative language such as:

"I *think* it is good . . ."

"I *believe* he is lazy . . ."

"It *looks to me like* a book . . ."

Such wording reminds us that what we describe is not "out there" but an experience inside ourselves. Recall from the opening scene when one of the committee members, Andrew, said, "Young children are just 'swingers' "; and Christopher countered, "You mean it looks that way to you."

The use of *is* also implies that we have examined the subject thoroughly and have determined how best to describe it. But in fact we have examined only a few possibilities and chosen one for personal reasons valid perhaps only for us. We hear the word *is* rendered with an air of finality about children, teachers, and educational practice, far beyond justification. To choose one characteristic is to imply that that's all there is to it (context-free). Instead one could say, "I've only seen the child four times, but he seems to be timid," rather than "He is timid." You can help students watch and qualify their own language and appraise the language of others, as did the children in the opening scene.

Thus the sentence patterns of persuasion vary. Some further examples follow: "That's not nice" (use of *is* mentioned earlier); "This is a warning"; "Too much rest is rust" (from Sir Walter Scott's "The Betrothed"); "All so and so are thus and sos"; "I wish you would. . . ."

Paralleling   Another grammatical feature of persuasive language is the rhythm of *paralleling* phrases, clauses, or sentence units in simple series. These often occur in units of three or four. The following is an example: "I am in earnest. I will not equivocate; I will not excuse; I will not retreat a single inch; and **I will be heard!**" (William Lloyd Garrison from "Salutatory of the Liberatory," January 1, 1931). Consider the illustrative activity in Box 10.11.

Teachers can guide children to see the variations that changes in grammar can effect and that these may be useful to a persuader. The facts in Box 10.11 could have been that the child had just had his eyes dilated and was not seeing too well; the glass door had just been cleaned, and in his hurry to get out, he thought it was open and had accidentally run into it. *Teachers and students can collect and analyze distortions through grammatical change (especially in an election year).* After style, consider organization.

ORGANIZATION of Persuasion   What kinds of *organizational* forms does persuasion have? Here again, it is important for teachers to know more than they plan to actually teach most children, but to be well prepared for the teachable moment. Consider first a two-part organization: the argument and the reasons. From the time of Aristotle (384–322 B.C.), two essentials to the organization of persuasion have been (1) stating your case (argument) and (2) proving it (reasons). Sometimes today, as indicated earlier in the logic section, the proving is omitted. Two additional organizational forms are brainwashing and modern-day advertising.

BOX 10.11 Grammar and Persuasive Language Use

Present examples (such as the ones that follow) to children; guide them to discover what's happening and to see that persuaders can build up judgmental emphases by changes in grammar. Have the children find and construct similar examples.

First provide instances that let the children discover buildup in the action part of the sentence (predication) with the addition of strong adjectives and adverbs ("crisis" words) and with use of words such as *very* to intensify further. A sample sentence to manipulate is "The child broke a glass door." See the example below.

GRAMMAR AND PERSUASION

Basic thought: "The child broke a glass door."

Grammatical manipulation	Examples
Add adjectives	*angry* "The *resentful* child broke a glass . . ." *wrathful*
Change nouns, and intrude personal pronouns	*hoodlum* "The *delinquent* broke a glass door, and *you* should do something." *brat*
Change verbs	*destroyed* "The child *smashed* a glass door." *annihilated*
Use verb *to be* to add judgment	"The child *is* a misfit because he broke a glass door."
Add adverbs	*spitefully* "The child broke the glass door *revengefully.*" *treacherously*
Subordinate a fact to hide it; change emphasis	*"The child,* who broke a glass door, *was the rescuer of the drowning child."*
Add another idea to make a compound sentence; confuse the issue	"The child broke a glass door and *interiors are too airtight and polluted, needing more ventilation anyway.*"

Brainwashing The brainwashing process may include the following organizational parts: (1) stripping of identity, (2) establishment of guilt, (3) self-betrayal, (4) period of lenience and opportunity, (5) confession, (6) channeling of guilt into a repudiation of former ideology, and (7) reeducation of viewpoint. The system is successful in separating one prisoner from another and forms a virtual monopoly on propagandistic ideas rather than a competition among persuaders, as in the advertising form (Brown, 1963).

In the case of some verbally abused children in this country, caseworkers can see the first three stages operating when nothing a child does seems to be accepted, much less praised. Such a child is made to feel unworthy and totally guilty or responsible for "shortcomings." Sometimes adults are treated in some of these ways by their peers, too, with devastating results. It is hoped that you have never and will never experience such dehumanizing treatment. But if you do, it may help to be able to recognize it and call it what it is.

Advertising Another example of organization in persuasive discourse is found in an advertising form:

Six-Point Sales Pitch

(1) get attention *(Hi),*

(2) demonstrate need and intensify desire *(You need . . .),*

(3) offer satisfaction for the need *(Our product does it.),*

(4) illustrate benefits of the product,

(5) inspire belief *(Trust us.),* and

(6) motivate action through challenge or appeal *(Hurry; buy!).*

Source: Adapted in part from Ehninger, Gronbeck, & Monroe, 1980.

Attention arousers in the first step might consist of things that are impressive and full of wonder, pleasant, humorous, personally interesting, and surprising. (Paralleling the surprise value of information in ads is the screaming headline from journalism.) The ad may have a stunning beginning or the clincher may be led up to gradually, as in the climax of a literary drama. In the intensifying of desire, *psychological needs* are addressed. Advertisers may try to latch onto human needs, even if irrelevant to the product. Examples of needs might be the following: protection or security, a sense of belonging, possessions, power, prestige, glamour, stimulation, well-being, recognition, control over one's life, and sex.

When it comes to organization, then, persuasion is not committed to any specific order. Organization is mainly psychological instead of logical. Persuasion may also be organized according to on-the-spot analysis of audience reaction. Such adaptive flexibility in an interpersonal situation can be more effective than written persuasion. You have probably dissolved one persuasive plan for a better approach, as revealed at the moment. Thus, persuasive discourse is flexibly organized and much a part of the present, ongoing context—far more so than is exposition or literature.

The activities in Box 10.12 not only reveal organization of persuasive language, but also can raise ethical questions for exploration in the classroom. They will illustrate how people use language in general and persuasion in particular. Agewise, teachers can adapt them upward and downward. They will require some extensive teacher and child preparation. These activities can follow and be integrated with role play and drama learnings

---

BOX 10.12 Ad Designer

In general, students can engage in several activities related to organization in advertising that are preliminary to a larger unit.

Taped ad collection and analysis: Have the children tape-record a series of current commercials; then play the tape and talk about the organization (style and logic also) used by the writers. Once children have made their own ads, they can intersperse the ads in a script for a program they produce. *(E.g., remember, one tree can make 3 million matches. One match can burn 3 million trees.)*

Book ads: Have the children design book reports in the form of advertisements using the six-point sales pitch described on page 364. Use a giant pretend TV screen or microphone as a prop. (See Chapter 9 of the activity book for related "book shower" and "book exchange" activities.)

School needs campaign: Have the children construct advertising and other persuasive discourse to improve some school condition such as litter, marking on walls or furniture, or noise. (Recall the committee in the opening scene involved in the planning of the new recreation area.)

Ads for school functions: Have the children design ad campaigns for promoting, say, a school clothing drive, a carnival, candidates for student council offices, school theatrical presentations, sports events, or a parents' workshop or meeting. Determine facts about the event or conditions and the audiences and their characteristics.

Stress the use of honest, straightforward facts, tastefulness, creativity in style, and accurate reasoning. Many ads are of this type; that is, they tell accurately what the product is, what it does, how much it costs, and where you can buy it.

(Chapter 5). Children can also apply brainstorming and problem-solving discussion strategies (Chapter 6). Teachers can relate them to the social studies area of economics. Keep each session to an appropriate length, stopping while interest is still high. Criteria for attainment of concepts rely on first-hand observation of children's behavior as a valid check. The first activity leads into others, and is best based on some previous experience with children as receivers and analyzers of language designed to influence. These activities allow children to integrate the logic, style, and organization of persuasive language. They put into practice our theme for this chapter: Children can learn that there are degrees of honesty, quality, and depth of scholarship in the language they receive and send.

One teacher reported the following advertising designer activity for a class needs campaign.

We worked in small committees, attempting to solve a perennial problem. The topic was respect for the belongings of others when you share the same desk. After fifteen minutes of small group discussion, recorders (keeping good notes this time) reported their findings to the large group. After we evaluated findings, we adopted one plan. It was an advertising

campaign aimed at educating all children using our room about the need for respect for
others and their belongings. At present this campaign is still being developed—with
posters, games, and activities constructed by the children. Our preliminary assessment
is that already fewer things are missing from desks.

After some of the previous experiences (including activities in Chapters 4, 5, and 6)
children will be ready for some role play representing an advertising company. (See the
activity book.) The general goals are to practice the verbal skills of valid persuasion they
have been studying (recall the right-hand column of Table 10.1, comparing lower-minded
and higher-minded persuasion). A further goal is to relate the study to the larger social
studies framework of economics. The matching activity book chapter has that and many
other related activities for developing children's critical thinking in an *integrative* way—the
next topic.

Integration of Critical and Creative Thinking into the Curriculum

This section stresses integration of thinking instruction with reading, literature, and written
composition. Consider reading first.

Reading and Literature   Teachers can exploit the vast resources of children's literature
to promote a creative and critical thinking environment. Literature documents how various
people at different times have found and solved a variety of human problems; thus it
stimulates children's creative problem-solving responses that use critical thought. Integration of literature and thinking means more than just cognitive evaluation of quality books
for children. It means welcoming children's minds and emotions as they come to own the
literature by creatively responding and gaining personal meanings from books.

Consider an example. If we had moved our attention in the opening scene to the pair
of students working next to Horace and Joel we would have found Gertrude and Loreen
sharing responses to a book, assessing how applicable and realistic it is:

GERTRUDE: My life is a little bit like this book—the divorce thing and my mom being a single
           parent. I could feel I was right alongside of Gigi, the main character.
  LOREEN: Yeah, I've known people like were in that book. I think it tells things like they really
           are, people that talk that way and do those things. I wonder what kind of life the
           author really led.
GERTRUDE: Why don't you write her?
  LOREEN: I will. I could plan it like a talk show. If she doesn't answer, I'll pretend to be the
           author and you can interview me. OK? We can do it as a response option.
GERTRUDE: OK.

We can see that Gertrude and Loreen thought about how the author developed
character, using criteria of reality ("Yeah, I've known people like were in that book.").
Gertrude transferred experience from her own life into and out of books. The pair was
reading creatively, for they were talking about their own past experiences and knowledge
to make meaning from what they read. At the same time such an experience helped them
to evaluate, to read critically.

Writing   Next consider how thought is integrated in written composition. In the struggle
to give shape to thought, your students need to reach for critical-thinking skills as they

search to find their own written meanings. Writing to learn also points the student's path to critical thinking. In composing, students need to distinguish the relevant from the irrelevant, classify, decide on the order of information and ideas, and look for relationships. They clarify their meanings by developing such criteria and asking themselves questions such as "Is this what I really want to say? In this order? Did I give enough information? Is this what my information really says?" (Norberg, 1987).

Throughout the composing process, students need to use convergent thinking; to use highly conscious standards; and judge, conclude, and act in light of these standards. They need to think critically. (And they do, that is, if their composition program resembles the one described in Chapter 8 encouraging child autonomy. In such programs one is unlikely to find students who think poorly and write well.)

For an example of thought in the composing process reconsider Naomi. After the opening scene, Naomi's teacher interviewed her about her process in writing her poem. (The poem is on page 337.) The teacher reported the following:

> Naomi had started the first line of her poem with *I run in the grass*, but had changed *grass* to *asphalt*, which was more true to her life. That phrasing also managed to introduce a black image, which would be part of the black theme to be developed in her poem. She played with the verb *run*, changing it to *dance*, which she then thought was too much like the Hughes poem; she changed it to *twirl*, and finally settled on *prance*. Naomi was intrigued by Chetin's poetic phrase *belly of a bee* and wanted to get it into her poem somehow. She could see it buzzing around in her mind's eye. She thought herself of the common black-eyed Susan that grew almost everywhere, even at the edges of her asphalt playground, and how she had gathered these flowers, skipping around with them in her arms. She had trouble working them in, pruning and trimming the too-long line. Then she wanted to save the word *black* for just the end of the poem. Bernice suggested the word *jet* instead of *black*, which Naomi used earlier in connection with *cone flower*. Naomi liked the sound of the word *cone*. Naomi knew a poem didn't have to rhyme, but she wanted to get as much rhyme in as she could because she liked it. So she hung on to *me* and *tree* and *bee*. First she just had *a tree*, then added the image of a "leafless" tree because there was a dead one near the asphalt, and its trunk and branches looked black and still beautiful to her. The theme of valuing and self-enjoyment was uppermost to her. She used her thinking to infer that Mamma liked the black-eyed Susan for the same reason that she did—its beautiful black cone. ("It's my mamma's favorite flower . . . I think I know why now.") Naomi's final creative thought was to arrange her poem in an inverted cone shape to match the "black cone of the flower."

In light of these ideas and this example, Box 10.13 displays some critical-thinking links in a writing process.

In essence, then, written (or spoken) composition gives us another area with which to address audience-related needs and rights. Knowing the presence of a critical audience, the writer (or speaker) can integrate information for the reader (or listener) in such a way as to clarify while logically and persuasively supporting the basic ideas offered (California State Department of Education, 1987). Self-monitoring (Chapter 3) of process, attitude, and habits can enhance critical thinking in all the language arts, transferring from one to another. Children who become critical processors judge the truth, worth, and validity of messages they receive or send. Such thoughtful students are likely to perform well as citizens, consumers, and voters. Using critical thinking in the language arts, the child may do the following: judge, rate, measure, decide, compare, estimate, conclude, and deduce. These actions may be *assessed*—the topic of the next section.

BOX 10.13 Critical-Thinking Links in a Writing Process

Prewriting

Considering the subject in general

Thinking about audience, voice, purpose, and medium

Examining beliefs and attitudes

Retrieving relevant information and experiences

Reading and reviewing additional information

Discovering divergent approaches

Brainstorming

Discussing ideas, asking questions

Planning

Narrowing focus of subject, including judging own purpose and competence

Selecting ideas and information to be included, including judging fact versus fantasy

Deciding about general organization

Making choices about voice, tone, and medium

Making notes, outlines, and diagrams, including checking facts using outside resources

Grouping points and evaluating conclusions in arguments

Writing

Choosing beginning strategy

Linking portions of piece, considering transitions

Maintaining consistent tone

Planning paragraph shape

Writing phrases and sentences

Searching for appropriate vocabulary, including analyzing and judging evocative language

Revising and Editing

Reading critically what has been written

Rethinking choices of structure and language

Making decisions about other orders, words, or sentences

Making changes: additions or deletions

Editing for usage, punctuation, capitalization, and spelling

Presenting product in appropriate format

Source: This material has been adapted from Nordberg (1987).

Informal Assessment and Formal Evaluation

This section deals with some assessment and suggestions for the classroom teacher, and then with some current happenings regarding evaluation of children's thinking at the national level.

How Teachers Can Assess Informally Teachers can use the kinds of informal observation, diagnosis, and record keeping stressed earlier in this book, being sure to include awareness of children's development of thinking. Remember that during in-class and out-of-class experiences your students can record their successes themselves as they engage in group reflection sessions, in their journal writing, and on other self-check devices they create.

By using the framework of goals and other ideas and activities described in this chapter, you can develop your own "tests" of thinking by holding individual conferences, by watching each child, and by asking a few carefully selected questions. (For example, "Is this passage you are using for solving your problem an opinion or a fact? What evidence do you have?")

You can use the framework of goals and objectives (Appendix 10A) to devise assessment checklists. Examples follow. The first, given in Box 10.14, is a checklist on student use of the critical process, the first goal in the framework. Teachers and students in conference could consider each item.

A checklist for student understanding of logic, style, and organization of persuasion is given in Box 10.15. This assessment relates to the second goal of the framework in Appendix 10A. (See the activity book for ways to extend these ideas into the classroom.)

BOX 10.14 Checklist on the Critical Process for Language Arts

Goal 1: Is this student aware of stages in critical **processes**, integrating and using them in all the language arts?

Subgoal: Does this student understand, engage in, and monitor a critical process, including the following:

☐ 1. *Intake.* Sustained, attentive intake of entire message or material (with questioning, analysis of material and context)

☐ 2. *Purpose spotting.* Identifying purpose(s)

☐ 3. *Standards* (or criteria).

☐   3.1. *Construction.* Autonomous construction, reconstructing, and labeling of criterion (or criteria) for judging—a standard that the student can explain and support

☐   3.2. *Standards application.* Applying criterion or standard(s) and knowledge background

☐ 4. *Evidence.* Applying evidence and principles of evidence (logical inquiry and reasoning)

☐ 5. *Judgment.* Constructing highly conscious judgment (identifying and controlling any tendency to snap judgment or bias—suspending judgment)

☐ 6. *Action.* Synthesizing, acting, concluding on judgment

BOX 10.15 Checklist on Student's Understanding of Logic, Organization, and Style in Persuasive Discourse for Language Arts

Goal 2: Is this student thinking critically for a variety of **purposes?**

Subgoal: Does this student receive and express critical purposes in listening, speaking, reading, and writing across the curriculum by understanding the characteristic *organization, style,* and *logic* of *persuasive* uses of language?

1. *Logic.* Understand the use of logic (or lack of logic) in persuasion
   - ☐ 1.1. Incomplete argument
   - ☐ 1.2. Single example
   - ☐ 1.3 Judging generalization, labeling, and stereotyping in arguments (including sexism)

2. *Organization.* Understand the organization of persuasive discourse (in the valid and invalid argument and its reasons, in the sales pitch with use of appeals to psychological needs, in brainwashing.) Some *reasons:*
   - ☐ 2.1. Propaganda devices as reasons
   - ☐ 2.2. Analogies as valid or invalid reasons
   - ☐ 2.3. Cause-effect validity or invalidity
   - ☐ 2.4. Inference strength or weakness
   - ☐ 2.5. Assumptions
   - ☐ 2.6. Credibility of fact, of opinion as reasons (objective and subjective viewpoints)
   - ☐ 2.7. Fallacies in reasons such as:
   - ☐ • self-contradictions
   - ☐ • failure to present all choices
   - ☐ • appeal to ignorance

3. *Style.* Separate style from content, understanding the persuasive style as using:
   - ☐ 3.1. Extremes
   - ☐ 3.2. Balances
   - ☐ 3.3. Repetitions
   - ☐ 3.4. Use of symbols
   - ☐ 3.5. Humor; figures of speech
   - ☐ 3.6. Grammar (e.g., subordination, intensifiers, verb *is*)
   - ☐ 3.7. Tone; use of connotation; euphemism
   - ☐ 3.8. Doublespeak—manipulation of language for deception

Note: Older students can use the above checklist as a group-work measure for collecting and analyzing examples, checking off items when they think they understand them.

The checklist in Box 10.16 examines an individual student's attitude about critical listening, the third goal in the framework. Again, such assessment can be used in student-teacher conferences, by the student, and in student groups.

Formal Evaluation at State and National Levels   A member of the Committee on Critical Thinking for the National Council of Teachers of English surveyed the chief education officers in each state (plus territories) to tap the relationship between the measurement of critical thinking and state testing programs, with a return of 70.9 percent (Lamb, 1987). The survey produced some interesting findings. In general, ideas are changing and developing. Of approximately 30 responses from state departments, about half indicated that critical thinking could or should be measured in the competency tests they were using. However, only six people responding said that their state competency tests actually included items designed to measure critical thinking. Almost a third indicated concerns that such tests should not include "critical thinking" items. On this point, there is little general agreement.

State departments designed sample test items to require students to detect organizational patterns, judge effective organization, and detect irrelevancies or insufficiency of information. Surprisingly in one case, younger students (grade 4) did well, while older students (grades 8 and 11) did not do well on items requiring them to make relatively fine distinctions, deal with abstractions, or engage in a multistep reasoning process (Lamb, 1987). The reasons for this are not clear but may be associated with the relative difficulty of items at different age levels. Generally speaking, state evaluation is still in developmental stages.

BOX 10.16 Checklist on Student's Attitude Toward Critical Thinking for Language Arts

Goal 3: Is this student developing a lasting, positive **attitude** toward the value of critical thinking and responsible use of persuasive speech?

Subgoals: Specifically, does this student display:

☐ 1. *Willingness and appreciation.* Develop a willingness to think creatively and critically, appreciating the value of these processes.

☐ 2. *Responsible use.* Use persuasive language logically, ethically, and with responsibility toward one's audience.

☐ 3. *Independent personal standards.* Establish personal standards independent of peer influence to evaluate speaker and message.

☐ 4. *Judicious attitude.* Develop neither a suspicious nor a predatory attitude, but a judicious one of careful analysis and judgment for self-protection, realizing that there are degrees of honesty, quality, and depth of scholarship in language sent one's way.

☐ 5. *Multiple perspectives.* Be open to many different perceptions of the world and many realities, realizing that one's own perspective is just one way of knowing.

Sources: California State Department of Education (1987), New York State Department of Education (1984), Wolvin (1985), and Lundsteen (1969, 1976, 1986).

What Some Test Publishers Are Doing   Judging from the responses of three publishers of standardized achievement tests, we may infer that publishers feel they are including items that require critical thinking. Sample items might require students to make inferences (such as inferring the motives and reasons for the actions of characters) or predicting outcomes after extracting information from a passage, interpreting the underlying theme, and making a judgment (Lamb, 1987).

None of the three publishers attempted to measure critical thinking before the third grade. Some of the items presented to students at the primary level, however, may require some critical thinking. Consider the ever-popular odd-one-out task, in which children are asked to consider a few words or pictures, determine a characteristic common to all or most, determine what category most of the words fall into (e.g., clothing, tools, food), then *judge* each choice to see if it is a member of that category. Anyone who has watched "Sesame Street" is familiar with this sort of activity, which uses pictures instead of words.

Test publishers seem to be aware of the significance and concern about critical thinking today. All those asked believed that critical thinking could and should be measured on achievement batteries (Lamb, 1987). They are also sensitive to testing those areas currently being taught, *so it is up to educators to inform test publishers of their expectations on tests and to choose tests that indicate valid increased attention to critical thinking.*

At the time of the survey, however, there was little agreement among chief education officers for the states about measuring critical thinking (Lamb, 1987). The picture of state and national testing of critical thinking is in flux and development. Keep informed. Beware of abuses and misuses of tests, for example, using only one way of knowing (Chapter 15).

The next two chapters, 11 and 12, move into the craft of editing thoughtful writing. The craft and study of language include the following: spelling, punctuation, handwriting, grammar, and usage. A reasonable practice is to put first things first. Craft without the uses of language elaborated in past chapters is a useless ritual. Written expression without the craft, however, blocks optimal communication.

SUMMARY

"Development of the mind is not a quick fix; it's a lifetime of effort."

Since freedom of speech ensures equal rights to both honest and dishonest communicators, children need to become effective thinkers in order to direct and control their own minds. Thus, this chapter emphasized the importance of critical thinking in the language arts and especially a critical appraisal of language designed to persuade. The opening scene showed child and teacher roles and activities designed for growth in thinking.

Critical thinking is characterized by its highly conscious judgmental aspect, with actions and conclusions drawn in terms of internal and external criteria. Critical listening uses the auditory language, and critical reading the visual mode. Both use the mental process of evaluation.

Both critical and creative thought are well used when harnessed to the solving of a genuine and significant challenge or problem in a child's life, academic or otherwise. Writing and speaking also profit from a knowledge of what critical thought processes and skills consist of and of audience-related needs and rights.

Teachers can help children use their oral and written language to improve their learning and thinking. Language can be a powerful way of inquiring, organizing, realizing, discovering, and interpreting meanings. Teaching thinking can integrate well into the language arts program.

Persuasive use of language can serve the greatest good for the greatest number or be exceedingly self-serving and detrimental to the welfare of the target audience in the long run—or function somewhere in between. A comparative analysis of persuasive language helps to clarify other major categories: self-expression, exposition, and literature. Persuasion borrows stylistic tendencies from these broad uses of language to serve its end—to get the receiver to do or believe something. The audience is the persuader's target. By using direct and indirect imperative, the persuader attempts to create an attractive image. All of us are propagandists at some time or another, and children catch on quickly, but sometimes not quickly enough. They need some help.

Developmental knowledge stands the teacher in good stead for getting the right environment and activity to the right child at the right time. Combining individualization with appropriate group-interactive stimulation is part of a teacher's craft and artistry. Teachers seem to be in greater danger of underestimating than overestimating children's ability to think autonomously. The admonition is to think big about the little and allow children's thinking strengths to flourish.

Goals in a framework were categorized mainly as to processes, uses, and attitudes, with emphasis on the recognition, analysis, and *judging* of persuasive language, while assessing and using evidence. An understanding of multiple contexts of goals sheds light on the origins of the bias and credibility of a speaker. Since no two people have exactly the same contexts, they rarely if ever have the same meanings. Asking and answering questions helps people get to shared meanings, a necessary (but not sufficient) base for cooperative, creative, and critical thought.

The teaching of critical and creative thinking depends on a thorough foundation of definition, rationale, developmental knowledge, knowledge about thought processes, uses, supportive attitude, and knowledge of persuasive discourse. A key instructional stance is that *teachers can help children to learn that there are degrees of creativity, honesty, straightforwardness, and scholarship in the language they receive and send.* Thus children aim for and demand the best. Teachers can also help children learn that how to think is different from what to think.

Some valuable curriculum inclusions concern the language of facts and inferences. Inference making requires an awareness of standards of probability and plausibility. Teachers can help children understand that both verbal and visual languages, such as those used in advertising and political euphemisms, can be powerful influences upon human thinking and behavior. Teachers can also help children discriminate varied purposes of language, achieve these purposes themselves, and do so keeping a firm grasp of personal ethics. Thus instructors help students recognize differences between fact and opinion and between clear thinking and propaganda.

Three features of persuasive language use are logic, style, and organization. *Logic* as used by persuaders may tend toward incomplete argument and single example. Misuse of logic, appeal to emotions, and repetition characterize many propaganda devices. Persuasive *style* has elements of symbolism, humor, figurative language, and paradox. Grammatically, persuaders manipulate sentence parts, with subordination and presumptive use of *is* being among the tricks. *Organization* in persuasive language is illustrated by argument and its reasons, brainwashing, and advertising.

At the state and national levels, ideas for evaluating children's thinking are changing and developing. Teachers, however, can assess children's strengths and needs while working integratively with significant goals of developing thought. They know that teaching thinking is a matter of developing children's applications of attitudes, knowledge, and skills.

APPENDIX 10A   Framework for Critical and Creative Thinking for the Language Arts

To think creatively and critically students need to:

GOAL 1: Be aware of, integrate, and use stages of creative and critical thinking **processes** *in all the language arts.*
SUBGOALS: Students need to understand, engage in, and monitor the
1.1. Creative process
    1.1.1. Sensory perception, identification, and incubation
    1.1.2. Revelation
    1.1.3. Synthesis (with sensory, reflective, intuitive, metaphorical, and divergent/convergent thought; and an attitude of openness, flexibility, and tolerance, with curiosity and risk taking)
    1.1.4. Evaluation and verification
1.2. Critical process (evaluative use of leftover thinking space)
    1.2.1. Sustained, attentive intake of entire message or material
    1.2.2. Questioning with analysis of material and context
    1.2.3. Identification of purpose(s) of material
    1.2.4. Autonomous construction, reconstruction, and labeling of criterion (or criteria) for judging (a standard that the student can explain and support)
    1.2.5. Application of criterion and knowledge background
    1.2.6. Application of evidence and principles of evidence (logical inquiry and reasoning)
    1.2.7. Identification and control of any tendency to snap judgment or bias (suspending judgment)
    1.2.8. Construction of highly conscious judgment
    1.2.9. Synthesis, and acting or concluding on the judgment made
GOAL 2: Think creatively and critically for a variety of **purposes.**
SUBGOALS:
2.1. Appreciate *creative* purposes (in the context of the language arts) used in listening, speaking, reading, writing, and their forms across the total curriculum (including literature, the arts, social studies, etc.)
    2.1.1. Understand the place of creative thinking in problem solving
    2.1.2. Understand the characteristic organization, style, and logic in creative uses of language, e.g., distinguish between fairy tale and nonfiction
    2.1.3. Experience vicariously the situation in a literary selection
        2.1.3.1. Express appropriate emotion
        2.1.3.2. Relate self to characters
        2.1.3.3. Respond to sensory, emotional, and descriptive power of literary language
    2.1.4. Synthesize ideas about how sound, diction, imagery, and symbolism combine to communicate multiple levels of meaning
    2.1.5. Respond creatively to oral and written literary language using various options (e.g., choral reading, story telling, discussion, music, art, drama, writing)

      2.1.6. Consider, synthesize, and to some degree internalize author's craft and artistry (e.g., connotative or symbolic meanings; liveliness of characters, dialect, colloquialisms; mood creation; provocative rhythm, rhyme, repetition, and figurative language)

      2.1.7. Appreciate the human, social, and cultural significance of a literary work

2.2. Appreciate *critical* purposes in the context of the language arts (used in listening, speaking, reading, writing, and their forms across the curriculum)

      2.2.1. Understand the place of critical thinking in problem solving

      2.2.2. Understand the characteristic organization, style, and logic of persuasive uses of language (in contrast to, say, exposition)

            2.2.2.1. Understand the *organization* of persuasive discourse (such as the argument and its reasons, for example, of the sales pitch, brainwashing, or appeals to psychological needs)

                  2.2.2.1.1. Propadanda devices as "reasons"

                  2.2.2.1.2. Analogies as "reasons"

                  2.2.2.1.3. Cause-effect validity

                  2.2.2.1.4. Inference strength

                  2.2.2.1.5. Assumptions

                  2.2.2.1.6. Credibility of fact, of opinion as reasons; objective and subjective viewpoints

                  2.2.2.1.7. Fallacies in reasons such as self-contradictions, failure to present all choices, appeal to ignorance

            2.2.2.2 Understand the persuasive *style* using, for example, extremes, balances, variations, repetitions, symbols, humor, figures of speech, grammar (subordination, intensifiers, verb *is*), tone, connotation, euphemism ("doublespeak"—manipulation of language in order to deceive)

            2.2.2.3 Be able to separate style from content of message.

            2.2.2.4. Understand the use of *logic* (or lack of logic) in the persuasive style (incomplete argument, single example)

                  2.2.2.4.1. Judging generalization labeling and stereotyping in arguments (including sexism)

      2.2.3. Establish and use criteria for evaluating literature and one's own writing (e.g., the appropriateness and appeal of one descriptive word over another)

      2.2.4 Establish and use criteria for assessing exposition, determining the value of information (e.g., practicality, usefulness in light of purpose, quality of evidence, relevance versus irrelevance, breadth, depth, and significance)

GOAL 3: Develop a lasting, positive **attitude** *toward the value of creative and critical thinking and responsible use of persuasive speech.*

SUBGOALS:

3.1. Develop a willingness to think creatively and critically, appreciating the value of these processes

3.2. Use persuasive language logically, ethically, and with responsibility toward one's audience

3.3. Establish personal standards independent of peer influence to evaluate speaker and message

3.4. Develop a judicious attitude of careful analysis and judgment for self-protection, realizing that there are degrees of honesty, quality, and depth of scholarship in language sent and received.

3.5. Be open to many different perceptions of the world, realizing that one's own perspective is just one way of knowing.

    Illustrative examples for this framework are found in the section on how to teach and in the corresponding chapter of the activity book.

Sources: California State Department of Education (1987), New York State Department of Education (1984), Wolvin Coakley (1985), and Lundsteen (1969, 1976, 1986).

CHAPTER 11

Spelling, Handwriting, and Other Writing Conventions

by Gail E. Tompkins

". . . Knowledge of all the conventions of writing gets into our head like much of our knowledge of spoken language . . . without awareness of the learning that is taking place. The learning is . . . incidental, vicarious, and collaborative. It is incidental because we learn when it is not our primary intention, vicarious because we learn from what someone else does, and collaborative because we learn through others helping us to achieve our own end."

Frank Smith

INTRODUCTION

The last editing job of the composer involves writing conventions—spelling, handwriting, punctuation, and usage (as distinguished from grammar). This chapter and the next shed new light on these areas. Premature overemphasis upon these conventions at any grade level is likely to hinder written expression, hinder the child's "Hey! I've really got something to say." Teachers best support conventions by encouraging children to write about things they care about and to audiences they wish to reach. Children's learning of conventions is also supported by teachers who have historical, scientific, and developmental knowledge.

OPENING SCENE: Collaboratively Using an Editing Checklist

The students in B. J. Ochs's third-grade classroom are writing science reports. A papier-mâché rendition of the solar system swings giddily from the ceiling. Mercury, Venus, Earth, Mars, and the other planets all orbit a gleaming, red-hot sun. The class has divided into small groups of three or four children in order to write research reports on their chosen planets. After doing their research, the students have written and revised several drafts of their reports. Today the groups are polishing their efforts for "publication" using an editing checklist (Figure 11.1). Moving from group to group, the teacher pauses by Timmy, Joe, and Aaron, who are writing a report on Jupiter.

    During the previous revising session, these boys noticed that almost all the sentences in their report began with *It*, and they corrected the problem. Now they are checking for mechanical errors—spelling, punctuation, and capitalization. Aaron gets out his pencil and says, "OK, number one says, 'Did you circle misspelled words?' " The three boys huddle together, moving their fingers in unison as they proofread, checking the spelling of each word. Each time they locate a word that might be misspelled, one of the boys circles that word. After they finish reading, Timmy goes to get a dictionary while Joe and Aaron begin correcting the misspelled words they are sure they know how to spell. When Timmy returns with the dictionary, the boys take turns looking up the correct spelling for the seven unknown words they spotted. Upon finishing, Aaron puts a checkmark in the box beside the first item. The teacher, still moving from group to group, has noticed their efforts and compliments the boys on their hard work.

    The process continues for another 10 or 15 minutes until Joe, Aaron, and Timmy have completed the checklist. Then they sign their names at the bottom of the sheet to verify they

Editing Checklist

☐   1. Did you circle misspelled words?

☐   2. Did you put punctuation marks at the ends of sentences?

☐   3. Did you put capital letters at the beginnings of sentences?

☐   4. Did you make paragraphs? How many? _____

☐   5. Did you write a title and the names of the authors?

Signatures of the authors:

_____   _____

_____   _____

Figure 11.1   A third-grade editing checklist.

have completed their editing responsibilities, staple the checklist to their edited draft, and return the report to their writing folder.

The next day each group chooses one member to put that group's edited report in final form and recopy it. Joe, Aaron, and Timmy choose Aaron to recopy their report on Jupiter because "he writes good." They mean that his handwriting is legible and that it incorporates most of the items listed on the chart "How Legible Is Your Handwriting?" posted in the classroom. A copy of the chart is presented in Box 11.1. All students judge the quality of their handwriting using these criteria as a part of B. J. Ochs's handwriting program. The boys realize that legible handwriting is a courtesy to readers. They are proud of their report, and by choosing Aaron to recopy it, they are sure the final copy will be legible and their

BOX 11.1 A Third-Grade Handwriting Checklist
How Legible Is Your Handwriting?

1. Are the letters formed correctly?

2. Do all letters touch the baseline?

3. Are letters the same size?

4. Is there enough space between letters and words?

5. Are letters parallel?

6. Are the lines smooth or are they shaky?

classmates will be able to read it easily. Later, groups will share the finished reports orally before compiling them into a class book.

Analysis of the Scene

In B. J. Ochs's class, spelling, handwriting, and other conventions such as capitalization and punctuation serve only one function: They are tools for writers. The ideas the students want to communicate are of primary importance in writing, but in order to communicate effectively, they must understand and use a set of commonly accepted writing conventions. As students write for a variety of purposes and audiences, they grow in their awareness of audience, and they acknowledge the need to write legibly and to correct spelling, punctuation, and other errors as a courtesy to their readers.

B. J. Ochs does not, however, expect all children to spell all words correctly in their first drafts, and consequently does not unintentionally restrict their writing to words they know how to spell. (Recall Chapter 8 on composition.) B. J. extends such support with respect to first draft work to their handwriting, too. This teacher also realizes that when the children see the correct form innumerable times in their wide reading, a powerful visual "teacher" of spelling is at work. We next consider this tool, spelling, in more depth.

SPELLING

> Ten-year-old Elaine with 23 consecutive errorless end-of-the-week spelling tests wrote in an independent writing assignment, "The ponys stoped comeing to."
>
> *L. M. Schell*

Again and again teachers find that while many students like Elaine earn 100 percent on weekly spelling tests, they do not apply what they have supposedly learned in their writing. After all, the purpose of spelling instruction is to prepare students to use spelling conventions correctly in their writing so that they can communicate effectively with their readers. This unfortunate situation raises many questions for elementary teachers: What is the nature of English spelling? How has the development of our language affected spelling? How do children learn to spell? How is spelling taught?

What Is the Nature of English Spelling?

As you learn about the English spelling system, your attitude toward spelling and how to teach it will probably change. You will gain a greater appreciation for our complex spelling system, or to borrow a computer term, spelling will become more "user friendly." Your new attitude will affect your students, too.

An Alphabetic System   English spelling, or orthography, is an alphabetic writing system in which *graphemes,* or letters, represent various *phonemes,* or speech sounds. In a "perfect" alphabetic system, each phoneme is represented by only one grapheme. In other words, there is a one-to-one correspondence between phonemes and graphemes, and each letter represents only one sound. For example the phoneme /b/ is always represented by the grapheme *b.* However, English is a modified alphabetic system and lacks a convenient one-to-one relationship between phonemes and graphemes.

Lack of Fit   This situation is known as a *lack of fit*. This lack of fit is especially true of vowel sounds, which can be represented by many different spellings. Mario Pei called English spelling "the world's most awful mess" (1952). While Pei's remark is an exaggeration, English does lack a seemingly ideal surface level correspondence. In English there are 26 letters, approximately 40–44 phonemes, and more than 500 different spellings for these 40–44 phonemes. For example, the grapheme *e* represents a variety of sounds. Long *e* is only one possible phoneme, and you can spell it in at least 14 different ways (E. Horn, 1957). For instance, you can spell /e/ as the *e* in *be, ee* in *feel, ea* in *meat,* and *ey* in *key.* These four spelling options are fairly common, but there are also some more unusual possibilities. Consider spelling /e/ as *eo* in *people, oe* in *phoenix, ie* in *chief, i* in *piano,* or *y* in *comedy.*

Prediction and Rules   Prediction is a problem and rules are often of little help. Moreover, the spelling of many of our most common words such as *because, come, head, is, said,* and *they* cannot be predicted by phoneme-grapheme correspondences, phonic generalizations, or spelling rules. For example, if *because* were spelled according to phoneme-grapheme correspondences, it might be spelled *becuz,* and in fact many children do attempt to spell the word this way. The phonic generalization that "when two vowels go walking, the first one does the talking" suggests that *head* be pronounced with a long *e* rather than a short *e* sound. However, only a small percentage of words containing adjacent vowels are pronounced correctly using the walking/talking rule.

Homophones add further confusion for spellers. These are words that sound alike but are spelled differently, such as *their-there-they're, sea-see,* and *eye-I.* These examples imply that English is a highly irregular, arbitrary, and even unpredictable language. In contrast, however, many words can be sounded out and spelled rather easily, such as *camp, dragnet,* and *hit.* With knowledge of long-vowel spelling rules, other words such as *feel, inside, mandate,* and *raincoat* can be spelled correctly. Also, *linguistic patterns* (e.g., bat-cat-fat and bill-fill-hill) provide evidence of regularity in English spelling.

Three Positions about Regularity of English Spelling   The controversy about whether English spelling is regular has been waged since the beginning of this century. At least three positions regarding the nature of our spelling system exist today: the highly irregular, the regular, and the deep structure. One group believes that English spelling is irregular enough so that it will not benefit children to study linguistic patterns or spelling rules. They cite the problem of fit and examples of spelling options as evidence of their position.

A second group believes that English orthography is far more regular than previously thought, and that a clear relationship exists between speech and print. For example, Paul and Jean Hanna (1965) argue that "a degree of regularity does exist in the relationship between phonological elements in the oral language and their graphic representation in the orthography." The Hannas and their colleagues (1966) used computer technology to analyze the phoneme/grapheme correspondences in over 17,000 words and then developed a computer program with 203 spelling rules developed through their analysis. Using these rules, the computer correctly spelled over 8,000 words or approximately 50 percent of the 17,000 words they analyzed and made only one error in another 37 percent of the words. Theorists arguing that English is a regular alphabetic system cite these results for their position, while others argue that the results support their claim that 50 percent regularity is actually irregularity! Hillerich (1977) adds that the computer programmed with 203 spelling rules did not spell as well as fifth-grade students!

Recently, linguists beginning to examine the deeper structure of language have been able to account for many of the seeming irregularities in English. These researchers, representing a third view, suggest that English spelling is indeed regular, not at the phoneme-grapheme level but at a deeper, more abstract level. In support of their position they note that spelling often remains consistent in meaning-related words even though pronunciations change. One example is the past tense marker *ed*. The spelling *ed* remains the same although it is pronounced in three different ways: It is pronounced /d/ in *nagged*, /t/ in *talked*, and /əd/ in *wanted*. Similarly, the spelling of the plural marker *s* remains the same even though it is sometimes pronounced /z/ as in *dogs* and /s/ as in *cats*. Also, spelling remains constant in different forms of the same *root word* even though the vowel sound shifts. For instance, this consistency is illustrated in *conve*ne-*conve*ntion, *na*tion-*na*tional, *wi*de-*wi*dth, and *defi*ne-*defi*nition. Similarly, consonant differences are not represented in spelling for related words such as electri*c*-electri*c*ity, si*g*n-si*g*nature. This new understanding about the deep-level consistencies in English spelling led Chomsky and Halle to state that "English orthography, despite its often cited inconsistencies, comes remarkably close to being an optimal orthographic system for English" (1968, p. 49).

How Has the Development of Our Language Affected Spelling?*

The development of our language has been influenced by geographic, political, economic, and social forces. Understanding its history helps to explain some of the seeming inconsistencies in English spelling. The word *island* is an example: In the Middle Ages, *island* was spelled *ilond*, reflecting the pronunciation of the word at that time, which has carried into our own pronunciation. The *s* was added to reflect a supposed origin from the French word *isle* (modern French *île*) even though *island* is actually a native English word and was not borrowed from French.

Consider other examples: the consonant digraph *ch*, which is pronounced in at least four different ways in English: /ch/ as in *children*, /sh/ as in *champagne*, /k/ as in *chaos*, and /kw/ as in *choir*. Moreover, the *c* in *cello* is pronounced /ch/ and there is no *h*. We can explain these inconsistencies using etymological (or word history) information available in most dictionaries. *Children* is a native English word, and the *ch* digraph is pronounced with the predictable English /ch/ sound, while the other *ch* words are **loan words** borrowed from languages around the world.

In fact, approximately 75 percent of English words are loan words. *Champagne* is a French loan word, and it retains the French /sh/ pronunciation. Other French *ch* words that are pronounced /sh/ include *chagrin, chalet, charlatan, charade, chef, chic, chiffon,* and *chivalry*. *Chaos* is a Greek loan word, and *ch* is spelled *kh* in Greek and typically pronounced /k/. Other examples of Greek *ch* words are *charisma, chloride,* and *chlorophyll*. Also, a few Latin source-words such as *chemist* are also pronounced /k/. *Choir* is an especially interesting word: In the Middle Ages, it was spelled *quer*, which reflects our modern pronunciation. The form *quer* is French, but the spelling was most likely changed through analogy to the Greek word *chorus*. While the spelling changed, the pronunciation did not, and *choir* has retained its French /kw/ sound.

*This section is adapted from Gail E. Tompkins and David B. Yaden, Jr., *Answering Students' Questions About Words*, Urbana, IL: ERIC Clearinghouse on Reading and Communication Skills and National Council of Teachers of English, 1986.

Three Periods of English Language Development: Old English, Middle English, and Modern English

Examining some of the influences on the development of English will provide even more information about why we spell words the way we do. Our discussion of English language development will be broken into three periods: Old English, 500–1100; Middle English, 1100–1500; and Modern English, 1500–present.

Old English   English is a Germanic language, dating back to 449 when the Angles, Saxons, and Jutes settled in Britain. Their language, known as Old English, was highly inflected and resembled Modern German more than Modern English. Many of our most basic words such as *ask, child, house,* and *sun* originated in this period. Children often ask why English has irregular plural forms (e.g., *mouse-mice*) and irregular verb forms (e.g., *eat-ate-eaten*). These irregular forms can be traced back to Old English.

Word borrowing also began in the Old English period. Christian missionaries brought Latin words such as *angel, candle,* and *hymn,* and the Vikings who invaded Britain in the ninth and tenth centuries contributed most of our *sc* and *sk* words (e.g., *scrape, skin, sky, wisk*) as well as hundreds of other common, everyday words including *husband, low, take,* and *window.*

Middle English   The most important event in the development of the English language occurred in 1066 when William of Normandy defeated the English King Harold and was crowned king of England. For the next 200 years, French replaced English as the official language in England. Although the peasants continued to speak English, the nobility and upper classes spoke and wrote French. One interesting result of this socioeconomic language split is that while the words for farm animals (e.g., *pig, sheep, steer*) are English, the words for their meat (e.g., *bacon, mutton, beef*) come from French.

After several hundred years, the French influence in England declined and English was restored as the official language. However, through contact with French, English was enriched with thousands of *loan* words reflecting almost every aspect of life (e.g., *army, blue, chair, collar, dinner, flower*). Also, French spelling replaced Old English spelling in some words. For instance, the Old English word *cwen* was changed to our word *queen,* and the Old English word *hus* (house) became *hous* in Middle English. More recently the final *e* was added.

Modern English   The establishment of the first printing press in England in 1476 ushered in the third period of language growth. The printing press accelerated the production of manuscripts and made books available to a far greater number of people. The invention served another function, too: It stabilized spelling. Before the invention of the printing press, scribes had some freedom in the way they spelled words, and more importantly, scribes often changed spellings to reflect changes they noted in pronunciation. Before the invention of the printing press, English spelling reflected pronunciation fairly well. Between 1500 and 1600, however, English spelling became stabilized while pronunciation continued to change. Dictionaries compiled by lexicographers, including Ben Johnson (1755) in England and Noah Webster (1828, 1841) in America, further served to standardize spelling by listing for the first time "correct" spellings for many words.

A second great effect on our language during this period resulted from the widespread trade and colonization. Through contact with people from around the world, words from nearly every language entered English. Box 11.2 gives some examples.

The native spellings of some of these borrowed words have been retained, and the spelling of other words has been anglicized. As a rule of thumb, the more recent the borrowing, the more likely it is that the word retains its native spelling. These native spellings have added many new spelling patterns, contributing to the lack of fit between phonemes and graphemes.

Learning the history of English will help students better understand the exceptions in English and why phonemes are often spelled in several different ways. While understanding the development of language and word lore may not make students better spellers, this knowledge and appreciation is valuable in developing a *positive attitude* toward spelling. Telling stories about how words entered English and how they changed through history brings the magic of storytelling to spelling and vocabulary study.

Who Are the Spellers in Your Classroom?

How does the spelling of children grow and change? And what perspective does this newer knowledge give to a teacher? Children learn to spell in much the same way that they learned to talk, using a *problem-solving* approach of successive approximations until they reach standard spelling. Their spelling, known as **invented spelling,** moves through clearly defined stages that parallel earlier stages of oral language development (see Chapter 2). As in oral language development, students use sets of rules in creating their spellings at each stage. Researchers have found that while all children do not develop spelling competence in exactly the same way, they do develop spelling strategies in roughly the same developmental stages (Beers, 1980; Beers & Henderson, 1977; Gentry, 1978, 1981, 1982; Henderson, 1980; Read, 1971, 1975). These stages move from a random ordering of letters in which children do not use sound-symbol correspondences, to phonetic spelling, and finally to standard or adult spelling. (The five stages presented here, as well as many of the samples of invented spellings cited, are drawn from the research of Gentry, 1978, 1981, 1982.)

BOX 11.2 Loan Words

alligator (Spanish)	egg (Scandinavian)	magazine (Arabic)
atom (Greek)	geyser (Icelandic)	paprika (Hungarian)
bagel (Yiddish)	horde (Turkish)	polka (Polish)
carnival (Italian)	igloo (Eskimo)	robot (Czech)
chauffeur (French)	judo (Japanese)	sauna (Finnish)
cherub (Hebrew)	jungle (Indian)	shamrock (Irish)
chipmunk (Native American)	kangaroo (Australian)	slogan (Scottish)
czar (Russian)	kindergarten (German)	tank (Portuguese)
divan (Persian)	luau (Hawaiian)	waffle (Dutch)

Stage 1: Precommunicative Spelling   In the first stage, writing appears to be random strings of letters or letterlike shapes, and sometimes the child also uses number symbols. Two examples of precommunicative spelling are:

MPRMRHM   btBpA

These examples demonstrate that young children's concept of the alphabetic principle is very primitive and shows no understanding of the relationship between phonemes and graphemes. Precommunicative spelling represents the natural expression of children's initial ideas about how alphabetic symbols represent words. Their spelling in this stage demonstrates that they are learning basic concepts about written language, including that writing moves from left to right and from top to bottom and that words are composed of letters.

Stage 2: Semiphonetic Spelling   Children's spellings are very abbreviated in the second stage and they use only one, two, or three letters to represent an entire word. Examples of stage-2 spelling include the following examples:

R	for	are
KLZ	for	closed
MSR	for	monster
SM	for	swimming

In these spellings, young writers accomplish a rudimentary understanding of the alphabetic principle: that a relationship or link exists between letters and sounds. They use the letter-name strategy in which letter names are used to spell words, and vowels are often omitted. Interestingly, their spellings represent some sound features while ignoring other equally important features.

Stage 3: Phonetic Spelling   In the third stage, children's understanding of phoneme-grapheme relationships is further refined. While they continue to use letter names to represent sounds, their ability to match letters and sounds is greatly improved. Children select letters to use in spelling words on the basis of sound alone without considering acceptable English letter sequences or other conventions. Their spellings usually do not resemble English words, and although their spelling does not look like standard adult spelling, teachers can decipher it. Examples of stage-3 spelling include the following:

LIV	live
DRAS	dress
PRD	purred
TIP	type
MONSTR	monster
MUZM	museum

Gentry also provides an interesting example of phonetic spelling: ADE LAFWITS KRAMD NTU A LAVATR for *Eighty elephants crammed into an elevator* (1981). These examples, typical of first graders' spelling, illustrate an ingenious and systematic step forward in this stage. In these examples, children not only include letters to represent *all* essential sound features in the words being spelled, but they also systematically develop particular spellings for various phonic and linguistic elements.

Stage 4: Transitional Spelling   In the fourth stage, students use both vowels and consonants in their spelling; they also apply many rules, but do not always apply them correctly. These rules include long-vowel rules, rules for forming plurals and rules for adding other suffixes. Examples of stage-4 spelling are:

RANE	rain
HUOSE	house
AFTERNEWN	afternoon
ELEFANT	elephant
MONSTUR	monster

These samples provide interesting information about the spelling strategies children use in the transitional stage. In the first word, RANE, the child chose the wrong vowel rule for marking a long vowel, and in the second word, HUOSE, two letters were reversed, perhaps because the writer relied primarily on visual clues. In the last three words, the writers made sophisticated, although incorrect, choices. In the word AFTERNEWN, the child chose the wrong homophone NEWN instead of NOON and in ELEFANT the writer chose the letter *f*, a more common spelling for /f/, instead of the letters *ph*. Finally, in MONSTUR, the child chose the wrong spelling for the *schwa* sound.

This stage is characterized by children's increased ability to represent a number of essential features of English spelling. First, they include a vowel in every syllable. For example, children typically use the letters EGL to represent *eagle* in the phonetic stage, but now they spell it EGUL. Next, children demonstrate knowledge of vowel patterns even though they make faulty decisions about which rule to use. For example, *toad* is often spelled TOD in stage-3 spelling and TODE in transitional spelling. Also, writers use common letter patterns in their spelling, including YOUNITED for *united* and HIGHCKED for *hiked*. Thus, in this stage, children use conventional alternatives for representing sounds, and although they continue to misspell words according to adult standards, transitional spelling resembles English words and it is easily read. As illustrated in these examples, children stop relying entirely on phonological information and begin to use visual clues and morphological information, or information about root words, prefixes, and suffixes as well.

Stage 5: Correct Spelling   As the name implies, children spell many words correctly in the fifth stage. However, not only do children in stage 5 spell words correctly, more importantly, they have internalized the alphabetic principle as well as basic spelling rules. Children's transition to this stage indicates that they are ready for formal spelling instruction.

In summary, children learn to spell by advancing through these five stages and acquiring a basic understanding of the alphabetic principle as well as other complex and abstract principles of our spelling system. The characteristics of the five stages are summarized in Box 11.3. While children's misspellings may at first appear to be errors, they are indicators of their stage of spelling development. In an amazingly short period, usually about four or five years (from age 4 to age 8 or 9), children move through these five stages. At the same time they are acquiring these spelling concepts, they are also learning to read and write. The three language abilities are naturally interwoven (Chapters 7 and 8). As they read,

BOX 11.3 Characteristics of the Stages of Invented Spelling

Stage 1: Precommunicative Spelling

- Children use letters and letterlike forms.
- Children show no understanding of phoneme-grapheme correspondence.
- Children show a preference for uppercase letters.
- Children mix uppercase and lowercase letters.
- Children often move from left to right across the page in writing.

Stage 2: Semiphonetic Spelling

- Children use abbreviated one-, two-, or three-letter spelling.
- Children omit some important letters in words.
- Children use letter-name strategy for spelling.

Stage 3: Phonetic Spelling

- Children match sounds to letter names.
- Children select letters on the basis of sound alone.
- Children's spelling represents all essential sound features.
- Children's spelling is readable.

Stage 4: Transitional Spelling

- Children use both consonants and vowels in spelling.
- Children include a vowel in every syllable.
- Children apply many spelling rules, although often incorrectly.
- Children use visual and morphological clues as well as phonological information.
- Children's spelling resembles English spelling.
- Children's spelling is easily read.

Stage 5: Correct Spelling

- Children spell words according to adult standards.
- Children have internalized the alphabetic principle.
- Children have learned basic spelling rules.

children see standard spelling and can compare their own spellings with the adult forms, and through writing they practice inventing and reformulating their own spellings. Most children's spelling spans two or three stages of spelling development, but with careful examination, a developmental level can be pinpointed and examples of words indicating movement toward the next stage can be identified. (For further examples of the developmental stages in spelling found in young children's compositions, see Box 11.4 and Chapters 2 and 8.)

BOX 11.4 Examples of Invented Words at Each Stage of Invented Spelling

Stages	Examples			
1. Precommunicative	btBpa	iBALI	LYilAWO	IDMitL
2. Semiphonetic	MTR	BTM	BD	U
3. Phonetic	MOSTR	BOTM	BRD	UNITID
4. Transitional	MONSTUR	BODUM	BRID	YOUNIGHTED
5. **Correct**	**MONSTER**	**BOTTOM**	**BIRD**	**UNITED**

Source: Adapted from Gentry, 1982b, pp. 52–61.

Spelling Miscues   Children's spelling mistakes are often indicative of their accomplishments as they move through developmental levels. Teachers, however, need to be alert to certain categories of error and possible teaching opportunities. Box 11.5 lists 12 common types of spelling miscues exhibited by students in the elementary grades. For example, when children's errors indicate confusion in using homonyms or in adding suffixes to root words, teachers can appropriately use the opportunity to work with individual students. Sometimes taking a minute or two to explain a spelling rule will solve the problem.

Invented Spelling as Problem Solving   Problem solving has been described as "a key motivation to mastery of language" Lundsteen (1976). The examples of invented spelling

---

BOX 11.5 Common Types of Spelling Mistakes

1. Mistaken choice of spelling rule — wead for weed
2. Omission of a pronounced letter — pay for play
3. Omission of silent letter — ofen for often
4. Insertion of a letter — molst for most
5. Reversal of letters — form for from
6. Use of inappropriate vowel in unaccented syllable — inturesting for interesting
7. Confusion in using homonyms — ware for wear
8. Confusion between words with similar pronunciations — except for accept
9. Suffixes — surly for surely
10. Double consonants — baloon for balloon
11. Plural forms involving es — brushs for brushes
12. Irregularly formed plurals — mouses for mice

provide ample evidence that children use problem solving as they experiment and test hypotheses about how to best represent spoken words in written language. Even before they enter school, young children experiment with letters and letterlike forms as the stage-1 examples indicate, recognizing that speech can be recorded. Through their exploration, they discover the alphabetic principle that sounds and letters are linked. While their understanding of the principle is very limited in stage-2 spelling, their writing indicates that they understand that letters represent specific speech sounds. They also segment their writing into groups, recognizing an essential writing convention that letters are grouped into words and that words are broken by spaces. In stage-3 spelling, children's understanding of the alphabetic principle is further elaborated as they include all important sound features of the word into their spelling. Next, in stage-4 spelling, they use typical English spelling patterns and rules, even though they sometimes choose the incorrect alternative. However, the outstanding accomplishment of this stage is that children recognize that English spelling involves more than just phoneme-grapheme relationships. Tracing the spelling of a single word through the five stages clearly illustrates this problem-solving approach as children grow in their ability to represent speech sounds and writing conventions. Consider, for example, one child's spellings of the word *monster:*

Stage 1: Precommunicative spelling	btBpa
Stage 2: Semiphonetic spelling	MSR
Stage 3: Phonetic spelling	MONSTR
Stage 4: Transitional spelling	MONSTUR
Stage 5: Correct spelling	MONSTER

Some of our basic assumptions about how children learn to spell have been refuted by the research on invented spelling. As the *monster* spellings indicate, children move from spelling words primarily on the basis of phonics to abstracting the principles of English spelling through experimenting and problem solving with written language. The process then is child-centered, not teacher-centered. Marino (1980) asked the question "What makes a good speller?" Through her research, she found that *good spellers use problem-solving strategies to reduce the alternatives* and *predict* the most likely spelling for an unknown word. These predictive abilities include those shown in Box 11.6.

In contrast, poor spellers do not make use of this information in predicting the spelling of unknown words. Marino suggests that the spelling game "Hangman" can be used to direct children's attention to these features of English spelling. In addition, students can generate lists of words that end with /k/ and from the list develop a rule about positional constraints.

BOX 11.6 Predictive Abilities

1. Awareness of letter frequency (e.g., f is a more commonly used spelling for /f/ than ph)

2. Awareness of pattern frequency (e.g., oke and ble are more frequently used than efe)

3. Awareness of positional constraints (e.g., words rarely if ever end in j or v, while e and st are commonly used at the ends of words)

In order to examine children's concepts about spelling and problem solving, try the activity given in Box 11.7. Word sorting is a valuable diagnostic tool, and it can be used again and again with students at any grade level. Through this activity, children reveal their current level of understanding of the alphabetic principle and spelling rules.

How Is Spelling Taught?

Commercial spelling textbooks form the basis of spelling programs in most elementary classrooms (Graves, 1977), but it is wrong to assume that spelling textbooks equal spelling programs. Teachers can modify spelling textbooks to meet the needs of their students or they can design individualized or contract spelling programs using words that students need to use in their writing. (Additional information on contract spelling is provided in the activity book that accompanies this textbook.)

Some Guidelines for Teaching Spelling   While spelling has been one of the most researched of the language arts, the research findings have not, for the most part, been applied by language arts teachers or in spelling textbooks. Often the strategies used to teach spelling are based on traditional practices rather than on research findings. The following guidelines for teaching spelling come from the results of spelling research (Fitzsimmons & Loomer, 1977; Graham, 1983; Hillerich, 1977, 1978; E. Horn, 1926, 1960; T. Horn, 1952; Rinsland, 1945).

1. *High-frequency words for spelling lists.* With more than 450,000 words included in unabridged dictionaries, it might seem difficult to choose the words for a spelling program. Again, the most important words for students to learn are the words they use most frequently in their own writing—including the high-frequency words. Researchers have identified these words. For instance, in a classic study E. Horn (1926) found that the three most frequently used words, *I, and,* and *the,* account for at least 10 percent of all words used, the ten most frequently used words account for 25 percent, and the top 100 words represent over 50 percent of all words children use in their writing. The 1000 most frequently used words account for 90 percent, 2000 words for 95.3 percent, 3000 words for 97.6 percent, 4000 words for 98.7 percent, and 5000 words for 99.2 percent. Thus, a relatively small number of words account for an amazingly large percentage of words children use in their writing.

BOX 11.7 Word-Sorting Activity

1. Have children compile collections of known words and write them on small cards.

2. Ask them to sort their word cards according to various categories, such as short vowels, one-syllable words, verbs ending in ing, adverbs, and so on. Either children or the teacher may determine the categories.

3. After the sorting is completed, ask children these questions and discuss their responses:
   - Why did you put these words together?
   - How are these words alike?
   - How are they different?
   - Is this a useful category for grouping words?

Using these statistics, some educators recommend that students learn to spell the 3000 most frequently used words by the end of sixth grade.

Lists of high-frequency words (e.g., Hillerich, 1978; Rinsland, 1945), the primary source of words that elementary students need to learn to spell, are the ones that students use most often in their writing. Hillerich's list of the 100 most frequently used words is presented in Box 11.8. Notice that a number of the words such as *you, they, would, said, because, do, know,* and *two* are inconsistent in sound/letter correspondence and thus difficult to spell. These words, known as spelling "demons," cannot be spelled phonetically, and some of them, such as *two,* are homophones. Teachers have tried highlighting hard spots in words, but this practice may not be helpful because a hard spot or even a demon word for one student is not necessarily difficult for another, especially one with good visual memory. A far better idea is to acknowledge to students that some words are indeed demons. Students can make small dictionaries or personal lists of their *own* problem words.

Again, another source of spelling words comes from the students themselves: the

---

BOX 11.8 The 100 Words Students Use Most Frequently in Their Writing

I	for	are	came	by
and	but	just	time	did
the	have	because	back	mother
a	up	what	will	our
to	had	if	can	don't
was	their	day	people	school
in	with	his	from	little
it	one	this	saw	into
of	be	not	now	who
my	so	very	or	after
he	all	to	know	no
is	said	do	your	am
you	were	about	home	well
that	then	some	house	two
we	like	her	an	put
when	went	him	around	man
they	them	could	see	didn't
on	she	as	think	us
would	out	get	down	things
me	at	got	over	too

Source: Hillerich, 1978, p. xiii.

words they misspell in their writing and the words they want to learn to spell. In addition to the high-frequency words that all students use in their writing, individual students have unique spelling needs based on their interests. For example, a student interested in dinosaurs will want to learn to spell different words than a student interested in astronauts and space. It is important to tailor the spelling program to meet these individual needs. Some teachers develop a master weekly spelling list with the spelling words the children have asked for during the previous week as well as words from the spelling textbook and seasonal or thematic words (from science and social studies units). From this master list, children *contract* with the teacher to learn to spell specific words during that week.

2. *A test-study-test approach.* Before asking students to study a list of words, administer a pretest to determine which words students already know how to spell. Then, ask them to study only the words they do not know. The opposite approach is the study-test method, in which students study all words whether they already know them or not, and then are tested on them. Common sense suggests that it is a *waste of time to have students study words they already know,* and this practice detracts from the time available for students to study the words they need to spell. One problem with spelling textbooks is that they are designed for students to study *all* spelling words through the practice activities regardless of whether or not students spelled the words correctly on the pretest.

3. *Students correcting their own spelling tests.* T. Horn (1947) found that having students immediately correct their own pretests (in the test-study-test method) accounted for 90–95 percent of the achievement resulting from word study. In fact, Horn stated that "the corrected test method may be the single most important factor contributing to spelling achievement" (p. 279). Teachers can write the list of spelling words on a transparency for the children to use in correcting their own tests, and having students correct their own tests certainly cuts down on the teacher's work load.

4. *An efficient strategy for learning spelling words.* It may be better to teach students a systematic and efficient strategy for learning unknown words rather than to have them adopt a haphazard and unproductive strategy. A productive strategy focuses on the whole word (and *not* word parts or syllables) and uses visual, auditory, and kinesthetic (i.e., using the body) components. The strategy in Box 11.9, used in the *Spelling for Word Mastery* program, is recommended (Cook, Esposito, Gabrielson, & Turner, 1984).

Begin by modeling this strategy for students who are unfamiliar with it, and then

---

BOX 11.9 Word Study Steps

1. LOOK at the word and say it.
2. READ each letter in the word.
3. CLOSE your eyes and spell the word to yourself.
4. LOOK at the word. Did you spell it correctly?
5. COPY the word from your list.
6. COVER the word and write it again.
7. LOOK at the word. Did you write it correctly?
8. If you made any mistakes, repeat the steps.

practice using the procedure until students understand how to use it to learn to spell unknown words independently. Also, list these steps on a student-illustrated chart to hang in the classroom for children to refer to.

Allow for individual differences, however, and for students to come up with *their own ideas* for studying spelling words. One example is the child who visualized his demon words nailed to a huge bulletin board. Another child molded her problem words using cookie dough. In this way she practiced her spelling words and ate the cookies, too.

5. *Approximately one hour per week on spelling instruction and practice.* The optimal amount of time to devote to spelling instruction and practice is approximately one hour per week, which breaks down to 10–12 minutes a day. Apparently, spending additional time on spelling does *not* significantly improve test results.

6. *Individualization of spelling instruction.* Just as students differ in their reading abilities, so do they exhibit a wide range of spelling abilities. Not all children learn to spell at the same rate, nor do they encounter the same problems in learning to spell. Spelling instruction needs to be individualized, that is, tailored to meet individual children's needs. Some begin by pretesting students and placing them at a level where they can spell 50–75 percent of the words correctly on a spelling list prior to study. It is essential that students not be overloaded by expecting them to learn 20 or more new words a week. The total number of spelling words depends on word frequency, word grouping, the degree of irregularity, and an individual child's skill in visual memory. Other factors to consider include the number of words presented each week, amount of practice and feedback, and interest level. It is amazing to see how quickly children learn to spell words such as *ghost, dinosaur,* and other high-interest words needed for genuine written communication.

7. *Realization that teaching spelling through phonic generalizations is of questionable value.* In addition to suggesting how to teach spelling, researchers also have one suggestion about how *not* to teach it. From their review of the literature, Johnson, Langford, and Quorn state that "the effectiveness of teaching spelling via phonic generalizations is highly questionable" (1981, p. 586). A phonic generalization commonly taught in first and second grade is that when two vowels are side by side in one-syllable words (such as *rain* and *meat*), the first vowel is long and the second is not pronounced. However, words such as *said* and *bread* are exceptions to this generalization. Ernest Horn (1960) lists five reasons why children should *not* be taught phonic generalizations and spelling rules:

Why *Not* to Teach Spelling Rules
1. Many sounds can be spelled in several different ways.
2. Most words that students spell incorrectly are phonetically correct.
3. More than one-third of our words have more than one accepted pronunciation.
4. More than half of English words contain unpronounced letters.
5. Sounds in unstressed syllables are hard to spell phonetically.

It seems clear that a majority of researchers in the area of spelling are opposed to teaching phonic generalizations and spelling rules with the possible exception of those rules that are highly consistent. Those generalizations and rules that are consistently regular may need to be taught at an appropriate level. For instance, rules for adding prefixes and suffixes are consistent. An example is *drop + ed = dropped,* which illustrates the rule for doubling the final consonant in one-syllable short vowel words before adding a suffix. The ten spelling rules listed in Box 11.10 are consistent enough to be useful to some spellers.

A review of spelling textbooks indicates that almost all textbooks group spelling words

BOX 11.10 Spelling Rules with Few Exceptions

1. Some rules governing the addition of suffixes and inflected endings are:

   a. Words ending in silent <u>e</u> drop the <u>e</u> when adding a suffix or ending beginning with a vowel, and keep the <u>e</u> when adding a suffix or ending beginning with a consonant.

bake	manage
baking	managing
baker	management

   b. When a root word ends in <u>y</u> preceded by a consonant, the <u>y</u> is changed to <u>i</u> in adding suffixes and endings unless the ending or suffix begins with <u>i</u>.

fly	study
flies	studying
flying	studious
	studies

   c. When a root word ends in <u>y</u> preceded by a vowel, the root word is not changed when adding suffixes or endings.

play	monkey
playful	monkeys

   d. When a one-syllable word ends in a consonant with one vowel before it, the consonant is doubled before adding a suffix or ending beginning with a vowel:

run	ship
running	shipping
	shipment

   e. In words of more than one syllable, the final consonant is doubled before adding a suffix or ending if: (1) the last syllable is accented, (2) the last syllable ends in a consonant with one vowel before it, and (3) the suffix or ending begins with a vowel.

begin	admit
beginning	admittance

2. The letter <u>q</u> is always followed by <u>u</u> in common English words.

queen	quiet

3. No English words end in <u>v</u>.

love	glove

(Continued)

4. Proper nouns and most adjectives formed from proper nouns should begin with capital letters.

   America   American

5. Most abbreviations end with a period.

   etc.   Nov.

6. The apostrophe is used to show the omission of letters in contractions.

   don't   haven't

7. The apostrophe is used to indicate the possessive form of nouns but not pronouns.

   boy's   its
   dog's   theirs

8. When adding <u>s</u> to words to form plurals or to change the tense of verbs, <u>es</u> must be added to words ending with the hissing sounds *(x, s, sh, ch)*.

   glass   watch
   glasses   watches

9. When <u>s</u> is added to words ending in a single <u>f</u>, the <u>f</u> is changed to <u>v</u> and <u>es</u> is added.

   half   shelf
   halves   shelves

10. When <u>ei</u> or <u>ie</u> are to be used, <u>i</u> usually comes before <u>e</u>, except after <u>c</u> or when sounded like <u>a</u>. (Note these exceptions: leisure, neither, seize, and weird.)

    believe   neighbor
    relieve   weigh

according to these generalizations and rules. Primary-grade students, however, have trouble with abstract generalizations; it is even difficult to find an adult who profits from them.

8. *Helping students develop a spelling conscience.* **Spelling conscience** can be described as a positive attitude toward spelling. Hillerich (1982) lists two dimensions of spelling conscience: (1) understanding that standard spelling is a courtesy to readers, and (2) developing the ability to proofread in order to spot and correct misspellings. Correct spelling—a courtesy to the reader—develops as children acquire audience awareness as they move from self-expressive to communicative writing. Teachers can facilitate audience awareness (or writing for the reader) by supporting meaningful writing activities directed to a variety of specific audiences. Too often school writing is written only for the teacher.

Proofreading for spelling errors is an essential component in all spelling programs. Too often children spell words correctly on weekly spelling tests, but spell incorrectly in their writing (as 10-year-old Elaine did). With the added demands of writing it is not surprising that students misspell words that they really do know how to spell. In addition, students often want to use words in their writing that they don't know how to spell. Certainly encourage them to do so. During the *translating stage* of the writing process students are concerned with expressing their ideas. However, it is important that they ultimately return to their rough drafts and proofread to correct spelling and other errors. Proofreading can be introduced in kindergarten and first grade rather than postponing it until the middle grades. Young children and their teachers can proofread group language experience charts together. As children begin dictating and writing their own compositions, modeling can encourage them to read over the piece and make any necessary corrections. With this beginning, children will accept proofreading as a natural part of the writing process, and with their growing awareness of audience, they will understand its value.

A teacher can use a large-group activity to introduce proofreading. Begin by presenting a piece of the teacher's writing with some spelling errors on an overhead projector or on the chalkboard. Explain that proofreading is a special kind of reading that has a specific purpose: to locate spelling and other mechanical errors. It is slow, word-by-word, and even letter-by-letter reading. Read slowly through the composition with the class, lightly circling each word that might be misspelled. Focus students' attention on homophones and other spelling demons. Next, correct the misspelled words that children know how to spell and have students check the correct spellings of other misspelled words in a dictionary or other references, such as personal card files of demon words, homophone charts, and so on. Then, correct these words as well. Many teachers prefer using small pocket dictionaries and paperback "word finders" for correcting misspellings located through proofreading rather than the large, cumbersome school dictionaries. ("Word finders" are elaborated on in the activity book.) After completing this exercise, cooperatively develop a chart to display in the classroom listing the steps in proofreading for spelling errors. Box 11.11 on page 396 presents an example of such a chart. Encourage students to refer to the chart as they proofread their writing (individually or cooperatively) throughout the year, as in the opening scene of this chapter. It may be worthwhile to review the procedure periodically, using the large-group approach described above.

9. *Teaching students how to locate unknown words in a dictionary.* Unabridged **dictionaries** include approximately 450,000 entry words, and by the end of sixth grade, students typically learn to spell approximately 3,000 of these words through spelling instruction. Subtracting 3,000 from 450,000 leaves 447,000 words unaccounted for. Obviously students may need to learn how to locate the correct spellings for these additional words. Dictionary study often includes a variety of skills including alphabetical order, dictionary respellings, entry words, guide words, parts of speech, pronunciation, syllabication, and word origins. However, only three of these skills—entry words and perhaps alphabetical order and word origins—are valuable to spelling. In fact, dictionary respelling, that is, spelling the word phonetically (e.g., *kul* for *cool*), may actually interfere with spelling performance by suggesting an alternative spelling form. The other dictionary skills can be learned incidentally in connection with whole language arts activities.

While it is relatively easy to find a known word in the dictionary, it is much harder to locate an unfamiliar word; and it is essential that students learn what to do when they don't know how to spell a word. They need to learn to use a *problem-solving* strategy to predict possible spellings for the word and then check their predictions by consulting a dictionary. The strategy involves five steps, as shown in Box 11.12.

Step 3 in Box 11.12 is undoubtedly the most difficult one in the strategy. While some sounds are represented by only one or two spelling options, others have ten or more possible

---

BOX 11.11 How to Proofread for Spelling Errors

Part I: Reading

1. Read only for spelling errors.
2. Read slowly, letter by letter in each word.
3. Lightly circle known misspelled words and words that might be misspelled.
4. Check spelling demons and words that are difficult for you to spell.
5. Check homonyms such as <u>there-their-they're</u> and <u>your-you're</u>.
6. Check for word endings such as -<u>s</u>, -<u>ed</u>, -<u>ing</u>.

Part II: Correcting Errors

1. Write the correct spelling above misspelled words that you are sure you know how to spell.
2. Check the spelling of misspelled words that you don't know how to spell in:
   • your spelling card file
   • the list of spelling demons
   • the dictionary

BOX 11.12 Problem-Solving Strategy for Predicting Spellings

1. Check for prefixes, suffixes, and root words.
2. Determine the sounds in the word.
3. Generate a list of possible spellings for each sound.
4. Select the most likely alternatives.
5. Consult a dictionary to check the correct spelling.

---

spellings. For example, while /b/ is always spelled *b*, /j/ can be spelled *g, ge, dge,* or *j*; and /sh/ can be spelled *ch, ti, ce, ci, s, ss, se, si,* and *sch* as well as *sh*.

A valuable spelling activity for upper-grade students is to have them construct lists of spelling options for each phoneme. As the lists are developed, hang them in the classroom or have students make copies for their own use in spelling unfamiliar words and store them in their individual writing files. A sample chart is shown in Box 11.13.

When students use a problem-solving strategy (Box 11.12) they are actually making educated guesses about probable spellings. In order to make these guesses, however, students must understand the basic relationships between phonemes and graphemes as well as common English spelling patterns. Also, *wide reading* helps students know the probabilities of each spelling pattern in English. (Recall an earlier section on invented spelling as problem solving and "Predictive Abilities" in Box 11.6.)

BOX 11.13 Ways to Spell the *SH* Sound

sh			ch
she	bushel	flash	chaperon
shadow	sunshine	smash	chauffeur
should	cushion	finish	chef
shell		Spanish	chiffon
sheik		leash	machine
shape		rush	

ti	se	si	ci
nation	nauseous	tension	mortician
fraction			delicious
election			special
vacation			ancient
dictionary			

s	ss	sch	ce
sure	mission	schwa	ocean
sugar	tissue		

Spelling Textbooks   Because of the widespread use of spelling textbooks in elementary classrooms, it is important to look at their approach to spelling instruction and to examine whether or not they applied the findings of spelling researchers in designing their programs. A list of possible questions to use in examining spelling textbooks is provided in Box 11.14. These questions examine five areas: (a) words and how they are selected and presented, (b) strategies for studying words, (c) testing procedures, (d) organization and skills included in the textbook, and (e) background information presented in the teacher's edition. Review sample spelling textbooks yourself and draw your own conclusions about the strengths and weaknesses of the textbooks. Compare yours with the conclusions drawn from the literature (e.g., Cohen, 1969; Hillerich, 1977). (Also see Chapter 13, the section on textbooks.)

A Textbook-Free Approach: Learning to Spell Through Written Composition

While teachers often equate spelling textbooks with their spelling programs, *textbooks are really not needed to teach spelling.* Instead teachers can design their own programs using these components:

Components for Designing a No-Textbook Program
1. Daily writing activities using a process approach in which students need to proofread their own writing.
2. A list of high-frequency words.
3. The test-study-test approach.
4. A strategy for learning to spell new words.

BOX 11.14 Questions to Use in Examining Spelling Textbooks

Part 1: Words

- How are words chosen for this textbook?
- How are words grouped into lessons?
- Are words presented in a list format?

Part 2: Word Study

- Does the textbook present a strategy for learning to spell new words?
- Do students study all words or only those they misspelled on the pretest?
- Do students study "hard spots" in words?

Part 3: Testing

- Is there an initial placement test?
- Are pretests administered prior to instruction?
- Are students directed to correct their own pretests and practice tests?
- How do students record their progress?

Part 4: Organization

- How are the units organized?
- Which dictionary skills are presented?
- Are proofreading activities included?
- What other language activities are included?
- What information is provided about individualizing the spelling program?

Part 5: Teacher's Guide

- Does the guide cite recent research on spelling?
- Is research reported on this program?
- Does the guide contain a bibliography?
- Are alternative management strategies suggested?
- Does the guide suggest how much time should be spent on spelling?

Source: Adapted from Boutin & Stetson, 1982.

5. Information about the development of the English language and word histories.
6. Dictionary study focusing on probabilities and how to locate unknown words.
7. An individual contract to learn to spell the words needed in written composition and from other appropriate sources, with the students involved having options and choices. (See the section on contract spelling in Chapter 11 of the activity book.)

These seven components provide an outlet for communicating, applying, and practicing the words students have learned how to spell. They provide a core spelling vocabulary, teach students how to find the correct spelling of all other words in English, and suggest strategies for helping students develop a *spelling conscience.*

In the quotation at the beginning of this spelling section, 10-year-old Elaine earned 100 percent on her weekly spellings tests, but she did not *apply* what she had learned in her writing. She may have had a problem with long-term visual memory, an important consideration with respect to the *who.* She could perhaps learn for those tests, but then forget, or she may not have developed a spelling conscience. She probably did not proofread her sentence "The ponys stoped comeing to." In any case, her classroom spelling program was probably incomplete. Teachers have an important supportive and creative role in helping children with their spelling.

HANDWRITING

> I had no idea that handwriting was for writing. . . . Handwriting was punishing, mindless, and mechanical whereas composing with ideas was lofty and worthwhile
>
> *D. H. Graves*

In recalling his own feelings about handwriting when he was a child, Graves describes an all too common reaction. Too often students in the elementary grades do not understand the functional role of handwriting. Handwriting can be defined as the physical act of making marks on paper to represent words and express thoughts. It is only one component of the writing process, and like spelling, handwriting is a tool for writers. It is important to note that the terms *handwriting* and *writing* are very different and cannot be used interchangeably. In previous generations, handwriting was considered almost an art form and the mark of an educated person. Now educators recognize the support function of handwriting, and the emphasis has shifted to helping students develop legible and fluent handwriting. Legibility is the ease with which a piece of writing can be read, and fluency is the speed or rate of writing. Comfort is an additional criterion; students need to develop a comfortable and relaxed way of holding the writing instrument so that handwriting will not be an overly fatiguing task.

This section will explore three areas related to students' handwriting development and handwriting instruction: the role of handwriting in the language arts program, the development of legible handwriting, and the teacher's role in facilitating students' growth in handwriting.

What Is the Role of Handwriting in the Language Arts Program?

Like spelling, handwriting is a tool students use in every written language activity, both in language arts and in other content areas. For example, students use handwriting when they write book reports, practice their spelling words, take notes on a science experiment, write letters to pen pals, and fill in the blanks on workbook pages. Although handwriting is a necessary tool, it plays a secondary role. Students need to develop legible and fluent handwriting in order to communicate their ideas effectively through written language. However, the ideas that students express about the books they read in their book reports and their accuracy in spelling their spelling words are of far greater importance than the correctness of their letter forms.

The key goal of handwriting instruction is to help students develop a comfortable style that is legible and allows them to write fluently. The importance of legible handwriting cannot be denied. For example, the quality of handwriting has been found to influence teachers' judgments about the quality of students' written compositions (Markham, 1976).

Too often teachers insist that students demonstrate their best handwriting every time they pick up a pencil or pen. This requirement is very unrealistic; certainly there are times when handwriting is important, but at other times speed or other considerations outweigh neatness. Children need to learn to recognize two basic types of writing occasions, **private writing** and **public writing.** Legibility counts in public writing, but when children make notes for themselves or write the first draft of a composition, they are doing private writing; they decide for themselves how important neatness is.

Today typewriters, word processors, and tape recorders provide alternatives to handwriting. Even so, handwriting remains an essential tool for both children and adults and an important component of language arts programs.

Handwriting Forms Elementary schools provide two forms of handwriting—manuscript, or printing, and cursive, or connected writing. These two forms are illustrated in Figure 11.2. Typically, students in kindergarten and the primary grades learn and use the manuscript form; they switch to the cursive form in the second or third grade. Then they use both manuscript and cursive handwriting forms throughout their school careers.

Until the 1920s students learned only cursive writing. Marjorie Wise is credited with introducing the manuscript form (Hildreth, 1960). Manuscript writing is considered better for young children because it is similar to the style of type used in reading textbooks. Only two letters, *a* and *g*, are significantly different in type.

There have been criticisms, however, of the manuscript form. A major complaint is the reversal problem caused by some of the lowercase letters, particularly *b* and *d*. Also, detractors have argued that the "circles and sticks" style of manuscript writing involves frequent stops and starts, inhibiting the smooth and rhythmic flow necessary for fluent writing.

A new style of handwriting called D'Nealian ® Handwriting after its developer, Donald Neal Thurber, appeared in 1968. Thurber, a teacher in Michigan, developed this program to ameliorate some of the problems associated with the manuscript form. In the D'Nealian manuscript form, letters are slanted as cursive letters are slanted, and all but five of the manuscript letters are formed in the same way the cursive letters are formed. Thus, the transition to cursive is simplified. D'Nealian ® Handwriting includes both manuscript and cursive forms, and both forms are presented in Figure 11.3. The unique characteristic of the D'Nealian cursive form is its simplicity. Compare the D'Nealian cursive form in Figure 11.3 on page 402 with the traditional cursive form in Figure 11.2.

How Do Students Develop Legible Handwriting, and What Is the Teacher's Role?

Clear-cut patterns similar to the stages of invented spelling have not been identified for children's handwriting development. Instead, their handwriting seems more dependent on instruction and teacher behaviors. In this section, characteristics of the handwriting of children (the *who*) will be discussed together with the teacher's role at the kindergarten,

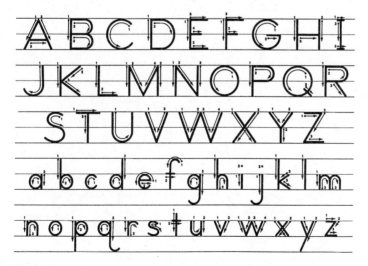

Figure 11.2 Manuscript and cursive handwriting forms. (Copyright © 1984, Zaner-Bloser, Inc.)

Figure 11.3 D'Nealian® Handwriting forms. (*Source:* From *D'Nealian® Handwriting* by Donald Thurber. Copyright © 1987 by Scott, Foresman and Company. Reprinted by permission.)

primary, and intermediate grade levels (the *how*). In addition, the special needs of left-handed writers will be examined.

Handwriting in Kindergarten   Children enter kindergarten with varying amounts of handwriting and handwriting-like experiences. Most 5-year-olds have used pens and crayons as well as paintbrushes, and some children already know how to print their names (often in all uppercase letters) and write some of the letters of the alphabet. Usually these young writers show a preference for using the uppercase letters and will even argue that their name is not their name when printed in lowercase letters. And, a few children still use both hands interchangeably for handwriting and other fine motor tasks.

In kindergarten, the teacher's role is threefold: (1) helping children develop hand dominance, (2) providing fine motor activities, and (3) teaching children how to form the manuscript letters. Before handwriting instruction can begin, children need to develop hand dominance, or a preference for using either the right or the left hand. While most children have made their preferences before entering kindergarten, often one or two children in a class will not have. The teacher's role is to provide a wide variety of fine motor activities and to chart the child's preference for using each hand in order to predict which hand will probably become dominant. Note which hand the child uses for coloring, rolling a ball, pushing open a door, turning on a light switch, eating, handing an object to someone, and so on. It is essential that children not be forced to use a particular hand, but through the typical kindergarten activities, children usually develop a preference for one hand or the other. Just as it is unwise to force young children into choosing a particular hand for writing activities, it is also unwise to force left-handed students to switch and use their right hands. When children do not demonstrate a clear preference for either hand, they probably need to be encouraged to use their right hands because we live in a right-handed world. In sum, knowledgeable educators now allow children to choose the hand they wish to use, but it is crucial that one hand become dominant before first grade, when the handwriting demands increase dramatically. No dominance may be a red flag indicating learning disabilities.

Kindergarten programs typically include many fine motor activities that focus on teaching students how to form manuscript letters. For example:

- Forming letters using clay
- Printing letters in finger paint, sand, and chocolate pudding
- Gluing macaroni or confetti on construction paper in the shape of a letter
- Bending pipe cleaners into letter shapes and tracing the formation of the letter

Kindergarten teachers also provide handwriting assistance by taking children's dictation. Five- and six-year-olds can easily be frustrated by the physical demands of writing; their ideas flow much faster than they can move their pencils. For many kindergartners, the teacher serves as a scribe, taking the children's dictation. Not only do teachers assume some of the physical demands of handwriting, but they also model how to hold a writing instrument, how to write from left to right and top to bottom, and how to form uppercase and lowercase letters. Interestingly, most children quickly learn to adjust the speed of their dictation to match the teacher's writing speed.

Handwriting in the Primary Grades   Children's handwriting needs increase dramatically in first grade and continue to increase throughout the elementary grades. As these demands grow to writing sentences, composing stories, and other expository uses, handwriting instruction becomes more formalized. In the primary grades, the teacher has a dual role: (1) to provide formal instruction in manuscript handwriting and (2) to encourage and provide meaningful, communicative writing activities in which students need to use their newly acquired handwriting skills.

The results of research in the area of handwriting (Askov, Otto, & Askov, 1970; Graves, 1978; Peck, Askov & Fairchild, 1980) offer the following suggestions about teaching handwriting:

1. *Teach handwriting in separate periods of direct instruction and teacher-supervised practice.* Research suggests that the teacher is an important variable in handwriting instruction. During short 10- to 15-minute periods several times a week, the teacher begins by demonstrating the handwriting skill and then walks around the classroom, supervising as students practice the skill. Research has shown that "moving models," such as the teacher demonstrating how a letter is formed, are far more valuable than "still models," such as letters drawn on a sheet of paper for the students to trace or copy.

2. *The use of beginner pencils or other writing aids does* **not** *improve students' handwriting.* Kindergartners and first graders commonly use "fat" beginner pencils, $13/32$ inch in diameter, because it has been assumed that they are easier for young children to hold. However, children seem to prefer to use regular size, $10/32$-inch pencils that older children and adults use. Moreover, regular pencils have erasers. Research now indicates that the beginner pencils are not better than regular pencils for young children (Lamme & Ayris, 1983). Likewise, there is no evidence that specially shaped pencils and little writing aids that slip onto pencils to improve children's grip are effective.

3. *The value of lined paper and the use of paper lined at specific intervals are still being debated.* There are many types of paper, both lined and unlined, available to use for writing. Paper companies manufacture lined paper in a range of sizes. For example, paper is typically lined at ⅞-inch intervals for first graders, ¾-inch intervals for second graders, ½-inch intervals for third graders, and ⅜-inch intervals for older students. The few research studies that have examined the value of lined paper in general and paper lined at these specific intervals offer conflicting results. While students' writing is often neater when they use lined paper, they can learn to write using either lined or unlined paper.

4. *Use a multisensory approach for teaching handwriting.* The best approach for teaching handwriting is a multisensory one, involving visual, auditory, and tactile components. The following strategy is recommended:

1. Demonstrate the skill (e.g., how to form a letter) on the chalkboard or on an overhead projector.
2. Repeat the demonstration and have the students describe it as you demonstrate.
3. Have students practice the skill at the chalkboard or with a variety of other materials. To practice letter formation, for instance, children can form letters with clay, finger paint, sand, or other material.
4. Have students practice the skill on paper.
5. Circulate among students, providing assistance and encouragement.
6. After students have practiced the skill, have them apply it in meaningful writing activities where they need to communicate in a legible manner.

Step 6 is the crucial one because students need to use handwriting in creative, imaginative, and meaningful activities. Too often these practice activities have been equated with copying daily news reports from the chalkboard, such as: "Today is Wednesday, October 14. We will go to the library at 10:50." This activity, as well as others requiring students to copy sentences or poems from the chalkboard, is intended to provide handwriting practice, but it is actually "busy work," and may indeed hinder the development of legible handwriting.

Too often primary-grade teachers place too great an emphasis on handwriting instruction and too little emphasis on having students apply what they have learned in meaningful writing activities. Handwriting is a tool for writers, and the goal of handwriting instruction at all levels is application in writing. In assignments, such as copying sentences and poems from the chalkboard, students may form letters incorrectly without the teacher being available to provide assistance; often children cannot even read what they are copying. In addition, far-point copying from the board is extremely difficult for many children. It is far better for students to create their own compositions or to copy very brief literary selections of their *own* choosing. For instance, a favorite handwriting practice activity for many primary-grade students is to copy self-selected jokes and riddles from books. These selections are short, easy to read, and full of meaning for children. Figure 11.4 is an example of a second-grader's handwriting practice from *Tyrannosaurus Wrecks* (1979), a dinosaur riddle book compiled by Noelle Sterne. (Check the activity book that accompanies this textbook for other handwriting activities.)

Almost as soon as students begin writing, they can assume a role in monitoring and assessing their own handwriting. They can check to see if they formed a particular letter correctly, if their letters touched the baseline, or if they left adequate space between letters and words. Kindergartners and first graders can look at a row of letters they have just printed, for example, and circle the two or three letters that were formed the best. Five elements of legibility are listed in Box 11.15, and students can assess their handwriting according to these elements. From these elements, checklists can be developed for second and third graders to use in assessing their own handwriting. An example of a checklist for assessing manuscript handwriting was presented in Box 11.1, but it would be preferable for teachers and students to develop their *own* checklists based on the elements of legibility. Include only a few items on the first checklist, and then add more items as handwriting skills are introduced and reviewed through the school year. Allowing students to assume responsibility for identifying their strengths and weaknesses is worthwhile because then they will show more willingness to work to improve their handwriting.

Transition to Cursive Writing   During the second half of second grade or during third grade, students are introduced to cursive writing. The switch is usually dictated by tradition rather than by sound educational theory. Students, however, are ready to make the change at different times—some as early as first grade and a few others not until fourth grade or later. Yet all students in a class or school typically make the change together.

Learning to write in cursive requires several skills. First students learn to read the cursive alphabet; next they learn to form and join the cursive letters; and finally they learn to position their bodies in a new way in order to slant their letters slightly to the right.

It makes sense to avoid asking students to read a written form that they cannot

What   are   dinosaur
children   afraid   of   at   nigth?

The   Boggy   Man.

by   Keneath   Steiner

Figure 11.4   A primary student's handwriting practice.

BOX 11.15 Elements of Legibility

Element 1: Letter Formation

- Letters are formed with specific strokes.
- Cursive letters are joined carefully.
- Letters touch the baseline.

Element 2: Size

- Letters are uniform in size.

Element 3: Spacing

- Adequate space is left between letters.
- Adequate space is left between words and sentences.

Element 4: Slant

- Letters are consistently parallel.
- Manuscript letters are vertical.
- Cursive letters are slanted slightly to the right.

Element 5: Line Quality

- Lines are of consistent thickness.
- Lines are not jerky or shaky.

---

decipher. Children need to learn to read the cursive letters before being taught to write the letters or they will not be able to read what they have written. However, as with manuscript writing, students are eager to write in cursive—the grown-up way—and they learn to write their names and a few other familiar words in the cursive form before it is taught in school. Often, they have to unlearn bad habits before they can learn how to form the letters and join them in a standard manner. The strategy for teaching the manuscript form is also used in teaching cursive writing, and the advice about having brief periods of direct instruction and providing many meaningful writing opportunities applies here as well.

The practice of changing students over to cursive handwriting only two or three years after they are introduced to the manuscript form is receiving increasing criticism from educators. The argument has been that students must learn the cursive form as early as possible because of their increasing need for writing speed. It has been assumed that because of its continuous flow, cursive is faster to form than manuscript. However, research suggests that manuscript writing can be written as quickly as cursive writing (Jackson, 1971). Also, the manuscript form has another advantage: It is more legible. Think how often people are asked to use the manuscript form when legibility counts, in filling out job applications, income tax returns, and other forms. The controversy over the benefits of the two forms as well as the best time to introduce cursive writing will most likely continue.

Handwriting in the Intermediate Grades By the intermediate grades, students have learned to form the manuscript and cursive letter forms, and they have firmly established writing habits. At this level, the emphasis is on helping students diagnose their handwriting trouble spots in order to develop a legible and fluent handwriting style. Older students both simplify letter forms as well as add unique flourishes to their handwriting to develop their own "trademark" styles. Allow them to do so as long as their handwriting remains legible and can be written fluently.

Working with students to improve their handwriting begins when they are able to recognize the strong and weak points of their handwriting and they indicate a desire to improve. This desire often develops as a part of the concept of *audience awareness,* as students learn to recognize the needs of those who will read their writing. Use a diagnostic, *problem-solving approach* in which students concentrate on their trouble spots. Research shows that some letters are more difficult than others to form. For instance, Horton (1970) found that the lowercase letter *r* is the most difficult of all cursive letters to form.

Intermediate-grade students can examine their own handwriting using the five elements of legibility presented in Box 11.15. As with primary-grade students, these older students can develop checklists based on the elements of legibility to use in assessing their own handwriting. Box 11.16 presents an example of a self-assessment checklist for cursive handwriting.

Older students are familiar with both manuscript and cursive handwriting forms. Encourage them to consider the two forms interchangeable, rather than cursive writing as the superior form. Actually, many students, especially boys, prefer the manuscript form and can be encouraged to continue to use it for many handwriting purposes.

Left-handed Writers Approximately 10 percent of the population is left-handed, and teachers can expect to have two or three left-handed writers in their classes. There seem to be more left-handed children than ever before, and this is probably due to the fact that children are now being allowed to use whichever hand they want for writing and other fine motor tasks. It is difficult for right-handed teachers to teach left-handed students because handwriting is taught differently for these students. Howell (1978) explains that "the act of writing for the left-handed is not merely the reverse of writing for the right-handed." The left-to-right direction of writing makes handwriting more problematic for left-handed stu-

---

BOX 11.16 Cursive Handwriting Checklist

1. Are my letters correctly formed?

2. Are my letters joined correctly?

3. Do my letters rest on the baseline?

4. Do I space letters evenly?

5. Do I leave enough space between words?

6. Do I slant my letters slightly to the right?

7. Are my letters parallel?

8. Are my letters uniform in size?

dents because they have difficulty seeing what they have written and they must avoid rubbing their hands across what they have just written and possibly smearing it.

Educators have concluded that it is not wise to try to change left-handed writers into right-handed ones. Research suggests that hand dominance is determined by the dominant hemisphere of the brain and is not an acquired habit. Handedness is usually well established by the time children enter school, but check kindergartners and primary-grade students at the beginning of the school year to be sure they have established a dominant hand. See the section on "Handwriting in Kindergarten" for information on how to help young children who have not yet developed handedness.

Little research-based information is available about how to teach handwriting to left-handed students, and most suggestions are based on tradition and opinions. Left-handed writers use the same letter formations and other handwriting guidelines, but their physical orientation is different. Related to their different physical orientation, left-handed writers need to make three major adjustments: (1) how they hold writing instruments, (2) how they position writing paper on their desks, and (3) how they slant their writing (Howell, 1978). First, left-handed writers should grip pencils or pens an inch or so farther back from the tip than right-handed writers do. This change will help them be able to see what they are writing and avoid smearing what they have just written. Also, it is crucial that left-handed students avoid "hooking" their wrists. Have left-handed students keep their wrists straight and elbows close to their bodies to avoid the awkward hooked position. Second, left-handed students slant their writing paper to the right, the opposite of right-handed children, who slant their paper to the left. If necessary, place a piece of masking tape on left-handed students' desks to indicate the correct paper position. Third, the slant of left-handed students' writing needs to be similar to the slant of right-handed writers. However, in practice, left-handed writers often slant their letters a little more backward than do right-handed students.

Special support is needed for the left-handed writers, and teachers need to carefully monitor them as they are forming writing habits because bad habits, such as hooking their wrists, are very hard to break. If you are right-handed, consider asking a left-handed teacher or an older left-handed student who has good handwriting skills to work with your left-handed writers. (See Figure 11.5 for pictures of correct pencil grip for a left-handed and for a right-handed writer.)

OTHER WRITING CONVENTIONS

Three other conventions that students need to learn to use in their writing are capitalization, punctuation, and formatting. Too often teachers overemphasize these conventions, and it cannot be stated too strongly that they are only tools for writers. As with spelling and handwriting, these conventions serve to facilitate effective written communication. In writing, the quality of students' ideas is of far greater importance. This section focuses on two fundamental questions: What other writing conventions do students need to learn? How can these conventions be taught?

What Other Writing Conventions Do Students Need to Learn?

Capitalization   The need to learn capitalization skills begins as soon as young children learn to write their names. They quickly learn to capitalize the first letter of their names,

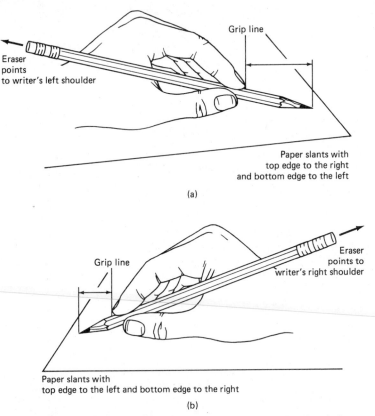

Grip line

Eraser points to writer's left shoulder

Paper slants with top edge to the right and bottom edge to the left

(a)

Grip line

Eraser points to writer's right shoulder

Paper slants with top edge to the left and bottom edge to the right

(b)

Figure 11.5 Correct pencil grip for (a) left-handed and (b) right-handed writers. (*Source:* Waveland Press.)

the pronoun *I,* and the first letter of sentences. Box 11.17 (p. 410) lists capitalization uses elementary students need to learn. Interestingly, the most common problem associated with capitalization is the tendency to capitalize too many words. Rules for using capital letters have changed through the years, just as they have for other conventions. And, they also differ in countries around the world. In the Declaration of Independence, for instance, Thomas Jefferson felt free to capitalize any words he wanted to emphasize. Now we only capitalize proper nouns, and that's a hard lesson for elementary students to learn. Naturally, they seem to follow Jefferson's approach and capitalize words either by choice or chance. (See corrolated activities in the activity book.)

Punctuation Punctuation may be described as "a set of signals showing the reader how to read the flow of words as the speaker would say them" (Moffett & Wagner, 1983). There is a clear connection between oral language and punctuation. To demonstrate this connection, repeat the same sentence three times: first as a statement, next as a question, and finally as an exclamation. For example, try repeating the following sentence with the three differing emphases:

The car is heading this way.

BOX 11.17 Uses of Capital Letters

Proper nouns, including names of people, days of week, months of year, and geographic names

Pronoun *I*

First word in a sentence

Titles such as Mr., Mrs., Dr.

Abbreviations

Initials

Important words in titles of stories and poems

First word of a greeting and closing of a letter

Commercial trade names

First word in a direct quote

Statement: The *car* is heading this way.

Question: The car is heading this *way?*

Exclamation: The car is heading *this way!*

When you said the sentence as a statement, did your voice drop at the end? It probably did. When you repeated the sentence as a question and as an exclamation, did your voice again drop at the end? No, we generally raise our voices at the end of a question and an exclamation. This connection between oral and written language is a crucial one for students to discover. As a general rule, each time we pause in oral language, a punctuation mark is needed in writing. The intonation of our voice provides a valuable clue to the correct punctuation mark to use. Without punctuation marks, readers could not adequately interpret the intended meaning.

Historical Storytelling About Punctuation   The ancient Greeks invented five of the punctuation marks used today to help their readers interpret the meaning of written messages (Farrant, 1977). The period began as a small circle written at the end of a sentence to indicate that the writer had "gone all around" the subject. Eventually the small circle was reduced to a dot. To indicate a question, the Greeks reduced their word *quaesto* to *Qo* and in time the circle came to be written under the *Q*. Later the Romans were responsible for shortening it to its present form. The exclamation point was developed from the Greek word *Io*, indicating excitement or surprise. As with the question mark, the circle became a dot and was written under the *I* rather than beside it. Finally, as many children guess, quotation marks were originally used to represent the two lips of the person speaking.

Children think of punctuation marks as abstract symbols without any real meaning. Knowing the story behind these marks adds a new dimension, and coordinating a unit on the history of our alphabet and writing with study of ancient Greece will demonstrate to students how interrelated our language, culture, and history are. (Other activities on punctuation, including a delightful poem, are found in the corresponding chapter of the activity book.)

Students are introduced to these nine punctuation marks during the elementary grades: period, question mark, exclamation point, quotation marks, apostrophe, comma, colon, parentheses, and hyphen. The uses that students learn for each punctuation mark are listed in Box 11.18 on page 412.

However, the nine punctuation marks do not always provide enough options for writers. In Figure 11.6 on page 413, Yetta Goodman (1979) shares a letter from an 8-year-old who invented a new punctuation mark to express sadness. This student's invention is a fine example of problem solving and using writing conventions in order to communicate more effectively.

Formatting   Formatting refers to "the arrangement of writing on a page" (Petty & Jensen, 1980). Included are general format elements such as writing on one side of a paper and paragraph indentation. A second dimension might include some specific format elements such as the scriptwriting format and the friendly letter form. The general format elements are common to most writing activities, while the specific format elements are unique to specific manuscript forms. For example, scripts are formatted very differently from haiku poems or stories. Box 11.19 (p. 414) outlines both the general and specific format elements.

How Can These Conventions Be Taught?

Traditionally, the most basic writing convention skills such as capitalizing the first letter of people's names and adding periods, question marks, and exclamation points at the end of sentences are introduced in first grade. They are then reinforced and elaborated at each succeeding grade level. Students typically practice the conventions through exercises in language arts textbooks, but often with little success. *A more effective way to teach these conventions is during the editing phase of the writing process,* when students want to use these conventions correctly in order to communicate more effectively through their writing. When students see a real purpose for the conventions, they are more likely to learn to use them correctly.

In a study of two classes of third graders, Calkins (1980) found that students in one class who learned punctuation marks as they needed to use them in their writing could define or explain many more marks than students in the other class who were taught in a traditional manner with lessons and practice exercises on each punctuation mark. Moreover, first graders who wrote frequently had many more opportunities to practice using punctuation marks than students who completed typical language arts textbook and worksheet activities (Cordeiro, Giacobbe, & Cazden, 1983). These two studies suggest a functional approach to teaching children to use punctuation marks correctly in the context of meaningful writing activities. While the studies examined only one writing convention, punctuation, the results seem to be applicable to capitalization and other writing conventions. Simply stated, providing for genuine, personal writing seems to be the answer to how to teach these conventions.

Winkeljohann (1981) points out that teachers need to be "in the right place at the right time" to teach writing conventions, and that *right place is while students are writing, specifically when they are refining and polishing their compositions.* In her article, Winkeljohann (p. 863) includes a number of observations about how to best teach these writing conventions:

BOX 11.18 Punctuation Marks and Their Uses

Period

- At the end of a sentence
- After most abbreviations
- After numbers in a list
- After an initial

Question Mark

- At the end of a question

Exclamation Point

- After words showing excitement

Quotation Marks

- Before and after direct quotations
- Around the title of a poem, short story, song, TV show

Apostrophe

- In contractions
- To show possession

Comma

- To separate words in a series
- Between day and year
- Between city and state
- After the greeting in a friendly letter
- After the closing of a letter
- After an initial yes or no
- After a noun of direct address
- To separate a quote from the speaker
- Before the conjunction in a compound sentence
- After a dependent clause at the beginning of a sentence

Colon

- Before a list
- In writing time
- After the greeting of a business letter
- After an actor's name in a script

Parentheses

- To enclose unimportant information
- To enclose stage directions in a script

Hyphen

- Between parts of a compound number
- To divide a word at the end of a line
- Between parts of some compound words

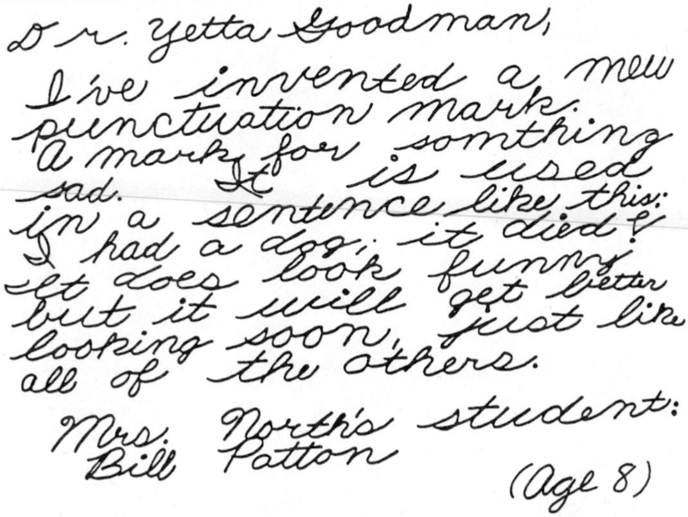

Dr. Yetta Goodman,
I've invented a new
punctuation mark.
A mark for something
sad. It is used
in a sentence like this:
I had a dog; it died?
It does look funny
but it will get better
looking soon, just like
all of the others.
Mrs. North's student:
Bill Patton
                    (Age 8)

Figure 11.6 A new punctuation mark. (*Source:* Goodman, 1979.)

Observational Notes on Teaching Conventions

1. Learning to observe the conventions of writing cannot be profitably separated from writing.
2. Mastery of conventions takes place most readily in the context of regular writing.
3. Mastery of conventions is also enhanced when students write about things they know about *and* care about.
4. Students learn about using writing conventions when they hear feedback from listeners and readers they have sought out who are interested in what they have said.
5. Students master conventions most readily when teachers see their task not as teaching conventions but as *supporting students' use* of them.
6. Students master conventions best when teachers *do not answer questions students have not asked.*

The last observation is particularly interesting: So often teachers provide more information than students need or, worse yet, information about an unrelated topic. Effective teachers are sensitive to their students' needs and let these needs determine what is presented. The

---

BOX 11.19 Formatting
General Format Elements

- Neat, attractive written work
- Writing on one side of a paper
- Left and right margins
- Top and bottom margins
- Paragraph indentation
- Space between title and body of the composition
- No crowding at the end of a line
- Use of appropriate paper

Specific Format Elements

- Narrative
- Script
- Poetry (haiku, diamante, etc.)
- Friendly letters
- Business letters

---

same observations can be made with respect to spelling and handwriting, in fact, to all conventions.

Assessment Checklists for Capitalization and Punctuation   The best way to teach these conventions is naturally, as students need them in their writing. Through one-on-one interaction during the revising and editing phases, teachers can provide short but intensive instruction in the conventions that students need to communicate more effectively in the compositions they are writing. Then students can help each other, sharing what they have learned about particular writing conventions.

As indicated in Chapter 8, teachers may keep capitalization and punctuation checklists in students' writing folders for indicating when initial or review instruction was provided on a particular convention. The form may also document when students demonstrated proficiency in using a particular convention correctly in a composition. A sample checklist for capitalization uses appropriate for second or third graders is presented in Figure 11.7. These checklists not only keep track of students' progress, but they can be used to identify students who are having problems with a particular usage. Then students with similar problems can be grouped together for special instruction.

Proofreader's Marks   As students reread their own papers as well as those of their classmates, checking for capitalization, punctuation, and other mechanical errors, they enjoy using actual proofreader's marks to indicate the errors they find. Figure 11.8 lists the proofreader's marks that elementary students learn to use easily.

CAPITALIZATION

Name _____

I = Skill introduced
R = Skill reviewed
D = Skill demonstrated

Writing activity and date	First letter of sentence	Names of people	Names of places	Days of week	Months of year	Abbreviations and initials
etc.						

Figure 11.7 Capitalization checklist.

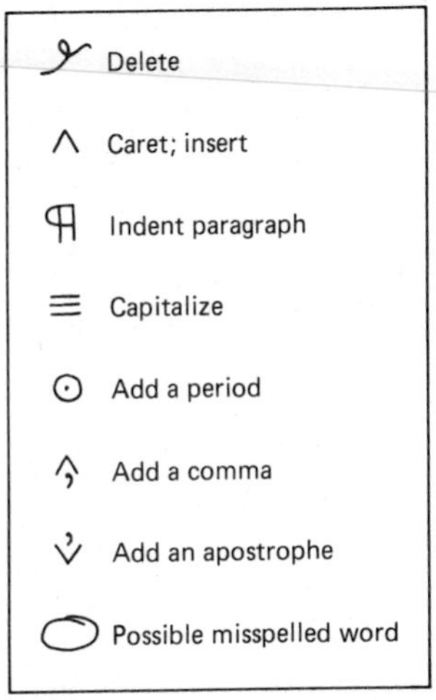

✗	Delete
∧	Caret; insert
¶	Indent paragraph
≡	Capitalize
⊙	Add a period
⌄	Add a comma
⌄	Add an apostrophe
◯	Possible misspelled word

Figure 11.8 Proofreader's marks.

Introduce the proofreader's marks by presenting them on a chart and explaining the use of each one. Choose a selection from a book of children's literature or a child's own volunteered writing and add appropriate "errors." Next, distribute copies of a writing sample with errors so that students can use each proofreader's mark on the chart at least once. Also, display a copy of the writing sample on the overhead projector. Ask students to read through the composition silently, and then read through it a second time together, adding the proofreader's marks to correct each error. After another large-group practice session, divide students into small groups for several additional practice sessions. Then students are prepared to use these proofreader's marks in revising and polishing their own writing.

Capitalization Activities   In addition to general writing activities, children have many opportunities to practice using capital letters in the activities to follow:

- Writing letters and addressing envelopes
- Compiling TV or movie guides
- Labeling maps
- Researching *eponyms* (people whose names have become words, e.g., Boycott, Maverick, Silhouette)
- Compiling class telephone or address directories

In these suggested activities, students have to make many decisions about whether or not to capitalize people's names, geographic locations, and titles. The eponyms activity is particularly challenging: The word *maverick* is not capitalized, but its eponym, *Samuel Maverick,* is!

Quotation Marks   Quotation marks are especially difficult for students to learn to use correctly. A three-step approach is effective: First, students use comic "talking balloons" to record dialogue. Second, they write the dialogue in script form using the name of the person speaking, a colon, and then the dialogue. Third, students rewrite the dialogue in narrative form using quotation marks. (See an example in the activity book.) As an alternative to cutting characters out of magazines or drawing them, students can add dialogue to comic strips or to wordless picture books. Two wordless picture books to try are Fernando Krahn's *The Great Ape* (1978) and *Frog Goes to Dinner* (1974) by Mercer Mayer. (Other activities for teaching quotation marks and other writing conventions are included in the activity book that accompanies this textbook.)

Chapter 12, "Grammar and Usage," moves to yet another set of conventions. The conventions of usage are distinguished from the study of grammar. The reader will find a fresh perspective, professionally important knowledge, and applications to classroom teaching.

SUMMARY

In a process-writing approach, students' learning of conventions takes place incidentally, when they are refining and polishing cared-about written composition that springs from many personal uses and aims. Teachers can further enhance instruction in the areas of spelling and other conventions indirectly with their own historical, theoretical, and developmental understandings. For example, educators disagree about whether or not English, a modified alphabetic system, is "regular." Research suggests that English words can be *spelled* according to phonic generalizations and spelling rules approximately half the time. Also, linguists suggest that English spelling is consistent or regular but at an underlying, abstract level.

Children develop a basic understanding of English spelling in much the same way they learn to talk. They move through a series of developmental stages of invented spelling as they elaborate and refine their understanding of the alphabetic principle and other factors influencing English spelling.

The purpose of spelling instruction emphasizes supporting students in becoming independent spellers who can communicate effectively through writing. Key components of a classroom spelling program include (1) many opportunities for students to apply spelling knowledge and develop courteous audience awareness through meaningful writing activities, (2) a list of high-frequency spelling words, (3) development of a *spelling conscience* through *proofreading* activities and learning about the development of the English language, and (4) dictionary study in which students learn how to locate unfamiliar words in the dictionary.

Although spelling instruction has been thoroughly researched, classroom practice and spelling textbooks still seem to reflect traditional ideas rather than research findings. Spelling textbooks provide an option for teachers, but spelling can be taught just as effectively by developing an individualized program using the key components delineated above. Teachers and students need not be controlled by textbooks; rather, texts can serve as references. Teachers have an important supportive and creative role in teaching spelling. They see their task not so much as formally teaching but as supporting student's *use* of these conventions.

When students realize the connection between *handwriting* and writing, and understand that readable handwriting is a courtesy to readers, they come to appreciate the need to develop legible and fluent handwriting styles and forms. There are two traditional handwriting forms, manuscript and cursive. Manuscript writing is taught in kindergarten and the primary grades, and the cursive form is typically introduced in second or third grade. There is growing controversy about the usefulness of the cursive form and the best time for students to change over to cursive writing. A new handwriting form, D'Nealian, has been developed to ease the transition from manuscript to cursive handwriting. In the D'Nealian manuscript form, letters are slanted to the right as they are in cursive, and all but five of the manuscript lowercase letters can be converted to cursive letters by adding connecting strokes.

A multisensory approach is best for teaching handwriting skills. According to the recommended procedure, the teacher begins by demonstrating and explaining the skill. Next the students who need to can practice it through a variety of visual, auditory, and tactile activities. The last step is the crucial one: After isolated, individualized skill practice, students apply the newly learned or reviewed handwriting skill in meaningful and internally motivated writing activities. Copying sentences and poems from the chalkboard for practice is not recommended. Many students, however, enjoy the practice of copying riddles or other short pieces of their own choice from word-play books.

Left-handed writers require special attention because of necessary adjustments including how they hold writing instruments, position their papers, and slant their writing. Right-handed teachers may want to ask a left-handed teacher or an older student with handwriting skills who is left-handed to work with their left-handed writers.

Young children begin to experiment with *capitalization, punctuation,* and *formatting* almost as soon as they start writing words. As students gain experience with writing, they develop an awareness of audience and recognize the need to use these writing conventions. Again, research and classroom experience suggest that capitalization, punctuation, and other conventions are best taught in the context of meaningful writing activities. Children master conventions most constructively when teachers see their task as supporting children's use of them and answering questions children have genuinely asked.

CHAPTER 12

Grammar and Usage:
A Story of Controversies

"A living language is like a man suffering incessantly from small haemorrhages, and what is needed above all else is constant transfusions of new blood from other tongues. The day the gates go up, that day it begins to die."

H. L. Mencken

"I live near a metropolitan area with a new Hispanic superintendent of schools. I'd like [anyone] to try to convince him there's no right or wrong! One of his platforms is to get students to speak more formal English, and for the schools not to be so accepting/tolerant!"

A reviewer

[English is a language that has] "its basis broad and low, close to the ground."

Walt Whitman

Building on Chapter 11, we will explore further the development of the English language and its systems for conveying meaning. While Chapter 11 dealt with one set of writing conventions, this chapter covers other conventions that we also use in oral language. The reason for such examination is straightforward: Observance of conventions of usage helps communication. Our language, an elevating gift of humankind, is a communication process central to human life and learning.

INTRODUCTION

The intent is to help you work toward a developmentally appropriate and carefully rationalized point of view for your teaching, one that grows from basic knowledge of this language area. Because of the new trends and controversies it is important to know where you are going, what you are doing, and why. We will begin with the question, "What does 'A Story of Controversies' mean?"

A Story of Controversies

"Language is a city, to the building of which every human being brought a stone."

Ralph Waldo Emerson

"An equally strong message for/from educators has to be a stronger adherence to 'right,' 'appropriate,' 'good,' 'acceptable,' . . . . It is not the majority that determines the standard!!!"

A reviewer

The history of English shows a contest between the forces of standardization and the forces that want to make language local, at both the written and spoken levels. The publication of the first major English dictionaries in the eighteenth century was a move to written standardization, but it was Victorian English that realized the ideal of "the Queen's English," a spoken standard to which "lesser breeds" could aspire (McCrum, Cran, & MacNeil, 1986). Not all agree with the Victorian view. Consider the following example. Interviewed in an issue of *Language Arts*, Anthony Adams, a linguist, commented on American teachers today.

Many teachers still have an immature view of language, having internalized a great deal of folk linguistics. Many of them feel that standard English, which literally means the language they themselves are speaking, is the only kind of oral language which should exist in the classroom. For many teachers, coming to terms with the variety of talk which can exist in a classroom is a very difficult business indeed, because they are being asked to change a lot of long-term and deeply held emotional attitudes about language.

We will revisit this controversy throughout this chapter, encouraging you to come to your own well-thought-out point of view to apply to individual cases.

Grammars—Old and New

The forerunner of our traditional school grammar entered the curriculum in England in medieval times, but it was Latin, not English. Since Latin was the language books were written in, students had to learn Latin grammar before they could participate in academic work. (Recall the section in Chapter 11 on the three periods of English language development.) In Shakespeare's time (1564–1616), English replaced Latin as the language of schools, but the subject of grammar lingered on. Trying to make the rigid Latin grammar fit English is something like a 6-year-old child trying to get into old baby shoes. Language changes as time passes. Some words become isolated and fall into disuse, new words are borrowed, pronunciations change, meanings change, and finally even conventions and grammar change.

Concern over the place of grammar in the schools continues today. Few topics can stimulate such ready or such extreme responses, from ill-concealed boredom to zeal for closely embraced views. The teaching of traditional grammar has long been a "must" in the schools. Reinforced by textbooks, such traditions tend to persist—unfortunately, for most young children. An understanding of language does contribute to effective communication. *Students gain this understanding, however, from experience in communicating, rather than from merely verbalizing facts about the language system.* Consider a quotation in support of this idea:

Perhaps the most widely ignored research finding is that the teaching of formal grammar, if divorced from the process of writing, has little or no effect on the writing ability of students. Studies from 1906 through 1976 have repeatedly reached this conclusion. (California State Department of Education, 1986)

The following opening scene illustrates a class involved excitedly in self-selected study and projects about their own language, including its usage and grammar. Their study is not divorced from their own listening, speaking, reading, and writing for genuine and important purposes. Since this scene will probably have more meaning for you after you have read the entire chapter, you may wish to read it twice.

OPENING SCENE: Creating a Word and Putting It in the News

Tommie Gunther, the teacher, had asked the fifth-grade class if they had ever invented words (themselves, among their friends, or in their families), what those words were, and how they came to be. Among other options, the teacher invited the children to "invent" objects by bringing in materials that would otherwise be thrown away. (The teacher furnished paper, tape, pins, and paint.) Then Tommie Gunther asked the children to give their invented objects names so that they became *new words* in their language.

The next optional step was to describe the inventions in sentences and put them into a class dictionary, "Grade 5A Lexicon of Neologisms" (*neologism* meaning a newly coined word). Some students then publicized an upcoming survey in the school newspaper. This survey was intended to gather response to photos of their creations. A group set up questions following the journalistic organization of the "who, what, when, where, and how" for roving reporters, who sampled fourth, fifth, and sixth-grade subscribers. Examples of their questions follow:

"Who invented the 'whopper machine'?"

"Just what is it?"

"When was it invented?"

"Where is it kept on display?"

"Have you used this new phrase?"

"How often do you talk or write about this new invention?"

Some children published results of the usage of their new terms in the next issue of their paper and planned a follow-up survey at the end of the year to note any change in use.

The activity led some to play with grammar as they changed their nouns to verbs, adjectives, or adverbs. For example:

"Is just about anything *whoppable?*"

"Is the person using it *whopping?*"

"Is it *whoppedly* changed?"

Some students added diacritical pronunciation marks to their entries in the dictionary, and photographs or diagrams. (Diacritical marks refer to the entry following a word, usually set off by slashes and indicating one or more phonetically transcribed pronunciations, for example: **whop** əˈhwäp ə.)

Finally, a few children switched and moved some of their newly invented words back into time. Related to their social studies, one group chose to create a cavern out of canvas and papier-mâché and role-play cave dwellers who wished to leave a message about their invention on the wall of their cave for the next cave dweller. As they role-played, these children discussed and left records about their inventions and themselves by using cave pictures.

Later this group of children copied and exchanged their "cave wall" pictures with partners. Their partners tried to translate the cave pictures into standard English. When the translations came back to the original creator, the children discussed the difficulties in communication, including the organization of the picture language.

In this way the teacher was able to help interested students attain some concepts about history, development, and change in language at the same time that they engaged in its expository use.

Analysis of the Scene

First think how *you* would analyze the scene. Then consider what one college student said:

To me the activity in the opening scene was about how words and language are formed, used, and how they change. Integrating with the history of language, it encouraged speculation on how words might have emerged from the beginnings of spoken languages. It also showed the students that language is a tool that we use because it is practical as well as beautiful. Language is invented through our power, because we need it. The scene also demonstrated how words and their usage can mean different things to different people.

Children in this scene were also studying concepts of usage as they observed how customary their new words were becoming. They studied grammar as they manipulated relationships in language. They saw language consisting of arbitrary, conventional symbols—their own created lexicon, expressed through a set of vocal symbols—and used their symbols in a framework of formal relationships (grammar).

They learned from their surveys that new words do not mean the same to all. As they made their new words function in sentences, they found out that they already knew quite a bit about grammar. They worked with identifying specific sounds for their words (phonology). From their project and survey, they understood some of the principles in language history: isolation and disuse of words; meaning change; and pronunciation change. They invented their words by imitating sounds, coining, borrowing, adapting, and fusing known words—just as many real words in their language had been formed historically. Finally, they found excitement in this investigative involvement with their language while learning terms such as *noun, verb, adjective,* and *adverb* in meaningful ways.

GRAMMAR—DEFINITION

"Language consists of arbitrary, conventional symbols (the vocabulary or lexicon) used in a *framework of formal relationships (the grammar),* and expressed through a set of vocal signals (the phonology)."

R. C. Troike

Everyone knows a great deal intuitively about grammar. You unconsciously obey the basic rules of English grammar in putting words together and in making sentences every day, just as the children did in the opening scene. We may define the grammar of a language as a system of word structures and word arrangements in expression, or the set of formal signals by which meaningful relationships of elements in sentences are shown. We may . . . but one definition or another does not really serve to clarify.

Lay people and even teachers are confused about the difference between *grammar* and *usage,* and between both of these terms and conventions of spelling, punctuation and handwriting. Other unclear terms are *standard English* and *dialects.* All of these (even spelling) may be popularly but erroneously lumped under *good grammar.*

To understand the meaning of grammar, consider its absence in the following sentence:

Rest this the of of life your day first the is.

If you find that each word above has meaning, but that the words as they stand fail to give you an idea, try changing them around as follows:

This is the first day of the rest of your life.

There you are! Now you have a grammatical sentence consisting of meaningful words in meaningful *relationships* to one another. *Grammar,* then, is that part of the study of language dealing not only with forms and structures of words (morphology), but also with their customary arrangement and relationships in phrases and sentences to convey meaning. In other words, the relationships among words in a language are called its grammar (Lodge & Trett, 1968). Grammar is also a theory of how language works, an explanatory study of its systems. In a school context it has often included naming parts of speech, diagramming, naming certain types of phrases and clauses, and naming sentence types (Hillocks, 1986).

Three Ways of Looking at Grammar

"Ignorant people think it's the noise which fighting cats make that is so aggravating, but it ain't so. It's the sickening grammar they use."

Mark Twain

What are the most common ways of looking at grammar in classrooms? Although not completely antagonistic, ways vary greatly. Some of the elements and terms are similar in the three, but the emphasis of each is different. These grammars are (1) *traditional* (old school), (2) *structural* (a product of descriptive linguistics), and (3) *transformational* (a more recent product of linguistics). All have made contributions to the understanding of how language works. At some point all have mistakenly been thought to provide the key activity for improving children's written and spoken language. Start with traditional school grammar.

Traditional School Grammar   Traditional school grammar, derived from Latin some 400 years ago, prescribes rules for how language is to be used, classifies words into eight parts of speech, emphasizes the subject-predicate relationship, and *inadequately* describes how English is used. In general the errors of traditional grammar are its false assumption that all languages have the same system and its failure to recognize that language grows and changes. Another problem is that it has generally been taught formally in a rule-, definition-, and diagram-laden way, removed from students' own speaking and writing.

Perhaps the main reason for the inadequacy of traditional school grammar lies in its ignoring of the significant English language feature: *word order.* Of the most widely used modern languages, only English and Chinese are characterized by word-order grammar. Other languages possess grammars that show relationships to a great extent through changes in the spelling of word endings (inflection). German is one example. Modern English is no longer primarily a word-ending language but is now positional. Take these sentences as an illustration.

The man killed the tigress.

The tigress killed the man.

In the first sentence we grasp who did what to whom (the subject and the object) by means of *position* in the sentence. In the English language, if you put the tigress in the man's place in the sentence, you have another story! In English, word order shows meaning and word meaning frequently depends on word order. In Latin or old Anglo-Saxon you could put the man and the tigress almost anywhere in a sentence and the inflected endings on the words helped you grasp the sense. Word order is the strongest signal system in English.

Other words in our English grammar must also be positioned; for example, we say, "a fierce tigress," rather than "a tigress fierce." Consider these examples using the word *pack:*

The *pack* of cards is new.

I want you to *pack* your trunk.

He rode the *pack-*horse.

Pack the ice around the bottle.

The dictionary meaning of *pack* is clear only if you know the grammatical meaning; that is, only if you know its context or position in a particular English sentence. English is becoming even more tied to word order; for example, *who* is slowly replacing the use of *whom* (an inflection vestige). Language rather resembles a person—changing, growing, and dependent on humanity.

It may help to distinguish between *linguistics* and *grammar.* Linguistics is the scientific study of language. The linguist may specialize in the study of:

Grammar (principles of word and sentence formation)

Rhetoric (the ways writers and speakers organize their "longer forms" of communication)

Usage (the changing fashions of "correctness" within regional or social dialects)

Grammar, then, is only one of several specialized studies within the general science of linguistics (Frazer & Hodson, 1978).

Shortcomings of Traditional Grammar   The way in which formal grammar study might help children with language use has been researched in this country, with repeated failure, for over 70 years. (Should instructors "hammer in the grammar"? The answer is emphatically "no.") For example, drill with traditional grammar was believed to do the following:

- Help children become more effective language users. (It won't.)
- Influence children to reduce errors in usage and speak in socially preferred ways. (It doesn't.)
- Give children knowledge and terminology resulting in effective revision of their compositions and oral discourse. (It hasn't yet.)

All the traditional practice of diagramming sentences produced was a few good diagrammers, not writers or "correct" speakers. (Documentation addressing the above points includes Hillocks, 1986; California State Department of Education, 1987; Braddock, Lloyd-Jones & Schoer, 1963; Oregon Department of Education, 1987; Petrosky, 1977.)

Although children have learned to write effectively while being taught grammar, they have probably learned in spite of traditional teaching rather than because of it. Since grammars are abstract constructs designed to explain how language works, students below high school age (and many even at that level) have difficulty understanding and do not know what to do with such knowledge if they do understand it.

If administrators mandate that grammar be taught in school, the teacher's attention is better placed on concrete manipulative experiences rather than on labels. For example, completing a sentence such as "Wild elephants . . ." is more helpful for concept attainment than is merely naming the part to be added, such as a *verb phrase* or a *predicate*. Children will attain the concept of a noun more quickly by finding and listing words that they can use after *the* than they will by trying to memorize abstract definitions for the label. Such concept attainment for nouns comes faster when children hunt for slot substitutes, such as *rocker* or *throne,* to take the place of the word *chair*. The boy in Figure 12.1 reflects the level of understanding that grammar study prompts in most children.

Structural Grammar Structural grammar avoids prescribing what is "correct" and emphasizes several concepts. Among them are the importance of word order, word forms, the idea of actual spoken language working to convey meaning, and a few sentence patterns. Although structural grammar has contributed to many areas, such as concepts of language growth and change, it is best known for explanations about sentence patterns and the simplification of word classes and their functions. Perhaps one of structural grammar's best gifts has been to steer teachers away from unproductively teaching parts of speech by handed-down, abstract definitions.

According to structural linguistic theory, English words fall into two major groups: (1) an almost infinite number of meaning-carrying words (form class), and (2) a small class of perhaps 300 words that connect and show relationships (structure words). Meaning-carrying words are referred to traditionally as nouns, verbs, adjectives, and adverbs. For example, a noun (or class 1 word) fits into the slots (or frame) represented by the blanks in the following pattern: The _____ scared the _____ . One can make many substitutions here. (Slot filling is another ritual that children are too often put through in excessive amounts.) One can inflect *nouns* to show plural number *(cat, cats)* and to form possessive case *(cat's)*. Or nouns may have a suffix (such as *ion—motion, precision*); and they "pattern after" the word *the* or after a preposition. In structural grammar, the 300 structure words connect in a variety of ways (e.g., a traditional label for one would be *preposition—to, of, for, on, over.*) These kinds of words "glue" the discourse together. They provide grammatical meaning by indicating how the other words are related in the sentence. Native speakers of a language have little trouble with them; it is a different story for nonnatives.

Basic sentence patterns Basic patterns, the foundation for any sentence we write or speak, can help us achieve variety by compounding, modifying, and subordinating our sentences. Box 12.1 presents five patterns—another contribution of structural grammar.

Figure 12.1 On grammatical terminology and usage. Copyright © 1973 by King Features Syndicate, Inc.

BOX 12.1 Some Basic Sentence Patterns

Pattern	Example
1. Noun-verb	The ghost floated.
2. Noun-verb-noun	The ghost scared the wizard.
3. Noun-verb-noun-noun	The ghost brought the wizard a hat.
4. Noun–linking verb–noun	The ghost is a spirit.
5. Noun–linking verb–adjective	The ghost is ghoulish.

Some elementary school textbooks have tried to incorporate this new scholarship by teaching these patterns and showing how to expand them by loading them with adjectives and other words. There is apparently no conclusive research evidence to date that such activity does anything to improve children's composition beyond adding some surface variation (Hillocks, 1986).

Transformational Grammar   Just as some teachers thought they were becoming able to cope with structural grammar, another grammar loomed on the horizon—transformational-generative grammar (as presented by N. Chomsky, 1965). While descriptive linguists emphasize observing and describing the language products (recording data, sorting it, classifying their findings), the transformational linguists are chiefly interested in the *process* by which the product comes to be, that is, in theory. They are also interested in this question: How does grammar represent orderliness of language meanings?

As mentioned in Chapter 2, young children can generate an almost infinite number of sentences that they have never heard before. Proponents of the transformational school of thought believe that the speaker becomes competent in transforming the basic sentence patterns (kernels) by the following: substituting, reordering, deleting, embedding, and combining parts. Thus, the transformational linguist sees all possible sentences as either kernel sentences or "transforms" of kernels.

Meaning, introspection, and inference are added to the investigative tools of the transformational grammarian. Moreover, this kind of linguist is concerned with competence, not just with performance. Briefly, transformational grammar consists of a set of rules for building sentences. It is not just a procedure for cutting up already formed sentences and labeling their parts and surface features (as both traditional and descriptive grammarians do.) Consider some aspects of transformational grammar—the kernel, the deep and surface structures—and their applications to the classroom writing program.

The kernel or basic sentence   A kernel sentence is a simple, affirmative, active, declarative sentence with no compound parts or elaboration. All the illustrations of the basic sentence patterns in Box 12.1 are kernel sentences. A basic sentence contains a subject and a predicate. Most English sentences have a noun followed by a verb.

Deep and surface structures   *Deep structure* and *surface structure* are two important concepts in transformational grammar. Every time you speak you are said to have a deep or underlying *meaning*. From this meaning you can derive a surface structure (through

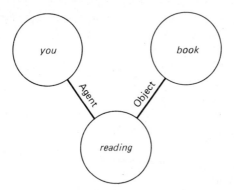

Figure 12.2 Map of deep assertions/meanings in grammar.

a series of transformations by means of rules). Deep structure contains those rules directly related to the meaningful content of a sentence. Transformational grammar assumes a deep-meaning structure system that leads to surface structure—sentences actually said and written.

For example, in the deep structure of the sentence *You are reading this book* there are three deep and meaningful elements: whatever *you, reading,* and *book* mean to us. These words contain a set of meaningful relations—a network of underlying assertions. The assertions in that sample sentence are that you are reading and that the book is being read. (See Figure 12.2.) Here we can see how transformational grammar represents orderliness of language *meanings.*

Surface structure contains those rules that are related to the sound, letter, or other tangible forms of the sentence. For example, here are two sentences that differ in surface structure but have the same deep structure.

You are reading this book.

This book was read by you.

In the second sentence a passive transformational rule was applied to the deep structure shown in the first sentence. The transformation resulted in several changes in the passive *was read* surface structure. For example, this *book* moved to the front position as the subject of the sentence; the verb *read* took on the structure word *was,* and *you* became the agent that *by* introduced. Again, a transformational grammar tries to show the connections between related sentences rather than to describe one separately. In other words, English sentences are based on distinct patterns that can be elaborated or compressed. You can create alternative sentences by resolving choice in these ways:

Transforms (passive, negative, question, imperative)

Modification (noun cluster, prepositional phrase, etc.)

Compounding (subject, predicate, whole sentences)

Apposition ("The reader, who knew . . .")

Subordination ("Yawning with boredom, the reader . . .")

Attempts to apply transformational grammar in the classroom   At the time transformational grammar was first introduced, some teachers hoped that it might give them steps for helping students put a series of simple kernel sentences together. They hoped to help students create more mature, complex, concise, tightly coiled sentences. In order to do this, they tried sentence combining and other means.

Sentence combining   *Sentence-combining* exercises, one of the attempts, emphasize methods for joining short sentences into longer, carefully constructed sentences. For example, *The ghost saw the goblin who hit the wizard* is a surface structure that combines two deep-structure sentences: *The ghost saw the goblin* and *The goblin hit the wizard.* (A relative-clause transformation changes the last sentence into a relative clause and embeds it in the surface-structure noun phrase.) The following example lays out these ideas:

Insert sentence: The goblin hit the wizard.

Relative clause: Who hit the wizard

The main sentence, the one into which the relative clause is to be inserted, follows:

Main sentence: The ghost saw the goblin.

The relative clause is inserted into the main sentence as follows:

                       who
The ghost saw the goblin(.) ~~The goblin~~ hit the wizard.

The resulting sentence, containing all the meaning of the two original sentences (called a transform) follows:

Transform: The ghost saw the goblin who hit the wizard.

Opinion on sentence-combining exercises is divided. On the plus side: "Over the past ten years several studies of classes, elementary school level through the first year in college, have shown that sentence-combining exercises, both oral and written, even when conducted with little or no grammatical terminology, can be effective in increasing the sentence-writing maturity of students" (California State Department of Education, 1982). On the negative side, while sentence combining offers a constructive approach to language manipulation, it is not without pitfalls. Students may make more errors as they practice and try out new combinations. An emphasis on sentence combining may lead students to conclude that longer sentences are always better, which could result in awkward and convoluted constructions (Hillocks, 1986; Oregon Department of Education, 1987). In relation to elementary school children, teaching these manipulations appears to the author to produce little or no genuine, long-term value for the quality of written composition. Again, we need to ask about the context and the individual case.

The following is a "before" example of uncombined language from a fifth-grade child for a journal activity in a social studies unit.

    I am a California Indian. I go to the sweathouse all the time. I go there with my friends after my chores are done. I race with my friends. They call me Small Lightning. I am small. I am the smallest one in my tribe.

Told to make a combined or more tightly coiled version, the student reluctantly rewrote the following.

> I am a California Indian named Small Lightning, the smallest one in my tribe. I got my name from racing with my friends. I go to the sweathouse all the time with my friends after my chores are done.

In this case one might argue that the uncombined language and "voice" of the first draft is more appropriate to the character who is supposed to be speaking—a small Native American boy of long ago.

Box 12.2 on page 430 offers a typical example of sentence-combining activities from a language arts textbook for children.

Other attempts to improve children's sentence structure   Some teachers have attempted to get children to achieve better "texture" in their threadbare sentences by adding modifier structures such as *ing* phrases to the end, *after* the subject and predicate (Christensen, 1967). That is, the teacher shows the children how to make cumulative sentences with free modifiers, without trying to explain and label all the grammatical structures. The teacher has the children "look" first at the scene for detail to verify the experience. For example:

> The boy looked at the dog, longingly, his eyes taking in the thin flanks and the droopy tail, his big toe of the right foot scratching his left leg as he thought about carrying the dog home to his mother.

Sometimes, however, efforts to produce expansions by embedding and extending can result in highly awkward sentences such as this one:

> The little girl on the tiny brown pony galloping across the green meadow comes from the south side of town by the old dilapidated cemetery next to Mr. Smith's house.

In this awful sentence, the young writer is striving for effect but is overloading the basic pattern of the sentence. As the sentence about the boy and the dog shows, the Christensen way does not overload the basic sentence. This is so because in the sentence modification follows the predicate. The following breakdown illustrates this idea:

> (A simple sentence) *The boy looked at the dog* . . .
>   (take)ing . . .
>   (scratch)ing . . .
>   (carry)ing . . .

An unfortunate traditional way of getting more sensory detail into a simple statement is to take a sentence such as *The boy looked at the dog* and elaborate it by adding adjective after adjective. Example: *The little barefooted boy looked at the grubby little dog.* A misguided teacher might ask the child to add even more vivid words: *The little barefooted waif gazed at the grubby, dingy little mongrel.*

When it comes to maturity in sentences, it is not how long you make them, but how you make them long. The best way to go is by reading and being read to from the well-crafted and memorable literature for children described in Chapter 9. In the elementary school, when children are ready to compact, they will compact; when children are ready to go the

BOX 12.2 Sentence-Combining Exercises

As Amanda revised her report on cats, she discovered that the ideas in some sentences were related. By joining related ideas, she could add variety and interest to her writing. Sometimes, Amanda combined parts of sentences. Other times, she joined whole sentences. In both cases, she ended with one sentence instead of two or more. In the following sentences, the words that Amanda joined are underlined.

Combine Single Words

<u>Panthera</u> is a category of cats.

<u>Felis</u> is another category of cats.

<u>Panthera</u> and <u>Felis</u> are two categories of cats.

Some domestic cats <u>purr</u>.

Other domestic cats <u>make</u> a high-pitched sound.

Domestic cats either <u>purr</u> or <u>make</u> a high-pitched sound.

Combine Groups of Words

Bones of cats have been found <u>in the cave dwellings of early humans</u>.

Bones of cats have also been found <u>in ancient Roman homes</u>.

Bones of cats have been found <u>in the cave dwellings of early humans</u> and <u>in ancient Roman homes</u>.

Combine Sentences

Cougars belong to the *Felis* category.

Lions belong to the *Panthera* category.

Cougars belong to the *Felis* category, but lions belong to the *Panthera* category.

In the first three sentences, Amanda joined similar words or groups of words with conjunctions. In her last example, she combined two related sentences to show contrast. In this case, she remembered to use a comma and a conjunction.

In revising, you can use conjunctions to combine words or word groups. You can also join related sentences.

Practice Revise these pairs of sentences by combining similar words or word groups or by combining sentences.

1. About 3000 B.C., the Egyptians first captured wild cats. The Egyptians tamed wild cats.

2. The hair of a Siamese cat is short and sleek. The eyes of a Siamese cat are blue.

Exercise Use a conjunction to combine ideas in each of the following groups of sentences.

1. Tigers are the largest members of the cat family. Lions are the second largest members.
2. Tigers are fierce hunters. Lions are fierce hunters.
3. Lions and tigers prefer to hunt large animals. Lions and tigers also will hunt small animals.
4. People are usually afraid of tigers. Tigers are shy and avoid contact with people.
5. House cats are afraid of water. Tigers are good swimmers.
6. The tiger's striped body blends in with the grass. The tiger's striped body allows it to get close to its prey.
7. Lions and tigers may live in the wild in certain areas. Lions and tigers may live in zoos around the world.
8. Lions can live in cool climates. Lions can live in hot, semidesert climates.

Activity Write six sentences about one of the following topics or a topic of your own. Revise your sentences, combining at least three groups of words or sentences.

Choose One   electronic games
             life in the city
             a historical period you are studying

Source: Holt English, Sixth Grade.

Christensen route, the chances are they will get a feel for this strategy and try it out—*if they get lots of chances to be read to, read, and write for real audiences. A child does not need to be taught lessons in formal grammar of any kind to communicate effectively in writing or in speaking.*

Other strategies with older children include (1) elimination of those words or phrases that garble meaning or repeat unnecessarily; (2) substitution of more specific, vivid, or concrete verbs and nouns; (3) some judicious additions of modifiers to focus on tone and texture. A *self-editing attitude* (described in Chapters 8, 11, and others) helps with decisions about usage and other conventions. While editing, children try to decide and discuss what they want to say and to whom. They do this before, during, and after they write, realizing that the first draft is mainly just to get the ideas down. Sometimes such group work sharpens observation. But sometimes it limits children's expression. An important and controversial question to consider is: How much of a child's composition remains his or her *own* after the group and teacher have scrutinized and attacked it?

Ideas of concern for the individual and evolvement of grammar take us into the developmentally oriented exploration of the *who* in our classrooms. Since Chapter 2 dealt mainly with early language learners, this next section deals mainly with later language learners.

WHO ARE THE GRAMMAR LEARNERS IN YOUR CLASSROOM?

Young children internalize much grammar even before schooling begins. We discussed such development in Chapter 2. Box 12.3 shows typical acquisition of sentence patterns at different ages (Loban, 1976).

BOX 12.3 Sentence Patterns at Different Ages

Ages 5 and 6: Use all the basic sentence patterns; use pronouns; use present, past, and future verb tenses (Black English speakers omit some inflectional endings). Average sentence length (speech): 6.8 words; most advanced children: 8 words; least advanced: 6 words.

Ages 6 and 7: Use more complex sentences, use more adjectives. Use *if . . . then* constructions or conditional dependent clauses: "If I have time then I will go." Average sentence length (speech): 7.5; most advanced children: 8.1; least advanced: 6.6.

Ages 7 and 8: Use adjectival clauses with *which:* "I have a plant which I water every day." Use adverbial subordinate clauses with *when, if,* and *because:* "I like it when we go to movies." Use gerund phrases (verbs + *-ing*) as objects of other verbs: "I like going to movies." Average sentence length (speech): 7.6; most advanced children: 8.3; least advanced: 7.

Ages 8, 9, and 10: Relate particular concepts to general ideas, using the connectors *meanwhile, unless, even if:* "She's a good dog, even if she snaps at people sometimes." About 50 percent of this age group use the subordinating connector *although* correctly: "Although I was tired, I stayed to watch the movie." Participles, both past and present, appear: "Turning around, I saw the bear." "Having lost the key, she couldn't get inside." Average sentence length (speech): 9; most advanced children: 9.3; least advanced: 7.5. Average sentence length (writing): 8; most advanced children: 9; least advanced: 6.

Ages 10, 11, and 12: More complex thinking patterns are reflected in complex relations between sentences. These connectors appear: *provided that, nevertheless, in spite of,* and *unless.* Auxiliary verbs *might, could,* and *should* are more frequent.
Problems remain with some verb tenses, especially the different uses of past, past perfect, future perfect, and present perfect.
Nouns modified by participles and participial phrases appear: "His clothes, faded by the sun, were the color of straw."
Compounds and coordinate predicates also appear: "We tried out and bought the bicycle."
Average sentence length (speech): 9.5; most advanced children: 10.5; least advanced: 8.
Average sentence length (writing): 9; most advanced children: 10.2; least advanced: 6.2.

Source: Loban, 1976.

At one time it was thought that children had done most of their learning about native-language sentence structures by age 5. Not so. For example, Chomsky (1969) studied the presence, or absence, of four sentence structures in the language of children from ages 5 to 10. Examples of the structures tested were: (1) *John is easy to see* (here the problem is the subject of the sentence and the subject of *see*); (2) *John promised Bill to go,* in which the problem is the subject of *go*; (3) *John asked Bill what to do,* in which the problem is the subject of *do*; and (4) *He knew that John was going to win the race,* in which the problem is the referent of *he.* "Structure 3 is still imperfectly learned by some children even at age ten, and structure 4 is acquired fairly uniformly at about age six" (p. 121). A child is likely to have fewer problems with complex structures if a great deal of literature is read to the child.

The following list reveals late language learnings from ages five to twelve (Wallach & Butler, 1984). The range of developmental aspects includes handling unusual word order, clauses, embeddings, and complements. In spite of its rather "bottom-up" approach, the material reminds us that children in the elementary school still have room to grow in language learning. Its inclusion is not intended as a suggestion for isolated skill teaching. Rushing and forcing children into mature sentence patterns before they have fully explored their own childlike ones is at best a risky business.

Students in Phases of Later Learning of the English Language Do the Following:

1. They learn analytic strategies for figuring out "who did what to whom" in complex sentences. For example, they learn how to deal with violations in typical word order, embedded clauses, passive reversibles *(The tree was hit by the lightning);* and relative clauses *(The lightning that struck the tree also hit the man).*
2. They learn inferential and integration strategies enabling them to "read between the lines" while combining sentences into complete ideas. For example, the child could not only infer that the lightning in the above examples used electricity for its strike but could combine the sentences into one tight one.
3. They learn pragmatic and metalinguistic strategies. For example, they learn that with ambiguity or sarcasm one sentence or structure can have more than one meaning *(Do you believe in clubs? Yes, when kindness fails);* they can make an ungrammatical sentence grammatical; and they can deal with figurative language in metaphor and humor.
4. They also become more and more adept in dealing with the language of the curriculum and of the classroom.

Levels of Abstraction

Consider four levels of abstraction required in typical study of grammar: (1) Language is an abstraction of experience, representing events and ideas through words. (2) Words are grouped to represent abstractly the relationships between and among those events and ideas. (3) To describe those relationships between words, teachers use a further abstraction, grammatical terminology. (4) Throw in diagramming—a symbolic representation of the description of those relationships—and students have four levels of abstraction with which to cope. Then teachers wonder why rather slow eighth-grade students have trouble with gerunds and participles. (Oregon Department of Education, 1987).

Need for Proficiency in Standard English

A final thought about the *who*—it *is* important for students to develop proficiency in standard English. Although many individual students come from uniquely rich cultures and speak a language that is linguistically different from standard English, they need eventually to move in larger contexts. Those contexts include the school setting and that of the larger society, including their economic and commercial communities (California State Department of Education, 1987). (Chapter 14 details further help for the unique child.) This goal of standard-English proficiency for all leads us in part to the next topic—usage and farther distinctions regarding grammar.

USAGE—DEFINITION

> "Language changes every eighteen or twenty miles."
>
> *Old Hindi Proverb*

> "Right now phrases such as 'you know' and 'I mean' are clearly 'majority use', yet they would NEVER be accepted in the mass media! . . . Even though minorities have the right to use their own dialects, . . . this is a right that exists outside of schools. . . . Schools are different from the streets, the playground, the home, etc."
>
> *A reviewer*

> "Slang is English with its sleeves rolled up."
>
> *Carl Sandburg*

Whereas grammar is concerned with the relationships and workings of language, usage is concerned with the conventions of language. **Usage** deals with *choices appropriate to a particular situation. These language choices need to be suited to (1) the speaker or writer, (2) the topic, and (3) the audience.* The standard is suitability of content. Usage primarily concerns the values we attach to pronunciation, vocabulary choice, and particular conventions (Fraser & Hodson, 1978). Many speak of usage as dealing with items such as agreement between subject and predicate *(he runs,* not *he run)* and singular and plural *(they are,* not *they is).* Rule consciousness of traditional grammar forces sentences that sound awkward to most of us, such as "That's the motorcycle on which I came" in place of the more natural "That's the motorcycle I came on." When one uses language such as "It is me" instead of "It is I," one has made a *usage* choice. Both choices are grammatical.

Changes in Usage

A school program growing out of the view of modern descriptive linguistics (structural grammar) accepts changes in usage. What was acceptable in the past may be unconventional today. What is acceptable today may have been inappropriate in the past. *People* make these changes. *If a language is not flexible enough to change, it dies.* The spoken language, however, tends to change more swiftly than the written language. An inflexible attitude toward usage in the classroom creates many problems. Effective English is language that creates genuine communication with the audience.

Situational Circles of Usage

How is context relevant to usage? There are various levels or circles of acceptable or appropriate usage. The diagram in Figure 12.3 is based on the situations in which one uses language: (1) formal, (2) general, and (3) nonstandard. These groupings, called *circles of usage,* represent occasions that most people encounter at some time during their lives. Vocabulary, sentence structure, and word forms (e.g., verbs and pronouns agreeing) of each area overlap into the other areas. For the general picture of written language, the circles are pushed further apart. When compared with circles for spoken language, there is much less overlap for written language. Whether you say "To whom do you wish to speak?" (formal), "Who do you want to talk to?" (general), or "Who y' be wantin'?" (nonstandard) may depend on your situational map.

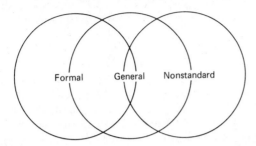

Figure 12.3 A situational diagram of English usage. (*Source:* Lodge & Trett, 1968.)

Thus, *usage* refers to choices appropriate to particular conventions. Some conventions (such as standard spelling, punctuation, and handwriting conventions) facilitate the communication of ideas to most literate people. Usage, however, is influenced by the idea from descriptive linguistics that the use of the majority of the speakers slowly moves to determine the standard. Usage in such a view is also influenced by the ideas of flexibility, of language to suit the occasion, and of the rights of minorities to use their own dialects in speech and in writing. On the other hand, the people who do most of the job hiring now speak standard English. Peter Elbow remarks that writing without errors doesn't make you anything, but writing with errors makes you a hick, a boob, a bumpkin (Elbow, 1981).

Keep in mind, however, that the language uses of young adults and children today will result in some changes in our language tomorrow. The computer industry has spread new words throughout the English-speaking world. Words such as *interface, software,* and *input* are already in the dictionary. *Diskette* and *modem* will go into future editions. Computer slang is gaining a toehold too, for example: "She's *high res*" for "She's on the ball" (McCrum et al., 1968). One day some of these slang terms may be in such common use that they, too, are in our dictionary. Some people, influenced by traditional school grammar, still believe that the dictionary should be the end-all in correctness of language. But modern dictionary makers have stopped subscribing to this valuational attitude, because a dictionary is a record book of how people use a word.

Dialects

Every person speaks a *dialect,* a specific branch of a language spoken in a given geographical area. A dialect (or variety of English) differs sufficiently from the standard in one or all features to be viewed as distinct, but not a separate language. Features include pronunciation, grammar, vocabulary, and use of words. TV and radio are breaking down some dialect differences, but some groups guard their dialect and special words zealously. Sometimes dialects in larger cities change within a few blocks, and sometimes they are far more widespread. Most people have a range of dialects or registers to use in different situations with various types of people.

No matter what socioeconomic, cultural, or linguistic background people are from, most can enlarge their ranges of communication. They can do this by learning more about the natural dignity of dialect varieties and various usages—alternative ways of saying things. For example, a friend says her grandmother from a section of North Carolina said, "I ken ye," meaning "I understand you." Actually this example, now almost faded away, can be traced back to Middle English.

The language arts classroom is a suitable place to explore the richness, diversity, and complexity of *varieties* of the English language. Older children can also explore the problems and realities of language acceptance and rejection among different age, sex, ethnic, occupational, and status groups.

To review, *grammar* reflects a list of possible ways to assemble sentences; *usage* is a smaller list of the socially preferred ways within a dialect. Usage may be trendy, arbitrary, and constantly changing like fashions in clothing, music, or cars (Fraser & Hodson, 1978). It is well to keep in mind the circles of usage and be able to choose appropriately to be formal when that mode communicates best, standard when that mode fits the context, and even nonstandard when that is the most communicative and appropriate. Most of us are multilingual creatures; we select from many "Englishes" the dialect that suits our audience, situation, and purpose. (For relevant dialect activities for the classroom, see the activity book.)

Older Children and Nonstandard Dialect   While most students have a highly developed linguistic competence within whatever dialect they use, not all share the same set of language rules. Teachers working with students who are not native English speakers and students who use a nonstandard dialect find that written communication requires attention to rules. Subjecting such children to isolated drill on grammar and mechanics, however, does not help—probably because students find it hard to draw upon abstract rules in actual writing situations (Oregon Department of Education, 1987).

How does a teacher respond? Nonmainstream students need to know which elements of their own oral dialect differ from standard English and to learn the standard form for use when they need it in writing. Such help does not mean making error the center of the curriculum or teaching standard English rules before students can write. Instead, it means helping students become skilled at reseeing and revising drafts of their own writing (Farr & Daniels, 1986). Such concern for the individual child leads into an exploration of goals— the next topic.

WHAT ARE SOME GOALS FOR LANGUAGE STUDY?

Goals for language study include those presented in Box 12.4, according to the Essentials of English statement of the National Council of Teachers of English (1983). The last item in the box was added by the author. These goals treat change, varieties, use, communication,

---

BOX 12.4 Goals for Language Study

- Learn how the English language has developed, continues to change, and survives because it is adaptable to new times.
- Understand that varieties of English usage are shaped by social, cultural, and geographical differences.
- Recognize that language is a powerful tool for thinking and learning.
- Become aware of how grammar represents the orderliness of language and makes meaningful communication possible.
- Recognize how context—topic, purpose, audience—influences the structure and use of language.
- Understand how language can act as a unifying force among citizens of a nation.

context, and national unity. Context includes the understanding that there is more than one level of appropriate spoken and written usage according to occasion, audience, and task.

Groupings of Language Concepts

The list in Box 12.5 (pp. 438, 439) groups some of the hundreds of concepts found in children's language texts and state frameworks. (The portion on meaning or semantics comes from the state of Maryland.) Offered as a summarization, it is also an example of information overload for some children.

HOW MIGHT A TEACHER RESPOND TO THE AREAS OF GRAMMAR AND USAGE?

How do you teach so that children learn? In the process of actually trying to communicate with written and oral expression, children *do* become sensitive to conventions, including those of grammar and usage. Children rarely if ever learn by memorizing rules that they are supposed to apply to producing "good" language. No authors that we know of have ever said that lessons in any kind of grammar made them into writers. *Grammar and usage are not learning topics in their own right, except for the language specialist.*

Of course conventions matter, but there is no point in learning them without producing language. Conventions of writing are tied to the *intentions* that lie behind them; conventions without actual intention are difficult to learn. Unless we make them too self-conscious, children who want to communicate use any grammar and usage that is available to them. They experiment with it, become increasingly sensitive through reading and listening, and interweave increasingly appropriate grammar and usage in their oral and written composition (Smith, 1982).

Both grammar and usage are *integrated*, not isolated, in the language arts program. Children can hear the grammar of well-written language when someone reads aloud or talks in that language. Again, young children who are read to become familiar with grammatical structures of well-written language without having to write or read for themselves in a standard way. (See suggestions, e.g., "Polly Parrot," in the activity book.) To write grammatically and with appropriate usage, a student needs more than demonstrations and motivation; a student needs editing (Chapters 8 and 11). Noun-verb agreement, for example, is a convention of English learned in the process of editing and "tidying up" the language the student has already produced.

Dealing with Usage

Helping children avoid usages such as *ain't* and *done went* preys on the minds of some teachers. Young children do not hear their deviations from standard English and do not want to change them. Their language may have a powerful hold on them, representing the normal way of talking among peers or in their social community. Generally, and referring to the primacy of oral language, you do not write what you do not speak.

What to Do   A teacher can provide children parallel, nonthreatening language alternatives, plenty of models of standard language in a variety of situations, and lots of chances to try out their own versions of appropriate talk and writing. Teachers can use what is best from television models and literature. (Chapters 4, 5, 9, and 14 elaborate on this idea.)

For change, older students need to do the following:

BOX 12.5 Sampling of Language Concepts

Grammar in General

- Everyone knows a great deal intuitively about grammar. You unconsciously obey the basic rules of English grammar in putting words together and in making sentences.

Morphology

- A morpheme is a meaningful unit of language that cannot be divided into smaller meaningful units.
- A morpheme can have one or more syllables.
- A morpheme can be a word or a part of a word.
- Morphology is the study of changes of word form, especially of those that affect meaning or function.
- A word part added to a word to change its meaning is an affix; prefixes come before, suffixes come after.
- Many words are members of word families, e.g., *direct, indirect, direction,* and *director.*
- Every English word has at least one vowel sound.

Syntax

- Language has structure.
- You can group English words according to their function in sentences. Some words may belong to more than one group.
- Word order helps to signal meaning; a different word order can give a sentence a different meaning. English is a word-order language.
- English sentences are based on distinct patterns that can be elaborated on or compressed.
- A basic sentence contains a subject and a predicate.

Usage

- Usage concerns the selection of specific words to be used in a certain speech or writing situation. The standard is suitability of context.
- There are various levels of acceptable or appropriate usage.
- Every person speaks a dialect. Speech dialects differ. Even standard English allows for variety of acceptable speech. Language is not the same in all places.
- TV and radio are beginning to break down dialect differences.
- Most English sentences have a noun followed by a verb.
- Sentence patterns include:
  N + V; N + V + N; N + LV + N; N + LV + A; N + V + N + N. (N, noun; V, verb; LV, linking verb; A, adjective.)
- Words are often added to basic sentences to give more information (modified).
- You can create alternative sentences by resolving choice in these ways:
  Transforms (passive, negative, question, imperative, etc.)
  Modification (noun cluster, prepositional phrase, adverbial phrase, participial phrase)

Compounding (subject, predicate, whole sentences)
Apposition
Subordination

- A phrase is a group of words that does not contain a subject and predicate working together.

Meaning

- Language conveys both explicit and implicit meaning in many ways.
- Speech and writing convey meaning differently.
- Language affects thoughts and feelings, clarifies and distorts—intentionally and unintentionally.

Essentials for Change

1. Have compelling motives to participate in the mainstream
2. Know precisely what differences to listen for
3. Have appropriate chances to try out standard pronunciations, word forms, and syntax

If students do not have these prerequisites for change, they will fail to successfully add standard to nonstandard language facility. It is unlikely that any students have ever modified their usage through trying to absorb a presentation of bewildering grammatical rules followed by written exercises for selecting "correct" grammatical forms. As the saying goes, "They do not need to know how to build a watch to tell time."

Teachers can also help children use language to think and understand in more varied and advanced ways, to express themselves with more precision and detail. Teachers can tell children to vary sentence beginnings or combinations, but unless children have a genuine reason they make no productive change. Working over someone else's worksheet sentences has consistently been of limited usefulness, and most teachers and students know it. Children need functional purposes and projects for developing usage and grammatical competence, just as they do for learning any of the language arts. Suggest to students that they forget grammar and usage while they are drafting. Let children pretend they will have an "editor" who will fix everything for them; then at the very end they hire *themselves* for the job (Elbow, 1975).

A Creative Problem-Solving Approach to Grammar Study for Older Children

A creative problem-solving approach can develop grammatical concepts (learning how language works). The teacher organizes this discovery activity around key questions or problems that children who are genuinely interested can seek to answer through their own experimentation (in the manner of linguists). The children as learners are not just acquiring concepts. In a traditional way, they memorize concepts repeated by the teacher, but more productively, they can acquire a sense of the structure of the discipline of linguistics through *using* its methods of inquiry. In the inquiry approach to learning about grammar, the children do the following:

Inquiry Approach

1. Try to answer questions that interest them.
2. Make observations and collect language data from themselves and from their own groups (e.g., family, friends, and class), as in the opening scene.
3. Search their observations and data for patterns. Compare and contrast forms heard on the playground, in the community, on trips, in the mass media, in business, and in antiquated literature.
4. Test their ideas (hypotheses) by trying them out in new situations.

The students can then begin a descriptive grammar for their own dialects or very own idiolects. An *idiolect* is one's personal variety of a community language system, one's own choice of words, at a given point in life.

The children can start with questions: "Why is it that some of the German words my grandmother speaks are a lot like our words?" "What would happen if we wrote every word the way it sounds and changed the spelling of all our words now?" "Why do we say 'bright blue sky,' but we don't say 'blue bright sky'?" "Does any language say 'blue bright'?"

With respect to the last question, children can discover what rules the English language uses for ordering adjectives. Students can begin to uncover the proposition that users follow the rules of their language that they have absorbed (Smith, Goodman, & Meredith, 1970; Fraser & Hodson, 1978).

Dependable Grammatical Patterns in Young Children's Literature

The predictable language patterns in delightful books for children help the young child experience the structure and working ways of language. The dependable patterns in literary models help them use the meaning context for developing strategies to handle unfamiliar words and grammatical structures. Such understandings may be important for reading.

With a story such as *Drummer Hoff*, children can join in on the noun-verb-noun pattern, develop a sense of sequence, and explore the rich pictorial detail and phonology of the rhymed couplets. Finally, they can enjoy ending this story with a tremendous, appropriate, and sanctioned amount of delicious noise. (The final illustration—award-winning with brilliant colors over the lines of the woodcuts—satisfactorily shows the cannon finally nestling in flowers.) Part of the text follows:

General Border
  gave the order,
Major Scott
  brought the shot,
Captain Bammer
  brought the rammer,
Sergeant Chowder
  brought the powder,
Corporal Farrell
  brought the barrel,
Private Parriage
  brought the carriage,
But Drummer Hoff fired it off.

BOX 12.6 Some Predictable Books for Beginning Readers: (Experiencing Grammatical Patterns)

Repetitive Sentences

Balian, L. (1972). *Where in the world is Henry?* Nashville, TN: Abingdon.

Brown, M. W. (1947). *Goodnight Moon.* New York: Harper & Row.

Brown, R. (1981). *A dark, dark tale.* New York: Dial.

Cauley, L. B. (1982). *The cock, the mouse, and the little red hen.* New York: Putnam.

Charlip, R. (1969). *What good luck! What bad luck!* New York: Scholastic.

Gag, W. (1956). *Millions of cats.* New York: Coward-McCann.

Galdone, P. (1973). *The little red hen.* New York: Seabury.

_____. (1973). *The three billy goats Gruff.* Boston: Houghton Mifflin.

Ginsburg, M. (1972). *The chick and the duckling.* New York: Macmillan.

Hill, E. (1980). *Where's Spot?* New York: Putnam.

Hutchins, P. (1972). *Good-night, owl!* New York: Macmillan.

Martin, B. (1983). *Brown bear, brown bear, what do you see?* New York: Holt.

Peek, M. (1981). *Roll over!* Boston: Houghton Mifflin.

Tafuri, N. (1984). *Have you seen my duckling?* New York: Greenwillow.

Viorst, J. (1972). *Alexander and the terrible, horrible, no good, very bad day.* New York: Atheneum.

Repetitive Sentences in a Cumulative Structure

Carle, E. (1971). *Do you want to be my friend?* New York: Crowell.

Ets, M. H. (1972). *Elephant in a well.* New York: Viking.

Continued on page 442

The text is then partially repeated as some of the characters are reintroduced with a full-page illustration in vivid color. After the story is read aloud, children can have fun when the reader pauses and lets them finish a verse. Then the children can look at the book and read it together. They can do a choral reading or tone poem with created sound effects. Finally, children can substitute other content words using the story pattern and structure words. For example, perhaps the theme could be making and using a birthday cake with verses such as the following:

Father Mandles
Lit the candles,

And with the following refrain:

But Betsey Stout blew them out.

The children can finish the story with everyone making the biggest, most delectable *blowing* noise possible. Then they can reread their newly written story. Chances are that the

Flack, M. (1932). *Ask Mr. Bear.* New York: Macmillan.

Galdone, P. (1975). *The gingerbread boy.* New York: Seabury.

Hutchins, P. (1968). *Rosie's walk.* New York: Macmillan.

Kellogg, S. (1974). *There was an old woman.* New York: Parents.

Peppe, R. (1970). *The house that Jack built.* New York: Delacorte.

Tolstoi, A. (1968). *The great big enormous turnip.* New York: Watts.

Westcott, N. B. (1980). *I know an old lady who swallowed a fly.* Boston: Little, Brown.

Zemach, H. & Zemach, M. (1966). *Mommy, buy me a china doll.* Chicago: Follett.

———. (1969). *The judge.* New York: Farrar.

Sequential Patterns

Alain. (1964). *One, two, three, going to sea.* New York: Scholastic.

Baskin, L. (1972). *Hosie's alphabet.* New York: Viking.

Carle, E. (1969). *The very hungry caterpillar.* Cleveland: Collins-World.

———. (1977). *The grouchy ladybug.* New York: Crowell.

Domanska, J. (1985). *Busy Monday morning.* New York: Greenwillow.

Keats, E. J. (1973). *Over in the meadow.* New York: Scholastic.

Mack, S. (1974). *10 bears in my bed.* New York: Pantheon.

Martin, B. (1970). *Monday, Monday, I like Monday.* New York: Holt.

Schulevitz, U. (1967). *One Monday morning.* New York: Scribner.

Sendak, M. (1975). *Seven little monsters.* New York: Harper & Row.

Source: Hoskisson & Tompkins, 1987, pp. 30, 31.

---

stories created in this pattern—and now child-owned—will be spontaneously picked up and shared again and again. This sort of activity represents a natural, delightful way to grasp the workings of English grammar to convey meaning, a way assessed by observation.

Other examples of literature for young children that have predictive, repetitive patterns are given in Box 12.6. These, too, offer natural grasp of grammar.

Assessment

"Someone needs to tell teachers that identifying parts of speech is not on any standardized test."

Overheard at the Committee on Resolutions, National Council of Teachers of English

The assessment of grammar and usage reemphasizes many of the goals and points of view already developed. In this section, we look at the assessment of grammatical features, but we do not give either grammar or usage a high priority for assessment in the elementary school.

Grammatical Features Return in thought for a moment to ideas of assessment developed in Chapters 4 and 7 for the British projects. Their results from varied assessments showed that grammatical structuring needs to be *appropriate to the demands of the task in hand* (National Foundation for Educational Research in England, MacLure & Hargreaves, 1986). For example, in the case of the task of telling anecdotes, 11-year-olds may select complex grammatical structures; but it is not necessary that they do so. The only requirement regarding grammar is that since anecdotes refer to past events, students need to adequately indicate the time of occurrence and the sequencing of events being related. That is, they just need to use grammatical structures such as adverbial clauses of time and consequence.

For the science experiment task, the students need to use very simple grammatical structures, mainly imperatives; for example: "Put that back in, and now get two plain marbles, and put them at the top." This simple grammatical form is entirely appropriate when the listener needs to clearly identify the action required. Students who used complex grammatical structures were liable to perform less successfully on this task; complex forms make instruction more difficult to interpret (MacLure & Hargreaves, 1986).

As in most of the earlier chapters, it is possible to take the goals and objectives presented in the *What* section and turn them into checklists for assessment purposes. For example, you might wish to check whether or not a student has fulfilled the goal on context translated:

- Understand that there is more than one level of appropriate spoken and written usage according to occasion, audience, and task.

In sum, assessment time is better spent on whole language, on listening, speaking, reading, and the quality of written composition. If the student has nothing to communicate, the grammar or usage could not matter less. The key in using conventions is power and flexibility in appropriateness.

How to Respond to Pressures

"Where is the diagramming of sentences I used to do?"

Irate parent

As a well-informed teacher, you will be able to deal with pressures from administrators and others to emphasize formal grammatical study and memorization of rules. Be prepared with information from this chapter and other sources related to educational goals. Be ready with your own well-thought-out position on improving the quality of written and oral composition.

Now that you are familiar with the terms, concepts, and attitudes presented in this chapter, you may choose to review the activity in the opening scene and explore the activity book for ideas to try with your students. Revisit the scene with more understanding of the teacher's point of view and goals. As you go on to Chapter 13, you will find it suggests that your program can take on an exciting new dimension by integrating technology and media into the study of language and literature. We explore, for example, controversial uses of computers in classrooms and some of the newly realized conventions of TV literacy.

SUMMARY

"If there is a 'new English,' it is to be found by reexamining and reinterpreting the child's experiences in language rather than by introducing new content."
Albert H. Marchwardt

"And finally, classrooms will be language-rich environments when they are planned and arranged by sensitive teachers who . . . understand the bankruptcy of grammar study and drillwork programs and of approaches that attempt to teach skills discretely and one at a time. . . ."
John C. Mellon (at Harvard, 1970)

Language, grammar, and usage change steadily over time, varying from place to place and culture to culture. Each of us is a part of this change and variation. Grammar is the study of systems used to explain the workings of the language. The difference between grammar study and writing is that knowledge of grammar is a theoretical understanding about language. The ability to speak and write flexibly and well, however, is a practical understanding of language (Holt, 1982).

Traditional grammar prescribes rules for language use, emphasizes subject-predicate relations, and classifies words into eight parts of speech (determined by function in the sentence). This Latin-derived grammar fails to describe adequately how English is used.

Structural grammar emphasizes the importance of word order, word forms or classes, the actual spoken English language, and a few basic sentence patterns. One can achieve variety with the sentence patterns through compounding, modifying, and subordinating. Grammatically essential sentence elements generally occupy fixed positions (e.g., subject, predicate). Grammatically less essential elements tend to be movable.

Transformational grammar emphasizes process and shows relationships among sentences by guessing at the source sentence (or kernel). Then the transformation process is to shift, delete, and insert words and phrases, or combine two or more sentences. Theoretically, this process is able to generate all the sentences in the English language. Children, however, do not need to be taught lessons in formal grammar to communicate effectively.

Rushing children into mature sentence patterns before they have fully explored their own childlike ones may be a risky business. Patterned methods to achieve sentence-form fluency may have some justification for children who appear to lack it as they move into middle school and high school. But exercises can be limiting to children, and may even have a negative effect on composition. Research into grammar instruction and learning development clearly shows that grade school students are not ready for the abstractions of grammar study.

Usage takes into account that most persons have a range of dialects or registers to use in different situations with various types of people. Usage concerns selection of language for certain speech or writing contexts, using a criterion of suitability. Visualizing usage as a series of overlapping circles—formal, standard, and nonstandard—clarifies these concepts. But unless students are motivated and have many chances to model after and try out roles, they will usually fail to broaden their circles of usage.

Dialect represents a mini-language within the larger language. The language of speakers or writers within a geographic region, socioeconomic class, or occupation shows certain distinctive and common features of usage. Most of us are not frozen within one dialect. Instead we choose and shift in our efforts to be comfortable, presentable, and effective

(Fraser & Hodson, 1978). Standard English may be thought of as the dialect used and understood by a majority of educated speakers and writers. Standard dialect changes by force of this majority's use.

How to work with children on grammar and usage has been and will continue to be subject to controversy. Up to the time of this writing, we can find no recent, verifiable evidence anywhere that the study of grammar (whatever kind it is) fosters correctness and sentence maturity in a fashion superior to far less time-consuming, more joyous, informal, creative, and naturalistic procedures. We can teach huge numbers of rules and still not have a composition program. Children need to spend their time learning how to form their *own* sentences in extended compositions, not merely analyzing the grammar and usage in the sentences of others.

How might one teach grammar? Teach as little as necessary in order to clarify a child's particular language question, task, or problem. Teach in relation to a writing (or reading) task or problem that a student cares about. Teach with clear connection to a larger system that can gradually be explored. Teach so as to avoid displacement of actual reading and writing. Finally, invite children to treat usage as a matter of very late editorial correcting.

PART 3

RESOURCES

CHAPTER 13

Creative Use of Computers, Textbooks, and Other Media

· —————— ·

by James L. Hoot and Sara W. Lundsteen

"A pen is just one voice . . . children need options of communicating with color, motion, and sound. . . . The media are like extension cords; they plug into a wider world."

Committee on Curriculum Bulletins, NCTE

The reader now enters the third part of this book, "Resources." In this part there are three chapters—this present one on media, Chapter 14 dealing with special children, and Chapter 15 dealing with evaluation and assessment. A theme is that the teacher is in control of resources, not the other way around.

It has been said that there are three literacies: print literacy, nonprint media literacy, and computer literacy. Many of the preceding chapters have stressed print literacy, but students live in a world with nonprint and nonverbal media as well. These new modes of communication demand a new kind of literacy. While reading comprehension rests on verbal language, comprehension of a medium such as TV depends mainly on recognizing and interpreting visual images. Video is a medium requiring that attention be paid to several simultaneously occurring processes. Radio and books are more serial in delivery of the messages; they have symbols following symbols in a more linear way. How does one best teach through combining these verbal and visual media? How does a teacher of the language arts evaluate, select, and use an array of textbooks, instructional media, and technological devices? Important questions such as these demand answers.

INTRODUCTION

The primary purpose of this chapter is the exploration of media and other resources in classroom instruction. The chapter encompasses the media of computers, textbooks, television, and film. The focus will be upon demonstrating the power they have over learning outcomes. Teachers and children are the masters of properly used media. When media are improperly used, teachers and children can easily become servants of the media and of commercial producers.

Teachers are aware of the behavior of media-saturated learners (i.e., "TV blotters"). Some teachers are concerned that print-oriented teaching methods are boring to learners used to "jazzy" computer programs, e.g., *Dungeons and Dragons* and *Up and Add 'Em*. Some are concerned that the use of slick, attention-getting production techniques in educational

TV programs such as "Sesame Street" may encourage short attention spans, hyperactivity, and disinterest in typical classroom presentations. But rather than feeling they must compete, teachers need to know that there is more to motivation than entertainment. Long-term motivation is not the product of a media gimmick. Chapters 1, 2, and 3 stressed that genuine, long-lasting motivation comes from within the child, beginning in the classroom as a joint effort by learner and teacher. Problems arise when we think genuine motivation comes preprogrammed inside the technology: It cannot. A youngster's discovery that marks on paper mean language brings tremendous excitement. We become media saturated ourselves and forget those first ecstasies (Barrett & Barrett, 1985).

Noisy, busy programs tend to distract children from learning. In *Up and Add 'Em*, a math software featuring lively, bouncing figures, children remembered nothing except the characters (Mackay-Smith, 1985). Newer software being produced all the time profits, of course, from past criticism to produce an improved product. In the near future there may be software and other media that avoid the problems mentioned in this chapter.

RATIONALE FOR INTEGRATING MEDIA INTO THE LANGUAGE ARTS PROGRAM

Why integrate media? Acquiring literacy now means taking into account a wide range of media communication. Throughout history we have hailed each new medium as a potentially revolutionary force for changing the forms and functions of communication. We can trace this stance beginning with the printing press to photography, radio, recordings, film, television, videotape, and now the computer. Language arts teachers have traditionally focused on communication through print. Meanwhile, students have grown up in environments including the newer auditory and visual electronic media. Teachers need to move beyond the early view of these media as mere support for print materials.

How can teachers justify devoting attention to the development of a broadly based literacy, especially if they are expected to focus exclusively on teaching the "basics" of reading and writing? They can argue that communication will mean the ability to understand, use, and control broader, electronically complex symbol systems. Students will need to know how a wide range of media acts on the development of language, thought, and knowledge in our culture.

Teachers can argue that integrating electronic media in the language arts means not only teaching through them but about them. Thus they can provide chances for students to use film, TV, texts, and computers. Their students can develop analytic composition processes through filmmaking as well as in written composition. They can develop process through discussion of TV narratives as well as through short stories. They can do it through critiquing stereotypes in TV commercials as well as in literature. Students can study oral and written language in the context of TV documentary narration, printed instruction on the screen, film production notes, stage directions for TV drama, and LOGO or other artificial computer languages.

Teachers can argue that thinking skills are best taught in the contexts of many media, both verbal and visual. When children understand the nature and power of media, they can better avoid being controlled. Finally, teachers can argue that not only daily life but also the job market in varied modes of informational processing require competence in new communication technologies (adapted from Commission on Media, National Council of Teachers of English, 1986).

COMPUTERS IN THE LANGUAGE ARTS

> "I like computers better than TV. With a computer you can make it do what
> *you* want it to do. TV does what *it* wants to do."
>
> *Child, Overheard by James Hoot*

Microcomputers, once devices of only the wealthiest industries, are becoming as common as pencils and paper in elementary schools. They might be thought of as a new realm of language providing an environment for communication, for structured group talk. The mere presence of these devices in classrooms, however, can no more assure improved language learning than a pile of bricks can assure the quality of a house to be built. The potential of computers as a tool for developing language competence can be realized only when competent school professionals are aware of the appropriate uses and limitations of computers in the language arts.

OPENING SCENE: A Computer in My Classroom?

"A computer in *my* classroom?" said Pat Beck, second-grade teacher. "Well, why not . . . I've never even touched a computer but . . . I'll try it! I've got a few questions, however. And I'm sure I'll have more later." That's the way it started the second Monday in January.

Question 1: One computer, 21 children?

Among Pat's first questions was one dealing with management. "One computer and 21 children? How do I manage that?" One week later, this problem was solved.

To begin, visualize a typical classroom with a computer placed in a corner, away from noise and classroom traffic. Surrounding the computer center is a painted partition cut from a large refrigerator box.

Near the entrance to the center, the teacher has put up a chart with the names of the jobs the children will be doing in order to develop their stories on the computer. Opposite each job is a slot for the children to put their names in. At the bottom is a holding packet to keep the name cards. The children can take out their name cards and place them next to the jobs they want to do. (See Figure 13.1.)

The jobs include keyboard, reader, and printer. The *keyboard* person is the child responsible for typing group stories into the computer and making revisions suggested by the three members of each group. The *reader's* task is to periodically read stories aloud to determine if they sound the way the authors intend. The *printer* has the job of printing out drafts for each member of the group.

Today, Joey (a gifted child) has come to school very excited about an idea he has for a story. This morning he ran over and looked for his name card. He was happy to find it still in the holding packet, as this meant he could have a turn. (The cards of people who have had turns recently are still in the teacher's possession.) He decided to be a reader today, since he knew he would have a hard time trying to concentrate on the keyboard and think of story events. (The teacher will note what job he did today on the back of his name card in order to ensure that he rotates with the other computer jobs.)

Amy has chosen to do the keyboard job, as she enjoys working with Joey. Surprisingly, April, who has been avoiding the computer, has put her name up to be the printer. Perhaps she feels it is the least threatening job. Pat, the teacher, smiled on seeing this; many a

Figure 13.1 Chart of computer jobs.

student in this class who has not wanted to work on the computer before has become quite intrigued after doing the printing job and has gone on to write well-composed stories on the computer.

Question 2: I know who does what. Now, when do they do it?

Pat's second question concerned how to find time for each group to use the computer. To solve this problem, each morning one of the self-chosen groups has its turn to create stories at the computer. This opportunity is provided during the entire language arts period. Children are also able to use the computer during free moments of the day and sometimes after school if an aide or volunteer is available.

Question 3: What's the next step?

After solving the above problems, Pat contacted the school district computer specialist to get help in finding programs that assist children in writing with computers. The consultant quickly provided programs to familiarize children with the keyboard. In addition, Pat spent a class session introducing children to the keyboard with the help of the district materials.

The district consultant also recommended a word processor program specifically developed for primary-grade children. This program required no previous experience with the computer and used pictures (icons) easily understood by children to explain program functions.

Young Writers at Work

Today it is four weeks since the class was introduced to computers; Joey, Amy, and April are taking their turns.

"I'm the keyboard," says Amy as she takes her seat at the computer and starts the program.

"Let's write about something exciting," suggests April. "I'm tired of stories about little animals picking raspberries."

"I've got a great idea!" says Joey. "Asbestos! Mom said they're tearing down a school because of asbestos. Those things can make you real sick! Last night I dreamed about an asbestos monster. Let's write about an asbestos monster."

"Yea!" says Amy. "Let's write about an asbestos monster! I'm ready. Give me some words to start the story."

"Type this," says Joey while adjusting his glasses. "Just then they heard a crash."

"But how did it start?" interrupts April.

"Oh, yeah, hmmm," pondered Joey. "It all started at the chemical lab in Dan Ford College. Eric Johnson and Leslie Wilborn were in the conference room with the principal. 'We have to get rid of the ceiling in the chemical room,' they said angrily. 'Somehow someone got illegal radiation.' "

"Now the crash part," April impatiently suggests.

"Just then they heard a crash. . . . And they walked outside to see what was the matter," continues Joey.

"Oh, boy," interrupts Amy, as she stops typing and turns around to look at Joey and April. "They could see a big monster outside."

"Yes, a fuzzy monster!" adds April delightedly.

"OK," says Joey with a nod. "Let me read what we have so far." He reads it.

"That's good; let's print it!" says April.

"But it's not done," says Joey. "We haven't told all of the things it did. And we have to tell how we stopped it."

"Well . . . do you know? What are all the things that happened?" asked April.

"I don't know yet. We'll find out as we write it," said Joey.

A lively and sometimes argumentative discussion ensues about the destructive exploits of the monster and how it met its demise by being sprayed with concrete. (See Figure 13.2 for the entire story.)

"Now let's print it!" says April, who now has a chance to do her job.

Three eager noses sway back and forth as the printer spews out each line of the story.

"That's it!" says Joey. "It looks even better than we wrote it!"

Analysis of the Scene

In this scene, the teacher was fortunate in having access to developmentally appropriate software programs for word processing. Not all school systems, however, have instructional computer specialists or appropriate programs. The children in the scene have many choices and options as they compose. They can interact socially and feed off each other's ideas, not always peacefully, but with engagement and motivation. Some people caution, however, that the polished look of the printout may make children view revision as unnecessary. Others say that the ease of revision (moving parts around, inserting, erasing) encourages far more revision than before.

In addition, a class of language arts students from a university had previously come to this opening-scene class. They encouraged the children to *dictate* stories to them, helping the children mount the stories in their own booklets. Then they provided the children with stapled blank paper and inspired them to plan, draft, respond, revise, and celebrate their own stories. It was with this background in a composing process that the children approached the computer and its word-processing software.

This scene showed how a computer-anxious child like April can warm up to the computer by beginning on the printer. It also showed part of a composing process ("I

Asbesos Monsters

It all started out at the chemical lab in Dan Ford Collage.Eric Johnson and Leslie Wilborn were in the conference room with the principal."We have to get rid of the ceiling in the chemical room." said angryly."Some ho someone got illegal radiation." Just then they heard a crash! They walked outdoors to see what was the matter. They saw a big fuzzy monster outside.

When it touched the mailbox the metal became a another monster!Leslie noticed that when the monster touched the mailbox,it didn"t do anything to the concrete or the wood.When it walked in the road,it melted the tar and turned it into a tar blob.When it walked on the grass it turned it into a grass monster.

The grass monster chewed on a telephone pole, the telephone pole fel down.When the grass monster chewed down the telephone pole it created a fire.The Asbesos monster walked through the fire,and turned it into a fire monster.When the fire monster walked on the grass it just burnt.Then they hit a dead end.

They all turned into a giant monster.It had a tar leg,a metal leg,a fire arm,a plant arm,and a Asbesos head an body.Just then Eric saw a concreate factory.He said,"Hey!Maybe we can sto it with concreate!""Of Course we can stop it with concreate!"Leslie said,"It can"t turn concreate into anything!

They went over to the concreat factor and mixed up some concreate.They sprayed it all over the monster and let it dry quickly on the monster.The tossed the monster into the sea.When they got back,the princpal said that he would take out the ceiling in the chemical room.

Figure 13.2 Asbestos monster story.

don't know yet—we'll find out as we write it.) It demonstrated how computer use encourages stimulating discussion, group work, organizational abilities, and excitement for writing and creating. If several classes had had to share one computer, the teachers might have just used it for demonstrations or as a central message center for communications. With one computer per classroom, each class has a publishing machine for group projects such as a cooperative story or a class newspaper. With older children, however, taking turns may involve much waiting time. With four or more computers, individual use becomes more realistic.

If our opening scene were to continue, we would see a classroom using all of the media discussed in this chapter—computer, textbook, TV, and film—all in a blend of learning materials. No one material can satisfy a child's needs.

In less fortunate circumstances, a school may be under strict contract with a software company. The contract may specify that if the manufacturer's instructions *are followed* and students' scores are *not* raised, then the school is not obligated to pay. Too often planning does not precede purpose.

The Other Side of the Coin   Picture, for example, a kindergarten class, actually witnessed by an observer, under the charge of aides. These aides had little understanding of the computer programs or of the children they were supposed to help. In an effort to adhere to the manufacturer's instructions, young children wearing earphones and sitting at cubicles were shuffled automatically every 15 minutes to the next station—from phonics, to spelling, to listening, to composing—like little automatons. Composing was only valued as a minor adjunct to measured reading.

The manufacturer's highly mechanical materials and instructions were being followed inflexibly for fear of voiding the contract. This ritual was imposed even though this meant children had to hear (again and again) tapes whose content they had already mastered, and they were at the writing station with no desire to write. The only ones to escape this routine were the ones at the "discipline" table. They were writing over and over, "I will follow directions."

This mindless school program had little or no rationale matching developmental goals for children and computer activities. The school had perhaps never realized what the opening-scene teacher, Pat Beck, had remembered: Teachers and children are the masters of properly used media.

SOFTWARE: THE KEY

Despite all the exaggerated claims about computers improving instruction in the elementary grades, computers themselves are not the real issue. Rather, the key to successful computer use may rest largely upon *software*, the programs providing the computer with specific instructions.

Major types of computer software currently in use with younger children are: (1) drill and practice, (2) tutorial, (3) tutee (in which a child teaches or programs a computer), (4) simulation, and (5) tool (Taylor, 1980; Hoot, 1986). Consider each in turn.

1. *Drill-and-practice* programs provide practice with concepts previously taught by the teacher. These programs, often described as computerized flash cards or workbooks on the screen, are currently the most common type. Drill-and-practice programs can either give children few if any options and choices or can allow them to move ahead (branch).

2. Like drill-and-practice programs, *tutorials* provide many opportunities for practice. They are also similar since emphasis is generally limited to concepts that are easily specified. Unlike drill and practice, however, tutorials move children through concepts not previously taught. The child supposedly learns something from the tutorial, for example, some aspect of reading such as visual discrimination. Brady and Hill (1984), however, reviewed the research and concluded that human adults do a better job of tutoring children.

3. With the *tutee* type of software, children learn to program computers and deal with the respective computer languages. The use of tutee software is open to many questions. When is it a developmentally appropriate time for children to learn such languages as LOGO? What skills are prerequisite? Conservation? Counting? Quantification? Linear

sequential thinking? Will using LOGO enhance children's creative problem solving (Brady & Hill, 1984)? These matters are still being researched.

4. *Simulations* are programs designed to provide imaginary environments relating to real-life situations, just as a book provides an imaginary depiction of possible events. The computer version of games such as Dungeons and Dragons is a rather violence-oriented example of a simulation. A child becomes a participant in a number of adventures that are altered depending upon given choices. While simulations may be beneficial for upper elementary children, their use with younger children is perhaps best minimized. Hands-on, concrete, manipulative activity is clearly superior to vicarious experiences as young children construct their knowledge.

5. A final and perhaps most promising type of computer program is *tool* software. Unlike other types of programs that encourage children to become consumers of information organized by a teacher or software developer, tool programs encourage children to become generators of ideas. Thus, these programs allow children to exploit computer technology toward *their* ends. The word processor used by the children in the opening scene is an example of such a program.

We can summarize here with an analogy. The invention of the horseless carriage at the turn of the century was a major technological breakthrough; yet this invention would have been of little use without an extensive system of roads and highways. Likewise, microcomputers have the potential to be an important resource for improving language arts instruction. This potential, however, is severely limited by the quality of software designed for younger children.

Selecting Language Arts Software

A wide variety of software designed to develop skill in areas such as alphabetization, vocabulary, letter recognition, spelling, punctuation, grammar, and writing is becoming increasingly available to language arts teachers. Availability, however, in no way assures quality or developmental appropriateness. The selection guidelines given in Box 13.1 are discussed below. These guidelines can help you choose appropriately.

1. Compatibility of Purpose and Goal   The first determination is some reasonable goals. Learnings in the language arts occur when teachers act to make them both interrelated and interdependent. That is, activities developing speaking abilities also develop listening abilities, and both of these result in improved reading and writing (Moffett & Wagner, 1983; Petty, Petty, & Becking, 1981). Thus, effective language arts software comprises programs that interrelate, rather than segment, the language arts.

Keeping the *purposes* of the software in the forefront while making selections is crucial when one understands that the prime purpose of much software is simply to sell programs. Software seldom includes evaluation concerning program effectiveness, since currently most software is neither field tested nor developed by teachers (Heard, 1982). Therefore, consider selecting only software supporting professionally justifiable language arts goals.

2. Interest Level   Because of TV and increased educational opportunities, today's children are much more academically sophisticated than those of previous generations. Many programs drill youngsters on concepts they have already learned, merely occupying minds rather than expanding them. Children are quickly bored by these programs.

BOX 13.1 Guidelines for Language Arts Software Selection

☐   1. <u>Purposes</u>. Do the purposes of the software package support predetermined and justifiable language arts goals?

☐   2. <u>Interest</u>. Is the program under consideration inherently interesting to K through elementary-grade children?

☐   3. <u>Content</u>. Is the content of the given program correct and appropriate?

☐   4. <u>Nonviolent format</u>. Is the content presented in a nonviolent format?

☐   5. <u>Stereotypes</u>. Does the program promote cultural or racial stereotypes?

☐   6. <u>Cost-effectiveness</u>. Does the use of the computer enhance achievement of a language arts objective better than use of a more traditional and less expensive format?

☐   7. <u>Level of difficulty</u>. Is the program's level of difficulty appropriate for children under consideration?

☐   8. <u>Choice of level of difficulty</u>. Does the program allow a child to choose the level of program difficulty?

---

3. Content   Watch the quality and accuracy of the content. A program designed to teach initial consonants to kindergarten and first-grade children had a picture of a fish with bubbles flashing from its mouth presented to the children. Students were then asked to type the letter that begins the word in the picture. The choices were f and b. Although f *(fish)* was deemed the one correct answer, a case could also be made for the b *(bubbles)*.

Another program was designed to teach the alphabet to kindergartners. Following the traditional textbook format, the computer simply began a is for *apple* followed by a picture of an apple. When the program arrived at the k, a *knife* was used as an example. Certainly other words are more appropriate for teaching the letter k, words that would relate to actual sound/letter associations, such as *kite*. Programs currently on the market are beset with inaccuracies and poor choices. Potential users need to identify these.

4. Nonviolence   A harmful trend emerging from the educational software industry is a preoccupation with violence. *MasterType,* for example, a typing tutor for children as young as 8 and one of the best-selling educational software programs, is typical of the state of the art. The publisher describes the program as follows:

> The program uses an arcade "shoot-em-up" format. The student is the planetary defender fighting off the deadly invaders from the planet "Lexicon." The invaders are depicted as letters or words in each corner of the screen. The words launch missiles toward the defender's planet in the center of the screen. The defender must destroy the missiles by typing them on the computer's keyboard. If the defender can destroy a missile near the invading word, the word itself is destroyed, to be quickly replaced by another word. The lesson ends when all 40 invading words have been destroyed. (Bockman, 1982.)

The goal of this program is useful since keyboard familiarity is likely to facilitate use of computer programs. However, we live in a world with more than enough violence without using aggressive formats for language arts instruction. Children can use other socialized formats that are just as interesting, surprising, and delightfully ridiculous without detracting from the educational/instructional purpose.

5. Freedom from Stereotypes   Stereotypes concerning race, religion, age, or sex clearly have no place in educational software. While computer educators are beginning to give serious attention to this issue, stereotypes remain (Marrapodi, 1984; Sanders, 1984).

6. Cost-effectiveness   Putting a lesson on a computer screen does not make it more appropriate than other methods of presentation. To be worthwhile, the program needs to be more effective in supporting educational purposes than less costly approaches.

For example, two experienced teachers in a university class were interested in kindergarten children's emerging written composition. One was using a set of expensive software *(Writing to Read)* designed to promote reading and writing readiness; the other used the language experience approach (LEA) described in Chapter 7. In both classes children were composing stories using invented (nonstandard) spelling. But in the LEA classroom, where the children were drawing their own pictures before they dictated or wrote, the children could read back their stories with invented spelling. In the computer group they could not read back, or only rarely. The children's creation of their own pictorial symbols possibly paved the way for better retention of their invented spelling symbols in the LEA group (Lundsteen, Penny, & Stewart, 1987).

7. Level of Difficulty   Current language arts software is replete with examples of inappropriate difficulty level. We recently viewed one program under development to familiarize kindergarten children with the computer keyboard. Although the goal may have been appropriate, the program suffered from an obvious problem—the first two frames of the software provided written directions for using the program. The fact that the majority of kindergarten children are not skillful readers was a major oversight.

8. Branching and Other Options   Since software is just beginning to attain sophisticated levels, programs currently on the market usually require the user always to start at the beginning of the program module. The program could allow learners who have attained some skills to select a more difficult level without starting at the beginning. This feature, which computer scientists call *branching,* is especially important for children with diverse language abilities and for fast learners. In addition, teachers can find out whether the software requires a high degree of interaction from the children by calling for thoughtful response and requiring children to make choices. (Several complete guideline checklists are available to assist beginning teachers in making software selections.)

Word Processing in the Elementary Grades

Of all the areas of the elementary curriculum, computers appear to have the most potential in the language arts. Word-processing programs are the literacy software apparently bringing about greatest optimism among teachers and researchers. A word processor is a software program allowing users to manipulate words easily. Students can erase words, insert text, move blocks of text to more appropriate locations, revise previous work without rewriting the entire document, correct spelling, and ultimately print out a completed letter-perfect manuscript. Computers used as word processors may have potential for improving writing abilities (Daiute, 1982; Toch, 1982; Watt, 1982). In many elementary classrooms, what is called *writing* is actually *handwriting* drill. Writing (written composition), as has been described in Chapter 8 and others, involves the creative process of children getting ideas, putting them down on paper, and forming them into clearly understandable communication units. This process involves thinking, composing, and rewriting (Vukelich, 1981; R. L. Graves, 1981; D. Graves, 1983).

Word processors handle all the technical aspects of composition with only a few simple manipulations of the computer keyboard. Although a wide variety of word-processing programs are available, most have been developed for the more lucrative industrial and professional markets. These highly complex, sophisticated programs have been generally inappropriate for elementary students. If a tutor presents small sets of needed commands, however, older children can learn to use even a complicated program. Several programs developed over the past few years have shown promise for the earlier elementary grades.

For children just breaking into print, programs that use synthesized speech, such as the *Talking Screen Textwriter* (Rosegrant, 1986), are gaining attention. By using speech, they help bridge the gap that makes it so difficult for children with very limited reading skills to use word processors. Other programs that have emerged for younger children are *Snoopy Writer* (Random House) and the *Primary Editor* (IBM). But, since availability does not ensure appropriateness, these and similar programs under development are in need of extensive research to determine their effectiveness with the young. Among other word processors appropriate for upper elementary students are *Bank Street Writer* (Scholastic), *Magic Slate*, (Sunburst), *Blackboard* (CTW), *Apple Writer II* (Apple Computer, Inc.), *Homeword* (Sierra On-Line, Inc.), and *Atari Writer* (Atari Inc.).

Although by no means conclusive, some research has been positive concerning the effects of word processing upon developing the writing abilities of some elementary children. At first older children are unlikely to write more in the same amount of time than they do with pen. However, children who use word processors may (1) stick to, return to, and revise their work more; (2) be less fearful of making mistakes; (3) write longer stories; (4) follow directions more carefully and pay more attention to detail; (5) have fewer fine-motor-control problems; and (6) take increased pride in their writing because their work looks much better than it could if they wrote the material out by hand (Collins, n.d.; Daiute, 1982; Daiute, 1985; Watt, 1982). While word processing appears to have positive effects, however, they are certainly limited by (1) the availability of competent writing teachers and (2) the ability of teachers to choose an appropriate word processor for a given group of children. As discussed in Chapter 8, two areas of the composing process most likely to be affected by word-processing programs and computers are planning and revision.

Clements (1985) has identified a number of questions that may be of help in choosing a developmentally appropriate word-processing program for older children, as shown in Box 13.2.

For an integrative classroom application of word-processor use, consider the following activity.

Computer Book Reviews—A Classroom Application   Some teachers have successfully used word-processing software to have older children keep a running set of book

---

BOX 13.2 Considerations in Choosing a Word-Processing Program

1. Are the commands simple (English, not jargon), logical, and generally limited to a single keystroke?

2. Does it include an on-line tutorial and easy-to-use menus and help screens?

3. Are uppercase and lowercase letters available? Are they easy to read?

4. Is the documentation easy to use for students yet complete enough for you?

5. Will it allow stories to be printed on paper?

6. Does it include (if you want them) such features as:
   windows or a split screen
   wrap around (as type appears on the screen, it automatically goes to the next line without the user having to hit a return key)
   indentation
   invisible lines (for comments the user does not want printed)
   search and find commands (and so on)

7. Can the program be used at several levels of difficulty, with children using only simple commands at first, then gradually learning additional powerful commands?

8. Does it have speech capability?

---

reviews. The students set up a file for each newly read book in a classroom. Children can browse through the series of reviews before reading the books and respond to the reviews after reading the books, agreeing or disagreeing and adding thoughts to this running commentary. Original book reviewers can insert additional thoughts and responses after a period of reflection and the reading of more books, and can interact with their respondents. Thus the dialogues continue. The children can print out a collection of book reviews and dialogues.

Other Support Programs for Language Arts

In addition to the word processor, many programs are available to check a given text for spelling errors. Words the computer does not understand are typically flagged in a different color, shade, or density. Children and teachers can easily put in additional words unfamiliar to the spelling programs' internal dictionary, such as student names, superheros, or places. It is not yet known whether these spelling checkers cause children to neglect spelling or help them become more aware of it.

Still other programs check punctuation, grammar, capitalization, and subject-verb agreement, and furnish a thesaurus (Collins, n.d.). Although research concerning these features is not yet available, their existence could suggest a need for rethinking the overemphasis given to spelling in some language arts curricula. Other programs supporting writing are mentioned in Chapters 8 and 9. Programs are likely to continue to proliferate in a social climate in which people are becoming more concerned with academic achievement.

The Future of Computers in Language Arts Instruction

Research on computers in the elementary schools is certainly in its infancy. For example, it is not known whether children accustomed to writing on a computer lose motivation and become unproductive when they enter a class that does not use them. Some data concerning the computer's use in helping children break into print and become better readers appears optimistic (Atkinson & Fletcher, 1972). Initial optimism, however, needs to be tempered with extensive research before teachers make substantial changes in language arts instruction. The best way, apparently, to integrate computers into the language arts is to focus on the student and the curriculum, not on the computer and its software. Computers can reach their potential as tools for improving language arts only if competent and informed teachers use these devices in a responsible, professional, and developmentally oriented manner. Furthermore, although microcomputers may supplement language arts education, they cannot substitute for it.

In concluding this section we might ask if attention to computers resembles "praise to the mechanical nightingale." Recall the Hans Christian Andersen tale about the emperor and the nightingale. The emperor brought a nightingale to court, and she sang her sweet, melodious songs to him every night. Then someone gave the emperor a bejeweled, mechanical one made of gold. It could be predictably wound up any time the emperor pleased, and the real nightingale was banished. On his death bed, the emperor longed for his natural nightingale and her ravishingly beautiful but unpredictable song. By analogy, we can become overly enamored with artificial technology, such as computers or even textbooks, and let them drive away natural joys and processes in learning and in composition.

TEXTBOOKS

"Textbooks don't equal the curriculum—at least not in the best programs. Teachers and kids and parents are the real resources."

Committee on Curriculum Bulletins, National Council of Teachers of English

When you get to your new classroom, you are likely to find that textbooks have already been adopted for you. In fact, the single resource that dominates language arts teaching is the adopted text and its supplementary material. What is this kind of media and what can you do with it? What criteria can teachers use to assess textbooks when they have a voice in their selection? How can they apply what they know about child development to the use of texts? These are some of the questions this section answers. The basic idea here is to encourage teachers to think of textbooks as resources instead of as the sum total for the year's lesson plans.

The Language Arts Textbook

A textbook generally contains a systematic presentation of the principles and vocabulary of a subject. It may be a collection of writings of various authors dealing with a specific area. Sets of language arts texts and workbooks are sequentially developed by levels to offer a basic program. From the classroom teacher's point of view, a textbook is a book that:

- Every student in your class can have (not a trade book or a reference book)
- Is designed to present at least the basic content, concepts, and skills of the language arts subject area to students

- Includes definitions, explanations, guided applications, a complimentary teachers' edition with instructional strategies, and often other companion items such as student practice materials and tests

Textbook Pluses and Minuses, Do's and Don'ts

To the extent that language arts textbooks bring together information that teachers and students could not obtain and organize on their own, they can be valuable learning tools. If textbooks communicate important ideas accurately and entice students to explore them more fully, they are useful resources.

Usually, however, language arts texts emphasize specific skills and conventions rather than expressive activities. Teachers need to be ready to supplement them. Excellent learning and teaching occur in many classrooms without textbooks. But since textbooks are generally a fact of school life, you will want to know ways to use them (not the other way around). No one book will meet the needs of all your children.

Avoid starting on page 1 and going through the whole language arts text (and its accompanying practice materials) with every child at the same time. Doing that might mean that children who already know what "sentences" are might have to study 12 pages on them, plus complete 6 workbook pages. They could have been reading or even beginning to write a novel instead. Going straight through a text inflexibly might mean that children who need a handbook of proofreading skills will not discover it until they reach the end of the book. By then, it might be June. Using a text inflexibly might mean that at midyear the children will be writing an invitation when they no longer have a real reason to do so—the class exposition was held a month ago.

In other words, it is well to use a language arts text flexibly. Some teachers get samples from several series and cut them up, categorizing material for individual packets and self-selection. They include texts from the level just above and just below.

Critical Examination of a Textbook

The next several sections relate to criteria for considering textbooks for classroom use: their philosophy, point of view, and treatment of the subject. A look at the language arts *scope and sequence chart* and the *index* in the teacher's guide gives the teacher a sense of the territory covered. The chart for the whole series gives a sense of what comes before the taught grade level and after, helping the teacher accommodate all manner of learners. A question to ask, however, is whether the scope and sequence chart is merely a way of trying to impress the unwary. Does it show the "mentioning" superficiality? This label refers to a concept or skill "mentioned" possibly only once in a text, leaving students with sparse, incomplete definitions and explanations, and concepts not connected to meaningful context. In this case students would be unable to do independent study (McCarthy, 1985).

Somewhere in the teacher's edition the author team and editors will probably put a *statement of their philosophy* of teaching language arts, maybe calling it their "English program." Hopefully the team is well qualified. See, for example, if grammar and usage are treated traditionally, out of context, and excessively. Note the point of view on composition. Check whether you could integrate the text with literature and mass media study.

As to *content*, see if the text has a wide range of genuinely useful personal and interpersonal varieties of formal and informal communication, tied into genuine uses of language by and for children. Note the text's range of language experiences and whether student responses are valued.

Try to figure out the text's *assumptions* about language and learners. Assumptions about *writing* in the textbook might include that students learn to write well: (1) through professional models; (2) through a building up from word, sentence, and paragraph; or (3) through working through a process of discovery, drafting, and revision. Assumptions about *literature* might be that its importance comes (1) from cultural heritage, (2) from an increase in aesthetic appreciation, or (3) because of self-understanding. Or there may be a hodge-podge of approaches implying an antiphilosophy to the effect that nothing really matters or can be known (Ad Hoc Committee on Textbook Selection).

Knowledge of the Encompassing Goals of Your Teaching Context

Know the goals of the parents for their children, the goals of the school district, and the goals of the state. Teachers need to see if the goals of the language arts textbook in the classroom are compatible with their own goals and those held by the school and community. Knowing goals will help with decisions about what to do with a textbook. As mentioned in Chapter 9, a student's language arts text is best used as a reference work, with the children's own writing and talking, and the literature and talk of others as the genuine content.

A Textbook Selection Checklist

Assume that you do have a voice in language arts textbook selection for your students, or even a larger context. What checklist might you use that is compatible with the point of view of this text? Consider the checklist given in Box 13.3 focusing on high priorities with sample language you might hope to find in the textbook. If such language is not present, you could simulate the language that might occur if the text authors were to actually talk to the students. If the text presentation is not designed to address students but only the teacher, then that is information to weigh, too.

Informed with these eight points, a teacher is almost ready to assess the student's language arts textbook. But consider one more aspect, knowledge of child development.

Who Are Your Textbook Users?

Teachers presumably go into teaching because they like children and enjoy seeing them learn. During textbook assessment we need to remind ourselves of the reasons for our professional existence; we need to remember and use the information we have about the development of learners.

Why should textbooks for preschool, primary, elementary, and middle school be different? Answers go beyond vocabulary, reading level, or scope and sequence of objectives to an understanding of where particular children are in their development of language and thought. Skilled teachers match materials to a child in a developmentally appropriate way. Some language arts texts, however, may demand that children do things inappropriate to their development. Why make the teaching job harder?

Take, for example, the use of the senses. In general, the younger the child, the more important sensory learning is. (We adults maintain this need in some situations.) Textbooks for young children need to support this sensory type of learning, for it is one of the things younger children do best. Ask if the materials provide means for getting the whole young

BOX 13.3 Criteria for Selecting a Language Arts Textbook

Does the text offer opportunities for:

☐ 1. **Integration.** The integration of reading, writing, talking, listening, literature, drama, and thinking activities. Is there a balance and provision for individual differences with integration of literature and writing?

Example of text language, speaking to student:
—"In this chapter you will have the opportunity to—
• Talk to each other about your experiences with . . .
• And then write your own story about . . .
• Then compare your writing to something you've read."

☐ 2. **Extended discourse for multiple purposes.** A range of extended discourse in various contexts, for various audiences and functions of language. Suggestions for talk and writing in transactional, expressive, and poetic forms, and for a range of purposes such as self-expression, exposition, or persuading. The substance is not just drill and practice with little bits of language.

Examples of text language, speaking to student:
—"Rewrite the story you just read or wrote and talked about as a story for younger children."
—"Think about how the story would be different if _____ had told it instead of _____ . Write or tell it from this point of view."

☐ 3. **Teaching conventions in context.** Teaching words, concepts, and conventions related to English language arts (not in isolation) but in a particular context, e.g., comparative, superlative adjectives in context.

Example of text language, speaking to student:
—"For the discussion and writing work coming up, make sure that you know the difference between: 'elder' and 'eldest' and between 'younger' and 'youngest.' This information will help you in the writing you will do next."

☐ 4. **A range of student response patterns.** Not just right/wrong answers, fill-in-the-blank, talking only to and for the teacher, e.g., use of students' own writing for response pattern.

Example of text language, speaking to student:
—"Make some notes to remind you of the most important points you have thought of.
—Share these notes with your group and write down any suggestions or questions they have."

(Continued)

☐ 5. **Encouragement of small-group work.** The whole class is not necessarily working on the same activities.

Example of text language, speaking to student:
—"Your teacher will organize the class so that you can visit another group in order to talk together about your findings. Then move on to the next option while. . . ."

☐ 6. **Some degree of self- and/or peer assessment.** All assessment is not necessarily measured against arbitrary normative standards with constricted right answers. Teacher and student, peer partners, or the student alone can evaluate a progression of learning: "Off to a start." "That's progress." "Moving right along." "I've got it now."

Example of text language, speaking to student:
—"You have now redrafted your story. Exchange your writing with some others to see how they have tackled the topic. Talk with some of the others in your group about your writing. Choose what it is about your piece of writing that pleases you most. Is there anything that you want to improve on next time?"

☐ 7. **Nonsexism, multicultural educational policy, and contemporary language.** Language used reflects a text for a democracy.

Example of text language, speaking to student:
—"Explain ways to correct these sentence *fragments.* Until age 78, Grandma Moses on the family farm. Then began a successful career as a painter."
—"Write an informative paragraph about an American woman or minority group member you admire. Review your draft in order to correct any sentence fragments."

☐ 8. **Field tests.** Examine whether or not a text has been well field-tested, continuously and thoroughly evaluated for effectiveness with students. Investigate whether or not field test data are available for examination and are not just a sales pitch.

Source: Based on ideas from the Australian Council of Teachers of English, N.D.

child actively involved in learning, rather than assuming that the child will passively receive knowledge. (Example of developmentally inappropriate text language for a young child: "Now, pick out the nouns from the following list.")

Ask if the materials allow process to be more important than product for the young child. Ask if the material takes away the right of children to be children. Each piece of material is only as good as the originator's understanding of children and how they learn, and only as effective as a teacher's discriminating use (Cohen, 1975). Developmental questions need to be asked about texts at each level. The specific question depends upon the age and development of the student.

Children learn language with their own rhythms. Teaching and texts can support and facilitate instead of hurry children. In all aspects of language, children need time to experiment and need to feel comfortable with the idea that it is acceptable, even necessary, to make mistakes.

With focus on the child, ask if the text is "user friendly." Would you want to study this student's language arts textbook for nine months? Is the text written in an interesting, interactive, connecting, positively stimulating, communicative manner? Do the objectives lead to gratifying, long-term, child-appropriate results? Or are the lessons organized according to adult logic so that only one isolated thing is being taught, removed from context so that there is little or no fit with children's minds? (Negative example of isolated textbook language: "Add the verb ending 'en' to words written in pronunciation symbols to make the words fit into sentences.")

Conclusions

In essence a textbook is not a language arts program but merely a teaching tool. Ultimately teachers need to ask if the text is designed for the kind of teaching they believe in. They can ask if it encourages higher-order thinking skills, not just remembering. Holding to individualized, child-appropriate learning, teachers can avoid letting the textbook (or any other medium) take over completely. Teachers can make use of such additional print resources as book clubs, newspapers, magazines, personal communications, and occasional print such as posters, notices, and greeting cards. Teachers can stay in command. Usually they will have opportunities for genuine choices, and they need to be prepared to make them.

TELEVISION AND THE LANGUAGE ARTS

"TV tells us what to wear, what to eat, and how to smell. It tells you what the president said after he just said it."

Overheard

"TV can give a window on wonders, on life in a global village visible to all."

ITV

"[The TV medium] is essentially a picture story-telling system that substitutes others' stories for the unfinished business, current concerns, and worries that constitute our private streams of consciousness."

Dorothy G. Singer

This section summarizes the form features of TV, such as camera shots, music, and pacing, and their possible impact on mental development. It also explores issues and makes recommendations for teachers.

The Impact of TV on Communication

Daily reliance on TV has probably led to a change in how we think, what we think, and how hard we are willing to work to extract information from other communication media (Singer, 1983). Magazines such as *Newsweek* and *Time* now include many more pictures, shorter paragraphs, and more articles dealing with TV stars.

Young children growing up in the United States have an environment in which they must not only process the shapes, contours, and objects of their own rooms and imitate the sounds and gestures of others around them, but also relate to miniature, rapid-fire, or all-at-once interactions of objects and figures displayed on a small box. These figures dance, laugh, scream, destroy each other, and urge purchases of food and toys. "In general, it is clear that children spend more time in this country watching TV than they will ever spend in school and, very likely, in direct communication with their parents" (Singer, 1983, p. 815). Given that American children from about 5 to 13 spend more time with their favorite medium than in any other waking activity, concern is justified (Huston & Wright, 1982). TV provides information, whether fictional or factual, about a supposed outside world. Thus its display becomes part of the so-called world knowledge of children and adults.

A New Kind of Literacy

TV as a communicative symbol system is different from other media because of its *form features* and formats, not its content. This section addresses this new kind of literacy, spurred by teacher education objectives of the NCTE and its Commission on Media. The topic is related to some of the production conventions belonging to this medium, including form features and how they are used to signal different kinds of content. Form features of TV include the following: physical action, pace (rates of scene and character change), and visual techniques such as zooms, cuts, pans, dissolves, and special effects. Additionally included are auditory features such as music, dialogue, laugh tracks, and sound effects. The presence or absence of dialogue and the amount of physical movement are also form features.

Show designers use these form features to present many types of messages, themes, and plots. What is said and the nature of the actions (flying, stabbing, hugging) are content. Form features, independent of content, have an impact on children's attention, comprehension, and social behavior.

Form Features in Children's TV   Commercial TV programs and children's educational TV programs differ in terms of form features. Commercial programs made for children, especially cartoons, hit the viewer's eyes and ears with high action, rapid pace, and barrages of visual and auditory presentations (strong perceptual features). Such programs have relatively little speech and often slapstick violence. Commercial producers apparently assume that the child's attention must be captured and held.

Educational programs use some of commercial TV's form features but include more child dialogue and a reflection cluster that may encourage thoughtful processing. This reflection cluster may contain long zooms of the camera and moderate action levels. Moderate action goes with the portions most important to advancing plot or providing key information. ("Moderate action" is somewhere between the frantic chase and the stationary talking head.) Long zooms give context. They tell the viewer where and how action is occurring and hint at the off-camera environment.

Part-Whole Understandings   Young viewers may not understand a camera "cut to close-up." They may not understand the part-whole relationship in a tight shot containing a small detail that had been part of an earlier long shot (e.g., a battle scene with a quick cut to the face of the drummer boy). When the designer, however, uses a long zoom to make the change from the wide to the tight shot, young children understand (Wright & Huston, 1983).

Attention   Children's attention to TV is guided by form features, such as animation, child (as opposed to adult male) voices, humorous segments, and high action. Animation, character voices, and sound effects signal to children that the content of the program is not only designed for them but is likely to be understandable, funny, interesting, or entertaining. *Such features as intensity, contrast, change, novelty, and surprise are more important in gaining children's attention than is violence.* It is to be hoped that this lesson is not lost on commercial producers (Wright & Huston, 1983, quoting from studies concerning the influences of television on children, conducted at the Center for Research).

Form Features as Structure Cues   Form features of TV, when grasped, also serve children as guides to the structure and types of content in a TV program. For a child who has learned how to use them, form features distinguish scenes, units of conflict, and their boundaries. They tell the TV-literate child how to go about understanding and how much effort and attention will be required. By analogy, this kind of literacy is learned as a sort of syntax or grammar; it is a way of representing information and structural relations in television.

For example, children may note that camera shots called "dissolves" come at major scene changes, or mark dreams or other states of altered consciousness. Slowing of pace may act as a spotlight does on a stage for signaling important content. Another example of form features that signal structure or content is the "wipe" pattern used to start and end an instant replay of TV baseball—an established marker for another type of content. Children's ability to use form cues has been employed in "Sesame Street"; for example, the song that starts "One of these things is not like the others" signals that a classification problem comes next. For some shows laugh tracks signal comedy to children. While form features of soft fuzzy images and background music can signal a content of feminine products, form features of high action, quick cuts, and loud sound may mean masculine ones.

Thus form features are not simply attention grabbers. Children may use TV forms in an active mental way to process content, relationships, and structure. The wise use of form features by program designers can aid children's comprehension of educational content.

TV and Reading

Can an adult viewing TV with a child stimulate the child's reading habits? There are similarities between some TV and reading elements, for example, conversation, character development, setting, and plot. TV can be a springboard to reading, as children relate reading to characters and themes shown on it. Such relating may be especially possible in the case of the 10- to 12-year-old range. For example, many children who watched the TV series "Little House on the Prairie" went on to read more of Laura Ingalls Wilder's books. Comparing books to programs may lead children to interesting generalizations. Prepared teachers can encourage parents to participate with their children in viewing and thus encourage related reading.

Classroom Instruction and TV

Teachers can guide students' viewing by keeping abreast of programs and making judicious recommendations. You can use well-designed series and prepare for specials. Find related books and articles. Plan discussions both before and after shows are broadcast to see what the children already know, to provide background and purposes, and to see what they learned. Box 13.4 gives some additional ideas.

A teacher also can point out language not used in the community and atypical words for vocabulary development. Upper-grade children can compare how TV, radio, newspapers, and newsmagazines report news. In this light, they can examine formats and features. Students can compare TV networks and public TV. They will probably discover that TV stresses the visual, radio depends on words to create images, and newspapers may use both photos and language with perhaps more discussion of the *who, what, where, when, why,* and *how.*

Teachers can bring TV programs right into the classroom, selecting special news events or shows on subjects the class is studying. (See the activity book sections matching this one, "Exploring Thought-Provoking Programming," and others.) You may be surprised at what your students know and can do relative to television. Work for understanding. Even young children can learn to recognize quality. When we educate enough viewers, programming will improve.

High Tech Needs High Touch   Carefully researched and planned, TV promises a rich future for educating children (Wright & Huston, 1983). As in the case of all media use, this promise may be especially true if wise adults are involved (high touch). Especially encouraging are built-in adult and peer interactions integrated with TV viewing. A co-viewing adult can aid children's comprehension. For example, children are not as good as adults in picking up time change cues such as change of dress and darkening of the sky.

As a final consideration, research on heavy TV viewing versus light viewing is beginning to appear in the literature. Heavy TV viewers ("TV blotters") appear more susceptible to ills associated with addiction to TV viewing—aggression, lack of imagination, gullibility (ITV, 1987). Adults still need to guide children in their bright new technological world. Thus, we conclude this section on TV with a poem by Shel Silverstein. Satirical humor or hyperbole sometimes gets the message across when admonition fails.

BOX 13.4 Teachers Use TV

- Watch some of the same TV programs your children watch. You need not watch all the episodes—most have predictable formats and you can quickly grasp characters and plots.

- Teach for active (not passive) viewing. Ask children to describe favorite TV characters. Pinpoint stereotyping.

- Ask children to log and categorize shows they have watched and look for balanced diets.

- Build upon sensory information gained by students from TV by asking them to tell someone else about what they saw and heard. Children will know a surprising amount about the West, for example, from watching westerns.

Jimmy Jack and His TV Set

I'll tell you the story of Jimmy Jack
    and you know what I tell you is true.

He loved to watch his TV set
    almost as much as you.

He watched all day and he watched all night
    till he grew pale and lean

From the early show to the late, late show
    and all the shows in between

He watched till his eyes grew open wide
    and his bottom grew into his chair

And his chin turned into a tuning dial
    and an antenna grew out of his hair

And his brain turned into TV tubes and his
    face to a TV screen

And two knobs saying vert and horiz
    grew where his ears had been

And he grew a plug that looked like a tail
    so we plugged in little Jim

And now instead of him watching TV
    we all sit around and watch him.
                Shel Silverstein

HOW TO TEACH: CREATIVE USE OF FILM AND ALTERNATIVE MEDIA

A film is a petrified fountain of thought.

Jean Cocteau

Ever since the film industry began over 80 years ago, films of all kinds have appealed to the child in us. Today children not only want to be observers but want to take part in filmmaking and video production. The visible language of media such as film, filmstrips, slides, transparencies, and photographs provides opportunities for children to practice many forms of the language arts.

Depending on the task, children making their own media need to organize and arrange ideas in order, make transitions, consider purpose and audience, edit, and plan concretely as they produce, say, a storyboard or other layout. Doesn't all this sound much like a composing process in written composition? All of these activities have a positive impact on thinking and communicating. During work with media, children read and research for ideas, take notes, spell captions, and write scripts. Moreover, this meaningful use of language arts can relate to all forms of children's literature (Cox, 1987).

Young media producers think creatively, solve problems, and profit from teamwork. They also better understand and critically evaluate what they see in films once they have produced one themselves. Media can sometimes encourage a child to attain improved levels of communication when all else seems to fail. Hollywood does not have to be the only place for filmmaking; it could be your classroom (Emerick, 1986).

Organize your film or video production unit using the following steps: (1) Get basic knowledge, (2) plan the movie or video, (3) film it, and (4) use postproduction activities (based on Emerick, 1986). One teacher said he had remarkable success simply videotaping, almost extemporaneously, a piece dramatized by his sixth graders. (See the activity book, Chapter 3, Section 3, "Making a Film," for details on steps, shots, treatments, storyboards, and resources.)

Do filmmaking and videotaping sound too complex? Simpler alternatives (also found in the activity book) include the following: children's hand-drawn films, animation, own script making, simple camera shots involving problem solving, self-made slides, and the working of found materials into collages with writings based on them. These activities show how even children who are hostile to words can be drawn into language arts through media. Teaching language arts by working with film and related media may sound complicated. But once teachers and children learn the knack of it, they are amply rewarded with imaginative and useful slide-tape shows, motion pictures, and animated films.

Media Production and a Creative Composing Process

> Creativity is so delicate a flower that praise tends to make it bloom while discouragement often nips it in the bud.
>
> *Alex Osborn*

In making media, children and teachers work not only with and through language arts and a composing process, but also with a highly creative process having seven components:

1. *Awareness, sensory perception, and identification.* The creative media makers are open, sensitive, and curious. They are more exposed to life than many. They draw from their environment more specifics than most—whispers, visions, facts, smells, quotations—the rich raw material of life.

2. *Caring and commitment.* The creative media makers are concerned and involved with what they learn about life. Life makes them amused, wondering, angry, elated, ecstatic, and empathetic. They can fully image and imagine the feelings of others, their contexts, and the implications of events. And they care.

3. *Incubation.* The creative media makers value that resting time while the subconscious is hard at work and play. They allow time while they go about their school and home business for the dream to swell, for unique combinations of ideas from earlier perceptions to mix in the far recesses of their minds.

4. *Discovery and revelation.* The creative media makers are discoverers; they construct order out of disorder. These individuals have to explore and build meanings on their own and have to find revelations on their own, no matter how many have tried before them. They use their language and craft to help dig for and mine their unique understandings in their contexts. In doing so they reveal and create themselves.

5. *Synthesis melding thought and attitude.* The creative media makers are synthesizers. They put things together in ways that are unique, at least for them. They combine sensory, reflective, intuitive, metaphorical, and divergent/convergent thought. They combine thought with attitudes of openness, caring, flexibility, tolerance with curiosity, and risk

taking. They take small, often far-flung parts of jumbled ideas and juxtapose them in a wonderful story, script, film, or collage.

6. *Detachment and assessment.* Creative media makers are detached assessors. After creating something, they force themselves to be their own toughest critic, to stand back and examine what they have made. Of course, there are some developmental constraints on the ability to see both what was accomplished and what was intended. Working this aspect of the creative process too early kills creativity. But for moving forward to discover more effective forms, abilities in detachment and self-assessment are crucial.

7. *Verification of effectiveness and communication.* Creative media makers verify communication and effectiveness. They want to know if their project gets across their information, feeling, and design; in other words, if the results work for the audience. (Adapted from ideas of Murray, 1973). Sample questions young creators might ask themselves regarding this last item are the following: Does the animation amuse my audience; does the photograph capture the spirit of the chase; does the video action capture the meanness of that character?

How does one *teach* for creative use of media? The teacher who understands a creative process has students who use it. This teacher establishes a classroom climate in which students can journey through a creative process at their own pace, in their own time, in their own sometimes lonely way. Throughout all seven aspects of the creative process runs the

---

BOX 13.5 Checklist for the Creative Process Using All Language Arts

Goal: Be aware of, integrate, and use stages of creative **processes** in all the language arts.

Subgoals: Does this student understand, engage in, and monitor a creative process including the following:

☐   1.1. Awareness, sensory perception, and identification
☐   1.2. Caring and commitment
☐   1.3. Incubation
☐   1.4. Discovery and revelation
☐   1.5. Synthesis, melding
       1.5.1. Thought
             1.5.1.1. Sensory
             1.5.1.2. Reflective
             1.5.1.3. Intuitive
             1.5.1.4. Metaphorical (appreciating/using similes and metaphors)
             1.5.1.5. Divergent/convergent
       1.5.2. Attitude
             1.5.2.1. Openness
             1.5.2.2. Flexibility
             1.5.2.3. Tolerance (with curiosity and risk taking)
☐   1.6. Detachment and assessment
☐   1.7. Verification of effectiveness and communication

strand of individuality. Creativity implies the personal and private. Consequently, the teacher responds to each child as one who deserves a personal reaction. The teacher is not in this case an instructor of the group, the class, the herd. The teacher encourages individuals to finally stand back and see the difference between what each of them has done and what they can do as they build their own meaning (Murray, 1973).

The teacher guiding a creative process does not initiate, but reacts and confers, prods, pulls, coaches, praises, and enters into the learning process with the student. The creative problem of finding something to communicate through media and ways of communicating it is ever new, and the teacher and student can be creative in solving it.

The checklist in Box 13.5 on page 473 charts the goal and subgoals for the creative process. It can be used for planning, assessment, and review of this important dimension of teaching and learning in the language arts.

Take time to nurture your own creative goals and resources as well as those of your students. These values will help you not only meet the needs of typical children to be creative, but also those of special children—the topic of upcoming Chapter 14.

SUMMARY

Resources such as nonprint and instructional media and new modes of communication can be integrated creatively into the language arts classroom. Professionals are moving beyond the view of nonprint media as mere audiovisuals used only to support print materials. Teachers and students need to understand the impact of technology on communication. They can recognize that electronic modes such as computers, TV, and film require special skills, though the basic process of creative use remains the same. These skills, in turn, enable teachers and students to understand the ways in which nonprint media present information and experience. Moreover, teachers need to understand how nonprint/nonverbal media *differ* from print/verbal media. Language arts teachers also need to know about technological devices and media in order to help their students learn effectively.

The opening scene showed children constructively using a *computer* and software for word processing—contrasted with other children found in a predicament. Next discussed was criteria teachers could use in selecting software and other support programs. Teachers cannot ignore computers. Teachers can use them. Teachers and children are the masters of properly used computers or any media—not the other way around.

Textbooks, by far the most frequently found media in the classroom, may be a little intimidating to new teachers because they are the traditional staples of the classroom. But it is important for teachers to know how to assess, select, and flexibly use an array of instructional materials (and equipment), including textbooks. Prospective elementary language arts teachers need to know instructional materials for a wide range at their teaching level. Developmental know-how is a key criterion for text or any media selection. A textbook is not a language arts program; it is a teaching tool to be made compatible with a teacher's goals and teaching style, and individual children's learning styles. Teachers need to be aware of both the appropriate uses and the limitations of textbooks. Evidence suggests that thinking abilities are better taught with the help of both verbal and visual media, not just a textbook.

Television in the context of the language arts means another new kind of literacy. TV, with its visual information and *form features,* differs from print media in the way it communicates messages and tells stories. The form features of TV have an impact on children's attention, comprehension, and social behavior. Form features in children's commercial programs differ from those in educational TV for children, but in all cases, they act as cues to content and structure. We are learning how to use TV to the advantage of children rather than letting it use them. We are also thoroughly realizing that high tech needs high touch and are findings ways to encourage parents and teachers to interact with children to achieve the best use of TV for learning.

Film and *related media* in the language arts again offer a new literacy. Steps for filmmaking somewhat parallel a written composing process. Teachers can encourage children to take advantage of the various media available. Alternative media give many joyful options that stimulate communication, especially for those not yet ready for narrative filmmaking with motion or for those looking for the right medium at the right time for the right child in order to boost communication skills.

Finally, the teacher who understands a *creative process* has students who use it with media and through the language arts. By creative process we mean awareness, caring, incubation, revelation, synthesis, and assessment with verification. The creative problem of communication through and about media is a renewing challenge, with the teacher as the senior learner.

CHAPTER 14

Children with Special Needs in the Language Arts

by Irene Rodriguez and Sara W. Lundsteen

"Every child needs to feel that they are special; but no more special than anybody else."

Burton White

All children are special. But some have needs that require unusual attention from the teacher and the school. This extra attention is important because children, all children, represent our nation's greatest wealth and most important investment. Looking at the crucial priorities, we realize we need to put our children first, to provide each special child with the best, most effective, and least restrictive educational setting and language arts instruction.

The key theme in this chapter is attitude. Can you accept children who are *different?* Can you assist with the necessary individualized planning? Are you willing to try? It won't hurt and it could further the growth of you and your "normal" children. Classrooms can profit from additional diversity. Much depends on a teacher's willingness to reach out, to be caring, enthusiastic, and prepared. It is a rewarding feeling to know that you prevented the destruction or brought about the building up of a child's positive self-concept in communication.

The primary objectives of this chapter are to raise your awareness regarding recognizing, understanding, and adapting instruction for teaching children from special groups with language or related problems. Teachers generally have the responsibility for identifying, referring for assessment, and implementing individually tailored instruction for those with these problems.

INTRODUCTION

The "special" children we need to consider are:

1. Gifted students
2. Less prepared students
3. Limited-English-proficient (LEP) students
4. Other special education students

This chapter answers questions about how a teacher might help students in each of the above groups get into the mainstream. It also includes some ideas for individualized education programs (IEPs).

One of the most important problems to solve creatively in teaching language arts lies in reaching students with widely diverse needs, talents, and backgrounds. Teachers need a broad repertoire of teaching strategies with special adaptations; some are suggested in this chapter.

A teacher's basic language arts program, however, remains the same: (1) quality literature; (2) integration of instruction in all the language arts; (3) encouragement of extended reading and writing in students' own areas of interest; and (4) the making of connections with language arts to the students' own lives (California State Department of Education, 1987). Focus on a core concept of creative problem solving also remains valuable.

The following opening scene highlights many of the major concepts in this chapter. The instructor is a student teacher and the characters engage in monologues that reflect their inner thoughts. Although there are many highly different children in this classroom, we will focus on the thoughts of the following: (1) a gifted child (Gertrude); (2) a combination less-prepared, language-delayed, and mildly retarded child (Ella) who has been mainstreamed; (3) a mildly handicapped child (Tim) with some learning disability, hearing, and visual problems; (4) a more typical child (Andy); and (5) a limited-English-proficient student (Sarom) who has just recently been brought to the classroom by her non-English-speaking mother, a Cambodian refugee.

Context of the Scene

A student teacher, Pat, wants to teach a lesson incorporating message reception (listening/reading), appreciation of artistic language, and poetry. Pat has selected Carl Sandburg's poem "Fog" for this creative listening lesson for the third-grade class where the student teaching takes place. Pat plans to read the poem aloud first and give a copy to each child to read and refer to later. The responses Pat will seek from the children relate to the head (cognition), the heart (emotion), and the hand (response activities). These three areas overlap, of course.

Pat, using the questioning circle described in Chapter 6, has also planned questions touching on content, self, and the external world. In spite of good intentions and hopes to impress the college supervisor who has come to observe, this student teacher makes a few mistakes. The scene provides insights into the children's thought processes, anxieties, and feelings toward each other and the student teacher. See what happens in a class with typical individual differences. (Remember: Characters reveal inner thoughts by talking to themselves as represented by italicized print.)

OPENING SCENE: We Never Promised You a Rose Garden

Pat, the student teacher, speaks first.

> PAT: Class, let me share one of my favorite poems with you. [Sits in large rocking chair provided in the classroom and gathers children around on the rug.] Gertrude, put your project away. Ella, give me your eyes and ears. Tim, sit up close so you can hear better.
>
> TIM: [To self] *I wish Pat wouldn't pick on me. The other kids look at me funny.*
>
> PAT: Andy, bring your new tutee, Sarom, over here with you. . . . I like the way Andy is ready to listen.
>
> ANDY: [To self] *I wonder why I got stuck with taking care of Sarom. Her slant eyes and smile make me feel creepy. And why didn't Pat choose a girl? Well, I'll give it my best shot.*
>
> PAT: Now we're all ready to listen with our heads and hearts. [Reads poem with animation, pauses, and gestures.]

FOG

by *Carl Sandburg*

The fog comes
on little cat feet.

It sits looking
over harbour and city
on silent haunches . . .
and then moves on.

ELLA: [To self] *Pat read it pretty. I like cats.* [Aloud] Read it again. [Others nod; student teacher does so with an equally dramatic performance.]

PAT: [To self] *Occasionally Ella comes in handy—glad she wanted it again. Ella's slow, slow, but sometimes there's a glimmer. At least she's not fidgeting now. I thought I read that rather well. Now for my prepared questions—I'm really well prepared. My college supervisor is going to be impressed with these!*] [To class] What is this poem all about? [To self] *Hope my supervisor noticed how I asked that content question of all the children, to hold their attention. Sarom is smiling—but she always smiles. I don't think she speaks a word of English. I'll call on my gifted child, Gertrude; I'll be sure to get a response.* [To Gertrude] Gertrude, what's this poem all about?

GERTRUDE: [To self] *That poem was written before 1926. I wish Pat would use more recent poetry. Many poets have used personification in their poems. Take James Reeves. He compared the sound of "The Sea" with howls of a hungry dog. Besides, his poem rhymes. My mentor likes Rachel Field's poem, "Skyscrapers . . . " "tired of holding themselves up high. . . . " This is going to be boring; I'd like to get back to my project. Anybody could have answered that question. But I'd better say something nice; I like Pat. . . .* [To Pat] What's the poem about—it's about how the fog might remind one of a little cat.

PAT: [To class] Now, how did it make you feel? Ella? Ella, are you paying attention? [To self] *Ella is so slow! I probably should have asked her the same question I asked Gertrude. I think Ella was listening back then.* [To Ella] Ella, how did the poem make you feel?

ELLA: [To self] *I'm afraid the kids will laugh at me. I know an answer, but I can't get started saying it. I could act it out better. I've got to say something.* [To Pat] My cat has fleas.

PAT: What?!

ELLA: The tom cat across the street . . . doesn't mind she has fleas. I think she's going to have kittens. [All laugh] [To self] *There, I knew they'd laugh. I wasn't trying to be funny. What was funny? I don't know how to be funny. I wish I had my cat here.*

PAT: [To self] *I should have called on Andy. He'd give a more typical response.* [To Andy] How did the poem make you feel? Andy?

ANDY: It made me feel like I could. . . . I could see the fog like a big, a really big white cat. I remembered my dad and I driving to school in the fog. We couldn't see any signs. I'd have been scared, I guess, if he wasn't along.

PAT: [To self] *Thank goodness for typical Andy. Now, here comes my "external-world-realities" question.* [To class] Class, besides yourself, what would you relate this poem to? [Silence . . . more silence] [To self] *I'd better rephrase it!* [Aloud] Class, we've talked about the content of the poem, fog likened to a cat. And we talked about our personal experience it called up. Can you relate it, can you relate the poem to something else in the world? Something else you've studied? Anything? Anybody? Gertrude?

ELLA: [To self] *I wish Pat said things slower. I wish Pat said things different. Relate, relation—my cousin???*

GERTRUDE: [To self] *I'd better help; Pat looks desperate.* [To Pat] If you wanted to relate the poem to science, you might say that fog is a cloud of condensed water vapor in the form of water droplets suspended in the atmosphere just over the surface of the earth. Kinds of fog are: advection, radiation, upslope, and precipitation fogs.

ANDY: [To self, raising his brow and folding his arms] *Showoff!*

ELLA: [Not even knowing that she doesn't understand] *I wish it was recess. I can run fast, and the kids don't laugh.*

GERTRUDE: [Sensitive to Andy's nonverbal reaction] I meant to relate to you and your father's experience, Andy. The kind of fog in your case was probably radiation fog. I'd be glad to explain it to you, if you'd like to try it out on your dad. [Andy nods and looks favorably inclined.]

PAT: [To self] *I won't ask that kind of question any more, especially if only Gertrude can respond. Now I've done my "head and heart" questions, here comes my "hand" question. My supervisor ought to like all my options and choices.* [To class] About our poem—what would each of you choose to do from the response list? Who would like to read the list? Ella? [Ella shakes her head no.]

GERTRUDE: [To self] *I'd really like to get back to my project. I have to be so careful of everyone. Everyone seems to have more fun than I do. I think too much.*

ANDY: I'll read it. [Reading] "Response to literature.

　　　1. Drama center. Use dramatic movement to ex . . . express the poem." [To Pat] You mean we could move like fog cats? [Pat nods while Ella wiggles and nods head up and down, as if she would like to do that option, but then looks scared. Andy continues reading.]

　　　"2. Art center. Make a picture about it." [Andy's face lights up.] I'd like to do that one; but how can I make a foggy cat? [Looks at Gertrude.]

GERTRUDE: Maybe you could tear white tissue paper and glue it on a dark gray background, or use cotton balls, or splatter very light gray paint with a toothbrush over screen and onto dark blue paper over a cutout of a cat, or . . .

ANDY: Gertrude, I'll try the tissue paper, thanks. [Andy continues reading.]

　　　"3. Reading/Writing center. Write your own poem. Use one thing compar . . . compared to another."

GERTRUDE: [To self] *That's the best one for me. I wish I could get started on it, but I'd really like to work on my project first today.*

ELLA: [To self] *I'm hungry. I wish I was home with my cat.*

TIM: [To self] *I wish that student teacher wouldn't sit in that rocker with her back to the light, it makes it hard for me to read lips. I could see better even closer, but I'm sure not going to say anything about it.*

SAROM: [To self] *I have no idea what they have been talking about. I wish they would show a picture. I must keep smiling. I can still hear the helicopter in the field overhead where we had been made to work . . . and the shots, and my father lying face down in the rice. I could make a picture of that. . . . The student teacher is looking at me. Keep smiling.*

PAT: Thank you, Andy. [To self] *I guess I should have called on Tim to read, too. But I can't take time with him right now.* [To class] Now class, raise your hand when I call the center number and I'll send you there, quietly, quietly, to work on your response to the poem. [To self] *I hope they are orderly. I thought I was well organized for these centers until Gertrude came up with all those ideas. Gifted kids are sometimes a pain. And I'll bet Ella is just going to sit there fidgeting, and it'll take me 30 minutes to get her started. And Tim, he'll start but he never seems to finish anything. Either he can't remember what to do, or he loses interest. He seems smart enough. I wish I had more Andys instead. They're easy to teach. I wonder when my college supervisor is going to leave!*

Analysis of the Scene

Federal and state laws and community demands now make it necessary for the schools to provide appropriate educational opportunities for all children, including those with special needs. The student teacher in the opening scene is feeling the impact of these demands and realities of wide differences—not exactly a rose garden, or maybe it is. Teachers need to remain patient, and to look beyond the topsoil, or surface, of children's behaviors to discover the roots of their inner turmoil, insecurities, desire for expression, and need for approval.

Briefly, the first thorn appears as Tim, who needs his hearing aid, heavy spectacles, and special positioning, but who also needs subtle and sensitive handling of his handicaps by a teacher who knows how to enlist peer acceptance. Without such handling, Tim may become a child who in later years sneaks off his glasses and hearing aid to be more like the others—and learns nothing. It would help the Tims if their teachers would remember simple techniques such as facing the light so that their facial expressions and lip movements are easier to see.

The next thorn, Ella, mildly language delayed and mildly mentally retarded, needs learnings broken down into smaller parts, language sent her way simplified, lots of time, physical avenues of learning, and freedom from fear of ridicule. In return for partner help, Ella, needing physical activity, might offer a game or skill in dramatic movement to others. The college supervisor will probably recommend the continuation of asking the same questions to more than one child, including Ella (and recommend conferencing firmly with any who laugh derisively at her). For example, the question asking children to use literature to see their own lives is worth asking to as many children as will respond. Pat might have rephrased it as "Does the poem remind you of something? A time in your life?"

Ella's opposite, Gertrude the gifted, needs acceleration, time for her own almost independent projects, and peers to share ideas with; yet she also needs opportunities to learn compassion and understanding of others for real-world, cooperative living. Gertrude has a million ideas tumbling at jet speed. She could make a fine contribution to the world, or she could become totally frustrated—a wasted rosebud in an educational desert. Perhaps the reader felt Gertrude's display of mental prowess was exaggerated. It wasn't. Even more astounding examples of talk by young, gifted children exist in the professional literature.

The thorny aspect of Sarom, the limited-English-speaking example, is not only no mainstream language at present, but possibly severe emotional disturbance. Emotional disturbance is not the province of this chapter or of the typical teacher, but hints that might be found in Sarom's drawings could give reason for referral. Her constant smile probably covers the great pain of witnessing her father's murder.

The teacher could do a lot to help Sarom, despite the language barrier. Use of pictures, of pantomime, of a roving aide who speaks Sarom's language are starters. The student teacher was on track with the partner or buddy system for limited-English speakers, and "typical Andys" are a good choice. But some groundwork and support for "first friends" are in order. In return for help, Sarom might teach or share some of her nonverbal artistic ability. Subsequent sections of this chapter deal with each of these major divisions of special needs: the less prepared, the gifted, the limited-English speakers, and the other special education students.

This classroom really can become a joyful rose garden. It takes a teacher who knows at least the rudiments of diagnosis, knows how to get help and implement it, has a basic attitude of valuing each learner, knows how to build democratic spirit in a classroom, and can bring out the best from the richness of children's diversity. That is what the rest of this chapter is about.

WHERE IS SUCCESS FACILITATED?

In general a facilitating environment for such a diverse group as we just saw in the opening scene has many authentic, fascinating, and developmentally oriented aspects. *Authentic* means any of the environments described in earlier chapters. *Nonauthentic* means, e.g., isolated use of flash cards or mindless dittos. Do use music: Encourage LEP children and those with other difficulties to make up their own songs to preserve and read in both English and in their dominant language. Interest centers, even computers, encourage tension-free speech. Toys and games such as tag and jump rope are often somewhat similar throughout the world; have some available. Specifics of optimal environments depend on the specifics of the special children served. Remember that teachers who specialize in English as a second language (ESL), special education, and gifted education are sources of information.

As important as the classroom environment is in helping a diverse group, it is even more important to ask questions about *who* they are—the next topic. Along with descriptions of the varied groups of special children are found some *how to*s.

WHO ARE YOUR SPECIAL STUDENTS AND HOW CAN YOU HELP THEM?

The following sections deal with the gifted, less prepared, LEP, and other special education students. These sections present ideas on what to do (and what not to do) in the mainstreamed language arts classroom.

Who are these special children? They are the ones who need our sensitive concern and help because they differ from the classroom norm in ways related to their culture, environment, economic level, language, intelligence, creativity, emotional stability, learning ability, and physical ability. Of course you may never have all possible kinds of special children in your class; and certainly you will not have all of them at one time. But you will need to make provisions for some. Although categories and labels play a part in diagnosis, we need to be cautious about stereotyping and overgeneralizing about special children. Otherwise, who they are can become constricted. First consider the gifted.

Gifted Students

"A mind is a terrible thing to waste!"

United Negro College Fund

The "Gertrudes" in your classroom come in many shapes, sizes, and colors, with a multitude of intellectual gifts, creativities, and talents. Although there are many types of giftedness, in this chapter we are talking of giftedness shown in the language arts. About the only thing gifted children have in common is a minimum base level of moderately high IQ (say at the very least around 120). Generally, gifted children are capable of reaching high-level abstraction quickly, but sometimes mainly in one specialized field. Then there are those who seem to be gifted in almost everything. Intellectual giftedness may mean, but does not necessarily mean, a totally balanced child. Some gifted children need help in developing balanced self-concepts and healthy social relationships. This section devotes much space to the gifted because the chances are that they are slighted in the mainstreaming and multicultural modules or courses that many readers will have had.

Creative talent and academic giftedness do not necessarily go together. The creative child may not necessarily have an exceptionally high IQ or unusually high achievement. Often, however, creative and gifted children do these (sometimes unwelcome) kinds of things (adapted from Torrance, 1969):

- Behave in ways that conflict with the teacher's expectations
- Question and challenge authority
- Become intensely absorbed in what they are doing
- Become extremely animated and physically involved
- Appear overly eager to share their discoveries with others
- Note relationships among apparently unrelated ideas
- Show curiosity, digging hard for information
- Take highly independent action
- Show willingness to consider strange ideas
- Seek alternatives and explore new possibilities
- Demonstrate a particular talent

Provisions vary. Some states have a clear qualifying level for gifted programs. Children enter programs on the basis of IQ scores, with teacher, parent, and peer recommendations. Programs that expand the existing curriculum provide, at the child's level, high-interest materials to be used at a pace set by the child. Some schools provide special classes or interest groups; some use grade advancement or combination classes where several grades are grouped for certain areas.

What to Do How does a teacher help those who are gifted in the language arts areas? How can a teacher help them explore the resources of their minds through rich experiences of reading, listening, writing, and speaking? For example, will they need help in developing support and documentation for their fluent written ideas? Many of the recommendations appropriate for the gifted apply to well-designed curricula for students in general. The gifted do not require a completely separate or changed curriculum. They do benefit from a teacher acknowledging their abilities, with the opportunity for the further development that encourages their curiosity and questioning. They benefit from a teacher willing to explore and accept their alternative solutions to problems (e.g., Gertrude's many ways to produce a foggy cat). Teachers need to encourage gifted children's higher levels of thinking with work drawing upon their abilities to analyze, synthesize, generalize, and solve problems creatively. The following are some further suggestions. Some the teacher can readily assimilate into an ongoing curriculum; the suggestions may already be part of it. Others require a bit more change in current methods, materials, or scope and sequence (e.g., technical writing).

Develop nonegocentric listening Help the gifted to listen thoughtfully and tolerantly to the opinions of others during discussion. Gifted children may become so verbal and excited about ideas that they may need to discipline themselves to focus on the topic of common interest. Encourage gifted children to accept their special gifts as a responsibility, not just a privilege. They need to learn to value the contribution of all people and on occasion to tutor or guide other children. (Refer to Chapter 6 on discussion and Chapter 3 on listening.)

Provide audience reality   Provide peer response groups to written composition for developing gifted children's understanding of audience. Gifted children may have unrealistic ideas about the world of audiences they wish to address. (Refer to Chapter 8, peer conferences on writing.)

Encourage long-term projects   Provide opportunities for individual language projects and their presentation. It is especially important for the gifted to engage in long-term projects that allow them to delve into a subject and express themselves on complex levels. They need large blocks of time for processes of research and related communication at complex levels. Allow time for them to let their minds wander through reflections and daydreams about their projects. Involve gifted children in special projects that benefit them and can be of value to the class or school.

Use curriculum adaptation   Adapt three areas: (1) individualized reading; (2) individualized writing, both creative and technical; and (3) drama for the gifted (Robinson, 1986). Consider each in turn.

1. *Individualized reading.* Rather than being bound by the content and controlled vocabulary of a basal reader, gifted students (given a choice) tend to choose material at an appropriate level of difficulty in complete pieces of literature. They let their interest propel them through material at a fast rate. (Refer to Baum, 1985; the activity book: its Chapter 9 on literature and Chapter 14 on the use of picture books with gifted children.)

2. *Individualized writing—creative and technical.* Writing programs allowing gifted students to engage in all sorts of discourse give them opportunities to write creative fiction, poetry, and all manner of informative and persuasive text. Using word-processing software, even young gifted children can grasp and remember relatively complex commands for revisions and let the computer print final versions. They can submit work for publication in the many magazines and other outlets for children. (Chapter 10 on critical and creative thinking offers many activities that teachers can adapt for the gifted.)

Perhaps you were curious about the creative poem Gertrude wrote, stimulated by the student teacher's lesson plan and response options in the opening scene. Here it is.

Fog

The sea pumped
and bellowed
the fog
in and upon the city.
It hugged and caressed
all that walked
upon the streets.

Gifted students can also write to learn via extensive reading and research for a technical report; they can accompany their presentation with graphs, tables, statistical forms, and diagrams. Such project writing done in technological, business, and scientific domains stimulates critical thought. Students can write concise research proposals in place of the more traditional independent study contract. You can help the gifted to learn specialized reference skills that will speed them through a lifetime of learning. (Refer to examples in Chapter 7 on expository uses of language.) A sample list of topics on communication generated by a gifted fifth- and sixth-grade class is shown in Box 14.1.

3. *Drama for the gifted.* Drama provides gifted children chances to further develop their imaginations, play with language, practice affective and social abilities, learn coopera-

---

BOX 14.1 Research Paper Topics

The following list of possible topics for a language arts research paper was generated by a gifted fifth- and sixth-grade class.

1. Helen Keller (nonverbal cues or body language, e.g., use of eyes, gestures, pupil dilation, touch, body lang.)
2. Egyptian pictographs
3. Sign language
4. Traffic signals around the world
5. "ese" words, education*ese*, engineer*ese*, computer*ese*, valley*ese*
6. ESP
7. Telecommunication
8. Laughter or humor
9. Cetaceans (dolphins, whales)
10. Prophecy
11. Intonation patterns
12. Media: TV, radio, film
13. Semaphores (flags)
14. Esperanto
15. Morse code
16. Indian languages
17. Advertising
18. Family jokes
19. Symbolic languages
20. Group processes
21. Sign languages
22. Graffiti
23. Poetry
24. Language of silence
25. Communication with animals

tion, and apply creative problem-solving processes. Drama creation is material for a long-term project (Robinson, 1986). For example, the special project of Gertrude in the opening scene happens to be a drama she is writing. It is an allegory/fantasy entitled *Anna and the Woodsman* that takes place mainly in a forest. She is designing the scenery, costumes, music, and lighting as well as writing the script. She plans to cast, direct, and present her drama in her garage this coming summer. Given opportunities for choice, gifted children will seek out their appropriate level of depth, complexity, and challenge.

Use curriculum compacting   Teachers can also adapt content for gifted students through the process of *curriculum compacting*. First they uncover what the student already knows, then they present the rest of the material quickly so that the student can go on to other topics (Renzulli, Smith, & Reis, 1982). A final way of adapting the content is by pulling in a *mentor*, such as Gertrude's mentor in poetry writing. These mentors are not necessarily educators; they can be professional members of the community who are willing to share some of their knowledge and expertise with a youngster who has an interest and/or talent related to the mentor's. Gertrude is fortunate that the school was able to locate a woman who is a poet herself and is willing to share interesting poems with Gertrude, as well as give her support and constructive criticism when she attempts to write them herself.

What *Not* to Do   Do not have the gifted spend time on unnecessary activities, such as decoding skills, the studying of already-known words, workbook skill exercises, and the answering of low-level questions (activities that we would want few, if any, children to do). Avoid repetition where grasp has been complete; avoid limiting choices; avoid fragmenting time; avoid exploitation (filling their time *only* with errands, clerical jobs, or helping others in the class), and avoid grinding them down to some supposed norm.

Last but not least, avoid being threatened by them—they are children who need your love, your common sense wrought from relatively long years of experience, and your command of resources. Afraid you are short on resources? Get busy combing the community and beyond. Do not feel threatened if you do not know the answers to some of their questions. Do be willing to help them search for the answers. For a humorists view on the intimidation of the gifted, see Figure 14.1.

Less Prepared Students

Children who are low achievers or underachievers, including such students as Ella, Tim, and Sarom, may need extra help with meaning. They struggle with the processes of reading, writing, and oral language to such an extent that they lose the joy of language. They may have dialects that differ greatly from the standard in the class. They may be from environments of low socioeconomic status compared to the rest. Being less prepared than other students can cut across many categories.

What to Do   The teacher can set a positive learning environment. Such an environment avoids or eases negative feelings and threats such as fear, frustration, and embarrassment. (Recall Ella's embarrassment.) How do teachers and class members establish a positive

Figure 14.1 On the intimidation of being gifted. Reprinted by permission of UFS, Inc.

climate for the language learning of those less prepared? Consider the overview of ideas listed in Box 14.2 and discussed below.

Draw less prepared students into activities Recall that Pat, the student teacher in the opening scene, rather ineptly invited Ella to participate, but not Tim. Examples of words and ideas for enticement that Pat might have used are the following: Using

---

BOX 14.2 Seven Ideas to Help the Less Prepared

1. Draw less-prepared students into activities.

2. Respect language and dialects different from standard English.

3. Show that each student's ideas and interests are important.

4. Develop attitudes of self-worth.

5. Use direct coaching and modeling.

6. Compromise and add.

7. Become acquainted with local, state, and national services available to the poor or less prepared.

language they understand, Pat could have set the stage for listening with auditory and visual images for the poem and with background questions ("What do you do . . . see . . . feel on a foggy day?" "Fog is what we're going to be talking about and acting out." "Ella, what is it we're going to be talking about?" "Good listening, Ella!"). As the less prepared students enact, they can dramatize the metaphor that might otherwise escape them ("Ella, show me how your cat could move as a regular cat . . . as a fog cat . . . Ella, it's all right if you can't say it now. I'll get back to you.") To Sarom: "You can help us with drawing so we can add *Fog* to our 'pictionary.' " "Even if you can just say your name again, I love to hear it . . . and your country . . . and city. Let's find them on the map." (Also refer to the activity book: its Chapter 5 on drama and Chapter 14.)

Respect language and dialects different from standard English Pat could learn at least a few words of Sarom's language, as could a volunteer to be her "first friend." In addition, a teacher could learn, for example, how gratitude is expressed in the child's different language—by an equivalent of *thank you,* or by a gesture, or not at all—and find out the social significance of the response or its absence. The different culture as well as the language may be used for appreciative comparison, without denigration and for the benefit of all students (NCTE Committee on Issues in ESL and Bilingual Education, n.d.). Also refer to Chapter 12, the section on usage and dialects, and the activity book.

Show that each student's ideas and interests are important Pat, the student teacher, basically had a promising learning situation with many options and choices for response. Sarom had undoubtedly experienced the early morning fog in her native Cambodia. The student teacher could have taken the trouble to research one simple Cambodian word, *ap,* meaning "fog," and Sarom would have understood at least one word used 13 times (including variants) during the lesson, and probably would have learned it. The class could have learned a Cambodian word.

The student teacher could also have photographed, videotaped, film-clipped, or selected a foggy day for the lesson and had the children create a little "fog" via steam right in the classroom for the less-prepared Ellas and Saroms, migrant children, and the very poor who maybe did not have many words for their misty experience. Creative problem-solving discussions about this topic and others are also particularly useful for providing situations where each student's ideas are recorded and respected (Chapter 6).

Pat could also let Ella know that whatever response she comes up with is okay. Some forget that such children have feelings. Accepting response is critical. Relevance to the basic topic can usually be found someplace in a response (even in "cat fleas"). Actually Ella's "motor" IQ is higher than Andy's, and she could make important contributions to the class in the psychomotor domain—which leads us to the fourth point.

Develop attitudes of self-worth Encourage feelings of self-confidence and a sense that no one student is less human and valuable than another. Pat could structure multiability group work at the centers so that no one would lose self-esteem by being isolated as "slow" (Chapter 6). Thus, the student teacher could provide activities for the less prepared that avoid impatience, rote-drilling, or condescending "special" textbooks. Or, Pat could have the children reproduce their names in as many variations as possible: using rubber stamps, plastic letters, yarn, beans, a typewriter, or different computer print styles.

The children's names could appear on ego-boosting lists for oral or written display, such as authors of the week.

Use direct coaching and modeling The low achievers like Ella and the under-achievers like Tim will generally need more direct coaching and modeling for writing processes, applying new listening strategies to reading, and applying their prior experience to language use. Pat's self-relating kinds of questions are likely to help the less prepared better understand.

Questions to help the less prepared students clarify and summarize what happens during reading might also promote learning. Questions to help these students separate the important ideas from the trivial would help their comprehension and pave the way to critical judgment. For example, if there is an attention deficit in listening, an inability regarding vigilance in sustained attention, the teacher can model an approach of reorienting and bringing oneself back into the task. By third grade, teachers can guide Ellas in being aware of their problems in vigilance, their need to keep looking back on their listening (metacognition). Teachers can give them a guide: "This is a way to do it, Ella." Thus, a teacher can offer such children challenges and problems at a level that causes them to grow.

The revision of writing, often a task completely avoided by the less prepared, can become easier in the coaching and modeling approaches of the multiability group. (Recall Chapter 8, the section on peer conferences.) Peers can help the less prepared realize, e.g., where they could use more examples and where a sentence gets into a maze. Well-prepared multiability groups allow language-delayed, language-different, and other less-prepared students opportunities to be drawn into enjoyable learning and communication, and chances to receive attention to their valued ideas (California State Department of Education, 1987).

Finally, through direct teaching, modeling, and parent involvement you can develop concepts needed in school that an impoverished child may lack, for example, a tradition of valuing literacy, books, and writing. Include concepts of learning how to learn—use of library, reference books, and resource people.

Compromise and add Your normal rate of speech may be fine for most of the children in the class, but it may be too fast for some of the less prepared, such as Ella. Yet if you slow down too much, you may lose the attention of the average and the gifted. Try compromising by adding some extra clues for the slower ones. For example, speak in your normal manner while giving and explaining assignments, but take the time to write key points on the board. These are the words on which the less prepared children can concentrate and focus. As you continue to elaborate and be chatty with the faster students, the less prepared can go back and review the key instructions and words to their heart's content. Because such words are left as a set of written guidelines, they do not create the same time pressure that the spoken words would (Erway et al., 1988).

Become acquainted with local, state, and national services available to the poor or less prepared Large school districts will have directories of free services available, for example, Lions' clubs for eyeglasses. Compile a list of sources for your area.

With some adaptation, nearly all of the foregoing suggestions apply equally well to limited-English-proficient students—the next topic.

Limited-English-Proficient Students

> "Success comes in all colors, shapes, and sizes. All children need to succeed in
> school."
>
> *NCTE Committee on Curriculum Bulletin*

Recall Sarom from the opening scene, speaking no English. One of the big challenges to teachers today is to extend language arts skills to the growing numbers of students for whom English is a second language. *Who* are they? The limited-English-proficient (LEP) students in your classroom come in a wide variety of native languages and diverse cultural backgrounds. LEPs show great individual differences in their gradual development and uses of English. They come to your classroom already knowing what language is, what it can do, and what it is for in their own communities (Lindfors, 1987). The speedy learners probably have the following characteristics. They will likely be willing to risk, be attentive, and identify with English speakers while making meaningful use of English. Their goal is clearly to understand and be understood.

Broad program goals (the *what*) include the following: (1) positive self-concept; (2) respect for the culture and values of others, by appreciating differences *and* similarities (the unique parts in a whole human community); and (3) interaction and cooperation in order to solve problems flexibly in a multicultural society.

Linguistically different students need to experience the same high-quality instruction and expectations for performance as native speakers. This book has stressed that genuine, useful, and interesting opportunities to read, speak, write, and listen are important for students learning language in your classroom; and these activities become even more important in the case of students already fluent in one language, yet needing to learn the mainstream one. Children from diverse linguistic and cultural backgrounds usually exhibit more similarities than differences.

A key principle is that language learners, whatever their nature, need to understand the *meaning* of messages about their own needs and purposes. Language learners who are meaning makers do not acquire language by drills unrelated to themselves. Whether the language learners are mainstream toddlers or older students learning another language, the grasp and use of messages is aided by the context of gestures, pictures, actions, and intrinsic rewards. Recall that Sarom in the opening scene unfortunately was in a highly abstract teaching-learning situation, unrelated to her past or present experience and needs.

Thus the communication of LEP students is hampered when what is listed in Box 14.3 occurs (California State Department of Education, 1987).

Visualize an experience as vividly as you can, real or imagined, of arriving at a place where you have extremely little command of the language. What are your first communication needs for getting things done? Is your first need to conjugate a verb? Make a plural noun? Or manipulate other surface forms of language? Highly unlikely. More likely is your need for transportation from the airport, a comfort station, or something to drink—meaningful content, concepts, and pragmatic uses of language. All of your energies go into making assumptions about meaning with regard to urgent uses of the new language.

The situation for the LEP children in your classroom is somewhat similar. Their meaning-making energy might be going into the talk associated with the cooperative making and hanging of a group storybook mobile, into cooperative improvisation for a dramatic scene, or any of the other authentic classroom activities suggested in this book.

BOX 14.3 Stumbling Blocks to Learning

1. The content is too abstract, and oriented to repetitive skill-based worksheets.

2. LEP children do not know the vocabulary and sentence structure, especially that needed for certain content areas.

3. The teacher delivers a lesson too rapidly.

4. They do not have the time provided nor the opportunity to use language in meaningful ways.

Source: California State Department of Education, 1987.

It helps if the teacher knows and understands the *particular language difficulties* the child is encountering. For example, did you know that there are only 10 possible ways for a word to end in Spanish? Contrast that with 40 possible endings in English. That makes 30 new sounds for Spanish-speaking children to hear and produce (Lundsteen & Tarrow, 1981). In addition, the Spanish-speaking child has come to expect that the vowel sounds will remain constant; in English the vowel *a* alone has at least 12 variations.

Sociocultural and Linguistic Differences   Children's culture may affect who they are as communicators. We need to avoid stereotyping, but some generalizations help explain differences. Some cultures do not value listening to females. Some peer cultures listen only to certain peers. Other cultures do not listen to peers in school but only to teachers. Some are people-oriented and ignore objects such as media of instruction. Again, it is important not to overgeneralize and label. But culture does make a difference in the communication of some individual children. Some cultures may be so preoccupied with getting language *right* that children avoid risking any interpretation or production. Some cultures may excel in empathetic listening, responding well to emotive use of language. Some cultures respond far more comfortably to objective, unemotional language. Some cultures communicate better when only one listener and speaker are involved ("I can't hear with more than one talking!"), whereas others are accustomed to multiparty communication ("everyone" talking and listening at once).

Some linguistically different children may unintentionally mislead a teacher's assessment. They may glibly pick up holistic phrases such as "Whaddoyoumean?" They do not know exactly what the separate parts mean, but they know that use of it gets attention. When linguistically different children have a number of these phrases, the teacher may be fooled into thinking that the children are understanding far more than they really are. Some children may not want to show that they do not understand. They sit politely and nod, and the teacher thinks, "Wonderful, they understand it all!" Maybe they don't. Watch it.

Overcoming differences in intonation patterns may plague your linguistically different listeners. You can try learning their intonation pattern and then, when speaking to them, alternating the standard English intonation pattern with theirs. When a language is difficult for people, just listening requires almost all their attention, leaving little "leftover thinking space." This kind of stressful demand on linguistically different children also needs to be taken into account.

What to Do   Certain teaching strategies can help unconscious and conscious learning of language. They can make it possible for LEP students even to find delight in discoveries about a new language. Again, teachers using such effective strategies minimize any study of rules of grammar. They may use ideas such as those in Box 14.4, which are elaborated upon below.

Use purposeful pairing   The teacher initially pairs the LEP student with native- or fluent-English speakers. Such a strategy (the buddy or first-friend system) also helps with adjustment to school. (Recall Andy and Sarom in the opening scene.) Pairs can start with "must talk," soon move to "fun talk" for sheer joy, then move on to "fact talk" related to "think talk" (Enright & McClosky, 1988).

Work from strengths   With respect to their native language, acknowledge LEP students' "already learned powers." Emphasize LEP students' strengths as they acquire another language—accentuate the positive. The student teacher in the opening scene might start with Sarom's drawing ability, for example. A demonstrated ability in mathematics can lead to an opportunity for the student to participate verbally in arithmetic lessons, once the names of numbers in English have been learned. In addition, teachers need to understand that a second culture is a bonus.

Work their oral language base   Make the most of their oral and thinking skills in whatever language they can use to expand understanding and fluency. Invite them to say what they have heard, read a transcription of what they have said, and write about what they have read. If you find some young children who come to school not even having much of a first language, you may need to find ways to help them build up that first language. Try to have aides, volunteers, parents, or older children available for your LEP children

---

BOX 14.4 Strategies to Help LEP Students

1. Use purposeful pairing.

2. Work from strengths.

3. Work their oral language base.

4. Make it easy with predictable, repetitive, and patterned stories.

5. Concretize with multisensory media, songs, and other forms.

6. Use functional and concrete situations.

7. Use and teach a variety of questioning techniques in and out of *multiability* groups.

8. Structure some lessons to preview and monitor learnings.

9. Share the richness of their culture.

10. Try to begin with some content area instruction in their native language.

11. Provide a nurturing environment for writing.

12. Involve parents in providing support.

to dictate stories to, and try to provide fascinating experiences to prompt dictation (in their language, in English, or in a combination of the two).

You might provide the students with relevant open-ended topics, such as "What is a pocket for?" After reading a provocative story, such as *A House Is a House for Me*, give the children a chance to make contributions. Record them in a class book, individual story, or group experience chart. For example: "A leaf is a house for a spider egg." "A mailbox is a house for a letter.") With older children you may want to photocopy story pages, covering up the words but leaving the pictures. Then the children may invent their own stories, matching their oral or written response to the pictures. (Refer to the LEA section in Chapter 7.)

Make it easy with predictable, repetitive, and patterned stories   In tune with the whole-language perspective for any child, use literary works with predictable story structures, language patterns, and repeated or cumulative events (e.g., based on the text "Brown bear, brown bear, what do you see? I see a . . . looking at me," let children substitute on their own, e.g., "Chalkboard, chalkboard, what do you see? I see a venetian blind looking at me," and so on). A categorized list of such predictable storybooks is found in Chapter 12. With the very young, the teacher can read to and with children from *enlarged books.* The teacher can then make student copies of a selected enlarged book for the children to take home and read to parents, siblings, and others. (Big books are available commercially or can be made by the teacher.)

Concretize with multisensory media, songs, and other forms   Frequently use audiovisual aids, recordings, pictures, films, videotapes, actual objects such as utensils, and other concrete media for vocabulary building. Let the children handle and name objects. Have bilingual aides or volunteers give labels in the child's first language, then in the mainstream language. The teacher can further extend the children's oral language by developing charts with songs, action rhymes, or poems. The children can follow along with the print version as the teacher says the language form. Thus the oral and written relationships are fostered.

Use functional and concrete situations   Take advantage of concrete situations, such as occur during outdoor and indoor play. Hispanics often have trouble with pronouns (confusing masculine and feminine), prepositions, and other troublesome speech parts. You can take advantage of naturally occurring situations to emphasize reflectively ("*He* is throwing the ball"; "*She* is building with blocks," etc.). *Leo, the Late Bloomer* is a children's book appropriate for emphasizing the pronoun *he.* "He couldn't do [this] . . . He couldn't do [that]." A piece of easily enacted literature for emphasizing prepositions is *The Bus Ride,* with all the characters getting *on* and *off.*

Use and teach a variety of question techniques in and out of **multiability groups**   Use a variety of well-designed questioning techniques ranging from factual to inferential. (Refer to Chapter 6 on discussion, the questioning section.) Some learners may initiate questions directly about a form or structure of the new language. The idea is to encourage cooperative learning among LEP students themselves and with native-English speakers for developing friendship with students of other backgrounds.

Bilingual children can be a valuable bridge in the group. They translate for both sets of monolinguals and offer help to the non- or limited-English-speaking students. As the year progresses, teachers can find children who understand another language, even though they cannot speak much of it as yet. For example, you might see a conversation between a Spanish- and an English-speaking child. Each is speaking in his or her own language but clearly understands the other (Cohen, 1986).

Working from their group activity card (described in Chapter 6), multiability groups can paraphrase several sentences for every two pages they read in textbooks, recognizing topic sentences in each paragraph and underlining key concepts. They can use the key concepts to make up their own table of contents for their version of the material. As in Chapter 6, children can play the roles of reader, recorder, and facilitator. Recall the group work motto: "No one will be good at all needed abilities, but *everyone* will be good at something." Be sure that someone makes clear exactly what the student has done well. The child with the most knowledge for the task is not always the one with the best English. In essence, then, group work can assist you in teaching to the highest level, not just to the lowest.

CPS activities for multiability groups. As part of the multiability group, children learn to help each other cross language barriers as they engage in creative problem solving (CPS). For example, the challenge may be to plan and carry out a drama activity. Or the children may create props for introducing a book on the school voting list to the rest of the group, then handle a polling on the book's popularity. Or the creative problem may be to examine folk tales from various countries for treatment of magic. Or the students may individually create pictures of animals with important parts missing, then come together in groups to figure out the missing parts. The previously silent creator is the final authority when all else fails, showing the original animal picture and indicating the missing part.

Structure some lessons to preview and monitor learnings   Plan lessons so that important vocabulary and concepts for subject areas are organized in advance and reviewed regularly. This practice may help to monitor LEP students' academic progress. In a unit about the Stone Age, for example, one could teach *cave, fire, hunt, fur,* and *flint.* Many of these concepts can be illustrated, pantomimed, or used in charades. As a further example, you might check to see if students are using their own language structures to grasp those of English. In English, for instance, the indirect object is expressed by the function word *to* or by a position before the object. *(He gave the book* **to** *Mary.)* How does the student's own language express it? (NCTE Committee on Issues in ESL and Bilingual Education, n.d.)

Share the richness of their culture   Recognize the importance of diverse languages and cultures through multicultural activities that prevent alienation and inhibitions about language. When introducing classroom topics that connect the students' experiences with the classroom, let them share and value their special culture—their folklore, tales, music, dance, food, customs, dwellings, values, arts, crafts, holidays, national events, architecture, and language. Provide opportunities for English-speaking children to learn some words of the different languages of their classmates by having them label objects in the classroom in both languages.

Teachers can choose and progress through the following levels of multicultural sharing.

Levels of Multicultural Sharing

1. The beginning level may be attending to self-concept and a few holidays (e.g., *Cinco de Mayo*).

2. Next teachers may go on to enlarge the children's cultural knowledge base with cooking and other above-mentioned traditional rituals, and field trips.
3. The above materials and activities (with the help of parents) may be integrated more closely into the curriculum, instead of being tacked on as an afterthought. Classroom physical space is actually set aside for this multicultural work.
4. The classroom environment at the next level is concerned with cultural validity in every aspect of the cultures, as opposed to a few mere surface stereotypes.
5. This level goes beyond the single classroom to a total school awareness.
6. The sixth level goes yet further with its additional concern with working for social justice among cultures (Kendall, 1983).

Student communication increases in depth as you progress from lower levels to higher levels.

Try to begin with some content area instruction in their native language

Although a classroom teacher is not likely to be fluent in the various languages that will become a part of the class, an aide, tutor, or parent can help the LEP student keep pace with important academic content ongoing in the classroom. A program needs to ensure that children are learning academic concepts and skills as they learn English as a second language (ESL). That is, instructors facing students in the process of becoming proficient in English need to offer these LEP students concept development in all subject areas, if at all possible, by *using the language they know best for instruction,* be it Spanish, French, Cambodian (as in the case of Sarom), or whatever. The idea is not simultaneous translation, which may slow progress (Krashen, 1982).

Instructors need to do this native-language instruction at a rate that compares well with what English-speaking students are doing. English-only instruction, of course, needs to begin as soon as possible. The availability of library materials written in both English and in the LEP students' native languages helps them find recreational reading and do research work appropriate to their level of mental proficiency.

This ideal of academic-area instruction in one's native language is sometimes difficult to coordinate and expensive to implement. But for most children it is less traumatic than total immersion in a strange language and better than relatively senseless language pattern drills.

Provide a nurturing environment for writing

While encouraging contributions from all students, allow peer *cooperative* interaction to support learning for a variety of audiences and purposes. Group experience stories (discussed in Chapter 7) are an example. Provide frequent, meaningful chances for students to create their own text (as described in Chapter 8). Respond supportively to the writing of students by acknowledging and validating their experiences, feelings, and ideas with your comments, assessing writing in a way that encourages critical thinking (presented in Chapters 8 and 10). Second-language growth increases the more that LEP students are read to and encouraged to read and write themselves (Task Force on Racism and Bias in the Teaching of English, 1986).

Involve parents in providing support

Parental support helps students' language and thought whether the home activity is in English or another language. Parents need to know that it is the *quality* of home language interaction with the child that is more important to their child's school success than whether or not they use English. Parents who read, talk, listen, tell stories, discuss news, and interact regarding television develop their children's language and thought. Rely on nonverbal creativity, too. Part of involving parents includes having them come to school for conferences. For those parents whose English resources or time-telling conventions differ, it may help to send home a *picture* of a clock indicating time of appointment.

One set of parents who barely spoke English was so conscientious about speaking it with their young children that they never used their native language at home. The quality of language and thought in the home was sadly lacking, therefore, and the child's development was actually hindered (Heath, 1986). It is the quality of communication in the home, making children stretch their powers, that counts the most. Therefore, parents do *not* need to be encouraged to speak to their children exclusively in English. If parents can find an out-of-school playmate who speaks English (and not the native language), that may afford their child one kind of natural and effective teacher. Some children are better at this role than others.

Have parents come into your classroom and read to LEP children in both languages with books from home. This idea may be your solution to those hard-to-find second-language materials. Again, the key is meaningfulness and helping children use language in literate and literary ways. (Note Harcourt's *HBJ Lectura* series and other references for this chapter, and the extensive bibliography in the activity book.)

OTHER SPECIAL EDUCATION STUDENTS

> "Dependency is learned, but so is independence."
>
> *NCTE Committee on Curriculum Bulletin*

The special education students mainstreamed in your classroom come in a great variety of classifications. Labels, changing almost yearly, have hurt a lot of children. But for funding, service, and academic discussion we have not figured out how to do without labels. Under Public Law 94-142, the handicapped include those with any physical or mental impairment substantially limiting one or more major activities. Children rarely fall into clear-cut categories. Some (such as Tim in the opening scene) are multiply handicapped. View exceptions against a background that includes a continuum of general individual differences, strengths, weaknesses, and learning styles. One important factor affecting exceptional students' participation, accomplishment of goals, and academic growth is their language competence and performance. For example, frequently the language performance of the slightly mentally retarded child is below age level, with problems in formation of sounds and monotonous expression (Jordan, 1976).

A key principle is that English-language arts teachers *work closely with special education staff* serving students with disabilities. Teachers work closely by discussing necessary changes of the curriculum and by cooperatively coordinating instruction and services. They receive copies of individualized education programs (IEPs) or attend meetings to develop IEPs when necessary. Optimally, a special education consultant may come to sit in a teacher's room for a day or so. Then the consultant offers helpful suggestions that are easy to implement, but that the teacher may not have thought of (e.g., the student teacher's position with respect to the light and Tim's visual needs in the opening scene).

General Helpful Concepts

Among the general concepts that are useful in helping the educationally handicapped are those previewed in Box 14.5 and discussed below.

BOX 14.5 Some Concepts for Working with Special Children

1. *Tension reduction:* Look for signs of tension in children during language arts activities and try to pinpoint causes. Make the environment more soothing.

2. *Perseverance:* Help children keep at their language arts tasks.

3. *Multisensory methods:* Use multisensory approaches to learning.

4. *Initial cuing:* Help children get blocked responses flowing by using the technique of initial cuing.

5. *Basic concepts:* Give just as much opportunity to develop basic language arts concepts, both literacy and literary knowledge, as regular students have.

6. *Study skills:* Provide "learn-how-to-learn" know-how, just as regular students receive.

Sources: California State Department of Education, 1987; and Cheek, 1978.

Tension Reduction   A teacher needs to find ways to relieve children who show signs of being tense: sweaty palms, upset stomach, and flushes behind the ears. In humans such reactions indicate readiness to flee or fight for survival. In such a state abstract thinking and learning come to a virtual standstill. Try soft music, deep breathing, relaxation games, and even just a reassuring pat on the shoulder to indicate the child is making progress.

Perseverance Assistance   Assisting the child to persevere requires more attention from the teacher and other helpers than would be the case for the "normal" child. Offer the child a task in small, nonthreatening, easily digested portions, one problem at a time, one task to a page, one explicit direction at a time. Helpful, too, is careful thought about interest and intrinsic rewards (not gold stars or other extrinsic bribes).

Multisensory Approach   Learning for educationally handicapped children can take place and be stored through and by all the senses. For example, let the children clap to their language, see their language, feel their language in sandpaper and clay shapes, even eat letter- and word-shaped cookies they have made. As emphasized in Chapter 2, relationships needed for lasting learning are constructed with layer upon layer of varied multisensory experiences.

Initial Cuing   Recall that Ella in the opening scene said, "I know an answer, but I can't get started saying it." It is important to be patiently willing to model and assist these children with strategies for getting started. Sometimes educationally handicapped children appear to block in responding to tasks or starting work. (Recall our student teacher said, "I'll bet Ella is just going to sit there fidgeting. . . .") This blocking does not necessarily mean that they cannot come up with an answer or do the work. Saying the first words in a text or doing the first part of a task in unison with the teacher may help. For example, a teacher may say, "Once upon a time there was . . . " instead of "How does your story start?", or "You use a capital at the beginning of a . . . " instead of "Where do you use a capital?" Aids such as these are called *initial cuing.*

Basic Concepts   We do not want special education students to miss out on the essence of the language arts curriculum—the core of literary language and the basic communication functions and processes. While they may show difficulties in listening, speaking, reading, and writing, we want to make sure we do not overrestrict their exposure to the wonderful experiences the language arts can afford. We do not want to be so caught up in getting them to learn the explicit mechanics of reading that we forget to expose them to *Charlotte's Web* and other classics.

Study Skills   We do not want to leave the Ellas and the Tims with a helpless attitude. Instead, we offer them some study skills so they can learn how to learn. Making use of a library, of a reference work, of a picture dictionary, and of resource people needs to be part of their education, too (California State Department of Education, 1987). Remember that special children can produce. Generally they do not want just the sympathy and leniency that permit them to avoid what the others in the class are doing. What they do want and need is the respect that comes from accomplishing a useful task, reasonable limits, and standards consistently adhered to—the encouragement and assistance to do what you and they know they can do.

With that overview in mind, consider three categories of special education students most relevant to the area of the language arts: (1) visually impaired, (2) hearing impaired, (3) learning disabled with several subcategories, including speech-language pathologies.

Visually Impaired

Dewdrops in a spider web, a bright evening star, the first scarlet tulip of spring—most of us are aware of the sights around us. But about 15 million Americans are seriously visually impaired and another 82,000 are legally blind and receiving supplemental security income (Bureau of the Census, 1987). A child with impaired vision needs to learn through other senses or through special materials prepared for the partially sighted. On the plus side, the visually impaired child may be able to hear language better and be even more motivated than sighted children since the impaired use language as a major way to communicate (Hallahan & Kauffman, 1978).

Some Clues to Detection   Some clues to visual impairment noted by the National Association for the Blind include those in Box 14.6.

BOX 14.6 Some Detection Clues for Visual Impairment

- Favors one eye by shutting or covering the other.
- Blinks or squints or moves eyes more than usual.
- Holds objects unusually close or far away.
- Complains of headaches or dizziness.
- Has problems with reading and with written assignments.
- Has eyes that are watery.
- Has learned to read, but reads only for short periods, and reads slowly and hesitantly.

BOX 14.7 Some Suggested Compensations for Visually Impaired Students

1. *Special materials:* specialized magnifying devices, books, and materials to be provided in large print, braille, or on tape; large-print typewriters; materials to encourage tactile, auditory, and kinesthetic exploring; games and puzzles with raised surfaces; unglazed paper, soft-leaded pencils and black felt-tip pens. Again, exceptional children need to manipulate in order to make sense out of their world, just as typical children do, but even more so.

2. *An adapted program:* a specialized listening skills and auditory program for the content area curriculum, and possibly speeded speech. (See the "generally helpful concepts" at the beginning of the special student section.)

3. *Environment:* placing partially sighted children so that they can see to their best advantage, using lighting that does not cause glare or cast shadows. Provide lowered noise levels when auditory cues are needed for orientation to what is going on. Provide helpers who can tape assignments and read directions aloud. Use touch and auditory contact. Remember that a child who cannot see you well will miss out on eye contact. Say the child's name and touch the child to acknowledge, for example, a job well done. Again, a buddy system where children help children is useful.

What to Do   Adaptations in your classroom necessary to meet the unique needs of a visually impaired student may include the following in Box 14.7.

Hearing Impaired

The crackling sound of the last leaves clinging to winter-blown trees, jingling keys turning clicking locks, caressing words—most of us are well aware of the sounds surrounding us. About 16 million Americans, however, have impaired hearing; about half a million are profoundly deaf. While a child with some hearing can use it in learning, a child unable to hear well has to learn through other senses. Other aspects affecting learning are age at which the hearing loss occurred, type of loss, and amount of correction possible.

With a slight loss, students miss faint or distant speech that is sometimes important to language arts activities. With mild loss (41–55 decibels), they may miss 50 percent of class discussion if voices are faint or speakers are out of their line of vision. With a marked degree of loss (56–70 decibels), not only is group discussion a problem, but also speech, language, vocabulary, and comprehension are impaired. Severe loss (71–90 decibels) still lets children hear loud environmental sounds and loud voices—possibly all vowels, but not all consonants (Hallahan & Kauffman, 1978).

Tim, in our opening scene, has a disorder of the middle and outer ear which was partially corrected through surgery and a hearing aid. Disorders of the inner ear and those related to brain damage are treated through therapy designed to teach compensatory skills. The teacher needs to know how the school district handles audiologic and medical referrals and to know the corrective program being used. Then the teacher can follow suggestions for appropriate classroom adaptations.

BOX 14.8 Some Detection Clues for Hearing Impairment

- Delayed, hard-to-understand, or unusually loud speech.
- Extremely limited vocabulary.
- Staring blankly when spoken to.
- Holding head to one side, attempting to hear.
- Inattentiveness; easily distracted.
- Unwillingness to join in activities.
- Inability to follow directions; responding physically to sound without understanding.
- Selective awareness of sound. Certain sounds are grasped while others are not (e.g., loss in higher-frequency sounds such as /s/, /t/, /th/, /sh/). The child may hear some speech as a jumbled mass of noise.
- Smiling and nodding peculiarly (i.e., struggling to look as though they understand).
- Variable response to sound (i.e., seeming to hear one day and not the next, partly because of variation in the pathology or in environmental noise).

Some Clues to Detection   Of course teachers are sensitive to a child coming to school with a hearing aid, but other signals that might indicate a hearing impairment and need for referral include those in Box 14.8.

What to Do   In working with hearing-impaired students, you may need to modify some of your auditory strategies and use visual media to accommodate special needs. Consider the ideas in Box 14.9.

Learning-Disabled, Language-Disordered, Delayed, and Hyperactive Children

The umbrella term of *learning disabilities* groups language disorder, delay, and hyperactivity. Why put topics of learning disability and language disorder and delay together? Some learning-disabled students can listen to and read words, but they show problems in recall for spontaneous use. Some cannot get easily started speaking (e.g., Ella in opening scene). Others stick to single words and phrases because of difficulty in planning and organizing. In sum, language disorders may be a central problem in learning-disabled children, including those with reading and attention problems (Bryan & Bryan, 1975). Accordingly, we consider learning disability and language disorder side by side. *Developmental delay* is subsumed under language disorder and refers to those children who develop language at a slower than average rate, but follow a normal progression (Bloom & Lahey, 1978).

Learning Disabled   The problem in trying to define *learning disabilities* is that it is a catchall term used to describe many different problems (Kirk & Gallagher, 1986). It does not include the other problems addressed in earlier sections of this chapter. It shows itself in imperfect ability to listen, think, speak, read, write, spell, or do math. *Learning disabled,*

BOX 14.9 Some Suggested Compensations for Hearing Impaired Students

1. *Varied visual media:* For reinforcement of learning you may use slides, overhead projectors, and captioned films and videotapes (refer to Chapter 13 and its chapter in the activity book).

2. *Hearing aids:* Learn to check the functioning of a child's hearing aid. Generally, professionals in the field will have recommended whatever technology the hearing-impaired child can use to improve hearing. From time to time, however, some otherwise normal children may develop temporary hearing loss due to illness or ear infection. In some cases, if the hearing loss will last for some time, a *temporary* hearing aid can help those children keep up with classroom activities and content presented orally. Since such children may not have been to a specialist, it is easy for such a problem to persist for some time without any remedy being applied. It may well be the classroom teacher who notices the problem and offers guidance to help the child bridge the gap until hearing is restored to normal.

3. *Program adaptations:* Teachers need to review their daily lesson plans with the child's special education teacher to determine where academic concepts and vocabulary may need to be made more clear. (Also see earlier "General Helpful Concepts.")

4. *Environment:* Teachers need to control background noise if possible. In some cases you may need to use signing interpreters (those able to use sign language for the deaf) and note takers to support the student in the mainstream English-language arts program. Unobtrusively seat the child in the middle and close to the front of the learning action. Keep the source of light behind the child to facilitate speech reading. Get the child's attention before speaking to him or her. Speak clearly and without exaggeration. Again, monitor hearing aids to make sure that they are turned on and working. A tension-free environment with rich interest centers will encourage, not force, exploration and joining in. And again, a system of children assisting children helps.

---

a term of the 1970s, encompassed earlier labels such as *minimal brain dysfunction or injury, special learning disabilities, perceptually disabled,* and *neurologically impaired* (Lundsteen & Tarrow, 1981). Children who demonstrate one year or more of delay on achievement tests and/or more than one standard deviation between verbal and nonverbal intelligence test scores are often identified as "learning disabled" (Erway et al., 1987).

Language Disordered   A language disorder has been defined as "any disruption in the learning of a native language" (Bloom & Lahey, 1978, p. 287). This umbrella term includes developmental delay and disorders of language surface form, of content (weak concepts), and of use (mismatch between form and content of concepts). Again, those with language delays and other disorders and those with learning disabilities are not necessarily separate groups.

Tim in the opening scene has a learning disability that shows itself as a language disorder in writing. He also shows a discrepancy between his potential intellectual ability and his achievement. Although a recent IQ test indicates that Tim has an IQ of around 110, he fluctuates in his performance, not succeeding on his expected level. In addition to Tim's other problems, recall that our student teacher also remarked, "Tim . . . never seems to finish anything. Either he can't remember what to do, or he loses interest. . . . He seems smart enough."

A child who is language disordered, learning disabled, or both is one who is not making achievements that go with his or her age and ability levels in one or more of the following areas: oral expression, listening comprehension, written expression including spelling, basic reading skill, reading comprehension, and math calculation or reasoning. The terms *language disabled* and *learning disabled* do *not* refer to children who exhibit a mismatch between ability and achievement that is primarily the result of physical, mental and emotional, or environmental handicaps. Instead, a psychological or neurological factor has inhibited the normal development of the child. Interference may be in mental operations, language, or academic schoolwork. Thusly excluded are children who are mentally retarded or sensory handicapped, or who lack the opportunity to learn (Kirk & Gallagher, 1986). The listening disabled child may have central auditory processing deficits, reduced competency in language, attention deficit disorders, and memory limitations (Erway et al., 1987).

Hyperactivity   Hyperactivity is one possible characteristic of the learning-disabled child, though this is usually more of Ella's problem than Tim's. Not all learning-disabled children are hyperactive. Hyperactivity is defined as a consistently high level of activity that is shown "in situations where it is clearly inappropriate *for the age of the child* and is coupled with an inability to inhibit activity on command" (Ross & Ross, 1976). What is normal for a 3-year-old may be "hyper" for a first or third grader.

The response to the term *hyperactive* has sometimes been unfortunate. Some teachers have fallen into the trap of attaching this label to children who are simply active, energetic, and curious. Be guided by reliable medical diagnosis with respect to use of this term. We have seen much controversy over the treatment of such children with drugs such as Ritalin. Researchers are not yet fully aware of the effects of drugs of this nature. Some stress dietary control of such substances as artificial coloring, food additives, and chocolate (e.g., Feingold, 1975).

Some Clues to Detection   Teachers working with children daily can spot clues to learning disabilities and language delays. A few of the signals follow in Box 14.10.

Some children in the past have not realized that they were learning disabled and have gone on to do quite well, with perhaps, for example, a residual tendency to reverse some letters when they are typing or to tap their foot a lot. Others could have used a lot of help, perhaps including self-help. Sapir (1985) suggests that there is no such thing as developmental delay or lag. *Learners simply need to learn how to compensate, to take difficulties on as a creative problem and learn another way.* They learn to use what they do well to help themselves. The goal (the *what*) is to find strategies for compensation.

What to Do   What are some of the things the teacher can do to meet the special needs of the learning-disabled child (the *how*)? See the suggestions in Box 14.11.

Next we move from the category called learning disabled to a different category considering those with speech-language pathologies. Those discussed here include problems of (1) articulation, (2) voice quality, and (3) stuttering.

BOX 14.10 Some Detection Clues for Learning Disabilities and Language Delays

- A short attention span for his or her age.
- Overly distractible for his or her age, impaired concentration, figure-ground discrimination problems.
- Tantrums frequently thrown when crossed, difficult relations with peers.
- Generally awkward.
- Difficulty remembering.
- Motor or verbal perseveration (e.g., once started, the child is unable to stop laughing).
- Academic difficulties (e.g., a fourth grader confuses similar words and letters; reverses letters, digits, words).
- Mismatch among abilities (e.g., the child talks well but can't put a puzzle together).

BOX 14.11 Some Suggested Compensations for Learning-Disabled Students

1. *Materials:* Again, use concrete materials provocative of multiple-sensory experiences. The older learning-disabled child may still have difficulty understanding abstract ideas in some areas. (Again, there will be a mismatch or discrepancy among abilities.)

2. *Environment:* Place the child close at hand so that teachers and others can give help easily. Minimize distractions since the learning-disabled child has a tendency to pay too much attention to everything. Along this line, simplify the child's surroundings, decreasing the number of choices he or she is faced with. Keep in mind, however, the principle of nothing in excess. While some learning-disabled children may profit from a simplification of their environment, avoid making their space bleak and barren, and consider the other children in your classroom. Many classrooms, however, would be more aesthetically pleasing for all with less clutter.

3. *Program suggestions:* Avoid unnecessary frustrations; for instance, avoid assigning tasks the child cannot do. Have reasonable expectations since it takes longer for a learning-disabled child to complete an assignment. Break the work into small segments if a large task overwhelms a learning-disabled child. Basic principles of appropriate teaching—working from the child's strengths, individualizing, and giving concise, well-thought-through directions—are just as important for the learning-disabled child as for any child. Along with guided self-assessment, direct tutoring, focused questions, and models for successful response, each aspect of approaches used with normal children is made explicit for the disabled (Erway et al., 1988).

Speech-Language Pathology

Slight speech defects can seem severe to a child because of the importance of communication and the pressure to be understood by others. Speech is abnormal when it deviates so far from the speech of other people that it calls attention to itself, interferes with communication, or causes the speaker or his or her listeners to be distressed (Van Riper, 1978). Speech-language pathologies are *not* learning disabilities.

Articulation   The powers to articulate are developed skills, just as are intellectual skills. As a child grows, speech pronunciation normally improves. If mispronunciations are typical of children that age, then the mistakes are generally developmental in nature and will be self-corrected in time with exposure to appropriate models.

Some speech errors, however, are not developmental. Some have a medical basis, while others come from faulty signals from the brain. Still other speech errors have inadequate hearing at their root. Children who usually make such errors need help from a speech pathologist.

Voice Quality   Voice quality disorders are not developmental in nature. Examples are persistent hoarseness, harshness, breathiness, stridency, high pitch, or nasality. Disorders can come from improper use of the voice or illness. Doctors can determine the cause of the problem and suggest medical treatment for correction. Speech therapists can help when disorders in vocal quality are from voice misuse.

Stuttering   Historians have recorded stuttering back to Greek and Roman times. Yet we continue to be puzzled as to its cause and remediation. In stuttering the forward flow of speech is interrupted abnormally by repetitions or prolongations of sound, syllable, or struggling behaviors (Van Riper, 1978).

Some Clues to Detection   Some signals that may reveal speech disorders include those in Box 14.12.

What to Do   Suggestions vary for the case of stuttering and articulation disorders. Early referral to a speech pathologist is advisable. Consider each in turn.

Stuttering: Very severe stuttering needs referral to a speech therapist. (Also see Gottwald, Goldbach, & Isack, 1985.) In Box 14.13 you will find some classroom ideas.

Articulation problems: Because of normal developmental aspects, schools usually make referrals for working with articulation problems after the end of first grade. Screening is usually done in grades K–one. The following four specific approaches are usually recommended:

- *Listen to it.* Help the child hear the error. Use a recorder and present the child with correct and incorrect examples. Have the child speak into the recorder.
- *Model it.* Provide a model for correct use. Encourage the parents to model, too.
- *Produce it.* Help the child produce the correct sound. Make rhyming lists; use puzzles and games.
- *Use it.* Use the correct model in familiar stories (Lundsteen & Tarrow, 1981).

Teachers need to be prepared to learn about various disabilities and their impact on the language arts, and to explore the best ways to meet the needs of those who have them. Each child has a right to remain in the mainstream until he or she demonstrates other needs.

BOX 14.12 Some Detection Clues for Speech Disorders

- Consistent mispronunciation or substitution, not appropriate to the child's age (e.g., /l/ or /w/ for /r/ (*wabbit* for *rabbit*); /f/ for /th/ (*firty* for *thirty*); /th/ for /sn/ (*thnow* for *snow*; sounds omitted or distorted).
- Omission (e.g., *cool* for *school*; *top* for *stop*).
- Distortion (e.g., *shtop* for *stop*).
- Shyness; absence or near absence of speech.
- Stuttering.
- Cleft palate, harelip, or both.
- Poor speech quality.

BOX 14.13 Classroom Do's and Don'ts Regarding Stuttering

- Avoid referring to the stuttering disorder.
- Help the child relax.
- Observe situations that increase the problem.
- When the child is comfortable, encourage participation.
- Reduce demands for speech when stress occurs.
- Capitalize on curriculum provisions for singing, choral speaking and reading, puppets, movement, and drama (Chapters 4 and 5).

Chapter 15 deals with evaluation and assessment, or how do we know we got there? Pat, the student teacher in the opening scene for this chapter, appears once again, this time as a wise and more experienced teacher who is adept at assessing student needs.

SUMMARY

"There is no single right method. Decisions must be made case by case, based on individual needs, not on . . . category of handicap."
Kirk & Gallagher (1986)

This chapter has moved through a thorny rose garden of special children needing sensitive, well-researched diagnosis, referral for help, and carefully planned education in the language arts—all analogous to soil analysis and enrichment, careful watering, fertilizing, and pest control. Various categories of children with special needs were presented, along with options for responding and behaviors to avoid.

All children are special. But some have needs that require unusual attention from the teacher and the school. This extra attention is important because children represent our nation's greatest wealth and most important investment. Looking at the crucial priorities, we realize that we need to put children first, providing each special child with the best, most effective, and least restrictive educational setting and language arts instruction.

Again, the key theme is *attitude*—accepting children who are different. Classrooms can profit from the additional diversity contributed by such children. Those with special needs discussed in this chapter encompassed the gifted (often lacking in appropriate educational opportunities), the "less prepared," the limited-English-proficient students, and other special education students. Those examined in this chapter included the visual and hearing impaired, the learning disabled (including the hyperactive) and language delayed, and those with speech-language pathologies—including articulation, stuttering, and voice quality.

For each category we talked about what the classroom teacher might do and, for categories needing it, gave some clues to detection so that you can refer the child for further study. Many of the teaching suggestions are consistent with positive teaching practices for any child, but are particularly important (or can be especially adapted) for the child with special needs. Some generally useful teaching concepts for the learning disabled were tension reduction, perseverance assistance, multisensory approach, initial cuing, inclusion of core language arts concepts, and study skills. Goals are in the area of *strategies for compensation.*

A key idea useful across most cases was students working as partners, learning together, and teaching each other. The theme was that no one is good at everything, but everyone can be good at something. Ideas for the less prepared and the LEP students were the following: to start with the child's strengths, providing needed additional experiences; to act as a resource for referring child and parent for help; to value and feature a balance of many cultures in the classroom; to understand a token level versus a deeper level of cultural involvement; and to build a bridge between home and school. For the LEP children, we suggested gaining an understanding of the language variation spoken by those children, even learning at least portions of another language yourself, and using a language experience approach for building all communication skills. Also suggested were relating the abstract to the concrete and enacting meanings. Differences in strengths of the creative and of the gifted child were clarified.

We stressed the importance of avoiding overgeneralizations, of watching out for stereotypes concerning all these categories of children, and of applying well-grounded knowledge of typical child development. With this basic understanding, you can know which expectations are reasonable in relation to the child and which are not. This chapter has not given all the answers: it has merely provided bare roots from which to grow in your relations with special children. Approach them with a sense of professional responsibility. Remember that all children are special—and so are the teachers who care. A diverse classroom can be a fine rose garden.

CHAPTER 15

Evaluation and Assessment of Language Learners, Teachers, and Programs

"Tested and measured
You were found wanting
So you left your school
Taking with you
your warmth
and decency
your grace
and poetry
We get to keep your scores."

Zlota Pacifici

The primary purpose of this chapter is to examine some basic ideas on assessment and evaluation in the language arts. The theme of the chapter is that testing be used *in the interests of children* (Scarr, 1981). With that principle in mind, two main guidelines for teacher preparation in the English language arts are the following:

1. Know assessment techniques (tools of the trade) for describing your students' progress
2. Understand the uses and abuses of testing instruments, tools, and procedures (National Council of Teachers of English, 1986).

Assessment techniques have great diversity and answer different kinds of questions. As for uses, this chapter looks at teachers' assessment of students, teachers' own self-assessment, and the influence of principals or other administrators. After meeting such interconnections in the opening scene, the reader will experience their development in the rest of the chapter. Briefly, *abuse* includes relying solely on one type of testing instrument and/or testing procedure in the language arts. More detail comes later in the chapter.

Each chapter in this book has had its particular look at assessment of children's growth in certain language arts areas. So what can this chapter add? Besides the promised review of tools and of abuses, the chapter also deals with assessment of the teacher's own language arts program and self as teacher. Moreover, the chapter does this with a creative problem-solving approach. In regard to self-assessment, you may wish to skip to the activity in Appendix 15A, "The *Me* in Measurement"; try it now, and then use it again when you have finished the chapter. The chapter concludes with an epilogue to the book, reviewing its basic themes and major points.

INTRODUCTION

Why Assess and Evaluate?

Why has so much attention generally been focused on evaluation, on testing? Why attend specifically to evaluation and assessment in a language arts text? First, teachers need to attend to the immediate classroom context wherein assessment helps them answer questions such as these:

- Where do my students stand as communicators when I begin teaching?
- Are my language arts objectives reasonable?
- Are my literature materials and activities effective?
- Do I need to try something different in regard to composition?
- Or is it best to continue just what I'm doing?

Why assess in the classroom? It would be at least a partial waste of time to select goals as shown in each chapter in this book, then painstakingly select delightful activities to develop processes and skills, and then never know whether your students learned anything. Ideally the purpose of assessment is to find out *what children have learned and determine the next steps.* Knowledge of progress, even the smallest bit, is rewarding. It is an important part of taking heart and trying again. The purpose is not to be educationally fashionable nor to appease a school district management bent on evaluating for cost-effectiveness.

Assessment can mean that no child is allowed to fall by the wayside. A question a teacher might ask is "Today how can I help a child I haven't been reaching to have a *successful experience* with language?" Such success usually depends on having clearly in mind the following factors:

1. The nature of the child's strength or difficulty
2. The way you made this assessment
3. The steps you are taking to continue to improve the child's process and performance

Few if any teachers can make the decisions involved without the help of some form of measurement. And emphatically, assessment does not always have to concern immediately observable, overt behavior or objective tests of low levels of thought.

There is nothing quite as apt to expose fuzzy-headed thinking as trying to set down goals and their assessment. With *clarified thought,* teachers sometimes uncover a wide gap between objectives desired and what actually happens in their classroom. Once the gap is uncovered, teachers can close it. For example, if a teacher's goal includes creative problem solving and/or critical listening, but children never get a chance to do either, the classroom has a gap the teacher can close.

A second reason to be aware of assessment and evaluation involves the larger context, which goes beyond the classroom but has an important impact on it. Many national, state, and local roles of evaluation ultimately affect the English language arts teacher, who *needs to keep informed.* Evaluation remains one of the most characteristic traits of our educational system and shapes much of what we ultimately do in our classrooms. Standardized testing for evaluation continues to be at the center of public controversy.

The impact of evaluation is so great in part because of its powerful and multifaceted role in the following: (1) the sorting of individuals for placement (sometimes highly inappropriately); (2) certification of student achievement; (3) teacher certification and recertification; (4) evaluation of the effectiveness of educational programs and of teacher effectiveness for merit pay; and (5) appeals for educational reform stressing standardized reading and writing test results as evidence (Linn, 1986). One of the best-known appeals for reform and for excellence is *A Nation at Risk: The Imperative for Educational Reform* (National Commission on Excellence in Education, 1983).

Issues of appropriate test roles, use, and interpretation, however, remain unresolved (Linn, 1986). Some critics see tests and testing as an example of science and technology run amok; others argue that they offer a hope of fairness in democratic treatment of all members of society. Thus criticism coexists with widespread demands for increased reliance on tests. As professionals, teachers need to develop a supportable point of view and keep informed about this larger context (Wigdor & Garner, 1982).

Assessment Compared to Evaluation

An understanding of the distinction between the terms *evaluation* and *assessment* is necessary to an appreciation of much of the rest of the chapter.

Evaluation When we *evaluate,* we make a value judgment of children's language development—"far above average," "failing," or "someplace in between"—that is, in comparison with other groups. We evaluate to make decisions about grading, placement, promotion or retention, and program and teaching effectiveness.

Assessment Alternatively, when we *assess,* we offer confirmation and help to students in their learning as opposed to impersonal evaluation (Dillon, 1987). Assessment can be a nonthreatening, helpful activity with which you and the children feel comfortable. With assessment, we make a specific, objective diagnosis based on observation of children's patterns, say, of language use (for example, "I see you have started to use dialogue in your stories"). Assessment, relatively free of controlling values, can form the basis for evaluation. The reader may look back in this book and note that in every chapter the term *assessment* has been carefully used, rarely the term *evaluation,* unless that was exactly what was meant.

A teacher making an assessment relies on observations of individual students, both as audience member and as participant. The teacher-assessor puts it all together—the child's content and the selected form, the child's process and product—be it improvised drama, poetic dialogue, or character sketch (Searle & Dillon, 1980).

Evaluation based on assessment can be more long-range and developmentally oriented, and more on target for children and their education. We will see such assessment operating in our opening scene. You might consider interviewing teachers in your community to see how they assess and what kinds of evaluation take place. You can ask them about how they deal with assessment and evaluation in their conferences with children and with parents. *After reading this chapter, try role-playing alternative ways of assessing with peers.* (Recall, e.g., Chapter 3 on assessing listening, Chapter 4 on assessing oral language, and Chapter 5 on assessing drama.)

Large-scale evaluation can be impersonal and can lead to negative labeling and unfortunate tracking; it can be fatalistic and unhelpful instead of promoting continuous progress. Because it is discrete and oriented toward a final product, testing can depress all the complexities that go into being a language user—a writer, reader, listener, and speaker. Any evaluation system functioning without knowledge of individual children will tend to ignore process and operate on a skills model with minutiae of mechanics. If the context is not taken into account, the evaluation may be invalid (Wilkinson, 1983; Samway, 1987). Context includes the range of behaviors and the child's multiple roles in the language he or she produces.

Examine your own state minimum competency tests for children in the language arts areas. You will probably find little or no correspondence between the total language arts curriculum as described in this textbook and such evaluative measures. We need to unite assessment, evaluation, and learning in the best interests of children.

Grading Grading, quantified reporting, is a common school practice, representing a teacher's summary estimate of a student's work. It is a composite of value judgments. Teachers may consider factors such as ability, improvement, effort, and attitude in relation to goals and objectives. Grading compositions that children write with joy makes the task wearisome for you and fearful for the children. There is no need to mark with a red pencil all over a child's composition or give it a grade. Assessment does not have to be a frightening, terminal experience for children. The brief, cozy, individual writing conference keeps a teacher from adopting a laissez-faire attitude of just letting children's writing grow like a weed. A conference can keep the assessment sensitive and emphasize constructive self-competency and motivation, yet encourage the risk taking that is so important to composition. We saw in Chapter 8 that there is much more to assess in composition than just spelling, punctuation, and usage as measured by some objective test.

In the glossary in the *Instructor's Manual* for this text is found expanded definitions of the term *test*, including a distinction between standardized and teacher-made tests, and also the terms *reliability* and *validity*. These definitions contain some crucial concepts for a well-rationalized point of view useful to a reader who is not already in command of them. The glossary also has a list of widely used standardized tests in connection with that term.

Context of the Scene

The following opening scene previews and illustrates many of the major concepts in this chapter. In particular, it highlights ongoing assessment of a teacher's own language arts program, day-to-day activities for language use and development. It also sets the stage for a creative problem-solving analysis to follow, and thoughts on communicating the needs of your children to "significant others," or to your principal.

Pat was a student teacher in the opening scene of Chapter 14 and is now a teacher of a combined second- and third-grade class. Pat has been capitalizing on children's natural interest in dinosaurs. The unit was prompted by some recent discoveries, the children's interest, a promising series of activities designed to integrate and develop many communication processes and skills, and a parental interest in excellence.

Randy, Katy, and Matthew have been listening to a teacher-prepared tape that has directed them to some previewed books (these books are listed under "Dinosaur Books for Children" in the reference section for Chapter 15). Teacher and children have participated cooperatively in some goal setting, a prerequisite for the program and learning assessment. Randy and his group want to know about the dinosaur finds closest to their home town. We will see how assessment works in this classroom, and how it may or may not relate to evaluation in the interests of children. Examples in this scene can serve as suggestions for the reader's classroom.

Pat is trying to implement learnings from supervisors, instructors, courses, and all the teachers visited in the other opening scenes of this book. To add to the challenge, the state and school are committed to mandated competency testing of students with a standardized instrument. Pat recalls the teacher's function from Chapter 1: to know the *why, who, what,* and *where,* and to let all of these understandings flow into the *how* of teaching. (Pat calls it the 4 *W*'s & *H* approach.) Following Pat's encouraging progress, you will see a person who has learned to be not too much a teacher and to let children construct much of their own learning. Pat has additionally learned that the parents' educational role is to be the child's first teacher and to know what's going on in school, being helpful and welcomed by the teacher to the enterprise. Such a communicative relationship sets the stage and holds hope for assessment and evaluation *in the interests of children.*

OPENING SCENE: How Is Large-Scale Testing Like a Dinosaur?

Pat has called for a time of silent reading. All the students are reading books or articles related to their present projects. Pat is meeting with students individually for reading conferences, and has just asked Randy to come over to the teacher's desk.

PAT: How is your book reading coming along?

RANDY: OK.

PAT: Have you been able to find out what you wanted to know about dinosaurs?

RANDY: I guess . . . I don't know.

Pat wonders if Randy is having trouble comprehending the book he has chosen. Perhaps he needs an easier book, or perhaps Pat can just help with a trouble spot.

PAT: Read me something from your dinosaur book. How about this page?

RANDY: [Reading] This dino-sa—uh, dinosaur—had a very large ja—jah? It must have looked a . . . away . . . ar-ful . . . oh-ful—what does this say?—to any smaller animal. Its name was "ty-ran-no-sa-rus." I don't get it.

As Randy reads the page, Pat notices that there are several words with *aw* or *au* giving him trouble. The teacher decides to help him with this troublesome vowel diphthong.

PAT: Randy, I've noticed you had trouble with this word—*jaw*—and this word—*awful*—and this one, *tyrannosaurus*. *Au* and *aw* usually make the sound /aw/, as when your mother wants you to do something, and you don't want to do it, and you say, "*Aw,* gee, Mom, do I have to?" [Randy smiles.] Let's make a list of words with these letters. [Pat gets a strip of paper from a stack on the desk, and writes *au* and *aw* at the top.] Let's think of some words we could put here. For example, *jaw* and *awful.* Can you think of any others?

RANDY: How about tyrannosau rus?

PAT: Good. What else? [They continue with some words and together think of some that were not in the book.] We've got a great list. Read the words back to me. [Randy does so.] This list is for you to keep. [Pat gets a work sheet from the teacher's file of different exercises to help students, as needed, with different diphthongs and consonant clusters.] Here's a sheet for you to work on later. It will give you practice and help you review what we just talked about. I think you can figure out what to do by reading the instructions. Bring it back to me by tomorrow morning. Now, do you want to continue reading this book, or do you think you need an easier one?

RANDY: I want to keep on trying with this one. I really like the pictures. I'll get help if I can't figure something out myself.

PAT: Good for you. I noticed you could read all those tricky words with *fl, cl,* and *bl* now. Your reading is really improving. We'll talk more about your book at our next conference.

After reading, the children are allowed to meet together in small groups to discuss what they have read and to assess how they are coming along in their projects and questions. Randy, Katy, and Matthew are talking about their dinosaur books and trying to see if anyone has found out where the closest dinosaur find is.

RANDY: There was a dinosaur found in Seymour, Texas! It says so right here on page 18 of my book. Now I wanna know about more . . . if there's more fossils closer to here, to where we live.

MATTHEW: So maybe we could even go see the place!

RANDY: [The "researcher"] Now this book, *Dinosaurs of North America,* has a list in the back. "Discoveries by location." There are six different ones in Texas listed. *But* it doesn't tell which city.

KATY: And Cotolosaur in Seymour, Texas, isn't even mentioned in that book.

MATTHEW: Look at the book's date, 1981, it was even written after the one that mentions Seymour, Texas, that 1966 one. I think we need some help that books don't give.

PAT: [To self, edging closer] *Matthew has certainly been picking up on that material we had stressing importance of dates for references—one of our framework objectives. I'll make a tally mark for that one.*

KATY: Yeah, we could talk to a person at the Dallas Museum of Natural History. Didn't our teacher say there was a palo . . . palo . . .

PAT: [No longer able to resist moving in] A paleontologist. Yes, you could communicate with him. You could write him a letter, after you've read a bit more. [Assessing] You've listened, read, and learned quite a lot this last week. You may be getting ready to set up an interview. [To self] *What a good chance for some useful listening/speaking/ reading/and writing.* [Goes to another work group.]

RANDY: [Continuing] How do we do it? How do we get our question into a letter?

KATY: How do we start the letter?

MATTHEW: Well, we start it with "Dear" . . .

KATY: Dear Mr. Paleontologist: . . . Then what?

RANDY: We could say, "We want to know the closest . . . the closest dinosaur find to our city."

KATY: But we can't just pop out with our question. We have to lead up to it.

MATTHEW: Let him know we've looked in a lot of books. We tried to find out ourselves. How would you say that? How to a paleon*li* go this?

KATY: Paleon*to*logist.

MATTHEW: I'm not sure we say, "Dear Mr. Paleo-whatever–it–is" at the beginning of the letter. It sounds funny to me.

RANDY: Would our language arts textbook tell us how?

KATY: Maybe, but let's take it to "writer's chair" next time consultation groups meet. You get good ideas there.

MATTHEW: We could ask our teacher what to say now.

RANDY: Let's try to figure it out ourselves first.

KATY: We can go ahead and set up the interview in a week or so by phone. Then we'll know how to say it . . . how to write the letter better.

RANDY: In the meantime we can continue reading and thinking up questions. I think this book *The Smallest Dinosaurs* has the best pictures. My dad's bought me one of these books for my birthday. You should see the picture my little brother in kindergarten drew about it. How would you like to have one of these small ones for a pet!

KATY: That's a good question to ask the paleontologist! "If they came back, which might make the best pet?"

RANDY: "And why!"

MATTHEW: [Speaking to Pat, who has moved back around to their group again] Could we please look at the calendar with you, and set a date for inviting the pale . . .

KATY: Paleontologist to come talk to our class—

RANDY: About dinosaur finds in Texas.

MATTHEW: We've already got two good questions for him. But we don't know how to get started with the letter. Dear what? What comes after "Dear"?

KATY: Then do we just put the questions? Or do we have to write something else first?

RANDY: If we could talk to him on the phone, we'd know better how to write him a letter.

PAT: I like your thinking, your problem solving. Let's see our school calendar [frowns, wrinkles nose, shakes head]. I'm really sorry. I didn't realize it was this close. How could it be this close! [The three children ask what Pat is talking about.] For the next four weeks it's time for preparation for the state testing. The scores for the district were down last year and the principal said we will be practicing for the test starting next week until the testing is over. Listening, speaking, reading, writing, and thinking about dinosaurs will have to wait while we do the test preparation exercises. We'll have to close our centers tomorrow. [To self] *Just as teaching was really getting to be rewarding! I wonder if that paleontologist needs an assistant. Well, anyway, now I've got to get skills-oriented, multiple-choice-oriented for this testing. I know this group of children doesn't need all that test practice. I wonder if I dare risk approaching my principal about this.*

Analysis of the Scene

Perhaps you can see yourself in the character of this teacher. In this scene Pat used ongoing, continuous assessment in the interests of the children. Teachers sometimes think of assessment as occurring after instruction, but we can see that it takes place before and during instruction.

Pat also showed ability in monitoring decoding skills (*au* in words for Randy). The reader has probably met the idea of individual reading conferences before and perhaps even role-played them. This new teacher also seems to have some grasp of observational techniques for assessment of higher-order thinking skills, such as reading for meaning and to learn. Pat confirmed the children's autonomy in problem solving. Indirectly, the intent of this scene was to show how a teacher can guide children into becoming fully participating members of our democratic society—where voluntary assessment of self and others is essential to its success.

This new teacher was creating an environment in which children could succeed. Parents supported their children's progress ("My dad's bought me one of these books"), and the children commended each other for their strengths ("That's a good question"; "You get good ideas there"). Finally, the teacher had some grasp of the abuse of testing when children are forced to spend large parts of their instructional year in preparation for state evaluation, whether they need to or not, wasting irretrievable time when they could have been learning something more significant.

Figure 15.1 shows an overview representation of instructional planning and assessment with a creative problem-solving perspective. Start in the center of the spiral with problem-solving step 1, and move outward.

Figure 15.2 (p. 516) gives details and examples for Figure 15.1. The first column shows the progression of activity and assessment. The next column is more descriptive of the first, and the third column gives examples, mainly of the composing process in both receptive and expressive language depicted in the opening scene.

Approaching Administrators   What about Pat's dilemma, depicted at the end of the scene? Did arbitrary treatment and large-scale testing close down communication and ruin the rest of the year?

After the children had gone home, Pat sat down in the empty classroom, dejected, worried, and thoughtful. *"What were some of the things my college supervisor said?"* mused Pat. *" 'Tension can lead to creativity'; 'Keep giving information'; 'Ask questions that get you*

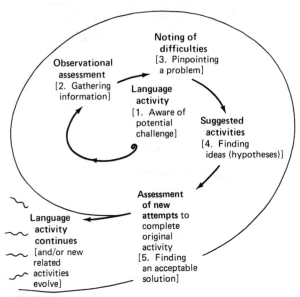

Figure 15.1 Overview of five steps in instructional planning and assessment: problem-solving perspective.

what you need'; 'In a democracy, we don't need to deal arbitrarily with each other'; 'As well-trained teachers, as professionals, we have special expertise'; 'Find a related short article and put it on your principal's desk with a note asking the principal to read the article and discuss it with you.'"

"Well, it had better be a short paragraph in this case," grumbled Pat. *"Maybe . . . I could bring in some photos, a bit of videotape. I should have started that newsletter the supervisor talked about . . . I know! I'll bring in our scrapbook to show my principal all the learning. 'Keep giving information.' That supervisor did have some good ideas. I'll be creative. We shall see."*

We leave Pat for a moment, but will return. We need a bit of perspective to put the dilemma into further focus.

Perspectives from the Past First, we need to realize that the fundamentals of the most widely used standardized tests have changed little during the last half-century. Advances in psychology, statistics, and supporting technology have resulted in few if any major changes in test items appearing on widely used ability and achievement tests. Any advances have led to few if any changes in uses or interpretation of scores. Little or nothing has been done to solve the problems of limitations and misuses of test results rooted in status quo and administrative convenience (Linn, 1986).

The rallying cry in the 1960s and 1970s addressed questions of equity and the disadvantaged. Finally managing to respond, testing identified children eligible for services and required the evaluation of programs designed to help them catch up in communication and other skills. During the latter half of the 1970s, however, a new movement gained strength. The states began requiring some form of minimum competency testing. Popular opinion that many graduates lacked basic skills led legislators to turn to tests as enforcement, with minimum performance standards (e.g., in reading and writing). By the early 1980s, equity's push had receded and "excellence," even beyond "basic skills," became the new

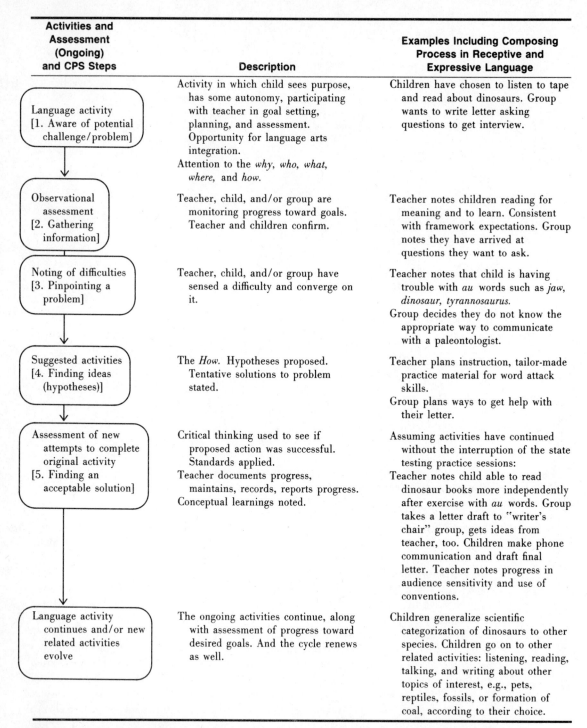

Activities and Assessment (Ongoing) and CPS Steps	Description	Examples Including Composing Process in Receptive and Expressive Language
Language activity [1. Aware of potential challenge/problem]	Activity in which child sees purpose, has some autonomy, participating with teacher in goal setting, planning, and assessment. Opportunity for language arts integration. Attention to the *why, who, what, where,* and *how.*	Children have chosen to listen to tape and read about dinosaurs. Group wants to write letter asking questions to get interview.
Observational assessment [2. Gathering information]	Teacher, child, and/or group are monitoring progress toward goals. Teacher and children confirm.	Teacher notes children reading for meaning and to learn. Consistent with framework expectations. Group notes they have arrived at questions they want to ask.
Noting of difficulties [3. Pinpointing a problem]	Teacher, child, and/or group have sensed a difficulty and converge on it.	Teacher notes that child is having trouble with *au* words such as *jaw, dinosaur, tyrannosaurus.* Group decides they do not know the appropriate way to communicate with a paleontologist.
Suggested activities [4. Finding ideas (hypotheses)]	The *How.* Hypotheses proposed. Tentative solutions to problem stated.	Teacher plans instruction, tailor-made practice material for word attack skills. Group plans ways to get help with their letter.
Assessment of new attempts to complete original activity [5. Finding an acceptable solution]	Critical thinking used to see if proposed action was successful. Standards applied. Teacher documents progress, maintains, records, reports progress. Conceptual learnings noted.	Assuming activities have continued without the interruption of the state testing practice sessions: Teacher notes child able to read dinosaur books more independently after exercise with *au* words. Group takes a letter draft to "writer's chair" group, gets ideas from teacher, too. Children make phone communication and draft final letter. Teacher notes progress in audience sensitivity and use of conventions.
Language activity continues and/or new related activities evolve	The ongoing activities continue, along with assessment of progress toward desired goals. And the cycle renews as well.	Children generalize scientific categorization of dinosaurs to other species. Children go on to other related activities: listening, reading, talking, and writing about other topics of interest, e.g., pets, reptiles, fossils, or formation of coal, according to their choice.

Figure 15.2 Ongoing, integrated assessment incorporating a creative problem-solving (CPS) perspective in instructional planning in the language arts.

slogan. Higher-order skills (e.g., critical thinking) came to the forefront. But large-scale testing is still lumbering along decidedly behind.

Throughout its history of trying to respond to varying emphases, testing still is far from being used consistently *in the interests of the children tested*. Such an emphasis is by far the most important. Testing in the language arts needs to be linked to developmentally appropriate instruction for children. It needs to show what independent young communicators can do, will do, really need to do, enjoy doing, and may do.

With this perspective from the past to the present, next consider the opening scene's subtitle, "How Is Large-Scale Testing Like a Dinosaur?"

How Is Large-Scale Testing Like a Dinosaur?   One problem shared by dinosaurs and large-scale evaluation seems to be slowness in adapting to changes in "climate"—physical climate probably in the case of the dinosaurs' extinction, social climate in the case of testing's inappropriateness for children. Large-scale evaluation seems too lumbering (like the brontosaurus) in responding to rallying calls, and by the time it finally catches up, there is a newer, more imperative rallying call. Like the dinosaurs, large-scale evaluation will probably be in existence a long, long time, struggling to perpetuate itself or those adults who profit from its employment. It is to be hoped that such cumbersome testing will evolve into a better partnership with the classroom environment and its assessment of developmental learning *in the interests of children*.

Also like the dinosaurs, large-scale evaluation takes many forms—from the horny-plated IQ tests, well protected with their studies of reliability and validity, to the huge population-normed standardized language tests, with a gigantic "body" of items, "long neck" reaching far across the nation, and relatively tiny "head and brain" for measuring the higher mental processes. You may be able to add to the dinosaur analogy as we turn to two important teacher competencies with respect to both evaluation and assessment: (1) knowledge of uses and abuses of testing instruments and procedures, and (2) use of tools in the classroom for describing students' progress in English.

USES AND ABUSES OF TESTING INSTRUMENTS AND PROCEDURES

Recall that one of the primary objectives of teacher preparation in the language arts is to know about uses and abuses of testing instruments. Consider *uses* first.

Uses

There are some appropriate applications of information from standardized tests. School districts may find the overview of students' skills and their employment of language conventions examined by objective instruments useful. If large-scale evaluation can reflect the goals of the language arts curriculum, it can help. Such goals are: listening and speaking that are interactive, vital, and meaningful; in-depth reading of literature; and extended discourse of written composition. Large-scale tests *can* integrate the language arts, as we saw in the British Assessment of Performance Units for listening/speaking in Chapter 4 and reading/writing examples in Chapter 7. Literature tests can focus on students' meanings, not just on formal features of plot and character. Tests can be designed to measure not simply weaknesses or failures in ability to write, but also students' strengths and accomplishments, thus giving direction for the teacher by identifying what the students have learned and what progress they have made.

Objective multiple-choice tests have some attractive features. They can provide broad indicators of students' performance and detail on particular skills such as listening, and they are easier to administer, less expensive, and more quickly scored. But they can measure only a small part of what children have learned and understood, what they can do, will do, and may do.

Alternatives to objective testing provide more *formative* data. That is, they form, inform, and re-form the program rather than fragment learnings into isolated elements (California State Department of Education, 1987). *Preassessment* helps a teacher to individualize instruction from the beginning, to confirm or modify already-chosen objectives. *Formative* assessment occurring during the learning process helps a teacher check a child's progress, decide what the child's next step might be, and guide instructional revision of material, activity, and sequence. (How well is Randy learning to read, and what might we change to improve his learning?) *Summative* assessment looks reflectively at the completed instructional sequence or program and helps the teacher with comparing, continuing, terminating, and grading for a finished unit. (How well did the child/children learn to monitor, analyze, and judge information by the end of the dinosaur unit?)

Keeping *purpose* in mind during assessment and evaluation is important. For example, the method used for assessing oral language appropriate for students learning a new skill may not be appropriate for evaluating students at the end of the year. One trend we noted in Chapter 3, for example, was to select assessment tasks reflecting a variety of settings (e.g., one to many, small group, and mass media). Another approach has been to focus communication assessment on varied purposes—to describe, inform, persuade, and solve problems (e.g., as in Chapter 8 on written composition). A third trend has been to focus on basic competencies needed for everyday life—giving and receiving directions or basic information for emergency situations (Rubin & Mead, 1985).

Abuses

Because the results of objective, standardized tests are subject to misuse, their employment demands caution. A crucial caution is to avoid relying solely on *one* type of testing instrument and/or testing procedure; and to make sure that there is a *match* between the professionally recommended language arts curriculum and the measure. Teachers need to be aware of the limitations as well as the uses of test data. They need to be aware of the negative impact of tests on curriculum and instruction. For example, the teaching and testing of reading subskills alone may interfere with students' understanding of a whole work (Anderson et al., 1984). Those features of composition most easy to measure reliably (the surface conventions of spelling, punctuation, and usage) tend to be those having the least to do with writers' true competence. A big dose of conventions in test-taking preparation and testing robs children of their ability to make and connect assertions, penetrate a subject, discover lines of reasoning, construct imaginative insights, and think well with language (Knoblauch & Brannon, 1984).

Even test publishers themselves bemoan the unwise misuse of the so-called *grade-level-equivalent score.* Some teachers assume—and tell parents, children, and others—that these tests provide a precise yardstick of each student's progress to points above or below grade level, for example, in reading. Such measurement designed for groups, not individuals—is imprecise. Moreover, because children differ so widely in classrooms, it is still nonsense to specify what a "fourth-grade" student will be able to do, say, in reading.

Furthermore, standardized, norm-referenced, paper-and-pencil tests are usually not appropriate for determining growth in interests, attitudes, appreciations, and values—the third goal in each framework for the various language arts chapters in this book. A highly important kind of learning for teachers to develop is students' *willingness* to initiate language activity. Again, such attitudinal learning has been stressed in the goals frameworks for listening, speaking, composition, drama, and critical and creative thinking in this book. Laughter, tears, and signs of embarrassment may give better evidence of affective listening and reading than any objective test yet designed.

In addition, test results are only as useful as teachers are *skillful in interpreting* them. (Ask: What do the results of those reading tests really mean?) Abuses of test results come from a misunderstanding of what the test measures, an exaggerated belief in the "truth" and infallibility of tests, or an unwarranted use of results to predict a child's future achievement (Lundsteen & Tarrow, 1981).

Experienced teachers have long understood the inadequacy of test scores for identifying the multitude of dimensions of students' success in communication. They have learned to rely on many other "tools of the trade"—as follows.

TOOLS OF THE TRADE: ASSESSMENT TECHNIQUES

Teachers need to become competent in applying a number of assessment techniques, including the use of individual conferences, for determining and reporting student performance. Chapter 8 on composition dealt with the writing conference, also mentioning holistic scoring. Let's examine some more informal means of assessment.

Informal Ways of Describing Student Progress

The complex nature of language acquisition and the multiple elements of language use demand the need for assessment tools and experiences beyond the limits of objective tests. Teachers need to be proficient at "child watching" and other informal ways of describing student progress in all language processes. The most useful information for assessing students' growth in the English language arts comes directly from students' classroom encounters with literature and writing, speaking, and listening activities, as was the case in the opening scene.

Informal assessment in English language arts needs to include frequent observation of children's responses to their own and their peers' communication (Chapters 3–8, 10, 13). Included are the teacher's own more formal assessments of children's participation and responses indicative of objectives identified in the curriculum. Teachers need to observe and record children's language use and learnings continually. Records of home visits, made at any time in narrative or diary form, are also appropriate.

Goals of Informal Assessment for the Language Arts Program   Goals of language arts informal assessment include:

1. Chances to observe students' broadening, deepening attitudes and understandings of literature and its values related to their own lives as they read widely and in depth (Chapter 9).
2. An ability to handle a variety of writing tasks with confidence, insight, clarity, liveliness, and ease. (Chapter 8 and other chapters throughout this book offer illustrations.)

BOX 15.1 Informal Classroom Assessment Ideas for the Language Arts Program

Literature and reading

☐ Monitor student understanding of a literary work during small-group or class-wide *discussion* (activity book, Chapter 9).

☐ Examine depth of understanding through improvisational *drama* based on literature, choral reading, or reader's theater (Chapter 5).

☐ Observe older students' use of the *vocabulary* of literary analysis, demonstrating growth during literary discussion and writing (activity book, Chapter 9).

☐ Note students' writing of *original endings* to literary works, revealing students' understanding of the work and their creativity (Chapter 8).

☐ Analyze a student's assuming the role of a literary character and writing an *in-character letter*, revealing insight into the character's values and motives (Chapter 9).

☐ Look at a student's rewriting of a piece in a *different genre* (e.g., a poem as narrative fiction or a story as a play, reflecting understanding of meaning, tone, character, and format (Chapter 8).

☐ Tally the student's *free-choice reading* of books, magazines, and newspapers, indicating reading as an activity of choice and pleasure.

☐ Observe a child's *taste development*, movement from predictable plots to more complex stories in free reading, indicating intellectual growth.

☐ Tally or diagram *variation in types* of material read, indicating the student's confidence in a wide variety of reading purposes (number, quality, and types of materials students read).

---

3. Facility with critical and thoughtful listening and speaking tasks. (Chapters 3, 4, 5, and 6 offer examples.)
4. A range of thinking skills including summarizing, analysis, interpretation, and problem solving. (Chapters 1, 10, and 13 give special emphasis here.)

All of these goals enable students to participate fully in a democratic society. Effective assessment focuses on identifying the extent to which programs have accomplished these goals.

Categorized Examples of Informal Assessment   Box 15.1 presents some categorized examples of informal classroom assessment for the language arts program (California State Department of Education, 1987). Related chapters from this text and its activity book are indicated. (Some items are elaborated upon later.)

Consider turning Box 15.1 into a *checklist* for keeping a watch on your own informal assessment in your classroom program. Keys to success in your language arts program (in the best interests of children) are informal ways of assessment that enhance student motivation, unifying both the testing and the learning process.

Oral language

☐ Analyze audiotape or videotape *recordings* of children's oral reading or other oral language samples made several times a year (also see assessment ideas in Chapters 3, 4, 5, 6, and 7).

Written composition

☐ Make notes about *work samples*, pieces worked on both in and out of class, giving children time to reexamine and revise as they grapple with understanding and communicating (Chapters 2, 8, 7, 10, and 13).

☐ Tally *frequency* of student writing.

☐ Tally *variety* of composition—autobiographical, narrative, persuasive.

☐ Report extent to which and in what ways student writing is *"published"* (Chapter 8 and activity book).

All the language arts

☐ Uncover students' understandings and problems during *individual consultation* (Chapters 3, 4, 6, 7, 8, 10, 13, and 14).

☐ Note results of *questioning* by teacher to focus on children's learnings, and by peers for each other. Look for their going beyond low-level "yes" or "no" answers where high-thinking processes can be observed (Chapters 4, 6, and 10 and activity book).

☐ Record extent of positive *parent support* and participation in language arts activities (reading programs, language fairs).

☐ Collect information about student *attitudes* recorded on checklists, in anecdotes, self-reports, and other observations.

Pat's Triumph   Now is an appropriate time to reveal that Pat, the teacher in the opening scene, did get to keep the center and invite the paleontologist. Why? Pat had the help of a combination of the following: information from class activities, bits of information slipped in from the preceding section on abuses for a rationale, some informal assessment using some of the tools just described, and some creative problem solving. We often have more freedom than we think we have (or sometimes are willing to take responsibility for, work for, and admit). Let's take a closer look at some of those informal tools Pat used. The first is *self-report*.

Self-Report   Self-assessment in one's use of language arts is important to anyone, including children. The self-report also gives the teacher valuable information about student interests and feelings. Examples of questions eliciting self-reports follow:

Questions for Eliciting Self-Report on Writing
- *What was the reason for your writing?*
- *Who was your audience?*

- *What do you think was the best part of your work?*
- *What choices did you make?*
- *What problems did you have when writing and what did you do?*
- *What would you do differently?*
- *What is your goal for next time you write?*

Chapter 6 developed ideas on peer reports designed to let children constructively help one another. The activity for the reader in Appendix 15A is another example of a self-report. Of course, bear in mind that children will increase in their ability to report on themselves and to plan goals as they increase in age and in the number of opportunities they have had to consider their own progress. Even kindergartners, however, can begin to gain valuable experience in self-reporting if one does not expect too much in the way of an abstract, global response.

Observation Scales and Structural Approaches with Rating Systems   Each chapter on a language art in this book has presented examples of observation scales. Each framework of goals can be turned into an observation scale. A scale for children on creative problem solving with descriptive examples is found in Chapter 15 of the activity book. With respect to assessing speaking skills, two methods are common: an unobtrusive observational approach and a structured approach. In the *observational* approach, the student's behavior is observed covertly and assessed unobtrusively. In the *structured* approach, the student is asked to perform one or more specific oral communication tasks. The teacher then evaluates the performance. The teacher can administer the task in a one-on-one setting or in a group or class setting. Either way, recall from Chapter 4 that students need to feel they are communicating meaningful content to a real audience with topics they can easily talk about or on which they can collect information (Rubin & Mead, 1985).

Both informal observational and structured approaches use a variety of rating systems. A *holistic* rating (covered in Chapter 8) captures a general impression of the student's performance. A *primary trait* score assesses the student's ability to achieve a specific communication purpose. An example might be a persuasive purpose for speaking, with argument supported by related, well-founded reasons. *Analytic* scales (also presented in Chapter 8) capture the student's performance in varied aspects of communication: content, organization, style, logic, delivery, and usage. Rating systems may describe varying degrees of competence along a scale of one to ten or may simply indicate the presence or absence of a characteristic (Rubin & Mead, 1985).

A third and final example in this structured observational category is the two-pole (or *bipolar*) assessment. It permits a wide-ranging, holistic view of a working system, say the quality of classroom discussion, so that teachers and students can see what problems need to be worked out. Two applications of bipolar assessment are to see whether a specific activity is included in class discussion (e.g., use of written resources) and to determine where that activity fits between two poles (e.g., highly direct use of written resources through a range to indirect use of written resources). The teacher observes to see where the classroom discussion fits in the range between the extremes and can mark it with an *X* along a line between the two—when the category applies (Alvermann, Dillon, & O'Brien, 1987).

For example, a teacher who sees material from a reference book used directly to verify a point during discussion would mark an *X* toward the "direct use" side of the continuum. Teachers can then make a profile among several categories examined, listing observed current practices on the left and possible activities to try on the right. For example, if the teacher observes during discussion that use of the category "written resources" is merely mentioned in passing, if at all, the teacher might list that category and by it write a suggested solution. The suggestion might be giving students specific discussion guides referring to specific resources or texts where they can find verification for material being discussed (Alvermann, Dillon, & O'Brien, 1987). See an example in Chapter 15 of the activity book.

Conclusions

Teacher development and use of varied observational skills is important for several reasons. They tell much about what a child has learned or accomplished in language and thought; they supplement standardized, objective test results by providing insights into the causes of behavior and emotional states that elude formal measures. Observations made by children, teachers, parents, and others each have a slightly different perspective and setting. The trained teacher can use records of observations to design more appropriate teaching *in the interest of individual children.* Table 15.1 on page 524 lists informal observational techniques just described and poses questions that each technique can answer. Updated assessment ideas remind us of the motto "If you are educated today, and quit learning tomorrow, you are uneducated the day after." (See the activity book for informal assessment ideas that are *fun* to do.)

ASSESSMENT OF TEACHERS

Professionally oriented teachers are concerned with self-assessment. In most instances, teachers are also evaluated by others—parents, children, colleagues, supervisors, and other people appointed by the district. Consider each in turn. The aim of this section is to give you some ideas and encourage your own creativity in cooperating and interacting with administrators and other teachers. (Also see Appendix 15A, a self-report device, if you have not already done so.)

Assessment by Parents

An informal network of parents usually shares information with each other about teachers in the school. Criteria sometimes reflect personal qualities and sometimes deal with motivational technique. Frequent and open communication between teacher and parents helps to increase the likelihood that parental judgments are based on *accurate* information. Try dialogue journals with *parents.*

Assessment by Children

While older children may tend to assess teachers directly, younger children may transmit assessment indirectly. Older children often share information with each other ("When she says something, she *means* it!"). Young children may transmit information about teachers to others in less direct ways ("Why did the teacher make Nick write it 100 times?"). A teacher can notice the assessment implicit in some of the following child behaviors.

Children's Indirect Assessment Behavior Regarding Teachers
- Do the children generally accept and use your suggestions in a writing conference and not view them as personal attacks?

Table 15.1 METHODS OF OBSERVING CHILDREN AND QUESTIONS ANSWERED FOR THE LANGUAGE ARTS

Technique	Questions Answered
Diary record	How does communication go each day for you as a teacher? How would you describe the language arts centers or classroom environment today?
Anecdotal record	What specific incidents are especially illustrative of the student communicator or the language program development in your educational setting? What critical incidents regarding progress in spelling, handwriting, and composition can you add to the file?
Selective record	What aspects, e.g., of the writing routines, are continually observable? How does a particular child behave in a given language routine or center from day to day? What does a tallying of language arts centers selected suggest?
Behavior scales, ratings, and checklists	How well developed is a child's fine muscle development for writing? How well (measured on a continuum or in terms of scaled behaviors) can the child solve a problem in regard to reference/library skills? Read directions? These scales may be completed by teachers, parents, and other program participants to give added perspectives. (See Chapter 8 for examples of scales concerning composition.)
Developmental histories	What can others tell you about a child's early language development that will assist you in understanding the child's behavior in the present?
Case studies	What formal and informal measures and records can help you create the most complete picture of a child's language development? How does a complete profile of this child's literature-reading choices for this year (compared to last year's) contribute to the total picture?
Home visits by the teacher	Can your relationship with a child's parents and family enhance your work in the English language arts classroom? Who are the significant language-contributing people in the child's home life that you may never meet in the educational setting?
Cumulative records	What information have past teachers and school personnel gathered regarding language learnings of an individual child? What implications can you draw from the following: reading scores, handwriting samples, language experience stories dictated, scores on listening comprehension tests, hearing acuity, and auditory perception?

- Do the children seem to like to listen to your voice?
- Do they look to you as a language resource, initiating contact with you and showing trust?
- Are they eager to share experiences with you, to dictate them to you?

Assessment by Colleagues

Teachers sometimes gossip about children, parents, and colleagues—a crime for which it is difficult to fire them. But your colleagues can also be a source of constructive criticism and guidance. You can check the impression you have made on them by the way they respond to your opinions, suggestions, and offerings; by whether or not they seek you out; and by their willingness to share their ideas and negotiate with you.

If you have developed mutual trust and respect, you can ask a colleague to observe you at work in your classroom. You could use the problem-solving checklist for teachers in Figure 15.3 on pages 526 and 527 as you conduct a creative problem-solving discussion with your children. It is compatible with the teaching concepts developed in *how* sections throughout this book. A big lift can be welcoming each other into classrooms to observe *whole-language* strategies and share materials. Modeling and demonstrating, always an effective means for growth, can be particularly helpful for a beginning teacher.

Assessment by Supervisors and Other Administrative Appointees

Wherever you teach, you are likely to find systematic observation and assessment of teachers by their principals and supervisors. Some schools have a set format and set number of written observations each year. Most teachers, especially new ones, feel some anxiety over these assessments. A copy of the observational instrument is typically given to each teacher beforehand. Some teachers want to know in advance exactly when the observer will come; some would rather not know. Some locations honor preferences.

Some separate the observational function into two parts: (1) in-service growth and (2) job security. If the function is in-service growth, the observer is likely to be a consultant upon whom teachers feel free to call for help and inspiration. Some supervisors use checklists with items describing subject, materials, and grouping; strong and weak areas; classroom control; use of state-adopted reading materials; compliance with district policies; and suggestions and recommendations. Others prefer to write a narrative.

Some principals say that they value the following:

- Being made to feel welcome in the room
- Being regarded as resource persons for teachers
- A consistent positive attitude generally, and in particular toward suggestions
- A teacher's ability to continue the classwork without frequent explanations to the principal
- Use of effective teaching/learning strategies

How can a teacher, especially a new one, reduce anxiety about assessment? Plan carefully and keep "significant others" current about your language arts plans. In the classroom, stay as enthusiastic and as free from anxiety as possible. Since you are always doing your best in the interests of children, you do not need generally to do anything differently during a visit. What you lack in experience and wisdom can be made up for by

Observer and/or Coder _____ Date _____

Time _____

Context _____

Type(s) of problem(s) _____ Teacher (or other leader) _____

Item	*Line or Tape Numbers and/or Comments*
Readiness	
00.0 Warm-up	
01.1 Openness	
01.2 Clarification [of whatever the child(ren) is (are) trying to say]	
01.3 Risk encouragement	
01.4 Pacing behavior 01.4.1 Focusing and/or refocusing 01.4.2 Extending 01.4.3 Lifting	
Promotion of problem-solving process	
02.1 Introduces problem(s) and seeks facts and conditions	
02.2 Prompts memory and recall	
02.3 Problem clarification	
02.4 Missing-information search	
02.5 Hypothesis making, decisions encouraged	
02.6 Planning behavior, encouraged	
Reinforcement and confirmation	
03.1 Neutral reflection	
03.2 Summarizing (neutral)	
03.3 Confirmation of desirable behaviors that child may be unable to verbalize	
03.4 Traditional positive and vague verbal rewarding ("That's good")	
Transfer-seeking behavior	
04.1 Looks for transfer possibilities and makes this focus clear to children participating while seeking application	
04.2 Finds similar elements in two situations and points out	

Figure 15.3 Checklist of teacher behaviors regarding the guidance of young children's problem solving.

Control (negative behavior)

05.1   Gives content or principle, or fishes for it; takes autonomy away
        from the children; forgoes guiding the process and gets into
        (however nicely) telling the children what to think and say

Unclassifiable

06.1   Not related to problem solving; might be social courtesy comment,
        management of routine, or incoherent

Individualizing behaviors

07.1   Differentiates treatment of child because of special needs

Modeling

08.1   Models various desirable aspects of problem solving; intends to
        serve as a model to the children

Room for further comments: (e.g., regarding the interaction of teacher moves and child moves)

Figure 15.3 (Continued)

BOX 15.2 Some Ideas for Teacher Self-Assessment

1. Keep a *scrapbook* for the year and use it as a monthly and end-of-year reflection device, as did the teacher in the opening scene. (Ask yourself if you would like to have been a student in this classroom.)

2. Make *audiotapes* and *videotapes* of your interaction with your class or individual students covering each language arts area and literature. Analyze the tapes and make a prioritized list to work on (include your own verbal skill). Put your top *goal* on one side of a card; and write a vivid, detailed, and concrete word image of your achievement of that goal on the other side. Referring to this card monthly, add to and revise the first steps.

3. Use a *checklist(s)* for various teaching skills such as those given in this book and others.

4. Keep a *diary* of your experiences and reactions, stressing interesting challenges and problems and telling how you solved them.

5. Keep a list of things you *like* about yourself, your strengths, and ways in which you keep them strong.

6. Keep a list of experiences that made you feel uncomfortable. Try to reflect and understand why.

7. Weigh and use information obtained from *observations* of supervisors, principal, colleagues, friends, or children.

8. Integrate all this information to feed into your own self-observational and prioritized list mentioned in item 3 above.

your fresh enthusiasm. Invite your supervisor and/or principal to observe, and explain your rationale beforehand, if you are trying out relatively new ideas or want to communicate about your own style and techniques of teaching. Then there will be few if any surprises during the assessment visits (Lundsteen & Tarrow, 1981).

Self-Assessment

Professionally oriented teachers are their own critics as they strive to work in the best interests of children. Ultimately, *the evaluation that optimally serves the needs of students and the teachers who serve them is self-assessment.* Information from any other source is filtered through the teacher (or child), to be assimilated, accommodated, and acted upon. Some ideas for self-assessment are given in Box 15.2 on page 527.

SUMMARY

"The development of language is more like climbing a tree than like climbing a ladder. If we are too dogmatic, we may push at the wrong places, or miss unexpected advances which need immediate support."

Andrew Stibbs

"Children, it's state test-taking time. This time you *don't* help someone who's having trouble."

Saddened teacher

This chapter has stressed that the more we know about types and methods of evaluation and assessment, the more of a key role we can play and the greater is our voice in the planning and evaluation/assessment of our teaching programs. Be informed, be articulate, be idealistic *in the interests of children.* Too often, evaluation is stuck on at the end of instruction for the purpose of reporting to parents or significant others.

Assessment before instruction (preassessment) can help you and the children find out each individual's starting point. This *rationale* applies whether assessment is objective or subjective, whether it is based on attitude scale or on teacher judgment, and whether the performance observed is role-playing, discussion, or writing a poem. In light of the goals and objectives selected by you and the child, assessment can set reasonable levels of aspiration. When children achieve their goals, they feel successful and competent. In the long run, assessment before, during, and at the end of instruction can help answer questions about the child, the materials, and even the nature of learning and teaching language arts.

On the more negative side, *abuses* of evaluation stem from a preoccupation with the unimportant. We need to ask whether a particular goal and its measurement prepare children to make choices and help themselves as communicators. We need to make sure that crucial goals of process, function, and attitude do not get lost in multiple-choice trivia. A steady dose of right-or-wrong, multiple-choice types of questions and answers may unintentionally teach the child that responses showing learning come only in the form of certain predictable conclusions. Programs and tests that only accept one answer limit children's perception and inhibit rather than extend their thinking. For example, engagement in creative problem solving (CPS) along with inquiry in pursuit of written thought (composition) is the height of learning behavior. It is also an area of much incidental learning that is difficult for a teacher to measure and report. When working with CPS it may be impossible to predict completely what children will learn and when, but we need to tolerate this uncertainty. Since language arts is a complex, process-oriented, and subtly integrated curriculum, evaluation devices today treat this area crudely and are to be viewed with caution. We teach better than we formally test.

Tools of assessment include individual conferences, tapes revealing patterns of language and thought development, cumulative files of written work, quality and quantity of literature read by the children, tabulation of levels of response to media and cultural events, examination of process (not just product), and self-report. The tool of observation has served well a range of persons from the skilled and experienced practitioner to the distinguished researcher, and it can serve you and the children in your classroom.

Some key thoughts in this chapter follow.

Key Thoughts
- Assess whole, individual children with their integrated use of language arts, instead of just testing them as a group.
- Provide motivation instead of anxiety during each stage of learning, with assessment occurring before, during, and after instruction.
- Do assessment (diagnostic, formative, and summative; standardized, norm-referenced, or informal) in the interests of children, rather than cause them boredom, pain, and misclassification.
- Keep in mind that the true test of a program occurs daily in the classroom and in later life, and that grade-level competency is an inaccurate abstraction.
- Give many children a chance to assess their own effective communication through your commitment to oral language and its use in creative problem solving.
- Boil down assessment and evaluation to insight into how you and your children are learning and what you are gaining from one another.

Finally, language arts education is a social process in which humans interact with other humans in creative ways that are imperfectly measurable, unpredictable, and never finished. This creative spirit is as valuable to science and to our governmental institutions as it is to the humanities. Nurturing it with tender assessment is not only in the best interests of children, but in the best interests of us all.

EPILOGUE

This book started with the assertion that behind the processes and skills of communication lie those of thinking—thinking that can be successfully motivated and integrated by creative problem solving (see Figure 15.4, p. 530). This thinking represents higher levels of conceptualization.

We considered the language arts as a network, and pulled up each major knot (listening, speaking, reading, and writing) for closer scrutiny, focusing on key uses of language in the real world. We cautioned that if any of the language arts knots in the network were weak, it would affect the others. We detailed each language arts area, thus reinforcing the larger net with a finer network of related concepts, as suggested in Figure 15.5, page 530.

Assignments Revisited   Although we used the analogy of a network to guide our approach, there are many other possibilities. The ideas of some past students are offered

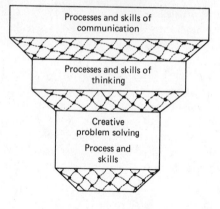

Figure 15.4 Relation of communication and thinking to problem solving revisited.

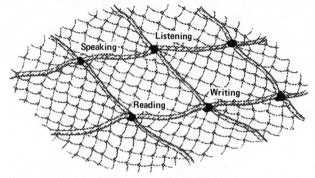

Figure 15.5 The language arts network revisited.

here to inspire you (Figure 15.6). We invite you to create your own analogy. Depicting the language arts as you will teach them, create your own "map." Recall also that in Chapter 1 we asked you to *define* language arts then and again at the end of this book. Additionally recall that in the first chapter we invited you to consider walking into your empty classroom and, using the *where* sections of all the chapters, to make drawings of how you might arrange your room at different times of the year for different purposes. This would be a suitable time to try these activities.

An underlying theme of this book has been democracy in the classroom. The concept of democracy instructs us to avoid dealing arbitrarily with each other and our students. It also teaches that our strength lies in understanding our freedoms and responsibilities as citizens and teachers. Thus, we understand the supremacy of the spirit of our laws, not just their letter. We most closely approach the democratic ideal in environments—including your classroom—where there is an open and vigorous exchange among all participants.

This book has emphasized that language use is more than the sum of its parts. Some experiences are communicated not just by words, but by a whisper, a glance, a dramatic gesture, laughter, or consciousness. Such communication can give us a treasure that can never be plundered, defiled, or destroyed. While some years bring a lot of questions about this treasure, some bring a lot of answers. May yours be filled with both. Finally, we would be interested in your reactions, experiences, and experiments with this book. If you write to us, we promise to answer. Good luck!

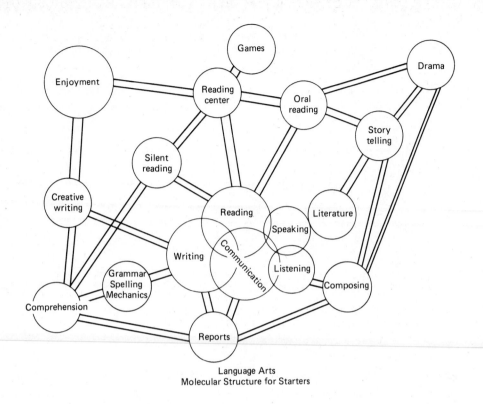

Language Arts
Molecular Structure for Starters

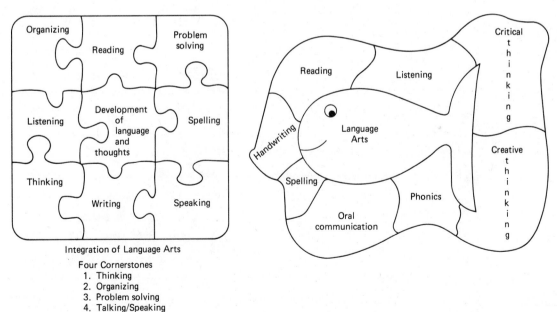

Integration of Language Arts

Four Cornerstones
1. Thinking
2. Organizing
3. Problem solving
4. Talking/Speaking

Figure 15.6 Sample student analogies and depictions of the language arts as they will teach them.

APPENDIX 15A   An Activity for the Reader: The *Me* in Measurement

Number a separate piece of paper and write your answers so that you can use this form both as a pretest and as a posttest. (Circle one.)

Pretest   Posttest

1. Evaluation tools and techniques now used with my class (or that are used in the class I observe) are _____

_____ .

2. To me, now, the purpose of assessment is _____

_____ .

The advantages or uses of assessment are _____

_____ .

The disadvantages or abuses of evaluation can be _____

_____ .

3. I know these tests in the language arts: _____

_____ .

4. This is the way I have learned to handle daily assessment of my students for language arts: _____

_____ .

5. For individual conferences I use (or would use) _____

_____ .

6. My students are (or would be) independently involved in assessment in these ways:

_____ .

7. This is the way I feel about assessment of myself: _____

_____ .

These are instances in which I have sought self-assessment of my skills: _____

_____ .

8. These are some references or other sources on measurement, evaluation, and assessment that I have found helpful with respect to my language arts program: _____

_____ .

References and Resources

CHAPTER 1

References

Bach, R. (1977). *Illusions.* London: Heinemann.

Brown, L. J. (1987, May). Developing thinking and problem-solving with children's books. *Childhood Education, 63*(2), 102–107.

Getzels, J. W. (1964). Creative thinking, problem solving and instruction. In E. R. Hilgard (Ed.), *Theories of learning and instruction.* The 63rd yearbook of the National Society for the Study of Education (pp. 240–267). Chicago: University of Chicago Press.

Goffin, S. G., & Tull, C. Q. (1985, March). Problem solving: Encouraging active learning. *Young Children,* pp. 28–32.

Green C. (1985, March). *A kindergarten compositional writing scale.* Paper presented at the meeting of the National Council of Teachers of English. Houston, TX.

Isaksen, S. G., & Treffinger, D. J. (1985). *Creative problem solving: The basic course.* Buffalo, NY: Bearly Ltd.

Klein, G. A., & Weitzenfeld, J. (1978). Improvement of skills for solving ill-defined problems. *Educational Psychologist, 13,* 31–41.

Lundsteen, S. W. (1976). *Children learn to communicate: Language arts through creative problem solving.* Englewood Cliffs, NJ: Prentice-Hall.

Lundsteen, S. W., & Tarrow, N. B. (1981). *Guiding young children's learning.* New York: McGraw-Hill.

National Council of Teachers of English (NCTE). (1982). *Essentials of English: A document for reflection and dialogue.* Urbana, IL: NCTE.

Raskin, E. (1969). *And it rained.* New York: Atheneum.

Russell, D. H. (1956). *Children's thinking.* Boston: Ginn.

Yashima, T. (1955). *Crow boy.* New York: Viking Press.

If You Want to Learn More

Gordon, T. (1977). *Leadership effectiveness training.* New York: Wyden.

Lindberg, R. (1980). *Dynamics of self image.* San Antonio, TX: Audio Specialities. (Cassette tapes.)

National Council of Teachers of English. (1982). *Essentials of English: A document for reflection and dialogue.* Urbana, IL: Author.

    The following quotation from the beginning serves as an annotation: "The study of English includes knowledge of the language itself, development of its use as a basic means of communication, and appreciation of its artistry as expressed in literature. Teachers of English trace the origins of the language in the past, study its development in the present, and recognize that continuing change in the future will keep the language and the literature alive, flexible and adaptable to the highest expression of which the human being is capable. The use of English involves skills in reading, writing, speaking, listening and observing."

Organization for the Essentials of Education. (n. d.) *The essentials of education: a call for dialog and action.* Urbana, IL: National Council of Teachers of English. (Pamphlet # 482.)

The statement "embodies the collective concern" of 24 endorsing professional associations in the field of education, a concern about oversimplification, fragmentation, and overuse of inneffective measurement of certain skills.

Pilon, B. (1978). *Teaching the language arts creatively in the elementary school.* Melbourne, FL: Krieger.

CHAPTER 2

References

Applebee, A. N. (1978). *The child's concept of story.* Chicago: University of Chicago Press.

Bosma, B. (1986, November). The nature of critical thinking: Its base and boundaries. Paper presented at the open meeting of the National Council of Teachers of English Committee on Critical Thinking. San Antonio, TX.

Bruner, J. (1983). *Child's talk: Learning to use language.* New York: Norton.

Bzoch, K. R., & League, R. (1970). *Receptive-expressive emergent language scale.* Baltimore: University Park Press.

Carlsson-Paige, N., & Levin, D. E. (1985). *Helping young children understand peace, war, and the nuclear threat.* Washington, D.C.: National Association for Young Children.

Chomsky, N. (1965). *Aspects of the theory of syntax.* Cambridge, MA: MIT Press.

Clay, M. (1975). *What did I write?* Exeter, NH: Heinemann.

Clay, M. (1980). Exploring with a pencil. *Theory into Practice, 16,* 334–341.

DeFord, D. (1980). Young children and their writing. *Theory into Practice, 19,* 157–162.

Donaldson, M. (1978). *Children's minds.* New York: Norton.

Dyson, A. H. (1981). Oral language: The rooting system for learning to write. *Language Arts, 59,* 126–131.

Fisher, C., & Natarella, M. (1979). Of cabbages and kings, or what kinds of poetry young children like. *Language Arts, 56*(4), 380–385.

Genishi, C., & Dyson, A. H. (1984). *Language assessment in the early years.* Norwood, NJ: Ablex.

Gentry, J. R. (1981). Learning to spell developmentally. *The Reading Teacher, 31,* 632–637.

Gibson. J. J. (1979). *The ecological approach to visual perception.* Boston: Houghton Mifflin.

Graves, D. (1975). An examination of the writing processes of seven-year-old-children. *Research in the Teaching of English, 9*(3), 227–242.

Graves, D. (1983). *Writing: Teachers and children at work.* Portsmouth, NH: Heinemann.

Green, C. (1985, March). A kindergarten compositional writing scale. Paper presented at the meeting of the National Council of Teachers of English. Houston, TX.

Harste, J. C., Woodward, V. A., & Burke, C. L. (1984). *Language stories and literacy lessons.* Portsmouth, NH: Heinemann.

Heald-Taylor, B. G. (1984). Scribble in first grade writing. *The Reading Teacher, 38*(1), 4–8.

Heath, S. B. (1986, February). A long look at being literate. Paper presented at the meeting of the Federation of North Texas Area Universities, Reading Committee, Dallas, TX.

International Reading Association. (1986). Literacy development and pre-first grade: A joint statement about present practices in pre-first grade reading instruction and recommendations for improvement. *Young Children, 4*(4), 10–13.

Lamme, L. L. (1985, March). Children's encounters with print in a play-oriented preschool. Paper given at the meeting of the National Council of Teachers of English, Houston, TX.

Lenneberg, E. H. (1966). The natural history of language. In F. Smith & G. A. Miller (Eds.), *The genesis of language.* Cambridge, MA: MIT Press.

Lundsteen, S. W. (1976). *Children learn to communicate.* Englewood Cliffs, NJ: Prentice-Hall.

Lundsteen, S. W. (1985, May 7). The impact of learning/solving styles and development on young children's performance of a prereading task. Paper given at the annual meeting of International Reading Association, New Orleans. (ERIC Document No. ED 264 523.)

Lundsteen, S. W., & Tarrow, N. B. (1981). *Guiding young children's learning.* New York: McGraw-Hill.

Moerk, E. L. (1986, July 17). Personal communication.

Nelson, K. (1973). Structure and strategy in learning to talk. *Monographs of the Society for Research in Child Development, 38*(1–2, Serial No. 149).

Nova #1207. (1985). *Baby talk.* Boston: WGBH transcripts (Feb. 26).

Palincsar, A. S. (1986). The role of dialogue in providing scaffolded instruction. *Educational Psychologist, 21*(1 & 2), 73–98.

Paul, R. (1976). Invented spelling in kindergarten. *Young Children, 31,* 195–200.

Piaget, J. (1955). *The language and thought of the child.* New York: Harcourt Brace Jovanovich.

Read, C. (1971). Pre-school children's knowledge of English phonology. *Harvard Educational Review, 41,* 1–34.

Rosenberg, M. (1968). *Diagnostic teaching.* Seattle: Special Child Publications.

Templin, M. C. (1957). *Certain language skills in children: their development and interrelationship,* Minneapolis: University of Minnesota Press.

Texas Association for the Education of Young Children. (n.d.). *Developmentally appropriate kindergarten reading programs: A position statement.* Denton, TX: Author.

Vygotsky, L. S. (1978). In M. Cole, V. John-Steiner, S. Scribner, & E. Souberman (Eds.), *Mind in society: The development of higher psychological processes.* Cambridge, MA: Harvard University Press.

Willert, M. K., & Kamii, C. (1985). Reading in kindergarten: Direct vs. indirect teaching. *Young Children, 40*(4), 3–9.

Wolfe, C. M. (1986, July 28). Personal communication.

Wood, P., Bruner, J., & Ross, G. (1976). The role of tutoring in problem solving. *Journal of Child Psychology and Psychiatry, 17,* 89–100.

Zidonis, F. (Ed.). (n.d.). *Instructor's guide to the language of children: Protocol materials on oral language acquisition.* Columbus: Ohio State University.

If You Want to Learn More

Green, C. (1985, March). A kindergarten compositional writing scale. Paper given at the spring meeting of the National Council of Teachers of English, Houston, TX.

Jaggar, A., & Smith-Burke, M. T. (Eds.). (1985). *Observing the language learner.* Urbana, IL: National Council of Teachers of English.

Moerk, E. L. (1986). Environmental factors in early language acquisition. In G. J. Whitehurst (Ed.), *Annals of child development: Vol. 3* (pp. 191–235). Greenwich, CT: JAI Press.

Nelson, K. (1985). *Making sense. The acquisition of shared meaning.* New York: Academic Press.

Schickedanz, J. A. (1986). *More than the ABCs: The early stages of reading and writing.* Washington, DC: National Association for the Education of Young Children.

Stewart, I. S. (1985, May/June). Kindergarten reading curriculum: Reading abilities, not reading readiness. *Childhood Education, 61,* 356–360.

Taylor, N. E., Blum, I. H., & Logsdon, D. M. (1986). The development of written language awareness: Environmental aspects and program characteristics. *Reading Research Quarterly, 21,* 132–149.

Vukelich, C. & Golden, J. (1984, January). Early writing: development and teaching strategies. *Young Children,* pp. 3–8.

Vygotsky, L. (1962). *Thought and language.* Cambridge, MA: MIT Press.

CHAPTER 3

References

Board of Education, Orange County, CA. (1966). *Children & listening centers: Why, how, what.* (EP-8273). Orange County, CA: Author.

Devine, T. (1984, November). Listening in 1984. Presentation on listening given before the National Council of Teachers of English, Detroit, MI.

Flavel, J. H. (1981). Cognitive monitoring. In W. P. Dickson (Ed.), *Children's oral communication skills.* (Ch. 2, Cognitive monitoring, pp. 35–58). New York: Academic Press.

Heath, S. B. (1985, November 25). Literate and illiterate faces. Paper presented at the Federation of North Texas Area Universities, Committee on Reading, Dallas, TX.

Holt, Rinehart and Winston. (1984). *Holt English.* New York: Author.

Illinois State Board of Education. (1982). *Basic listening skills.* Springfield, IL: Author.

Nichols, R., & Stevens, L. A. (1957). *Are you listening?* New York: McGraw-Hill. The first full-length book on listening.

Rankin, P. T. (1952). The measurement of the ability to understand spoken language. Doctoral dissertation, University of Michigan, 1926. *Dissertation Abstracts International, 12,* 847.

Revelle, G. L., Wellman, H. M., & Karabenick, J. D. (1985). Comprehension monitoring in preschool children. *Child Development, 56*(3), 654–663.

Robinson, E. J., & Robinson, W. P. (1982). Knowing when you don't know enough: Children's judgments about ambiguous information. *Cognition, 12,* 267–280. (The Netherlands: Elsevier Sequoia.)

Texas Education Agency. (1984). English language arts: K–grade 12. *State board of education rules for curriculum* (TEA Publication GE4 450 01). Chapter 75 Curriculum, Subchapter B. Essential Elements 75.21. Austin, TX: Author.

Tompkins, G. E., Friend, M., & Smith, P. L. (1987). Strategies for more effective listening. In C. R. Personke & D. D. Johnson (Eds.), *Language arts and beginning teacher* (pp. 30–41). Englewood Cliffs, NJ: Prentice-Hall.

Wolvin, A. D., Fogler, C. L., Brownell, L., Cochran, K., Denniston, C., McDonough, J., Moffitt, F., & Slaughter, P. (1985). *Illustrative objectives for listening.* Frederick County, MD: State of Maryland.

If You Want to Learn More

Curriculum Review. (1984), February. Volume *23*(1), almost whole issue on listening. Lundsteen reviews standardized tests, pp. 32–33; 35–36.

Lundsteen, S. W. (1979). *Listening: Its impact at all levels on reading and the other language arts.* Urbana, IL: National Council of Teachers of English.

Lundsteen, S. W., and Goode, L. (1981, January). Listening: An integrated approach to developing listening skills (Some how to's and why to's for teachers). *Early Years,* 60–63, 85.

Flavell, J. H., Speer, J. R., Green, F. L., & August, D. L. (1981). The development of comprehension monitoring and knowledge about communication. *Monographs of the Society for Research in Child Development, 46* (5, Serial No. 192).

International Listening Association. (Any issue). Quarterly *Newsletter.* Executive Office: Charles Roberts, McNeese State University, Lake Charles, LA 70609-0340.

Pearson, D. P., & Fielding, L. (1983, March). Instructional implications of listening comprehension research. Reading Education Report No. 39. University of Illinois at Urbana-Champaign.

Rubin, D. L., Daly, J., McCroskey, J. C., & Mead, N. A. (1982). A review and critique of procedures for assessing speaking and listening skills among preschool through grade twelve students. *Communication Education, 31,* 285–303.

Wolvin, A. D., & Coakley, C. G. (1985). *Listening* (2nd ed.). Dubuque, IA: Brown.

Listening in Children's Literature: Three Categories of Themes

I. Awareness of Sounds

Alyesworth, J. (1981). *Tonight's the night.* Chicago: Whitman.
   A little boy learns what the night sounds are like around his house—noises he was not aware of during the day.

Aylesworth, J. (1983). *Siren in the night.* Chicago: Whitman.
   A siren can be a scary noise—especially at night.

Baylor, B. (1971). *Plink, plink, plink.* Boston: Houghton Mifflin.
   In verse the author speculates on what sounds seem like at night.

Behrens, J. (1976). *What I hear.* Chicago: Children's Press.
   Photographs depict young children listening to the everyday sounds of their school environment.

Brown, M. W. (1947). *The noisy book.* New York: Harper & Row.
   Muffin must wear a bandage over his eyes. He listens to sounds and even tires to guess a special sound.

Brown, M. W. (1940). *Country noisy book.* New York: Harper & Row.
   Muffin goes to the farm and hears a variety of interesting animal and country noises.

Brown, M. W. (1942). *Indoor noisy book.* New York: Harper & Row.
   Muffin has to stay inside and hear all the indoor sounds.

Brown, M. (1947). *The winter noisy book.* New York: Harper & Row.
   Brown is more poetic in this book as Muffin hears the soft sounds of winter.

Carlson, B. W. (1965). *Listen! And help tell the story.* New York: Abingdon Press.
   Children are encouraged to supply sound effects to this story.

de Regniers, Beatrice Schenk. (1961). *Going for a walk.* New York: Harper & Row.
   This book depicts the sights and sounds of the homey experience of a walk in the country.

Kuskin, K. (1962). *All sizes of noises.* New York: Harper & Row.
   Just as objects can be seen to come in different sizes, so do noises, which can be heard at different volumes.

LeTord, B. (1981). *An alphabet of sounds.* New York: Four Winds Press.
   A sound is given for each letter of the alphabet: art, boo, click, etc.

Mathews, G. B. (1975). *What was that!* New York: Golden Press.
   Three young bears are frightened by noises they hear in the night. Each time they are reassured that the noises are the small sounds of little bugs going to bed.

Myller, R. (1981). *A very noisy day.* New York: Atheneum.
   Encourages reader- (or listener-) generated sounds. A dog in a city and park setting has a multitude of noisy adventures, culminating in his catching a bank robber. Preschool to age 7.

Ogle, L., & Thoburn, T. (1971). *I hear: sounds in a child's world.* New York: American Heritage.
   The title makes the content of this book self-evident.

Rand, A. (1970). *Listen! Listen!* New York: Harcourt Brace Jovanovich.
   Different sounds are described. Children are invited to guess a sound.

Spier, P. (1972). *Crash! Bang! Boom!* Garden City, NY: Doubleday.
   Like a picture dictionary, words depicting sounds are written close to illustrations that portray those sounds.

Sussman, S. (1982). *Hippo thunder.* Chicago: Whitman.
   This counting book teaches children to count off the time between lightning and thunder by counting, "one hippopotamus, two hippopotamus," etc.

(Continued)

Ziefert, H., & Gorbaty, N. (1984). *Baby Ben's noise book.* New York: Random House.
This cardboard book is for the very young to enjoy sounds.

II. Valuing of Quieter Sounds

Baylor, B., & Parnall, P. (1978). *The other way to listen.* New York: Scribner.
When you are close to nature and yourself, you can hear the rocks murmuring and the hills singing.

Elkin, B. (1954). *The loudest noise in the world.* New York: Viking Press.
A young prince wants the loudest noise in the world for a birthday present. He is surprised by the silence he gets, and consequently enjoys for the first time the singing of a bird.

Fisher, A. (1964). *Listen, rabbit.* New York: Crowell.
A young boy describes to a rabbit the many things a very still animal with good ears can hear. This book is written in a very poetic manner, and it is beautifully illustrated.

Garelick, M. (1963). *Sounds of a summer night.* Reading, MA: Addison-Wesley.
Description of sounds between sunset and sunrise: frogs, clocks.

Hopkins, L. B. (1980). *Morning, noon, and nighttime, too.* New York: Harper & Row.
Children will enjoy this collection of poems that take the listener through a day of amazing and amusing sounds.

Zolotow, C. (1980). *If you listen.* New York: Harper & Row.
A mother reassures a little girl that she can feel her father's love from far away by being still and receptive to sounds and feelings that come to one across a long distance.

III. Listening to Others

Berger, T. (1974). *A friend can help.* Milwaukee, WI: Raintree Editions.
A girl tells her friend about her feelings in relation to her parents' divorce and finds that talking to a good listener makes her feel better.

Breitner, S. (1981). *The bookseller's advice.* New York: Viking Press.
A bookseller who is getting a little deaf recommends highly inappropriate books when his customers seek advice. Somehow it all works out to their benefit.

Brown, M. W. (1942). *The runaway bunny.* New York: Harper & Row.
Mother Bunny listens to her child's plans to run away and adjusts her plans for staying with him, thus reassuring him of her constant presence and love.

Cosgrove, S. (1982). *Kartusch.* Los Angeles: Price/Stern/Sloan.
A little blind snake teaches the Furry Eyefuls to listen.

Geisel, T. (Dr. Seuss). (1954). *Horton hears a who!* New York: Random House.
Horton the elephant believes that even the smallest beings have a right to be heard and protected from harm.

Heide, P. (1970). *Sound of sunshine, sound of rain.* New York: Parents.
A blind boy finds a friend.

Hurd, T. (1984). *Mama don't allow.* New York: Harper & Row.
The noise of Miles's new saxophone is driving everyone crazy until he teams up to form a band with three other musicians.

Hutchins, P. (1969). *The surprise party.* New York: Macmillan.
Rabbit has a hard time getting people to come to his party, as they have heard and understood incorrectly what his plans are.

Hutchins, P. (1972). *Good-night, owl!* New York: Macmillan.
An owl is kept awake all day by the noises of the animals that share his tree with him. Wonderful illustrations.

McGovern, A. (1967). *Too much noise.* New York: Scholastic Book Services.

    In the folk-tale genre, an old man finally follows advice to get rid of his animals, who made home too noisy. Colorful.

Minarik, E. H. (1957). *Little bear.* New York: Harper & Row.

    Mother Bear listens to Little Bear's account of his pretence—a trip to the moon—and joins in, being careful to follow his flight into fantasy and return to reality according to what Little Bear tells her. In this way she fosters their relationship.

Orgel, D. (1970). *The uproar.* New York: McGraw-Hill.

    A child thinks his mother said she was going to the "uproar" rather than the "opera."

Peterson, J. W. (1977). *I have a sister. My sister is deaf.* New York: Harper & Row.

    A little girl describes her life with her five-year-old deaf sister, telling how they both cope with her deafness.

Robinson, V. (1966). *David in silence.* Philadelphia: Lippincott.

    This is a book for older elementary school children. A deaf boy is isolated until a friend reaches out to him.

Vandrell, C. S. (1983). *The moon.* (Victor & Maria series.) London: Blackie.

    The esthetic experience of going out to look at the moon is marred by Otto's attempts to practice on the trombone.

CHAPTER 4

References

Alberta Department of Education, Edmonton, Canada. (1985). *Elementary drama curriculum guide* (ERIC Document Reproduction Service No. ED 257 156).

Burrows, A. T. (1986, November 21). Personal communication.

California State Department of Education. (1986). English language framework (Draft 3-27–86). Sacramento, CA: Author.

Dillon, D. & Pinnell, G. (1985, November). The place of oral language activities in the English classroom. Tape #TE85-25, E.5. Session presented at the Annual Convention of the National Council of Teachers of English. Philadelphia, PA.

Edelsky, C. (1978). Teaching oral language. *Language Arts, 55,* 291–296.

Eliot, T. S. (1939, 1967). *Old Possum's book of practical cats.* New York: Harcourt Brace Jovanovich.

Fairweather, T. A. (1986, November 2). Encouraging creative writing at home. Paper presented at the meeting of the National Association for Gifted Children, Las Vegas, NV.

Flavell, J. H., Botkin, P. T., Fry, C. L., Wright, J. W., & Jarvis, P. E. (1968). *The development of role-taking and communication skills in children.* New York: Wiley.

Fowler, R. (1983). *A squirrel's tale.* Tulsa, OK: Educational Development Corporation.

Fox, S. E., & Allen, V. G. (1983). *The language arts: an integrated approach.* New York: Holt, Rinehart and Winston.

Genishi, C., & Dyson, A. H. (1984). *Language assessment in the early years.* Norwood, NJ: Ablex.

Halliday, M. A. K. (1976). *Explorations in the functions of language.* London: Edward Arnold.

Juntune, J. E. (1986). *Creative thinking fun with a squirrel's tale.* Circle Pines, MN: 120 Creative Corner.

Lundsteen, S. W. (1976). *Children learn to communicate.* Englewood Cliffs, NJ: Prentice-Hall.

Lundsteen, S. W., & Tarrow, N. B. (1981). *Guiding young children's learning.* New York: McGraw-Hill.

McAfee, O. D. (1985, September). Circle time: Getting past "two little pumpkins." *Young Children,* pp. 24–29.

McCroskey, J. C. (1977). Oral communication apprehension: A summary of recent theory and research. *Human Communication Research, 4,* 78–96.

McCrum, R., Cran, W., & MacNeil, R. (1986). *The story of English.* New York: Viking Press.

MacLure, M., & Hargreaves, M. (1986). *Speaking and listening: Assessment at age 11.* Windsor, Berkshire, England: NFER-NELSON.

Marshall, R., & Paul, K. (1982). *Cats up.* New York: Simon & Schuster.

Miccinati, J. L. (1985). Using prosodic cues to teach oral reading fluency. *The Reading Teacher, 39,* 206–212.

Morrow, L. M. (1985). Reading and retelling stories: Strategies for emergent readers. *The Reading Teacher, 38,* 870–875.

National Council of Teachers of English. (1983). Forum: Essentials of English. *Language Arts, 60,* 244–248.

Nelson, K. (1985). *Making sense: The acquisition of shared meaning.* New York: Academic Press.

New York State Education Department. (1984 draft). Draft: Listening and speaking in the English language arts curriculum K–12. Albany: Author.

Norton, D. E. (1985). *The effective teaching of language arts.* Columbus, OH: Merrill.

Ross, R. (1980). *Storyteller* (2nd ed.). Columbus, OH: Merrill.

Schickendanz, J. A., York, M. E., Stewart, I. S., & White, D. A. (1983). *Strategies for teaching young children* (2nd ed.). Englewood Cliffs, NJ: Prentice-Hall.

Silverstein, S. (1974). *Where the sidewalk ends.* New York: Harper & Row.

Stewig, J. W. (1980). Planning environments to promote language growth. In G. S. Pinnell (Ed.), *Discovering language with children.* Urbana, IL: National Council of Teachers of English.

Texas Education Agency. (1984). English language arts: K–grade 12. *State board of education rules for curriculum. TEA Publication GE4 450 01. Chapter 75 Curriculum, Subchapter B. Essential Elements 75.21.* Austin, TX: Author.

Wells, G. (1975). *Coding manual for the description of child speech.* Bristol, England: University of Bristol School of Education.

Wilkinson, L. C. (1984). Research currents: Peer group talk in elementary school. *Language Arts, 61,* 164–169.

Wolvin, A. D., et al. (1985). *Draft of goals and subgoals for speaking.* State of Maryland.

Wood, B. S. (Ed.). (1977). *Development of functional communication competencies: Pre-K–Grade 6.* Urbana, IL: ERIC Clearinghouse on Reading and Communication Skills & Speech Communication Association.

Ylisto, I. (1984, November). Appraisal of talking and listening. Paper presented at the meeting of the National Council of Teachers of English, Detroit, MI.

If You Want to Learn More

Collins, C. (1986). Is the cart before the horse? Effects of preschool reading instruction on 4 year olds. *The Reading Teacher, 40,* 332–339.

Flatley, J. K., & Rutland, A. D. (1986). Using wordless picture books to teach linguistically/culturally different students. *The Reading Teacher, 40,* 276–281.

Geller, L. G. (1985). *Word play and language learning for children.* Urbana, IL: National Council of Teachers of English.

Rondal, J. A. (1985). *Adult-child interaction and the process of language acquisition.* New York: Praeger.

Seaver, J. A. T., & Botel, M. (1983). A first-grade teacher teaches reading, writing, and oral communication across the curriculum. *The Reading Teacher, 36,* 656–664.

Tough, J. (1983). *Listening to children talking.* Cardiff, Wales: Ward Lock Educational Associates. *Deals with informal ways of assessing classroom language that are informal: Provides useful information for improving teaching while maintaining the spontaneous, natural use of language and its development.*

Wishon, P. M., Brazee, P., & Eller, B. (1986, December). Facilitating oral language competence: The natural ingredients. *Childhood Education,* pp. 91–94.
Describes the informal ways in which children are helped to increase their language competence in relational contexts that are meaningful to them.

Some Wordless Picture Books

Anno, M. (1979). *Anno's journey.* New York: Collins.
Anno, M. (1980). *Anno's Italy.* New York: Collins.
Briggs, R. (1978). *The snowman.* New York: Random House.
Carle, E. (1971). *Do you want to be my friend?* New York: Crowell.
Carroll, R. (1932). *What Whiskers did.* New York: Macmillan.
Day, A. (1985). *Good dog, Carl.* La Jolla, CA: Green Tiger Press.
dePaola, T. (1981). *The hunter and the animals.* New York: Holiday House.
Goodall, J. S. (1968). *The adventures of Paddy Pork.* New York: Harcourt Brace Jovanovich.
Goodall, J. S. (1977). *The surprise picnic.* New York: Atheneum.
Heller, L. (1979). *Lily at the table.* New York: Macmillan.
Hutchins, P. (1971). *Changes, changes.* New York: Macmillan.
Krahn, F. (1970). *A flying saucer full of spaghetti.* New York: Dutton.
Krahn, F. (1975). *Who's seen the scissors?* New York: Dutton.
Mari, I. (1967). *The magic balloon.* New York: S. G. Phillips.
Mayer, M. (1969). *Frog, where are you?* New York: Dial Press.
Mayer, M. (1973). *Bubble bubble.* New York: Parents Magazine Press.
Mayer, M. (1974). *Frog goes to dinner.* New York: Dial Press.
Mayer, M., & Mayer, M. (1971). *A boy, a dog, a frog and a friend.* New York: Dial Press.
Mayer, M., & Mayer, M. (1975). *One frog too many.* New York: Dial Press.
Ward, L. (1973). *The silver pony: A story in pictures.* Boston: Houghton Mifflin.

Some Folktales for Storytelling

Appiah, P. (1966). *Ananse the spider: Tales from an Ashanti village.* New York: Pantheon Books.
Bryan, A. (1980). *Beat the story-drum, pum-pum.* New York: Atheneum.
Ginsburg, M. (1970). *Three rolls and one doughnut: Fables from Russia.* New York: Dial Press.
Gittans, A. (1977). *Tales from the South Pacific islands.* Owing Mills, MD: Stemmer House.
Jugendorf, M. A., & Weng, V. (1980). *The magic boat and other Chinese folk stories.* New York: Vanguard.
Lofgren, U. (1978). *The boy who ate more than the giant and other Swedish folktales* (LaFarge, S., translator). New York: Collins.
Wolkstein, D. (1972). *8,000 stones: A Chinese folktale.* Garden City, NY: Doubleday.

CHAPTER 5

References

Alberta Department of Education, Edmonton, Canada. (1985). *Elementary drama curriculum guide.* (ERIC document Reproduction Service No. ED 257 156.)
Agency for Instructional Television. (n. d.). *A guide for teachers: Creative dramatics.* Bloomington, IN: Author.

Bruner, J. (1973, February). On the continuity of learning. *Saturday Review of Education,* pp. 21–24.

DeHaven, E. P. (1983). *Teaching and learning the language arts* (3rd ed.). (Ch. 6, "Creative Drama," pp. 160–201.) Boston: Little, Brown.

Fox, S. E., & Allen, V. G. (1983). *The language arts: An integrated approach.* New York: Holt, Rinehart and Winston.

Hoberman, M. A. (1978). *A house is a house for me.* New York: Viking.

Loch, M. A. (1985, March). Readers theatre: An enjoyable means to the art of languaging. Paper presented at the spring meeting of the National Council of Teachers of English, Houston, TX.

Lundsteen, S. W. (1976). *Children learn to communicate.* Englewood Cliffs, NJ: Prentice-Hall.

NCTE/CTA (Joint Committee of the National Council of Teachers of English and Children's Theatre Association). (1983, March). Forum: Informal classroom drama. *Language Arts, 60,* 370–372.

O'Neill, C., & Lambert, A. (1982). *Drama structures.* London: Hutchinson, 1982.

Rosenberg, H. S. (1985, November). Creative drama and imagination: Transforming ideas into action. Paper presented at the meeting of the National Council of Teachers of English, Philadelphia, PA.

Stewig, J. W. (1983). *Informal drama in the elementary language arts program.* New York: Teachers College Press.

Temple, C., & Gillet, J. W. (1984). *Language arts: Learning processes and teaching practices.* Boston: Little, Brown.

Texas Education Agency. (1984). English language arts: K–grade 12. *State Board of Education Rules for Curriculum,* TEA Publication GE4 450 01. Chapter 75 Curriculum, Subchapter B. Essential Elements 75.21 Austin, TX: Author.

Verriour, P. (1986). Creating worlds of dramatic discourse. *Language Arts, 63,* 253–263.

Wagner, B. J. (1983). The expanding circle of classroom drama. In B. A. Busching & J. I. Schwartz (Eds.), *Integrating the language arts in the elementary school.* Urbana, IL: National Council of Teachers of English.

Way, Brian. (1967). *Development through drama.* New York: Humanities Press.

If You Want to Learn More

Crosscup, R. (1966). *Children and dramatics.* New York: Scribner.

Cullum, A. (1967). *Push back the desks.* New York: Citation Press.

Duke, C. R. (1974). *Creative dramatics and English teaching.* Urbana, IL: National Council of Teachers of English.

Durland, F. C. (1975). *Creative dramatics for children: A practical manual for teachers and leaders* (rev. ed.). Kent, OH: Kent State University.

Gillies, E. (1973). *Creative dramatics for all children.* Washington: Association for Childhood Education International.

Koste, V. G. (1978). *Dramatic play in childhood: Rehearsal for life.* New Orleans: Anchorage Press.

Maley, A. (1982). *Drama techniques in language learning: A resource book of communication activities for language teachers* (rev. ed.). New York: Cambridge University Press.

Robinson, K. (1980). *Exploring theatre and education.* London: Heinemann Educational.

Rosenberg, H. S. (1987). *Creative drama and imagination.* New York: Holt, Rinehart and Winston.

Scher, A. (1976). *100+ ideas for drama.* London: Heinemann Educational.

Siks, G. B. (1961). *Children's theatre and creative dramatics.* Seattle: University of Washington Press.

Siks, G. B. (1977). *Drama with children.* New York: Harper & Row.

Sloyer, S. (1982). *Reader's theatre: Story dramatization in the classroom.* Urbana, IL: National Council of Teachers of English.

Texas Education Agency. (1978). *Creative dramatics in the elementary school.* Austin, TX: Author. (ED 154 434.)

Tyas, B. (1971). *Child drama in action: a practical manual for teachers.* Scarborough, Ontario: Gage Educational Publishing.

Wootton, M. (1982). *New directions in drama teaching.* London: Heinemann Educational.

Enactive Way of Knowing: Some Children's Books to Stimulate Dramatic Movement

Beyer, E. (1951). Jump or jiggle. In M. H. Arbuthnot (Ed.), *Time for poetry.* New York: Scott, Foresman.
A simple poem about animals and their ways of knowing. Teachers can use it to have children imitate action and develop interest in word meaning and rhyme.

Brown, M. (1957). *The three billy goats gruff.* New York: Harcourt Brace Jovanovich.
Using the illustrations children can also imitate the action as they relate events in sequence. The child can learn to take a role and be a cooperative part of an enactment.

Ets, M. H. (1965). *Just me.* New York: Viking Press.
In using this story about a child who imitates animal walks—until at the end he runs like nobody else at all, just himself—the teacher can encourage children to enact. It is also useful for developing importance of self, placing characters in order, adding to a series, and knowing about different types of illustrations, such as photos and woodcuts.

Ets, M. H. (1968). *Talking without words.* New York: Viking Press.
Captioned pictures convey how to express feelings and thoughts through facial expressions, body gestures. Provides opportunity to imitate story action.

Galdone, P. (1968). *Henny Penny.* New York: Seabury Press.
Illustrations for this old tale of the chicken who thought the sky was falling are outstanding. Teachers can encourage children to enact the story in a sequence of events while reciting the refrain.

Keats, E. J. (1970). *Hi, cat!* New York: Macmillan.
After a little boy meeting a strange cat in his neighborhood says "Hi," it follows him around, managing to ruin a neighborhood production that the boy and a friend are trying to put on. But at the end the boy decides that the cat likes him. Children could enact this story and various endings. After gaining familiarity with it, they can enact parts, or the whole, in pantomime while it is being read adaptively or in improvisation.

Kohn, B. (1970). *Chipmunks.* Englewood Cliffs, NJ: Prentice-Hall.

Parramon, J. M. (1985). *The four elements: Fire, earth, water, and air.* New York: Barron's.

Wagner, J. (1962). *Hurrah for hats.* Chicago: Children's Press. Illustrated by Frances Eckart.
Different hats can tell about what a person does; e.g., a hat might say, "I belong to the man who puts out fires." Teachers can use this book to promote classification of objects. Use can lead into pantomime and dramatic play with a partner. Children can be invited to choose a hat from a collection and then choose a partner wearing a different hat, assume the character, and carry on a conversation.

CHAPTER 6

References

Alvermann, D. E., Dillon, D. R., & O'Brien, D. G. (1987). *Using discussion to promote reading comprehension.* Newark, DE: International Reading Association.

Christenbury, L., & Kelly, P. P. (1983). *Questioning: A path to critical thinking.* Urbana, IL: ERIC/ NCTE.

Cohen, E. G. (1986). *Designing groupwork.* New York: Teachers College, Columbia University.

Deutsch, M. (1968). The effects of cooperation and competition upon group process. In D. Cartwright & A. Zander (Eds.), *Group dynamics.* New York: Harper & Row.

Dillon, J. T. (1984). Research on question and discussion. *Educational Leadership, 42,* 50–56.

Dreikurs, R., & Cassel, P. (1972). *Discipline without tears* (2nd ed.). New York: Hawthorn Books.

Fisher, R., & Ury, W. (1981). *Getting to yes.* Boston: Houghton Mifflin.

Goble, P. (1984). *Buffalo woman.* Scarsdale, NY: Bradbury Press.

Lundsteen, S. W. (1976). *Children learn to communicate.* Englewood Cliffs, NJ: Prentice-Hall.

MacLure, M., & Hargreaves, M. (1986). *Speaking and listening assessment at age 11* (Report of the Assessment of Performance Unit, APU, Department of Education and Science). Windsor, Berkshire, England: Nfer-Nelson.

Maier, N. R. F. (1963). *Problem solving discussion and conference: Leadership methods and skills.* New York: McGraw-Hill, 1963.

Manzo, A. V., & Casale, U. P. (1985). Listen-read-discuss: A content heuristic. *Journal of Reading, 28,* 732–734.

Rosenholtz, S. J. (1985). Treating problems of academic status. In J. Berger & M. Zelditch, Jr. (Eds.), *Status, rewards, and influence.* San Francisco: Jossey-Bass.

Taba, H., Levine, S., & Freeman, F. E. (1964). *Thinking in elementary school children* (USOE Cooperative Research Project No. 1574). San Francisco: San Francisco State College.

Tammivaara, J. (1982). The effects of task structure on beliefs about competence and participation in small groups. *Sociology of Education, 55,* 211–222.

If You Want to Learn More

Bloom, B. S. (Ed.). (1956). *Taxonomy of Educational Objectives.* New York: McKay.

Davidson County Metropolitan Public Schools, Nashville, TN. (1980). *Communication skills handbook: Phases I & II.* (ERIC Document Reproduction Service No. ED 195 592.)
Teaching guide includes effective group and communication skills, definitions, group processes for consensus, skills for participants, leaders, recorders, plans for centers, and integration of writing.

Dillon, J. T. (1983). *Teaching and the art of questioning.* Bloomington, IN: Phi Delta Kappa Educational Foundation.
Gives and elaborates on seven alternatives in place of questions to encourage student discussion: contribution of (1) a factual statement, (2) a reflective or summary statement, or (3) a state-of-mind statement; (4) invitation to elaborate; (5) encouragement to formulate student thoughts into a question; (6) encouragement of mutual question asking; (7) deliberate silence.

Farrar, M. T. (1984). Asking better questions. *The Reading Teacher, 38*(1), 10–15.

Foley, J. P., & Bagley, M. T. (1984). *Suppose the wolf were an octopus?* New York: Trillium Press.
A guide for creative questioning for primary-grade literature, this book demonstrates procedures for building different levels of questions, based on Bloom's taxonomy.

Hersey, P., & Blanchard, K. (1977). *Management of organizational behavior.* Englewood Cliffs, NJ: Prentice-Hall.
Gives interesting leadership model applied to low- to higher-maturity/skill groups, with four functions as follows: (1) Telling (for low-maturity groups) as high directive, firm, specific, decisive, authoritative and assertive (if appropriately used) and dictatorial and low supportive if not; (2) Selling (for moderate/low-maturity groups) as high directive and high supportive, consultative, collaborative (if appropriate) and manipulating if not; (3) Participating (for moderate/high-maturity groups) as facilitative, encouraging, active listening (if appropriate) and meddling, condescending if not; (4) Delegating (for high-maturity/skill groups) as enabling, allowing to take major

responsibility for problem solving and for decisions (if appropriate) and avoiding, escaping work if not.

Madden, N. A., Slavin, R. E., & Stevens, R. J. (1986). *Cooperative integrated reading and composition.* Baltimore, MD: Johns Hopkins Team Learning Project.

Slavin, R. E. (1986). Learning together. *American Educator, 10,* 6–13.

Describes how to structure learning so that students will root for one another to succeed and will help each other to do so, with higher academic achievement.

Newsletter

The Question Exchange. J. T. Dillon (Ed.). University of California, Riverside, CA 92521.

CHAPTER 7

References

Allen, R. R., Brown, K. L., & Yatvin, J. (1986). *Learning language through communication: A functional approach.* Belmont, CA: Wadsworth.

Allen, R. V. (1976). *Language experiences in communication.* Boston: Houghton Mifflin.

Chambers, B. (1987, April). Books for children. *Teachers Networking: The Whole Language Newsletter,* pp. 6–7.

Goodman, K. S., Goodman, Y. M., & Hood, W. J. (1989). *The whole language evaulation book.* Portsmouth, NH: Heineman.

Gorman, T. (1986). *The framework for the assessment of language.* (Assessment of Performance Unit, Department of Education and Science, National Foundation for Educational Research.) Windsor, Berkshire, England: Nfer-Nelson.

Haley-James, S. M. (1980). Interviewing: A means of encouraging the drive to communicate. *Language Arts, 57,* 497–503.

Hall, M. A. (1978). *The language experience approach for teaching reading: A research perspective.* Newark, DE: International Reading Association.

Heimlich, J. E., & Pittelman, S. D. (1986). *Semantic mapping: Classroom applications.* Newark, DE: International Reading Association.

Hoberman, M. A. (1978). *A house is a house for me.* New York: Viking.

Hurst, C. O., Healy, J., Witherell, L., & Alouise, M. (1983, May). Books in all directions. *Early Years,* pp. 23–32.

Indrisano, R. (1984). *Reading and writing revisited.* Ginn Occasional Papers No. 18, Writings in reading and language arts. Columbus, OH: Ginn.

Jacobson, D. (1987, April). Dialogue. *Teachers Networking: The Whole Language Newsletter,* pp. 4, 9.

Kinney, M. A. (1985). A language experience approach to teaching expository text structure. *The Reading Teacher, 38,* 854–856.

McCrum, R., Cran W., & MacNeil, R. (1986). *The story of English.* New York: Viking Press.

McGee, L. M. (1982). Awareness of text structure: Effects on children's recall of expository text. *Reading Research Quarterly, 17,* 581–590.

Mallon, B., & Berglund, R. (1984). The language experience approach to reading: Recurring questions and their answers. *The Reading Teacher, 37,* 867–871.

May, F. B. (1982). *Reading as communication.* Columbus, OH: Merrill.

Meyer, B. J. F., Brandt, D. M., & Bluth, G. J. (1980). Use of top-level structure in text: Key for reading comprehension of ninth-grade students. *Reading Research Quarterly, 16,* 72–103.

Morreale, C. J. (1987, March 16). Personal Communication.

Moss, J. F. (1984). *Focus units in literature: A handbook for elementary school teachers.* Urbana, IL: National Council of Teachers of English.

Ohio State University. (1987). *The Web: Wonderfully exciting books.* (Available from: The Web, Ohio State University College of Education, 200 Ramseyer Hall, 29 West Woodruff, Columbus, Ohio 43210-1177).

> *A quarterly pamphlet selecting a core theme and webbing related children's books and activities radiating outward from a central word or phrase.*

Parramon, J. M. (1985). *The four elements: fire, earth, water, and air.* New York: Barrons.

Pearson, P. D., Gallagher, M., Gouvdis, A., & Johnston, P. (1981). What kinds of expository material are occurring in elementary school children's textbooks? Paper presented at the National Reading Conference, Dallas, TX.

Taylor, B. M. (1980). Children's memory for expository text after reading. *Reading Research Quarterly, 15,* 399–411.

Young, S. L. (1985, May). Using children's books to teach mathematical concepts: Grades K–6. Paper presented at the national meeting of the International Reading Association, New Orleans, LA.

Children's Books Mentioned

Anno, M., & Anno, M. (1983). *Anno's mysterious publishing jar.* New York: Putnam.

Brenner, B. (1966). *Mr. Tall and Mr. Small.* Reading, MA: Addison-Wesley.

Carle, E. (1969). *The very hungry caterpillar.* Cleveland, OH: Collins and World.

de Paola, T. (1973). *Charlie needs a cloak.* Englewood Cliffs, NJ: Prentice-Hall.

> *Describes the steps involved in making a piece of clothing.*

de Paola, T. (1975). *The cloud book.* New York: Holiday House.

> *Different clouds and their weather implications are described, along with folk beliefs about them.*

de Paola, T. (1977). *The quicksand book.* New York: Holiday House.

> *Describes characteristics of quicksand and ways of surviving it.*

de Paola, T. (1978). *The popcorn book.* New York: Holiday House.

> *Shows how popcorn is made, and includes recipes.*

de Paola, T. (1979). *The kid's cat book.* New York: Holiday House.

> *Interesting facts about cats.*

Geisel, T. (1938). *The 500 hats of Bartholomew Cubbins.* New York: Vanguard Press.

Hoberman, M. A. (1978). *A house is a house for me.* New York: Viking Press.

Kohn, B. (1970). *Chipmunks.* Englewood Cliffs, NJ: Prentice-Hall. Ages 5–8.

Lauber, P. (1986). *Volcano: The eruption and healing of Mount St. Helens.* New York: Bradbury.

> *Engrossing, readable description with memorable, even beautiful, clear full-color photos, ages 8–12.*

Lionni, L. (1968). *The biggest house in the world.* New York: Pantheon Books.

Mathews, L. (1979). *Gator pie.* New York: Dodd, Mead.

Mathews, L. (1980). *The great take-away.* New York: Dodd, Mead.

Parramon, M. (1985). The four elements: Fire, earth, water, and air. New York: Barrons.

Seingobosc, F. (1951, 1957). *Jeanne-Marie counts her sheep.* New York: Scribner.

Selsan, M. E. (1986). *Mushrooms.* New York: Morrow. History, structure, and cultivation of common edible mushrooms, ages 9–11.

Simon, S. (1985). *Jupiter.* New York: Morrow.

> *Fine photographs and information on this planet, ages 8 and up.*

If You Want to Learn More

Britton, J. (1971). What's the use? A schematic account of language functions. *Education Review, 23*(3), 205–219.

> *Details "transactional" (informational) uses of language, such as language to record and report, or language that is narrative/descriptive, analogic, speculative, and tautologic (theorizing).*

Buckley, M. H., & Boyle, O. (1981). *Mapping the writing journey* (Curriculum Publication No. 15). Berkeley. CA: Bay Area Writing Project, University of California.

Dillon, D. (Ed.). (1983). Reading and writing across the curriculum (Whole issue). *Language Arts, 60*(6).
  Stresses the importance of reading and writing to learn across the curriculum.

Goodman, K. S. (1986). *What's whole in whole education?* Portsmouth, NH: Heinemann Educational Books.

Hall, M. (1981). *Teaching reading as a language experience.* Columbus, OH: Merrill.
  Explains philosophy and procedures for teaching in a language experience reading program.

Hansen-Krening, N. (1983). *Language experience . . . fiction and fact.* (ERIC Document Reproduction Service No. ED 233 367.)
  Explores six misconceptions that prevail about LEA, although research and practical experience have proven them false.

Harris, T. L., & Hodges, R. E. (Eds.). (1981). *A dictionary of reading and related terms.* Newark, DE: International Reading Association

McCarthy, M. (1981). *Language experience integration into the primary classroom.* (ERIC Document Reproduction Service No. ED 207 015.)
  Annotated bibliography of 63 items.

Mayher, J. S., & Lester, N. B. (1983). Putting learning first in writing to learn. *Language Arts, 60,* 719.

Thaiss, C. (1986). *Language across the curriculum in the elementary grades.* Urbana, IL: National Council of Teachers of English.
  Talking, writing, listening, and reading are shown to play critical roles in teaching all subject matters.

Veatch, J. (1983). *The case for the language experience approach and individualized reading.* (ERIC Document Reproduction Service No. ED 232 124.)
  Describes LEA as a reading methodology that is structured, organized, and systematic.

Some Children's Informational Books for the Young

Cole, J. (1983). *Cars and how they go.* New York: Crowell.

Gibbons, G. (1979). *Clocks and how they go.* New York: Crowell.

Gibbons, G. (1982). *The post office book: Mail and how it moves.* New York: Crowell.

Gibbons, G. (1984). *Fire! Fire!* New York: Crowell.

Gibbons, G. (1985). *Check it out! The book about libraries.* New York: Harcourt Brace Jovanovich.

CHAPTER 8

References

Applebee, A. N. (1978). *The child's concept of story: Ages two to seventeen.* Chicago: University of Chicago Press.

Applebee, A. N. (1984). Writing and reasoning. *Review of Educational Research, 54,* 577–596.

Benton, S. L., Glover, J. A., & Plake, B. S. (1984). Employing adjunct aides to facilitate elaboration in writing. *Research in the Teaching of English, 18(2),* 189–200.

Bissex, G. L. (1980). *GNYS AT WRK: A child learns to write and read.* Cambridge, MA: Harvard University Press.

Bridwell, L. S. (1980). Revising strategies in twelfth grade students' transactional writing. *Research in the Teaching of English, 14,* 197–222.

Britton, J. L., Burgess, T., Martin, N., McLeod, A., & Rosen, H. (1975). *The development of writing abilities (11–18).* London: Macmillian Education.

Burns, P. C., & Broman, B. L. (1983). *The language arts in childhood education* (2nd ed.). Skokie, IL: Rand McNally.

Calkins, L. M. (1986). *The art of teaching writing.* Portsmouth, NH: Heinemann.

Carlson, R. K. (1963). Recent research in originality. *Elementary English, 40,* 583–589.

Collerson, J. (1983). One child and one genre: Development in letter writing. In B. Kroll & A. Wells (Eds.), *Explorations in the development of writing: Theory, research, and practice.* New York: Wiley.

Connors, R. J. (1981). The rise and fall of the modes of discourse. *College Composition and Communication, 32,* 444–455.

Daiute, C. (1984). Can the computer stimulate writer's inner dialogues? In W. Wresch (Ed.), *The computer in composition instruction.* Urbana, IL: National Council of Teachers of English.

Daiute, C. (1985). *Writing and computers.* Reading, MA: Addison-Wesley.

Diederich, P. B. (1974). *Measuring growth in English.* Urbana, IL: National Council of Teachers of English.

Emig, J. (1971). *The composing process of twelfth graders.* (Research Report No. 13). Urbana, IL: National Council of Teachers of English.

Emig, J. (1977). Writing as a mode of learning. *College Composition and Communication, 28,* 122–128.

Faigley, L., & Witte, S. (1981). Analyzing revision. *College Composition and Communication, 32,* 400–414.

Fisher, C. J., & Natarella, M. A. (1982). Young children's preferences in poetry: A national survey of first, second, and third graders. *Research in the Teaching of English, 16*(4), 339–354.

Fisher, C. J., & Terry, C. A. (1977). *Children's language and the language arts.* New York: McGraw-Hill.

Flavell, J. H., Botkin, P. T., Fry, C. L., Wright, J. W., & Jarvis, P. E. (1968). *The development of role-taking and communication skills in children.* New York: Wiley.

Flower, L., & Hayes, J. R. (1980). The cognition of discovery: Defining a rhetorical problem. *College Composition and Communication, 23,* 2–32.

Flower, L., & Hayes, J. R. (1981). A cognitive process theory of writing. *College Composition and Communication, 32,* 365–387.

Frederick County Board of Education. (1988). *The writing process and suggested topics and activities (K-6E).* Frederick, MD.

Gardner, J. (1984). *The art of fiction.* New York: Knopf.

Gentry, L. A. (1980). *A new look at young writers: The writing process approach of Donald Graves.* (ERIC Document Reproduction Service No. ED 192 354.)

Goldberg, M. F. (1984). An update on the National Writing Project. *Phi Delta Kappan,* 356–357.

Graves, D. H. (1983). *Writing: Teachers and children at work.* Portsmouth, NH: Heinemann Educational Books.

Graves, D. H., & Murray, D. M. (1980). Revision: In the writer's workshop and in the classroom. *Journal of Education, 162,* 38–56.

Harste, J. C., Woodward, V. A., & Burke, C. L. (1984). *Language stories and literary lessons.* Portsmouth, NH: Heinemann.

Humes, A. (1983). Research on the composing process. *Review of Educational Research, 53*(2), 201–216.

Inhelder, B., & Piaget, J. (1958). *The growth of logical thinking from childhood to adolescence.* New York: Basic Books.

Klein, M. L. (1985). *The development of writing in children: Pre-K through grade 8.* Englewood Cliffs, NJ: Prentice-Hall.

Langer, J. A. (1980). The effects of available information on responses to school writing tasks. *Research in the Teaching of English, 18*(1), 26–44.

Lundsteen, S. W. (1976a). *Children learn to communicate: Language arts through creative problem-solving.* Englewood Cliffs, NJ: Prentice-Hall.

Lundsteen, S. W. (Ed.). (1976b). *Help for the teacher of written composition.* Urbana, IL: National Council of Teachers of English.

McKenzie, L., & Tompkins, G. E. (1984). Evaluating students' writing: A process approach. *Journal of Teaching Writing, 3,* 201–212.

Mandler, J. M., & Johnson, M. S. (1977). Remembrance of things parsed: Story structure and recall. *Cognitive Psychology, 9,* 111–115.

Mayer, J. S., & Lester, N. B. (1983). Putting learning first in writing to learn. *Language Arts, 60*(6), 717–722.

Moffett, J. (1968). *Teaching the universe of discourse.* Boston: Houghton Mifflin.

Newkirk, T. (1987). The non-narrative writing of young children. *Research in the Teaching of English, 21*(2), 121–143.

Nold, E. W. (1981). Revising. In C. H. Frederiksen, M. F. Whiteman, & J. F. Dominic (Eds.), *Writing: The nature, development, and teaching of written communication.* Hillsdale, NJ: Lawrence Erlbaum.

Osborn, A. F. (1963). *Applied imagination: Principles and procedures of creative problem-solving* (3rd rev. ed.). New York: Scribner.

Petty, W. T., & Jensen, J. M. (1980). *Developing children's language.* Boston: Allyn & Bacon.

Phenix, W. T., & Hannan, E. (1984). Word processing in the grade one classroom. *Language Arts, 61*(8), 804–812.

Pianko, S. (1979). A description of the composing process of college freshman writers. *Research in the Teaching of English, 13*(5), 5–22.

Read, C. (1980). Creative spelling by young children. In T. Shapen & J. M. Williams (Eds.), *Standards and dialects in English.* Cambridge, MA: Winthrop Publications.

Robinson, A., & Feldhusen, J. F. (1984). Don't leave them alone: The effects of probing on gifted children's imaginative explanations. *Journal for the Education of the Gifted, 7*(3), 156–163.

Rodrigues, R. J., & Rodrigues, D. W. (1984). Computer-based invention: Its place and potential. *College Composition and Communication, 35,* 78–87.

Scardamalia, M. (1981). How children cope with the cognitive demands of writing. In C. H. Frederiksen, M. F. Whiteman, & J. F. Dominic (Eds.), *Writing: The nature, development and teaching of written composition.* Hillsdale, NJ: Lawrence Erlbaum.

Schwartz, M. (1982). Computers and the teaching of writing. *Educational Technology, 22,* 27–29.

Sommers, N. (1980). Revision strategies of student writers and experienced adult writers. *College Composition and Communication, 31,* 378–388.

Sowers, S. (1980). KDS CN RIT SUNR THN WE THINGK. *Learning, 93,* 14–18.

Stallard, C. K. (1974). An analysis of the behavior of good student writers. *Research in the Teaching of English, 8,* 206–218.

Temple, C. A., Nathan, R. J., & Burris, N. A. (1982). *The beginnings of writing.* Boston: Allyn & Bacon.

Terry, A. (1974). *Children's poetry preferences: A national survey of upper elementary grades.* Urbana, IL: National Council of Teachers of English.

Tiedt, S. W., & Tiedt, I. M. (1978). *Language arts for the classroom.* Boston: Allyn & Bacon.

Tierney, R. (1981). Using expressive writing to teach biology. In A. M. Wotring & R. Tierney (Eds.), *Two studies of writing in high school science.* Berkeley, CA: Bay Area Writing Project.

Toth, M. D. (1984). *The writing teacher's survival kit.* Morristown, NJ: Silver Burdett (pamphlet).

Tway, E. (1984). *Time for writing in the elementary school.* Urbana, IL: National Council of Teachers of English.

Weiss, R. H., & Walters, S. A. (1980). *Writing to learn.* (ERIC Document Reproduction Service No. ED 191 056.)

Wilkensen, A., Barnsley, J., Hanna, P., & Swan, M. (1980). *Assessing language development.* Oxford, England: Oxford University Press.

Zinsser, W. K. (1980). *On writing well* (3rd ed.). New York: Harper & Row.

If You Want to Learn More

Burrows, A. T., Jackson, D. C., & Saunders, D. O. (1984). *They all want to write* (4th ed.). Hamden, CT: Library Professional Publications.

Calkins, L. M. (1986). *The art of teaching writing.* Portsmouth, NH: Heinemann Educational Books.

Clay, M. M. (1979). *What did I write? Beginning writing behavior.* Portsmouth, NH: Heinemann Educational Books.

Clements, D. H. (1985). *Computers in early and primary education.* Englewood Cliffs, NJ: Prentice-Hall.

Ferreiro, E., & Teberosky, A. (1982). *Literacy before schooling.* Portsmouth, NH: Heinemann Educational Books.

National writing project. (n. d.). Berkeley, CA: University of California, School of Education.

Scardamalia, M., & Bereiter, C. (1986). Research on written composition. In M. C. Wittrock (Ed.), *Handbook of research on teaching* (3rd ed.). New York: Macmillan.

Some Poetry Books

Hopkins, L. B. (Ed.) (1986). *Best friends.* New York: Harper & Row.

Kennedy, X. J. (1986). *Brats.* New York: Atheneum.

Livingston, M. C. (1985). *Worlds I know and other poems.* New York: Atheneum.

Prelutsky, J. (Ed.) (1983). *Random House book of poetry.* New York: Random House.

CHAPTER 9

References

Children's Reading Roundtable, 1321 E. 56th Street, Chicago, IL 60637.

Christensen, J. (Ed.). (1983). *Your reading.* Urbana, IL: National Council of Teachers of English.

Clay, M. (1975). *What did I write?* Auckland, New Zealand: Heinemann.

Colbath, M. L. (1971, December) Worlds as they should be. *Elementary English, 48,* 937–945.

Coody, B. & Nelson, D. (1982). *Teaching elementary language arts: A literature approach.* Belmont, CA: Wadsworth.

Cullinan, B. E., Jaggar, A., & Strickland, D. (1974, January). Language expansion for black children in the primary grades: A research report. *Young Children, 29,* 98–112.

Cullinan, B. E. (1981). *Literature and the child.* New York: Harcourt Brace Jovanovich.

de la Mare, W. (1960). Quoted in P. Hazard, *Books, children, and men.* Boston: The Horn Book, Inc.

Dreyer, S. S. (Ed.). (1981). *The bookfinder. A guide to children's literature about the needs and problems of youth aged 2–15.* 2 volumes. Circle Pines, MN: American Guidance.

Early I-Can-Read Books. New York: Harper & Row.

Gillespie, J. T. (Ed.). (1985). *The elementary school paperback collection.* Chicago: American Library Association.

The Horn Book Magazine. Boston: The Horn Book, Inc.

Huck, C. (1976). *Children's literature in the elementary school* (3rd ed.). New York: Holt, Rinehart and Winston.

Johnston, W. (1962). You can't write writing. In S. I. Hayakawa, *The use and misuse of language.* Greenwich, CT: Fawcett.

Judy, S. (1975). *Explorations in the teaching of secondary English.* New York: Dodd, Mead.

Just-Beginning-to-Read Books. Chicago: Follett.

Lamme, L. L. (1980). *Raising readers.* New York: Walker.

Language Arts. The Elementary Journal of the National Council of Teachers of English, Urbana, IL.

Larrick, N. (1975). *A parent's guide to children's reading.* (4th ed., rev.). Garden City, New York: Doubleday.

Let's-Read-and-Find-Out Science Books. New York: Crowell.

Lima, C. W. (1986). *A to zoo: Subject access to children's picture books* (2nd ed.). New York: Bowker.

Lukens, R. (1983). Literature: What is it? In J. P. May (Ed.), *Children and their literature: A reading book.* West Lafayette, IN: Children's Literature Association.

Lundsteen, S. W. (1976). *Children learn to communicate.* Englewood Cliffs, NJ: Prentice-Hall.

May, J. P. (1983). *Children and their literature: A reading book.* West Lafayette, IN: The Children's Literature Association.

Mayher, J. S., Lester, N., & Pradl, G. M. (1983). *Learning to write/writing to learn.* Upper Montclair, NJ: Boynton/Cook.

The McGuffey Writer, 401A McGuffey Hall, Miami University, Oxford, OH 45056. This magazine of children's writings salutes a different school or regional magazine of children's writing in each issue.

Monson, D. (Ed.). (1985). *Adventuring with books.* Urbana, IL: National Council of Teachers of English.

Moss, J. (1984). *Focus units in literature.* Urbana, IL: National Council of Teachers of English.

The Reading Teacher. Elementary Journal of the International Reading Association, Newark, DE.

Rees, D. (1984). *Painted desert, green shade: Essays on contemporary writers of fiction for children and young adults.* Boston: Horn Book.

Sims, R. (1982). *Shadow and substance: Afro-American experience in contemporary children's fiction.* Urbana, IL: National Council of Teachers of English.

Sloan, G. D. (1984). *The child as critic: Teaching literature in the elementary school* (2nd ed.). New York: Teachers College Press.

Tierney, R. J., & Pearson, D. P. (1983, May). Toward a composing model of reading. *Language Arts, 60,* 568–580.

Townsend, J. R. (1979). *A sounding of storytellers.* Philadelphia: Lippincott.

Trelease, J. (1982). *The read-aloud handbook.* New York: Penguin Books.

Tway, E. (Ed.). (1981). *Reading ladders for human relations.* Urbana, IL: National Council of Teachers of English with the American Council on Education.

UNESCO's Bibliography of Books for Handicapped Children. (1981). Munich, Germany: The International Youth Library.

The Web. Columbus, Ohio: The Ohio State University College of Education.

Winkeljohann, R., & Gallant, R. (1981). Growing into self. In *Reading ladders for human relations.* Urbana, IL: National Council of Teachers of English with American Council on Education.

Children's Books Mentioned in Text

Alexander, L. (1969). *The book of three.* New York: Dell.

Andersen, H. C. (1982). *The emperor's new clothes.* New York: Crowell,

Anno, M. (1978). *Anno's journey.* New York: Philomel.

Anno, M. (1980). *Anno's Italy.* Philadelphia: Collins.

Anno, M. (1982). *Anno's Britain.* New York: Philomel.

Arnosky, J. (1982). *Mouse numbers and letters.* New York: Harcourt Brace Jovanovich.

Arnosky, J. (1983). *Mouse writing.* New York: Harcourt Brace Jovanovich.

Aruego, J. (1971). *Look what I can do.* New York: Scribner.

Aylesworth, J. (1981). *Tonight's the night.* Chicago: Whitman.

Babbitt, N. (1969). *The search for delicious.* New York: Farrar, Straus & Giroux.

Babbitt, N. (1975). *Tuck everlasting.* New York: Bantam Books.

Bacon, M. H. (1974). *I speak for my slave sister: The life of Abby Kelley Foster.* New York: Crowell.

Behn, H. (Trans.). (1964). *Cricket songs.* New York: Harcourt Brace Jovanovich.

Behn, H. (Trans.). (1971). *More cricket songs.* New York: Harcourt Brace Jovanovich.

Blume, J. (1978). Tales of a fourth grade nothing. New York: Dell.

Branley, F. M. (1984). *Is there life in outer space?* New York: Crowell.

Bridgers, S. E. (1984). *Notes for another life.* New York: Bantam Books.

Bulla, C. R. (1975). *Shoeshine girl.* New York: Scholastic.

Bulla, C. R. (1981). *A lion to guard us.* New York: Crowell.

Burningham, J. (1975). *The baby.* New York: Crowell.

Burns, M. (1981). *The Hanukkah book.* New York: Four Winds Press.

Butterworth, O. (1978). *The enormous egg.* New York: Dell.

Byars, B. (1976). *After the goat man.* New York: Avon Camelot.

Byars, B. (1981). *The 18th emergency.* New York: Puffin.

Cleary, B. (1975). *Ramona the brave.* New York: Morrow.

Cleary, B. (1981). Ramona Quimby, age 8. New York: Morrow.

Cleary, B. (1983). *Dear Mr. Henshaw.* New York: Morrow.

Clymer, E. (1978). *The getaway car.* New York: Dutton.

Collier, J. L., & Collier, C. (1974). *My brother Sam is dead.* New York: Four Winds, Scholastic Book Services.

Colum, P. (1953). *The Arabian nights.* New York: Macmillan.

Corbett, S. (1964). *The limerick trick.* Boston: Little, Brown.

Crews, D. (1980). *Truck.* New York: Greenwillow.

Degen, B. (1983). *Jamberry.* New York: Harper & Row.

de Regniers, B. S. (1961). *Going for a walk.* New York: Harper & Row.

Dragonwagon, C. (1977). *Will it be okay?* New York: Harper & Row.

du Bois, W. P. (1969). *The twenty-one balloons.* New York: Dell.

Elkin, B. (1964). *The loudest noise in the world.* New York: Viking Press.

Esbensen, B. J. (1986). *Words with wrinkled knees.* New York: Crowell.

Estes, E. (1977). *The hundred dresses.* New York: Harcourt Brace Jovanovich.

Fadiman, C. (1983). *Wally the wordworm.* Owing Mills, MD: Stemmer House.

Fitzhugh, L. (1975). *Nobody's family is going to change.* New York: Dell.

Frasconi, A. (1958). *The house that Jack built.* New York: Harcourt Brace Jovanovich.

Fritz, J. (1982). *Homesick: My own story.* New York: Putnam.

Galdone, P. (1973). The three billy goats gruff. New York: Seabury Press.

Geller, M. (1986). *My life in the seventh grade.* New York: Harper & Row.

Goldreich, G., & Goldreich, E. (1981). *What can she be? A scientist.* Holt, Rinehart and Winston.

Goodall, J. S. (1982). *Paddy goes traveling.* New York: Atheneum.

Goor, R., & Goor, N. (1983). *Signs.* New York: Crowell.

Gordon, S. (1980). *The boy who wanted a family.* New York: Harper & Row.

Grimm, J., & Grimm, W. (1972). *Mother Holly.* (Mother Holle). Retold and illustrated by Bernadette Watts. New York: Crowell.

Grimm, J., & Grimm, W. (1982). The Bremen Town musicians. In *Favorite tales from Grimm.* Illustrated by Mercer Mayer. New York: Four Winds Press.

Guilfoile, E. (1957). *Nobody listens to Andrew.* Chicago: Follett.

Gundersheimer, K. (1984). *A, B, C say with me.* New York: Harper & Row.

Heide, F. P. (1982). *The problem with Pulcifer.* Philadelphia: Lippincott.

Hoban, T. (1976). *Push-pull, empty-full.* New York: Collier. 1976.

Hoff, S. (1969). *Danny and the dinosaur.* New York: Harper & Row.

Hoff, S. (1963) *Grizzwold.* New York: Harper & Row.

Hoff, S. (1959) *Sammy the seal.* New York: Harper & Row.

Hoff, S. (1962). *Stanley.* New York: Harper & Row.

Hopkins, L. B. (Ed.). (1980). *Morning, noon, and nighttime, too.* New York: Harper & Row.

Hopkins, L. B. (Ed.). (1982). *Circus! circus!* New York: Knopf.

Hopkins, L. B. (Ed.). (1983). *How to make an elephant float.* Chicago: Whitman.

Horwitz, E. L. (1975). *When the sky is like lace.* Philadelphia: Lippincott.

Howe, J. (1984). *The celery stalks at midnight.* New York: Atheneum.

Jewell, N. (1983). *ABC cat.* New York: Harper & Row.

Johnson, C. (1955). *Harold and the purple crayon.* New York: Harper & Row.

Jones, T. (1986). *Skindeep.* New York: Harper & Row.

Keats, E. J. (1974). *Dreams.* New York: Macmillan.

Keats, E. J. (1984). *A letter to Amy.* New York: Harper Trophy.

Keegan, M. (1975). *The Taos Indians and their sacred blue lake.* New York: Julian Messner.

Kehoe, M. (1982). *The puzzle of books.* Minneapolis: Carolrhoda Books.

Keller, C. (1982). *Ohm on the range.* Englewood Cliffs, NJ: Prentice-Hall.

Kennedy, R. (1985). *Amy's eyes.* New York: Harper & Row.

Kent, J. (1981). *The scribble monster.* New York: Harcourt Brace Jovanovich.

Konigsburg, E. L. (1976). *Father's arcane daughter.* New York: Atheneum.

Kuskin, K. (1980). *Dogs and dragons, trees and dreams.* New York: Harper & Row.

Kwitz, M. D. (1983). *Little Chick's breakfast.* New York: Harper & Row.

Landin, J. (1981). *The long way to a new land.* New York: Harper & Row.

Larrick, N. (Ed.) (1970). *I heard a scream in the street.* Philadelphia: Lippincott.

Lewis, C. S. (1950). *The lion, the witch, and the wardrobe.* New York: Macmillan.

Lionni, L. (1963). *Swimmy.* New York: Pantheon Books.

Lionni, L. (1963). *Tico and the golden wings.* New York: Pantheon Books.

Lipsyte, R. (1984). *Assignment: Sports.* New York: Harper & Row.

Livingston, M. C. (1979). *O sliver of liver.* New York: Atheneum.

Lobel, A. (1973). *Frog and Toad together.* New York: Harper & Row.

Lowry, L. (1979). *Anastasia Krupnik.* Boston: Houghton Mifflin.

Maestro, B., & Maestro, G. (1982). *The key to the kingdom.* New York: Harcourt Brace Jovanovich.

Mayer, M. (1974). *Frog goes to dinner.* New York: Dial Press.

Minarik, E. H. (1957). *Little bear.* New York: Harper & Row.

O'Brien, R. (1971). *Mrs. Frisby and the rats of NIMH.* New York: Atheneum.

Parish, P. (1963). *Amelia Bedelia.* New York: Harper & Row.

Paterson, K. (1977). *Bridge to Terabithia.* New York: Crowell.

Paterson, K. (1978). *The great Gilly Hopkins.* New York: Crowell.

Pearce, P. (1984). *Tom's midnight garden.* Philadelphia: Lippincott.

Petersen, P. (1977). *Sally can't see.* New York: John Day.

Rawls, W. (1974). *Where the red fern grows.* New York: Bantam Books.

Rodgers, M. (1972). *Freaky Friday.* New York: Harper & Row.

Ronan, M. (1978). *All about our 50 states.* New York: Random House.

Rosario, I. (1981). *Idalia's project ABC.* New York: Holt, Rinehart and Winston.

Schlein, M. (1980). *Antarctica: The great white continent.* New York: Hastings House.

Seuss, Dr. (Theodor Geisel). (1954). *Horton hears a who.* New York: Random House.

Silverstein, S. (1974). *Where the sidewalk ends.* New York: Harper & Row.

Simon, N. (1982). *Elly the elephant.* Chicago: Whitman.

Slote, A. (1973). *Hang tough, Paul Mather.* Philadelphia: Lippincott.

Speare, E. G. (1983). *The sign of the beaver.* Boston: Houghton Mifflin.

Sperry, A. (1940, 1971). *Call it courage.* New York: Macmillan.

Spier, P. (1977). *Noah's ark.* Garden City, NY: Doubleday.

Stadler, J. (1984). *Hooray for snail!* New York: Crowell.

Steig, W. (1982). *Dr. de Soto.* New York: Farrar, Straus & Giroux.

Strickland, D. (1982). *Listen, children.* New York: Bantam Books.

Sussman, S. (1982). *Hippo thunder.* Chicago: Whitman.

Sussman, S. (1983). *There's no such thing as a Chanukah bush, Sandy Goldstein.* Chicago: Whitman.

Taylor, M. (1977). *Roll of thunder, hear my cry.* New York: Dial Press.

Terban, M. (1983). *In a pickle and other funny idioms.* New York: Clarion.

Tresselt, A. (1965). *Hide and seek fog.* New York: Lothrop.

Turkle, B. (1976). *Deep in the forest.* New York: Dutton.

Turnill, R. (1980). *Space age.* New York: Frederick Warne.

Viereck, P. (1972). *Terror on the mountain (the summer I was lost).* New York: Scholastic.

Voigt, C. (1983). *Dicey's song.* New York: Atheneum.

Watson, J. W. (1976). *Living together in tomorrow's world.* New York: Abelard-Schuman.

Weiss, A. E. (1980). *What's that you said? How words change.* New York: Harcourt Brace Jovanovich.

White, E. B. (1952). *Charlotte's web.* New York: Harper & Row.

Wilder, L. I. (1953). *Little house* series. *Little house in the big woods.* New York: Harper & Row.

Wolf, J. (1982). *Her book.* New York: Harper & Row.

Wood, A. (1984). *The napping house.* New York: Harcourt Brace Jovanovich.

Young, E. (1983). *Up a tree.* New York: Harper & Row.

Young, E. (1984). *The other bone.* New York: Harper & Row.

Zindel, P. (1968). *Pigman.* New York: Harper & Row.

If You Want to Learn More

Burke, E. M. (1986). *Early childhood literature.* Boston: Allyn & Bacon.

Huck, C. S., Hepler, S., & Hickman, J. (1987). *Children's literature in the elementary school* (4th ed.). New York: Holt, Rinehart and Winston.

Kingman, L. (Ed.). (1986). *Newbery and Caldecott Medal books, 1976–1985.* Boston: The Horn Book, Inc.

McCracken, R. A., & McCracken, M. J. (1986). *Stories, songs, and poetry to teach reading and writing: Literacy through language.* Chicago: American Library Association.

Tway, E. (1985). *Writing is reading: 26 ways to connect.* Urbana, IL: NCTE/ERIC.

CHAPTER 10

References

Brown, J. A. C. (1963). *Techniques of persuasion from propaganda to brainwashing.* Baltimore, MD: Penguin Books.

Brown, R. (1958). *Words and things.* New York: Free Press.

California State Department of Education. (1987). *English/Language arts framework.* Sacramento, CA.: Author.

College Board. (1983). *Academic preparation for college.* New York: College Board.

Cooke, J. K., & Haipt, M. (1986). *Thinking with the whole brain: An integrative teaching/learning model (K–8).* West Haven, CT: National Educational Association (NEA Professional Library).

Cowan, G., & Avants, S. K. (1987). *Children's influence strategies: Structure, gender differences, and bilateral mother-child influence.* Manuscript submitted for publication.

Cowan, G., Drinkard, J., & MacGavin, L. (1984). The effects of target, age, and gender on use of power strategies. *Journal of Personality and Social Psychology, 47,* 1391–1398.

Delia, J. G., Kline, S. L., & Burleson, B. R. (1979, November). The development of persuasive communication strategies in kindergartners through twelfth-graders. *Communication Monographs, 46* (whole issue).

Ehninger, D., Gronbeck, B. E., & Monroe, A. H. (1980). *Principles and types of speech communication* (8th brief ed.). Glenview, IL: Scott, Foresman.

Goodlad, J. (1984). *A place called school.* New York: McGraw-Hill.

Hughes, L. (1959). Dream variations. In *Selected poems of Langston Hughes* New York: Knopf.

Kaiser Aluminum and Chemical Corporation. (1965). *Communications. Kaiser Aluminum News, 23*(3) (whole issue).

Kinneavy, J. (1971). *A theory of discourse.* Englewood Cliffs, NJ: Prentice-Hall.

Lamb, P. (1987, November). Exploring accountability in connection with the teaching of thinking. Paper presented for the Critical Thinking Committee (Also Report to the Committee on Critical Thinking and the Language Arts Committee Workshop for the National Council of Teachers of English, Los Angeles.).

Lundsteen, S. W. (1969). Critical listening and thinking: A recommended goal for future research. *Journal of Research and Development in Education, 3,* 119–133.

Lundsteen, S. W. (1976). *Children learn to communicate.* Englewood Cliffs, NJ: Prentice-Hall.

Lundsteen, S. W. (1986, March). Critical listening. Paper given at the annual spring meeting, International Listening Association, San Diego, CA.

MacLure, M., & Hargreaves, M. (1986). Speaking and listening: Assessment at age 11 (Report of the Assessment of Performance Unit (APU), Department of Education and Science). Windsor, Berkshire, England: Nfer-Nelson.

Moffett, J. (1986, October 3). From personal experience to impersonal essay. Paper presented at Colorado State Department of Education conference on writing, Denver, CO.

National Assessment of Educational Progress. (1981a). *Reading, thinking, and writing: Results from the 1979–80 National Assessment of Reading and Literature* (Report No. 11-L-01). Denver, CO: Education Commission of the States. (ED 209 641.)

National Assessment of Educational Progress. (1981b). *Three National Assessments of Reading: Changes in Performance 1979–80.* Denver, CO: Education Commission of the States. (ED 200 898.)

National Assessment of Educational Progress. (1986). NAEP Data Report. *Reading Today, 3*(1), 1.

National Commission on Excellence in Education. (1983). *A nation at risk.* Washington, DC: U. S. Department of Education.

National Council of Teachers of English. (1982). *Essentials of English: A document for reflection and dialogue.* Urbana, IL: Author.

National Council of Teachers of English (1986a, October). *Newsletter of the National Council of Teachers of English Committee on Public Doublespeak.* Urbana, IL: Author.

National Council of Teachers of English and the NCTE Standing Committee on Teacher Preparation and Certification. (1986b). *Guidelines for the preparation of teachers of English language arts.* Urbana, IL: Author.

New York State Department of Education. (1984). *Listening, speaking, and reading in the English language arts curriculum, K–12.* Albany, NY: Author.

Norberg, B. (1987, November). Whispers of the mind: Holding on to ownership of writing. Paper presented for the Critical Thinking and the Language Arts Committee Workshop for the National Council of Teachers of English, Los Angeles.

Saadeh, I. Q. (1969). The teacher and the development of critical thinking. *Journal of Research and Development in Education, 3,* 87–99.

Sternberg, R. (1985). Teaching critical thinking, Part 1: Are we making critical mistakes? *Phi Delta Kappan, 67*(3), 194–198.

Suhor, C. (1984). Thinking skills in English—and across the curriculum. *ERIC Digest.* Urbana, IL: ERIC/RCS.

Traeger, H. C., & Yarrow, M. R. (1952). *They learn what they live: Prejudice in young children.* New York: Harper & Row.

Tutolo, D. (1981). Critical listening/reading of advertisements. *Language Arts, 58,* 679–683.

VanCamp, M. E. (1987, November). Propaganda and persuasion: Getting beyond the textbook. Paper presented for the Critical Thinking and the Language Arts Committee Workshop for the National Council of Teachers of English, Los Angeles.

Wolvin, A. D., & Coakley, C. G. (1985). *Listening* (2nd ed.). Dubuque, IO: Brown.

Children's Books Mentioned

Chetin, H. (1970). *Tales of an African drum.* New York: Harcourt Brace Jovanovich.

Gordon, S. (1980). *The boy who wanted a family.* New York: Harper & Row.

Lifton, B. J. (1970). *Return to Hiroshima.* New York: Atheneum.

Saxe, J. G. (1963). *Six blind men and the elephant.* New York: McGraw-Hill.

Zolotow, C. (1972). *William's doll.* New York: Harper & Row.

If You Want to Learn More

Bender, D. L. (1982–1984). *Opposing viewpoints series.* (See highlights from the series and sample critical thinking activities.) St. Paul, MN: Greenhaven Press.

Bordelon, K. W. (1985). Sexism in reading materials. *The Reading Teacher, 38,* 792–797.

Brown, L. J. (1986). Developing thinking and problem-solving skills with children's books. *Childhood Education, 63*(22), 102–107.

California Assessment Program. (n. d.). *Critical thinking vocabulary list.* Sacramento, CA: California Department of Education.

Dinkmeyer, D., McRay, G. D., & Dinkmeyer, D., Jr. (1980). *Systematic training for effective teaching.* (See chapters on "Communication: Problem solving conferences" and "Communication: Listening.") Circle Pines, MN: American Guidance Service.

Engel, S. M. (1984). *The language trap, or how to defend yourself against the tyranny of words.* Englewood Cliffs, NJ: Prentice-Hall.

Ennis, R. (1985). *Goals for a thinking/reasoning curriculum.* Champaign-Urbana, IL: University of Illinois.

Harris, L. A., & Smith, C. B. (1986). *Reading instruction: Diagnostic teaching in the classroom* (4th ed.). (See Chapter 10, "Critical and Creative Reading.") New York: Macmillan.

Kimmel, S., & MacGinitie, W. H. (1985). Helping students revise hypotheses while reading. *The Reading Teacher, 38,* 768–771.

Lambdin, W. (1979). *Doublespeak dictionary.* New York: Pinnacle Books.

Lee, D., Bingham, A., & Woelfel, S. (1968). *Critical reading develops early.* Newark, DE: International Reading Association.

McIntosh, M. E. (1985). What do practitioners need to know about current inference research? *The Reading Teacher, 38,* 755–761.

Marzano, R. J. (1984). *Language/interaction based model for teaching thinking skills.* (ERIC Document Reproduction Service No. ED 252 814.)

Miller, C. R. (1952). *What everybody should know about propaganda: How it works and why* (4th ed.). New York: Commission for Propaganda Analysis, Methodist Federation for Social Action.

Norris, S. P. (1985). Synthesis of research on critical thinking. *Educational Leadership, 42*(8), 40–45.

Paul, R. W. (1985). Bloom's taxonomy and critical thinking instruction. *Educational Leadership, 42*(8), 36–39.

Petty, R. R. (1986). *Communication and persuasion.* New York: Springer-Verlag.

Poindexter, C. A., & Prescott, S. (1986). A technique for teaching students to draw inferences from text. *The Reading Teacher, 39,* 908–911.

Postman, N. (1985). *Amusing ourselves to death: Public discourse in the age of show business.* New York: Elizabeth Sifton/Viking.

Vestergaard, T., & Schroder, K. (1985). *The language of advertising.* New York: Blackwell.

Whitmer, J. E. (1986). Pickles will kill you: Use humorous literature to teach critical reading. *The Reading Teacher, 39,* 530–534.

Wright, J. P., & Laminack, L. (1982). First graders can be critical listeners and readers. *Language Arts, 59,* 133–136.

Some Critical Thinking Tests

Cornell Critical Thinking Test, Level X (1985), by Robert H. Ennis and Jason Millman. Midwest Publications, PO Box 448, Pacific Grove, CA 93950.

> *Aimed at grades 4–12; sections on induction, credibility, observation, deduction, and assumption identification.*

New Jersey Test of Reasoning Skills (1983), developed by Virginia Shipman. IAPC, Test Division, Montclair State College, Upper Montclair, NJ 07043.

> *Aimed at grades 4–college; syllogism (including A.E.I.O. statements) heavily represented; several items apiece on assumption identification, induction, good reasons, and kind and degree. Listed but not reviewed in the Ninth Mental Measurements Yearbook.*

Ross Test of Higher Cognitive Processes (1976), by John D. Ross and Catherine M. Ross. Academic Therapy Publications, 20 Commercial Blvd., Novato, CA 94947.

> *Aimed at grades 4–college; sections on verbal analogies, deduction, assumption identification, word relationships, sentence sequencing, interpreting answers to questions, information sufficiency and relevance in mathematics problems, and analysis of attributes of complex stick figures. Listed but not reviewed in the Ninth Mental Measurements Yearbook.*

CHAPTER 11

References

Allred, R. A. (1977). *Spelling: An application of research findings.* Washington, DC: National Educational Association.

Askov, E., Otto, W., & Askov, W. (1970, November). A decade of research in handwriting: Progress and prospect. *The Journal of Educational Research, 64*(3), 100–111.

Beers, J. W. (1980) Developmental strategies of spelling competencies in primary school children. In E. Henderson & J. Beers (Eds.), *Developmental and cognitive aspects of learning to spell: A reflection of word knowledge.* Newark, DE: International Reading Association.

Beers, J. W., & Henderson, E. H. (1977, Fall). A study of developing orthographic concepts among first graders. *Research in the Teaching of English, 11,* 133–148.

Beers, J. W. & Beers, C. S. (1980). Vowel spelling strategies among first and second graders: A growing awareness of written words. *Language Arts, 57,* 166–172.

Boutin, F. J., & Stetson, E. G. (1982, December 4). The Spelling Program Effectiveness Rating Scale (SPERS): An evaluation of twelve spelling programs. Paper presented at the National Reading Conference, Clearwater, FL.

Calkins, L. M. (1980, May). When children want to punctuate: Basic skills belong in context. *Language Arts, 57,* 567–573.

Chomsky, N. & Halle, M. (1968). *The sound pattern of English.* New York: Harper & Row.

Cohen, L. A. (1969). Evaluating structural analysis methods used in spelling books. Doctoral dissertation, Boston University.

Cook, G. E., Esposito, M., Gabrielson, T., & Turner, G. R. (1984). *Spelling for word mastery.* Columbus, OH: Merrill.

Cordeiro, P., Giacobbe, M. E., & Cazden, C. (1983, March). Apostrophes, quotation marks, and periods: Learning punctuation in the first grade. *Language Arts, 60,* 323–332.

DeHaven, E. P. (1983). *Teaching and learning the language arts* (2nd ed.). Boston: Little, Brown.

Doggett, M. (1982, March). The pocket dictionary: A textbook for spelling. *English Journal, 71,* 47–50.

Farrant, A. (1977, March). Punctuation: In the beginning. *Teacher,* p. 93.

Fitzsimmons, R. J., & Loomer, B. M. (1977). *Spelling research and practice.* Iowa City: University of Iowa Press.

Fox, S. E., & Allen, V. G. (1983). *The language arts: An integrated approach.* New York: Holt, Rinehart and Winston.

Gentry, J. R. (1978, November). Early spelling strategies. *The Elementary School Journal, 79,* 88–92.

Gentry, J. R. (1981, January). Learning to spell developmentally. *The Reading Teacher, 34,* 378–381.

Gentry, J. R. (1982a, November). An analysis of developmental spelling in GNYS AT WRK. *The Reading Teacher, 36,* 192–200.

Gentry, J. R. (1982b). Developmental spelling: Assessment. *Diagnostique, 8,* 52–61.

Goodman, Y. (1979, May). The sadlamation point. *Language Arts, 56,* 482.

Graham, S. (1983, May). Effective spelling instruction. *The Elementary School Journal, 83,* 560–567.

Graves, D. H. (1977, January). Research update: Spelling texts and structural analysis methods. *Language Arts, 54,* 86–90.

Graves, D. H. (1978, March). Research update: Handwriting is for writing. *Language Arts, 55,* 393–399.

Hanna, P. R., & Hanna, J. S. (1965, November). The teaching of spelling. *The National Elementary Principal, 45,* 19–28.

Hanna, P. R., Hanna, J. S., Hodges, R. E., & Rudorf, E. H. (1966). *Phoneme-grapheme correspondences as cues to spelling improvement.* Washington, DC: Government Printing Office, U.S. Office of Education.

Henderson, E. H. (1980). Developmental concepts of word. In E. Henderson & J. Beers (Eds.), *Developmental and cognitive aspects of learning to spell: A reflection of word knowledge.* Newark, DE: International Reading Association.

Hildreth, G. (1960, January). Manuscript writing after sixty years. *Elementary English, 37,* 3–13.

Hillerich, R. L. (1977, March). Let's teach spelling—not phonetic misspelling. *Language Arts, 54,* 301–307.

Hillerich, R. L. (1978). *A writing vocabulary of elementary children.* Springfield, IL: Thomas.

Hillerich, R. L. (1982, November). Spelling: What can be diagnosed? *The Elementary School Journal, 83,* 138–147.

Horn, E. (1926). *A basic writing vocabulary.* Iowa City: University of Iowa Press.

Horn, E. (1957). Phonetics and spelling. *Elementary School Journal, 57,* 233–235, 246.

Horn, E. (1960). Spelling. In C. W. Harris (Ed.), *Encyclopedia of educational research* (3rd ed.). New York: Macmillan, pp. 1337–1354.

Horn, T. D. (1947). The effect of the corrected test on learning to spell. *The Elementary School Journal, 47,* 277–285.

Horn, T. D. (1952, May). That straw man: The spelling list. *Elementary English, 29,* 265–267.

Horton, L. W. (1970, May). Illegibilities in the cursive handwriting of sixth graders. *Elementary School Journal, 70,* 446–450.

Howell, H. (1978, October). Write on, you sinistrals! *Language Arts, 55,* 852–856.

Jackson, A. D. (1971). A comparison of speed and legibility of manuscript and cursive handwriting of intermediate grade pupils. *Dissertation Abstracts, 31,* 4383A–4384A.

Johnson, T. D., Langford, K. G., & Quorn, K. C. (1981, May). Characteristics of an effective spelling program. *Language Arts, 58,* 581–588.

Krahn, F. (1978). *The great ape.* New York: Penguin Books.

Lamme, L. L., & Ayris, B. M. (1983, Fall). Is the handwriting of beginning writers influenced by writing tools? *Journal of Research and Development in Education, 17,* 32–38.

Lundsteen, S. W. (1976). *Children learn to communicate.* Englewood Cliffs, NJ: Prentice-Hall.

Marino, J. L. (1980, February). What makes a good speller? *Language Arts, 57,* 173–177.

Markham, L. R. (1976, Fall). Influences of handwriting quality on teacher evaluation of written work. *American Educational Research Journal, 13,* 277–283.

Mayer, M. (1974). *Frog goes to dinner.* New York: Dial Press.

Moffett, J., & Wagner, B. J. (1983). *Student-centered language arts and reading, K–13: A handbook for teachers* (3rd ed.). Boston: Houghton Mifflin.

Peck, M., Askov, E. A., & Fairchild, S. H. (1980, May/June). Another decade of research in handwriting: Progress and prospect in the 1970's. *Journal of Educational Research, 73,* 283–298.

Pei, M. (1952). *The story of English.* Philadelphia: Lippincott.

Petty, W. T., & Jensen, J. M. (1980). *Developing children's language.* Boston: Allyn & Bacon.

Read, C. (1971, February). Pre-school children's knowledge of English phonology. *Harvard Educational Review, 41,* 1–34.

Read, C. (1975). *Children's categorization of speech sounds in English.* (Research Report No. 14). Urbana, IL: National Council of Teachers of English.

Rinsland, H. D. (1945). *A basic writing vocabulary of elementary school children.* New York: Macmillan.

Schell, L. M. (1975, February). B+ in composition: C— in spelling. *Elementary English, 52,* 239–242, 257.

Smith, F. (1983). Reading like a writer. *Language Arts, 60,* 558–567.

Sterne, N. (1979). *Tyrannosaurus wrecks: A book of dinosaur riddles.* New York: Crowell, 1979.

Winkeljohann, R. (1981, October). How do we help children with the conventions of writing? *Language Arts, 58,* 862–863.

Zaner-Bloser Handwriting, Grades K–8. Columbus, OH: Zaner-Bloser, Inc., 1984.

If You Want to Learn More

Applebee, A. N., Langer, J. A., & Mullis, I. V. S. (1987). *Grammar, punctuation and spelling: Controlling the conventions of written English at ages 9, 13, and 17.* The Nation's Report Card, National Assessment of Educational Progress. Princeton, NJ: Educational Testing Service.
Finds that (1) older students use a greater proportion of complex sentences, fewer fragments and run-ons; (2) spelling improves markedly at the older ages and all three ages make few errors in word choice or capitalization; (3) the majority make very few punctuation errors. Concludes classroom or large-group drill activities to be inappropriate.

Oregon Department of Education, with Masters, D. G. (1987). *Handwriting* (English Language Arts Concept Paper, No. 3). Salem, OR: Author.
Confirms ideas in this chapter. Reviews possible applications of new computer technology and videotape for instant diagnosis for the future.

Oregon Department of Education, with Mazzio, F. (1987). *Spelling* (English Language Arts Concept Paper, No. 3). Salem, OR: Author.

Suggests that teachers provide reinforcement for that portion of a word that is spelled correctly and help for the portion of the word that is not; and that regardless of grade level, students need to feel free to use invented spellings during drafting stages of writing to keep uninterrupted flow of ideas going. Recommends only noncompetitive games such as word search puzzles.

Smith, P. (1987). Handwriting in the United Kingdom. *The Reading Teacher, 41*(1), 27–31.

Templeton, S. (1986, March). Synthesis of research on the learning and teaching of spelling. *Educational Leadership, 43*(6), 73–78.

Describes learning to spell as a conceptual process growing from student interaction with other language arts of reading, writing, and vocabulary development.

Some Spelling Software for Computers

Electric Webster (Cornucopia Software).
Random House Proofreader (Digital Marketing).
Lexicheck (Quark Engineering).

CHAPTER 12

References

Braddock, R., Lloyd-Jones, R., & Schoer, L. (1963). *Research in written composition.* Urbana, IL: National Council of Teachers of English.

Reviews literature on teaching grammar and concludes that the teaching of formal grammar has a negligible or, because it usually displaces some instruction and practice in actual composition, even a harmful effect on the improvement of writing (pp. 37–38). George Hillocks, in his 1986 update of this work, Research on written composition, *reached the same conclusion. See Hillocks reference.*

California State Department of Education. (1982). *Handbook for planning an effective writing program, K–12.* Sacramento, CA: Author.

California State Department of Education. (1986). *Handbook for planning an effective writing program.* Sacramento, CA: Author.

California State Department of Education. (1987). *Preliminary English language framework (K–12).* Sacramento, CA: Author.

Chomsky, N. (1965). *Aspects of the theory of syntax.* New York: Holt, Rinehart and Winston.

Chomsky, C. S. (1969). *The acquisition of syntax in children from 5 to 10.* Cambridge, MA: MIT Press.

Christensen, F. (1967). *Notes toward a new rhetoric.* New York: Harper & Row.

Elbow, P. (1975). *Writing without teachers.* New York: Oxford University Press.

Elbow, P. (1981). Techniques for mastering the writing process. New York: Oxford University Press, 1981.

Farr, M., & Daniels, H. (1986). *Language diversity and writing instruction.* New York: ERIC Clearinghouse on Urban Education.

Fraser, I. S., & Hodson, L. M. (1978). Twenty-one kicks at the grammar horse. *English Journal, 67*(9), 49–54.

Hillocks, G. (1986). *Research on written composition: New directions for teaching.* Urbana, IL: National Council of Teachers of English.

Reports the results of a meta-analysis of over 2000 studies of writing instruction. Contains a chapter called "Grammar and the Manipulation of Syntax." Concludes that none of the studies reviewed provides any support for teaching grammar as a means of improving compositional skills. If schools insist upon teaching the identification of parts of speech, the parsing or diagramming of sentences, or other concepts of traditional school grammar, they cannot defend it as a means of improving the quality of writing.

Holt, J. R. (1982, May). In defense of formal grammar. *Curriculum Review,* pp. 173–178.

Hoskisson, K., & Tompkins, G. E. (1987). *Language arts: Content and strategies.* Columbus, OH: Merrill, pp. 30–31.

Loban, W. (1976). *Language development: Kindergarten through grade 12.* Urbana, IL: National Council of Teachers of English.

Lodge, H. C., & Trett, G. L. (1968). *New ways in English.* Englewood Cliffs, NJ: Prentice-Hall.

McCrum, R., Cran, W., & MacNeil, R. (1986). *The story of English.* New York: Viking Press.

MacLure, M., & Hargreaves, M. (1986). *Speaking and listening: Assessment at age 11.* Windsor, Berkshire, England: Nfer-Nelson.

Mellon, J. C. (1967). *Transformational sentence combining: A method for enhancing the development of syntactic fluency in English composition.* Urbana, IL: National Council of Teachers of English.

Mellon, J. C. (1970, November). Linguistics, language development, and the concept of language-rich classroom environments. Paper presented at the annual meeting of the National Council of Teachers of English, Atlanta, GA.

National Council of Teachers of English. (1983). Forum: Essentials of English. *Language Arts, 60,* 244–248.

Oregon Department of Education, with Shinkle, C. R. (1987, September). *Grammar.* (English Language Arts Concept Paper, No. 6.) Salem, OR: Author.

Petrosky, A. R. (1977). Research roundup—grammar instruction: What we know. *English Journal, 66*(9), 86–88.

Small, R. (1985). Why I'll never teach grammar again. *English Education, 17*(3), 174–178.

Smith, E. B., Goodman, K. S., & Meredith, R. (1970). *Language and thinking in the elementary school.* New York: Holt, Rinehart and Winston.

Smith, F. (1982). *Writing and the writer.* New York: Holt, Rinehart and Winston.

Talk and learning in the classroom: An interview with Anthony Adams. (1984, February). *Language Arts, 16*(2): 119–124.

Wallach, G. P., & Butler, K. G. (Eds.). (1984). *Language learning disabilities in school-age children.* Baltimore, MD: Williams & Wilkins.

Children's Book Mentioned

Emberly, E., & Emberly, B. (1967). *Drummer Hoff.* Englewood Cliffs, NJ: Prentice-Hall. (Also see Box 12.5, pp. 441 and 442.)

If You Want to Learn More

Applebee, A. N., et al. (1978). *Grammar, punctuation, and spelling: Controlling the conventions of written English at ages 9, 13, and 17.* Princeton, NJ: National Assessment of Educational Progress (NAEP).

Hartwell, P. (1985). Grammar, grammars, and the teaching of grammar. *College English, 47*(2), 105–127.

Examines the controversy over grammar study. Concludes that it is time for teachers and researchers to move on to more interesting inquiries, knowing that research has clearly shown teaching grammar to be ineffective.

National Council of Teachers of English, Committee on Resolutions. (1986). Resolutions. Resolution on the study of grammar. Urbana, IL: author.

"Resolved, that the National Council of Teachers of English affirm the position that the use of isolated grammar and usage exercises not supported by theory and research is a deterrent to the improvement of students' speaking and writing, and that, in order to improve both of these, class time at all levels must be devoted to opportunities for meaningful listening, speaking, reading, and

writing; and that NCTE urge the discontinuance of testing practices that encourage the teaching of grammar rather than English language arts instruction."

Weaver, C. (1979). *Grammar for teachers: Perspectives and definitions.* Urbana, IL: National Council of Teachers of English. (No. 18763) (ED 168 053.)

CHAPTER 13

General References

Barrett, B., & Barrett, C. M. (1985, May). The motivational experience: Maximizing the in-school influence. Paper presented at the convention of the International Reading Association, New Orleans, LA.

Commission on Media, National Council of Teachers of English. (1983, November). Rationale for integrating media into English and the language arts. Statement distributed at a session (Talk's not cheap: Fostering growth in literature, writing, and media through talk) at the meeting of the National Council of Teachers of English, San Antonio, TX.

Children's Books Mentioned

Andersen, H. C. (1965). *The nightingale.* (Translated by Eva leGallienne, version illustrated by Nancy Ekholm Burkert). New York: Harper & Row.

Andersen, H. C. (1984). *The nightingale.* (Translated by Anthea Bell, version illustrated by Lisbeth Zwerger). USA: Picture Book Studio.

Computer Section References

Atkinson, R., & Fletcher, J. D. (1972). Teaching children to read with a computer. *The Reading Teacher, 25,* 319–327.

Bockman, F. (1982). MasterType: The typing instruction game. *The Apple Journal of Courseware Review* (Educator's Resource Guide, Issue 1).

Brady, E. H., & Hill, S. (1984, March). Young children and microcomputers: Research issues and directions. *Young Children,* pp. 49–61.

Clements, D. H. (1985). *Computers in early and primary education.* Englewood Cliffs, NJ: Prentice-Hall.

Collins, A. (n. d.) *Teaching reading and writing with personal computers.* Cambridge, MA: Bolt, Beranek and Newman.

Daiute, C. (1982, March/April). Word processing. Can it make good writers better? *Electronic Learning,* pp. 29–31.

Daiute, C. (1985). *Writing and computers.* Reading, MA: Addison-Wesley.

Graves, D. (1983). *Writing: Teachers and children at work.* Exeter, NH: Heinemann Educational Books.

Graves, R. L. (1981). Renaissance and reform in the composition curriculum. *Phi Delta Kappan, 62,* 417–420.

Heard, A. (1982, February 2). U.S. unlikely to develop national strategy on educational use of computer technology. *Education Week,* p. 16.

Hoot, J. L. (1986). Computers in early childhood education. In J. L. Hoot (Ed.), *Computers in early childhood education: Issues and practices* (pp. 1–5). Englewood Cliffs, NJ: Prentice-Hall.

Lundsteen, S. W., Penny, A., & Stewart, K. (1987, August). Selected areas of children's aesthetic development: Teachers as ethnographers. Paper presented at the meeting of the International Council of Psychologists, New York.

Mackay-Smith, A. (1985, February 13). A computer can hone a child's writing and creativity, but don't expect all A's. *Wall Street Journal,* p. 32.

Marrapodi, M. (1984, April). Females and computers? Absolutely! *The Computing Teacher*, pp. 57–58.

Moffett, J., & Wagner, B. J. (1983). *Student-centered language arts and reading, K–13: A handbook for teachers* (3rd ed.). Boston: Houghton Mifflin.

Murray, D. M. (1973). Why creative writing isn't—or is. *Elementary English, 50,* 523–525, 556.

Petty, W. T., Petty, D. C., & Becking, M. F. (1981). *Experiences in language* (3rd. ed.). Boston: Allyn & Bacon.

Rosegrant, T. J. (1986). Using the microcomputer as a scaffold for assisting beginning readers and writers. In J. L. Hoot (Ed.), *Computers in early childhood education: Issues and practices* (pp. 128–143). Englewood Cliffs, NJ: Prentice-Hall.

Sanders, J. S. (1984, April). The computer: Male, female or adrogynous? *The Computing Teacher*, pp. 31–34.

Taylor, R. P. (Ed.). (1980). *The computer in the school: Tutor, tool, tutee.* New York: Teachers College Press.

Toch, T. (1982, February 2). Huge potential seen in largely underdeveloped field: Sophisticated microcomputers used to teach students to write. *Education Week*, pp. 2, 13.

Vukelich, C. (1981). The development of writing in young children: Review of the literature. *Childhood Education, 57,* 167–170.

Watt, D. (1982, June). Word processors and writing. *Popular Computing*, pp. 124–126.

If You Want to Learn More About Computers

Jones, N. B., & Vaughan, L. (Eds.). (1983, January). *Evaluation of educational software: A guide to guides.* (ERIC Document Reproduction Service No. ED 237 064.)

Daiute, C. (1985). Using microcomputers in elementary language arts instruction. *ERIC Digest: A product of ERIC Clearinghouse on Reading and Communication Skills.* Available from 1111 Kenyon Rd., Urbana, IL.

Phenix, J., & Hannan, E. (1984). Word processing in the grade one classroom. *Language Arts, 61,* 804–812.
Described are observations of the effects of the computer's word processor on the ability of six first-grade children at different writing levels to compose and transcribe.

Directories

Courseware Report Card
150 W. Carob Street
Compton, CA 90220

1985 Classroom Computer News Directory of Educational Computing Resources
Intentional Educations, Inc.
341 Mount Auburn Street
Watertown, MA 02172

Swift's Directory of Educational Software for the IBM P.C. or Apple Computer
Sterling Swift Publishing Company
7901 South Interstate Highway 35
Austin, TX 78744

Software Reports Editor
2101 Las Palkmas Drive
Carlsbad, CA 92008

Journals

Childhood Education (Software Reviews for Elementary Grades)
Journal of the Association for Childhood Education International
11141 Georgia Avenue, Suite 200
Wheaton, MD 20902

Classroom Computer News
Intentional Educations, Inc.
341 Mt. Auburn St.
Watertown, MA 02172

The Computing Teacher
International Council for Computers in Education
University of Oregon
1787 Agtate St.
Eugene, OR 97403

Educational Computer Magazine
3199 De la Cruz Blvd.
Santa Clara, CA 95050

Electronic Learning
Scholastic, Inc.
902 Sylvan Ave.
Box 2001
Englewood Cliffs, NJ 07632

TLC (Teaching, Learning, Computing)
P.O. Box 9159
Brea, CA 92621

Textbooks

Ad Hoc Committee on Textbook Selection, National Council of Teachers of English. (1985–1987). Unpublished statement. (Members: Sara Lundsteen, Chair; Kenneth Bradford, Editor; Darrell Garber; Judith Gilbert; Rosalie Kiah; Raymond Rodrigues.)

Cohen, D. H. (1975). *Criteria for the evaluation of language arts materials in early childhood.* New York: Early Childhood Education Council of New York.
   A ten-page pamphlet, based on research, with clearly stated ideas.

McCarthy, M. (1985, April 15). Personal communication. (Consultant, Curriculum Framework and Textbook Development Unit, California State Dept. of Education.)

If You Want to Learn More About Textbooks

Antell, L. (1981). *Indian education: Guidelines for evaluating textbooks from an American Indian perspective* (Report No. 143). Denver, CO: Education Commission of the States.
   Content, language, and illustration guidelines are given as well as forms for textbook evaluation.

Association for Supervision and Curriculum Development. (1985). *The pitfalls of textbook adoption— and how to avoid them.* Alexandria, VA: Author.
   This 40-minute videotape explains how publishers determine content based on consumer demands, also steps and problems in the textbook adoption process.

Australian Council of Teachers of English (N.D.). Curriculum paper written by Sawyer, W., & Bernhardt, S. Printed by Kingsway Printers Pty Ltd., Caringbab, N.S.W.

Barton, T. L. (1979, December). Textbook selection. *Slate Newsletter* (Newsletter of the NCTE/SLATE

Steering Committee on Social and Political Concerns). Urbana, IL: National Council of Teachers of English.

After discussing issues and opinions, 11 guidelines are given, along with resources.

Bernstein, H. T. (1985, March). The new politics of textbook adoption. *Phi Delta Kappan,* pp. 364–466.

The effects of various types of special-interest groups on textbook development are explored.

Brandt, R. (Ed.). (1985, April). *Educational Leadership* (Whole issue). Alexandria, VA: Association for Supervision and Curriculum Development.

The weaknesses of current learning materials are discussed in a variety of articles.

Bridgman, A. (1984, March 28). States to work on improving text selection, adoption policies. *Education Week,* pp. 1, 15–16.

Education officials and others from 22 states convene to pressure publishers into improving text materials.

Bridgman, A. (1984, September 5). "Dumbing down": The cost of aiming low may be high. *Education Week.*

Other articles in this issue point to problems associated with publishers competing for the market and trying to keep to textbooks that are not too challenging.

Campbell, A. (1979). How readability formulae fall short in matching content to text in the content areas. *Journal of Reading, 22,* 683–688.

The inadequacies of using readability formulae are discussed, as well as possible solutions.

Center for Performance Assessment. (1985, November). Do tests and textbooks match? *Captrends.*

Four mathematics textbooks, standardized tests, and teachers' actual teaching are compared.

Davis, J. E. (Ed.). (1979). *Dealing with censorship.* Urbana, IL: National Council of Teachers of English.

Articles analyze censorship from a variety of perspectives and suggest ways to handle censorship within the school context. Excellent models, processes, and bibliography.

Doyle, D. P. (1984, Summer). The "sacred" texts: Market forces that work too well. *American Educator,* pp. 8–13.

Political and economic realities related to textbook publication and selection are discussed.

Grindstaff, G. (1984, April). Textbooks: Friends with varied faces. *Clearing House,* pp. 362–363.

Teacher use of textbooks is explored along with opinions as to priorities in criteria selection.

Tierney, R. J., et al. (1980). *Some classroom applications of text analysis: Toward improving text selection and use* (Reading Education Report No. 17). (ERIC Document Reproduction Service No. ED 192 251.)

Teachers need to concentrate on the ideational and structural properties of texts, rather than on readability formulae when choosing texts. A framework is suggested for examining a text, considering the functions the text is designed to serve.

Weiner, L. (1979, December). Warning: Textbooks are not made—or used—in heaven. *English Journal,* pp. 7–10.

Processes for sensible selection are outlined: determining what is needed, gathering information, and deciding what to buy.

Television Section References

Huston, A. C., & Wright, J. C. (1982). Effects of communication media on children. In C. B. Kopp & J. B. Krakow (Eds.), *The child: Development in a social context.* Reading, MA: Addison-Wesley.

ITV (Instructional Television). (1987). Childhood socialization and television. "Focus on Society." Dallas County Community College. (Aired in Dallas, TX, on February 9.)

Singer, D. G. (1983). A time to reexamine the role of television in our lives. *American Psychologist, 38,* 815–816.

Wright, A. C., & Huston, A. C. (1983). A matter of form: Potentials of television for young viewers. *American Psychologist, 38,* 835–843.

If You Want to Learn More About TV

Clark, R. E. (1978). *Children's television: The best of ERIC.* (ERIC Document Reproduction Service No. ED 152 254.)

   Annotated listing of research reviews, position papers, and planning documents, 1974–1977.

Foster, H. (1979). *The new literacy: The language of film and television.* Urbana, IL: National Council of Teachers of English.

   Defines filmmaking and describes the teaching of visual literacy skills as part of the high school English curriculum.

Freeman-Towner, R. J. (1981). *What research says about the effects of television viewing on the reading achievement of elementary school children.* (ERIC Document Reproduction Service No. ED 219 742.)

   Reports inconclusive evidence and calls for more research on specific types of programming and their effects on reading.

Liebert, R. M., & Sprafkin, J. (1988). *The early window: Effects of television on children and youth* (3rd. ed.). Elmsford, NY: Pergamon Books.

Morison, P., et al. (1978). *Exploring the realities of television with children.* (ERIC Document Reproduction Service No. ED 165 804.)

   Elementary-age children's ability to differentiate reality and fantasy are examined in light of familiarity with various TV programs. Implications are found for teaching children about TV conventions.

Neuman, S. B. (1982). *Television viewing and leisure reading: A qualitative analysis.* (ERIC Document Reproduction Service No. ED 214 106.)

   Study relates students' choices to view television or read and quality of their leisure reading choices. Students who were heavy viewers and light readers tended to choose books of lower quality.

Neuman, S. B. (1981). *The effects of television viewing on reading behavior.* (ERIC Document Reproduction Service No. ED 205 941.)

   Presents a study of upper elementary school children's reading achievement, leisure reading, and television viewing. No clear relationship was found between amount of time viewing and reading, but there was some indication that adventure programs might be negatively related to reading scores.

Rankin, P. M., & Roberts, C. W. (1981). Television and teaching. *The Reading Teacher, 35,* 30–32.

   Gives specific ideas for using television as a springboard to instruction in various areas: televised books, scripts of TV shows, writing exercises, note taking, and interpretive writing.

Singer, J. L. (1981). *Television, imagination, and aggression: A study of preschoolers.* Hillsdale, NJ: Erlbaum Associates.

Sirota, D. R. (1978). *The development of critical television viewing skills in students: Proceed with caution.* (ERIC Document Reproduction Service No. ED 175 417.)

   Discusses various recommendations made to the federal government in relation to developing critical television viewing skills. Examines the difference in demands made on viewer when watching easily absorbed entertainment and when watching programs that require thought and analysis.

Agencies

ACT (Action for Children's Television) (Citizen action group to improve programming)
46 Austin St.; Newtonville, MA 02160

ABC Community Relations (re Guides)
1330 Avenue of the Americas; New York, NY 10019

CBS Educational Relations (re Guides & scripts)
51 W. 52 St.; New York, NY 10019

Critical Television Viewing Skills Curriculum (K–5)
Southwest Educational Development Laboratory
211 East 7th St.; Austin, TX 78701

Prime Time School Television (CBS)
120 S. La Salle, Rm. 810; Chicago, IL 60603

Teacher's Guides to Television
699 Madison Avenue; New York, NY 10021

The Television Reading Program,
Capitol Cities Communications, Inc.
4100 City Lane Ave.; Philadelphia, PA 19131

Film and Alternative Media

Cox, C. (1985). Filmmaking as a composing process. *Language Arts, 62*(1), 60–69.

Cox, C. (1987). Making and using media as a language art. In C. R. Personke, & D. D. Johnson (Eds.), *Language arts instruction and the beginning teacher.* Englewood Cliffs, NJ: Prentice-Hall, pp. 199–207.

Cox, D. (1986, November). Teaching talking in connection to television programs and films. Paper presented at the National Council of Teachers of English, San Antonio, TX.

Emerick, L. (1986). Lights! Camera! Learn! *Gifted Child Today, 9,* 29–31.

Weiss, M. R. (1967, June 17). Learning through the lens. *Saturday Review,* p. 49.

If You Want to Learn More About Film and Alternative Media

Belgrano, G. (1987). *Let's make a movie.* Mansfield Center, CT: Creative Learning Press.
This is a step-by-step how-to on moviemaking for elementary age children, complete with drawings and photographs.

Culhane, J. (1981). *Special effects in the movies: How they do it.* New York: Ballantine Books.

Davis, R. E. (1975). *Introduction to film making* (a Theory into Practice booklet). Urbana, IL: ERIC Clearinghouse on Reading and Communication Skills.
Included are various exercises designed to give students a feel for different aspects of making a film.

Foster, H. (1979). *The new literacy: The language of film and television.* Urbana, IL: National Council of Teachers of English.

Gaskill, A. L., & Englander, D. A. (1985). *How to shoot a movie and video story.* Dobbs Ferry, NY: Morgan & Morgan, Inc.

Kohler, A. D. (1976). *Project MOPPET (media oriented program promoting exploration in teaching): A 4–6 grade humanities program.* (ERIC Document Reproduction Service No. ED 169 554.)
Lesson plans for the upper elementary grades, including art and film among other forms of expression.

McGee, L. M., & Tompkins, G. C. (1981). The videotape answer to independent reading comprehension activities. *The Reading Teacher, 34,* 427–433.
Discusses the use of videotaping activities in analyzing story structure and explains why such activities improve reading comprehension.

Mattingly, E. G. (1983). *Expert techniques for home video production.* Blue Ridge Summit, PA: Tab Books, Inc.

Schneiderman, P. (1979). Homemade talking books. *Reading Teacher, 33,* 205.

Describes instructional techniques for students making their own taped books. Readers choose their own books, rehearse, and then record as a group.

Seminoff, N. W. (1986). Children's periodicals throughout the world: An overlooked educational resource. *The Reading Teacher, 39,* 889–895.
Magazines written for children provide numerous benefits, including material at a variety of reading levels.

Sinatra, R. (1981). Using visuals to help the second language learner. *Reading Teacher, 34,* 539–546.
Explores the relationship of visualization in the teaching of English to the bilingual learner. Practical suggestions are given for classroom use of visual stories using photography, filmstrips, and slides.

Super-8 Filmmaker Magazine (Eds.). (1980). *Film maker's guide to Super-8.* San Francisco, CA: Sheptow Publishing.

Tidhar, C. E. (1984). Children communicating in cinematic codes: Effects on cognitive skills. *Journal of Educational Psychology, 76,* 957–965.
Filmmaking, in this study, had a positive effect on the development of eight different cognitive skills, including spatial aptitude and logical inference. Editing activities seemed to be particularly beneficial.

If You Want to Learn More about Creative Thinking

Bookbinder, J. (1975). Art and reading. *Language Arts, 52,* 783–785, 796.

Cagle, M. (1985). A general abstract-concrete model of creative thinking. *Journal of Creative Behavior, 19,* 104–109.

Feldhusen, J. F., & Clinkenbeard, P. R. (1986). Creativity instructional materials: A review of research. *The Journal of Creative Behavior, 20,* 153–182.

Froese, V. (1978, November). The "arts" in language arts. Paper presented at the annual meeting of the National Council of Teachers of English, New York, NY.

Garner, W. I. (1984). Reading is a problem-solving process. *The Reading Teacher, 37,* 36–39.

Geller, L. G. (1984). Exploring metaphor in language development and learning. *Language Arts, 61,* 151–161.

Labuda, M. (Ed.). (1985). *Creative reading for gifted learners: A design for excellence.* Newark, DE: International Reading Association.

Lehr, F. (1983). ERIC/RCS report: Developing critical and creative reading and thinking skills. *Language Arts, 60,* 1031–1035.

Moran, III, J. D. (1982). *Measuring creativity in preschool children.* (ERIC Document Reproduction Service No. ED 224 584.)

Semple, Jr., E. E., & Semple, P. M. (1979). *Creativity in the elementary curriculum.* (ERIC Document Reproduction Service No. ED 222 281.)

Shaw, J. M., & Cliatt, M. J. P. (1986). A model for training teachers to encourage divergent thinking in young children. *The Journal of Creative Behavior, 20,* 81–88.

Sinatra, R., & Stahl-Gemake, J. (1983). *How curriculum leaders can involve the right brain in active reading and writing development.* (ERIC Document Reproduction Service No. ED 232 127.)

Stievater, S. M. (1985). Bibliography of recent books on creativity and problem solving (Supplement XXIII). *The Journal of Creative Behavior, 20,* 276–282.

Torrance, E. P., & Safter, H. T. (1986). Are children becoming more creative? *The Journal of Creative Behavior, 20,* 1–13.

Yawkey, T. D., (1986). Creative dialogue through sociodramatic play and its uses. *The Journal of Creative Behavior, 20,* 52–60.

Young, J. G. (1985). What is creativity? *The Journal of Creative Behavior, 20,* 77–87.

CHAPTER 14

References

Baum, S. (1985, April). How to use picture books to challenge the gifted. *Early Years*, pp. 48–50.

Bloom, L., & Lahey, M. (1978). *Language development and language disorders.* New York: Wiley.

Bryan, T., & Bryan, J. (1975). *Understanding learning disabilities.* New York: Knopf.

Bureau of the Census. (1987). *Statistical abstracts of the U. S.* (Table #619, p. 363). Washington, DC: Government Printing Office.

California State Department of Education. (1987). *Preliminary English-language arts framework for California public schools, kindergarten through grade 12.* Sacramento, CA: Author.

Cheek, C. W. (1978, November 20). Personal communication. (Special Education Department, University of North Texas.)

Cohen, E. G. (1986). *Designing groupwork: strategies for the heterogeneous classroom.* New York: Teacher's College, Columbia University.

Enright, D. S., & McCloskey, M. L. (1988). *Integrating English: Developing classroom language and literacy communities.* Reading, MA: Addison-Wesley.

Erway, E., Berkheimer, S., Lundsteen, S., Palmer, B., & Wolvin, A. (March, 1988). Strategies for teaching listening/reading: typical and unique listeners. Session presented at the International Listening Association, Scottsdale, AZ.

Feingold, F. (1975). Hyperkinesis and learning disabilities linked to artificial food flavors and colors. *American Journal of Nursing, 75,* 797–803.

Gottwald, S. R., Goldbach, P, & Isack, A. H. (1985, November). Stuttering: Prevention and detection. *Young children,* pp. 9–19.

Hallahan, D., & Kauffman, J. (1978). *Exceptional children: Introduction to special education.* Englewood Cliffs, NJ: Prentice-Hall.

Heath, S. B. (1986, February). A long look at being literate. Paper presented at the meeting of the Federation of North Texas Area Universities, Reading Committee, Dallas, TX.

Jordan, T. (1976). *The mentally retarded* (4th ed.). Columbus, OH: Merrill.

Kendall, F. (1983). *Diversity in the classroom: A multicultural approach to the education of young children.* New York: Teachers College Press.

Kirk, S. A., & Gallagher, J. J. (1986). *Educating exceptional children* (5th ed.). Boston: Houghton Mifflin.

Krashen, S. (1982). *Principles and practices in second language acquisition.* Elmsford, NY: Pergamon Press.

Lindfors, J. (1987). *Children's language and learning* (2nd ed.). Englewood Cliffs, NJ: Prentice-Hall.

Lundsteen, S. W., & Tarrow, N. B. (1981). *Guiding young children's learning.* New York: McGraw-Hill.

NCTE Committee on issues in ESL and bilingual education. (n. d.). Position statement. Urbana, Il: National Council of Teachers of English.

Renzulli, J., Smith, L., & Reis, S. (1982). Curriculum compacting: An essential strategy for working with gifted students. *Elementary School Journal, 82,* 185–194.

Robinson, A. (1986). Elementary language arts for the gifted: Assimilation and accommodation in the curriculum. *Gifted Child Quarterly, 30*(4), 178–181.

Ross, D. M., & Ross, S. A. (1976). *Hyperactivity: Research, theory, action.* New York: Wiley.

Sapir, S. (1985). *Clinical insights and strategies for the learning-disabled child.* New York: Brunner/Mazel.

Task Force on Racism and Bias in the Teaching of English, 1986. (1986). Expanding opportunities: Academic success for culturally and linguistically diverse students. (Position statement). Urbana, IL: National Council of Teachers of English.

Torrance, P. E. (1969). *Creativity.* Belmont, CA: Fearon.

Van Riper, C. (1978). *Speech correction principles and methods.* Englewood Cliffs, NJ: Prentice-Hall.

West, R. (ed.) (1926). *Selected poems of Carl Sandburg.* New York: Harcourt Brace.

If You Want to Learn More

Gifted

Clark, B. (1983). *Growing up gifted* (2nd ed.). Columbus, OH: Merrill.

Ehrlich, V. Z. (1985). *Gifted children, a guide for parents and teachers.* New York: Trillium Press.
> *Identifies (with sound common sense) terms applied to gifted children, such as* identification, *and also treats problems, schools, and expectations.*

Greenlaw, M. J., & McIntosh, M. E. (1986). Literature for use with gifted children. *Childhood Education, 62,* 281–286.

Greenlaw, M. J., & McIntosh, M. E. (1988) *Educating the gifted: A sourcebook.* Chicago: American Library Association.

Horowitz, F. D., & O'Brien, M. (1986). Gifted and talented children. *American Psychologist, 41,* 1147–1152.
> *Discusses the need for further research to more fully determine the worth of various approaches to the gifted, including the acceleration and enrichment programs.*

Howell, H. (1987). Language, literature, and vocabulary development for gifted students. *The Reading Teacher, 40,* 500–504.
> *Strategies, along with children's books, are described, providing challenging vocabulary development activities for gifted readers.*

Knight, L. N. (1974). *Language arts for the exceptional: The gifted and the linguistically different.* Itasca, IL: Peacock.

Parker, J. (1988). *Instructional strategies for teaching the gifted.* Boston: Allyn & Bacon. (Esp. Chapter 11, Challenging the gifted reader.)

Torrance, E. P. (1984). The role of creativity in identification of the gifted and talented. *Gifted Child Quarterly, 28,* 153–156.

West, W. W. (1980). *Teaching the gifted and talented in the English classroom.* Washington, D. C.: National Educational Association.
> *After describing characteristics of the gifted, discusses how lessons and units can be developed to further develop the abilities of the gifted.*

Varied Backgrounds

Canadian Children's Literature Association. (1984). *Canadian Children's Literature* [Whole issue], 35/36 (issue number). (Address: Box 335, Guelph, Ontario N1H 6K5, Canada.)
> *Articles reflect literature for children that describe the experiences of immigrants adjusting to a new land and culture.*

Corder, L. J., & Quisenberry, N. L. (1987). Early education and Afro-Americans: History, assumptions and implications for the future. *Childhood Education, 63,* 154–158.

Dillon, D. (Ed.). Language arts in multicultural education [Special issue]. *Language Arts, 63* (5).

Edmonds, R. (1979). Effective schools for the urban poor. *Educational Leadership, 3,* 22–23.

Harcourt Brace Jovanovich. (1987). *HBJ Lectura.* New York: Author.
> *An independent Spanish reading program, culturally relevant, thematic, with lesson plans, teachers' editions, tests (placement, unit, end of book), levels 1–11.*

Meier, T. R., & Cazden, C. B. (1982). Research update: A focus on oral language and writing from a multicultural perspective. *Language Arts, 59,* 504–512.

Ramsey, P. G. (1987). *Teaching and learning in a diverse world: Multicultural education for young children.* New York: Teachers College Press.

Turner, A. (1986). *Street talk.* Boston: Houghton Mifflin.

Twenty-nine poems about city life through a child's perspective. Good for 8–12 year olds.

West, B. (1986). Culture before ethnicity. *Childhood Education, 62,* 175–181.

LEP

Dillon, D. (Ed.). (1986). English for everyone? [Special issue]. *Language Arts, 63*(1).

Enright, D. S., & McCloskey, M. (1985). Yes, talking!: Organizing the classroom to promote second language acquisition. *TESOL Quarterly, 19,* 431–453.

Norton, D. (1985). Language and cognitive development through multicultural literature. *Childhood Education, 62,* 103–108.

Sinatra, R. (1981). Using visuals to help the second language learner. *Reading Teacher, 34,* 539–546.

Describes the use of visual stories (using photography, filmstrips, and slides) to help teach English as a second language. Relates the importance of visualization to the learning of English.

Urzua, C. (1986). A children's story. In P. Rigg & D. S. Enright (Eds.), *Children and ESL: Integrating perspectives,* pp. 95–112. Washington, DC: Teachers of English to Speakers of Other Languages.

Other Special Education

Association for Childhood Education International/Children's Book Council Joint Committee. (1981, March/April). Children's books about special children: A selected bibliography. *Childhood Education,* pp. 205–208.

D'Angelo, K. (1980). Wordless picture books and the learning disabled. In National Council of Teachers of English (Ed.), *Dealing with differences.* Urbana, IL: National Council of Teachers of English.

Wordless picture books are used to encourage reading readiness in the learning disabled, by developing oral language, developing an understanding of story development, and providing success experiences with books.

Epps, S., Ysseldyke, J. E., & McGue, M. (1984). "I know one when I see one"—differentiating LD and non-LD students. *Learning Disability Quarterly, 7,* 89–99.

Ferguson, A. M. (1981). *Children's literature—for all handicapped children.* (ERIC Document Reproduction Service No. ED 234 541.)

Describes 14 books dealing realistically with a variety of handicaps. Useful for teachers and for nonhandicapped children to better empathize with the handicapped.

Sinatra, R. C., Stahl-Gemake, J., & Berg, D. N. (1984). Improving reading comprehension of disabled readers through semantic mapping. *The Reading Teacher, 38,* 22–29.

Story elements can be presented visually as a map, revealing the structure of the story. This approach is presented as an aid to comprehension.

CHAPTER 15

References

Alvermann, D. E., Dillon, D. R., & O'Brien, D. G. (1987). *Using discussion to promote reading comprehension.* Newark, DE: International Reading Association.

Anderson, R. C., et al. (1984). *Becoming a nation of readers: The report of the commission on reading.* Washington, DC: The National Institute of Education, U.S. Department of Education.

California State Department of Education. (1987). *Preliminary English-language arts framework for California public schools, kindergarten through grade 12.* Sacramento, CA: Author.

Dillon, D. (1987). [Editorial introduction of thematic issue *Evaluation of language and learning*]. *Language Arts, 64*(3), 271.

Knoblauch, C. H., & Brannon, L. (1984). *Rhetorical traditions and the teaching of writing.* Upper Montclair, NJ: Boynton Cook.

Linn, R. L. (1986). Educational testing and assessment: Research needs and policy issues. *American Psychologist, 41,* 1153–1160.

Lundsteen, S. W., & Tarrow, N. B. (1981). *Guiding young children's learning.* New York: McGraw-Hill.

National Commission on Excellence in Education. (1983). *A nation at risk: The imperative for educational reform.* Washington, DC: Government Printing Office.

National Council of Teachers of English (Standing Committee on Teacher Preparation and Certification). (1986). *Guidelines for the preparation of teachers of English language arts.* Urbana, IL: Author.

Rubin, D. L., & Mead, N. A. (1985). Assessing listening and speaking skills. *ERIC Digest.* Urbana, IL: A product of the ERIC Clearinghouse on Reading and Communication Skills.

Samway, K. (1987). Formal evaluation of children's writing: An incomplete story. *Language Arts, 64*(3), 289–298.

Scarr, S. (1981). Testing for children: Assessment and the many determinants of intellectual competence. *American Psychologist, 36,* 1159–1166.

Searle, D., & Dillon, D. (1980). Responding to student writing: What is said or how it is said. *Language Arts, 57,* 773–781.

Stibbs, A. (1979). *Assessing children's language: Guidelines for teachers.* London: Ward Lock Educational/National Association for the Teaching of English.

Wigdor, A. K., & Garner, W. R. (Eds.). (1982). *Ability testing: Uses, consequences, and controversies. Part I: Report of the Committee.* Washington, DC: National Academic Press.

Wilkinson, A. (1983). Assessing language development: The Credition Project. In A. Freedman, I. Pringle, & J. Yalden (Eds.), *Learning to write: First language/second language.* New York: Longman.

If You Want to Learn More

Clay, M. (1972). *Sand: A diagnostic survey and concepts of print test.* Exeter, NH: Heinemann Educational Books. (A new version, called *Stones,* was published in 1979.)

Clay, M. (1979). *What did I write?* Exeter, NH: Heinemann Educational Books.

Cooper, C. R., & Odell, L. (1977). *Evaluating writing: Describing, measuring, judging.* Buffalo, NY: State University of New York.

Dillon, D. (Ed.). (1984). Assessment [Special issue]. *Language Arts, 61*(4).

Dillon, D. (Ed.). (1987). Evaluation of language and learning [Special issue]. *Language Arts, 64*(3).

Goodman, Y. M. (1978, June). Kid watching: An alternative to testing. *National Elementary Principal,* pp. 41–45.

Goodman, Y. M., & Burke, C. L. (1972). *Reading miscue inventory manual: Procedure for diagnosis and evaluation.* New York: Richard C. Owen.

Gray, P. A. (1984). *Assessment of basic oral communication skills: A selected, annotated bibliography.* Distributed by the Speech Communication Module—ERIC Clearinghouse on Reading and Communication Skills, 5105 Backlick Road, Annandale, VA 22003.

Jaggar, A. M., & Smith-Burke, T., (Eds.). (1985). *Observing the language learner.* Newark, DE: International Reading Association and National Council of Teachers of English.

Langer, J. A., & Pradl, G. M. (1984). Standardized testing: A call for action. *Language Arts, 61,* 764–767.

Lehr, F. (1984). *Responses of English language arts professionals to A Nation at Risk.* Urbana, IL: ERIC Clearinghouse on Reading and Communication Skills.

McPike, E. (Ed.). (1987). Education for democracy: Passing on the knowledge and values that sustain us [Special issue]. *American Educator, 11*(2).

Marek, A. M, et al. (1984). *A kid-watching guide: Evaluation for whole language classrooms* (Occasional Paper No. 9, Program in Language and Literacy, Arizona Center for Research and Development). Tucson, AZ: University of Arizona.

Mitchell, B. C. (n. d.). *Test service notebook 13: A glossary of measurement terms.* New York: Harcourt Brace Jovanovich.

Myers, M. (1980). *Procedure for writing assessment and holistic scoring.* Urbana, IL: National Council of Teachers of English/ERIC.

National Council of Teachers of English. (1974). *Uses, abuses, misuses of standardized tests in English: A first-aid kit for the test-wounded.* Urbana, IL: Author.

O'Donnell, H. (1984). *Large scale writing assessment.* Urbana, IL: ERIC Clearinghouse on Reading and Communication Skills.

Summarizes three approaches to scoring. Holistic scoring of a writing sample is based upon the reader's overall impression of the effectiveness of a piece of writing, usually comparing the paper with others. Primary-trait scoring focuses on a specific rhetorical characteristic or trait of a given piece of writing, usually comparing papers to an external criterion. Importance of audience to a piece of writing is often stressed. Analytical scoring is a thorough trait-by-trait analysis, in which traits considered important to any writing are examined. Components need to be explicit and well defined.

Oklahoma State Department of Education. (1982). *Study skills: Study your way to success. Kindergarten–6th.* (ERIC Document Reproduction Service No. ED 235 125.)

Shuy, R. W. (1981). What the teacher knows is more important than text or test. *Language Arts, 58,* 919–930.

Wilkinson, A., Barnsley, G., Hanna, P., & Swan, M. (1983). More comprehensive assessment of writing development. *Language Arts, 60,* 871–881.

Explains how to use and report on primary trait, analytical, and discourse scoring.

Witkin, B. R. (1986, February). *Resources for assessing listening* (Report to International Listening Association Committee on Research, Goal #7). Unpublished report.

Some Dinosaur Books for Children

Burton, J. (1984). *Time exposure: A photographic record of the dinosaur age.* (Text by Dougal Dixon). New York: Beaufort Books.

Davidson, R. (1969). *Dinosaurs: The terrible lizards.* San Carlos, CA.

Greene, C. (1966). *How to know dinosaurs.* Indianapolis! Bobbs-Merrill.

Huck, C., & Hickman, J. (Eds.). (1988, Spring). Dinosaurs and digs web. *The Web: Wonderfully Exciting Books, vol. II* (3). Ohio State University, Columbus, Ohio 43210.

A reference for teachers about children's books, subscription issued quarterly. The web with seven concepts mentions 44 related books.

Sattler, H. R. (1981). *Dinosaurs of North America.* New York: Lothrop, Lee & Shepard Books.

Service, W. (1981). *The Dinosaurs.* New York: Bantam Books. (William Stout illustrator)

A must. Well-qualified paleontologist, phenomenal illustrations, renowned writer provide a highly sensory vicarious experience.

Simon, S. (1982). *The smallest dinosaurs.* New York: Crown.

Text and Illustration Credits

The use of the following text, quotations, figures, and tables is gratefully acknowledged:*

Chapter 2: Page 27, quotation, from *Baby Talk*, NOVA transcript #1207 (February 26, 1985). Page 30, Figure 2.1, from B. G. Heald-Taylor, "Scribble in first-grade writing," *The Reading Teacher* 38(1) 4–8. Courtesy of B. G. Heald-Taylor. Page 37, Table 2.1, from E. H. Lenneberg, "The natural history of language," in F. Smith and G. A. Miller (eds.), *The Genesis of Language.* Copyright © 1966 by MIT Press. Reproduced by permission. Page 40, Table 2.2, courtesy of C. Green and the National Council of Teachers of English. Pages 41–42, Box 2.1, from C. Genishi and A. H. Dyson, *Language Assessment in the Early Years.* Copyright © 1984 by Ablex Publishing Company. Reprinted with permission of the publisher. Page 43, Table 2.3, from M. C. Templin, *Certain Language Skills in Children: Their Development and Relationship.* Copyright © 1957 by the University of Minnesota Press. Reproduced by permission of the University of Minnesota Press.

Chapter 4: Page 104, Figure 4.2, J. A. Schickendanx, M. E. York, I. S. Stewart, and D. A. White, *Strategies for Teaching Young Children*, 2nd edition. Copyright © 1983 by Prentice-Hall, Inc. Reproduced by permission of Prentice-Hall, Inc. Page 105, Figure 4.3, from *Guiding Young Children's Learning* by S. Lundsteen and N. B. Tarrow. Copyright © 1981 by McGraw-Hill Book Company. Reprinted by permission of McGraw-Hill Book Company. Page 106, Figure 4.4, from *The Effective Teaching of Language Arts*, 2nd ed., by Donna Norton. Copyright © 1985 Merrill Publishing Company, Columbus, Ohio. Reproduced by permission. Page 116, "Invitation," from *Where the Sidewalk Ends* by Shel Silverstein. Copyright © 1974 by Evil Eye Music, Inc. Reprinted by permission of Harper & Row, Publishers. Page 127, Figure 4.6, from C. Genishi and A. H. Dyson, *Language Assessment in the Early Years.* Copyright © 1984 by Ablex Publishing Company.

Chapter 5: Page 138, Figure 5.1, from Alberta Department of Education, *Elementary Drama Curriculum Guide* (ERIC Document Reproduction Service No. ED 257 156), 1985. Courtesy of the Alberta Department of Education, Edmonton, Canada. Pages 143–144, Table 5.1, from Alberta Department of Education, *Elementary Drama Curriculum Guide* (ERIC Document Reproduction Service No. ED 257 156), 1985. Courtesy of the Alberta Department of Education, Edmonton, Canada. Page 145,

*An attempt has been made to obtain permission from all sources of figures, tables, and quoted material used in this edition. Some sources have not been located, but permission will be requested from them upon notification to us of their ownership of the material.

Figure 5.2, from B. Way, *Development Through Drama* (1967). Reprinted courtesy of Humanities Press International, Inc. Atlantic Highlands, NJ 07716. Page 146, Figure 5.4, from Alberta Department of Education, *Elementary Drama Curriculum Guide* (ERIC Document Reproduction Service No. ED 257 156), 1985. Courtesy of the Alberta Department of Education, Edmonton, Canada. Page 149, Figure 5.5, from Alberta Department of Education, *Elementary Drama Curriculum Guide* (ERIC Document Reproduction Service No. ED 257 156), 1985. Courtesy of the Alberta Department of Education, Edmonton, Canada. Page 158, Figure 5.7, from Alberta Department of Education, *Elementary Drama Curriculum Guide* (ERIC Document Reproduction Service No. ED 257 156), 1985. Courtesy of the Alberta Department of Education, Edmonton, Canada. Page 160, Figure 5.8, from Alberta Department of Education, *Elementary Drama Curriculum Guide* (ERIC Document Reproduction Service No. ED 257 156), 1985. Courtesy of the Alberta Department of Education, Edmonton, Canada.

Chapter 6: Page 184, Figure 6.7, courtesy D. Jim Laney, University of North Texas. Page 185, Table 6.1, from *Designing Groupwork* by E. G. Cohen. Copyright © 1986 by Teachers College Press. Reprinted by permission. Pages 194–195, Table 6.2, from *Speaking and Listening Assessment at Age 11* (Report of the Assessment of Performance Unit, APU, Department of Education and Science), by M. MacLure and M. Hargreaves. Reproduced by permission of NFER-Nelson, Berkshire, England. Page 203, Figure 6.11, from H. Taba, S. Levine, and F. E. Freeman, *Thinking in Elementary School Children* (USOE Cooperative Research Project # 1574), 1964. Reprinted by permission. Page 204, Figure 6.12, copyright © 1983 by the NCTE. Reprinted by permission.

Chapter 7: Page 217, Figure 7.1, adapted from *Reading and Writing Revisited* by Roselmina Indrisano, Number 18 of the *Ginn Occasional Papers*, copyright © 1984 by Ginn and Company. Used by permission of Silver, Burdett & Ginn, Inc. Page 218, Table 7.1, adapted from *Reading and Writing Revisited* by Roselmina Indrisano, Number 18 of the *Ginn Occasional Papers*, copyright © 1984 by Ginn and Company. Used by permission of Silver, Burdett & Ginn, Inc. Page 237, Figure 7.6, from *Learning Language Through Communication: A Functional Approach* by R. R. Allen, K. L. Brown, and J. Yatvin. Copyright © 1986 by Wadsworth Publishing Company. Reproduced by permission of Wadsworth Publishing Company. Pages 237–240, Figure 7.7, reproduced by permission of the International Reading Association. Page 240, Figure 7.8, adapted from *Reading and Writing Revisited* by Roselmina Indrisano, Number 18 of the *Ginn Occasional Papers*, copyright © 1984 by Ginn and Company. Used by permission of Silver, Burdett & Ginn, Inc. Page 241, Figure 7.9, reproduced courtesy of *Early Years* and J. Healy. Page 256, Table 7.2, from *The Framework for the Assessment of Language* (Assessment of Performance Unit, Dept. of Education and Science, National Foundation for Educational Research), by T. Gorman. Reproduced by permission of NFER-Nelson, Berkshire, England. Page 257, Figure 7.12, from *The Framework for the Assessment of Language* (Assessment of Performance Unit, Dept. of Education and Science, National Foundation for Educational Research), by T. Gorman. Reproduced by permission of NFER-Nelson, Berkshire, England.

Chapter 8: Page 274, Figure 8.2, from *New Directions in Creativity, Mark B* by J. Renzulli, L. Smith, G. F. Barbare, and M. J. Renzulli. Copyright © 1976 by Harper & Row, Publishers. Reprinted by permission of Harper & Row, Publishers, Inc. Page 299, Figure 8.13, from L. McKenzie and G. E. Tompkins, "Evaluating students' writing," *Journal of Teaching Writing* (1984) 3, 201–212. Reproduced by permission of *Journal of Teaching Writing*, 425 Agnew St., Indianapolis, IN 46202. Page 300, Figure 8.14, from *Children Learn to Communicate: Language Arts Through Creative Problem-Solving,* by S. Lundsteen. Copyright © 1976 by Prentice-Hall, Inc. Reprinted by permission of Prentice-Hall, Inc. Page 301, Figure 8.15, by permission of the Department of Instruction, Grosse Pointe Public School System, Grosse Pointe, MI.

Chapter 9: Page 312, Figure 9.1, from *Dear Mr. Henshaw* by Beverly Cleary. Copyright © 1983 by Beverly Cleary. Reproduced by permission of Dell Publishing Company.

Chapter 10: Page 334, poem, copyright 1926 by Alfred A. Knopf, Inc. and renewed 1954 by Langston Hughes. Reprinted from *Selected Poems of Langston Hughes* by permission of the publisher.

Name Index

Subject Index

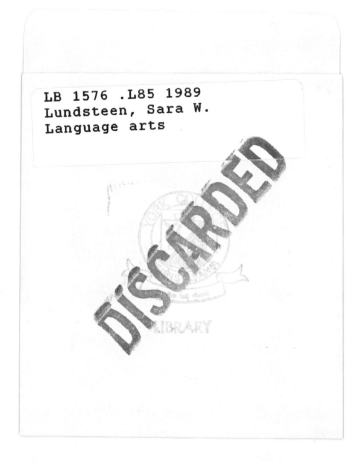